Sears List of
Subject Headings

Sears List of Subject Headings

18th Edition

JOSEPH MILLER

Editor

JOAN GOODSELL

Associate Editor

Haverstraw King's Daughters
Public Library
85 Main Street
Haverstraw, NY 10927

New York • Dublin

The H. W. Wilson Company

2004

Printed in the United States of America

ISBN 0-8242-1040-9

Contents

CONTENTS

Preface

The year 2003 marked the eightieth anniversary of the Sears List of Subject Headings. For eight decades the Sears List has served the needs of small and medium-sized libraries, suggesting headings appropriate for use in their catalogs and providing patterns and instructions for adding new headings as they are required. The successive editors of the List have faced the need to accommodate change while maintaining a sound continuity. The new and revised headings in each edition reflect developments in the literature and in the use of the English language, while the changes in the form of the headings and in the structure and display of the List reflect shifts in the prevailing philosophy of subject cataloging.

There are three major features of this new edition of the Sears List. The first is the inclusion of five hundred new subject headings. The second is the revision of the classification numbers to conform to the usage of the 14th edition of the *Abridged Dewey Decimal Classification* (2004). The third is a small but important addition to the Principles of the Sears List.

The Principles of the Sears List, which follows this Preface, is intended both as a statement of the theoretical foundations of the Sears List and as a concise introduction to subject cataloging in general. It has been expanded in this edition to provide guidance to libraries that choose to assign topical and geographic headings to individual works of fiction, drama, and poetry. This difficult area of cataloging has been much discussed in recent years in the library community and in the committees and subcommittees of the American Library Association.

The List of Commonly Used Subdivisions, which was omitted in the previous edition of the Sears in favor of a more exhaustive treatment of subdivisions within the body of the List, has been restored in this edition and renamed List of Subdivisions Provided for in the Sears List. It now lists, for the purpose of easy reference, every subdivision for which there is a provision in Sears, no matter how specialized. At the same time, for every subdivision there is an entry in the alphabetical List with full instructions for the use of that particular subdivision.

A History of the Sears List

Minnie Earl Sears prepared the first edition of this work in response to demands for a list of subject headings that was better suited to the needs of the small library than the existing American Library Association and Library of Congress lists. Published in 1923, the *List of Subject Headings for Small Libraries* was based on the headings used by nine small libraries that were known to be well cataloged. Minnie Sears used only *See* and "refer from" references in the first edition. In the second edition (1926) she added *See also* references at the request of teachers of cataloging who were using the List as a textbook. To make the List more useful for that purpose, she wrote a chapter on "Practical Suggestions for the Beginner in Subject Heading Work" for the third edition (1933).

Isabel Stevenson Monro edited the fourth (1939) and fifth (1944) editions. A new feature of the fourth edition was the inclusion of Dewey Decimal Classification numbers as applied in the *Standard Catalog for Public Libraries*. The new subjects added to the List were based on those used in the Standard Catalog Series and on the catalog cards issued by the

H.W. Wilson Company. Consequently, the original subtitle "Compiled from Lists used in Nine Representative Small Libraries" was dropped.

The sixth (1950), seventh (1954), and eighth (1959) editions were prepared by Bertha M. Frick. In recognition of the pioneering and fundamental contribution made by Minnie Sears the title was changed to *Sears List of Subject Headings* with the sixth edition. Since the List was being used by medium-sized libraries as well as small ones, the phrase "for Small Libraries" was deleted from the title. The symbols *x* and *xx* were substituted for the "Refer from (see ref.)" and "Refer from (see also ref.)" phrases to conform to the format adopted by the Library of Congress.

The ninth edition (1965), the first of four to be prepared by Barbara M. Westby, continued the policies of the earlier editions. With the eleventh edition, the "Practical Suggestions for the Beginner in Subject Heading Work" was retitled "Principles of the Sears List of Subject Headings" to emphasize "principles," and a section dealing with nonbook materials was added.

The thirteenth edition (1986), prepared by Carmen Rovira and Caroline Reyes, was the first to take advantage of computer validation capabilities. It also responded to the changing theory in subject analysis occasioned by the development of online public access catalogs. This effort was taken further in the fourteenth edition (1991) under the editorship of Martha T. Mooney, who reduced the number of compound terms, simplified many subdivisions, and advanced the work of uninverting inverted headings.

In accord with a suggestion of the Cataloging of Children's Materials Committee of the American Library Association, many of the headings from *Subject Headings for Children's Literature* (Library of Congress) were incorporated into the Sears List with the thirteenth edition. Since the Sears List is intended for both adult and juvenile collections, wherever the Library of Congress has two different headings for adult and juvenile approaches to a single subject, a choice of a single term was made for Sears. In cases where the Sears List uses the adult form, the cataloger of children's materials may prefer to use the juvenile form found in *Subject Headings for Children's Literature*.

In the fifteenth edition (1994), the first edited by Joseph Miller, the interval between publication of editions was shortened to provide a more timely updating of subject headings. In keeping with prevailing thinking in the field of library and information science, all remaining inverted headings were canceled in favor of the uninverted form. Likewise, the display of the List on the page was changed to conform to the NISO standards for thesauri approved in 1993. While Sears remains a list of subject headings and not a true thesaurus, it uses the labels BT, NT, RT, SA, and UF for broader terms, narrower terms, related terms, See Also, and Used for. A List of Canceled and Replacement Headings was added to facilitate the updating of catalogs, and the legend "[*Former heading*]" was introduced within the List to identify earlier forms of headings. Also in the fifteenth edition many headings were added to enhance access to individual works of fiction, poetry, drama, and other imaginative works, such as films and radio and television programs, based on the *Guidelines on Subject Access to Individual Works of Fiction, Drama, etc.* prepared by a subcommittee of the Subject Analysis Committee of the ALA.

In the sixteenth edition (1997) the suggested classification numbers were revised to conform to the 13th edition of the Abridged Dewey Decimal Classification, further instructions were added for the application of subdivisions, and the headings in the field of religion were extensively revised to reduce their exclusively Christian application and make them more useful for cataloging materials on other religions.

PREFACE

The major feature of the seventeenth edition (2000) was the revision of the headings for the native peoples of the Western Hemisphere. The headings **Indians, Indians of North America, Indians of Mexico,** etc., were cancelled in favor of **Native Americans,** which may be subdivided geographically by continent, region, country, state, or city. Subdivisions formerly used under **Indians of North America** for classes of persons, such as *Women* or *Children,* and for things distinctly ethnic, such as *Medicine* or *Music,* were canceled in favor of phrase headings, such as **Native American women, Native American children, Native American medicine,** and **Native American music.** Subdivisions for things not of an ethnic nature, such as *Housing* or *Social conditions,* remain subdivisions under **Native Americans.** The heading **Native Americans** is now the pattern heading for all ethnic groups

In further revisions in the seventeenth edition, many headings that formerly incorporated the word "modern" were simplified and clarified, such as **Modern history** and **Modern art,** and headings for government policy were revised and regularized, so that all headings for policies are either phrase headings, such as **Economic policy** and **Environmental policy,** or topics subdivided by *Government policy,* such as **Homeless persons—Government policy** and **Genetic engineering—Government policy,** all subdivided geographically.

The Scope of the Sears List

No list can possibly provide a heading for every idea, object, process, or relationship, especially not within the scope of a single volume. What Sears hopes to offer instead is a basic list that includes many of the headings most likely to be needed in small libraries together with patterns and examples that will guide the cataloger in creating additional headings as needed. New topics appear every day, and books on those topics require new subject headings. Headings for new topics can be developed from the Sears List in two ways, by establishing new terms as needed and by subdividing the headings already in the List. Instructions for creating new headings based on the pattern in Sears and sources for establishing the wording of new headings are given in the Principles of the Sears List. The various kinds of subdivisions and the rules for their application are also discussed in the Principles of the Sears List.

It is only by being flexible and expandable that Sears has been able over the years to fill the needs of various kinds of libraries. The degree or level of specificity required for a collection depends entirely on the material being collected. While a small library is unlikely to need very narrow topics of a technical or scientific nature, it is not at all unlikely that a small library might have a children's book on a single concept such as **Triangle** or a gardening book on **Irises.** Neither of these terms is in Sears, but the first would be added as a narrower term under **Shape** and the second as a narrower term under **Flowers.**

New Headings in this Edition

The abundance of new subject headings in the present edition represents a major enhancement to the List. The new terms reflect developments in many different areas, especially computers, personal relations, politics, and popular culture. Among the new headings in the field of technology are **Bar coding, Digital cameras, Digital libraries, DVDs, Intranets, MP3 players, Nanotechnology, Optical scanners, V-chips,** and **Web databases.** Among the new headings in other fields are **Alien labor, Aromatherapy, Braids (Hairstyling), Cheating (Education), Fanzines, Fetal alcohol syndrome, Journaling, Pilates method, Racially mixed people, Test bias, Tree houses,** and **Word problems (Mathematics).** In many cases the new headings in Sears conform to the usage of the Library of Congress Subject Headings, while in other cases, such as **Tattling** for **Talebearing,** or **Mountain biking** for **All terrain cycling,** the Sears form varies from the form found in LCSH. In other cases, such as **Hearing in animals** and **Fractured fairy tales,** the concept is not represented in LCSH.

Many of the headings new to this edition were suggested by librarians representing various sizes and types of libraries, by commercial vendors of bibliographic records, and by the catalogers, indexers, and subject specialists at the H.W. Wilson Company.

Revised Headings in this Edition

Revisions to existing headings have been kept to a minimum in this edition. The most significant is the replacement of the subdivision *Description* by *Description and travel*. In the 17th edition of the Sears List the subdivision *Travel* was established, to be used under names of individuals and categories of persons. The subdivision *Description and travel* under names of places, replacing the subdivision *Description* in all cases, should now be an unambiguous descriptor for both geographic descriptive material and various forms of travel writings about countries, regions, cities, etc.. It also conforms to the usage of the Library of Congress Subject Headings and other thesauri.

As in previous editions, certain headings of decreasing interest and some unnecessary examples, such as **Margarine, Van life**, and **Iran-Contra Affair, 1985-1990**, have been deleted from the List. Such headings are not invalid and may be maintained in the catalog. Other headings that have been deleted are no longer valid and are now used as cross-references to other headings. Earlier forms of headings revised in this edition appear in the alphabetical List after the UF [Used for] label under the established headings with the label "[*Former heading*]" and also in the List of Canceled and Replacement Headings

Form of Headings

It was the policy of Minnie Sears to use the Library of Congress form of subject headings with some modification, chiefly the simplification of phrasing. The Sears List still reflects the usage of the Library of Congress unless there is some compelling reason to vary, but those instances of variation have become numerous over the years. A major difference between the two lists is that in Sears the direct form of entry has replaced the inverted form, on the theory that most library users search for multiple-word terms in the order in which they occur naturally in the language. In most cases cross-references have been made from the inverted form and from the Library of Congress form where it otherwise varies.

Scope Notes

As in previous editions, all the new and revised headings in this edition have been provided with scope notes where such notes are required. Scope notes are intended to clarify the specialized use of a term or to distinguish between terms that might be confused. If there is any question of what a term means, the cataloger should simply consult a dictionary. There are times, however, when subject headings require a stricter limitation of a term than the common usage given in a dictionary would allow, as in the case of **Marketing**, a term in business and economics, not to be confused with **Grocery shopping**. Here a scope note is required. Some scope notes distinguish between topics and forms, such as **Encyclopedias and dictionaries** for critical and historical materials and the subdivisions –**Encyclopedias** and –**Dictionaries** under topics for items that are themselves encyclopedias or dictionaries. There are also scope notes in Sears that identify any headings in the area of literature that may be assigned to individual works of drama, fiction, poetry, etc.

Classification

The classification numbers in this edition of Sears are taken from the 14th edition of the *Abridged Dewey Decimal Classification* (2004). The numbers are intended only to direct the cataloger to a place in the DDC schedules where material on that subject is often found. They are not intended as a substitute for consulting the schedules, notes, and manual of the DDC itself when classifying a particular item. The relationship between subject headings and classification is further discussed in the Principles of the Sears List.

Usually only one number is assigned to a subject heading. In some cases, however, when a subject can be treated in more than one discipline, the subject is then given more than one number in the List. The heading **Chemical industry**, for example, is given two numbers, **338.4** and **660**, which represent possible classification numbers for materials dealing with the chemical industry from the viewpoints of economics and technology respectively. Classification numbers are not assigned to a few very general subject headings, such as **Charters, Exhibitions, Hallmarks**, and **Identification**, which cannot be classified unless a specific application is identified. The alphabetic notation of B for individual biographies is occasionally provided in addition to Dewey classification numbers for such materials. Numbers in the 810s and 840s prefixed by a C are given as optional numbers for topics in Canadian literature.

The Dewey numbers given in Sears are extended as far as is authorized by the *Abridged Dewey Decimal Classification*, which is seldom more than four places beyond the decimal point. When an item being classified has a particular form or geographic specificity, the number may be extended by adding form and geographic subdivisions from the Dewey tables. Only a few examples of built numbers are given in Sears, such as **940.53022** for **World War, 1939-1945—Pictorial Works**. No library should feel the need to extend classification numbers beyond what is practical for the size of the library's collection. For a discussion of close and broad classification and for instructions on building numbers from the Dewey tables, the cataloger should consult the introduction to the most recent edition of the *Abridged Dewey Decimal Classification and Relative Index*.

Style, Filing, Etc.

For spelling and definitions the editor has relied upon *Webster's Third New International Dictionary of the English Language, Unabridged* (1961) and the *Random House Webster's Unabridged Dictionary*, 2nd ed., revised and updated (1997). Capitalization and the forms of corporate and geographic names used as examples are based on the *Anglo-American Cataloguing Rules*, 2nd ed., 2002 revision. The filing of entries follows the *ALA Filing Rules* (1980).

Every term in the List that may be used as a subject heading is printed in boldface type whether it is a main term; a term in a USE reference; a broader, narrower, or related term; or an example in a scope note or general reference. If a term is not printed in boldface type, it is not used as a heading.

Acknowledgments

The editors wish to acknowledge with gratitude the contributions to this edition of the individual catalogers, reference librarians, and vendors of cataloging services who have offered suggestions for headings to be added to the List.

The Cataloging of Children's Materials Committee of the American Library Association has been, as ever, an important source of advice in the editorial work on the Sears List. ALA's Subject Analysis Committee, especially its subcommittee on Fiction Guidelines, has provided useful guidance in the revision of the Principles of the Sears List in this edition.

Thanks are extended to the editors and catalogers of the H.W. Wilson Company; especially to Patricia Kuhr, Editor, Subject Authority Files, for her help in formulating subject headings, and to Jan Borodkin, Assistant Editor, Bibliographic Index, for his research and editorial assistance.

Very special thanks are extended to Frances E. Corcoran, a long-time friend of the Sears List, for sharing with us her cataloging problems and solutions in a school environment. She is now the librarian at the St. Andrew's Priory Elementary School in Honolulu, where she continues to be one of the world's most thoughtful and innovative catalogers.

The classification numbers given in this edition of Sears conform to the *Abridged Dewey Decimal Classification Edition 14*, published in 2004, by OCLC. We extend special thanks to Joan S. Mitchell, editor in chief of the Dewey Decimal Classification (DDC), for providing advance information that made it possible for us to include the most recent Dewey numbers in this edition of the Sears List. The assistant editors of the DDC, Julianne Beall, Winton E. Matthews, Giles Martin, and Gregory R. New, have also been generous and helpful in this endeavor.

Every edition of the Sears List represents the work of many hands, especially those of the previous editors over the years. The contributions of the users of the List have also been invaluable. Every comment, suggestion, question, or request from a user represents an opportunity for improvement and is greatly valued.

J. Miller

Principles of the Sears List of
Subject Headings

Certain principles and practices of subject cataloging should be understood before an attempt is made to assign subject headings to library materials. The discussion that follows makes reference to the *Sears List of Subject Headings,* henceforth referred to as the Sears List or the List, but the principles are applicable to other lists of subject headings as well.

1. THE PURPOSE OF SUBJECT CATALOGING

All library work is a matter of the storage and retrieval of information, and cataloging is that aspect of library work devoted to storage. The best cataloging is simply that which facilitates the most accurate and complete retrieval. The two basic branches of cataloging are descriptive cataloging and subject cataloging. Descriptive cataloging makes possible the retrieval of materials in a library by title, author, date, etc.—in short all the searchable elements of a cataloging record except the subjects. Only by conforming to the standards for descriptive cataloging can a librarian assure the user accurate retrieval on the descriptive elements, and those standards are codified in the *Anglo-American Cataloguing Rules,* which is now in its second revised edition (commonly known as *AACR2*).

Until the second half of the nineteenth century, descriptive cataloging was the only library cataloging that was found necessary. Libraries were much smaller than they are today, and scholarly librarians then were able, with the aid of printed bibliographies, to be familiar with everything available on a given subject and guide the users to it. With the rapid growth of knowledge in many fields in the course of the nineteenth century and the resulting increase in the volume of books and other library materials, it became desirable to do a preliminary subject analysis of such works and then to represent them in the catalog in such a way that they would be retrievable by subject.

Subject cataloging deals with what a book or other library item is about, and the purpose of subject cataloging is to list under one uniform word or phrase all the materials on a given topic that a library has in its collection. A subject heading is that uniform word or phrase used in the library catalog to express a topic. The use of authorized words or phrases only, with cross-references from unauthorized synonyms, is the essence of bibliographic control in subject cataloging. The purpose of a subject authority, such as the Sears List, is to provide a basic vocabulary of authorized terms together with suggestions for useful cross-references.

The two most common types of subject authorities are the thesaurus and the subject heading list. A true thesaurus, in the realm of information science, is a comprehensive controlled vocabulary of discrete unit terms, called descriptors, arranged is such a way as to display the hierarchical and associative relationships among terms. It is usually limited to a particular realm of knowledge, as in the case of the *Art and Architecture Thesaurus.* The American national standards for thesauri are spelled out in the NISO *Guidelines for the Construction, Format, and Management of Monolingual Thesauri.* A subject heading list, such as the Sears List or the *Library of Congress Subject Headings,* is simply an alphabetical list of terms that have been established over time as warranted by the materials being cataloged. A subject heading list also indicates relationships among terms but does not attempt to establish any comprehensive hierarchies. In addition to simple descriptors, a subject heading list can include pre-coordinated strings composed of subject terms with subdivisions.

The *Library of Congress Subject Headings*, which in print now comprises five large volumes, is primarily a list of headings that have been used in the Library. Likewise *Medical Subject Headings* derives from the holdings of the National Library of Medicine. The Sears List is unique among subject heading lists in that it does not attempt to be a complete list of terms used in any single library but only a list of headings most likely to be needed in a typical small library and a skeleton or pattern for creating other headings as needed. By using the Sears List as a foundation, the cataloger in a small library can develop a local authority list that is consistent in form and comprehensive for that library. This has proven over the years to be a practical and economical solution to the cataloging needs of small libraries. In other ways, such as the use of uninverted headings only and of popular rather than technical vocabulary, the Sears List is specifically tailored to the needs of small libraries of any kind, including school libraries, small public libraries, church libraries, etc.

Because the Sears List is not a complete authority list, the cataloger using the Sears List must take an active part in developing a larger vocabulary of terms. As an aid in this process we offer the following discussion of the basic principles of subject analysis and the construction and control of subject headings.

2. DETERMINING THE SUBJECT OF THE WORK

The first and most important step in subject cataloging is to ascertain the true subject of the material being cataloged. This concept of "aboutness" should never be far from a subject cataloger's thoughts. It is a serious mistake to think of subject analysis as a matter of sorting through material and fitting it into the available categories, like sorting the mail, rather than focusing first on the material and determining what it is really about.

Many times the subject of a work is readily determined. **Hummingbirds** is obviously the subject of a book entitled *The Complete Book of Hummingbirds*. In others cases the subject is not so easy to discern, because it may be a complex one or the author may not express it in a manner clear to someone unfamiliar with the subject. The subject of a work cannot always be determined from the title alone, which is often uninformative or misleading, and undue dependence on it can result in error. A book entitled *Great Masters in Art* immediately suggests the subject **Artists**, but closer examination may reveal the book to be only about painters, not about artists in general. After reading the title page, the cataloger should examine the table of contents and skim the preface and introduction, and then, if the subject is still not clear, examine the text carefully and read parts of it, if necessary. In the case of nonbook materials, the cataloger should examine the container, the label, any accompanying guides, etc., and view or listen to the contents if possible. Only after this preliminary examination has been made is it possible to determine the subject of a work. If the meaning of technical terminology is not clearly understood, reference sources should be consulted, not only an unabridged dictionary and general encyclopedia, but specialized reference books as well.

Only when the cataloger has determined the subject content of a work and identified it with explicit words can the Sears List be used to advantage. The List is consulted to determine one of three possibilities. If the word the cataloger chose to describe the subject content of the work is an established heading in the List, then that heading should be assigned to the work. If the word the cataloger chose is a synonym or alternate form of an established heading in the List, then the cataloger forgoes the word that first came to mind in favor of the term from the List. A third possibility is that there is no heading in the List for the subject of the work at hand, in which case the cataloger must formulate the appropriate heading, add it to the library's subject authority file with its attendant references, and then assign it to the work.

Many books are about more than one subject. In that case a second or third subject heading would be necessary. Theoretically there is no limit to the number of subject entries that could be made for one work, but in practice an excess of entries is a disservice to the user of the catalog. More than three subject headings should be assigned to a single item only after careful consideration. The need for more than three may be due to the cataloger's inability to identify precisely the single broader heading that would cover all the topics in the work. Similarly, a subject heading should not be assigned for a topic that comprises less than one third of a work. The commonest practice, known as the Rule of Three, may be stated as follows: As many as three specific subject headings in a given area may be assigned to a work, but if the work treats of more than three subjects, then a broader heading is used instead and the specific headings are omitted. A work about snakes and lizards, for example, would be assigned the headings **Snakes** and **Lizards**. If the work also included material on turtles, a third heading **Turtles** would be added. But if the work discussed alligators and crocodiles as well, the only subject heading assigned would be **Reptiles**.

Subject headings are used for materials that have definite, definable subjects. There are always a few works so indefinite in their subject content that it is better not to assign a heading at all. Such a work might be a collection of materials produced by several individuals on a variety of topics or one person's random thoughts and ideas. If a cataloger cannot determine a definite subject, the reader is unlikely to find the item under a makeshift or general heading. The headings **Human behavior** and **Happiness**, for example, would be misleading when assigned to a book titled *Appreciation*, which is a personal account of the sources of the author's pleasure in life. The book has no specific subject and so it should be assigned no subject headings.

3. SPECIFIC AND DIRECT ENTRY

The principle of specific and direct entry is fundamental in modern subject cataloging. According to that rule a work is entered in the catalog directly under the most specific subject heading that accurately represents its content. This term should be neither broader nor narrower but co-extensive in scope with the subject of the work cataloged. The principle was definitively formulated by Charles A. Cutter (1837-1903) in his *Rules for a Dictionary Catalog*. Cutter wrote: "Enter a work under its subject-heading, not under the heading of a class which includes that subject." His example is: "Put Lady Cust's book on 'The Cat' under Cat, not under Zoology or Mammals, or Domestic animals; and put Garnier's 'Le Fer' under Iron, not under Metals or Metallurgy." The reason this principle has become sacred to modern cataloging is simply that there is no other way to insure uniformity. In subject cataloging uniformity means simply that all materials on a single topic are assigned the same subject heading. If the headings **Cats**, **Zoology**, **Mammals**, and **Domestic animals** were all equally correct for a book on cats, as they would be without Cutter's rule, there would be no single heading for that topic and consequently no assurance of uniformity. One cataloger could assign the heading **Cats** to Lady Cust's book, another cataloger could assign the heading **Mammals** to another book on cats, and a third cataloguer could assign the heading **Domestic animals** or **Pets** to yet another book on cats. There would then be no simple way to retrieve all the materials on cats in the library's collection.

The principle of specific entry holds that a work is always entered under a specific term rather than under a broader heading that includes the specific concept. This principle is of particular importance to the cataloguer using the Sears List, since the heading of appropriate specificity must be added if it is not already there. If, for example, a work being catalogued is about penguins, it should be entered only under the most specific term that is not narrower than the scope of the book itself, that is, **Penguins**. It should not be assigned the heading **Birds** or **Water birds**. This is true even though the heading **Penguins** does not appear in the List. When a specific subject is not found in the List, the heading for the larger group or category to which it belongs should be consulted, in this case **Birds**. There the cataloger finds a general reference that reads: "SA [See also] types of birds, e.g. **Birds of prey**; **Canaries**; etc. {to be added as needed}." The cataloger must establish the heading **Penguins** as a narrower term under the heading **Birds** and then assign it to the book on penguins. In many cases the most specific entry will be a general subject. A book entitled

Birds of the World would have the subject heading **Birds**. Even though **Birds** is a very broad term, it is the narrowest term that comprehends the subject content of that work.

Having assigned a work the most specific subject heading that is applicable, the cataloger should not then make an additional entry under a broader heading. A work with the title *Birds of the Ocean* should not be entered under both **Birds** and **Water birds** but only under **Water birds**. To eliminate this duplication, the *See also* references in the public catalog direct the user from the broader subject headings to the more specific ones. At **Birds**, for example, the reference would read: "See also **Birds of Prey; Canaries; Pelicans; Penguins; Water birds**," etc.

The principle of direct entry holds that a subject heading should stand as a separate term rather than as a subdivision under a broader heading. If the reader wants information about owls, the direct approach is to consult the catalog under the heading **Owls**, not under the broader subject **Birds** subdivided by the narrower topic **Owls**. In other words, the cataloger has entered the book directly under **Owls**, not indirectly under "Birds—Owls," or under "Birds—Birds of prey—Owls." The latter two subject strings are both specific, but they are not direct.

4. TYPES OF SUBJECT HEADINGS

There are four types of subject headings: topical headings, form headings, geographic headings, and proper names.

4. A. TOPICAL HEADINGS

Topical subject headings are simply the words or phrases for common things or concepts that represent the content of various works. In choosing the word or phrase that makes the best subject heading several things should be considered. The first and most obvious is the literary warrant, or the language of the material being cataloged. The word most commonly used in the literature is most likely the word that best represents the item cataloged. If nine out of ten books on the subject use the phrase "Gun control," there is no reason to use any word or phrase other than **Gun control** as a subject heading, so long as that phrase meets certain other criteria.

A second consideration, and one of the criteria that a subject heading should meet, is that of common usage. In so far as possible a subject heading should represent the common usage of the English language. In American libraries this means current American spelling and terminology: **Labor** not Labour; **Elevators** not Lifts. (In British libraries these choices would be reversed.) Foreign terms such as **Film noir** are not used unless they have been fully incorporated into the English language. By the same token contemporary usage gradually should replace antiquated words or phrases. The heading **Blacks**, for example, replaced Negroes as common usage changed. In time the heading **African Americans** was added to the Sears List for greater specificity, as the use of that term stabilized. What is common usage depends, in part, upon who the users of a library are. In most small libraries the popular or common word for a thing is to be preferred to the scientific or technical word, when the two are truly synonymous. For example, **Desert animals** is preferable in most small libraries to Desert fauna. In such a case the scientific term should be a *See* reference to the established term.

In order to maintain uniformity in a library catalog two things are necessary. The first is abiding by Cutter's rule of specificity, and the second is choosing a single word or phrase from among its synonyms or near-synonyms in establishing a subject heading. If **Desert animals** and Desert fauna were both allowed as established headings, the material on one subject would end up in two places. Sometimes a single word or phrase must be chosen from among several choices that do not mean exactly the same thing but are too close to be easily distinguished. In the Sears List, for example, **Regional planning** is an established heading with *See* references from County planning, Metropolitan planning, and State planning. The term chosen as the established heading is the one that is most inclusive.

Another important consideration in establishing topical subject headings is that they should be clear and unambiguous. Sometimes the most common term for a topic is not suitable as a subject heading because it is ambiguous. Civil War, for example, must be rejected in favor of **United States—History—1861-1865, Civil War**, since not all civil wars are the American Civil War. The term **Civil war** could itself become a heading, if it were needed for general materials on rebellions or internal revolutions.

When a single word has several meanings, that word can be used as a subject heading only when it is somehow rendered unambiguous. The word Depression, for example, can mean either an economic or a mental state, but as subject headings one is formulated **Depressions** and the other **Depression (Psychology)**. Stress can mean either stress on materials or stress on the mind, and the two headings are **Strength of materials** and **Stress (Psychology)**. Notice that the ambiguous word is qualified even when the other meaning is expressed in other words. Furthermore, an ambiguous term such as Feedback should be qualified, **Feedback (Psychology)**, even when the other meaning, **Feedback (Electronics)**, does not yet exist in the catalog. Whenever identical words with different meanings are used in the catalog, both require a parenthetical qualifier, which is usually either a broader term or discipline of study, as in the case of **Seals (Animals)** and **Seals (Numismatics)**.

In choosing one term as a subject heading from among several possibilities the cataloger must also think of the spelling, number, and connotations of the various forms. When variant spellings are in use, one must be selected and uniformly applied, such as **Archeology** rather than Archaeology. A decision also must be made between the singular and plural form, which will be further discussed under Grammar of Subject Headings below. Sometimes variant forms of words can have different connotations, as with Arab, Arabian, and Arabic. It may seem inconsistent to use all three forms in subject headings, but, in fact, they are used consistently in the following ways: Arab relating to the people; Arabian referring to the geographical area and to horses; and Arabic for the language, script, or literature.

4. B. FORM HEADINGS

The second kind of heading that is found in a library catalog is the form heading, which describes not the subject content of a work but its form. In other words, a form heading tells us not what a work is about but what it is. Form in this context means intellectual form of the materials rather than the physical form of the item. The physical forms of such nonbook materials as videorecordings, electronic resources, etc., are considered general material designations (GMD), a part of the descriptive cataloging, rather than subject headings.

Some form headings describe the general arrangement of the material and the purpose of the work, such as **Almanacs, Directories, Gazetteers**, and **Encyclopedias and dictionaries**. These headings are customarily assigned to individual works as well as to materials about such forms. Theoretically, at least, any form can also be a topic, since it is possible for someone to write a book about almanacs or gazetteers.

Other form headings are the names of literary forms and genres. Headings for the major literary forms, **Fiction, Poetry, Drama**, and **Essays**, are usually used as topical subject headings. As form headings they are used for collections only rather than for individual literary works. Minor literary forms, also known as genres, such as **Science fiction, Epistolary poetry**, and **Children's plays**, are much more numerous and are often assigned to individual literary works. These headings will be discussed at greater length below under Literature. The distinction between form headings and topical headings in literature can sometimes be made by using the singular form for the topical heading and the plural for the form heading. **Short story**, for example, is topical, for materials about the short story as a literary form, while **Short stories** is a form. Likewise, **Essay** is topical, while **Essays** is a form. The peculiarities of language, however, do not always permit this distinction.

4. C. GEOGRAPHIC HEADINGS

Many works in a library's collection are about geographic areas, countries, cities, etc. The appropriate subject heading for such a work is the name of the place in question. Geographic headings are the established names of individual places, from places as large as **Africa** to places as small as **Walden Pond (Mass.)**. They signify not only physical places but also political jurisdictions. These headings differ from topical subject headings in that they refer to a unique entity rather than to an abstraction or category of things.

The Sears List does not attempt to provide geographic headings, which are numerous far beyond the scope of a single volume. The geographic headings that are found in Sears, such as **United States**, **Ohio**, and **Chicago (Ill.)**, are offered only as examples. The cataloger using the Sears List must establish geographic headings as needed with the aid of standard references sources. Some suggested sources are the most current editions of *The Columbia Gazetteer of the World*; *National Geographic Atlas of the World*; *Statesman's Year-book*; *Times Atlas of the World*; and *Merriam-Webster's Geographical Dictionary*. The geographic headings and geographic subdivisions found in Sears follow the form of abbreviation for qualifying states, provinces, etc., found in Appendix B (Abbreviations) of *AACR2*.

4. D. NAMES

Still other materials in a library's collection are about individual persons, families, corporate bodies, literary works, motion pictures, etc. The appropriate heading for such material is the unique name of the entity in question. The three major types of name headings are personal names, corporate names, and uniform titles. Individual or personal name headings are usually established in the inverted form, with dates if necessary, and with *See* references from alternate forms. The heading **Clinton, Bill**, for example, would require a *See* reference from "Clinton, William Jefferson," and if the library had material about any other person called Bill Clinton, the name heading for the president would need to take the form **Clinton, Bill, 1946-** . Corporate name headings are the commonly established names of corporate bodies, such as business firms, institutions, buildings, sports teams, performing groups, etc. Materials about a corporate body, such as **Rockefeller Center** or **Fort Lauderdale International Boat Show**, are entered directly under the corporate name heading as a subject. Uniform titles are the established names of sacred scriptures, anonymous literary works, periodicals, motion pictures, radio and television programs, etc. Materials about a particular motion picture or about an anonymous literary work, for example, are entered directly under the uniform title, such as **Gone with the wind (Motion picture)** or **Beowulf**, as a subject. Materials about a literary work with a known author are entered under a name-title heading consisting of the author's name followed by the title, such as **Shakespeare, William, 1564-1616. Hamlet** for a book about Shakespeare's play.

Like geographic headings, name headings are numerous beyond the scope of the Sears List and must be established by the cataloger as needed. Suggested sources for personal and corporate names are *Who's Who*; *Who's Who in America*; *Merriam-Webster's Biographical Dictionary*; *The Dictionary of National Biography*; and the *Encyclopedia of Associations*. General encyclopedias and standard reference works limited to specific fields are also useful sources for names.

5. THE GRAMMAR OF SUBJECT HEADINGS

While many subject headings are simple terms like **Reptiles** or **Electricity**, other subjects can be very complex, in some cases involving several levels of subdivision. In order to construct subject headings consistently the cataloger should understand the grammar of subject headings.

5. A. THE FORMS OF HEADINGS

5. A. i. Single Nouns

A single noun is the ideal type of subject heading when the language supplies it. Such terms are not only the simplest in form but often the easiest to comprehend. A choice must be made between the singular and plural forms of a noun. The plural is the more common, but in practice both are used. Abstract ideas and the names of disciplines of study are usually stated in the singular, such as **Biology** or **Existentialism**. An action, such as **Editing** or **Child abuse**, is also expressed in the singular. Headings for concrete things are most commonly in the plural form, when those things can be counted, such as **Playgrounds** or **Children**. Concrete things that cannot be counted, such as **Steel** or **Milk**, obviously remain in the singular. In most cases common sense can be relied upon. In some instances both the singular and the plural of a word can be subject headings when they have two different meanings, such as **Theater** for the activity and **Theaters** for the buildings. In the case of **Arts** and **Art**, the one means the arts in general, while the other means the fine and decorative arts specifically.

5. A. ii. Compound Headings

Subject headings that consist of two nouns joined by "and" are of several types. Some headings link two things because together they form a single concept or topic, such as **Bow and arrow** or **Good and evil**; because they are so closely related they are rarely treated separately, such as **Forests and forestry** or **Publishers and publishing**; or because they are so closely synonymous they are seldom distinguished, such as **Cities and towns** or **Rugs and carpets**. Other headings that link two words with "and" stand for the relationship between the two things, such as **Church and state** or **Television and children**. Compound headings of this type should not be made without careful consideration. Often there is a better way to formulate the heading. A heading like "Medicine and religion," for example, is less accurate that the form established in Sears, which is **Medicine—Religious aspects**. (There is not likely to be material on the medical aspects of religion.) One question that arises in forming compound headings is word order. The only rule is that common usage takes precedence (no one says "Arrow and bow"), and, where there is no established common usage, alphabetic order is preferred. Whatever the order, a *See* reference should be made from either the second term or from the pair of terms reversed, as in Forestry, *See* **Forests and forestry**, or Children and television, *See* **Television and children**.

5. A. iii. Adjectives with Nouns

Often a specific concept is best expressed by a noun with an adjective, such as **Unemployment insurance** or **Buddhist art**. In the past the expression was frequently inverted (Insurance, Unemployment; Art, Buddhist). There were two possible reasons for inversion: 1) an assumption was made that the searcher would think first of the noun; or 2) the noun was placed first in order to keep all aspects of a broad subject together in an alphabetical listing, as in a card catalog. In recent years these arguments have been abandoned in favor of the direct order because users have become more and more accustomed to searching in the order of natural language. The only headings that have been retained in Sears in the inverted form are proper names, including the names of battles and massacres.

5. A. iv. Phrase Headings

Some concepts that involve two or more elements can be expressed only by more or less complex phrases. These are the least satisfactory headings, as they offer the greatest variation in wording, are often the longest, and may not be thought of readily by either the maker or the user of the catalog, but for many topics the English language seems to offer no more compact terminology. Examples are **Insects as carriers of disease** and **Violence in popular culture**.

5. B. SUBDIVISIONS

Specific entry in subject headings is achieved in two basic ways. The first, as noted above, is the creation of narrower terms as needed. The second is the use of subdivisions under an established term to designate aspects of that term, such as **Birds—Eggs** or **Food—Analysis**, or the form of the item itself, such as **Agriculture—Bibliography**. The scope of the Sears List can be expanded far beyond the actual headings printed through the use of subdivisions. Some subdivisions are applicable to only a few subjects. *Eggs*, for example, is applicable only under headings for oviparous animals. Other subdivisions, such as *Analysis*, are applicable under many subjects. Still other subdivisions, such as *Bibliography*, are applicable under nearly any heading. The Sears List does not attempt to list all possible subdivisions, but all those that are most likely to be used in a small library are included. For every subdivision included there is an instruction in the List for the use of that subdivision. Some subdivisions are also headings, such as **Bibliography**, and in such cases the instruction is given in a general reference as part of the entry for that heading. Other subdivisions, such as *Economic aspects*, are not themselves headings, and in such cases the instruction for the use of the subdivision is a free-standing general reference in the alphabetical List.

5. B. i. Topical Subdivisions

Topical subdivisions are those subdivisions that brings out the aspect of a subject or point of view presented in a particular work. A work may be a history of the subject, as in **Clothing and dress—History**; or it may deal with the philosophy of the subject, as in **Religion—Philosophy**; research in the field, as in **Oceanography—Research**; the laws about it, as in **Automobiles—Law and legislation**; or how to study and teach the subject, as in **Mathematics—Study and teaching**. The advantage of subdivisions over phrase headings for complex subjects is that uniformity can be more readily achieved with subdivisions. Once the subdivisions have been established, they can be appended to any applicable subject heading without guessing or straining the language for a suitable phrase. Subject strings with topical subdivisions can be read backwards: **Clothing and dress—History**, for example, means the history of clothing and dress, and **Oceanography—Research—Ethical aspects** means ethical aspects of research in the field of oceanography.

5. B. ii. Geographic Subdivisions

Another aspect of subjects that can be brought out in subdivisions is geographic specificity. The unit used as a subdivision may be the name of a country, state, city, or other geographic area. A topical heading with a geographic subdivision means simply that topic in a particular place. **Bridges—France**, for example, is the appropriate subject string for a work on bridges in France, and **Agriculture—Ohio** for a work on agriculture in Ohio.

Not every topical heading lends itself logically or practically to geographic subdivision. Some topics, such as **Internet addresses** or **Intuition**, are either non-physical or too abstract to have a geographic location. Other headings, such as **Pet therapy** or **Parenting**, are unlikely to be dealt with geographically, at least in works that would be found in a small library. Still other headings, such as **Exploration** or **Church history**, are not subdivided geographically because the same term is used instead as a subdivision under the geographic heading, as in **Arctic regions—Exploration** or **United States—Church history**.

Many subject headings in the Sears List are followed by the parenthetical phrase (May subdiv. geog.). In application this means that if the work in hand deals with that subject in general, only the heading itself is used; but if it deals with the subject in a particular place, the heading may be subdivided geographically. Some small libraries limit the use of geographic subdivision to countries other than the United States, since most of their material will be concerned with the United States. Furthermore, if a library prefers geographic subdivisions for subjects that are not so indicated in the List, the library should feel free to add them, provided, of course, that the heading is not itself used as a subdivision under geographic headings.

Some subjects, mostly in the fields of art and music, have general references that read: "SA [See also] art of particular countries or regions, e.g. **Greek art**." For these headings the geographic qualification is conveyed by a modifying adjective rather than by a subdivision. The Sears List historically has never distinguished between French art and Art in France (which is not necessarily French). Should a library have sufficient material to warrant such a distinction, **Art—France** could be established in addition to **French art**, which is suggested, and the art of particular countries could also be subdivided by other countries, as in **Italian art—Great Britain**. Such a decision should be based on the materials at hand and the purpose and needs of the library.

Geographic subdivisions can be either direct or indirect. The Sears List uses the direct form of subdivision, whereby topics are subdivided directly by cities, counties, metropolitan areas, etc., as in **Theater—Paris (France)** or **Hospitals—Chicago (Ill.)**. The indirect form of subdivision, used by the Library of Congress and certain other subject heading systems, interposes the name of the country or state (the larger geographic area) between the topical subject and the smaller area, as in "Theater—France—Paris" and "Hospitals—Illinois—Chicago."

5. B. iii. Chronological Subdivisions

In any catalog, large or small, there will be many works on American history. If these works are all entered under the general heading **United States—History**, the library user is required to look through many entries to find materials about any specific period of American history. Chronological subdivisions, which correspond to generally accepted periods of a country's history or to the spans of time most frequently treated in the literature, make such a search much simpler by bringing together all works on a single period of history, such as **United States—History—1945-1953**. If a chronological period has been given a name, this name is included in the heading following the dates, as in **United States—History—1600-1775, Colonial period**.

Historical periods vary from one country to another and usually correspond to major dynastic or governmental changes. The Sears List includes chronological subdivisions only for those countries about which a small library is likely to have much historical material, with the greatest number of period subdivisions under **United States, Canada, Great Britain, France, Germany**, and **Italy**, and a few subdivisions only under several other countries. Whenever there is only a small amount of material on the history of a country, it should simply be entered under the name of the country with the subdivision *History*, without a chronological subdivision. For most small libraries in North America the heading **Turkey—History** will suffice for all historical material about Turkey, even though Turkey has a very long history. If, however, a library should acquire a large amount of historical material about any such country or region, period subdivisions should be established beyond those spelled out in the Sears List. For these the cataloger may wish to consult *LC Period Subdivisions under Names of Places*.

The same chronological subdivisions that are used under a country's history may also be used under that country with the subdivision *Politics and government*. Other kinds of subjects, especially those relating to literature and the arts, may also be subdivided chronologically as appropriate, usually by century.

5. B. iv. Form Subdivisions

The most common item found in a library is an expository prose treatise on a subject. Many works, however, present their material in other forms, such as lists, tables, maps, pictures, etc. Form subdivisions specify the form an item takes. Like form headings they tell what an item is rather than what it is about. Some of the most common form subdivisions are *Bibliography*; *Catalogs*; *Dictionaries*; *Directories*; *Gazetteers*; *Handbooks, manuals, etc.*; *Indexes*; *Maps*; *Pictorial works*; *Portraits*; *Registers*; and *Statistics*.

Topical headings with form subdivisions, such as **Children's literature—Bibliography** or **Geology—Maps**, render such works retrievable by form and separate them from expository treatises. Apart from a few examples, these combinations of subject heading with form subdivision are not given in the Sears List but are to be added by the cataloger as needed. Form subdivisions are particularly valuable under headings for the large fields of knowledge that are represented by many entries in a library's catalog. In applying form subdivisions the cataloger should be guided by the character of an item itself, not by the title. Many works with titles beginning with Outline of, Handbook of, or Manual of, are in fact expository works. For example, H. G. Wells's *Outline of History* and H. J. Rose's *Handbook of Latin Literature* are lengthy, comprehensive treatises, and to use the form subdivisions that the titles suggest would be inaccurate. Other so-titled Outlines or Manuals or Handbooks may prove to be bibliographies, dictionaries, or statistics of the subject.

5. B. v. The Order of Subdivisions

At the Subject Subdivision Conference that took place at Airlie House, Virginia, in May 1991, organized by the Library of Congress, it was recommended that subdivisions follow the standard order of **[Topical]—[Geographic]—[Chronological]—[Form]**. Since that time the library community has endeavored to implement that recommendation. Only in a few subject areas, especially in the field of art, have exceptions been made. A cataloger using the Sears List can safely assume that subject strings made in the recommended order will provide the greatest uniformity. By following this standard the cataloger will know, for example, to prefer **Railroads—Rates—United States** to "Railroads—United States—Rates," and **Sports—United States—Statistics** to "Sports—Statistics—United States."

5. B. vi. Geographic Headings Subdivided by Topic

A longstanding exception to the practice of subdividing topics geographically, and one that remains apart from the Airlie House recommendation, is that of subdividing geographic headings by topics, when those topics pertain to the history, geography, or politics of a place. For works discussing the history of California, a census of Peru, the government of Italy, the boundaries of Bolivia, the population of Paris, or the climate of Alaska, the appropriate subject strings would be **California—History; Peru—Census; Italy—Politics and government; Bolivia—Boundaries; Paris (France)—Population;** and **Alaska—Climate**.

Many subdivisions, such as *Defenses* or *Race relations*, are used only under geographic headings; many subdivisions are never used under geographic headings; and others, such as *History* or *Biography*, are used under geographic headings exactly as they are under topical subjects. Specific instructions for the application of subdivisions are given at the general reference for the subdivision in the List. For example, at **Census** in the List the general reference reads: "SA [See also] names of countries, cities, etc., with the subdivision *Census* {to be added as needed}." Similar instructions appear under **Boundaries; Climate; Population;** etc. Some topics that are used as subdivisions under geographic headings are applicable to countries only. The subdivision *Foreign relations*, for example, can be used only under countries, since only countries have foreign relations. The instructions for applications are explicit. At *Foreign relations* in the List, for example, the general reference reads: "USE names of countries with the subdivision *Foreign relations*, e.g. **United States—Foreign relations** {to be added as needed}."

A list of suggested topical subdivisions that may be used under the name of any city is given in the List under **Chicago (Ill.)**; those that may be used under the name of any state are listed under **Ohio**; and those that may be used under the name of any country or region, except for *History* further subdivided chronologically, are given under **United States**. Since each country's history is unique, the period subdivisions for its history are also unique.

5. B. vii. Local Materials

If for any reason a library wishes to keep state, local, or community area materials together in the catalog, those materials may constitute an exception to the practice of geographic subdivision. All local materials are then entered under the name of the place with all topics as subdivisions. If, for example, a library in Honolulu chose this option, the headings **Public buildings—Honolulu (Hawaii)** and **Bridges—Honolulu (Hawaii)** would become **Honolulu (Hawaii)—Public buildings** and **Honolulu (Hawaii)—Bridges**. Materials with geographic specificity other than local materials would still be treated in the ordinary way, with most topics subdivided geographically.

6. SOME DIFFICULT AREAS OF APPLICATION

In many areas the application of subject headings and their appropriate subdivisions is a simple and straightforward matter. There are, however, areas in which either the complexity of the material or the vagaries of the English language create persistent problems. Even in these areas, by maintaining sound principles, following instructions carefully, and using common sense, it is possible to catalog library materials in such a way that users can find what they need. Some of these problem areas are dealt with here.

6. A. BIOGRAPHY

Discussions of biography as a form of writing are given the topical subject heading **Biography as a literary form**. Works that are themselves biographies are given either the form heading **Biography** or the form subdivision *Biography*. Such works are considered here in two groups, collective biographies and individual biographies.

6. A. i. Collective Biographies

Collective biographies are works containing biographies of more than three persons. Works consisting of biographies of three persons or fewer are treated as individual biographies and given headings for the names of the persons individually. Collective biographies not limited to any area or to any class of persons, such as *Lives of Famous Men and Women*, are simply assigned the heading **Biography**. Often collective biographies are devoted to persons of a single country or geographic area, such as *Who's Who in the Arab World*, or *Dictionary of American Biography*; or to ethnic groups, such as *Who's Who among Hispanic Americans*. For such works the appropriate subject heading is the name of the geographic area or ethnic group with the subdivision *Biography*, in this case **Arab countries—Biography; United States—Biography**; and **Hispanic Americans—Biography**. If there are many entries under any such heading, the biographical dictionaries, which list a large number of names in alphabetical order, may be separated from the works with longer articles intended for continuous reading by adding the form subdivision *Dictionaries*. The heading for such a work as *Dictionary of American Biography* or *Who's Who in America* would then be **United States—Biography—Dictionaries**.

Some collective biographies are devoted to lives of a particular class of persons, such as women, or persons of a particular occupation or profession, such as librarians. These are entered under the heading for the class of persons or occupational group with the subdivision *Biography*, such as **Women—Biography** or **Librarians—Biography**. Still other collective biographies are devoted to any or all persons connected with a particular industry, institution, or field of endeavor. For these works the appropriate heading is the heading for that industry, institution, or field with the subdivision *Biography*, such as **Computer industry—Biography**; **Catholic Church—Biography**; or **Baseball—Biography**. A subject is usually broader in scope than a single category of persons associated with that subject, and likewise **Baseball—Biography** is broader than **Baseball players—Biography** and would be more suitable for a collective biography that includes managers, owners of teams, and other persons associated with the sport.

6. A. ii. Individual Biographies

Usually the only subject heading needed for the life of an individual is the name of the person, established in the same way as an author entry. The rules for establishing names are in *AACR2*. If a work is an autobiography, the author's name is entered in the bibliographic record twice, once as the author and again as the subject. There are a few individual persons about whom much has been written other than biographical material, such as works about their writings or other activities. In such cases, subdivisions are added to the person's name to specify the various aspects treated, among them *Biography*. As examples of such persons, the Sears List includes **Jesus Christ** and **Shakespeare, William, 1564-1616**, with subdivisions appropriate to material written about them. The subdivisions listed under Shakespeare may also be used, if needed, under the name of any voluminous author. The subdivisions provided under **Presidents—United States** may also be used under the name of any president or other ruler, if applicable. The subdivisions needed will vary from one individual to another. Different topics will be applicable, for example, to the material on Martin Luther, Napoleon, and Sigmund Freud. It should be noted that this use of subdivisions represents the exceptional, not the usual, treatment. For most individual biographies the name alone is sufficient.

Occasionally a biography will include enough material about the field in which the person worked that a second subject heading is required in addition to the personal name. A life of Mary Baker Eddy, for example, may include an account of the development of Christian Science substantial enough to warrant the subject heading **Christian Science—History**. The additional subject headings should be used only when the work contains a significant amount of material about the field of endeavor in addition to the subject's personal life, not simply because the subject was prominent in that field.

It is not customary practice to categorize the subjects of individual biographies by race, sex, occupation, etc. with the subdivision *Biography*. Headings such as **African American musicians—Biography** or **Women politicians—Biography** are appropriate only to collective biographies. Some catalogers are tempted to assign such headings to individual biographies as well, but there are several compelling reasons for not doing so. The first and most obvious is that in the case of a collective biography it is the author or compiler of the work who classifies or categorizes the persons included, not the cataloger. For a book such as *Black Women Scientists in the United States*, the subject heading **African American women scientists** is applicable because the author has selected the subjects of the biographies expressly for being African Americans, women, and scientists. For a collective biography entitled *Just as I Am: Famous Men and Women with Disabilities*, the subject string **Handicapped—Biography** would be appropriate because the author has written about several handicapped persons with their handicapped condition as the common feature. It would be impertinent, however, for a cataloger to assign the subject string **Handicapped—Biography** to a biography of an individual person who happened to be handicapped, even if that condition were an important element of the person's story. In other words, three or more handicapped persons constitute the category Handicapped, but a single person can never constitute a category.

Another reason for not assigning categories of persons to individual biographies is that there is no way of controlling them. Consider the case of Maya Angelou, who is a woman, an African American, an author, a poet, a memoirist, a novelist, and a filmmaker, among other things. Given those seven categories alone, the number of subject headings that could be assigned to a biography of Maya Angelou would number in the dozens if not scores: **Women, American women, African Americans, African American women, Women authors**, etc. Unless the cataloger thought of every possible combination and made a heading for that category with the subdivision *Biography*, the catalog would be inconsistent and retrieval unreliable.

The real reason for not entering individual biographies under categories of persons is that it violates the principle of specific entry. The wisdom of Cutter's rule prevails. Any of dozens of categories would apply equally to a biography of Maya Angelou simply because none of them applies. The only heading that is neither broader nor narrower but is co-extensive in scope with the subject content of the work is the personal name heading **Angelou, Maya**. *See also* references can be made, if such references are deemed useful, from a category of persons to the names of individuals about whom the library has material. At the heading **African American women authors**, for example, one would then find any books that are really about African American women authors, followed by a reference: "See also **Angelou, Maya; McMillan, Terry; Morrison, Toni**," etc. Any inconsistencies in these *See also* references would limit retrieval but would not compromise the essential integrity of the catalog.

6. B. NATIONALITIES

An aspect of subject headings fraught with confusion is that of nationalities. Even though some headings are given national adjectives, the general rule is that the national aspects of subjects are expressed by geographic subdivisions under the topical subject headings. Headings for things that are always stationary are never given national adjectives but are instead subdivided geographically, such as **Architecture—France**. Things that are not stationary are also usually expressed as topical headings with a geographic subdivision, such as **Automobiles—Germany** or **Corporations—Japan**. When those things are replicated or transported to foreign countries, however, they are given national adjectives to express national style, ownership, or origin, and subdivided by the place where they are found, such as **German automobiles—United States** or **Japanese corporations—France**.

Headings for topics in literature and the arts are given national adjectives to express national character, such as **American literature, Spanish art**, etc. These headings may then be subdivided geographically by any place except for the country expressed in the national adjective. **American literature—Southern States** is therefore allowable, but not "Spanish art—Spain."

In the area of people, all headings for categories of persons are subdivided geographically in the Sears List with the exception of **Authors, Novelists, Dramatists**, and **Poets**, which are given national adjectives. All other categories of writers, such as **Biographers, Journalists**, etc., are subdivided geographically. A collective biography of American poets would be entered under **American poets—Biography**, but a collective biography of American composers or journalists would be given the heading **Composers—United States—Biography** or **Journalists—United States—Biography**. When a book deals with a category of persons from one country living or working in a foreign country, such as American composers in France, the book requires two subject strings rather than one, in this case **Composers—United States** and **Americans—France**.

6. C. LITERATURE

The field of literature presents special difficulties in cataloging because it includes two distinct types of material. The first consists of works about literature, and such works are assigned topical subject headings for whatever they are about. The second consists of literary works themselves, and those works are assigned form headings to describe what the item is rather than what it is about.

6. C. i. Works about Literature

The subject headings for works about the various literary forms are the headings for those forms, such as **Drama, Fiction**, and **Poetry**. A work about poetry is simply given the heading **Poetry**. Topical subdivisions are added to such headings as needed. A work about the history of poetry or about the criticism of poetry would be entered under **Poetry—History and criticism**. A work about the technique of writing plays would be entered under **Drama—Technique**. Form subdivisions may also be used under these headings to indicate the form the work takes, such as **Drama—Dictionaries** or **Poetry—Indexes**. In addition to the major forms of literature there are also lesser genres, which are subsets of the major literary forms, such as **Science fiction** or **Epic poetry**. These headings are also applicable to works about literature, with topical and form subdivisions added as needed.

Literary works are commonly studied and written about according to categories characterized by nationality, language, religions, etc. The primary consideration in discussing literature is nationality, as in **American literature, Mexican literature**, and **Brazilian literature**. These topics are never dealt with as subsets of **English literature, Spanish literature**, or **Portuguese literature** simply because they are written in the English, Spanish, and Portuguese languages. Nationality takes precedence over language. Only a few national literatures are included in the List, and others are to be added as needed. Works about the major literary forms of national literatures are entered under the direct phrase, such as **Italian poetry** or **Russian fiction**, and again specific aspects or forms are expressed by subdivisions, as in **Italian poetry—History and criticism** or **Russian fiction—Dictionaries**. The subdivisions that appear under **English literature** may be used under any national literature, and headings for the major literary forms for any national literature may be formulated by substituting its national name for the word English.

Apart from national literatures there are also literatures characterized by areas larger than countries, such as **Latin American literature** or **African literature**; by languages not limited to or identified with a single country, such as **Latin literature** or **Arabic literature**; or by religions, such as **Catholic literature** or **Buddhist literature**. All these kinds of literature are treated in the same way as national literatures. Where a national literature is written in two or more prominent languages, the language is identified in parentheses after the name of the literature for material specifically limited to literature in that language, such as **Canadian literature (French)**. Materials about the literatures of minority groups within a country, written in the predominant language of that country's literature, are identified by subdivisions indicating the author group under the name of the literature, such as **American literature—African American authors**. Materials about the literatures of indigenous minority groups written in their own language are given the name of the language, such as **Navajo literature**.

6. C. ii. Literary Works

Items that are literary works themselves are of two types: collections of several authors, or anthologies, and works by a single author, or individual literary works. Literary anthologies are given a heading for the most specific literary form that includes every item in the anthology. Very general anthologies are given broad headings, such as **Literature—Collections; Poetry—Collections;** or **Drama—Collections**. Anthologies of national literatures and the forms of national literatures are given the headings for those literatures or forms with the subdivision *Collections*, such as **American literature—Collections** and **Italian poetry—Collections**. Headings for minor literary genres, such as **Science fiction** or **Pastoral poetry**, are usually assigned to anthologies without any subdivision.

Traditionally the literary works of individual authors receive no subject headings. Literary works are best known by author and title, and readers usually want a specific novel or play, or poetry by a specific poet—material that can be located in the catalog by the author and title entries. Headings describing the major literary forms (such as **Drama**, **Fiction**, and **Poetry**) and the headings for the major forms of a national literature (such as **Irish drama**, **Russian fiction**, and **Italian poetry**) are never assigned to an individual work or to a collection by a single author. It would be counterproductive, for example, to assign the heading **Fiction** to every novel in a library's collection, since the numbers of records with the same heading would be impracticably large. Furthermore, the form and national origin of a work are expressed in the classification.

In recent years, however, many libraries have felt the need for access by genre to individual works of imaginative literature. In the Sears List the headings for minor literary forms and genres—such as **Ballads**, **Fables**, **Fairy tales**, **Horror fiction**, **Science fiction**, etc.—are identified in the scope notes as applicable to individual works as well as to collections and materials about the topic. If there is no scope note indicating that a literature heading can be applied to an individual work, it can be assumed that it is not intended to be so applied. This policy is in accordance with the *Guidelines on Subject Access to Individual Works of Fiction, Drama, etc.* prepared by the Subcommittee on Subject Access to Individual Works of Fiction, Drama, etc., of the ALA Subject Analysis Committee (ALA, 1990). It varies from the usage of the Library of Congress *Subject Cataloging Manual* in that it allows form and genre access to certain kinds of literary works that are often requested in libraries. Genre headings with national or linguistic adjectives, such as **Australian science fiction** or **Latin epic poetry**, are applicable to collections but are never assigned to individual works. If they were assigned to individual works, since all authors fall into the purview of one nationality or another, there would be nothing remaining under the heading **Science fiction** or **Epic poetry** but collections of international scope. Likewise, the cataloger is discouraged from adding the qualifier "juvenile" to the genre headings. The subdivision —*Juvenile literature* may be added to genre headings in libraries where it is necessary to distinguish juvenile materials from adult materials, that is, in libraries not devoted exclusively or primarily to children's materials, or where juvenile material is not indicated in the shelf number. No other subdivision is ever applicable to genre headings, as applied to individual works.

The cataloger is also discouraged, except in the most unusual cases, from devising new genre terms. The *Guidelines on Subject Access* of the ALA aim to limit the number of genre terms in order to bring like material together, while the proliferation of genres and sub-genres would only scatter like material and do the user a disservice. As stated on page 4 of the *Guidelines*, "Genre terms are determined by convention, as set by the bibliographic community of publishers, booksellers, librarians, and readers." It is only by conforming to these conventions that the application of genre headings to individual works is really useful.

In some libraries subject access is provided to works of literature by using any applicable subject heading from the List with the subdivision *Fiction*, *Drama*, or *Poetry*. Hence a collection of stories all set in Los Angeles could be assigned the heading **Los Angeles (Calif.)—Fiction**; a collections of plays in which the main characters are all nurses could be assigned the heading **Nurses—Drama**; and a volume of poems by several authors all on the theme of baseball could be assigned the heading **Baseball—Poetry**. Personal and corporate names can always be added to the List in order to be used with the subdivisions *Fiction*, *Drama*, and *Poetry* to provide subject access to literary collections that deal with real persons or corporate entities.

Providing the same kind of access by setting, character, or theme to individual works of fiction, drama, or poetry is more problematic. For the collection of stories set in Los Angeles, the appropriate level of specificity can be determined by finding what is common to all the stories. The plays about nurses may be about a variety of nurses, one elderly, one Hispanic American, one male, etc., but their being nurses is what they have in common. The topic **Nurses**, then, is of equal specificity with the collection itself. In individual stories or plays, however, the characters and settings are unique. For a novel in which the main character is an Italian American woman who is anorexic and a Buddhist, drives a truck for a living, and runs for political office, the number of applicable subject headings could run to a dozen or more. These headings are all less specific than the unique character and the unique situation, and to assign any of them is to violate the principle of specificity and abandon uniformity in cataloging. To assign headings for those topics also violates the principle of "aboutness." The novel is not really about truck drivers or Buddhists or political candidates at all.

It is the case, nonetheless, that some libraries, for the purpose of readers' advisory or for curriculum enhancement, require the application of topical subjects and geographic headings to individual works of fiction, drama, and poetry. In this endeavor they leave behind the logic of subject analysis and embrace a kind of tagging or labeling that is approximate and pragmatic and not subject to hard rules. Even without the principles of specificity and uniformity, however, there are still some guidelines that may be useful in the application of topical subject and geographic headings to individual literary works:

1)   Use only terms that come readily to mind. Only if a novel is extensively set in the milieu of the motion picture industry, for example, would the heading **Motion picture industry—Fiction** be suitable. The less central a topic is to the novel the less useful it will be to the user, who, for whatever purpose, wants fiction on that topic.

2)   Use only terms that are specific enough to limit retrieval in a meaningful way. Headings such as **Family life—Fiction** or **Popular culture—Fiction** are dubiously useful, since they would apply equally to innumerable novels.

3)   Use only discrete terms, not terms that combine two or more concepts. Use two headings, such as **Hispanic Americans—Fiction** and **Nurses—Fiction** instead of **Hispanic American nurses—Fiction**. The user who is interested in novels about Hispanic Americans may also want the novel about Hispanic American nurses, and there is no way that *See also* references from broader terms in fiction to narrower terms in fiction can function in a catalog.

4)   Apply headings for categories of persons only when the main character or several principal characters are representative of that category in a more than incidental way. If the main character of a novel is a lawyer, but the novel is mostly concerned with his love life and very little with his occupation, the heading **Lawyers—Fiction** would be a disservice to the user.

5)   Use geographic headings only when the setting of a novel is prominent and central to the work. The history and geography of New Mexico, for example, are central in Willa Cather's *Death Comes for the Archbishop*, while in many novels the setting is incidental. All novels, after all, are set somewhere, but many novels have very little in the way of local color.

6)   In applying geographic headings, use only place names of intermediate specificity. In libraries in the United States this would mean using only the names of states or regions and those of a few very large cities. **United States—Fiction** would clearly be useless, because most American novels are set in the United States. At the same times the names of towns and villages would be useless to most users, except for the towns and villages of their own state. For novels set in foreign countries, the name of the country is to be preferred, except for a few large cities, such as London, Paris, or Moscow.

7)   If both a topical subject and a geographic location are central to a work, they should be expressed separately rather than as a subject string. A novel about organized crime in Florida in which both the topic and the setting are central, for example, should be given the subjects **Organized crime—Fiction** and **Florida—Fiction**. A person looking for novels set in Florida may want this book and might not find it when Florida is appended to another subject.

8)   Historical novels should be given headings only for the broadest historical periods under a place name, usually a century. Specifying narrower historical periods would only scatter the material and frustrate retrieval. The only exception to this rule would be for a few distinct periods or events that have stimulated a great number of literary works, such as **United States—History—1861-1865, Civil War—Fiction**.

9)   Do not hesitate to catalog an individual work of fiction, drama, or poetry without topical or geographic headings. Many literary works do not lend themselves to this kind of treatment, and to go beyond the obvious will only lead users to items that do not satisfy their needs.

In applying topical and geographic headings to individual works of fiction, drama, and poetry, the most important rule is to remember or imagine the needs of the users in a particular library setting, either readers who want novels, plays, etc., with a particular theme or setting, or teachers who need fictional materials on curriculum topics.

6. C. iii. Themes in Literature

Some libraries have a significant amount of material about topics, locales, or themes in imaginative literature. The appropriate headings for such material is simply "Topic in literature," according to the pattern found in the Sears List under **Literature—Themes**, such as **Dogs in literature, Ohio in literature**, etc.   Headings of this type are for critical discussions only, not for literary works. Materials about the depiction of historical persons in drama, fiction, or poetry are entered under the person's name with the subdivision *In literature*, such as **Napoleon I, Emperor of the French, 1769-1821—In literature**. Materials about the depiction of a particular war in drama, fiction, or poetry are entered under the heading for the war with the subdivision *Literature and the war*, such as **World War, 1939-1945—Literature and the war**.

6. D. WARS AND EVENTS

Catalogers are often called upon to formulate headings as needed for wars and current events, when those wars or events generate books and other library materials. Wars fought between two or more nations are given a name, followed by a date or dates, as appropriate, such as **War of 1812; Israel-Arab War, 1967; World War, 1939-1945**; etc. Civil wars, insurrections, and invasions are entered under the history of the country involved (following the dates, as with other historical periods), such as **United States—History—1861-1865, Civil War; Cuba—History—1961, Invasion**; etc.

Events of short duration, including battles, are dealt with as isolated topics rather than as periods in a country's history. Events that have names are given a heading for the name, followed by the place, and then by the date, such as **Tiananmen Square Incident, Beijing (China), 1989**, and **World Trade Center Bombing, New York (N.Y.), 1993**. Battles are entered under the name of the battle, but in the inverted form, with the place of the battle qualified as needed, such as **Hastings (East Sussex, England), Battle of, 1066**, and **Gettysburg (Pa.), Battle of, 1863**. Recurring events, such as games, festivals, etc., are given the recurring name, followed by the date, with the place in parentheses, if the place changes, such as **Olympic Games, 1996 (Atlanta, Ga.)**. Unnamed events, such as individual riots or tornadoes, are entered under the kind of event subdivided by the place of the event, such as **Riots—Washington (D.C.)** or **Tornadoes—Moore (Okla.).**

6. E. NONBOOK MATERIALS

The assignment of subject headings for electronic media and for audiovisual and special instructional materials should follow the same principles that are applied to books. The uniform application of the same headings to book and nonbook materials alike is especially important in an integrated catalog, which brings all materials on one subject together regardless of format. Because nonbook materials often concentrate on very small aspects of larger subjects, the cataloger may not find in the List the specific heading that should be used. In such instances the cataloger should be generous in adding new subjects as needed. There are many form and genre headings that apply equally to nonbook materials and to books about such materials, such as **Biographical films**; **Comedy television programs**; and **Science fiction comic books, strips, etc.**

Topical subject headings assigned to nonbook materials should not include form subdivisions to describe physical format, such as motion pictures, slides, sound recordings, etc. For libraries using integrated catalogs, *AACR2* provides the option of using general material designations (GMD) at the end of the title proper to alert users to the general class of material to which an item belongs. Additional information on this aspect of descriptive cataloging can be found in the most recent edition of *AACR2* and in the ALA's *Guidelines for Bibliographic Description of Interactive Multimedia*.

7. CLASSIFICATION AND SUBJECT HEADINGS

The cataloger should recognize a fundamental difference between classification and subject headings for the library catalog. In any system of classification that determines the arrangement of items on the shelves, a work can obviously have only one class number and stand in only one place, but in a catalog the same work can be entered, if necessary, under as many different points of entry as there are distinct subjects in the work (usually, however, not more than three). Classification is used to gather in one numerical place on the shelf works that give similar treatment to a subject. Subject headings gather in one alphabetical place in a catalog all treatments of a subject regardless of shelf location.

Another difference between classification and subject cataloging is that classification is frequently less precise than the subject entries for the catalog. Material on floriculture in general as well as on specific kinds of garden flowers are classed together in 635.9 in the Dewey Decimal Classification. A book on flower gardening, one on perennial gardening, and one on rose gardening will all three be classified in one number, while in the catalog each book will have its own specific subject heading: **Flower gardening**, **Perennials**, or **Roses**.

Library materials are classified by discipline, not by subject. A single subject may be dealt with in many disciplines. The Dewey classification numbers given with a heading in the Sears List are intended only to direct the cataloger to the disciplines where that subject is most likely to be treated. They are not meant to be absolute or cover all possibilities and should be used together with the Dewey Decimal Classification schedules. The cataloger must examine the work at hand and determine the discipline in which the author is writing. On the basis of that decision the cataloger classifies the work, not by the subject of the work alone.

8. MAINTAINING A CATALOG

The library catalog is a vital function at the very center of a library, and as such it is always growing and changing to reflect the growing collection and to meet the changing needs of the users. It is a challenge to the cataloger to add new records, revise existing records, and make all the appropriate references, and at the same time maintain the integrity of the catalog.

8. A. ADDING NEW HEADINGS

When a cataloger has determined what an item to be cataloged is about and formulated that concept into words, the next step is to find the subject heading that expresses that concept. The first thing to be determined is whether or not there is already an existing heading in the List for that concept. If, for example, there is a book on lawsuits, the cataloger may think of the terms Lawsuits, Suing, and Suits. Upon consulting the List it becomes clear that those words are not headings but references to the established heading **Litigation. Litigation** is slightly broader than Suing, but is more suitable as a subject heading because it includes the matter of defending oneself against lawsuits. In this case the cataloger enters the book into the catalog under the heading **Litigation**. A new heading is not necessary.

At other times the appropriate heading for a book is not a new heading but a new combination of an established heading and a subdivision. If, for example, there is a book on the use and abuse of alcohol on college campuses, the cataloger may first think of the term Drunkenness. In the Sears List Drunkenness is an unpreferred term and a reference to two established headings: **Alcoholism** and **Temperance**. The scope note at **Temperance** reads: "Use for materials on the virtue of temperance or on the temperance movement." The book is not about drunkenness in relation to either vice and virtue or the temperance movement, so that heading can be eliminated. Neither is the book really about alcoholism, but at the heading **Alcoholism**, there is a general reference that reads: "SA [See also] classes of persons with the subdivision *Alcohol use*, e.g. **Employees—Alcohol use; Youth—Alcohol use**; etc., {to be added as needed}." At this point the cataloger realizes that the appropriate Sears subject heading for the book at hand would be **College students—Alcohol use. College students** is already an established heading in the List, but it could be added if it were not.

The cataloger should always keep in mind that it is not only appropriate but essential that types of things and examples of things not found in the List be established as headings and added to the List locally as needed. If there is a book on gloves, for example, and there is no heading in the Sears List for Gloves, the cataloger thinks of the concept or category of thing that would include gloves. Clothing comes to mind. At the heading **Clothing and dress** in the List there is a general reference: "SA [See also] types of clothing articles and accessories {to be added as needed}." The cataloger then establishes the heading **Gloves** and enters the book into the catalog under **Gloves**. It would be inappropriate to enter the book under the heading **Clothing and dress** simply because **Clothing and dress** is in the List and **Gloves** is not. It would mean that a user looking in the catalog under Gloves would find nothing. The general references in the List should reinforce the point that the List does not aim at completeness and must be expanded. Even where there is no general reference, narrower terms for types of things and examples and instances of things must be added as needed.

At times it is nearly impossible to determine what broader concept or category a new subject might be included under. This should not deter the cataloger from establishing any heading that is needed. Take, for example, the case of a book on thumb sucking, a common phenomenon among small children. The nearest terms in the List might be **Child psychology**, **Child rearing**, or **Human behavior**, but they are none too near. Nowhere is there a general reference instructing the cataloger to add headings for common childhood phenomena, and still the only appropriate heading for the book would be **Thumb sucking**. Here the intrepid cataloger, thinking how useless the headings **Child psychology**, **Child rearing**, or **Human behavior** would be on such a book, adds the heading **Thumb sucking** to the List and enters the book into the catalog under that heading.

There are resources that a cataloger can turn to for help in establishing subject headings that are not in the List. Other available databases and catalogs in which books are listed by subject can always be consulted, such as the Standard Catalog Series; *American Book Publishing Record*; *Subject Guide to Books in Print*; and the *National Union Catalog: Books*. Periodical indexes, such as *Readers' Guide to Periodical Literature* or *Applied Science & Technology Index,* are especially helpful in establishing headings for current events and very new topics and trends. The index and the schedules of the *Dewey Decimal Classification* are a useful source of subject terminology as well as a way of seeing a topic in its relation to other topics. The Library of Congress issues lists of new subject headings in *Library of Congress Subject Headings Weekly Lists* on its World Wide Web site and includes new subject headings of current interest in its quarterly *Cataloging Service Bulletin.* Library of Congress cataloging information, including subject headings, emanating from its Cataloging in Publication (CIP) program, is available in various online databases and is also printed on the title page verso of many books.

8. B. REVISING SUBJECT HEADINGS

Because the English language does not stand still, neither do subject headings. It would be impossible today for a catalog to maintain the headings Negroes or Dinosauria, since common usage has relegated these terms to history. The prevailing thinking about the form of subject headings also changes, and as a result whole groups of headings need to be revised. All the inverted headings in the Sears List, for example, were eventually revised to the uninverted form, such as **Health insurance** for "Insurance, Health." With each new edition of the Sears List a library should consult the List of Canceled and Replacement Headings in the front of the volume and revise its catalog accordingly. Any headings created locally based on the pattern set by a Sears heading, and strings consisting of a Sears heading and a subdivision, must also be revised if that heading is revised in Sears. If, for example, a library had added the headings "Insurance, Title" and "Insurance, Health—Law and legislation," those headings would need to be revised to **Title insurance** and **Health insurance—Law and legislation**.

How a library revises its catalog depends upon the kind of catalog. In a card catalog the subjects are physically erased and retyped, either on all the cards on which they appear or on the subject entry cards alone. If in a card catalog replacement of a term is desirable but the number of bibliographic records to be revised is prohibitive, a history note can be used instead. A history note is simply a card at both the old and the new form indicating the change. When, for example, the heading "Insurance, Health" is changed in Sears to **Health insurance**, the two cards would read as follows:

> **Insurance, Health**. For materials issued after [date] consult the following heading:
> **Health insurance**

and

> **Health insurance**. For materials issued before [date] consult the following heading:
> **Insurance, Health**.

In an online catalog the revision process depends upon the software employed in the catalog. If the software provides global update capability, the revision of many bibliographic records at once is simple. If they must be revised one by one, the process is still immensely easier than revising cards in a card catalog. There is also the option, provided the software allows for it, of displaying a history note in an online catalog in lieu of revising the bibliographic records.

8. C. MAKING REFERENCES

Once an item has been assigned a subject heading, either a heading found in the List or one added as needed, attention must be directed to insuring that the reader who is searching for this material will not fail to find it because of insufficient references to the proper heading. References direct the user from terms not used as headings to the term that is used, and from broader and related terms to the term chosen to represent a given subject. The Sears List uses the symbols found in most thesauri to point out the relationships among the terms found in the List and to assist the cataloger in establishing appropriate references in the public catalog based upon these relationships. There are three types of references: *See* references, *See also* references, and general references.

8. C. i. *See* References

In the public catalog *See* references direct the user from unpreferred or unestablished terms and phrases to the preferred or established terms that are used as subject headings. Under most headings in the Sears List, following the UF [Used for] label, is one or more suggested terms for *See* references in the public catalog. A cataloger may want to use some or all of them as references, and many catalogers add other *See* references they deem useful. In theory there is no limit to the number of *See* references to a particular term, but in practice there may well be, especially in a card catalog. The references will be more useful if the cataloger considers materials from the reader's point of view. The reader's profile depends on age, background, education, occupation, and geographical location, and takes into account the type of library, such as school, public, university, or special.

The following are some types of unpreferred terms that might be used as *See* references in a catalog:

1) Synonyms or terms so nearly synonymous that they would cover the same material. For example, **Instructional materials centers** requires a reference from School media centers.

2) The second part of compound headings. For example, **Antique and vintage motorcycles** requires a reference from Vintage motorcycles.

3) The inverted form of a heading, either an adjective-noun combination or a phrase heading, especially if the word brought forward is not also the broader term. For example, **Theory of knowledge** requires a reference from "Knowledge, Theory of," there being no heading Knowledge.

4) Variant spellings. For example, **Archeology** requires a reference from Archaeology.

5) The opposite of a term, when it is included in the meaning of a term without being specifically mentioned. For example, **School attendance** requires a reference from Absence from school and from Absenteeism (Schools), and **Equality** requires a reference from Inequality.

6) The former forms of headings revised to reflect common usage, when the older term still has any currency. For example, Negroes remains as a reference to **Blacks** and to **African Americans**, but Dinosauria is no longer retained as a reference to **Dinosaurs**.

The first time a heading from the List is assigned to a work in the collection, the terms in the UF field in the List are entered, at the cataloger's discretion, as *See* references in the public catalog. When the same heading is subsequently assigned to other works, the references are already in place. When the cataloger adds a heading to the authority file as needed, all the appropriate *See* references are entered as well the first time the heading is used. For the heading **College students—Alcohol use**, for example, suitable *See* references might be Campus drinking, College drinking, and Drinking on campus.

8. C. ii. *See also* References

In the public catalog *See also* references direct the user from one established heading to another established heading. Under most headings in the Sears List, following the BT [Broader term] label, is a term that is broader in scope than the heading itself. As a rule, a term has only one broader term, unless it is an example or aspect of two or more things. The broader term serves two functions in the List. The first is to aid the cataloger in finding the best term to assign to a work. If the first term the cataloger thinks of to describe the contents of the work does not cover all aspects of work, the broader term may be the more appropriate heading for that work. The second function is to indicate where *See also* references should be made in the public catalog. A *See also* reference is made from a broader term to a narrower term, but not from a narrower term to a broader term. Take, for example, the broader term **Clothing and dress** on the heading **Gloves**. When the heading **Gloves** is assigned for the first time to a work in the collection, a reference is made at **Clothing and dress** "See also **Gloves**." If **Clothing and dress** has never been assigned to a work in the collection, it is entered in the catalog for the sake of the reference, and the reference "See also **Gloves**" is made. The point is that the user who is interested in works on clothing and dress in general may also be interested in works limited to gloves. The book on gloves need not be entered under both **Clothing and dress** and **Gloves**, but only under the appropriately specific heading, because the *See also* reference will direct the user from the broader to the narrower term. If the book on gloves were entered under both **Clothing and dress** and **Gloves**, the catalog would first list the book under the heading **Clothing and dress** and then direct the user to look as well under **Gloves** only to find the same book.

Under many headings in the Sears List, following the RT [Related term] label, one or more terms are listed that represent similar or associated subjects. These related terms are neither broader nor narrower than the main term but roughly equal in specificity. The term **Pardon**, for example, is related to **Amnesty**. The cataloger or the user may easily look first to one term only to realize that the other is the more precise term for the material being cataloged or being sought in the catalog. Related terms are reciprocal. When the term **Pardon** is assigned for the first time to a work in the collection, a reference is made in the catalog at **Amnesty** "See also **Pardon**." The reciprocal reference at **Pardon** "See also **Amnesty**" is also made, but only if **Amnesty** has also been assigned to a work in the collection. A reference is never made to a heading until there is a work entered under that heading in the collection, and if the only work entered under a heading is lost or discarded the references to that heading must be deleted. References to headings under which there is no material in the collection are called blind references and are to be avoided.

8. C. iii. General References

Under many headings in the Sears List, following the SA [See also] label, there is what is called a general reference, not to a specific heading but to a general group or category of things that may be established as headings as needed. In the example of **Clothing and dress** given above, the general reference is to "types of clothing articles and accessories, {to be added as needed}." This reference is addressed to the cataloger as a reminder not to be limited to the types of clothing and dress items given as examples in the List—**Hats, Hosiery, Shoes**, etc.—but to create a heading for any other clothing item, such as **Gloves**, when the need arises.

A second function of general references is to provide instruction in the application of subdivisions. Only a few subdivisions are universally applicable. All others apply only to certain types of headings. For every subdivision provided in the List, except those of unique application, there is a general reference spelling out the use of that subdivision. If the subdivision is also a heading, the general reference is given under the heading. **Folklore**, for example, is both a heading and a subdivision. Under the heading **Folklore** the general reference reads: "SA [See also] topics as themes in folklore with the subdivision *Folklore*, e.g.

Plants—Folklore; names of ethnic or occupational groups with the subdivision *Folklore*, e.g. **Inuit—Folklore**; and names of individual legendary characters, e.g. **Bunyan, Paul (Legendary character)** {to be added as needed}." When the subdivision is not also a heading, there is a free-standing general reference in the alphabetical List with instructions on the use of that subdivision. For example, at *Industrial applications*, which is not a heading but only a subdivision, there is a general reference that reads: "USE types of scientific phenomena, chemicals, plants, and crops with the subdivision *Industrial applications*, e.g. **Ultrasonic waves—Industrial applications** {to be added as needed}."

Some libraries also display general references in the public catalog. Rather than make a specific *See also* reference from the broader term to every narrower term, they adapt the general reference in the List to address it to the user of the catalog. At **Flowers**, for example, rather than a specific *See also* reference to **Day lilies, Orchids, Peonies, Poppies, Roses, Tulips,** and **Violets,** there would be a general reference "See also types of flowers." The drawback of this procedure and the reason it is not recommended is that the user who wants to see all the books on specific flower types would have to think of every type of flower and look in dozens of places in the catalog. Many online catalogs are now able to provide the user with an expanded display of all the narrower terms under **Flowers** that have been used in the catalog.

8. D. RECORDING HEADINGS AND REFERENCES

The cataloger should keep a record of all the subject headings used in the catalog and all the references made to and from them. This local authority file may be kept on cards or on a computer. Some catalogers are tempted to forgo this process and merely consult the catalog whenever there is a question of previous practice. Without a local authority file, however, there can be no consistency in the cataloging. It is not possible to consult the catalog at the heading **Teachers—Ethics**, for example, and find what *See also* references were made to that term from any broader or related terms or what *See* references were made from unpreferred terms. Since **Teachers—Ethics** is not in the Sears List but was added as needed, consulting the List is not the answer. When a book appears on the ethics of psychologists, the cataloger will create **Psychologists—Ethics**, but without knowing what references were made to the heading **Teachers—Ethics**, there is no way the cataloger can create similar and consistent references for the new term. Likewise, if there is only one book entered under **Teachers—Ethics**, and if that book is lost or discarded, without a local authority file there would be no way of knowing what to delete in order to avoid blind references.

Many libraries today do little original cataloging but instead get their cataloging records from outside sources, either from computerized cooperative cataloging utilities or from vendors, often the same companies that sell them their books and other library materials. This procurement of cataloging from outside sources can save libraries a great deal of money, but it does not mean that there is no work for the cataloger in the library. Someone must order the cataloging, specifying to the vendor the particular needs of the library. If a library is devoted largely or entirely to children's materials, for example, a librarian will need to specify that the library does not want the subdivision *Juvenile literature* on every subject heading. A library using Sears subject headings will need to apprise the vendor of that fact. When the cataloging records arrive in the library, only a cataloger can check them to be sure they are what was ordered. And lastly, only a cataloger can made the appropriate references in the local catalog, tailored to that library's particular collection, which make the records useful to the users.

9. CATALOGING IN THE TWENTY-FIRST CENTURY

It is useful to view modern cataloging practice in an historical perspective. In the nineteenth century, as libraries grew and cataloging became more thorough, it was clear that some form of cooperation among libraries was desirable. For many years the distribution of printed library cards was the principal method of cooperative cataloging. Later computerized utilities replaced printed cards. From the beginning it was clear that without principles and standards guaranteeing uniformity, cooperative cataloging would be impossible. In the very first volume of the American Library Association's *Library Journal* (1876-77) there are several lengthy discussions of cooperative cataloging, including an article on the topic by Melvil Dewey. It was out of these discussions and the voluminous correspondence that ensued that the modern standards of cataloging developed, both the rules for descriptive cataloging and Cutter's *Rules for a Dictionary Catalog*. These rules are not arbitrary but are firmly grounded in logic. They have stood unchallenged for nearly a hundred years because they have served to facilitate accurate and comprehensive retrieval in the modern library.

The world of libraries in the twenty-first century is certain to be quite different from what it has been heretofore. More information will be available in machine-readable form, and ready access to the Internet will no doubt change the way many users seek and find information. Traditional methods of storage and retrieval in libraries will likely be supplemented by new methods engendered by artificial intelligence. The challenge of catalogers in the future is to approach every new technology and theory knowledgeably and fearlessly, judge them against what we know are the soundest principles, and embrace the good and reject the spurious, always keeping in mind the ultimate goal of meeting, even anticipating, the changing needs of the library users.

10. BIBLIOGRAPHY

American Library Association. Filing Committee. *ALA Filing Rules*. Chicago: American Library Association, 1980.

American Library Association. Subject Analysis Committee. *Guidelines on Subject Access to Individual Works of Fiction, Drama, etc.* 2nd ed. Chicago: American Library Association, 2000.

American Library Association. Interactive Multimedia Guidelines Review Task Force. *Guidelines for Bibliographic Description of Interactive Multimedia*. Chicago: American Library Association, 1994.

Anglo-American Cataloguing Rules. 2nd ed., 2002 Revision. Chicago: American Library Association, 2002.

Chan, Lois Mai. *Cataloging and Classification: an Introduction*. 2nd ed. New York: McGraw-Hill, 1994.

Chan, Lois Mai, Phyllis A. Richmond, and Elaine Svenonius, eds. *Theory of Subject Analysis: a Sourcebook*. Englewood, Colo.: Libraries Unlimited, 1985. [Contains excerpts from Charles A. Cutter's *Rules for a Dictionary Catalog*]

Dewey, Melvil. *Abridged Dewey Decimal Classification and Relative Index*. 14th ed. Edited by Joan S. Mitchell, et al. Dublin, Ohio: OCLC, 2004.

Foskett, A. C. *The Subject Approach to Information*. 5th ed. London: Library Association Pub., 1996.

Hoffman, Herbert H. *Small Library Cataloging*. 3rd ed. Lanham, Md.: Scarecrow Press, 2002.

Intner, Sheila S., and Jean Riddle Weihs. *Standard Cataloging for School and Public Libraries*. 3rd ed. Englewood, Colo.: Libraries Unlimited, 2001.

Library Literature & Information Science. New York: The H. W. Wilson Co., 1921-

Library of Congress. Cataloging Policy and Support Office. *Subject Cataloging Manual: Subject Headings*. 5th ed. Washington, D.C.: Library of Congress, 1996-

Library of Congress. Office for Subject Cataloging Policy. *LC Period Subdivisions under Names of Places*. 5th ed. Washington, D.C.: Library of Congress, 1994.

Lighthall, Lynne, ed. *Sears List of Subject Headings: Canadian Companion*. 6th ed. New York: The H. W. Wilson Co., 2001.

Taylor, Arlene G. *The Organization of Information*. 2nd ed. Westport, Conn.: Libraries Unlimited, 2003.

Taylor, Arlene G. *Wynar's Introduction to Cataloging and Classification*. 9th ed. Englewood, Colo.: Libraries Unlimited, 2000.

Zuiderveld, Sharon, ed. *Cataloging Correctly for Kids: An Introduction to the Tools*. 3rd ed. Chicago: American Library Association, 1998.

Headings to be Added by the Cataloger

Sears is not intended to be a complete list of subject headings but only a list of many of the most commonly used headings and a pattern for creating other headings as needed. Types of things and names of individual things must always be added when they are not already provided in the List. The general references in the List explicitly instruct the cataloger to create headings in areas where the need for such additions is most obvious (such as under **Flowers**, where the general reference reads "SA [See also] types of flowers, e.g. **Roses** {to be added as needed}"). Where there is no general reference the same instruction is implicit. A further discussion of adding headings can be found in the Principles of the Sears List. Some of the additional headings most likely to be needed are the following:

Topical Subjects
1. Types of common things—foods, tools, sports, musical instruments, etc.
2. Types of plants and animals—fruits, flowers, birds, fishes, etc.
3. Types of chemicals and minerals
4. Types of enterprises and industries
5. Types of diseases
6. Names of organs and regions of the body
7. Names of languages, language groups, and national literatures
8. Names of ethnic groups and nationalities
9. Names of wars, battles, treaties, etc.

Geographic Headings
1. Names of political jurisdictions—countries, states, cities, provinces, etc.
2. Groups of states, groups of countries, alliances, etc.
3. Names of geographic features—regions, mountain ranges, island groups, individual mountains, individual islands, rivers, river valleys, oceans, lakes, etc.

Names
1. Personal names—individual persons and families
2. Corporate names—associations, societies, government bodies, religious denominations, business firms, performing groups, colleges, libraries, hospitals, hotels, ships, etc.
3. Uniform titles—anonymous literary works, newspapers, periodicals, sacred scriptures, motion pictures, etc.

The Key Headings on the following page can be used as a guide in applying subdivisions to any similar headings. Subdivisions not provided for in the Sears List may also be established and used as needed.

"Key" Headings

Certain headings in the Sears List have been chosen to serve as examples, at which the subdivisions particularly applicable to certain categories of headings are given. If a subdivision is provided under the "key" heading, it may also be used under any heading of that type.

Authors: **Shakespeare, William, 1564-1616** (to illustrate the subdivisions that may be used under any voluminous author, and in some cases other individual persons)

Ethnic groups: **Native Americans** (to illustrate the subdivisions that may be used under any ethnic group or native people)

Languages: **English language** (to illustrate the subdivisions that may be used under any language or group of languages)

Literature: **English literature** (to illustrate the subdivisions that may be used under any literature)

Places: **United States**
       Ohio
       Chicago (Ill.)
(to illustrate the subdivisions—except for historical periods—that may be used under any country, state, or city)

Public figures: **Presidents—United States** (to illustrate the subdivisions that may be used under the presidents, prime ministers, governors, and rulers of any country, state, etc., and in some cases under the names of individual presidents, prime ministers, etc.)

Wars: **World War, 1939-1945** (to illustrate the subdivisions that may be used under any war, and in some cases individual battles)

List of Canceled and Replacement Headings

CANCELED HEADINGS	REPLACEMENT HEADINGS
American periodicals	Periodicals—United States
Australian aborigines	Aboriginal Australians
Chicago—Description	Chicago—Description and travel
Database management—Computer programs	Database management—Computer software
Greece—Description	Greece—Description and travel
Greece—Description—0-323	Greece—Description and travel—0-323
Ohio—Description	Ohio—Description and travel
Rome—Description	Rome—Description and travel
Rome (Italy)—Description	Rome (Italy)—Description and travel
Soviet Union—History—1953-1985	Soviet Union—History—1953-1991
Soviet Union—History—1985-1991	Soviet Union—History 1953-1991
United States—Description	United States—Description and travel
Utilities (Computer programs)	Utilities (Computer software)

Revisions of Specifically Canadian Interest

The following revisions apply to headings found in the Sixth edition of **Sears List of Subject Headings—Canadian Companion**, edited by Lynne Lighthall (H. W. Wilson, 2001).

CANCELED HEADINGS	REPLACEMENT HEADINGS
Canada--Description	Canada—Description and travel
Manitoba—Description	Manitoba—Description and travel
Newfoundland	Newfoundland and Labrador
Newfoundland—History	Newfoundland and Labrador—History
Newfoundland—History—0-1855	Newfoundland and Labrador—History—0-1855
Newfoundland—History—19th century	Newfoundland and Labrador—History—19th century
Newfoundland—History—1855-1934	Newfoundland and Labrador—History—1855-1934
Newfoundland—History—20th century	Newfoundland and Labrador—History—20th century
Newfoundland—History—1934-1949	Newfoundland and Labrador—History—1934-1949
Newfoundland—History—1949-	Newfoundland and Labrador—History—1949-
Newfoundland—House of Assembly	Newfoundland and Labrador—House of Assembly
Newfoundland—Politics and government	Newfoundland and Labrador—Politic and government
Newfoundland—History—21st century	Newfoundland and Labrador—History—21st century
Vancouver (B.C.)—Description	Vancouver (B.C.)—Description and travel

The Use of Subdivisions in the Sears List

To allow for a standardized formulation of many complex subjects, there are a large number of topical and form subdivisions that may be used under a variety of subjects as needed. There are provisions and examples for more than five hundred subdivisions in the Sears List. The List of Subdivisions found on the following pages is meant for handy reference only. For each of the subdivisions provided for in Sears there is also a general reference in the alphabetical List with specific instructions as to what types of headings that subdivision can be used under.

SUBDIVISIONS OF BROAD APPLICATION

Some subdivisions are of very broad application and can be used under nearly any subject heading. The following are examples of two general references for such subdivisions—one for a topical subdivision, *Computer simulation*, which is also a heading, and one for a form subdivision, *Interactive multimedia*, which is only a subdivision:

Computer simulation
SA subjects with the subdivision *Computer simulation*, e.g. **Psychology—Computer simulation** [to be added as needed]

Interactive multimedia
USE subjects with the subdivision *Interactive multimedia*, e.g. **Geology—Interactive multimedia** [to be added as needed]

SUBDIVISIONS OF LIMITED APPLICATION

Some subdivisions are of limited application and can be used only under certain categories of subject heading. The following are examples of two general references for such subdivisions—one for a topical subdivision, *Satellites*, which is also a heading, and one for a form subdivision, *Facsimiles*, which is only a subdivision:

Satellites
SA names of planets with the subdivision *Satellites*, e.g. **Mars (Planet)—Satellites** [to be added as needed]

Facsimiles
USE types of printed or written materials, documents, etc., with the subdivision *Facsimiles*, e.g. **Autographs—Facsimiles** [to be added as needed]

List of Subdivisions Provided for in the Sears List

The following is a list of every subdivision for which there is a specific provision in the Sears List. This list is meant for handy reference only. For instructions on the use of a particular subdivision, see the entry for that subdivision in the main body of the alphabetical List. The following list is not exhaustive. It does not, for example, contain geographic or chronological subdivisions, which should be established by the cataloger as needed. Further topical and form subdivisions may also be required in libraries that contain specialized material, and they too should be established as needed and used consistently.

Accidents
Accounting
Accreditation
Adaptations
Administration
Aerial operations
African American authors
Agriculture
Air conditioning
Alcohol use
Allusions
Alphabet
Amphibious operations
Analysis
Anatomy
Anecdotes
Anniversaries
Antiquities
Apologetic works
Appointments and retirements
Appropriations and expenditures
Archives
Armed forces
Armistices
Army
Art and the war
Art collections
Assassination
Atlases
Atrocities
Attitudes
Audiences
Audiovisual aids
Auditing
Autographs
Authorship
Automation
Awards
Battlefields

Behavior
Biblical teaching
Bio-bibliography
Biography
Black authors
Blockades
Book reviews
Books and reading
Boundaries
Brakes
Breeding
Buildings
Calendars
Campaigns
Captivities
Care
Cartoons and caricatures
Case studies
Catalogs
Catechisms
Catholic Church
Causes
Censorship
Census
Centennial celebrations, etc.
Chaplains
Characters
Charities
Charts, diagrams, etc.
Chemical warfare
Children
Christian missions
Chronology
Church history
Citizen participation
Civil rights
Civilian relief
Civilization
Claims

Classification
Cleaning
Clergy
Climate
Clothing
Coaching
Collaborationists
Collectibles
Collection and preservation
Collections
Collectors and collecting
Colonies
Color
Comic books, strips, etc.
Commentaries
Commerce
Communication systems
Comparative studies
Comparison
Competitions
Composition
Composition and exercises
Computer networks
Computer software
Computer simulation
Computer-assisted instruction
Concordances
Conduct of life
Conference proceedings
Conferences
Conscientious objectors
Conservation and restoration
Control
Controversial literature
Conversation and phrase books
Correspondence
Corrupt practices
Cost effectiveness
Costs
Counseling of
Courts and courtiers
Creeds
Cross-cultural studies
Curricula
Customs and practices
Data processing
Databases
Death
Death and burial
Defenses
Demobilization
Dental care
Deregulation
Description and travel
Desertions

Design
Design and construction
Designs and plans
Destruction and pillage
Dialects
Diaries
Dictionaries
Diet therapy
Diplomatic history
Directories
Discography
Diseases
Diseases and pests
Doctrines
Documentation
Draft resisters
Drama
Dramatic production
Drug testing
Drug therapy
Drug use
Drying
Dwellings
Early works to 1800
Earthquake effects
Ecology
Economic aspects
Economic conditions
Editing
Education
Education and the war
Eggs
Election
Employees
Employment
Encyclopedias
Endowments
Engineering and construction
Entrance examinations
Entrance requirements
Environmental aspects
Equipment and supplies
Errors of usage
Estimates
Ethical aspects
Ethics
Ethnic identity
Ethnic relations
Ethnobiology
Ethnobotany
Ethnozoology
Etymology
Evacuation of civilians
Evaluation
Evolution

Examinations
Exhibitions
Experiments
Exploration
Exploring expeditions
Facsimiles
Faculty
Family
Fiction
Filmography
Finance
Finishing
Fires and fire prevention
First editions
Flight
Folklore
Food
Forced repatriation
Forecasting
Foreign countries
Foreign economic relations
Foreign influences
Foreign opinion
Foreign relations
Foreign words and phrases
Forgeries
Friends and associates
Fuel consumption
Funeral customs and rites
Gazetteers
Genealogy
Genetic aspects
Geographical distribution
Geography
Geology
Gold discoveries
Government
Government ownership
Government policy
Government relations
Governments in exile
Grammar
Grooming
Growth
Guidebooks
Habitations
Handbooks, manuals, etc.
Health and hygiene
Health aspects
Heating and ventilation
Hispanic American authors
Historical geography
Historiography
History
History and criticism

History of doctrines
Home care
Homes
Homonyms
Housing
Humor
Identification
Identity
Idioms
Illustrations
Immigration and emigration
Impeachment
In art
Inaugural addresses
Inauguration
Indexes
Industrial applications
Industries
Infinitive
Influence
Information resources
Information services
In literature
In-service training
Insignia
Inspection
Institutional care
Intellectual life
Interactive multimedia
International cooperation
Internet resources
Interviews
Jargon
Juvenile drama
Juvenile fiction
Juvenile literature
Juvenile poetry
Kings and rulers
Kinship
Knowledge
Labeling
Laboratory manuals
Labor productivity
Language
Languages
Law and legislation
Legal status, laws, etc.
Legends
Library resources
Licenses
Life cycles
Life skills guides
Lighting
Lists
Literary collections

Literature and the war
Liturgy
Local history
Localisms
Maintenance and repair
Malpractice
Management
Manpower
Manuscripts
Maps
Marketing
Marks
Material culture
Materials
Mathematical models
Mathematics
Measurement
Medals, badges, decorations, etc.
Medical care
Medical examinations
Meditations
Memorizing
Mental health
Mergers
Messages
Methodology
Mexican American authors
Microbiology
Migration
Military history
Military intelligence
Military life
Militia
Miscellanea
Missing in action
Missions
Models
Monuments
Moral conditions
Mortality
Motion pictures and the war
Motors
Museums
Name
Names
Naval history
Naval operations
Navy
Nazi persecution
Nests
Noise
Nomenclature
Nomenclature (Popular)
Nomination

Nursing
Nutrition
Obituaries
Occupied territories
Ordnance
Officers
Officials and employees
Origin
Outlines, syllabi, etc.
Packaging
Painting
Parachute troops
Paralysis
Parasites
Parodies, imitations, etc.
Parts of speech
Patients
Patterns
Peace
Pensions
Periodicals
Persecutions
Personal finance
Personal narratives
Personnel management
Philosophy
Physical therapy
Physiological aspects
Physiological effect
Physiology
Pictorial works
Piloting
Planning
Poetry
Political activity
Political aspects
Politics and government
Population
Portraits
Posters
Practice
Prayers
Preservation
Press coverage
Press relations
Prevention
Prices
Prisoners and prisons
Problems, exercises, etc.
Production standards
Programmed instruction
Pronunciation
Prophecies
Protection

Protest movements
Provincialisms
Psychological aspects
Psychology
Public opinion
Publishing
Purchasing
Quality control
Queens
Quotations
Race identity
Race relations
Rates
Rating
Reading materials
Recruiting
Recruiting, enlistment, etc.
Recycling
Refugees
Regimental histories
Registers
Rehabilitation
Relations with Congress
Religion
Religious aspects
Religious life
Relocation
Remedial teaching
Remodeling
Repairing
Reparations
Research
Reservations
Resignation
Reviews
Rhyme
Riots
Rites and ceremonies
Romances
Rural conditions
Safety devices
Safety measures
Safety regulations
Salaries, wages, etc.
Sanitation
Satellites
Scholarships
Secret service
Security measures
Segregation
Services for
Sexual behavior
Signaling
Slang

Social aspects
Social conditions
Social life and customs
Societies
Songs
Sources
Specifications
Spelling
Staff
Stage history
Standards
Statistics
Storage
Stories
Stories, plots, etc.
Strategic aspects
Study and teaching
Study guides
Succession
Suffrage
Suicide
Supply and demand
Surgery
Surveys
Synonyms and antonyms
Tables
Tank warfare
Taxation
Technique
Technological innovations
Telephone directories
Terminology
Terms and phrases
Territorial expansion
Territorial questions
Territories and possessions
Testing
Textbooks
Texts
Theater and the war
Therapeutic use
Thermodynamics
Tombs
Tournaments
Toxicology
Trademarks
Training
Transplantation
Transportation
Travel
Treaties
Tropical conditions
Tropics
Tuning

LIST OF SUBDIVISIONS PROVIDED FOR IN THE SEARS LIST

Underground movements
Uniforms
Usage
Vaccination
Vocational guidance
War use

War work
Wars
Waste disposal
Weight
Women authors
Wounds and injuries

Symbols Used

UF = Used for

SA = See also

BT = Broader term

NT = Narrower term

RT = Related term

[Former heading] = Term that was once used as a heading and is no longer

(May subdiv. geog.) = Heading that may be subdivided by name of place

Sears List of Subject Headings

3-D photography
  USE **Three dimensional photogra-**
      phy
4-H clubs **630.6**
  UF Four-H clubs
  BT **Agriculture—Societies**
      Agriculture—Study and teach-
      ing
      Boys' clubs
      Girls' clubs
4th of July
  USE **Fourth of July**
100 years' war
  USE **Hundred Years' War, 1339-**
      1453
Abacus **513.028**
  BT **Calculators**
Abandoned children (May subdiv. geog.)
      362.73
  UF Exposed children
  BT **Child welfare**
      Children
  RT **Orphans**
Abandoned towns
  USE **Extinct cities**
      Ghost towns
Abandonment of family
  USE **Desertion and nonsupport**
Abbeys (May subdiv. geog.) **271; 726**
  SA names of individual abbeys [to
      be added as needed]
  BT **Church architecture**
      Monasteries
  NT **Westminster Abbey**
  RT **Cathedrals**
Abbreviations **411**
  UF Contractions
      Symbols
  BT **Writing**
  NT **Acronyms**
      Code names
  RT **Ciphers**
      Shorthand
      Signs and symbols

ABCs
  USE **Alphabet**
Abduction
  USE **Kidnapping**
Abduction of humans by aliens
  USE **Alien abduction**
Abilities
  USE **Ability**
Ability **153.9**
  UF Abilities
      Aptitude
      Skill
      Skills
      Talent
      Talents
  SA types of ability [to be added as
      needed]
  NT **Creative ability**
      Executive ability
      Leadership
      Mathematical ability
      Musical ability
  RT **Success**
Ability grouping in education **371.2**
  UF Grouping by ability
  BT **Education**
      Educational psychology
      Grading and marking (Educa-
      tion)
  NT **Nongraded schools**
Ability—Testing **153.9; 371.26**
  UF Aptitude testing
  BT **Educational tests and measure-**
      ments
      Intelligence tests
      Psychological tests
ABMs
  USE **Antimissile missiles**
Abnormal children
  USE **Exceptional children**
      Handicapped children
Abnormal growth
  USE **Growth disorders**

Abnormal psychology   616.89

Use for systematic descriptions of mental disorders. Materials on clinical aspects of mental disorders, including therapy, are entered under **Psychiatry.** Popular materials and materials on regional or social aspects of mental disorders are entered under **Mental illness.**

UF   Mental diseases
      Pathological psychology
      Psychology, Pathological
      Psychopathology
      Psychopathy
BT   **Mind and body**
      Nervous system
NT   **Codependency**
      Compulsive behavior
      Depression (Psychology)
      Eating disorders
      Hallucinations and illusions
      Mental illness
      Mental retardation
      Multiple personality
      Neuroses
      Panic disorders
      Personality disorders
      Psychosomatic medicine
      Self-mutilation
RT   **Criminal psychology**
      Mental health
      Psychiatry
      Psychoanalysis

Abnormalities, Human
USE   **Birth defects**
       Growth disorders

Abolition of capital punishment
USE   **Capital punishment**

Abolition of slavery
USE   **Abolitionists**
       Slavery
       Slaves—Emancipation

Abolitionists (May subdiv. geog.)   326; 920

UF   Abolition of slavery
      Antislavery
BT   **Reformers**
RT   **Slavery**
      Slaves—Emancipation

Abominable snowman
USE   **Yeti**

Aboriginal Australians   305.89

UF   Australian aborigines *[Former heading]*

BT   **Australians**
      Native peoples

Aborigines
USE   **Native peoples**

Abortion (May subdiv. geog.)   618.8

UF   Induced abortion
      Termination of pregnancy

Abortion—Ethical aspects   179.7

UF   Abortion—Moral and religious aspects
BT   **Ethics**
RT   **Pro-choice movement**
      Pro-life movement

Abortion—Law and legislation (May subdiv. geog.)   344; 363.46

BT   **Law**
      Legislation

Abortion—Moral and religious aspects
USE   **Abortion—Ethical aspects**
       Abortion—Religious aspects

Abortion—Religious aspects   205

May be further subdivided by religion or sect.

UF   Abortion—Moral and religious aspects
RT   **Pro-choice movement**
      Pro-life movement

Abortion—Religious aspects—Catholic Church   241

Abortion rights movement
USE   **Pro-choice movement**

Abrasives   553.6

BT   **Ceramics**

Absence from school
USE   **School attendance**

Absenteeism (Labor)   331.25; 658.3

UF   Employee absenteeism
      Labor absenteeism
BT   **Hours of labor**
      Personnel management
RT   **Employee morale**

Absenteeism (Schools)
USE   **School attendance**

Abstinence
USE   **Fasting**
       Temperance

Abstinence, Sexual
USE   **Sexual abstinence**

Abstract art (May subdiv. geog.)   709.04; 759.06

UF   Abstract painting
      Geometric art

Abstract art—*Continued*
    Nonobjective art
  BT **Art**
Abstract painting
  USE **Abstract art**
Abuse of animals
  USE **Animal welfare**
Abuse of children
  USE **Child abuse**
Abuse of medications
  USE **Medication abuse**
Abuse of medicines
  USE **Medication abuse**
Abuse of persons
  USE **Offenses against the person**
Abuse of the elderly
  USE **Elderly abuse**
Abuse of wives
  USE **Wife abuse**
Abuse, Verbal
  USE **Invective**
Abused aged
  USE **Elderly abuse**
Abused children
  USE **Child abuse**
Abused wives
  USE **Abused women**
        Wife abuse
Abused women   **362.82**
  UF Abused wives
        Battered wives
        Battered women
  BT **Victims of crimes**
      Women
  RT **Wife abuse**
Academic achievement (May subdiv.
  geog.)   **370.1; 371.2**
  UF Academic failure
        Achievement, Academic
        Educational achievement
        Scholastic achievement
        Student achievement
  BT **Success**
  NT **Achievement tests**
Academic advising
  USE **Educational counseling**
Academic degrees   **378.2**
  UF College degrees
        Degrees, Academic
        Doctors' degrees
        Honorary degrees
        University degrees

  BT **Colleges and universities**
Academic dishonesty
  USE **Cheating (Education)**
Academic dissertations
  USE **Dissertations**
Academic failure
  USE **Academic achievement**
Academic freedom (May subdiv. geog.)
      371.1; 378.1
    Use for materials on the freedom of teach-
  ers and students to teach, discuss, or investi-
  gate controversial subjects without penalty or
  restraint from officials, governments, or orga-
  nized groups.
  UF Educational freedom
        Freedom, Academic
        Freedom of teaching
        Teaching, Freedom of
  BT **Intellectual freedom**
      Toleration
Academic libraries (May subdiv. geog.)
      027.7
  UF College and university libraries
        College libraries
        University libraries
  BT **Libraries**
Accelerated reading
  USE **Speed reading**
Accident insurance   **368.38**
  UF Insurance, Accident
  BT **Casualty insurance**
  NT **Workers' compensation**
Accidents (May subdiv. geog.)   **363.1**
  UF Emergencies
        Injuries
        Wrecks
  SA types of accidents, e.g. **Railroad
        accidents;** subjects with the
        subdivision *Accidents,* e.g.
        **Chemical industry—Acci-
        dents; Nuclear power
        plants—Accidents;** etc.; and
        groups and classes of persons,
        animals, organs of the body,
        and plants and crops with the
        subdivision *Wounds and inju-
        ries,* e.g. **Horses—Wounds
        and injuries; Foot—Wounds
        and injuries** [to be added as
        needed]
  NT **Aircraft accidents**
      Explosions
      Fires

Accidents—*Continued*
>> Home accidents
>> Industrial accidents
>> Poisons and poisoning
>> Railroad accidents
>> Shipwrecks
>> Space vehicle accidents
>> Traffic accidents
>> Wounds and injuries
> RT **Disasters**
>> **First aid**

Accidents—Prevention   363.1; 658.3
> UF   Prevention of accidents
>> Safety measures
> SA   subjects with the subdivision *Safety devices* or *Safety measures,* e.g. **Railroads—Safety devices; Radiation—Safety measures;** etc. [to be added as needed]
> NT   **Aeronautics—Safety measures**
>> **Radiation—Safety measures**
>> **Railroads—Safety devices**
>> **Safety education**
>> **Safety regulations**
>> **Water safety**
> RT   **Safety devices**

Acclimatization
> USE   **Adaptation (Biology)**
>> **Environmental influence on humans**

Accompaniment, Musical
> USE   **Musical accompaniment**

Accountability
> USE   **Liability (Law)**
>> **Responsibility**

Accountants   657.092; 920
> UF   Bookkeepers
>> Certified public accountants
> RT   **Accounting**

Accounting (May subdiv. geog.)   657
> UF   Financial accounting
> SA   types of industries, professions, and organizations with the subdivision *Accounting* [to be added as needed]
> BT   **Business**
>> **Business education**
>> **Business mathematics**
> NT   **Corporations—Accounting**
>> **Cost accounting**

> RT   **Accountants**
>> **Auditing**
>> **Bookkeeping**

Accounting machines
> USE   **Calculators**

Accounts, Collecting of
> USE   **Collecting of accounts**

Accreditation
> USE   types of hospitals and service institutions, types of educational institutions, and names of individual institutions with the subdivision *Accreditation,* e.g. **Colleges and universities—Accreditation;** and subjects with the subdivision *Study and teaching,* for accreditation of programs of study in those subjects, e.g. **Mathematics—Study and teaching** [to be added as needed]

Accreditation (Education)
> USE   **Schools—Accreditation**

Acculturation (May subdiv. geog.)   303.48
> UF   Culture contact
> BT   **Anthropology**
>> **Civilization**
>> **Culture**
>> **Ethnology**
> NT   **Ethnic relations**
>> **Multicultural education**
>> **Race relations**
>> **Socialization**
> RT   **East and West**

Achievement, Academic
> USE   **Academic achievement**

Achievement motivation   153.8
> UF   Performance motivation
> BT   **Educational psychology**
>> **Motivation (Psychology)**
>> **Performance**

Achievement tests (May subdiv. geog.)   371.26
> UF   Scholastic achievement tests
>> School achievement tests
> BT   **Academic achievement**
>> **Educational tests and measurements**

4

Acid precipitation
USE **Acid rain**
Acid rain 363.738; 628.5
UF Acid precipitation
BT **Rain**
Water pollution
Acids 546; 661
SA types of acids [to be added as needed]
BT **Chemicals**
Chemistry
NT **Carbolic acid**
Acne 616.5
UF Blackheads (Acne)
Pimples (Acne)
BT **Skin—Diseases**
ACOAs
USE **Adult children of alcoholics**
Acoustics
USE **Architectural acoustics**
Hearing
Music—Acoustics and physics
Sound
Acquaintance rape
USE **Date rape**
Acquired immune deficiency syndrome
USE **AIDS (Disease)**
Acquisitions, Corporate
USE **Corporate mergers and acquisitions**
Acquisitions (Libraries)
USE **Libraries—Acquisitions**
Acrobats and acrobatics 791.3; 796.47
SA types of acrobatic activities, e.g.
Tumbling [to be added as needed]
BT **Circus**
NT **Tumbling**
RT **Gymnastics**
Acronyms 411
UF English language—Acronyms
Initialisms
BT **Abbreviations**
Code names
Acting 791.4; 792
Use for materials on the art and technique of acting in any medium (stage, television, etc.) and on acting as a profession. Materials limited to the presentation of plays are entered under **Amateur theater** or **Theater—Production and direction.**
UF Dramatic art
Stage

BT **Drama**
Public speaking
NT **Commedia dell'arte**
Mime
Pageants
Pantomimes
RT **Actors**
Amateur theater
Drama in education
Theater
Acting—Costume
USE **Costume**
Actions and defenses
USE **Litigation**
Activities curriculum
USE **Creative activities**
Activity schools
USE **Education—Experimental methods**
Actors (May subdiv. geog.) 791.4; 792; 920
Use for materials on several persons of the acting profession, whether male or female. Materials on several female actors that emphasize their identity as women are entered under **Actresses.** Materials on several male actors that emphasize their identity as men are entered under **Male actors.**
UF Actors and actresses
Motion picture actors and actresses
Television actors
SA names of individual actors [to be added as needed]
BT **Entertainers**
NT **Actors—United States**
Actresses
African American actors
Black actors
Comedians
Male actors
Stunt performers
RT **Acting**
Actors and actresses
USE **Actors**
Actors, Black
USE **Black actors**
Actors—United States 791.4; 792; 920
UF American actors
American actors and actresses
BT **Actors**

5

Actresses (May subdiv. geog.)   **791.4;**
   792; 920
   Use for materials on several female actors
   that emphasize their identity as women. Gen-
   eral materials on persons of the acting profes-
   sion, whether male or female, are entered un-
   der **Actors.**
   UF   Female actors
        Women actors
   BT   **Actors**
Acupressure   615.8
   UF   Finger pressure therapy
        Myotherapy
   BT   **Alternative medicine**
        Massage
   RT   **Acupuncture**
Acupuncture   615.8
   BT   **Alternative medicine**
   RT   **Acupressure**
Adages
   USE   **Proverbs**
Adaptability (Psychology)
   USE   **Adjustment (Psychology)**
Adaptation (Biology)   578.4; 581.4;
   591.4
   UF   Acclimatization
   BT   **Biology**
        Ecology
        Genetics
        Variation (Biology)
   NT   **Environmental influence on**
        humans
        Stress (Physiology)
Adaptation (Psychology)
   USE   **Adjustment (Psychology)**
Adaptations
   USE   **Film adaptations**
        Television adaptations
        and   names of authors, titles of
        anonymous literary works,
        types of literature, and types
        of musical compositions with
        the subdivision *Adaptations,*
        for individual works, collec-
        tions, or criticism and inter-
        pretation of literary, cinemat-
        ic, video, or television adapta-
        tions, e.g., **Shakespeare, Wil-**
        liam, 1564-1616—Adapta-
        tions; Beowulf—Adaptations;
        Arthurian romances—Adap-
        tations; etc. [to be added as
        needed]

Addiction
   USE   types of addiction, e.g. **Alcohol-**
        ism; Drug abuse; Exercise
        addiction; etc. [to be added
        as needed]
Addiction to alcohol
   USE   **Alcoholism**
Addiction to drugs
   USE   **Drug abuse**
Addiction to exercise
   USE   **Exercise addiction**
Addiction to gambling
   USE   **Compulsive gambling**
Addiction to nicotine
   USE   **Tobacco habit**
Addiction to tobacco
   USE   **Tobacco habit**
Addiction to work
   USE   **Workaholism**
Addictive behavior
   USE   **Compulsive behavior**
Addicts
   USE   **Drug addicts**
Adding machines
   USE   **Calculators**
Additives, Food
   USE   **Food additives**
Addresses
   USE   **Lectures and lecturing**
        Speeches
Adhesives   620.1; 668; 691
   SA   types of adhesives [to be added
        as needed]
   BT   **Materials**
   NT   **Cement**
        Glue
        Mortar
Adjustment (Psychology)   155.2
   UF   Adaptability (Psychology)
        Adaptation (Psychology)
        Coping behavior
        Maladjustment (Psychology)
   BT   **Psychology**
Adjustment, Social
   USE   **Social adjustment**
Administration
   USE   **Civil service**
        Management
        Public administration
        and   types of institutions in the
        sphere of health, education,

Administration—*Continued*

and social services, and names of individual institutions with the subdivision *Administration,* e.g. **Libraries—Administration; Schools—Administration;** etc.; types of management, e.g. **Office management;** types of industries, types of industrial plants and processes, and names of individual corporate bodies, with the subdivision *Management,* e.g. **Information systems—Management;** and names of countries, cities, etc., with the subdivision *Politics and government,* e.g. **United States—Politics and government** [to be added as needed]

Administration of criminal justice (May subdiv. geog.) **353.4**

UF   Criminal justice, Administration of

BT   **Administration of justice**
      Criminal law

NT   **Amnesty**
      Clemency
      Corrections
      Crime
      Law enforcement
      Pardon
      Parole
      Police
      Prisons
      Punishment

Administration of justice (May subdiv. geog.) **347; 353.4**

UF   Justice, Administration of

BT   **Law**

NT   **Administration of criminal justice**
      Due process of law
      Governmental investigations
      Impeachments

RT   **Courts**

Administrative ability

USE   **Executive ability**

Administrative agencies (May subdiv. geog.) **351**

Use for materials on governmental bodies, such as boards, commissions, departments,

etc., responsible for implementing and administering legislation.

UF   Administrative agencies—Law and legislation
      Executive agencies
      Government agencies
      Regulatory agencies

SA   names of administrative agencies [to be added as needed]

BT   **Administrative law**
      Public administration

NT   **Executive departments**

Administrative agencies—Law and legislation

USE   **Administrative agencies**

Administrative agencies—Reorganization (May subdiv. geog.) **351**

UF   Executive departments—Reorganization
      Executive reorganization
      Government reorganization
      Reorganization of administrative agencies

Administrative agencies—Reorganization—Ohio 352.2

UF   Ohio—Executive departments—Reorganization

Administrative agencies—Reorganization—United States 352.2

UF   United States—Executive departments—Reorganization

Administrative law (May subdiv. geog.) **342**

BT   **Law**

NT   **Administrative agencies**
      Civil service
      Local government
      Ombudsman

RT   **Constitutional law**
      Public administration

Administrators and executors

USE   **Executors and administrators**

Admirals 359.0092; 920

BT   **Military personnel**
      Navies

Admissions applications

USE   **College applications**

Admissions essays

USE   **College applications**

Adolescence 155.5; 305.235

Use for materials on the process or the state of growing to maturity. Materials on the time

Adolescence—*Continued*

of life between thirteen and twenty-five years, and on people in this general age range, are entered under **Youth.** Materials limited to teen youth are entered under **Teenagers.** Materials limited to people in the general age range of eighteen through twenty-five years are entered under **Young men** or **Young women.**

  UF Teen age
      Teenagers—Development
  BT **Age**
  RT **Puberty**
      Youth

Adolescence—Psychology
  USE **Adolescent psychology**

Adolescent fathers
  USE **Teenage fathers**

Adolescent mothers
  USE **Teenage mothers**

Adolescent pregnancy
  USE **Teenage pregnancy**

Adolescent prostitution
  USE **Juvenile prostitution**

Adolescent psychiatry   616.89
  UF Teenagers—Psychiatry
  BT **Psychiatry**

Adolescent psychology   155.5
  UF Adolescence—Psychology
      Behavior of teenagers
      Teenage behavior
      Teenagers—Psychology
  BT **Psychology**

Adolescents
  USE **Teenagers**

Adopted children   306.87; 362.82
  BT **Adoptees**
      Children
  RT **Adoption**
      Orphans

Adoptees   346.01; 362.73

Use for materials on anyone formally adopted as a dependent.

  UF Adult adoptees
  NT **Adopted children**
  RT **Adoption**
      Birthparents

Adoption (May subdiv. geog.)   346.01; 362.734
  UF Child placing
      Children—Adoption
      Children—Placing out
  BT **Parent-child relationship**
  NT **Interracial adoption**
  RT **Adopted children**
      Adoptees
      Foster home care

Adoption—Corrupt practices   364.1
  UF Black market children
      Sale of infants
      Selling of infants
  BT **Criminal law**

Adult adoptees
  USE **Adoptees**

Adult child abuse victims   362.76
  UF Adult survivors of child abuse
      Adults abused as children
      Child abuse survivors
      Grown-up abused children
  BT **Victims of crimes**
  NT **Adult child sexual abuse victims**
  RT **Child abuse**

Adult child sexual abuse victims   362.76
  UF Adult survivors of child sexual abuse
      Adults sexually abused as children
  BT **Adult child abuse victims**
  RT **Child sexual abuse**

Adult children of alcoholics   362.292
  UF ACOAs
      Alcoholic parents
  BT **Children of alcoholics**
  RT **Alcoholics**

Adult education (May subdiv. geog.)   374
  UF Education of adults
      Lifelong education
  BT **Education**
      Higher education
      Secondary education
      University extension
  NT **Agricultural extension work**
      Prisoners—Education
  RT **Continuing education**
      Evening and continuation schools

Adult fiction
  USE **Erotic fiction**

Adult films
  USE **Erotic films**

Adult survivors of child abuse
    USE **Adult child abuse victims**
Adult survivors of child sexual abuse
    USE **Adult child sexual abuse victims**
Adulteration of food
    USE **Food adulteration and inspection**
Adultery   176; 306.73; 363.4
    UF Extramarital relationships
        Marital infidelity
    BT **Sexual ethics**
Adults abused as children
    USE **Adult child abuse victims**
Adults and children
    USE **Child-adult relationship**
Adults sexually abused as children
    USE **Adult child sexual abuse victims**
Adventure and adventurers (May subdiv. geog.)   904; 904.092; 910.4; 920
    NT **Escapes**
        Exploration
        Explorers
        Frontier and pioneer life
        Heroes and heroines
        Safaris
        Sea stories
        Seafaring life
        Shipwrecks
    RT **Voyages and travels**
Adventure and adventurers—Fiction
    USE **Adventure fiction**
Adventure fiction   808.3; 808.83
    May be used for individual works, collections, or materials about adventure fiction.
    UF Adventure and adventurers—Fiction
        Adventure stories
        Suspense novels
        Swashbucklers
        Thrillers
    BT **Fiction**
    NT **Robinsonades**
        Romantic suspense novels
        Science fiction
        Sea stories
        Spy stories
        Western stories
Adventure films   791.43
    May be used for individual works, collections, or materials about adventure films.

    UF Suspense films
        Swashbucklers
        Thrillers
    BT **Motion pictures**
    NT **Superhero films**
        Western films
    RT **Adventure television programs**
Adventure radio programs   791.44
    May be used for individual works, collections, or materials about adventure radio programs.
    BT **Radio programs**
    NT **Superhero radio programs**
Adventure stories
    USE **Adventure fiction**
Adventure television programs   791.45
    May be used for individual works, collections, or materials about adventure television programs.
    BT **Television programs**
    NT **Superhero television programs**
    RT **Adventure films**
Advertisement writing
    USE **Advertising copy**
Advertising (May subdiv. geog.)   659.1
    May be subdivided by topic, e.g. **Advertising—Cosmetics;** to specify the thing advertised.
    BT **Business**
        Retail trade
    NT **Advertising and children**
        Advertising copy
        Advertising layout and typography
        Commercial art
        Commercial catalogs
        Coupons (Retail trade)
        Deceptive advertising
        Electric signs
        Fashion models
        Market surveys
        Newspaper advertising
        Packaging
        Posters
        Printing—Specimens
        Radio advertising
        Show windows
        Sign painting
        Signs and signboards
        Television advertising
    RT **Marketing**
        Propaganda
        Public relations

Advertising—*Continued*
>> Publicity
>> Selling
Advertising and children   659.1
> UF   Children and advertising
> BT   Advertising
>> Children
Advertising art
> USE   Commercial art
Advertising copy   659.13
> UF   Advertisement writing
>> Copy writing
> BT   Advertising
>> Authorship
Advertising—Cosmetics   659.1
> UF   Cosmetics—Advertising
Advertising layout and typography
659.13
> BT   Advertising
>> Printing
>> Typography
Advertising, Newspaper
> USE   Newspaper advertising
Advertising—Newspapers   659.1
> Use for materials on the advertising of newspapers. Materials on advertising in newspapers are entered under **Newspaper advertising.**
> UF   Newspapers—Advertising
Advice columns   070.4
> BT   Counseling
>> Newspapers—Sections, columns, etc.
Advisors
> USE   Consultants
Aerial bombs
> USE   Bombs
Aerial navigation
> USE   Navigation (Aeronautics)
Aerial operations
> USE   names of wars with the subdivision *Aerial operations,* e.g. **World War, 1939-1945—Aerial operations** [to be added as needed]
Aerial photography   778.3
> BT   Photography
> NT   Remote sensing
Aerial propellers   629.134
> UF   Airplanes—Propellers
>> Propellers, Aerial
> BT   Airplanes

Aerial reconnaissance   355.4; 358.4
> UF   Reconnaissance, Aerial
> BT   Military aeronautics
>> Remote sensing
Aerial rockets
> USE   Rockets (Aeronautics)
Aerial spraying and dusting
> USE   Aeronautics in agriculture
Aerobatics
> USE   Stunt flying
Aerobic dancing
> USE   Aerobics
Aerobic exercises
> USE   Aerobics
Aerobics   613.7
> UF   Aerobic dancing
>> Aerobic exercises
> BT   Exercise
> NT   Walking
> RT   Dance
Aerobiology
> USE   Air—Microbiology
Aerodromes
> USE   Airports
Aerodynamics   533; 629.132
> UF   Streamlining
> BT   Air
>> Dynamics
>> Pneumatics
> NT   Supersonic aerodynamics
> RT   Aeronautics
Aerodynamics, Supersonic
> USE   Supersonic aerodynamics
Aeronautical instruments   629.135
> UF   Airplanes—Instruments
>> Instruments, Aeronautical
> SA   types of instruments, e.g. **Gyroscope** [to be added as needed]
> BT   Scientific apparatus and instruments
> NT   Airplanes—Electric equipment
>> Gyroscope
>> Instrument flying
Aeronautical sports   797.5
> SA   types of aeronautical sports [to be added as needed]
> BT   Aeronautics
>> Sports
> NT   Airplane racing
>> Skydiving

Aeronautics (May subdiv. geog.) **629.13**

Use for materials dealing collectively with various types of aircraft and for materials on the scientific or technical aspects of aircraft and their construction and operation. Materials on companies engaged in commercial aviation are entered under **Airlines.**

UF   Air routes

Airways

Aviation

SA   aeronautics in particular industries or fields of endeavor,
e.g. **Aeronautics in agriculture** [to be added as needed]

BT   **Engineering**

Locomotion

NT   **Aeronautical sports**

Aeronautics and civilization

Aeronautics in agriculture

Air pilots

Airplanes

Airports

Airships

Astronautics

Balloons

Gliders (Aeronautics)

Gliding and soaring

Helicopters

High speed aeronautics

Kites

Lasers in aeronautics

Meteorology in aeronautics

Military aeronautics

Navigation (Aeronautics)

Parachutes

Radio in aeronautics

Rocketry

Rockets (Aeronautics)

Unidentified flying objects

RT   **Aerodynamics**

Flight

Aeronautics—Accidents

USE   **Aircraft accidents**

Aeronautics and civilization   **306**

UF   Civilization and aeronautics

BT   **Aeronautics**

Civilization

NT   **Astronautics and civilization**

Aeronautics, Commercial

USE   **Commercial aeronautics**

Aeronautics—Flights   **387.7; 629.13**

UF   Aeronautics—Voyages

Flights around the world

Transatlantic flights

BT   **Voyages and travels**

NT   **Space flight**

Aeronautics in agriculture   **631.3**

UF   Aerial spraying and dusting

Airplanes in agriculture

Crop dusting

Crop spraying

BT   **Aeronautics**

Agriculture

Spraying and dusting

RT   **Agricultural pests**

Aeronautics—Medical aspects

USE   **Aviation medicine**

Aeronautics, Military

USE   **Military aeronautics**

Aeronautics—Navigation

USE   **Navigation (Aeronautics)**

Aeronautics—Piloting

USE   **Airplanes—Piloting**

Aeronautics—Safety measures   **387.7;
629.134**

BT   **Accidents—Prevention**

NT   **Air traffic control**

**Aeronautics—Study and teaching
629.1307**

UF   Flight training

NT   **Airplanes—Piloting**

Aeronautics—Voyages

USE   **Aeronautics—Flights**

Aeroplanes

USE   **Airplanes**

Aerosol sniffing

USE   **Solvent abuse**

Aerosols   **541; 551.51; 660**

BT   **Air pollution**

Aerospace industries

USE   **Aerospace industry**

Aerospace industry (May subdiv. geog.)
338.4

UF   Aerospace industries

Aircraft production

BT   **Industries**

NT   **Airplane industry**

Aerospace law

USE   **Space law**

Aerospace medicine

USE   **Aviation medicine**

Space medicine

Aerothermodynamics   629.132; 629.4
  UF   Thermoaerodynamics
  BT   **Astronautics**
       High speed aeronautics
       Supersonic aerodynamics
       Thermodynamics
Aesthetics   111; 701; 801
  UF   Beauty
       Esthetics
       Taste (Aesthetics)
  SA   styles and movements in the
       arts, e.g. **Classicism; Post-**
       modernism; etc., and aesthet-
       ics of particular countries, e.g.
       Japanese aesthetics [to be
       added as needed]
  BT   **Philosophy**
  NT   **Art appreciation**
       Classicism
       Color
       Criticism
       Japanese aesthetics
       Kitsch
       Modernism (Aesthetics)
       Postmodernism
       Rhythm
       Romanticism
       Values
  RT   **Arts**
Aesthetics, Japanese
  USE   **Japanese aesthetics**
Affection
  USE   **Friendship**
        Love
Affirmative action programs (May
       subdiv. geog.)   331.13; 658.3
  UF   Equal employment opportunity
       Equal opportunity in employ-
       ment
  BT   **Discrimination in employment**
       Personnel management
Affliction
  USE   **Joy and sorrow**
        Suffering
Affluent people
  USE   **Rich**
Affordable housing
  USE   **Housing**
Africa   960
  NT   **Central Africa**
       East Africa

       North Africa
       Northeast Africa
       Northwest Africa
       Pan-Africanism
       South Africa
       Southern Africa
       Sub-Saharan Africa
       West Africa
  RT   **Africans**
Africa, Central
  USE   **Central Africa**
Africa—Civilization   306.096; 960
  UF   African civilization
  BT   **Civilization**
Africa, East
  USE   **East Africa**
Africa, Eastern
  USE   **East Africa**
Africa, French-speaking Equatorial
  USE   **French-speaking Equatorial Af-**
        rica
Africa, French-speaking West
  USE   **French-speaking West Africa**
Africa—History   960
Africa—History—1960-   960.3
Africa, North
  USE   **North Africa**
Africa, Northeast
  USE   **Northeast Africa**
Africa, Northwest
  USE   **Northwest Africa**
Africa, Southern
  USE   **Southern Africa**
Africa—Study and teaching   960.07
  UF   African studies
  BT   **Area studies**
Africa, Sub-Saharan
  USE   **Sub-Saharan Africa**
Africa, West
  USE   **West Africa**
African American actors   791.4; 792;
       920
  UF   African American actors and ac-
       tresses
       Afro-American actors
  BT   **Actors**
       Black actors
African American actors and actresses
  USE   **African American actors**

African American art (May subdiv. geog.)   **704**

Use for materials on works of art by several African American artists. Materials on African Americans depicted in works of art are entered under **African Americans in art.**

UF   Afro-American art

BT   **Art**

    Black art

NT   **Harlem Renaissance**

RT   **African American artists**

African American artists   709.2; 920

Use for materials on several African Americans artists.

UF   Afro-American artists

BT   **Artists**

    Black artists

RT   **African American art**

African American athletes   796.092; 920

UF   Afro-American athletes

BT   **Athletes**

    Black athletes

African American authors   810.9; 920

Use for materials on several African American authors.

UF   Afro-American authors

SA   genres of American literature with the subdivision *African American authors,* e.g. **American poetry—African American authors;** etc. [to be added as needed]

BT   **American authors**

    Black authors

African American business people

USE   **African American businesspeople**

African American businesspeople   338.092; 658.0092; 920

UF   African American business people

    Afro-American businesspeople

BT   **Black businesspeople**

    Businesspeople

African American children   305.23

UF   Afro-American children

BT   **Black children**

    Children

African American elderly   305.26

BT   **Elderly**

African American folklore

USE   **African Americans—Folklore**

African American librarians   020.92; 920

UF   Afro-American librarians

BT   **Black librarians**

    Librarians

African American literature

USE   **American literature—African American authors**

African American men   305.38

UF   Afro-American men

BT   **Men**

African American music (May subdiv. geog.)   **780.089**

Use for materials on the music of African Americans. Materials on the music of Blacks not limited to the United States are entered under **Black music.**

UF   African American songs

    Afro-Americans—Music

    Songs, African American

BT   **Black music**

    Music

NT   **Blues music**

    Gospel music

    Harlem Renaissance

    Rap music

RT   **African American musicians**

    Spirituals (Songs)

African American musicians   780.92; 920

UF   Afro-American musicians

BT   **Black musicians**

    Musicians

RT   **African American music**

African American poetry

USE   **American poetry—African American authors**

African American songs

USE   **African American music**

African American suffrage

USE   **African Americans—Suffrage**

African American women   305.48

UF   Afro-American women

BT   **Black women**

    Women

African American youth   305.235

BT   **Youth**

African Americans (May subdiv. geog. by cities, states, or regions of the U.S.)   **305.896; 973**

Use for materials dealing collectively with Blacks in the United States. General materials

African Americans—*Continued*
and materials on Blacks in places other than
the United States are entered under **Blacks.**

UF   Afro-Americans

      Black Americans

      Blacks—United States

      Negroes

SA   African Americans in various
      occupations and professions,
      e.g. **African American art-
      ists; African American li-
      brarians;** etc. [to be added as
      needed]

BT   **Blacks**

NT   **Libraries and African Ameri-
      cans**

      **World War, 1939-1945—
      African Americans**

African Americans and libraries

USE   **Libraries and African Ameri-
       cans**

African Americans—Biography   **920**

BT   **Blacks—Biography**

**African Americans—Chicago (Ill.)
305.896; 977.3**

African Americans—Civil rights (May
subdiv. geog.)   **323.1196; 342**

BT   **Blacks—Civil rights**

      Civil rights

NT   **African Americans—Suffrage**

African Americans—Economic conditions
(May subdiv. geog.)   **330.973**

BT   **Blacks—Economic conditions**

      Economic conditions

African Americans—Education (May
subdiv. geog.)   **370.89; 371.829**

BT   **Blacks—Education**

      Education

African Americans—Employment (May
subdiv. geog.)   **331.6**

BT   **Blacks—Employment**

      Employment

African Americans—Folklore   **398**

UF   African American folklore

BT   **Blacks—Folklore**

      Folklore

African Americans—Housing (May
subdiv. geog.)   **307.3; 363.5**

BT   **Blacks—Housing**

      Housing

African Americans in art   **704.9**

Use for materials on African Americans depicted in works of art. Materials on the attainments of several African Americans in the
area of art are entered under **African
American artists.** Materials on works of art
by several African American artists are entered under **African American art.**

UF   Afro-Americans in art

BT   **Art—Themes**

African Americans in literature   **809**

Use for materials on the theme of African
Americans in works of literature. Materials on
several African American authors are entered
under **African American authors.** Materials
on works of literature by several African
American authors are entered under **American
literature—African American authors** and
the various forms of American literature with
the subdivision *African American authors,* e.g.
**American poetry—African American au-
thors.**

UF   Afro-Americans in literature

BT   **Literature—Themes**

**African Americans in motion pictures
791.43**

Use for materials on the depiction of
African Americans in motion pictures. Materials on several African American actors are entered under **African American actors.** Materials discussing all aspects of African Americans' involvement in motion pictures are entered under **African Americans in the motion picture industry.**

BT   **Blacks in motion pictures**

      Motion pictures

African Americans in television

USE   **African Americans on televi-
       sion**

**African Americans in television broad-
casting**   **791.45**

Use for materials on all aspects of African
Americans' involvement in the television industry. Materials on the portrayal of African
Americans in television programs are entered
under **African Americans on television.**

UF   African Americans in the televi-
      sion industry

      Afro-Americans in television
      broadcasting

BT   **Television broadcasting**

**African Americans in the motion picture
industry**   **791.43092**

Use for materials on all aspects of African
Americans' involvement in motion pictures.
Materials on the depiction of African Ameri-
cans in motion pictures are entered under
African Americans in motion pictures.

BT   **Blacks in the motion picture
      industry**

      Motion picture industry

African Americans in the television indus-
try
USE **African Americans in television
broadcasting**
African Americans—Intellectual life
(May subdiv. geog.) **305.896**
BT **Blacks—Intellectual life
Intellectual life**
**African Americans—Ohio 305.896;
977.1**
African Americans on television 791.45
Use for materials on the portrayal of
African Americans in television programs.
Materials on all aspects of African Americans'
involvement in the television industry are en-
tered under **African Americans in television
broadcasting.**
UF African Americans in television
Afro-Americans on television
BT **Television**
African Americans—Political activity
(May subdiv. geog.) **322.4; 324**
BT **Blacks—Political activity
Political participation**
NT **Black nationalism
Black power**
**African Americans—Race identity
305.896**
BT **Blacks—Race identity
Race awareness**
NT **Black nationalism**
**African Americans—Religion 270.089;
299.6**
BT **Blacks—Religion
Religion**
NT **Black Muslims**
African Americans—Segregation (May
subdiv. geog.) **305.896**
BT **Blacks—Segregation
Segregation**
African Americans—Social conditions
(May subdiv. geog.) **305.896**
BT **Blacks—Social conditions
Social conditions**
**African Americans—Social life and cus-
toms** (May subdiv. geog.)
305.896
BT **Blacks—Social life and cus-
toms
Manners and customs**

**African Americans—Southern States
305.896; 975**
UF Southern States—African Ameri-
cans
African Americans—Suffrage (May
subdiv. geog.) **324.6**
UF African American suffrage
BT **African Americans—Civil
rights
Blacks—Suffrage
Suffrage**
African civilization
USE **Africa—Civilization**
African diaspora 304.8096
UF Black diaspora
Diaspora, African
BT **Human geography**
African literature (English) 820
BT **Literature**
African peoples
USE **Africans**
African relations
USE **Pan-Africanism**
African songs 782.42096
UF Songs, African
BT **Songs**
African studies
USE **Africa—Study and teaching**
Africans 305.896; 960
UF African peoples
SA names of African peoples, e.g.
Yoruba (African people) [to
be added as needed]
NT **Blacks—Africa
Yoruba (African people)**
RT **Africa**
Afrikaaners
USE **Afrikaners**
Afrikaners 305.83; 968
UF Afrikaaners
Boers
South African Dutch
South Africans, Afrikaans-
speaking
Afro-American actors
USE **African American actors**
Afro-American art
USE **African American art**
Afro-American artists
USE **African American artists**

Afro-American athletes
    USE   **African American athletes**
Afro-American authors
    USE   **African American authors**
Afro-American businesspeople
    USE   **African American businesspeople**
Afro-American children
    USE   **African American children**
Afro-American librarians
    USE   **African American librarians**
Afro-American men
    USE   **African American men**
Afro-American musicians
    USE   **African American musicians**
Afro-American women
    USE   **African American women**
Afro-Americans
    USE   **African Americans**
Afro-Americans and libraries
    USE   **Libraries and African Americans**
Afro-Americans in art
    USE   **African Americans in art**
Afro-Americans in literature
    USE   **African Americans in literature**
Afro-Americans in television broadcasting
    USE   **African Americans in television broadcasting**
Afro-Americans—Music
    USE   **African American music**
Afro-Americans on television
    USE   **African Americans on television**
After dinner speeches   808.5; 808.85
    BT   **Speeches**
    RT   **Toasts**
After school day care
    USE   **After school programs**
After school programs   362.71; 372.12
    UF   After school day care
    BT   **Student activities**
Afterlife
    USE   **Future life**
Afternoon teas   641.5
    UF   Teas
    BT   **Cooking**
    RT   **Entertaining**
            Tea

Age   305.2
    UF   Age groups
    SA   types of animals, plants, and crops with the subdivision *Age* [to be added as needed]
    NT   **Adolescence**
            Age and employment
            Aging
            Children
            Drinking age
            Elderly
            Life expectancy
            Longevity
            Middle age
            Middle aged persons
            Old age
            Teenagers
            Youth
Age and employment   331.3
    UF   Employment and age
    BT   **Age**
            Employment
    NT   **Career changes**
            Child labor
            Teenagers—Employment
            Youth—Employment
Age discrimination   305.2
    BT   **Discrimination**
Age groups
    USE   **Age**
Age—Physiological effect
    USE   **Aging**
Aged
    USE   **Elderly**
Aged men
    USE   **Elderly men**
Aged parents
    USE   **Aging parents**
Aged—Pensions
    USE   **Old age pensions**
Aged women
    USE   **Elderly women**
Ageing
    USE   **Aging**
Agent Orange   363.17; 615.9
    BT   **Herbicides**
Aggregates
    USE   **Set theory**
Aggressive behavior
    USE   **Aggressiveness (Psychology)**

Aggressiveness (Psychology)   152.4;
    155.2
  UF Aggressive behavior
  BT **Human behavior**
      Psychology
  NT **Assertiveness (Psychology)**
      Bullies
      Teasing
      Violence
Aging 571.8; 612.6
  UF Age—Physiological effect
      Ageing
      Senescence
  SA types of animals, organs of the
      body, plants, and crops with
      the subdivision *Aging* [to be
      added as needed]
  BT **Age**
      Elderly
      Gerontology
      Longevity
      Middle age
      Old age
  NT **Male climacteric**
      Menopause
Aging parents (May subdiv. geog.)
    306.874
  UF Aged parents
      Elderly parents
  BT **Elderly**
      Parents
Aging persons
  USE **Elderly**
Agnosticism 149; 211
  BT **Free thought**
      Religion
  RT **Atheism**
      Belief and doubt
      Positivism
      Rationalism
      Skepticism
Agoraphobia 616.85
  UF Fear of open spaces
  BT **Phobias**
Agrarian question
  USE **Agriculture—Economic aspects**
      Agriculture—Government poli-
      cy
      Land tenure
Agrarian reform
  USE **Land reform**

Agreements
  USE **Contracts**
      Covenants
Agribusiness
  USE **Agricultural industry**
Agricultural bacteriology 630.2
  UF Bacteriology, Agricultural
      Diseases and pests
  SA types of crops, plants, trees, etc.,
      with the subdivision *Diseases*
      and pests, e.g. **Fruit—Dis-**
      eases and pests [to be added
      as needed]
  BT **Bacteriology**
  RT **Soil microbiology**
Agricultural botany
  USE **Economic botany**
Agricultural chemicals 631.8; 668
  SA types of agricultural chemicals
      and names of individual
      chemicals [to be added as
      needed]
  BT **Agricultural chemistry**
      Chemicals
  NT **Fertilizers**
      Herbicides
      Insecticides
      Pesticides
Agricultural chemistry 630.2
  BT **Chemistry**
  NT **Agricultural chemicals**
  RT **Soils**
Agricultural clubs
  USE **Agriculture—Societies**
Agricultural cooperation
  USE **Cooperative agriculture**
Agricultural credit (May subdiv. geog.)
    332.7
  UF Farm credit
      Farm loans
      Rural credit
  BT **Agriculture—Economic aspects**
      Banks and banking
      Credit
Agricultural economics
  USE **Agriculture—Economic aspects**
Agricultural education
  USE **Agriculture—Study and teach-**
      ing

Agricultural engineering (May subdiv. geog.) **630**
UF Agricultural mechanics
Farm mechanics
BT **Engineering**
NT **Drainage**
Electricity in agriculture
Irrigation
RT **Agricultural machinery**
Agricultural experiment stations (May subdiv. geog.) **630.7**
UF Experimental farms
BT **Agriculture—Government policy**
Agriculture—Research
Agriculture—Study and teaching
RT **Agricultural extension work**
Agricultural extension work (May subdiv. geog.) **630.7**
BT **Adult education**
Agriculture—Government policy
NT **County agricultural agents**
RT **Agricultural experiment stations**
Agriculture—Study and teaching
Community development
Agricultural industries
USE **Agricultural industry**
Agricultural industry (May subdiv. geog.) **338.1**
UF Agribusiness
Agricultural industries
BT **Agriculture—Economic aspects**
Industries
NT **Food industry**
Agricultural laborers (May subdiv. geog.) **331.7**
UF Farm laborers
BT **Labor**
RT **Migrant labor**
Peasantry
Agricultural machinery **631.3**
UF Agricultural tools
Farm engines
Farm equipment
Farm implements
Farm machinery
Farm mechanics

SA types of farm machinery [to be added as needed]
BT **Machinery**
Tools
NT **Electricity in agriculture**
Harvesting machinery
Plows
Tractors
RT **Agricultural engineering**
Agricultural mechanics
USE **Agricultural engineering**
Agricultural pests **632**
UF Diseases and pests
Garden pests
SA types of crops, plants, trees, etc., with the subdivision *Diseases and pests,* e.g. **Fruit—Diseases and pests** [to be added as needed]
BT **Economic zoology**
Pests
NT **Fruit—Diseases and pests**
Fungi
Pest control
Plant diseases
Spraying and dusting
Weeds
RT **Aeronautics in agriculture**
Insect pests
Agricultural policy
USE **Agriculture—Government policy**
Agricultural products
USE **Farm produce**
Agricultural research
USE **Agriculture—Research**
Agricultural societies
USE **Agriculture—Societies**
Agricultural subsidies (May subdiv. geog.) **338.9**
UF Farm subsidies
BT **Subsidies**
RT **Agriculture—Government policy**
Agricultural tools
USE **Agricultural machinery**
Agriculture (May subdiv. geog.) **338.1; 630**
UF Agronomy
Farming
Planting

Agriculture—*Continued*

SA   types of agriculture, e.g. **Truck farming;** types of agricultural products, e.g. **Corn;** and ethnic groups with the subdivision *Agriculture,* e.g. **Native Americans—Agriculture** [to be added as needed]

BT   **Life sciences**

NT   **Aeronautics in agriculture**
    Aquaculture
    Beekeeping
    Cooperative agriculture
    Crop rotation
    Cultivated plants
    Dairying
    Dry farming
    Economic botany
    Farmers
    Forests and forestry
    Fruit culture
    Gardening
    Horticulture
    Livestock industry
    Native Americans—Agriculture
    Organic farming
    Pastures
    Plant breeding
    Reclamation of land
    Soils
    Truck farming

RT   **Farms**
    Food supply

Agriculture and state
    USE **Agriculture—Government policy**

Agriculture—Bibliography   016.63

Agriculture, Cooperative
    USE **Cooperative agriculture**

Agriculture—Documentation   025
    BT **Documentation**

Agriculture—Economic aspects (May subdiv. geog.)   338.1

UF   Agrarian question
    Agricultural economics

BT   **Economics**

NT   **Agricultural credit**
    Agricultural industry
    Land tenure

RT   **Farm management**
    Farm produce—Marketing

Agriculture—Government policy (May subdiv. geog.)   **338.9**

UF   Agrarian question
    Agricultural policy
    Agriculture and state
    State and agriculture

BT   **Industrial policy**

NT   **Agricultural experiment stations**
    Agricultural extension work
    Rural development

RT   **Agricultural subsidies**
    Land reform

Agriculture—Research   630.7

UF   Agricultural research

BT   **Research**

NT   **Agricultural experiment stations**

Agriculture—Societies   630.6

UF   Agricultural clubs
    Agricultural societies

SA   names of agricultural societies [to be added as needed]

BT   **Associations**
    Country life
    Societies

NT   **4-H clubs**
    Grange

Agriculture—Statistics   338.1; 630.2

UF   Crop reports

BT   **Statistics**

Agriculture—Study and teaching   630.7

UF   Agricultural education

BT   **Vocational education**

NT   **4-H clubs**
    Agricultural experiment stations
    County agricultural agents

RT   **Agricultural extension work**

Agriculture—Tenant farming
    USE **Farm tenancy**

Agriculture—Tropics   630.913
    BT **Tropics**

Agriculture—United States   630.973

Agronomy
    USE **Agriculture**

AI (Artificial intelligence)
    USE **Artificial intelligence**

Aid to dependent children
    USE **Child welfare**

Aid to developing areas
    USE **Foreign aid**
            Technical assistance
AIDS (Disease) (May subdiv. geog.)
       616.97
    UF Acquired immune deficiency
          syndrome
         HIV disease
    BT **Communicable diseases**
         Diseases
AIDS (Disease)—Prevention **616.97**
    Use for materials on AIDS prevention in
general not limited to safe sexual practices.
Materials limited to safe sexual practices in
the prevention of AIDS are entered under
Safe sex in AIDS prevention.
    NT **Safe sex in AIDS prevention**
AIDS (Disease)—Treatment **615.5**
    BT **Therapeutics**
Air **533; 546**
    Use for materials dealing with air in general
and with its chemical and physical properties.
Materials on the body of air surrounding the
earth are entered under **Atmosphere.**
    BT **Meteorology**
    NT **Aerodynamics**
         Atmosphere
         Bubbles
         Ventilation
    RT **Atmosphere**
Air bases (May subdiv. geog.) **358.4**
    UF Military air bases
         Naval air bases
    BT **Airports**
         Military aeronautics
Air cargo
    USE **Commercial aeronautics**
Air carriers
    USE **Airlines**
Air charters
    USE **Airlines—Chartering**
Air conditioning **644; 697.9**
    SA subjects with the subdivision *Air
         conditioning* [to be added as
         needed]
    NT **Automobiles—Air conditioning**
    RT **Refrigeration**
         Ventilation
Air crashes
    USE **Aircraft accidents**
Air-cushion vehicles **629.3**
    UF Ground effect machines
         Hovercraft
    BT **Vehicles**

Air defenses (May subdiv. geog.) **363.3**
    Use for materials on military defense
against air attack. Materials on the protection
of civilians from enemy attack are entered un-
der **Civil defense.**
    UF Air raid defensive measures
    BT **Military aeronautics**
    NT **Radar defense networks**
Air freight
    USE **Commercial aeronautics**
Air lines
    USE **Airlines**
Air mail service **383**
    BT **Commercial aeronautics**
         Postal service
Air—Microbiology **579**
    UF Aerobiology
    BT **Microbiology**
Air, Moisture of
    USE **Humidity**
Air navigation
    USE **Navigation (Aeronautics)**
Air pilots **629.13092; 920**
    UF Airplane pilots
         Aviators
         Pilots
         Test pilots
    BT **Aeronautics**
    NT **Astronauts**
         Women air pilots
Air piracy
    USE **Hijacking of airplanes**
Air pollution (May subdiv. geog.)
       363.739; 628.5
    UF Atmosphere—Pollution
         Pollution of air
    BT **Environmental health**
         Pollution
    NT **Aerosols**
         Dust
         Indoor air pollution
Air pollution—Measurement **363.739;
       628.5**
    BT **Measurement**
Air pollution—United States **363.739;
       628.5**
Air power **358.4**
    BT **Military aeronautics**
Air raid defensive measures
    USE **Air defenses**

Air raid shelters 363.3
    UF   Blast shelters
           Bomb shelters
           Fallout shelters
           Nuclear bomb shelters
           Public shelters
           Shelters, Air raid
    BT   **Civil defense**
Air rights law
    USE **Airspace law**
Air routes
    USE **Aeronautics**
Air-ships
    USE **Airships**
Air space law
    USE **Airspace law**
Air surfing
    USE **Gliding and soaring**
Air terminals
    USE **Airports**
Air traffic control 387.7
    UF   Airports—Traffic control
    BT   **Aeronautics—Safety measures**
Air transport
    USE **Commercial aeronautics**
Air warfare
    USE **Military aeronautics**
          Military airplanes
Aircraft
    USE **Airplanes**
          Airships
          Balloons
          Gliders (Aeronautics)
          Helicopters
Aircraft accidents (May subdiv. geog.)
    363.12; 629.13
    UF   Aeronautics—Accidents
           Air crashes
           Airplane accidents
           Airplane crashes
           Airplanes—Accidents
           Aviation accidents
           Plane crashes
    BT   **Accidents**
    RT   **Survival after airplane accidents, shipwrecks, etc.**
Aircraft carriers 359.3; 623
    UF   Airplane carriers
    BT   **Military aeronautics**
          Warships

Aircraft industry
    USE **Airplane industry**
Aircraft production
    USE **Aerospace industry**
          Airplane industry
Airdromes
    USE **Airports**
Airline hostesses
    USE **Flight attendants**
Airline stewardesses
    USE **Flight attendants**
Airline stewards
    USE **Flight attendants**
Airlines (May subdiv. geog.) **387.7**
    Use for materials on companies engaged in commercial aviation. Materials on various types of aircraft and on the scientific or technical aspects of aircraft and their construction and operation are entered under **Aeronautics.**
    UF   Air carriers
           Air lines
    BT   **Commercial aeronautics**
    NT   **Flight attendants**
Airlines—Chartering 387.7
    UF   Air charters
           Airplanes—Chartering
           Charter flights
Airlines—Hijacking
    USE **Hijacking of airplanes**
Airplane accidents
    USE **Aircraft accidents**
Airplane carriers
    USE **Aircraft carriers**
Airplane crashes
    USE **Aircraft accidents**
Airplane engines 629.134
    UF   Airplane motors
           Airplanes—Engines
           Airplanes—Motors
    BT   **Engines**
    NT   **Jet propulsion**
Airplane hijacking
    USE **Hijacking of airplanes**
Airplane industry (May subdiv. geog.)
    338.4; 387.7
    UF   Aircraft industry
           Aircraft production
    BT   **Aerospace industry**
Airplane motors
    USE **Airplane engines**
Airplane pilots
    USE **Air pilots**

Airplane racing 797.5
　　UF　Airplanes—Racing
　　BT　**Aeronautical sports**
　　　　Racing
Airplane spotting
　　USE　**Airplanes—Identification**
Airplanes 387.7; 629.133
　　UF　Aeroplanes
　　　　Aircraft
　　SA　types of airplanes and specific
　　　　makes of airplanes [to be
　　　　added as needed]
　　BT　**Aeronautics**
　　NT　**Aerial propellers**
　　　　Bombers
　　　　Gliders (Aeronautics)
　　　　Helicopters
　　　　Jet planes
　　　　Military airplanes
Airplanes—Accidents
　　USE　**Aircraft accidents**
Airplanes—Chartering
　　USE　**Airlines—Chartering**
Airplanes—Design and construction
　　　629.134
Airplanes—Electric equipment 629.135
　　UF　Airplanes—Instruments
　　BT　**Aeronautical instruments**
Airplanes—Engines
　　USE　**Airplane engines**
Airplanes—Flight testing
　　USE　**Airplanes—Testing**
Airplanes—Hijacking
　　USE　**Hijacking of airplanes**
Airplanes—Identification 623.74;
　　　629.133
　　UF　Airplane spotting
　　　　Airplanes—Recognition
　　BT　**Identification**
Airplanes in agriculture
　　USE　**Aeronautics in agriculture**
Airplanes—Inspection 387.7; 629.134
Airplanes—Instruments
　　USE　**Aeronautical instruments**
　　　　Airplanes—Electric equipment
Airplanes—Maintenance and repair
　　　629.134
　　UF　Airplanes—Repair
Airplanes—Materials 629.134
　　BT　**Materials**

Airplanes, Military
　　USE　**Military airplanes**
Airplanes—Models 629.133
　　UF　Model airplanes
　　　　Paper airplanes
　　BT　**Models and modelmaking**
Airplanes—Motors
　　USE　**Airplane engines**
Airplanes—Noise 629.132
　　BT　**Noise**
　　　　Noise pollution
Airplanes—Operation
　　USE　**Airplanes—Piloting**
Airplanes—Piloting 629.132
　　UF　Aeronautics—Piloting
　　　　Airplanes—Operation
　　　　Flight training
　　SA　types and names of airplanes
　　　　with the subdivision *Piloting*
　　　　[to be added as needed]
　　BT　**Aeronautics—Study and teach-
　　　　ing**
　　　　Navigation (Aeronautics)
　　NT　**Helicopters—Piloting**
　　　　Instrument flying
　　　　Stunt flying
Airplanes—Propellers
　　USE　**Aerial propellers**
Airplanes—Racing
　　USE　**Airplane racing**
Airplanes—Recognition
　　USE　**Airplanes—Identification**
Airplanes—Repair
　　USE　**Airplanes—Maintenance and
　　　　repair**
Airplanes, Rocket propelled
　　USE　**Rocket planes**
Airplanes—Testing 629.134
　　UF　Airplanes—Flight testing
　　　　Test pilots
Airports (May subdiv. geog.) 387.7;
　　　629.136
　　UF　Aerodromes
　　　　Air terminals
　　　　Airdromes
　　SA　names of individual airports [to
　　　　be added as needed]
　　BT　**Aeronautics**
　　NT　**Air bases**
　　　　Heliports
Airports—Security measures 363.28

Airports—Traffic control
USE **Air traffic control**
Airships   629.133
    Use for materials on self-propelled aircraft that are lighter than air and steerable. Materials on aircraft held aloft by hot air or light gases that are nondirigible and propelled only by the wind are entered under **Balloons.**
  UF   Air-ships
          Aircraft
          Balloons, Dirigible
          Blimps
          Dirigible balloons
          Zeppelins
  BT   **Aeronautics**
  RT   **Balloons**
Airspace law   341.4
  UF   Air rights law
          Air space law
  BT   **Property**
Airways
USE   **Aeronautics**
Alaska Highway (Alaska and Canada)
    388.1; 979.8
  BT   **Roads**
Alchemy   540.1
    Use for materials on medieval attempts to change base metals into gold. Materials on the transmutation of metals in nuclear physics are entered under **Transmutation (Chemistry).**
  UF   Hermetic art and philosophy
          Philosophers' stone
          Transmutation of metals
  BT   **Chemistry**
          Occultism
  RT   **Transmutation (Chemistry)**
Alcohol   547; 661
  UF   Alcohol use
          Intoxicants
  SA   classes of persons with the subdivision *Alcohol use,* e.g. **Employees—Alcohol use; Youth—Alcohol use;** etc. [to be added as needed]
  BT   **Chemicals**
  NT   **Alcohol as fuel**
          Alcoholic beverages
          Denatured alcohol
  RT   **Alcoholism**
          Distillation
Alcohol and employees
USE   **Employees—Alcohol use**
Alcohol and teenagers
USE   **Teenagers—Alcohol use**

Alcohol and youth
USE   **Youth—Alcohol use**
Alcohol as fuel   662
  UF   Alcohol fuel
          Ethanol
          Ethyl alcohol fuel
  SA   types of alcohol fuels, e.g. **Gasohol** [to be added as needed]
  BT   **Alcohol**
          Fuel
  NT   **Gasohol**
Alcohol consumption
USE   **Drinking of alcoholic beverages**
Alcohol, Denatured
USE   **Denatured alcohol**
Alcohol fuel
USE   **Alcohol as fuel**
Alcohol in the workplace
USE   **Employees—Alcohol use**
Alcohol—Physiological effect   615
Alcohol use
USE   **Alcohol**
          Alcoholism
          Drinking of alcoholic beverages
          and classes of persons with the subdivision *Alcohol use,* e.g. **Employees—Alcohol use; Youth—Alcohol use;** etc. [to be added as needed]
Alcoholic beverage consumption
USE   **Drinking of alcoholic beverages**
Alcoholic beverages   641.2
  UF   Drinks
          Intoxicants
  BT   **Alcohol**
          Beverages
  NT   **Liquors**
          Wine and wine making
  RT   **Drinking of alcoholic beverages**
Alcoholic parents
USE   **Adult children of alcoholics**
          Children of alcoholics
Alcoholics   362.292; 616.86
  UF   Drunkards
  NT   **Recovering alcoholics**
  RT   **Adult children of alcoholics**
          Alcoholism
          Children of alcoholics

Alcoholism (May subdiv. geog.)
  362.292; 616.86
  UF Addiction to alcohol
      Alcohol use
      Drinking problem
      Drunkenness
      Intemperance
      Intoxication
      Liquor problem
      Problem drinking
  SA classes of persons with the sub-
      division *Alcohol use,* e.g. **Em-
      ployees—Alcohol use;
      Youth—Alcohol use;** etc. [to
      be added as needed]
  BT **Social problems**
  RT **Alcohol
      Alcoholics
      Drinking of alcoholic beverages
      Temperance
      Twelve-step programs**
Alfalfa   583; 633.3
  BT **Forage plants**
Algae   579.8
  UF Sea mosses
      Seaweeds
  BT **Marine plants**
Algebra   512
  BT **Mathematical analysis
      Mathematics**
  NT **Graph theory
      Group theory
      Linear algebra
      Logarithms
      Number theory
      Probabilities
      Sequences (Mathematics)**
Algebra, Boolean
  USE **Boolean algebra**
Alien abduction (May subdiv. geog.)
  001.942
  UF Abduction of humans by aliens
      Extraterrestrial abduction
      UFO abduction
  BT **Human-alien encounters**
Alien encounters with humans
  USE **Human-alien encounters**
Alien labor (May subdiv. geog.)   331.6
  BT **Labor**
  RT **Migrant labor**

Alienation (Social psychology)   302.5
  UF Estrangement (Social psycholo-
      gy)
      Rebels (Social psychology)
      Social alienation
  BT **Social psychology**
Aliens (May subdiv. geog.)   323.6
  UF Foreign population
      Foreigners
      Noncitizens
      Nonnationals
  SA national groups subdivided by
      the place of their residence,
      e.g. **Mexicans—United States**
      [to be added as needed]
  BT **Minorities**
  NT **Illegal aliens
      Refugees**
  RT **Citizenship
      Immigrants
      Immigration and emigration
      Naturalization**
Aliens from outer space
  USE **Extraterrestrial beings**
Aliens—United States   325.73
  UF United States—Foreign popula-
      tion
  NT **Mexicans—United States**
  RT **United States—Immigration
      and emigration**
All Fools' Day
  USE **April Fools' Day**
All Hallows' Eve
  USE **Halloween**
All terrain bicycles
  USE **Mountain bikes**
All terrain cycling
  USE **Mountain biking**
All terrain vehicles   629.22
  UF ATVs
  SA types of vehicles, e.g. **Snowmo-
      biles** [to be added as needed]
  BT **Vehicles**
  NT **Mountain bikes
      Snowmobiles**
Allegories   808.88
  May be used for individual works or for
  collections of allegories. Materials on allegory
  as a literary form or on allegory in the fine
  and decorative arts are entered under **Allego-
  ry.**

Allegories—*Continued*
   BT   Fiction
   RT   Fables
        Parables
Allegory   704.9; 808
   Use for materials on allegory as a literary form as well as for allegory in the fine and decorative arts. Individual allegories and collections of allegories are entered under **Allegories.**
   BT   Arts
        Fiction
   RT   Symbolism in literature
Allergies
   USE   **Allergy**
Allergies, Food
   USE   **Food allergy**
Allergy   616.97
   UF   Allergies
   SA   types of allergies [to be added as needed]
   BT   Immunity
   NT   Asthma
        Food allergy
        Hay fever
Allergy, Food
   USE   **Food allergy**
Alleys
   USE   **Streets**
Allied health personnel   610.69
   UF   Paramedical personnel
   SA   types of allied health personnel [to be added as needed]
   NT   **Emergency medical technicians**
        Medical technologists
        Nurse practitioners
Alligators   597.98
   BT   Reptiles
   RT   Crocodiles
Allocation of time
   USE   **Time management**
Allowances, Children's
   USE   **Children's allowances**
Alloys   669
   SA   types of alloys [to be added as needed]
   BT   Industrial chemistry
        Metals
   NT   Aluminum alloys
        Brass
        Pewter
   RT   Metallurgy

Allusions   031.02; 803
   SA   names of individual persons with the subdivision *Allusions,* for materials on allusions to that person, e.g. **Shakespeare, William, 1564-1616—Allusions** [to be added as needed]
   RT   **Terms and phrases**
Almanacs   030
   UF   Annuals
   BT   Serial publications
   NT   Nautical almanacs
   RT   Calendars
        Chronology
        Yearbooks
Alphabet   411
   Use for materials on the series of characters that form the elements of a written language and for materials to be used in teaching children the ABCs. Materials on the styles of alphabets used by artists, etc., are entered under **Alphabets.**
   UF   ABCs
        Alphabet books
        Letters of the alphabet
   SA   names of languages with the subdivision *Alphabet,* e.g. **English language—Alphabet** [to be added as needed]
   BT   Writing
   NT   Alphabets
Alphabet books
   USE   **Alphabet**
Alphabetizing
   USE   **Files and filing**
Alphabets   745.6
   Use for materials on the styles of alphabets used by artists, etc. Materials on the series of characters that form the elements of a written language and for materials to be used in teaching children the ABCs are entered under **Alphabet.**
   UF   Ornamental alphabets
   BT   Alphabet
        Sign painting
   NT   Monograms
   RT   Illumination of books and manuscripts
        Initials
        Lettering
Alpine animals
   USE   **Mountain animals**
Alpine fauna
   USE   **Mountain animals**

Alpine flora
  USE **Mountain plants**
Alpine plants
  USE **Mountain plants**
Alternate energy resources
  USE **Renewable energy resources**
Alternate work sites
  USE **Telecommuting**
Alternating current machinery
  USE **Electric machinery—Alternat-
        ing current**
Alternating currents
  USE **Alternating electric currents**
Alternating electric currents   621.31
  UF Alternating currents
       Electric currents, Alternating
  BT **Electric currents**
Alternative energy resources
  USE **Renewable energy resources**
Alternative histories   808.3; 808.83
  May be used for individual works, collec-
  tions, or materials about imaginative works
  featuring key changes in historical facts.
  BT **Fantasy fiction**
Alternative lifestyles (May subdiv. geog.)
       306
  Use for materials on ways of living regard-
  ed as unacceptable by conventional standards,
  especially those that reject consumerism, the
  work ethic, etc.
  BT **Lifestyles**
  RT **Counter culture**
Alternative medicine (May subdiv. geog.)
       610; 613; 615.5
  UF Therapeutic systems
  SA types of alternative medicine [to
       be added as needed]
  BT **Medicine**
  NT **Acupressure**
       Acupuncture
       Chiropractic
       Health self-care
       Holistic medicine
       Homeopathy
       Mental healing
       Naturopathy
       Reflexology
Alternative military service
  USE **National service**
Alternative press (May subdiv. geog.)
       070.4
  Use for materials about publications issued
  clandestinely and contrary to government reg-

ulation and for materials about publications is-
sued legally (and usually serially) and pro-
duced by radical, anti-establishment, or coun-
ter-culture groups.
  UF Underground literature
       Underground press
  BT **Press**
Alternative schools
  USE **Experimental schools**
Alternative universities
  USE **Free universities**
Alternative work schedules
  USE **Flexible hours of labor**
       Part-time employment
Altitude, Influence of
  USE **Environmental influence on
        humans**
Altruism   171
  UF Altruistic behavior
       Unselfishness
  BT **Conduct of life**
  RT **Charity**
       Helping behavior
Altruistic behavior
  USE **Altruism**
Altruists
  USE **Philanthropists**
Aluminum   669; 673
  BT **Metals**
  NT **Aluminum foil**
Aluminum alloys   669; 673
  BT **Alloys**
Aluminum foil   673
  BT **Aluminum**
       Packaging
Aluminum—Recycling   628.4; 673
  BT **Recycling**
Alzheimer's disease   616.8
  BT **Brain—Diseases**
Amateur films   778.5; 791.43
  May be used for individual works, collec-
  tions, or materials about amateur films.
  UF Amateur motion pictures
       Home movies
       Home video movies
       Personal films
  BT **Motion pictures**
  RT **Camcorders**
       Motion picture cameras
Amateur motion pictures
  USE **Amateur films**

Amateur radio stations   384.54;
   621.3841
   UF   Ham radio stations
   BT   Radio stations
        Shortwave radio
Amateur theater (May subdiv. geog.)
   792
   UF   Non-professional theater
        Play production
        Private theater
   BT   Amusements
        Theater
   NT   Charades
        Children's plays
        College and school drama
        One act plays
        Pantomimes
        Shadow pantomimes and plays
   RT   Acting
        Drama in education
        Little theater movement
Ambassadors (May subdiv. geog.)
   327.2092
   BT   Diplomats
Amendments, Equal rights
   USE   Equal rights amendments
America   970
   Use for general materials on the Western
   Hemisphere.
   SA   names of individual countries of
        the Western Hemisphere [to
        be added as needed]
   NT   Latin America
        North America
        South America
America—Antiquities   970.01
   BT   Antiquities
America—Civilization   970; 980
   Use for general materials on the civilization
   of the Western Hemisphere in modern times.
   Materials on ancient civilizations in America
   are entered under America—Antiquities; un-
   der a region, country, city, etc., with the sub-
   division Antiquities; or under the name of an
   ancient people. Materials limited to the civili-
   zation of the United States are entered under
   United States—Civilization.
   UF   American civilization
   BT   Civilization
America—Discovery and exploration
   USE   America—Exploration
America—Exploration   970.01
   UF   America—Discovery and explo-
        ration

   BT   Exploration
   NT   Northwest Passage
        United States—Exploration
America—History   970
   UF   American history
America—Politics and government   970
   RT   Pan-Americanism
American actors
   USE   Actors—United States
American actors and actresses
   USE   Actors—United States
American architecture
   USE   Architecture—United States
American art   709.73
   UF   Art, American
   BT   Art
   NT   American folk art
American artificial satellites   629.43;
   629.46
   UF   Artificial satellites, American
   BT   Artificial satellites
American artists
   USE   Artists—United States
American arts
   USE   Arts—United States
American authors   810.9; 920
   UF   Authors, American
   BT   Authors
   NT   African American authors
        American dramatists
        American novelists
        American poets
        Hispanic American authors
American ballads   811
   BT   American poetry
American Bicentennial
   USE   American Revolution Bicenten-
        nial, 1776-1976
American Bill of rights
   USE   United States. Constitution.
        1st-10th amendments
American bison
   USE   Bison
American characteristics
   USE   American national characteris-
        tics
American Civil War
   USE   United States—History—1861-
        1865, Civil War
American civilization
   USE   America—Civilization

American colonial style in architecture
       724
   UF   Colonial architecture
   BT   **Architecture**
American colonies
   USE   **United States—History—1600-
       1775, Colonial period**
American color prints   769.973
   UF   Color prints, American
   BT   **Color prints**
American composers
   USE   **Composers—United States**
American constitution
   USE   **United States. Constitution**
American cooking   641.5973
   Use for materials on cooking limited to
American national and regional styles.
   UF   Cookery, American
   SA   styles of regional American
       cooking, e.g. **Southern cook-
       ing** [to be added as needed]
   BT   **Cooking**
American decoration and ornament
   USE   **Decoration and ornament—
       United States**
American diaries   809; 920
   Use for collections of American diaries and
for materials about American diaries.
   BT   **American literature
       Diaries**
American diplomatic and consular ser-
       vice (May subdiv. geog.)   327.73;
       353.1
   UF   Diplomatic and consular service,
       American
       United States—Diplomatic and
       consular service
   BT   **Diplomatic and consular ser-
       vice**
American drama   812
   Use for general materials about American
drama, not for individual works.
   BT   **American literature
       Drama**
American drama—Collections   812.008
American drama—History and criticism
       812.009
American dramatists   812.009; 920
   UF   Dramatists, American
   BT   **American authors
       Dramatists**

American drawing   741.973
   UF   Drawing, American
   BT   **Drawing**
American economic assistance
   USE   **American foreign aid**
American engraving   760; 769
   UF   Engraving, American
   BT   **Engraving**
American espionage   327.1273; 355.3
   UF   Espionage, American
   BT   **Espionage**
American essays   814; 814.008
   BT   **American literature
       Essays**
American ethics
   USE   **Ethics—United States**
American exploring expeditions
   USE   **United States—Exploring expe-
       ditions**
American fables   813
   BT   **Fables**
American fiction   813
   May be used for collections or materials
about American fiction, not for individual
works.
   BT   **American literature
       Fiction**
American films
   USE   **Motion pictures—United States**
American flag
   USE   **Flags—United States**
American folk art   745.0973
   UF   Folk art, American
   BT   **American art
       Folk art**
American folk dancing
   USE   **Folk dancing—United States**
American folk music
   USE   **Folk music—United States**
American folk songs
   USE   **Folk songs—United States**
American foreign aid (May subdiv. geog.)
       338.91; 361.6
   UF   American economic assistance
       Economic assistance, American
   BT   **Foreign aid**
American furniture   684.100973;
       749.09073
   UF   Furniture, American
   SA   styles of American furniture [to
       be added as needed]
   BT   **Furniture**

American government
  USE **United States—Politics and
        government**
American graphic arts
  USE **Graphic arts—United States**
American historians
  USE **Historians—United States**
American history
  USE **America—History
        United States—History**
American hostages (May subdiv. geog.
  except U.S.) **920**
  BT **Hostages**
American hostages—Iran 920
  NT **Iran hostage crisis, 1979-1981**
American illustrators
  USE **Illustrators—United States**
American Indian authors
  USE **Native American authors**
American Indians
  USE **Native Americans**
American letters 816; 816.008
  BT **American literature
        Letters**
American literature (May subdiv. geog.
  by state or region) **810**
  May be subdivided by the topical subdivi-
  sions and literary forms used under **English
  literature;** or geographically by states or re-
  gions of the United States for works by or
  about several authors from a state or region or
  writing about a state or region, e.g. **American
  literature—Massachusetts; American literature—Southern States;** etc.
  SA various forms of American liter-
        ature, e.g. **American poetry;
        American satire;** etc. [to be
        added as needed]
  BT **Literature**
  NT **American diaries
        American drama
        American essays
        American fiction
        American letters
        American literature (Spanish)
        American poetry
        American prose literature
        American satire
        American speeches
        American wit and humor
        Beat generation**

**American literature—17th and 18th cen-
  turies 810**
  UF American literature—Colonial
        period
American literature—19th century 810
American literature—20th century 810
American literature—21st century 810
**American literature—African American
  authors 810.8; 810.9**
  May be used for collections or materials
  about American literature by several African
  American authors, not for individual works.
  Use same pattern for literatures and literary
  forms written by other ethnic groups or class-
  es of authors.
  UF African American literature
        American literature—Afro-
          American authors
        American literature—Black au-
          thors
        Black literature (American)
  SA particular forms of American lit-
        erature with the subdivision
        African American authors;
        e.g., **American poetry—
        African American authors**
        [to be added as needed]
  NT **Harlem Renaissance**
American literature—Afro-American authors
  USE **American literature—African
        American authors**
American literature—American Indian au-
  thors
  USE **American literature—Native
        American authors**
American literature—Black authors
  USE **American literature—African
        American authors**
American literature—Collections 810.8
  Use for collections of both poetry and prose
  by several American authors. Collections con-
  sisting of prose only are entered under
  American prose literature; collections of po-
  etry are entered under **American poetry—
  Collections.**
American literature—Colonial period
  USE **American literature—17th and
        18th centuries**
**American literature—Hispanic American
  authors 810**
  Use for materials on American literature in
  English written by American authors of Span-
  ish or Latin American origins. Materials on
  American literature written in Spanish are en-
  tered under **American literature (Spanish).**

American literature—Hispanic American authors—*Continued*
- UF   American literature—Latin American authors
  - Hispanic American literature (English)
- SA   genres of American literature with the subdivision *Hispanic American authors;* and **American literature** and genres of American literature with subdivisions for specific groups of Hispanic American authors, e.g. **American literature—Mexican American authors** [to be added as needed]
- NT   **American literature—Mexican American authors**

American literature—Latin American authors
- USE   **American literature—Hispanic American authors**

American literature—Massachusetts 810

American literature—Mexican American authors   810

Use for materials on American literature written in English by American authors of Mexican origins.
- UF   Chicano literature (English)
  - Mexican American literature (English)
- SA   genres of American literature with the subdivision *Mexican American authors* [to be added as needed]
- BT   **American literature—Hispanic American authors**

American literature—Native American authors   810.8; 810.9

May be used for collections or materials about American literature written in English by several Native American authors, not for individual works. Collections or materials about literature written in Native American languages by several Native American authors are entered under **Native American literature.**
- UF   American literature—American Indian authors

American literature—Southern States 810
- UF   Southern literature

American literature (Spanish)   860

Use for materials on American literature written in Spanish. Materials on American literature in English written by American authors of Spanish or Latin American origins are entered under **American literature—Hispanic American authors.**
- UF   Hispanic American literature (Spanish)
  - Spanish American literature
- SA   genres of American literature with the qualifier (Spanish) [to be added as needed]
- BT   **American literature**

American literature—Women authors 810.8; 810.9

May be used for collections or for materials about several American women authors.

American Loyalists   973.3
- UF   Loyalists, American
  - Tories, American
- BT   **United States—History—1775-1783, Revolution**

American military assistance (May subdiv. geog.)   **355**
- UF   Military assistance, American
- BT   **Military assistance**

American motion pictures
- USE   **Motion pictures—United States**

American music   780.973
- UF   Music, American
- BT   **Music**

American musicians
- USE   **Musicians—United States**

American national characteristics 306.0973; 973
- UF   American characteristics
  - National characteristics, American
  - United States—National characteristics
- BT   **National characteristics**

American national songs
- USE   **National songs—United States**

American newspapers
- USE   **Newspapers—United States**

American novelists   813.009; 920
- UF   Novelists, American
- BT   **American authors**
  - **Novelists**

American orations
- USE   **American speeches**

American painters
USE **Painters—United States**
American painting   759.13
UF   Painting, American
BT   **Painting**
American periodicals
USE   **Periodicals—United States**
American personal names
USE   **Personal names—United States**
American philosophers
USE   **Philosophers—United States**
American philosophy   191
UF   Philosophy, American
BT   **Philosophy**
American poetry   811
Use for general materials about American poetry, not for individual works.
BT   **American literature**
Poetry
NT   **American ballads**
American poetry—African American authors   811
May be used for collections or materials about American poetry by several African American authors, not for individual works.
UF   African American poetry
American poetry—Afro-American authors
American poetry—Black authors
Black poetry (American)
American poetry—Afro-American authors
USE   **American poetry—African American authors**
American poetry—Black authors
USE   **American poetry—African American authors**
American poetry—Collections   811.008
American poetry—History and criticism   811.009
American poets   811.009; 920
UF   Poets, American
BT   **American authors**
Poets
American politicians
USE   **Politicians—United States**
American politics
USE   **United States—Politics and government**
American pottery   738.0973
UF   Pottery, American
BT   **Pottery**

American prints   769.973
UF   Prints, American
BT   **Prints**
American propaganda   303.3; 327.1
UF   Propaganda, American
BT   **Propaganda**
American prose literature   818
Use for collections of prose writings by several American authors that may include a variety of literary forms, such as essays, fiction, orations, etc. May also be used for general materials about such prose writings.
UF   Prose literature, American
BT   **American literature**
American Revolution
USE   **United States—History—1775-1783, Revolution**
American Revolution Bicentennial, 1776-1976   973.3
UF   American Bicentennial
Bicentennial celebrations—United States—1976
United States—Bicentennial celebrations
United States—History—1775-1783, Revolution—Centennial celebrations, etc.
BT   **United States—Centennial celebrations, etc.**
American Revolution Bicentennial, 1776-1976—Collectibles   973.3075
BT   **Collectors and collecting**
American satire   817; 817.008
UF   Satire, American
BT   **American literature**
Satire
American schools
USE   **Schools—United States**
American sculptors
USE   **Sculptors—United States**
American sculpture   730.973
BT   **Sculpture**
American songs   782.420973
BT   **Songs**
NT   **Folk songs—United States**
National songs—United States
American-Spanish War, 1898
USE   **Spanish-American War, 1898**
American speeches   815; 815.008
UF   American orations
Speeches, addresses, etc., American

American speeches—*Continued*
    BT   American literature
           Speeches
American technical assistance (May
      subdiv. geog.)   338.91; 361.6
    UF   Technical assistance, American
    BT   Technical assistance
American teenagers
    USE   Teenagers—United States
American tourists
    USE   American travelers
American travelers   910.92; 920
    UF   American tourists
    BT   Travelers
American wit and humor   817;
      817.008; 817.009

Use for collections by several authors or for materials about American wit and humor. Individual works by American humorists are entered under **Wit and humor.**

    BT   American literature
           Wit and humor
American youth
    USE   Youth—United States
Americana   069; 973

Use for materials about American objects of interest to collectors for their historical value, such as documents, relics, etc., including items of little intrinsic value. Materials about old American objects that have aesthetic as well as financial value, usually furniture or decorative arts, are entered under **Antiques—United States.**

    BT   Collectors and collecting
           Popular culture—United States
           United States—Civilization
           United States—History
    RT   Antiques—United States
Americanisms   427

Use for materials on words and expressions peculiar to the United States.

    UF   English language—Americanisms
    BT   English language—Dialects
Americanization   305.813; 306.0973
    BT   Socialization
    NT   United States—Immigration
           and emigration
    RT   Immigration and emigration
           Naturalization
Americans (May subdiv. geog. except
      U.S.)   305.813; 920; 973

Use for materials on citizens of the United States.

    RT   United States

Americans—Foreign countries   305.813;
      920; 973
Americans—Greece   305.813
Amish   289.7
    BT   Christian sects
           Mennonites
Ammunition   623.4
    SA   types of ammunition, e.g.
           Bombs [to be added as need-
           ed]
    BT   Explosives
           Ordnance
           Projectiles
    NT   Bombs
    RT   Firearms
           Gunpowder
Amnesty   364.6
    BT   Administration of criminal jus-
           tice
           Executive power
    RT   Clemency
           Forgiveness
           Pardon
Amniocentesis   618.3
    BT   Prenatal diagnosis
Amphetamines   615
    UF   Pep pills
    SA   types of amphetamines, e.g.
           Methamphetamine [to be
           added as needed]
    BT   Stimulants
    NT   Methamphetamine
Amphibians (May subdiv. geog.)   567;
      597.8
    SA   types of amphibians [to be add-
           ed as needed]
    BT   Animals
    NT   Frogs
           Salamanders
Amphibious operations
    USE   names of wars with the subdivi-
           sion *Amphibious operations,*
           e.g. **World War, 1939-**
           1945—Amphibious opera-
           tions [to be added as needed]
Amplifiers (Electronics)   621.3815
    SA   types of amplifiers [to be added
           as needed]
    BT   Electronics
    NT   Masers
           Transistor amplifiers

Amplifiers, Transistor
USE **Transistor amplifiers**
Amusement parks (May subdiv. geog.)
791.06
UF Theme parks
SA names of specific parks [to be
added as needed]
BT **Parks**
NT **Walt Disney World (Fla.)**
RT **Carnivals**
Amusements (May subdiv. geog.) **790**
UF Entertainments
Pastimes
SA types of amusements, e.g. **Car-
nivals** [to be added as need-
ed]
NT **Amateur theater**
Carnivals
Charades
Children's parties
Christmas entertainments
Church entertainments
Circus
Concerts
Creative activities
Dance
Fireworks
Fortune telling
Hobbies
Juggling
Literary recreations
Magic tricks
Mathematical recreations
Puzzles
Riddles
Roller coasters
Scientific recreations
Shadow pictures
Skits
Theater
Toys
Tricks
Vaudeville
Ventriloquism
RT **Entertaining**
Games
Indoor games
Play
Recreation
Sports

Anabolic steroids
USE **Steroids**
Anaesthetics
USE **Anesthetics**
Analysis
USE types of chemicals and sub-
stances with the subdivision
Analysis, e.g. **Water—Analy-
sis; Milk—Analysis;** etc., for
materials on methods of ana-
lyzing those items [to be add-
ed as needed]
Analysis (Chemistry)
USE **Analytical chemistry**
Analysis (Mathematics)
USE **Calculus**
Functions
Mathematical analysis
Analysis of food
USE **Food adulteration and inspec-
tion**
Food—Analysis
Analytic geometry 516.3
UF Geometry, Analytic
BT **Geometry**
Analytical chemistry 543
UF Analysis (Chemistry)
Chemical analysis
Chemistry, Analytic
Qualitative analysis
Quantitative analysis
SA types of substances with the
subdivision *Analysis,* e.g. **Wa-
ter—Analysis** [to be added as
needed]
BT **Chemistry**
NT **Distillation**
Food—Analysis
Water—Analysis
Anarchism and anarchists 320.5; 335
BT **Freedom**
Political crimes and offenses
Political science
RT **Terrorism**
Anatomy 571.3; 611
SA names of organs and regions of
the body and subjects with
the subdivision *Anatomy,* e.g.
**Heart—Anatomy; Birds—
Anatomy;** etc. [to be added
as needed]

Anatomy—*Continued*
  BT   Biology
       Medicine
  NT   Animals—Anatomy
       Artistic anatomy
       Birds—Anatomy
       Cardiovascular system
       Comparative anatomy
       Foot
       Glands
       Head
       Heart—Anatomy
       Human anatomy
       Immune system
       Musculoskeletal system
       Nervous system
       Plants—Anatomy
       Reproductive system
       Respiratory system
       Skin
       Stomach
       Throat
  RT   Physiology
Anatomy, Artistic
  USE Artistic anatomy
Anatomy, Comparative
  USE Comparative anatomy
Anatomy of animals
  USE Animals—Anatomy
Anatomy of plants
  USE Plants—Anatomy
Ancestor worship (May subdiv. geog.)
    202
  UF   Worship of the dead
  BT   Religion
Ancestry
  USE Genealogy
       Heredity
Ancient architecture (May subdiv. geog.)
    722
  UF   Architecture, Ancient
  BT   Archeology
       Architecture
  NT   Byzantine architecture
       Greek architecture
       Pyramids
       Roman architecture
Ancient art (May subdiv. geog.)   709.01
  UF   Art, Ancient
  BT   Art
  NT   Byzantine art
       Greek art

       Roman art
Ancient civilization   306.093; 930
  UF   Civilization, Ancient
  BT   Ancient history
       Civilization
  NT   Classical civilization
Ancient geography   913
    Use for materials on the geography of the ancient world in general. Materials on the ancient geography of one country or region still existing in modern times are entered under the name of the place with the subdivision *Historical geography*. Materials on the geography of regions or countries of antiquity that no longer exist as such in modern times are entered under the name of the place with the subdivision *Geography*.
  UF   Classical geography
       Geography, Ancient
  SA   names of modern countries with the subdivision *Historical geography,* e.g. **Greece—Historical geography;** and names of places of antiquity with the subdivision *Geography,* e.g. **Gaul—Geography** [to be added as needed]
  BT   Ancient history
       Historical geography
  NT   Gaul—Geography
       Greece—Historical geography
       Rome—Geography
Ancient Greece
  USE Greece—History—0-323
Ancient Greece—Description
  USE Greece—Description and travel—0-323
Ancient history   930
    Use for materials on the history of the ancient world up to the fall of Rome not limited to a single country or region.
  UF   History, Ancient
  SA   names of ancient peoples, e.g. **Hittites;** and names of countries of antiquity, with the subdivision *History* [to be added as needed]
  BT   World history
  NT   Ancient civilization
       Ancient geography
       Bible
       Classical dictionaries
       Hittites
       Inscriptions
       Numismatics

Ancient philosophy   180
    UF   Greek philosophy
           Philosophy, Ancient
           Roman philosophy
    BT   **Philosophy**
    NT   **Stoics**
Androgyny   155.3; 305.3
    BT   **Sex differences (Psychology)**
           Sex role
Anecdotes   808.88
    May be used for collections of anecdotes
and for materials about anecdotes.
    UF   Facetiae
           Stories
    SA   subjects with the subdivision *An-
           ecdotes* [to be added as need-
           ed]
    NT   **Music—Anecdotes**
    RT   **Wit and humor**
Anesthetics   615; 617.9
    UF   Anaesthetics
    BT   **Materia medica**
    RT   **Pain**
           Surgery
Angels   235
    BT   **Heaven**
           Spirits
Anger   152.4
    UF   Rage
           Wrath
    BT   **Emotions**
Angina pectoris   616.1
    BT   **Heart diseases**
Anglican Church
    USE   **Church of England**
Angling
    USE   **Fishing**
Anglo-American law
    USE   **Common law**
Anglo-French intervention in Egypt, 1956
    USE   **Sinai Campaign, 1956**
Anglo-Saxon language
    USE   **English language—Old English
           period**
Anglo-Saxon literature
    USE   **English literature—Old English
           period**
Anglo-Saxons   305.82; 941.01
    BT   **Great Britain—History—0-1066
           Teutonic peoples**
Animal abuse
    USE   **Animal welfare**

Animal attacks   591.6
    UF   Attacks by animals
    BT   **Dangerous animals**
Animal babies   591.3
    Use for materials on baby animals of sever-
al species. Baby animals of a particular species are entered under the name of the species.
    UF   Animals—Infancy
           Baby animals
    BT   **Animals**
Animal behavior   591.5
    UF   Animals—Behavior
           Behavior
           Habits of animals
    SA   types of specific behavior, e.g.
           **Animals—Migration; Hiber-
           nation; Sexual behavior in
           animals;** etc.; and types of
           animals with the subdivision
           Behavior, e.g. **Birds—Behav-
           ior** [to be added as needed]
    BT   **Animals**
           Zoology
    NT   **Animal communication**
           Animal courtship
           Animal defenses
           Animal sounds
           Animals—Food
           Animals—Migration
           Birds—Behavior
           Hibernation
           Instinct
           Monkeys—Behavior
           Nest building
           Primates—Behavior
           Sexual behavior in animals
    RT   **Animal intelligence**
           Tracking and trailing
Animal camouflage
    USE   **Camouflage (Biology)**
Animal communication   591.59
    UF   Animal language
           Animals—Language
           Communication among animals
    BT   **Animal behavior**
    RT   **Animal sounds**
Animal courtship   591.56
    UF   Animals—Courtship
           Courtship (Animal behavior)
           Courtship of animals
           Mate selection in animals

Animal courtship—*Continued*
    Mating behavior
  BT **Animal behavior**
      Sexual behavior in animals
Animal defenses 591.47
  UF Defense mechanisms of animals
      Self-defense in animals
      Self-protection in animals
  BT **Animal behavior**
  NT **Camouflage (Biology)**
Animal drawing
  USE **Animal painting and illustration**
Animal embryos, Frozen
  USE **Frozen embryos**
Animal experimentation 616
  UF Experimentation on animals
      Laboratory animal experimentation
  BT **Research**
  NT **Vivisection**
  RT **Animal welfare**
Animal exploitation
  USE **Animal welfare**
Animal-facilitated therapy
  USE **Pet therapy**
Animal flight 573.7
  UF Animals—Flight
  SA types of animals with the subdivision *Flight,* e.g. **Birds—Flight** [to be added as needed]
  BT **Animal locomotion**
      Flight
  NT **Birds—Flight**
Animal food
  USE **Animals—Food**
      Food of animal origin
Animal habitations
  USE **Animals—Habitations**
Animal homes
  USE **Animals—Habitations**
Animal housing 636.08
  Use for materials on houses or habitations provided by humans for either wild or domestic animals. Materials on the natural shelters and homes animals build for themselves, such as burrows, dens, lairs, etc., are entered under **Animals—Habitations.**
  UF Animals—Housing
      Domestic animal dwellings
      Domestic animals—Housing
      Habitations of domestic animals

  SA types of animals with the subdivision *Housing,* e.g. **Pets—Housing** [to be added as needed]
  BT **Animals**
  NT **Beehives**
      Birdhouses
      Pets—Housing
  RT **Animals—Habitations**
Animal husbandry
  USE **Livestock industry**
Animal industry
  USE **Livestock industry**
Animal instinct
  USE **Instinct**
Animal intelligence 591.5
  UF Animal psychology
      Intelligence of animals
  SA types of animals with the subdivision *Psychology* [to be added as needed]
  BT **Animals**
  NT **Dogs—Psychology**
      Psychology of learning
  RT **Animal behavior**
      Comparative psychology
      Instinct
Animal kingdom
  USE **Zoology**
Animal language
  USE **Animal communication**
      Animal sounds
Animal light
  USE **Bioluminescence**
Animal locomotion 573.7; 591.57
  UF Animals—Movements
      Movements of animals
  BT **Animals**
      Locomotion
  NT **Animal flight**
Animal lore
  USE **Animals—Folklore**
      Animals in literature
      Mythical animals
      Natural history
Animal luminescence
  USE **Bioluminescence**
Animal magnetism
  USE **Hypnotism**
Animal migration
  USE **Animals—Migration**

Animal oils
USE **Oils and fats**
**Animal painting and illustration   704.9;
743.6; 758**
Use for materials on the art of painting or
drawing animals. Materials on the depiction of
animals in works of art are entered under **An-
imals in art.** Popular materials consisting
chiefly of photographs or illustrations of ani-
mals are entered under **Animals—Pictorial
works.**
UF   Animal drawing
BT   **Painting**
RT   **Animals in art
Animals—Pictorial works
Photography of animals**
Animal parasites
USE   **Parasites**
Animal photography
USE   **Photography of animals**
Animal physiology
USE   **Zoology**
Animal pictures
USE   **Animals—Pictorial works**
Animal pounds
USE   **Animal shelters**
Animal products   338.1; 338.4
UF   Products, Animal
SA   types of animal products [to be
added as needed]
BT   **Commercial products**
NT   **Dairy products
Hides and skins
Ivory
Leather
Wool**
Animal psychology
USE   **Animal intelligence
Comparative psychology**
Animal reproduction   571.8
UF   Animals—Birth
Animals—Reproduction
BT   **Animals
Reproduction**
Animal rights (May subdiv. geog.)   **179**
Use for materials on the inherent rights at-
tributed to animals. Materials on the protec-
tion and treatment of animals are entered un-
der **Animal welfare.** Materials on the political
movement to promote the idea of animal
rights are entered under **Animal rights move-
ment.**
UF   Animals' rights
Rights of animals

RT   **Animal rights movement
Animal welfare**
Animal rights movement (May subdiv.
geog.)   **179**
UF   Animal rights movements
Animal welfare movement
Antivivisection movement
BT   **Social movements**
RT   **Animal rights
Animal welfare**
Animal rights movements
USE   **Animal rights movement**
Animal sexual behavior
USE   **Sexual behavior in animals**
Animal shelters   179; 636.08
UF   Animal pounds
BT   **Animal welfare**
Animal signs
USE   **Animal tracks**
Animal sounds   573.9; 591.59
UF   Animal language
Animals—Sounds
BT   **Animal behavior**
NT   **Birdsongs**
RT   **Animal communication**
Animal stories
USE   **Animals—Fiction**
Animal tracks   590
UF   Animal signs
Tracks of animals
BT   **Tracking and trailing**
Animal training
USE   **Animals—Training**
Animal welfare   179
Use for materials on the protection and
treatment of animals. Materials on the inher-
ent rights attributed to animals are entered un-
der **Animal rights.** Materials on the political
movement to promote the idea of animal
rights are entered under **Animal rights move-
ment.**
UF   Abuse of animals
Animal abuse
Animal exploitation
Animals—Mistreatment
Animals—Protection
Animals—Treatment
Cruelty to animals
Humane treatment of animals
Laboratory animal welfare
Prevention of cruelty to animals
Protection of animals

Animal welfare—*Continued*
  NT Animal shelters
  RT Animal experimentation
      Animal rights
      Animal rights movement
Animal welfare movement
  USE Animal rights movement
Animals (May subdiv. geog.) 590
    Use for nonscientific materials. Materials on
  the science of animals are entered under **Zool-
  ogy.** Subdivisions used under this heading
  may be used under the names of orders, class-
  es, or individual species of animals.
  UF Beasts
      Fauna
      Wild animals
  SA names of orders and classes of
        the animal kingdom; kinds of
        animals characterized by their
        environments; and names of
        individual species [to be add-
        ed as needed]
  NT Amphibians
      Animal babies
      Animal behavior
      Animal housing
      Animal intelligence
      Animal locomotion
      Animal reproduction
      Aquatic animals
      Birds
      Carnivorous animals
      Dangerous animals
      Desert animals
      Domestic animals
      Extinct animals
      Forest animals
      Furbearing animals
      Game and game birds
      Insects
      Invertebrates
      Jungle animals
      Mammals
      Mountain animals
      Pets
      Poisonous animals
      Predatory animals
      Prehistoric animals
      Rare animals
      Reptiles
      Spiders
      Stream animals
      Swamp animals

      Ticks
      Vertebrates
      Wildlife
      Wildlife attracting
      Working animals
      Worms
  RT Zoology
      Zoos
Animals—Anatomy 571.3
  UF Anatomy of animals
      Structural zoology
      Zoology—Anatomy
  BT Anatomy
      Zoology
  NT Fur
Animals and the handicapped 636.088
  UF Handicapped and animals
      Pets and the handicapped
  BT Animals—Training
  NT Guide dogs
      Hearing ear dogs
      Pet therapy
Animals as food
  USE Food of animal origin
Animals—Behavior
  USE Animal behavior
Animals—Birth
  USE Animal reproduction
Animals—Camouflage
  USE Camouflage (Biology)
Animals—Color 573.5; 591.47
  BT Color
Animals—Courtship
  USE Animal courtship
Animals—Diseases 571.9; 636.089
  UF Diseases of animals
      Domestic animals—Diseases
  SA types of animals with the subdi-
        vision *Diseases* [to be added
        as needed]
  BT Diseases
  NT Horses—Diseases
  RT Veterinary medicine
Animals, Edible
  USE Food of animal origin
Animals—Fiction 808.83
    Use for collections of stories about animals.
  Materials about the portrayal of animals in lit-
  erature are entered under **Animals in litera-
  ture.**

Animals—Fiction—*Continued*
  UF Animal stories
  SA types of animals with the subdi-
        vision *Fiction,* e.g. **Dogs—**
        Fiction [to be added as need-
        ed]
  RT **Animals in literature**
       Fables
Animals—Filmography   016.591
Animals—Flight
  USE **Animal flight**
Animals—Folklore   398.24
  UF Animal lore
  BT **Folklore**
  NT **Dragons**
       Ethnozoology
       Monsters
  RT **Mythical animals**
Animals—Food   591.5
    Use for materials on the food and food hab-
  its of animals. Materials on human food of
  animal origin are entered under **Food of ani-**
  mal origin.
  UF Animal food
       Feeding behavior in animals
  SA types of animals and species of
        animals with the subdivision
        Food [to be added as needed]
  BT **Animal behavior**
       Food
  NT **Feeds**
       Food chains (Ecology)
Animals—Habitations   591.56
    Use for materials on the natural shelters and
  homes animals build for themselves, such as
  burrows, dens, lairs, etc. Materials on houses
  or habitations provided by humans for either
  wild or domestic animals are entered under
  Animal housing.
  UF Animal habitations
       Animal homes
       Habitations of wild animals
       Wild animal dwellings
  SA types of animals and individual
        species of animals with the
        subdivision *Habitations,* or
        Nests, e.g. **Beavers—Habita-**
        tions; Birds—Nests; etc. [to
        be added as needed]
  NT **Nest building**
  RT **Animal housing**
Animals—Hibernation
  USE **Hibernation**

Animals—Housing
  USE **Animal housing**
Animals in art   704.9
    Use for materials on the depiction of ani-
  mals in works of art. Materials on the art of
  painting or drawing animals are entered under
  Animal painting and illustration. Materials
  consisting chiefly of photographs or illustra-
  tions of animals are entered under **Animals—**
  Pictorial works.
  BT **Art—Themes**
  RT **Animal painting and illustra-**
       tion
       Animals—Pictorial works
Animals in literature   809
    Use for materials on the theme of animals
  in literature. Collections of poems or stories
  about animals are entered under **Animals—**
  Poetry or **Animals—Fiction.**
  UF Animal lore
  SA phrase headings for specific ani-
        mals in literature, e.g. **Dogs**
        in literature [to be added as
        needed]
  BT **Literature—Themes**
  RT **Animals—Fiction**
       Animals—Poetry
Animals in motion pictures   791.43
  BT **Motion pictures**
Animals in police work   363.2; 636.088
  BT **Police**
       Working animals
Animals—Infancy
  USE **Animal babies**
Animals—Language
  USE **Animal communication**
Animals—Migration   591.56
  UF Animal migration
       Migration
  SA types of animals with the subdi-
        vision *Migration,* e.g. **Birds—**
        Migration [to be added as
        needed]
  BT **Animal behavior**
Animals—Mistreatment
  USE **Animal welfare**
Animals—Movements
  USE **Animal locomotion**
Animals, Mythical
  USE **Mythical animals**
Animals—Photography
  USE **Photography of animals**

Animals—Pictorial works   590.22

   Use for popular materials consisting chiefly of photographs or illustrations of animals. Materials on the art of painting or drawing animals are entered under **Animal painting and illustration**. Materials on the depiction of animals in works of art are entered under **Animals in art.**

   UF   Animal pictures

   RT   **Animal painting and illustration**

         Animals in art

         Photography of animals

Animals—Poetry   808.81

   Use for collections of poetry about animals. Materials on the theme of animals in literature are entered under **Animals in literature.**

   RT   **Animals in literature**

Animals, Prehistoric

   USE   **Prehistoric animals**

Animals—Protection

   USE   **Animal welfare**

Animals—Reproduction

   USE   **Animal reproduction**

Animals' rights

   USE   **Animal rights**

Animals—Sexual behavior

   USE   **Sexual behavior in animals**

Animals—Sounds

   USE   **Animal sounds**

Animals—Temperature

   USE   **Body temperature**

Animals—Training   636.088

   UF   Animal training

         Training of animals

   SA   types of animals with the subdivision *Training*, e.g. **Horses—Training** [to be added as needed]

   NT   **Animals and the handicapped**

         Dogs—Training

Animals—Treatment

   USE   **Animal welfare**

Animals—United States   591.973

   UF   Zoology—United States

Animals, Useful and harmful

   USE   **Economic zoology**

Animals—War use   355.4

   UF   War use of animals

   BT   **Working animals**

   NT   **Dogs—War use**

Animated cartoons

   USE   **Animated films**

Animated films   741.5; 791.43

   May be used for individual works, collections, or materials about animated films.

   UF   Animated cartoons

         Cartoons, Animated

         Motion picture cartoons

   BT   **Cartoons and caricatures**

         Motion pictures

   RT   **Animation (Cinematography)**

Animated television programs   791.45

   May be used for individual works, collections, or materials about animated television programs.

   UF   Cartoons, Television

         Television cartoons

   BT   **Television programs**

Animation (Cinematography)   741.5; 778.5

   BT   **Cinematography**

   RT   **Animated films**

Anniversaries   394.2

   UF   Celebrations, anniversaries, etc.

         Commemorations

   SA   ethnic groups, classes of persons, individuals, corporate bodies, places, religious denominations, historic or social movements, and historic events with the subdivision *Anniversaries*, for materials about anniversary celebrations, e.g. **Shakespeare, William, 1564-1616—Anniversaries**, and names of places, corporate bodies, and historical events with the subdivision *Centennial celebrations, etc.*, e.g. **United States—History—1861-1865, Civil War—Centennial celebrations, etc.** [to be added as needed]

   BT   **Manners and customs**

   NT   **Birthdays**

   RT   **Days**

         Festivals

         Holidays

Annual income guarantee

   USE   **Guaranteed annual income**

Annuals

   USE   **Almanacs**

         Calendars

         Periodicals

Annuals—*Continued*
> School yearbooks
> Yearbooks
> and subjects and names of countries, cities, etc., individual persons, families, and corporate bodies with the subdivision *Periodicals,* e.g. **Engineering—Periodicals** [to be added as needed]

Annuals (Plants)   582.1; 635.9
> BT   Cultivated plants
> Flower gardening
> Flowers

Annuities   368.3
> BT   Investments
> Retirement income
> NT   Pensions
> RT   Life insurance

Annulment of marriage
> USE   Marriage—Annulment

Anointing of the sick   265
> UF   Extreme unction
> Last rites (Sacraments)
> Last sacraments
> BT   Sacraments

Anonyms
> USE   Pseudonyms

Anorexia nervosa   616.85
> BT   Eating disorders

Answers to questions
> USE   Questions and answers

Antarctic expeditions
> USE   Antarctica—Exploration

Antarctic regions
> USE   Antarctica

Antarctica   998
> Use for materials on the continent of Antarctica and the regions adjacent to it.
> UF   Antarctic regions
> BT   Earth
> Polar regions
> RT   South Pole

Antarctica—Exploration   919.8
> UF   Antarctic expeditions
> Polar expeditions
> SA   names of expeditions, e.g. **Byrd Antarctic Expedition** [to be added as needed]
> BT   Exploration
> Scientific expeditions
> NT   Byrd Antarctic Expedition

Antenuptial contracts
> USE   Marriage contracts

Anthologies   080; 808.8
> Use for collections of general interest by several authors not limited to works of literature or focused on a single subject.
> UF   Collected papers (Anthologies)
> Collected works
> Collections (Anthologies)
> Collections of literature
> Literary collections
> Readings (Anthologies)
> SA   form headings for minor literary forms that represent collections of works of several authors, e.g. **Essays; American essays; Parodies; Short stories;** etc.; major literary forms and national literatures with the subdivision *Collections,* e.g. **Poetry—Collections; English literature—Collections;** etc.; and subjects with the subdivision *Literary collections,* for collections focused on a single subject by two or more authors involving two or more literary forms, e.g. **Cats—Literary collections** [to be added as needed]
> BT   Books

Anthropogeography
> USE   Human geography

Anthropology (May subdiv. geog.)   301; 599.9
> UF   Human race
> SA   names of races and peoples, e.g. **Navajo Indians** [to be added as needed]
> BT   Social sciences
> NT   Acculturation
> Anthropometry
> Ethnopsychology
> Human geography
> Language and languages
> National characteristics
> Physical anthropology
> Social change
> RT   Civilization
> Culture
> Ethnology
> Human beings

Anthropometry 599.9
  UF Skeletal remains
  BT Anthropology
     Ethnology
     Human beings
  NT Fingerprints
Anti-abortion movement
  USE Pro-life movement
Anti-Americanism
  USE United States—Foreign opinion
Anti-apartheid movement 172; 320.5;
     323.1
  BT Civil rights
     Social movements
     South Africa—Race relations
  RT Apartheid
Anti-fascist movements
  USE World War, 1939-1945—Un-
     derground movements
Anti-Nazi movement
  USE World War, 1939-1945—Un-
     derground movements
Anti-poverty programs
  USE Domestic economic assistance
Anti-Reformation
  USE Counter-Reformation
Anti-terrorism
  USE Terrorism—Prevention
Anti-utopias
  USE Dystopias
Anti-war films
  USE War films
Anti-war poetry
  USE War poetry
Anti-war stories
  USE War stories
Antiabortion movement
  USE Pro-life movement
Antiamericanism
  USE United States—Foreign opinion
Antiballistic missiles
  USE Antimissile missiles
Antibiotics 615
  SA names of specific antibiotics [to
     be added as needed]
  BT Drug therapy
  NT Penicillin
Antibusing
  USE Busing (School integration)

Anticommunist movements (May subdiv.
     geog.) 322.4
  BT Communism
Anticorrosive paint
  USE Corrosion and anticorrosives
Antimissile missiles 358.1; 623.4
  UF ABMs
     Antiballistic missiles
  BT Guided missiles
Antinuclear movement (May subdiv.
     geog.) 303.48; 327.1; 363.17
  UF Nuclear freeze movement
  BT Arms control
     Nuclear weapons
     Social movements
  RT Nuclear power plants—Envi-
     ronmental aspects
Antipoverty programs
  USE Domestic economic assistance
Antiquarian books
  USE Rare books
Antique and classic cars (May subdiv.
     geog.) 629.222
  UF Antique automobiles
     Antique cars
     Classic automobiles
     Classic cars
     Vintage automobiles
     Vintage cars
  BT Automobiles
Antique and vintage motorcycles (May
     subdiv. geog.) 629.227
  UF Antique motorcycles
     Classic motorcycles
     Vintage motorcycles
  BT Motorcycles
Antique automobiles
  USE Antique and classic cars
Antique cars
  USE Antique and classic cars
Antique motorcycles
  USE Antique and vintage motorcy-
     cles
Antiques (May subdiv. geog.) 745.1
  Use for materials on old decorative or utili-
  tarian objects that have aesthetic or historical
  importance and financial value. Materials on
  any objects of interest to collectors, including
  mass produced items of little intrinsic value,
  are entered under Collectibles.
  SA subjects and names with the
     subdivision Collectibles, e.g.
     American Revolution Bicen-

Antiques—*Continued*

tennial, 1776-1976—**Collectibles;** and types of objects collected, excluding antiquities and natural objects, with the subdivision *Collectors and collecting,* e.g. **Boxes—Collectors and collecting** [to be added as needed]

- BT **Antiquities**
  Collectors and collecting
  Decoration and ornament
  Decorative arts
- NT **Art objects**
  Collectors and collecting
  Victoriana

Antiques—United States   745.10973

Use for materials about old American objects that have aesthetic as well as financial value, usually furniture or decorative arts. Materials about American objects of interest to collectors for their historical value, such as documents, relics, etc., including items of little intrinsic value, are entered under **Americana.**

- RT **Americana**

Antiquities   930.1

Use for general materials on the relics or monuments of ancient times. Materials on the relics or monuments of an extinct city or town are entered under the name of the city or town.

- UF Archeological specimens
  Ruins
- SA names of extinct cities, e.g. **Delphi (Extinct city);** and names of groups of people extant in modern times and names of cities (except extinct cities), countries, regions, etc., with the subdivision *Antiquities,* e.g. **Native Americans—Antiquities; United States—Antiquities;** etc. [to be added as needed]
- NT **America—Antiquities**
  Antiques
  Bible—Antiquities
  Chicago (Ill.)—Antiquities
  Christian antiquities
  Classical antiquities
  Egypt—Antiquities
  Jews—Antiquities
  Native Americans—Antiquities
  Ohio—Antiquities

Prehistoric peoples
United States—Antiquities
- RT **Archeology**

Antiquities—Collection and preservation   069
- UF Preservation of antiquities
- BT **Collectors and collecting**

Antiquity of man
- USE **Human origins**

Antisemitism (May subdiv. geog.)   **305.892**
- BT **Prejudices**
- NT **Holocaust, 1933-1945**
  Jews—Persecutions

Antiseptics   614.4; 617.9
- BT **Therapeutics**
- RT **Disinfection and disinfectants**
  Surgery

Antislavery
- USE **Abolitionists**
  Slavery
  Slaves—Emancipation

Antistalking laws
- USE **Stalking**

Antitank warfare
- USE **Tank warfare**

Antitrust law (May subdiv. geog.)   **343.07**
- UF Industrial trusts—Law and legislation
- BT **Commercial law**
- RT **Industrial trusts**

Antivivisection movement
- USE **Animal rights movement**

Antiwar movements
- USE **Peace movements**

Antonyms
- USE **Opposites**
  and names of languages with the subdivision *Synonyms and antonyms,* e.g. **English language—Synonyms and antonyms** [to be added as needed]

Ants   595.79
- BT **Insects**

Anxieties
- USE **Anxiety**

Anxiety   152.4
- UF Anxieties
  Anxiousness

Anxiety—*Continued*
  BT Emotions
       Neuroses
       Stress (Psychology)
  NT Post-traumatic stress disorder
       Separation anxiety in children
  RT Fear
       Worry
Anxiousness
  USE Anxiety
Apartheid   320.5
   Use for materials on the economic, political,
   and social policies of the government of
   South Africa designed to segregate racial
   groups in South Africa and Namibia.
  UF Separate development (Race re-
       lations)
  BT Segregation
       South Africa—Race relations
  RT Anti-apartheid movement
Apartment houses (May subdiv. geog.)
       647; 728
  BT Buildings
       Domestic architecture
       Houses
       Housing
  NT Apartments
       Condominiums
       Tenement houses
Apartments (May subdiv. geog.)   643
  UF Flats
  BT Apartment houses
Apiculture
  USE Beekeeping
Apocalyptic fantasies
  USE Fantasy fiction
       Fantasy films
       Fantasy television programs
       Robinsonades
       Science fiction
       War films
       War stories
Apollo project   629.45
  UF Project Apollo
  BT Life support systems (Space
       environment)
       Orbital rendezvous (Space
       flight)
       Space flight to the moon

Apologetic works
  USE Apologetics
       and religions and denominations
       with the subdivision *Apologet-
       ic works,* for materials de-
       fending those religions or de-
       nominations, e.g. **Christiani-
       ty—Apologetic works** for
       materials defending Christiani-
       ty; and religions, denomina-
       tions, religious orders, and sa-
       cred works with the subdivi-
       sion *Controversial literature,*
       for materials that argue
       against or express opposition
       to those groups or works, e.g.
       **Christianity—Controversial
       literature** for materials attack-
       ing Christianity [to be added
       as needed]
Apologetics   202; 239
  UF Apologetic works
  SA religions and denominations with
       the subdivision *Apologetic
       works,* for materials defending
       those religions or denomina-
       tions, e.g. **Christianity—
       Apologetic works** for materi-
       als defending Christianity; and
       religions, denominations, reli-
       gious orders, and sacred
       works with the subdivision
       Controversial literature, for
       materials that argue against or
       express opposition to those
       groups or works, e.g. **Chris-
       tianity—Controversial litera-
       ture** for materials attacking
       Christianity [to be added as
       needed]
  BT Theology
  NT Christianity—Apologetic works
       Natural theology
Apoplexy
  USE Stroke
Apostles   225.92
  UF Disciples, Twelve
  BT Christian saints
       Church history—30-600, Early
       church

Apostles' Creed   238
  BT   Creeds
Apostolic Church
  USE   Church history—30-600, Early
         church
Apparatus, Chemical
  USE   Chemical apparatus
Apparatus, Electric
  USE   Electric apparatus and appli-
         ances
Apparatus, Electronic
  USE   Electronic apparatus and ap-
         pliances
Apparatus, Scientific
  USE   Scientific apparatus and in-
         struments
Apparitions   133.1
  UF   Phantoms
       Specters
  BT   Parapsychology
       Spirits
  NT   Ghosts
  RT   Hallucinations and illusions
       Spiritualism
       Visions
Appearance, Personal
  USE   Personal appearance
Apperception   153.7
  BT   Educational psychology
       Psychology
  NT   Attention
       Consciousness
       Number concept
  RT   Perception
       Theory of knowledge
Apple
  USE   Apples
Apple Macintosh (Computer)
  USE   Macintosh (Computer)
Apples   641.3
  UF   Apple
  BT   Fruit
Appliances, Electric
  USE   Electric apparatus and appli-
         ances
         Electric household appliances
Appliances, Electronic
  USE   Electronic apparatus and ap-
         pliances
Applications for college
  USE   College applications

Applications for positions   331.12;
      650.14
  UF   Employment applications
       Employment references
       Job applications
       Letters of recommendation
       Recommendations for positions
  BT   Job hunting
       Personnel management
  NT   Interviewing
       Résumés (Employment)
Applied arts
  USE   Decorative arts
Applied mechanics   620.1
    Use for materials on the application of the
  principles of mechanics to engineering struc-
  tures other than machinery. Materials on the
  application of the principles of mechanics to
  the design, construction, and operation of ma-
  chinery are entered under **Mechanical engi-
  neering.**
  UF   Mechanics, Applied
  BT   Mechanics
Applied psychology   158
  UF   Industrial psychology
       Practical psychology
       Psychology, Applied
  SA   subjects with the subdivision
       Psychological aspects, e.g.
       Drugs—Psychological aspects
       [to be added as needed]
  BT   Psychology
  NT   Behavior modification
       Counseling
       Drugs—Psychological aspects
       Employee morale
       Human engineering
       Negotiation
       Organizational behavior
       Pastoral psychology
       Psychological warfare
  RT   Educational psychology
       Interviewing
       Social psychology
Applied science
  USE   Technology
Appliqué   746.44
  BT   Needlework
Appointment
  USE   types of public officials and
         names of individual public of-
         ficials with the subdivision

Appointment—*Continued*

        Appointment, e.g. **Presidents—United States—Appointment** [to be added as needed]

Appointments and retirements
    USE   names of armed forces with the subdivision *Appointments and retirements,* e.g. **United States. Army—Appointments and retirements** [to be added as needed]

Apportionment (Election law) (May subdiv. geog.)   **324; 328.3; 342**
    UF   Legislative reapportionment
          Reapportionment (Election law)
    BT   **Representative government and representation**

Appraisal
    USE   **Tax assessment**
           Valuation

Appraisal of books
    USE   **Book reviewing**
           Books and reading
           Criticism
           Literature—History and criticism

Appreciation of art
    USE   **Art appreciation**

Appreciation of music
    USE   **Music appreciation**

Apprentices   **331.5**
    BT   **Labor**
           Technical education
    RT   **Employees—Training**

Apprenticeship novels
    USE   **Bildungsromans**

Appropriations and expenditures
    USE   names of countries and names of individual government departments, agencies, etc., with the subdivision *Appropriations and expenditures,* e.g. **United States—Appropriations and expenditures** [to be added as needed]

Approximate computation   **372.7; 511**
    UF   Arithmetic—Estimation
           Computation, Approximate
           Estimation (Mathematics)
    BT   **Numerical analysis**

April First
    USE   **April Fools' Day**

April Fools' Day   **394.262**
    UF   All Fools' Day
           April First
    BT   **Holidays**

Aptitude
    USE   **Ability**

Aptitude testing
    USE   **Ability—Testing**

Aquaculture   **639**
    UF   Aquiculture
           Freshwater aquaculture
           Mariculture
           Marine aquaculture
           Ocean farming
           Sea farming
    BT   **Agriculture**
           Marine resources
    NT   **Fish culture**

Aquarian Age movement
    USE   **New Age movement**

Aquariums   **597.073; 639.34**
    SA   names of specific aquariums [to be added as needed]
    BT   **Freshwater biology**
           Natural history
    NT   **Marine aquariums**
    RT   **Fish culture**
           Fishes

Aquatic animals (May subdiv. geog.)   **591.76**
    UF   Aquatic fauna
           Water animals
    BT   **Animals**
    NT   **Fishes**
           Freshwater animals
           Marine animals
           Shellfish
           Sponges

Aquatic birds
    USE   **Water birds**

Aquatic fauna
    USE   **Aquatic animals**

Aquatic plants
    USE   **Freshwater plants**
           Marine plants

Aquatic sports
    USE   **Water sports**

Aquatic sports—Safety measures
    USE   **Water safety**

Aqueducts   628.1
   UF   Water conduits
   BT   **Civil engineering**
         Hydraulic structures
         Water supply
Aquiculture
   USE **Aquaculture**
Arab civilization   306.0917; 909
   UF   Civilization, Arab
   BT   **Civilization**
Arab countries   956
   Use for materials on several Arabic-speaking countries. Materials on the region consisting of northeastern Africa and Asia west of Afghanistan are entered under **Middle East.**
   BT   **Islamic countries**
         Middle East
Arab countries—Foreign relations—Israel
   956
   UF   Arab-Israel relations
         Arab-Israeli relations
         Israel-Arab relations
         Israeli-Arab relations
   NT   **Israel-Arab conflicts**
   RT   **Israel—Foreign relations—**
         Arab countries
         Jewish-Arab relations
Arab countries—Politics and government
   956
   BT   **Politics**
   NT   **Pan-Arabism**
Arab-Israel conflicts
   USE **Israel-Arab conflicts**
Arab-Israel relations
   USE **Arab countries—Foreign rela-**
         tions—Israel
         Israel—Foreign relations—
         Arab countries
Arab-Israel War, 1948-1949
   USE **Israel-Arab War, 1948-1949**
Arab-Israel War, 1956
   USE **Sinai Campaign, 1956**
Arab-Israel War, 1967
   USE **Israel-Arab War, 1967**
Arab-Israel War, 1973
   USE **Israel-Arab War, 1973**
Arab-Israeli conflict, 1987-
   USE **Intifada, 1987-**
Arab-Israeli conflicts
   USE **Israel-Arab conflicts**

Arab-Israeli relations
   USE **Arab countries—Foreign rela-**
         tions—Israel
         Israel—Foreign relations—
         Arab countries
Arab-Jewish relations
   USE **Jewish-Arab relations**
Arab refugees (May subdiv. geog.)
   305.9
   UF   Refugees, Arab
   BT   **Refugees**
Arabia
   USE **Arabian Peninsula**
Arabian Peninsula   953
   UF   Arabia
   BT   **Peninsulas**
Arabs (May subdiv. geog.)   **305.892; 909**
   SA   names of specific Arab peoples
         [to be added as needed]
   NT   **Bedouins**
         Jewish-Arab relations
         Palestinian Arabs
Arabs—Palestine
   USE **Palestinian Arabs**
Arbitration and award   347
   Use for materials on the settlement of civil disputes by arbitration instead of a court trial.
   UF   Awards (Law)
         Mediation
   BT   **Commercial law**
         Courts
   RT   **Litigation**
Arbitration, Industrial
   USE **Industrial arbitration**
Arbitration, International
   USE **International arbitration**
Arboriculture
   USE **Forests and forestry**
         Fruit culture
         Trees
Arc light
   USE **Electric lighting**
Arc welding
   USE **Electric welding**
Archaeology
   USE **Archeology**
Archeological specimens
   USE **Antiquities**
Archeologists   920; 930.1092
   BT   **Historians**

Archeology (May subdiv. geog.) **930.1**

Use for materials on the discipline of archeology. General materials on the relics or monuments of ancient times are entered under **Antiquities.** Materials on the relics or monuments of an extinct city or town are entered under the name of the city or town.

UF   Archaeology

        Prehistory

SA   names of extinct cities, e.g. **Delphi (Extinct city)** [to be added as needed]; and names of groups of people and of cities (except extinct cities), countries, regions, etc., with the subdivision *Antiquities,* e.g. **Native Americans—Antiquities; United States—Antiquities;** etc. [to be added as needed]

BT   **History**

NT   **Ancient architecture**

        Bible—Antiquities

        Brasses

        Bronzes

        Burial

        Buried treasure

        Cliff dwellers and cliff dwellings

        Excavations (Archeology)

        Extinct cities

        Fossil hominids

        Gems

        Heraldry

        Historic sites

        Industrial archeology

        Inscriptions

        Mounds and mound builders

        Mummies

        Numismatics

        Obelisks

        Prehistoric peoples

        Pyramids

        Radiocarbon dating

        Rock drawings, paintings, and engravings

        Tombs

RT   **Antiquities**

Archery   **799.3**

BT   **Martial arts**

        Shooting

RT   **Bow and arrow**

Architects (May subdiv. geog.)   **720.92; 920**

BT   **Artists**

Architectural acoustics   **729; 690**

UF   Acoustics

BT   **Sound**

NT   **Soundproofing**

Architectural decoration and ornament 729

UF   Architecture—Decoration and ornament

        Decoration and ornament, Architectural

BT   **Architecture**

        Decoration and ornament

NT   **Gargoyles**

Architectural design   **720**

Use for materials on the process and methodology of designing buildings.

BT   **Architecture**

        Design

Architectural designs

USE   **Architecture—Designs and plans**

Architectural details

USE   **Architecture—Details**

Architectural drawing   **720.28**

BT   **Drawing**

Architectural engineering

USE   **Building**

        Structural analysis (Engineering)

        Structural engineering

Architectural features

USE   **Architecture—Details**

Architectural metalwork   **721**

BT   **Metalwork**

Architectural perspective

USE   **Perspective**

Architecture (May subdiv. geog.)   **720**

Use for materials on the design and style of structures. Materials on the process of construction are entered under **Building.** General materials on buildings are entered under **Buildings.**

UF   Building design

        Construction

SA   styles of architecture, e.g. **Byzantine architecture;** and types of buildings, e.g. **Farm buildings** [to be added as needed]

Architecture—*Continued*
- BT   Art
- NT   American colonial style in architecture
  - Ancient architecture
  - Architectural decoration and ornament
  - Architectural design
  - Asian architecture
  - Baroque architecture
  - Byzantine architecture
  - Church architecture
  - Classicism in architecture
  - Domestic architecture
  - Gothic revival (Architecture)
  - Greek architecture
  - Industrial buildings—Design and construction
  - Islamic architecture
  - Landscape architecture
  - Library architecture
  - Lost architecture
  - Medieval architecture
  - Modernism in architecture
  - Monuments
  - Native American architecture
  - Naval architecture
  - Obelisks
  - Roman architecture
  - Romanesque architecture
  - Spires
  - Sustainable architecture
  - Tombs
  - Underground architecture
- RT   Building
  - Buildings

Architecture—15th and 16th centuries
(May subdiv. geog.)   **724**
- UF   Architecture, Renaissance
  - Renaissance architecture

Architecture—17th and 18th centuries
(May subdiv. geog.)   **724**
- UF   Architecture, Modern—17th-18th centuries
  - Modern architecture—1600-1799 (17th and 18th centuries)

Architecture—19th century (May subdiv. geog.)   **724**
- UF   Architecture, Modern—19th century
  - Modern architecture—1800-1899 (19th century)

Architecture—20th century (May subdiv. geog.)   **724**
- UF   Architecture, Modern—20th century
  - Modern architecture—1900-1999 (20th century)

Architecture—21st century (May subdiv. geog.)   **724**
- UF   Architecture, Modern—21st century
  - Modern architecture—2000-2099 (21st century)

Architecture, American
- USE   **Architecture—United States**

Architecture, Ancient
- USE   **Ancient architecture**

Architecture and the handicapped   **720**
- UF   Barrier free design
  - Handicapped and architecture
- BT   **Handicapped**

Architecture—Awards   **720.79**

Architecture, Baroque
- USE   **Baroque architecture**

Architecture, Byzantine
- USE   **Byzantine architecture**

Architecture—Composition, proportion, etc.   **720; 729**
- UF   Architecture—Proportion
  - Proportion (Architecture)
- BT   **Composition (Art)**

Architecture—Conservation and restoration   **690; 720.28**
- UF   Architecture—Restoration
  - Buildings, Restoration of
  - Conservation of buildings
  - Preservation of buildings
  - Restoration of buildings
- RT   **Buildings—Maintenance and repair**

Architecture—Decoration and ornament
- USE   **Architectural decoration and ornament**

Architecture—Designs and plans   **720.28; 729**
- UF   Architectural designs
  - Architecture—Plans
  - Designs, Architectural
- NT   **Domestic architecture—Designs and plans**

Architecture—Details   721; 729
  UF   Architectural details
       Architectural features
  SA   types of architectural features,
          e.g. **Windows; Fireplaces;**
          etc. [to be added as needed]
  NT   **Chimneys**
       Doors
       Fireplaces
       Floors
       Foundations
       Gargoyles
       Roofs
       Windows
       Woodwork
Architecture, Domestic
  USE   **Domestic architecture**
Architecture, Gothic
  USE   **Gothic architecture**
Architecture, Greek
  USE   **Greek architecture**
Architecture, Islamic
  USE   **Islamic architecture**
Architecture, Medieval
  USE   **Medieval architecture**
Architecture, Modern
  USE   **Modernism in architecture**
Architecture, Modern—17th-18th centuries
  USE   **Architecture—17th and 18th**
          centuries
Architecture, Modern—19th century
  USE   **Architecture—19th century**
Architecture, Modern—20th century
  USE   **Architecture—20th century**
Architecture, Modern—21st century
  USE   **Architecture—21st century**
Architecture—Plans
  USE   **Architecture—Designs and**
          plans
Architecture—Proportion
  USE   **Architecture—Composition,**
          proportion, etc.
Architecture, Renaissance
  USE   **Architecture—15th and 16th**
          centuries
Architecture—Restoration
  USE   **Architecture—Conservation**
          and restoration
Architecture, Roman
  USE   **Roman architecture**

Architecture, Romanesque
  USE   **Romanesque architecture**
Architecture, Rural
  USE   **Farm buildings**
Architecture—United States   720.973
  UF   American architecture
       Architecture, American
Architecture—United States—1600-1775,
  Colonial period   720.973
  UF   Colonial architecture
Archives (May subdiv. geog.)   **026; 027**
  UF   Documents
       Government records—Preserva-
          tion
       Historical records—Preservation
       Preservation of historical records
       Public records—Preservation
       Records—Preservation
  SA   subjects, ethnic groups, classes
          of persons, individuals, fami-
          lies, schools, and military ser-
          vices with the subdivision *Ar-*
          chives [to be added as need-
          ed]
  BT   **Bibliography**
       Documentation
       History—Sources
       Information services
  NT   **Manuscripts**
       Presidents—United States—Ar-
          chives
  RT   **Charters**
       Libraries
Archives—United States   027.0973;
  353.0071
  UF   United States—Archives
Arctic expeditions
  USE   **Arctic regions—Exploration**
Arctic regions   919.8; 998
  UF   Far north
  BT   **Earth**
       Polar regions
  NT   **Northeast Passage**
       Northwest Passage
  RT   **North Pole**
Arctic regions—Exploration   919.8
  UF   Arctic expeditions
       Polar expeditions
  SA   names of expeditions [to be add-
          ed as needed]

Arctic regions—Exploration—*Continued*
BT Exploration
Scientific expeditions
Ardennes, Battle of the, 1944-1945
940.54
UF Bastogne, Battle of
Battle of the Bulge
Bulge, Battle of the
BT World War, 1939-1945—Campaigns
Area studies   940-999
Use for general materials on area studies.
UF Foreign area studies
SA continents, countries, and geographic regions with the subdivision *Study and teaching* [to be added as needed]
BT Education
NT Africa—Study and teaching
Arena theater   725; 792
UF Round stage
Theater-in-the-round
BT Theater
Argentine rummy
USE Canasta (Game)
Argumentation
USE Debates and debating
Logic
Arid regions (May subdiv. geog.)
551.41
UF Arid zones
Semiarid regions
BT Earth
Arid zones
USE Arid regions
Aristocracy (May subdiv. geog.)   305.5
BT Political science
Upper class
RT Nobility
Arithmetic   513
UF Computation (Mathematics)
SA types of arithmetic operations [to be added as needed]
BT Mathematics
Set theory
NT Average
Calculators
Cube root
Fractions
Mental arithmetic
Metric system
Multiplication

Percentage
Ratio and proportion
Square root
Subtraction
RT Numbers
Arithmetic, Commercial
USE Business mathematics
Arithmetic—Estimation
USE Approximate computation
Arithmetic—Study and teaching   372.7; 513.07
NT Counting
Mathematical readiness
Number games
Arithmetic—Textbooks   513
Arithmetical ability
USE Mathematical ability
Arithmetical readiness
USE Mathematical readiness
Armada, 1588
USE Spanish Armada, 1588
Armaments
USE Military readiness
Military weapons
Armaments industries
USE Defense industry
Armed forces   343; 355
UF Armed services
Military forces
SA specific branches of the armed forces under names of countries, e.g. United States. Army; and names of countries, regions, and international organizations with the subdivision *Armed forces,* e.g. United States—Armed forces; United Nations—Armed forces; etc. [to be added as needed]
BT Military art and science
NT Armies
Military personnel
Navies
Ohio—Militia
Recruiting and enlistment
United Nations—Armed forces
United States—Armed forces
United States—Militia
Voluntary military service

Armed forces—*Continued*
    RT   **Military readiness**
          War
Armed forces—Recruiting, enlistment, etc.
    USE **Recruiting and enlistment**
Armed services
    USE **Armed forces**
Armies   355.3
    UF   Army
          Military power
    SA   names of countries with the sub-
          head *Army,* e.g. **United
          States. Army** [to be added as
          needed]
    BT   **Armed forces**
          Military personnel
    NT   **Draft**
          Soldiers
          United States. Army
    RT   **Military art and science**
Armies—Medical care   355.3
    SA   names of wars with the subdivi-
          sion *Health aspects* or *Medi-
          cal care,* e.g. **World War,
          1939-1945—Health aspects;
          World War, 1939-1945—
          Medical care;** etc. [to be
          added as needed]
    BT   **Medical care**
          Military medicine
    RT   **Military personnel—Health
          and hygiene**
Armistice Day
    USE **Veterans Day**
Armistices
    USE names of wars with the subdivi-
          sion *Armistices,* e.g. **World
          War, 1939-1945—Armistices**
          [to be added as needed]
Armor   355.8; 623.4; 739.7
    Use for materials on protective covering
    worn as a defense against weapons.
    UF   Arms and armor
          Suits of armor
    BT   **Art metalwork**
          Costume
          Military art and science
    RT   **Weapons**
Armored cars (Tanks)
    USE **Military tanks**

Arms and armor
    USE **Armor**
          Weapons
Arms control (May subdiv. geog.)
          327.1; 341.7
    UF   Disarmament
          Limitation of armament
          Non-proliferation of nuclear
            weapons
          Nuclear non-proliferation
          Nuclear test ban
    BT   **International relations**
          International security
          War
    NT   **Antinuclear movement**
          Arms race
    RT   **International arbitration**
          Military readiness
          Peace
Arms proliferation
    USE **Arms race**
Arms race (May subdiv. geog.)   327.1;
          355
    Use for materials on the competitive in-
    crease in the military power of two or more
    nations or blocs.
    UF   Arms proliferation
          Proliferation of arms
    BT   **Arms control**
          International security
    RT   **Arms transfers**
          Military readiness
          Military weapons
Arms sales
    USE **Arms transfers**
          Defense industry
          Military assistance
          Military weapons
Arms traffic
    USE **Arms transfers**
Arms transfers (May subdiv. geog.)
          327.1; 382
    UF   Arms sales
          Arms traffic
          Foreign military sales
          Military sales
    BT   **International trade**
    RT   **Arms race**
          Defense industry
          Military assistance

Army
  USE   **Armies**
        Military art and science
        and names of countries with the
        subhead *Army,* e.g. **United
        States. Army** [to be added as
        needed]
Army bases
  USE   **Military bases**
Army desertion
  USE   **Military desertion**
Army life
  USE   **Soldiers**
        and names of armies with the
        subdivision *Military life,* e.g.
        **United States. Army—Mili-
        tary life** [to be added as
        needed]
Army posts
  USE   **Military bases**
Army schools
  USE   **Military education**
Army tests
  USE   **United States. Army—Exami-
        nations**
Army vehicles
  USE   **Military vehicles**
Aromatherapy   615
  BT   **Therapeutics**
Aromatic plant products
  USE   **Essences and essential oils**
Aromatic plants (May subdiv. geog.)
        582; 635.9
  BT   **Plants**
  RT   **Essences and essential oils**
        Fragrant gardens
Arrow
  USE   **Bow and arrow**
Art   700
    Use for materials on the visual arts only
  (architecture, painting, etc.). Materials on the
  arts in general, including the visual arts, liter-
  ature, and the performing arts, are entered un-
  der **Arts.**
  SA   types of art, e.g. **Commercial
        art;** art of particular religions,
        e.g. **Christian art;** move-
        ments in art, e.g. **Romanti-
        cism in art;** art and other
        subjects, e.g. **Art and my-
        thology;** subjects and themes
        in art, e.g. **Animals in art;**

        and art of particular countries,
        regions, or ethnic groups, e.g.
        **American art; Greek art;
        Native American art;** etc. [to
        be added as needed]
  BT   **Arts**
  NT   **Abstract art**
        African American art
        American art
        Ancient art
        Architecture
        Art and mythology
        Art and religion
        Art and society
        Art objects
        Artistic anatomy
        Artistic photography
        Artists' models
        Arts and crafts movement
        Asian art
        Baroque art
        Black art
        Botanical illustration
        Bronzes
        Buddhist art
        Byzantine art
        Children's art
        Christian art
        Collage
        Collectors and collecting
        Commercial art
        Composition (Art)
        Computer art
        Copy art
        Cubism
        Decoration and ornament
        Drawing
        Earthworks (Art)
        Engraving
        Erotic art
        Etching
        Ethnic art
        Expressionism (Art)
        Folk art
        Futurism (Art)
        Gems
        Gothic revival (Art)
        Graphic arts
        Greek art
        **Illumination of books and
          manuscripts**

Art—*Continued*
        Illustration of books
        Impressionism (Art)
        Interior design
        Islamic art
        Kinetic art
        Medieval art
        Modernism in art
        Municipal art
        Native American art
        Painting
        Performance art
        Pictures
        Portraits
        Postimpressionism (Art)
        Prehistoric art
        Realism in art
        Religious art
        Roman art
        Romanticism in art
        Sculpture
        Symbolism
        Video art
        World War, 1939-1945—Art
          and the war
  RT Artists
Art—15th and 16th centuries   709.02;
    709.03
  UF Art, Renaissance
      Renaissance art
Art—17th and 18th centuries   709.03
  UF Art, Modern—17th-18th centu-
      ries
Art—19th century   709.03
  UF Art, Modern—19th century
      Modern art—1800-1899 (19th
      century)
Art—20th century   709.04
  UF Art, Modern—20th century
      Modern art—1900-1999 (20th
      century)
  SA types of twentieth-century art,
      e.g. **Cubism** [to be added as
      needed]
Art—21st century   709.05
  UF Art, Modern—21st century
      Modern art—2000-2099 (21st
      century)
Art, American
  USE **American art**

Art—Analysis, interpretation, appreciation
  USE **Art appreciation**
        Art criticism
        Art—Study and teaching
Art, Ancient
  USE **Ancient art**
Art and mythology   704.9
  UF Mythology in art
  BT **Art**
      Mythology
  RT **Art and religion**
Art and religion   201; 246; 701
  UF Arts in the church
      Religion and art
  BT **Art**
      Religion
  RT **Art and mythology**
      Religious art
Art and society (May subdiv. geog.)
    701
  UF Art and sociology
      Society and art
      Sociology and art
  BT **Art**
  NT **Art patronage**
      Art—Political aspects
      Folk art
Art and sociology
  USE **Art and society**
Art and the war
  USE names of wars with the subdivi-
      sion *Art and the war,* e.g.
      World War, 1939-1945—Art
      and the war [to be added as
      needed]
Art appreciation   701
  UF Appreciation of art
      Art—Analysis, interpretation, ap-
      preciation
  BT **Aesthetics**
      Art criticism
Art, Asian
  USE **Asian art**
Art, Baroque
  USE **Baroque art**
Art, Black
  USE **Black art**
Art, Buddhist
  USE **Buddhist art**
Art, Byzantine
  USE **Byzantine art**

Art collections (May subdiv. geog.)　**708**
　　UF　Art—Collections
　　　　Art—Private collections
　　　　Collections of art, painting, etc.
　　　　Private art collections
　　SA　names of collectors or of the
　　　　original owners of private art
　　　　collections with the subdivi-
　　　　sion *Art collections* [to be
　　　　added as needed]
　　RT　**Art museums**
　　　　Collectors and collecting
Art—Collections
　　USE　**Art collections**
Art—Composition
　　USE　**Composition (Art)**
Art criticism　**701; 709**
　　UF　Art—Analysis, interpretation, ap-
　　　　preciation
　　BT　**Criticism**
　　NT　**Art appreciation**
Art education
　　USE　**Art—Study and teaching**
Art—Exhibitions　**707.4**
　　BT　**Exhibitions**
Art—Federal aid
　　USE　**Federal aid to the arts**
Art—Forgeries　**702.8; 751.5**
　　UF　Art forgeries
　　　　Forgery of works of art
　　BT　**Counterfeits and counterfeiting**
　　　　Forgery
Art forgeries
　　USE　**Art—Forgeries**
Art galleries
　　USE　**Art museums**
　　　　Commercial art galleries
Art, Gothic
　　USE　**Gothic art**
Art, Greek
　　USE　**Greek art**
Art—History　**709**
　　BT　**History**
Art in advertising
　　USE　**Commercial art**
Art in motion
　　USE　**Kinetic art**
Art industries and trade
　　USE　**Decorative arts**
Art, Islamic
　　USE　**Islamic art**

Art, Kinetic
　　USE　**Kinetic art**
Art, Medieval
　　USE　**Medieval art**
Art metalwork　**739; 745.56**
　　UF　Decorative metalwork
　　SA　types of art metalwork [to be
　　　　added as needed]
　　BT　**Decorative arts**
　　　　Metalwork
　　NT　**Armor**
　　　　Brasses
　　　　Bronzes
　　　　Goldwork
　　　　Pewter
　　　　Silverwork
Art, Modern—17th-18th centuries
　　USE　**Art—17th and 18th centuries**
Art, Modern—19th century
　　USE　**Art—19th century**
Art, Modern—20th century
　　USE　**Art—20th century**
Art, Modern—21st century
　　USE　**Art—21st century**
Art, Municipal
　　USE　**Municipal art**
Art museums (May subdiv. geog.)　**708**
　　UF　Art galleries
　　　　Collections of art, painting, etc.
　　　　Picture galleries
　　SA　names of individual art museums
　　　　[to be added as needed]
　　BT　**Museums**
　　RT　**Art collections**
Art objects　**700; 745**
　　Use for general materials about decorative
　　articles of artistic merit such as snuff boxes,
　　brasses, pottery, needlework, glassware, etc.
　　Materials on old decorative objects having
　　historical or financial value are entered under
　　Antiques.
　　UF　Objets d'art
　　SA　types of art objects, e.g. **Furni-
　　　　ture; Pottery;** etc. [to be
　　　　added as needed]
　　BT　**Antiques**
　　　　Art
　　　　Decoration and ornament
　　　　Decorative arts
　　NT　**Miniature objects**
Art, Oriental
　　USE　**Asian art**

Art patronage (May subdiv. geog.)   **700**

    Use for materials on patronage of the arts by individuals or corporations. Materials on government support of the arts are entered under **Arts—Government policy** or **Federal aid to the arts.**

  UF Art patrons

        Business patronage of the arts

        Corporate patronage of the arts

        Corporations—Art patronage

        Funding for the arts

        Patronage of the arts

        Private funding of the arts

  BT **Art and society**

  RT **Arts—Government policy**

        Federal aid to the arts

Art patrons

  USE **Art patronage**

Art—Political aspects (May subdiv. geog.) **701**

  BT **Art and society**

Art, Prehistoric

  USE **Prehistoric art**

Art—Prices **707.5**

  BT **Prices**

Art—Private collections

  USE **Art collections**

Art, Renaissance

  USE **Art—15th and 16th centuries**

Art robberies

  USE **Art thefts**

Art, Roman

  USE **Roman art**

Art, Romanesque

  USE **Romanesque art**

Art schools

  USE **Art—Study and teaching**

Art—Study and teaching **707**

  UF Art—Analysis, interpretation, appreciation

        Art education

        Art schools

Art—Technique **702.8**

Art thefts (May subdiv. geog.) **364.16**

  UF Art robberies

  BT **Theft**

Art—Themes **704.9**

  UF Iconography

        Themes in art

  SA topics in art, e.g. **Dogs in art;** and names of persons, families, and corporate bodies

with the subdivision *In art,* e.g. **Napoleon I, Emperor of the French, 1769-1821—In art** [to be added as needed]

  NT **African Americans in art**

        Animals in art

        Blacks in art

        Children in art

        Dogs in art

        Flowers in art

        Napoleon I, Emperor of the French, 1769-1821—In art

        Nude in art

        Plants in art

        Women in art

Art—Therapeutic use

  USE **Art therapy**

Art therapy **615.8; 616.89**

  UF Art—Therapeutic use

  BT **Therapeutics**

Arthritis **616.7**

  BT **Diseases**

  NT **Gout**

Arthritis—Physical therapy **616.7**

Arthur, King—Romances

  USE **Arthurian romances**

Arthurian romances **398.22; 808.8; 809**

    May be used for individual works, collections, or materials about Arthurian romances.

  UF Arthur, King—Romances

        Knights of the Round Table

  BT **Romances**

  RT **Grail—Legends**

Arthurian romances—Adaptations 808.8

Articles of war

  USE **Military law**

Articulation (Education) **371.2**

    Use for materials that discuss the integration of various elements of the school system, between levels, between schools, between subjects, or between the school's programs and outside activities, aimed at promoting a continuous advancement by the student.

  BT **Education—Curricula**

        Schools—Administration

Artificial flies **688.7; 799.1**

  UF Fishing flies

        Flies, Artificial

  BT **Fishing**

        Fly casting

Artificial flowers   745.594
  UF Flowers, Artificial
  BT **Decoration and ornament**
Artificial foods   641.3; 664
  UF Synthetic foods
  BT **Food**
      Synthetic products
Artificial fuels
  USE **Synthetic fuels**
Artificial heart   617.4
  BT **Artificial organs**
      Heart
Artificial insemination   636.08

Use for general materials on artificial insemination and materials specifically on the artificial insemination of livestock and other animals. Materials limited to artificial insemination in humans are entered under **Human artificial insemination.**

  BT **Reproduction**
  NT **Human artificial insemination**
Artificial insemination, Human
  USE **Human artificial insemination**
Artificial intelligence   006.3
  UF AI (Artificial intelligence)
      Machine intelligence
  BT **Computer science**
  NT **Expert systems (Computer science)**
Artificial limbs   617.5
  UF Limbs, Artificial
      Prosthesis
  BT **Orthopedics**
Artificial organs   617.9
  UF Organs, Artificial
      Prosthesis
  SA names of artificial organs, e.g. **Artificial heart** [to be added as needed]
  BT **Surgery**
  NT **Artificial heart**
Artificial reality
  USE **Virtual reality**
Artificial respiration   617.1
  UF Pulmonary resuscitation
      Respiration, Artificial
      Resuscitation, Pulmonary
  BT **First aid**
Artificial satellites   629.43; 629.46
  UF Orbiting vehicles
      Satellites, Artificial

  SA satellites of particular countries, e.g. **American artificial satellites;** types of satellites; and names of specific satellites [to be added as needed]
  BT **Astronautics**
  NT **American artificial satellites**
      Explorer (Artificial satellite)
      Meteorological satellites
      Space stations
  RT **Space vehicles**
Artificial satellites, American
  USE **American artificial satellites**
Artificial satellites—Control systems 629.46
Artificial satellites in telecommunication 384.5; 621.382
  UF Communication satellites
      Communications relay satellites
      Global satellite communications systems
      Satellite communication systems
  SA names of specific satellites or projects [to be added as needed]
  BT **Telecommunication**
  NT **Telstar project**
Artificial satellites—Launching   629.43
  UF Launching of satellites
  BT **Rockets (Aeronautics)**
Artificial satellites—Law and legislation
  USE **Space law**
Artificial satellites—Orbits   629.4
  BT **Astrodynamics**
Artificial satellites—Tracking   629.43
  UF Tracking of satellites
Artificial selection
  USE **Breeding**
Artificial sweeteners
  USE **Sugar substitutes**
Artificial weather control
  USE **Weather control**
Artillery   355.8; 623.4
  BT **Military art and science**
  RT **Ordnance**
Artistic anatomy   704.9; 743.4
  UF Anatomy, Artistic
      Human anatomy in art
      Human figure in art
  BT **Anatomy**
      Art

Artistic anatomy—*Continued*
    Drawing
    Nude in art
  NT **Figure drawing**
    Figure painting
Artistic photography   770; 779
  UF Photography—Aesthetics
    Photography, Artistic
  BT **Art**
    Photography
Artists (May subdiv. geog.) **709.2; 920**
  SA types of artists and names of in-
      dividual artists [to be added
      as needed]
  NT **African American artists**
    Architects
    Black artists
    Child artists
    Designers
    Engravers
    Etchers
    Illustrators
    Lithographers
    Painters
    Photographers
    Potters
    Sculptors
    Women artists
  RT **Art**
    Arts
Artists, American
  USE **Artists—United States**
Artists, Black
  USE **Black artists**
Artists' materials   741.2; 751.2
  UF Drawing materials
    Painters' materials
  SA types of artists' materials [to be
      added as needed]
  BT **Materials**
Artists' models   702.8
  UF Models
    Models, Artists'
    Models (Persons)
  BT **Art**
Artists—United States   709.2; 920
  UF American artists
    Artists, American
Arts (May subdiv. geog.) **700**
  Use for materials on the arts in general,
  including the visual arts, literature, and the

performing arts. Materials on the visual arts
only (architecture, painting, etc.) are entered
under **Art.**
  BT **Humanities**
  NT **Allegory**
    Art
    Decorative arts
    Handicraft
    Performing arts
    Surrealism
    Visual literacy
  RT **Aesthetics**
    Artists
Arts, American
  USE **Arts—United States**
Arts and crafts movement (May subdiv.
    geog.) **745**
  Use for materials on the movement originat-
  ing in England in the nineteenth century that
  promoted a return to craftsmanship in the ap-
  plied and decorative arts.
  UF Crafts (Arts)
  BT **Art**
    Decoration and ornament
    Decorative arts
    Industrial arts
  RT **Folk art**
    Handicraft
Arts and state
  USE **Arts—Government policy**
    Federal aid to the arts
Arts—Federal aid
  USE **Federal aid to the arts**
Arts—Government policy (May subdiv.
    geog.) **353.7; 700**
  UF Arts and state
    Funding for the arts
    State encouragement of the arts
  BT **Social policy**
  RT **Art patronage**
    Federal aid to the arts
Arts, Graphic
  USE **Graphic arts**
Arts in the church
  USE **Art and religion**
Arts—United States   700.973
  UF American arts
    Arts, American
Asbestos   553.6; 620.1; 666; 691
  BT **Minerals**
Asceticism   204; 248.4
  May be subdivided by religion or sect.

Asceticism—*Continued*
    BT   **Ethics**
          Religious life
    NT   **Fasting**
          Sexual abstinence
Asceticism—Catholic Church   248.4
Asia   950
    UF   East
          Orient
    SA   areas of Asia [to be added as
          needed]
    NT   **Central Asia**
          East Asia
          Middle East
          Southeast Asia
Asia, Central
    USE **Central Asia**
Asia—Civilization   306.095; 950
    UF   Asian civilization
          Civilization, Oriental
          Oriental civilization
    BT   **Civilization**
          East and West
Asia—Politics and government   950
    BT   **Politics**
Asia, Southeastern
    USE **Southeast Asia**
Asian architecture   720.95
    UF   Oriental architecture
    BT   **Architecture**
Asian art   709.5
    UF   Art, Asian
          Art, Oriental
          Oriental art
    BT   **Art**
Asian civilization
    USE **Asia—Civilization**
Asphyxiating gases
    USE **Poisonous gases**
Assassination   364.15
    SA   classes of persons and names of
          individuals with the subdivi-
          sion *Assassination* [to be add-
          ed as needed]
    BT   **Crime**
          Homicide
          Political crimes and offenses
    NT   **Presidents—United States—As-**
          sassination
Assault, Criminal
    USE **Offenses against the person**

Assault, Sexual
    USE **Rape**
Assembly programs, School
    USE **School assembly programs**
Assembly, Right of
    USE **Freedom of assembly**
Assertive behavior
    USE **Assertiveness (Psychology)**
Assertiveness (Psychology)   155.2; 158.2
    UF   Assertive behavior
    BT   **Aggressiveness (Psychology)**
          Psychology
    RT   **Self-confidence**
Assessment
    USE **Tax assessment**
Assessment, Tax
    USE **Tax assessment**
Assistance in emergencies
    USE **Helping behavior**
Assistance to developing areas
    USE **Foreign aid**
          Technical assistance
Assisted reproduction
    USE **Reproductive technology**
Association, Freedom of
    USE **Freedom of association**
Associations (May subdiv. geog.)   **060;**
          302.3; 366
    UF   Associations, institutions, etc.
          Networks (Associations, institu-
          tions, etc.)
          Organizations
          Voluntary associations
          Voluntary organizations
    SA   types of associations; subjects,
          classes of persons, ethnic
          groups, and names of individ-
          ual persons, families, and cor-
          porate bodies, with the subdi-
          vision *Societies;* and names of
          specific associations [to be
          added as needed]
    NT   **Agriculture—Societies**
          Charity organization
          Clubs
          Community life
          Cooperation
          Financial institutions
          Nonprofit organizations
          Religious institutions
          Societies

Associations—*Continued*
>> **Trade and professional associations**

Associations, institutions, etc.
>> USE **Associations**

Associations, International
>> USE **International agencies**

Asteroids   523.44
>> UF   Minor planets
>> Planetoids
>> BT   **Astronomy**
>> **Solar system**
>> RT   **Planets**

Asthma (May subdiv. geog.)   **616.2**
>> UF   Bronchial asthma
>> BT   **Allergy**
>> **Lungs—Diseases**

Astral projection   133.9
>> UF   Astral travel
>> Out-of-body experiences
>> BT   **Parapsychology**

Astral travel
>> USE   **Astral projection**

Astrobiology
>> USE   **Life on other planets**
>> **Space biology**

Astrochemistry
>> USE   **Space chemistry**

Astrodynamics   521; 629.4
>> BT   **Dynamics**
>> NT   **Artificial satellites—Orbits**
>> **Navigation (Astronautics)**
>> RT   **Astronautics**
>> **Space flight**

Astrogeology   559.9
>> SA   names of planets with the subdivision *Geology* [to be added as needed]
>> BT   **Geology**
>> NT   **Lunar geology**
>> **Mars (Planet)—Geology**

Astrology   133.5
>> UF   Hermetic art and philosophy
>> BT   **Astronomy**
>> **Divination**
>> **Occultism**
>> NT   **Horoscopes**
>> **Zodiac**
>> RT   **Constellations**

Astronautical accidents
>> USE   **Space vehicle accidents**

Astronautical communication systems
>> USE   **Astronautics—Communication systems**

Astronautical instruments   629.4
>> UF   Instruments, Astronautical
>> Space vehicles—Instruments
>> BT   **Navigation (Astronautics)**
>> **Space optics**
>> RT   **Astronautics—Communication systems**

Astronautics (May subdiv. geog.)   **629.4**
>> BT   **Aeronautics**
>> NT   **Aerothermodynamics**
>> **Artificial satellites**
>> **Astronautics and civilization**
>> **Interplanetary voyages**
>> **Navigation (Astronautics)**
>> **Outer space**
>> **Rocketry**
>> **Space flight**
>> **Space flight to the moon**
>> **Space stations**
>> **Unidentified flying objects**
>> RT   **Astrodynamics**
>> **Space sciences**
>> **Space vehicles**

Astronautics—Accidents
>> USE   **Space vehicle accidents**

Astronautics and civilization   306.4
>> UF   Civilization and astronautics
>> Outer space and civilization
>> Space age
>> Space power
>> BT   **Aeronautics and civilization**
>> **Astronautics**
>> **Civilization**
>> NT   **Space colonies**
>> **Space law**

Astronautics—Communication systems   629.47
>> UF   Astronautical communication systems
>> Space communication
>> BT   **Interstellar communication**
>> **Telecommunication**
>> NT   **Radio in astronautics**
>> RT   **Astronautical instruments**

Astronautics—International cooperation   629.4
>> UF   International space cooperation
>> BT   **International cooperation**

Astronautics—Law and legislation
    USE   **Space law**

Astronautics—United States   629.40973
    NT   **Project Voyager**

Astronauts   629.450092; 920
    UF   Cosmonauts
    BT   **Air pilots**
          Space flight
    NT   **Space vehicles—Piloting**

Astronauts—Clothing
    USE   **Space suits**

Astronauts—Nutrition   629.47
    UF   Space nutrition
    BT   **Nutrition**

Astronavigation
    USE   **Navigation (Astronautics)**

Astronomers   520.92; 920
    BT   **Scientists**

Astronomical instruments   522
    UF   Instruments, Astronomical
    SA   types of instruments, e.g. **Telescopes** [to be added as needed]
    BT   **Scientific apparatus and instruments**
          Space optics
    NT   **Astronomical photography**
          Telescopes

Astronomical observatories   522
    UF   Observatories, Astronomical
    RT   **Astronomy**

Astronomical photography   522
    UF   Astrophotography
    BT   **Astronomical instruments**
          Photography

Astronomical physics
    USE   **Astrophysics**

Astronomy   520
    BT   **Physical sciences**
          Science
          Universe
    NT   **Asteroids**
          Astrology
          Astrophysics
          Bible—Astronomy
          Black holes (Astronomy)
          Chronology
          Comets
          Galaxies
          Life on other planets
          Lunar eclipses
          Meteorites
          Meteors
          Moon
          Nautical astronomy
          Outer space
          Planetariums
          Planets
          Pulsars
          Quasars
          Radio astronomy
          Seasons
          Sky
          Solar eclipses
          Solar system
          Space environment
          Spectrum analysis
          Sun
          Zodiac
    RT   **Astronomical observatories**
          Constellations
          Space sciences
          Stars

Astronomy—Atlases
    USE   **Stars—Atlases**

Astronomy—Mathematics   520.1
    BT   **Mathematics**

Astrophotography
    USE   **Astronomical photography**

Astrophysics   523.01
    UF   Astronomical physics
    BT   **Astronomy**
          Physics
    NT   **Black holes (Astronomy)**
          Spectrum analysis

Astros (Baseball team)
    USE   **Houston Astros (Baseball team)**

Asylum   323.6; 342.08
    UF   Asylum, Right of
          Political asylum
          Right of asylum
          Sanctuary (Law)
    BT   **International law**
    NT   **Political refugees**
          Sanctuary movement

Asylum, Right of
    USE   **Asylum**

Asylums
    USE   **Institutional care**

At-home employment
    USE   **Home-based business**

At risk students   371.93

Use for materials on students considered prone to academic failure or other problems.

  UF   Disadvantaged students

        High risk students

        Students with problems

        Underprivileged students

  BT   **Students**

  RT   **Dropouts**

        Socially handicapped children

Atheism   211

  BT   **Religion**

        Secularism

        Theology

  RT   **Agnosticism**

        Deism

        Rationalism

        Theism

Athletes (May subdiv. geog.)   **796.092; 920**

  SA   types of athletes, e.g. **Baseball players** [to be added as needed]

  NT   **African American athletes**

        Baseball players

        Black athletes

  RT   **Sports**

Athletes, Black

  USE **Black athletes**

Athletes—Drug use   362.29; 796

  UF   Drugs and sports

        Sports and drugs

  RT   **Steroids**

Athletic coaching

  USE **Coaching (Athletics)**

Athletic medicine

  USE **Sports medicine**

Athletics (May subdiv. geog.)   **796**

  SA   types of athletic activities [to be added as needed]

  NT   **Boxing**

        Coaching (Athletics)

        Gymnastics

        Martial arts

        Olympic games

        Rowing

        Track athletics

        Walking

        Weight lifting

        Wrestling

  RT   **Physical education**

        Sports

Atlantic Ocean   910.9163

  BT   **Ocean**

  NT   **Bermuda Triangle**

Atlantic States   974; 975

  UF   Eastern Seaboard

        Middle Atlantic States

        South Atlantic States

  BT   **United States**

Atlantis   001.94; 398.23

  BT   **Geographical myths**

        Lost continents

Atlas (Missile)   623.4; 629.47

  BT   **Ballistic missiles**

        Intercontinental ballistic missiles

Atlases   912

Use as a form heading for geographical atlases of world coverage. General materials about maps and their history are entered under **Maps.**

  UF   Geographical atlases

  SA   scientific and technical subjects with the subdivision *Atlases,* for materials consisting of comprehensive, often systematically arranged, collections of illustrative plates, charts, etc., usually with explanatory captions, e.g. **Human anatomy—Atlases;** and names of countries, cities, etc., with the subdivision *Maps,* e.g. **United States—Maps** [to be added as needed]

  BT   **Geography**

        Maps

  NT   **Bible—Geography**

        Historical atlases

        Human anatomy—Atlases

        Stars—Atlases

        United States—Maps

Atlases, Astronomical

  USE **Stars—Atlases**

Atmosphere   551.5

Use for materials on the body of air surrounding the earth. Materials on the chemical and physical properties of air are entered under **Air.**

  BT   **Air**

        Earth

  NT   **Clouds**

        Fog

        Sky

Atmosphere—*Continued*
Upper atmosphere
RT **Meteorology**
Atmosphere—Pollution
USE **Air pollution**
Atmosphere, Upper
USE **Upper atmosphere**
Atmospheric chemistry   551.51
BT **Physical chemistry**
Atmospheric dust
USE **Dust**
Atmospheric greenhouse effect
USE **Greenhouse effect**
Atmospheric humidity
USE **Humidity**
Atolls
USE **Coral reefs and islands**
Atom smashing
USE **Cyclotrons**
Atomic bomb   355.8; 623.4
BT **Bombs**
Nuclear weapons
NT **Radioactive fallout**
RT **Hydrogen bomb**
Atomic bomb—Physiological effect
616.9
RT **Radiation—Physiological effect**
Atomic bomb—Testing   623.4
Atomic bomb victims   940.54
UF Victims of atomic bombings
Atomic energy
USE **Nuclear energy**
Atomic industry
USE **Nuclear industry**
Atomic medicine
USE **Nuclear medicine**
Atomic nuclei
USE **Nuclear physics**
Atomic power
USE **Nuclear energy**
Atomic power plants
USE **Nuclear power plants**
Atomic-powered vehicles
USE **Nuclear propulsion**
Atomic submarines
USE **Nuclear submarines**
Atomic theory   539.7; 541
BT **Physical chemistry**
RT **Quantum theory**
Atomic warfare
USE **Nuclear warfare**

Atomic weapons
USE **Nuclear weapons**
Atoms   539.7; 541
BT **Physical chemistry**
NT **Cyclotrons**
Electrons
Isotopes
Neutrons
Protons
Transmutation (Chemistry)
Atonement—Christianity   232; 234
UF Jesus Christ—Atonement
Vicarious atonement
BT **Christianity**
Jesus Christ
Sacrifice
Salvation
Atonement, Day of
USE **Yom Kippur**
Atonement—Judaism   296.3
UF Atonement (Judaism)
BT **Judaism**
Atonement (Judaism)
USE **Atonement—Judaism**
Atrocities (May subdiv. geog.)   **909**
UF Military atrocities
SA names of wars with the subdivi-
sion *Atrocities,* e.g. **World**
War, 1939-1945—Atrocities;
and names of specific atroci-
ties [to be added as needed]
BT **Crime**
Cruelty
NT **Massacres**
Persecution
World War, 1939-1945—Atroc-
ities
Attacks by animals
USE **Animal attacks**
Attempted suicide
USE **Suicide**
Attendance, School
USE **School attendance**
Attention   153.1; 153.7
UF Concentration
BT **Apperception**
Educational psychology
Memory
Psychology
Thought and thinking
NT **Listening**

Attention-seeking
    USE **Showing off**
Attitude (Psychology)   **152.4**
    UF Attitudes
    SA ethnic groups and classes of persons with the subdivision *Attitudes,* e.g. **Teenagers—Attitudes** [to be added as needed]
    BT **Emotions**
          Psychology
    NT **Conformity**
          Empathy
          Frustration
          Job satisfaction
          Prejudices
          Racism
          Sexism
          Stereotype (Psychology)
          Teenagers—Attitudes
          Trust
    RT **Public opinion**
Attitudes
    USE **Attitude (Psychology)**
          and ethnic groups and classes of persons with the subdivision *Attitudes,* e.g. **Teenagers—Attitudes** [to be added as needed]
Attorneys
    USE **Lawyers**
Attracting birds
    USE **Bird attracting**
Attracting wildlife
    USE **Wildlife attracting**
ATVs
    USE **All terrain vehicles**
Auction bridge
    USE **Bridge (Game)**
Auctions   **658.8**
    UF Sales, Auction
    BT **Selling**
Audiences (May subdiv. geog.)   **302.3**
    SA types of performances or events with the subdivision *Audiences,* e.g. **Performing arts—Audiences** [to be added as needed]
    BT **Communication**
          Social psychology
    NT **Performing arts—Audiences**
          Sports spectators

Television viewers
Audio amplifiers, Transistor
    USE **Transistor amplifiers**
Audio cassettes
    USE **Sound recordings**
Audiobooks   **028**
    Use for materials on sound recordings of books, including but not limited to materials recorded specifically for the blind.
    UF Books on cassette
          Books on tape
          Cassette books
          Recorded books
          Talking books
    BT **Sound recordings**
    RT **Blind—Books and reading**
Audiodisc players
    USE **Compact disc players**
Audiotapes
    USE **Sound recordings**
Audiovisual aids
    USE subjects with the subdivision *Audiovisual aids,* e.g. **Library education—Audiovisual aids;** and subjects with the subdivisions *Study and teaching—Audiovisual aids,* for the use of audiovisual aids in the teaching of those subjects, e.g. **Science—Study and teaching—Audiovisual aids** [to be added as needed]
Audiovisual education   **371.33**
    UF Visual instruction
    SA subjects with the subdivision *Audiovisual aids* [to be added as needed]
    BT **Education**
    NT **Audiovisual materials**
          Library education—Audiovisual aids
          Motion pictures in education
          Radio in education
          Television in education
Audiovisual materials   **025.17; 371.33**
    UF Multimedia materials
          Nonbook materials
          Nonprint materials
    SA subjects with the subdivision *Audiovisual aids;* and names of specific audiovisual materials [to be added as needed]

Audiovisual materials—*Continued*
    BT   **Audiovisual education**
           Teaching—Aids and devices
    NT   **Filmstrips**
           Library education—Audiovisual aids
           Manipulatives
           Motion pictures
           Sound recordings
           Videodiscs
           Videotapes
Audiovisual materials centers
    USE   **Instructional materials centers**
Auditing (May subdiv. geog.)   **657**
    SA   topics and names of corporate bodies with the subdivision *Auditing* [to be added as needed]
    BT   **Bookkeeping**
    RT   **Accounting**
Auditoriums (May subdiv. geog.)   **725**
    BT   **Buildings**
           Centers for the performing arts
    NT   **Concert halls**
Auricular confession
    USE   **Confession**
Aurora australis
    USE   **Auroras**
Aurora borealis
    USE   **Auroras**
Auroras   **538**
    UF   Aurora australis
           Aurora borealis
           Northern lights
           Polar lights
           Southern lights
    BT   **Geophysics**
           Meteorology
Australia   **994**
    May be subdivided like United States except for *History*.
    NT   **Australians**
Australian aborigines
    USE   **Aboriginal Australians**
Australians   **305.82; 994**
    BT   **Australia**
    NT   **Aboriginal Australians**
Author and publisher
    USE   **Authors and publishers**

Authoring programs for computer-assisted instruction
    USE   **Computer-assisted instruction—Authoring programs**
Authoritarianism
    USE   **Fascism**
           Totalitarianism
Authority   **303.3**
    BT   **Political science**
Authors   **809; 920**
    UF   Writers
    SA   authors of particular countries, e.g. **American authors;** types of writers, e.g. **Poets;** names of national literatures with the subdivision for a particular kind of author, e.g. **American literature—Women authors; American literature—African American authors;** etc.; subjects and names of countries, cities, etc. with the subdivision *Bio-bibliography;* and names of individual authors [to be added as needed]
    NT   **American authors**
           Black authors
           Child authors
           Dramatists
           English authors
           Historians
           Journalists
           Native American authors
           Novelists
           Poets
           Women authors
    RT   **Books**
           Literature—Bio-bibliography
Authors, American
    USE   **American authors**
Authors and publishers   **070.5**
    Use for materials on the relations between author and publisher.
    UF   Author and publisher
           Publishers and authors
    BT   **Authorship**
           Contracts
           Publishers and publishing
    RT   **Copyright**
Authors, Black
    USE   **Black authors**

Authors—Correspondence   808.6;
        808.86
    BT   Letters
Authors, English
    USE   English authors
Authors—Homes and haunts
    USE   Literary landmarks
Authors—Interviews   809
    BT   Interviews
Authorship   808
    Use for general materials on being or be-
    coming an author. Materials concerning the
    composition of special types of literature are
    entered under more specific headings such as
    Fiction—Technique; Biography as a liter-
    ary form; Short story; etc.
    UF   Writing (Authorship)
    SA   individual writers, titles of liter-
            ary works, and sacred works
            with the subdivision *Author-
            ship;* e.g. **Shakespeare, Wil-
            liam, 1564-1616—Authorship**
            [to be added as needed]
    BT   Literature
    NT   Advertising copy
            Authors and publishers
            Biography as a literary form
            Creative writing
            Drama—Technique
            Editing
            Fiction—Technique
            Historiography
            Journaling
            Journalism
            Love stories—Technique
            Radio authorship
            Report writing
            Short story
            Technical writing
            Television authorship
            Travel writing
            Versification
Authorship—Handbooks, manuals, etc.
        808
    RT   Printing—Style manuals
Autism   616.85; 618.92
    BT   Child psychiatry
Autobiographical fiction   808.3; 808.83
    May be used for individual works, collec-
    tions, or materials about autobiographical fic-
    tion.
    UF   Autobiographical novels
    BT   Biographical fiction

Autobiographical novels
    USE   **Autobiographical fiction**
Autobiographies   920
    Use for collections of autobiographies. Ma-
    terials about autobiography as a literary form
    are entered under **Autobiography.**
    UF   Memoirs
            Personal narratives
    SA   ethnic groups, classes of per-
            sons, and subjects with the
            subdivision *Biography* or *Cor-
            respondence,* e.g. **Women—
            Biography; Authors—Corre-
            spondence;** etc.; and names
            of diseases, events, and wars
            with the subdivision *Personal
            narratives* [to be added as
            needed]
    BT   Biography
    NT   Holocaust, 1933-1945—Personal
            narratives
            United States—History—1861-
            1865, Civil War—Personal
            narratives
            World War, 1939-1945—Per-
            sonal narratives
    RT   Diaries
Autobiography   809
    Use for materials on autobiography as a lit-
    erary form. Collections of autobiographies are
    entered under **Autobiographies.**
    UF   Autobiography as a literary form
            Autobiography—History and crit-
            icism
            Autobiography—Technique
            Memoirs
    BT   **Biography as a literary form**
    NT   **Slave narratives**
Autobiography as a literary form
    USE   **Autobiography**
Autobiography—History and criticism
    USE   **Autobiography**
Autobiography—Technique
    USE   **Autobiography**
Autographed copies
    USE   **Autographed editions**
Autographed editions   016
    UF   Autographed copies
            Signed editions
    BT   **Autographs**
            Editions

Autographs   929.8
   SA   classes of persons, ethnic
         groups, wars, and names of
         individual persons with the
         subdivision *Autographs,* or
         Autographs—Facsimiles [to be
         added as needed]
   BT **Biography**
        Writing
   NT **Autographed editions**
   RT **Manuscripts**
Autographs—Facsimiles   929.8
   SA   classes of persons, ethnic
         groups, wars, and names of
         individual persons with the
         subdivisions *Autographs—Fac-*
         similes [to be added as need-
         ed]
Automata
   USE **Robots**
Automated cataloging   025.3
   UF Cataloging—Data processing
   BT **Cataloging**
Automatic bread machines
   USE **Bread machines**
Automatic control
   USE **Automation**
         Cybernetics
         Electric controllers
         Servomechanisms
Automatic data processing
   USE **Data processing**
Automatic drafting
   USE **Computer graphics**
Automatic drawing
   USE **Computer graphics**
Automatic machinery
   USE **Automation**
Automatic speech recognition   006.4
   UF Mechanical speech recognition
        Speech recognition, Automatic
   BT **Speech processing systems**
        Voice
Automation   629.8; 670.42
   UF Automatic control
        Automatic machinery
        Computer control
   SA   subjects with the subdivision *Au-*
         tomation, e.g. **Libraries—Au-**
         tomation [to be added as
         needed]

   BT **Industrial equipment**
        Machinery in the workplace
   NT **Feedback control systems**
        Industrial robots
        Libraries—Automation
        Servomechanisms
        Systems engineering
        Telecommuting
Automatons
   USE **Robots**
Automobile accidents
   USE **Traffic accidents**
Automobile design
   USE **Automobiles—Design and con-**
          struction
Automobile driver education (May
     subdiv. geog.)   **629.28**
   UF Automobile drivers—Education
        Car driver education
        Driver education
   BT **Education**
Automobile drivers   629.28
   UF Automobile driving
        Automobiles—Driving
        Car drivers
        Drivers, Automobile
Automobile drivers—Education
   USE **Automobile driver education**
Automobile drivers' licenses
   USE **Drivers' licenses**
Automobile driving
   USE **Automobile drivers**
Automobile engines
   USE **Automobiles—Motors**
Automobile guides
   USE **Automobile travel—Guidebooks**
Automobile industry (May subdiv. geog.)
     338.4; 388.3
   UF Automotive industry
        Car industry
        Motor vehicle industry
   BT **Industries**
   NT **Service stations**
Automobile industry—Production stan-
     dards   658.5
   BT **Production standards**
Automobile insurance   368
   UF Car insurance
        Insurance, Automobile
   BT **Insurance**

Automobile motors
USE **Automobiles—Motors**
Automobile parts   **629.28**
UF Automobiles—Parts
Car parts
BT **Automobiles**
Automobile pools
USE **Car pools**
Automobile racing (May subdiv. geog.)
796.72
UF Automobiles—Racing
Car racing
SA types of automobile racing and
names of specific races [to be
added as needed]
BT **Racing**
NT **Karts and karting**
Stock car racing
Automobile repairs
USE **Automobiles—Maintenance and
repair**
Automobile touring
USE **Automobile travel**
Automobile transmission
USE **Automobiles—Transmission de-
vices**
Automobile travel (May subdiv. geog.)
796.7
UF Automobile touring
Automobiles—Touring
Car travel
Motoring
BT **Travel**
Automobile travel—Guidebooks   **912**
UF Automobile guides
Automobiles—Road guides
Travel guides
BT **Maps**
RT **Road maps**
Automobiles (May subdiv. geog.)   **388.3;
629.222**
UF Cars (Automobiles)
Motor cars
SA names of specific makes and
models of automobiles, e.g.
Ford automobile [to be add-
ed as needed]
BT **Highway transportation
Vehicles**
NT **Antique and classic cars
Automobile parts**

**Buses
Compact cars
Diesel automobiles
Electric automobiles
Ford automobile
Foreign automobiles
Sports cars
Trucks**
Automobiles—Accidents
USE **Traffic accidents**
Automobiles—Air conditioning   **629.2**
BT **Air conditioning**
Automobiles—Brakes   **629.2**
BT **Brakes**
**Automobiles—Conservation and restora-
tion**   **629.28**
UF Automobiles—Restoration
Restoration of automobiles
Automobiles—Construction
USE **Automobiles—Design and con-
struction**
Automobiles—Design
USE **Automobiles—Design and con-
struction**
Automobiles—Design and construction
629.222
UF Automobile design
Automobiles—Construction
Automobiles—Design
Automotive engineering
Car design
BT **Industrial design**
Automobiles—Drivers' licenses
USE **Drivers' licenses**
Automobiles—Driving
USE **Automobile drivers**
Automobiles, Electric
USE **Electric automobiles**
Automobiles—Electric equipment
629.25
UF Electric equipment of automo-
biles
Automobiles—Engines
USE **Automobiles—Motors**
Automobiles, Foreign
USE **Foreign automobiles**
Automobiles—Fuel consumption   **629.28**
BT **Energy consumption
Fuel**

Automobiles—Gearing
  USE **Automobiles—Transmission de-**
       vices
Automobiles—Inspection (May subdiv.
  geog.) **353.9**
Automobiles—Law and legislation (May
  subdiv. geog.) **343.09**
  BT **Law**
       Legislation
  RT **Traffic regulations**
Automobiles—Maintenance and repair
  629.28
  UF Automobile repairs
       Automobiles—Repairing
       Car maintenance
       Car repair
Automobiles—Models 629.22
  UF Model cars
  BT **Models and modelmaking**
Automobiles—Motors 629.25
  UF Automobile engines
       Automobile motors
       Automobiles—Engines
       Car engines
  SA types of automobiles and makes
       and models of automobiles
       with the subdivision *Motors*
       [to be added as needed]
  BT **Engines**
Automobiles—Painting 667
  UF Car painting
  BT **Industrial painting**
Automobiles—Parts
  USE **Automobile parts**
Automobiles—Pollution control devices
  629.25
  UF Pollution control devices (Motor
       vehicles)
  BT **Pollution control industry**
Automobiles—Purchasing (May subdiv.
  geog.) **381**
Automobiles—Racing
  USE **Automobile racing**
Automobiles—Repairing
  USE **Automobiles—Maintenance and**
       repair
Automobiles—Restoration
  USE **Automobiles—Conservation**
       and restoration
Automobiles—Road guides
  USE **Automobile travel—Guidebooks**

Automobiles—Technological innovations
  629.22
  BT **Technological innovations**
Automobiles—Touring
  USE **Automobile travel**
Automobiles—Trailers
  USE **Travel trailers and campers**
Automobiles—Transmission devices
  629.2
  UF Automobile transmission
       Automobiles—Gearing
       Car transmissions
       Transmissions, Automobile
  BT **Gearing**
Automotive engineering
  USE **Automobiles—Design and con-**
       struction
Automotive industry
  USE **Automobile industry**
Autosuggestion
  USE **Hypnotism**
       Mental suggestion
Autumn 508; 525
  UF Fall
  BT **Seasons**
Avant-garde churches
  USE **Non-institutional churches**
Avant-garde films
  USE **Experimental films**
Avant-garde theater
  USE **Experimental theater**
Avarice 178; 205
  Use for materials on an inordinate desire
  for wealth. Materials on any excessive desire
  for food, personal possessions, etc. are entered
  under **Greed.**
  UF Covetousness
  BT **Sin**
  RT **Greed**
Avenues
  USE **Streets**
Average 519.5
  BT **Arithmetic**
       Probabilities
       Statistics
Aviation
  USE **Aeronautics**
Aviation accidents
  USE **Aircraft accidents**
Aviation medicine 616.9
  UF Aeronautics—Medical aspects
       Aerospace medicine

Aviation medicine—*Continued*
　　BT　Medicine
　　NT　Jet lag
　　RT　Space medicine
Aviators
　　USE　Air pilots
Avocations
　　USE　Hobbies
Awakening, Religious
　　USE　Religious awakening
Awards　001.4
　　UF　Competitions
　　　　Prizes (Rewards)
　　　　Rewards (Prizes, etc.)
　　SA　types of awards and prizes; sub-
　　　　jects, corporate entities, per-
　　　　sons, and military services
　　　　with the subdivision *Awards,*
　　　　e.g. **Architecture—Awards;**
　　　　and names of specific awards
　　　　and prizes, e.g. **Nobel Prizes**
　　　　[to be added as needed]
　　NT　Literary prizes
　　　　Nobel Prizes
　　RT　Contests
Awards (Law)
　　USE　Arbitration and award
Axiology
　　USE　Values
Aztecs　972.004
　　BT　Native Americans—Mexico
B-52 bomber　623.74
　　BT　Bombers
B and B accommodations
　　USE　Bed and breakfast accommo-
　　　　dations
Babies
　　USE　Infants
Baby animals
　　USE　Animal babies
Baby boom generation (May subdiv.
　　geog.)　305.2
　　UF　Baby boomers
　　BT　Population
Baby boomers
　　USE　Baby boom generation
Baby care
　　USE　Infants—Care
Baby clothes
　　USE　Infants' clothing
Baby names
　　USE　Personal names

Baby sitters
　　USE　Babysitters
Baby sitting
　　USE　Babysitting
Babysitters　649
　　UF　Baby sitters
　　　　Sitters (Babysitters)
　　RT　Babysitting
Babysitting　649
　　UF　Baby sitting
　　BT　Child care
　　　　Infants—Care
　　RT　Babysitters
Back packing
　　USE　Backpacking
Backpack cycling
　　USE　Bicycle touring
Backpacking　796.51
　　UF　Back packing
　　　　Pack transportation
　　BT　Camping
　　　　Hiking
Bacon-Shakespeare controversy
　　USE　Shakespeare, William, 1564-
　　　　1616—Authorship
Bacon's Rebellion, 1676　973.2
　　BT　United States—History—1600-
　　　　1775, Colonial period
Bacteria　579.3
　　Use for general materials on bacteria. Mate-
　　rials on the science of studying bacteria are
　　entered under **Bacteriology.**
　　UF　Disease germs
　　　　Germs
　　　　Microbes
　　BT　Microorganisms
　　　　Parasites
　　RT　Bacteriology
Bacterial warfare
　　USE　Biological warfare
Bacteriology　579.3
　　Use for materials on the science of studying
　　bacteria. General materials on bacteria are en-
　　tered under **Bacteria.**
　　SA　types of bacteriology, e.g. **Agri-
　　　　cultural bacteriology;** types
　　　　of microbiology, e.g. **Soil mi-
　　　　crobiology;** and subjects with
　　　　the subdivision *Microbiology,*
　　　　e.g. **Cheese—Microbiology**
　　　　[to be added as needed]

Bacteriology—*Continued*
    BT   **Microbiology**
    NT   **Agricultural bacteriology**
    RT   **Bacteria**
Bacteriology, Agricultural
    USE **Agricultural bacteriology**
Bad behavior   179; 302.3; 395
    UF   Meanness
          Rudeness
    BT   **Human behavior**
Bad breath   616.3
    UF   Halitosis
    BT   **Mouth—Diseases**
Bad sportsmanship
    USE **Sportsmanship**
Badges of honor
    USE **Decorations of honor**
          Insignia
          Medals
Baggage
    USE **Luggage**
Bahai Faith   297.9
    UF   Bahaism
    BT   **Religions**
Bahaism
    USE **Bahai Faith**
Baking   641.7
    SA   types of baked products [to be
          added as needed]
    BT   **Cooking**
    NT   **Bread**
          Cake
          Pastry
    RT   **Bread machines**
Balance of nature
    USE **Ecology**
Balance of payments (May subdiv. geog.)
    382
    BT   **International economic rela-**
          tions
    RT   **Balance of trade**
Balance of power   327.1
    UF   Power politics
    BT   **International relations**
Balance of trade (May subdiv. geog.)
    382
    UF   Trade, Balance of
          Trade deficits
          Trade surpluses
    BT   **International trade**
    RT   **Balance of payments**

Ball bearings
    USE **Bearings (Machinery)**
Ball games   796.3
    SA   types of games, e.g. **Baseball;**
          and names of competitions [to
          be added as needed]
    BT   **Games**
    NT   **Baseball**
          Basketball
          Billiards
          Bowling
          Football
          Soccer
          Softball
          Table tennis
          Volleyball
Ball room dancing
    USE **Ballroom dancing**
Ballads   808.1; 808.81
    May be used for individual works, collec-
tions, or materials about ballads. Materials on
the folk tunes associated with these ballads
and collections that include both words and
music are entered under **Folk songs.**
    BT   **Literature**
          Poetry
          Songs
    RT   **Folk songs**
Ballet (May subdiv. geog.)   792.8
    Use for musical works composed for the
ballet and for materials about the ballet. Individual ballet plots or collections of ballet plots
are entered under **Ballet—Stories, plots, etc.**
    UF   Ballets
    BT   **Dance**
          Drama
          Performing arts
          Theater
    RT   **Pantomimes**
Ballet dancers   792.8092; 920
    BT   **Dancers**
Ballet plots
    USE **Ballet—Stories, plots, etc.**
Ballet—Stories, plots, etc.   792.8
    UF   Ballet plots
Ballets
    USE **Ballet**
Ballistic missiles   358.1; 623.4
    Use for materials on high-altitude, high-
speed missiles that are self-propelled and
guided in the first stage of flight only and lat-
er have a natural and uncontrolled trajectory.

Ballistic missiles—*Continued*
UF Missiles, Ballistic
SA types of ballistic missiles and
      names of specific missiles [to
      be added as needed]
BT **Guided missiles**
      Nuclear weapons
      Rockets (Aeronautics)
NT **Atlas (Missile)**
      **Intercontinental ballistic mis-
      siles**
Balloons 629.133
Use for materials on aircraft held aloft by
hot air or light gases that are nondirigible and
propelled only by the wind. Materials on self-
propelled aircraft that are lighter than air and
steerable are entered under **Airships.**
UF Aircraft
BT **Aeronautics**
RT **Airships**
Balloons, Dirigible
USE **Airships**
Ballot
USE **Elections**
Ballparks
USE **Stadiums**
Ballroom dancing (May subdiv. geog.)
      793.3
UF Ball room dancing
BT **Dance**
Band music   784
BT **Instrumental music**
      Military music
Bandages   616.02
UF Bandages and bandaging
BT **First aid**
Bandages and bandaging
USE **Bandages**
Bandits
USE **Thieves**
Bandmasters
USE **Conductors (Music)**
Bands (Music)   784
SA types of bands and names of in-
      dividual bands [to be added
      as needed]
NT **Drum majoring**
      **Instrumentation and orchestra-
      tion**
RT **Conducting**
      Orchestra
Bank credit cards
USE **Credit cards**

Bank debit cards
USE **Debit cards**
Bank failures (May subdiv. geog.)   **332.1**
UF Failure of banks
BT **Bankruptcy**
      Banks and banking
      Business failures
Bank robberies (May subdiv. geog.)
      364.15
BT **Theft**
Banking
USE **Banks and banking**
Bankruptcy (May subdiv. geog.)   **332.7;
      336.3; 346.07**
UF Business mortality
      Failure in business
      Insolvency
BT **Business failures**
      Commercial law
      Debtor and creditor
      Finance
NT **Bank failures**
Banks and banking (May subdiv. geog.)
      332.1
UF Banking
      Savings banks
SA names of individual banks [to be
      added as needed]
BT **Business**
      Capital
      Commerce
      Finance
NT **Agricultural credit**
      Bank failures
      Consumer credit
      Cooperative banks
      Debit cards
      Federal Reserve banks
      Foreign exchange
      Interest (Economics)
      Investments
      Negotiable instruments
      Savings and loan associations
RT **Credit**
      Money
      Trust companies
Banks and banking, Cooperative
USE **Cooperative banks**
Banks and banking—Credit cards
USE **Credit cards**

Banks and banking—Data processing
      332.10285
  BT   Data processing
Banks and banking—United States
      332.10973
Banned books
  USE Books—Censorship
Banners
  USE Flags
Banquets
  USE Dining
      Dinners
Baptism   234; 265
  UF   Christening
  BT   Sacraments
Baptists   286
  BT   Christian sects
Bar
  USE Lawyers
Bar coding   006.4; 658.7
  BT   Identification
Barbary States
  USE North Africa
Barbecue cookery
  USE Barbecue cooking
Barbecue cooking   641.7
  UF   Barbecue cookery
      Grill cooking
  BT   Outdoor cooking
Barbering
  USE Hair
Barbie dolls   688.7
  BT   Dolls
Bargaining
  USE Negotiation
Barns   631.2; 728
  BT   Farm buildings
Barometers   551.5; 681
  BT   Meteorological instruments
Baroque architecture (May subdiv. geog.)
      724
  UF   Architecture, Baroque
  BT   Architecture
Baroque art (May subdiv. geog.)   709.03
  UF   Art, Baroque
  BT   Art
Barrier free design
  USE Architecture and the handi-
      capped
Barristers
  USE Lawyers

Barrooms
  USE Bars
Barrows
  USE Mounds and mound builders
Bars (May subdiv. geog.)   647.95
    Use for materials on public drinking estab-
lishments.
  UF   Barrooms
      Pubs
      Restaurants, bars, etc.
      Saloons
      Taverns
  BT   Liquor industry
  RT   Restaurants
Bartending   641.8
  UF   Mixology
  BT   Food service
Barter (May subdiv. geog.)   332
  UF   Exchange, Barter
  BT   Commerce
      Economics
      Money
      Subsistence economy
      Underground economy
Basal readers   372.41; 418
    Use for readers providing controlled vocab-
ulary in a series of books intended to be read
sequentially and for materials about such read-
ers.
  UF   English language—Basal readers
  BT   Reading materials
Baseball (May subdiv. geog.)   796.357
  BT   Ball games
      Sports
  NT   Baseball teams
      Little League baseball
      Negro leagues
      Softball
  RT   Baseball players
Baseball cards   769
  BT   Sports cards
Baseball clubs
  USE Baseball teams
Baseball—Fiction   808.83
    Use for collections of baseball stories.
  UF   Baseball stories
Baseball players (May subdiv. geog.)
      796.357; 920
  BT   Athletes
  RT   Baseball
Baseball stories
  USE Baseball—Fiction

Baseball teams (May subdiv. geog.)
    796.35706
    UF   Baseball clubs
    SA   names of individual baseball
            teams, e.g. **Houston Astros**
            (Baseball team) [to be added
            as needed]
    BT   **Baseball**
          Sports teams
    NT   **Houston Astros (Baseball**
          team)
Basements 721
    UF   Cellars
    BT   **Foundations**
          Underground architecture
Bases (Chemistry) 546; 661
    BT   **Chemistry**
Bashfulness
    USE **Shyness**
Basic education (May subdiv. geog.)
    370.11
    UF   Basic skills education
          Fundamental education
    BT   **Education**
Basic life skills
    USE **Life skills**
Basic needs (May subdiv. geog.) **306**
    Use for materials on human needs such as
  food, shelter, education, health, water, em-
  ployment, etc., that provide a minimum quali-
  ty of life.
    RT   **Poverty**
          Quality of life
Basic rights
    USE **Civil rights**
          Human rights
Basic skills education
    USE **Basic education**
Basket making 746.41
    BT   **Weaving**
Basketball (May subdiv. geog.) **796.323**
    BT   **Ball games**
          Sports
    NT   **Basketball teams**
          Wheelchair basketball
Basketball for women (May subdiv.
    geog.) **796.323**
    BT   **Sports for women**

Basketball teams (May subdiv. geog.)
    796.323
    SA   names of individual basketball
          teams, e.g. **New York Knicks**
          (Basketball team) [to be add-
          ed as needed]
    BT   **Basketball**
          Sports teams
    NT   **New York Knicks (Basketball**
          team)
Baskets (May subdiv. geog.) **746.41**
    BT   **Containers**
Bastogne, Battle of
    USE **Ardennes, Battle of the, 1944-**
          1945
Baths 613; 615.8
    BT   **Cleanliness**
          Hygiene
          Physical therapy
    RT   **Hydrotherapy**
Bathyscaphe 387.2; 623.8
    BT   **Oceanography—Research**
          Submersibles
Batik 746.6
    BT   **Dyes and dyeing**
Baton twirling 791.6
    RT   **Drum majoring**
Bats 599.4
    BT   **Mammals**
Battered elderly
    USE **Elderly abuse**
Battered wives
    USE **Abused women**
Battered women
    USE **Abused women**
Batteries, Electric
    USE **Electric batteries**
          Storage batteries
Batteries, Solar
    USE **Solar batteries**
Battering of wives
    USE **Wife abuse**
Battle of the Bulge
    USE **Ardennes, Battle of the, 1944-**
          1945
Battle ships
    USE **Warships**
Battle songs
    USE **War songs**

Battlefields (May subdiv. geog.)   **904**
  UF   Battlegrounds
  SA   names of wars with the subdivision *Battlefields,* e.g. **World War, 1939-1945—Battlefields;** and names of individual battlefields [to be added as needed]
  BT   **Battles**
Battlegrounds
  USE   **Battlefields**
Battles (May subdiv. geog.)   **355.4; 904; 909**
  UF   Fighting
     Sieges
  SA   names of wars with the subdivision *Campaigns,* e.g. **United States—History—1861-1865, Civil War—Campaigns;** and names of individual battles, e.g. **Ardennes, Battle of the, 1944-1945** [to be added as needed]
  BT   **Military art and science**
     Military history
     War
  NT   **Battlefields**
     Naval battles
Battleships
  USE   **Warships**
Bay of Pigs invasion
  USE   **Cuba—History—1961, Invasion**
Bazaars
  USE   **Fairs**
BBBs (Better business bureaus)
  USE   **Better business bureaus**
Beaches (May subdiv. geog.)   **551.45**
  BT   **Seashore**
Beadwork   **746.5**
  BT   **Crocheting**
     Embroidery
     Weaving
Bearings (Machinery)   **621.8**
  UF   Ball bearings
  BT   **Machinery**
  RT   **Lubrication and lubricants**
Beasts
  USE   **Animals**
Beat generation   **810.9**
  UF   Beatniks
     Beats

  BT   **American literature**
     Bohemianism
Beatniks
  USE   **Beat generation**
Beats
  USE   **Beat generation**
Beautification of landscape
  USE   **Landscape protection**
Beauty
  USE   **Aesthetics**
Beauty parlors
  USE   **Beauty shops**
Beauty, Personal
  USE   **Personal appearance**
     Personal grooming
Beauty salons
  USE   **Beauty shops**
Beauty shops   **646.7**
  UF   Beauty parlors
     Beauty salons
  BT   **Business enterprises**
Beavers   **599.37**
  BT   **Furbearing animals**
     Mammals
Beavers—Habitations   **599.37**
Bed and breakfast accommodations (May subdiv. geog.)   **910.46**
  UF   B and B accommodations
  BT   **Hotels and motels**
Bedouins (May subdiv. geog.)   **305.892; 909**
  BT   **Arabs**
Bedspreads   **643; 746.9**
  UF   Coverlets
  BT   **Interior design**
Bedtime   **306.4; 392.3**
  UF   Getting ready for bed
  BT   **Night**
     Sleep
  NT   **Lullabies**
Bee culture
  USE   **Beekeeping**
Bee hives
  USE   **Beehives**
Bee houses
  USE   **Beehives**
Beef   **641.3; 664**
  BT   **Meat**

Beef cattle   636.2
  UF   Steers
  SA   names of breeds of beef cattle
        [to be added as needed]
  BT   **Cattle**
  NT   **Hereford cattle**
Beehives   638
  UF   Bee hives
        Bee houses
        Bees—Housing
  BT   **Animal housing**
  RT   **Beekeeping**
Beekeeping   638
  UF   Apiculture
        Bee culture
        Honeybee culture
  BT   **Agriculture**
  RT   **Beehives**
        Bees
Beer making
  USE   **Brewing**
Bees   595.79; 638
  BT   **Insects**
  RT   **Beekeeping**
        Honey
Bees—Housing
  USE   **Beehives**
Begging   362.5
  UF   Mendicancy
        Panhandling
  BT   **Poor**
  RT   **Tramps**
Beginning reading materials
  USE   **Easy reading materials**
Behavior
  USE   **Animal behavior**
        Human behavior
        and types of specific behavior,
        e.g. **Sexual behavior;** and
        types of animals with the
        subdivision *Behavior,* e.g.
        Birds—Behavior [to be add-
        ed as needed]
Behavior genetics   155.7
  UF   Psychogenetics
  BT   **Genetics**
        Psychology
Behavior, Helping
  USE   **Helping behavior**
Behavior in organizations
  USE   **Organizational behavior**

Behavior modification   153.8
  BT   **Applied psychology**
        Human behavior
        Psychology of learning
  NT   **Brainwashing**
        Twelve-step programs
Behavior of children
  USE   **Child psychology**
        Children—Conduct of life
        Etiquette for children and
          teenagers
Behavior of teenagers
  USE   **Adolescent psychology**
        Etiquette for children and
          teenagers
        Teenagers—Conduct of life
Behavior problems (Children)
  USE   **Emotionally disturbed children**
Behavioral psychology
  USE   **Psychophysiology**
Behaviorism   150.19
    Use for materials on empirical psychology
    dealing with the observable actions of organ-
    isms rather than with mental phenomena.
  UF   Behavioristic psychology
        Interbehaviorial psychology
  BT   **Human behavior**
        Psychology
        Psychophysiology
Behavioristic psychology
  USE   **Behaviorism**
Beijing Massacre, 1989
  USE   **Tiananmen Square Incident,**
          Beijing (China), 1989
Belief and doubt   121
    Use for materials on belief and doubt from
    the philosophical standpoint. Materials on reli-
    gious belief and doubt are entered under
    Faith.
  UF   Doubt
  BT   **Philosophy**
        Theory of knowledge
  NT   **Truth**
  RT   **Agnosticism**
        Faith
        Rationalism
        Skepticism
Bell System Telstar satellite
  USE   **Telstar project**
Belles lettres
  USE   **Literature**

Bells 786.8
UF Carillons
Chimes
Church bells
BT **Musical instruments**
Belts and belting 621.8
UF Chain belting
BT **Machinery**
RT **Power transmission**
Beneficial insects 591.6
UF Helpful insects
Useful insects
SA types of beneficial insects, e.g.
Silkworms [to be added as
needed]
BT **Economic zoology**
Insects
NT **Silkworms**
Benefit cost analysis
USE **Cost effectiveness**
Benefits, Employee
USE **Fringe benefits**
Benefits, Fringe
USE **Fringe benefits**
Benevolent institutions
USE **Institutional care**
Beowulf—Adaptations 829
Bequests
USE **Gifts**
Inheritance and succession
Wills
Bereavement 155.9; 248.8
Use for materials on the suffering of those
who have lost a loved one. Materials on men-
tal suffering or sorrow from other causes, es-
pecially loss or remorse, are entered under
Grief.
UF Mourning
Sorrow
Sympathy
BT **Emotions**
RT **Consolation**
Grief
Bermuda Triangle 001.9
UF Devil's Triangle
BT **Atlantic Ocean**
Berries 634
SA types of berries, e.g. **Strawber-
ries** [to be added as needed],
in the plural form
BT **Fruit**
Fruit culture
NT **Strawberries**

Best-book lists
USE **Best books**
Best books 011
Use for lists of recommended books and
materials about recommended books. Materi-
als on the principles of book selection for li-
braries are entered under **Book selection.**
UF Best-book lists
Bibliography—Best books
Book lists
Books and reading—Best books
Choice of books
Evaluation of literature
Literature—Evaluation
BT **Books**
RT **Book selection**
Best sellers (Books) 028; 070.5
UF Books—Best sellers
BT **Books and reading**
Better business bureaus (May subdiv.
geog.) **381.3**
UF BBBs (Better business bureaus)
BT **Consumer protection**
Betting
USE **Gambling**
Bevel gearing
USE **Gearing**
Beverage industry (May subdiv. geog.)
338.4
SA types of beverage industries, e.g.
Coffee industry [to be added
as needed]
BT **Food industry**
NT **Coffee industry**
Liquor industry
Tea industry
Beverages 613; 641.2; 641.8; 663
UF Drinks
SA types of beverages and names of
specific beverages [to be add-
ed as needed]
BT **Diet**
Food
NT **Alcoholic beverages**
Cocoa
Coffee
Liquors
Tea
Bi-racial people
USE **Racially mixed people**
Bias attacks
USE **Hate crimes**

Bias crimes
USE **Hate crimes**
Bias in testing
USE **Test bias**
Bias (Psychology)
USE **Prejudices**
Bible   220

The subdivisions provided under **Bible** may also be used with any part of the Bible, with single books of the Bible, and with groups of books, e.g. **Bible. O.T.—Biography; Bible. O.T. Pentateuch—Commentaries; Bible. O.T. Psalms—History; Bible. N.T. Gospels—Inspiration;** etc.

UF   Holy Scriptures
Scriptures, Holy
BT   **Ancient history**
Hebrew literature
Jewish literature
Sacred books
NT   **Bible stories**
Bible and science   220.8
UF   Bible—Science
Science and the Bible
BT   **Religion and science**
Science
RT   **Creationism**
Bible—Animals
USE   **Bible—Natural history**
Bible—Antiquities   220.9
UF   Biblical archeology
BT   **Antiquities**
Archeology
NT   **Christian antiquities**
Bible as literature   809
UF   Bible—Language, style, etc.
Bible—Literary character
NT   **Bible—Criticism**
Bible—Parables
RT   **Religious literature**
Bible—Astronomy   220.8
BT   **Astronomy**
Bible—Biography   220.92
UF   Biblical characters
BT   **Biography**
NT   **Women in the Bible**
Bible—Birds
USE   **Bible—Natural history**
Bible—Botany
USE   **Bible—Natural history**
Bible—Catechism, question books
USE   **Bible—Catechisms**

Bible—Catechisms   220
UF   Bible—Catechism, question
books
Bible—Question books
BT   **Bible—Study and teaching**
Catechisms
Bible—Chronology   220.9

Use for materials on the dates of events related in the Bible and their correlation with the dates of general history.

UF   Bible—History of biblical
events—Chronology
Chronology, Biblical
BT   **Chronology**
Bible classes
USE   **Bible—Study and teaching**
Religious summer schools
Sunday schools
Bible—Commentaries   220.7
UF   Bible—Interpretation
Commentaries, Biblical
Bible—Concordances   220.3

Use for works that list the words of the Bible and give the passages where each word occurs. Works that list topics or names found in the Bible and give the passages where those topics or names rather than exact words are found are entered under **Bible—Indexes.**

Bible—Cosmology
USE   **Biblical cosmology**
Bible—Criticism   220.6
UF   Bible—Criticism, interpretation,
etc.
Bible—Exegesis
Bible—Hermeneutics
Bible—Interpretation
Exegesis, Biblical
Hermeneutics, Biblical
Higher criticism
BT   **Bible as literature**
Bible—Criticism, interpretation, etc.
USE   **Bible—Criticism**
Bible—Dictionaries   220.3
BT   **Encyclopedias and dictionaries**
Bible—Drama
USE   **Bible plays**
Bible—Evidences, authority, etc.   220.1

Use for materials that attempt to establish the truth of statements in the Bible or the authority of its precepts. Materials on the divine inspiration of the Bible are entered under **Bible—Inspiration.**

UF   Evidences of the Bible
BT   **Bible—Inspiration**

Bible—Exegesis
USE **Bible—Criticism**
Bible fiction   808.3; 808.83
> May be used for individual works, collections, or materials about imaginative fiction in which characters and settings are taken from the Bible. Stories that are retold or adapted from the Bible while remaining faithful to the original are entered under **Bible stories.**

UF   Bible—History of biblical
>   events—Fiction

SA   names of biblical characters with
>   the subdivision *Fiction* [to be
>   added as needed]

BT   **Fiction**
RT   **Bible stories**
Bible films   791.43
> May be used for individual works, collections, or materials about bible films.

UF   Biblical films
BT   **Motion pictures**
RT   **Bible plays**
Bible—Flowers
USE   **Bible—Natural history**
Bible games and puzzles   220.07;
>   **793.73**

UF   Bible puzzles
BT   **Games**
>   **Puzzles**
Bible—Gardens
USE   **Bible—Natural history**
Bible—Geography   220.91
UF   Bible—Maps
>   Biblical geography
BT   **Atlases**
>   **Geography**
Bible—Hermeneutics
USE   **Bible—Criticism**
Bible—History   220.9
> Use for materials on the origin, authorship, and composition of the Bible as a book. Materials on historical events as described in the Bible are entered under **Bible—History of biblical events.**

Bible—History of biblical events   220.9
> Use for materials on historical events as described in the Bible. Materials on the origin, authorship, and composition of the Bible as a book are entered under **Bible—History.**

UF   History, Biblical
Bible—History of biblical events—Chronology
USE   **Bible—Chronology**
Bible—History of biblical events—Fiction
USE   **Bible fiction**

Bible—Illustrations
USE   **Bible—Pictorial works**
Bible in literature   809
> Use for materials that discuss the Bible as a theme in literature.

BT   **Literature**
RT   **Religion in literature**
Bible in the schools
USE   **Religion in the public schools**
Bible—Indexes   220.3
> Use for works that list topics or names found in the Bible and give the passages where those topics or names rather than exact words are found. Works that list the words of the Bible and give the passages where the exact word occurs are entered under **Bible—Concordances.**

Bible—Inspiration   220.1
> Use for materials on the divine inspiration of the Bible. Materials that attempt to establish the truth of statements in the Bible or the authority of its precepts are entered under **Bible—Evidence, authority, etc.**

UF   Inspiration, Biblical
NT   **Bible—Evidences, authority,**
>   **etc.**
Bible—Interpretation
USE   **Bible—Commentaries**
>   **Bible—Criticism**
Bible—Introductions
USE   **Bible—Study and teaching**
Bible—Language, style, etc.
USE   **Bible as literature**
Bible—Literary character
USE   **Bible as literature**
Bible—Maps
USE   **Bible—Geography**
Bible. N.T.   225
> Use same subdivisions as those given under **Bible.** They may also be used for groups of books, e.g. **Bible. N.T. Gospels—Inspiration;** and for single books, e.g. **Bible. N.T. Matthew—Commentaries.**

UF   New Testament
Bible—Natural history   220.8
UF   Bible—Animals
>   Bible—Birds
>   Bible—Botany
>   Bible—Flowers
>   Bible—Gardens
>   Bible—Plants
>   Bible—Zoology
>   Botany of the Bible
>   Nature in the bible
>   Zoology of the Bible
BT   **Natural history**

Bible. O.T.   221

Use same subdivisions as those given under **Bible.** They may also be used for groups of books, e.g. **Bible. O.T. Pentateuch—Commentaries;** and for single books, e.g. **Bible. O.T. Psalms—History.**

UF   Old Testament

NT   **Ten commandments**

Bible—Parables   226.8

BT   **Bible as literature**
       Parables

NT   **Jesus Christ—Parables**

Bible—Pictorial works   220.022

UF   Bible—Illustrations

RT   **Jesus Christ—Art**

Bible—Plants

USE   **Bible—Natural history**

Bible plays   808.82

May be used for individual plays, collections, or materials about dramatizations of biblical events.

UF   Bible—Drama
       Biblical plays
       Plays, Bible

SA   names of biblical characters with the subdivision *Drama* [to be added as needed]

BT   **Religious drama**

NT   **Mysteries and miracle plays**
       Passion plays

RT   **Bible films**

Bible—Prophecies   220.1

UF   Prophecies (Bible)

NT   **Jesus Christ—Prophecies**

Bible—Psychology   220.8

UF   Biblical psychology

BT   **Psychology**

Bible puzzles

USE   **Bible games and puzzles**

Bible—Question books

USE   **Bible—Catechisms**

Bible—Reading   220.5

BT   **Books and reading**

Bible—Science

USE   **Bible and science**

Bible stories   220.9

May be used for individual works, collections, or materials about stories that are retold or adapted from the Bible while remaining faithful to the original. Imaginative fiction in which characters and settings are taken from the Bible is entered under **Bible fiction.**

UF   Stories

BT   **Bible**

RT   **Bible fiction**

Bible—Study

USE   **Bible—Study and teaching**

Bible—Study and teaching   220.07

UF   Bible classes
       Bible—Introductions
       Bible—Study

BT   **Christian education**
       Sunday schools

NT   **Bible—Catechisms**

Bible—Use   220.6

Use for materials that show how the Bible is used as a guide to living, to cultivation of a spiritual life, and to problems of doctrine.

Bible—Versions   220.4; 220.5

Use for materials on the various versions and translations of the Bible.

Bible—Women

USE   **Women in the Bible**

Bible—Zoology

USE   **Bible—Natural history**

Biblical archeology

USE   **Bible—Antiquities**

Biblical characters

USE   **Bible—Biography**

Biblical cosmology   202; 231.7; 296.3

UF   Bible—Cosmology

BT   **Cosmology**

RT   **Creation**

Biblical films

USE   **Bible films**

Biblical geography

USE   **Bible—Geography**

Biblical plays

USE   **Bible plays**

Biblical psychology

USE   **Bible—Psychology**

Biblical teaching

USE   religious or secular topics with the subdivision *Biblical teaching,* e.g. **Salvation—Biblical teaching; Family—Biblical teaching;** etc. [to be added as needed]

Bibliographic control   025.3

UF   Universal bibliographic control

BT   **Documentation**

NT   **Cataloging**
       Indexing
       Information systems
       MARC formats

Bibliographic data in machine readable
form
    USE **Machine readable bibliographic
data**
Bibliographic instruction   025.5

Use for materials on the instruction of readers in library use. Materials on the education
of librarians are entered under **Library education.**

    UF   Library instruction
          Library orientation
          Library skills
          Library user orientation
    BT   **Library services**
Bibliography   010
    SA   subjects and names of persons
          and places with the subdivi-
          sion *Bibliography,* e.g. **Agri-
          culture—Bibliography;
          Shakespeare, William, 1564-
          1616—Bibliography; United
          States—Bibliography;** etc. [to
          be added as needed]
    BT   **Documentation**
    NT   **Archives
          Editions
          Indexes
          Indexing
          Manuscripts
          Printing
          Reference books
          Serial publications**
    RT   **Books
          Cataloging
          Library science**
Bibliography—Best books
    USE **Best books**
Bibliography—Bilingual books
    USE **Bilingual books**
Bibliography—Editions
    USE **Editions**
Bibliography—First editions
    USE **First editions**
Bibliography—Rare books
    USE **Rare books**
Bibliography—Reprint editions
    USE **Reprints (Publications)**
Bibliomania
    USE **Book collecting**
Bibliophily
    USE **Book collecting**

Bicentennial celebrations—United States—
1976
    USE **American Revolution Bicenten-
          nial, 1776-1976**
Biculturalism (May subdiv. geog.)
    305.8; 306.44

Use for materials on the presence of two
distinct cultures within a single country or region. Materials on the coexistence of several
distinct ethnic, religious, or cultural groups
within one society are entered under **Pluralism (Social sciences).** Materials on policies or
programs that foster the preservation of various cultures or cultural identities within a unified   society   are   entered   under
Multiculturalism.

    BT   **Pluralism (Social sciences)**
    RT   **Multiculturalism**
**Biculturalism—United States   305.8;
    306.44**
Bicycle camping
    USE **Bicycle touring**
Bicycle racing (May subdiv. geog.)
    796.6
    BT   **Cycling
          Racing**
    RT   **Bicycle touring
          Bicycles**
Bicycle touring (May subdiv. geog.)
    796.6
    UF   Backpack cycling
          Bicycle camping
          Touring, Bicycle
    BT   **Camping
          Cycling
          Travel**
    RT   **Bicycle racing
          Bicycles**
Bicycles   629.227
    UF   Bicycles and bicycling
          Bikes
    BT   **Vehicles**
    NT   **Minibikes
          Motorcycles
          Mountain bikes**
    RT   **Bicycle racing
          Bicycle touring
          Cycling**
Bicycles and bicycling
    USE **Bicycles
          Cycling**
Bicycling
    USE **Cycling**

Big bang cosmology
USE **Big bang theory**
Big bang theory   **523.1**
  UF   Big bang cosmology
  BT   **Cosmology**
Big books   **372.41**
    Use for books produced in an oversize format and intended for use in shared-reading learning experiences or for materials about such books.
  UF   Enlarged texts for shared reading
       Oversize books
       Oversized books for shared reading
       Shared reading books
  BT   **Children's literature**
       Reading materials
  RT   **Large print books**
Big foot
USE   **Sasquatch**
Big game hunting (May subdiv. geog.)
  799.2
  BT   **Hunting**
Bigfoot
USE   **Sasquatch**
Bigotry
USE   **Prejudices**
       Toleration
Bigotry-motivated crimes
USE   **Hate crimes**
Bikes
USE   **Bicycles**
Biking
USE   **Cycling**
Bildungsromans   **808.3**
    May be used for individual works, collections, or materials about fiction in which the theme is the development of a character from youth to adulthood.
  UF   Apprenticeship novels
       Coming of age stories
  BT   **Fiction**
Bilingual books   **002; 011**
    Use for materials about bilingual books. As a form heading for the bilingual materials themselves, use this heading subdivided by the languages, e.g. **Bilingual books—English-Spanish.**
  UF   Bibliography—Bilingual books
       Books—Bilingual editions
  BT   **Books**
       Editions
Bilingual books—English-Spanish
    Use as a form heading for bilingual materials in English and Spanish.

  UF   Bilingual books—Spanish-English
Bilingual books—Spanish-English
  USE   **Bilingual books—English-Spanish**
Bilingual education (May subdiv. geog.)
  370.117
  UF   Education, Bilingual
  BT   **Bilingualism**
       Multicultural education
Bilingualism (May subdiv. geog.)
  306.44; 400
  BT   **Language and languages**
  NT   **Bilingual education**
Bilingualism—United States   **306.44;**
  420
Bill collecting
  USE   **Collecting of accounts**
Bill of rights (U.S.)
  USE   **United States. Constitution.**
       1st-10th amendments
Billboards
  USE   **Signs and signboards**
Billiards   **794.92**
  BT   **Ball games**
  NT   **Pool (Game)**
Bills and notes
  USE   **Negotiable instruments**
Bills of credit
  USE   **Credit**
       Negotiable instruments
Bills of fare
  USE   **Menus**
Binary system (Mathematics)   **513.5**
  UF   Pair system
  BT   **Mathematics**
       Numbers
Binding of books
  USE   **Bookbinding**
Binge eating behavior
  USE   **Bulimia**
Binge-purge behavior
  USE   **Bulimia**
Bio-bibliography
  USE   subjects, groups and classes of persons, names of places, and names of individual persons with the subdivision *Bio-bibliography*, e.g. **English literature—Bio-bibliography; United States—Bio-**

Bio-bibliography—*Continued*
　　　　　bibliography; etc. [to be add-
　　　　　ed as needed]
Bioastronautics
　　USE　**Space medicine**
Biochemistry　572
　　UF　Biological chemistry
　　　　Physiological chemistry
　　BT　**Biology**
　　　　Chemistry
　　　　Medicine
　　NT　**Clinical chemistry**
　　　　Metabolism
　　　　Molecular biology
　　　　Nucleic acids
　　　　Proteins
　　　　Steroids
Bioconversion
　　USE　**Biomass energy**
Biodiversity
　　USE　**Biological diversity**
Bioethics　174
　　UF　Biological ethics
　　　　Biology—Ethical aspects
　　　　Biomedical ethics
　　　　Life sciences ethics
　　BT　**Ethics**
　　NT　**Medical ethics**
　　　　Transplantation of organs, tis-
　　　　　sues, etc.—Ethical aspects
Biofeedback training　152.1
　　UF　Visceral learning
　　BT　**Feedback (Psychology)**
　　　　Mind and body
　　　　Psychology of learning
　　　　Psychotherapy
Biogeography (May subdiv. geog.)
　　　　578.09
　　Use for materials on the geographical distri-
　bution of animals and plants collectively or of
　animals only. Materials on the geographical
　distribution of plants are entered under
　Plants—Geographical distribution.
　　UF　Distribution of animals and
　　　　　plants
　　　　Geographical distribution of ani-
　　　　　mals and plants
　　SA　types of plants and animals with
　　　　　the subdivision *Geographical*
　　　　　distribution, e.g. **Fishes—Geo-**
　　　　　graphical distribution [to be
　　　　　added as needed]

　　BT　**Ecology**
　　　　Geography
　　NT　**Fishes—Geographical distribu-**
　　　　　tion
　　　　Plants—Geographical distribu-
　　　　　tion
　　RT　**Natural history**
Biographical dictionaries
　　USE　**Biography—Dictionaries**
Biographical fiction　808.3; 808.83
　　May be used for individual works, collec-
　tions, or materials about fictionalized accounts
　of the lives of real persons.
　　UF　Biographical novels
　　SA　names of real persons with the
　　　　　subdivision *Fiction,* e.g. **Na-**
　　　　　poleon I, Emperor of the
　　　　　French, 1769-1821—Fiction;
　　　　　or *In literature,* e.g. **Napoleon**
　　　　　I, Emperor of the French,
　　　　　1769-1821—In literature; [to
　　　　　be added as needed]
　　BT　**Fiction**
　　NT　**Autobiographical fiction**
　　RT　**Historical fiction**
Biographical films　791.43
　　May be used for individual works, collec-
　tions, or materials about films depicting the
　lives of real persons.
　　BT　**Motion pictures**
Biographical novels
　　USE　**Biographical fiction**
Biographical radio programs　791.44
　　May be used for individual works, collec-
　tions, or materials about radio programs re-
　counting the lives of real persons.
　　BT　**Radio programs**
Biographical television programs
　　　　791.45
　　May be used for individual works, collec-
　tions, or materials about television programs
　depicting the lives of real persons.
　　BT　**Television programs**
Biography　920
　　Use for collections of biographies not limit-
　ed to one country or to one group or class of
　persons. Materials on the writing of biography
　are entered under **Biography as a literary**
　form.
　　UF　Life histories
　　　　Memoirs
　　　　Personal narratives
　　SA　subjects and names of places
　　　　　and corporate bodies with the
　　　　　subdivision *Biography;* ethnic

Biography—*Continued*

　　groups and classes of persons with the subdivision *Biography* or *Correspondence;* and names of diseases, events, and wars with the subdivision *Personal narratives* [to be added as needed]

　BT　**History**
　NT　**Autobiographies**
　　　Autographs
　　　Bible—Biography
　　　Blacks—Biography
　　　Chicago (Ill.)—Biography
　　　Christian biography
　　　Epitaphs
　　　Greece—Biography
　　　Medicine—Biography
　　　Men—Biography
　　　Motion pictures—Biography
　　　Musicians—Biography
　　　Obituaries
　　　Ohio—Biography
　　　Portraits
　　　Religious biography
　　　Rome—Biography
　　　United States. Army—Biography
　　　United States—Biography
　　　United States—History—1861-1865, Civil War—Biography
　　　United States—History—1861-1865, Civil War—Personal narratives
　　　United States. Navy—Biography
　　　United States. Supreme Court—Biography
　　　Women—Biography
　　　World War, 1939-1945—Biography
　　　World War, 1939-1945—Personal narratives
　RT　**Genealogy**
Biography (as a literary form)
　USE　**Biography as a literary form**
Biography as a literary form　809
　Use for materials on the writing of biography.
　UF　Biography (as a literary form)
　　　Biography—History and criticism
　　　Biography—Technique

　BT　**Authorship**
　　　Literature
　NT　**Autobiography**
Biography—Dictionaries　920.02
　Use for collections of biographies in dictionary form not limited to one group or class of persons.
　UF　Biographical dictionaries
　　　Dictionaries, Biographical
　SA　subjects, groups or classes of persons, and names of places with the subdivisions *Biography—Dictionaries,* e.g. **Women—Biography—Dictionaries; United States—Biography—Dictionaries;** etc. [to be added as needed]
　BT　**Encyclopedias and dictionaries**
Biography—History and criticism
　USE　**Biography as a literary form**
Biography—Technique
　USE　**Biography as a literary form**
Biological anthropology
　USE　**Physical anthropology**
Biological chemistry
　USE　**Biochemistry**
Biological clocks
　USE　**Biological rhythms**
Biological diversification
　USE　**Biological diversity**
Biological diversity (May subdiv. geog.)　**333.95**
　Use for materials on the variety and variability among living organisms and the ecological complexes in which they occur, including ecosystem diversity, species diversity, and genetic diversity.
　UF　Biodiversity
　　　Biological diversification
　　　Diversity, Biological
　BT　**Biology**
　RT　**Ecology**
Biological diversity conservation (May subdiv. geog.)　**333.95**
　UF　Conservation of biological diversity
　　　Maintenance of biological diversity
　　　Preservation of biological diversity
　BT　**Conservation of natural resources**

Biological ethics
    USE **Bioethics**
Biological form
    USE **Morphology**
Biological parents
    USE **Birthparents**
Biological physics
    USE **Biophysics**
Biological rhythms   571.7
    UF   Biological clocks
          Biology—Periodicity
          Biorhythms
    BT   **Cycles**
    NT   **Jet lag**
Biological structure
    USE **Morphology**
Biological warfare (May subdiv. geog.)
    358; 623.4
    UF   Bacterial warfare
          Germ warfare
    BT   **Military art and science**
          Tactics
Biologists (May subdiv. geog.)   **570.92;**
    920
    BT   **Naturalists**
          Scientists
Biology   570
    BT   **Life sciences**
          Science
    NT   **Adaptation (Biology)**
          Anatomy
          Biochemistry
          Biological diversity
          Biomathematics
          Biophysics
          Botany
          Cells
          Cryobiology
          Death
          Ecology
          Embryology
          Ethnobiology
          Fossils
          Freshwater biology
          Gaia hypothesis
          Genetics
          Heredity
          Life (Biology)
          Life cycles (Biology)
          Marine biology
          Microbiology

          Physiology
          Protoplasm
          Radiobiology
          Reproduction
          Sex (Biology)
          Space biology
          Symbiosis
          Variation (Biology)
          Zoology
    RT   **Evolution**
Biology—Ecology
    USE **Ecology**
Biology—Ethical aspects
    USE **Bioethics**
Biology, Molecular
    USE **Molecular biology**
Biology—Periodicity
    USE **Biological rhythms**
Biology—Social aspects
    USE **Sociobiology**
Bioluminescence   572
    UF   Animal light
          Animal luminescence
          Light production in animals
    BT   **Luminescence**
Biomass energy   333.95
    Use for materials on organic matter that can
    be converted to fuel and is therefore regarded
    as a potential energy source.
    UF   Bioconversion
          Energy, Biomass
          Energy conversion, Microbial
          Microbial energy conversion
    SA   types of matter as fuels, e.g.
          Waste products as fuel [to
             be added as needed]
    BT   **Energy resources**
          Fuel
    RT   **Waste products as fuel**
Biomathematics   570.1
    BT   **Biology**
          Mathematics
Biomechanics
    USE **Human engineering**
          Human locomotion
Biomedical ethics
    USE **Bioethics**
Bionics   003
    Use for materials on the science of techno-
    logical systems that function in the manner of
    living systems.
    BT   **Biophysics**
          Cybernetics

Bionics—*Continued*
> Systems engineering

Biophysics   571.4
> UF   Biological physics
> BT   **Biology**
> **Physics**
> NT   **Bionics**
> **Molecular biology**
> **Radiobiology**

Biorhythms
> USE   **Biological rhythms**

Biosciences
> USE   **Life sciences**

Biotechnology   620.8; 660.6
> Use for materials on the application of living organisms or their biological systems or processes to the manufacture of products.
> BT   **Chemical engineering**
> **Microbiology**
> NT   **Reproductive technology**
> RT   **Genetic engineering**

Bipolar depression
> USE   **Manic-depressive illness**

Bipolar disorder
> USE   **Manic-depressive illness**

Bird attracting   639.9
> UF   Attracting birds
> BT   **Wildlife attracting**

Bird decoys (Hunting)
> USE   **Decoys (Hunting)**

Bird eggs
> USE   **Birds—Eggs**

Bird houses
> USE   **Birdhouses**

Bird photography
> USE   **Photography of birds**

Bird song
> USE   **Birdsongs**

Bird watching   598.07
> BT   **Natural history**

Birdbanding   598.07
> UF   Birds—Banding
> Birds—Marking
> BT   **Wildlife conservation**

Birdhouses   690
> UF   Bird houses
> BT   **Animal housing**

Birds (May subdiv. geog.)   **598**
> SA   types of birds, e.g. **Birds of prey; Canaries;** etc. [to be added as needed]

> BT   **Animals**
> NT   **Birds of prey**
> **Cage birds**
> **Canaries**
> **Ducks**
> **Eagles**
> **Game and game birds**
> **Geese**
> **Peacocks**
> **Pheasants**
> **Poultry**
> **Robins**
> **State birds**
> **Terns**
> **Turkeys**
> **Water birds**

Birds—Anatomy   598
> BT   **Anatomy**

Birds—Banding
> USE   **Birdbanding**

Birds—Behavior   598.15
> UF   Birds—Habits and behavior
> BT   **Animal behavior**

Birds—Collection and preservation 598.075
> BT   **Zoological specimens—Collection and preservation**

Birds—Color   598.147
> BT   **Color**

Birds—Eggs   598.14
> UF   Bird eggs
> Birds' eggs
> Birds—Eggs and nests
> BT   **Eggs**

Birds' eggs
> USE   **Birds—Eggs**

Birds—Eggs and nests
> USE   **Birds—Eggs**
> **Birds—Nests**

Birds—Flight   591.5; 598.15
> BT   **Animal flight**

Birds—Habits and behavior
> USE   **Birds—Behavior**

Birds—Marking
> USE   **Birdbanding**

Birds—Migration   598.156
> UF   Migration of birds

Birds—Nests   598.156
> UF   Birds—Eggs and nests
> Birds' nests

Birds' nests
USE **Birds—Nests**
Birds of prey 598.9
SA names of specific birds of prey
[to be added as needed]
BT **Birds**
Predatory animals
NT **Eagles**
Birds—Photography
USE **Photography of birds**
Birds—Protection 333.95; 639.9
UF Protection of birds
BT **Wildlife conservation**
RT **Game protection**
Birds—Song
USE **Birdsongs**
Birds—United States 598.0973
Birdsongs 598.159
UF Bird song
Birds—Song
BT **Animal sounds**
Birth
USE **Childbirth**
Birth attendants
USE **Midwives**
Birth control (May subdiv. geog.)
353.5; 363.9; 613.9
UF Conception—Prevention
Contraception
Family planning
Fertility control
Planned parenthood
BT **Population**
Sexual hygiene
NT **Sterilization (Birth control)**
RT **Birth rate**
Childlessness
Family size
Human fertility
Infertility
Birth control—Ethical aspects 176
UF Birth control—Moral and reli-
gious aspects
BT **Ethics**
Birth control—Moral and religious aspects
USE **Birth control—Ethical aspects**
Birth control—Religious as-
pects

Birth control—Religious aspects 205;
248.4
UF Birth control—Moral and reli-
gious aspects
Birth customs
USE **Childbirth**
Birth defects 616
UF Abnormalities, Human
Birth injuries
Deformities
Human abnormalities
Infants—Birth defects
Malformations, Congenital
BT **Medical genetics**
Pathology
RT **Fetal alcohol syndrome**
Growth disorders
Birth injuries
USE **Birth defects**
Birth, Multiple
USE **Multiple birth**
Birth order 306.87
UF Firstborn child
Middle child
Oldest child
Sibling sequence
Youngest child
BT **Children**
Family
Birth rate (May subdiv. geog.) **304.6**
UF Birthrate
BT **Vital statistics**
NT **Human fertility**
RT **Birth control**
Population
Birth records
USE **Registers of births, etc.**
Birthday books 394.2
Use for books with birthdays of famous
persons for every day or month of the year
and for similar books with space for recording
birthdays of acquaintances.
BT **Birthdays**
Calendars
Birthdays 394.2
BT **Anniversaries**
Days
NT **Birthday books**
Birthparents 306.874
Use for materials on natural, i.e. biological,
parents who relinquished their children for
adoption.

Birthparents—*Continued*
  UF Biological parents
       Natural parents
       Parents, Biological
  BT **Parents**
  RT **Adoptees**
Birthrate
  USE **Birth rate**
Births, Registers of
  USE **Registers of births, etc.**
Bison   599.64; 636.2
  UF American bison
       Buffalo, American
  BT **Mammals**
Black actors   791.4; 792; 920
  UF Actors, Black
       Black actors and actresses
  BT **Actors**
  NT **African American actors**
Black actors and actresses
  USE **Black actors**
Black Africa
  USE **Sub-Saharan Africa**
Black Americans
  USE **African Americans**
Black art (May subdiv. geog.)   **704.03**
  Use for materials on works of art by several
  Black artists. Materials on Blacks depicted in
  works of art are entered under **Blacks in art.**
  UF Art, Black
       Blacks—Art
  BT **Art**
  NT **African American art**
  RT **Black artists**
Black art (Magic)
  USE **Magic**
       Witchcraft
Black artists (May subdiv. geog.)   **709.2;
  920**
  Use for materials on several Black artists.
  UF Artists, Black
  BT **Artists**
  NT **African American artists**
  RT **Black art**
Black athletes (May subdiv. geog.)
  796.092; 920
  UF Athletes, Black
  BT **Athletes**
  NT **African American athletes**
Black authors   809; 920
  Use for collections and for materials on
  several Black authors not limited to a single
  national literature or literary form.

  UF Authors, Black
  SA names of national literatures oth-
       er than American literature
       and forms of literature with
       the subdivision *Black authors,*
       e.g. **French literature—Black
       authors; French poetry—
       Black authors;** etc. [to be
       added as needed]
  BT **Authors**
  NT **African American authors**
Black business people
  USE **Black businesspeople**
Black businesspeople (May subdiv. geog.)
  338.092; 658.0092; 920
  UF Black business people
  BT **Businesspeople**
  NT **African American businesspeo-
       ple**
Black children (May subdiv. geog.)
  305.23
  UF Blacks—Children
       Children, Black
  BT **Children**
  NT **African American children**
Black comedy (Literature)
  USE **Black humor (Literature)**
Black death
  USE **Plague**
Black diaspora
  USE **African diaspora**
Black folk songs
  USE **Black music**
Black folklore
  USE **Blacks—Folklore**
Black Hawk War, 1832   973.5
  BT **Native Americans—Wars**
       **United States—History—1815-
       1861**
Black holes (Astronomy)   523.8
  UF Frozen stars
  BT **Astronomy**
       Astrophysics
       Stars
Black humor (Literature)   808.7; 808.87
  May be used for individual works, collec-
  tions, or materials about literary works charac-
  terized by a desperate, sardonic humor intend-
  ed to induce laughter as the appropriate re-
  sponse to the apparent meaninglessness and
  absurdity of existence.
  UF Black comedy (Literature)
       Dark humor (Literature)

Black humor (Literature)—*Continued*
BT Fiction
Literature
Wit and humor
Black lead
USE **Graphite**
Black librarians   020.92; 920
BT Librarians
NT African American librarians
Black literature (American)
USE **American literature—African
American authors**
Black literature (French)
USE **French literature—Black au-
thors**
Black magic (Witchcraft)
USE **Magic
Witchcraft**
Black market (May subdiv. geog.)   381
Use for materials on illegal trade aimed at avoiding government regulations, such as fixed prices or rationing. Materials on goods and services that are produced and sold legally but not reported or taxed are entered under **Underground economy.**
UF Grey market
BT **Commerce**
RT **Underground economy**
Black market children
USE **Adoption—Corrupt practices**
Black music (May subdiv. geog.)
780.089
Use for general materials and for materials on the music of Blacks not in the United States. Materials on the music of African Americans are entered under **African American music.**
UF Black folk songs
Black songs
Blacks—Music
Blacks—Songs and music
BT **Music**
NT **African American music**
RT **Black musicians**
Black musicians (May subdiv. geog.)
780.92; 920
UF Musicians, Black
BT **Musicians**
NT **African American musicians**
RT **Black music**
Black Muslims   297.8
UF Nation of Islam
BT **African Americans—Religion
Black nationalism**

Muslims—United States
Black nationalism   320.54
UF Black separatism
Nationalism, Black
Separatism, Black
BT **African Americans—Political
activity
African Americans—Race iden-
tity
Blacks—Political activity
Blacks—Race identity**
NT **Black Muslims**
RT **Black power**
Black poetry (American)
USE **American poetry—African
American authors**
Black poetry (French)
USE **French poetry—Black authors**
Black power   322.4
BT **African Americans—Political
activity
Blacks—Political activity**
RT **Black nationalism**
Black separatism
USE **Black nationalism**
Black songs
USE **Black music**
Black suffrage
USE **Blacks—Suffrage**
Black women (May subdiv. geog.)
305.48
UF Women, Black
BT **Women**
NT **African American women**
Blackboard drawing
USE **Chalk talks
Crayon drawing**
Blackheads (Acne)
USE **Acne**
Blackouts, Electric power
USE **Electric power failures**
Blacks (May subdiv. geog. except U.S.)
305.896
Use for materials on the Black race in general or for materials on Blacks as an element in the population, especially in countries where they are a minority. Works on Black people in countries with a population predominantly Black are assigned headings appropriate for the country without the use of the heading **Blacks,** except when the works discuss Blacks as distinct from other groups in the country. Materials on Blacks in the United States are entered under **African Americans.**

Blacks—*Continued*

   UF   Negroes

   SA   Blacks in various occupations
          and professions, e.g. **Black
          artists; Black librarians;** etc.
          [to be added as needed]

   NT   **African Americans**

Blacks—Africa   305.896; 960

   BT   **Africans**

Blacks—Art

   USE   **Black art**

Blacks—Biography   920

   BT   **Biography**

   NT   **African Americans—Biography**

Blacks—Children

   USE   **Black children**

Blacks—Civil rights (May subdiv. geog.)
     323.1196; 342

   BT   **Blacks—Political activity**
         Civil rights

   NT   **African Americans—Civil
         rights**

Blacks—Economic conditions (May
     subdiv. geog.)   **330.9**

   BT   **Economic conditions**

   NT   **African Americans—Economic
         conditions**

Blacks—Education (May subdiv. geog.)
     370.89; 371.829

   BT   **Education**

   NT   **African Americans—Education**

Blacks—Employment (May subdiv. geog.)
     331.6

   BT   **Employment**

   NT   **African Americans—Employ-
         ment**

Blacks—Folklore   398

   UF   Black folklore

   BT   **Folklore**

   NT   **African Americans—Folklore**

Blacks—France   305.896; 944

   UF   France—Blacks

Blacks—Housing (May subdiv. geog.)
     307.3; 363.5

   BT   **Housing**

   NT   **African Americans—Housing**

Blacks in art   704.9

   Use for materials on Blacks depicted in
works of art. Materials on African Americans
depicted in works of art are entered under
African Americans in art. Materials on the
attainments of several Blacks in the area of
art are entered under **Black artists.** Materials
on the attainments of several African Americans in the area of art are entered under
African American artists. Materials on
works of art by several Black artists are entered under **Black art.** Materials on works of
art by several African American artists are entered under **African American art.**

   BT   **Art—Themes**

Blacks in literature   809

   Use for materials on the theme of Blacks in
works of literature. Materials on the attainments of several Blacks in the area of literature are entered under **Black authors.** Materials on works of literature by several Black authors are entered under individual literatures
and forms of literature with the subdivision
Black authors, e.g. **French literature—Black
authors; French poetry—Black authors;** etc.
Materials on the theme of African Americans
in works of literature are entered under
African Americans in literature. Materials
on the attainments of several African Americans in the area of literature are entered under
African American authors. Materials on
works of literature by several African
American authors are entered under **American
literature—African American authors** and
the various forms of American literature with
the subdivision *African American authors,* e.g.
**American poetry—African American au-
thors.**

   BT   **Literature—Themes**

Blacks in motion pictures   791.43

   Use for materials on the depiction of Blacks
in motion pictures. Materials on several Black
actors are entered under **Black actors.** Materials discussing all aspects of Blacks' involvement in motion pictures are entered under
Blacks in the motion picture industry.

   BT   **Motion pictures**

   NT   **African Americans in motion
         pictures**

**Blacks in the motion picture industry
     791.43092**

   Use for materials on all aspects of Blacks'
involvement in motion pictures. Materials on
the depiction of Blacks in motion pictures are
entered under **Blacks in motion pictures.**

   BT   **Motion picture industry**

   NT   **African Americans in the mo-
         tion picture industry**

Blacks—Intellectual life (May subdiv.
     geog.)   **305.896**

   BT   **Intellectual life**

   NT   **African Americans—Intellectu-
         al life**

Blacks—Music

   USE   **Black music**

Blacks—Political activity (May subdiv. geog.) 322.4; 324
    BT   Political participation
    NT   African Americans—Political activity
        Black nationalism
        Black power
        Blacks—Civil rights
Blacks—Race identity 305.896
    UF   Negritude
    BT   Race awareness
    NT   African Americans—Race identity
        Black nationalism
Blacks—Religion 270.089; 299.6
    BT   Religion
    NT   African Americans—Religion
Blacks—Segregation (May subdiv. geog.) 305.896
    BT   Segregation
    NT   African Americans—Segregation
Blacks—Social conditions (May subdiv. geog.) 305.896
    BT   Social conditions
    NT   African Americans—Social conditions
Blacks—Social life and customs (May subdiv. geog.) 305.896
    BT   Manners and customs
    NT   African Americans—Social life and customs
Blacks—Songs and music
    USE   Black music
Blacks—Suffrage 324.6
    UF   Black suffrage
    BT   Suffrage
    NT   African Americans—Suffrage
Blacks—United States
    USE   African Americans
Blacksmithing 682
    BT   Ironwork
    NT   Welding
    RT   Forging
Blast furnaces 669
    BT   Furnaces
        Smelting
Blast shelters
    USE   Air raid shelters

Bleaching 667
    BT   Cleaning
        Industrial chemistry
        Textile industry
    RT   Dyes and dyeing
Blessed Virgin Mary
    USE   Mary, Blessed Virgin, Saint
Blimps
    USE   Airships
Blind 362.4
    BT   Physically handicapped
        Vision disorders
Blind—Books and reading 011.63; 027.6; 028
    UF   Books for the blind
    BT   Books and reading
    NT   Large print books
    RT   Audiobooks
        Braille books
Blind—Education (May subdiv. geog.) 371.91
    UF   Education of the blind
    BT   Education
Blind—Institutional care 362.4
    BT   Institutional care
Blizzards 551.55
    BT   Storms
    RT   Snow
Block printing
    USE   Color prints
        Linoleum block printing
        Textile printing
        Wood engraving
        Woodcuts
Block signal systems
    USE   Railroads—Signaling
Blockades
    USE   names of wars with the subdivision *Blockades*, e.g. **World War, 1939-1945—Blockades** [to be added as needed]
Blood 573.1; 612.1
    BT   Physiology
    NT   Blood groups
        Blood pressure
Blood—Circulation 573.1; 612.1
    UF   Circulation of the blood
    RT   Blood pressure
        Cardiovascular system

Blood—Diseases 616.1
UF Diseases of the blood
SA types of blood diseases, e.g.
Leukemia [to be added as
needed]
BT Diseases
NT Leukemia
Blood groups 612.1
UF Rh factor
BT Blood
RT Blood—Transfusion
Blood pressure 612.1
BT Blood
NT Hypertension
RT Blood—Circulation
Blood—Transfusion 615
RT Blood groups
Blowing the whistle
USE Whistle blowing
Blowouts, Oil well
USE Oil wells—Blowouts
Blue collar workers
USE Labor
Working class
Blue prints
USE Blueprints
Blueprints 604.2; 692
UF Blue prints
BT Mechanical drawing
Blues music 781.643; 782.421643
UF Blues songs
BT African American music
Folk music—United States
Popular music
RT Jazz music
Blues songs
USE Blues music
Board games 794
BT Games
NT Checkers
Chess
Board sailing
USE Windsurfing
Boarding houses
USE Hotels and motels
Boarding schools
USE Private schools
Boards of education
USE School boards
Boards of health
USE Health boards

Boards of trade
USE Chambers of commerce
Boards of trustees
USE Trusts and trustees
Boat building
USE Boatbuilding
Boat racing (May subdiv. geog.) 797.1
UF Regattas
SA types of boat racing and names
of specific races [to be added
as needed]
BT Boats and boating
Racing
Boatbuilding 623.8
UF Boat building
Boats—Construction
BT Naval architecture
NT Yachts and yachting
RT Boats and boating
Shipbuilding
Boating
USE Boats and boating
Boats and boating 797.1
UF Boating
BT Water sports
NT Boat racing
Canoes and canoeing
Catamarans
Houseboats
Hydrofoil boats
Iceboats
Marinas
Motorboats
Rowing
Steamboats
Tugboats
Yachts and yachting
RT Boatbuilding
Sailing
Ships
Boats—Construction
USE Boatbuilding
Body
USE Human body
Body and mind
USE Mind and body
Body building
USE Bodybuilding
Body care
USE Hygiene

Body heat
　USE　**Body temperature**
Body image　128; 155.2
　　Use for materials on the visual, mental, or memory image of one's own body or another's body, and one's attitude towards that image.
　BT　**Human body**
　　　Mind and body
　　　Personality
　　　Self-perception
Body language　153.6; 302.2
　BT　**Nonverbal communication**
Body surfing
　USE　**Surfing**
Body temperature　571.7; 612
　UF　Animals—Temperature
　　　Body heat
　　　Temperature, Animal and human
　　　Temperature, Body
　BT　**Diagnosis**
　　　Physiology
　RT　**Fever**
Body weight　613
　BT　**Human body**
　　　Weight
　NT　**Obesity**
　　　Weight loss
Bodybuilding　646.7
　UF　Body building
　　　Physique
　BT　**Exercise**
　　　Physical fitness
　RT　**Weight lifting**
Boers
　USE　**Afrikaners**
Bogs (May subdiv. geog.)　**551.41**
　BT　**Wetlands**
Bohemianism (May subdiv. geog.)　**306**
　BT　**Counter culture**
　　　Manners and customs
　NT　**Beat generation**
　　　Hippies
Bolshevism
　USE　**Communism**
Bomb attacks
　USE　**Bombings**
Bomb shelters
　USE　**Air raid shelters**

Bombers　358.4; 623.74
　SA　types of bombers, e.g. **B-52 bomber** [to be added as needed]
　BT　**Airplanes**
　　　Military airplanes
　NT　**B-52 bomber**
Bombings (May subdiv. geog.)　**364.1**
　　Use for materials on the use of explosive devices for the purposes of political terrorism or protest. Materials on bombs in general and on bombs launched from aircraft are entered under **Bombs**.
　UF　Bomb attacks
　　　Terrorist bombings
　SA　names of individual bombings incidents [to be added as needed]
　BT　**Offenses against public safety**
　　　Political crimes and offenses
　　　Terrorism
Bombs　355.8; 623.4
　　Use for materials on bombs in general and and on bombs launched from aircraft. Materials on the use of explosive devices for the purposes of political terrorism or protest are entered under **Bombings**.
　UF　Aerial bombs
　SA　types of bombs, e.g. **Atomic bomb** [to be added as needed]
　BT　**Ammunition**
　　　Explosives
　　　Ordnance
　　　Projectiles
　NT　**Atomic bomb**
　　　Guided missiles
　　　Hydrogen bomb
　　　Incendiary bombs
　　　Neutron bomb
Bonds　332.63
　BT　**Finance**
　　　Investments
　　　Negotiable instruments
　　　Securities
　　　Stock exchanges
　NT　**Junk bonds**
　RT　**Public debts**
　　　Stocks
Bonds—Rating　332.63
Bones　573.7; 611; 612.7
　　Use for comprehensive and systematic materials on the anatomy of bones. Materials limited to the morphology or mechanics of the

Bones—*Continued*
skeleton, human or animal, are entered under
Skeleton.
- BT **Musculoskeletal system**
- NT **Fractures**
- RT **Skeleton**

Bonsai   635.9
- BT **Dwarf trees**

Book arts—Exhibitions
- USE **Books—Exhibitions**

Book awards
- USE **Literary prizes**
  and names of awards, e.g.
  **Caldecott Medal; Newbery
  Medal;** etc. [to be added as
  needed]

Book buying (Libraries)
- USE **Libraries—Acquisitions**

Book catalogs   017; 025.3
Use for materials on library catalogs in
book form. Retail book catalogs and book
auction catalogs and materials about such cat-
alogs are entered under **Booksellers' catalogs.**
Publishers' book catalogs and materials about
such catalogs are entered under **Publishers'
catalogs.**
- UF Books—Catalogs
  Catalogs, Book
  Catalogs in book form
- BT **Library catalogs**

Book collecting   002.075
- UF Bibliomania
  Bibliophily
  Books—Collectors and collecting
- BT **Book selection**
  Collectors and collecting
- RT **Bookplates**
  Books

Book fairs
- USE **Books—Exhibitions**

Book illustration
- USE **Illustration of books**

Book industries
- USE **Book industry**

Book industries and trade
- USE **Book industry**

Book industries—Exhibitions
- USE **Books—Exhibitions**

Book industry (May subdiv. geog.)   **686**
- UF Book industries
  Book industries and trade
  Book trade

- BT **Industries**
- NT **Bookbinding**
  Booksellers and bookselling
  Printing
- RT **Publishers and publishing**

Book lending
- USE **Library circulation**

Book lists
- USE **Best books**

Book numbers, Publishers' standard
- USE **Publishers' standard book
  numbers**

Book plates
- USE **Bookplates**

Book prices
- USE **Books—Prices**

Book prizes
- USE **Literary prizes**
  and names of prizes, e.g.
  **Caldecott Medal; Newbery
  Medal;** etc. [to be added as
  needed]

Book rarities
- USE **Rare books**

Book reviewing   028.1; 808
Use for materials on the technique of reviewing books. Collections of miscellaneous
book reviews are entered under **Book reviews.**
- UF Appraisal of books
  Books—Appraisal
  Evaluation of books
  Literature—Evaluation
  Reviewing (Books)
- SA types of books with the subdivision *Reviews,* and topics,
  types of literature, ethnic
  groups, classes of persons,
  and names of places with the
  subdivision *Book reviews;* for
  collections of book reviews
  devoted to a particular type
  of book or subject, e.g. **Reference books—Reviews; Sociology—Book reviews; Children's literature—Book reviews;** etc. [to be added as
  needed]
- BT **Books and reading**
  Criticism
- RT **Book reviews**

Book reviews   028.1; 808.8

  Use for collections of book reviews. Materials on the technique of reviewing books are entered under **Book reviewing.**

  UF   Books—Reviews

  SA   types of books with the subdivision *Reviews,* and topics, types of literature, ethnic groups, classes of persons, and names of places with the subdivision *Book reviews;* for collections of book reviews devoted to a particular type of book or subject, e.g. **Reference books—Reviews; Sociology—Book reviews; Children's literature—Book reviews;** etc. [to be added as needed]

  NT   **Book talks**

  RT   **Book reviewing**

Book sales

  USE **Books—Prices**

Book selection   025.2

  Use for materials on the principles of book selection for libraries. Lists of recommended books and materials about recommended books are entered under **Best books.**

  UF   Books—Selection

       Choice of books

  BT   **Libraries—Acquisitions**

       Libraries—Collection development

  NT   **Book collecting**

  RT   **Best books**

Book talks   021.7; 028.1

  UF   Booktalking

       Booktalks

  BT   **Book reviews**

       Libraries—Public relations

       Public speaking

Book trade

  USE **Book industry**

       Booksellers and bookselling

       Publishers and publishing

Book trade—Exhibitions

  USE **Books—Exhibitions**

Book Week, National

  USE **National Book Week**

Bookbinding (May subdiv. geog.)   **025.7; 095; 686.3**

  UF   Binding of books

  BT   **Book industry**

       Books

Bookkeepers

  USE **Accountants**

Bookkeeping   657

  SA   types of industries, professions, and organizations with the subdivision *Accounting* [to be added as needed]

  BT   **Business**

       Business education

       Business mathematics

  NT   **Auditing**

       Corporations—Accounting

       Cost accounting

       Office equipment and supplies

  RT   **Accounting**

Bookmobiles   027.4

  BT   **Library extension**

Bookplates   025.7; 769.5

  UF   Book plates

       Ex libris

  BT   **Prints**

  RT   **Book collecting**

Books   002

  NT   **Anthologies**

       Best books

       Bilingual books

       Bookbinding

       Books of hours

       Braille books

       Chapbooks

       Early printed books

       Electronic books

       Illumination of books and manuscripts

       Illustration of books

       Incunabula

       Librettos

       Manuscripts

       Paperback books

       Rare books

       Reference books

       Reprints (Publications)

       Textbooks

  RT   **Authors**

       Bibliography

       Book collecting

Books—*Continued*
>Literature
>Printing
>Publishers and publishing

Books and reading (May subdiv. geog.)
>028

>Use for general materials on reading for information and culture, advice to readers, and surveys of reading habits.

>UF Appraisal of books
>>Books—Appraisal
>>Choice of books
>>Evaluation of literature
>>Literature—Evaluation
>>Reading interests

>SA names of individuals and classes of persons with the subdivision *Books and reading*, e.g. **Blind—Books and reading** [to be added as needed]

>BT **Communication**
>>**Education**
>>**Reading**

>NT **Best sellers (Books)**
>>**Bible—Reading**
>>**Blind—Books and reading**
>>**Book reviewing**
>>**Children—Books and reading**
>>**National Book Week**
>>**Reference books**
>>**Teenagers—Books and reading**

>RT **Reading materials**

Books and reading—Best books
>USE **Best books**

Books and reading for children
>USE **Children—Books and reading**

Books and reading for teenagers
>USE **Teenagers—Books and reading**

Books and reading for young adults
>USE **Teenagers—Books and reading**

Books—Appraisal
>USE **Book reviewing**
>>**Books and reading**
>>**Criticism**
>>**Literature—History and criticism**

Books—Best sellers
>USE **Best sellers (Books)**

Books—Bilingual editions
>USE **Bilingual books**

Books—Catalogs
>USE **Book catalogs**
>>**Booksellers' catalogs**
>>**Publishers' catalogs**

Books—Censorship 025.2; 323.44
>UF Banned books
>>Index librorum prohibitorum
>>Prohibited books

>BT **Censorship**

Books—Classification
>USE **Library classification**

Books—Collectors and collecting
>USE **Book collecting**

Books—Exhibitions (May subdiv. geog.)
>070.5074; 686.074

>UF Book arts—Exhibitions
>>Book fairs
>>Book industries—Exhibitions
>>Book trade—Exhibitions
>>Library book fairs
>>Publishers and publishing—Exhibitions

>BT **Exhibitions**

Books—First editions
>USE **First editions**

Books for children
>USE **Children's literature**

Books for sight saving
>USE **Large print books**

Books for teenagers
>USE **Young adult literature**

Books for the blind
>USE **Blind—Books and reading**
>>**Braille books**

Books in machine-readable form
>USE **Electronic books**

Books—Large print
>USE **Large print books**

Books of hours (May subdiv. geog.)
>242; 745.6

>BT **Books**
>RT **Illumination of books and manuscripts**

Books of lists 030

>Use as a form heading for books consisting of miscellaneous lists of facts, names, etc.

>UF Facts, Miscellaneous
>>List books
>>Lists
>>Miscellanea
>>Miscellaneous facts

Books of lists—*Continued*
SA topics with the subdivision *Lists,*
     e.g. **Sports—Lists** [to be add-
     ed as needed]
Books on cassette
USE **Audiobooks**
Books on tape
USE **Audiobooks**
Books—Preservation
USE **Library resources—Conserva-
     tion and restoration**
Books—Prices   002.075
UF Book prices
     Book sales
BT **Booksellers and bookselling
     Prices**
Books—Reviews
USE **Book reviews**
Books—Selection
USE **Book selection**
Booksellers and bookselling (May subdiv.
    geog.)   **070.5; 381; 658.8**
UF Book trade
BT **Book industry**
NT **Books—Prices
     Booksellers' catalogs**
RT **Publishers and publishing**
Booksellers' catalogs   017
    Use for retail book catalogs and book auc-
tion catalogs and materials about such cata-
logs. Materials on library catalogs in book
form are entered under **Book catalogs.** Pub-
lishers' book catalogs and materials about
such catalogs are entered under **Publishers'
catalogs.**
UF Books—Catalogs
     Catalogs
     Catalogs, Booksellers'
BT **Booksellers and bookselling**
Booktalking
USE **Book talks**
Booktalks
USE **Book talks**
Boolean algebra   511.3
UF Algebra, Boolean
BT **Group theory
     Set theory
     Symbolic logic**
Boots
USE **Shoes**
Border life
USE **Frontier and pioneer life**

Borders (Geography)
USE **Boundaries**
Boring
USE **Drilling and boring (Earth and
     rocks)
     Drilling and boring (Metal,
     wood, etc.)**
Born again Christianity
USE **Regeneration (Christianity)**
Borrowing
USE **Loans**
Boss rule
USE **Political corruption**
Bossiness   155.2
BT **Personality**
Botanic gardens
USE **Botanical gardens**
Botanical chemistry   572
UF Plant chemistry
BT **Chemistry**
NT **Plants—Analysis**
Botanical classification
USE **Botany—Classification**
Botanical gardens (May subdiv. geog.)
    580.73
UF Botanic gardens
SA names of individual botanical
     gardens [to be added as need-
     ed]
BT **Gardens
     Parks**
Botanical illustration (May subdiv. geog.)
    758
UF Flower painting and illustration
     Fruit painting and illustration
BT **Art
     Illustration of books**
RT **Botany
     Plants in art**
Botanical specimens—Collection and pres-
    ervation
USE **Plants—Collection and preser-
     vation**
Botanists (May subdiv. geog.)   **580.92;
    920**
BT **Naturalists**
Botany   580
    Use for materials on the science of plants.
Nonscientific materials on plants are entered
under **Plants.**
UF Flora
     Vegetable kingdom

Botany—*Continued*
  BT **Biology**
        Science
  NT **Economic botany**
        Medical botany
        Photosynthesis
        Plant physiology
        Plants—Anatomy
  RT **Botanical illustration**
        Natural history
        Plants

Botany—Anatomy
  USE **Plants—Anatomy**

Botany—Classification 580.1
  UF Botanical classification
        Botany—Taxonomy
        Classification—Botany
        Classification—Plants
        Plant classification
        Plant taxonomy
        Plants—Classification
        Systematic botany
        Taxonomy (Botany)
  BT **Classification**

Botany—Ecology
  USE **Plant ecology**

Botany, Economic
  USE **Economic botany**

Botany, Medical
  USE **Medical botany**

Botany—Nomenclature 580.1
Use for systematically derived lists of names or designations of plants and for materials about such names. Materials on the common or vernacular names of plants are entered under **Popular plant names.**
  UF Plants—Names
        Plants—Nomenclature
        Scientific names of plants
        Scientific plant names
  RT **Botany—Terminology**
        Popular plant names

Botany of the Bible
  USE **Bible—Natural history**

Botany—Pathology
  USE **Plant diseases**

Botany—Physiology
  USE **Plant physiology**

Botany—Structure
  USE **Plants—Anatomy**

Botany—Taxonomy
  USE **Botany—Classification**

Botany—Terminology 580.1
Use for lists or discussions of words and expressions in the field of botany. Systematically derived lists of names or designations of plants and materials about such names are entered under **Botany—Nomenclature.** Materials on the common or vernacular names of plants are entered under **Popular plant names.**
  RT **Botany—Nomenclature**
        Popular plant names

Botany—United States
  USE **Plants—United States**

Boulder Dam (Ariz. and Nev.)
  USE **Hoover Dam (Ariz. and Nev.)**

Boulevards
  USE **Streets**

Boundaries 320.1; 341.4
  UF Borders (Geography)
        Frontiers
        Political boundaries
        Political geography
  SA names of wars with the subdivision *Territorial questions,* and countries, cities, etc., with the subdivision *Boundaries* [to be added as needed]
  BT **Geography**
        International law
        International relations
  NT **Chicago (Ill.)—Boundaries**
        Ohio—Boundaries
        United States—Boundaries
        World War, 1914-1918—Territorial questions
        World War, 1939-1945—Territorial questions
  RT **Geopolitics**

Bourgeoisie
  USE **Middle class**

Boutique breweries
  USE **Microbreweries**

Bow and arrow 799.2028
  UF Arrow
  BT **Weapons**
  RT **Archery**

Bow and arrow hunting
  USE **Bowhunting**

Bowed instruments
  USE **Stringed instruments**

Bowhunting (May subdiv. geog.)
   799.2028
   UF   Bow and arrow hunting
   BT   **Hunting**
Bowling   794.6; 796.31
   UF   Tenpins
   BT   **Ball games**
Boxes   688.8; 745.593
   UF   Crates
   BT   **Containers**
Boxes—Collectors and collecting
   745.593
   BT   **Collectors and collecting**
Boxing   796.83
   UF   Fighting
         Prize fighting
         Pugilism
         Sparring
   BT   **Athletics**
         Self-defense
Boy Scouts (May subdiv. geog.)   369.43
   UF   Cub Scouts
   BT   **Boys' clubs**
         Scouts and scouting
Boycott
   USE   **Boycotts**
Boycotts (May subdiv. geog.)   327.1;
         331.89; 338.6; 341.5
   UF   Boycott
         Consumer boycotts
   BT   **Commerce**
         Consumers
         Passive resistance
   RT   **Restraint of trade**
Boys   155.43; 305.23081
   BT   **Children**
   RT   **Teenagers**
         Young men
Boys' clubs   369.42
   UF   Boys—Societies
   BT   **Clubs**
         Societies
   NT   **4-H clubs**
         Boy Scouts
Boys—Education (May subdiv. geog.)
         371.823
   BT   **Education**
   RT   **Coeducation**
Boys—Employment
   USE   **Youth—Employment**

Boys—Societies
   USE   **Boys' clubs**
Boys' towns
   USE   **Children—Institutional care**
Brahmanism   294.5
   BT   **Religions**
   RT   **Hinduism**
Braids (Hairstyling)   646.7
   BT   **Hair**
Braille   411
   BT   **Writing**
Braille books   011.63; 411
   UF   Books for the blind
   BT   **Books**
   RT   **Blind—Books and reading**
Brain   573.8; 611; 612.8
   BT   **Head**
         Nervous system
   NT   **Memory**
         Mind and body
         Phrenology
         Psychology
         Sleep
Brain damaged children   618.92
   BT   **Exceptional children**
         Handicapped children
Brain death   616.07
   UF   Irreversible coma
   BT   **Death**
Brain—Diseases   616.8
   BT   **Diseases**
   NT   **Alzheimer's disease**
         Cerebral palsy
         Dementia
         Stroke
Brain storming
   USE   **Group problem solving**
Brainwashing   153.8
   Use for materials on the forcible indoctrina-
   tion of an individual or group in order to alter
   basic political, social, religious, or moral be-
   liefs.
   UF   Deprogramming
         Forced indoctrination
         Indoctrination, Forced
         Mind control
         Thought control
         Will
   BT   **Behavior modification**
         Mental suggestion
         Psychological warfare
         Psychology of learning

Brakes   **625.2; 629.2**
   SA   types of vehicles with the subdi-
          vision *Brakes*, e.g. **Automo-
          biles—Brakes** [to be added
          as needed]
   NT   **Automobiles—Brakes**
Branch stores
   USE   **Chain stores**
Brand name products   381; 658.8
   UF   Branded merchandise
   BT   **Commercial products
          Manufactures**
   RT   **Trademarks**
Branded merchandise
   USE   **Brand name products**
Brass   669; 673
   BT   **Alloys
          Metals**
   NT   **Brasses**
Brass instruments   788.9
   BT   **Wind instruments**
Brasses   739.5
   UF   Monumental brasses
          Sepulchral brasses
   BT   **Archeology
          Art metalwork
          Brass
          Inscriptions
          Sculpture
          Tombs**
Bravery
   USE   **Courage**
Brazilian literature   869
   May use same subdivisions and names of
   literary forms as for **English literature.**
   BT   **Latin American literature
          Literature**
Bread   641.8; 664
   BT   **Baking
          Cooking
          Food**
   RT   **Bread machines**
Bread machines   641.7
   UF   Automatic bread machines
   BT   **Kitchen utensils**
   RT   **Baking
          Bread**
Break dancing   793.3
   BT   **Dance**
Breakers
   USE   **Ocean waves**

Breakfast cereals
   USE   **Prepared cereals**
Breakfasts   642
   BT   **Cooking
          Menus**
   NT   **Prepared cereals**
Breakthroughs, Scientific
   USE   **Discoveries in science**
Breast—Cancer
   USE   **Breast cancer**
Breast cancer   616.99
   UF   Breast—Cancer
   BT   **Cancer
          Women—Diseases**
Breast feeding   649
   UF   Nursing (Infant feeding)
   BT   **Infants—Nutrition**
Breathing
   USE   **Respiration**
Breeding (May subdiv. geog.)   **631.5;
          636.08**
   Use for materials on the controlled propaga-
   tion of plants and animals with the purpose of
   producing or maintaining desired characteris-
   tics.
   UF   Artificial selection
          Selection, Artificial
   SA   types of animals with the subdi-
          vision *Breeding* [to be added
          as needed]
   BT   **Reproduction**
   NT   **Dogs—Breeding
          Heredity
          Horses—Breeding
          Livestock breeding
          Mendel's law
          Plant breeding**
   RT   **Genetics**
Breeding behavior
   USE   **Sexual behavior in animals**
Breweries (May subdiv. geog.)   **663**
   BT   **Factories**
   NT   **Microbreweries**
   RT   **Brewing**
Brewing   641.8; 663
   UF   Beer making
   RT   **Breweries
          Liquors**
Bricklaying   693
   BT   **Building**
   RT   **Bricks
          Masonry**

Bricks   666; 691
  BT **Building materials**
  RT **Bricklaying**
Bridal customs
  USE **Marriage customs and rites**
Bridge (Game)   795.41
  UF Auction bridge
      Contract bridge
      Duplicate bridge
  BT **Card games**
Bridges (May subdiv. geog.)   **624.2; 725**
  This heading may be subdivided by the names of rivers, lakes, canals, etc. as well as by countries, states, cities, etc.
  UF Viaducts
  SA types of bridges and names of individual bridges [to be added as needed]
  BT **Civil engineering**
      Transportation
  NT **Golden Gate Bridge (San Francisco, Calif.)**
Bridges—Chicago (Ill.)   624.209773
  UF Chicago (Ill.)—Bridges
Bridges—Hudson River (N.Y. and N.J.)   624.20973
  UF Hudson River (N.Y. and N.J.)—Bridges
Brigands
  USE **Thieves**
Bright children
  USE **Gifted children**
British Commonwealth countries
  USE **Commonwealth countries**
British Commonwealth of Nations
  USE **Commonwealth countries**
British Dominions
  USE **Commonwealth countries**
British Empire
  USE **Great Britain—Colonies**
Broadcast journalism (May subdiv. geog.)   **070.4**
  UF Radio journalism
      Television journalism
  BT **Broadcasting**
      Journalism
      Press
  NT **Radio broadcasting of sports**
      Television broadcasting of news
      Television broadcasting of sports

Broadcasting (May subdiv. geog.)   **384.54**
  BT **Telecommunication**
  NT **Broadcast journalism**
      Equal time rule (Broadcasting)
      Fairness doctrine (Broadcasting)
      Minorities in broadcasting
      Radio broadcasting
      Television broadcasting
Bronchial asthma
  USE **Asthma**
Bronze Age (May subdiv. geog.)   **930.1**
  BT **Civilization**
Bronzes (May subdiv. geog.)   **739.5**
  BT **Archeology**
      Art
      Art metalwork
      Decoration and ornament
      Metalwork
      Sculpture
Brothers   306.875
  BT **Men**
      Siblings
Brothers and sisters
  USE **Siblings**
Brownies (Girl Scouts)
  USE **Girl Scouts**
Brownouts
  USE **Electric power failures**
Brutality
  USE **Cruelty**
Bubbles   530.4
  BT **Air**
      Gases
Bubonic plague
  USE **Plague**
Buccaneers
  USE **Pirates**
Bucolic poetry
  USE **Pastoral poetry**
Buddhism (May subdiv. geog.)   **294.3**
  BT **Religions**
  NT **Zen Buddhism**
Buddhism—Prayers   294.3
  UF Buddhist prayers
  BT **Prayers**
Buddhist art (May subdiv. geog.)   **294.3; 704.9**
  UF Art, Buddhist
  BT **Art**

Buddhist prayers
USE **Buddhism—Prayers**
Budget (May subdiv. geog.)   **352.4**

Use for materials on government budgets or reports on governmental appropriations and expenditures. Materials on business budgets are entered under **Business budgets.** Materials on household budgets are entered under **Household budgets.** Materials on personal budgets are entered under **Personal finance.**

UF   Government budgets
SA   names of countries and names
    of individual government de-
    partments, agencies, etc., with
    the subdivision *Appropriations*
    and expenditures, e.g. **United**
    States—Appropriations and
    expenditures [to be added as
    needed]
BT   **Public finance**
Budget—United States   352.4
UF   Federal budget
    United States—Budget
NT   **United States—Appropriations**
    and expenditures
Budgets, Business
USE   **Business budgets**
Budgets, Household
USE   **Household budgets**
Budgets, Personal
USE   **Personal finance**
Buffalo, American
USE   **Bison**
Buffing
USE   **Grinding and polishing**
Bugging, Electronic
USE   **Eavesdropping**
Building   690

Use for materials on the process of constructing buildings and other structures. Materials on the design and style of structures are entered under **Architecture.** General materials on buildings and materials on buildings in a particular place are entered under **Buildings.**

UF   Architectural engineering
    Construction
SA   types of buildings with the sub-
    division *Design and construc-*
    tion, e.g. **Industrial build-**
    ings—Design and construc-
    tion [to be added as needed]
BT   **Structural engineering**
NT   **Bricklaying**
    Carpentry
    Concrete construction

    House construction
    Industrial buildings—Design
    and construction
    Masonry
    Plumbing
    Steel construction
RT   **Architecture**
    Building materials
Building and earthquakes
USE   **Buildings—Earthquake effects**
Building and loan associations
USE   **Savings and loan associations**
Building contracts
USE   **Construction contracts**
Building—Contracts and specifications
USE   **Construction contracts**
Building design
USE   **Architecture**
Building—Estimates   692
Building failures   690
BT   **Structural failures**
Building, Iron and steel
USE   **Steel construction**
Building machinery
USE   **Construction equipment**
Building materials   691
UF   Structural materials
SA   types of building materials, e.g.
    Bricks [to be added as need-
    ed]
BT   **Materials**
NT   **Bricks**
    Cement
    Concrete
    Glass
    Glass construction
    Reinforced concrete
    Stone
    Structural steel
    Stucco
    Terra cotta
    Tiles
    Wood
RT   **Building**
    Strength of materials
Building nests
USE   **Nest building**
Building repair
USE   **Buildings—Maintenance and**
    repair

Building—Repair and reconstruction
   USE   **Buildings—Maintenance and repair**
Building security
   USE   **Burglary protection**
Building—Tropical conditions   690
Buildings (May subdiv. geog.)   **690; 720**

   Use for general materials on buildings and, with geographic subdivisions, for materials on buildings in a particular place. Materials on the design and style of structures are entered under **Architecture.** Materials on the process of constructing buildings and other structures are entered under **Building.**

   UF   Edifices
          Structures
   SA   types of building features, e.g. **Doors; Windows;** etc.; types of buildings and construction, e.g. **Farm buildings;** types of institutions and names of individual institutions and corporate bodies with the subdivision *Buildings,* e.g. **Colleges and universities—Buildings;** and names of specific buildings [to be added as needed]
   NT   **Apartment houses**
          Auditoriums
          Castles
          Children's playhouses
          Chimneys
          Church buildings
          Colleges and universities— Buildings
          Commercial buildings
          Doors
          Farm buildings
          Fireplaces
          Floors
          Foundations
          Garden structures
          Historic buildings
          Houses
          Industrial buildings
          Office buildings
          Palaces
          Prefabricated buildings
          Public buildings
          Roofs
          Rooms
          School buildings
          Skyscrapers
          Synagogues
          Temples
          Theaters
          Tree houses
          Walls
          Windows
   RT   **Architecture**
Buildings—Earthquake effects   693.8

   Use for materials on the design and construction of buildings to withstand earthquakes.

   UF   Building and earthquakes
          Earthquakes and building
   BT   **Earthquakes**
   NT   **Skyscrapers—Earthquake effects**
Buildings, Industrial
   USE   **Industrial buildings**
Buildings—Maintenance and repair 690
   UF   Building repair
          Building—Repair and reconstruction
          Buildings—Remodeling
   SA   types of buildings with the subdivision *Maintenance and repair,* e.g. **Houses—Maintenance and repair;** and types of buildings and parts of buildings with the subdivision *Remodeling,* e.g. **Houses—Remodeling; Kitchens—Remodeling;** etc. [to be added as needed]
   RT   **Architecture—Conservation and restoration**
Buildings, Office
   USE   **Office buildings**
Buildings, Prefabricated
   USE   **Prefabricated buildings**
Buildings—Remodeling
   USE   **Buildings—Maintenance and repair**
Buildings, Restoration of
   USE   **Architecture—Conservation and restoration**
Buildings, School
   USE   **School buildings**
Buildings—Security
   USE   **Burglary protection**
Built-in furniture   645; 684.1; 749
   BT   **Furniture**

Bulbs   584; 635.9
    BT   **Flower gardening**
            Plants
Bulge, Battle of the
    USE **Ardennes, Battle of the, 1944-**
            1945
Bulimia   616.85
    UF   Binge eating behavior
           Binge-purge behavior
           Gorge-purge syndrome
    BT   **Eating disorders**
Bulletin boards   371.33
    BT   **Teaching—Aids and devices**
    NT   **Computer bulletin boards**
Bullfights   791.8
    UF   Fighting
    BT   **Sports**
Bullies   155.4; 302.3
    UF   Bullying
           Bullyism
    BT   **Aggressiveness (Psychology)**
Bullion
    USE **Precious metals**
Bullying
    USE **Bullies**
Bullyism
    USE **Bullies**
Bunnies
    USE **Rabbits**
Bunny rabbits
    USE **Rabbits**
Bunyan, Paul (Legendary character)
    398.22
    UF   Paul Bunyan
    BT   **Folklore—United States**
Bureaucracy (May subdiv. geog.)   302.3
    BT   **Political science**
           Public administration
    RT   **Civil service**
           Organizational sociology
Burglar alarms   621.389
    BT   **Burglary protection**
           Electric apparatus and appli-
           ances
Burglars
    USE **Thieves**
Burglary protection   621.389; 643
    UF   Building security
           Buildings—Security
           Protection against burglary
           Residential security

    SA   types of protective devices, e.g.
           Burglar alarms; and types of
           buildings with the subdivision
           Security measures, e.g. **Nucle-**
           ar power plants—Security
           measures [to be added as
           needed]
    BT   **Crime prevention**
    NT   **Burglar alarms**
           Locks and keys
Burial (May subdiv. geog.)   363.7; 393
    UF   Burial customs
           Burying grounds
           Graves
           Interment
    SA   names of individual persons and
           groups of notable persons
           with the subdivision *Death*
           and burial, e.g. **Presidents—**
           United States—Death and
           burial [to be added as need-
           ed]
    BT   **Archeology**
           Public health
    NT   **Catacombs**
           Cemeteries
           Cryonics
           Mounds and mound builders
           Mummies
           Tombs
    RT   **Cremation**
           Death
           Funeral rites and ceremonies
Burial customs
    USE **Burial**
Burial statistics
    USE **Mortality**
           Registers of births, etc.
           Vital statistics
Buried cities
    USE **Extinct cities**
Buried treasure   622; 910.4
    UF   Hidden treasure
           Sunken treasure
           Treasure trove
    BT   **Archeology**
           Underwater exploration
Burn out (Psychology)   158.7
    UF   Burnout syndrome
    BT   **Job satisfaction**
           Job stress

Burn out (Psychology)—*Continued*
      Mental health
      Motivation (Psychology)
      Occupational health and safety
      Stress (Psychology)
Burnout syndrome
  USE **Burn out (Psychology)**
Burnt offering
  USE **Sacrifice**
Bursaries
  USE **Scholarships**
Burying grounds
  USE **Burial**
      Cemeteries
Buses **388.4; 629.222**
  UF Motor buses
  BT **Automobiles**
      Highway transportation
      Local transit
Bush survival
  USE **Wilderness survival**
Business **650**
  UF Trade
  BT **Commerce**
      Economics
  NT **Accounting**
      Advertising
      Banks and banking
      Bookkeeping
      Business budgets
      Business enterprises
      Business failures
      Businesspeople
      Competition
      Customer relations
      Department stores
      Economic conditions
      Entrepreneurship
      Home-based business
      Installment plan
      Mail-order business
      Management
      Marketing
      Markets
      Office management
      Profit
      Real estate business
      Selling
      Small business
      Social responsibility of business
      Trust companies

Business administration
  USE **Management**
Business and government
  USE **Economic policy**
Business and politics (May subdiv. geog.)
    322
  UF Business—Political activity
      Politics and business
  BT **Politics**
Business arithmetic
  USE **Business mathematics**
Business budgets **658.15**
  UF Budgets, Business
  BT **Business**
Business colleges
  USE **Business schools**
Business correspondence
  USE **Business letters**
Business cycles (May subdiv. geog.)
    338.5
  UF Economic cycles
      Stabilization in industry
  SA types of business cycles, e.g.
      Depressions [to be added as
      needed]
  BT **Cycles**
      Economic conditions
  NT **Depressions**
      Economic forecasting
      Recessions
  RT **Financial crises**
Business—Databases **650**
  BT **Databases**
Business depression, 1929-1939
  USE **Great Depression, 1929-1939**
Business depressions
  USE **Depressions**
Business education (May subdiv. geog.)
    650.07
  UF Business—Study and teaching
      Clerical work—Training
      Commercial education
      Office work—Training
  BT **Education**
  NT **Accounting**
      Bookkeeping
      Keyboarding (Electronics)
      Shorthand
      Typewriting

Business English
    USE   **English language—Business English**
Business enterprises (May subdiv. geog.)
    338.7
    Use for materials on business concerns as legal entities, regardless of the form of organization.
    UF   Business organizations
          Businesses
          Companies
          Enterprises
          Firms
    SA   types of businesses [to be added as needed]
    BT   **Business**
    NT   **Beauty shops**
          Commercial art galleries
          Corporations
          Government business enterprises
          Joint ventures
          Minority business enterprises
          Money-making projects for children
          Multinational corporations
          New business enterprises
          Partnership
Business enterprises—Computer networks **004.6; 658**
    BT   **Computer networks**
    NT   **Intranets**
Business entertaining   **395.3; 658**
    BT   **Entertaining**
          Public relations
Business ethics (May subdiv. geog.)   **174**
    BT   **Ethics**
          Professional ethics
    NT   **Competition**
          Deceptive advertising
          Social responsibility of business
          Success
Business etiquette   **395.5**
    UF   Office etiquette
    BT   **Etiquette**
Business failures (May subdiv. geog.)
    338; 658
    UF   Business mortality
          Failure in business
    BT   **Business**
    NT   **Bank failures**
          Bankruptcy

Business forecasting (May subdiv. geog.)
    338.5
    BT   **Economic forecasting**
          Forecasting
Business—Government policy
    USE   **Economic policy**
Business—Information resources   **650**
    BT   **Information resources**
Business—Information services (May subdiv. geog.)   **658.4**
    BT   **Information services**
Business—International aspects
    USE   **Multinational corporations**
Business—Internet resources   **650**
    BT   **Internet resources**
Business—Internet resources—Directories
    650.025
Business Japanese
    USE   **Japanese language—Business Japanese**
Business language
    USE   names of languages with unique language subdivisions, e.g. **English language—Business English; Japanese language—Business Japanese;** etc. [to be added as needed]
Business law
    USE   **Commercial law**
Business—Law and legislation
    USE   **Commercial law**
Business letters   **651.7**
    UF   Business correspondence
          Commercial correspondence
          Correspondence
    BT   **Letter writing**
Business libraries   **026**
    Use for materials on libraries with a subject focus on business. Materials on libraries located within companies, firms, or private businesses, covering any subject area, are entered under **Corporate libraries.**
    UF   Libraries, Business
    BT   **Special libraries**
Business machines
    USE   **Office equipment and supplies**
Business management
    USE   **Management**
Business math
    USE   **Business mathematics**
Business mathematics   **650.01**
    UF   Arithmetic, Commercial
          Business arithmetic

Business mathematics—*Continued*
      Business math
      Commercial arithmetic
      Commercial mathematics
      Finance—Mathematics
  BT **Mathematics**
  NT **Accounting**
      Bookkeeping
      Interest (Economics)
Business mortality
  USE **Bankruptcy**
      Business failures
Business organizations
  USE **Business enterprises**
Business patronage of the arts
  USE **Art patronage**
Business people
  USE **Businesspeople**
Business—Political activity
  USE **Business and politics**
Business recessions
  USE **Recessions**
Business schools 650.071
  UF Business colleges
  BT **Schools**
Business secrets
  USE **Trade secrets**
Business—Social responsibility
  USE **Social responsibility of business**
Business—Study and teaching
  USE **Business education**
Businesses
  USE **Business enterprises**
Businessmen (May subdiv. geog.)
      338.092; 658.0092; 920
  UF Men in business
  BT **Businesspeople**
Businesspeople (May subdiv. geog.)
      338.092; 658.0092; 920
  UF Business people
  BT **Business**
  NT **African American businesspeople**
      Black businesspeople
      Businessmen
      Businesswomen
      Capitalists and financiers
      Entrepreneurs
      Merchants
      Self-employed

Businesswomen (May subdiv. geog.)
      338.092; 658.0092; 920
  UF Women in business
  BT **Businesspeople**
      Women
Busing (School integration) 379.2
  UF Antibusing
      School busing
      Student busing
  BT **School children—Transportation**
      School integration
Butter 637; 641.3
  BT **Dairy products**
Butterflies 595.78
  UF Cocoons
      Lepidoptera
  BT **Insects**
  NT **Caterpillars**
  RT **Moths**
Buttons 646; 687
  BT **Clothing and dress**
Buy American policy
  USE **Buy national policy—United States**
Buy national policy (May subdiv. geog.)
      352.5
    Use for materials on the requirement that a national government procure goods produced domestically.
  UF Government policy
  BT **Commercial policy**
      Government purchasing
Buy national policy—United States
      352.5
  UF Buy American policy
Buyers' guides
  USE **Consumer education**
      Shopping
Buying
  USE **Purchasing**
Buyouts, Corporate
  USE **Corporate mergers and acquisitions**
Buyouts, Leveraged
  USE **Leveraged buyouts**
By-products
  USE **Waste products**
Byrd Antarctic Expedition 919.8
  BT **Antarctica—Exploration**

Byzantine architecture (May subdiv. geog.) **723**
  UF Architecture, Byzantine
  BT **Ancient architecture**
      Architecture
      Medieval architecture
Byzantine art 709.02
  UF Art, Byzantine
  BT **Ancient art**
      Art
      Medieval art
Byzantine Empire 949.5
  UF Eastern Empire
Cabala 135; 296.1
  UF Cabbala
      Kabbala
  BT **Hebrew literature**
      Jewish literature
      Judaism
      Mysticism
      Occultism
  RT **Symbolism of numbers**
Cabarets
  USE **Night clubs, cabarets, etc.**
Cabbala
  USE **Cabala**
Cabinet officers (May subdiv. geog.)
      352.24; 920
  UF Ministers of state
  NT **Prime ministers**
Cabinet work
  USE **Cabinetwork**
Cabinetwork 684.1
  Use for materials on the making and finishing of fine woodwork, such as furniture or interior details. Materials on the construction of a wooden building or the wooden portion of any building are entered under **Carpentry.**
  UF Cabinet work
  BT **Carpentry**
  NT **Veneers and veneering**
  RT **Furniture**
      Woodwork
Cabins
  USE **Log cabins and houses**
Cable railroads (May subdiv. geog.)
      385; 625.5
  UF Funicular railroads
      Railroads, Cable
  BT **Railroads**
  RT **Street railroads**

Cable television (May subdiv. geog.)
      384.55
  BT **Television broadcasting**
Cables 384.6; 621.319; 624.1
  BT **Power transmission**
      Rope
Cables, Submarine
  USE **Submarine cables**
Cactus 583; 635.9
  BT **Desert plants**
CAD
  USE **Computer-aided design**
CAD/CAM software
  USE **Computer-aided design software**
CAD software
  USE **Computer-aided design software**
Cafes
  USE **Coffeehouses**
      Restaurants
Cage birds 636.6
  SA types of cage birds [to be added as needed]
  BT **Birds**
  NT **Canaries**
CAI
  USE **Computer-assisted instruction**
Cake 641.8; 664
  BT **Baking**
      Confectionery
      Cooking
      Desserts
  RT **Pastry**
Cake decorating 641.8
  BT **Confectionery**
Calculating machines
  USE **Calculators**
Calculators 510.28; 651.8; 681
  Use for materials on present-day calculators or on calculators and mechanical computers made before 1945. Materials on modern electronic computers developed after 1945 are entered under **Computers.**
  UF Accounting machines
      Adding machines
      Calculating machines
      Pocket calculators
  BT **Arithmetic**
      Office equipment and supplies
  NT **Abacus**
      Slide rule
  RT **Computers**

Calculus 515
UF Analysis (Mathematics)
BT **Mathematical analysis**
Mathematics
NT **Differential equations**
RT **Functions**
Caldecott Awards
USE **Caldecott Medal**
Caldecott Medal 028.5
UF Caldecott Awards
Caldecott Medal books
BT **Children's literature**
Illustration of books
Literary prizes
Caldecott Medal books
USE **Caldecott Medal**
Calendars 529
UF Annuals
SA subjects, corporate bodies, and
names of countries, cities,
etc., with the subdivision *Cal-
endars,* for works that list re-
curring, coming, or past
events in those places or re-
lated to those topics or orga-
nizations [to be added as
needed]
BT **Time**
NT **Birthday books**
Church year
Days
Devotional calendars
Months
Week
RT **Almanacs**
California—Gold discoveries 979.4
UF California gold rush
California gold rush
USE **California—Gold discoveries**
Calisthenics
USE **Gymnastics**
Physical education
Calligraphy 745.6
BT **Decorative arts**
Handwriting
Writing
Caloric content of foods
USE **Food—Caloric content**
Calories (Food)
USE **Food—Caloric content**

Calvinism (May subdiv. geog.) **284**
BT **Reformation**
RT **Congregationalism**
Puritans
Camcorders 621.388; 778.59
UF Home video cameras
Video cameras, Home
BT **Cameras**
Home video systems
Video recording
RT **Amateur films**
Camels 599.63; 636.2
UF Dromedaries
BT **Desert animals**
Mammals
Cameras 681; 771.3
SA types of cameras and names of
individual makes of cameras
[to be added as needed]
BT **Photography**
**Photography—Equipment and
supplies**
NT **Camcorders**
Digital cameras
Kodak camera
Motion picture cameras
Camouflage (Biology) 591.47
UF Animal camouflage
Animals—Camouflage
BT **Animal defenses**
**Camouflage (Military science) 355.4;
623**
BT **Military art and science**
Naval art and science
Camp cooking
USE **Outdoor cooking**
Camp Fire Girls 369.47
BT **Girls' clubs**
Camp sites
USE **Campgrounds**
Campaign funds (May subdiv. geog.)
324.7
UF Elections—Finance
Political parties—Finance
BT **Elections**
Politics
Campaign funds—United States 324.7
UF Elections—United States—Fi-
nance
United States—Campaign funds

Campaign literature (May subdiv. geog.)
   324.2
   UF   Political campaign literature
   BT   **Literature**
        Politics
Campaigns
   USE   names of wars with the subdivision *Campaigns,* e.g. **World War, 1939-1945—Campaigns;** which may be further subdivided geographically [to be added as needed]
Campaigns, Political
   USE   **Politics**
Campaigns, Presidential—United States
   USE   **Presidents—United States—Election**
Campers and trailers
   USE   **Travel trailers and campers**
Campgrounds (May subdiv. geog.)
   796.54
   UF   Camp sites
   NT   **Trailer parks**
   RT   **Camping**
Camping (May subdiv. geog.)   **796.54**
   Use for materials on the technique of camping. Materials on camps with a definite program of activities are entered under **Camps.**
   BT   **Outdoor recreation**
   NT   **Backpacking**
        Bicycle touring
        Outdoor cooking
        Tents
        Travel trailers and campers
        Wilderness survival
   RT   **Campgrounds**
        Outdoor life
Camps (May subdiv. geog.)   **796.54**
   Use for materials on camps with a definite program of activities. Materials on the technique of camping are entered under **Camping.**
   UF   Summer camps
   BT   **Recreation**
Camps (Military)
   USE   **Military camps**
Campus disorders
   USE   **College students—Political activity**
Canada   **971**
   May be subdivided like United States except for *History.*

SA   names of individual provinces, territories, or regions [to be added as needed]
Canada—English-French relations
   305.811; 306.44
   UF   Canada—French-English relations
Canada—French-English relations
   USE   **Canada—English-French relations**
Canada—History—0-1763 (New France)
   971.01
   UF   New France—History
Canada—History—1755-1763   **971.01**
Canada—History—1763-1791   **971.02**
Canada—History—1763-1867   **971.02**
Canada—History—1775-1783   **971.02**
Canada—History—1791-1841   **971.03**
Canada—History—19th century   **971.03**
Canada—History—1841-1867   **971.04**
Canada—History—1867-   **971.05**
Canada—History—1867-1914   **971.05**
Canada—History—20th century   **971.06**
Canada—History—1914-1945   **971.06**
Canada—History—1945-   **971.06**
Canada—History—21st century   **971.07**
Canadian Indians
   USE   **Native Americans—Canada**
Canadian Invasion, 1775-1776   **973.3**
   BT   **United States—History—1775-1783, Revolution**
Canadian literature (May subdiv. geog.)
   810; C810
   Use for general materials not limited to literature in a particular language or form. May use same subdivision and names of literary forms as for **English literature;** e.g. **Canadian poetry;** etc.
   BT   **Literature**
   NT   **Canadian literature (English)**
        Canadian literature (French)
        Canadian poetry
Canadian literature (English) (May subdiv. geog.)   **810; C810**
   May use same subdivisions and names of literary forms as for **English literature;** e.g. **Canadian poetry (English);** etc.
   UF   English Canadian literature
   BT   **Canadian literature**
   NT   **Canadian poetry (English)**
Canadian literature (French) (May subdiv. geog.)   **840; C840**
   May use same subdivisions and names of literary forms as for **English literature;** e.g. **Canadian poetry (French);** etc.

Canadian literature (French)—*Continued*
   UF   French Canadian literature
         French literature—Canada
   BT   **Canadian literature**
   NT   **Canadian poetry (French)**
Canadian poetry (May subdiv. geog.)
     811; C811
   Use for general materials about Canadian poetry not limited to a particular language, not for individual works.
   BT   **Canadian literature**
   NT   **Canadian poetry (English)**
         Canadian poetry (French)
Canadian poetry (English) (May subdiv. geog.)   **811; C811**
   Use for general materials about Canadian poetry in English, not for individual works.
   UF   English Canadian poetry
   BT   **Canadian literature (English)**
         Canadian poetry
Canadian poetry (French) (May subdiv. geog.)   **841; C841**
   Use for general materials about Canadian poetry in French, not for individual works.
   UF   French Canadian poetry
   BT   **Canadian literature (French)**
         Canadian poetry
Canadians   **305.811; 971**
   NT   **French Canadians**
Canals (May subdiv. geog.)   **386; 627**
   SA   names of individual canals [to be added as needed]
   BT   **Civil engineering**
         Hydraulic structures
         Transportation
         Waterways
   NT   **Panama Canal**
   RT   **Inland navigation**
Canaries   **598.8; 636.6**
   BT   **Birds**
         Cage birds
Canasta (Game)   **795.41**
   UF   Argentine rummy
   BT   **Card games**
Cancer (May subdiv. geog.)   **616.99**
   UF   Carcinoma
         Malignant tumors
   SA   types of cancer [to be added as needed]
   BT   **Diseases**
         Tumors
   NT   **Breast cancer**
         Leukemia

         Lung cancer
Cancer—Chemotherapy   **616.99**
   UF   Chemotherapy
   BT   **Drug therapy**
Cancer—Diet therapy   **616.99**
   BT   **Diet therapy**
Cancer—Genetic aspects   **616.99**
   BT   **Medical genetics**
Cancer—Nursing   **616.99**
   BT   **Nursing**
Cancer patients
   USE   **Cancer—Patients**
Cancer—Patients   **616.99**
   UF   Cancer patients
   BT   **Patients**
Cancer—Surgery   **616.99**
   BT   **Surgery**
Candies
   USE   **Candy**
Candles   **621.32; 745.593**
   BT   **Lighting**
Candy   **641.8**
   UF   Candies
         Sweets
   BT   **Confectionery**
Caning of chairs
   USE   **Chair caning**
Cannabis
   USE   **Marijuana**
Canned goods
   USE   **Canning and preserving**
Cannibalism   **394**
   BT   **Ethnology**
         Human behavior
Canning and preserving   **641.4; 664**
   UF   Canned goods
         Food, Canned
         Pickling
         Preserving
   SA   types of foods with the subdivision *Preservation* [to be added as needed]
   BT   **Cooking**
         Food—Preservation
         Industrial chemistry
   NT   **Fruit—Preservation**
         Vegetables—Preservation
Cannon
   USE   **Ordnance**

Canoes and canoeing   797.122
   BT   Boats and boating
        Water sports
   NT   Kayaking
Canon law
   USE   Ecclesiastical law
Canons, fugues, etc.
   USE   Fugue
Cantatas   782.2
     Use for musical scores and for materials on
   the cantata as a musical form.
   BT   Choral music
        Vocal music
Canvas embroidery
   USE   Needlepoint
Capital (May subdiv. geog.)   332
   BT   Economics
        Finance
   NT   Banks and banking
        Human capital
        Industrial trusts
        Interest (Economics)
        Investments
        Profit
        Saving and investment
   RT   Capitalism
        Wealth
Capital accumulation
   USE   Saving and investment
Capital and labor
   USE   Industrial relations
Capital equipment
   USE   Industrial equipment
Capital formation
   USE   Saving and investment
Capital goods
   USE   Industrial equipment
Capital market   332
   BT   Finance
        Financial institutions
        Loans
        Securities
   NT   Euro
Capital punishment (May subdiv. geog.)
     179.7; 364.6
   UF   Abolition of capital punishment
        Death penalty
        Hanging
   BT   Criminal law
        Punishment
   RT   Executions and executioners

Capital punishment—United States
     364.6
Capitalism (May subdiv. geog.)   330.12
   BT   Economics
        Labor
        Profit
   NT   Entrepreneurship
   RT   Capital
        Capitalists and financiers
        Free enterprise
Capitalists and financiers (May subdiv.
    geog.)   332.092; 920
   UF   Financiers
   BT   Businesspeople
   RT   Capitalism
Capitalization (Finance)
   USE   Corporations—Finance
        Securities
        Valuation
Capitals (Cities)   307.76
     Use for materials on the capital cities of
   several countries or states.
   BT   Cities and towns
   NT   Capitols
Capitols   725
   BT   Capitals (Cities)
        Public buildings
Captivities
   USE   ethnic groups with the subdivi-
          sion Captivities, e.g. Native
          Americans—Captivities [to
          be added as needed]
Car accidents
   USE   Traffic accidents
Car design
   USE   Automobiles—Design and con-
          struction
Car driver education
   USE   Automobile driver education
Car drivers
   USE   Automobile drivers
Car engines
   USE   Automobiles—Motors
Car industry
   USE   Automobile industry
Car insurance
   USE   Automobile insurance
Car maintenance
   USE   Automobiles—Maintenance and
          repair
Car painting
   USE   Automobiles—Painting

Car parts
    USE   **Automobile parts**
Car pools   388.4
    UF   Automobile pools
         Carpools
         Ride sharing
         Van pools
    BT   **Traffic engineering**
         Transportation
Car racing
    USE   **Automobile racing**
Car repair
    USE   **Automobiles—Maintenance and**
         repair
Car transmissions
    USE   **Automobiles—Transmission de-**
         vices
Car travel
    USE   **Automobile travel**
Car wheels
    USE   **Wheels**
Car wrecks
    USE   **Traffic accidents**
Carbines
    USE   **Rifles**
Carbolic acid   547; 661
    BT   **Acids**
         Chemicals
Carbon   540; 660
    BT   **Chemical elements**
    NT   **Diamonds**
         Graphite
Carbon 14 dating
    USE   **Radiocarbon dating**
Carbon dioxide greenhouse effect
    USE   **Greenhouse effect**
Carburetors   621.43
    BT   **Internal combustion engines**
Carcinoma
    USE   **Cancer**
Card catalogs   025.3
    UF   Catalogs, Card
    BT   **Library catalogs**
Card games   795.4
    SA   types of card games [to be add-
         ed as needed]
    BT   **Games**
    NT   **Bridge (Game)**
         Canasta (Game)
         Card tricks
         Collectible card games

         Poker
         Solitaire (Game)
         Tarot
    RT   **Playing cards**
Card tricks   795.4
    BT   **Card games**
         Magic tricks
         Tricks
Cardiac diseases
    USE   **Heart diseases**
Cardiac resuscitation   616.1
    UF   Heart resuscitation
         Resuscitation, Heart
    BT   **Emergency medicine**
    RT   **CPR (First aid)**
Cardinals   262
    BT   **Catholic Church—Clergy**
Cardiopulmonary resuscitation
    USE   **CPR (First aid)**
Cardiovascular system   612.1
    UF   Circulatory system
         Vascular system
    BT   **Anatomy**
         Physiology
    NT   **Heart**
    RT   **Blood—Circulation**
Cards, Debit
    USE   **Debit cards**
Cards, Greeting
    USE   **Greeting cards**
Cards, Playing
    USE   **Playing cards**
Cards, Sports
    USE   **Sports cards**
Care
    USE   parts of the body, classes of
         persons, and types of animals
         with the subdivision *Care,*
         e.g. **Foot—Care; Infants—**
         Care; Dogs—Care; etc.;
         classes of persons with the
         subdivisions *Medical care, In-*
         stitutional care, and *Home*
         care, e.g. **Elderly—Medical**
         care; Elderly—Institutional
         care; Elderly—Home care;
         etc.; ethnic groups and classes
         of persons with the subdivi-
         sion *Health and hygiene,* e.g.
         Infants—Health and hy-
         giene; and inanimate things

Care—*Continued*

　　　　with the subdivision *Mainte-*
　　　　nance and repair, e.g. **Auto-**
　　　　mobiles—Maintenance and
　　　　repair [to be added as need-
　　　　ed]

Care givers
　　USE　**Caregivers**

Care of children
　　USE　**Child care**

Care of the dying
　　USE　**Terminal care**

Career changes　650.14; 658.4
　　UF　Changing careers
　　　　Mid-career changes
　　SA　fields of knowledge, professions,
　　　　industries, and trades with the
　　　　subdivision *Vocational guid-*
　　　　ance [to be added as needed]
　　BT　**Age and employment**
　　　　Vocational guidance

Career counseling
　　USE　**Vocational guidance**

Career development
　　USE　**Personnel management**
　　　　Vocational guidance

Career education
　　USE　**Vocational education**

Career guidance
　　USE　**Vocational guidance**

Careers
　　USE　**Occupations**
　　　　Professions
　　　　Vocational guidance

Caregivers　362; 649.8
　　Use for materials on family and friends
　　who on a voluntary basis provide personal
　　home care for the elderly, ill, or handicapped.
　　UF　Care givers
　　　　Family caregivers
　　BT　**Volunteer work**
　　RT　**Home care services**

Caricatures and cartoons
　　USE　**Cartoons and caricatures**

Carillons
　　USE　**Bells**

Carnival (May subdiv. geog.)　**394.25**
　　Use for materials on festivals, merrymaking,
　　and revelry before Lent. Materials on travel-
　　ing amusement enterprises, consisting of side-
　　shows, games of chance, etc., are entered un-
　　der **Carnivals.**

UF　Mardi Gras
　　Pre-Lenten festivities
BT　**Festivals**

Carnivals (May subdiv. geog.)　**394.26;**
　　791
　　Use for materials on traveling amusement
　　enterprises, consisting of sideshows, games of
　　chance, merry-go-rounds, etc. Materials on
　　festivals, merrymaking, and revelry before
　　Lent are entered under **Carnival.**
　　BT　**Amusements**
　　　　Festivals
　　RT　**Amusement parks**
　　　　Circus
　　　　Fairs

Carnivora
　　USE　**Carnivorous animals**

Carnivores
　　USE　**Carnivorous animals**

Carnivorous animals　599.7
　　UF　Carnivora
　　　　Carnivores
　　　　Meat-eating animals
　　SA　types of carnivorous animals [to
　　　　be added as needed]
　　BT　**Animals**

Carnivorous plants　583; 635.9
　　UF　Insect-eating plants
　　　　Insectivorous plants
　　BT　**Plants**

Carols　782.28
　　UF　Christmas carols
　　　　Easter carols
　　BT　**Church music**
　　　　Folk songs
　　　　Hymns
　　　　Songs
　　　　Vocal music

Carpentry　694
　　Use for materials on the construction of a
　　wooden building or the wooden portion of
　　any building. Materials on the making and
　　finishing of fine woodwork, such as furniture
　　or interior details, are entered under **Cabinet-**
　　work.
　　BT　**Building**
　　NT　**Cabinetwork**
　　　　Turning
　　RT　**Woodwork**

Carpentry—Tools
　　USE　**Carpentry tools**

Carpentry tools   694
   UF   Carpentry—Tools
   SA   types of carpentry tools [to be
            added as needed]
   BT   **Tools**
   NT   **Saws**
Carpet cleaning
   USE   **Rugs and carpets—Cleaning**
Carpetbag rule
   USE   **Reconstruction (1865-1876)**
Carpets
   USE   **Rugs and carpets**
Carpools
   USE   **Car pools**
Carriages and carts   388.3; 688.6
   UF   Carts
            Stagecoaches
            Wagons
   BT   **Vehicles**
Cars (Automobiles)
   USE   **Automobiles**
Cartels
   USE   **Industrial trusts**
Cartography
   USE   **Map drawing**
            Maps
Cartooning   741.5
   BT   **Cartoons and caricatures**
            Wit and humor
Cartoons and caricatures   741.5
   Use for collections of pictorial humor and
   for materials about caricatures and cartoons.
   UF   Caricatures and cartoons
   SA   subjects, classes of persons,
            names of individuals, and
            names of wars with the sub-
            division *Cartoons and carica-*
            tures [to be added as needed]
   BT   **Pictures**
            Portraits
   NT   **Animated films**
            Cartooning
            Computers—Cartoons and car-
            icatures
            World War, 1939-1945—Car-
            toons and caricatures
   RT   **Comic books, strips, etc.**
Cartoons, Animated
   USE   **Animated films**
Cartoons, Television
   USE   **Animated television programs**

Carts
   USE   **Carriages and carts**
Carts (Midget cars)
   USE   **Karts and karting**
Carving (Arts)
   USE   **Carving (Decorative arts)**
Carving (Decorative arts) (May subdiv.
      geog.)   **731.4; 736**
   UF   Carving (Arts)
   SA   types of carving, e.g. **Wood**
            carving [to be added as need-
            ed]
   BT   **Decorative arts**
   NT   **Wood carving**
   RT   **Sculpture**
Carving (Meat, etc.)   642
   BT   **Dining**
            Entertaining
            Meat
Carving, Wood
   USE   **Wood carving**
Case studies
   USE   subjects with the subdivision
            Case studies, e.g. **Juvenile**
            delinquency—Case studies
            [to be added as needed]
Case work, Social
   USE   **Social case work**
Cassette books
   USE   **Audiobooks**
Cassette recorders and recording
   USE   **Magnetic recorders and re-**
            cording
Cassette tapes, Audio
   USE   **Sound recordings**
Castaways
   USE   **Survival after airplane acci-**
            dents, shipwrecks, etc.
Caste (May subdiv. geog.)   **305.5**
   BT   **Manners and customs**
   NT   **Social classes**
Casting
   USE   **Founding**
            Plaster casts
Castles (May subdiv. geog.)   **728.8**
   UF   Chateaux
   BT   **Buildings**
   RT   **Medieval architecture**
Casts, Plaster
   USE   **Plaster casts**

Casualty insurance 368.5
  UF Insurance, Casualty
  BT **Insurance**
  NT **Accident insurance**
CAT scan
  USE **Tomography**
Catacombs 393; 726
  BT **Burial**
      Cemeteries
      Christian antiquities
      Tombs
  RT **Church history—30-600, Early church**
Cataloging 025.3
  UF Cataloguing
      Libraries—Cataloging
      Library cataloging
  SA cataloging of particular subjects, e.g., **Cataloging of music** [to be added as needed]
  BT **Bibliographic control**
      Documentation
      Library science
      Library technical processes
  NT **Automated cataloging**
      Cataloging of music
      International Standard Bibliographic Description
      Library classification
      Machine readable bibliographic data
      Subject headings
  RT **Bibliography**
      Indexing
      Library catalogs
Cataloging data in machine readable form
  USE **Machine readable bibliographic data**
Cataloging—Data processing
  USE **Automated cataloging**
Cataloging—Music
  USE **Cataloging of music**
Cataloging of music 025.3
  UF Cataloging—Music
      Music—Cataloging
  BT **Cataloging**
Catalogs
  USE **Booksellers' catalogs**
      Commercial catalogs
      Library catalogs
      Publishers' catalogs

and subjects and names of museums with the subdivision *Catalogs,* e.g. **Motion pictures—Catalogs** [to be added as needed]
Catalogs, Book
  USE **Book catalogs**
Catalogs, Booksellers'
  USE **Booksellers' catalogs**
Catalogs, Card
  USE **Card catalogs**
Catalogs, Classified
  USE **Classified catalogs**
Catalogs, Film
  USE **Motion pictures—Catalogs**
Catalogs in book form
  USE **Book catalogs**
Catalogs, Library
  USE **Library catalogs**
Catalogs, Online
  USE **Online catalogs**
Catalogs, Publishers'
  USE **Publishers' catalogs**
Catalogs, Subject
  USE **Subject catalogs**
Cataloguing
  USE **Cataloging**
Catalysis 541
  BT **Physical chemistry**
  RT **Catalytic RNA**
Catalytic RNA 572.8
  UF Ribozymes
  BT **Enzymes**
      RNA
  RT **Catalysis**
Catamarans 797.1
  BT **Boats and boating**
Catastrophes
  USE **Disasters**
Catechisms 202; 238
  SA names of religions and sects and titles of sacred works with the subdivision *Catechisms* [to be added as needed]
  BT **Theology—Study and teaching**
  NT **Bible—Catechisms**
  RT **Creeds**
Categories of persons
  USE **Persons**
      and classes of persons, e.g. **Elderly; Handicapped; Explor-**

Categories of persons—*Continued*
ers; **Drug addicts;** etc. [to be
added as needed]
Caterers and catering
USE **Catering**
Catering 642
UF Caterers and catering
BT **Cooking**
Food service
RT **Menus**
Caterpillars 595.78
UF Cocoons
BT **Butterflies**
Moths
Cathedrals (May subdiv. geog.) **726.6**
SA names of individual cathedrals
[to be added as needed]
BT **Church buildings**
RT **Abbeys**
Church architecture
Gothic architecture
Medieval architecture
Cathedrals—United States 726.60973
Cathode ray tubes 537.5; 621.3815
UF CRTs
BT **Vacuum tubes**
Catholic charismatic movement 282
UF Charismatic movement
Charismatic renewal movement
BT **Catholic Church**
Episcopal Church
RT **Pentecostalism**
Spiritual gifts
Catholic Church (May subdiv. geog.)
282
UF Roman Catholic Church
SA religious subjects with the subdi-
vision *Catholic Church,* e.g.
**Asceticism—Catholic
Church; Laity—Catholic
Church;** etc., and other sub-
jects with the subdivisions
*Religious aspects—Catholic
Church;* e.g. **Abortion—Reli-
gious aspects—Catholic
Church** [to be added as
needed]
BT **Christian sects**
Christianity
NT **Catholic charismatic movement
Inquisition
Laity—Catholic Church**

Papacy
RT **Catholics**
Catholic Church—Charities 361.7
BT **Charities**
Catholic Church—Clergy 253
BT **Clergy**
Priests
NT **Cardinals**
Ex-priests
Catholic Church—Converts
USE **Converts to Catholicism**
Catholic Church—Creeds 238
Use for materials about the concise, formal,
authorized statements of Catholic doctrine and
for the texts of such statements.
UF Catholic creeds
BT **Creeds**
Catholic Church—Foreign relations (May
subdiv. geog.) **282; 327.456**
Use for materials on diplomatic relations
between the Catholic Church and various gov-
ernments or political bodies. When this head-
ing is subdivided geographically, an additional
entry is provided with the Catholic Church
and the place in reversed positions. Materials
on the relations between the Catholic Church
and other churches or religions are entered
under **Catholic Church—Relations.**
UF Catholic Church—Relations
(Diplomatic)
Vatican City—Foreign relations
BT **International relations**
Catholic Church—Liturgy 264
Use for materials on the forms of prayers,
rituals, and ceremonies used in the official
public worship of the Catholic Church. Texts
of Catholic liturgies are entered under **Catho-
lic Church—Liturgy—Texts.**
UF Catholic liturgies
BT **Liturgies**
Rites and ceremonies
Catholic Church—Liturgy—Texts 264
Catholic Church—Missions 266
BT **Christian missions**
Catholic Church—Relations 282
Use for materials on relations between the
Catholic Church and other churches or reli-
gions. This heading may be further subdivided
by church or religion, in which case an addi-
tional entry is provided with the two churches
or religions in reversed positions. Materials on
diplomatic relations between the Catholic
Church and various governments or political
bodies are entered under **Catholic Church—
Foreign relations.**
Catholic Church—Relations (Diplomatic)
USE **Catholic Church—Foreign relations**

Catholic Church—United States 282

Catholic colleges and universities (May subdiv. geog.) **378**
UF Catholic universities and colleges
BT **Colleges and universities**

Catholic converts
USE **Converts to Catholicism**

Catholic creeds
USE **Catholic Church—Creeds**

Catholic ex-nuns
USE **Ex-nuns**

Catholic ex-priests
USE **Ex-priests**

Catholic laity
USE **Laity—Catholic Church**

Catholic literature 282; 808; 809
BT **Christian literature**
     Literature

Catholic liturgies
USE **Catholic Church—Liturgy**

Catholic universities and colleges
USE **Catholic colleges and universities**

Catholics (May subdiv. geog.) **282.092; 305.6**
NT **Converts to Catholicism**
RT **Catholic Church**

Catholics—United States 282.092; 305.6

Cats (May subdiv. geog.) **599.75; 636.8**
Use for materials on domestic cats. Materials on non-domesticated species of cats or domestic cats living in a wild state are entered under **Wild cats.**
UF Kittens
SA names of specific breeds of cat [to be added as needed]
BT **Domestic animals**
     Mammals
RT **Wild cats**

Cats—Literary collections 808.8

Cattle 599.64; 636.2
UF Cows
BT **Domestic animals**
     Mammals
NT **Beef cattle**
     Dairy cattle

Cattle brands 636.2

Cattle—Vaccination 636.089
BT **Vaccination**

Causality
USE **Causation**

Causation 122
UF Causality
     Cause and effect
BT **Metaphysics**
     Philosophy

Cause and effect
USE **Causation**

Causes
USE names of wars with the subdivision *Causes,* e.g. **World War, 1939-1945—Causes** [to be added as needed]

Cautionary tales and verse
USE **Fables**
     Parables

Cautionary tales and verses
USE **Didactic fiction**
     Didactic poetry

Cave drawings
USE **Cave drawings and paintings**

Cave drawings and paintings (May subdiv. geog.) **743; 759.01**
UF Cave drawings
     Cave paintings
BT **Rock drawings, paintings, and engravings**

Cave dwellers 569.9; 930.1
BT **Prehistoric peoples**

Cave paintings
USE **Cave drawings and paintings**

Caves 551.44
UF Grottoes
     Speleology

CB radio
USE **Citizens band radio**

CD-I technology 006.7
UF CDI technology
     Compact disc interactive technology
     Interactive CD technology
BT **Compact discs**
     Optical storage devices

CD players
USE **Compact disc players**

CD-ROM
USE **CD-ROMs**

CD-ROMs 004.5
UF CD-ROM
     CDROM
     CDROMs
     Compact disc read-only memory

CD-ROMs—*Continued*
  BT **Compact discs**
       Optical storage devices
CDI technology
  USE **CD-I technology**
CDROM
  USE **CD-ROMs**
CDROMs
  USE **CD-ROMs**
CDs (Compact discs)
  USE **Compact discs**
Celebrations, anniversaries, etc.
  USE **Anniversaries**
Celebrities (May subdiv. geog.) **920**
  UF Famous people
       Public figures
  SA types of celebrities, e.g. **Actors;**
       Television personalities; and
       names of individual celebrities
       [to be added as needed]
  BT **Persons**
  NT **Television personalities**
  RT **Fame**
Celebrity
  USE **Fame**
Celery **635; 641.3**
  BT **Vegetables**
Celibacy **204; 248.4**
    Use for materials on the renunciation of
  marriage for religious reasons. Materials on
  the virtue that moderates and regulates the
  sexual appetite in human beings are entered
  under **Chastity.** Materials on abstinence from
  sexual activity are entered under **Sexual absti-
  nence.**
  UF Clerical celibacy
  BT **Clergy**
       Religious life
  RT **Chastity**
       Sexual abstinence
Cell phones
  USE **Cellular telephones**
Cellars
  USE **Basements**
Cellists
  USE **Violoncellists**
Cello
  USE **Violoncellos**
Cello players
  USE **Violoncellists**

Cells **571.6**
  UF Cytology
  BT **Biology**
       Physiology
       Reproduction
  NT **DNA**
  RT **Embryology**
       Protoplasm
Cells, Electric
  USE **Electric batteries**
Cellular phones
  USE **Cellular telephones**
Cellular telephones **384.5**
  UF Cell phones
       Cellular phones
  BT **Telephone**
Celtic legends **398.208991**
  BT **Legends**
Celtic mythology **299; 936.4**
  UF Mythology, Celtic
  BT **Mythology**
Celts (May subdiv. geog.) **305.891;
       936.4**
  UF Gaels
  BT **France—History—0-1328**
       Great Britain—History—0-1066
  NT **Druids and Druidism**
Cement **620.1; 666; 691**
  UF Hydraulic cement
  BT **Adhesives**
       Building materials
       Ceramics
       Masonry
       Plaster and plastering
  RT **Concrete**
Cemeteries (May subdiv. geog.) **393;
       718**
  UF Burying grounds
       Churchyards
       Graves
       Graveyards
  SA types of cemeteries and names
       of individual cemeteries [to
       be added as needed]
  BT **Burial**
       Public health
       Sanitation
  NT **Catacombs**
       Epitaphs
  RT **Tombs**

Censorship (May subdiv. geog.)   303.3;
363.31

Use for general materials on the limitation of freedom of expression in various fields.

    SA   subjects and names of wars with the subdivision *Censorship,* e.g. **Books—Censorship** [to be added as needed]

    BT   **Intellectual freedom**

    NT   **Books—Censorship**
          Freedom of speech
          Libraries—Censorship
          Motion pictures—Censorship
          Television—Censorship
          World War, 1939-1945—Censorship

    RT   **Freedom of information**
          Freedom of the press

Census   304.6; 310; 352.7

    SA   names of countries, cities, etc., with the subdivision *Census* [to be added as needed]

    BT   **Population**
          Statistics
          Vital statistics

    NT   **Chicago (Ill.)—Census**
          Ohio—Census
          United States—Census

Centennial celebrations, etc.

    USE   names of places, wars, and historical events with the subdivision *Centennial celebrations, etc.,* e.g. **United States—History—1861-1865, Civil War—Centennial celebrations, etc.**; and ethnic groups, classes of persons, individuals, corporate bodies, places, religious denominations, historic or social movements, and historic events with the subdivision *Anniversaries,* for materials about anniversary celebrations, e.g. **Shakespeare, William, 1564-1616—Anniversaries** [to be added as needed]

Centers for the performing arts   725;
790.2

    SA   names of individual centers [to be added as needed]

    BT   **Performing arts**

    NT   **Auditoriums**
          Theaters

Central Africa   967

Use for materials dealing collectively with the region of Africa that includes the Central African Republic, Equatorial Guinea, Gabon, Congo (Republic), and Congo (Democratic Republic).

    UF   Africa, Central

    BT   **Africa**

    NT   **French-speaking Equatorial Africa**

Central America   972.8

    BT   **North America**

Central Asia   958

    UF   Asia, Central

    BT   **Asia**

Central Asia—History   958

Central Asia—History—1991-   958

Central Europe   943

Use for materials on the area included in the basins of the Danube, Elbe and Rhine rivers.

    UF   Europe, Central

Central planning

    USE   **Economic policy**

Central States

    USE   **Middle West**

Centralization of schools

    USE   **Schools—Centralization**

Centralized processing (Libraries)

    USE   **Library technical processes**

Ceramic industries

    USE   **Ceramic industry**

Ceramic industry (May subdiv. geog.)
338.4

    UF   Ceramic industries

    SA   types of ceramic industries, e.g. **Glass manufacture** [to be added as needed]

    BT   **Industries**

    NT   **Clay industry**
          Glass manufacture

    RT   **Ceramics**

Ceramic materials

    USE   **Ceramics**

Ceramic tiles

    USE   **Tiles**

Ceramics   666

Use for materials on the technology of fired earth products or on ceramic products intended for industrial use. Materials on ceramic

Ceramics—*Continued*
products intended for the table or decorative use are entered under **Pottery** or **Porcelain**.
- UF   Ceramic materials
- BT   **Industrial chemistry**
  - **Materials**
- NT   **Abrasives**
  - **Cement**
  - **Clay**
  - **Glass**
  - **Glazes**
  - **Pottery**
  - **Tiles**
- RT   **Ceramic industry**

Cereals
- USE   **Grain**

Cereals, Prepared
- USE   **Prepared cereals**

Cerebral palsy   616.8
- UF   Paralysis, Cerebral
- BT   **Brain—Diseases**

Cerebrovascular disease
- USE   **Stroke**

Ceremonies
- USE   **Etiquette**
  - **Manners and customs**
  - **Rites and ceremonies**

Certainty   121
- BT   **Logic**
  - **Theory of knowledge**
- RT   **Truth**

Certified public accountants
- USE   **Accountants**

Chain belting
- USE   **Belts and belting**

Chain stores   658.8
- UF   Branch stores
- BT   **Retail trade**
  - **Stores**

Chair caning   684.1
- UF   Caning of chairs
- BT   **Handicraft**

Chairs   645; 684.1; 749
- BT   **Furniture**
- NT   **Wheelchairs**

Chalk talks   741.2
- UF   Blackboard drawing
- BT   **Public speaking**

Challenger (Space shuttle)
- USE   **Challenger (Spacecraft)**

Challenger (Spacecraft)   629.44
- UF   Challenger (Space shuttle)
- BT   **Space shuttles**

Chamber music   785
- BT   **Instrumental music**
  - **Music**
- NT   **Quintets**

Chambers of commerce (May subdiv. geog.)   **380.106; 381.06**
- UF   Boards of trade
  - Trade, Boards of
- BT   **Commerce**

Change   116
- BT   **Metaphysics**

Change of life in men
- USE   **Male climacteric**

Change of life in women
- USE   **Menopause**

Change of sex
- USE   **Transsexualism**

Change, Organizational
- USE   **Organizational change**

Change, Social
- USE   **Social change**

Changing careers
- USE   **Career changes**

Chanties
- USE   **Sea songs**

Chants (Plain, Gregorian, etc.)   782.32
Use for books of chants and for materials about chants.
- UF   Gregorian chant
  - Plain chant
  - Plainsong
- BT   **Church music**

Chanukah
- USE   **Hanukkah**

Chaos (Science)   003
- UF   Chaotic behavior in systems
- BT   **Dynamics**
  - **Science**
  - **System theory**

Chaotic behavior in systems
- USE   **Chaos (Science)**

Chap-books
- USE   **Chapbooks**

Chapbooks   398
May be used for individual works, collections, or materials about chapbooks.
- UF   Chap-books
  - Jestbooks

Chapbooks—*Continued*
 BT **Books**
  Folklore
  Literature
  Pamphlets
  Periodicals
  Wit and humor
 RT **Comic books, strips, etc.**
Chaplains 253
 SA corporate bodies and institutions
  with the subdivision *Chap-
  lains,* e.g. **United States.
  Army—Chaplains** [to be
  added as needed]
 BT **Clergy**
 NT **United States. Army—Chap-
  lains**
Character 155.2
 BT **Ethics**
  Personality
 NT **Human behavior**
 RT **Temperament**
Character assassination
 USE **Libel and slander**
Character education
 USE **Moral education**
Characters
 USE **Characters and characteristics
  in literature**
  and names of authors with the
  subdivision *Characters;* e.g.
  **Shakespeare, William, 1564-
  1616—Characters** [to be add-
  ed as needed]
**Characters and characteristics in litera-
  ture 809**
 UF Characters
  Fictional characters
  Fictitious characters
  Literary characters
 SA names of authors with the subdi-
  vision *Characters;* e.g.
  **Shakespeare, William, 1564-
  1616—Characters;** racial and
  ethnic groups and classes of
  persons in literature, e.g.
  **African Americans in litera-
  ture; Children in literature;**
  etc.; names of persons, families, and corporate bodies
  with the subdivision *In litera-*

ture, e.g. **Napoleon I, Em-
  peror of the French, 1769-
  1821—In literature;** and in-
  dividual literary characters es-
  tablished in the inverted form
  with the qualifier (Fictitious
  character), e.g. **Holmes, Sher-
  lock (Fictitious character)**
  [to be added as needed]
 BT **Literature**
 RT **Literature—Themes**
Charades 793.2
 BT **Amateur theater**
  Amusements
  Literary recreations
  Riddles
Charcoal 662
 BT **Fuel**
Charismata
 USE **Spiritual gifts**
Charismatic movement
 USE **Catholic charismatic movement**
  Pentecostalism
Charismatic renewal movement
 USE **Catholic charismatic movement**
  Pentecostalism
Charitable institutions
 USE **Charities**
  Institutional care
  Orphanages
Charities (May subdiv. geog.) **361.7**
 Use for materials on privately supported
 welfare activities. Materials on tax supported
 welfare activities are entered under **Public
 welfare.** Materials on the methods employed
 in welfare work, public or private, are entered
 under **Social work.** General materials on the
 various policies, programs, services, and facil-
 ities to meet basic human needs, such as
 health, education, and welfare, are entered un-
 der **Human services.**
 UF Charitable institutions
  Endowed charities
  Homes (Institutions)
  Institutions, Charitable and philanthropic
  Poor relief
  Social welfare
  Welfare agencies
  Welfare work
 SA names of appropriate corporate
  bodies with the subdivision
  Charities, e.g. **Catholic**

Charities—*Continued*

    Church—Charities; and names of wars with the subdivision *Civilian relief,* e.g. World War, 1939-1945—Civilian relief [to be added as needed]

BT Human services
      Social work

NT Catholic Church—Charities
      Child welfare
      Disaster relief
      Food relief
      Institutional care
      Medical charities
      Orphanages
      Social settlements
      World War, 1939-1945—Civilian relief

RT Charity organization
      Endowments
      Philanthropy
      Public welfare
      Volunteer work

Charities, Medical
  USE Medical charities

Charity   177
  BT Ethics
      Virtue
  RT Altruism
      Love—Religious aspects

Charity organization   361
  BT Associations
  RT Charities
      Philanthropy

Charlatans
  USE Impostors and imposture

Charms   133.4
  UF Spells
      Talismans
  BT Folklore
      Superstition

Charter flights
  USE Airlines—Chartering

Charter schools (May subdiv. geog.)   371.01

Use for materials on legislatively authorized, independent, and innovative public schools that operate under the authority of a charter.

  BT Schools

Charters
  UF Documents
  BT **History—Sources**
  NT **Magna Carta**
  RT **Archives**
      Manuscripts

Chartography
  USE **Maps**

Charts
  USE **Charts, diagrams, etc.**

Charts, diagrams, etc.   912
  UF Charts
  SA topics with the subdivision *Charts, diagrams, etc.,* for works consisting of charts or diagrams illustrating those topics, e.g. **Electric wiring—Charts, diagrams, etc.** [to be added as needed]
  RT **Maps**

Charts, Nautical
  USE **Nautical charts**

Chasidism
  USE **Hasidism**

Chastity   176

Use for materials on the virtue that moderates and regulates the sexual appetite in human beings. Materials on the renunciation of marriage for religious reasons are entered under **Celibacy**. Materials on abstinence from sexual activity are entered under **Sexual abstinence**.

  BT Sexual ethics
      Virtue
  RT Celibacy
      Sexual abstinence

Chat groups, Online
  USE **Online chat groups**

Chat rooms, Online
  USE **Online chat groups**

Chateaux
  USE **Castles**

Cheating (Education) (May subdiv. geog.)   371.26; 371.5
  UF Academic dishonesty
      Student cheating
      Student dishonesty
  BT Honesty

Cheating in sports
  USE **Sports—Corrupt practices**

Checkers   794.2
  UF Draughts
  BT Board games

Cheerleaders
  USE **Cheerleading**
Cheerleading   371.8; 791.6
  UF Cheerleaders
      Cheers and cheerleading
  BT **Student activities**
Cheers and cheerleading
  USE **Cheerleading**
Cheese   637; 641.3
  BT **Dairy products**
Cheese—Bacteriology
  USE **Cheese—Microbiology**
Cheese—Microbiology   637
  UF Cheese—Bacteriology
  BT **Microbiology**
Chemical analysis
  USE **Analytical chemistry**
Chemical apparatus   542
  UF Apparatus, Chemical
      Chemistry—Apparatus
  BT **Scientific apparatus and in-
       struments**
Chemical elements   546
  UF Elements, Chemical
  SA names of chemical elements [to
      be added as needed]
  BT **Chemistry**
  NT **Carbon**
      Gold
      Helium
      Hydrogen
      Iron
      Mercury
      Oxygen
      Radium
      Silver
      Sulphur
      Tin
      Uranium
      Zinc
  RT **Periodic law**
Chemical engineering (May subdiv. geog.)
      660
  UF Chemistry, Industrial
      Chemistry, Technical
  BT **Engineering**
  NT **Biotechnology**
      Fermentation
  RT **Industrial chemistry**
      Metallurgy

Chemical equations   540
  UF Equations, Chemical
  BT **Chemical reactions**
Chemical geology
  USE **Geochemistry**
Chemical industries
  USE **Chemical industry**
Chemical industry (May subdiv. geog.)
      338.4; 660
  Use for materials about industries that pro-
  duce chemicals or are based on chemical pro-
  cesses. General materials on chemicals,
  including their manufacture, are entered under
  Chemicals.
  UF Chemical industries
      Chemistry, Industrial
      Chemistry, Technical
  SA types of industries, e.g. **Plastics
       industry** [to be added as
       needed]
  BT **Industries**
  NT **Plastics industry**
  RT **Chemicals**
      Industrial chemistry
Chemical industry—Accidents   363.11
  BT **Industrial accidents**
Chemical industry—Employees   331.11
  UF Chemical workers
  BT **Employees**
Chemical industry—Employees—Diseases
      616.9
  UF Chemical workers' diseases
  BT **Occupational diseases**
Chemical industry—Employees—Pensions
      331.25
**Chemical industry—Employees—Salaries,
  wages, etc.** (May subdiv. geog.)
      331.2
  BT **Salaries, wages, etc.**
**Chemical industry—Employees—Supply
  and demand**   331.12
  BT **Supply and demand**
Chemical industry—Law and legislation
      (May subdiv. geog.)   343
  BT **Law**
      Legislation
Chemical industry—Waste disposal
      363.72; 628.4
  BT **Refuse and refuse disposal**
Chemical landfills
  USE **Hazardous waste sites**
Chemical pollution
  USE **Pollution**

Chemical reactions　541
　　UF　Reactions, Chemical
　　BT　Chemistry
　　NT　Chemical equations
Chemical societies
　　USE　Chemistry—Societies
Chemical technology
　　USE　Industrial chemistry
Chemical warfare　358; 623.4
　　UF　Gas warfare
　　　　Poisonous gases—War use
　　SA　names of wars with the subdivi-
　　　　sion *Chemical warfare* [to be
　　　　added as needed]
　　BT　Military art and science
　　　　War
　　NT　Incendiary weapons
　　　　World War, 1914-1918—Chem-
　　　　ical warfare
　　　　World War, 1939-1945—Chem-
　　　　ical warfare
Chemical workers
　　USE　Chemical industry—Employees
Chemical workers' diseases
　　USE　Chemical industry—Employ-
　　　　ees—Diseases
Chemicals　540; 661
　　Use for general materials on chemicals,
　　including their manufacture. Materials about
　　industries that produce chemicals or are based
　　on chemical processes are entered under
　　Chemical industry.
　　SA　types of chemicals, e.g. **Acids;**
　　　　Agricultural chemicals; etc.;
　　　　and names of individual
　　　　chemicals [to be added as
　　　　needed]
　　NT　Acids
　　　　Agricultural chemicals
　　　　Alcohol
　　　　Carbolic acid
　　　　Deuterium oxide
　　　　Nitrates
　　　　Organic compounds
　　　　Petrochemicals
　　RT　Chemical industry
　　　　Industrial chemistry
Chemicals—Toxicology
　　USE　Toxicology
Chemistry　540
　　BT　Physical sciences
　　　　Science

　　NT　Acids
　　　　Agricultural chemistry
　　　　Alchemy
　　　　Analytical chemistry
　　　　Bases (Chemistry)
　　　　Biochemistry
　　　　Botanical chemistry
　　　　Chemical elements
　　　　Chemical reactions
　　　　Color
　　　　Combustion
　　　　Explosives
　　　　Fermentation
　　　　Fire
　　　　Geochemistry
　　　　Industrial chemistry
　　　　Inorganic chemistry
　　　　Microchemistry
　　　　Organic chemistry
　　　　Pharmaceutical chemistry
　　　　Pharmacy
　　　　Photographic chemistry
　　　　Physical chemistry
　　　　Space chemistry
　　　　Spectrum analysis
Chemistry, Analytic
　　USE　Analytical chemistry
Chemistry—Apparatus
　　USE　Chemical apparatus
Chemistry, Diagnostic
　　USE　Clinical chemistry
Chemistry—Dictionaries　540.3
　　BT　Encyclopedias and dictionaries
Chemistry—Experiments　540; 542
Chemistry, Industrial
　　USE　Chemical engineering
　　　　Chemical industry
Chemistry, Inorganic
　　USE　Inorganic chemistry
Chemistry—Laboratory manuals
　　540.78
Chemistry, Medical
　　USE　Clinical chemistry
Chemistry of food
　　USE　Food—Analysis
　　　　Food—Composition
Chemistry, Organic
　　USE　Organic chemistry
Chemistry, Physical and theoretical
　　USE　Physical chemistry

Chemistry—Problems, exercises, etc.
540.76
Chemistry—Societies   540.6
    UF   Chemical societies
    BT   **Societies**
Chemistry, Synthetic
    USE   **Organic compounds—Synthesis**
Chemistry, Technical
    USE   **Chemical engineering**
            Chemical industry
            Industrial chemistry
Chemistry, Textile
    USE   **Textile chemistry**
Chemists (May subdiv. geog.)   540.92;
    920
    BT   **Scientists**
Chemists' shops
    USE   **Drugstores**
Chemotherapy
    USE   **Cancer—Chemotherapy**
            Drug therapy
Chess   794.1
    BT   **Board games**
Chicago (Ill.)   917.73; 977.3
    The subdivisions under **Chicago (Ill.)** may
    be used under the name of any city. The sub-
    divisions under **United States** may be further
    consulted as a guide for formulating other
    headings as needed.
Chicago (Ill.)—Antiquities   977.3
    BT   **Antiquities**
Chicago (Ill.)—Bibliography   015.773;
    016.9773
Chicago (Ill.)—Bio-bibliography   012
Chicago (Ill.)—Biography   920.0773
    BT   **Biography**
Chicago (Ill.)—Biography—Portraits
    920.0773
Chicago (Ill.)—Boundaries   977.3
    BT   **Boundaries**
Chicago (Ill.)—Bridges
    USE   **Bridges—Chicago (Ill.)**
Chicago (Ill.)—Census   317.73
    BT   **Census**
Chicago (Ill.)—City planning
    USE   **City planning—Chicago (Ill.)**
Chicago (Ill.)—Civil defense
    USE   **Civil defense—Chicago (Ill.)**
Chicago (Ill.)—Climate   551.69773
    BT   **Climate**
Chicago (Ill.)—Commerce   381
    BT   **Commerce**

Chicago (Ill.)—Description
    USE   **Chicago (Ill.)—Description and**
            travel
Chicago (Ill.)—Description and travel
    917.73
    UF   Chicago (Ill.)—Description *[For-*
            mer heading]
Chicago (Ill.)—Description and travel—
    Guidebooks
    USE   **Chicago (Ill.)—Guidebooks**
Chicago (Ill.)—Description and travel—
    Views
    USE   **Chicago (Ill.)—Pictorial works**
Chicago (Ill.)—Directories   917.73
    Use for lists of names and addresses. Lists
    of names without addresses are entered under
    Chicago (Ill.)—Registers.
    BT   **Directories**
    NT   **Chicago (Ill.)—Telephone di-**
            rectories
    RT   **Chicago (Ill.)—Registers**
Chicago (Ill.)—Directories—Telephone
    USE   **Chicago (Ill.)—Telephone di-**
            rectories
Chicago (Ill.)—Economic conditions
    330.9773
    BT   **Economic conditions**
Chicago (Ill.)—Employees
    USE   **Chicago (Ill.)—Officials and**
            employees
Chicago (Ill.)—Government
    USE   **Chicago (Ill.)—Politics and**
            government
Chicago (Ill.)—Government employees
    USE   **Chicago (Ill.)—Officials and**
            employees
Chicago (Ill.)—Government publications
    USE   **Government publications—Chi-**
            cago (Ill.)
Chicago (Ill.)—Guidebooks   917.73
    UF   Chicago (Ill.)—Description and
            travel—Guidebooks
Chicago (Ill.)—Historic buildings
    USE   **Historic buildings—Chicago**
            (Ill.)
Chicago (Ill.)—History   977.3
Chicago (Ill.)—History—Societies
    977.3006
    BT   **History—Societies**
Chicago (Ill.)—Industries
    USE   **Industries—Chicago (Ill.)**

Chicago (Ill.)—Intellectual life   977.3
   BT   Intellectual life
Chicago (Ill.)—Manufactures
   USE   Manufactures—Chicago (Ill.)
Chicago (Ill.)—Maps   912.773
   BT   Maps
Chicago (Ill.)—Moral conditions   977.3
   BT   Moral conditions
Chicago (Ill.)—Occupations
   USE   Occupations—Chicago (Ill.)
Chicago (Ill.)—Officials and employees
   352.1773
   UF   Chicago (Ill.)—Employees
        Chicago (Ill.)—Government em-
        ployees
Chicago (Ill.)—Pictorial works   917.73
   UF   Chicago (Ill.)—Description and
        travel—Views
Chicago (Ill.)—Politics and government
   977.3
   UF   Chicago (Ill.)—Government
   BT   Municipal government
        Politics
Chicago (Ill.)—Popular culture
   USE   Popular culture—Chicago (Ill.)
Chicago (Ill.)—Population   304.609773
   BT   Population
Chicago (Ill.)—Public buildings
   USE   Public buildings—Chicago (Ill.)
Chicago (Ill.)—Public works
   USE   Public works—Chicago (Ill.)
Chicago (Ill.)—Race relations
   305.8009773
   BT   Race relations
Chicago (Ill.)—Registers   917.73
      Use for lists of names without addresses.
   Lists of names that include addresses are en-
   tered under Chicago (Ill.)—Directories.
   RT   Chicago (Ill.)—Directories
Chicago (Ill.)—Social conditions   977.3
   BT   Social conditions
Chicago (Ill.)—Social life and customs
   977.3
   BT   Manners and customs
Chicago (Ill.)—Social policy
   USE   Social policy—Chicago (Ill.)
Chicago (Ill.)—Statistics   317.73
   BT   Statistics
Chicago (Ill.)—Streets
   USE   Streets—Chicago (Ill.)
Chicago (Ill.)—Suburbs and environs
   USE   Chicago Suburban Area (Ill.)

Chicago (Ill.)—Telephone directories
   917.73
   UF   Chicago (Ill.)—Directories—
        Telephone
   BT   Chicago (Ill.)—Directories
Chicago (Ill.)—Urban renewal
   USE   Urban renewal—Chicago (Ill.)
Chicago Metropolitan Area (Ill.)   977.3
   RT   Chicago Suburban Area (Ill.)
Chicago Metropolitan Area (Ill.)—Poli-
   tics and government   977.3
   BT   Metropolitan government
Chicago Suburban Area (Ill.)   977.3
   UF   Chicago (Ill.)—Suburbs and en-
        virons
   RT   Chicago Metropolitan Area
        (Ill.)
Chicanas
   USE   Mexican American women
Chicanery
   USE   Deception
Chicano literature (English)
   USE   American literature—Mexican
        American authors
Chicanos
   USE   Mexican Americans
Chicken pox
   USE   Chickenpox
Chickenpox   616.9
   UF   Chicken pox
   BT   Diseases
        Viruses
Chief justices
   USE   Judges
Child abuse (May subdiv. geog.)
   305.23086; 362.76; 364.15
   UF   Abuse of children
        Abused children
        Child neglect
        Children—Abuse
        Cruelty to children
   BT   Child welfare
        Domestic violence
        Parent-child relationship
   NT   Child sexual abuse
   RT   Adult child abuse victims
Child abuse survivors
   USE   Adult child abuse victims

Child-adult relationship   305.23; 362.7;
   649
   UF   Adults and children
          Children and adults
   BT   **Children**
   NT   **Child rearing**
          Children and strangers
          Conflict of generations
          Parent-child relationship
          Teacher-student relationship
Child and father
   USE   **Father-child relationship**
Child and mother
   USE   **Mother-child relationship**
Child and parent
   USE   **Parent-child relationship**
Child artists   704; 709.2; 920
   Use for materials on children as artists and
   on works of art by children.
   UF   Children as artists
   BT   **Artists**
          Gifted children
   NT   **Finger painting**
Child authors   809; 920
   Use for materials on children as authors and
   discussions of literary works written by chil-
   dren. Individual literary works and collections
   of literary works written by children are en-
   tered under the form heading **Children's
   writings.**
   UF   Children as authors
   BT   **Authors**
          Gifted children
   RT   **Children's writings**
Child behavior
   USE   **Child psychology**
          Children—Conduct of life
          **Etiquette for children and
             teenagers**
Child birth
   USE   **Childbirth**
Child care (May subdiv. geog.)   **649**
   UF   Care of children
          Children—Care
   NT   **Babysitting**
          Child rearing
          Day care centers
          Infants—Care
          Nannies
Child care centers
   USE   **Day care centers**

Child custody   306.89; 346.01; 362.7
   UF   Children—Custody
          Custody of children
          Joint custody of children
          Parental custody
          Shared custody
   BT   **Divorce mediation**
          Parent-child relationship
   NT   **Parental kidnapping**
   RT   **Visitation rights (Domestic re-
             lations)**
Child death
   USE   **Children—Death**
Child development   155.4; 305.231;
   612.6
   UF   Child study
          Children—Development
   BT   **Children**
   NT   **Children—Growth**
   RT   **Child psychology**
          Child rearing
Child labor (May subdiv. geog.)   331.3
   UF   Children—Employment
          Employment of children
          Working children
   BT   **Age and employment**
          Child welfare
          Labor
          Social problems
Child labor—United States   331.3
Child molesting
   USE   **Child sexual abuse**
Child mortality
   USE   **Children—Mortality**
Child neglect
   USE   **Child abuse**
Child placing
   USE   **Adoption**
          Foster home care
Child prostitution
   USE   **Juvenile prostitution**
Child psychiatry   616.89; 618.92
   Use for materials on the clinical and thera-
   peutic aspects of mental disorders in children.
   Materials on children suffering from mental or
   emotional illnesses are entered under **Emo-
   tionally distrubed children.**
   UF   Children—Mental health
          Pediatric psychiatry
   BT   **Psychiatry**
   NT   **Autism**
          Mentally handicapped children

128

Child psychiatry—*Continued*
RT Child psychology
Emotionally disturbed children
Child psychology 155.4
UF Behavior of children
Child behavior
Child study
Children—Psychology
BT Psychology
NT Cognitive styles in children
Emotions in children
Fear in children
Imaginary playmates
Intelligence tests
Moral development
Psychology of learning
Separation anxiety in children
Sibling rivalry
RT Child development
Child psychiatry
Child rearing
Educational psychology
Child raising
USE Child rearing
Child rearing 392.1; 649
Use for materials on the principles and techniques of rearing children. Materials on the psychological and social interaction between parents and their minor children are entered under **Parent-child relationship.** Materials on the skills, attributes, and attitudes needed for parenthood are entered under **Parenting.**
UF Child raising
Children—Management
Children—Training
Discipline of children
Training of children
BT Child-adult relationship
Child care
Parent-child relationship
NT Children's allowances
Socialization
Toilet training
RT Child development
Child psychology
Parenting
Child sex abuse
USE Child sexual abuse
Child sexual abuse (May subdiv. geog.)
362.76; 364.15
UF Child molesting
Child sex abuse
Children—Molesting

Molesting of children
Sexual abuse
Sexually abused children
BT Child abuse
Incest
Sex crimes
RT Adult child sexual abuse victims
Child snatching by parents
USE Parental kidnapping
Child study
USE Child development
Child psychology
Child support 346.01
UF Support of children
BT Child welfare
Desertion and nonsupport
Divorce mediation
Child welfare (May subdiv. geog.)
362.7
Use for materials on the aid, support, and protection of children, by the state or by private welfare organizations.
UF Aid to dependent children
Children—Charities, protection, etc.
Mothers' pensions
Protection of children
BT Charities
Public welfare
Social work
NT Abandoned children
Child abuse
Child labor
Child support
Children—Institutional care
Day care centers
Foster home care
RT Children's hospitals
Juvenile delinquency
Orphanages
Childbirth (May subdiv. geog.) 612.6;
618.2
UF Birth
Birth customs
Child birth
Labor (Childbirth)
Obstetrics
NT Midwives
Multiple birth
Natural childbirth
RT Pregnancy

Childhood diseases
USE **Children—Diseases**
Childlessness   306.85
    BT   **Children**
          Family size
    RT   **Birth control**
          Human fertility
          Infertility
Children (May subdiv. geog.)   **305.23**

    Use for materials on people from birth through age twelve. Materials limited to the first two years of a child's life are entered under **Infants.**

    UF   Preschool children
    SA   children of particular racial or ethnic groups, e.g. **African American children;** children and other subjects, e.g. **Children and war;** and names of wars with the subdivision *Children,* e.g. **World War, 1939-1945—Children** [to be added as needed]
    BT   **Age**
          Family
    NT   **Abandoned children**
          Adopted children
          Advertising and children
          African American children
          Birth order
          Black children
          Boys
          Child-adult relationship
          Child development
          Childlessness
          Children and war
          Children of alcoholics
          Children of drug addicts
          Children of immigrants
          Computers and children
          Exceptional children
          Father-child relationship
          Foster children
          Girls
          Handicapped children
          Infants
          Internet and children
          Missing children
          Mother-child relationship
          Motion pictures and children
          Native American children
          Only child

          Orphans
          Parent-child relationship
          Runaway children
          School children
          Television and children
Children, Abnormal
    USE   **Handicapped children**
Children—Abuse
    USE   **Child abuse**
Children—Adoption
    USE   **Adoption**
Children and adults
    USE   **Child-adult relationship**
Children and advertising
    USE   **Advertising and children**
Children and death   155.9

    Use for materials on children's experiences with, conceptions of, and reactions to death. Materials on the death of children are entered under **Children—Death.** Materials on children's death rates and causes are entered under **Children—Mortality.**

    UF   Death and children
    BT   **Death**
Children and motion pictures
    USE   **Motion pictures and children**
Children and strangers   362.7
    UF   Infants and strangers
          Strangers and children
    BT   **Child-adult relationship**
Children and television
    USE   **Television and children**
Children and the Internet
    USE   **Internet and children**
Children and war (May subdiv. geog.)   **305.23**
    UF   War and children
    SA   names of particular wars with the subdivision *Children,* e.g. **World War, 1939-1945—Children** [to be added as needed]
    BT   **Children**
          War
    NT   **World War, 1939-1945—Children**
Children as artists
    USE   **Child artists**
Children as authors
    USE   **Child authors**
Children as consumers
    USE   **Young consumers**

Children, Black
  USE **Black children**
**Children—Books and reading   011.62;
      028.5**
    Use for materials on the reading interests of
  children and lists of books for children. Collections or materials about literature published
  for children are entered under **Children's lit-
  erature.** Individual literary works and collec-
  tions of literary works written by children are
  entered under **Children's writings.** Materials
  about works written by children and materials
  about children as authors are entered under
  Child authors.
  UF   Books and reading for children
       Children's reading
       Reading interests of children
  BT   **Books and reading**
Children—Care
  USE **Child care**
Children—Charities, protection, etc.
  USE **Child welfare**
Children—Civil rights   323.3; 342
  BT   **Civil rights**
Children—Clothing
  USE **Children's clothing**
Children—Conduct of life   173
  UF   Behavior of children
       Child behavior
  BT   **Conduct of life**
  NT   **Etiquette for children and
       teenagers**
Children—Costume
  USE **Children's costumes**
Children, Crippled
  USE **Physically handicapped chil-
       dren**
Children—Custody
  USE **Child custody**
Children—Day care
  USE **Day care centers**
Children—Death   306.9
    Use for materials on the death of children.
  Materials on children's experiences with, con-
  ceptions of, and reactions to death are entered
  under **Children and death.** Materials on chil-
  dren's death rates and causes are entered un-
  der **Children—Mortality.**
  UF   Child death
  BT   **Death**
  RT   **Terminally ill children**
Children—Death—Causes
  USE **Children—Mortality**
Children—Death rate
  USE **Children—Mortality**

Children—Defense
  USE **Self-defense for children**
Children—Dental care   617.6
Children—Development
  USE **Child development**
Children—Diseases   618.92
  UF   Childhood diseases
       Children's diseases
       Diseases of children
       Medicine, Pediatric
       Pediatrics
  SA   types of diseases, e.g.
       Chickenpox [to be added as
       needed]
  BT   **Diseases**
  RT   **Children—Health and hygiene**
Children—Education
  USE **Elementary education**
       Preschool education
Children—Employment
  USE **Child labor**
Children—Etiquette
  USE **Etiquette for children and
       teenagers**
Children—Food
  USE **Children—Nutrition**
Children, Gifted
  USE **Gifted children**
Children—Growth   155.4; 612.6
  BT   **Child development**
Children—Health and hygiene (May
    subdiv. geog.)   613
  UF   Children—Hygiene
       Pediatrics
  BT   **Health**
       Hygiene
  NT   **Children—Nutrition**
       Children—Physical fitness
       School hygiene
  RT   **Children—Diseases**
       Children's hospitals
       Health education
Children—Hospitals
  USE **Children's hospitals**
Children—Hygiene
  USE **Children—Health and hygiene**
Children, Hyperactive
  USE **Hyperactive children**
Children in art   704.9
    Use for materials on children depicted in
  works of art. Materials on children as artists
  are entered under **Child artists.**

Children in art—*Continued*

    BT   Art—Themes

Children in literature   **809**

    Use for materials on the theme of children in works of literature. Individual literary works or collections of literary works written by children are entered under the form heading **Children's writings**. Materials about children as authors and about works written by children are entered under **Child authors**.

    BT   Literature—Themes

Children—Institutional care (May subdiv. geog.)   **362.73**

    UF   Boys' towns

          Children's homes

    BT   Child welfare

          Institutional care

    NT   Day care centers

          Orphanages

          Reformatories

    RT   Foster home care

Children—Language   **155.4**

    BT   Language and languages

Children—Management

    USE   Child rearing

Children—Medical examinations   **616.07**

    UF   Medical inspection in schools

          School children—Medical examinations

Children—Mental health

    USE   Child psychiatry

Children—Molesting

    USE   Child sexual abuse

Children—Mortality (May subdiv. geog.)   **304.6**

    Use for material on children's death rates and causes. Material on children's experiences with, conceptions of, and reactions to death are entered under **Children and death**. Materials on the death of children are entered under **Children—Death**.

    UF   Child mortality

          Children—Death—Causes

          Children—Death rate

    BT   Mortality

Children—Nutrition   **613.2083; 641.1083; 649**

    UF   Children—Food

          Children's food

    BT   Children—Health and hygiene

          Nutrition

    NT   School children—Food

Children of alcoholics   **362.292**

    UF   Alcoholic parents

          COAs

    BT   Children

    NT   Adult children of alcoholics

    RT   Alcoholics

Children of divorced parents   **306.874; 646.7**

    BT   Divorce

          Parent-child relationship

    RT   Part-time parenting

Children of drug addicts   **362.29**

    UF   Children of narcotic addicts

          Cocaine babies

          Crack babies

    BT   Children

          Drug addicts

Children of immigrants   **305.23**

    UF   First generation children

    BT   Children

          Immigration and emigration

Children of narcotic addicts

    USE   Children of drug addicts

Children of single fathers

    USE   Children of single parents

Children of single mothers

    USE   Children of single parents

Children of single parents   **306.874**

    UF   Children of single fathers

          Children of single mothers

          Single parents' children

    BT   Single parents

Children of working parents   **306.874; 362.7**

    UF   Working parents' children

    BT   Parent-child relationship

    NT   Latchkey children

Children—Physical fitness   **613.7**

    BT   Children—Health and hygiene

          Physical fitness

Children—Placing out

    USE   Adoption

          Foster home care

Children—Psychology

    USE   Child psychology

Children, Retarded

    USE   Mentally handicapped children

Children—Self-defense

    USE   Self-defense for children

Children—Socialization

    USE   Socialization

Children—Surgery   **617**

    UF   Pediatric surgery

    BT   Surgery

Children—Training
USE **Child rearing**
Children—United States 305.230973
Children's allowances 332.024; 649
UF Allowances, Children's
BT **Child rearing**
Money
Personal finance
RT **Money-making projects for children**
Children's art (May subdiv. geog.)
704.083
BT **Art**
Children's books
USE **Children's literature**
Children's clothing 391; 646.4
Use for materials on children's clothing that is worn from day to day, including historical materials. Works on children's costumes for fancy dress of theatricals are entered under **Children's costumes.**
UF Children—Clothing
BT **Clothing and dress**
NT **Infants' clothing**
RT **Children's costumes**
Children's costumes 646.4; 792
Use for materials on children's costumes for fancy dress or theatricals. Materials on children's clothing that is worn from day to day are entered under **Children's clothing.**
UF Children—Costume
BT **Costume**
RT **Children's clothing**
Children's courts
USE **Juvenile courts**
Children's day care centers
USE **Day care centers**
Children's diseases
USE **Children—Diseases**
Children's food
USE **Children—Nutrition**
Children's homes
USE **Children—Institutional care**
Children's hospitals 362.11
UF Children—Hospitals
BT **Hospitals**
RT **Child welfare**
Children—Health and hygiene
Children's libraries 027.62
UF Libraries and children
Library services to children
BT **Libraries**
RT **Libraries and schools**

Children's literature 808.8
Use for collections or materials about literature published for children. Materials on the reading interests of children and lists of books for children are entered under **Children—Books and reading.** Individual literary works and collections of literary works written by children are entered under **Children's writings.** Materials about works written by children and materials about children as authors are entered under **Child authors.**
UF Books for children
Children's books
Juvenile literature
SA subjects and personal, corporate, and place names with the subdivision *Juvenile literature,* for non-fiction materials e.g. **Computers—Juvenile literature;** and with the subdivisions *Juvenile fiction; Juvenile poetry;* and *Juvenile drama;* for materials in those forms, e.g. **Christmas—Juvenile fiction; Christmas—Juvenile poetry; Christmas—Juvenile drama;** etc. [to be added as needed]
BT **Literature**
NT **Big books**
Caldecott Medal
Children's plays
Children's poetry
Children's stories
Coretta Scott King Award
Easy reading materials
Fairy tales
Newbery Medal
Picture books for children
Plot-your-own stories
Reading materials
Storytelling
Children's literature—Book reviews
808.8
Children's literature—History and criticism 809
Children's moneymaking projects
USE **Money-making projects for children**
Children's parties 395.3; 793.2
BT **Amusements**
Entertaining
Parties

Children's playhouses 690

    BT   **Buildings**

Children's plays 808.82

    May be used for individual works, collections, or materials about plays for children. Materials about plays for production in colleges and schools are entered under **College and school drama.** Individual works and collections of plays written by children are entered under **Children's writings.** Materials about plays written by children are entered under **Child authors.**

    UF   Plays for children

          School plays

    SA   subjects and personal, corporate, and place names with the subdivision *Juvenile drama,* e.g. **Christmas—Juvenile drama** [to be added as needed]

    BT   **Amateur theater**

          Children's literature

          Drama

          Theater

Children's poetry 808.81

    Use for individual poems, collections, or materials about poetry written for children. Individual works and collections of poetry written by children are entered under **Children's writings.** Materials about poetry written by children are entered under **Child authors.**

    UF   Poetry for children

    SA   subjects and personal, corporate, and place names with the subdivision *Juvenile poetry;* e.g. **Christmas—Juvenile poetry** [to be added as needed]

    BT   **Children's literature**

          Poetry

    NT   **Children's songs**

          Lullabies

          Nonsense verses

          Nursery rhymes

          Tongue twisters

Children's reading

    USE   **Children—Books and reading**

           Reading

Children's secrets 155.4

    BT   **Secrecy**

Children's songs 782.42

    Use for collections of songs that contain both words and music, and for materials about songs for children. Collections of songs without the music are entered under **Children's poetry.**

    UF   Songs for children

    BT   **Children's poetry**

          School songbooks

          Songs

    NT   **Lullabies**

          Nursery rhymes

Children's stories 808.3; 808.83

    Use for individual stories and collections of stories written for children. Individual works and collections of stories written by children are entered under **Children's writings.** Materials about stories written by children are entered under **Child authors.**

    UF   Fiction for children

          Stories for children

    SA   subjects and personal, corporate, and place names with the subdivision *Juvenile fiction,* e.g. **Christmas—Juvenile fiction** [to be added as needed]

    BT   **Children's literature**

          Fiction

Children's writings 808.8

    Use for individual literary works or collections of literary works written by children. Materials on children as authors and discussions of literary works written by children are entered under **Child authors.** Collections of works published for children are entered under **Children's literature.**

    UF   School prose

          School verse

    RT   **Child authors**

          College and school journalism

Chimes

    USE   **Bells**

Chimneys 697; 721

    UF   Smoke stacks

    BT   **Architecture—Details**

          Buildings

    RT   **Fireplaces**

China 951

    Use as a heading or as a geographic subdivision for materials dealing with mainland China, regardless of time period, or with the People's Republic of China, or for comprehensive materials on China including Taiwan. Materials dealing with the island of Taiwan, regardless of time period, or with the post-1948 Republic of China are entered under **Taiwan.** May be subdivided like United States except for *History.*

    UF   China (People's Republic of China)

          People's Republic of China

China—History 951

China—History—1912-1949 951.04

China—History—1949- 951.05
China—History—1949-1976 951.05
China—History—1976- 951.05
China—History—1989, Tiananmen Square
    Incident
  USE   **Tiananmen Square Incident,**
        Beijing (China), 1989
China painting   738.1
  UF   Porcelain painting
  BT   **Decoration and ornament**
       Painting
       Porcelain
China (People's Republic of China)
  USE   **China**
China (Porcelain)
  USE   **Porcelain**
China (Republic)
  USE   **Taiwan**
Chinaware
  USE   **Porcelain**
Chinese Americans (May subdiv. geog.)
    305.895; 973
Chinese satellite countries
  USE   **Communist countries**
Chipmunks   599.36
  BT   **Mammals**
       Squirrels
Chiropody
  USE   **Podiatry**
Chiropractic   615.5
  BT   **Alternative medicine**
       Massage
  RT   **Naturopathy**
       Osteopathic medicine
Chivalry   394
  BT   **Manners and customs**
  NT   **Medieval tournaments**
  RT   **Crusades**
       Feudalism
       Heraldry
       Knights and knighthood
       Medieval civilization
       Romances
Chivalry—Romances
  USE   **Romances**
Chocolate   641.3
  BT   **Food**
  RT   **Cocoa**
       Desserts
Choice, Freedom of
  USE   **Free will and determinism**

Choice of books
  USE   **Best books**
       Book selection
       Books and reading
Choice of college
  USE   **College choice**
Choice of profession, occupation, vocation,
    etc.
  USE   **Vocational guidance**
Choice of school
  USE   **School choice**
Choice (Psychology)   153.8
  BT   **Psychology**
  RT   **Decision making**
Choirs (Music)   782.5
  BT   **Church music**
  RT   **Choral conducting**
       Choral music
       Choral societies
       Singing
Cholesterol content of food
  USE   **Food—Cholesterol content**
Choose-your-own story plots
  USE   **Plot-your-own stories**
Choral conducting   782.5
  UF   Conducting, Choral
  BT   **Conducting**
  RT   **Choirs (Music)**
       Choral music
       Conductors (Music)
Choral music   782.5
  UF   Music, Choral
  BT   **Church music**
       Vocal music
  NT   **Cantatas**
  RT   **Choirs (Music)**
       Choral conducting
       Choral societies
Choral societies   782.506
  UF   Singing societies
  BT   **Societies**
  RT   **Choirs (Music)**
       Choral music
Choral speaking   808.5
  UF   Speaking choirs
       Unison speaking
  BT   **Drama**
       Recitations
Christ
  USE   **Jesus Christ**

Christening
USE **Baptism**
Christian antiquities (May subdiv. geog.)
225.9; 270; 930.1
UF   Christian archeology
Church antiquities
Ecclesiastical antiquities
BT   **Antiquities**
Bible—Antiquities
NT   **Catacombs**
RT   **Christian art**
Christian archeology
USE   **Christian antiquities**
Christian art (May subdiv. geog.)   **246;**
704.9
UF   Christian art and symbolism
Ecclesiastical art
BT   **Art**
Religious art
NT   **Icons (Religion)**
Jesus Christ—Art
Mary, Blessed Virgin, Saint—
Art
RT   **Christian antiquities**
Christian symbolism
Gothic art
Christian art and symbolism
USE   **Christian art**
Christian symbolism
Christian biography   **270.092; 920**
UF   Christianity—Biography
Christians—Biography
Ecclesiastical biography
BT   **Biography**
Religious biography
NT   **Fathers of the church**
Christian civilization   **270; 909**
UF   Civilization, Christian
BT   **Christianity**
Civilization
Christian denominations
USE   **Christian sects**
Christian devotional calendars
USE   **Devotional calendars**
Christian doctrinal theology
USE   **Christianity—Doctrines**
Christian doctrine
USE   **Christianity—Doctrines**
Christian education (May subdiv. geog.)
268
Use for materials on the instruction of
Christian religion in schools and private life.

General materials on the instruction of religion in schools and private life are entered
under **Religious education.** Materials on the
relation of the church to education and materi-
als on the history of the part that the church
has taken in secular education are entered un-
der **Church and education.** Materials on
church supported and controlled elementary
and secondary schools are entered under
Church schools.
UF   Education, Christian
BT   **Religious education**
NT   **Bible—Study and teaching**
RT   **Church and education**
Christian ethics   **241**
UF   Christian moral theology
Moral theology, Christian
BT   **Ethics**
NT   **Conscience**
RT   **Christian life**
Christian fasts and feasts
USE   **Christian holidays**
Christian fiction   **808.83**
Use for individual works, collections, or
materials about fiction that promotes Christian
teachings or exemplifies a Christian way of
life.
BT   **Fiction**
Religious fiction
Christian fundamentalism   **230; 270.8**
Use for materials on the modern conserva-
tive movement in Protestantism emphasizing
literal interpretation of the Bible, as opposed
to religious liberalism, modernism, or evolu-
tionism.
UF   Fundamentalism
Modernist-fundamentalist contro-
versy
BT   **Christianity—Doctrines**
Religious fundamentalism
RT   **Modernism (Theology)**
Christian heresies (May subdiv. geog.)
273
UF   Heresies, Christian
BT   **Doctrinal theology**
Heresy
Christian holidays   **263; 394.266**
UF   Christian fasts and feasts
Christian holy days
Fasts and feasts—Christianity
SA   names of Christian holidays, e.g.
Christmas [to be added as
needed]
BT   **Church year**
Religious holidays

Christian holidays—*Continued*
  NT   **Christmas**
       Easter
       Good Friday
Christian holy days
  USE **Christian holidays**
Christian-Jewish relations
  USE **Christianity—Relations—Judaism**
        Judaism—Relations—Christianity
Christian life   248.4
  UF Religious life (Christian)
  BT **Religious life**
  RT **Christian ethics**
Christian life—Sermons   252
  BT **Sermons**
Christian literature   230
  BT **Religious literature**
  NT **Catholic literature**
       Early Christian literature
       Papal encyclicals
       Sermons
Christian literature—30-600, Early
  USE **Early Christian literature**
Christian literature, Early
  USE **Early Christian literature**
Christian ministry   253
  BT **Ministry**
Christian missionaries   266.0092; 920
  UF Missionaries, Christian
  RT **Christian missions**
Christian missions (May subdiv. geog.)   266
  UF Foreign missions, Christian
       Home missions, Christian
       Missions, Christian
  SA names of Christian churches, denominations, religious orders, etc., with the subdivision *Missions,* e.g. **Catholic Church—Missions;** and names of peoples evangelized with the subdivision *Christian missions,* e.g. **Native Americans—Christian missions** [to be added as needed]
  BT **Christianity**
       Church history
       Church work
  NT **Catholic Church—Missions**
       Native Americans—Christian missions
       Salvation Army
  RT **Christian missionaries**
       Evangelistic work
Christian moral theology
  USE **Christian ethics**
Christian names
  USE **Personal names**
Christian philosophy   190; 230.01
    Use for materials on philosophy as practiced by Christian philosophers or on the nature, origins, or validity of Christian beliefs from a philosophical point of view.
  UF Christianity—Philosophy
  BT **Philosophy**
Christian saints   270.092; 920
  BT **Saints**
  NT **Apostles**
Christian Science   289.5
  UF Church of Christ, Scientist
  BT **Christian sects**
  RT **Spiritual healing**
Christian sects (May subdiv. geog.)   280
  UF Christian denominations
       Church denominations
       Denominations, Christian
  SA names of Christian sects, e.g. **Presbyterian Church** [to be added as needed]
  BT **Christianity**
       Church history
       Sects
  NT **Amish**
       Baptists
       Catholic Church
       Christian Science
       Christian union
       Church of England
       Church of Jesus Christ of Latter-day Saints
       Community churches
       Congregationalism
       Eastern churches
       Ecumenical movement
       Episcopal Church
       Greek Orthodox Church
       Huguenots
       Interdenominational cooperation
       Mennonites

Christian sects—*Continued*
>> Moravians
>> Non-institutional churches
>> Orthodox Eastern Church
>> Pentecostal churches
>> Presbyterian Church
>> Protestant churches
>> Puritans
>> Russian Orthodox Church
>> Salvation Army
>> Shakers
>> Society of Friends
>> Unitarianism

Christian sects—Government
>> USE **Church polity**

Christian sociology (May subdiv. geog.)
>> **261**

>> Use for materials on social theory from a Christian point of view. Materials on religious sociology in general are entered under **Religion and sociology**. Materials on the practical treatment of social problems from the point of view of the church are entered under **Church and social problems**.

>> UF Sociology, Christian
>> BT **Religion and sociology**
>> **Sociology**
>> RT **Christianity and economics**
>> **Church and social problems**

Christian symbolism (May subdiv. geog.)
>> **246; 704.9**

>> UF Christian art and symbolism
>> BT **Symbolism**
>> RT **Christian art**

Christian union (May subdiv. geog.)
>> **280**

>> Use for materials on prospective and actual mergers within and across denominational lines. Materials on unity as one of the marks of the church are entered under **Church—Unity**. Materials on a movement originating in the twentieth century aimed at promoting church cooperation and unity are entered under **Ecumenical movement**. Materials on religious activities planned and conducted cooperatively by two or more Christian sects are entered under **Interdenominational cooperation**.

>> UF Christian unity
>> Christianity—Union between churches
>> Ecumenism
>> BT **Christian sects**
>> **Church**
>> RT **Ecumenical movement**

Christian unity
>> USE **Christian union**
>> **Church—Unity**
>> **Ecumenical movement**
>> **Interdenominational cooperation**

Christian year
>> USE **Church year**

Christianity (May subdiv. geog.) **230**

>> SA names of Christian churches and sects, e.g. **Catholic Church; Huguenots;** etc.; and Christianity and other subjects, e.g. **Christianity and economics** [to be added as needed]

>> BT **Religions**
>> NT **Atonement—Christianity**
>> **Catholic Church**
>> **Christian civilization**
>> **Christian missions**
>> **Christian sects**
>> **Christianity and economics**
>> **Councils and synods**
>> **Counter-Reformation**
>> **Eastern churches**
>> **Pentecostalism**
>> **Protestantism**
>> **Reformation**
>> RT **Christians**
>> **Church**
>> **Jesus Christ**

Christianity and economics **261.8**
>> UF Economics and Christianity
>> BT **Christianity**
>> **Economics**
>> RT **Christian sociology**
>> **Church and labor**

Christianity and evolution
>> USE **Creationism**

Christianity and other religions **261.2**

>> Use for materials on the relations between Christianity and several other religions. Materials on the relations between Christianity and one other religion are entered under **Christianity** subdivided by *Relations* further subdivided by the other religion, and also under the other religion subdivided by *Relations—Christianity*, e.g. **Christianity—Relations—Judaism** and **Judaism—Relations—Christianity**. The same pattern is followed for sects and denominations.

Christianity and other religions—*Continued*

UF Comparative religion
BT **Religions**
NT **Christianity—Relations—Judaism**
    Judaism—Relations—Christianity
    Paganism

Christianity and other religions—Judaism
USE **Christianity—Relations—Judaism**
    Judaism—Relations—Christianity

Christianity and politics 261.7; 322

UF Christianity—Political aspects
    Politics and Christianity
BT **Church and state**
    Religion and politics

Christianity—Apologetic works 239

Use for materials defending Christianity. Materials attacking Christianity are entered under **Christianity—Controversial literature.**

BT **Apologetics**

Christianity—Biography
USE **Christian biography**

Christianity—Controversial literature 239

Use for materials attacking Christianity. Materials defending Christianity are entered under **Christianity—Apologetic works.**

Christianity—Doctrines 230

UF Christian doctrinal theology
    Christian doctrine
BT **Doctrinal theology**
NT **Christian fundamentalism**
    Creationism
    God—Christianity
    Liberation theology
    Modernism (Theology)
    Regeneration (Christianity)
    Trinity

Christianity—Government
USE **Church polity**

Christianity—History
USE **Church history**

Christianity—Origin
USE **Church history—30-600, Early church**

Christianity—Philosophy
USE **Christian philosophy**

Christianity—Political aspects
USE **Christianity and politics**

Christianity—Polity
USE **Church polity**

Christianity—Psychology 230.01; 253.5

BT **Psychology of religion**

Christianity—Relations—Judaism 261.2; 296.3

Use for materials on the relations between Christianity and Judaism. When assigning this heading, provide an additional subject entry under **Judaism—Relations—Christianity.**

UF Christian-Jewish relations
    Christianity and other religions—Judaism
    Jewish-Christian relations
BT **Christianity and other religions**
    Judaism

Christianity—Union between churches
USE **Christian union**

Christians (May subdiv. geog.) 270.092

RT **Christianity**

Christians—Biography
USE **Christian biography**

Christians—Persecutions (May subdiv. geog.) 272

BT **Church history**
    Persecution

Christmas (May subdiv. geog.) 263; 394.2663

BT **Christian holidays**
    Holidays
NT **Christmas entertainments**
    Santa Claus
RT **Jesus Christ—Nativity**

Christmas cards 741.6; 745.594

BT **Greeting cards**

Christmas carols
USE **Carols**

Christmas cooking (May subdiv. geog.) 641.5

BT **Cooking**

Christmas decorations 394.2663; 745.594

UF Christmas ornaments
BT **Decoration and ornament**
NT **Christmas trees**

Christmas—Drama 394.2663; 792; 808.82

Use for collections of plays about Christmas.

UF Christmas plays

Christmas entertainments   394.2663;
791
   BT   **Amusements**
         Christmas
Christmas—Fiction   808.83
    Use for collections of stories about Christmas.
   UF   Christmas stories
Christmas—Juvenile drama   808.82
    Use for collections of plays about Christmas written for children.
Christmas—Juvenile fiction   808.83
    Use for collections of stories about Christmas written for children.
Christmas—Juvenile poetry   808.81
    Use for collections of poems about Christmas written for children.
Christmas ornaments
   USE   **Christmas decorations**
Christmas plays
   USE   **Christmas—Drama**
Christmas poetry
   USE   **Christmas—Poetry**
Christmas—Poetry   808.81
    Use for collections of poems about Christmas.
   UF   Christmas poetry
Christmas stories
   USE   **Christmas—Fiction**
Christmas tree growing   635.9
   UF   Growing of Christmas trees
   BT   **Forests and forestry**
   RT   **Christmas trees**
         Tree planting
Christmas trees   394.2663; 745.594
   BT   **Christmas decorations**
         Trees
   RT   **Christmas tree growing**
Christmas—United States   394.2663
Christology
   USE   **Jesus Christ**
Chromosome mapping
   USE   **Gene mapping**
Chromosomes   572.8
   BT   **Genetics**
         Heredity
   NT   **Genetic recombination**
Chronic diseases   616
   UF   Diseases, Chronic
   BT   **Diseases**
   NT   **Chronic pain**

Chronic pain   616
   UF   Persistent pain
   BT   **Chronic diseases**
         Pain
Chronicle history (Drama)
   USE   **Historical drama**
Chronicle plays
   USE   **Historical drama**
Chronology   529
    Use for materials on the science that deals with measuring time by regular divisions and that assigns proper dates to events.
   SA   individual persons, wars, sacred works, topics that are inherently historical, and topics not subdivided by *History,* such as art, music, literature, etc., with the subdivision *Chronology,* e.g. **Bible—Chronology;** and ethnic groups, corporate bodies, military services, topics not inherently historical, and names of places with the subdivision *History—Chronology,* e.g. **Native Americans—History—Chronology** [to be added as needed]
   BT   **Astronomy**
         History
         Time
   NT   **Bible—Chronology**
         Day
         Historical chronology
         Months
         Night
         Week
   RT   **Almanacs**
Chronology, Biblical
   USE   **Bible—Chronology**
Chronology, Historical
   USE   **Historical chronology**
Church   260
    Use for materials on the concept and function of the Christian Church as a whole.
   SA   church and other subjects, e.g. **Church and education** [to be added as needed]
   BT   **Theology**
   NT   **Christian union**
         Church and education
         Church and social problems
         Church and state

Church—*Continued*
        Church polity
        Church work
        Clergy
        Ecclesiastical law
        Ecumenical movement
        Laity
        Sacraments
  RT   Christianity

Church and education   261

Use for materials on the relation of the church to education in general, and for materials on the history of the part that the church has taken in secular education. Materials on church supported and controlled elementary and secondary schools are entered under **Church schools.** Materials on the instruction of religion in schools and private life are entered under **Religious education,** and of Christian religion under **Christian education.**

  UF   Education and church
         Education and religion
         Fundamentalism and education
         Religion and education
  BT   **Church**
         Education
  NT   **Religion in the public schools**
  RT   **Christian education**

Church and labor   261.8
  UF   Labor and the church
  BT   **Labor**
  RT   **Christianity and economics**

Church and race relations   261.8
  UF   Integrated churches
         Race relations and the church
  BT   **Church work**

Church and social problems   261.8

Use for materials on the practical treatment of social problems from the point of view of the church. Materials on social theory from a Christian point of view are entered under **Christian sociology.** Materials on religious sociology in general are entered under **Religion and sociology.**

  UF   Religion and social problems
         Social problems and the church
  BT   **Church**
         Social problems
  NT   **Liberation theology**
         Sanctuary movement
  RT   **Christian sociology**
         Church work

Church and state (May subdiv. geog.)
        201; 261.7; 322
  UF   Church—Government policy
         Religion and state

         Religion—Government policy
         Separation of church and state
  BT   **Church**
         State, The
  NT   **Christianity and politics**
         Religion in the public schools

Church and state—United States   322
  UF   United States—Church and state

Church antiquities
  USE **Christian antiquities**

Church architecture (May subdiv. geog.)
        726.5
  UF   Ecclesiastical architecture
  BT   **Architecture**
  NT   **Abbeys**
         Monasteries
         Mosques
         Spires
         Temples
  RT   **Cathedrals**
         Church buildings
         Gothic architecture

Church attendance
  USE **Public worship**

Church bells
  USE **Bells**

Church buildings (May subdiv. geog.)
        726.5

Use for general descriptive and historical materials on church buildings that cannot be entered under **Church architecture.**

  UF   Churches
  SA   names of individual churches,
           e.g. **Westminster Abbey** [to
           be added as needed]
  BT   **Buildings**
  NT   **Cathedrals**
         Westminster Abbey
  RT   **Church architecture**

Church buildings—United States
        726.50973

Church councils
  USE **Councils and synods**

Church denominations
  USE **Christian sects**
         Sects

Church entertainments   253.7
  UF   Church sociables
         Socials
  BT   **Amusements**
         Church work

Church fathers
    USE **Fathers of the church**
Church festivals
    USE **Religious holidays**
Church finance   254; 262.0068
    BT **Finance**
    NT **Tithes**
Church furniture   247
    UF Ecclesiastical furniture
    BT **Furniture**
Church government
    USE **Church polity**
Church—Government policy
    USE **Church and state**
Church history   270
    Use for materials dealing with the develop-
ment of Christianity and church organization.
    UF Christianity—History
        Ecclesiastical history
        Religious history
    SA names of countries, states, etc.
        with the subdivision *Church
        history,* e.g. **United States—
        Church history;** and names
        of individual denominations,
        sects, churches, etc. [to be
        added as needed]
    BT **History**
    NT **Christian missions**
        Christian sects
        Christians—Persecutions
        Councils and synods
        Martyrs
        Monasteries
        Ohio—Church history
        Papacy
        Popes
        Popes—Temporal power
        Protestant churches
        Protestantism
        Sects
        United States—Church history
**Church history—30-600, Early church
    270.1**
    UF Apostolic Church
        Christianity—Origin
        Early church history
        Primitive Christianity
    NT **Apostles**
        Gnosticism
    RT **Catacombs**
        Early Christian literature

**Church history—600-1500, Middle Ages
    270.3**
    UF Medieval church history
    BT **Middle Ages**
    NT **Crusades**
**Church history—1500-, Modern period
    270.6**
    UF Modern church history
    NT **Counter-Reformation**
        Reformation
Church history—Ohio
    USE **Ohio—Church history**
Church history—United States
    USE **United States—Church history**
Church law
    USE **Ecclesiastical law**
Church libraries   027.6
    UF Parish libraries
    BT **Libraries**
Church music (May subdiv. geog.)
    781.71
    This heading may be subdivided by religion
or denomination as needed.
    UF Religious music
        Sacred music
    SA types of church music, e.g.
        Hymns [to be added as need-
        ed]
    BT **Music**
    NT **Carols**
        Chants (Plain, Gregorian, etc.)
        Choirs (Music)
        Choral music
        Gospel music
        Hymnals
        Hymns
        Oratorio
        Organ music
    RT **Liturgies**
Church of Christ, Scientist
    USE **Christian Science**
Church of England (May subdiv. geog.)
    283
    UF Anglican Church
        England, Church of
    BT **Christian sects**
Church of England—Government   283
Church of England—United States   283
    Use for materials on the Episcopal Church
in the United States prior to 1789. Materials
on the Episcopal Church in the United States
after 1789 are entered under **Episcopal
Church.**

Church of England—United States—_Continued_

RT   **Episcopal Church**

       Puritans

Church of Jesus Christ of Latter-day Saints (May subdiv. geog.)   **289.3**

UF   Latter-day Saints

      Mormon Church

BT   **Christian sects**

RT   **Mormons**

Church polity   **262**

UF   Christian sects—Government

      Christianity—Government

      Christianity—Polity

      Church government

      Ecclesiastical polity

      Polity, Ecclesiastical

SA   names of church denominations with the subdivision _Government,_ e.g. **Church of England—Government** [to be added as needed]

BT   **Church**

Church schools (May subdiv. geog.)   **371.07**

Use for materials on church supported and controlled elementary and secondary schools. Materials on the relation of the church to education and on the history of the part that the church has taken in secular education are entered under **Church and education.** Materials on the instruction of religion in schools and private life are entered under **Religious education,** and of Christian religion under **Christian education.**

UF   Denominational schools

      Nonpublic schools

      Parochial schools

BT   **Private schools**

      Schools

Church service books

USE   **Liturgies**

Church settlements

USE   **Social settlements**

Church sociables

USE   **Church entertainments**

Church—Unity   **262**

Use for materials on unity as one of the marks of the church. Materials on prospective and actual mergers within and across denominational lines are entered under **Christian union.** Materials on a movement originating in the twentieth century aimed at promoting church cooperation and unity are entered under **Ecumenical movement.** Materials on religious activities planned and conducted cooperatively by two or more Christian sects are entered under **Interdenominational cooperation.**

UF   Christian unity

Church work   **200; 253**

SA   church work with particular groups of persons, e.g. **Church work with the sick** [to be added as needed]

BT   **Church**

NT   **Christian missions**

      Church and race relations

      Church entertainments

      Church work with the sick

      Church work with youth

      Evangelistic work

      Interdenominational cooperation

      Lay ministry

      Ministry

      Pastoral psychology

      Rural churches

      Sunday schools

RT   **Church and social problems**

      Pastoral theology

Church work with the sick   **259; 362.1023**

BT   **Church work**

      Sick

Church work with youth   **259**

BT   **Church work**

      Youth

Church year   **263**

Use for materials on the seasons of observance and Christian festivals with their cycles, as making up the Christian or church year. Works on the origins of Christian festivals and fasts are entered under **Christian holiday.**

UF   Christian year

      Ecclesiastical year

      Liturgical year

SA   festival seasons and seasons of the church year, e.g. **Lent** [to be added as needed]

BT   **Calendars**

      Religious holidays

      Worship

NT   **Christian holidays**

      Holy Week

      Lent

Churches

USE   **Church buildings**

      Religious institutions

Churches, Community
USE **Community churches**
Churches, Country
USE **Rural churches**
Churches, Non-institutional
USE **Non-institutional churches**
Churches, Rural
USE **Rural churches**
Churches, Undenominational
USE **Community churches**
Churchyards
USE **Cemeteries**
Cigarettes 679
BT **Smoking**
Tobacco
Cigars 679
BT **Smoking**
Tobacco
Cinema
USE **Motion pictures**
Cinematography 778.5
Use for materials on the technical aspects of making motion pictures and their projection onto a screen. General materials on motion pictures, including motion pictures as an art form, are entered under **Motion pictures.**
UF Motion picture photography
Photography—Motion pictures
BT **Photography**
NT **Animation (Cinematography)**
Motion picture cameras
Cinesiology
USE **Kinesiology**
Cipher and telegraph codes 384.1
UF Codes, Telegraph
Morse code
Telegraph codes
BT **Ciphers**
Telegraph
Ciphers 652
UF Codes
Contractions
BT **Signs and symbols**
NT **Cipher and telegraph codes**
RT **Abbreviations**
Cryptography
Writing
Ciphers (Lettering)
USE **Monograms**
Circuits, Electric
USE **Electric circuits**
Circulation of library materials
USE **Library circulation**

Circulation of the blood
USE **Blood—Circulation**
Circulatory system
USE **Cardiovascular system**
Circumcision (May subdiv. geog.) **392.1**
UF Male circumcision
BT **Initiation rites**
Circumcision, Female
USE **Female circumcision**
Circumnavigation
USE **Voyages around the world**
Circus (May subdiv. geog.) **791.3**
BT **Amusements**
NT **Acrobats and acrobatics**
Clowns
RT **Carnivals**
CIS
USE **Commonwealth of Independent States**
Cities and towns (May subdiv. geog.)
307.76
Use for general materials on cities and towns. For materials on large cities and their surrounding areas use **Metropolitan areas.** General materials on the government of cities are entered under **Municipal government.** General materials on local government other than that of cities are entered under **Local government.**
UF Municipalities
Towns
Urban areas
SA names of individual cities and towns [to be added as needed]
BT **Sociology**
NT **Capitals (Cities)**
City and town life
Extinct cities
Inner cities
Markets
Municipal art
Parks
Streets
Urbanization
Villages
RT **Urban sociology**
Cities and towns—Civic improvement
307.3; 354.3
UF Civic improvement
Municipal improvements
NT **City planning**
Community centers

Cities and towns—Finance
USE **Municipal finance**
Cities and towns—Government
USE **Municipal government**
Cities and towns—Growth   307.76
UF   Cities and towns, Movement to
Urban development
BT   **Internal migration**
Population
NT   **Metropolitan areas**
Suburbs
RT   **Urbanization**
Cities and towns—Lighting
USE   **Streets—Lighting**
Cities and towns, Movement to
USE   **Cities and towns—Growth**
Urbanization
Cities and towns—Planning
USE   **City planning**
Cities and towns—United States
307.760973; 973
UF   United States—Cities and towns
Cities, Imaginary
USE   **Geographical myths**
Citizen participation
USE   **Political participation**
and subjects designating govern-
ment activity with the subdi-
vision *Citizen participation,*
e.g. **City planning—Citizen**
participation [to be added as
needed]
Citizens band radio   384.5; 621.3845
UF   CB radio
Citizens radio service
BT   **Shortwave radio**
Citizen's defender
USE   **Ombudsman**
Citizens radio service
USE   **Citizens band radio**
Citizenship (May subdiv. geog.)   **172;**
323.6
UF   Civics
Franchise
Nationality (Citizenship)
BT   **Constitutional law**
Political ethics
Political science
NT   **Patriotism**
Suffrage

RT   **Aliens**
Naturalization
Citrus
USE   **Citrus fruits**
Citrus fruit
USE   **Citrus fruits**
Citrus fruits   634
Names of particular fruits may be used for
either the fruit or the tree.
UF   Citrus
Citrus fruit
SA   types of citrus fruits, e.g. **Lem-**
ons [to be added as needed]
BT   **Fruit**
NT   **Lemons**
Limes
Oranges
City and town life (May subdiv. geog.)
307.76
UF   City life
Town life
Urban life
BT   **Cities and towns**
Urban sociology
NT   **Street life**
Urban policy
City-federal relations
USE   **Federal-city relations**
City government
USE   **Municipal government**
City life
USE   **City and town life**
City manager
USE   **Municipal government by city**
manager
City planning (May subdiv. geog.)
307.1; 354.3; 711
Use for materials on the architectural and
engineering aspects of urban redevelopment.
Materials on the economic, sociological, and
political aspects are entered under **Urban re-**
newal.
UF   Cities and towns—Planning
Municipal planning
Town planning
Urban development
Urban planning
BT   **Cities and towns—Civic im-**
provement
Planning
NT   **Planned communities**
Suburbs
Zoning

145

City planning—*Continued*
  RT   Community development
        Housing
        Municipal art
        Public works
        Regional planning
        Urban policy
        Urban renewal
City planning—Chicago (Ill.)   307.1;
    354.3; 711
  UF   Chicago (Ill.)—City planning
City planning—Citizen participation
    (May subdiv. geog.)   307.1
  BT   Political participation
        Social action
City planning—United States   307.1;
    354.3; 711
City planning—Zone system
  USE Zoning
City schools
  USE Urban schools
City-state relations
  USE State-local relations
City traffic   388.4
  UF   Local traffic
        Street traffic
        Traffic, City
        Urban traffic
  BT   Streets
        Traffic engineering
City transit
  USE Local transit
Civic art
  USE Municipal art
Civic improvement
  USE Cities and towns—Civic im-
       provement
Civic involvement
  USE Political participation
       and subjects with the subdivi-
       sion *Citizen participation*, e.g.
       City planning—United
       States—Citizen participation
       [to be added as needed]
Civics
  USE Citizenship
        Political science
Civil defense (May subdiv. geog.)
    363.35
    Use for materials on the protection of civil-
  ians from enemy attack. Materials on military

defenses against air attack are entered under
Air defenses.
  UF   Civilian defense
  SA   names of wars with the subdivi-
       sion *Evacuation of civilians*
       [to be added as needed]
  BT   Military art and science
  NT   Air raid shelters
        Rescue work
        Survival skills
        World War, 1939-1945—Evac-
       uation of civilians
Civil defense—Chicago (Ill.)   363.35
  UF   Chicago (Ill.)—Civil defense
Civil defense—United States   363.35
  UF   United States—Civil defense
Civil disobedience (May subdiv. geog.)
    303.6; 322.4
  BT   Resistance to government
Civil disorders
  USE Riots
Civil engineering (May subdiv. geog.)
    624
  BT   Engineering
  NT   Aqueducts
        Bridges
        Canals
        Dams
        Drainage
        Dredging
        Excavation
        Extraterrestrial bases
        Harbors
        Highway engineering
        Hydraulic engineering
        Lunar bases
        Marine engineering
        Mechanical engineering
        Military engineering
        Mining engineering
        Public works
        Railroad engineering
        Reclamation of land
        Roads
        Streets
        Structural engineering
        Structural steel
        Surveying
        Tunnels
        Walls
        Water supply engineering

Civil government
  USE **Political science**
Civil law suits
  USE **Litigation**
Civil liberty
  USE **Freedom**
Civil procedure (May subdiv. geog.)
  347
  BT **Courts**
  NT **Probate law and practice**
  RT **Litigation**
Civil rights (May subdiv. geog.) **323;**
  342

Use for materials on citizens' rights as established by law or protected by a constitution. Materials on the rights of persons regardless of their legal, socioeconomic, or cultural status and as recognized by the international community are entered under **Human rights.**

  UF Basic rights
      Constitutional rights
      Fundamental rights
  SA ethnic groups and classes of persons with the subdivision *Civil rights* [to be added as needed]
  BT **Constitutional law**
      Human rights
      Political science
  NT **African Americans—Civil rights**
      Anti-apartheid movement
      Blacks—Civil rights
      Children—Civil rights
      Due process of law
      Employee rights
      Fair trial
      Freedom of assembly
      Freedom of association
      Freedom of information
      Freedom of movement
      Freedom of religion
      Freedom of speech
      Freedom of the press
      Right of privacy
      Right of property
      Women's rights
  RT **Civil rights demonstrations**
      Discrimination
      Freedom

Civil rights demonstrations (May subdiv. geog.) **322.4**
  UF Demonstrations for civil rights
      Freedom marches for civil rights
      Marches for civil rights
      Sit-ins for civil rights
  BT **Demonstrations**
  RT **Civil rights**
Civil rights (International law)
  USE **Human rights**
Civil servants
  USE **Civil service**
Civil service (May subdiv. geog.) **342;**
  351; 352.6

Use for general materials on career government service and the laws governing it. Materials on civil service employees are entered under the name of the country, state, city, corporate body, or government agency with the subdivision *Officials and employees.*

  UF Administration
      Civil servants
      Employees and officials
      Government employees
      Government service
      Officials and employees
      Tenure of office
  SA names of countries, states, cities, etc., and corporate bodies with the subdivision *Officials and employees,* e.g. **United States—Officials and employees; Ohio—Officials and employees; Chicago (Ill.)—Officials and employees; United Nations—Officials and employees;** etc. [to be added as needed]
  BT **Administrative law**
      Political science
      Public administration
  NT **Municipal officials and employees**
  RT **Bureaucracy**
      Public officers
Civil service—Examinations **351.076**
  BT **Examinations**
Civil service—United States **351.73**
  UF United States—Civil service
  RT **United States—Officials and employees**

Civil War—England
    USE   Great Britain—History—1642-
           1660, Civil War and Com-
           monwealth
Civil War—United States
    USE   United States—History—1861-
           1865, Civil War
Civilian defense
    USE   Civil defense
Civilian evacuation
    USE   World War, 1939-1945—Evac-
           uation of civilians
Civilian relief
    USE   names of wars with the subdivi-
           sion *Civilian relief,* e.g.
           **World War, 1939-1945—Ci-
           vilian relief** [to be added as
           needed]
Civilization   306; 909
    Use for materials on civilization in general
and on the development of social customs, art,
industry, religion, etc., of several countries or
peoples.
    SA   names of continents, regions,
          countries, states, etc., with the
          subdivision *Civilization,* e.g.
          United States—Civilization;
          and the civilizations of peo-
          ples not confined to a single
          place, e.g. **Arab civilization;
          Western civilization;** etc. [to
          be added as needed]
    NT   **Acculturation
          Aeronautics and civilization
          Africa—Civilization
          America—Civilization
          Ancient civilization
          Arab civilization
          Asia—Civilization
          Astronautics and civilization
          Bronze Age
          Christian civilization
          Computers and civilization
          Education
          Iron Age
          Jewish civilization
          Learning and scholarship
          Manners and customs
          Medieval civilization
          Modern civilization
          Ohio—Civilization
          Primitive societies**

**Progress
          Religions
          Renaissance
          Science and civilization
          Social sciences
          Stone Age
          Technology and civilization
          United States—Civilization
          War and civilization
          Western civilization**
    RT   **Anthropology
          Culture
          Ethnology
          History
          Sociology**
Civilization, Ancient
    USE   **Ancient civilization**
Civilization and aeronautics
    USE   **Aeronautics and civilization**
Civilization and astronautics
    USE   **Astronautics and civilization**
Civilization and computers
    USE   **Computers and civilization**
Civilization and science
    USE   **Science and civilization**
Civilization and technology
    USE   **Technology and civilization**
Civilization and war
    USE   **War and civilization**
Civilization, Arab
    USE   **Arab civilization**
Civilization, Christian
    USE   **Christian civilization**
Civilization, Classical
    USE   **Classical civilization**
Civilization, Greek
    USE   **Greece—Civilization**
Civilization, Medieval
    USE   **Medieval civilization**
Civilization, Modern
    USE   **Modern civilization**
Civilization, Oriental
    USE   **Asia—Civilization**
Civilization, Western
    USE   **Western civilization**
Claims
    USE   ethnic groups, places, and wars
           with the subdivision *Claims,*
           e.g. **Native Americans—
           Claims** [to be added as need-
           ed]

Clairvoyance   133.8
   BT   Extrasensory perception
         Occultism
   RT   Telepathy
Clairvoyants
   USE Psychics
Clans (May subdiv. geog.)   306.85;
     941.1
   SA   names of clans or of families
        [to be added as needed]
   BT   Family
   NT   Tartans
   RT   Kinship
Clans—Scotland   941.1
   UF   Highland clans
        Scottish clans
Class action lawsuits
   USE Class actions (Civil procedure)
Class actions (Civil procedure) (May
     subdiv. geog.)   347
   UF   Class action lawsuits
   BT   Litigation
Class conflict
   USE Social conflict
Class consciousness   305.5
   BT   Social classes
        Social psychology
   RT   Marxism
Class distinction
   USE Social classes
Class struggle
   USE Social conflict
Classed catalogs
   USE Classified catalogs
Classes (Mathematics)
   USE Set theory
Classes of persons
   USE Persons
        and classes of persons, e.g. El-
        derly; Handicapped; Explor-
        ers; Drug addicts; etc. [to be
        added as needed]
Classic automobiles
   USE Antique and classic cars
Classic cars
   USE Antique and classic cars
Classic motorcycles
   USE Antique and vintage motorcy-
        cles

Classical antiquities   937; 938
   UF   Classical archeology
        Greek antiquities
        Roman antiquities
   SA   names of extinct cities of Greek
        and Roman antiquity e.g. Del-
        phi (Extinct city); and names
        of groups of people extant in
        modern times and names of
        cities (except extinct cities),
        countries, regions, etc., with
        the subdivision *Antiquities* [to
        be added as needed]
   BT   Antiquities
   NT   Greece—Antiquities
        Greek art
        Roman art
        Rome—Antiquities
        Rome (Italy)—Antiquities
Classical antiquities—Dictionaries
   USE Classical dictionaries
Classical archeology
   USE Classical antiquities
Classical art
   USE Greek art
        Roman art
Classical biography
   USE Greece—Biography
        Rome—Biography
Classical civilization (May subdiv. geog.)
     937

     Use for materials on both ancient Greek
and Roman civilizations. Materials on the
spread of Greek civilization throughout the
ancient world following the conquests of Al-
exander the Great are entered under Helle-
nism.
   UF   Civilization, Classical
   BT   Ancient civilization
   NT   Greece—Civilization
        Rome—Civilization
   RT   Classicism
Classical dictionaries   937.003; 938.003
   UF   Classical antiquities—Dictionaries
        Dictionaries, Classical
   BT   Ancient history
        Encyclopedias and dictionaries
Classical education   370.11
   BT   Education
   RT   Humanism
        Humanities

Classical geography
USE **Ancient geography**
Greece—Historical geography
Rome—Geography
Classical languages
USE **Greek language**
Latin language
Classical literature   870; 880
BT **Literature**
RT **Greek literature**
Latin literature
Classical music
USE **Music**
Classical mythology   292.1
UF Mythology, Classical
BT **Mythology**
NT **Greek mythology**
Roman mythology
Classicism   709; 809
BT **Aesthetics**
Literature
NT **Classicism in architecture**
RT **Classical civilization**
Classicism in architecture   723; 724
BT **Architecture**
Classicism
Classification   001
Use for materials on the organization of knowledge into a systematic arrangement of topics or categories. Materials on the classification of library materials are entered under **Library classification,** which may be subdivided by the type of literature or the subject of the materials classified.
UF Classification of knowledge
SA subjects with the subdivision
Classification, e.g. **Botany—Classification** [to be added as needed]
NT **Botany—Classification**
Library classification
Classification—Books
USE **Library classification**
Classification—Botany
USE **Botany—Classification**
Classification, Dewey Decimal
USE **Dewey Decimal Classification**
Classification of knowledge
USE **Classification**
Classification—Plants
USE **Botany—Classification**

Classified catalogs   017; 025.3
UF Catalogs, Classified
Classed catalogs
BT **Library catalogs**
RT **Library classification**
Classroom management   371.102
BT **School discipline**
Teaching
Clay   553.6; 666; 738.1
BT **Ceramics**
Soils
NT **Modeling**
Clay industries
USE **Clay industry**
Clay industry (May subdiv. geog.)
338.4; 666
UF Clay industries
BT **Ceramic industry**
NT **Pottery**
Clay modeling
USE **Modeling**
Cleaning   648; 667
SA topics with the subdivision
Cleaning, e.g. **Rugs and carpets—Cleaning** [to be added as needed]
BT **Sanitation**
NT **Bleaching**
Cleaning compounds
Dry cleaning
House cleaning
Laundry
Street cleaning
Cleaning compounds   648; 667
BT **Cleaning**
NT **Detergents**
Soap
Cleanliness   391.6; 613
UF Neatness
BT **Hygiene**
Sanitation
NT **Baths**
Clearing of land
USE **Reclamation of land**
Clemency   364.6
BT **Administration of criminal justice**
Executive power
RT **Amnesty**
Forgiveness
Pardon

Clergy (May subdiv. geog.)   **200.92;
270.092**
- UF   Curates
      Ministers of the gospel
      Pastors
      Preachers
      Rectors
- SA   church denominations with the
       subdivision *Clergy,* e.g. **Cath-
       olic Church—Clergy** [to be
       added as needed]
- BT   **Church**
- NT   **Catholic Church—Clergy**
       Celibacy
       Chaplains
       Priests
       Rabbis
       Women clergy
- RT   **Ministry**
       Ordination
       Pastoral theology

Clergy—Office
- USE   **Ministry**

Clergy—Political activity   201; 261.7
- BT   **Political participation**

Clerical celibacy
- USE   **Celibacy**

Clerical employees
- USE   **Office workers**

Clerical personnel
- USE   **Office workers**

Clerical psychology
- USE   **Pastoral psychology**

Clerical work—Training
- USE   **Business education**

Clerks
- USE   **Office workers**

Clerks (Retail trade)
- USE   **Sales personnel**

Cliff dwellers and cliff dwellings (May
   subdiv. geog.)   **979**
- BT   **Archeology**
       **Native Americans—Southwest-
       ern States**

Climacteric, Female
- USE   **Menopause**

Climacteric, Male
- USE   **Male climacteric**

Climate   551.6

Use for materials on climate as it relates to
humans and to plant and animal life, including

the effects of changes of climate. Materials
limited to the climate of a particular region
are entered under the name of the place with
the subdivision *Climate.* Materials on the state
of the atmosphere at a given time and place
with respect to heat or cold, wetness or dryness, calm or storm, are entered under
Weather. Scientific materials on the atmosphere, especially weather factors, are entered
under **Meteorology.**
- UF   Climatology
- SA   names of countries, cities, etc.,
       with the subdivision *Climate*
       [to be added as needed]
- BT   **Earth sciences**
- NT   **Chicago (Ill.)—Climate**
       Desertification
       Forest influences
       Greenhouse effect
       Ohio—Climate
       Seasons
       United States—Climate
- RT   **Meteorology**
       Weather

Climate and forests
- USE   **Forest influences**

Climatology
- USE   **Climate**

Climbing plants   582.1; 635.9
- UF   Vines
- BT   **Gardening**
       Plants

Clinical chemistry   616.07

Use for materials on the chemical diagnosis
of disease and health monitoring.
- UF   Chemistry, Diagnostic
       Chemistry, Medical
       Diagnostic chemistry
       Medical chemistry
- BT   **Biochemistry**
       Diagnosis

Clinical drug trials
- USE   **Drugs—Testing**

Clinical genetics
- USE   **Medical genetics**

Clinical trials of drugs
- USE   **Drugs—Testing**

Clinics
- USE   **Health facilities**
        Medical practice

Clip art   741.6

Use for materials on clipping art work from
published sources to use in creating documents, posters, newsletters, etc. Materials on
the use of photocopying machines to create

Clip art—*Continued*
original works of art are entered under **Copy art.**
BT **Graphic arts**
Clipper ships   387.2; 623.82
BT **Ships**
**Clippings (Books, newspapers, etc.)
025.17**
UF   Newspaper clippings
Press clippings
BT **Newspapers**
Clitoridotomy
USE **Female circumcision**
Clocks and watches (May subdiv. geog.)
681.1; 739.3
UF   Horology
Watches
BT **Time**
NT **Sundials**
Clog dancing   793.3
UF   Clog-dancing
Clogging (Dance)
BT **Dance**
Clog-dancing
USE **Clog dancing**
Clogging (Dance)
USE **Clog dancing**
Cloisters
USE **Convents**
Monasteries
Clones and cloning
USE **Cloning**
Cloning   571.8; 660.6
UF   Clones and cloning
BT **Genetic engineering**
NT **Human cloning**
Molecular cloning
Cloning—Ethical aspects   174
BT **Ethics**
Closed caption television   384.55
BT **Deaf**
Television
Closed caption video recordings   384.55
UF   Video recordings, Closed caption
Video recordings for the hearing
impaired
BT **Deaf**
Videodiscs
Videotapes

Closed-circuit television   384.55
UF   Television, Closed-circuit
BT **Intercommunication systems**
Microwave communication systems
Television
Closed shop
USE **Open and closed shop**
Closing of factories
USE **Plant shutdowns**
Cloth
USE **Fabrics**
Clothes
USE **Clothing and dress**
Clothiers
USE **Clothing industry**
Clothing
USE   types of clothing articles and accessories; costume of particular ethnic groups, e.g. **Native American costume;** and professions and classes of persons with the subdivision *Clothing,* e.g. **Handicapped—Clothing** [to be added as needed]
Clothing and dress (May subdiv. geog.)
391; 646.4
Use for materials on clothing and the art of dress from day to day in practical situations, including historical dress and the clothing of various professions or classes of persons. Materials on the characteristic costume of ethnic groups and on fancy dress and theatrical costumes are entered under **Costume.** Materials on the prevailing mode or style of dress are entered under **Fashion.**
UF   Clothes
Dress
Garments
Style in dress
SA   types of clothing articles and accessories; costume of particular ethnic groups, e.g. **Native American costume;** and professions and classes of persons with the subdivision *Clothing,* e.g. **Handicapped—Clothing** [to be added as needed]
BT **Manners and customs**
NT **Buttons**
Children's clothing
Dress accessories

Clothing and dress—*Continued*
    Dressmaking
    Fans
    Fashion
    Handicapped—Clothing
    Hats
    Hosiery
    Infants' clothing
    Jewelry
    Leather garments
    Men's clothing
    Shoes
    T-shirts
    Tailoring
    Umbrellas and parasols
    Uniforms
    Wigs
    Women's clothing
  RT Clothing industry
    Costume
    Personal appearance
    Personal grooming
Clothing and dress—Dry cleaning
  USE Dry cleaning
Clothing and dress—France 391
    Use for materials on day to day dress in France.
Clothing and dress—France—History
    391
    Use for materials on day to day dress in France in the past.
Clothing and dress—History 391
    Use for materials on day to day dress in the past.
Clothing and dress—Repairing 646.2
  UF Mending
Clothing designers
  USE Fashion designers
Clothing industry (May subdiv. geog.)
    338.4; 687
  UF Clothiers
    Clothing trade
    Fashion industry
    Garment industry
  BT Industries
  NT Dressmaking
    Fashion design
    Shoe industry
    Tailoring
  RT Clothing and dress
Clothing trade
  USE Clothing industry

Cloud seeding
  USE Weather control
Clouds 551.57
  BT Atmosphere
    Meteorology
Clowns 791.3; 791.3092; 920
  BT Circus
    Entertainers
Clubs (May subdiv. geog.) 367
  BT Associations
  NT Boys' clubs
    Girls' clubs
    Men—Societies
    Scouts and scouting
    Women—Societies
  RT Societies
Co-dependence
  USE Codependency
Co-dependency
  USE Codependency
Co-ops
  USE Cooperative societies
Co-ops (Housing)
  USE Cooperative housing
Co-parenting
  USE Part-time parenting
Coaching
  USE Coaching (Athletics)
    Horsemanship
    and types of sports with the subdivision *Coaching* [to be added as needed]
Coaching (Athletics) 796.07
  UF Athletic coaching
    Coaching
    Sports coaching
  SA types of sports with the subdivision *Coaching* [to be added as needed]
  BT Athletics
    Physical education
    Sports
  NT Football—Coaching
Coal (May subdiv. geog.) 553.2
  BT Fuel
  NT Coal gasification
    Coal liquefaction
    Coal mines and mining
Coal gas
  USE Gas

Coal gasification   665.7
   UF   Gasification of coal
   BT   **Coal**
Coal liquefaction   622
   UF   Liquefaction of coal
   BT   **Coal**
Coal miners   622; 920
   BT   **Miners**
Coal mines and mining (May subdiv.
     geog.)   622
   BT   **Coal**
       Mines and mineral resources
   NT   **Mining engineering**
Coal oil
   USE   **Petroleum**
Coal tar products   547; 661
   BT   **Petroleum**
   RT   **Gas**
COAs
   USE   **Children of alcoholics**
Coast ecology
   USE   **Coastal ecology**
Coast pilot guides
   USE   **Pilot guides**
Coastal ecology (May subdiv. geog.)
     577.5
   UF   Coast ecology
       Coastal zone ecology
   BT   **Ecology**
Coastal landforms
   USE   **Coasts**
Coastal signals
   USE   **Signals and signaling**
Coastal zone ecology
   USE   **Coastal ecology**
Coastal zone management (May subdiv.
     geog.)   333.91
   BT   **Coasts**
       Regional planning
Coasts (May subdiv. geog.)   551.45
   UF   Coastal landforms
   BT   **Landforms**
   NT   **Coastal zone management**
   RT   **Seashore**
Coats of arms
   USE   **Heraldry**
Cocaine   362.29; 615
   BT   **Narcotics**
   NT   **Crack (Drug)**
Cocaine babies
   USE   **Children of drug addicts**

Cocoa   633.7; 641.3
   BT   **Beverages**
   RT   **Chocolate**
Cocoons
   USE   **Butterflies**
         Caterpillars
         Moths
         Silkworms
Code deciphering
   USE   **Cryptography**
Code enciphering
   USE   **Cryptography**
Code names   423
   BT   **Abbreviations**
       Names
   NT   **Acronyms**
Codependency   616.86
   UF   Co-dependence
       Co-dependency
       Codependent behavior
   BT   **Abnormal psychology**
Codependent behavior
   USE   **Codependency**
Codes
   USE   **Ciphers**
Codes, Penal
   USE   **Criminal law**
Codes, Telegraph
   USE   **Cipher and telegraph codes**
Coeducation (May subdiv. geog.)
     371.822
   BT   **Education**
   RT   **Boys—Education**
       Girls—Education
       Men—Education
       Women—Education
Coffee   633.7; 641.8
   BT   **Beverages**
   RT   **Coffee industry**
Coffee bars
   USE   **Coffeehouses**
Coffee houses
   USE   **Coffeehouses**
Coffee industry (May subdiv. geog.)
     338.1; 338.4
   UF   Coffee trade
   BT   **Beverage industry**
   NT   **Coffeehouses**
   RT   **Coffee**
Coffee shops
   USE   **Restaurants**

Coffee trade

USE **Coffee industry**

Coffeehouses (May subdiv. geog.)
647.95

Use for materials on public establishments devoted primarily to serving coffee. Materials on coffee shops and cafes as small inexpensive restaurants are entered under **Restaurants.**

UF Cafes

Coffee bars

Coffee houses

BT **Coffee industry**

Restaurants

Cog wheels

USE **Gearing**

Cognition

USE **Theory of knowledge**

Cognitive styles 153; 370.15

BT **Intellect**

Theory of knowledge

Cognitive styles in children 155.4;
370.15

BT **Child psychology**

Cohabitation

USE **Unmarried couples**

Cohousing

USE **Cooperative housing**

Coiffure

USE **Hair**

Coin collecting

USE **Coins—Collectors and collecting**

Coinage (May subdiv. geog.) 332.4

Use for materials on the processing and history of metal money. Lists of coins and general materials about coins are entered under **Coins.**

BT **Money**

NT **Counterfeits and counterfeiting**

RT **Gold**

Mints

Silver

Coinage of words

USE **New words**

Coins (May subdiv. geog.) 737.4

Use for lists of coins and general materials about coins. Materials on coins from the point of view of art and archeology are entered under **Numismatics.** Materials on the processing of metal money are entered under **Coinage.**

UF Specie

BT **Money**

Coins—Collectors and collecting 737.4

UF Coin collecting

RT **Numismatics**

Cold 536; 551.5

NT **Cryobiology**

Ice

RT **Low temperatures**

Temperature

Cold (Disease) 616.2

UF Common cold

BT **Communicable diseases**

Diseases

NT **Influenza**

Cold—Physiological effect 613

BT **Cryobiology**

Cold storage 641.4; 664

BT **Food—Preservation**

NT **Compressed air**

RT **Refrigeration**

Cold—Therapeutic use 615.8

UF Cryotherapy

BT **Therapeutics**

NT **Cryosurgery**

Cold war 909.82

Use for materials on the rivalry between capitalist and communist nations following World War II.

UF Power politics

BT **World politics—1945-1991**

Collaborationists (May subdiv. geog.)
364.1

UF Collaborators (Traitors)

SA names of wars with the subdivision *Collaborationists,* e.g. **World War, 1939-1945— Collaborationists** [to be added as needed]

BT **Traitors**

NT **World War, 1939-1945—Collaborationists**

Collaborators (Traitors)

USE **Collaborationists**

Collage 702.8; 751.4

BT **Art**

Handicraft

Collapse of structures

USE **Structural failures**

Collectables

USE **Collectibles**

Collected papers (Anthologies)

USE **Anthologies**

Collected works
    USE **Anthologies**
         Literature—Collections
         Storytelling—Collections
         and form headings for minor
         literary forms that represent
         collections of works of sever-
         al authors, e.g. **Essays;**
         American essays; Parodies;
         Short stories; etc.; major lit-
         erary forms and national liter-
         atures with the subdivision
         Collections, e.g. **Poetry—Col-**
         lections; English literature—
         Collections; etc.; and subjects
         with the subdivision *Literary*
         collections, for collections fo-
         cused on a single subject by
         two or more authors involving
         two or more literary forms,
         e.g. **Cats—Literary collec-**
         tions [to be added as needed]
Collectible card games   795.4
    UF Trading card games
    BT **Card games**
Collectibles (May subdiv. geog.)   **745.1**
    Use for materials on any objects of interest
    to collectors, including mass produced items
    of little intrinsic value. Materials on old deco-
    rative or utilitarian objects that have aesthetic
    or historical importance and financial value
    are entered under **Antiques.**
    UF Collectables
        Memorabilia
    SA subjects and names with the
        subdivision *Collectibles,* e.g.
        American Revolution Bicen-
        tennial, 1776-1976—Collect-
        ibles; and types of objects
        collected, excluding antiquities
        and natural objects, with the
        subdivision *Collectors and*
        collecting, e.g. **Boxes—Col-**
        lectors and collecting [to be
        added as needed]
    BT **Collectors and collecting**
    NT **Trading cards**
        Victoriana
Collecting
    USE **Collectors and collecting**
Collecting of accounts   658.8
    UF Accounts, Collecting of
        Bill collecting

Collection of accounts
    BT **Commercial law**
        Credit
        Debt
        Debtor and creditor
Collection and preservation
    USE types of antiquities and types of
         natural objects, including ani-
         mal specimens and plant
         specimens, with the subdivi-
         sion *Collection and preserva-*
         tion, e.g. **Birds—Collection**
         and preservation; for materi-
         als on methods of collecting
         and preserving those objects
         [to be added as needed]
Collection development (Libraries)
    USE **Libraries—Collection develop-**
         ment
Collection of accounts
    USE **Collecting of accounts**
Collections
    USE form headings for minor literary
         forms that represent collec-
         tions of works of several au-
         thors, e.g. **Essays; American**
         essays; Parodies; Short sto-
         ries; etc.; major literary forms
         and national literatures with
         the subdivision *Collections,*
         e.g. **Poetry—Collections; En-**
         glish literature—Collections;
         etc.; and subjects with the
         subdivision *Literary collec-*
         tions, for collections focused
         on a single subject by two or
         more authors involving two or
         more literary forms, e.g.
         Cats—Literary collections [to
         be added as needed]
Collections (Anthologies)
    USE **Anthologies**
Collections of art, painting, etc.
    USE **Art collections**
         Art museums
Collections of literature
    USE **Anthologies**
         Literature—Collections
         Storytelling—Collections
         and form headings for minor
         literary forms that represent

Collections of literature—*Continued*
collections of works of several authors, e.g. **Essays; American essays; Parodies; Short stories;** etc.; major literary forms and national literatures with the subdivision *Collections,* e.g. **Poetry—Collections; English literature—Collections;** etc.; and subjects with the subdivision *Literary collections,* for collections focused on a single subject by two or more authors involving two or more literary forms, e.g. **Cats—Literary collections** [to be added as needed]

Collections of natural specimens
  USE **Plants—Collection and preservation**
      Zoological specimens—Collection and preservation
      and types of natural specimens with the subdivision *Collection and preservation,* e.g. **Birds—Collection and preservation** [to be added as needed]

Collections of objects
  USE **Collectors and collecting**
      and subjects and names with the subdivision *Collectibles,* e.g. **American Revolution Bicentennial, 1776-1976—Collectibles;** and types of objects collected, excluding antiquities and natural objects, with the subdivision *Collectors and collecting,* e.g. **Boxes—Collectors and collecting** [to be added as needed]

Collective bargaining (May subdiv. geog.)
    331.89; 658.3
  May be subdivided by groups of professional or nonprofessional workers, e.g. **Collective bargaining—Librarians.**
  UF Labor negotiations
  BT **Industrial relations**
      Labor
      Labor disputes
      Negotiation

  RT **Industrial arbitration**
      Labor contract
      Labor unions
      Participative management
      Strikes

Collective bargaining—Librarians
    331.89
  UF Librarians—Collective bargaining
      Libraries—Collective bargaining

Collective farms
  USE **Collective settlements**
      Cooperative agriculture

Collective identity
  USE **Group identity**

Collective labor agreements
  USE **Labor contract**

Collective security
  USE **International security**

Collective settlements (May subdiv. geog.)
    307.77; 335
  Use for materials on traditional, formally organized communal ventures, usually based on ideological, political, or religious affiliation. Materials on arrangements in voluntary cooperative living, usually informal, are entered under **Communal living.**
  UF Collective farms
      Communal settlements
      Communes
      Cooperative living
  SA names of individual collective settlements [to be added as needed]
  BT **Communism**
      Cooperation
      Socialism
  RT **Communal living**
      Cooperative agriculture
      Counter culture
      Utopias

Collective settlements—Israel   **307.77**
  UF Israel—Collective settlements
      Kibbutz

Collective settlements—United States
    307.77

Collectivism (May subdiv. geog.)
    320.53; 335
  BT **Economics**
      Political science
  NT **Communism**
      Socialism

Collectors and collecting (May subdiv. geog.)   **790.1**

   UF   Collecting

         Collections of objects

   SA   types of collecting, e.g. **Book collecting;** types of objects collected, excluding antiquities and natural objects, with the subdivision *Collectors and collecting,* e.g. **Postcards— Collectors and collecting;** names of original owners of private art collections with the subdivision *Art collections;* subjects and names with the subdivision *Collectibles,* e.g. **American Revolution Bicentennial, 1776-1976—Collectibles;** and antiquities and types of natural objects with the subdivision *Collection and preservation,* e.g. **Birds—Collection and preservation** [to be added as needed]

   BT   **Antiques**

         Art

         Hobbies

   NT   **American Revolution Bicentennial, 1776-1976—Collectibles**

         Americana

         Antiques

         Antiquities—Collection and preservation

         Book collecting

         Boxes—Collectors and collecting

         Collectibles

         Plants—Collection and preservation

         Stamp collecting

         Zoological specimens—Collection and preservation

   RT   **Art collections**

Collects

   USE   **Prayers**

College admissions essays

   USE   **College applications**

College and school drama   **371.8; 792**

    Use for materials about college and school drama. Individual works, collections, and materials about plays for children are entered under **Children's plays.** Plays for children on a particular theme are entered under subjects and personal, corporate, and place names with the subdivision *Juvenile drama.*

   UF   College drama

         School plays

   BT   **Amateur theater**

         Drama

         Student activities

   RT   **Drama in education**

College and school journalism   **371.8**

   UF   College journalism

         College periodicals

         School journalism

         School newspapers

   BT   **Journalism**

         Student activities

   RT   **Children's writings**

College and university libraries

   USE   **Academic libraries**

College applications   **378.1**

   UF   Admissions applications

         Admissions essays

         Applications for college

         College admissions essays

         Colleges and universities—Applications

   RT   **Colleges and universities—Entrance requirements**

College athletics

   USE   **College sports**

College choice   **378**

   UF   Choice of college

         Colleges and universities—Selection

   BT   **Colleges and universities**

         School choice

College costs   **378.3**

   UF   Tuition

   BT   **Colleges and universities—Finance**

   NT   **Student aid**

         Student loan funds

College degrees

   USE   **Academic degrees**

College drama

   USE   **College and school drama**

College dropouts

   USE   **Dropouts**

College entrance examinations

   USE   **Colleges and universities—Entrance examinations**

College entrance requirements
    USE   **Colleges and universities—Entrance requirements**
College fraternities
    USE   **Fraternities and sororities**
College graduates (May subdiv. geog.)
    305.5; 378
    UF   Graduates, College
          University graduates
    BT   **Professions**
    RT   **College students**
College journalism
    USE   **College and school journalism**
College libraries
    USE   **Academic libraries**
College life
    USE   **College students**
College periodicals
    USE   **College and school journalism**
College songs
    USE   **Students' songs**
College sororities
    USE   **Fraternities and sororities**
College sports (May subdiv. geog.)
    371.8; 796
    UF   College athletics
          Intercollegiate athletics
          Varsity sports
    SA   types of sports [to be added as needed]
    BT   **Sports**
          Student activities
    RT   **School sports**
College students (May subdiv. geog.)
    371.8; 378
    UF   College life
          Colleges and universities—Students
          Student life
          Undergraduates
          University students
    BT   **Students**
    RT   **College graduates**
College students, Foreign
    USE   **Foreign students**
College students—Political activity
    371.8; 378
    UF   Campus disorders
    BT   **Political participation**

College students—Sexual behavior
    371.8; 378
    BT   **Sexual behavior**
College teachers
    USE   **Colleges and universities—Faculty**
          Educators
          Teachers
College yearbooks
    USE   **School yearbooks**
Colleges and universities (May subdiv. geog.) **378**
    UF   Universities
          Universities and colleges
    SA   types of colleges and universities, e.g. **Catholic colleges and universities;** and names of individual colleges and universities [to be added as needed]
    BT   **Education**
          Higher education
          Professional education
          Schools
    NT   **Academic degrees**
          Catholic colleges and universities
          College choice
          Commencements
          Fraternities and sororities
          Free universities
          Junior colleges
          Law schools
          Medical colleges
          Teachers colleges
          United States Military Academy
          University extension
Colleges and universities—Accreditation
    378; 379.1
Colleges and universities—Applications
    USE   **College applications**
Colleges and universities—Buildings
    727
    BT   **Buildings**
Colleges and universities—Curricula
    378.1
    UF   Core curriculum
    SA   types of education and schools with the subdivision *Curricula,* e.g. **Library education—**

Colleges and universities—Curricula—
Continued

Curricula [to be added as needed]
　BT　Education—Curricula
Colleges and universities—Employees
　(May subdiv. geog.)　378.1
　BT　Employees
Colleges and universities—Employees—
　Salaries, wages, etc. (May subdiv.
　geog.)　331.2
　BT　Salaries, wages, etc.
Colleges and universities—Endowments
　378
　BT　Endowments
Colleges and universities—Entrance ex-
　aminations　378.1
　UF　College entrance examinations
　　　Entrance examinations for col-
　　　leges
　BT　Educational tests and measure-
　　　ments
　　　Examinations
　NT　Graduate Record Examination
　　　Scholastic Aptitude Test
Colleges and universities—Entrance re-
　quirements　378.1
　UF　College entrance requirements
　　　Entrance requirements for col-
　　　leges and universities
　SA　names of individual colleges and
　　　universities with the subdivi-
　　　sion *Entrance requirements*
　　　[to be added as needed]
　BT　Examinations
　RT　College applications
Colleges and universities—Faculty
　378.1
　UF　College teachers
　　　Faculty (Education)
　BT　Teachers
Colleges and universities—Faculty—Pen-
　sions　331.25
Colleges and universities—Finance
　378.1
　UF　Tuition
　BT　Finance
　NT　College costs
　RT　Federal aid to education
Colleges and universities—Insignia
　378.2
　BT　Insignia

Colleges and universities—Selection
　USE　College choice
Colleges and universities—Students
　USE　College students
Colleges and universities—United States
　378.73
Collies　636.737
　BT　Dogs
Collisions, Railroad
　USE　Railroad accidents
Colloids　541
　BT　Physical chemistry
Colonial architecture
　USE　American colonial style in ar-
　　　chitecture
　　　Architecture—United States—
　　　1600-1775, Colonial period
Colonial history (U.S.)
　USE　United States—History—1600-
　　　1775, Colonial period
Colonialism
　USE　Colonies
　　　Imperialism
Colonies　321; 325

　　Use for materials on general colonial poli-
　cy. Materials on the policy of settling immi-
　grants or nationals abroad are entered under
　Colonization. Materials on migration from
　one country to another are entered under **Im-
　migration and emigration**. Materials on the
　movement of population within a country for
　permanent settlement are entered under **Inter-
　nal migration**.

　UF　Colonialism
　　　Dependencies
　SA　names of countries with the sub-
　　　division *Colonies,* or *Territo-
　　　ries and possessions,* e.g.
　　　**Great Britain—Colonies;
　　　United States—Territories
　　　and possessions;** etc. [to be
　　　added as needed]
　BT　Imperialism
　NT　Great Britain—Colonies
　　　Land settlement
　　　Penal colonies
　RT　Colonization
Colonies, Space
　USE　Space colonies
Colonization　325

　　Use for materials on the policy of settling
　immigrants or nationals abroad. Materials on
　general colonial policy are entered under **Col-
　onies**. Materials on migration from one coun-

Colonization—*Continued*

try to another are entered under **Immigration and emigration.** Materials on the movement of population within a country for permanent settlement are entered under **Internal migration.**

SA   names of countries with the subdivision *Immigration and emigration,* e.g. **United States— Immigration and emigration** [to be added as needed]

BT   **Imperialism**
      Land settlement

NT   **Internal migration**
      Land grants
      Public lands

RT   **Colonies**
      Immigration and emigration

Color   535.6; 701; 752

UF   Colour

SA   subjects with the subdivision *Color,* and names of specific colors [to be added as needed]

BT   **Aesthetics**
      Chemistry
      Light
      Optics
      Painting
      Photometry

NT   **Animals—Color**
      Birds—Color
      Dyes and dyeing
      Red

RT   **Pigments**

Color blindness   617.7

BT   **Color sense**
      Vision disorders

Color etchings
USE   **Color prints**

Color photography   778.6

UF   Color slides
      Photography, Color

BT   **Photography**

Color printing   686.2

Use for materials on practical printing in color. Materials on hand-colored prints or on pictures printed in color are entered under **Color prints.**

SA   types of color printing processes [to be added as needed]

BT   **Printing**

NT   **Illustration of books**
      Lithography

Silk screen printing

RT   **Color prints**

Color prints   769

Use for materials on hand-colored prints or on pictures printed in color. Materials on practical printing in color are entered under **Color printing.**

UF   Block printing
      Color etchings
      Painting—Color reproductions

SA   color prints of particular countries, e.g. **American color prints** [to be added as needed]

BT   **Prints**

NT   **American color prints**
      Japanese color prints

RT   **Color printing**

Color prints, American
USE   **American color prints**

Color prints, Japanese
USE   **Japanese color prints**

Color—Psychological aspects   152.14

UF   Psychology of color

BT   **Color sense**
      Psychology

Color sense   152.14

BT   **Psychophysiology**
      Senses and sensation
      Vision

NT   **Color blindness**
      Color—Psychological aspects

Color slides
USE   **Color photography**
      Slides (Photography)

Color television   621.388

BT   **Television**

Colorado River—Hoover Dam
USE   **Hoover Dam (Ariz. and Nev.)**

Coloring books   372.5

UF   Painting books

BT   **Picture books for children**

Colour
USE   **Color**

Columnists
USE   **Journalists**

Combustion   541; 621.402

BT   **Chemistry**

NT   **Fuel**

RT   **Fire**
      Heat

Comedians (May subdiv. geog.) **791;
792.2; 920**
- BT **Actors
Entertainers**
- NT **Fools and jesters**

Comedies 808.82

May be used for individual works or for collections. Materials about comedy as a literary form are entered under **Comedy.**
- UF Comic drama
Comic plays
Humorous plays
Slapstick comedies
- BT **Drama
Wit and humor**
- NT **Comedy films
Comedy television programs
Farces**

Comedy 792.2; 809.2

Use for materials on comedy as a literary form. Individual works and collections of comedies are entered under **Comedies.**
- UF Comic drama
Comic literature
- BT **Drama
Wit and humor**
- NT **Commedia dell'arte**

Comedy films 791.43

May be used for individual works, collections, or materials about comedy films.
- UF Comic films
Humorous films
Slapstick comedies
- SA types of comedy films, e.g.
Three Stooges films [to be added as needed]
- BT **Comedies
Motion pictures**
- NT **Three Stooges films**
- RT **Comedy television programs**

Comedy radio programs 791.44

May be used for individual works, collections, or materials about comedy radio programs.
- UF Radio comedies
Radio comedy programs
- BT **Radio programs**

Comedy television programs 791.45

May be used for individual works, collections, or materials about television comedies.
- UF Comic television programs
Sitcoms
Situation comedies
Slapstick comedies
Television comedies
Television comedy programs
- BT **Comedies
Television programs**
- RT **Comedy films**

Comets 523.6
- BT **Astronomy
Solar system**
- NT **Halley's comet**

Comic book novels
- USE **Graphic novels**

Comic books, strips, etc. (May subdiv. geog.) **741.5**

May be used for individual works, collections, or materials about printed comic strips, i.e. groups of cartoons in narrative sequence, and books and magazines consisting of comic strips, etc.
- UF Comic strips
Funnies
Humorous pictures
- SA ethnic groups, classes of persons, corporate bodies, individual persons, literary authors, or sacred works with the subdivision *Comic books, strips, etc.;* and names of comic books, comic strips, and comic strip characters [to be added as needed]
- BT **Wit and humor**
- NT **Graphic novels
Mystery comic books, strips, etc.
Science fiction comic books, strips, etc.
Superhero comic books, strips, etc.
Western comic books, strips, etc.**
- RT **Cartoons and caricatures
Chapbooks**

Comic drama
- USE **Comedies
Comedy**

Comic epic literature
- USE **Mock-heroic literature**

Comic films
- USE **Comedy films**

Comic literature
- USE **Comedy
Parody
Satire**

Comic novels
USE **Humorous fiction**
Comic opera
USE **Opera**
Operetta
Comic plays
USE **Comedies**
Comic strips
USE **Comic books, strips, etc.**
Comic television programs
USE **Comedy television programs**
Comic verse
USE **Humorous poetry**
Coming of age stories
USE **Bildungsromans**
Commedia dell'arte 792.2
BT **Acting**
Comedy
Farces
Commemorations
USE **Anniversaries**
Commencements 394.2
UF Graduation
BT **Colleges and universities**
High schools
School assembly programs
Commentaries
USE names of sacred works, includ-
ing named parts of sacred
works, with the subdivision
Commentaries, e.g. **Bible—**
Commentaries [to be added
as needed]
Commentaries, Biblical
USE **Bible—Commentaries**
Commerce 381
Use for general materials on foreign and
domestic commerce. Materials limited to com-
merce between states are entered under **Inter-**
state commerce.
UF Distribution (Economics)
Trade
SA names of countries, cities, etc.,
with the subdivision *Com-*
merce, e.g. **United States—**
Commerce; and names of ar-
ticles of commerce, e.g. **Cot-**
ton [to be added as needed]
BT **Economics**
Finance
NT **Banks and banking**
Barter

Black market
Boycotts
Business
Chambers of commerce
Chicago (Ill.)—Commerce
Commercial geography
Commercial products
Competition
Contracts
Cooperation
Developing countries—Com-
merce
Electronic commerce
Exchange
Industrial trusts
International trade
Interstate commerce
Marine insurance
Markets
Monopolies
Multinational corporations
Ohio—Commerce
Prices
Profit sharing
Restraint of trade
Retail trade
Stocks
Tourist trade
Trade routes
Trademarks
United States—Commerce
RT **Transportation**
Commerce—Law and legislation
USE **Commercial law**
Commercial aeronautics (May subdiv.
geog.) 387.7
UF Aeronautics, Commercial
Air cargo
Air freight
Air transport
Commercial aviation
BT **Freight**
Transportation
NT **Air mail service**
Airlines
Commercial arithmetic
USE **Business mathematics**
Commercial art (May subdiv. geog.)
741.6
UF Advertising art
Art in advertising

Commercial art—*Continued*
   BT   **Advertising**
        Art
        Drawing
   NT   **Fashion design**
        Posters
        Textile design
Commercial art galleries (May subdiv.
        geog.)   **338.7; 708**
   UF   Art galleries
        Picture galleries
   BT   **Business enterprises**
Commercial aviation
   USE   **Commercial aeronautics**
Commercial buildings (May subdiv.
        geog.)   **333.33; 725**
   UF   Mercantile buildings
        Store buildings
   BT   **Buildings**
   NT   **Shopping centers and malls**
        Stores
Commercial catalogs   **380.1029; 659.13**
   UF   Catalogs
        Commercial products—Catalogs
        Mail order catalogs
        Trade catalogs
   SA   types of merchandise, objects,
        products, etc., and names of
        individual companies with the
        subdivision *Catalogs* [to be
        added as needed]
   BT   **Advertising**
Commercial correspondence
   USE   **Business letters**
Commercial education
   USE   **Business education**
Commercial employees
   USE   **Office workers**
Commercial endeavors in space
   USE   **Space industrialization**
Commercial fishing (May subdiv. geog.)
        338.3; 639.2
   Use for materials on the fishing industry.
   Materials on the cultivation of fish in captivi-
   ty are entered under **Fish culture.** Materials
   on fishing as a sport are entered under **Fish-
   ing.**
   UF   Fisheries
        Fishing, Commercial
        Fishing industry
        Sea fisheries

   BT   **Industries**
   NT   **Pearl fisheries**
        Whaling
Commercial fishing—**United States**
        338.3; 639.2
Commercial geography   **330.9**
   UF   Economic geography
        World economics
   BT   **Commerce**
        Geography
   NT   **Trade routes**
   RT   **Economic conditions**
Commercial law (May subdiv. geog.)
        346.07
   UF   Business law
        Business—Law and legislation
        Commerce—Law and legislation
        Mercantile law
   BT   **Law**
   NT   **Antitrust law**
        Arbitration and award
        Bankruptcy
        Collecting of accounts
        Contracts
        Corporation law
        Debtor and creditor
        Fraud
        Insider trading
        Landlord and tenant
        Licenses
        Negotiable instruments
        Restraint of trade
        Unfair competition
   RT   **Maritime law**
Commercial mathematics
   USE   **Business mathematics**
Commercial paper
   USE   **Negotiable instruments**
Commercial photography   **778**
   BT   **Photography**
   NT   **Photojournalism**
Commercial policy (May subdiv. geog.)
        381.3; 382
   Use for general materials on the various
   regulations by which governments seek to
   protect and increase the commerce of a coun-
   try, such as subsidies, tariffs, free ports, etc.
   UF   Government policy
        Government regulation of com-
          merce
        Reciprocity
        Trade barriers

Commercial policy—*Continued*
    World economics
  BT **Economic policy**
      International economic relations
  NT **Buy national policy**
      Commercial products
      Free trade
      Protectionism
      Tariff
Commercial policy—United States
    381.3; 382
  UF United States—Commercial policy
Commercial products (May subdiv. geog.)
    338; 381
  UF Merchandise
      Products, Commercial
  SA types of products and names of
      specific products [to be added
      as needed]
  BT **Commerce**
  NT **Animal products**
      Brand name products
      Consumer goods
      Forest products
      Generic products
      Manufactures
      Marine resources
      New products
      Raw materials
      Substitute products
Commercial products—Catalogs
  USE **Commercial catalogs**
Commercial products recall
  USE **Product recall**
Commercial secrets
  USE **Trade secrets**
Commercials, Radio
  USE **Radio advertising**
Commercials, Television
  USE **Television advertising**
Commission government
  USE **Municipal government by commission**
Commission government with city manager
  USE **Municipal government by city manager**
Common cold
  USE **Cold (Disease)**
Common currencies
  USE **Monetary unions**

Common law (May subdiv. geog.) **340.5**
  UF Anglo-American law
  BT **Law**
Common law marriage
  USE **Unmarried couples**
Common market
  USE **European Union**
Commonplaces
  USE **Terms and phrases**
Commonwealth countries **909**
    Use for materials dealing collectively with
the member countries of the international organization that was founded in 1931 as the
British Commonwealth of Nations, changed
its name to the Commonwealth of Nations in
1950, and became known as the Commonwealth in 1969.
  UF British Commonwealth countries
      British Commonwealth of Nations
      British Dominions
      Commonwealth of Nations
      Dominions, British
  RT **Great Britain—Colonies**
Commonwealth of England
  USE **Great Britain—History—1642-1660, Civil War and Commonwealth**
Commonwealth of Independent States
    947.086
    Use for materials specifically on the federation of independent former Soviet republics
that was established in December 1991 and
does not include the Baltic states. General materials on several or all of the countries that
emerged from the dissolution of the Soviet
Union in 1991 are entered under **Former Soviet republics.**
  UF CIS
  RT **Former Soviet republics**
      Russia (Federation)
      Soviet Union
Commonwealth of Nations
  USE **Commonwealth countries**
Commonwealth, The
  USE **Political science**
      Republics
      State, The
Communal living (May subdiv. geog.)
    307.77
    Use for materials on arrangements in voluntary cooperative living, usually informal. Materials on traditional, formally organized communal ventures, usually based on ideological,
political, or religious affiliation are entered
under **Collective settlements.**

Communal living—*Continued*
- UF Communal settlements
  - Communes
  - Cooperative living
  - Group living
- BT Cooperation
- RT Collective settlements
  - Cooperative housing
  - Counter culture

Communal settlements
- USE **Collective settlements**
  - **Communal living**

Communes
- USE **Collective settlements**
  - **Communal living**

Communicable diseases (May subdiv. geog.) **614.4; 616.9**
- UF Contagion and contagious diseases
  - Contagious diseases
  - Infection and infectious diseases
  - Quarantine
- SA names of communicable diseases [to be added as needed]
- BT **Diseases**
  - **Public health**
- NT **AIDS (Disease)**
  - **Cold (Disease)**
  - **Fumigation**
  - **Germ theory of disease**
  - **Influenza**
  - **Plague**
  - **Rabies**
  - **Sexually transmitted diseases**
- RT **Epidemics**
  - **Immunity**
  - **Insects as carriers of disease**

Communicable diseases—Prevention **614.4**
- BT **Preventive medicine**

Communication 302.2
  Use for general materials on communication in its broadest sense, including the use of the spoken and written word, signs, symbols, or behavior.
- UF Mass communication
- BT **Sociology**
- NT **Audiences**
  - **Books and reading**
  - **Conversation**
  - **Cybernetics**

Deaf—Means of communication
- **Information science**
- **Language and languages**
- **Language arts**
- **Mass media**
- **Nonverbal communication**
- **Persuasion (Psychology)**
- **Popular culture**
- **Postal service**
- **Public speaking**
- **Signals and signaling**
- **Signs and symbols**
- **Telecommunication**
- **Writing**

Communication among animals
- USE **Animal communication**

Communication arts
- USE **Language arts**

Communication disorders (Medicine)
- USE **Communicative disorders**

Communication in marriage 646.7
- UF Marital communication
- BT **Marriage**

Communication satellites
- USE **Artificial satellites in telecommunication**

Communication systems
- USE subjects with the subdivision *Communication systems,* e.g. **Astronautics—Communication systems** [to be added as needed]

Communication systems, Wireless
- USE **Wireless communication systems**

Communications relay satellites
- USE **Artificial satellites in telecommunication**

Communicative disorders 616.85
- UF Communication disorders (Medicine)
  - Disorders of communication
- BT **Nervous system—Diseases**
- NT **Language disorders**
  - **Speech disorders**

Communion
- USE **Eucharist**

Communism (May subdiv. geog.)   **320.5;**
    321.9; 324.1; 335.43
  UF   Bolshevism
  SA   communism and other subjects,
          e.g. **Communism and litera-
          ture** [to be added as needed]
  BT   **Collectivism**
       Political science
       Totalitarianism
  NT   **Anticommunist movements**
       Collective settlements
       Communism and literature
       Communism and religion
       Dialectical materialism
  RT   **Marxism**
       Socialism
Communism and literature   **335.4; 809**
  UF   Literature and communism
  BT   **Communism**
       Literature
Communism and religion   **261.7; 335.4**
  UF   Communism—Religious aspects
       Religion and communism
  BT   **Communism**
       Religion
Communism—Religious aspects
  USE   **Communism and religion**
Communism—Soviet Union   **320.5;**
    335.430947; 947.084
  UF   Russian communism
       Soviet communism
       Soviet Union—Communism
Communism—United States   **320.5;**
    335.43; 973
Communist countries   **909**
  UF   Chinese satellite countries
       Iron curtain countries
       People's democracies
       Russian satellite countries
       Soviet bloc
Communities, Space
  USE   **Space colonies**
Community action
  USE   **Political participation**
Community and libraries
  USE   **Libraries and community**
Community and school (May subdiv.
    geog.)   **371.19**
  UF   School and community
  BT   **Community life**
  NT   **Parent-teacher associations**

Community based residences
  USE   **Group homes**
Community centers (May subdiv. geog.)
    374; 790.06
  UF   Neighborhood centers
       Play centers
       Recreation centers
       School buildings as recreation
          centers
       Schools as social centers
  BT   **Cities and towns—Civic im-
          provement**
       Community life
       Community organization
       Recreation
       Social settlements
  NT   **Youth hostels**
  RT   **Playgrounds**
Community chests
  USE   **Fund raising**
Community churches (May subdiv. geog.)
    254
    Use for materials on local churches that
  have no denominational affiliations.
  UF   Churches, Community
       Churches, Undenominational
       Nondenominational churches
       Undenominational churches
       Union churches
  BT   **Christian sects**
Community colleges
  USE   **Junior colleges**
Community councils
  USE   **Community organization**
Community development (May subdiv.
    geog.)   **307.1; 361.6**
  UF   Neighborhood development
       Regional development
  BT   **Domestic economic assistance**
       Social change
       Urban renewal
  NT   **Rural development**
  RT   **Agricultural extension work**
       City planning
       Technical assistance
Community health services (May subdiv.
    geog.)   **362.12**
  BT   **Community services**
       Public health
Community history
  USE   **Local history**

Community identity
  USE **Group identity**
Community life (May subdiv. geog.)
      307
  BT **Associations**
  NT **Community and school**
      Community centers
      Community organization
      Neighborhood
      Scouts and scouting
Community organization (May subdiv.
      geog.) **307**
  UF Community councils
  BT **Community life**
      Social work
  NT **Community centers**
      Local government
  RT **Urban renewal**
Community services (May subdiv. geog.)
      361.7; 361.8
  SA types of services, e.g. **Commu-**
      nity health services [to be
      added as needed]
  BT **Social work**
  NT **Community health services**
Community surveys
  USE **Social surveys**
Community theater
  USE **Little theater movement**
Compact automobiles
  USE **Compact cars**
Compact cars   **629.222**
  UF Compact automobiles
      Compacts (Automobiles)
      Economy cars
      Small cars
  SA names of specific makes and
      models of compact cars [to
      be added as needed]
  BT **Automobiles**
Compact disc interactive technology
  USE **CD-I technology**
Compact disc players   **621.389**
  UF Audiodisc players
      CD players
      Digital audio disc players
  BT **Phonograph**
      Sound—Recording and repro-
        ducing
Compact disc read-only memory
  USE **CD-ROMs**

Compact discs   **621.389; 780.26**
  Use for materials on small optical discs in
  general and on the compact disc format for
  sound recordings. Materials about sound
  recordings that emphasize the content of the
  recording rather than the format are entered
  under **Sound recordings.**
  UF CDs (Compact discs)
      Compact disks
      Digital compact discs
  BT **Optical storage devices**
      Sound recordings
  NT **CD-I technology**
      CD-ROMs
Compact disks
  USE **Compact discs**
Compacts (Automobiles)
  USE **Compact cars**
Companies
  USE **Business enterprises**
      Corporations
      Partnership
Companion-animal partnership
  USE **Pet therapy**
Company libraries
  USE **Corporate libraries**
Company symbols
  USE **Trademarks**
Comparative anatomy   **571.3**
  UF Anatomy, Comparative
  BT **Anatomy**
      Zoology
  NT **Morphology**
Comparative government   **320.3**
  UF Government, Comparative
  SA names of countries, cities, etc.,
      with the subdivision *Politics*
      and government, e.g. **United**
      States—Politics and govern-
      ment [to be added as needed]
  BT **Political science**
Comparative linguistics
  USE **Linguistics**
Comparative literature   **809**
  UF Literature, Comparative
  BT **Literature**
Comparative morphology
  USE **Morphology**
Comparative philology
  USE **Linguistics**
Comparative philosophy   **100**
  BT **Philosophy**

Comparative physiology   571.1
  UF   Physiology, Comparative
  BT   **Physiology**
Comparative psychology   156
  UF   Animal psychology
       Psychology, Comparative
  SA   types of animals with the subdivision *Psychology,* e.g.
       Dogs—Psychology [to be added as needed]
  BT   **Zoology**
  NT   **Dogs—Psychology**
       Sociobiology
  RT   **Animal intelligence**
       Instinct
Comparative religion
  USE   **Christianity and other religions**
        Religions
Comparative studies
  USE   religious topics and names of sacred works and individual Christian denominations with the subdivision *Comparative studies,* e.g. **Mysticism—Comparative studies** [to be added as needed]
Comparison
  USE   names of languages with the subdivision *Comparison,* e.g. **English language—Comparison** [to be added as needed]
Comparison (English grammar)
  USE   **English language—Comparison**
Comparison of cultures
  USE   **Cross-cultural studies**
Compass   538; 623.8
  UF   Magnetic needle
       Mariner's compass
  BT   **Magnetism**
       Navigation
Compassion
  USE   **Consolation**
Compensation
  USE   **Pensions**
        Salaries, wages, etc.
        Workers' compensation
Compensatory spending
  USE   **Deficit financing**
Competence
  USE   **Performance**

Competition (May subdiv. geog.)   338.6
  BT   **Business**
       Business ethics
       Commerce
  RT   **Industrial trusts**
       Monopolies
       Supply and demand
Competition, International
  USE   **International competition**
Competition, Unfair
  USE   **Unfair competition**
Competitions
  USE   **Awards**
        Contests
        and   subjects with the subdivision *Competitions,* e.g. **Literature—Competitions** [to be added as needed]
Composers (May subdiv. geog.)   780.92; 920
  UF   Songwriters
  BT   **Musicians**
Composers, American
  USE   **Composers—United States**
Composers—United States   780.92; 920
  UF   American composers
       Composers, American
Composition
  USE   types of natural substances of unfixed composition, including soils, plants and crops, animals, farm products, etc., with the subdivision *Composition,* for the results of analyses of those substances, e.g. **Food—Composition** [to be added as needed]
Composition and exercises
  USE   names of languages with the subdivision *Composition and exercises,* e.g. **English language—Composition and exercises** [to be added as needed]
Composition (Art)   701
  UF   Art—Composition
  BT   **Art**
  NT   **Architecture—Composition, proportion, etc.**
  RT   **Painting**

Composition (Music) 781.3
UF Music—Composition
   Musical composition
   Song writing
   Songwriting
BT **Music**
   Music—Theory
NT **Counterpoint**
   Harmony
   Instrumentation and orchestration
   Musical accompaniment
   Musical form
   Popular music—Writing and publishing
Composition of natural substances
USE types of natural substances of unfixed composition, including soils, plants and crops, animals, farm products, etc., with the subdivision *Composition* for the results of analyses of those substances, e.g. **Food—Composition** [to be added as needed]
Composition (Printing)
USE **Typesetting**
Composition (Rhetoric)
USE **Rhetoric**
   and names of languages with the subdivision *Composition and exercises,* e.g. **English language—Composition and exercises** [to be added as needed]
Compost 631.8
BT **Fertilizers**
   Soils
RT **Organic gardening**
Comprehensive health care organizations
USE **Health maintenance organizations**
Compressed air 621.5
UF Pneumatic transmission
BT **Cold storage**
   Pneumatics
   Power (Mechanics)
Compulsion (Psychology)
USE **Compulsive behavior**

Compulsive behavior 616.85
UF Addictive behavior
   Compulsion (Psychology)
SA types of compulsive behavior [to be added as needed]
BT **Abnormal psychology**
   Human behavior
NT **Compulsive gambling**
   Exercise addiction
   Workaholism
RT **Obsessive-compulsive disorder**
   Twelve-step programs
Compulsive exercising
USE **Exercise addiction**
Compulsive gambling 616.85
UF Addiction to gambling
BT **Compulsive behavior**
   Gambling
Compulsive working
USE **Workaholism**
Compulsory education 379.2
UF Compulsory school attendance
   Education, Compulsory
BT **Education—Government policy**
NT **Evening and continuation schools**
RT **School attendance**
Compulsory labor
USE **Forced labor**
Compulsory military service
USE **Draft**
Compulsory school attendance
USE **Compulsory education**
   School attendance
Computation, Approximate
USE **Approximate computation**
Computation (Mathematics)
USE **Arithmetic**
Computer-aided design 620
   Use for materials on the use of computer graphics to design tools, vehicles, buildings, etc.
UF CAD
   Computer aided design
   Computer-assisted design
   Electronic design
BT **Computer graphics**
   Design
RT **Computer-aided design software**
Computer aided design
USE **Computer-aided design**

Computer-aided design software   006.6

    UF   CAD/CAM software

           CAD software

    BT   **Computer software**

    RT   **Computer-aided design**

Computer art (May subdiv. geog.)   700; 760; 776

Use for materials on the use of computer graphics to create artistic designs, drawings, or other works of art.

    BT   **Art**

           Computer graphics

Computer-assisted design

    USE   **Computer-aided design**

Computer-assisted instruction   371.33

Use for materials on automated instruction in which a student interacts directly with a computer.

    UF   CAI

           Computer assisted instruction

           Computers—Educational use

           Education—Automation

           Education—Data processing

           Teaching—Data processing

    SA   subjects with the subdivision

           Computer-assisted instruction

           [to be added as needed]

    BT   **Programmed instruction**

    NT   **Mathematics—Computer-assisted instruction**

Computer assisted instruction

    USE   **Computer-assisted instruction**

Computer-assisted instruction—Authoring programs   005.5; 371.33

Use for materials on computer programs that allow the user with comparatively little expertise to design customized computer programs for educational purposes.

    UF   Authoring programs for computer-assisted instruction

    BT   **Computer software**

Computer awareness

    USE   **Computer literacy**

Computer-based information systems

    USE   **Information systems**

           Management information systems

Computer-based multimedia information systems

    USE   **Multimedia**

Computer bulletin boards   004.693; 384.3

Use for materials on services that allow users to post messages and retrieve messages from others who have some common interest. Materials on services that allow users to engage in conversations in real time are entered under **Online chat groups**. Materials on services, commonly called newsgroups or LISTSERV lists, that allow subscribers to post messages that are then distributed to other subscribers are entered under **Electronic discussion groups**.

    UF   Electronic bulletin boards

    BT   **Bulletin boards**

    RT   **Electronic discussion groups**

           Online chat groups

Computer control

    USE   **Automation**

Computer crimes (May subdiv. geog.)   364.16

    UF   Computer fraud

    BT   **Crime**

    NT   **Computer viruses**

    RT   **Computer security**

Computer drafting

    USE   **Computer graphics**

Computer drawing

    USE   **Computer graphics**

Computer fonts   686.2

    BT   **Type and type-founding**

Computer fraud

    USE   **Computer crimes**

Computer games   794.8

    BT   **Computer software**

           Games

Computer graphics   006.6

Use for materials on the production of drawings, pictures, or diagrams, as distinct from letters and numbers, on a computer screen or hard-copy output devices. Materials on the use of computer graphics to create artistic designs, drawings, or other works of art are entered under **Computer art**. Materials on the use of computer graphics to design tools, vehicles, buildings, etc., are entered under **Computer-aided design**.

    UF   Automatic drafting

           Automatic drawing

           Computer drafting

           Computer drawing

           Electronic drafting

           Electronic drawing

           Graphics, Computer

    BT   **Data processing**

    NT   **Computer-aided design**

           Computer art

Computer hardware

    USE   **Computers**

Computer industry (May subdiv. geog.)
  338.7
  BT **Industries**
  RT **Computers**
Computer input-output equipment
  USE **Computer peripherals**
Computer interfaces   004.6; 621.39
  Use for materials on equipment and techniques linking computers to peripheral devices or to other computers.
  UF Interfaces, Computer
  BT **Computer peripherals**
Computer keyboarding
  USE **Keyboarding (Electronics)**
Computer keyboards
  USE **Keyboards (Electronics)**
Computer languages
  USE **Programming languages**
Computer literacy   004
  Use for materials on the basic knowledge of computers a person needs in order to function in a computer-based society.
  UF Computer awareness
  BT **Computers and civilization**
      Literacy
Computer memory systems
  USE **Computer storage devices**
Computer modeling
  USE **Computer simulation**
Computer models
  USE **Computer simulation**
Computer monitors   004.7
  Use for materials on video display devices connected to a personal computer.
  UF CRT display terminals
      Video display terminals
  BT **Computer peripherals**
Computer music   786.7
  BT **Music**
  RT **Computer sound processing**
      Electronic music
Computer network resources
  USE **Internet resources**
Computer networks   004.6; 384.3
  Use for materials on systems consisting of two or more interconnected computers.
  UF Information superhighway
      Networks, Computer
  SA types of computer networks, names of specific computer networks, and subjects with the subdivision *Computer net-*

works, e.g. **Business enterprises—Computer networks** [to be added as needed]
  BT **Data transmission systems**
      Telecommunication
  NT **Business enterprises—Computer networks**
      Cyberspace
      Internet
      Local area networks
  RT **Information networks**
Computer operating systems   005.4
  UF Computers—Operating systems
      Operating systems (Computers)
  BT **Computer software**
Computer peripherals   004.7; 621.39
  UF Computer input-output equipment
      Input equipment (Computers)
      Output equipment (Computers)
  SA types of computer peripherals [to be added as needed]
  BT **Computers**
  NT **Computer interfaces**
      Computer monitors
      Computer storage devices
      Computer terminals
      Keyboards (Electronics)
      Optical scanners
Computer program languages
  USE **Programming languages**
Computer programming   005.1
  UF Computers—Programming
      Programming (Computers)
  SA subjects with the subdivision *Computer software,* e.g. **Database management—Computer software** [to be added as needed]
  BT **Computer science**
      Data processing
  RT **Computer software**
      Programming languages
Computer programs
  USE **Computer software**
Computer science   004
  Use for materials discussing collectively the disciplines that deal with the general theory and application of computers.
  BT **Science**
  NT **Artificial intelligence**
      Computer programming
      Database management

Computer science—*Continued*
RT   **Computers**
Computer science—Dictionaries   004.03
   UF   Computer terms
          Computers—Dictionaries
   BT   **Encyclopedias and dictionaries**
Computer security   005.8
   Use for materials on protecting computer hardware and software from accidental or malicious access, use, modification, disclosure, or destruction.
   UF   Computers—Access control
          Computers—Security measures
   BT   **Computers**
   RT   **Computer crimes**
          Computer viruses
Computer sex   306.7
   UF   Cybersex
          On-line sex
          Online sex
   BT   **Sexual behavior**
Computer simulation   003
   UF   Computer modeling
          Computer models
          Simulation, Computer
   SA   subjects with the subdivision *Computer simulation,* e.g. **Psychology—Computer simulation** [to be added as needed]
   BT   **Mathematical models**
   NT   **Psychology—Computer simulation**
          Virtual reality
Computer software   005.3
   UF   Computer programs
          Programs, Computer
          Software, Computer
   SA   types of computer software, e.g. **Computer games; Spreadsheet software;** etc.; subjects with the subdivision *Computer software,* e.g. **Oceanography—Computer software;** and names of individual computer programs qualified by *(Computer software),* e.g. **Microsoft Word (Computer software)** [to be added as needed]
   NT   **Computer-aided design software**

          Computer-assisted instruction—Authoring programs
          Computer games
          Computer operating systems
          Computer viruses
          Database management—Computer software
          Educational software
          Free computer software
          Image processing software
          Internet software
          Microsoft Word (Computer software)
          Multimedia
          Oceanography—Computer software
          Programming languages
          Shareware (Computer software)
          Spreadsheet software
          Utilities (Computer software)
          Word processing software
   RT   **Computer programming**
          Computer software industry
          Computers
Computer software industry (May subdiv. geog.)   **338.4**
   BT   **Industries**
   RT   **Computer software**
Computer sound processing   006.5
   UF   Sound processing, Computer
   BT   **Computers**
          Sound
   NT   **MP3 players**
   RT   **Computer music**
          Speech processing systems
Computer speech processing systems
   USE   **Speech processing systems**
Computer storage devices   004.5; 621.39
   UF   Computer memory systems
          Computers—Memory systems
          Computers—Storage devices
          Memory devices (Computers)
          Storage devices, Computer
   BT   **Computer peripherals**
   NT   **Optical storage devices**
Computer terminals   004.7; 621.39
   Use for materials on video display devices connected to a mainframe computer.
   UF   Terminals, Computer
   BT   **Computer peripherals**

Computer terms
  USE **Computer science—Dictionaries**
Computer utility programs
  USE **Utilities (Computer software)**
Computer viruses   005.8
  UF Software viruses
      Viruses, Computer
  BT **Computer crimes**
      Computer software
  RT **Computer security**
Computerized tomography
  USE **Tomography**
Computers   004; 621.39
      Use for materials on modern electronic
  computers developed after 1945. Materials on
  present-day calculators and on calculating ma-
  chines and mechanical computers made before
  1945 are entered under **Calculators.**
  UF Computer hardware
  SA types of computers, e.g.
        Microcomputers; and names
        of specific computers, e.g.
        IBM 7090 (Computer) [to be
        added as needed]
  BT **Electronic apparatus and ap-**
      pliances
  NT **Computer peripherals**
      Computer security
      Computer sound processing
      Computers and children
      Computers and civilization
      Data processing
      IBM 7090 (Computer)
      Information systems
      Macintosh (Computer)
      Microcomputers
      Microprocessors
      Portable computers
      Supercomputers
  RT **Calculators**
      Computer industry
      Computer science
      Computer software
Computers—Access control
  USE **Computer security**
Computers and children   004.083
  BT **Children**
      Computers
Computers and civilization   004; 303.48
  UF Civilization and computers
  BT **Civilization**
      Computers
      Technology and civilization

  NT **Computer literacy**
Computers—Cartoons and caricatures
      621.39; 741.5
  BT **Cartoons and caricatures**
Computers—Dictionaries
  USE **Computer science—Dictionaries**
Computers—Educational use
  USE **Computer-assisted instruction**
Computers—Juvenile literature   004
Computers—Memory systems
  USE **Computer storage devices**
Computers—Operating systems
  USE **Computer operating systems**
Computers—Programming
  USE **Computer programming**
Computers—Security measures
  USE **Computer security**
Computers—Storage devices
  USE **Computer storage devices**
Computers—Utility programs
  USE **Utilities (Computer software)**
Con artists
  USE **Swindlers and swindling**
Con game
  USE **Swindlers and swindling**
Concealment
  USE **Secrecy**
Concentration
  USE **Attention**
Concentration camps (May subdiv. geog.)
      365
  UF Internment camps
  SA names of wars with the subdivi-
        sion *Prisoners and prisons;*
        and names of individual
        camps [to be added as need-
        ed]
  BT **Military camps**
      Political crimes and offenses
  NT **World War, 1939-1945—Pris-**
      oners and prisons
  RT **Prisoners of war**
Concept formation
  USE **Concept learning**
Concept learning   153.2; 370.15
      Use for materials on the process of discov-
  ering the distinguishing features of particular
  concepts and the ensuing ability to use the
  concepts appropriately.
  UF Concept formation
  BT **Concepts**
      Psychology of learning

Conception—Prevention
USE **Birth control**
Concepts **153.2**
SA types of concepts and images,
e.g. **Size; Shape;** etc. [to be
added as needed]
BT **Perception**
NT **Concept learning**
Opposites
Shape
Size
Concert halls (May subdiv. geog.) **725**
UF Music-halls
BT **Auditoriums**
Concerto **784.18**
Use for musical scores and for materials on
the concerto as a musical form.
UF Concertos
BT **Musical form**
Orchestral music
Concertos
USE **Concerto**
Concerts **780.78**
BT **Amusements**
Music
RT **Music festivals**
Concordances **010**
Use for works that list words with refer-
ences to passages in a text where the exact
word occurs. Works that list topics or names
with references to books, articles, or passages
where those topics or name are to be found
are entered under **Indexes.**
SA names of individual authors, lit-
erary works, sacred works, lit-
eratures, and literary forms,
with the subdivision *Concor-
dances,* e.g. **Shakespeare,
William, 1564-1616—Concor-
dances; Bible—Concor-
dances;** etc. [to be added as
needed]
BT **Indexes**
Concrete **691; 693**
BT **Building materials**
Foundations
Masonry
Plaster and plastering
NT **Reinforced concrete**
RT **Cement**
Concrete construction
Concrete building
USE **Concrete construction**

Concrete construction **693**
UF Concrete building
Construction, Concrete
BT **Building**
RT **Concrete**
Concrete—Testing **620.1**
BT **Strength of materials**
Condemnation of land
USE **Eminent domain**
Condensers (Electricity) **621.31**
UF Electric condensers
BT **Induction coils**
Condensers (Steam) **621.1**
BT **Steam engines**
Condominium timesharing
USE **Timesharing (Real estate)**
Condominiums (May subdiv. geog.)
346.04; 643
BT **Apartment houses**
NT **Timesharing (Real estate)**
Conduct of life **170**
Use for materials on standards of behavior
and materials containing moral guidance and
advice to the individual.
UF Morals
Personal conduct
SA classes of persons with the sub-
division *Conduct of life,* e.g.
Children—Conduct of life;
and names of vices and vir-
tues [to be added as needed]
BT **Ethics**
Human behavior
Life skills
NT **Altruism**
Children—Conduct of life
Fairness
Pride and vanity
Simplicity
Teenagers—Conduct of life
Vice
Virtue
Conducting **781.45**
Use for materials on orchestral conducting
or a combination of orchestral and choral con-
ducting. Materials limited to choral conduct-
ing are entered under **Choral conducting.**
BT **Music**
NT **Choral conducting**
RT **Bands (Music)**
Conductors (Music)
Orchestra

Conducting, Choral
  USE **Choral conducting**
Conductors, Electric
  USE **Electric conductors**
Conductors (Music) (May subdiv. geog.)
      784.2092; 920
  UF Bandmasters
      Music conductors
  BT **Musicians**
      Orchestra
  RT **Choral conducting**
      Conducting
Confectionary
  USE **Confectionery**
Confectionery **641.8; 664**
  UF Confectionary
      Sweets
  BT **Cooking**
  NT **Cake**
      Cake decorating
      Candy
Confederacies
  USE **Federal government**
Confederate States of America **973.7**
  BT **United States—History—1861-**
      1865, Civil War
Confederation of American colonies
  USE **United States—History—1783-**
      1809
Conference calls (Teleconferencing)
  USE **Teleconferencing**
Conference papers
  USE **Conference proceedings**
Conference proceedings (May subdiv.
    geog.) **060**
    Use for materials about the papers and other documents stemming from a conference and for collections of various conference proceedings. Materials about conferences apart from the proceedings are entered under **Conferences.**
  UF Conference papers
  SA topics and names of corporate
      bodies with the subdivision
      Conference proceedings [to be
      added as needed]
  BT **Documentation**
  RT **Conferences**
Conferences **060**
    Use for materials about conferences, congresses, or conventions. Materials about the papers and other documents stemming from a conference and collections of various confer-

ence proceedings are entered under **Conference proceedings.**
  UF Congresses
      Congresses and conventions
      Conventions
      International conferences
  SA subjects and names of corporate
      bodies with the subdivision
      Conferences, e.g. **World**
      War, 1939-1945—Confer-
      ences; Physics—Conferences;
      names of specific conferences,
      congresses, or conventions;
      and subjects and names of
      corporate bodies with the sub-
      division *Conference proceed-*
      ings [to be added as needed]
  BT **Intellectual cooperation**
      International cooperation
  NT **Constitutional conventions**
      Political conventions
      World War, 1939-1945—Con-
      ferences
  RT **Conference proceedings**
Conferences, Parent-teacher
  USE **Parent-teacher conferences**
Confession **265**
  UF Auricular confession
  RT **Forgiveness of sin**
      Penance
Confessions of faith
  USE **Creeds**
Confidence game
  USE **Swindlers and swindling**
Configuration (Psychology)
  USE **Gestalt psychology**
Confirmation **265**
  BT **Sacraments**
Conflict management (May subdiv. geog.)
      303.6
  UF Conflict resolution
      Dispute settlement
      Management of conflict
  BT **Management**
      Negotiation
      Problem solving
      Social conflict
  RT **Crisis management**
Conflict of cultures
  USE **Culture conflict**

Conflict of generations   306.874
- UF   Generation gap
- BT   **Child-adult relationship**
  Interpersonal relations
  Parent-child relationship
  Social conflict

Conflict of interests (May subdiv. geog.)
   172; 353.4
- BT   **Political ethics**
- NT   **Misconduct in office**
  Political corruption

Conflict resolution
- USE   **Conflict management**

Conflict, Social
- USE   **Social conflict**

Conformity   **153.8; 302.5; 303.3**
- UF   Nonconformity
  Social conformity
- BT   **Attitude (Psychology)**
  Freedom
- NT   **Persuasion (Psychology)**
- RT   **Deviant behavior**
  Dissent
  Individuality

Confucianism (May subdiv. geog.)   **181;
   299.5**
- BT   **Religions**

Congenital diseases
- USE   **Medical genetics**

Conglomerate corporations (May subdiv.
   geog.)   **338.8**
- UF   Diversified corporations
- BT   **Corporations**
- RT   **Corporate mergers and acqui-
   sitions**

Congregationalism (May subdiv. geog.)
   285.8
- BT   **Christian sects**
- NT   **Unitarianism**
- RT   **Calvinism**
  Puritans

Congregations
- USE   **Religious institutions**

Congress (U.S.)
- USE   **United States. Congress**

Congresses
- USE   **Conferences**
  and subjects with the subdivision *Conferences,* e.g. **World
  War, 1939-1945—Confer-
  ences; Physics—Conferences;**

  and names of specific conferences, congresses, or conventions [to be added as needed]

Congresses and conventions
- USE   **Conferences**

Congressional investigations
- USE   **Governmental investigations**

Conjuring
- USE   **Magic tricks**

Conscience   **170; 241**
- BT   **Christian ethics**
  Duty
  Ethics
- NT   **Freedom of conscience**
  Guilt

Conscientious objectors (May subdiv.
   geog.)   **343; 355.2**
- SA   names of wars with the subdivi-
  sion *Conscientious objectors*
  [to be added as needed]
- BT   **Freedom of conscience**
  War—Religious aspects
- NT   **World War, 1939-1945—Con-
   scientious objectors**
- RT   **Draft resisters**
  Pacifism

Consciousness   **126; 153**
- BT   **Apperception**
  Mind and body
  Perception
  Psychology
- NT   **Gestalt psychology**
  Individuality
  Personality
  Self
  Theory of knowledge
- RT   **Subconsciousness**

Consciousness expanding drugs
- USE   **Hallucinogens**

Conscript labor
- USE   **Forced labor**

Conscription, Military
- USE   **Draft**

Conservation and restoration
- USE   types of art objects, library materials, architecture, and land
  vehicles with the subdivision
  Conservation and restoration,
  e.g. **Automobiles—Conservation and restoration** [to be
  added as needed]

Conservation movement
USE **Environmental movement**
Conservation of biological diversity
USE **Biological diversity conservation**
Conservation of buildings
USE **Architecture—Conservation and restoration**
Conservation of energy
USE **Energy conservation**
Force and energy
Conservation of forests
USE **Forest conservation**
Conservation of natural resources (May subdiv. geog.) **333.72; 639.9**
UF Preservation of natural resources
Resource management
SA types of conservation, e.g. **Soil conservation** [to be added as needed
BT **Environmental protection**
Natural resources
NT **Biological diversity conservation**
Energy conservation
Forest conservation
Nature conservation
Plant conservation
Soil conservation
Water conservation
Wildlife conservation
RT **Environmental policy**
National parks and reserves
Wilderness areas
Conservation of nature
USE **Nature conservation**
Conservation of photographs
USE **Photographs—Conservation and restoration**
Conservation of plants
USE **Plant conservation**
Conservation of power resources
USE **Energy conservation**
Conservation of the soil
USE **Soil conservation**
Conservation of water
USE **Water conservation**
Conservation of wildlife
USE **Wildlife conservation**

Conservation of works of art, books, etc.
USE subjects with the subdivision *Conservation and restoration,* e.g. **Library resources—Conservation and restoration; Painting—Conservation and restoration;** etc. [to be added as needed]
Conservatism (May subdiv. geog.) **320.5**
UF Reaction (Political science)
Right (Political science)
BT **Political science**
Social sciences
RT **Right and left (Political science)**
Conservatories, Home
USE **Garden rooms**
Consolation **152.4; 155.9**
UF Compassion
Solace
Sympathy
BT **Emotions**
Human behavior
RT **Bereavement**
Grief
Consolidation and merger of corporations
USE **Corporate mergers and acquisitions**
Consolidation of schools
USE **Schools—Centralization**
Consortia, Library
USE **Library cooperation**
Constellations **523.8**
SA names of constellations [to be added as needed]
BT **Sky**
RT **Astrology**
Astronomy
Stars
Constitution (U.S.)
USE **United States. Constitution**
Constitutional amendments (May subdiv. geog.) **342**
Use for texts of constitutional amendments and materials about constitutional amendments and the amending process.
SA subjects dealt with in constitutional amendments with the subdivision *Law and legislation,* or *Legal status, laws, etc.* [to be added as needed]

Constitutional amendments—*Continued*
  BT Constitutional law
       Constitutions
Constitutional conventions (May subdiv.
  geog.) 342
  UF Conventions, Constitutional
  BT Conferences
Constitutional history (May subdiv. geog.)
  342

    Use for materials on the history of constitutions. Texts of constitutions are entered under **Constitutions.**
  UF Constitutional law—History
  BT History
  NT Democracy
       Monarchy
       Representative government and
         representation
       Republics
  RT Constitutions
Constitutional history—Ohio   342.771;
  977.1
  UF Ohio—Constitutional history
  BT Ohio—History
Constitutional history—United States
  342.73; 973
  UF United States—Constitutional
        history
  BT United States—History
Constitutional law (May subdiv. geog.)
  342

    Use for materials on constitutions or constitutional law. Texts of constitutions are entered under **Constitutions.**
  BT Law
  NT Citizenship
       Civil rights
       Constitutional amendments
       Democracy
       Election law
       Eminent domain
       Executive power
       Federal government
       Injunctions
       Legislative bodies
       Magna Carta
       Monarchy
       Proportional representation
       Referendum
       Representative government and
        representation
       Republics
       Separation of powers

       Suffrage
       War and emergency powers
  RT Administrative law
       Constitutions
Constitutional law—History
  USE Constitutional history
Constitutional law—Ohio   342.771
  UF Ohio—Constitutional law
Constitutional law—United States
  342.73
  UF United States—Constitutional
        law
Constitutional rights
  USE Civil rights
Constitutions (May subdiv. geog.)   342

    Use for texts of constitutions. Materials about constitutions are entered under either **Constitutional law** or **Constitutional history.**
  UF State constitutions
  BT Law
  NT Constitutional amendments
       Equal rights amendments
  RT Constitutional history
       Constitutional law
Constitutions—Ohio   342.771
  UF Ohio—Constitution
Constitutions—United States   342.73;
  973

    Use for collections of texts of several state or federal constitutions. Materials about constitutions are entered under either **Constitutional history** or **Constitutional law.** Materials on the United States Constitution alone are entered under **United States—Constitution.**
  UF State constitutions
       United States—Constitutions
Construction
  USE Architecture
       Building
       Engineering
Construction, Concrete
  USE Concrete construction
Construction contracts   692
  UF Building contracts
       Building—Contracts and specifi-
        cations
  BT Contracts
Construction equipment   621.8
  UF Building machinery
  BT Machinery
  NT Road machinery
Construction, House
  USE House construction

Construction of roads
　USE　**Roads**
Consular service
　USE　**Diplomatic and consular ser-
　　　　vice**
Consulates
　USE　**Diplomatic and consular ser-
　　　　vice**
Consuls (May subdiv. geog.)　**327.2092**
　BT　**Diplomats**
Consultants　001
　UF　Advisors
　SA　types of consultants [to be add-
　　　　ed as needed]
　BT　**Counseling**
　NT　**Educational consultants**
Consultative management
　USE　**Participative management**
Consumer behavior
　USE　**Consumers**
Consumer boycotts
　USE　**Boycotts**
Consumer credit　332.7
　BT　**Banks and banking
　　　　Credit
　　　　Personal finance**
　NT　**Credit cards
　　　　Installment plan
　　　　Personal loans**
Consumer demand
　USE　**Consumption (Economics)**
Consumer education (May subdiv. geog.)
　　　　640.73
　　　Use for materials on the selection and effi-
　　cient use of consumer goods and services and
　　on methods of educating consumers. Materials
　　on the decision-making processes, external
　　factors, and individual characteristics of con-
　　sumers that determine their purchasing behav-
　　ior are entered under **Consumers**. Materials
　　on the economic theory of consumption and
　　on consumerism or consumer demand are en-
　　tered under **Consumption (Economics)**.
　UF　Buyers' guides
　　　　Consumers' guides
　　　　Shoppers' guides
　BT　**Education
　　　　Home economics**
　RT　**Consumers
　　　　Shopping**
Consumer goods (May subdiv. geog.)
　　　　338.4
　　　Use for materials on products that are pur-
　　chased for personal or household purposes.

　UF　Consumer products
　　　　Merchandise
　BT　**Commercial products
　　　　Manufactures**
　RT　**Consumption (Economics)**
Consumer loans
　USE　**Personal loans**
Consumer organizations
　USE　**Cooperative societies**
Consumer price indexes　338.5
　UF　Cost of living indexes
　　　　Price indexes, Consumer
　BT　**Cost and standard of living
　　　　Prices**
Consumer products
　USE　**Consumer goods**
Consumer protection (May subdiv. geog.)
　　　　343.07; 381.3
　　　Use for materials on governmental and pri-
　　vate activities that guard consumers against
　　dangers to their health, safety, or economic
　　well-being.
　UF　Consumerism
　BT　**Industrial policy**
　NT　**Better business bureaus
　　　　Drugs—Testing
　　　　Food adulteration and inspec-
　　　　tion
　　　　Product recall
　　　　Product safety**
Consumer spending
　USE　**Consumption (Economics)**
Consumerism
　USE　**Consumer protection
　　　　Consumption (Economics)**
Consumers (May subdiv. geog.)　**640.73;
　　　　658.8**
　　　Use for materials on the decision-making
　　processes, external factors, and individual
　　characteristics of consumers that determine
　　their purchasing behavior. Materials on the se-
　　lection and efficient use of consumer goods
　　and services and on methods of educating
　　consumers are entered under **Consumer edu-
　　cation**. Materials on the economic theory of
　　consumption and on consumerism or consum-
　　er demand are entered under **Consumption
　　(Economics)**.
　UF　Consumer behavior
　NT　**Boycotts
　　　　Young consumers**
　RT　**Consumer education
　　　　Consumption (Economics)
　　　　Shopping**

Consumers' cooperative societies
    USE **Cooperative societies**
Consumers' guides
    USE **Consumer education**
Consumers—Information services (May
    subdiv. geog.) **658.8**
    BT **Information services**
Consumption (Economics) (May subdiv.
    geog.) **339.4**

Use for materials on the economic theory of
consumption and on consumerism or consumer demand. Materials on the decision-making
processes, external factors, and individual
characteristics of consumers that determine
their purchasing behavior are entered under
Consumers. Materials on the selection and efficient use of consumer goods and services
and on methods of educating consumers are
entered under **Consumer education.**

    UF Consumer demand
          Consumer spending
          Consumerism
    BT **Economics**
    NT **Prices**
    RT **Consumer goods**
          Consumers
Consumption of alcoholic beverages
    USE **Drinking of alcoholic beverages**
Consumption of energy
    USE **Energy consumption**
Contact lenses **617.7**
    BT **Eyeglasses**
          Lenses
Contagion and contagious diseases
    USE **Communicable diseases**
Contagious diseases
    USE **Communicable diseases**
Container gardening **635.9**
    BT **Gardening**
    RT **Flower gardening**
          House plants
          Indoor gardening
          Miniature gardens
          Window gardening
Containers **688.8**
    BT **Implements, utensils, etc.**
    NT **Baskets**
          Boxes
          Luggage
    RT **Packaging**
Contaminated food
    USE **Food contamination**
Contamination of environment
    USE **Pollution**

Contests **001.4; 790.1**
    UF Competitions
    SA types of contests and names of
          specific contests, e.g. **Olym-**
          pic games; and subjects with
          the subdivision *Competitions*
          or *Tournaments,* e.g. **Litera-**
          ture—Competitions; Ten-
          nis—Tournaments [to be
          added as needed]
    NT **Literature—Competitions**
          Olympic games
          Sports tournaments
    RT **Awards**
Continental drift **551.1**
    UF Drifting of continents
    BT **Continents**
          Geology
    RT **Plate tectonics**
Continental shelf **551.41**
    BT **Geology**
    RT **Territorial waters**
Continents **551.41**
    BT **Earth**
    NT **Continental drift**
          Lost continents
Continuation schools
    USE **Evening and continuation**
          schools
Continuing care communities
    USE **Life care communities**
Continuing care retirement communities
    USE **Life care communities**
Continuing education (May subdiv. geog.)
    374
    UF Lifelong education
          Permanent education
          Recurrent education
    BT **Education**
    NT **Evening and continuation**
          schools
    RT **Adult education**
Contraband trade
    USE **Smuggling**
Contraception
    USE **Birth control**
Contract bridge
    USE **Bridge (Game)**

Contract labor (May subdiv. geog.)
    331.5
  UF Indentured servants
  BT **Labor**
  RT **Peonage**
Contractions
  USE **Abbreviations**
       Ciphers
Contracts 346.02
  UF Agreements
  SA types of contracts, e.g. **Construction contracts** [to be added as needed]
  BT **Commerce**
       Commercial law
  NT **Authors and publishers**
       Construction contracts
       Covenants
       Labor contract
       Liability (Law)
       Marriage contracts
       Negotiable instruments
       Trusts and trustees
Contrition
  USE **Penance**
Control
  USE types of control, e.g. **Flood control; Weather control;** etc., and animals, plants, or processes with the subdivision *Control,* e.g. **Mosquitoes—Control** [to be added as needed]
Control of guns
  USE **Gun control**
Controversial literature
  USE types of religions, denominations, religious orders, and sacred works with the subdivision *Controversial literature,* for materials that argue against or express opposition to those groups or works, e.g. **Christianity—Controversial literature** for materials attacking Christianity; and religions and denominations with the subdivision *Apologetic works,* for materials defending those religions or denominations, e.g. **Christianity—Apologetic**

works for materials defending Christianity [to be added as needed]
Conundrums
  USE **Riddles**
Convenience cooking
  USE **Quick and easy cooking**
Convenience foods 641.3; 664
    Use for materials on prepackaged foods that are easy to prepare for eating.
  UF Fast foods
  BT **Food**
  NT **Fast food restaurants**
Conventions
  USE **Conferences**
       and subjects with the subdivision *Conferences,* e.g. **World War, 1939-1945—Conferences; Physics—Conferences;** and names of specific conferences, congresses, or conventions [to be added as needed]
Conventions, Constitutional
  USE **Constitutional conventions**
Conventions, Political
  USE **Political conventions**
Convents (May subdiv. geog.) **271; 726**
  UF Cloisters
       Nunneries
  BT **Monasteries**
  NT **Monasticism and religious orders for women**
Conversation 808.56
  UF Discussion
       Table talk
       Talking
  BT **Communication**
       Language and languages
  NT **Discussion groups**
       Interviews
       Online chat groups
Conversation and phrase books
  USE **Modern languages—Conversation and phrase books**
       and names of languages and groups of languages with the subdivision *Conversation and phrase books,* e.g. **English language—Conversation and phrase books** [to be added as needed]

Conversation in foreign languages
　　USE　**Modern languages—Conversation and phrase books**
Conversations and phrases
　　USE　**Modern languages—Conversation and phrase books**
Conversion　204; 248.2
　　BT　**Evangelistic work**
　　　　Salvation
　　　　Spiritual life
　　NT　**Converts**
　　RT　**Regeneration (Christianity)**
Conversion of saline water
　　USE　**Sea water conversion**
Conversion of waste products
　　USE　**Recycling**
Converts　204; 248.2
　　Use for materials on converts from one religion or denomination to another.
　　SA　converts to a particular religion or denomination, e.g. **Converts to Catholicism** [to be added as needed]
　　BT　**Conversion**
　　NT　**Converts to Catholicism**
Converts to Catholicism　282
　　UF　Catholic Church—Converts
　　　　Catholic converts
　　BT　**Catholics**
　　　　Converts
Conveying machinery　621.8
　　UF　Conveyors
　　BT　**Machinery**
　　　　Materials handling
　　RT　**Hoisting machinery**
Conveyors
　　USE　**Conveying machinery**
Convict labor (May subdiv. geog.)　331.5; 365
　　UF　Prison labor
　　BT　**Forced labor**
　　　　Prisoners
Convicts
　　USE　**Criminals**
　　　　Prisoners
Cook books
　　USE　**Cooking**
Cookbooks
　　USE　**Cooking**
Cookery
　　USE　**Cooking**

Cookery, American
　　USE　**American cooking**
Cookery for the sick
　　USE　**Cooking for the sick**
Cookery, French
　　USE　**French cooking**
Cooking (May subdiv. geog.)　641.5
　　Use a phrase heading, e.g. **French cooking; Southern cooking;** etc., for distinctive national or regional styles of cooking. For cooking as it is practiced in a particular city, state, province, etc., subdivide **Cooking** geographically.
　　UF　Cook books
　　　　Cookbooks
　　　　Cookery
　　　　Food preparation
　　　　Recipes
　　SA　types of cooking, e.g. **Microwave cooking;** cooking of particular countries or regions, e.g. **French cooking; American cooking; Southern cooking;** etc.; and, for materials on the cooking of specific foods or kinds of food, **Cooking** with a subdivision for the food, e.g. **Cooking—Vegetables; Cooking—Natural foods;** etc. [to be added as needed]
　　BT　**Home economics**
　　NT　**Afternoon teas**
　　　　American cooking
　　　　Baking
　　　　Bread
　　　　Breakfasts
　　　　Cake
　　　　Canning and preserving
　　　　Catering
　　　　Christmas cooking
　　　　Confectionery
　　　　Cooking for the sick
　　　　Desserts
　　　　Dinners
　　　　Fish as food
　　　　Flavoring essences
　　　　French cooking
　　　　Holiday cooking
　　　　Luncheons
　　　　Menus
　　　　Microwave cooking
　　　　Outdoor cooking

Cooking—*Continued*
    Pastry
    Quantity cooking
    Quick and easy cooking
    Salads
    Sandwiches
    Sauces
    Soups
    Southern cooking
    Vegetarian cooking
    Wok cooking
  RT Diet
    Food
    Gastronomy

Cooking for institutions
  USE **Food service**

Cooking for large numbers
  USE **Quantity cooking**

Cooking for the sick **641.5**
  UF Cookery for the sick
    Food for invalids
    Invalid cooking
  SA types of diets, e.g. **Salt-free diet**
    [to be added as needed]
  BT **Cooking**
    Diet in disease
    Nursing
    Sick
  NT **Diet therapy**
    Salt-free diet

Cooking—Natural foods **641.5**
  UF Natural food cooking
  RT **Natural foods**

Cooking utensils
  USE **Kitchen utensils**

Cooking—Vegetables **641.6**
  BT **Vegetables**
  RT **Salads**
    Vegetarian cooking

Cooling appliances
  USE **Refrigeration**

Cooperation (May subdiv. geog.) **334**
  Use for general materials on the theory and history of cooperation and the cooperative movement. Materials dealing specifically with cooperative enterprises are entered under **Cooperative societies.**
  UF Cooperative distribution
    Distribution, Cooperative
  BT **Associations**
    Commerce
    Economics

  NT **Collective settlements**
    Communal living
    Cooperative agriculture
    Cooperative banks
    Cooperative housing
    Cooperative societies
    International cooperation
    Savings and loan associations
  RT **Profit sharing**

Cooperation, Intellectual
  USE **Intellectual cooperation**

Cooperation, Interchurch
  USE **Interdenominational cooperation**

Cooperation, Interdenominational
  USE **Interdenominational cooperation**

Cooperation (Psychology)
  USE **Cooperativeness**

Cooperative agriculture (May subdiv. geog.) **334**
  Use for materials on cooperation in the production and disposal of agricultural products.
  UF Agricultural cooperation
    Agriculture, Cooperative
    Collective farms
    Farmers' cooperatives
  BT **Agriculture**
    Cooperation
  RT **Collective settlements**

Cooperative banks (May subdiv. geog.) **334**
  UF Banks and banking, Cooperative
    People's banks
  BT **Banks and banking**
    Cooperation
    Cooperative societies
    Personal loans
  NT **Credit unions**
  RT **Savings and loan associations**

Cooperative distribution
  USE **Cooperation**
    Cooperative societies

Cooperative education (May subdiv. geog.) **371.2**
  UF Education, Cooperative
    Study-work plan
    Work-based learning
  BT **Vocational education**

Cooperative housing (May subdiv. geog.)
334
- UF Co-ops (Housing)
    Cohousing
    Housing, Cooperative
- BT **Cooperation**
    Housing
- RT **Communal living**

Cooperative learning   371.3
Use for materials on the method of education that involves having students work together on projects in a structured manner.
- UF Group method in teaching
    Group teaching
    Group work in education
- BT **Education**
    Teaching

Cooperative living
- USE **Collective settlements**
    Communal living

Cooperative societies (May subdiv. geog.)
334; 658.8
Use for materials dealing specifically with cooperative enterprises. General materials on the theory and history of cooperation and the cooperative movement are entered under **Cooperation.**
- UF Co-ops
    Consumer organizations
    Consumers' cooperative societies
    Cooperative distribution
    Cooperative stores
    Cooperatives
- SA types of cooperative societies,
    e.g. **Credit unions** [to be
    added as needed]
- BT **Cooperation**
    Corporations
    Societies
- NT **Cooperative banks**
    Savings and loan associations

Cooperative stores
- USE **Cooperative societies**

Cooperativeness   158
- UF Cooperation (Psychology)
- BT **Social psychology**

Cooperatives
- USE **Cooperative societies**

Copiers
- USE **Copying machines**

Coping behavior
- USE **Adjustment (Psychology)**

Coping skills
- USE **Life skills**

Copper engraving
- USE **Engraving**

Copperwork   673; 739.5
- BT **Metalwork**

Copy art (May subdiv. geog.)   **760**
Use for materials on the use of photocopying machines to create original works of art. Materials on clipping art work from published sources to use in creating documents, posters, newsletters, etc., are entered under **Clip art.**
- UF Copying machine art
    Reprographic art
    Xerographic art
- BT **Art**
- RT **Photocopying**

Copy writing
- USE **Advertising copy**

Copying machine art
- USE **Copy art**

Copying machines   681
- UF Copiers
    Copying processes and machines
    Duplicating machines
    Photocopying machines
- BT **Office equipment and supplies**
- RT **Copying processes**

Copying processes   686
- UF Copying processes and machines
    Duplicating processes
    Reproduction processes
    Reprography
- SA names of specific processes [to
    be added as needed]
- BT **Documentation**
- NT **Photocopying**
- RT **Copying machines**

Copying processes and machines
- USE **Copying machines**
    Copying processes

Copyright (May subdiv. geog.)   **346.04;**
352.7
May be subdivided by topic, e.g. **Copyright—Sound recordings.**
- UF International copyright
    Literary property
- NT **Fair use (Copyright)**
- RT **Authors and publishers**
    Intellectual property

Copyright—Sound recordings (May
subdiv. geog.)   **346.04**
- UF Sound recordings—Copyright

Coral reefs and islands (May subdiv.
　　geog.)　**551.42**
　UF　Atolls
　BT　**Geology**
　　　Islands
Corals　563; 593.6
　BT　**Marine animals**
Cordials (Liquor)
　USE　**Liquors**
Core curriculum
　USE　**Colleges and universities—Cur-**
　　　ricula
　　　Education—Curricula
Coretta Scott King Award　028.5
　UF　King Award
　BT　**Children's literature**
　　　Literary prizes
Corn (May subdiv. geog.)　**633.1; 633.2**
　UF　Maize
　BT　**Forage plants**
　　　Grain
Coronary heart diseases
　USE　**Heart diseases**
Corporate accountability
　USE　**Social responsibility of business**
Corporate acquisitions
　USE　**Corporate mergers and acqui-**
　　　sitions
Corporate culture (May subdiv. geog.)
　　　302.3
　UF　Culture, Corporate
　　　Organizational culture
　BT　**Corporations**
Corporate downsizing
　USE　**Downsizing of organizations**
Corporate libraries　027.6
　　Use for materials on libraries located within
　companies, firms, or private businesses, cover-
　ing any subject areas. Materials on libraries
　with a subject focus on business are entered
　under **Business libraries.**
　UF　Company libraries
　　　Industrial libraries
　　　Libraries, Corporate
　BT　**Special libraries**
Corporate mergers and acquisitions
　　(May subdiv. geog.)　**338.8; 658.1**
　UF　Acquisitions, Corporate
　　　Buyouts, Corporate
　　　Consolidation and merger of
　　　　corporations
　　　Corporate acquisitions
　　　Corporate takeovers

　　　Industrial mergers
　　　Mergers
　　　Takeovers, Corporate
　SA　types of institutions and types of
　　　industries and businesses with
　　　the subdivision *Mergers,* e.g.
　　　Railroads—Mergers [to be
　　　added as needed]
　NT　**Leveraged buyouts**
　　　Railroads—Mergers
　RT　**Conglomerate corporations**
　　　Industrial trusts
Corporate patronage of the arts
　USE　**Art patronage**
Corporate responsibility
　USE　**Social responsibility of business**
Corporate symbols
　USE　**Trademarks**
Corporate takeovers
　USE　**Corporate mergers and acqui-**
　　　sitions
Corporate welfare
　USE　**Subsidies**
Corporation law (May subdiv. geog.)
　　　346
　BT　**Commercial law**
　　　Corporations
　　　Law
　NT　**Limited liability companies**
　　　Public service commissions
　RT　**Industrial trusts**
　　　Monopolies
　　　Restraint of trade
Corporations (May subdiv. geog.)
　　　338.7; 658.1
　UF　Companies
　BT　**Business enterprises**
　　　Stocks
　NT　**Conglomerate corporations**
　　　Cooperative societies
　　　Corporate culture
　　　Corporation law
　　　Limited liability companies
　　　Multinational corporations
　　　Municipal ownership
　　　Public service commissions
　　　Trust companies
　RT　**Industrial trusts**
Corporations—Accounting　657; 658.15
　BT　**Accounting**
　　　Bookkeeping

Corporations—Art patronage
USE **Art patronage**
Corporations—Finance 658.15
UF   Capitalization (Finance)
BT   **Finance**
Corporations, Multinational
USE   **Multinational corporations**
Corporations, Nonprofit
USE   **Nonprofit organizations**
Corporations—Social responsibility
USE   **Social responsibility of business**
Corpulence
USE   **Obesity**
Correctional institutions (May subdiv.
geog.)   **365**
UF   Penal institutions
SA   types of correctional institutions
[to be added as needed]
BT   **Punishment**
NT   **Halfway houses**
Penal colonies
Prisons
Reformatories
Correctional services
USE   **Corrections**
Corrections (May subdiv. geog.)   **364.6**
Use for materials on the rehabilitation and
treatment of offenders through parole, penal
custody, and probation programs, and on the
administration of such programs.
UF   Correctional services
Criminals—Rehabilitation pro-
grams
Penology
Reform of criminals
BT   **Administration of criminal jus-
tice**
NT   **Parole**
Probation
Punishment
Correspondence
USE   **Business letters**
Letter writing
Letters
and ethnic groups, classes of
persons, and names of indi-
vidual persons and families
with the subdivision *Corre-
spondence,* e.g. **Authors—
Correspondence** [to be added
as needed]

Correspondence schools and courses
(May subdiv. geog.)   **374.35**
UF   Home education
Home study courses
BT   **Distance education**
Schools
Technical education
University extension
RT   **Self-instruction**
Corrosion and anticorrosives   620.1
UF   Anticorrosive paint
Rust
Rustless coatings
BT   **Industrial chemistry**
RT   **Paint**
Corrupt practices
USE   subjects with the subdivision
Corrupt practices, e.g. **Adop-
tion—Corrupt practices;
Sports—Corrupt practices;**
etc. [to be added as needed]
Corruption in politics
USE   **Political corruption**
Corruption in sports
USE   **Sports—Corrupt practices**
Corruption, Police
USE   **Police corruption**
Corsairs
USE   **Pirates**
Cosmetic surgery
USE   **Plastic surgery**
Cosmetics   646.7
UF   Makeup (Cosmetics)
SA   types of cosmetics [to be added
as needed]
BT   **Personal grooming**
NT   **Perfumes**
Theatrical makeup
RT   **Toiletries**
Cosmetics—Advertising
USE   **Advertising—Cosmetics**
Cosmic rays   539.7
UF   Millikan rays
BT   **Nuclear physics**
Radiation
Radioactivity
Space environment
Cosmobiology
USE   **Space biology**
Cosmochemistry
USE   **Space chemistry**

Cosmogony
USE **Cosmology**
Universe
Cosmography
USE **Cosmology**
Universe
Cosmology   113; 523.1
Use for general or theoretical materials on the science or philosophy of the universe. Materials limited to the physical description of the universe are entered under **Universe.**
UF   Cosmogony
Cosmography
BT   **Universe**
NT   **Biblical cosmology**
Big bang theory
Cosmonauts
USE   **Astronauts**
Cost accounting   657
BT   **Accounting**
Bookkeeping
Cost and standard of living (May subdiv. geog.)   **339.4**
UF   Cost of living
Food, Cost of
Household finances
Standard of living
BT   **Economics**
Home economics
Quality of life
Social conditions
Wealth
NT   **Consumer price indexes**
Household budgets
Subsistence economy
RT   **Prices**
Salaries, wages, etc.
Cost benefit analysis
USE   **Cost effectiveness**
Cost effectiveness   658.15
UF   Benefit cost analysis
Cost benefit analysis
SA   topics with the subdivision *Cost effectiveness,* e.g. **Electric automobiles—Cost effectiveness** [to be added as needed]
BT   **Economics**
NT   **Electric automobiles—Cost effectiveness**
Cost of living
USE   **Cost and standard of living**

Cost of living indexes
USE   **Consumer price indexes**
Cost of medical care
USE   **Medical care—Costs**
Costs
USE   subjects with the subdivision *Costs,* e.g. **Medical care—Costs** [to be added as needed]
Costume (May subdiv. geog.)   **391; 792**
Use for materials on the characteristic costume of ethnic or national groups and for materials on fancy dress and theatrical costumes. For the traditional national costume of a particular country subdivide geographically. Materials on clothing and the art of dress from day to day in practical situations, including historical dress and the clothing of various professions or classes of persons, are entered under **Clothing and dress.** Materials on the prevailing mode or style of dress are entered under **Fashion.**
UF   Acting—Costume
Fancy dress
Style in dress
Theatrical costume
SA   costume of particular ethnic groups, e.g. **Native American costume;** and professions and classes of persons with the subdivision *Clothing,* e.g. **Handicapped—Clothing** [to be added as needed]
BT   **Decorative arts**
Ethnology
Manners and customs
NT   **Armor**
Children's costumes
Disguise
Fans
Hats
Jewelry
Masks (Facial)
Native American costume
Theatrical makeup
Uniforms
Wigs
RT   **Clothing and dress**
Cot death
USE   **Sudden infant death syndrome**
Cottage industry
USE   **Home-based business**
Cotton   633.5; 677
BT   **Economic botany**
Fabrics

Cotton—*Continued*
    Fibers
    Yarn
Cotton manufacture 677
    BT   **Textile industry**
Councils and synods 262
    UF   Church councils
          Ecumenical councils
          Synods
    SA   names of specific councils and
          synods, e.g. **Vatican Council**
          (2nd : 1962-1965) [to be
          added as needed]
    BT   **Christianity**
          Church history
    NT   **Vatican Council (2nd : 1962-**
          1965)
Counseling 361; 371.4
    UF   Guidance
    SA   types of counseling; and ethnic
          groups and classes of persons
          with the subdivision *Counsel-*
          ing of, e.g. **Employees—**
          Counseling of [to be added
          as needed]
    BT   **Applied psychology**
          Helping behavior
          Personnel management
    NT   **Advice columns**
          Consultants
          Crisis centers
          Drug abuse counseling
          Educational counseling
          Elderly—Counseling of
          Employees—Counseling of
          Family therapy
          Health counseling
          Hotlines (Telephone counseling)
          Marriage counseling
          Mentoring
          Peer counseling
          School counseling
          Self-help groups
          Social group work
          Vocational guidance
    RT   **Interviewing**
          Social case work
Counseling of
    USE   classes of persons and ethnic
          groups with the subdivision
          Counseling of, e.g. **Elderly—**

Counseling of [to be added
    as needed]
Counseling of the elderly
    USE   **Elderly—Counseling of**
Counseling with the aged
    USE   **Elderly—Counseling of**
Counter culture (May subdiv. geog.)
    306
    UF   Counterculture
          Nonconformity
          Subculture
    BT   **Lifestyles**
          Social conditions
    NT   **Bohemianism**
    RT   **Alternative lifestyles**
          Collective settlements
          Communal living
          Radicalism
Counter-Reformation (May subdiv. geog.)
    270.6
    UF   Anti-Reformation
    BT   **Christianity**
          Church history—1500-, Mod-
          ern period
    RT   **Reformation**
Counter-terrorism
    USE   **Terrorism—Prevention**
Counterculture
    USE   **Counter culture**
Counterespionage
    USE   **Intelligence service**
Counterfeits and counterfeiting 332;
    364.1
    BT   **Coinage**
          Crime
          Forgery
          Impostors and imposture
          Money
          Swindlers and swindling
    NT   **Art—Forgeries**
          Literary forgeries
Counterintelligence
    USE   **Intelligence service**
Counterpoint 781.2
    BT   **Composition (Music)**
          Music—Theory
    NT   **Fugue**
Counting 513.2
    Use for materials on counting, including
counting books. Materials on numbers, num-
bering, and systems of numeration are entered

Counting—*Continued*
under **Numbers.** Materials on the conceptualization of numbers are entered under **Number
concept.**

    UF   Counting books
    BT   **Arithmetic—Study and teach-
         ing**
    NT   **Number games**
    RT   **Numbers**

Counting books
    USE **Counting**

Country and western music
    USE **Country music**

Country churches
    USE **Rural churches**

Country life (May subdiv. geog.)
    307.72; 630

    Use for descriptive, popular, and literary
materials on living in the country. Materials
on social organization and conditions in rural
communities are entered under **Rural sociology.**

    UF   Rural life
    BT   **Manners and customs**
    NT   **Agriculture—Societies
         Farm life
         Mountain life
         Plantation life**
    RT   **Outdoor life
         Rural sociology**

**Country life—United States   307.72;
630**

Country music   781.642
    UF   Country and western music
         Hillbilly music
    BT   **Folk music—United States
         Popular music**

Country schools
    USE **Rural schools**

Country stores
    USE **General stores**

County agricultural agents   630.7
    BT   **Agricultural extension work
         Agriculture—Study and teach-
         ing**

County government (May subdiv. geog.)
    320.8; 352.15
    UF   County officers
    BT   **Local government**

County libraries
    USE **Public libraries
         Regional libraries**

County officers
    USE **County government**

County planning
    USE **Regional planning**

Coupons (Retail trade)   659
    BT   **Advertising**

Coups d'état
    USE **Revolutions**

Courage   179
    UF   Bravery
         Heroism
    BT   **Virtue**
    NT   **Encouragement
         Morale**
    RT   **Heroes and heroines**

Courses of study
    USE **Education—Curricula**

Court fools
    USE **Fools and jesters**

Court life
    USE **Courts and courtiers**

Court martial
    USE **Courts martial and courts of
         inquiry**

Courtesy   177; 395
    UF   Manners
         Politeness
    BT   **Etiquette
         Virtue**

Courtiers
    USE **Courts and courtiers**

Courting
    USE **Courtship**

Courtroom drama
    USE **Legal drama (Films)
         Legal drama (Radio programs)
         Legal drama (Television pro-
         grams)**

Courts (May subdiv. geog.)   **347**
    UF   Judiciary
    BT   **Law**
    NT   **Arbitration and award
         Civil procedure
         Courts martial and courts of
         inquiry
         Criminal procedure
         Jury
         Juvenile courts
         United States. Supreme Court**
    RT   **Administration of justice
         Judges**

Courts and courtiers   394; 929.7
  UF   Court life
        Courtiers
  SA   names of countries, cities, etc.,
        with the subdivision *Courts
        and courtiers* [to be added as
        needed]
  BT   **Manners and customs**
  NT   **Fools and jesters**
        Princes
        Princesses
  RT   **Kings and rulers**
        Queens
Courts martial and courts of inquiry
  343
  UF   Court martial
        Military courts
  BT   **Courts**
        Trials
  RT   **Military law**
Courts—United States   347.73
  UF   Federal courts
        United States—Courts
Courtship (May subdiv. geog.)   306.73;
  392.4
  UF   Courting
  BT   **Love**
  NT   **Dating (Social customs)**
  RT   **Marriage**
Courtship (Animal behavior)
  USE   **Animal courtship**
Courtship of animals
  USE   **Animal courtship**
Cousins   306.87
  BT   **Family**
Couturiers
  USE   **Fashion designers**
Covenants   202; 231.7

  Use for materials on religious covenants.
  May be subdivided by religion as needed. Ma-
  terials on non-religious covenants are entered
  under **Contracts.**
  UF   Agreements
  BT   **Contracts**
        Theology
Covens
  USE   **Witches**
Coverlets
  USE   **Bedspreads**
        Quilts
Covetousness
  USE   **Avarice**

Cowboys
  USE   **Cowhands**
Cowgirls
  USE   **Cowhands**
Cowhands (May subdiv. geog.)   636.2;
  978
  UF   Cowboys
        Cowgirls
        Gauchos
  BT   **Frontier and pioneer life**
        Ranch life
  RT   **Rodeos**
Cowhands—Songs   782.42
  UF   Cowhands—Songs and music
  BT   **Music**
        Songs
Cowhands—Songs and music
  USE   **Cowhands—Songs**
Cows
  USE   **Cattle**
CPR (First aid)   616.1
  UF   Cardiopulmonary resuscitation
  BT   **First aid**
  RT   **Cardiac resuscitation**
Crabs   565; 595.3
  BT   **Crustacea**
        Shellfish
Crack babies
  USE   **Children of drug addicts**
Crack cocaine
  USE   **Crack (Drug)**
Crack (Drug)   362.29; 615
  UF   Crack cocaine
  BT   **Cocaine**
Cradle songs
  USE   **Lullabies**
Craft festivals
  USE   **Craft shows**
Craft shows   745
  UF   Craft festivals
  BT   **Exhibitions**
        Festivals
        Handicraft
Crafts (Arts)
  USE   **Arts and crafts movement**
        Handicraft
Cranes, derricks, etc.   621.8
  UF   Derricks
  BT   **Hoisting machinery**
Crank (Drug)
  USE   **Ice (Drug)**

Cranks
USE **Eccentrics and eccentricities**
Crashes (Finance)
USE **Financial crises**
Crates
USE **Boxes**
Crayon drawing   741.2
UF   Blackboard drawing
BT   **Drawing**
RT   **Pastel drawing**
Crazes
USE   **Fads**
Creation   213; 231.7
BT   **Natural theology**
RT   **Biblical cosmology**
Creationism
Evolution
Universe
Creation (Literary, artistic, etc.)   153.3
UF   Inspiration
BT   **Genius**
Imagination
Intellect
Inventions
NT   **Creative writing**
Planning
RT   **Creative ability**
Creation—Study and teaching
USE   **Creationism**
Evolution—Study and teaching
Creationism   231.7
Use for materials on the doctrine that the universe was created by God out of nothing in the initial seven days of time and that all biological species were created rather than evolving from pre-existing types through modifications in successive generations.
UF   Christianity and evolution
Creation—Study and teaching
Evolution and Christianity
Fundamentalism and education
Fundamentalism and evolution
Scientific creationism
BT   **Christianity—Doctrines**
RT   **Bible and science**
Creation
Evolution
Evolution—Study and teaching
Religion and science

Creative ability   153.3; 701; 801
UF   Creativity
BT   **Ability**
NT   **Creative thinking**
RT   **Creation (Literary, artistic, etc.)**
Creative activities   372.5
Use for materials on activities for children that result in some form of personal expression such as painting, cooking, drama, etc.
UF   Activities curriculum
BT   **Amusements**
Elementary education
Kindergarten
RT   **Handicraft**
Creative movement
USE   **Movement education**
Creative thinking   153.4
BT   **Creative ability**
Creative writing   808
UF   Writing (Authorship)
BT   **Authorship**
Creation (Literary, artistic, etc.)
Language arts
Creativity
USE   **Creative ability**
Creature films
USE   **Horror films**
Credibility
USE   **Truthfulness and falsehood**
Credit (May subdiv. geog.)   332.7
UF   Bills of credit
Letters of credit
BT   **Finance**
Money
NT   **Agricultural credit**
Collecting of accounts
Consumer credit
Installment plan
Negotiable instruments
RT   **Banks and banking**
Debtor and creditor
Loans
Credit card crimes
USE   **Credit card fraud**
Credit card fraud   364.16
UF   Credit card crimes
BT   **Fraud**
Swindlers and swindling

Credit cards 332.7
  UF Bank credit cards
      Banks and banking—Credit
        cards
  BT **Consumer credit**
Credit unions (May subdiv. geog.) **334**
  Use for materials on cooperative associations that make small loans to its members at low interest rates.
  BT **Cooperative banks**
Creditor
  USE **Debtor and creditor**
Creeds 202; 238
  Use for materials about the concise, formal, and authorized statements of doctrines and for the texts of those statements.
  UF Confessions of faith
  SA names of religions and individual denominations with the subdivision *Creeds,* e.g. **Catholic Church—Creeds** [to be added as needed]
  BT **Doctrinal theology**
  NT **Apostles' Creed**
      Catholic Church—Creeds
      Nicene Creed
  RT **Catechisms**
Cremation 363.7; 393; 614
  UF Incineration
      Mortuary customs
  BT **Public health**
      Sanitation
  RT **Burial**
      Funeral rites and ceremonies
Creole folk songs 782.42162
  UF Folk songs, Creole
  BT **Folk songs**
Creoles (May subdiv. geog.) **305.84; 972.9; 976**
  BT **Ethnic groups**
Crests
  USE **Heraldry**
Crew (Rowing)
  USE **Rowing**
Crewelwork 746.44
  BT **Embroidery**
Crib death
  USE **Sudden infant death syndrome**
Crime (May subdiv. geog.) **364**
  UF Crimes
      Criminology
      Felony

  SA types of crimes, e.g. **Computer crimes** [to be added as needed]
  BT **Administration of criminal justice**
      Social problems
  NT **Assassination**
      Atrocities
      Computer crimes
      Counterfeits and counterfeiting
      Crime prevention
      Crimes against humanity
      Crimes without victims
      Criminals
      Drugs and crime
      Drunk driving
      Forgery
      Fraud
      Hate crimes
      Homicide
      Impostors and imposture
      Juvenile delinquency
      Lynching
      Offenses against property
      Offenses against public safety
      Offenses against the person
      Organized crime
      Racketeering
      Riots
      School shootings
      Sex crimes
      Smuggling
      Swindlers and swindling
      Theft
      Treason
      Victims of crimes
      Vigilance committees
      White collar crimes
  RT **Criminal law**
      Police
      Punishment
      Trials
      Vice
Crime and drugs
  USE **Drugs and crime**
Crime and narcotics
  USE **Drugs and crime**
Crime comics
  USE **Mystery comic books, strips, etc.**

Crime films
USE **Film noir**
Gangster films
Mystery films
Crime plays
USE **Mystery and detective plays**
Crime prevention (May subdiv. geog.)
364.4
UF Prevention of crime
BT **Crime**
NT **Burglary protection**
Crime prevention—Citizen participation
(May subdiv. geog.) **364.4**
BT **Political participation**
Crime programs
USE **Mystery radio programs**
Mystery television programs
Crime stories
USE **Mystery fiction**
Crime syndicates
USE **Organized crime**
Racketeering
Crime—United States **364.973**
Crime victims
USE **Victims of crimes**
Crimean War, 1853-1856 **947**
UF Great Britain—History—1853-
1856, Crimean War
Russo-Turkish War, 1853-1856
Crimes
USE **Crime**
Crimes against humanity (May subdiv.
geog.) **364.1**
BT **Crime**
NT **Forced labor**
Genocide
Slavery
War crimes
Crimes against public safety
USE **Offenses against public safety**
Crimes against the person
USE **Offenses against the person**
Crimes, Military
USE **Military offenses**
Crimes of hate
USE **Hate crimes**
Crimes, Political
USE **Political crimes and offenses**
Crimes without victims **364.1**
UF Non-victim crimes
Nonvictim crimes

Victimless crimes
BT **Crime**
Criminal law
Criminal assault
USE **Offenses against the person**
Criminal behavior
USE **Criminal psychology**
Criminal investigation (May subdiv.
geog.) **363.25**
BT **Law enforcement**
NT **Criminals—Identification**
Eavesdropping
Fingerprints
Lie detectors and detection
Missing persons
Wiretapping
RT **Detectives**
Forensic sciences
Police
Criminal justice, Administration of
USE **Administration of criminal jus-
tice**
Criminal law (May subdiv. geog.) **345**
UF Codes, Penal
Misdemeanors (Law)
Penal codes
Penal law
SA types of crimes, e.g. **Homicide**
[to be added as needed]
BT **Law**
NT **Administration of criminal jus-
tice**
Adoption—Corrupt practices
Capital punishment
Crimes without victims
Executions and executioners
Homicide
Insanity defense
Jury
Kidnapping
Military offenses
Misconduct in office
Obscenity (Law)
Offenses against property
Offenses against public safety
Offenses against the person
Political crimes and offenses
Probation
Prohibition
Sports—Corrupt practices
Tax evasion

194

Criminal law—*Continued*

      Trials

      Vigilance committees

  RT **Crime**

      Criminal procedure

      Punishment

Criminal procedure (May subdiv. geog.) **345**

  BT **Courts**

  NT **Executions and executioners**

      Torture

  RT **Criminal law**

Criminal psychiatry

  USE **Criminal psychology**

Criminal psychology **364.3**

  UF Criminal behavior

      Criminal psychiatry

  BT **Psychology**

  RT **Abnormal psychology**

Criminalistics

  USE **Forensic sciences**

Criminals (May subdiv. geog.) **364.3; 364.6**

  UF Convicts

      Delinquents

      Outlaws

  BT **Crime**

  NT **Gangs**

      Impostors and imposture

      Pirates

      Prisoners

      Serial killers

      Swindlers and swindling

      Thieves

Criminals and drugs

  USE **Criminals—Drug use**

Criminals and narcotics

  USE **Criminals—Drug use**

Criminals—Drug use **362.29; 364.3**

  UF Criminals and drugs

      Criminals and narcotics

      Drugs and criminals

      Narcotics and criminals

  RT **Drugs and crime**

Criminals—Identification **363.25**

  BT **Criminal investigation**

      Identification

  NT **Fingerprints**

Criminals—Rehabilitation programs

  USE **Corrections**

Criminology

  USE **Crime**

Crippled children

  USE **Physically handicapped children**

Crippled people

  USE **Physically handicapped**

Crisis centers **361.3; 362**

  UF Crisis intervention centers

  SA types of crisis centers, e.g. **Hotlines (Telephone counseling)** [to be added as needed]

  BT **Counseling**

      Social work

  RT **Hotlines (Telephone counseling)**

Crisis counseling

  USE **Hotlines (Telephone counseling)**

Crisis intervention centers

  USE **Crisis centers**

Crisis intervention (Mental health services) (May subdiv. geog.) **362.2; 616.89**

  UF Crisis intervention (Psychiatry)

      Emergency mental health services

  BT **Mental health services**

Crisis intervention (Psychiatry)

  USE **Crisis intervention (Mental health services)**

Crisis intervention telephone service

  USE **Hotlines (Telephone counseling)**

Crisis management **658.4**

  BT **Management**

      Problem solving

  RT **Conflict management**

Critical thinking **153.4; 160**

Use for materials on thinking that is based on sound logic and the careful evaluation of all pertinent evidence.

  BT **Decision making**

      Logic

      Problem solving

      Reasoning

      Thought and thinking

Criticism **801**

Use for materials on the history, principles, methods, etc., of criticism in general and of literary criticism in particular. Materials that are themselves histories or criticisms of literature are entered under **Literature—History and criticism.** Criticism of the work of an individual author, artist, composer, etc., is entered under that person's name as a subject; only in the case of voluminous authors is it necessary to add the subdivision *Criticism.* Criticism of a single work is entered under the name of the author, artist, or composer, followed by the title of the work.

Criticism—*Continued*
UF Appraisal of books
Books—Appraisal
Criticism and interpretation
Criticism, interpretation, etc.
Evaluation of literature
Literary criticism
Literature—Evaluation
SA literature, film, and music subjects with the subdivision *History and criticism*, e.g. **English poetry—History and criticism**; and names of voluminous authors and of sacred works with the subdivision *Criticism*, e.g. **Shakespeare, William, 1564-1616—Criticism; Bible—Criticism**; etc. [to be added as needed]
BT **Aesthetics**
Literature
Rhetoric
NT **Art criticism**
Book reviewing
Dramatic criticism
Feminist criticism
RT **Literary style**
Criticism and interpretation
USE **Criticism**
and literature, film, and music subjects with the subdivision *History and criticism*, e.g. **English poetry—History and criticism**; and names of voluminous authors and of sacred works with the subdivision *Criticism*, e.g. **Shakespeare, William, 1564-1616—Criticism; Bible—Criticism**; etc. [to be added as needed]
Criticism, Feminist
USE **Feminist criticism**
Criticism, interpretation, etc.
USE **Criticism**
and literature, film, and music subjects with the subdivision *History and criticism*, e.g. **English poetry—History and criticism**; and names of voluminous authors and of sacred works with the subdivision

Criticism, e.g. **Shakespeare, William, 1564-1616—Criticism; Bible—Criticism**; etc. [to be added as needed]
Cro-Magnons   569.9; 930.1
UF Cromagnons
BT **Prehistoric peoples**
Crocheting   746.43
BT **Needlework**
NT **Beadwork**
Lace and lace making
Crockery
USE **Pottery**
Crocodiles (May subdiv. geog.)   **597.98**
BT **Reptiles**
RT **Alligators**
Cromagnons
USE **Cro-Magnons**
Crop dusting
USE **Aeronautics in agriculture**
Crop reports
USE **Agriculture—Statistics**
Crop rotation   631.5
UF Rotation of crops
BT **Agriculture**
Crop spraying
USE **Aeronautics in agriculture**
Crops
USE **Farm produce**
Cross cultural conflict
USE **Culture conflict**
Cross-cultural psychology
USE **Ethnopsychology**
Cross-cultural studies   306
Use for materials on the systematic comparison of two or more cultural groups, either within the same country or in separate countries.
UF Comparison of cultures
Cross cultural studies
Intercultural studies
Transcultural studies
SA topics with the subdivision *Cross-cultural studies*, e.g. **Marriage—Cross-cultural studies** [to be added as needed]
BT **Culture**
Social sciences
Cross cultural studies
USE **Cross-cultural studies**

Cross-examination
  USE **Witnesses**
Cross-stitch 746.44
  BT **Embroidery**
Crossword puzzles 793.73
  BT **Puzzles**
      Word games
Crowds 302.3
  UF Mobs
  NT **Demonstrations**
      Riot control
  RT **Riots**
      Social psychology
Crown lands
  USE **Public lands**
CRT display terminals
  USE **Computer monitors**
CRTs
  USE **Cathode ray tubes**
Crucifixion of Jesus Christ
  USE **Jesus Christ—Crucifixion**
Crude oil
  USE **Petroleum**
Cruelty 179
  UF Brutality
  BT **Ethics**
  NT **Atrocities**
      Torture
Cruelty to animals
  USE **Animal welfare**
Cruelty to children
  USE **Child abuse**
Cruises
  USE **Ocean travel**
Crusades 909.07
  BT **Church history—600-1500,**
      Middle Ages
  RT **Chivalry**
Crushes 152.4; 177
  UF Romantic crushes
  BT **Friendship**
      Love
Crustacea 565; 595.3
  SA names of specific crustaceans,
      e.g. **Lobsters** [to be added as
      needed]
  BT **Shellfish**
  NT **Crabs**
      Lobsters

Cryobiology 571.4
  UF Freezing
      Low temperature biology
  BT **Biology**
      Cold
      Low temperatures
  NT **Cold—Physiological effect**
      Frozen embryos
Cryogenic interment
  USE **Cryonics**
Cryogenic surgery
  USE **Cryosurgery**
Cryogenics
  USE **Low temperatures**
Cryonics 621.5
  UF Cryogenic interment
      Freezing of human bodies
      Human cold storage
  BT **Burial**
Cryosurgery 617
  UF Cryogenic surgery
  BT **Cold—Therapeutic use**
      Surgery
Cryotherapy
  USE **Cold—Therapeutic use**
Cryptography 652
  UF Code deciphering
      Code enciphering
      Secret writing
  BT **Signs and symbols**
      Writing
  RT **Ciphers**
Crystal gazing
  USE **Divination**
Crystal meth (Drug)
  USE **Ice (Drug)**
Crystallization
  USE **Crystals**
Crystallography
  USE **Crystals**
Crystals 548
  UF Crystallization
      Crystallography
  SA types of crystals, e.g. **Quartz** [to
      be added as needed]
  BT **Physical chemistry**
      Solids
  NT **Quartz**
  RT **Minerals**
Cub Scouts
  USE **Boy Scouts**

Cuba 972.91
    May be subdivided like United States except for *History.*
    BT **Islands**
Cuba—History 972.91
Cuba—History—1958-1959, Revolution
    972.9106
Cuba—History—1959- 972.9106
Cuba—History—1961, Invasion
    972.9106
    UF   Bay of Pigs invasion
          Cuban invasion, 1961
          Invasion of Cuba, 1961
Cuban invasion, 1961
    USE **Cuba—History—1961, Invasion**
Cube root 513.2
    BT **Arithmetic**
Cubic measurement
    USE **Volume (Cubic content)**
Cubism (May subdiv. geog.) 709.04;
    759.06
    BT **Art**
Cultivated plants (May subdiv. geog.)
    581.6; 631.5
    UF   Plants, Cultivated
    BT   **Agriculture**
          Gardening
          Plants
    NT   **Annuals (Plants)**
          House plants
          Ornamental plants
          Perennials
Cultivated plants—United States 581.6;
    631.5
Cults (May subdiv. geog.) 209; 306.6
    Use for materials on groups or movements whose beliefs or practices differ significantly from the traditional religions and are often focused upon a charismatic leader. Materials on the major world religions are entered under **Religions.** Materials on independent religious groups whose teachings or practices fall within the normative bounds of the major world religions are entered under **Sects.**
    UF   Religious cults
    BT   **Religions**
    NT   **New Age movement**
    RT   **Sects**
Cultural anthropology
    USE **Ethnology**
Cultural change
    USE **Social change**
Cultural diversity in the workplace
    USE **Diversity in the workplace**

Cultural exchange programs
    USE **Exchange of persons programs**
Cultural heritage
    USE **Cultural property**
Cultural life
    USE **Intellectual life**
Cultural patrimony
    USE **Cultural property**
Cultural policy (May subdiv. geog.) 306
    Use for materials on official government policy toward educational, artistic, intellectual, or other cultural activities and organizations in general.
    UF   Government policy
          Intellectual life—Government
            policy
          State encouragement of science,
            literature, and art
    SA   types of artistic or intellectual
            activities with the subdivision
            Government policy [to be
            added as needed]
    BT   **Culture**
          Intellectual life
    NT   **Cultural property—Protection**
Cultural policy—United States 306
    UF   United States—Cultural policy
Cultural property (May subdiv. geog.)
    344
    Use for materials on property that is considered essential to a nation's cultural heritage.
    UF   Cultural heritage
          Cultural patrimony
          Heritage property
          National heritage
          National patrimony
          National treasure
    BT   **Property**
Cultural property—Protection (May
    subdiv. geog.) 344
    Use for materials on protecting cultural heritage property from theft, misappropriation, or exportation. Materials on identifying and preserving historically important towns, buildings, sites, etc., are entered under **Historic preservation.**
    UF   Cultural property—Protection—
            Government policy
          Cultural resources management
    BT   **Cultural policy**
    RT   **Historic preservation**
Cultural property—Protection—Government
    policy
    USE **Cultural property—Protection**

Cultural relations 303.48; 306; 344
  UF Intercultural relations
  BT **Intellectual cooperation**
      International cooperation
      International relations
  NT **Exchange of persons programs**
      Interfaith relations
Cultural resources management
  USE **Cultural property—Protection**
Cultural tourism (May subdiv. geog.)
      910
  UF Heritage tourism
      Historical tourism
      History tourism
  BT **Tourist trade**
Culturally deprived
  USE **Socially handicapped**
Culturally deprived children
  USE **Socially handicapped children**
Culturally handicapped
  USE **Socially handicapped**
Culturally handicapped children
  USE **Socially handicapped children**
Culture 306; 909
  Use for materials on the sum total of ways of living or thinking established by a group of human beings and transmitted from one generation to the next, including a concern for what is regarded as excellent in the arts, manners, scholarship, etc.
  SA regions, countries, states, etc., with the subdivisions *Intellectual life; Civilization;* or *Social life and customs,* e.g. **United States—Intellectual life; United States—Civilization; United States—Social life and customs;** etc. [to be added as needed]
  NT **Acculturation**
      Cross-cultural studies
      Cultural policy
      Humanism
      Intellectual life
      Language and culture
      Material culture
      Multiculturalism
      Pluralism (Social sciences)
      Popular culture
  RT **Anthropology**
      Civilization
      Education
      Learning and scholarship

Sociology
Culture conflict (May subdiv. geog.)
      155.8; 306; 155.8
  UF Conflict of cultures
      Cross cultural conflict
      Culture shock
      Future shock
  BT **Ethnic relations**
      Ethnopsychology
      Race relations
Culture contact
  USE **Acculturation**
Culture, Corporate
  USE **Corporate culture**
Culture shock
  USE **Culture conflict**
Curates
  USE **Clergy**
Curiosities and wonders (May subdiv. geog.)   030
  UF Enigmas
      Facts, Miscellaneous
      Miscellanea
      Miscellaneous facts
      Oddities
      Trivia
      Wonders
  SA subjects with the subdivision *Miscellanea,* e.g. **Medicine—Miscellanea** [to be added as needed]
  NT **Eccentrics and eccentricities**
      Medicine—Miscellanea
      Monsters
      World records
Curiosity 155.2
  UF Exploratory behavior
      Inquisitiveness
  BT **Human behavior**
Currency
  USE **Money**
Currency devaluation
  USE **Monetary policy**
Current events 909.82
  Use for materials on the study and teaching of current events. Accounts or discussions of the events themselves are entered under the appropriate heading for historical period or history of a place. Periodicals and yearbooks devoted to current events are entered under **History—Periodicals.**
  BT **Modern history—Study and teaching**

Currents, Electric
  USE **Electric currents**
Currents, Ocean
  USE **Ocean currents**
Curricula
  USE **Education—Curricula**
     and types of education and
     schools with the subdivision
     Curricula, e.g. **Library edu-**
     cation—Curricula [to be
     added as needed]
Curriculum development
  USE **Curriculum planning**
Curriculum materials centers
  USE **Instructional materials centers**
Curriculum planning (May subdiv. geog.)
    375
  UF Curriculum development
  BT **Education—Curricula**
      Planning
  NT **Interdisciplinary approach in**
      education
Curtains
  USE **Draperies**
Custody kidnapping
  USE **Parental kidnapping**
Custody of children
  USE **Child custody**
Custom duties
  USE **Tariff**
Customer relations 658.8
  BT **Business**
      Public relations
  NT **Customer services**
Customer service
  USE **Customer services**
Customer services 658.8
  UF Customer service
      Service, Customer
      Service (in industry)
      Services, Customer
      Technical service
  BT **Customer relations**
Customs and practices
  USE religions, denominations, reli-
     gious orders, and religious
     holidays with the subdivision
     Customs and practices, e.g.
     Judaism—Customs and
     practices [to be added as
     needed]

Customs, Social
  USE **Manners and customs**
Customs (Tariff)
  USE **Tariff**
Cybercommerce
  USE **Electronic commerce**
Cybernetics 003
  UF Automatic control
      Mechanical brains
  BT **Communication**
      Electronics
      System theory
  NT **Bionics**
      System analysis
      Systems engineering
Cybersex
  USE **Computer sex**
Cybershopping
  USE **Internet shopping**
Cyberspace 006
    Use for materials on the non-physical envi-
    ronment created by the Internet or other com-
    puter networks.
  BT **Computer networks**
      Space and time
Cycles 115
  UF Cyclic theory
      Natural cycles
      Periodicity
  NT **Biological rhythms**
      Business cycles
      Life cycles (Biology)
  RT **Rhythm**
      Time
Cyclic theory
  USE **Cycles**
Cycling 796.6
  UF Bicycles and bicycling
      Bicycling
      Biking
  BT **Exercise**
      Outdoor recreation
      Sports
  NT **Bicycle racing**
      Bicycle touring
      Motorcycling
      Mountain biking
  RT **Bicycles**
      Tricycles
Cyclones (May subdiv. geog.) **551.55**
    Use for materials on large-scale storms that
    involve high winds rotating around a center of

Cyclones—*Continued*

low atmospheric pressure. Materials on the cyclones of the West Indies are entered under **Hurricanes.** Materials on the cyclones of the China Seas and the Philippines are entered under **Typhoons.**

BT   Meteorology

Storms

Winds

NT   Hurricanes

Typhoons

Cyclopedias

USE   **Encyclopedias and dictionaries**

Cyclotron

USE   **Cyclotrons**

Cyclotrons   539.7

UF   Atom smashing

Cyclotron

Magnetic resonance accelerator

BT   Atoms

Nuclear physics

Transmutation (Chemistry)

Cytology

USE   **Cells**

Czech Republic   943.71

Use for materials on this part of the former country of Czechoslovakia since its becoming independent on January 1, 1993. May be subdivided like United States except for *History.*

RT   **Czechoslovakia**

Czechoslovakia   943.703

Use for materials on the former country of Czechoslovakia through December 31, 1992. Materials on the two parts of the former country of Czechoslovakia, which became independent on January 1, 1993, are entered under **Czech Republic** and **Slovakia.**

RT   **Czech Republic**

Slovakia

Czechoslovakia—History—1918-1968   943.703

Czechoslovakia—History—1945-1992   943.704

UF   Czechoslovakia—History—1989-1992

Czechoslovakia—History—1968-1989   943.704

Czechoslovakia—History—1989-1992

USE   **Czechoslovakia—History—1945-1992**

D.D.T. (Insecticide)

USE   **DDT (Insecticide)**

D Day

USE   **Normandy (France), Attack on, 1944**

Daily readings (Spiritual exercises)

USE   **Devotional calendars**

Dairies

USE   **Dairying**

Dairy cattle   636.2

SA   names of breeds of dairy cattle [to be added as needed]

BT   Cattle

Dairying

NT   Holstein-Friesian cattle

Dairy farming

USE   **Dairying**

Dairy industry

USE   **Dairying**

Dairy products   637; 641.3

UF   Products, Dairy

SA   types of dairy products [to be added as needed]

BT   **Animal products**

NT   **Butter**

Cheese

Milk

Dairying (May subdiv. geog.)   **636.2; 637**

Use for materials on the production and marketing of milk and milk products and for general materials on dairy farming.

UF   Dairies

Dairy farming

Dairy industry

BT   Agriculture

Livestock industry

NT   Dairy cattle

Milk

Dams (May subdiv. geog.)   **627**

SA   names of dams, e.g. **Hoover Dam (Ariz. and Nev.)** [to be added as needed]

BT   **Civil engineering**

Hydraulic structures

Water supply

NT   Hoover Dam (Ariz. and Nev.)

Dance (May subdiv. geog.)   **792.8; 793.3**

Use for materials on recreational dancing as well as performance dance.

UF   Dances

Dancing

SA   types of dances and dancing [to be added as needed]

BT   Amusements

Performing arts

Dance—*Continued*
    NT   **Ballet**
            Ballroom dancing
            Break dancing
            Clog dancing
            Folk dancing
            Modern dance
            Tap dancing
    RT   **Aerobics**
            Dance music
Dance music (May subdiv. geog.)   **781.5;**
    784.18
    BT   **Music**
    RT   **Dance**
Dance—United States   **792.80973;**
    793.30973
Dancers (May subdiv. geog.)   **792.8092;**
    793.3092; 920
    SA   types of dancers, e.g. **Ballet**
            dancers [to be added as
            needed]
    BT   **Entertainers**
    NT   **Ballet dancers**
Dances
    USE   **Dance**
Dancing
    USE   **Dance**
Dangerous animals   **591.6**
    BT   **Animals**
    NT   **Animal attacks**
            Poisonous animals
Dangerous materials
    USE   **Hazardous substances**
Dangerous occupations
    USE   **Hazardous occupations**
Danish language   **439.8**
    May be subdivided like **English language.**
    BT   **Language and languages**
            Norwegian language
            Scandinavian languages
Danish literature   **839.81**
    May use same subdivisions and names of
    literary forms as for **English literature.**
    BT   **Literature**
            Scandinavian literature
Dark Ages
    USE   **Middle Ages**
Dark humor (Literature)
    USE   **Black humor (Literature)**
Dark matter (Astronomy)   **523.1**
    BT   **Matter**

Dark night of the soul
    USE   **Mysticism**
Darkroom technique in photography
    USE   **Photography—Processing**
Darwinism
    USE   **Evolution**
Data banks
    USE   **Databases**
Data base design
    USE   **Database design**
Data bases
    USE   **Databases**
Data processing (May subdiv. geog.)
    004
    UF   Automatic data processing
            Electronic data processing
    SA   subjects with the subdivision
            Data processing, e.g. **Banks**
            and banking—Data process-
            ing [to be added as needed]
    BT   **Computers**
            Information systems
    NT   **Banks and banking—Data pro-**
            cessing
            Computer graphics
            Computer programming
            Database management
            Expert systems (Computer sci-
            ence)
            Optical data processing
    RT   **Computer science**
Data processing—Keyboarding
    USE   **Keyboarding (Electronics)**
Data retrieval
    USE   **Information retrieval**
Data storage and retrieval systems
    USE   **Information systems**
Data transmission systems   **004.6;**
    621.38; 621.39
    UF   Transmission of data
    BT   **Telecommunication**
    NT   **Computer networks**
            Electronic mail systems
            Fax transmission
            Instant messaging
            Teletext systems
            Video telephone
            Videotex systems
Databanks
    USE   **Databases**

Database design   005.74
   UF   Data base design
   BT   **System design**
Database management   005.74
   UF   Systems, Database management
   BT   **Computer science**
          Data processing
          Information systems
Database management—Computer programs
   USE **Database management—Computer software**
Database management—Computer software   005.74
   UF   Database management—Computer programs *[Former heading]*
   BT   **Computer software**
Databases   025.04

Use for materials on any type of organized body of information, including written, numerical, and visual information, not limited to a particular subject.

   UF   Data banks
          Data bases
          Databanks
   SA   subjects with the subdivision *Databases,* for materials about data files on a subject regardless of the medium of distribution, e.g. **Business—Databases;** subjects with the subdivision *Information resources,* for general materials about information on a subject, e.g. **Business—Information resources;** subjects with the subdivision *Internet resources,* for materials about information available on the Internet on a subject, e.g. **Business—Internet resources;** and headings for the providers or the users of information with the subdivision *Information services,* for materials about organizations that provide information services, e.g. **United Nations—Information services; Consumers—Information services;** etc. [to be added as needed]

   BT   **Information resources**
   NT   **Business—Databases**
          Web databases
Date etiquette
   USE **Dating (Social customs)**
Date rape   362.883; 364.15
   UF   Acquaintance rape
          Dating violence
   BT   **Dating (Social customs)**
          Rape
Dates, Historical
   USE **Historical chronology**
Dating etiquette
   USE **Dating (Social customs)**
Dating, Radiocarbon
   USE **Radiocarbon dating**
Dating (Social customs) (May subdiv. geog.)   306.73; 392.4; 646.7
   UF   Date etiquette
          Dating etiquette
   BT   **Courtship**
          Etiquette
          Manners and customs
   NT   **Date rape**
   RT   **Man-woman relationship**
Dating violence
   USE **Date rape**
Daughters   306.874
   BT   **Family**
          Women
   NT   **Father-daughter relationship**
          Mother-daughter relationship
Daughters and fathers
   USE **Father-daughter relationship**
Daughters and mothers
   USE **Mother-daughter relationship**
Day   529
   BT   **Chronology**
          Time
   RT   **Night**
Day care centers (May subdiv. geog.)   362.71
   UF   Child care centers
          Children—Day care
          Children's day care centers
          Day nurseries
          Nurseries, Day
   BT   **Child care**
          Child welfare
          Children—Institutional care
   RT   **Nursery schools**

Day dreams
USE **Fantasy**

Day nurseries
USE **Day care centers**

Day of Atonement
USE **Yom Kippur**

Day trading (Securities) 332.64
BT **Securities**

Days 394.2
UF Days of the week
SA types of days and names of particular days [to be added as needed]
BT **Calendars**
NT **Birthdays**
Holidays
RT **Anniversaries**
Festivals
Week

Days of the week
USE **Days**

DDT (Insecticide) 668
UF D.D.T. (Insecticide)
Dichloro-diphenyl-trichloroethane
BT **Insecticides**

Dead Sea scrolls 221.4; 229; 296.1
UF Qumran texts
RT **Essenes**

Deaf (May subdiv. geog.) 362.4
BT **Hearing impaired**
Physically handicapped
NT **Closed caption television**
Closed caption video recordings

Deaf—Education (May subdiv. geog.) 371.91
UF Education of the deaf
BT **Education**

Deaf—Institutional care 362.4
BT **Institutional care**

Deaf—Means of communication 362.4; 419
Use for general materials on communication in the broadest sense by people who are deaf. Materials on language systems based on hand gestures are entered under **Sign language**.
UF Finger alphabet
BT **Communication**
NT **Hearing ear dogs**
Lipreading
RT **Nonverbal communication**
Sign language

Deaf—Sign language
USE **Sign language**

Deafness 362.4; 617.8
BT **Ear**
NT **Hearing aids**
RT **Hearing**

Death (May subdiv. geog.) 128; 236; 306.9; 571.9
SA ethnic groups and classes of persons with the subdivision *Death*, e.g. **Infants—Death;** and names of individual persons and groups of notable persons with the subdivision *Death and burial*, e.g. **Presidents—United States—Death and burial** [to be added as needed]
BT **Biology**
Eschatology
Life
NT **Brain death**
Children and death
Children—Death
Future life
Infants—Death
Near-death experiences
Right to die
RT **Burial**
Mortality
Terminal care
Terminally ill

Death and burial
USE names of individual persons and groups of notable persons with the subdivision *Death and burial*, e.g. **Presidents—United States—Death and burial** [to be added as needed]

Death and children
USE **Children and death**

Death masks
USE **Masks (Sculpture)**

Death notices
USE **Obituaries**

Death penalty
USE **Capital punishment**

Death rate
USE **Mortality**
Vital statistics

Deaths, Registers of
USE **Registers of births, etc.**
Debates and debating   808.53
UF   Argumentation
Discussion
Speaking
BT   **Public speaking**
Rhetoric
NT   **Parliamentary practice**
Radio addresses, debates, etc.
RT   **Discussion groups**
Debit cards   332.1
UF   Bank debit cards
Cards, Debit
BT   **Banks and banking**
Debris in space
USE   **Space debris**
Debt (May subdiv. geog.)   **332.7**
Use for economic and statistical materials
on debt. Legal materials regarding debtor and
creditor are entered under **Debtor and credi-
tor.**
UF   Indebtedness
BT   **Finance**
NT   **Collecting of accounts**
Public debts
RT   **Debtor and creditor**
Debtor
USE   **Debtor and creditor**
Debtor and creditor (May subdiv. geog.)
346.07
Use for legal materials regarding debtor and
creditor. Economic and statistical materials on
debt are entered under **Debt.**
UF   Creditor
Debtor
BT   **Commercial law**
NT   **Bankruptcy**
Collecting of accounts
RT   **Credit**
Debt
Debts, Public
USE   **Public debts**
Decalogue
USE   **Ten commandments**
Deceit
USE   **Deception**
Fraud
Decentralization of schools
USE   **Schools—Decentralization**
Deception   001.9; 177
UF   Chicanery
Deceit

Subterfuge
BT   **Truthfulness and falsehood**
NT   **Disguise**
Deceptive advertising   343.07
UF   False advertising
Fraudulent advertising
Misleading advertising
Misrepresentation in advertising
Truth in advertising
BT   **Advertising**
Business ethics
Decimal system   513.5
BT   **Numbers**
RT   **Metric system**
Decision making (May subdiv. geog.)
153.8; 302.3; 658.4
NT   **Critical thinking**
Group decision making
RT   **Choice (Psychology)**
Problem solving
Decks (Domestic architecture)
USE   **Patios**
Declamations
USE   **Monologues**
Recitations
Declaration of independence (U.S.)
USE   **United States—Declaration of
independence**
Decoration and ornament (May subdiv.
geog.)   **745.4**
Use for general materials on the forms and
styles of decoration in various fields of fine
arts or applied art and on the history of vari-
ous styles of ornament. In addition to geo-
graphic subdivision, this heading may be sub-
divided by date or by style of ornament, e.g.
**Decoration and ornament—15th and 16th
centuries; Decoration and ornament—Goth-
ic style;** etc. Materials limited to the decora-
tion of houses are entered under **Interior de-
sign.**
UF   Decorative art
Decorative design
Decorative painting
Ornament
Painting, Decorative
BT   **Art**
Decorative arts
NT   **Antiques**
**Architectural decoration and
ornament**
Art objects
Artificial flowers
Arts and crafts movement

Decoration and ornament—*Continued*
> Bronzes
> China painting
> Christmas decorations
> Decoupage
> Design
> Egg decoration
> Embroidery
> Enamel and enameling
> Flower arrangement
> Furniture
> Garden ornaments and furniture
> Gems
> Glass painting and staining
> Holiday decorations
> Illumination of books and manuscripts
> Illustration of books
> Interior design
> Ironwork
> Leather work
> Lettering
> Metalwork
> Monograms
> Mosaics
> Mural painting and decoration
> Needlework
> Picture frames and framing
> Pottery
> Sculpture
> Show windows
> Stencil work
> Stucco
> Table setting and decoration
> Tapestry
> Terra cotta
> Textile design
> Wood carving
>
> RT   Handicraft
>   Painting

Decoration and ornament—15th and 16th centuries (May subdiv. geog.) **745.4**
> UF   Decoration and ornament, Renaissance
>   Renaissance decoration and ornament

Decoration and ornament, American
> USE   **Decoration and ornament— United States**

Decoration and ornament, Architectural
> USE   **Architectural decoration and ornament**

Decoration and ornament, Gothic
> USE   **Decoration and ornament— Gothic style**

Decoration and ornament—Gothic style (May subdiv. geog.) **745.4**
> UF   Decoration and ornament, Gothic
>   Gothic decoration and ornament

Decoration and ornament, Renaissance
> USE   **Decoration and ornament— 15th and 16th centuries**

Decoration and ornament—United States **745.4**
> UF   American decoration and ornament
>   Decoration and ornament, American

Decoration Day
> USE   **Memorial Day**

Decorations, Holiday
> USE   **Holiday decorations**

Decorations of honor (May subdiv. geog.) **355.1; 929.8**
> UF   Badges of honor
>   Emblems
> SA   names of medals [to be added as needed]
> RT   **Heraldry**
>   **Insignia**
>   **Medals**

Decorative art
> USE   **Decoration and ornament**
>   **Decorative arts**

Decorative arts (May subdiv. geog.) **745**

Use for general materials on the various applied art forms having some utilitarian as well as decorative purpose, including furniture, silverware, the decoration of buildings, etc.

> UF   Applied arts
>   Art industries and trade
>   Decorative art
>   Minor arts
> SA   types of decorative arts [to be added as needed]
> BT   **Arts**
> NT   **Antiques**
>   **Art metalwork**
>   **Art objects**
>   **Arts and crafts movement**

Decorative arts—*Continued*
> Calligraphy
> Carving (Decorative arts)
> Costume
> Decoration and ornament
> Decoupage
> Enamel and enameling
> Fabrics
> Furniture
> Glassware
> Jewelry
> Lacquer and lacquering
> Leather work
> Mosaics
> Needlework
> Porcelain
> Pottery
> Rugs and carpets
> Silverware
> Tapestry
> Woodwork
> RT Folk art
> Handicraft

Decorative arts—United States
> 745.0973

Decorative design
> USE **Decoration and ornament**

Decorative metalwork
> USE **Art metalwork**

Decorative painting
> USE **Decoration and ornament**

Decoupage 745.54
> BT **Decoration and ornament**
> **Decorative arts**
> **Paper crafts**

Decoys (Hunting) (May subdiv. geog.)
> 745.593; 799.2
> UF Bird decoys (Hunting)
> BT **Hunting**
> **Shooting**

Deduction (Logic)
> USE **Logic**

Deep diving (May subdiv. geog.) **627**
> Use for materials on underwater diving with equipment. Materials on diving from a board or platform are entered under **Diving**.
> UF Deep sea diving
> Submarine diving
> Underwater diving
> BT **Underwater exploration**
> **Water sports**

> NT Scuba diving
> Skin diving
> RT **Diving**

Deep sea diving
> USE **Deep diving**

Deep sea drilling (Petroleum)
> USE **Offshore oil well drilling**

Deep sea engineering
> USE **Ocean engineering**

Deep sea mining
> USE **Ocean mining**

Deep-sea photography
> USE **Underwater photography**

Deer (May subdiv. geog.) **599.65**
> UF Fawns
> BT **Game and game birds**
> **Mammals**
> NT **Reindeer**

Defamation
> USE **Libel and slander**

Defective speech
> USE **Speech disorders**

Defective vision
> USE **Vision disorders**

Defectors (May subdiv. geog.) **325;**
> **327.12**
> UF Political defectors
> Turncoats
> BT **Political refugees**

Defense industries
> USE **Defense industry**

Defense industry (May subdiv. geog.)
> 338.4
> Use for materials on the industries producing the implements of war. Materials on the implements of war themselves are entered under **Ordnance** or under **Military weapons**.
> UF Armaments industries
> Arms sales
> Defense industries
> Military sales
> Military supplies industry
> Munitions
> Weapons industry
> BT **Industries**
> RT **Arms transfers**
> **Military readiness**
> **Military weapons**
> **Ordnance**

Defense (Law)
> USE **Litigation**

Defense mechanisms of animals
  USE **Animal defenses**
Defense mechanisms of plants
  USE **Plant defenses**
Defense policy
  USE **Military policy**
Defense readiness
  USE **Military readiness**
Defense research
  USE **Military research**
Defenses
  USE types of defenses, e.g. **Air defenses;** and names of continents, regions, countries, and individual colonies with the subdivision *Defenses,* e.g. **United States—Defenses** [to be added as needed]
Defenses, Radar
  USE **Radar defense networks**
Deficit financing (May subdiv. geog.)
       336.3
  UF Compensatory spending
       Deficit spending
  BT **Public finance**
  RT **Public debts**
Deficit spending
  USE **Deficit financing**
Defoliants
  USE **Herbicides**
Deforestation (May subdiv. geog.)   **634.9**
  UF Forest depletion
  BT **Forests and forestry**
Deformities
  USE **Birth defects**
Degrees, Academic
  USE **Academic degrees**
Degrees of latitude and longitude
  USE **Geodesy**
       Latitude
       Longitude
Dehydrated foods
  USE **Dried foods**
Dehydrated milk
  USE **Dried milk**
Deism (May subdiv. geog.)   **211**
  BT **Religion**
       Theology
  RT **Atheism**
       Free thought
       Positivism

       Rationalism
       Theism
Deities
  USE **Gods and goddesses**
Dejection
  USE **Depression (Psychology)**
Delayed memory
  USE **Recovered memory**
Delinquency, Juvenile
  USE **Juvenile delinquency**
Delinquents
  USE **Criminals**
Delivery of health care
  USE **Medical care**
Delivery of medical care
  USE **Medical care**
Delphi (Ancient city)
  USE **Delphi (Extinct city)**
Delphi (Extinct city)   **938**
  UF Delphi (Ancient city)
  BT **Extinct cities—Greece**
       Greece—Antiquities
Delusions
  USE **Hallucinations and illusions**
Dementia   **616.8**
  BT **Brain—Diseases**
Demobilization
  USE names of armed forces with the subdivision *Demobilization,* e.g. **United States. Army—Demobilization** [to be added as needed]
Democracy (May subdiv. geog.)   **321.8**
  UF Popular government
       Self-government
  BT **Constitutional history**
       Constitutional law
       Political science
  NT **Freedom**
       Referendum
       Suffrage
  RT **Equality**
       Representative government and representation
       Republics
Democratic Party (U.S.)   **324.2736**
  BT **Political parties**
Demography
  USE **Population**

Demoniac possession 133.4
  BT **Demonology**
  RT **Devil**
      Exorcism
Demonology (May subdiv. geog.) 133.4
  UF Evil spirits
  BT **Occultism**
  NT **Demoniac possession**
  RT **Devil**
      Exorcism
      Spirits
Demonstrations (May subdiv. geog.)
      322.4; 361.2
  Use for materials on public gatherings,
  marches, etc., organized for nonviolent protest
  even though incidental disturbances or rioting
  may occur.
  UF Marches (Demonstrations)
      Protest marches and rallies
      Protests, demonstrations, etc.
      Public demonstrations
      Rallies (Protest)
  SA names of specific wars or other
      objects of protest with the
      subdivision *Protest move-*
      ments, e.g. **World War,**
      1939-1945—Protest move-
      ments [to be added as need-
      ed]
  BT **Crowds**
      Public meetings
  NT **Civil rights demonstrations**
      Hunger strikes
  RT **Peace movements**
      Protest movements
      Riots
Demonstrations—Chicago (Ill.)
      322.409773
Demonstrations for civil rights
  USE **Civil rights demonstrations**
Demonstrations—United States
      322.40973; 361.2
Denationalization
  USE **Privatization**
Denatured alcohol 661
  UF Alcohol, Denatured
      Industrial alcohol
  BT **Alcohol**
Denominational schools
  USE **Church schools**
Denominations, Christian
  USE **Christian sects**

Denominations, Protestant
  USE **Protestant churches**
Denominations, Religious
  USE **Sects**
Dental care (May subdiv. geog.) **617.6**
  Use for materials on the organization of
  services and facilities for dental care. Materi-
  als on the technical and medical aspects of
  dental care are entered under **Dentistry.**
  SA ethnic groups, classes of per-
      sons, and military services
      with the subdivision *Dental*
      care, e.g. **Children—Dental**
      care [to be added as needed]
  BT **Medical care**
  RT **Dentistry**
Dentistry (May subdiv. geog.) **617.6**
  Use for materials on the technical and med-
  ical aspects of dental care. Materials on the
  organization of services and facilities for den-
  tal care are entered under **Dental care.**
  SA ethnic groups, classes of per-
      sons, and military services
      with the subdivision *Dental*
      care, e.g. **Children—Dental**
      care [to be added as needed]
  BT **Medicine**
  RT **Dental care**
      Teeth
Deoxyribonucleic acid
  USE **DNA**
Department stores (May subdiv. geog.)
      658.8
  BT **Business**
      Retail trade
      Stores
Dependencies
  USE **Colonies**
Depression, Mental
  USE **Depression (Psychology)**
Depression (Psychology) **616.85**
  UF Dejection
      Depression, Mental
      Depressive psychoses
      Melancholia
      Mental depression
      Mentally depressed
  BT **Abnormal psychology**
      Neuroses
  RT **Manic-depressive illness**
Depressions (May subdiv. geog.) **338.5**
  UF Business depressions
      Economic depressions

Depressions—*Continued*
SA   names of countries, states, cities, etc., with the subdivision *Economic conditions* [to be added as needed]
BT   **Business cycles**
NT   **Great Depression, 1929-1939**
Depressions—1929
USE   **Great Depression, 1929-1939**
Depressive psychoses
USE   **Depression (Psychology)**
Deprogramming
USE   **Brainwashing**
Derailments
USE   **Railroad accidents**
Deregulation (May subdiv. geog.)   **338.9; 352.8**
UF   Industries—Deregulation
SA   types of industry with the subdivision *Deregulation*, e.g. **Petroleum industry—Deregulation** [to be added as needed]
BT   **Industrial policy**
Dermatitis
USE   **Skin—Diseases**
Derricks
USE   **Cranes, derricks, etc.**
Desalination of water
USE   **Sea water conversion**
Desalting of water
USE   **Sea water conversion**
Descent
USE   **Genealogy**
       Heredity
Description
USE   names of cities (except extinct cities), countries, states, and regions with the subdivision *Description and travel*, e.g. **Chicago (Ill.)—Description and travel; United States—Description and travel;** etc., for descriptive materials and accounts of travel, including the history of travel, in those places; names of places with the subdivision *Geography* for broad geographical materials about a specific place, e.g. **United States—Geography;** and names of extinct cities or towns, without further subdivision, for general descriptive materials on those places, e.g. **Delphi (Extinct city)** [to be added as needed]
Description and travel
USE   names of cities (except extinct cities), countries, states, etc., with the subdivision *Description and travel,* e.g. **Chicago (Ill.)—Description and travel; United States—Description and travel;** etc., for descriptive materials and accounts of travel, including the history of travel, in those places; names of places with the subdivision *Geography* for broad geographical materials about a specific place, e.g. **United States—Geography;** names of extinct cities or towns, without further subdivision, for general descriptive materials on those places, e.g. **Delphi (Extinct city);** and ethnic groups, classes of persons, and names of individuals with the subdivision *Travel,* e.g. **Handicapped—Travel** [to be added as needed]
Descriptive geometry   **516**
UF   Geometry, Descriptive
BT   **Geometrical drawing**
       Geometry
NT   **Perspective**
Desegregated schools
USE   **School integration**
Desegregation
USE   **Segregation**
Desegregation in education
USE   **School integration**
Desert animals (May subdiv. geog.)   **578.754**
UF   Desert fauna
SA   types of desert animals, e.g. **Camels** [to be added as needed]
BT   **Animals**
       Deserts

Desert animals—*Continued*
  NT **Camels**
Desert fauna
  USE **Desert animals**
Desert plants (May subdiv. geog.) **581.7**
  SA types of desert plants, e.g. **Cactus** [to be added as needed]
  BT **Deserts**
       Plant ecology
       Plants
  NT **Cactus**
Desertification (May subdiv. geog.)
  333.73
  BT **Climate**
       Deserts
Desertion
  USE **Desertion and nonsupport**
       Military desertion
Desertion and nonsupport **306.88;**
  346.01
  UF Abandonment of family
       Desertion
       Nonsupport
  BT **Divorce**
       Domestic relations
  NT **Child support**
       Runaway adults
Desertion, Military
  USE **Military desertion**
Desertions
  USE names of wars with the subdivision *Desertions,* e.g. **World War, 1939-1945—Desertions** [to be added as needed]
Deserts **551.41**
  BT **Physical geography**
  NT **Desert animals**
       Desert plants
       Desertification
Design (May subdiv. geog.) **745.4**
  SA types of design, e.g. **Industrial design; Fashion design;** etc.; types of objects, structures, machines, equipment, etc., and types of educational tests and examinations with the subdivision *Design and construction,* e.g. **Automobiles—Design and construction;** topical headings with which the subdivision *Design and construc-*

tion would be inappropriate with the subdivision *Design,* e.g. **Quilts—Design; Pamphlets—Design;** etc.; and types of architecture and landscape with the form subdivision *Designs and plans,* for materials containing designs and drawings, e.g. **Domestic architecture—Designs and plans** [to be added as needed]
  BT **Decoration and ornament**
  NT **Architectural design**
       Computer-aided design
       Fashion design
       Garden design
       Industrial design
       Interior design
       Machine design
       Pamphlets—Design
       Quilts—Design
       Textile design
       Web sites—Design
  RT **Designers**
       Patternmaking
Design and construction
  USE types of objects, structures, machines, equipment, etc., and types of educational tests and examinations with the subdivision *Design and construction,* e.g. **Airplanes—Design and construction** [to be added as needed]
Design, Industrial
  USE **Industrial design**
Design perception
  USE **Pattern perception**
Designed genetic change
  USE **Genetic engineering**
Designer drugs **362.29; 615**
  Use for materials on illicit drugs manufactured by altering the molecular structure of existing drugs to mimic the effects of standard narcotics, stimulants, or hallucinogens.
  UF Synthetic drugs of abuse
  SA types of designer drugs, e.g. **Ice (Drug)** [to be added as needed]
  BT **Drugs**
  NT **Ice (Drug)**

Designers (May subdiv. geog.)　**709.2**
  BT　**Artists**
  NT　**Fashion designers**
  RT　**Design**
Designs and plans
  USE　types of architecture and land-
      scape with the form subdivi-
      sion *Designs and plans,* for
      materials containing designs
      and drawings, e.g. **Domestic
      architecture—Designs and
      plans** [to be added as needed]
Designs, Architectural
  USE　**Architecture—Designs and
      plans**
Designs, Floral
  USE　**Flower arrangement**
Desktop computers
  USE　**Microcomputers**
Desktop publishing　070.5; 686.2
  Use for materials on the use of a personal
  computer with writing, graphics, and page lay-
  out software to produce printed material for
  publication. Materials on the process of pub-
  lishing by which books and articles or any
  kind of data are made available as an elec-
  tronic product are entered under **Electronic
  publishing.**
  RT　**Electronic publishing
      Word processing**
Desserts　641.8
  SA　types of desserts and names of
      specific desserts [to be added
      as needed]
  BT　**Cooking**
  NT　**Cake
      Ice cream, ices, etc.**
  RT　**Chocolate**
Destiny
  USE　**Fate and fatalism**
Destitution
  USE　**Poverty**
Destruction and pillage
  USE　names of wars with the subdivi-
      sion *Destruction and pillage,*
      e.g. **World War, 1939-
      1945—Destruction and pil-
      lage** [to be added as needed]
Destruction of property
  USE　**Vandalism**
Destructive insects
  USE　**Insect pests**

Detective and mystery comic books, strips,
    etc.
  USE　**Mystery comic books, strips,
      etc.**
Detective and mystery films
  USE　**Mystery films**
Detective and mystery plays
  USE　**Mystery and detective plays**
Detective and mystery radio programs
  USE　**Mystery radio programs**
Detective and mystery stories
  USE　**Mystery fiction**
Detective and mystery television programs
  USE　**Mystery television programs**
Detective comics
  USE　**Mystery comic books, strips,
      etc.**
Detective fiction
  USE　**Mystery fiction**
Detective stories
  USE　**Mystery fiction**
Detectives (May subdiv. geog.)　**363.25;
    920**
  BT　**Police**
  RT　**Criminal investigation
      Secret service**
Detergent pollution of rivers, lakes, etc.
  USE　**Water pollution**
Detergents　668
  UF　Synthetic detergents
  BT　**Cleaning compounds**
  RT　**Soap**
Determinism and indeterminism
  USE　**Free will and determinism**
Deuterium oxide　546
  UF　Heavy water
  BT　**Chemicals**
Devaluation of currency
  USE　**Monetary policy**
Developing countries　330.9
  Use for comprehensive materials on coun-
  tries that are not fully modernized or industri-
  alized. This heading may be subdivided by the
  topical subdivisions used under countries, re-
  gions, etc., and may also be used as a geo-
  graphic subdivision e.g. **Education—Develop-
  ing countries.**
  UF　Less developed countries
      Third World
      Underdeveloped areas
  BT　**Economic conditions
      Industrialization**
  NT　**New states**

Developing countries—Commerce
338.91; 382
  BT   Commerce
Developing countries—Education
  USE Education—Developing coun-
          tries
Development
  USE Embryology
       Evolution
       Growth disorders
       Modernization (Sociology)
Development, Economic
  USE Economic development
Developmental psychology   155
  BT   Psychology
Deviancy
  USE Deviant behavior
Deviant behavior   155.2; 302.5
  UF   Deviancy
       Social deviance
  BT   Human behavior
  RT   Conformity
       Social adjustment
Deviation, Sexual
  USE Sexual deviation
Devices (Heraldry)
  USE Heraldry
       Insignia
Devil   235
  UF   Satan
  RT   Demoniac possession
       Demonology
Devil's Triangle
  USE Bermuda Triangle
Devotion
  USE Prayer
       Worship
Devotional calendars   242
  UF   Christian devotional calendars
       Daily readings (Spiritual exer-
         cises)
       Devotional exercises (Daily read-
         ings)
  BT   Calendars
       Devotional literature
Devotional exercises   242; 248.3
    Use for general materials on acts of private
prayer and private worship and for materials
on religious practices other than the corporate
worship of a congregation. Materials on the
religious literature used as aids in devotional
exercises are entered under **Devotional literature.**

  UF   Devotional theology
       Devotions
       Family devotions
       Family prayers
  BT   Worship
  NT   Meditation
  RT   Prayer
Devotional exercises (Daily readings)
  USE Devotional calendars
Devotional literature   242
    Use for materials on the religious literature
used as aids in devotional exercises. General
materials on acts of private prayer and private
worship and materials on religious practices
other than the corporate worship of a congregation are entered under **Devotional exercises.**

  BT   Religious literature
  NT   Devotional calendars
       Devotional literature for chil-
         dren
       Meditations
       Prayers
Devotional literature for children   242
  BT   Devotional literature
Devotional theology
  USE Devotional exercises
       Prayer
Devotions
  USE Devotional exercises
Dewey Decimal Classification   025.4
  UF   Classification, Dewey Decimal
  BT   Library classification
Diabetes   616.4
  BT   Diseases
Diagnosis   616.07
  UF   Medical diagnosis
       Symptoms
  BT   Medicine
  NT   Body temperature
       Clinical chemistry
       Magnetic resonance imaging
       Pain
       Prenatal diagnosis
  RT   Pathology
Diagnostic chemistry
  USE Clinical chemistry
Dialectical materialism   335.4
  UF   Historical materialism
  BT   Communism
       Socialism
  RT   Marxism

Dialectics
    USE   **Logic**
Dialects
    USE   names of languages with the
           subdivision *Dialects,* e.g. **English language—Dialects** [to be added as needed]

Diamonds   553.8
    BT   **Carbon**
          Precious stones

Diaries   808; 920
    Use for collections of diaries from various countries and for materials about diaries in general.
    UF   Journals (Diaries)
    SA   diaries of particular countries, e.g. **American diaries;** and classes of persons, ethnic groups, and names of individual persons and families with the subdivision *Diaries* [to be added as needed]
    BT   **Literature**
    NT   **American diaries**
          Journaling
    RT   **Autobiographies**

Diaspora, African
    USE   **African diaspora**
Diaspora, Jewish
    USE   **Jewish diaspora**
Dichloro-diphenyl-trichloroethane
    USE   **DDT (Insecticide)**

Dictators   321.9092; 920
    BT   **Heads of state**
          Totalitarianism

Dictionaries
    USE   **Encyclopedias and dictionaries** and subjects, names of languages, and names of voluminous authors with the subdivision *Dictionaries,* e.g. **English language—Dictionaries; Biography—Dictionaries; Shakespeare, William, 1564-1616—Dictionaries** etc. [to be added as needed]

Dictionaries, Biographical
    USE   **Biography—Dictionaries**
Dictionaries, Classical
    USE   **Classical dictionaries**
Dictionaries, Machine readable
    USE   **Machine readable dictionaries**

Dictionaries, Multilingual
    USE   **Polyglot dictionaries**
Dictionaries, Picture
    USE   **Picture dictionaries**
Dictionaries, Polyglot
    USE   **Polyglot dictionaries**

Didactic drama   808.82
    May be used for individual works, collections, or materials about didactic drama.
    BT   **Drama**

Didactic fiction   808.3; 808.83
    May be used for individual works, collections, or materials about didactic fiction.
    UF   Cautionary tales and verses
          Moral and philosophic stories
          Morality stories
    BT   **Fiction**
    RT   **Fables**
          Parables

Didactic poetry   808.1; 808.81
    May be used for individual works, collections, or materials about didactic poetry.
    UF   Cautionary tales and verses
    BT   **Poetry**
    RT   **Fables**
          Parables

Dies (Metalworking)   621.9; 671.2
    BT   **Metalwork**

Diesel automobiles   629.222
    UF   Diesel cars
    BT   **Automobiles**
Diesel cars
    USE   **Diesel automobiles**

Diesel engines   621.43
    BT   **Engines**
          Internal combustion engines

Diet (May subdiv. geog.)   613.2
    UF   Dietetics
    SA   types of diets, e.g. **Salt-free diet** [to be added as needed]
    BT   **Health**
          Hygiene
    NT   **Beverages**
          Dietetic foods
          Eating customs
          Fasting
          Gastronomy
          Menus
          Salt-free diet
          School children—Food
          Vegetarianism

Diet—*Continued*
  RT **Cooking**
      Digestion
      Food
      Nutrition
      Weight loss
Diet in disease   613.2; 616.3
  SA types of diets, e.g. **Salt-free diet**
        [to be added as needed]
  BT **Therapeutics**
  NT **Cooking for the sick**
      Diet therapy
      Salt-free diet
Diet—Therapeutic use
  USE **Diet therapy**
Diet therapy   615.8
  UF Diet—Therapeutic use
      Invalid cooking
  SA names of diseases with the sub-
        division *Diet therapy,* e.g.
        Cancer—Diet therapy; and
        types of food with the subdi-
        vision *Therapeutic use,* e.g.
        Herbs—Therapeutic use [to
        be added as needed]
  BT **Cooking for the sick**
      Diet in disease
      Therapeutics
  NT **Cancer—Diet therapy**
Dietary fiber
  USE **Food—Fiber content**
Dietetic foods   641.3; 664
  BT **Diet**
      Food
Dietetics
  USE **Diet**
Dieting
  USE **Weight loss**
Diets, Reducing
  USE **Weight loss**
Differential equations   515
  BT **Calculus**
  NT **Functions**
Digestion   573.3; 612.3
  BT **Physiology**
  NT **Indigestion**
  RT **Diet**
      Nutrition
      Stomach
Digital audio disc players
  USE **Compact disc players**

Digital cameras   771.3
  BT **Cameras**
Digital circuits
  USE **Digital electronics**
Digital compact discs
  USE **Compact discs**
Digital electronics   621.381
  UF Digital circuits
  BT **Electronics**
  NT **Digital photography**
Digital libraries   025.00285
  UF Electronic libraries
      Virtual libraries
  BT **Information systems**
      Libraries
Digital photography   775
  UF Photography—Digital techniques
  BT **Digital electronics**
      Photography
Dimension, Fourth
  USE **Fourth dimension**
Dining (May subdiv. geog.)   **641.01**
    Use for materials on dining customs and
  gastronomic travel. Materials on menus and
  recipes for dinners are entered under **Dinners.**
  UF Banquets
      Dinners and dining
      Eating
  BT **Food**
  NT **Carving (Meat, etc.)**
  RT **Dinners**
      Eating customs
      Entertaining
      Gastronomy
      Table etiquette
Dinners   642
    Use for materials on menus and recipes for
  dinners. Materials on dining customs and gas-
  tronomic travel are entered under **Dining.**
  UF Banquets
      Dinners and dining
  BT **Cooking**
      Menus
  RT **Dining**
Dinners and dining
  USE **Dining**
      Dinners
Dinosaur eggs
  USE **Dinosaurs—Eggs**
Dinosaurs (May subdiv. geog.)   **567.9**
  SA types of dinosaurs and names of
        specific dinosaurs [to be add-
        ed as needed]

Dinosaurs—*Continued*
    BT   **Fossil reptiles**
           Prehistoric animals
Dinosaurs—**Eggs**   567.9
    UF   Dinosaur eggs
    BT   **Eggs**
Dioptrics
    USE   **Refraction**
Diphtheria   616.9
    BT   **Diseases**
Diplomacy   327.2; 341.3
    SA   names of countries with the sub-
           division *Foreign relations* [to
           be added as needed]
    BT   **International relations**
    NT   **Diplomats**
           Treaties
           United States—Foreign rela-
           tions
    RT   **Diplomatic and consular ser-**
           vice
Diplomatic and consular service (May
    subdiv. geog.)   **327.2**
    Use for materials on diplomatic and consul-
ar service in general or on the diplomatic and
consular officials of various countries stationed abroad in various countries. Materials
on the diplomatic and consular officials of
various countries stationed in a specific country are entered under **Diplomatic and consular service** subdivided by the country where
they are stationed. Materials on the diplomatic
and consular officials of a specific country,
regardless of where they are stationed, are entered under the appropriately modified heading, e.g. **American diplomatic and consular
service.** Materials on the diplomatic and consular officials of a specific country stationed
in a specific country are entered under the appropriately modified heading subdivided by
the place where they are stationed.
    UF   Consular service
           Consulates
           Embassies
           Foreign service
           Legations
    SA   diplomatic and consular services
           of particular countries, e.g.
           **American diplomatic and
           consular service** [to be added
           as needed]
    BT   **International relations**
    NT   **American diplomatic and con-
           sular service**
    RT   **Diplomacy**
           Diplomats

Diplomatic and consular service, American
    USE   **American diplomatic and con-**
           sular service
Diplomatic history
    USE   names of wars with the subdivi-
           sion *Diplomatic history,* e.g.
           **World War, 1939-1945—
           Diplomatic history** [to be
           added as needed]
Diplomats (May subdiv. geog.)
           327.2092; 920
    UF   Ministers (Diplomatic agents)
    BT   **Diplomacy**
           International relations
           Statesmen
    NT   **Ambassadors**
           Consuls
    RT   **Diplomatic and consular ser-**
           vice
Direct current machinery
    USE   **Electric machinery—Direct
           current**
Direct legislation
    USE   **Referendum**
Direct mail campaigns
    USE   **Direct marketing**
Direct marketing (May subdiv. geog.)
           381; 658.8
    UF   Direct mail campaigns
    BT   **Mail-order business**
           Marketing
    RT   **Direct selling**
Direct primaries
    USE   **Primaries**
Direct selling   658.8
    BT   **Marketing**
           Retail trade
           Selling
    NT   **Mail-order business**
           Peddlers and peddling
           Telemarketing
    RT   **Direct marketing**
Direct taxation
    USE   **Taxation**
Direction sense   152.1; 912
    UF   Orientation
           Sense of direction
    NT   **Left and right (Direction)**
    RT   **Navigation**
           Orienteering

Direction (Theater)
 USE **Theater—Production and di-**
       rection
Directories   910.25
   Use for materials about directories and for
   bibliographies of directories.
   SA subjects and names of countries,
        cities, etc., with the subdivi-
        sion *Directories,* for lists of
        persons, organizations, objects,
        etc., together with addresses
        or other identifying data [to
        be added as needed]
   NT **Chicago (Ill.)—Directories**
        Junior colleges—Directories
        Ohio—Directories
        Physicians—Directories
        United States—Directories
Directories—Telephone
 USE names of cities with the subdivi-
        sion *Telephone directories,*
        e.g. **Chicago (Ill.)—Tele-**
        phone directories [to be add-
        ed as needed]
Directors
 USE types of producers and directors
        in specific media, e.g. **Motion**
        picture producers and direc-
        tors; Theatrical producers
        and directors; etc. [to be
        added as needed]
Directory, French, 1795-1799
 USE **France—History—1789-1799,**
        Revolution
Dirigible balloons
 USE **Airships**
Disability income insurance
 USE **Disability insurance**
Disability insurance   368.38
   UF Disability income insurance
        Insurance, Disability
   BT **Insurance**
Disability law
 USE **Handicapped—Legal status,**
        laws, etc.
Disabled
 USE **Handicapped**
Disadvantaged
 USE **Socially handicapped**
Disadvantaged children
 USE **Socially handicapped children**

Disadvantaged students
 USE **At risk students**
Disappointment   152.4
   BT **Emotions**
Disarmament
 USE **Arms control**
Disaster preparedness
 USE **Disaster relief**
Disaster relief (May subdiv. geog.)
       363.34
   UF Disaster preparedness
        Emergency preparedness
        Emergency relief
   BT **Charities**
        Public welfare
   NT **Food relief**
Disasters (May subdiv. geog.)   **904**
   UF Catastrophes
        Emergencies
   SA types of disasters [to be added
        as needed]
   NT **Fires**
        Natural disasters
        Railroad accidents
        Shipwrecks
   RT **Accidents**
Disciples, Twelve
 USE **Apostles**
Discipline
 USE **Punishment**
Discipline of children
 USE **Child rearing**
        School discipline
Discography
 USE **Sound recordings**
        and subjects and names of per-
        sons with the subdivision *Dis-*
        cography, e.g. **Music—Dis-**
        cography; Shakespeare, Wil-
        liam, 1564-1616—Discogra-
        phy; etc., for lists or catalogs
        of sound recordings [to be
        added as needed]
Discount stores   381; 658.8
   BT **Retail trade**
        Stores
Discoverers
 USE **Explorers**
Discoveries and exploration
 USE **Exploration**

Discoveries in geography
　USE　**Exploration**
Discoveries in science (May subdiv. geog.)
　　500
　UF　Breakthroughs, Scientific
　　　Discoveries, Scientific
　　　Scientific breakthroughs
　　　Scientific discoveries
　BT　**Research**
　　　Science
Discoveries, Scientific
　USE　**Discoveries in science**
Discrimination (May subdiv. geog.)
　　177; 305
　　　Use for general materials on discrimination
　　by race, religion, sex, age, social status, or
　　other factors, including reverse discrimination.
　SA　phrase headings for discrimina-
　　　tion in particular realms of
　　　activity, e.g. **Discrimination**
　　　in employment; or discrimi-
　　　nation against particular ethnic
　　　groups or classes of persons,
　　　e.g. **Discrimination against**
　　　the handicapped; and ethnic
　　　groups and classes of persons
　　　with the subdivision *Civil*
　　　rights, or *Legal status, laws,*
　　　etc., e.g. **African Ameri-**
　　　cans—Civil rights; Handi-
　　　capped—Legal status, laws,
　　　etc. [to be added as needed]
　BT　**Ethnic relations**
　　　Interpersonal relations
　　　Prejudices
　　　Race relations
　　　Social problems
　　　Social psychology
　NT　**Age discrimination**
　　　Discrimination against the
　　　handicapped
　　　Discrimination in education
　　　Discrimination in employment
　　　Discrimination in housing
　　　Discrimination in public ac-
　　　commodations
　　　Hate crimes
　　　Race discrimination
　　　Sex discrimination
　RT　**Civil rights**
　　　Minorities
　　　Segregation

　　　Toleration
Discrimination against disabled persons
　USE　**Discrimination against the**
　　　handicapped
Discrimination against handicapped persons
　USE　**Discrimination against the**
　　　handicapped
Discrimination against the disabled
　USE　**Discrimination against the**
　　　handicapped
Discrimination against the handicapped
　　305.9; 362.4
　UF　Discrimination against disabled
　　　persons
　　　Discrimination against handi-
　　　capped persons
　　　Discrimination against the dis-
　　　abled
　BT　**Discrimination**
　　　Handicapped
Discrimination in education (May subdiv.
　　geog.)　379.2
　BT　**Discrimination**
　NT　**Test bias**
　RT　**Segregation in education**
Discrimination in employment (May
　　subdiv. geog.)　331.13
　UF　Employment discrimination
　　　Equal employment opportunity
　　　Equal opportunity in employ-
　　　ment
　　　Fair employment practice
　　　Job discrimination
　SA　ethnic groups and classes of per-
　　　sons with the subdivision *Em-*
　　　ployment, e.g. **African Amer-**
　　　icans—Employment [to be
　　　added as needed]
　BT　**Discrimination**
　NT　**Affirmative action programs**
　　　Equal pay for equal work
Discrimination in housing (May subdiv.
　　geog.)　363.5
　UF　Fair housing
　　　Open housing
　　　Segregation in housing
　BT　**Discrimination**
　　　Housing

218

Discrimination in public accommodations
    (May subdiv. geog.)   **305**
    UF   Public accommodations, Discrim-
          ination in
          Segregation in public accommo-
          dations
    BT   **Discrimination**
Discussion
    USE **Conversation**
         Debates and debating
         Negotiation
Discussion groups   **374**
    UF   Forums (Discussions)
         Great books program
         Group discussion
         Panel discussions
    BT   **Conversation**
    NT   **Electronic discussion groups**
    RT   **Debates and debating**
Disease germs
    USE **Bacteria**
         Germ theory of disease
Disease (Pathology)
    USE **Pathology**
Diseases (May subdiv. geog.)   **614.4; 616**
    UF   Illness
         Sickness
    SA   types of diseases, e.g. **Commu-**
         nicable diseases; names of
         specific diseases, e.g. **Influen-**
         za; and types of animals,
         classes of persons, and parts
         of the body with the subdivi-
         sion *Diseases,* e.g. **Nervous**
         system—Diseases [to be add-
         ed as needed]
    NT   **AIDS (Disease)**
         Animals—Diseases
         Arthritis
         Blood—Diseases
         Brain—Diseases
         Cancer
         Chickenpox
         Children—Diseases
         Chronic diseases
         Cold (Disease)
         Communicable diseases
         Diabetes
         Diphtheria
         Elderly—Diseases
         Epidemics

         Heart diseases
         Hyperactivity
         Infants—Diseases
         Influenza
         Lungs—Diseases
         Lyme disease
         Malaria
         Men—Diseases
         Mental illness
         Mouth—Diseases
         Nervous system—Diseases
         Occupational diseases
         Plant diseases
         Poliomyelitis
         Rheumatism
         Skin—Diseases
         Teeth—Diseases
         Typhoid fever
         Women—Diseases
    RT   **Health**
         Medicine
         Pathology
         Sick
Diseases and pests
    USE **Agricultural bacteriology**
         Agricultural pests
         Fungi
         Household pests
         Insect pests
         Parasites
         Plant diseases
         and names of individual pests,
         e.g. **Locusts;** and types of
         crops, plants, trees, etc., with
         the subdivision *Diseases and*
         pests, e.g. **Fruit—Diseases**
         and pests [to be added as
         needed]
Diseases, Chronic
    USE **Chronic diseases**
Diseases of animals
    USE **Animals—Diseases**
Diseases of children
    USE **Children—Diseases**
Diseases of plants
    USE **Plant diseases**
Diseases of the blood
    USE **Blood—Diseases**
Diseases of women
    USE **Women—Diseases**

Diseases—Prevention
  USE **Preventive medicine**
Diseases—Treatment
  USE **Therapeutics**
Diseases, Tropical
  USE **Tropical medicine**
Disguise **306.4**
  BT **Costume**
      Deception
Dishes
  USE **Porcelain**
      Pottery
      Tableware
Dishonesty
  USE **Honesty**
Disinfection and disinfectants **614.4**
  UF Germicides
  BT **Hygiene**
      Pharmaceutical chemistry
      Public health
      Sanitation
  RT **Antiseptics**
      Fumigation
Disney World (Fla.)
  USE **Walt Disney World (Fla.)**
Disobedience
  USE **Obedience**
Disorderliness
  USE **Messiness**
Disorders of communication
  USE **Communicative disorders**
Displaced persons
  USE **Political refugees**
      Refugees
Disposal of medical waste
  USE **Medical wastes**
Disposal of refuse
  USE **Refuse and refuse disposal**
Dispute settlement
  USE **Conflict management**
Dissent (May subdiv. geog.) **303.48;**
      361.2
  UF Nonconformity
      Protest
  BT **Freedom of conscience**
      Freedom of religion
  RT **Conformity**
Dissertations **378.2; 808**
  Use for materials about academic theses and
  dissertations.
  UF Academic dissertations
      Dissertations, Academic

Doctoral theses
  Theses
  BT **Research**
Dissertations, Academic
  USE **Dissertations**
Distance education (May subdiv. geog.)
      371.35
  Use for materials on the various forms of
  long-distance instruction, usually in the field
  of adult education, made possible by written,
  audiovisual, or electronic communication be-
  tween a student and a teacher.
  UF Distance learning
  BT **Education**
  NT **Correspondence schools and**
      courses
      University extension
Distance learning
  USE **Distance education**
Distillation **641.2; 663**
  UF Stills
  BT **Analytical chemistry**
      Industrial chemistry
      Technology
  NT **Essences and essential oils**
  RT **Alcohol**
      Liquors
Distribution, Cooperative
  USE **Cooperation**
Distribution (Economics)
  USE **Commerce**
      Marketing
Distribution of animals and plants
  USE **Biogeography**
Distribution of wealth
  USE **Economics**
      Wealth
District libraries
  USE **Regional libraries**
District schools
  USE **Rural schools**
Districting (in city planning)
  USE **Zoning**
Diversified corporations
  USE **Conglomerate corporations**
Diversity, Biological
  USE **Biological diversity**
Diversity in the workplace (May subdiv.
      geog.) **331.11; 658.3**
  UF Cultural diversity in the
      workplace
      Multicultural diversity in the
      workplace

Diversity in the workplace—*Continued*
Workforce diversity
BT **Multiculturalism**
Personnel management
Diversity movement
USE **Multiculturalism**
Dividends
USE **Securities**
Stocks
Divination (May subdiv. geog.)   133.3
UF Crystal gazing
Necromancy
Soothsaying
BT **Occultism**
NT **Astrology**
Feng-shui
Fortune telling
Palmistry
RT **Oracles**
Prophecies
Divine healing
USE **Spiritual healing**
Diving   797.2
Use for materials on diving from a board or platform. Materials on underwater diving with equipment are entered under **Deep diving.**
BT **Swimming**
Water sports
RT **Deep diving**
Divinity of Jesus Christ
USE **Jesus Christ—Divinity**
Division of powers
USE **Separation of powers**
Divorce (May subdiv. geog.)   173;
306.89; 346.01
UF Separation (Law)
BT **Family**
NT **Children of divorced parents**
Desertion and nonsupport
Divorce mediation
RT **Divorced people**
Domestic relations
Divorce counseling
USE **Divorce mediation**
Divorce mediation   362.82
UF Divorce counseling
Mediation, Divorce
BT **Divorce**
NT **Child custody**
Child support
RT **Marriage counseling**

Divorced men (May subdiv. geog.)
306.892
BT **Divorced people**
Single men
Divorced people (May subdiv. geog.)
306.89
UF Divorced persons
BT **Single people**
NT **Divorced men**
Divorced women
RT **Divorce**
Divorced persons
USE **Divorced people**
Divorced women (May subdiv. geog.)
306.893
BT **Divorced people**
Single women
DNA   572.8
UF Deoxyribonucleic acid
BT **Cells**
Heredity
Nucleic acids
NT **Recombinant DNA**
DNA cloning
USE **Molecular cloning**
DNA fingerprinting   614
UF DNA fingerprints
DNA identification
DNA profiling
Genetic fingerprinting
Genetic fingerprints
Genetic profiling
BT **Identification**
Medical jurisprudence
DNA fingerprints
USE **DNA fingerprinting**
DNA identification
USE **DNA fingerprinting**
DNA profiling
USE **DNA fingerprinting**
Docks   386; 387.1; 627
BT **Hydraulic structures**
Marinas
RT **Harbors**
Doctor films
USE **Medical drama (Films)**
Doctor novels
USE **Medical novels**
Doctor radio programs
USE **Medical drama (Radio programs)**

Doctor television programs
 USE **Medical drama (Television programs)**
Doctoral theses
 USE **Dissertations**
Doctors
 USE **Physicians**
Doctors' degrees
 USE **Academic degrees**
Doctrinal theology (May subdiv. geog.) **202; 230**
 UF Dogmatic theology
  Dogmatics
  Systematic theology
  Theology, Doctrinal
 SA names of religions or individual denominations with the subdivision *Doctrines*, e.g. **Christianity—Doctrines; Judaism—Doctrines;** etc., and religious topics with the subdivision *History of doctrines,* e.g. **Salvation—History of doctrines** [to be added as needed]
 BT **Theology**
 NT **Christian heresies**
  Christianity—Doctrines
  Creeds
  Grace (Theology)
  Human beings (Theology)
  Judaism—Doctrines
  Salvation
  Salvation—History of doctrines
Doctrine of fairness (Broadcasting)
 USE **Fairness doctrine (Broadcasting)**
Doctrines
 USE names of religions or individual denominations with the subdivision *Doctrines,* e.g. **Christianity—Doctrines; Judaism—Doctrines;** etc. [to be added as needed]
Documentaries (Motion pictures)
 USE **Documentary films**
Documentary films (May subdiv. geog.) **070.1**
 UF Documentaries (Motion pictures)
  Nonfiction films
 BT **Motion pictures**

Documentation   025
 SA subjects with the subdivision *Documentation,* e.g. **Agriculture—Documentation** [to be added as needed]
 BT **Information science**
 NT **Agriculture—Documentation**
  Archives
  Bibliographic control
  Bibliography
  Cataloging
  Conference proceedings
  Copying processes
  Information retrieval
  Libraries
  Library science
 RT **Information services**
Documents
 USE **Archives**
  Charters
  Government publications
Dog
 USE **Dogs**
Dog breeding
 USE **Dogs—Breeding**
Dog care
 USE **Dogs—Care**
Dog guides
 USE **Guide dogs**
Dogmatic theology
 USE **Doctrinal theology**
Dogmatics
 USE **Doctrinal theology**
Dogs (May subdiv. geog.)   **599.77; 636.7**
 UF Dog
  Puppies
 SA types of dogs, e.g. **Guide dogs;** and names of specific breeds of dogs [to be added as needed]
 BT **Domestic animals**
  Mammals
 NT **Collies**
  Working dogs
Dogs—Breeding   636.7
 UF Dog breeding
 BT **Breeding**
Dogs—Care   636.7
 UF Dog care

Dogs—Fiction   808.83

Use for collections of stories about dogs. Materials about dog stories are entered under **Dogs in literature.**

Dogs for the blind

USE   **Guide dogs**

Dogs for the deaf

USE   **Hearing ear dogs**

Dogs in art   704.9

BT   **Art—Themes**

Dogs in literature   809

Use for materials about the depiction of dogs in literary works. Collections of dog stories are entered under **Dogs—Fiction.**

BT   **Literature—Themes**

Dogs—Psychology   636.7

BT   **Animal intelligence**

Comparative psychology

Psychology

Dogs—Training   636.7

BT   **Animals—Training**

Dogs—War use   355.4

UF   War use of dogs

BT   **Animals—War use**

Doll

USE   **Dolls**

Doll furniture (May subdiv. geog.)
688.7; 745.592

BT   **Miniature objects**

Toys

Dollhouses   688.7

BT   **Miniature objects**

Toys

Dollmaking   745.592

BT   **Dolls**

Dolls (May subdiv. geog.)   **688.7**

UF   Doll

BT   **Toys**

NT   **Barbie dolls**

Dollmaking

Domesday book   942.02

UF   Doomsday book

BT   **Great Britain—History—1066-1154, Norman period**

Domestic animal dwellings

USE   **Animal housing**

Domestic animals (May subdiv. geog.)
636

Use for general materials on farm animals. Materials limited to animals as pets are entered under **Pets.** Materials on stock raising as an industry are entered under **Livestock industry.**

UF   Domestication

Farm animals

Livestock

SA   types of domestic animals, e.g. **Cattle** [to be added as needed]

BT   **Animals**

NT   **Cats**

Cattle

Dogs

Pigs

Poultry

Reindeer

Sheep

Working animals

RT   **Livestock industry**

Pets

Domestic animals—Diseases

USE   **Animals—Diseases**

Domestic animals—Housing

USE   **Animal housing**

Domestic appliances

USE   **Electric household appliances**

Household equipment and supplies

Domestic architecture (May subdiv. geog.)   **728**

Use for materials on residential buildings from the standpoint of style and design. General materials on buildings in which people live are entered under **Houses.**

UF   Architecture, Domestic

Dwellings

Residences

SA   types of residential buildings, e.g. **Apartment houses** [to be added as needed]

BT   **Architecture**

NT   **Apartment houses**

House construction

Prefabricated houses

Solar homes

RT   **Houses**

Domestic architecture—Designs and plans   728

UF   Home designs

House plans

BT   **Architecture—Designs and plans**

Domestic economic assistance (May
   subdiv. geog.) **338.9**
   UF Anti-poverty programs
       Antipoverty programs
       Economic assistance
       Economic assistance, Domestic
       Poor relief
   BT **Economic policy**
   NT **Community development**
       Government lending
       Public works
       Subsidies
       Transfer payments
   RT **Grants-in-aid**
       Poverty
       Unemployed
Domestic finance
   USE **Household budgets**
       Personal finance
Domestic relations (May subdiv. geog.)
   346.01
   UF Family relations
   BT **Interpersonal relations**
   NT **Desertion and nonsupport**
       Visitation rights (Domestic re-
       lations)
   RT **Divorce**
       Family
       Family life education
       Marriage
Domestic violence (May subdiv. geog.)
   362.82
   UF Family violence
       Household violence
   BT **Violence**
   NT **Child abuse**
       Elderly abuse
       Wife abuse
Domestic workers
   USE **Household employees**
Domestication
   USE **Domestic animals**
Dominion of the sea
   USE **Sea power**
Dominions, British
   USE **Commonwealth countries**
Donation of organs, tissues, etc. **362.1**
   UF Organ donation
       Tissue donation

   BT **Gifts**
   RT **Transplantation of organs, tis-**
       sues, etc.
Donations
   USE **Gifts**
Doomsday book
   USE **Domesday book**
Door to door selling
   USE **Peddlers and peddling**
Doors **721**
   BT **Architecture—Details**
       Buildings
Double consciousness
   USE **Multiple personality**
Doubt
   USE **Belief and doubt**
Down syndrome **616.85**
   UF Down's syndrome
   BT **Mental retardation**
Down's syndrome
   USE **Down syndrome**
Downsizing of organizations **658.1**
   UF Corporate downsizing
       Organizational downsizing
       Organizational retrenchment
       Retrenchment of organizations
   BT **Organizational change**
   RT **Employees—Dismissal**
Draft **355.2**
   UF Compulsory military service
       Conscription, Military
       Military conscription
       Military draft
       Military service, Compulsory
       Military training, Universal
       Selective service
       Universal military training
   BT **Armies**
       Military law
       Recruiting and enlistment
   RT **Draft resisters**
Draft dodgers
   USE **Draft resisters**
Draft evaders
   USE **Draft resisters**
Draft resisters **355.2**
   UF Draft dodgers
       Draft evaders
   SA names of wars with the subdivi-
       sion *Draft resisters* [to be
       added as needed]

Draft resisters—*Continued*
   NT   World War, 1939-1945—Draft
           resisters
   RT   Conscientious objectors
           Draft
           Military desertion
Drafting, Mechanical
   USE Mechanical drawing
Dragons   398.24
   BT   Animals—Folklore
           Folklore
           Monsters
           Mythical animals
Drainage (May subdiv. geog.)   **631.6**
   Use for materials on land drainage. Materials on house drainage are entered under **House drainage.**
   UF   Land drainage
   BT   Agricultural engineering
           Civil engineering
           Hydraulic engineering
           Municipal engineering
           Reclamation of land
           Sanitary engineering
   RT   Sewerage
Drainage, House
   USE House drainage
Drama   **808.2; 808.82**
   Use for general materials on drama, not for individual works. Materials on the history and criticism of drama as literature are entered under **Drama—History and criticism.** Materials on criticism of drama as presented on the stage are entered under **Dramatic criticism.** Materials on the presentation of plays are entered under **Acting; Amateur theater;** or **Theater—Production and direction.** Collections of plays are entered under **Drama—Collections; American drama—Collections; English drama—Collections;** etc.
   UF   Stage
   SA   subjects, historical events, names of countries, cities, etc., ethnic groups, classes of persons, and names of individual persons with the subdivision *Drama,* to express the theme or subject content of collections of plays, e.g. **Easter—Drama; United States—History—1861-1865, Civil War—Drama; Napoleon I, Emperor of the French, 1769-1821—Drama;** etc. [to be added as needed]

   BT   Literature
   NT   Acting
           American drama
           Ballet
           Children's plays
           Choral speaking
           College and school drama
           Comedies
           Comedy
           Didactic drama
           Drama in education
           Dramatists
           English drama
           Folk drama
           Historical drama
           Horror plays
           Masks (Plays)
           Melodrama
           Morality plays
           Motion picture plays
           Mystery and detective plays
           One act plays
           Opera
           Pantomimes
           Pastoral drama
           Puppets and puppet plays
           Radio plays
           Religious drama
           Science fiction plays
           Television plays
           Tragedies
           Tragedy
   RT   Dramatic criticism
           Theater
Drama—Collections   **808.82**
   Use for collections of plays by several authors.
   UF   Plays
Drama—History and criticism   **809.2**
   Use for materials on criticism of drama as a literary form. Materials on criticism of drama as presented on the stage are entered under **Dramatic criticism.**
   NT   English drama—History and criticism
   RT   Dramatic criticism
Drama in education   **372.66**
   BT   Drama
   RT   Acting
           Amateur theater
           College and school drama
           School assembly programs

Drama—Technique   808.2
   UF   Play writing
          Playwriting
   BT   **Authorship**
   NT   **Motion picture plays—Technique**
          Radio plays—Technique
          Television plays—Technique
Dramatic art
   USE **Acting**
Dramatic criticism   792.9

   Use for materials on criticism of drama as presented on the stage. Materials on criticism of drama as a literary form are entered under **Drama—History and criticism; American drama—History and criticism;** etc.

   UF   Theater criticism
   BT   **Criticism**
   RT   **Drama**
          Drama—History and criticism
          Theater
Dramatic music
   USE **Musicals**
          Opera
          Operetta
Dramatic plots
   USE **Stories, plots, etc.**
Dramatic production
   USE names of dramatists with the subdivision *Dramatic production,* e.g. **Shakespeare, William, 1564-1616—Dramatic production** [to be added as needed]
Dramatists   809.2; 920

   Use for materials on the personal lives of several playwrights, not limited to a single national literature. Materials dealing with their literary work are entered under **Drama—History and criticism; English drama—History and criticism;** etc.

   UF   Playwrights
   SA   dramatists of particular countries, e.g. **American dramatists** [to be added as needed]
   BT   **Authors**
          Drama
   NT   **American dramatists**
Dramatists, American
   USE **American dramatists**
Draperies   645; 684
   UF   Curtains
          Drapery

   BT   **Interior design**
          Upholstery
Drapery
   USE **Draperies**
Draughts
   USE **Checkers**
Drawing   741; 743
   UF   Drawings
          Sketching
   SA   drawing of particular countries, e.g. **American drawing** [to be added as needed]
   BT   **Art**
          Graphic arts
   NT   **American drawing**
          Architectural drawing
          Artistic anatomy
          Commercial art
          Crayon drawing
          Figure drawing
          Geometrical drawing
          Graphic methods
          Landscape drawing
          Map drawing
          Mechanical drawing
          Pastel drawing
          Pen drawing
          Pencil drawing
          Shades and shadows
          Topographical drawing
   RT   **Illustration of books**
          Painting
          Perspective
Drawing, American
   USE **American drawing**
Drawing materials
   USE **Artists' materials**
Drawings
   USE **Drawing**
Drawn work   746.44
   BT   **Embroidery**
          Needlework
   NT   **Hardanger needlework**
Dream interpretation
   USE **Dreams**
Dreaming
   USE **Dreams**
Dreams   154.6
   UF   Dream interpretation
          Dreaming

Dreams—*Continued*
- BT Visions
- NT Fantasy
- RT Sleep
       Subconsciousness

Dredging 627
- BT Civil engineering
       Hydraulic engineering

Dress
- USE **Clothing and dress**

Dress accessories 391.4; 646
- BT **Clothing and dress**

Dressage
- USE **Horsemanship**

Dressing of ores
- USE **Ore dressing**

Dressmaking 646.4; 687
- UF Garment making
- BT **Clothing and dress**
       Clothing industry
- RT **Needlework**
       Sewing
       Tailoring

Dressmaking—Patterns 646.4; 687

Dried flowers
- USE **Flowers—Drying**

Dried foods 641.4; 664
- UF Dehydrated foods
- BT **Food**
- NT **Dried milk**
       Freeze-dried foods
- RT **Food—Preservation**

Dried milk 637
- UF Dehydrated milk
       Powdered milk
- BT **Dried foods**
       Milk

Drifting of continents
- USE **Continental drift**

Drill and minor tactics 355.5
- UF Military drill
       Minor tactics
- BT **Tactics**
- RT **Military art and science**

Drill (Nonmilitary)
- USE **Marching drills**

Drilling and boring
- USE **Drilling and boring (Earth and rocks)**
       Drilling and boring (Metal, wood, etc.)

Drilling and boring (Earth and rocks) 622

Use for materials on the operation of cutting holes in earth or rock. Materials on workshop operations in metal, wood, etc., are entered under **Drilling and boring (Metal, wood, etc.)**.

- UF Boring
       Drilling and boring
       Shaft sinking
       Well boring
- BT **Hydraulic engineering**
       Mining engineering
       Water supply engineering
- NT **Oil well drilling**
- RT **Tunnels**
       Wells

Drilling and boring (Metal, wood, etc.) 621.9

Use for materials on workshop operations in metal, wood, etc. Materials on the operation of cutting holes in earth or rock are entered under **Drilling and boring (Earth and rocks)**.

- UF Boring
       Drilling and boring
- BT **Machine shop practice**
- RT **Machine tools**

Drilling, Oil well
- USE **Oil well drilling**

Drilling platforms 627
- UF Marine drilling platforms
       Ocean drilling platforms
       Oil drilling platforms
       Platforms, Drilling
- BT **Ocean engineering**
       Offshore oil well drilling

Drills, Marching
- USE **Marching drills**

Drinking age (May subdiv. geog.) **344; 363.4**
- UF Minimum drinking age
- BT **Age**
       Teenagers—Alcohol use
       Youth—Alcohol use

Drinking and employees
- USE **Employees—Alcohol use**

Drinking and teenagers
- USE **Teenagers—Alcohol use**

Drinking and youth
- USE **Youth—Alcohol use**

Drinking in the workplace
- USE **Employees—Alcohol use**

Drinking of alcoholic beverages (May
  subdiv. geog.)   178; 363.4; 394.1;
  613.81
  Use for materials on drinking in its social
aspects and as a social problem.
  UF   Alcohol consumption
        Alcohol use
        Alcoholic beverage consumption
        Consumption of alcoholic bever-
          ages
        Drinking problem
        Liquor problem
        Social drinking
  SA   classes of persons and ethnic
          groups with the subdivision
          Alcohol use, e.g. **Employ-
          ees—Alcohol use; Youth—
          Alcohol use;** etc. [to be add-
          ed as needed]
  NT   **Drunk driving**
  RT   **Alcoholic beverages**
        Alcoholism
        Temperance
Drinking problem
  USE   **Alcoholism**
        Drinking of alcoholic beverages
Drinking water (May subdiv. geog.)
  363.6; 628.1
  UF   Potable water
        Tap water
  BT   **Water**
        Water supply
Drinks
  USE   **Alcoholic beverages**
        Beverages
        Liquors
Driver education
  USE   **Automobile driver education**
Drivers, Automobile
  USE   **Automobile drivers**
Drivers' licenses (May subdiv. geog.)
  353.9; 629.28
  UF   Automobile drivers' licenses
        Automobiles—Drivers' licenses
        Motor vehicles—Drivers' li-
          censes
  BT   **Safety regulations**
Driving under the influence of alcohol
  USE   **Drunk driving**
Driving while intoxicated
  USE   **Drunk driving**

Dromedaries
  USE   **Camels**
Drop forging
  USE   **Forging**
Dropouts (May subdiv. geog.)   371.2
  UF   College dropouts
        Elementary school dropouts
        High school dropouts
        School dropouts
        Student dropouts
        Teenage dropouts
  BT   **Students**
        Youth
  RT   **At risk students**
        Educational counseling
        School attendance
Droughts (May subdiv. geog.)   551.57;
  632
  BT   **Meteorology**
  NT   **Dust storms**
  RT   **Rain**
Drowning prevention
  USE   **Water safety**
Drug abuse (May subdiv. geog.)   362.29;
  613.8; 616.86
  Use for general materials on the misuse or
abuse of drugs. Materials on the abuse of a
particular drug or kind of drugs are entered
under this heading and also under the drug or
kind of drugs, e.g. **Cocaine; Hallucinogens;**
etc.
  UF   Addiction to drugs
        Drug addiction
        Drug habit
        Drug misuse
        Drug use
        Drugs—Abuse
        Drugs—Misuse
        Narcotic abuse
        Narcotic addiction
        Narcotic habit
        Substance abuse
  SA   classes of persons with the sub-
          division *Drug use,* e.g. **Crim-
          inals—Drug use;** and types
          of drug abuse, e.g. **Medica-
          tion abuse** [to be added as
          needed]
  BT   **Social problems**
  NT   **Medication abuse**
  RT   **Drug addicts**
        Drugs
        Solvent abuse

Drug abuse—*Continued*

        Twelve-step programs

Drug abuse counseling   **362.29; 613.8**

   UF   Drug addiction counseling

         Drug counseling

         Narcotic addiction counseling

   BT   **Counseling**

   NT   **Drug addicts—Rehabilitation**

Drug abuse education

   USE   **Drug education**

Drug abuse—Physiological effect

   USE   **Drugs—Physiological effect**

Drug abuse screening

   USE   **Drug testing**

Drug abuse—Study and teaching

   USE   **Drug education**

Drug abuse—Testing

   USE   **Drug testing**

Drug abuse—Treatment   **362.29**

   BT   **Therapeutics**

Drug abusing physicians

   USE   **Physicians—Drug use**

Drug addicted physicians

   USE   **Physicians—Drug use**

Drug addiction

   USE   **Drug abuse**

Drug addiction counseling

   USE   **Drug abuse counseling**

Drug addiction education

   USE   **Drug education**

Drug addicts (May subdiv. geog.)

        362.29; 616.86

   UF   Addicts

         Narcotic addicts

   SA   classes of persons with the sub-

         division *Drug use,* e.g. **Crim-**

         inals—Drug use [to be added

         as needed]

   NT   **Children of drug addicts**

         Recovering addicts

   RT   **Drug abuse**

Drug addicts—Rehabilitation   **362.29;**

        613.8; 616.86

   BT   **Drug abuse counseling**

Drug counseling

   USE   **Drug abuse counseling**

Drug dealing

   USE   **Drug traffic**

Drug education (May subdiv. geog.)

        362.29; 371.7; 613.8

   Use for materials on the study of drugs, including their source, abuse, chemical com-

position, and social, physical, and personal effects.

   UF   Drug abuse education

         Drug abuse—Study and teaching

         Drug addiction education

   BT   **Health education**

Drug habit

   USE   **Drug abuse**

Drug misuse

   USE   **Drug abuse**

Drug plants

   USE   **Medical botany**

Drug pushers

   USE   **Drug traffic**

Drug stores

   USE   **Drugstores**

Drug testing   **344; 658.3**

   Use for materials on testing to identify personal use or misuse of drugs. Materials on the testing of drugs for safety or effectiveness are entered under **Drugs—Testing.**

   UF   Drug abuse screening

         Drug abuse—Testing

         Screening for drug abuse

         Testing for drug abuse

   SA   classes of persons with the sub-

         division *Drug testing,* e.g.

         Employees—Drug testing [to

         be added as needed]

   NT   **Employees—Drug testing**

Drug testing in the workplace

   USE   **Employees—Drug testing**

Drug therapy   **615.5**

   UF   Chemotherapy

         Pharmacotherapy

   SA   names of diseases other than

         cancer with the subdivision

         Drug therapy, e.g. **Mental ill-**

         ness—Drug therapy [to be

         added as needed]

   BT   **Therapeutics**

   NT   **Antibiotics**

         Cancer—Chemotherapy

         Mental illness—Drug therapy

   RT   **Drugs**

         Pharmacology

Drug trade, Illicit

   USE   **Drug traffic**

Drug traffic (May subdiv. geog.)

        363.45; 364.1

   UF   Drug dealing

         Drug pushers

         Drug trade, Illicit

Drug traffic—*Continued*
>> Narcotic traffic
>> Smuggling of drugs
>> Trafficking in drugs
>> Trafficking in narcotics
> BT **Drugs and crime**

Drug use
> USE **Drug abuse**
>> **Drugs**
>> and classes of persons with the subdivision *Drug use,* e.g.
>>> **Criminals—Drug use; Employees—Drug use; Teenagers—Drug use; Youth—Drug use;** etc. [to be added as needed]

Drugs 615
> UF Drug use
>> Pharmaceuticals
> SA classes of persons with the subdivision *Drug use,* e.g. **Criminals—Drug use;** types of drugs, e.g. **Amphetamines; Hallucinogens; Narcotics; Stimulants;** etc.; and names of individual drugs, e.g. **Crack (Drug); Marijuana;** etc. [to be added as needed]
> BT **Pharmacy**
>> **Therapeutics**
> NT **Designer drugs**
>> **Drugs and crime**
>> **Generic drugs**
>> **Hallucinogens**
>> **Narcotics**
>> **Nonprescription drugs**
>> **Orphan drugs**
>> **Psychotropic drugs**
>> **Steroids**
>> **Stimulants**
>> **Sulfonamides**
> RT **Drug abuse**
>> **Drug therapy**
>> **Materia medica**
>> **Pharmacology**

Drugs—Abuse
> USE **Drug abuse**

Drugs—Adulteration and analysis
> USE **Pharmacology**

Drugs and crime (May subdiv. geog.)
> **364.1**
>> Use for general materials on the relationship of drugs and crime. Materials on the illicit drug trade are entered under **Drug traffic.** Materials on the use of drugs by criminals are entered under **Criminals—Drug use.**
> UF Crime and drugs
>> Crime and narcotics
>> Narcotics and crime
> BT **Crime**
>> **Drugs**
> NT **Drug traffic**
> RT **Criminals—Drug use**

Drugs and criminals
> USE **Criminals—Drug use**

Drugs and employees
> USE **Employees—Drug use**

Drugs and sports
> USE **Athletes—Drug use**

Drugs and teenagers
> USE **Teenagers—Drug use**

Drugs and youth
> USE **Youth—Drug use**

Drugs—Chemistry
> USE **Pharmaceutical chemistry**

Drugs—Generic substitution
> USE **Generic drugs**

Drugs in the workplace
> USE **Employees—Drug use**

Drugs—Misuse
> USE **Drug abuse**

Drugs, Nonprescription
> USE **Nonprescription drugs**

Drugs—Physiological effect 615; 616.86
>> Use for materials limited to the effect of drugs on the functions of living organisms.
> UF Drug abuse—Physiological effect
> SA names of drugs with the subdivision *Physiological effect* [to be added as needed]
> BT **Pharmacology**
> NT **Opium—Physiological effect**

Drugs—Psychological aspects 615; 616.86
> BT **Applied psychology**

Drugs—Testing 363.19
>> Use for materials on the testing of drugs for safety or effectiveness. Materials on testing to identify the personal use or misuse or drugs are entered under **Drug testing.**
> UF Clinical drug trials
>> Clinical trials of drugs

  BT   **Consumer protection**
         Pharmacology
Drugstores   381
  Use for materials on business establishments that sell drugs. Materials on the art or practice of preparing, preserving, and dispensing drugs are entered under **Pharmacy.**
  UF   Chemists' shops
         Drug stores
         Pharmacies
  BT   **Retail trade**
         Stores
Druids and Druidism   299
  BT   **Celts**
         Religions
Drum
  USE   **Drums**
Drum majoring   784.9; 791.6
  BT   **Bands (Music)**
  RT   **Baton twirling**
Drums   786.9
  UF   Drum
  BT   **Musical instruments**
         Percussion instruments
Drunk driving   363.12; 364.1
  UF   Driving under the influence of
            alcohol
         Driving while intoxicated
  BT   **Crime**
         Drinking of alcoholic beverages
Drunkards
  USE   **Alcoholics**
Drunkenness
  USE   **Alcoholism**
         Temperance
Dry cleaning   667
  UF   Clothing and dress—Dry cleaning
  BT   **Cleaning**
Dry farming (May subdiv. geog.)   **631.5**
  UF   Farming, Dry
  BT   **Agriculture**
Dry goods
  USE   **Fabrics**
Drying   660
  SA   materials, products, or objects
            dried with the subdivision
            Drying, e.g. **Flowers—Drying**
            [to be added as needed]
  BT   **Industrial chemistry**

Dual-career couples
  USE   **Dual-career families**
Dual-career families   306.85; 646.7
  Use for materials on families in which both the husband and wife are pursuing careers.
  UF   Dual-career couples
         Dual career family
         Dual-career marriage
         Dual-income couples
         Two-career couples
         Two-career families
         Two-career family
         Two-income families
         Working couples
  BT   **Family**
  RT   **Work and family**
Dual career family
  USE   **Dual-career families**
Dual-career marriage
  USE   **Dual-career families**
Dual-income couples
  USE   **Dual-career families**
Ducks   598.4; 636.5
  BT   **Birds**
         Poultry
Ductless glands
  USE   **Endocrine glands**
Due process of law (May subdiv. geog.)
         347
  Use for materials on the regular administration of the law, according to which citizens may not be denied their legal rights and all laws must conform to fundamental and accepted legal principles. Materials on legal hearings before an impartial and disinterested tribunal are entered under **Fair trial.**
  UF   Procedural due process
         Substantive due process
  BT   **Administration of justice**
         Civil rights
  NT   **Fair trial**
Dueling (May subdiv. geog.)   **179.7; 394**
  UF   Fighting
  BT   **Manners and customs**
         Martial arts
  NT   **Fencing**
Dumps, Toxic
  USE   **Hazardous waste sites**
Dunes
  USE   **Sand dunes**
Duplicate bridge
  USE   **Bridge (Game)**
Duplicating machines
  USE   **Copying machines**

Duplicating processes
  USE **Copying processes**
Durable power of attorney
  USE **Power of attorney**
Dust 551.51
  UF Atmospheric dust
      Dust particles
  BT **Air pollution**
Dust particles
  USE **Dust**
Dust, Radioactive
  USE **Radioactive fallout**
Dust storms 551.55
  BT **Droughts**
      Erosion
      Storms
Dusting and spraying
  USE **Spraying and dusting**
Duties
  USE **Tariff**
      Taxation
Duty 170
  BT **Ethics**
      Human behavior
  NT **Conscience**
      Vocation
DVDs 004.5
  BT **Optical storage devices**
Dwarf trees 582.16; 635.9
  SA types of dwarf trees, e.g. **Bonsai**
      [to be added as needed]
  BT **Trees**
  NT **Bonsai**
Dwarfism 616.4
  UF Growth retardation
  BT **Growth disorders**
Dwellings
  USE **Domestic architecture**
      Houses
      Housing
      and ethnic groups and classes
      of persons with the subdivi-
      sion *Dwellings,* for materials
      on the residential buildings of
      a group from the standpoint
      of architecture, construction,
      or ethnology, e.g. **Native**
      Americans—Dwellings; and
      ethnic groups and classes of
      persons with the subdivision
      Housing, for materials on the

social and economic aspects
of providing housing for the
group, e.g. **Physically handi-**
capped—Housing [to be add-
ed as needed]
Dyes and dyeing 646.6; 667; 746.6
  SA types of dyes and types of dye-
      ing [to be added as needed]
  BT **Color**
      Pigments
      Textile chemistry
      Textile industry
  NT **Batik**
      Tie dyeing
  RT **Bleaching**
Dying children
  USE **Terminally ill children**
Dying patients
  USE **Terminally ill**
Dynamics 531
  UF Kinetics
  BT **Mathematics**
      Mechanics
  NT **Aerodynamics**
      Astrodynamics
      Chaos (Science)
      Hydrodynamics
      Kinematics
      Matter
      Motion
      Quantum theory
      Thermodynamics
  RT **Force and energy**
      Physics
      Statics
Dynamite 662
  BT **Explosives**
Dynamos
  USE **Electric generators**
Dyslexia 371.91; 616.85
  BT **Reading disability**
Dyspepsia
  USE **Indigestion**
Dysphasia
  USE **Language disorders**
Dystopias 808.3
  May be used for individual works, collec-
  tions, or materials about dystopias.
  UF Anti-utopias
  BT **Fantasy fiction**
      Science fiction
  RT **Utopian fiction**

E-mail
USE **Electronic mail systems**
E-mail discussion groups
USE **Electronic discussion groups**
Eagles   598.9
BT **Birds**
Birds of prey
Ear   611; 612.8
BT **Head**
NT **Deafness**
RT **Hearing**
Early childhood education (May subdiv.
geog.)   **372.21**
Use for materials on formal or informal education of children up to grade 3.
BT **Education**
Early Christian literature   270.1
Use for individual works or collections of the writings of early Christian authors. Materials on the lives and thought of the leaders of the Christian church up to the time of Gregory the Great in the West and John of Damascus in the East are entered under **Fathers of the church.**
UF Christian literature—30-600, Early
Christian literature, Early
BT **Christian literature**
Literature
Medieval literature
RT **Church history—30-600, Early church**
Fathers of the church
Latin literature
Early church history
USE **Church history—30-600, Early church**
Early printed books (May subdiv. geog.)
094
SA subjects with the subdivision
Early works to 1800, for materials on those subjects written before 1800, e.g. **Political science—Early works to 1800** [to be added as needed]
BT **Books**
Early printed books—15th century
USE **Incunabula**
Early works to 1800
USE subjects with the subdivision
Early works to 1800, for materials on those subjects written before 1800, e.g. **Political**

science—Early works to
1800 [to be added as needed]
Earth   525; 550
Use for general materials on the whole planet. Materials limited to the structure and composition of the earth and the physical changes it has undergone and is still undergoing are entered under **Geology.**
UF World
BT **Planets**
Solar system
NT **Antarctica**
Arctic regions
Arid regions
Atmosphere
Continents
Earthquakes
Gaia hypothesis
Geodesy
Geography
Ice age
Latitude
Longitude
Ocean
Tropics
RT **Earth sciences**
Geology
Physical geography
Earth—Age   551.7
Earth—Chemical composition
USE **Geochemistry**
Earth—Crust   551.1
BT **Earth—Internal structure**
NT **Plate tectonics**
RT **Earth—Surface**
Earth, Effect of man on
USE **Human influence on nature**
Earth fills
USE **Landfills**
Earth-friendly technology
USE **Green technology**
Earth—Gravity
USE **Gravity**
Earth—Internal structure   551.1
NT **Earth—Crust**
Earth magnetic field
USE **Geomagnetism**
Earth—Magnetism
USE **Geomagnetism**
Earth sciences   550
UF Geoscience
BT **Physical sciences**
Science

233

Earth sciences—*Continued*
  NT Climate
      Geochemistry
      Geography
      Geology
      Geophysics
      Meteorology
      Oceanography
      Water
  RT Earth
Earth sheltered houses   690; 728
  UF Underground houses
  BT House construction
      Houses
      Underground architecture
Earth—Surface   551.1
  UF Surface of the earth
  NT Landforms
  RT Earth—Crust
Earthenware
  USE Pottery
Earthly paradise
  USE Paradise
Earthquake effects
  USE types of structures with the sub-
       division *Earthquake effects,*
       e.g. **Skyscrapers—Earth-
       quake effects** [to be added as
       needed]
Earthquake sea waves
  USE Tsunamis
Earthquakes (May subdiv. geog.)
      551.22
  UF Seismography
      Seismology
  SA types of structures subject to
      earthquake forces with the
      subdivision *Earthquake effects,*
      e.g. **Skyscrapers—Earth-
      quake effects** [to be added as
      needed]
  BT Earth
      Geology
      Natural disasters
      Physical geography
  NT Buildings—Earthquake effects
      Skyscrapers—Earthquake ef-
      fects
Earthquakes and building
  USE Buildings—Earthquake effects
Earthquakes—California   551.2209794
Earthquakes—United States   551.220973

Earthworks (Archeology)
  USE Excavations (Archeology)
Earthworks (Art) (May subdiv. geog.)
      709.04
  UF Landscape sculpture
      Site oriented art
  BT Art
East
  USE Asia
East Africa   967.6
      Use for materials dealing collectively with
      the eastern regions of Africa. The term usual-
      ly includes the areas now occupied by Burun-
      di, Kenya, Rwanda, Tanzania, Uganda, and
      Somalia, and sometimes Malawi and Mozam-
      bique as well.
  UF Africa, East
      Africa, Eastern
      Eastern Africa
  BT Africa
East and West   306; 909
      Use for materials on both acculturation and
      cultural conflict between Asian and Occidental
      civilizations.
  BT International relations
  NT Asia—Civilization
      Orientalism
      Western civilization
  RT Acculturation
East Asia   950
      Use for materials that deal collectively with
      the eastern regions of Asia including China,
      Japan, Korea, and Taiwan.
  UF East (Far East)
      Far East
      Orient
  BT Asia
  RT Pacific rim
East (Far East)
  USE East Asia
East Germany
  USE Germany (East)
East Goths
  USE Goths
East Indians   305.891; 954
  UF Indians (of India)
Easter (May subdiv. geog.)   263;
      394.2667
  BT Christian holidays
      Holy Week
  RT Lent
Easter carols
  USE Carols

Easter—Drama 808.82
> Use for collections of plays about Easter.
> BT **Religious drama**

Easter egg decoration
> USE **Egg decoration**

Eastern Africa
> USE **East Africa**

Eastern churches 281
> BT **Christian sects**
> **Christianity**
> NT **Orthodox Eastern Church**

Eastern Empire
> USE **Byzantine Empire**

Eastern Europe 947
> UF Europe, Eastern

Eastern Europe—History 947

Eastern Europe—History—1989-
> **947.085; 947.086**

Eastern Seaboard
> USE **Atlantic States**

Easy and quick cooking
> USE **Quick and easy cooking**

Easy reading materials 372.41
> UF Beginning reading materials
> Preprimers
> Preschool reading materials
> Primers
> BT **Children's literature**
> **Reading materials**

Eating
> USE **Dining**
> **Gastronomy**

Eating customs (May subdiv. geog.)
> **394.1**
> UF Food customs
> Food habits
> BT **Diet**
> **Human behavior**
> **Nutrition**
> NT **Table etiquette**
> RT **Dining**

Eating disorders 616.85
> SA types of eating disorders [to be added as needed]
> BT **Abnormal psychology**
> NT **Anorexia nervosa**
> **Bulimia**

Eavesdropping 363.25
> UF Bugging, Electronic
> Electronic bugging
> Electronic eavesdropping
> Electronic listening devices
> Listening devices
> BT **Criminal investigation**
> **Right of privacy**
> RT **Wiretapping**

Eccentrics and eccentricities (May subdiv. geog.) 920
> UF Cranks
> BT **Curiosities and wonders**
> **Personality**
> NT **Hermits**

Ecclesiastical antiquities
> USE **Christian antiquities**

Ecclesiastical architecture
> USE **Church architecture**

Ecclesiastical art
> USE **Christian art**

Ecclesiastical biography
> USE **Christian biography**

Ecclesiastical fasts and feasts
> USE **Religious holidays**

Ecclesiastical furniture
> USE **Church furniture**

Ecclesiastical history
> USE **Church history**

Ecclesiastical institutions
> USE **Religious institutions**

Ecclesiastical law 262.9
> UF Canon law
> Church law
> BT **Church**
> **Law**
> NT **Tithes**

Ecclesiastical polity
> USE **Church polity**

Ecclesiastical rites and ceremonies
> USE **Rites and ceremonies**

Ecclesiastical year
> USE **Church year**

Eclipses, Lunar
> USE **Lunar eclipses**

Eclipses, Solar
> USE **Solar eclipses**

Eclogues
> USE **Pastoral poetry**

Eco-development
> USE **Economic development—Environmental aspects**

Ecodevelopment
> USE **Economic development—Environmental aspects**

Ecological movement
  USE **Environmental movement**
Ecological tourism
  USE **Ecotourism**
Ecology (May subdiv. geog.) **577**
  UF Balance of nature
      Biology—Ecology
      Ecosystems
  SA types of ecology, e.g. **Marine
      ecology;** and types of ani-
      mals, plants, and crops with
      the subdivision *Ecology* [to be
      added as needed]
  BT **Biology**
      Environment
  NT **Adaptation (Biology)**
      Biogeography
      Coastal ecology
      Environmental protection
      Fishes—Ecology
      Food chains (Ecology)
      Gaia hypothesis
      Habitat (Ecology)
      Marine ecology
      Plant ecology
      Symbiosis
  RT **Biological diversity**
      Environmental sciences
Ecology, Human
  USE **Human ecology**
Ecology, Social
  USE **Human ecology**
Economic aid
  USE **Foreign aid**
Economic aspects
  USE subjects with the subdivision
      Economic aspects, e.g. **Agri-
      culture—Economic aspects**
      [to be added as needed]
Economic assistance
  USE **Domestic economic assistance**
      Foreign aid
Economic assistance, American
  USE **American foreign aid**
Economic assistance, Domestic
  USE **Domestic economic assistance**
Economic biology
  USE **Economic botany**
      Economic zoology

Economic botany 581.6
  UF Agricultural botany
      Botany, Economic
      Economic biology
  BT **Agriculture**
      Botany
  NT **Cotton**
      Edible plants
      Forage plants
      Forest products
      Plant conservation
      Plant introduction
      Poisonous plants
      Weeds
Economic conditions 330.9
  Use for general materials on some or all of
  the following: natural resources, business,
  commerce, industry, labor, manufactures, fi-
  nancial conditions. Materials on the history of
  the economic development of several coun-
  tries are entered under **Economic development.**
  UF Economic history
      National resources
      World economics
  SA racial and ethnic groups, classes
      of persons, and names of
      countries, cities, areas, etc.,
      with the subdivision *Economic
      conditions,* e.g. **African
      Americans—Economic condi-
      tions; United States—Eco-
      nomic conditions;** etc. [to be
      added as needed]
  BT **Business**
      Economics
      Social conditions
      Wealth
  NT **African Americans—Economic
      conditions**
      Blacks—Economic conditions
      Business cycles
      **Chicago (Ill.)—Economic con-
      ditions**
      Developing countries
      Great Depression, 1929-1939
      Industrial revolution
      Jews—Economic conditions
      Labor supply
      **Native Americans—Economic
      conditions**
      Natural resources
      Ohio—Economic conditions

Economic conditions—*Continued*
      Poverty
      Quality of life
      United States—Economic conditions
  RT Commercial geography
      Economic development
Economic cycles
  USE Business cycles
Economic depressions
  USE Depressions
Economic development   338.9
    Use for materials on the theory and policy of economic development. Materials restricted to a particular place are entered under the name of the country, city, or area with the subdivisions *Economic conditions; Economic policy;* or *Industries.*
  UF Development, Economic
      Economic growth
  BT Economic policy
      Economics
  NT Infrastructure (Economics)
      Rural development
      Sustainable development
  RT Economic conditions
Economic development—Environmental aspects   333.71; 338.9
    Use for general materials on the environmental impact of economic development. Materials on economic development that satisfies the needs of the present generation without depleting natural resources for the future or having adverse environmental effects are entered under **Sustainable development.**
  UF Eco-development
      Ecodevelopment
Economic equilibrium
  USE Equilibrium (Economics)
Economic forecasting   338.5
  BT Business cycles
      Economics
      Forecasting
  NT Business forecasting
      Employment forecasting
Economic geography
  USE Commercial geography
Economic geology   553
  UF Geology, Economic
  SA types of geological products, e.g. **Asbestos; Gypsum;** etc. [to be added as needed]
  BT Geology
  NT Mines and mineral resources
      Petroleum geology

      Quarries and quarrying
      Soils
      Stone
Economic growth
  USE Economic development
Economic history
  USE Economic conditions
Economic mobilization
  USE Industrial mobilization
Economic planning
  USE Economic policy
Economic policy (May subdiv. geog.)   338.9
    Use for materials on the policy of government in economic affairs.
  UF Business and government
      Business—Government policy
      Central planning
      Economic planning
      Government and business
      Government policy
      National planning
      State planning
  SA subjects with the subdivision *Government policy,* e.g. **Agriculture—Government policy;** and types of activities, facilities, industries, services, and undertakings with the subdivision *Planning,* e.g. **Transportation—Planning** [to be added as needed]
  BT Economics
      Planning
  NT Commercial policy
      Domestic economic assistance
      Economic development
      Fiscal policy
      Foreign aid
      Free enterprise
      Government lending
      Government ownership
      Industrial mobilization
      Industrial policy
      Industrialization
      International economic relations
      Labor policy
      Land reform
      Monetary policy
      Municipal ownership
      Privatization

Economic policy—*Continued*
    Sanctions (International law)
    Subsidies
    Tariff
    Transfer payments
    Urban policy
    Welfare state
  RT National security
    Social policy
Economic policy—Ohio 338.9771
  UF Ohio—Economic policy
Economic policy—United States
    338.973
  UF United States—Economic policy
Economic recessions
  USE **Recessions**
Economic relations, Foreign
  USE **International economic relations**
Economic sanctions
  USE **Sanctions (International law)**
Economic sustainability
  USE **Sustainable development**
Economic zones (Maritime law)
  USE **Territorial waters**
Economic zoology 591.6
  Use for general materials on animals injurious or beneficial to agriculture, and for materials on the extermination of wild animals, venomous snakes, etc.
  UF Animals, Useful and harmful
    Economic biology
    Zoology, Economic
  BT **Zoology**
  NT **Agricultural pests**
    Beneficial insects
    Furbearing animals
    Insect pests
    Livestock industry
    Pest control
    Pests
    Poisonous animals
    Wildlife conservation
    Working animals
Economics (May subdiv. geog.) 330
  Use for materials on the science of economics. This heading may be subdivided geographically for materials on this branch of learning in a particular place. Materials on the economic conditions of a particular place are entered under the name of the place with the subdivision *Economic conditions*.
  UF Distribution of wealth
    Political economy

    Production
  SA subjects with the subdivision *Economic aspects,* e.g. **Agriculture—Economic aspects;** and countries, states, cities, regions, etc., with the subdivision *Economic conditions,* e.g. **United States—Economic conditions** [to be added as needed]
  BT **Social sciences**
  NT **Agriculture—Economic aspects**
    Barter
    Business
    Capital
    Capitalism
    Christianity and economics
    Collectivism
    Commerce
    Consumption (Economics)
    Cooperation
    Cost and standard of living
    Cost effectiveness
    Economic conditions
    Economic development
    Economic forecasting
    Economic policy
    Employment
    Equilibrium (Economics)
    Finance
    Gross national product
    Income
    Individualism
    Industrial trusts
    Industries
    Labor
    Land use
    Macroeconomics
    Marxism
    Medical economics
    Microeconomics
    Money
    Monopolies
    Population
    Prices
    Profit
    Property
    Risk
    Saving and investment
    Socialism
    Statistics

Economics—*Continued*
>> Supply and demand
>> Underground economy
>> Waste (Economics)
>> Wealth

Economics and Christianity
> USE **Christianity and economics**

Economics—History   330.09; 330.1
> Use for materials describing the development of economic theories. Materials on the economic conditions and development of countries are entered under **Economic conditions.**

Economics of war
> USE **War—Economic aspects**

Economy
> USE **Saving and investment**

Economy cars
> USE **Compact cars**

Economy, Underground
> USE **Underground economy**

Ecosystems
> USE **Ecology**

Ecotourism (May subdiv. geog.)   338.4
> UF   Ecological tourism
> Environmental tourism
> Green tourism
> Nature tourism
> BT   **Tourist trade**

Ecumenical councils
> USE **Councils and synods**

Ecumenical movement (May subdiv.
>> geog.)   280
> Use for materials on a movement originating in the twentieth century aimed at promoting church cooperation and unity. Materials on unity as one of the marks of the church are entered under **Church—Unity.** Materials on prospective and actual mergers within and across denominational lines are entered under **Christian union.** Materials on religious activities planned and conducted cooperatively by two or more Christian sects are entered under **Interdenominational cooperation.**
> UF   Christian unity
> Ecumenism
> BT   **Christian sects**
> **Church**
> RT   **Christian union**

Ecumenism
> USE **Christian union**
> **Ecumenical movement**

Eddas   839
> May be used for individual works, collections, or materials about eddas.

> BT   **Old Norse literature**
> **Poetry**
> **Scandinavian literature**

Eden
> USE **Paradise**

Edgar Allan Poe Awards   808.3
> UF   Edgars
> BT   **Literary prizes**
> **Mystery fiction**

Edgars
> USE **Edgar Allan Poe Awards**

Edible plants   581.6
> UF   Food plants
> Plants, Edible
> BT   **Economic botany**
> **Food**
> **Plants**

Edifices
> USE **Buildings**

Editing   070.5; 808
> Use for materials on the editing of books and texts. Materials on the editing of newspapers and periodicals are entered under **Journalism—Editing.**
> SA   subjects and types of literature with the subdivision *Editing,* e.g. **Poetry—Editing;** etc. [to be added as needed]
> BT   **Authorship**
> **Publishers and publishing**
> NT   **Journalism—Editing**
> **Poetry—Editing**

Editions   016
> UF   Bibliography—Editions
> BT   **Bibliography**
> NT   **Autographed editions**
> **Bilingual books**
> **First editions**
> **Paperback books**
> **Reprints (Publications)**

Education (May subdiv. geog.)   370
> Subdivisions listed under this heading may be used under other education headings where applicable.
> UF   Instruction
> Pedagogy
> Study and teaching
> SA   types of education [to be added as needed], e.g. **Vocational education;** classes of persons and social and ethnic groups with the subdivision *Educa-*

Education—*Continued*

    tion, e.g. **Deaf—Education;**
    African Americans—Educa-
    tion; etc.; and subjects with
    the subdivision *Study and*
    teaching, e.g. **Science—Study**
    and teaching [to be added as
    needed]

BT   **Civilization**

NT   **Ability grouping in education**
    Adult education
    African Americans—Education
    Area studies
    Audiovisual education
    Automobile driver education
    Basic education
    Blacks—Education
    Blind—Education
    Books and reading
    Boys—Education
    Business education
    Church and education
    Classical education
    Coeducation
    Colleges and universities
    Consumer education
    Continuing education
    Cooperative learning
    Deaf—Education
    Distance education
    Early childhood education
    Educational evaluation
    Educational games
    Educational technology
    Educational tests and measure-
    ments
    Educators
    Elementary education
    Evening and continuation
    schools
    Family life education
    Foreign study
    Girls—Education
    Health education
    Higher education
    Home and school
    Home schooling
    International education
    Internet in education
    Labor—Education
    Library education
    Literacy

    Mainstreaming in education
    Men—Education
    Mentally handicapped chil-
    dren—Education
    Military education
    Moral education
    Multicultural education
    Native Americans—Education
    Nature study
    Naval education
    Outdoor education
    Physical education
    Preschool education
    Professional education
    Psychology of learning
    Religious education
    Scholarships
    School choice
    Secondary education
    Self-instruction
    Simulation games in education
    Socialization
    Special education
    Study skills
    Teaching
    Technical education
    Veterans—Education
    Vocational education
    Women—Education
    World War, 1939-1945—Edu-
    cation and the war

RT   **Culture**
    Learning and scholarship
    Schools

Education—Aims and objectives   370.11

Education and church
   USE   **Church and education**

Education and radio
   USE   **Radio in education**

Education and religion
   USE   **Church and education**

Education and state
   USE   **Education—Government policy**

Education and television
   USE   **Television in education**

Education and the war
   USE   names of wars with the subdivi-
       sion *Education and the war,*
       e.g. **World War, 1939-**
       1945—Education and the
       war [to be added as needed]

Education associations
  USE **Education—Societies**
Education—Automation
  USE **Computer-assisted instruction**
Education, Bilingual
  USE **Bilingual education**
Education, Christian
  USE **Christian education**
Education, Compulsory
  USE **Compulsory education**
Education—Computer software
  USE **Educational software**
Education, Cooperative
  USE **Cooperative education**
Education—Curricula   375
  UF Core curriculum
      Courses of study
      Curricula
      Schools—Curricula
  SA types of education and schools
      with the subdivision *Curricu-*
      la, e.g. **Library education—**
      Curricula [to be added as
      needed]
  NT **Articulation (Education)**
      Colleges and universities—Cur-
      ricula
      Curriculum planning
      Library education—Curricula
Education—Data processing
  USE **Computer-assisted instruction**
Education—Developing countries
      370.9172
  UF Developing countries—Education
Education, Elementary
  USE **Elementary education**
Education—Experimental methods
      371.3
  UF Activity schools
      Experimental methods in educa-
      tion
      Progressive education
      Teaching—Experimental methods
  SA types of experimental methods,
      e.g. **Nongraded schools;**
      Open plan schools; etc. [to
      be added as needed]
  NT **Experimental schools**
      Nongraded schools
      Open plan schools
      Whole language

Education—Federal aid
  USE **Federal aid to education**
Education—Finance   371.2; 379.1
  UF School finance
      School taxes
      Tuition
  BT **Finance**
  NT **Educational vouchers**
      Government aid to education
  RT **Federal aid to education**
Education for librarianship
  USE **Library education**
Education—Government aid
  USE **Government aid to education**
Education—Government policy (May
      subdiv. geog.)   **379**
  UF Education and state
      Educational policy
  BT **Social policy**
  NT **Compulsory education**
      Federal aid to education
      Government aid to education
Education, Higher
  USE **Higher education**
Education, Industrial
  USE **Industrial arts education**
Education—Integration
  USE **School integration**
      Segregation in education
Education of adults
  USE **Adult education**
Education of children
  USE **Elementary education**
Education of criminals
  USE **Prisoners—Education**
Education of men
  USE **Men—Education**
Education of prisoners
  USE **Prisoners—Education**
Education of the blind
  USE **Blind—Education**
Education of the deaf
  USE **Deaf—Education**
Education of veterans
  USE **Veterans—Education**
Education of women
  USE **Women—Education**
Education of workers
  USE **Labor—Education**

Education—Parent participation (May subdiv. geog.) **371.19**

  UF Parent participation in children's education

      Parental involvement in children's education

  RT **Home schooling**

Education—Personnel service

  USE **Educational counseling**

Education, Preschool

  USE **Preschool education**

Education, Primary

  USE **Elementary education**

Education, Secondary

  USE **Secondary education**

Education—Segregation

  USE **Segregation in education**

Education—Societies **370.6**

  UF Education associations

      Educational associations

  BT **Societies**

  NT **Parent-teacher associations**

Education—State aid

  USE **Government aid to education**

Education—Statistics **370**

  BT **Statistics**

Education—Study and teaching **370.7**

Use for materials on the study of education as a discipline. Materials on the history and methods of training teachers, including the educational functions of teachers colleges, are entered under **Teachers—Training.** Materials on the art of teaching and methods of teaching are entered under **Teaching.**

  UF Pedagogy

  NT **Teachers colleges**

      Teachers—Training

Education, Theological

  USE **Theology—Study and teaching**

Education—United States **370.973**

Educational accreditation

  USE **Schools—Accreditation**

Educational achievement

  USE **Academic achievement**

Educational administration

  USE **Schools—Administration**

Educational assessment

  USE **Educational evaluation**

Educational associations

  USE **Education—Societies**

Educational consultants (May subdiv. geog.) **370.7**

  BT **Consultants**

Educational counseling (May subdiv. geog.) **371.4**

Use for materials on the assistance given to students by schools, colleges, or universities in the selection of a program of studies suited to their abilities, interests, future plans, and general circumstances. Materials on the assistance given to students in understanding and coping with adjustment problems are entered under **School counseling.** Materials on the activities and programs designed to help people plan, choose, and succeed in their careers are entered under **Vocational guidance.**

  UF Academic advising

      Education—Personnel service

      Educational guidance

      Guidance counseling, Educational

      Personnel service in education

      Student guidance

      Students—Counseling

  BT **Counseling**

  RT **Dropouts**

      School counseling

      Vocational guidance

Educational evaluation (May subdiv. geog.) **370.7; 379.1**

  UF Educational assessment

      Educational program evaluation

      Evaluation research in education

      Instructional systems analysis

      Program evaluation in education

      Self-evaluation in education

  SA topics in education with the subdivision *Evaluation,* e.g. **Science—Study and teaching—Evaluation** [to be added as needed]

  BT **Education**

Educational films

  USE **Libraries and motion pictures**

      Motion pictures in education

Educational freedom

  USE **Academic freedom**

Educational games **371.33**

  UF Instructional games

      Instructive games

  BT **Education**

      Games

  NT **Simulation games in education**

Educational gaming

  USE **Simulation games in education**

Educational guidance

  USE **Educational counseling**

Educational measurements
USE **Educational tests and measurements**
Educational media
USE **Teaching—Aids and devices**
Educational media centers
USE **Instructional materials centers**
Educational policy
USE **Education—Government policy**
Educational program evaluation
USE **Educational evaluation**
Educational psychology   370.15
BT **Psychology**
Teaching
NT **Ability grouping in education**
Achievement motivation
Apperception
Attention
Imagination
Intelligence tests
Listening
Memory
Psychology of learning
Thought and thinking
RT **Applied psychology**
Child psychology
Educational reports
USE **School reports**
Educational simulation games
USE **Simulation games in education**
Educational sociology (May subdiv. geog.)
306.43
UF   Social problems in education
BT **Sociology**
Educational software   005.3
UF   Education—Computer software
BT **Computer software**
Educational surveys (May subdiv. geog.)
370
UF   School surveys
BT **Surveys**
Educational technology (May subdiv.
geog.)   **371.33**
UF   Instructional technology
BT **Education**
RT **Teaching—Aids and devices**
Educational television
USE **Public television**
Television in education

Educational tests and measurements
(May subdiv. geog.)   **371.26**
UF   Educational measurements
Tests
BT **Education**
NT **Ability—Testing**
Achievement tests
Colleges and universities—Entrance examinations
Grading and marking (Education)
Test bias
RT **Examinations**
Intelligence tests
Psychological tests
Educational vouchers   379.1
UF   School vouchers
Vouchers, Educational
BT **Education—Finance**
Educators (May subdiv. geog.)   370.92;
920
Use for materials on people engaged professionally in the field of education in general. Materials on educators engaged in classroom or other instruction are entered under **Teachers.**
UF   College teachers
Faculty (Education)
Professors
BT **Education**
NT **Teachers**
EEC
USE **European Union**
Efficiency, Industrial
USE **Industrial efficiency**
Egg decoration   745.59
UF   Easter egg decoration
BT **Decoration and ornament**
Handicraft
Eggs   636.5; 641
Use for materials on chicken eggs or on animal eggs in general.
SA   types of animals other than
chickens with the subdivision
Eggs, e.g. **Dinosaurs—Eggs**
[to be added as needed]
BT **Food**
NT **Birds—Eggs**
Dinosaurs—Eggs
Ego (Psychology)   154.2
BT **Personality**
Psychoanalysis
Psychology

Ego (Psychology)—*Continued*
    Self
    RT   **Identity (Psychology)**
Egypt   962
    May be subdivided like United States except for *History*.
Egypt—Antiquities   932
    UF   Egyptology
    BT   **Antiquities**
Egypt—History   932; 962
    NT   **Sinai Campaign, 1956**
Egypt—History—1970-   962.05
Egyptology
    USE **Egypt—Antiquities**
Eight-hour day
    USE **Hours of labor**
Eighteenth century
    USE **World history—18th century**
El Niño Current   551.46
    BT   **Ocean currents**
Elder abuse
    USE **Elderly abuse**
Elder care
    USE **Elderly—Care**
Elderly (May subdiv. geog.)   **155.67; 305.26**
    UF   Aged
          Aging persons
          Elderly persons
          Older persons
          Senior citizens
    SA   elderly of particular racial or ethnic groups [to be added as needed]
    BT   **Age**
          Gerontology
    NT   **African American elderly**
          Aging
          Aging parents
          Elderly men
          Elderly women
          Libraries and the elderly
          Social work with the elderly
    RT   **Old age**
          Retirees
Elderly abuse   362.6
    UF   Abuse of the elderly
          Abused aged
          Battered elderly
          Elder abuse
          Elderly—Mistreatment
          Elderly neglect

          Parent abuse
    BT   **Domestic violence**
Elderly and libraries
    USE **Libraries and the elderly**
Elderly—Care (May subdiv. geog.)   **362.6**
    Use for general materials on the care of the dependent elderly.
    UF   Elder care
    NT   **Elderly—Home care**
          Elderly—Institutional care
          Elderly—Medical care
Elderly—Counseling of   362.6
    UF   Counseling of the elderly
          Counseling with the aged
    BT   **Counseling**
Elderly—Diseases   618.97
    UF   Geriatrics
    BT   **Diseases**
    RT   **Elderly—Health and hygiene**
Elderly—Health and hygiene (May subdiv. geog.)   **618.97**
    UF   Geriatrics
    BT   **Health**
          Hygiene
    RT   **Elderly—Diseases**
Elderly—Home care (May subdiv. geog.)   **362.14; 362.6; 649.8**
    BT   **Elderly—Care**
          Home care services
Elderly—Housing (May subdiv. geog.)   **362.6**
    UF   Housing for the elderly
    BT   **Housing**
    NT   **Retirement communities**
Elderly—Institutional care (May subdiv. geog.)   **362.61**
    UF   Homes for the elderly
          Old age homes
    BT   **Elderly—Care**
          Institutional care
Elderly—Life skills guides   362.6; 646.7
    BT   **Life skills**
    RT   **Retirement**
Elderly—Medical care (May subdiv. geog.)   **362.1; 618.97**
    UF   Medical care for the elderly
    BT   **Elderly—Care**
          Medical care
    NT   **Medicare**

Elderly men (May subdiv. geog.)   **305.26**
    UF   Aged men
    BT   **Elderly**
Elderly—Mistreatment
    USE **Elderly abuse**
Elderly neglect
    USE **Elderly abuse**
Elderly parents
    USE **Aging parents**
Elderly persons
    USE **Elderly**
Elderly—Recreation   **790.084**
    BT   **Recreation**
Elderly—Societies   **367**
    BT   **Societies**
Elderly—United States   **305.260973**
Elderly women (May subdiv. geog.)
    305.26
    UF   Aged women
    BT   **Elderly**
Elected officials
    USE **Public officers**
Election
    USE **Elections**
          and types of public officials
          and names of individual pub-
          lic officials with the subdivi-
          sion *Election,* e.g. **Presi-**
          dents—United States—Elec-
          tion [to be added as needed]
Election law (May subdiv. geog.)   **342**
    UF   Law, Election
    BT   **Constitutional law**
Election (Theology)
    USE **Predestination**
Electioneering
    USE **Politics**
Elections (May subdiv. geog.)   **324**
    UF   Ballot
           Election
           Franchise
           Polls
           Voting
    SA   types of public officials and
          names of individual public of-
          ficials with the subdivision
          Election, e.g. **Presidents—**
          United States—Election [to
          be added as needed]

    BT   **Politics**
    NT   **Campaign funds**
          Presidents—United States—
          Election
          Primaries
          Referendum
          Suffrage
          Voter registration
    RT   **Proportional representation**
          Representative government and
          representation
Elections—Finance
    USE **Campaign funds**
Elections—United States   **324.973**
    UF   United States—Elections
Elections—United States—Finance
    USE **Campaign funds—United**
          States
Electoral college
    USE **Presidents—United States—**
          Election
Electric apparatus and appliances
    621.3028; 643
    Use for materials on small electrical ma-
    chines and appliances. Materials on large ma-
    chines powered by electricity are entered un-
    der **Electric machinery.**
    UF   Apparatus, Electric
           Appliances, Electric
           Electric appliances
    SA   types of electric apparatus and
          appliances, e.g. **Burglar**
          alarms [to be added as need-
          ed]
    BT   **Scientific apparatus and in-**
          struments
    NT   **Burglar alarms**
          Electric batteries
          Electric generators
          Electric household appliances
          Electric lamps
          Induction coils
          Storage batteries
Electric appliances
    USE **Electric apparatus and appli-**
          ances
          Electric household appliances
Electric automobiles   **629.222**
    UF   Automobiles, Electric
           Electric cars
    BT   **Automobiles**

Electric automobiles—Cost effectiveness
388.3
  BT Cost effectiveness
Electric batteries   621.31
  UF Batteries, Electric
      Cells, Electric
  BT Electric apparatus and appli-
      ances
      Electrochemistry
  NT Fuel cells
      Solar batteries
  RT Storage batteries
Electric cars
  USE Electric automobiles
Electric circuits   621.319
  UF Circuits, Electric
  BT Electric lines
      Electricity
  NT Electronic circuits
Electric companies
  USE Electric utilities
Electric condensers
  USE Condensers (Electricity)
Electric conductors   621.319
  UF Conductors, Electric
  BT Electronics
  NT Semiconductors
      Superconductors
Electric controllers   629.8
  UF Automatic control
  BT Electric machinery
Electric currents   537.6; 621.31
  UF Currents, Electric
  BT Electricity
  NT Alternating electric currents
      Electric measurements
      Electric transformers
Electric currents, Alternating
  USE Alternating electric currents
Electric distribution
  USE Electric lines
      Electric power distribution
Electric engineering
  USE Electrical engineering
Electric equipment of automobiles
  USE Automobiles—Electric equip-
      ment
Electric eye
  USE Photoelectric cells

Electric generators   621.31
  UF Dynamos
      Generators, Electric
  BT Electric apparatus and appli-
      ances
      Electric machinery
Electric heating   621.402; 644; 697
  UF Electricity in the home
  BT Heating
Electric household appliances   643
  UF Appliances, Electric
      Domestic appliances
      Electric appliances
      Electricity in the home
      Household appliances, Electric
      Labor saving devices, Household
  SA types of specific appliances [to
      be added as needed]
  BT Electric apparatus and appli-
      ances
      Household equipment and sup-
      plies
Electric industries
  USE Electric products industry
Electric lamps   621.32; 645
  UF Incandescent lamps
  BT Electric apparatus and appli-
      ances
      Lamps
  RT Electric lighting
Electric light
  USE Electric lighting
      Photometry
      Phototherapy
Electric light and power industry
  USE Electric utilities
Electric lighting   621.32
  UF Arc light
      Electric light
      Electricity in the home
      Light, Electric
  BT Lighting
  NT Fluorescent lighting
  RT Electric lamps
Electric lighting, Fluorescent
  USE Fluorescent lighting
Electric lines   621.319
    Use for materials on power transmission
  lines, their construction and properties.
  UF Electric distribution
      Electric power transmission
      Electric transmission

Electric lines—*Continued*
        Electricity—Distribution
        Power transmission, Electric
        Transmission of power
  BT **Electric power distribution**
  NT **Electric circuits**
        Electric wiring
Electric machinery   621.31
    Use for materials on large machines powered by electricity. Materials on smaller machines and appliances are entered under **Electric apparatus and appliances.**
  BT **Machinery**
  NT **Electric controllers**
        Electric generators
        Electric motors
        Electric transformers
Electric machinery—Alternating current
        621.319
  UF Alternating current machinery
Electric machinery—Direct current
        621.319
  UF Direct current machinery
Electric measurements   621.37
  UF Measurements, Electric
  BT **Electric currents**
        Weights and measures
  NT **Electric meters**
  RT **Electric testing**
Electric meters   621.37
  UF Meters, Electric
  BT **Electric measurements**
Electric motors   621.46
  UF Induction motors
        Motors
  BT **Electric machinery**
  NT **Electric transformers**
Electric power   621.31
  BT **Electricity**
        Energy resources
        Power (Mechanics)
Electric power development
  USE **Electrification**
Electric power distribution   621.319
  UF Electric distribution
        Electric power transmission
        Electric transmission
        Electricity—Distribution
        Power transmission, Electric
        Transmission of power
  BT **Electrical engineering**
        Power transmission

  NT **Electric lines**
        Electric utilities
        Electric wiring
Electric power failures   621.319
  UF Blackouts, Electric power
        Brownouts
        Electric power interruptions
        Power blackouts
        Power failures
Electric power in mining
  USE **Electricity in mining**
Electric power industry
  USE **Electric utilities**
Electric power interruptions
  USE **Electric power failures**
Electric power plants (May subdiv. geog.)
        621.31
  UF Power plants
        Power stations
  SA types of electric power plants,
        e.g. **Nuclear power plants**
        [to be added as needed]
  NT **Hydroelectric power plants**
        Nuclear power plants
        Steam power plants
Electric power transmission
  USE **Electric lines**
        Electric power distribution
Electric products industry (May subdiv. geog.)   **338.4**
    Use for materials on industries producing products that contain electrical motors or otherwise employ electricity.
  UF Electric industries
  BT **Industries**
Electric railroads (May subdiv. geog.)
        385; 621.33; 625.1
  UF Interurban railroads
  BT **Railroads**
  RT **Street railroads**
Electric signs   621.32; 659.13
  BT **Advertising**
        Signs and signboards
  NT **Neon tubes**
Electric smelting
  USE **Electrometallurgy**
Electric testing   621.37
  BT **Testing**
  RT **Electric measurements**
Electric toys   688.7
  BT **Toys**

Electric transformers 621.31
UF Transformers, Electric
BT **Electric currents**
Electric machinery
Electric motors
Electric transmission
USE **Electric lines**
Electric power distribution
Electric utilities (May subdiv. geog.)
333.793
Use for materials on businesses that sell and distribute electricity to customers.
UF Electric companies
Electric light and power industry
Electric power industry
BT **Electric power distribution**
Public utilities
NT **Electrification**
Electric utilities—Government ownership
(May subdiv. geog.) **333.793**
Electric waves 537; 621.381
UF Hertzian waves
Radio waves
BT **Electricity**
Waves
NT **Electromagnetic waves**
Microwaves
Electric welding 671.5
UF Arc welding
Resistance welding
Spot welding
Welding, Electric
BT **Welding**
Electric wiring 621.319
UF Wiring, Electric
BT **Electric lines**
Electric power distribution
Electric wiring—Charts, diagrams, etc.
621.319
Electrical engineering (May subdiv. geog.)
621.3
UF Electric engineering
BT **Engineering**
Mechanical engineering
NT **Electric power distribution**
Electricity in mining
Electrification
Electricity 537; 621.3
SA electricity in various endeavors,
e.g. **Electricity in agriculture**
[to be added as needed]

BT **Physics**
NT **Electric circuits**
Electric currents
Electric power
Electric waves
Electricity in agriculture
Electricity in mining
Lightning
RT **Magnetism**
Electricity—Distribution
USE **Electric lines**
Electric power distribution
Electricity in agriculture 333.79; 631.3
UF Electricity on the farm
BT **Agricultural engineering**
Agricultural machinery
Electricity
RT **Rural electrification**
Electricity in medicine
USE **Electrotherapeutics**
Electricity in mining 622
UF Electric power in mining
Mining, Electric
BT **Electrical engineering**
Electricity
RT **Mining engineering**
Electricity in the home
USE **Electric heating**
Electric household appliances
Electric lighting
Electricity on the farm
USE **Electricity in agriculture**
Electrification (May subdiv. geog.)
621.319
UF Electric power development
BT **Electric utilities**
Electrical engineering
NT **Rural electrification**
Electrochemistry 541; 660
BT **Industrial chemistry**
Physical chemistry
NT **Electric batteries**
Electrometallurgy
Electroplating
Electrotyping
Fuel cells
Electromagnetic waves 539.2
UF Waves, Electromagnetic
BT **Electric waves**
Radiation

Electromagnetic waves—*Continued*
- NT **Gamma rays**
  - **Heat**
  - **Infrared radiation**
  - **Light**
  - **Microwaves**
  - **Ultraviolet rays**
  - **X-rays**

Electromagnetism   621.34
- BT **Magnetism**
- NT **Masers**

Electromagnets   621.34
- UF Magnet winding
- BT **Magnetism**
  - **Magnets**

Electrometallurgy   669.028
- UF Electric smelting
- BT **Electrochemistry**
  - **Metallurgy**
  - **Smelting**
- RT **Electroplating**
  - **Electrotyping**

Electron microscope and microscopy
- USE **Electron microscopes**

Electron microscopes   502.8
- UF Electron microscope and microscopy
- BT **Microscopes**

Electron tubes
- USE **Vacuum tubes**

Electronic apparatus and appliances   621.381
- UF Apparatus, Electronic
  - Appliances, Electronic
- SA types of electronic apparatus and appliances, e.g. **Computers** [to be added as needed]
- BT **Electronics**
  - **Scientific apparatus and instruments**
- NT **Computers**
  - **Electronic toys**
  - **Intercommunication systems**
  - **Magnetic recorders and recording**
  - **Vacuum tubes**

Electronic art
- USE **Video art**

Electronic books   070.5
- UF Books in machine-readable form
  - Online books
- BT **Books**

Electronic bugging
- USE **Eavesdropping**

Electronic bulletin boards
- USE **Computer bulletin boards**

Electronic circuits   621.319; 621.3815
- BT **Electric circuits**
  - **Electronics**

Electronic commerce (May subdiv. geog.)
  381; 658
  Use for materials on the exchange of goods and services and the transfer of funds through electronic communications.
- UF Cybercommerce
  - Internet commerce
  - Online commerce
- BT **Commerce**
- NT **Internet marketing**
  - **Internet shopping**

Electronic data processing
- USE **Data processing**

Electronic design
- USE **Computer-aided design**

Electronic discussion groups   004.692
  Use for materials on services, commonly called newsgroups or LISTSERV lists, that allow subscribers to post messages that are then distributed to other subscribers. Materials on services that allow users to engage in conversations in real time are entered under **Online chat groups.** Materials on services that allow users to post messages and retrieve messages from others who have some common interest are entered under **Computer bulletin boards.**
- UF E-mail discussion groups
  - Electronic newsgroups
  - Internet discussion groups
  - Internet newsgroups
  - LISTSERV lists
  - Newsgroups, Electronic
  - Online discussion groups
  - Online newsgroups
  - Usenet newsgroups
- BT **Discussion groups**
- RT **Computer bulletin boards**
  - **Online chat groups**

Electronic drafting
- USE **Computer graphics**

Electronic drawing
- USE **Computer graphics**

Electronic eavesdropping
- USE **Eavesdropping**

Electronic games
- USE **Video games**

Electronic libraries
- USE **Digital libraries**

Electronic listening devices
USE **Eavesdropping**
Electronic mail systems   004.692; 384.3
Use for materials on the electronic transmission of letters, messages, etc., primarily through the use of computers.
UF E-mail
Email
BT **Data transmission systems**
Telecommunication
Electronic marketing
USE **Telemarketing**
Electronic music   786.7
UF Synthesizer music
BT **Music**
RT **Computer music**
Electronic musical instruments   786.7
UF Musical instruments, Electronic
SA types of instruments, e.g. **Synthesizer (Musical instrument)**
[to be added as needed]
BT **Musical instruments**
NT **Synthesizers (Musical instruments)**
Electronic newsgroups
USE **Electronic discussion groups**
Electronic publishing (May subdiv. geog.)
070.5; 686.2
Use for materials on the process of publishing by which books and articles or any kind of data are made available as an electronic product. Materials on the use of a personal computer with writing, graphics, and page layout software to produce printed material for publication are entered under **Desktop publishing.**
UF Online publishing
Web publishing
BT **Information services**
Publishers and publishing
NT **Teletext systems**
RT **Desktop publishing**
Electronic speech processing systems
USE **Speech processing systems**
Electronic spreadsheets
USE **Spreadsheet software**
Electronic surveillance   621.389
UF Surveillance, Electronic
BT **Remote sensing**
Electronic toys   688.7
BT **Electronic apparatus and appliances**
Toys
NT **Video games**

Electronics   537.5; 621.381
BT **Engineering**
Physics
Technology
NT **Amplifiers (Electronics)**
Cybernetics
Digital electronics
Electric conductors
Electronic apparatus and appliances
Electronic circuits
High-fidelity sound systems
Microelectronics
Semiconductors
Superconductors
Transistors
Electrons   539.7
BT **Atoms**
Particles (Nuclear physics)
Electroplating   671.7
BT **Electrochemistry**
Metalwork
RT **Electrometallurgy**
Electrotherapeutics   615.8
UF Electricity in medicine
Medical electricity
BT **Massage**
Physical therapy
Therapeutics
NT **Radiotherapy**
Electrotyping   686.2
BT **Electrochemistry**
Printing
RT **Electrometallurgy**
Elegiac poetry   808.1; 808.81
May be used for individual works, collections, or materials about elegiac poetry.
UF Elegies
Lamentations
BT **Poetry**
Elegies
USE **Elegiac poetry**
Elementary education (May subdiv. geog.)   **372**
UF Children—Education
Education, Elementary
Education of children
Education, Primary
Grammar schools
Primary education

Elementary education—*Continued*
   BT   Education
   NT   Creative activities
        Exceptional children
        Kindergarten
        Montessori method of education
        Nursery schools
        Readiness for school
Elementary particles (Physics)
   USE Particles (Nuclear physics)
Elementary school dropouts
   USE Dropouts
Elementary school libraries   027.8
   BT   School libraries
Elementary schools (May subdiv. geog.)
       373.236
   UF   Grade schools
   BT   Schools
   RT   Middle schools
Elements, Chemical
   USE Chemical elements
Elephants (May subdiv. geog.)   599.67
   BT   Mammals
Elevators   621.8
   UF   Lifts
   BT   Hoisting machinery
Elite (Social sciences) (May subdiv. geog.)
       305.5
   BT   Leadership
        Power (Social sciences)
        Social classes
        Social groups
Elizabeth II, Queen of Great Britain,
      1926-   92; B
   BT   Queens—Great Britain
Elocution
   USE Public speaking
Elves   398.21
   BT   Folklore
Email
   USE Electronic mail systems
Emancipation
   USE Freedom
Emancipation of slaves
   USE Slaves—Emancipation
Emancipation of women
   USE Women's rights
Embarrassment
   USE Self-consciousness

Embassies
   USE Diplomatic and consular service
Emblems
   USE Decorations of honor
        Heraldry
        Insignia
        Mottoes
        National emblems
        Seals (Numismatics)
        Signs and symbols
Emblems, State
   USE State emblems
Embracing
   USE Hugging
Embroidery (May subdiv. geog.)   746.44
   SA   types of embroidery [to be added as needed]
   BT   Decoration and ornament
        Needlework
        Sewing
   NT   Beadwork
        Crewelwork
        Cross-stitch
        Drawn work
        Hardanger needlework
        Needlepoint
        Samplers
Embryology   571.8; 612.6
   UF   Development
   BT   Biology
        Zoology
   NT   Fetus
        Frozen embryos
        Genetics
   RT   Cells
        Protoplasm
        Reproduction
Embryos, Frozen
   USE Frozen embryos
Emergencies
   USE Accidents
        Disasters
        First aid
Emergency assistance
   USE Helping behavior
Emergency medical technicians   610.69; 616.02
   UF   Emergency paramedics
        EMTs (Medicine)
        Paramedical personnel

Emergency medical technicians—*Continued*

    Paramedics, Emergency
  BT **Allied health personnel**

Emergency medicine 616.02
  BT **Medicine**
  NT **Cardiac resuscitation**

Emergency mental health services
  USE **Crisis intervention (Mental health services)**

Emergency paramedics
  USE **Emergency medical technicians**

Emergency powers
  USE **War and emergency powers**

Emergency preparedness
  USE **Disaster relief**

Emergency relief
  USE **Disaster relief**

Emergency survival
  USE **Survival skills**

Emigrants
  USE **Immigrants**

Emigration
  USE **Immigration and emigration**

Eminent domain 333.1; 343
  UF Condemnation of land
      Expropriation
  BT **Constitutional law**
      Land use
      Property

Emotional stress
  USE **Stress (Psychology)**

Emotionally disturbed children 155.4; 362.2; 371.94; 618.92

Use for general materials on children suffering from mental or emotional illnesses. Materials on the clinical and therapeutic aspects of mental disorders in children are entered under **Child psychiatry.**

  UF Behavior problems (Children)
      Maladjusted children
      Mentally ill children
      Neurotic children
      Problem children
      Psychotic children
  BT **Exceptional children**
      Mentally ill
  RT **Child psychiatry**
      Juvenile delinquency

Emotions 152.4
  UF Feelings
      Passions

  SA types of emotions [to be added as needed]
  BT **Psychology**
      Psychophysiology
  NT **Anger**
      Anxiety
      Attitude (Psychology)
      Bereavement
      Consolation
      Disappointment
      Emotions in children
      Empathy
      Fanaticism
      Fear
      Frustration
      Gratitude
      Grief
      Guilt
      Happiness
      Hate
      Hope
      Horror
      Jealousy
      Joy and sorrow
      Laughter
      Loneliness
      Love
      Pain
      Pleasure
      Prejudices
      Self-confidence
      Shame
      Shyness
      Temper tantrums
      Trust
      Worry

Emotions in children 155.4
  BT **Child psychology**
      Emotions

Empathy 152.4
  BT **Attitude (Psychology)**
      Emotions
      Social psychology

Emperors (May subdiv. geog.) **920; 929.7**
  UF Rulers
      Sovereigns
  SA names of emperors, e.g. **Nero, Emperor of Rome, 37-68** [to be added as needed]
  BT **Kings and rulers**

Emperors—Rome 920; 937
    UF   Roman emperors
    SA   names of Roman emperors, e.g.
            Nero, Emperor of Rome, 37-68 [to be added as needed]
    NT   **Nero, Emperor of Rome, 37-68**
Empiricism 146
    UF   Experience
    BT   **Philosophy**
          Rationalism
          Theory of knowledge
    RT   **Pragmatism**
Employee absenteeism
    USE **Absenteeism (Labor)**
Employee assistance programs 658.3
    BT   **Personnel management**
Employee benefits
    USE **Fringe benefits**
Employee counseling
    USE **Employees—Counseling of**
Employee drinking
    USE **Employees—Alcohol use**
Employee drug testing
    USE **Employees—Drug testing**
Employee fringe benefits
    USE **Fringe benefits**
Employee health services
    USE **Occupational health services**
Employee morale 158.7; 658.3
    BT   **Applied psychology**
          Morale
          Personnel management
    NT   **Job satisfaction**
    RT   **Absenteeism (Labor)**
Employee rights (May subdiv. geog.) **331.01**
    UF   Employees—Civil rights
          Labor rights
          Rights of employees
    BT   **Civil rights**
          Labor laws and legislation
Employees 331.11; 920
    UF   Workers
    SA   types of employees, e.g. **Office workers;** types of industries, services, establishments, or institutions, with the subdivision *Employees;* e.g. **Chemical industry—Employees; Railroads—Employees;** etc.; and names of countries, states, cit-

ies, etc., and corporate bodies with the subdivision *Officials and employees,* e.g. **United States—Officials and employees; Ohio—Officials and employees; Chicago (Ill.)—Officials and employees; United Nations—Officials and employees;** etc. [to be added as needed]
    BT   **Labor**
    NT   **Chemical industry—Employees**
          Colleges and universities—Employees
          Medical personnel
          Migrant labor
          Office workers
          Railroads—Employees
    RT   **Personnel management**
Employees—Accidents
    USE **Industrial accidents**
Employees—Alcohol use 331.25; 658.3
    UF   Alcohol and employees
          Alcohol in the workplace
          Drinking and employees
          Drinking in the workplace
          Employee drinking
          Employees and alcohol
Employees and alcohol
    USE **Employees—Alcohol use**
Employees and drugs
    USE **Employees—Drug use**
Employees and narcotics
    USE **Employees—Drug use**
Employees and officials
    USE **Civil service**
Employees—Civil rights
    USE **Employee rights**
Employees—Counseling of 658.3
    UF   Employee counseling
          Industrial counseling
    BT   **Counseling**
Employees—Dismissal 331.25; 658.3
    BT   **Job security**
          Personnel management
    RT   **Downsizing of organizations**
Employees—Drug testing 331.25; 658.3
    UF   Drug testing in the workplace
          Employee drug testing
    BT   **Drug testing**

Employees—Drug use   331.25; 658.3
   UF   Drugs and employees
       Drugs in the workplace
       Employees and drugs
       Employees and narcotics
Employees—Pensions
   USE   **Old age pensions**
Employees—Rating   331.25; 658.3
Employees' representation in management
   USE   **Participative management**
Employees—Salaries, wages, etc.
   USE   **Salaries, wages, etc.**
Employees—Training   331.25; 658.3
   Use for materials discussing on-the-job training. Materials on teaching people a skill during the educational process are entered under **Vocational education.** Materials on teaching people a skill after formal education are entered under **Occupational training.** Materials on retraining are entered under **Occupational retraining.**
   UF   In-service training
       Inservice training
       Training of employees
   SA   types of employees or personnel with the subdivision *Training,* e.g. **Teachers—Training;** or with the subdivision *In-service training,* e.g. **Librarians—In-service training** [to be added as needed]
   BT   **Occupational training**
       Personnel management
       Vocational education
   NT   **Occupational retraining**
   RT   **Apprentices**
       Technical education
Employer-employee relations
   USE   **Industrial relations**
Employers' liability
   USE   **Workers' compensation**
Employment   331.1
   Use for materials on the economic theory of employment.
   SA   racial and ethnic groups and classes of persons with the subdivision *Employment,* e.g. **African Americans—Employment; Veterans—Employment;** etc. [to be added as needed]
   BT   **Economics**
       Labor

   NT   **African Americans—Employment**
       Age and employment
       Blacks—Employment
       Labor supply
       Men—Employment
       Part-time employment
       Summer employment
       Teenagers—Employment
       Temporary employment
       Unemployment
       Veterans—Employment
       Women—Employment
       Youth—Employment
   RT   **Occupations**
       Vocational guidance
Employment agencies (May subdiv. geog.)   **331.12**
   BT   **Labor**
       Labor turnover
       Personnel management
       Recruiting of employees
       Unemployment
   NT   **Job hunting**
   RT   **Labor supply**
Employment and age
   USE   **Age and employment**
Employment applications
   USE   **Applications for positions**
Employment discrimination
   USE   **Discrimination in employment**
Employment forecasting (May subdiv. geog.)   **331.1**
   UF   Occupational forecasting
   BT   **Economic forecasting**
   RT   **Labor supply**
Employment guidance
   USE   **Vocational guidance**
Employment management
   USE   **Personnel management**
Employment of children
   USE   **Child labor**
Employment references
   USE   **Applications for positions**
Employment security
   USE   **Job security**
Employment, Supplementary
   USE   **Supplementary employment**
Employment, Temporary
   USE   **Temporary employment**

Empresses (May subdiv. geog.) **920**

  SA   names of empresses; and countries, cities, etc., with the subdivision *Kings and rulers* [to be added as needed]

  BT   **Monarchy**

  RT   **Queens**

EMTs (Medicine)

  USE **Emergency medical technicians**

Enamel and enameling 738.4

  UF   Porcelain enamels

  BT   **Decoration and ornament**

        Decorative arts

Encounter groups

  USE **Group relations training**

Encouragement 158

  BT   **Courage**

        Helping behavior

Encyclicals, Papal

  USE **Papal encyclicals**

Encyclopedias

  USE **Encyclopedias and dictionaries** and subjects, groups or classes of persons, and names of places with the subdivision *Encyclopedias,* e.g. **Philosophy—Encyclopedias; Jews—Encyclopedias;** etc., for materials that provide topical information usually in alphabetical order [to be added as needed]

Encyclopedias and dictionaries 030; 403

    Use for general materials about encyclopedias and dictionaries.

  UF   Cyclopedias

        Dictionaries

        Encyclopedias

        Glossaries

        Subject dictionaries

  SA   subjects and names of languages with the subdivision *Dictionaries,* for materials in alphabetical order that define terms or identify things, e.g. **Chemistry—Dictionaries; English language—Dictionaries;** etc.; subjects, groups or classes of persons, and names of places with the subdivision *Biography—Dictionaries,* for biographical dictionaries, e.g. **Women—Biography—Dictionaries; Ohio—Biography—Dictionaries;** etc.; and subjects, groups or classes of persons, and names of places with the subdivision *Encyclopedias,* e.g. **Philosophy—Encyclopedias; Jews—Encyclopedias;** etc., for materials that provide topical information usually in alphabetical order [to be added as needed]

  BT   **Reference books**

  NT   **Bible—Dictionaries**

        Biography—Dictionaries

        Chemistry—Dictionaries

        Classical dictionaries

        Computer science—Dictionaries

        English language—Dictionaries

        English language—Dictionaries—French

        French language—Dictionaries—English

        Geography—Dictionaries

        History—Dictionaries

        Jews—Encyclopedias

        Literature—Dictionaries

        Machine readable dictionaries

        Philosophy—Encyclopedias

        Picture dictionaries

        Polyglot dictionaries

        Shakespeare, William, 1564-1616—Dictionaries

        Technology—Dictionaries

End of the earth

  USE **End of the world**

End of the world 001.9; 202; 236; 523.1

    Use for materials on the end of the world from an eschatological point of view (including Judgment Day, signs, fulfillments of prophecies, etc.) or from a scientific point of view.

  UF   End of the earth

        End of the world (Astronomy)

  BT   **Eschatology**

End of the world (Astronomy)

  USE **End of the world**

End-of-the-world fantasies

  USE **Fantasy fiction**

        Fantasy films

End-of-the-world fantasies—*Continued*
>> Fantasy television programs
>> **Robinsonades**
>> Science fiction
>> War films
>> War stories

Endangered species (May subdiv. geog.)
>> **333.95; 578.68**
> UF Threatened species
>> Vanishing species
> BT **Environmental protection**
>> **Nature conservation**
> NT **Plant conservation**
>> **Wildlife conservation**
> RT **Rare animals**
>> **Rare plants**

Endocrine glands   616.4
> UF Ductless glands
>> Glands, Ductless
> BT **Endocrinology**
> RT **Hormones**

Endocrinology   616.4
> BT **Medicine**
> NT **Endocrine glands**
>> **Hormones**

Endorphins   612.8; 615

Endowed charities
> USE **Charities**
>> **Endowments**

Endowments (May subdiv. geog.)   **001.4;**
>> **361.6; 361.7**
> UF Endowed charities
>> Foundations (Endowments)
> SA disciplines, types of corporate
>> bodies, and names of individ-
>> ual corporate bodies with the
>> subdivision *Endowments*, e.g.
>> **Colleges and universities—**
>> **Endowments** [to be added as
>> needed]
> BT **Finance**
> NT **Colleges and universities—En-**
>> **dowments**
>> **Scholarships**
> RT **Charities**
>> **Philanthropy**

Endurance, Physical
> USE **Physical fitness**

Energy
> USE **Energy resources**
>> **Force and energy**

Energy and state
> USE **Energy policy**

Energy, Biomass
> USE **Biomass energy**

Energy conservation (May subdiv. geog.)
>> **333.791**
> UF Conservation of energy
>> Conservation of power resources
>> Power resources conservation
> SA types of energy conservation,
>> e.g. **Recycling** [to be added
>> as needed]
> BT **Conservation of natural re-**
>> **sources**
>> **Energy resources**
> NT **Recycling**
> RT **Energy consumption**
>> **Energy policy**

Energy consumption (May subdiv. geog.)
>> **333.79**
> UF Consumption of energy
> SA subjects with the subdivision
>> *Fuel consumption*, e.g. **Auto-**
>> **mobiles—Fuel consumption**
>> [to be added as needed]
> BT **Energy resources**
> NT **Automobiles—Fuel consump-**
>> **tion**
> RT **Energy conservation**

Energy consumption—Forecasting
>> **333.79**

Energy conversion from waste
> USE **Waste products as fuel**

Energy conversion, Microbial
> USE **Biomass energy**

Energy development (May subdiv. geog.)
>> **333.79**
> UF Energy resources development
>> Power resources development
> BT **Energy resources**
> NT **Water resources development**

Energy policy (May subdiv. geog.)
>> **333.79; 354.3**
> UF Energy and state
>> Energy resources—Government
>> policy
>> Government policy
> BT **Energy resources**
>> **Industrial policy**
> RT **Energy conservation**

Energy resources (May subdiv. geog.)
    333.79

    Use for materials on the available sources of mechanical power in general. Materials on the physics and engineering aspects of power are entered under **Power (Mechanics)**.

  UF   Energy

        Power resources

        Power supply

  BT   **Natural resources**

        Power (Mechanics)

  NT   **Biomass energy**

        Electric power

        Energy conservation

        Energy consumption

        Energy development

        Energy policy

        Fuel

        Ocean energy resources

        Renewable energy resources

        Solar energy

        Water power

        Wind power

Energy resources development

  USE **Energy development**

Energy resources—Government policy

  USE **Energy policy**

Energy technology

  USE **Power (Mechanics)**

Engineering (May subdiv. geog.)   **620**

  UF   Construction

  SA   types of engineering, e.g. **Chemical engineering** [to be added as needed]

  BT   **Industrial arts**

        Technology

  NT   **Aeronautics**

        Agricultural engineering

        Chemical engineering

        Civil engineering

        Electrical engineering

        Electronics

        Genetic engineering

        Highway engineering

        Human engineering

        Hydraulic engineering

        Marine engineering

        Mechanical drawing

        Military engineering

        Mining engineering

        Minorities in engineering

        Municipal engineering

        Nuclear engineering

        Ocean engineering

        Railroad engineering

        Reliability (Engineering)

        Sanitary engineering

        Steam engineering

        Structural engineering

        Systems engineering

        Traffic engineering

        Water supply engineering

  RT   **Engineers**

        Materials

Engineering and construction

  USE names of wars with the subdivision *Engineering and construction,* e.g. **World War, 1939-1945—Engineering and construction** [to be added as needed]

Engineering drawing

  USE **Mechanical drawing**

Engineering, Genetic

  USE **Genetic engineering**

Engineering instruments   620.0028

  UF   Instruments, Engineering

  BT   **Scientific apparatus and instruments**

Engineering materials

  USE **Materials**

Engineering—Periodicals   620.005

Engineering—Study and teaching
    620.007

  BT   **Technical education**

Engineers (May subdiv. geog.)
    620.0092; 920

  RT   **Engineering**

        Inventors

Engines   621.4

  UF   Motors

  SA   types of engines and motors, e.g. **Steam engines; Electric motors;** etc., and types of vehicles and makes and models of vehicles with the subdivision *Motors,* e.g. **Automobiles—Motors** [to be added as needed]

  BT   **Machinery**

  NT   **Airplane engines**

        Automobiles—Motors

        Diesel engines

Engines—*Continued*
>> Fire engines
>> Fuel
>> Heat engines
>> Internal combustion engines
>> Marine engines
>> Pumping machinery
>> Solar engines
>> Steam engines
>> Turbines

England   942

> May be subdivided like United States except for *History,* and *Politics and government,* or any subdivisions relating to history or politics and government. Such materials are entered instead under **Great Britain.**

> BT **Great Britain**

England, Church of
> USE **Church of England**

England—History
> USE **Great Britain—History**

English as a foreign language
> USE **English as a second language**

English as a second language   420.7; 428

> UF   English as a foreign language
> English for foreigners
> English language as a second language
> English language—Study and teaching, Foreign
> English language—Texts for foreigners

> BT **English language—Study and teaching**

> NT **English language—Conversation and phrase books**

English authors   820.9; 920

> UF   Authors, English
> BT **Authors**

English authors—First editions
> USE **English literature—First editions**

English authors—Homes (May subdiv. geog.)   820.9; 920

> BT **Literary landmarks**

English Canadian literature
> USE **Canadian literature (English)**

English Canadian poetry
> USE **Canadian poetry (English)**

English composition
> USE **English language—Composition and exercises**

English drama   822

> Use for general materials about English drama, not for individual works.

> BT **Drama**
> **English literature**

> NT **Morality plays**
> **Mysteries and miracle plays**

English drama—Collections   822.008

English drama—History and criticism   822.009

> BT **Drama—History and criticism**

English essays   824; 824.008

> Use for collections of literary essays by several authors.

> BT **English literature**
> **Essays**

English fiction   823

> May be used for collections or materials about English fiction, not for individual works.

> BT **English literature**
> **Fiction**

English fiction—History and criticism   823.009

English for foreigners
> USE **English as a second language**
> **English language—Conversation and phrase books**

English grammar
> USE **English language—Grammar**

English history
> USE **Great Britain—History**

English language (May subdiv. geog.)   420

> Subdivisions used under this heading may be used under other languages unless otherwise specified.

> BT **Language and languages**

English language—0-1100
> USE **English language—Old English period**

English language—Acronyms
> USE **Acronyms**

English language—Alphabet   421

English language—Americanisms
> USE **Americanisms**

English language—Antonyms
> USE **English language—Synonyms and antonyms**

English language as a second language
> USE **English as a second language**

English language—Basal readers
> USE **Basal readers**

English language—Business English
428

Business English is a unique subdivision for **English language.** Use same pattern with unique subdivisions for other languages, e.g. **Japanese language—Business Japanese**; etc.

UF   Business English

English language—Comparison   425

UF   Comparison (English grammar)

English language—Composition and exercises   428

UF   English composition

RT   **Rhetoric**

English language—Conversation and phrase books   428

UF   English for foreigners

English language—Conversations and phrases

BT   **English as a second language**

English language—Conversations and phrases

USE   **English language—Conversation and phrase books**

English language—Dialects   427

NT   **Americanisms**

English language—Dictionaries   423

Use for English language dictionaries. Dictionaries from English to another language are entered under this heading further subdivided by the other language, e.g. **English language—Dictionaries—French.** French-English dictionaries are entered under **French language—Dictionaries—English.** Combined English-French and French-English dictionaries are entered under both headings.

BT   **Encyclopedias and dictionaries**

RT   **English language—Terms and phrases**

English language—Dictionaries—French   443

Use for English-French dictionaries. French-English dictionaries are entered under **French language—Dictionaries—English.** Combined English-French and French-English dictionaries are entered under both headings.

UF   Foreign language dictionaries

BT   **Encyclopedias and dictionaries**

RT   **French language—Dictionaries—English**

English language—Errors

USE   **English language—Errors of usage**

English language—Errors of usage   428

UF   English language—Errors

English language—Etymology   422

BT   **English language—History**

English language—Examinations   420.76

BT   **Examinations**

English language—Examinations—Study guides   420.76

English language—Figures of speech

USE   **Figures of speech**

English language—Foreign words and phrases   422

Use for materials on foreign words and phrases incorporated into the English language.

UF   Foreign language phrases

English language—Grammar   425

UF   English grammar

SA   **English language** subdivided by topics in the study of grammar, e.g. **English language—Parts of speech; English language—Infinitive;** etc. [to be added as needed]

BT   **Grammar**

NT   **English language—Usage**

English language—History   420.9

NT   **English language—Etymology**

English language—Homonyms   423

English language—Idioms   428

RT   **English language—Provincialisms**

English language—Infinitive   425

English language—Jargon   427

English language—Middle English period   420

UF   Middle English language

English language—Old English period   429

UF   Anglo-Saxon language

English language—0-1100

Old English language

English language—Orthography

USE   **English language—Spelling**

English language—Parts of speech   425

English language—Phonetics

USE   **English language—Pronunciation**

English language—Phrases and terms

USE   **English language—Terms and phrases**

English language—Programmed instruction   420.7

BT   **Programmed instruction**

English language—Pronunciation 421
UF   English language—Phonetics
BT   **Phonetics**
NT   **Reading—Phonetic method**
English language—Provincialisms 427
RT   **English language—Idioms**
English language—Punctuation
USE   **Punctuation**
English language—Reading materials
USE   **Reading materials**
English language—Rhetoric
USE   **Rhetoric**
English language—Rhyme 428.1
BT   **Rhyme**
English language—Slang 427
English language—Social aspects 420
English language—Spelling 421
UF   English language—Orthography
NT   **Spellers**
Spelling reform
RT   **Word skills**
English language—Spelling reform
USE   **Spelling reform**
English language—Study and teaching 420.7
NT   **English as a second language**
English language—Study and teaching, Foreign
USE   **English as a second language**
English language—Synonyms and antonyms 423
UF   English language—Antonyms
RT   **Opposites**
English language—Terms and phrases 420

Use for general lists of words and phrases and for lists that are applicable to certain situations (collective nouns, curious expressions, etc.) rather than to specific subjects. Lists of words and phrases limited to specific subjects are entered under the subject with the subdivision *Dictionaries*, e.g. **Chemistry—Dictionaries.**

UF   English language—Phrases and terms
RT   **English language—Dictionaries**
English language—Texts for foreigners
USE   **English as a second language**
English language—Usage 428
BT   **English language—Grammar**
English language—Versification
USE   **Versification**

English language—Vocabulary
USE   **Vocabulary**
English letters 826; 826.008
BT   **English literature**
Letters
English literature 820

Subdivisions used under this heading may be used under other literatures.

BT   **Literature**
NT   **English drama**
English essays
English fiction
English letters
English poetry
English prose literature
English satire
English sermons
English speeches
English wit and humor
English literature—0-1100
USE   **English literature—Old English period**
English literature—16th and 17th centuries 820
UF   English literature—Early modern, 1500-1700
Renaissance English literature
English literature—18th century 820
English literature—19th century 820
UF   Victorian literature
English literature—20th century 820
English literature—21st century 820
English literature—Bibliography 016.82
English literature—Bio-bibliography 820.9
English literature—Collections 820.8

Use for collections of English literature by several authors in more than one genre. Collections of prose are entered under **English prose literature.** Collections of poetry are entered under **English poetry—Collections.** Collections of drama are entered under **English drama—Collections.**

English literature—Criticism
USE   **English literature—History and criticism**
English literature—Dictionaries 820.3
BT   **Literature—Dictionaries**
English literature—Early modern, 1500-1700
USE   **English literature—16th and 17th centuries**

English literature—Examinations
820.76
BT **English literature—Study and teaching**

English literature—First editions   820
UF   English authors—First editions

English literature—History and criticism
820.9
UF   English literature—Criticism

English literature—Indexes   016.82

English literature—Middle English period   820
UF   Middle English literature

English literature—Old English period
829
UF   Anglo-Saxon literature
English literature—0-1100
Old English literature

English literature—Outlines, syllabi, etc.
820.2
BT   **Literature—Outlines, syllabi, etc.**
RT   **English literature—Study and teaching**

English literature—Study and teaching
820.7
NT   **English literature—Examinations**
RT   **English literature—Outlines, syllabi, etc.**

English newspapers
USE   **Newspapers—Great Britain**

English orations
USE   **English speeches**

English periodicals   052
BT   **Periodicals**

English poetry   821
Use for general materials about English poetry, not for individual works.
BT   **English literature**
Poetry

English poetry—Collections   821.008

English poetry—History and criticism
821.009

English prose literature   828
Use for collections of prose writings that may include several literary forms, such as essays, fiction, orations, etc.
UF   Prose literature, English
BT   **English literature**

English public schools   373.2
Use for materials on British endowed secondary schools that are open to public admis-

sion but are not financed or administered by any government body.
UF   Public schools, Endowed (Great Britain)
Public schools, English
BT   **Private schools**

English satire   827; 827.008
UF   Satire, English
BT   **English literature**
Satire

English sermons   252
BT   **English literature**
Sermons

English speeches   825; 825.008
UF   English orations
Speeches, addresses, etc., English
BT   **English literature**
Speeches

English wit and humor   827; 827.008; 827.009
Use for collections by several authors or for materials about English wit and humor. Individual works by English humorists are entered under **Wit and humor.**
BT   **English literature**
Wit and humor

Engravers (May subdiv. geog.)   760.92; 920
BT   **Artists**
NT   **Etchers**

Engraving   760; 765
UF   Copper engraving
Engravings
Line engraving
Steel engraving
SA   engraving of particular countries, e.g. **American engraving** [to be added as needed]
BT   **Art**
Graphic arts
Illustration of books
Pictures
NT   **American engraving**
Gems
Mezzotint engraving
Photoengraving
Wood engraving
RT   **Etching**

Engraving, American
USE   **American engraving**

Engravings
USE   **Engraving**

Enhanced radiation weapons
USE **Neutron weapons**
Enigmas
USE **Curiosities and wonders**
Riddles
Enlarged texts for shared reading
USE **Big books**
Enlarging (Photography)
USE **Photography—Enlarging**
Enlightenment (May subdiv. geog.) **190;**
909.7; 940.2

Use for materials on the philosophic movement of the 18th century marked by the questioning of traditional doctrines and values, naturalistic and individualistic tendencies, and an emphasis on the empirical method in science and the free use of reason.

BT **Modern civilization**
Modern philosophy
Rationalism
Enlistment
USE **Recruiting and enlistment**
Enneagram   155.2
BT **Typology (Psychology)**
Ensemble playing
USE **Ensembles (Music)**
Ensembles (Mathematics)
USE **Set theory**
Ensembles (Music)   782; 784

Use for materials on small instrumental or vocal groups and for the music written for such groups.

UF Ensemble playing
Instrumental ensembles
Musical ensembles
Vocal ensembles
SA types of vocal or instrumental ensembles, e.g. **Jazz ensembles** [to be added as needed]
BT **Music**
Musical form
Musicians
NT **Jazz ensembles**
RT **Orchestra**
Ensigns
USE **Flags**
Enteric fever
USE **Typhoid fever**
Enterprises
USE **Business enterprises**

Entertainers (May subdiv. geog.)
791.092; 920
SA types of entertainers and names of individual entertainers [to be added as needed]
NT **Actors**
Clowns
Comedians
Dancers
Fools and jesters
Entertaining (May subdiv. geog.)   **395.3;**
642

Use for materials on hospitality and the art of entertaining guests.

UF Guests
Hospitality
BT **Etiquette**
Home economics
NT **Business entertaining**
Carving (Meat, etc.)
Children's parties
Games
Parties
RT **Afternoon teas**
Amusements
Dining
Luncheons
Entertainments
USE **Amusements**
Entozoa
USE **Parasites**
Entrance examinations
USE types of educational institutions and names of individual institutions with the subdivision *Entrance examinations,* e.g. **Colleges and universities— Entrance examinations** [to be added as needed]
Entrance examinations for colleges
USE **Colleges and universities—Entrance examinations**
Entrance requirements
USE types of educational institutions and names of individual institutions with the subdivision *Entrance requirements,* e.g **Colleges and universities— Entrance requirements** [to be added as needed]

Entrance requirements for colleges and universities
    USE **Colleges and universities—Entrance requirements**

Entrepreneurs (May subdiv. geog.)   **338; 920**
    BT **Businesspeople**
         Self-employed

Entrepreneurship (May subdiv. geog.)
    338; 658.4
    BT **Business**
         Capitalism
         Small business

Environment (May subdiv. geog.)
    304.2; 333.7; 363.7
    Use for materials on the habitat or surroundings of a population or on all factors external to the individual.
    SA subjects with the subdivision *Environmental aspects,* e.g. **Nuclear power plants—Environmental aspects** [to be added as needed]
    NT **Ecology**
         Environmental degradation
         Environmental movement
         Environmental policy
         Environmental protection
         Nuclear power plants—Environmental aspects
         Pesticides—Environmental aspects
         Work environment
    RT **Environmental sciences**

Environment and pesticides
    USE **Pesticides—Environmental aspects**

Environment and state
    USE **Environmental policy**

Environment—Government policy
    USE **Environmental policy**

Environment, Space
    USE **Space environment**

Environmental aspects
    USE subjects with the subdivision *Environmental aspects,* e.g. **Nuclear power plants—Environmental aspects; Economic development—Environmental aspects** [to be added as needed]

Environmental control
    USE **Environmental law**

Environmental damages, Liability for
    USE **Liability for environmental damages**

Environmental degradation (May subdiv. geog.)   **333.7; 363.7**
    UF Environmental destruction
         Environmental deterioration
    BT **Environment**
         Natural disasters

Environmental destruction
    USE **Environmental degradation**

Environmental deterioration
    USE **Environmental degradation**

Environmental ethics   **179**
    UF Environmental quality—Ethical aspects
         Human ecology—Ethical aspects
    BT **Ethics**

Environmental health (May subdiv. geog.)
    616.9
    UF Health—Environmental aspects
    SA subjects with the subdivision *Environmental aspects,* e.g. **Nuclear power plants—Environmental aspects** [to be added as needed]
    BT **Environmental influence on humans**
         Public health
    NT **Air pollution**
         Nuclear power plants—Environmental aspects
         Occupational health and safety
         Pollution
         Water pollution

Environmental health engineering
    USE **Sanitary engineering**

Environmental influence on humans (May subdiv. geog.)   **304.2; 599.9**
    UF Acclimatization
         Altitude, Influence of
         Man—Influence of environment
    BT **Adaptation (Biology)**
         Human ecology
         Human geography
    NT **Environmental health**
         Survival skills
         Weightlessness

Environmental law (May subdiv. geog.)
344
  UF Environmental control
       Environmental protection—Law
         and legislation
  BT **Environmental policy**
      Environmental protection
      Law
  NT **Liability for environmental**
        damages
Environmental lobby
  USE **Environmental movement**
Environmental movement (May subdiv.
    geog.) **320.5; 322.4; 363.7**
  UF Conservation movement
       Ecological movement
       Environmental lobby
       Environmentalism
       Green movement
  BT **Environment**
      Social movements
Environmental policy (May subdiv. geog.)
    344; 354.3; 363.7
  UF Environment and state
       Environment—Government poli-
         cy
       Environmental quality—Govern-
         ment policy
       Government policy
       State and environment
  BT **Environment**
  NT **Environmental law**
  RT **Conservation of natural re-**
      sources
Environmental policy—United States
    344; 354.30973; 363.7
  UF United States—Environmental
       policy
Environmental pollution
  USE **Pollution**
Environmental protection (May subdiv.
    geog.) **344; 363.7**
  UF Environmentalism
       Protection of environment
  BT **Ecology**
      Environment
  NT **Conservation of natural re-**
      sources
      Endangered species
      Environmental law
      Landscape protection

      Soil conservation
      Wildlife conservation
  RT **Pollution**
Environmental protection—Law and legisla-
    tion
  USE **Environmental law**
Environmental protection—Standards
    (May subdiv. geog.) **354.3**
Environmental quality—Ethical aspects
  USE **Environmental ethics**
Environmental quality—Government policy
  USE **Environmental policy**
Environmental radioactivity
  USE **Radioactive pollution**
Environmental sciences **304.2; 333.7;**
    363.7
  BT **Science**
  RT **Ecology**
      Environment
Environmental technology
  USE **Green technology**
Environmental tourism
  USE **Ecotourism**
Environmentalism
  USE **Environmental movement**
      Environmental protection
Environmentally friendly architecture
  USE **Sustainable architecture**
Enzymes **547; 572**
  BT **Proteins**
  NT **Catalytic RNA**
Eolithic period
  USE **Stone Age**
Epic films **791.43**
    May be used for individual works, collec-
  tions, or materials about epic films.
  UF Film epics
  BT **Motion pictures**
Epic literature **800**
    May be used for individual works, collec-
  tions, or materials about epic literature.
  BT **Literature**
  NT **Epic poetry**
  RT **Mock-heroic literature**
Epic poetry **808.1; 808.81**
    May be used for individual works, collec-
  tions, or materials about epic poetry.
  BT **Epic literature**
      Narrative poetry
  RT **Romances**

Epidemics (May subdiv. geog.) **614.4**
  UF Pestilences
  SA names of contagious diseases,
        e.g. **AIDS (Disease)** [to be
        added as needed]
  BT **Diseases**
        Public health
  NT **Plague**
  RT **Communicable diseases**
Epigrams 808.88
  May be used for collections of epigrams
  and for materials about epigrams.
  UF Sayings
  BT **Wit and humor**
  NT **Quotations**
        Toasts
  RT **Proverbs**
Epigraphy
  USE **Inscriptions**
Epilepsy 616.8
  BT **Nervous system—Diseases**
Episcopal Church (May subdiv. geog.)
  283
  Use for materials on the Episcopal Church
  in the United States after 1789. Materials on
  the Episcopal Church in the United States pri-
  or to 1789 are entered under **Church of Eng-
  land—United States.**
  UF Protestant Episcopal Church in
        the U.S.A.
  BT **Christian sects**
  NT **Catholic charismatic movement**
  RT **Church of England—United
        States**
Epistemology
  USE **Theory of knowledge**
Epistolary fiction 808.3
  May be used for individual works, collec-
  tions, or materials about novels written in the
  form of a series of letters.
  UF Epistolary novels
        Novels in letters
  BT **Fiction**
Epistolary novels
  USE **Epistolary fiction**
Epistolary poetry 808.1; 808.81
  May be used for individual works, collec-
  tions, or materials about epistolary verse.
  UF Verse epistles
  BT **Poetry**
Epitaphs 929
  UF Graves
  BT **Biography**
        Cemeteries

Inscriptions
Tombs
Epithets
  USE **Names**
        Nicknames
Epizoa
  USE **Parasites**
Equal employment opportunity
  USE **Affirmative action programs**
        Discrimination in employment
Equal opportunity in employment
  USE **Affirmative action programs**
        Discrimination in employment
Equal pay for equal work 331.2; 658.3
  UF Pay equity
  BT **Discrimination in employment**
        Salaries, wages, etc.
        Women—Employment
Equal rights amendments (May subdiv.
  geog.) **305.42; 323.4; 342**
  UF Amendments, Equal rights
        ERAs
  BT **Constitutions**
        Sex discrimination
Equal time rule (Broadcasting) 324
  Use for materials on the requirement that
  all qualified candidates for public office be
  granted equal broadcast time if one of one
  such candidates is permitted to broadcast. Ma-
  terials on the requirement that, if one side of
  a controversial issue of public importance is
  aired, the same opportunity must be given for
  the presentation of contrasting views are en-
  tered under **Fairness doctrine (Broadcast-
  ing.)**
  UF Rule of equal time (Broadcast-
        ing)
  BT **Broadcasting**
        Television and politics
  RT **Fairness doctrine (Broadcast-
        ing)**
Equality (May subdiv. geog.) **323.42**
  UF Inequality
        Social equality
  BT **Political science**
        Sociology
  NT **Individualism**
  RT **Democracy**
        Freedom
Equations, Chemical
  USE **Chemical equations**
Equestrianism
  USE **Horsemanship**

Equilibrium (Economics)   339.5
  UF   Economic equilibrium
  BT   **Economics**
Equipment and supplies
  USE subjects and names of wars with
         the subdivision *Equipment*
         and supplies, e.g. **Televi-**
         sion—Equipment and sup-
         plies; World War, 1939-
         1945—Equipment and sup-
         plies [to be added as needed]
ERAs
  USE **Equal rights amendments**
Ergonomics
  USE **Human engineering**
Erosion   551.3
  SA   types of erosion, e.g. **Soil ero-**
        sion [to be added as needed]
  BT   **Geology**
  NT   **Dust storms**
        Soil erosion
  RT   **Soil conservation**
Erotic art (May subdiv. geog.)   **704.9**
  UF   Sex in art
  BT   **Art**
        Erotica
Erotic fiction   808.3; 808.83
  May be used for individual works, collec-
  tions, or materials about erotic fiction.
  UF   Adult fiction
        Erotic novels
        Erotic stories
  BT   **Erotic literature**
        Fiction
Erotic films   791.43
  May be used for individual works, collec-
  tions, or materials about erotic films.
  UF   Adult films
  BT   **Motion pictures**
Erotic literature   808.8; 809
  UF   Literature, Erotic
  BT   **Erotica**
        Literature
  NT   **Erotic fiction**
        Erotic poetry
Erotic novels
  USE **Erotic fiction**
Erotic poetry   808.1; 808.81
  May be used for individual works, collec-
  tions, or materials about erotic poetry.
  BT   **Erotic literature**
        Poetry

  RT   **Love poetry**
Erotic stories
  USE **Erotic fiction**
Erotica   704.9; 809
  SA   types of erotica, e.g. **Erotic art;**
        Erotic literature; etc. [to be
        added as needed]
  NT   **Erotic art**
        Erotic literature
  RT   **Obscenity (Law)**
        Pornography
Errors   001.9; 153.7; 165
  Use for materials on errors of judgment, er-
  rors of observation, scientific errors, popular
  misconceptions, etc. Errors in language are
  entered under names of languages with the
  subdivision *Errors of usage,* e.g. **English lan-**
  guage—Errors of usage.
  UF   Fallacies
        Medical errors
        Mistakes
        Scientific errors
  RT   **Superstition**
Errors of usage
  USE names of languages with the
         subdivision *Errors of usage,*
         e.g. **English language—Er-**
         rors of usage [to be added as
         needed]
Erudition
  USE **Learning and scholarship**
Eruptions
  USE **Geysers**
Escapes (May subdiv. geog.)   **365; 904**
  UF   Hostage escapes
        Prison escapes
  BT   **Adventure and adventurers**
        Prisons
Eschatology   202; 236
  UF   Intermediate state
        Last things (Theology)
  BT   **Theology**
  NT   **Death**
        End of the world
        Future life
        Heaven
        Hell
        Immortality
        Millennium
        Purgatory
        Second Advent
Eskimos
  USE **Inuit**

ESP
  USE **Extrasensory perception**
Esperanto **499**
  BT **Universal language**
Espionage (May subdiv. geog.) **327.12**
  UF Spying
  SA espionage practiced by particular
        countries, e.g. **American espi-**
        onage [to be added as need-
        ed]
  BT **Intelligence service**
        Secret service
        Subversive activities
  NT **American espionage**
        Spies
Espionage, American
  USE **American espionage**
Espionage films
  USE **Spy films**
Espionage stories
  USE **Spy stories**
Espionage television programs
  USE **Spy television programs**
Esquimaux
  USE **Inuit**
Essay **808.4**
    Use for materials on the appreciation of the
essay and on the technique of writing essays.
Collections of essays are entered under **Es-**
says; American essays; etc.
  BT **Literature**
Essays **808.4; 808.84**
    Use for collections of literary essays by au-
thors of several nationalities. Collections of
literary essays by American authors are en-
tered under **American essays;** by English au-
thors, under **English essays;** etc. Essays limit-
ed to a particular subject, by one or more authors, are entered under that subject. Materials
on the appreciation of the essay and on the
technique of writing essays are entered under
Essay.
  NT **American essays**
        English essays
Essences and essential oils **664; 668**
  UF Aromatic plant products
        Essential oils
        Vegetable oils
        Volatile oils
  BT **Distillation**
        Oils and fats
  NT **Flavoring essences**
        Perfumes
  RT **Aromatic plants**

Essenes **296.8**
  BT **Jews**
  RT **Dead Sea scrolls**
Essential oils
  USE **Essences and essential oils**
Estate planning (May subdiv. geog.)
        332.024; 343.05; 346.05
  BT **Personal finance**
        Planning
  NT **Inheritance and transfer tax**
        Insurance
  RT **Investments**
        Tax planning
        Trusts and trustees
Estate tax
  USE **Inheritance and transfer tax**
Esthetics
  USE **Aesthetics**
Estimates
  USE types of engineering, technical
        processes, industries, etc.,
        with the subdivision *Esti-*
        mates, e.g. **Building—Esti-**
        mates [to be added as need-
        ed]
Estimation (Mathematics)
  USE **Approximate computation**
Estrangement (Social psychology)
  USE **Alienation (Social psychology)**
Etchers (May subdiv. geog.) **769.92;**
        920
  BT **Artists**
        Engravers
Etching **767**
  UF Etchings
  BT **Art**
        Pictures
  NT **Pyrography**
  RT **Engraving**
Etchings
  USE **Etching**
Eternal life
  USE **Eternity**
        Future life
        Immortality
Eternal punishment
  USE **Hell**
Eternity **115**
    Use for materials on the philosophical con-
cept of eternity. Materials on the character
and form of a future life are entered under

Eternity—*Continued*
  Future life. Materials on the question of the endless existence of the soul are entered under **Immortality.**
  UF   Eternal life
  RT   **Future life**
Ethanol
  USE   **Alcohol as fuel**
Ethical aspects
  USE   subjects with the subdivision
          Ethical aspects, e.g. **Birth control—Ethical aspects** [to be added as needed]
Ethical development
  USE   **Moral development**
Ethical education
  USE   **Moral education**
Ethics (May subdiv. geog.)   **170**
  UF   Moral philosophy
          Morality
          Morals
  SA   types of ethics, e.g. **Business ethics;** ethics of particular religions, e.g. **Christian ethics;** names of individual persons, classes of persons, types of professions, and types of professional personnel with the subdivision *Ethics,* e.g. **Librarians—Ethics; Shakespeare, William, 1564-1616—Ethics;** etc., and subjects with the subdivision *Ethical aspects,* e.g. **Birth control—Ethical aspects** [to be added as needed]
  BT   **Philosophy**
  NT   **Abortion—Ethical aspects**
          Asceticism
          Bioethics
          Birth control—Ethical aspects
          Business ethics
          Character
          Charity
          Christian ethics
          Cloning—Ethical aspects
          Conduct of life
          Conscience
          Cruelty
          Duty
          Environmental ethics
          Feminist ethics

Golden rule
Good and evil
Guilt
Honesty
Human cloning—Ethical aspects
Jewish ethics
Justice
Legal ethics
Loyalty
Medical ethics
Moral education
Motion pictures—Ethical aspects
Natural law
Perseverance
Political ethics
Professional ethics
Promises
Responsibility
Secularism
Sexual ethics
Sin
Social ethics
Stoics
Utilitarianism
Values
Vice
Virtue
Vocation
Work ethic
World War, 1939-1945—Ethical aspects
  RT   **Human behavior**
Ethics—United States   170.973
  UF   American ethics
Ethiopian-Italian War, 1935-1936
  USE   **Italo-Ethiopian War, 1935-1936**
Ethnic art (May subdiv. geog.)   **709**
  BT   **Art**
          Ethnic groups
Ethnic cleansing
  USE   **Genocide**
Ethnic conflict
  USE   **Ethnic relations**
Ethnic diversity
  USE   **Pluralism (Social sciences)**
Ethnic groups (May subdiv. geog.)
          305.8
  Use for materials on groups of people bound together by common ancestry and cul-

Ethnic groups—*Continued*

ture. Materials on indigenous minorities are entered under **Native peoples.** Materials on the subjective sense of belonging to a particular ethnic group are entered under **Ethnicity.** Materials on several ethnic groups in a particular region or country are entered under **Ethnology** subdivided geographically. Materials on individual ethnic groups are entered under the name of the group, e.g. **Mexican Americans.**

- UF People
- SA names of individual ethnic groups [to be added as needed]
- BT **Ethnology**
- NT **Creoles**
  Ethnic art
  Hispanic Americans
  Mexican Americans
  Racially mixed people
- RT **Ethnic relations**
  Ethnicity

Ethnic identity
- USE **Ethnicity**
  and ethnic groups with the subdivision *Ethnic identity,* e.g. **Mexican Americans—Ethnic identity** [to be added as needed]

Ethnic psychology
- USE **Ethnopsychology**

Ethnic relations 305.8
- UF Ethnic conflict
  Relations among ethnic groups
- SA names of regions, countries, cities, etc., with the subdivision *Ethnic relations;* e.g. **United States—Ethnic relations** [to be added as needed]
- BT **Acculturation**
  Ethnology
  Sociology
- NT **Culture conflict**
  Discrimination
- RT **Ethnic groups**
  Minorities
  Multiculturalism
  Pluralism (Social sciences)
  Race relations

Ethnic relations—Political aspects 305.8

Ethnic relations—Religious aspects 305.8

Ethnicity (May subdiv. geog.) **305.8**

Use for materials on the subjective sense of belonging to a particular ethnic group. Materials on groups of people bound together by a common ancestry or culture are entered under **Ethnic groups.** Materials on several ethnic groups in a particular region or country are entered under **Ethnology.**

- UF Ethnic identity
- SA ethnic groups with the subdivision *Ethnic identity,* e.g. **Mexican Americans—Ethnic identity;** and racial groups with the subdivision *Race identity,* e.g. **African Americans—Race identity** [to be added as needed]
- BT **Identity (Psychology)**
- RT **Ethnic groups**
  Multiculturalism
  Pluralism (Social sciences)

Ethnobiology (May subdiv. geog.) **306.4; 578.6**
- UF Folk biology
- SA names of ethnic groups with the subdivision *Ethnobiology,* e.g. **Native Americans—Ethnobiology** [to be added as needed]
- BT **Biology**
  Ethnology
- NT **Ethnobotany**
  Ethnozoology
  Native Americans—Ethnobiology

Ethnobotany (May subdiv. geog.) **581.6**
- SA names of ethnic groups with the subdivision *Ethnobotany,* e.g. **Native Americans—Ethnobotany** [to be added as neede]
- BT **Ethnobiology**
  Ethnology
  Plants—Folklore
- NT **Native Americans—Ethnobotany**

Ethnocentrism (May subdiv. geog.) **305.8**
- BT **Ethnopsychology**
  Nationalism
  Prejudices
  Race

Ethnocide
USE **Genocide**
Ethnography
USE **Ethnology**
Ethnology (May subdiv. geog.)   **305.8;
306; 599.97**

Use for materials on the disciplines of ethnology and cultural anthropology, and, with
appropriate geographic subdivisions, for materials on the origin, distribution, and characteristics of the elements of the population of a
particular region or country. General materials
on groups of people who are bound together
by common ties of ancestry and culture are
entered under **Ethnic groups.** Materials on individual racial or ethnic groups are entered
under the name of the group, e.g. **Aboriginal
Australians.**

UF   Cultural anthropology
      Ethnography
      Races of people
      Social anthropology
SA   names of countries with the sub-
      division *Social life and cus-
      toms,* e.g. **United States—So-
      cial life and customs;** and
      names of individual ethnic
      groups [to be added as need-
      ed]
BT   **Human beings**
NT   **Acculturation
      Anthropometry
      Cannibalism
      Costume
      Ethnic groups
      Ethnic relations
      Ethnobiology
      Ethnobotany
      Ethnopsychology
      Ethnozoology
      Folklore
      Human geography
      Kinship
      Language and languages
      Manners and customs
      Mountain people
      Native peoples
      Physical anthropology
      Primitive societies
      Race
      Race relations
      Semitic peoples
      Totems and totemism**
RT   **Anthropology
      Archeology**

Civilization
Ethnology—United States   305.813
UF   United States—Ethnology
      United States—Peoples
SA   names of individual ethnic
      groups [to be added as need-
      ed]
Ethnopsychology (May subdiv. geog.)
155.8
UF   Cross-cultural psychology
      Ethnic psychology
      Folk psychology
      National psychology
      Race psychology
SA   names of racial or ethnic groups
      with the subdivision *Psycholo-
      gy* [to be added as needed]
BT   **Anthropology
      Ethnology
      Psychology
      Sociology**
NT   **Culture conflict
      Ethnocentrism
      Native Americans—Psychology**
RT   **National characteristics
      Social psychology**
Ethnozoology (May subdiv. geog.)   **591.6**
UF   Folk zoology
SA   names of ethnic groups with the
      subdivision *Ethnozoology,* e.g.
      **Native Americans—
      Ethnozoology** [to be added as
      needed]
BT   **Animals—Folklore
      Ethnobiology
      Ethnology**
NT   **Native Americans—
      Ethnozoology**
Ethyl alcohol fuel
USE   **Alcohol as fuel**
Etiquette (May subdiv. geog.)   **395**
UF   Ceremonies
      Manners
      Politeness
      Salutations
SA   types of etiquette, e.g. **Table et-
      iquette;** and names of coun-
      tries with the subdivision *So-
      cial life and customs,* e.g.
      United States—Social life

Etiquette—*Continued*

        and customs [to be added as needed]

BT   **Human behavior**

NT   **Business etiquette**

      Courtesy

      Dating (Social customs)

      Entertaining

      Excuses

      Letter writing

      Table etiquette

RT   **Manners and customs**

Etiquette for children and teenagers
177.1; 395.1

UF   Behavior of children

      Behavior of teenagers

      Child behavior

      Children—Etiquette

      Etiquette for teenagers

      Teenage behavior

      Teenagers—Etiquette

BT   **Children—Conduct of life**

      Teenagers—Conduct of life

Etiquette for teenagers

USE   **Etiquette for children and teenagers**

Etymology

USE   **Language and languages—Etymology**

      and names of languages with the subdivision *Etymology,* e.g. **English language—Etymology** [to be added as needed]

Eucharist   234; 264

   May be subdivided by Christian sect or denomination.

UF   Communion

      Holy communion

      Lord's Supper

BT   **Liturgies**

      Sacraments

RT   **Mass (Liturgy)**

Eugenics (May subdiv. geog.)   **363.9**

BT   **Genetics**

      Population

RT   **Heredity**

Euro   332.4

BT   **Capital market**

      Money

Europe   940

UF   Europe, Western

      Western Europe

Europe, Central

USE   **Central Europe**

Europe, Eastern

USE   **Eastern Europe**

Europe—History   940

NT   **Holy Roman Empire**

Europe—History—0-476   936; 937

Europe—History—476-1492   940.1; 940.2

NT   **Hundred Years' War, 1339-1453**

RT   **Middle Ages**

Europe—History—1492-1789   940.2

NT   **Seven Years' War, 1756-1763**

      Thirty Years' War, 1618-1648

Europe—History—18th century   940.2

Europe—History—1789-1815   940.2

NT   **Napoleonic Wars, 1800-1815**

Europe—History—1789-1900   940.2

UF   Europe—History—19th century

Europe—History—19th century

USE   **Europe—History—1789-1900**

Europe—History—1815-1848   940.2

Europe—History—1848-1871   940.2

Europe—History—1871-1918   940.2

NT   **World War, 1914-1918**

Europe—History—20th century   940.5

Europe—History—1918-1945   940.5

NT   **Russo-Finnish War, 1939-1940**

      World War, 1939-1945

Europe—History—1945-   940.55

Europe—History—21st century   940.56

Europe—Politics and government   940

   May be subdivided by period using the same subdivisions as are listed under **Europe—History.**

NT   **European federation**

Europe, Western

USE   **Europe**

European Common Market

USE   **European Union**

European Community

USE   **European Union**

European Economic Community

USE   **European Union**

European federation   321; 940

   Use for general materials on the political or economic union of European countries. Materials on the corporate body formerly known as

European federation—*Continued*
the European Economic Community and the
European Community, which became known
as the European Union upon ratification of the
Treaty of European Union on October 29,
1993, are entered under **European Union.**

UF Federation of Europe

BT **Europe—Politics and government**

Federal government

International organization

NT **European Union**

European Union   341.242; 382

Use for materials on the corporate body formerly known as the European Economic
Community and the European Community,
which became known as the European Union
upon ratification of the Treaty on European
Union on October 29, 1993. General materials
on the political or economic union of European countries are entered under **European federation.**

UF Common market

EEC

European Common Market

European Community

European Economic Community

BT **European federation**

Euthanasia (May subdiv. geog.)   **179.7**

UF Mercy killing

BT **Homicide**

Medical ethics

RT **Right to die**

Evacuation of civilians

USE names of wars with the subdivision *Evacuation of civilians,*
e.g. **World War, 1939-
1945—Evacuation of civil-
ians** [to be added as needed]

Evaluation

USE types of evaluation, e.g. **Educational evaluation;** and names
of corporate bodies and types
of institutions, products, services, equipment, activities,
projects, and programs with
the subdivision *Evaluation,*
e.g. **Public health—Evaluation; Science—Study and
teaching—Evaluation;** etc.
[to be added as needed]

Evaluation of books

USE **Book reviewing**

Evaluation of literature

USE **Best books**

Books and reading

Criticism

**Literature—History and criti-
cism**

Evaluation research in education

USE **Educational evaluation**

Evangelism

USE **Evangelistic work**

Evangelistic healing

USE **Spiritual healing**

Evangelistic work (May subdiv. geog.)
253; 269

UF Evangelism

Revival (Religion)

BT **Church work**

NT **Conversion**

Revivals

RT **Christian missions**

Evening and continuation schools   374

UF Continuation schools

Evening schools

Night schools

BT **Compulsory education**

Continuing education

Education

Public schools

Schools

Secondary education

Technical education

RT **Adult education**

Evening schools

USE **Evening and continuation
schools**

Evergreens   582.1; 635.9

BT **Landscape gardening**

Shrubs

Trees

Evidences of the Bible

USE **Bible—Evidences, authority,
etc.**

Evil

USE **Good and evil**

Evil spirits

USE **Demonology**

Evolution   576.8

UF Darwinism

Development

Mutation (Biology)

Origin of species

Evolution—*Continued*

    SA   types of animals, plants, crops, chemicals, and organs of the body with the subdivision *Evolution* [to be added as needed]

    BT   **Philosophy**

    NT   **Life—Origin**

    RT   **Biology**

          Creation

          Creationism

          Human origins

          Natural selection

          Religion and science

          Variation (Biology)

Evolution and Christianity

    USE **Creationism**

Evolution—Study and teaching   576.807

    UF   Creation—Study and teaching

    RT   **Creationism**

Ex libris

    USE **Bookplates**

Ex-nuns   305.48

    UF   Catholic ex-nuns

          Former nuns

    BT   **Nuns**

Ex-priests   305.33; 920

    UF   Catholic ex-priests

          Former priests

    BT   **Catholic Church—Clergy**

          Priests

Ex-Soviet republics

    USE **Former Soviet republics**

Ex-Soviet states

    USE **Former Soviet republics**

Examinations (May subdiv. geog.)
    371.26

Use for general materials on examinations. Materials discussing the requirements for examinations in particular branches of study, or compilations of questions and answers for such examinations, are entered under the subject with the subdivision *Examinations.*

    UF   Tests

    SA   branches of study with the subdivision *Examinations,* e.g. **English language—Examinations;** and names of individual examinations [to be added as needed]

    BT   **Questions and answers**

          Teaching

    NT   **Civil service—Examinations**

          Colleges and universities—Entrance examinations

          Colleges and universities—Entrance requirements

          English language—Examinations

          Graduate Record Examination

          Music—Examinations

          Scholastic Aptitude Test

          United States. Army—Examinations

    RT   **Educational tests and measurements**

Examinations—Design and construction
    371.26

Examinations—Study guides   371.26

Use for materials that provide directions on how to prepare for and pass examinations, usually with practice questions and answers included.

    UF   Preparation guides for examinations

          Study guides for examinations

          Test preparation guides

    SA   subjects, educational levels, and names of educational institutions with the subdivisions *Examinations—Study guides,* e.g. **English language—Examinations—Study guides;** and named examinations with the subdivision *Study guides,* e.g. **Graduate Record Examination—Study guides** [to be added as needed]

    BT   **Study skills**

Excavation   624.1

    BT   **Civil engineering**

          Tunnels

Excavations (Archeology) (May subdiv. geog.)   930.1

    UF   Earthworks (Archeology)

          Ruins

    BT   **Archeology**

    RT   **Extinct cities**

          Mounds and mound builders

Excavations (Archeology)—United States
    973

Exceptional children   155.45
UF   Abnormal children
BT   **Children**
      Elementary education
NT   **Brain damaged children**
      Emotionally disturbed children
      Gifted children
      Handicapped children
      Mainstreaming in education
      Slow learning children
      Wild children
Excess government property
USE   **Surplus government property**
Exchange   332.4; 332.64
BT   **Commerce**
NT   **Foreign exchange**
      Money
RT   **Supply and demand**
Exchange, Barter
USE   **Barter**
Exchange of persons programs   327.1;
      370.116
UF   Cultural exchange programs
      Interchange of visitors
      Specialists exchange programs
      Visitors' exchange programs
SA   types of exchange programs for
        particular classes of persons,
        e.g. **Teacher exchange** [to be
        added as needed]
BT   **Cultural relations**
      International cooperation
NT   **Student exchange programs**
      Teacher exchange
Exchange of prisoners of war
USE   **Prisoners of war**
Exchange of students
USE   **Student exchange programs**
Exchange of teachers
USE   **Teacher exchange**
Exchange programs, Student
USE   **Student exchange programs**
Exchange rates
USE   **Foreign exchange**
Excuses   395
BT   **Etiquette**
      Manners and customs
Executions and executioners (May subdiv.
      geog.)   **364.66**
BT   **Criminal law**
      Criminal procedure

RT   **Capital punishment**
Executive ability   658.4
UF   Administrative ability
BT   **Ability**
NT   **Leadership**
      Planning
Executive agencies
USE   **Administrative agencies**
Executive departments (May subdiv.
      geog.)   **351**
   Use for materials on major administrative
divisions of the executive branch of govern-
ment, usually headed by an officer of cabinet
rank.
UF   Government departments
      Government ministries
      State ministries
SA   names of executive departments
        [to be added as needed]
BT   **Administrative agencies**
Executive departments—Ohio   352.2
UF   Ohio—Executive departments
SA   names of executive departments
        [to be added as needed]
Executive departments—Reorganization
USE   **Administrative agencies—Reor-**
      ganization
Executive departments—United States
      352.2
UF   United States—Executive depart-
      ments
SA   names of executive departments
        [to be added as needed]
NT   **Presidents—United States—**
      Staff
Executive investigations
USE   **Governmental investigations**
Executive power (May subdiv. geog.)
      351
   Use for materials on the powers of the ex-
ecutive or administrative branch of govern-
ment.
UF   Presidents—Powers
BT   **Constitutional law**
      Political science
NT   **Amnesty**
      Clemency
      Heads of state
      Monarchy
      Pardon
      Prime ministers
      Separation of powers
      War and emergency powers

Executive power—*Continued*
   RT   **Presidents**
Executive power—United States
      352.230973
   UF   Presidents—United States—Power
      United States—Executive power
Executive reorganization
   USE   **Administrative agencies—Reorganization**
Executors and administrators (May
      subdiv. geog.)   **346.05**
   UF   Administrators and executors
   BT   **Inheritance and succession**
   RT   **Trusts and trustees**
      Wills
Exegesis, Biblical
   USE   **Bible—Criticism**
Exemption from taxation
   USE   **Tax exemption**
Exercise (May subdiv. geog.)   **613.7**
   SA   types of exercises and physical
      activities [to be added as
      needed]
   BT   **Health**
      Hygiene
   NT   **Aerobics**
      Bodybuilding
      Cycling
      Gymnastics
      Hatha yoga
      Physical fitness
      Pilates method
      Rowing
      Tai chi
      Weight lifting
   RT   **Physical education**
      Weight loss
Exercise addiction   **616.85**
   UF   Addiction to exercise
      Compulsive exercising
   BT   **Compulsive behavior**
Exercises, problems, etc.
   USE   subjects with the subdivision
      Problems, exercises, etc., for
      compilations of practice prob-
      lems or exercises for use in
      the study of a topic, e.g.
      Chemistry—Problems, exercises, etc. [to be added as
      needed]

Exhaustion
   USE   **Fatigue**
Exhibitions
   UF   Exhibits
      Expositions
      International exhibitions
      World's fairs
   SA   types of exhibitions, e.g. **Flower
      shows;** subjects and names of
      individual persons with the
      subdivision *Exhibitions,* e.g.
      Printing—Exhibitions; and
      names of particular exhibi-
      tions, e.g. **Expo 92 (Seville,
      Spain)** [to be added as need-
      ed]
   NT   **Art—Exhibitions**
      Books—Exhibitions
      Craft shows
      Expo 92 (Seville, Spain)
      Fashion shows
      Flower shows
      Printing—Exhibitions
      Science—Exhibitions
      Trade shows
   RT   **Fairs**
Exhibits
   USE   **Exhibitions**
Exiles
   USE   **Refugees**
Existentialism   **142**
   BT   **Metaphysics**
      Modern philosophy
      Phenomenology
Exorcism   **133.4; 203**
   BT   **Supernatural**
   RT   **Demoniac possession**
      Demonology
Expansion (United States politics)
   USE   **United States—Territorial expansion**
Expectancy of life
   USE   **Life expectancy**
Expectation of life
   USE   **Life expectancy**
Expeditions, Scientific
   USE   **Scientific expeditions**
Experience
   USE   **Empiricism**

Experimental farms
USE **Agricultural experiment stations**
Experimental films (May subdiv. geog.)
791.43

May be used for individual works, collections, or materials about experimental films.

UF Avant-garde films
Personal films
Underground films
BT **Motion pictures**
Experimental methods in education
USE **Education—Experimental methods**
Experimental schools (May subdiv. geog.)
371.04

Use for materials on schools in which new teaching methods, organizations of subject matter, educational theories, personnel practices, etc., are tested.

UF Alternative schools
Free schools
Nonformal schools
Project schools
Schools, Nonformal
BT **Education—Experimental methods**
Schools
RT **Open plan schools**
Experimental theater (May subdiv. geog.)
792

UF Avant-garde theater
BT **Theater**
Experimental universities
USE **Free universities**
Experimentation on animals
USE **Animal experimentation**
Experimentation on humans, Medical
USE **Human experimentation in medicine**
Experiments
USE scientific subjects with the subdivision *Experiments,* e.g. **Chemistry—Experiments** [to be added as needed]
Experiments, Scientific
USE **Science—Experiments**
Expert systems (Computer science)
006.3

UF Knowledge-based systems (Computer science)
BT **Artificial intelligence**
Data processing

Information systems
Exploration 910.9

Use for materials on voyages and explorations that have advanced geographic knowledge.

UF Discoveries and exploration
Discoveries in geography
Explorations
Maritime discoveries
SA names of celestial bodies, continents, regions, countries, states, etc., with the subdivision *Exploration* for materials on the exploration of those areas when they were unsettled or sparsely settled and largely unknown to the world at large, e.g. **America—Exploration;** or with the subdivision *Description and travel* for materials on later and recent travels is those areas, e.g. **United States—Description and travel;** and names of countries, states, etc., with the subdivision *Exploring expeditions* for materials on explorations sponsored by those governments, e.g. **United States—Exploring expeditions** [to be added as needed]
BT **Adventure and adventurers**
Geography
History
NT **America—Exploration**
Antarctica—Exploration
Arctic regions—Exploration
Northeast Passage
Outer space—Exploration
Underwater exploration
United States—Exploration
RT **Explorers**
Scientific expeditions
Voyages and travels
Exploration of space
USE **Outer space—Exploration**
Exploration—United States
USE **United States—Exploration**
Explorations
USE **Exploration**
Exploratory behavior
USE **Curiosity**

Explorer (Artificial satellite) 629.46
   BT   Artificial satellites
Explorers (May subdiv. geog.) 910.92;
   920
   UF   Discoverers
        Navigators
        Voyagers
   SA   names of places explored with
        the subdivision *Exploration,*
        e.g. **America—Exploration;**
        names of countries with the
        subdivisions *Description* and
        Exploring expeditions; and
        names of individual explorers
        [to be added as needed]
   BT   **Adventure and adventurers**
        Heroes and heroines
   NT   **United States—Exploring expe-**
        ditions
   RT   **Exploration**
        Travelers
        Voyages and travels
Exploring expeditions
   USE names of countries sponsoring
        exploring expeditions with the
        subdivision *Exploring expedi-*
        tions, e.g. **United States—Ex-**
        ploring expeditions; etc.; and
        names of expeditions, e.g.
        Lewis and Clark Expedition
        (1804-1806) [to be added as
        needed]
Explosions 904
   BT   **Accidents**
Explosives 363.17; 363.33; 623.4; 662
   SA   types of explosives and explo-
        sive devices [to be added as
        needed]
   BT   **Chemistry**
   NT   **Ammunition**
        Bombs
        Dynamite
        Gunpowder
        Land mines
        Torpedoes
Expo 92 (Seville, Spain) 909.82
   UF   Seville (Spain). World's Fair,
        1992
        World's Fair (1992 : Seville,
        Spain)

   BT   **Exhibitions**
        Fairs
Exports (May subdiv. geog.) 382
   BT   **International trade**
Exposed children
   USE **Abandoned children**
Expositions
   USE **Exhibitions**
Express highways (May subdiv. geog.)
   388.1; 625.7
   UF   Freeways
        Interstate highways
        Limited access highways
        Motorways
        Parkways
        Superhighways
        Toll roads
        Turnpikes (Modern)
   BT   **Roads**
        Traffic engineering
Express service 388
   BT   **Railroads**
        Transportation
   NT   **Pony express**
Expressionism (Art) (May subdiv. geog.)
   709.04; 759.06
   BT   **Art**
Expropriation
   USE **Eminent domain**
Expulsion
   USE **Penal colonies**
Extended care facilities
   USE **Long-term care facilities**
Extermination of pests
   USE **Pest control**
Extinct animals (May subdiv. geog.)
   560
   SA   types of extinct animals [to be
        added as needed]
   BT   **Animals**
   NT   **Mastodon**
   RT   **Fossils**
        Prehistoric animals
        Rare animals
Extinct cities (May subdiv. geog.) 930
   UF   Abandoned towns
        Buried cities
        Ruins
        Sunken cities

Extinct cities—*Continued*
  SA names of extinct cities and
        towns, e.g. **Delphi (Extinct
        city)** [to be added as needed]
  BT **Archeology**
        Cities and towns
  NT **Ghost towns**
  RT **Excavations (Archeology)**
Extinct cities—Greece   938
  NT **Delphi (Extinct city)**
Extinct plants
  USE **Fossil plants**
Extracurricular activities
  USE **Student activities**
Extragalactic nebulae
  USE **Galaxies**
Extramarital relationships
  USE **Adultery**
Extrasensory perception   133.8
  UF ESP
  BT **Parapsychology**
  NT **Clairvoyance**
        Telepathy
Extrasolar planetary systems
  USE **Extrasolar planets**
Extrasolar planets   523.2
  UF Extrasolar planetary systems
  BT **Planets**
Extraterrestrial abduction
  USE **Alien abduction**
Extraterrestrial bases   629.44
  Use for materials on bases established on
  natural extraterrestrial bodies for specific
  functions other than colonization. Materials on
  communities established in space or on natural
  extraterrestrial bodies are entered under **Space
  colonies.** Materials on manned installations
  orbiting in space for specific functions, such
  as servicing space ships, are entered under
  Space stations.
  BT **Civil engineering**
  RT **Space colonies**
Extraterrestrial beings   576.8
  UF Aliens from outer space
        Interplanetary visitors
  BT **Life on other planets**
  RT **Human-alien encounters**
Extraterrestrial communication
  USE **Interstellar communication**
Extraterrestrial encounters with humans
  USE **Human-alien encounters**
Extraterrestrial environment
  USE **Space environment**

Extraterrestrial life
  USE **Life on other planets**
**Extravehicular activity (Space flight)
        629.45**
  UF Space vehicles—Extravehicular
        activity
        Space walk
        Walking in space
  BT **Space flight**
Extreme sports (May subdiv. geog.)
        796.04
  BT **Sports**
Extreme unction
  USE **Anointing of the sick**
Extremism (Political science)
  USE **Radicalism**
Eye   611; 612.8
  BT **Face**
        Head
  RT **Optometry**
        Vision
Eyeglasses   617.7; 681
  UF Glasses
        Spectacles
  SA types of eyeglasses, e.g. **Contact
        lenses** [to be added as need-
        ed]
  NT **Contact lenses**
Fables   398.24; 808.8
  May be used for individual works, collec-
  tions, or materials about short tales intended
  to teach moral lessons, often with animals or
  inanimate objects speaking and acting like hu-
  man beings, and usually with the lesson stated
  briefly at the end.
  UF Cautionary tales and verse
        Moral and philosophic stories
        Tales
  SA fables of particular countries,
        e.g. **American fables** [to be
        added as needed]
  BT **Fiction**
        Literature
  NT **American fables**
  RT **Allegories**
        Animals—Fiction
        Didactic fiction
        Didactic poetry
        Folklore
        Legends
        Parables
        Romances

Fabric design
    USE **Textile design**
Fabrics (May subdiv. geog.)   677
    UF   Cloth
          Dry goods
          Textiles
    SA   types of fabrics [to be added as
          needed]
    BT   **Decorative arts**
    NT   **Cotton**
          Linen
          Silk
          Synthetic fabrics
          Wool
    RT   **Weaving**
Face   611; 612
    BT   **Head**
    NT   **Eye**
          Mouth
          Nose
    RT   **Physiognomy**
Facetiae
    USE **Anecdotes**
          Wit and humor
Facsimile transmission
    USE **Fax transmission**
Facsimiles
    USE   types of printed or written mate-
          rials, documents, etc., with
          the subdivision *Facsimiles,*
          e.g. **Autographs—Facsimiles**
          [to be added as needed]
Factories (May subdiv. geog.)   338.6;
          670; 725
    UF   Industrial plants
          Mill and factory buildings
          Plants, Industrial
    SA   types of factories [to be added
          as needed]
    BT   **Industrial buildings**
    NT   **Breweries**
          Plant shutdowns
    RT   **Factory management**
          Mills
Factories—Management
    USE **Factory management**
Factory and trade waste
    USE **Industrial waste**
Factory management   658.5
    Use for materials on the technical aspects
    of manufacturing processes. Materials on gen-

eral principles of management of industries
are entered under **Management.**
    UF   Factories—Management
          Production engineering
          Shop management
    BT   **Management**
    NT   **Job analysis**
          Motion study
          Office management
          Participative management
          Supervisors
          Time study
    RT   **Factories**
          Personnel management
Factory waste
    USE **Industrial waste**
Factory workers
    USE **Labor**
          Working class
Facts, Miscellaneous
    USE **Books of lists**
          Curiosities and wonders
Faculty
    USE   types of educational institutions
          and names of individual edu-
          cational institutions with the
          subdivision *Faculty,* e.g. **Col-
          leges and universities—Fac-
          ulty** [to be added as needed]
Faculty (Education)
    USE **Colleges and universities—Fac-
          ulty**
          Educators
          Teachers
Fads   306
    UF   Crazes
    BT   **Manners and customs**
          Popular culture
Faience
    USE **Pottery**
Failure in business
    USE **Bankruptcy**
          Business failures
Failure of banks
    USE **Bank failures**
Failure to thrive syndrome
    USE **Growth disorders**
Failures, Structural
    USE **Structural failures**
Fair employment practice
    USE **Discrimination in employment**

Fair housing
USE **Discrimination in housing**
Fair trade
USE **Unfair competition**
Fair trade (Tariff)
USE **Free trade**
Fair trial (May subdiv. geog.) **345**

Use for materials on legal hearings before an impartial and disinterested tribunal. Materials on the regular administration of the law, according to which citizens may not be denied their legal rights and all laws must conform to fundamental and accepted legal principles, are entered under **Due Process of law.**

UF   Right to a fair trial
BT   **Civil rights**
      Due process of law
NT   **Freedom of the press and fair trial**
Fair trial and free press
USE   **Freedom of the press and fair trial**
Fair use (Copyright) (May subdiv. geog.)
      346.04
BT   **Copyright**
Fairies   398.21
BT   **Folklore**
Fairness   179
UF   Impartiality
BT   **Conduct of life**
RT   **Justice**
Fairness doctrine (Broadcasting)   343.09

Use for materials on the requirement that, if one side of a controversial issue of public importance is aired, the same opportunity must be given for the presentation of contrasting views. Materials on the requirement that all qualified candidates for public office be granted equal broadcast time if any one such candidate is permitted to broadcast are entered under **Equal time rule (Broadcasting).**

UF   Doctrine of fairness (Broadcasting)
BT   **Broadcasting**
      Television and politics
RT   **Equal time rule (Broadcasting)**
Fairs (May subdiv. geog.)   **381; 394;**
      607; 907.4

Use for general materials on public showings that suggest a variety of kinds of display and entertainment, usually in an outdoor setting, sometimes for the promotion of sales and sometimes in competition for prizes of excellence.

UF   Bazaars
      World's fairs

SA   names of fairs, e.g. **Expo 92 (Seville, Spain)** [to be added as needed]
NT   **Expo 92 (Seville, Spain)**
      Trade shows
RT   **Carnivals**
      Exhibitions
      Markets
Fairy tales (May subdiv. geog.)   **398.2;**
      808.83

May be used for individual works, collections, or materials about short, simple narratives, often of folk origin and usually intended for children, involving fantastic forces and magical beings such as dragons, elves, fairies, goblins, witches, and wizards.

UF   Stories
      Tales
BT   **Children's literature**
      Fiction
NT   **Fractured fairy tales**
RT   **Folklore**
Fairy tales—Parodies, imitations, etc.
USE   **Fractured fairy tales**
Faith   121; 201; 234

Use for materials on religious belief and doubt. Materials on belief and doubt from the philosophical standpoint are entered under **Belief and doubt.**

UF   Religious belief
BT   **Religion**
      Salvation
      Spiritual life
      Theology
      Virtue
RT   **Belief and doubt**
Faith cure
USE   **Spiritual healing**
Faith healing
USE   **Spiritual healing**
Faith—Psychology   200.1; 248; 253.5
BT   **Psychology of religion**
Faithfulness
USE   **Loyalty**
Falconry   799.2
UF   Hawking
BT   **Game and game birds**
      Hunting
Fall
USE   **Autumn**
Fallacies
USE   **Errors**
      Logic

Falling stars
  USE **Meteors**
Fallout, Radioactive
  USE **Radioactive fallout**
Fallout shelters
  USE **Air raid shelters**
False advertising
  USE **Deceptive advertising**
False memories
  USE **False memory syndrome**
False memory syndrome   **616.85**
  UF False memories
  BT **Memory**
  RT **Recovered memory**
Falsehood
  USE **Truthfulness and falsehood**
Fame   **306.4**
  UF Celebrity
       Renown
  RT **Celebrities**
Family (May subdiv. geog.)   **306.85**
     Use for materials stressing the sociological
     concept and structure of the family. Materials
     stressing the everyday life, interaction, and re-
     lationships of family members are entered un-
     der **Family life.**
  SA types of family members, e.g.
       Children; Fathers; Mothers;
       etc., types of family relation-
       ships, e.g. **Mother-son rela-**
       tionship; and names of indi-
       vidual persons with the subdi-
       vision *Family* [to be added as
       needed]
  BT **Interpersonal relations**
       Sociology
  NT **Birth order**
       Children
       Clans
       Cousins
       Daughters
       Divorce
       Dual-career families
       Family life
       Family size
       Farm family
       Fathers
       Grandparent-grandchild rela-
       tionship
       Husbands
       Kinship
       Marriage
       Married people

       Mothers
       Parent-child relationship
       Parenthood
       Parents
       Siblings
       Single-parent families
       Sons
       Stepfamilies
       Wives
       Work and family
  RT **Domestic relations**
       Family reunions
       Home
Family and work
  USE **Work and family**
Family—Biblical teaching   **248.4; 261.8**
Family budget
  USE **Household budgets**
Family caregivers
  USE **Caregivers**
Family counseling
  USE **Family therapy**
Family devotions
  USE **Devotional exercises**
       Family—Religious life
Family farms (May subdiv. geog.)
                338.1; 630
  BT **Farms**
  RT **Farm family**
       Farm life
Family finance
  USE **Personal finance**
Family group therapy
  USE **Family therapy**
Family histories
  USE **Genealogy**
Family leave
  USE **Parental leave**
Family life (May subdiv. geog.)   **306.85;**
                392.3; 646.7
     Use for materials stressing the everyday
     life, interaction, and relationships of family
     members. Materials on the sociological con-
     cept and structure of the family are entered
     under **Family.**
  UF Family relations
       Home life
  BT **Family**
  NT **Family traditions**

Family life education (May subdiv. geog.)
    306.85; 362.82; 372.82
    BT   **Education**
    NT   **Home economics**
          Marriage counseling
          Sex education
    RT   **Domestic relations**
Family medicine   **610**
    UF   Family practice (Medicine)
          General practice (Medicine)
    BT   **Medicine**
Family names
    USE   **Personal names**
Family planning
    USE   **Birth control**
Family practice (Medicine)
    USE   **Family medicine**
Family prayers
    USE   **Devotional exercises**
          Family—Religious life
Family psychotherapy
    USE   **Family therapy**
Family relations
    USE   **Domestic relations**
          Family life
Family—Religious life   **204; 248.4; 249**
    UF   Family devotions
          Family prayers
          Family worship
    BT   **Religious life**
Family reunions   **394.2**
    UF   Reunions, Family
    RT   **Family**
Family size (May subdiv. geog.)   **304.6**
    BT   **Family**
    NT   **Childlessness**
          Only child
    RT   **Birth control**
Family social work
    USE   **Social case work**
Family therapy   **616.89**
    UF   Family counseling
          Family group therapy
          Family psychotherapy
          Problem families—Counseling of
    BT   **Counseling**
          Psychotherapy
Family traditions (May subdiv. geog.)
    306.85; 392.3
    BT   **Family life**
          Manners and customs

Family trees
    USE   **Genealogy**
Family—United States   **306.850973**
Family violence
    USE   **Domestic violence**
Family worship
    USE   **Family—Religious life**
Famines (May subdiv. geog.)   **904**
    BT   **Food supply**
          Starvation
Famines—United States   **363.80973; 973**
Famous people
    USE   **Celebrities**
Fan magazines
    USE   **Fanzines**
Fanaticism   **152.4; 200.1; 303**
    UF   Intolerance
    BT   **Emotions**
Fancy dress
    USE   **Costume**
Fans   **391.4**
    BT   **Clothing and dress**
          Costume
Fantastic fiction
    USE   **Fantasy fiction**
Fantastic films
    USE   **Fantasy films**
Fantastic poetry
    USE   **Fantasy poetry**
Fantastic radio programs
    USE   **Fantasy radio programs**
Fantastic television programs
    USE   **Fantasy television programs**
Fantasy   **154.3**
    Use for materials on fantasy as an aspect of
psychology. Literary fantasies are entered under **Fantasy fiction.**
    UF   Day dreams
    BT   **Dreams**
          Imagination
    RT   **Hallucinations and illusions**
Fantasy fiction   **808.3; 808.83**
    May be used for individual works, collections, or materials about imaginative fiction with strange settings, grotesque or fanciful characters, and supernatural or impossible events or forces.
    UF   Apocalyptic fantasies
          End-of-the-world fantasies
          Fantastic fiction
    BT   **Fiction**
    NT   **Alternative histories**
          Dystopias

Fantasy fiction—*Continued*
  Ghost stories
  Imaginary voyages
  Utopian fiction
 RT Horror fiction
  Interplanetary voyages
  Occult fiction
  Science fiction
Fantasy films   791.43
  May be used for individual works, collections, or materials about fantasy films.
 UF Apocalyptic fantasies
  End-of-the-world fantasies
  Fantastic films
 BT **Motion pictures**
 RT **Horror films**
  Science fiction films
Fantasy games   793.93
 UF Fantasy role playing games
  Role playing games
 BT **Games**
  Role playing
Fantasy poetry   808.1; 808.81
  May be used for individual works, collections, or materials about fantasy poetry.
 UF Fantastic poetry
 BT **Poetry**
Fantasy radio programs   791.44
  May be used for individual works, collections, or materials about fantasy radio programs.
 UF Fantastic radio programs
 BT **Radio programs**
Fantasy role playing games
 USE **Fantasy games**
Fantasy television programs   791.45
  May be used for individual works, collections, or materials about fantasy television programs.
 UF Apocalyptic fantasies
  End-of-the-world fantasies
  Fantastic television programs
 BT **Television programs**
 RT **Horror television programs**
  Science fiction television programs
Fanzines (May subdiv. geog.)   **070.4**
 UF Fan magazines
  Zines
 BT **Periodicals**
Far East
 USE **East Asia**
Far north
 USE **Arctic regions**

Farces   808.2; 808.82
  May be used for individual works, collections, or materials about farces.
 BT **Comedies**
 NT **Commedia dell'arte**
Farm animals
 USE **Domestic animals**
Farm buildings (May subdiv. geog.)
  631.2; 728
 UF Architecture, Rural
  Rural architecture
 SA types of farm buildings [to be added as needed]
 BT **Buildings**
 NT **Barns**
Farm credit
 USE **Agricultural credit**
Farm crops
 USE **Farm produce**
Farm engines
 USE **Agricultural machinery**
Farm equipment
 USE **Agricultural machinery**
Farm family (May subdiv. geog.)
  306.85
 UF Rural families
 BT **Family**
 RT **Family farms**
  Farm life
  Rural sociology
Farm implements
 USE **Agricultural machinery**
Farm laborers
 USE **Agricultural laborers**
Farm life (May subdiv. geog.)   **306.3; 630**
 UF Rural life
 BT **Country life**
  Farmers
 NT **Ranch life**
 RT **Family farms**
  Farm family
  Rural sociology
Farm life—United States   306.3; 630
Farm loans
 USE **Agricultural credit**
Farm machinery
 USE **Agricultural machinery**
Farm management   630
 BT **Farms**
  Management
 RT **Agriculture—Economic aspects**

Farm mechanics
  USE **Agricultural engineering**
          Agricultural machinery
Farm produce (May subdiv. geog.)
      338.1; 630; 631.5
  UF Agricultural products
      Crops
      Farm crops
      Products, Agricultural
  SA types of farm products [to be
      added as needed]
  BT **Food**
      Raw materials
  NT **Hay**
Farm produce—Marketing 338.1
  UF Marketing of farm produce
  BT **Marketing**
      Prices
  RT **Agriculture—Economic aspects**
Farm subsidies
  USE **Agricultural subsidies**
Farm tenancy (May subdiv. geog.)
      333.5
  Use for materials on the economic and so-
cial aspects of farm tenancy. Materials on the
legal aspects are entered under **Landlord and
tenant.**
  UF Agriculture—Tenant farming
      Tenant farming
  BT **Farms**
      Land tenure
  NT **Sharecropping**
  RT **Landlord and tenant**
Farmers (May subdiv. geog.) **305.9;**
      630.92; 920
  BT **Agriculture**
  NT **Farm life**
Farmers' cooperatives
  USE **Cooperative agriculture**
Farming
  USE **Agriculture**
Farming, Dry
  USE **Dry farming**
Farming, Organic
  USE **Organic farming**
Farms 333.76; 630; 636
  BT **Land use**
      Real estate
  NT **Family farms**
      Farm management
      Farm tenancy
      Plantations

      Vineyards
  RT **Agriculture**
Fascism (May subdiv. geog.) **320.53;**
      321.9; 335.6
  Use for materials on the political philoso-
phy, movements, or regimes that advocate a
centralized autocratic government, severe eco-
nomic and social regimentation, and the exal-
tation of nation and race over the individual.
Materials on fascism in Germany during the
Nazi regime are entered under **National socialism.**
  UF Authoritarianism
      Neo-fascism
  BT **Totalitarianism**
  NT **National socialism**
      Neo-Nazis
Fascism—United States 320.5; 973.9
Fashion (May subdiv. geog.) **391**
  Use for materials on the prevailing mode or
style of dress. Materials on the characteristic
costume of ethnic or national groups and for
materials on fancy dress and theatrical cos-
tumes are entered under **Costume.** Materials
on clothing and the art of dress from day to
day in practical situations, including historical
dress and the clothing of various professions
or classes of persons, are entered under
Clothing and dress.
  UF Style in dress
  BT **Clothing and dress**
  RT **Fashion design**
Fashion design (May subdiv. geog.)
      746.9
  BT **Clothing industry**
      Commercial art
      Design
  RT **Fashion**
Fashion designers (May subdiv. geog.)
      746.9
  UF Clothing designers
      Couturiers
  BT **Designers**
Fashion industry
  USE **Clothing industry**
Fashion models 659.1; 746.9
  UF Manikins (Fashion models)
      Mannequins (Fashion models)
      Models
      Models (Persons)
      Style manikins
  BT **Advertising**
Fashion shows 391; 659.1
  BT **Exhibitions**
Fashionable society
  USE **Upper class**

Fast food restaurants (May subdiv. geog.)
647.95
  BT **Convenience foods**
      Restaurants
Fast foods
  USE **Convenience foods**
Faster reading
  USE **Speed reading**
Fasting   178; 204; 248.4; 296.7; 613.2
  UF Abstinence
  BT **Asceticism**
      Diet
  NT **Hunger strikes**
  RT **Hunger**
      Religious holidays
      Starvation
Fasts and feasts
  USE **Religious holidays**
Fasts and feasts—Christianity
  USE **Christian holidays**
Fasts and feasts—Judaism
  USE **Jewish holidays**
Fatally ill children
  USE **Terminally ill children**
Fatally ill patients
  USE **Terminally ill**
Fate and fatalism   149
  UF Destiny
      Fortune
  BT **Philosophy**
  RT **Free will and determinism**
      Predestination
Father and child
  USE **Father-child relationship**
Father-child relationship   306.874
  UF Child and father
      Father and child
  BT **Children**
      Fathers
      Parent-child relationship
  NT **Father-daughter relationship**
      Father-son relationship
Father-daughter relationship   306.874
  UF Daughters and fathers
      Fathers and daughters
  BT **Daughters**
      Father-child relationship
      Fathers
Father-son relationship   306.874
  UF Fathers and sons
      Sons and fathers

  BT **Father-child relationship**
      Fathers
      Sons
Fatherhood   306.874
  BT **Parenthood**
  RT **Fathers**
Fathers (May subdiv. geog.)   306.874
  BT **Family**
      Men
  NT **Father-child relationship**
      Father-daughter relationship
      Father-son relationship
      Stepfathers
    · **Teenage fathers**
      Unmarried fathers
  RT **Fatherhood**
Fathers and daughters
  USE **Father-daughter relationship**
Fathers and sons
  USE **Father-son relationship**
Fathers of the church   270.1; 920
      Use for materials on the lives and thought
      of the leaders of the Christian church up to
      the time of Gregory the Great in the West and
      John of Damascus in the East. Individual
      works or collections of the writings of early
      Christian authors are entered under **Early
      Christian literature.**
  UF Church fathers
      Patristic philosophy
      Patristics
  BT **Christian biography**
  RT **Early Christian literature**
Fatigue   152.1; 612; 613.7
  UF Exhaustion
      Weariness
  BT **Physiology**
  NT **Jet lag**
  RT **Rest**
Fatness
  USE **Obesity**
Fats
  USE **Oils and fats**
Faults (Geology) (May subdiv. geog.)
      551.8
  BT **Geology**
Fauna
  USE **Animals**
      Zoology
Fawns
  USE **Deer**
Fax machines
  USE **Fax transmission**

Fax transmission   384.1; 621.382
   Use for the machines, the processes, and
the products of facsimile transmission.
   UF   Facsimile transmission
        Fax machines
   BT   Data transmission systems
        Telecommunication
Fear   152.4
   BT   Emotions
   NT   Fear in children
        Fear of the dark
        Horror
        Phobias
   RT   Anxiety
Fear in children   155.41246
   BT   Child psychology
        Fear
   NT   Fear of the dark
Fear of open spaces
   USE   Agoraphobia
Fear of the dark   152.4
   BT   Fear
        Fear in children
Feast days
   USE   Religious holidays
Feast of Dedication
   USE   Hanukkah
Feast of Lights
   USE   Hanukkah
Fecundity
   USE   Fertility
Federal aid (May subdiv. geog.)   336
   Use for materials on central government aid
in federal systems. Materials on aid from gov-
ernments at any level in non-federal systems
and on aid from states, provinces, or local
governments in federal systems are entered
under Government aid.
   SA   federal aid to specific endeavors,
         e.g. Federal aid to the arts
         [to be added as needed]
   BT   Public finance
   NT   Federal aid to education
        Federal aid to libraries
        Federal aid to minority busi-
        ness enterprises
        Federal aid to the arts
   RT   Government aid
Federal aid to education (May subdiv.
   geog.)   379.1
   UF   Education—Federal aid
   BT   Education—Government policy
        Federal aid

   RT   Colleges and universities—Fi-
        nance
        Education—Finance
Federal aid to libraries (May subdiv.
   geog.)   021.8
   UF   Libraries—Federal aid
   BT   Federal aid
        Libraries—Government policy
   RT   Library finance
Federal aid to minority business enter-
   prises (May subdiv. geog.)   338.6
   UF   Minority business enterprises—
        Federal aid
   BT   Federal aid
        Subsidies
Federal aid to the arts (May subdiv.
   geog.)   353.7; 700
   UF   Art—Federal aid
        Arts and state
        Arts—Federal aid
        Funding for the arts
        State and the arts
        State encouragement of the arts
   BT   Federal aid
   RT   Art patronage
        Arts—Government policy
Federal budget
   USE   Budget—United States
Federal-city relations   351.09
   UF   City-federal relations
        Federal-municipal relations
        Municipal-federal relations
        Urban-federal relations
   BT   Federal government
        Municipal government
Federal courts
   USE   Courts—United States
Federal debt
   USE   Public debts
Federal government   321.02; 351
   UF   Confederacies
        Federalism
   BT   Constitutional law
        Political science
        Republics
   NT   European federation
        Federal-city relations
        Federal-state relations
   RT   State governments

Federal-Indian relations
    USE   **Native Americans—Govern-**
           ment relations
Federal libraries
    USE   **Government libraries**
Federal-municipal relations
    USE   **Federal-city relations**
Federal Republic of Germany
    USE   **Germany**
           Germany (West)
Federal Reserve banks   332.1
    BT   **Banks and banking**
Federal revenue sharing
    USE   **Revenue sharing**
Federal spending policy
    USE   **United States—Appropriations**
           and expenditures
Federal-state relations   321.02
    UF   State-federal relations
    BT   **Federal government**
           State governments
Federal-state tax relations
    USE   **Intergovernmental tax relations**
Federalism
    USE   **Federal government**
Federation of Europe
    USE   **European federation**
Feedback control systems   629.8
    BT   **Automation**
    NT   **Servomechanisms**
Feedback (Psychology)   153.1
    BT   **Psychology of learning**
    NT   **Biofeedback training**
Feeding behavior in animals
    USE   **Animals—Food**
Feeds   633.2; 633.3
    UF   Fodder
    SA   types of feeds, e.g. **Oats** [to be
           added as needed]
    BT   **Animals—Food**
    NT   **Forage plants**
           Oats
           Silage and silos
    RT   **Grasses**
           Hay
           Root crops
Feeling
    USE   **Perception**
           Touch
Feelings
    USE   **Emotions**

Fees
    USE   **Salaries, wages, etc.**
Feet
    USE   **Foot**
Felidae
    USE   **Wild cats**
Fellowships
    USE   **Scholarships**
Felony
    USE   **Crime**
Female actors
    USE   **Actresses**
Female circumcision (May subdiv. geog.)
           392.1
    UF   Circumcision, Female
           Clitoridotomy
           Female genital mutilation
           Genital mutilation, Female
           Mutilation, Female genital
    BT   **Initiation rites**
Female climacteric
    USE   **Menopause**
Female friendship   302.4
    UF   Friendship between women
           Friendship in women
           Women's friendship
    BT   **Friendship**
Female genital mutilation
    USE   **Female circumcision**
Female identity
    USE   **Women—Identity**
Female-male relationship
    USE   **Man-woman relationship**
Female role
    USE   **Sex role**
Feminine identity
    USE   **Women—Identity**
Feminine psychology
    USE   **Women—Psychology**
Femininity (May subdiv. geog.)   **155.3**
    UF   Femininity (Psychology)
    BT   **Sex (Psychology)**
    RT   **Women**
Femininity of God   212; 231
    UF   God—Femininity
    BT   **God**
Femininity (Psychology)
    USE   **Femininity**
Feminism (May subdiv. geog.)   **305.42;**
           323.3
    Use for materials on the theory of the polit-
    ical and social equality of the sexes and wom-

Feminism—*Continued*

en's perspectives on various subjects. Materials on activities aimed at obtaining equal rights and opportunities for women are entered under **Women's movement.**

UF   Feminist theory

SA   types of feminist endeavors, e.g.
       Feminist criticism; Feminist theology; etc. [to be added as needed]

NT   **Feminist ethics**
       Women—History

RT   **Suffragists**
       Women's movement
       Women's rights

Feminist criticism   801

UF   Criticism, Feminist

BT   **Criticism**

Feminist ethics (May subdiv. geog.)   **170**

BT   **Ethics**
       Feminism

Feminist fiction   808.3; 808.83

BT   **Fiction**

Feminist theology   230

Use for materials on the feminist critique of traditional theology and on alternative theology from a feminist perspective.

BT   **Theology**

Feminist theory

USE   **Feminism**

Fencing   796.86

UF   Fighting

BT   **Dueling**

Feng-shui (May subdiv. geog.)   **133.3**

BT   **Divination**

Feral animals

USE   **Wildlife**

Feral cats

USE   **Wild cats**

Feral children

USE   **Wild children**

Fermentation   547; 660; 663

UF   Ferments

BT   **Chemical engineering**
       Chemistry
       Microbiology

Ferments

USE   **Fermentation**

Ferns   587; 635.9

BT   **Plants**

Fertility   573.6; 591.1

Use for general materials on fertility in animals, including humans. Materials limited to fertility in humans are entered under **Human fertility.**

UF   Fecundity

BT   **Reproduction**

NT   **Human fertility**

RT   **Infertility**

Fertility control

USE   **Birth control**

Fertility, Human

USE   **Human fertility**

Fertilization in vitro   176; 618.1; 636.089

UF   Fertilization in vitro, Human
       Fertilization, Test tube
       In vitro fertilization
       Laboratory fertilization
       Test tube babies
       Test tube fertilization

BT   **Genetic engineering**
       Reproduction

Fertilization in vitro, Human

USE   **Fertilization in vitro**

Fertilization of plants   575.6

UF   Plants—Fertilization
       Pollination

BT   **Plant physiology**
       Plants

Fertilization, Test tube

USE   **Fertilization in vitro**

Fertilizers   631.8; 668

UF   Fertilizers and manures
       Manures

BT   **Agricultural chemicals**
       Soils

NT   **Compost**
       Lime
       Nitrates
       Phosphates
       Potash

Fertilizers and manures

USE   **Fertilizers**

Festivals (May subdiv. geog.)   **394.26**

Use for materials on occasions other than holidays devoted to festive community observances or to programs of cultural events. Materials on days of general exemption from work or days publicly dedicated to the commemoration of some person, event, or principle are entered under **Holidays.** Materials on religious fasts and feasts are entered under **Religious holidays.**

Festivals—*Continued*
UF Fiestas
SA types of festivals and names of specific festivals, e.g. **Carnival** [to be added as needed]
BT **Manners and customs**
NT **Carnival**
Carnivals
Craft shows
Film festivals
Music festivals
Parades
Powwows
RT **Anniversaries**
Days
Holidays
Pageants
Religious holidays
Festivals—United States 394.260973
Fetal alcohol syndrome 618.3
BT **Social problems**
RT **Birth defects**
Growth disorders
Fetal death
USE **Miscarriage**
Fetus 571.8; 612.6
UF Unborn child
BT **Embryology**
Reproduction
Feudalism (May subdiv. geog.) 321
UF Fiefs
Vassals
BT **Land tenure**
Medieval civilization
NT **Peasantry**
RT **Chivalry**
Fever 616
SA types of fevers, e.g. **Malaria** [to be added as needed]
BT **Pathology**
NT **Malaria**
Typhoid fever
RT **Body temperature**
Fiber content of food
USE **Food—Fiber content**
Fiber glass
USE **Glass fibers**
Fiberglass
USE **Glass fibers**

Fibers 677
UF Textile fibers
NT **Cotton**
Flax
Glass fibers
Hemp
Linen
Paper
Silk
Wool
Fibers, Glass
USE **Glass fibers**
Fiction 808.3
Use for collections and materials about fiction from several countries and for materials on fiction as a literary form, not for individual works.
UF Novels
Stories
SA fiction of particular national literatures, e.g. **American fiction**; genres of fiction, e.g. **Fantasy fiction**; and subjects, names of places, and personal and corporate names with the subdivision *Fiction,* to express the theme or subject content of collections of fiction, e.g. **Slavery—United States—Fiction; United States—History—1861-1865, Civil War—Fiction; Ohio—Fiction; Napoleon I, Emperor of the French, 1769-1821—Fiction;** etc. [to be added as needed]
BT **Literature**
NT **Adventure fiction**
Allegories
Allegory
American fiction
Bible fiction
Bildungsromans
Biographical fiction
Black humor (Literature)
Children's stories
Christian fiction
Didactic fiction
English fiction
Epistolary fiction
Erotic fiction
Fables

Fiction—*Continued*
     Fairy tales
     Fantasy fiction
     Feminist fiction
     Folklore
     Graphic novels
     Historical fiction
     Horror fiction
     Humorous fiction
     Interplanetary voyages
     Jewish religious fiction
     Legal stories
     Legends
     Love stories
     Medical novels
     Movie novels
     Mystery fiction
     Occult fiction
     Pastoral fiction
     Picaresque literature
     Plot-your-own stories
     Radio and television novels
     Religious fiction
     Romances
     Romans à clef
     School stories
     Science fiction
     Sea stories
     Short stories
     Short story
     War stories
     Western stories
Fiction for children
   USE   Children's stories
Fiction—History and criticism   **809.3**
Fiction—Technique   **808.3**
   BT   Authorship
Fictional characters
   USE   Characters and characteristics
       in literature
Fictional plots
   USE   Stories, plots, etc.
Fictitious characters
   USE   Characters and characteristics
       in literature
Fictitious names
   USE   Pseudonyms
Fictitious places
   USE   Geographical myths
Fiddle
   USE   Violins

Fiduciaries
   USE   Trusts and trustees
Fiefs
   USE   Feudalism
       Land tenure
Field athletics
   USE   Track athletics
Field hockey   **796.35**
   BT   Sports
Field hospitals
   USE   Military hospitals
       Military medicine
Field photography
   USE   Outdoor photography
Field trips   **069; 371.3**
   UF   School excursions
       School trips
   BT   Student activities
Fiestas
   USE   Festivals
Fifteenth century
   USE   World history—15th century
Fifth column
   USE   Subversive activities
       World War, 1939-1945—Col-
       laborationists
Fighting
   USE   Battles
       Boxing
       Bullfights
       Dueling
       Fencing
       Gladiators
       Military art and science
       Naval art and science
       Self-defense
       Self-defense for women
       War
Figure drawing   **743.4**
   UF   Human figure in art
   BT   Artistic anatomy
       Drawing
   RT   Figure painting
Figure painting   **757**
   UF   Human figure in art
   BT   Artistic anatomy
       Painting
   RT   Figure drawing
       Portrait painting
Figure skating
   USE   Ice skating

Figures of speech   808
    UF   English language—Figures of
           speech
           Imagery
           Tropes
    BT   **Rhetoric**
           Symbolism
Files and filing   005.74; 025.3; 651.5
    UF   Alphabetizing
           Filing systems
    BT   **Office management**
    RT   **Indexing**
Filing systems
    USE **Files and filing**
Filling stations
    USE **Service stations**
Fills (Earthwork)
    USE **Landfills**
Film adaptations   791.43
    May be used for individual works, collec-
    tions, or materials about film adaptations of
    material from other media.
    UF   Adaptations
           Filmed books
           Films from books
           Literature—Film and video adap-
           tations
           Motion picture adaptations
    SA   names of authors, titles of anon-
           ymous literary works, types of
           literature, and types of musi-
           cal compositions with the
           subdivision *Adaptations,* for
           individual works, collections,
           or criticism and interpretation
           of literary, cinematic, video,
           or television adaptations, e.g.,
           Shakespeare, William, 1564-
           1616—Adaptations;
           Beowulf—Adaptations; Ar-
           thurian romances—Adapta-
           tions; etc. [to be added as
           needed]
    BT   **Motion pictures**
Film catalogs
    USE **Motion pictures—Catalogs**
Film direction
    USE **Motion pictures—Production**
          and direction
Film directors
    USE **Motion picture producers and**
          directors

Film epics
    USE **Epic films**
Film festivals   791.43
    UF   Motion picture festivals
           Movie festivals
    BT   **Festivals**
Film industry (Motion pictures)
    USE **Motion picture industry**
Film noir   791.43
    UF   Crime films
           Films noirs
    BT   **Motion pictures**
    RT   **Mystery films**
Film posters   741.6; 791.43
    UF   Motion picture posters
           Motion pictures—Posters
           Movie posters
           Playbills
    BT   **Posters**
Film producers
    USE **Motion picture producers and**
          directors
Film production
    USE **Motion pictures—Production**
          and direction
Film projectors
    USE **Projectors**
Film scripts
    USE **Motion picture plays**
Filmed books
    USE **Film adaptations**
Filmmaking
    USE **Motion pictures—Production**
          and direction
Filmography
    USE **Motion pictures—Catalogs**
          and types of motion pictures
          with the subdivision *Catalogs,*
          e.g. **Science fiction films—**
          Catalogs; and subjects, class-
          es of persons, corporate enti-
          ties, and names of individual
          persons with the subdivision
          Filmography, e.g. **Animals—**
          Filmography; Shakespeare,
          William, 1564-1616—Filmog-
          raphy; etc. [to be added as
          needed]
Films
    USE **Filmstrips**
          Motion pictures

Films from books
   USE **Film adaptations**
Films noirs
   USE **Film noir**
Filmstrips   371.33; 778.2
   UF Films
         Strip films
   BT **Audiovisual materials**
         Photography
   RT **Slides (Photography)**
Finance (May subdiv. geog.)   **332**
   Use for general materials on the management of money and credit. Materials on the raising and expenditure of funds in the public sector are entered under **Public finance.**
   UF Funding
         Funds
   SA subjects, ethnic groups, names of wars, and names of corporate bodies with the subdivision *Finance*, e.g. **Education—Finance** [to be added as needed]
   BT **Economics**
   NT **Bankruptcy**
         Banks and banking
         Bonds
         Capital
         Capital market
         Church finance
         Colleges and universities—Finance
         Commerce
         Corporations—Finance
         Credit
         Debt
         Education—Finance
         Endowments
         Financial crises
         Foreign exchange
         Fund raising
         Income
         Inflation (Finance)
         Insurance
         Interest (Economics)
         Investments
         Library finance
         Loans
         Money
         Personal finance
         Prices
         Public finance

         Railroads—Finance
         Securities
         Speculation
         Stock exchanges
         United Nations—Finance
         Wealth
   RT **Monetary policy**
Finance, Household
   USE **Household budgets**
Finance—Mathematics
   USE **Business mathematics**
Finance, Municipal
   USE **Municipal finance**
Finance, Personal
   USE **Personal finance**
Finance, Public
   USE **Public finance**
Finance—United States   **332.0973; 336.73**
Financial accounting
   USE **Accounting**
Financial aid to students
   USE **Student aid**
Financial crashes
   USE **Financial crises**
Financial crises (May subdiv. geog.)   **338 5**
   UF Crashes (Finance)
         Financial crashes
         Financial panics
         Panics (Finance)
         Stock exchange crashes
         Stock market panics
   BT **Finance**
   RT **Business cycles**
Financial institutions (May subdiv. geog.)   **332.1**
   UF Lending institutions
   BT **Associations**
   NT **Capital market**
Financial panics
   USE **Financial crises**
Financial planning, Personal
   USE **Personal finance**
Financiers
   USE **Capitalists and financiers**
Finding things
   USE **Lost and found possessions**
Finger alphabet
   USE **Deaf—Means of communication**

Finger games
    USE **Finger play**
Finger marks
    USE **Fingerprints**
Finger painting   751.4
    UF Painting, Finger
    BT **Child artists**
        Painting
Finger play   793.4
    UF Finger games
    BT **Play**
Finger pressure therapy
    USE **Acupressure**
Finger prints
    USE **Fingerprints**
Fingerprints   363.25
    UF Finger marks
        Finger prints
    BT **Anthropometry**
        Criminal investigation
        Criminals—Identification
        Identification
Finishes and finishing   667; 684.1; 698;
    745.7
    UF Finishing
        Finishing materials
    SA topics with the subdivision *Fin-*
        ishing, e.g. **Metals—Finish-**
        ing; or with the subdivision
        Painting, e.g. **Automobiles—**
        Painting [to be added as
        needed]
    BT **Materials**
    NT **Industrial painting**
        Lacquer and lacquering
        Metals—Finishing
        Paint
        Varnish and varnishing
        Wood finishing
Finishing
    USE **Finishes and finishing**
        and topics with the subdivision
        Finishing, e.g. **Metals—Fin-**
        ishing [to be added as need-
        ed]
Finishing materials
    USE **Finishes and finishing**
Finno-Russian War, 1939-1940
    USE **Russo-Finnish War, 1939-1940**

Fire   536; 541
    BT **Chemistry**
    NT **Fires**
        Fuel
    RT **Combustion**
        Heat
Fire bombs
    USE **Incendiary bombs**
Fire departments (May subdiv. geog.)
    628.9
    UF Fire stations
    RT **Fire fighters**
Fire engines   628.9
    BT **Engines**
        Fire fighting
Fire etching
    USE **Pyrography**
Fire fighters (May subdiv. geog.)
    363.37092; 920
    UF Firemen and firewomen
    RT **Fire departments**
Fire fighting (May subdiv. geog.)   628.9
    BT **Fire prevention**
        Fires
    NT **Fire engines**
Fire insurance   368.1
    UF Insurance, Fire
    BT **Insurance**
    NT **Fireproofing**
Fire prevention (May subdiv. geog.)
    363.37; 628.9
    UF Prevention of fire
    SA types of institutions, buildings,
        industries, and vehicles with
        the subdivision *Fires and fire*
        prevention, e.g. **Nuclear pow-**
        er plants—Fires and fire
        prevention [to be added as
        needed]
    BT **Fires**
    NT **Fire fighting**
        Fireproofing
        Nuclear power plants—Fires
          and fire prevention
Fire stations
    USE **Fire departments**
Firearms (May subdiv. geog.)   623.4;
    739.7
    UF Guns
        Small arms

Firearms—*Continued*
    SA   types of firearms [to be added
          as needed]
    BT   **Weapons**
    NT   **Gunpowder**
          Handguns
          Rifles
          Shotguns
    RT   **Ammunition**
          Shooting
Firearms control
    USE **Gun control**
Firearms industry (May subdiv. geog.)
        338.4; 683.4
    Use for materials on the small arms indus-
    try. Materials on the production of military
    weapons are entered under **Defense industry.**
    UF   Firearms industry and trade
          Firearms trade
          Gunsmithing
          Weapons industry
    BT   **Industries**
Firearms industry and trade
    USE **Firearms industry**
Firearms—Law and legislation
    USE **Gun control**
Firearms trade
    USE **Firearms industry**
Firemen and firewomen
    USE **Fire fighters**
Fireplaces   **697; 749**
    BT   **Architecture—Details**
          Buildings
          Heating
          Space heaters
    RT   **Chimneys**
Fireproofing   **628.9; 693.8**
    BT   **Fire insurance**
          Fire prevention
Fires (May subdiv. geog.)   **363.37; 904**
    SA   types of institutions, buildings,
          industries, and vehicles with
          the subdivision *Fires and fire
          prevention,* e.g. **Nuclear pow-
          er plants—Fires and fire
          prevention** [to be added as
          needed]
    BT   **Accidents**
          Disasters
          Fire
    NT   **Fire fighting**
          Fire prevention

      Forest fires
      **Nuclear power plants—Fires
         and fire prevention**
Fires and fire prevention
    USE types of institutions, buildings,
          industries, and vehicles with
          the subdivision *Fires and fire
          prevention,* e.g. **Nuclear pow-
          er plants—Fires and fire
          prevention** [to be added as
          needed]
Fireworks   **662**
    BT   **Amusements**
Firms
    USE **Business enterprises**
First aid   **362.18; 616.02**
    UF   Emergencies
          Injuries
          Wounded, First aid to
    BT   **Health self-care**
          Home accidents
          Medicine
          Nursing
          Rescue work
          Sick
    NT   **Artificial respiration**
          Bandages
          CPR (First aid)
    RT   **Accidents**
          Lifesaving
First editions   **094**
    UF   Bibliography—First editions
          Books—First editions
    SA   types of publications, types of
          literature, and names of au-
          thors and composers with the
          subdivision *First editions,* e.g.
          **English literature—First edi-
          tions** [to be added as needed]
    BT   **Editions**
First generation children
    USE **Children of immigrants**
First ladies—United States
    USE **Presidents' spouses—United
         States**
First names
    USE **Personal names**
First nations
    USE **Native Americans—Canada**
First World War
    USE **World War, 1914-1918**

Firstborn child
    USE   **Birth order**
Fiscal policy (May subdiv. geog.)   **336.3**
    UF   Government policy
    BT   **Economic policy**
         Public finance
    RT   **Monetary policy**
Fiscal policy—United States   **336.73**
    UF   United States—Fiscal policy
Fish
    USE   **Fish as food**
          Fishes
Fish as food   **641.3**
    UF   Fish
    BT   **Cooking**
         Fishes
         Food
    RT   **Seafood**
Fish culture (May subdiv. geog.)   **639.3**
    Use for materials on the cultivation of fish in captivity. Materials on fishing as an industry are entered under **Commercial fishing.**
    UF   Fish farming
         Fish hatcheries
    BT   **Aquaculture**
    RT   **Aquariums**
Fish farming
    USE   **Fish culture**
Fish hatcheries
    USE   **Fish culture**
Fisheries
    USE   **Commercial fishing**
Fishes (May subdiv. geog.)   **597**
    UF   Fish
         Ichthyology
    SA   types of fishes, e.g. **Salmon** [to be added as needed]
    BT   **Aquatic animals**
    NT   **Fish as food**
         Goldfish
         Salmon
         Tropical fish
    RT   **Aquariums**
Fishes—Ecology (May subdiv. geog.)   **597**
    BT   **Ecology**
Fishes—Geographical distribution   **597.09**
    BT   **Biogeography**
Fishes—Photography
    USE   **Photography of fishes**
Fishes—United States   **597.0973**

Fishing (May subdiv. geog.)   **799.1**
    Use for materials on fishing as a sport. Materials on fishing as an industry are entered under **Commercial fishing.**
    UF   Angling
    SA   types of fishing [to be added as needed]
    BT   **Sports**
    NT   **Artificial flies**
         Fly casting
         Saltwater fishing
         Spear fishing
         Trout fishing
Fishing, Commercial
    USE   **Commercial fishing**
Fishing—Equipment and supplies   **799.1**
    UF   Fishing tackle
Fishing flies
    USE   **Artificial flies**
Fishing industry
    USE   **Commercial fishing**
Fishing tackle
    USE   **Fishing—Equipment and supplies**
Fishing—United States   **799.10973**
Fitness
    USE   **Physical fitness**
Five-day work week
    USE   **Hours of labor**
Fixed ideas
    USE   **Obsessive-compulsive disorder**
Fixing
    USE   **Repairing**
Flags (May subdiv. geog.)   **929.9**
    UF   Banners
         Ensigns
    BT   **Heraldry**
    RT   **National emblems**
         Signals and signaling
Flags—United States   **929.9**
    UF   American flag
         United States—Flags
Flats
    USE   **Apartments**
Flatware, Silver
    USE   **Silverware**
Flavoring essences   **664**
    BT   **Cooking**
         Essences and essential oils
         Food

Flax   633.5; 677
   BT   Fibers
        Yarn
   RT   Linen
Flea markets (May subdiv. geog.)   658.8
   BT   Markets
        Secondhand trade
Flexible hours of labor   331.25
   UF   Alternative work schedules
        Flexible work hours
        Flextime
        Four-day week
        Hours of labor, Flexible
   BT   Hours of labor
Flexible work hours
   USE   Flexible hours of labor
Flextime
   USE   Flexible hours of labor
Flies   595.77
   UF   Fly
        House flies
   SA   types of flies [to be added as
        needed]
   BT   Household pests
        Insects
        Pests
   NT   Fruit flies
Flies, Artificial
   USE   Artificial flies
Flight   629.13
   UF   Flying
   SA   types of animals with the subdi-
        vision *Flight*, e.g. **Birds—**
        Flight [to be added as need-
        ed]
   BT   Locomotion
   NT   Animal flight
   RT   Aeronautics
Flight attendants   387.7
   UF   Airline hostesses
        Airline stewardesses
        Airline stewards
        Stewardesses, Airline
        Stewards, Airline
   BT   Airlines
Flight to the moon
   USE   Space flight to the moon
Flight training
   USE   Aeronautics—Study and teach-
         ing
         Airplanes—Piloting

Flights around the world
   USE   Aeronautics—Flights
Flint implements
   USE   Stone implements
Floating hospitals
   USE   Hospital ships
Floats (Parades)
   USE   Parades
Flood control (May subdiv. geog.)   627
   UF   Flood prevention
   BT   Hydraulic engineering
   RT   Forest influences
Flood prevention
   USE   Flood control
Floods (May subdiv. geog.)   363.34;
            551.48; 904
      May also be subdivided by names of rivers
      or river valleys, e.g. **Floods—Mississippi**
      River.
   BT   Meteorology
        Natural disasters
        Rain
        Water
   RT   Rivers
Floods and forests
   USE   Forest influences
Floods—Mississippi River   363.34
Floors   690; 721
   BT   Architecture—Details
        Buildings
Flora
   USE   Botany
        Plants
Floral decoration
   USE   Flower arrangement
Floriculture
   USE   Flower gardening
Florists' designs
   USE   Flower arrangement
Flour   641.3; 664
   RT   Grain
Flour mills   664
   UF   Grist mills
        Milling (Flour)
   BT   Mills
Flow charts
   USE   Graphic methods
        System analysis
Flowcharting
   USE   Graphic methods
        System analysis

Flower arrangement   745.92

Use for materials on the artistic arrangement of flowers, including decoration of houses, churches, etc., with flowers.

UF   Designs, Floral
       Floral decoration
       Florists' designs
       Flowers—Arrangement
BT   **Decoration and ornament**
       Flowers
       Table setting and decoration
Flower drying
USE   **Flowers—Drying**
Flower gardening (May subdiv. geog.)
       635.9

Use for practical materials on the cultivation of flowering plants for either commercial or private purposes.

UF   Floriculture
SA   types of flowers, e.g. **Roses** [to
       be added as needed]
BT   **Gardening**
       Horticulture
NT   **Annuals (Plants)**
       Bulbs
       Greenhouses
       House plants
       Ornamental plants
       Perennials
RT   **Container gardening**
       Flowers
       Window gardening
Flower language
USE   **Language of flowers**
Flower painting and illustration
USE   **Botanical illustration**
       Flowers in art
Flower prints
USE   **Flowers in art**
Flower shows   635.9074
UF   Flowers—Exhibitions
BT   **Exhibitions**
Flowers (May subdiv. geog.)   **575.6;**
       582.13

Use for general materials on flowers. Materials limited to the cultivation of flowers are entered under **Flower gardening.**

SA   types of flowers, e.g. **Roses** [to
       be added as needed]
BT   **Plants**
NT   **Annuals (Plants)**
       Flower arrangement
       Perennials

Roses
State flowers
Wild flowers
RT   **Flower gardening**
Flowers—Arrangement
USE   **Flower arrangement**
Flowers, Artificial
USE   **Artificial flowers**
Flowers, Drying
USE   **Flowers—Drying**
Flowers—Drying   745.92
UF   Dried flowers
       Flower drying
       Flowers, Drying
BT   **Plants—Collection and preservation**
Flowers—Exhibitions
USE   **Flower shows**
Flowers in art   758
UF   Flower painting and illustration
       Flower prints
BT   **Art—Themes**
Flowers—United States   582.130973
Flu
USE   **Influenza**
Fluid mechanics   532; 620.1

Use for materials on the branch of mechanics dealing with the properties of liquids or gases, either at rest or in motion.

UF   Hydromechanics
BT   **Mechanics**
NT   **Gases**
       Hydraulic engineering
       Hydraulics
       Hydrodynamics
       Hydrostatics
       Liquids
Fluorescent lighting   621.32
UF   Electric lighting, Fluorescent
BT   **Electric lighting**
Fluoridation of water
USE   **Water fluoridation**
Flute
USE   **Flutes**
Flutes   788.3
UF   Flute
BT   **Wind instruments**
Fly
USE   **Flies**

Fly casting   799.12
    UF   Fly fishing
    BT   **Fishing**
    NT   **Artificial flies**
Fly fishing
    USE   **Fly casting**
Flying
    USE   **Flight**
Flying saucers
    USE   **Unidentified flying objects**
FM radio
    USE   **Radio frequency modulation**
Foals
    USE   **Horses**
         Ponies
Fodder
    USE   **Feeds**
Fog   551.57
    BT   **Atmosphere**
         Meteorology
Fog signals
    USE   **Signals and signaling**
Folding of napkins
    USE   **Napkin folding**
Foliage
    USE   **Leaves**
Folk art   745
    Use for materials on objects of fine or decorative art produced in a peasant, popular, or naive style, often in cultural isolation and by unschooled artists or artisans.
    UF   Peasant art
    SA   folk art of particular countries or ethnic groups, e.g. **American folk art** [to be added as needed]
    BT   **Art**
         Art and society
    NT   **American folk art**
    RT   **Arts and crafts movement**
         Decorative arts
         Handicraft
Folk art, American
    USE   **American folk art**
Folk beliefs
    USE   **Folklore**
         Superstition
Folk biology
    USE   **Ethnobiology**
Folk dances
    USE   **Folk dancing**

Folk dancing (May subdiv. geog.)   **793.3**
    UF   Folk dances
         National dances
    SA   dance of particular ethnic groups, e.g. **Native American dance** [to be added as needed]
    BT   **Dance**
    NT   **Native American dance**
         Square dancing
Folk dancing—United States   793.3
    UF   American folk dancing
Folk drama   808.2; 808.82
    May be used for collections or materials about folk drama, not for individual works.
    UF   Folk plays
    BT   **Drama**
    NT   **Puppets and puppet plays**
Folk literature   398.2
    SA   types of folk literature, e.g. **Jewish folk literature** [to be added as needed]
    BT   **Folklore**
         Literature
    NT   **Jewish folk literature**
Folk lore
    USE   **Folklore**
Folk medicine
    USE   **Traditional medicine**
Folk music (May subdiv. geog.)   **781.62**
    BT   **Music**
Folk music—United States   781.6200973
    UF   American folk music
    NT   **Blues music**
         Country music
Folk plays
    USE   **Folk drama**
Folk psychology
    USE   **Ethnopsychology**
Folk songs (May subdiv. geog.)
         782.42162
    Use for materials about folk songs and collections of folk songs that include both words and music. Materials about ballads and collections of ballads without music are entered under **Ballads.**
    SA   folk songs of particular ethnic groups, e.g. **Creole folk songs** [to be added as needed]
    BT   **Folklore**
         Songs
         Vocal music

Folk songs—*Continued*
   NT   **Carols**
         Creole folk songs
   RT   **Ballads**
         National songs
Folk songs, Creole
   USE **Creole folk songs**
Folk songs—France   782.4216200944
   UF   Folk songs, French
         France—Folk songs
         French folk songs
Folk songs, French
   USE **Folk songs—France**
Folk songs—Ohio   782.42162009771
Folk songs—United States
         782.4216200973
   UF   American folk songs
   BT   **American songs**
   NT   **Spirituals (Songs)**
Folk tales
   USE **Folklore**
         Legends
Folk zoology
   USE **Ethnozoology**
Folklore (May subdiv. geog.)   **398**
   Use for general materials on folklore. May
   also be used for individual works, collections,
   and materials about stories based on spoken
   rather than written traditions.
   UF   Folk beliefs
         Folk lore
         Folk tales
         Tales
         Traditions
   SA   topics as themes in folklore with
         the subdivision *Folklore,* e.g.
         Plants—Folklore; names of
         ethnic or occupational groups
         with the subdivision *Folklore,*
         e.g. **Inuit—Folklore;** types of
         folkloric creatures, e.g. **Elves;**
         and names of individual leg-
         endary characters, e.g. **Bun-**
         yan, Paul (Legendary char-
         acter) [to be added as need-
         ed]
   BT   **Ethnology**
         Fiction
         Manners and customs
   NT   **African Americans—Folklore**
         Animals—Folklore
         Blacks—Folklore

         Chapbooks
         Charms
         Dragons
         Elves
         Fairies
         Folk literature
         Folk songs
         Ghosts
         Giants
         Gnomes
         Goblins
         Grail
         Inuit—Folklore
         Jews—Folklore
         Monsters
         Native Americans—Folklore
         Nursery rhymes
         Plants—Folklore
         Proverbs
         Roland (Legendary character)
         Sagas
         Superstition
         Tall tales
         Tongue twisters
         Urban folklore
         Vampires
         Weather—Folklore
         Wicca
         Witchcraft
   RT   **Fables**
         Fairy tales
         Legends
         Material culture
         Mythology
         Storytelling
Folklore, Medical
   USE **Traditional medicine**
Folklore—United States   398.0973
   NT   **Bunyan, Paul (Legendary char-**
         acter)
Folkways
   USE **Manners and customs**
Food   **641; 641.3; 664**
   SA   types of foods, names of specif-
         ic foods, and subjects with
         the subdivision *Food* [to be
         added as needed]
   BT   **Home economics**
   NT   **Animals—Food**
         Artificial foods
         Beverages

Food—*Continued*

        Bread
        Chocolate
        Convenience foods
        Dietetic foods
        Dining
        Dried foods
        Edible plants
        Eggs
        Farm produce
        Fish as food
        Flavoring essences
        Food of animal origin
        Frozen foods
        Fruit
        Honey
        Meat
        Milk
        Natural foods
        Nuts
        Prepared cereals
        School children—Food
        Seafood
        Snack foods
        Spices
        Sugar
        Vegetables
        Vitamins
  RT Cooking
        Diet
        Food industry
        Gastronomy
        Grocery trade
        Nutrition

Food additives   **641.3; 664**
  UF Additives, Food
  BT Food—Analysis
        Food—Preservation

Food adulteration and inspection (May
    subdiv. geog.)   **363.19**
  UF Adulteration of food
        Analysis of food
        Food inspection
        Inspection of food
        Pure food
  BT Consumer protection
        Public health
  NT Food contamination
        Meat inspection
        Milk supply
  RT Food—Law and legislation

Food allergies
  USE **Food allergy**
Food allergy   616.97
  UF Allergies, Food
        Allergy, Food
        Food allergies
  SA types of food allergies [to be
        added as needed]
  BT **Allergy**
Food—Analysis   664
  Use for materials on methods of analyzing
foods. Materials presenting the results of the
analysis of foods are entered under **Food—
Composition.**
  UF Analysis of food
        Chemistry of food
        Food chemistry
  SA types of foods with the subdivi-
        sion *Analysis,* e.g. **Milk—
        Analysis** [to be added as
        needed]
  BT **Analytical chemistry
        Industrial chemistry**
  NT **Food additives**
  RT **Food—Composition**
Food assistance programs
  USE **Food relief**
Food—Bacteriology
  USE **Food—Microbiology**
Food banks (May subdiv. geog.)   **363.8**
  BT **Food relief**
Food buying
  USE **Grocery shopping**
Food—Caloric content   613.2
  UF Caloric content of foods
        Calories (Food)
        Food calories
  BT **Food—Composition**
Food calories
  USE **Food—Caloric content**
Food, Canned
  USE **Canning and preserving**
Food chains (Ecology)   **577**
  BT **Animals—Food
        Ecology**
Food chemistry
  USE **Food—Analysis
        Food—Composition**
Food—Cholesterol content   613.2
  UF Cholesterol content of food
  BT **Food—Composition**

Food—Composition   641; 664
> Use for materials presenting the results of the analysis of foods. Materials on methods of analyzing foods are entered under **Food—Analysis.**

UF   Chemistry of food
  Food chemistry

SA   food and types of food with subdivisions to indicate the particular content being analyzed, e.g. **Food—Cholesterol content** [to be added as needed]

NT   **Food—Caloric content**
  Food—Cholesterol content
  Food—Fiber content
  Food—Sodium content

RT   **Food—Analysis**

Food contamination (May subdiv. geog.)
  363.19

UF   Contaminated food

BT   **Food adulteration and inspection**

Food contamination—Press coverage
  (May subdiv. geog.)   **070.4**

Food control
  USE   **Food supply**

Food, Cost of
  USE   **Cost and standard of living**

Food coupons
  USE   **Food stamps**

Food customs
  USE   **Eating customs**

Food—Fiber content   613.2

UF   Dietary fiber
  Fiber content of food
  Roughage

BT   **Food—Composition**

Food for invalids
  USE   **Cooking for the sick**

Food for school children
  USE   **School children—Food**

Food, Freeze dried
  USE   **Freeze-dried foods**

Food habits
  USE   **Eating customs**

Food industry (May subdiv. geog.)
  338.1
> Use for materials on the processing and marketing of food.

UF   Food preparation
  Food preparation industry
  Food processing

  Food processing industry
  Food trade

SA   type of food industries, e.g.
  Beverage industry [to be added as needed]

BT   **Agricultural industry**

NT   **Beverage industry**
  Food service
  Grocery trade
  Meat industry

RT   **Food**

Food inspection
  USE   **Food adulteration and inspection**

Food—Labeling   363.19; 641

UF   Food labels

Food labels
  USE   **Food—Labeling**

Food—Law and legislation (May subdiv. geog.)   **344**

UF   Food laws

BT   **Law**
  Legislation

RT   **Food adulteration and inspection**

Food laws
  USE   **Food—Law and legislation**

Food—Microbiology   664

UF   Food—Bacteriology

BT   **Microbiology**

Food of animal origin   641.3
> Use for materials on human food of animal origin. Materials on the food and food habits of animals are entered under **Animals—Food.**

UF   Animal food
  Animals as food
  Animals, Edible

BT   **Food**

Food—Packaging   664

UF   Groceries—Packaging

BT   **Packaging**

Food plants
  USE   **Edible plants**

Food poisoning   615.9

BT   **Poisons and poisoning**

Food preparation
  USE   **Cooking**
    Food industry

Food preparation industry
  USE   **Food industry**

Food—Preservation   641.4; 664
UF   Preservation of food
SA   types of foods with the subdivision *Preservation* [to be added as needed]
NT   **Canning and preserving**
    Cold storage
    Food additives
    Fruit—Preservation
RT   **Dried foods**
    Frozen foods
Food processing
USE   **Food industry**
Food processing industry
USE   **Food industry**
Food—Purchasing
USE   **Grocery shopping**
Food relief (May subdiv. geog.)   **363.8**
UF   Food assistance programs
SA   types of food relief, e.g. **Meals on wheels programs;** and names of wars with the subdivision *Civilian relief* or *Food supply* [to be added as needed]
BT   **Charities**
    Disaster relief
    Public welfare
    Unemployed
NT   **Food banks**
    Food stamps
    Meals on wheels programs
    World War, 1939-1945—Civilian relief
    World War, 1939-1945—Food supply
Food service   642; 647.95
Use for materials on the preparation, delivery, and serving of ready-to-eat foods in large quantities outside of the home. Materials solely on the preparation of food in large quantities are entered under **Quantity cooking.**
UF   Cooking for institutions
    Mass feeding
    Volume feeding
BT   **Food industry**
    Service industries
NT   **Bartending**
    Catering
    Restaurants
    Waiters and waitresses
RT   **Quantity cooking**

Food—Sodium content   613.2
UF   Sodium content of food
BT   **Food—Composition**
Food stamp program
USE   **Food stamps**
Food stamps (May subdiv. geog.)   **363.8**
UF   Food coupons
    Food stamp program
BT   **Food relief**
Food supply (May subdiv. geog.)   **363.8**
Use for economic materials on the availability of food in general and on the conservation of food in wartime.
UF   Food control
SA   names of wars with the subdivision *Food supply,* e.g. **World War, 1939-1945—Food supply** [to be added as needed]
NT   **Famines**
RT   **Agriculture**
Food trade
USE   **Food industry**
Fools and jesters   791.092; 920
UF   Court fools
    Jesters
BT   **Comedians**
    Courts and courtiers
    Entertainers
Foot   611; 612
UF   Feet
BT   **Anatomy**
Foot—Care   617.5
UF   Foot—Care and hygiene
BT   **Podiatry**
Foot—Care and hygiene
USE   **Foot—Care**
Foot injuries
USE   **Foot—Wounds and injuries**
Foot—Paralysis   616.8
BT   **Paralysis**
Foot—Wounds and injuries   617.5
UF   Foot injuries
RT   **Podiatry**
Football (May subdiv. geog.)   **796.332**
BT   **Ball games**
    Sports
NT   **Soccer**
Football—Coaching   796.33207
BT   **Coaching (Athletics)**
Footwear
USE   **Shoes**

Forage plants (May subdiv. geog.)
633.2
SA names of forage plants [to be
added as needed]
BT **Economic botany**
Feeds
Plants
NT **Alfalfa**
Corn
Hay
Silage and silos
Soybean
RT **Grasses**
Force and energy 531
UF Conservation of energy
Energy
BT **Power (Mechanics)**
RT **Dynamics**
Mechanics
Motion
Quantum theory
Forced indoctrination
USE **Brainwashing**
Forced labor (May subdiv. geog.)
331.11
UF Compulsory labor
Conscript labor
BT **Crimes against humanity**
Labor
NT **Convict labor**
Peonage
RT **Slavery**
Forced migration (May subdiv. geog.)
325
BT **Internal migration**
Forced removal of Indians
USE **Native Americans—Relocation**
Forced repatriation
USE names of wars with the subdivi-
sion *Forced repatriation,* e.g.
World War, 1939-1945—
Forced repatriation [to be
added as needed]
Ford automobile 629.222
BT **Automobiles**
Forecasting 003
UF Forecasts
Futurology
Predictions

SA types of forecasting, e.g. **Weath-**
er forecasting; and subjects
and names of countries, cities,
etc., with the subdivision
Forecasting, e.g. **Energy con-**
sumption—Forecasting [to be
added as needed]
NT **Business forecasting**
Economic forecasting
Weather forecasting
Forecasts
USE **Forecasting**
Foreign affairs
USE **International relations**
Foreign aid (May subdiv. geog.) **338.91**
Use for general materials on international
economic aid given in the form of gifts, loans,
relief grants, etc. Materials limited to foreign
aid in the form of technical expertise are en-
tered under **Technical assistance.**
UF Aid to developing areas
Assistance to developing areas
Economic aid
Economic assistance
Foreign aid program
Foreign assistance
SA foreign aid from particular coun-
tries, e.g. **American foreign**
aid [to be added as needed]
BT **Economic policy**
International cooperation
International economic rela-
tions
NT **American foreign aid**
Technical assistance
World War, 1939-1945—Civil-
ian relief
RT **Reconstruction (1914-1939)**
Reconstruction (1939-1951)
Foreign aid program
USE **Foreign aid**
Military assistance
Technical assistance
Foreign area studies
USE **Area studies**
Foreign assistance
USE **Foreign aid**
Foreign automobiles (May subdiv. geog.)
629.222
UF Automobiles, Foreign
Foreign cars

Foreign automobiles—*Continued*
- SA names of specific makes and models [to be added as needed]
- BT **Automobiles**

Foreign cars
- USE **Foreign automobiles**

Foreign commerce
- USE **International trade**

Foreign countries
- USE ethnic and national groups, individual languages and literatures, military services, and types of publications qualified by language or nationality with the subdivision *Foreign countries,* e.g. **Americans—Foreign countries** [to be added as needed]

Foreign economic relations
- USE **International economic relations**
- and names of countries with the subdivision *Foreign economic relations,* e.g. **United States—Foreign economic relations** [to be added as needed]

Foreign economic relations—United States
- USE **United States—Foreign economic relations**

Foreign exchange (May subdiv. geog.)
332.4
- UF Exchange rates
  International exchange
- BT **Banks and banking**
  Exchange
  Finance
  Money

Foreign influences
- USE subjects, ethnic groups, and literatures with the subdivision *Foreign influences,* e.g. **United States—Civilization—Foreign influences** [to be added as needed]

Foreign investments (May subdiv. geog.)
332.6
- UF International investment
  Investments, Foreign
- BT **Investments**
  Multinational corporations

Foreign language dictionaries
- USE **English language—Dictionaries—French**
  French language—Dictionaries—English

Foreign language laboratories
- USE **Language laboratories**

Foreign language phrases
- USE **English language—Foreign words and phrases**
  Modern languages—Conversation and phrase books

Foreign military sales
- USE **Arms transfers**

Foreign missions, Christian
- USE **Christian missions**

Foreign opinion
- USE names of countries with the subdivision *Foreign opinion,* which may be further subdivided by the country holding the opinion, e.g. **United States—Foreign opinion; United States—Foreign opinion—France;** etc. [to be added as needed]

Foreign policy
- USE **International relations**

Foreign population
- USE **Aliens**
  Immigrants
  Immigration and emigration
  Minorities
  Population
- and names of countries with the subdivision *Population,* e.g. **United States—Population;** or with the subdivision *Immigration and emigration,* e.g. **United States—Immigration and emigration** [to be added as needed]

Foreign public opinion
- USE names of countries with the subdivision *Foreign opinion,* which may be further subdivided by the country holding the opinion, e.g. **United States—Foreign opinion; United States—Foreign opin-**

Foreign public opinion—*Continued*
        ion—**France;** etc. [to be add-
        ed as needed]
Foreign relations
    USE   **International relations**
        and names of countries with the
        subdivision *Foreign relations,*
        e.g. **United States—Foreign
        relations** [to be added as
        needed]
Foreign service
    USE   **Diplomatic and consular ser-
        vice**
Foreign students (May subdiv. geog.)
        370.116
    UF   College students, Foreign
        Students, Foreign
    BT   **Students**
Foreign study (May subdiv. geog.)
        370.116
    UF   Overseas study
        Study abroad
        Study, Foreign
        Study overseas
    BT   **Education**
Foreign trade
    USE   **International trade**
Foreign words and phrases
    USE   names of languages with the
        subdivision *Foreign words
        and phrases,* e.g. **English lan-
        guage—Foreign words and
        phrases** [to be added as
        needed]
Foreigners
    USE   **Aliens**
        Immigrants
Foremen
    USE   **Supervisors**
Forensic medicine
    USE   **Medical jurisprudence**
Forensic science
    USE   **Forensic sciences**
Forensic sciences   363.25
    Use for materials on science as applied in
courts of law or in criminal investigations.
    UF   Criminalistics
        Forensic science
    BT   **Science**
    NT   **Medical jurisprudence**
    RT   **Criminal investigation**

Foreordination
    USE   **Predestination**
Forest animals (May subdiv. geog.)
        578.73
    UF   Forest fauna
    BT   **Animals**
    NT   **Jungle animals**
Forest conservation (May subdiv. geog.)
        333.75
    UF   Conservation of forests
        Forest preservation
        Preservation of forests
    BT   **Conservation of natural re-
        sources**
    RT   **Forest reserves**
        Forests and forestry
Forest depletion
    USE   **Deforestation**
Forest fauna
    USE   **Forest animals**
Forest fires   634.9
    BT   **Fires**
Forest influences   577.3
    UF   Climate and forests
        Floods and forests
        Forests and climate
        Forests and floods
        Forests and rainfall
        Forests and water supply
        Rainfall and forests
    BT   **Climate**
        Water supply
    RT   **Flood control**
        Forests and forestry
        Plant ecology
        Rain
Forest plants (May subdiv. geog.)   **581.7**
    BT   **Forests and forestry**
        Plant ecology
        Plants
Forest preservation
    USE   **Forest conservation**
Forest products (May subdiv. geog.)
        634.9; 674
    BT   **Commercial products**
        Economic botany
        Raw materials
    NT   **Gums and resins**
        Lumber and lumbering
        Rubber
        Wood

Forest reserves (May subdiv. geog.)
     333.75; 719
  UF   National forests
  BT   **Public lands**
  NT   **Wilderness areas**
  RT   **Forest conservation**
       Forests and forestry
       National parks and reserves

Forestry
  USE **Forests and forestry**

Forests and climate
  USE **Forest influences**

Forests and floods
  USE **Forest influences**

Forests and forestry (May subdiv. geog.)
     577.3; 578.73; 634.9
  UF   Arboriculture
       Forestry
       Timber
       Woods
  BT   **Agriculture**
       Natural resources
  NT   **Christmas tree growing**
       Deforestation
       Forest plants
       Jungles
       Logging
       Lumber and lumbering
       Pruning
       Rain forests
       Reforestation
       Tree planting
  RT   **Forest conservation**
       Forest influences
       Forest reserves
       Trees
       Wood

Forests and forestry—United States
     577.30973; 634.90973

Forests and rainfall
  USE **Forest influences**

Forests and water supply
  USE **Forest influences**

Forgeries
  USE names of individual persons and
       types of art objects, docu-
       ments, etc., with the subdivi-
       sion *Forgeries,* e.g. **Art—**
       Forgeries [to be added as
       needed]

Forgery   **332; 364.16**
  SA   names of individual persons and
       types of art objects, docu-
       ments, etc., with the subdivi-
       sion *Forgeries,* e.g. **Art—**
       Forgeries [to be added as
       needed]
  BT   **Crime**
       Fraud
       Impostors and imposture
  NT   **Art—Forgeries**
       Counterfeits and counterfeiting
       Literary forgeries

Forgery of works of art
  USE **Art—Forgeries**

Forgetfulness   **153.1**
  BT   **Memory**
       Personality

Forging   **671.3; 682**
  UF   Drop forging
  BT   **Manufacturing processes**
       Metalwork
  NT   **Welding**
  RT   **Blacksmithing**
       Ironwork

Forgiveness   **179**
  BT   **Virtue**
  RT   **Amnesty**
       Clemency
       Pardon

Forgiveness of sin   **234**
  UF   Sin, Forgiveness of
  RT   **Penance**
       Sin

Form in biology
  USE **Morphology**

Formal gardens
  USE **Gardens**

Former nuns
  USE **Ex-nuns**

Former priests
  USE **Ex-priests**

Former Soviet republics   **947.086**
    Use for general materials on several or all
  of the countries that emerged from the dissolution of the Soviet Union in 1991. Materials
  specifically on the federation of independent
  former Soviet republics that was established in
  1991 and does not include the Baltic states
  are entered under **Commonwealth of Inde-**
  pendent States.
  UF   Ex-Soviet republics
       Ex-Soviet states

Former Soviet republics—*Continued*
      Former Soviet states
  RT **Commonwealth of Independent States**
      Soviet Union
Former Soviet states
  USE **Former Soviet republics**
Formosa
  USE **Taiwan**
Formula translation (Computer language)
  USE **FORTRAN (Computer language)**
Fortification (May subdiv. geog.) **623**
  UF Forts
  SA names of countries with the subdivision *Defenses* [to be added as needed]
  BT **Military art and science**
  RT **Military engineering**
FORTRAN (Computer language)
      005.13
  UF Formula translation (Computer language)
      FORTRAN (Computer program language)
  BT **Programming languages**
FORTRAN (Computer program language)
  USE **FORTRAN (Computer language)**
Forts
  USE **Fortification**
Fortune
  USE **Fate and fatalism**
      Probabilities
      Success
Fortune telling **133.3**
  BT **Amusements**
      Divination
  NT **Palmistry**
      Tarot
Fortunes
  USE **Income**
      Wealth
Forums (Discussions)
  USE **Discussion groups**
Fossil botany
  USE **Fossil plants**
Fossil hominids (May subdiv. geog.)
      569.9
  UF Hominids, Fossil
      Human fossils
      Human paleontology

      Man, Prehistoric
      Prehistoric man
      Prehistory
  BT **Archeology**
      Fossils
  RT **Human origins**
Fossil mammals (May subdiv. geog.)
      569
  UF Mammals, Fossil
  SA types of extinct mammals [to be added as needed]
  BT **Fossils**
      Mammals
  NT **Mastodon**
Fossil plants (May subdiv. geog.) **561**
  UF Extinct plants
      Fossil botany
      Paleobotany
      Plants, Extinct
      Plants, Fossil
  BT **Fossils**
      Plants
Fossil reptiles (May subdiv. geog.)
      567.9
  UF Reptiles, Fossil
  SA types of fossil reptiles, e.g. **Dinosaurs** [to be added as needed]
  BT **Fossils**
      Reptiles
  NT **Dinosaurs**
Fossils (May subdiv. geog.) **560**
  BT **Biology**
      Natural history
      Science
      Stratigraphic geology
  NT **Fossil hominids**
      Fossil mammals
      Fossil plants
      Fossil reptiles
      Prehistoric animals
  RT **Extinct animals**
      Paleontology
Foster children **306.874**
  BT **Children**
  RT **Foster home care**
Foster grandparents **362.73**
  BT **Grandparents**
      Volunteer work

Foster home care 362.73
　　UF　Child placing
　　　　Children—Placing out
　　BT　**Child welfare**
　　RT　**Adoption**
　　　　Children—Institutional care
　　　　Foster children
　　　　Group homes
Foundations 624.1; 721
　　BT　**Architecture—Details**
　　　　Buildings
　　　　Structural engineering
　　NT　**Basements**
　　　　Concrete
　　RT　**Soil mechanics**
Foundations (Endowments)
　　USE　**Endowments**
Founding 671.2
　　Use for materials on the melting and casting of metals.
　　UF　Casting
　　　　Foundry practice
　　　　Molding (Metal)
　　　　Moulding (Metal)
　　BT　**Manufacturing processes**
　　　　Metalwork
　　NT　**Type and type-founding**
　　RT　**Patternmaking**
Foundlings
　　USE　**Orphans**
Foundry practice
　　USE　**Founding**
Four-day week
　　USE　**Flexible hours of labor**
Four-H clubs
　　USE　**4-H clubs**
Fourteenth century
　　USE　**World history—14th century**
Fourth dimension 530.11
　　UF　Dimension, Fourth
　　　　Hyperspace
　　BT　**Mathematics**
　　NT　**Space and time**
　　　　Time travel
Fourth of July 394.2634
　　UF　4th of July
　　　　Independence Day (United
　　　　　States)
　　　　July Fourth
　　BT　**Holidays**
　　　　**United States—History—1775-
　　　　1783, Revolution**

Fractal geometry
　　USE　**Fractals**
Fractals 514
　　Use for materials on shapes or mathematical sets that have fractional, i.e. irregular, dimensions as opposed to the regular dimensions of Euclidean geometry.
　　UF　Fractal geometry
　　　　Sets, Fractal
　　　　Sets of fractional dimension
　　BT　**Geometry**
　　　　Mathematical models
　　　　Set theory
　　　　Topology
Fractions 513.2
　　BT　**Arithmetic**
　　　　Mathematics
Fractured fairy tales 398.2; 808.83
　　UF　Fairy tales—Parodies, imitations,
　　　　etc.
　　BT　**Fairy tales**
　　　　Parodies
Fractures 617.1
　　BT　**Bones**
　　　　Wounds and injuries
Fragrant gardens (May subdiv. geog.)
　　635.9
　　UF　Gardening for fragrance
　　　　Scented gardens
　　BT　**Gardens**
　　RT　**Aromatic plants**
Framing of pictures
　　USE　**Picture frames and framing**
France 944
　　May be subdivided like United States except for *History*.
France—Blacks
　　USE　**Blacks—France**
France—Folk songs
　　USE　**Folk songs—France**
France—History 944
France—History—0-1328 944
　　NT　**Celts**
**France—History—1328-1589, House of
　　Valois** 944
　　NT　**Hundred Years' War, 1339-
　　　　1453**
　　　　**Saint Bartholomew's Day,
　　　　Massacre of, 1572**
France—History—1589-1789, Bourbons
　　944

France—History—1789-1799, Revolution 944.04
    UF   Directory, French, 1795-1799
           French Revolution
           Reign of Terror
           Revolution, French
           Terror, Reign of
    BT   **Revolutions**
France—History—1799-1815   944.05
    NT   **Napoleonic Wars, 1800-1815**
France—History—1815-1914   944.06
France—History—20th century   944.081
France—History—1914-1940   944.081
France—History—1940-1945, German oc-
cupation   944.081
    UF   German occupation of France,
           1940-1945
France—History—1945-   944.082
France—History—1945-1958   944.082
France—History—1958-   944.083
    UF   France—History—1958-1969
           France—History—1969-
France—History—1958-1969
    USE   **France—History—1958-**
France—History—1969-
    USE   **France—History—1958-**
France—History—21st century   944.084
Franchise
    USE   **Citizenship**
          Elections
          Suffrage
Franchises (Retail trade) (May subdiv.
    geog.)   **658.8**
    UF   Franchising
          Retail franchises
    BT   **Retail trade**
Franchising
    USE   **Franchises (Retail trade)**
Franciscans   271
    UF   Friars Minor
          Gray Friars
          Grey Friars
          Mendicant orders
          Minorites
          Saint Francis, Order of
          St. Francis, Order of
    BT   **Monasticism and religious or-**
          ders
Fraternities and sororities   371.8
    UF   College fraternities
          College sororities

          Greek letter societies
          Sororities
    BT   **Colleges and universities**
          Students—Societies
    RT   **Secret societies**
Fraud (May subdiv. geog.)   **364.16**
    UF   Deceit
          Ripoffs
    BT   **Commercial law**
          Crime
          Offenses against property
          White collar crimes
    NT   **Credit card fraud**
          Forgery
          Securities fraud
    RT   **Impostors and imposture**
          Swindlers and swindling
Frauds, Literary
    USE   **Literary forgeries**
Fraudulent advertising
    USE   **Deceptive advertising**
Free agency
    USE   **Free will and determinism**
Free coinage
    USE   **Monetary policy**
Free computer software   005.3
    UF   Free software
          Freeware
          Public domain software
    BT   **Computer software**
          Free material
Free diving
    USE   **Scuba diving**
          Skin diving
Free enterprise (May subdiv. geog.)
    330.12
    UF   Free markets
          Laissez-faire
          Private enterprise
    BT   **Economic policy**
    RT   **Capitalism**
Free fall
    USE   **Weightlessness**
Free love   176; 306.7
    BT   **Sexual ethics**
Free markets
    USE   **Free enterprise**
Free material
    UF   Freebies
          Giveaways

Free material—*Continued*
  BT Gifts
  NT Free computer software
Free press
  USE Freedom of the press
Free press and fair trial
  USE Freedom of the press and fair
       trial
Free schools
  USE Experimental schools
Free software
  USE Free computer software
Free speech
  USE Freedom of speech
Free thought   211
  BT Freedom of conscience
  NT Agnosticism
       Skepticism
  RT Deism
       Rationalism
Free time (Leisure)
  USE Leisure
Free trade (May subdiv. geog.) **382**
  UF Fair trade (Tariff)
       Free trade and protection
  BT Commercial policy
       International trade
  RT Protectionism
       Tariff
Free trade and protection
  USE Free trade
       Protectionism
Free universities (May subdiv. geog.)
      378
  UF Alternative universities
       Experimental universities
       Open universities
  BT Colleges and universities
Free verse   808.1; 808.81
  May be used for collections or materials
about free verse, not for individual works.
  UF Vers libre
  BT Poetry
Free will and determinism   123
  UF Choice, Freedom of
       Determinism and indeterminism
       Free agency
       Freedom of choice
       Freedom of the will
       Indeterminism
       Liberty of the will
       Will

  BT Philosophy
  RT Fate and fatalism
       Predestination
Freebies
  USE Free material
Freedom (May subdiv. geog.)   **323.4**
  UF Civil liberty
       Emancipation
       Liberty
       Personal freedom
  BT Democracy
       Political science
  NT Anarchism and anarchists
       Conformity
       Freedom of assembly
       Freedom of association
       Freedom of conscience
       Freedom of movement
       Freedom of religion
       Freedom of speech
       Freedom of the press
       Intellectual freedom
       Slaves—Emancipation
  RT Civil rights
       Equality
Freedom, Academic
  USE Academic freedom
Freedom marches for civil rights
  USE Civil rights demonstrations
Freedom of assembly (May subdiv. geog.)
      323.4
  UF Assembly, Right of
       Right of assembly
  BT Civil rights
       Freedom
  NT Public meetings
       Riots
  RT Freedom of association
       Freedom of speech
Freedom of association (May subdiv.
  geog.)   **323.4**
  UF Association, Freedom of
       Right of association
  BT Civil rights
       Freedom
  RT Freedom of assembly
Freedom of choice
  USE Free will and determinism
Freedom of choice movement
  USE Pro-choice movement

Freedom of conscience (May subdiv. geog.) **323.44**
- UF Liberty of conscience
- BT **Conscience**
     Freedom
     Toleration
- NT **Conscientious objectors**
     Dissent
     Free thought
     Public opinion
- RT **Freedom of religion**

Freedom of information (May subdiv. geog.) **323.44**
- UF Information, Freedom of
     Right to know
- BT **Civil rights**
     Intellectual freedom
- NT **Press—Government policy**
- RT **Censorship**
     Freedom of speech
     Freedom of the press

Freedom of movement (May subdiv. geog.) **323.4**
- UF Movement, Freedom of
- BT **Civil rights**
     Freedom

Freedom of religion (May subdiv. geog.) **201; 261.7; 323.44**
- UF Freedom of worship
     Religious freedom
     Religious liberty
- BT **Civil rights**
     Freedom
     Toleration
- NT **Dissent**
- RT **Freedom of conscience**
     Persecution

Freedom of speech (May subdiv. geog.) **323.44**
- UF Free speech
     Liberty of speech
     Speech, Freedom of
- BT **Censorship**
     Civil rights
     Freedom
     Intellectual freedom
- RT **Freedom of assembly**
     Freedom of information
     Libel and slander

Freedom of teaching
- USE **Academic freedom**

Freedom of the press (May subdiv. geog.) **323.44**
- UF Free press
     Liberty of the press
     Press censorship
- BT **Civil rights**
     Freedom
     Intellectual freedom
     Press
- NT **Freedom of the press and fair trial**
- RT **Censorship**
     Freedom of information
     Libel and slander

Freedom of the press and fair trial **323.42; 323.44; 342**
- UF Fair trial and free press
     Free press and fair trial
     Prejudicial publicity
     Trial by publicity
- BT **Fair trial**
     Freedom of the press
     Press

Freedom of the will
- USE **Free will and determinism**

Freedom of worship
- USE **Freedom of religion**

Freelancers
- USE **Self-employed**

Freemasons **366**
- UF Masonic orders
     Masons (Secret order)
- BT **Secret societies**

Freeware
- USE **Free computer software**

Freeways
- USE **Express highways**

Freeze-dried foods **641.4; 664**
- UF Food, Freeze dried
- BT **Dried foods**

Freezing
- USE **Cryobiology**
     Frost
     Ice
     Refrigeration

Freezing of human bodies
- USE **Cryonics**

Freight **388**
- UF Freight and freightage
- BT **Maritime law**
     Materials handling

Freight—*Continued*
      Railroads
      Transportation
  NT Commercial aeronautics
      Trucking
  RT Railroads—Rates
Freight and freightage
  USE Freight
French and Indian War
  USE United States—History—1755-
      1763, French and Indian
      War
French Canadian literature
  USE Canadian literature (French)
French Canadian poetry
  USE Canadian poetry (French)
French Canadians (May subdiv. geog.)
      305.811; 971
  BT Canadians
French cookery
  USE French cooking
French cooking   641.5944
  UF Cookery, French
      French cookery
  BT Cooking
French Equatorial Africa
  USE French-speaking Equatorial Af-
      rica
French folk songs
  USE Folk songs—France
French language   440
    May be subdivided like **English language.**
  BT Language and languages
      Romance languages
French language—Conversation and
    phrase books   448
  UF French language—Conversations
      and phrases
French language—Conversations and
    phrases
  USE French language—Conversation
      and phrase books
French language—Dictionaries—English
    443
    Use for French-English dictionaries. En-
glish-French dictionaries are entered under
English language—Dictionaries—French.
Combined French-English and English-French
dictionaries are entered under both headings.
  UF Foreign language dictionaries
  BT Encyclopedias and dictionaries
  RT English language—Diction-
      aries—French

French language—Reading materials
    448.6
French literature   840
    May use same subdivisions and names of
literary forms as for **English literature.**
  BT Literature
      Romance literature
  NT French poetry
French literature—Black authors
    840.8; 840.9
    May be used for collections or materials
about French literature by several Black au-
thors, not for individual works.
  UF Black literature (French)
French literature—Canada
  USE Canadian literature (French)
French poetry   841
  BT French literature
      Poetry
  NT Troubadours
French poetry—Black authors   841
    May be used for collections or materials
about French poetry by several Black authors,
not for individual works.
  UF Black poetry (French)
French Revolution
  USE France—History—1789-1799,
      Revolution
French-speaking Equatorial Africa   967
    Use for materials dealing collectively with
the region of Africa that includes Central
African Republic, Chad, Congo (Republic),
and Gabon. The former name for the region
was French Equatorial Africa.
  UF Africa, French-speaking Equato-
      rial
      French Equatorial Africa
  BT Central Africa
French-speaking West Africa   966
    Use for materials dealing collectively with
the region of Africa that includes Benin,
Burkina Faso, Guinea, Ivory Coast, Mali,
Mauritania, Niger, Senegal, and Togo.
  UF Africa, French-speaking West
      French West Africa
  BT West Africa
French West Africa
  USE French-speaking West Africa
Frequency modulation, Radio
  USE Radio frequency modulation
Fresco painting
  USE Mural painting and decoration

Freshwater animals (May subdiv. geog.) **591.76**
UF Freshwater fauna
SA types of freshwater animals [to be added as needed]
BT **Aquatic animals**
RT **Freshwater biology**
Freshwater aquaculture
USE **Aquaculture**
Freshwater biology 578.76
BT **Biology**
NT **Aquariums**
     Freshwater plants
RT **Freshwater animals**
Freshwater fauna
USE **Freshwater animals**
Freshwater plants (May subdiv. geog.) **581.7**
UF Aquatic plants
     Water plants
BT **Freshwater biology**
     Plants
RT **Marine plants**
Friars Minor
USE **Franciscans**
Friendly fire (Military science) (May subdiv. geog.) **355.4**
BT **Military art and science**
Friends
USE **Friendship**
Friends and associates
USE names of individuals with the subdivision *Friends and associates* [to be added as needed]
Friends, Society of
USE **Society of Friends**
Friendship 177
UF Affection
     Friends
BT **Human behavior**
NT **Crushes**
     Female friendship
RT **Love**
Friendship between women
USE **Female friendship**
Friendship in women
USE **Female friendship**
Friesian cattle
USE **Holstein-Friesian cattle**

Fringe benefits 331.25
UF Benefits, Employee
     Benefits, Fringe
     Employee benefits
     Employee fringe benefits
     Non-wage payments
     Nonwage payments
BT **Salaries, wages, etc.**
Frogs (May subdiv. geog.) **597.8**
UF Tadpoles
BT **Amphibians**
Frontier and pioneer life (May subdiv. geog.) **978**
UF Border life
     Pioneer life
BT **Adventure and adventurers**
NT **Cowhands**
     Native Americans—Captivities
     Overland journeys to the Pacific
     Ranch life
Frontiers
USE **Boundaries**
Frost 551.57
UF Freezing
BT **Meteorology**
     Water
NT **Ice**
     Refrigeration
Frozen animal embryos
USE **Frozen embryos**
Frozen embryos 176; 571.8; 612.6
UF Animal embryos, Frozen
     Embryos, Frozen
     Frozen animal embryos
     Frozen human embryos
     Human embryos, Frozen
BT **Cryobiology**
     Embryology
Frozen foods 641.4; 664
BT **Food**
NT **Ice cream, ices, etc.**
RT **Food—Preservation**
Frozen human embryos
USE **Frozen embryos**
Frozen stars
USE **Black holes (Astronomy)**
Fruit (May subdiv. geog.) **634; 641.3**
   Names of tree fruits may be used for either the fruit or the tree.

Fruit—*Continued*

SA   types of fruits, e.g. **Berries; Apples; Citrus fruits;** etc. [to be added as needed]

BT   **Food**
       Plants

NT   **Apples**
       Berries
       Citrus fruits
       Fruit culture
       Grapes

Fruit—Canning

USE   **Fruit**—**Preservation**

Fruit culture (May subdiv. geog.)   **634**

Names of tree fruits may be used for either the fruit or the tree.

UF   Arboriculture
       Orchards

BT   **Agriculture**
       Fruit
       Gardening
       Horticulture
       Trees

NT   **Berries**
       Nurseries (Horticulture)
       Plant propagation
       Pruning

Fruit—**Diseases and pests**   **634**

BT   **Agricultural pests**
       Insect pests
       Pests
       Plant diseases

NT   **Spraying and dusting**

Fruit flies (May subdiv. geog.)   **595.77**

BT   **Flies**

Fruit painting and illustration

USE   **Botanical illustration**

Fruit—**Preservation**   **641.4; 664**

UF   Fruit—Canning

BT   **Canning and preserving**
       Food—**Preservation**

Frustration   **152.4**

UF   Futility

BT   **Attitude (Psychology)**
       Emotions

Fuel (May subdiv. geog.)   **333.8; 662**

SA   types of fuel; and subjects with the subdivision *Fuel consumption* [to be added as needed]

BT   **Combustion**
       Energy resources
       Engines
       Fire
       Home economics

NT   **Alcohol as fuel**
       Automobiles—**Fuel consumption**
       Biomass energy
       Charcoal
       Coal
       Gas
       Gasoline
       Natural gas
       Petroleum as fuel
       Synthetic fuels
       Wood

RT   **Heating**

Fuel cells   **621.31**

BT   **Electric batteries**
       Electrochemistry

Fuel consumption

USE   subjects with the subdivision *Fuel consumption,* e.g. **Automobiles**—**Fuel consumption** [to be added as needed]

Fuel oil

USE   **Petroleum as fuel**

Fugitive slaves (May subdiv. geog.)   **306.3**

UF   Runaway slaves

BT   **Slaves**

Fugue   **784.18**

Use for musical scores and for materials on the fugue as a musical form.

UF   Canons, fugues, etc.
       Fugues
       Prelude and fugue
       Preludes and fugues

BT   **Counterpoint**
       Musical form

Fugues

USE   **Fugue**

Fulfillment, Self

USE   **Self-realization**

Fumigation   **614.4; 648**

BT   **Communicable diseases**
       Insecticides

RT   **Disinfection and disinfectants**

Functional competencies

USE   **Life skills**

Functional literacy   **302.2; 374**

UF   Occupational literacy

BT   **Literacy**

Functions 511.3
  UF Analysis (Mathematics)
  BT **Differential equations**
      Mathematical analysis
      Mathematics
      Set theory
  RT **Calculus**
Fund raising (May subdiv. geog.)
      361.7068; 658.15
  UF Community chests
      Money raising
  BT **Finance**
  RT **Gifts**
Fundamental education
  USE **Basic education**
Fundamental life skills
  USE **Life skills**
Fundamental rights
  USE **Civil rights**
      Human rights
Fundamentalism
  USE **Christian fundamentalism**
      Islamic fundamentalism
      Religious fundamentalism
Fundamentalism and education
  USE **Church and education**
      Creationism
      Religion in the public schools
Fundamentalism and evolution
  USE **Creationism**
Fundamentalist movements
  USE **Religious fundamentalism**
Funding
  USE **Finance**
Funding for the arts
  USE **Art patronage**
      Arts—Government policy
      Federal aid to the arts
Funds
  USE **Finance**
Funeral customs and rites
  USE **Funeral rites and ceremonies**
      and ethnic groups and native
      peoples with the subdivision
      Funeral customs and rites [to
      be added as needed]
Funeral directors
  USE **Undertakers and undertaking**

Funeral rites and ceremonies (May
      subdiv. geog.) **393**
  UF Funeral customs and rites
      Graves
      Mortuary customs
      Mourning customs
  SA ethnic groups and native peoples
      with the subdivision *Funeral
      customs and rites* [to be add-
      ed as needed]
  BT **Manners and customs**
      Rites and ceremonies
  RT **Burial**
      Cremation
Fungi 579.5
  UF Diseases and pests
      Mycology
  BT **Agricultural pests**
      Pests
      Plants
  NT **Molds (Fungi)**
      Plant diseases
      Yeast
  RT **Mushrooms**
Fungicides 632; 668
  UF Germicides
  BT **Pesticides**
  RT **Spraying and dusting**
Funicular railroads
  USE **Cable railroads**
Funnies
  USE **Comic books, strips, etc.**
Fur 675; 685
  BT **Animals—Anatomy**
  RT **Hides and skins**
Fur-bearing animals
  USE **Furbearing animals**
Fur trade (May subdiv. geog.) 338.3
  BT **Trapping**
Furbearing animals (May subdiv. geog.)
      599.7; 636.97
  UF Fur-bearing animals
  SA types of furbearing animals, e.g.
      Beavers [to be added as
      needed]
  BT **Animals**
      Economic zoology
  NT **Beavers**

Furnaces   697
   BT   Heating
   NT   Blast furnaces
        Smelting
Furniture   645; 749
   SA furniture of particular countries,
        e.g. **American furniture;**
        types of furniture, and names
        of specific articles of furni-
        ture, e.g. **Tables; Chairs;** etc.
        [to be added as needed]
   BT   **Decoration and ornament**
        Decorative arts
        Interior design
   NT   **American furniture**
        Built-in furniture
        Chairs
        Church furniture
        Furniture making
        **Garden ornaments and furni-
        ture**
        **Libraries—Equipment and
        supplies**
        Mirrors
        **Schools—Equipment and sup-
        plies**
        Tables
        Veneers and veneering
   RT   **Cabinetwork**
        Upholstery
Furniture, American
   USE **American furniture**
Furniture building
   USE **Furniture making**
Furniture—Conservation and restoration
   USE **Furniture finishing**
        Furniture—Repairing
Furniture finishing   684.1; 749
   UF Furniture—Conservation and res-
        toration
        Furniture—Refinishing
        Furniture—Restoration
        Refinishing furniture
        Restoration of furniture
   BT   **Furniture making**
        Handicraft
        Wood finishing
   RT   **Furniture—Repairing**

Furniture making   684.1; 749
   UF Furniture building
   BT   **Furniture**
        Woodwork
   NT   **Furniture finishing**
        Furniture—Repairing
Furniture—Refinishing
   USE **Furniture finishing**
Furniture—Repairing   684.1; 749
   UF Furniture—Conservation and res-
        toration
        Furniture—Restoration
        Restoration of furniture
   BT   **Furniture making**
   RT   **Furniture finishing**
Furniture—Restoration
   USE **Furniture finishing**
        Furniture—Repairing
Futility
   USE **Frustration**
Future life   129; 236
     Use for materials on the character and form
of a future existence. Materials on the ques-
tion of the endless existence of the soul are
entered under **Immortality.** Materials on the
philosophical concept of eternity are entered
under **Eternity.**
   UF Afterlife
        Eternal life
        Intermediate state
        Life after death
        Life, Future
        Resurrection
        Retribution
   BT   **Death**
        Eschatology
   NT   **Heaven**
        Hell
        Paradise
        Soul
   RT   **Eternity**
        Immortality
Future shock
   USE **Culture conflict**
Futures (May subdiv. geog.)   **332.64**
   UF Futures contracts
        Futures trading
   BT   **Investments**
        Securities
Futures contracts
   USE **Futures**
Futures trading
   USE **Futures**

Futurism (Art) (May subdiv. geog.)
    709.04; 759.06
  BT Art
Futurology
  USE Forecasting
Fuzzy logic
  USE Fuzzy systems
Fuzzy systems 629.8
  UF Fuzzy logic
      Systems, Fuzzy
  BT System analysis
Gadgets
  USE Implements, utensils, etc.
Gaels
  USE Celts
Gaia concept
  USE Gaia hypothesis
Gaia hypothesis 550.1; 570.1
  UF Gaia concept
      Gaia principle
      Gaia theory
      Living earth theory
  BT Biology
      Earth
      Ecology
      Life (Biology)
Gaia principle
  USE Gaia hypothesis
Gaia theory
  USE Gaia hypothesis
Galaxies 523.1
  UF Extragalactic nebulae
      Nebulae, Extragalactic
  BT Astronomy
      Stars
Gales
  USE Winds
Gambling (May subdiv. geog.) 306.4;
    795
  UF Betting
      Gaming
  SA types of gambling, e.g. Lotteries
      [to be added as needed]
  BT Games
  NT Compulsive gambling
      Internet gambling
      Lotteries
      Sports betting

Game and game birds (May subdiv.
  geog.) 636.6
  UF Wild fowl
  SA types of animals and birds, e.g.
      Deer; Pheasants; etc. [to be
      added as needed]
  BT Animals
      Birds
      Wildlife
  NT Deer
      Falconry
      Game protection
      Pheasants
  RT Hunting
      Trapping
Game preserves
  USE Game reserves
Game protection (May subdiv. geog.)
    333.95; 636.9
  UF Game wardens
      Protection of game
  BT Game and game birds
      Hunting
      Wildlife conservation
  RT Birds—Protection
Game reserves (May subdiv. geog.)
    333.95
  UF Game preserves
  BT Hunting
      Wildlife conservation
Game theory 519.3
  UF Games, Theory of
      Theory of games
  BT Mathematical models
      Mathematics
      Probabilities
  NT Simulation games in education
Game wardens
  USE Game protection
Games (May subdiv. geog.) 790
  UF Pastimes
  SA types of games and names of
      individual games [to be added
      as needed]
  BT Entertaining
      Physical education
      Recreation
  NT Ball games
      Bible games and puzzles
      Board games
      Card games

Games—*Continued*
>> **Computer games**
>> **Educational games**
>> **Fantasy games**
>> **Gambling**
>> **Indoor games**
>> **Native American games**
>> **Olympic games**
>> **Singing games**
>> **Video games**
>> **Word games**
> RT **Amusements**
>> **Play**
>> **Sports**

Games, Theory of
> USE **Game theory**

Gaming
> USE **Gambling**

Gaming, Educational
> USE **Simulation games in education**

Gamma rays 537.5; 539.7
> BT **Electromagnetic waves**
>> **Radiation**
>> **X-rays**

Gangs (May subdiv. geog.) 302.3; 364.106
> UF Gangsters
>> Street gangs
>> Teenage gangs
> BT **Criminals**
>> **Juvenile delinquency**
>> **Organized crime**

Gangster films 791.43
> May be used for individual works, collections, or materials about gangster films.
> UF Crime films
> BT **Motion pictures**
> RT **Mystery films**

Gangsters
> USE **Gangs**

Garage sales 381
> UF Yard sales
> BT **Secondhand trade**

Garbage
> USE **Refuse and refuse disposal**

Garbage disposal
> USE **Refuse and refuse disposal**

Garden architecture
> USE **Garden structures**

Garden design (May subdiv. geog.) **712**
> UF Gardens—Design
> BT **Design**
>> **Gardening**
> RT **Landscape gardening**

Garden farming
> USE **Truck farming**

Garden furniture
> USE **Garden ornaments and furniture**

Garden of Eden
> USE **Paradise**

Garden ornaments and furniture **717**
> UF Garden furniture
> BT **Decoration and ornament**
>> **Furniture**
>> **Gardens**
>> **Landscape architecture**
> NT **Sundials**

Garden pests
> USE **Agricultural pests**
>> **Insect pests**
>> **Plant diseases**

Garden rooms **643**
> UF Conservatories, Home
>> Home conservatories
> BT **Houses**
>> **Rooms**
> RT **Greenhouses**

Garden structures **690**
> UF Garden architecture
>> Structures, Garden
> BT **Buildings**
>> **Landscape architecture**

Gardening (May subdiv. geog.) **635**
> Use for materials on the practical aspects of creating gardens and cultivating flowers, fruits, vegetables, etc. Materials on the design or rearrangement of extensive gardens or estates are entered under **Landscape gardening.** Materials on the scientific and economic aspects of the cultivation of plants are entered under **Horticulture.** General materials about gardens, the history of gardens, various types of gardens, etc., are entered under **Gardens.**
> UF Planting
> BT **Agriculture**
> NT **Climbing plants**
>> **Container gardening**
>> **Cultivated plants**
>> **Flower gardening**
>> **Fruit culture**
>> **Garden design**
>> **Gardening in the shade**

Gardening—*Continued*
> Greenhouses
> Grounds maintenance
> Indoor gardening
> Landscape gardening
> Nurseries (Horticulture)
> Organic gardening
> Plant propagation
> Pruning
> Truck farming
> Vegetable gardening
> Weeds
> Window gardening
> Winter gardening
>> RT   **Gardens**
>> **Horticulture**
>> **Plants**

Gardening for fragrance
>> USE   **Fragrant gardens**

Gardening in the shade   635
> UF   Gardens, Shade
> Shade gardens
> Shady gardens
> BT   **Gardening**

Gardens (May subdiv. geog.)   **635; 712**

> Use for general materials about gardens, the history of gardens, various types of gardens, etc. Materials on the design or rearrangement of extensive gardens or estates are entered under **Landscape gardening.** Materials on the practical aspects of creating gardens and cultivating flowers, fruits, vegetables, etc., are entered under **Gardening.**

> UF   Formal gardens
> SA   types of gardens, e.g. **Botanical gardens; Islamic gardens** etc., and names of individual gardens [to be added as needed]
> NT   **Botanical gardens**
> **Fragrant gardens**
> **Garden ornaments and furniture**
> **Islamic gardens**
> **Miniature gardens**
> **Rock gardens**
> RT   **Gardening**

Gardens—Design
> USE   **Garden design**

Gardens, Miniature
> USE   **Miniature gardens**

Gardens, Shade
> USE   **Gardening in the shade**

Gargoyles (May subdiv. geog.)   **729**
> BT   **Architectural decoration and ornament**
> **Architecture—Details**

Garment industry
> USE   **Clothing industry**

Garment making
> USE   **Dressmaking**
> **Tailoring**

Garments
> USE   **Clothing and dress**

Gas   **665.7**
> UF   Coal gas
> BT   **Fuel**
> RT   **Coal tar products**

Gas and oil engines
> USE   **Internal combustion engines**

Gas companies (May subdiv. geog.)   **363.6**

> Use for materials on the sale and distribution of gas to consumers.

> UF   Natural gas companies
> Natural gas utilities
> BT   **Public utilities**

Gas engines
> USE   **Internal combustion engines**

Gas stations
> USE   **Service stations**

Gas turbines   **621.43**
> BT   **Turbines**

Gas warfare
> USE   **Chemical warfare**

Gases   **530.4; 533**
> SA   types of gases, e.g. **Nitrogen** [to be added as needed]
> BT   **Fluid mechanics**
> **Hydrostatics**
> **Physics**
> NT   **Bubbles**
> **Helium**
> **Natural gas**
> **Nitrogen**
> **Oxygen**
> **Poisonous gases**
> RT   **Pneumatics**

Gases, Asphyxiating and poisonous
> USE   **Poisonous gases**

Gasification of coal
> USE   **Coal gasification**

Gasohol   **662**
> BT   **Alcohol as fuel**

Gasoline 665.5
BT Fuel
Petroleum
Gasoline engines
USE Internal combustion engines
Gastronomy 641.01
UF Eating
BT Diet
RT Cooking
Dining
Food
Gauchos
USE Cowhands
Gaul—Geography 914.4
BT Ancient geography
Historical geography
Gay liberation movement (May subdiv.
geog.) 306.76
BT Homosexuality
Gay lifestyle
USE Homosexuality
Gay marriage
USE Same-sex marriage
Gay men (May subdiv. geog.) 306.76
UF Gays, Male
Homosexuals, Male
BT Men
NT Gays and lesbians in the mili-
tary
RT Gay men's writings
Homosexuality
Gay men's writings 808.8
Use for collections of gay men's writings
by more than one author and for materials
about such writings.
UF Writings of gay men
BT Literature
RT Gay men
Gay women
USE Lesbians
Gay women's writings
USE Lesbians' writings
Gays and lesbians in the military
355.008
UF Gays in the military
Lesbians and gays in the mili-
tary
Lesbians in the military
United States—Armed forces—
Gays
BT Gay men
Lesbians

Military personnel
Gays, Female
USE Lesbians
Gays in the military
USE Gays and lesbians in the mili-
tary
Gays, Male
USE Gay men
Gazetteers 910.3
SA names of countries, states, etc.,
with the subdivision *Gazet-
teers,* e.g. United States—
Gazetteers [to be added as
needed]
BT Geography
NT Ohio—Gazetteers
United States—Gazetteers
RT Geographic names
Gearing 621.8
UF Bevel gearing
Cog wheels
Gears
Spiral gearing
BT Machinery
Power transmission
Wheels
NT Automobiles—Transmission de-
vices
RT Mechanical movements
Gears
USE Gearing
Geese (May subdiv. geog.) 598.4; 636.5
UF Goose
BT Birds
Poultry
Water birds
Gemini project 629.45
UF Project Gemini
BT Orbital rendezvous (Space
flight)
Space flight
Gems (May subdiv. geog.) 736
Use for materials on cut and polished pre-
cious stones treated from the point of view of
art or antiquity. Materials on gem stones treat-
ed from a mineralogical or technological point
of view are entered under **Precious stones.**
Materials on gems in which the emphasis is
on the setting are entered under **Jewelry.**
UF Jewels
BT Archeology
Art
Decoration and ornament

Gems—*Continued*
        Engraving
        Minerals
  RT **Jewelry**
        Precious stones
Gemstones
  USE **Precious stones**
Gender identity
  USE **Sex role**
Gene mapping   572.8
  UF Chromosome mapping
       Genetic mapping
       Genome mapping
  BT **Genetics**
Gene splicing
  USE **Genetic engineering**
Gene therapy   616
    Use for materials on therapeutic efforts involving the replacement or supplementation of genes in order to cure diseases caused by genetic defects.
  UF Therapy, Gene
  BT **Genetic engineering**
      Therapeutics
Gene transfer
  USE **Genetic engineering**
Genealogy   929
  UF Ancestry
       Descent
       Family histories
       Family trees
       Pedigrees
  SA countries, cities, etc., corporate bodies, ethnic groups, and classes of persons with the subdivision *Genealogy;* names of individual persons with the subdivision *Family;* and names of families, e.g. **Lincoln family** [to be added as needed]
  BT **History**
  NT **Registers of births, etc.**
      Wills
  RT **Biography**
      Heraldry
General practice (Medicine)
  USE **Family medicine**

General stores (May subdiv. geog.)
    381.1
  UF Country stores
  BT **Retail trade**
      Stores
Generals (May subdiv. geog.)   **355.0092; 920**
  BT **Military personnel**
Generation gap
  USE **Conflict of generations**
Generative organs
  USE **Reproductive system**
Generators, Electric
  USE **Electric generators**
Generic drugs   615
  UF Drugs—Generic substitution
  BT **Drugs**
      Generic products
Generic products   658.8
  UF Products, Generic
  BT **Commercial products**
      Manufactures
  NT **Generic drugs**
Generosity   179
  UF Giving
Genes
  USE **Heredity**
Genetic aspects
  USE types of diseases with the subdivision *Genetic aspects,* e.g. **Cancer—Genetic aspects** [to be added as needed]
Genetic code   572.8
  BT **Molecular biology**
Genetic counseling   616; 618
  BT **Medical genetics**
      Prenatal diagnosis
Genetic engineering (May subdiv. geog.)
    660.6
  UF Designed genetic change
       Engineering, Genetic
       Gene splicing
       Gene transfer
       Genetic intervention
       Genetic surgery
       Splicing of genes
       Transgenics
  BT **Engineering**
      Genetic recombination
  NT **Cloning**
      Fertilization in vitro

Genetic engineering—*Continued*
    Gene therapy
    Molecular cloning
    Recombinant DNA
  RT Biotechnology
Genetic engineering—Government policy
    (May subdiv. geog.) 353.7; 660.6
Genetic engineering—Social aspects
    306.4
Genetic fingerprinting
  USE DNA fingerprinting
Genetic fingerprints
  USE DNA fingerprinting
Genetic intervention
  USE Genetic engineering
Genetic mapping
  USE Gene mapping
Genetic profiling
  USE DNA fingerprinting
Genetic recombination 572.8
  UF Recombination, Genetic
  BT Chromosomes
  NT Genetic engineering
    Genetic transformation
    Recombinant DNA
Genetic surgery
  USE Genetic engineering
Genetic transformation 576.5
  UF Transformation (Genetics)
  BT Genetic recombination
Genetics 576.5
  SA types of diseases with the subdivision *Genetic aspects,* e.g. **Cancer—Genetic aspects** [to be added as needed]
  BT Biology
    Embryology
    Life (Biology)
    Mendel's law
    Reproduction
  NT Adaptation (Biology)
    Behavior genetics
    Chromosomes
    Eugenics
    Gene mapping
    Medical genetics
    Natural selection
    Variation (Biology)
  RT Breeding
    Heredity
Genital mutilation, Female
  USE Female circumcision

Genitalia
  USE Reproductive system
Genius 153.9
  UF Talent
  BT Psychology
  NT Creation (Literary, artistic, etc.)
Genocide (May subdiv. geog.) 179.7; 364.1
  UF Ethnic cleansing
    Ethnocide
  BT Crimes against humanity
Genome mapping
  USE Gene mapping
Geochemistry 551.9
  UF Chemical geology
    Earth—Chemical composition
    Geological chemistry
  BT Chemistry
    Earth sciences
    Petrology
  NT Geothermal resources
Geodesy 526
  UF Degrees of latitude and longitude
  BT Earth
    Measurement
  NT Latitude
    Longitude
  RT Surveying
Geographic names (May subdiv. geog.) 910
  UF Names, Geographical
    Place names
  BT Names
  RT Gazetteers
Geographic names—United States 917.3
  UF United States—Geographic names
Geographical atlases
  USE Atlases
Geographical distribution
  USE types of plants and animals with the subdivision *Geographical distribution,* e.g. **Fishes—Geographical distribution** [to be added as needed]
Geographical distribution of animals and plants
  USE Biogeography

Geographical distribution of people
  USE **Human geography**
Geographical distribution of plants
  USE **Plants—Geographical distribution**
Geographical myths   398.23
  UF Cities, Imaginary
      Fictitious places
      Imaginary places
      Islands, Imaginary
      Places, Imaginary
  BT **Mythology**
  NT **Atlantis**
      Lost continents
Geography   910
  Use for general materials, frequently school materials, that describe the surface of the earth and its interrelationship with various peoples, animals, natural products, and industries. Materials limited to a particular place are entered under the name of the place with the subdivision *Geography*. General descriptive materials and travel materials limited to a particular place are entered under the name of the place (except extinct cities) with the subdivision *Description and travel*. Materials on the physical features of the earth's surface and its atmosphere are entered under **Physical geography.**
  UF Social studies
  SA names of countries, states, etc.,
      with the subdivisions *Description and travel* and *Geography;* and sacred works with the subdivision *Geography,* e.g. **Bible—Geography** [to be added as needed]
  BT **Earth**
      Earth sciences
      World history
  NT **Atlases**
      Bible—Geography
      Biogeography
      Boundaries
      Commercial geography
      Exploration
      Gazetteers
      Greece—Geography
      Historical geography
      Human geography
      Maps
      Military geography
      Physical geography
      Regionalism
      Surveying

United States—Description and travel
United States—Geography
Voyages and travels
Geography, Ancient
  USE **Ancient geography**
Geography—Dictionaries   910.3
  Use for dictionaries of geographic terms. Materials listing names and descriptions of places are entered under **Gazetteers.**
  BT **Encyclopedias and dictionaries**
Geography, Historical
  USE **Historical geography**
Geography, Political
  USE **Geopolitics**
Geological chemistry
  USE **Geochemistry**
Geological physics
  USE **Geophysics**
Geologists (May subdiv. geog.)   **551.092; 920**
  BT **Scientists**
Geology (May subdiv. geog.)   **550**
  Use for materials limited to the structure and composition of the earth and the physical changes it has undergone and is still undergoing. General materials on the whole planet are entered under **Earth.**
  UF Geoscience
  SA names of planets and types of ore with the subdivision *Geology* [to be added as needed]
  BT **Earth sciences**
      Science
  NT **Astrogeology**
      Continental drift
      Continental shelf
      Coral reefs and islands
      Earthquakes
      Economic geology
      Erosion
      Faults (Geology)
      Geysers
      Glaciers
      Historical geology
      Landforms
      Minerals
      Ore deposits
      Physical geography
      Stratigraphic geology
      Submarine geology
      Volcanoes

Geology—*Continued*
  RT Earth
      Petrology
      Rocks
Geology, Dynamic
  USE **Geophysics**
Geology, Economic
  USE **Economic geology**
Geology—Interactive multimedia   551
Geology, Lunar
  USE **Lunar geology**
Geology—Maps   550.22
  BT **Maps**
Geology—Moon
  USE **Lunar geology**
Geology, Petroleum
  USE **Petroleum geology**
Geology, Stratigraphic
  USE **Stratigraphic geology**
Geology—United States   557.3
Geomagnetic field
  USE **Geomagnetism**
Geomagnetism (May subdiv. geog.)   **538**
  UF Earth magnetic field
      Earth—Magnetism
      Geomagnetic field
  BT **Geophysics**
      Magnetism
Geometric art
  USE **Abstract art**
Geometric patterns
  USE **Patterns (Mathematics)**
Geometrical drawing   516; 604.2
  UF Mathematical drawing
      Plans
  BT **Drawing**
      Geometry
  NT **Descriptive geometry**
      Graphic methods
      Perspective
  RT **Mechanical drawing**
Geometry   516
  BT **Mathematics**
  NT **Analytic geometry**
      Descriptive geometry
      Fractals
      Geometrical drawing
      Plane geometry
      Projective geometry
      Ratio and proportion
      Shape
      Solid geometry

      Square
      Topology
      Trigonometry
      Volume (Cubic content)
Geometry, Analytic
  USE **Analytic geometry**
Geometry, Descriptive
  USE **Descriptive geometry**
Geometry, Plane
  USE **Plane geometry**
Geometry, Projective
  USE **Projective geometry**
Geometry, Solid
  USE **Solid geometry**
Geophysics   550
  UF Geological physics
      Geology, Dynamic
      Physics, Terrestrial
      Terrestrial physics
  BT **Earth sciences**
      Physics
  NT **Auroras**
      Geomagnetism
      Plate tectonics
Geopolitics   320.1; 327.101
  UF Geography, Political
      Political geography
  BT **International relations**
      Political science
  RT **Boundaries**
      Human geography
      World politics
Geoscience
  USE **Earth sciences**
      Geology
Geothermal resources (May subdiv.
      geog.)   **333.8**
  UF Natural steam energy
      Thermal waters
  SA types of geothermal resources,
        e.g. **Geysers** [to be added as
        needed]
  BT **Geochemistry**
      Ocean energy resources
      Renewable energy resources
  NT **Geysers**
Geriatrics
  USE **Elderly—Diseases**
      Elderly—Health and hygiene
Germ theory
  USE **Life—Origin**

Germ theory of disease 616
　　UF　Disease germs
　　　　Germs
　　　　Microbes
　　BT　**Communicable diseases**
Germ warfare
　　USE　**Biological warfare**
German Democratic Republic
　　USE　**Germany (East)**
German Federal Republic
　　USE　**Germany (West)**
German language 430
　　May be subdivided like **English language.**
　　BT　**Language and languages**
German literature 830
　　May use same subdivisions and names of literary forms as for **English literature.**
　　BT　**Literature**
German occupation of France, 1940-1945
　　USE　**France—History—1940-1945, German occupation**
German occupation of Netherlands, 1940-1945
　　USE　**Netherlands—History—1940-1945, German occupation**
Germany 943
　　Use for materials on Germany before or after the division of the country following World War II and for materials on East and West Germany discussed collectively as occupied zones or countries. Materials limited to the eastern part of Germany from 1945 to 1990, the Russian occupation zone, or the German Democratic Republic, are entered under **Germany (East).** Materials limited to the western part of Germany from 1945 to 1990, the American, British, and French occupation zones, or the German Federal Republic, are entered under **Germany (West).** May be subdivided like United States except for *History.*
　　UF　Federal Republic of Germany
　　NT　**Germany (East)**
　　　　Germany (West)
Germany (Democratic Republic)
　　USE　**Germany (East)**
Germany (East) 943
　　Use for materials limited to the eastern part of Germany from 1945 to 1990, the Russian occupation zone, or the German Democratic Republic. Materials on Germany before or after the division of the country following World War II and materials on East and West Germany discussed collectively as occupied zones or countries are entered under **Germany.**
　　UF　East Germany
　　　　German Democratic Republic
　　　　Germany (Democratic Republic)

　　BT　**Germany**
Germany (Federal Republic)
　　USE　**Germany (West)**
Germany—History 943
Germany—History—0-1517 943
Germany—History—1517-1740 943
　　NT　**Thirty Years' War, 1618-1648**
Germany—History—1740-1815 943
Germany—History—1815-1866 943
Germany—History—1848-1849, Revolution 943
Germany—History—1866-1918 943.08
Germany—History—1918-1933 943.085
Germany—History—1933-1945 943.086
Germany—History—1945-1990 943.087
Germany—History—1990- 943.088
　　UF　Germany—History—Unification, 1990
Germany—History—Unification, 1990
　　USE　**Germany—History—1990-**
Germany (West) 943.087
　　Use for materials limited to the western part of Germany from 1945 to 1990, the American, British, and French occupation zones, or the German Federal Republic. Materials on Germany before or after the division of the country following World War II and materials on East and West Germany discussed collectively as occupied zones or countries are entered under **Germany.**
　　UF　Federal Republic of Germany
　　　　German Federal Republic
　　　　Germany (Federal Republic)
　　　　West Germany
　　BT　**Germany**
Germicides
　　USE　**Disinfection and disinfectants**
　　　　Fungicides
Germination 571.8
　　UF　Seeds—Germination
　　BT　**Plant physiology**
Germs
　　USE　**Bacteria**
　　　　Germ theory of disease
　　　　Microorganisms
Gerontology 305.26; 362.6; 612.6
　　BT　**Social sciences**
　　NT　**Aging**
　　　　Elderly
　　RT　**Old age**
Gestalt psychology 150.19
　　UF　Configuration (Psychology)
　　　　Psychology, Structural
　　　　Structural psychology

Gestalt psychology—*Continued*
  BT **Consciousness**
      Perception
      Psychology
      Senses and sensation
      Theory of knowledge
Getting ready for bed
  USE **Bedtime**
Gettysburg (Pa.), Battle of, 1863   973.7
  BT **United States—History—1861-**
      1865, Civil War—Campaigns
Geysers (May subdiv. geog.)   **551.2**
  UF Eruptions
      Thermal waters
  BT **Geology**
      Geothermal resources
      Physical geography
      Water
Ghettoes, Inner city
  USE **Inner cities**
Ghost stories   808.3; 808.83
      May be used for individual works, collec-
      tions, or materials about ghost stories.
  UF Ghosts—Fiction
      Terror tales
  BT **Fantasy fiction**
      Horror fiction
      Occult fiction
  RT **Gothic novels**
      Mystery fiction
Ghost towns (May subdiv. geog.)
      307.76
  UF Abandoned towns
      Towns, Abandoned
  BT **Extinct cities**
Ghosts (May subdiv. geog.)   **133.1**
  UF Phantoms
      Poltergeists
      Specters
  BT **Apparitions**
      Folklore
      Spirits
  RT **Haunted houses**
      Parapsychology
Ghosts—Fiction
  USE **Ghost stories**
Giantism   616.4
      Use for materials on excessive growth in
      humans. Materials on beings with a human
      form but with superhuman size or strength in
      folklore or imaginative literature are entered
      under **Giants.**

  UF Gigantism
  BT **Growth disorders**
Giants   398.21
      Use for materials on beings with a human
      form but with superhuman size or strength in
      folklore or imaginative literature. Materials on
      excessive growth in humans are entered under
      Giantism.
  BT **Folklore**
      Monsters
Gift of tongues
  USE **Glossolalia**
Gift wrapping   745.54
  UF Wrapping of gifts
  BT **Packaging**
      Paper crafts
Gifted children   155.45
  UF Bright children
      Children, Gifted
      Precocious children
  BT **Exceptional children**
  NT **Child artists**
      Child authors
Gifts   306.4; 361.7
  UF Bequests
      Donations
      Presents
  BT **Manners and customs**
  NT **Donation of organs, tissues,**
      etc.
      Free material
  RT **Fund raising**
Gifts of grace
  USE **Spiritual gifts**
Gifts of the Holy Spirit
  USE **Spiritual gifts**
Gifts, Spiritual
  USE **Spiritual gifts**
Gigantism
  USE **Giantism**
Gipsies
  USE **Gypsies**
Girl Scouts (May subdiv. geog.)
      369.463
  UF Brownies (Girl Scouts)
  BT **Girls' clubs**
      Scouts and scouting
Girls (May subdiv. geog.)   **155.43;**
      305.23082
  BT **Children**
  RT **Teenagers**
      Young women

Girls' clubs (May subdiv. geog.)   369.46
    UF   Girls—Societies and clubs
    BT   **Clubs**
         Societies
    NT   **4-H clubs**
         Camp Fire Girls
         Girl Scouts
Girls—Education (May subdiv. geog.)
    371.822
    BT   **Education**
    RT   **Coeducation**
Girls—Employment
    USE   **Women—Employment**
         Youth—Employment
Girls—Societies and clubs
    USE   **Girls' clubs**
GIs
    USE   **Soldiers—United States**
Giveaways
    USE   **Free material**
Giving
    USE   **Generosity**
Glacial epoch
    USE   **Ice age**
Glaciers (May subdiv. geog.)   **551.3**
    BT   **Geology**
         Ice
         Physical geography
Gladiators   796.8092; 920
    UF   Fighting
Gladness
    USE   **Happiness**
Glands   571.7; 573.4; 611; 612.4
    BT   **Anatomy**
         Physiology
Glands, Ductless
    USE   **Endocrine glands**
Glass   666
    BT   **Building materials**
         Ceramics
    NT   **Glass fibers**
Glass construction   693
    BT   **Building materials**
Glass fibers   666
    UF   Fiber glass
         Fiberglass
         Fibers, Glass
         Glass, Spun
         Spun glass
    BT   **Fibers**
         Glass

Glass industry
    USE   **Glass manufacture**
Glass manufacture (May subdiv. geog.)
    666
    UF   Glass industry
    BT   **Ceramic industry**
Glass painting and staining (May subdiv.
    geog.)   **748.5**
    UF   Glass, Stained
         Painted glass
         Stained glass
         Windows, Stained glass
    BT   **Decoration and ornament**
         Painting
Glass, Spun
    USE   **Glass fibers**
Glass, Stained
    USE   **Glass painting and staining**
Glasses
    USE   **Eyeglasses**
Glassware (May subdiv. geog.)   **642;**
    748.2
    BT   **Decorative arts**
         Tableware
    RT   **Vases**
Glassware—Trademarks   748.2
    BT   **Trademarks**
Glazes   666; 738.1
    BT   **Ceramics**
         Pottery
Gliders (Aeronautics)   629.133
    UF   Aircraft
         Sailplanes (Aeronautics)
    BT   **Aeronautics**
         Airplanes
Gliding and soaring   797.5
    UF   Air surfing
         Hang gliding
         Soaring flight
    BT   **Aeronautics**
Global Positioning System   526; 623.89
    UF   GPS (Navigation system)
    BT   **Navigation**
Global satellite communications systems
    USE   **Artificial satellites in telecom-**
         munication
Global warming
    USE   **Greenhouse effect**
Globalization   303.48; 337
    UF   Internationalization
    BT   **International relations**

Globes   912
  BT   Maps
Glossaries
  USE   Encyclopedias and dictionaries
Glossolalia   234
  UF   Gift of tongues
       Speaking in tongues
       Speaking with tongues
  BT   Spiritual gifts
  RT   Pentecostalism
Glow-in-the-dark books
  UF   Luminescent books
       Luminous books
  BT   Picture books for children
       Toy and movable books
Glue   668
  BT   Adhesives
Glue sniffing
  USE   Solvent abuse
Gnomes   398.21
  BT   Folklore
Gnosticism   273; 299
  BT   Church history—30-600, Early
       church
       Philosophy
       Religions
GNP
  USE   Gross national product
Go-karts
  USE   Karts and karting
Goblins   398.21
  BT   Folklore
God   211; 212; 231
       May subdivide by religion as needed, e.g.
       God—Christianity.
  NT   Femininity of God
       Providence and government of
       God
       Revelation
  RT   Metaphysics
       Monotheism
       Religion
       Theism
       Theology
God—Christianity   231
  BT   Christianity—Doctrines
  NT   Holy Spirit
       Jesus Christ
       Trinity
God—Femininity
  USE   Femininity of God

God—Providence and government
  USE   Providence and government of
       God
God—Sovereignty
  USE   Providence and government of
       God
Goddess movement
  USE   Goddess religion
Goddess religion (May subdiv. geog.)
       201
  UF   Goddess movement
       Mother Goddess religion
  BT   Paganism
  RT   Gods and goddesses
       Wicca
       Women—Religious life
Goddesses
  USE   Gods and goddesses
Gods
  USE   Gods and goddesses
Gods and goddesses   201
  UF   Deities
       Goddesses
       Gods
  SA   names of gods and goddesses,
       e.g. Zeus (Greek deity); Ves-
       ta (Roman deity); etc. [to be
       added as needed]
  NT   Vesta (Roman deity)
       Zeus (Greek deity)
  RT   Goddess religion
       Mythology
       Religions
Gold (May subdiv. geog.)   332.4; 553.4;
       669
  BT   Chemical elements
       Precious metals
  NT   Goldwork
  RT   Coinage
       Gold mines and mining
       Money
Gold articles
  USE   Goldwork
Gold discoveries
  USE   names of places with the subdi-
       vision Gold discoveries, e.g.
       California—Gold discoveries
       [to be added as needed]
Gold fish
  USE   Goldfish

Gold mines and mining (May subdiv. geog.) **622**
  UF   Gold rush
         Gold rushes
  SA   names of places with the subdivision *Gold discoveries,* e.g.
         California—Gold discoveries [to be added as needed]
  BT   **Mines and mineral resources**
  NT   **Prospecting**
  RT   **Gold**
Gold plate
  USE **Plate**
Gold rush
  USE **Gold mines and mining**
Gold rushes
  USE **Gold mines and mining**
Gold work
  USE **Goldwork**
Golden Gate Bridge (San Francisco, Calif.) **624.209794; 979.4**
  BT   **Bridges**
Golden rule **170**
  UF   Rule, Golden
  BT   **Ethics**
Goldfish **597.5**
  UF   Gold fish
  BT   **Fishes**
Goldsmithing
  USE **Goldwork**
Goldwork (May subdiv. geog.) **739.2**
  UF   Gold articles
         Gold work
         Goldsmithing
  BT   **Art metalwork**
         Gold
         Metalwork
  NT   **Plate**
Golf courses **796.352**
  BT   **Sports facilities**
Good and evil **170; 214; 241**
  UF   Evil
         Wickedness
  BT   **Ethics**
         Philosophy
         Theology
  NT   **Guilt**
         Sin
Good Friday **263**
  BT   **Christian holidays**
         Holy Week

       Lent
  RT   **Jesus Christ—Crucifixion**
Good grooming
  USE **Personal grooming**
Goose
  USE **Geese**
Gorge-purge syndrome
  USE **Bulimia**
Gospel music **781.71; 782.25**
  UF   Music, Gospel
         Revivals—Music
  BT   **African American music**
         Church music
         Popular music
  RT   **Spirituals (Songs)**
Gossip **070.4; 177; 302.2**
  BT   **Journalism**
         Libel and slander
  NT   **Tattling**
Gothic architecture (May subdiv. geog.) **723**
  UF   Architecture, Gothic
  BT   **Medieval architecture**
  RT   **Cathedrals**
         Church architecture
         Gothic art
Gothic art (May subdiv. geog.) **709.02**
  UF   Art, Gothic
  BT   **Medieval art**
  RT   **Christian art**
         Gothic architecture
Gothic decoration and ornament
  USE **Decoration and ornament—Gothic style**
Gothic fiction
  USE **Gothic novels**
Gothic novels **808.3**
    May be used for individual works, collections, or materials about contemporary novels that have a medieval setting and usually include castles and ghosts. For materials on literature of the eighteenth and nineteenth centuries featuring medieval settings and romantic gloom, use **Gothic revival (Literature).**
  UF   Gothic fiction
  BT   **Historical fiction**
         Horror fiction
         Occult fiction
  RT   **Ghost stories**
         Love stories
         Romantic suspense novels

Gothic revival (Architecture) (May
    subdiv. geog.) **724.3**
  BT **Architecture**
Gothic revival (Art) (May subdiv. geog.)
    700.41
  BT **Art**
Gothic revival (Literature) (May subdiv.
    geog.) **808.83; 823.08**
    Use for materials on literature of the
eighteenth and nineteenth centuries featuring
medieval settings and romantic gloom. For
contemporary novels that have a medieval set-
ting and usually include castles and ghosts use
Gothic novels.
  BT **Literature**
Goths **305.83**
  UF East Goths
      Ostrogoths
  BT **Teutonic peoples**
Gout **616.3**
  BT **Arthritis**
      Rheumatism
Government
  USE **Political science**
      and names of countries, cities,
      etc., with the subdivision *Pol-*
      itics and government, e.g.
      United States—Politics and
      government and names of
      Christian denominations with
      the subdivision *Government,*
      e.g. **Church of England—**
      Government [to be added as
      needed]
Government agencies
  USE **Administrative agencies**
Government aid (May subdiv. geog.)
    336
    Use for materials on aid from governments
at any level in non-federal systems and on aid
from state, provincial, or local governments in
federal systems. Materials on central govern-
ment aid in federal systems are entered under
Federal aid.
  SA government aid to specific en-
      deavors, e.g. **Government aid**
      to libraries [to be added as
      needed]
  BT **Public finance**
  NT **Government aid to education**
      Government aid to libraries
  RT **Federal aid**

Government aid to education (May
    subdiv. geog.) **379.1**
  UF Education—Government aid
      Education—State aid
      State aid to education
  BT **Education—Finance**
      Education—Government policy
      Government aid
Government aid to libraries (May subdiv.
    geog.) **021.8**
  UF Libraries—Government aid
      Libraries—State aid
      State aid to libraries
  BT **Government aid**
      Libraries—Government policy
      Library finance
Government and business
  USE **Economic policy**
Government and the press
  USE **Press—Government policy**
Government budgets
  USE **Budget**
Government buildings
  USE **Public buildings**
Government business enterprises (May
    subdiv. geog.) **338.7**
  UF Government companies
      Nationalized companies
      Public enterprises
  SA types of industries with the sub-
      division *Government owner-*
      ship, e.g. **Electric utilities—**
      Government ownership;
      which may be further subdi-
      vided geographically [to be
      added as needed]
  BT **Business enterprises**
Government by commission
  USE **Municipal government by com-**
      mission
Government companies
  USE **Government business enter-**
      prises
Government, Comparative
  USE **Comparative government**
Government debts
  USE **Public debts**
Government departments
  USE **Executive departments**
Government documents
  USE **Government publications**

Government employees
USE **Civil service**
Government health insurance
USE **National health insurance**
Government housing
USE **Public housing**
Government investigations
USE **Governmental investigations**
Government lending (May subdiv. geog.)
332.7; 354.8
BT **Domestic economic assistance**
Economic policy
Loans
Public finance
Government libraries (May subdiv. geog.)
027.5
Use for materials on special libraries maintained by government funds.
UF Federal libraries
Libraries, Governmental
BT **Special libraries**
NT **National libraries**
State libraries
Government, Local
USE **Local government**
Government, Military
USE **Military government**
Government ministries
USE **Executive departments**
Government, Municipal
USE **Municipal government**
Government officials
USE **Public officers**
Government ownership (May subdiv.
geog.) **333.1; 338.9**
UF Nationalization
Public ownership
Socialization of industry
State ownership
SA types of industries with the subdivision *Government ownership*, e.g. **Electric utilities— Government ownership;** which may be further subdivided geographically [to be added as needed]
BT **Economic policy**
Industrial policy
Socialism
NT **Municipal ownership**
Railroads—Government policy
RT **Privatization**

Government ownership of railroads
USE **Railroads—Government policy**
Government policy
USE **Buy national policy**
Commercial policy
Cultural policy
Economic policy
Energy policy
Environmental policy
Fiscal policy
Industrial policy
Labor policy
Military policy
Monetary policy
Social policy
Wage-price policy
and subjects, ethnic groups, and classes of persons with the subdivision *Government policy,* e.g. **Genetic engineering—Government policy; Homeless persons—Government policy;** etc., which may be further subdivided geographically [to be added as needed]
Government procurement
USE **Government purchasing**
Government property, Surplus
USE **Surplus government property**
Government publications (May subdiv. geog.) **011; 015; 025.17**
UF Documents
Government documents
Official publications
Public documents
BT **Library resources**
Government publications—Chicago (Ill.)
015.773
UF Chicago (Ill.)—Government publications
Government publications—Ohio
015.771
UF Ohio—Government publications
Government publications—United States
015.73; 025.17
UF United States—Government publications

331

Government purchasing (May subdiv. geog.) **352.5**
 UF Government procurement
  Procurement, Government
  Public procurement
  Public purchasing
 BT **Purchasing**
 NT **Buy national policy**
Government records—Preservation
 USE **Archives**
Government regulation of commerce
 USE **Commercial policy**
  Industrial laws and legislation
  Interstate commerce
Government regulation of industry
 USE **Industrial policy**
Government regulation of railroads
 USE **Railroads—Government policy**
Government relations
 USE ethnic groups with the subdivision *Government relations,* e.g. **Native Americans—Government relations** [to be added as needed]
Government reorganization
 USE **Administrative agencies—Reorganization**
Government, Resistance to
 USE **Resistance to government**
Government service
 USE **Civil service**
Government spending policy
 USE **United States—Appropriations and expenditures**
Government subsidies
 USE **Subsidies**
Government surveys
 USE **Surveys**
Government transfer payments
 USE **Transfer payments**
Governmental investigations (May subdiv. geog.) **328.3; 353.4**
 Use for materials on investigations initiated by the legislative, executive, or judicial branches of the government, usually of some particular problem of public interest.
 UF Congressional investigations
  Executive investigations
  Government investigations
  Judicial investigations
  Legislative investigations
 BT **Administration of justice**

Governmental investigations—United States 328.3; 353.4
 UF United States—Governmental investigations
Governments in exile
 USE names of wars with the subdivision *Governments in exile,* e.g. **World War, 1939-1945—Governments in exile** [to be added as needed]
Governors (May subdiv. geog.) **352.23; 920**
 BT **State governments**
GPS (Navigation system)
 USE **Global Positioning System**
Grace (Theology) 202; 234
 BT **Doctrinal theology**
  Salvation
 NT **Sacraments**
  Spiritual gifts
Grade repetition
 USE **Promotion (School)**
Grade retention
 USE **Promotion (School)**
Grade schools
 USE **Elementary schools**
Grading and marking (Education) 371.27
 UF Grading and marking (Students)
  Marking and grading (Education)
  Students—Grading and marking
 BT **Educational tests and measurements**
 NT **Ability grouping in education**
  Promotion (School)
 RT **School reports**
Grading and marking (Students)
 USE **Grading and marking (Education)**
Graduate Record Examination 378.1
 UF GRE
 BT **Colleges and universities—Entrance examinations**
  Examinations
Graduate Record Examination—Study guides 378.1
Graduates, College
 USE **College graduates**
Graduation
 USE **Commencements**

Graffiti (May subdiv. geog.) 080;
808.88
  BT **Inscriptions**
      Vandalism
Graft in politics
  USE **Political corruption**
Grafting 631.5
  BT **Plant propagation**
Grail 398
  UF Holy Grail
  BT **Folklore**
Grail—Legends 398; 809
  RT **Arthurian romances**
Grain 633.1
  UF Cereals
  SA types of cereal plants, e.g.
      Corn; Wheat; etc. [to be
      added as needed]
  NT **Corn**
      Wheat
  RT **Flour**
Grain—Storage (May subdiv. geog.)
633.1
Grammar 415
  SA names of languages with the
      subdivision *Grammar* [to be
      added as needed]
  BT **Language and languages**
      Linguistics
  NT **English language—Grammar**
Grammar schools
  USE **Elementary education**
Gramophone
  USE **Phonograph**
Grandparent and child
  USE **Grandparent-grandchild rela-**
       tionship
Grandparent-grandchild relationship
306.874
    Use for materials on the interaction between
grandparents and their grandchildren. Materi-
als restricted to the legal right of grandparents
to visit their grandchildren are entered under
Visitation rights (Domestic relations). Mate-
rials on the skills, etc., needed for being an
effective grandparent are entered under
Grandparenting.
  UF Grandparent and child
  BT **Family**
      Grandparents
Grandparenting 306.874
    Use for materials on the skills, etc., needed
for being an effective grandparent. Materials

on the interaction between grandparents and
their grandchildren are entered under **Grand-
parent-grandchild relationship.**
  BT **Grandparents**
      Parenting
Grandparents 306.874
  BT **Parents**
  NT **Foster grandparents**
      Grandparent-grandchild rela-
        tionship
      Grandparenting
      Grandparents as parents
Grandparents as parents 306.874
  UF Parenting by grandparents
  BT **Grandparents**
      Parenting
Grange 334
  BT **Agriculture—Societies**
Granite 552; 553.5
  BT **Rocks**
      Stone
Grants
  USE **Grants-in-aid**
       Subsidies
Grants-in-aid (May subdiv. geog.)
336.1; 352.73
    Use for materials on grants of money made
from a central government to a local govern-
ment.
  UF Grants
  SA federal aid to particular endeav-
      ors, e.g. **Federal aid to edu-**
      cation [to be added as need-
      ed]
  BT **Public finance**
  RT **Domestic economic assistance**
Grapes 634.8; 641.3
  UF Viticulture
  BT **Fruit**
  RT **Vineyards**
      Wine and wine making
Graph theory 511
  UF Graphs, Theory of
      Theory of graphs
  BT **Algebra**
      Mathematical analysis
      Topology
Graphic arts (May subdiv. geog.) 760
  UF Arts, Graphic
  SA types of graphic arts [to be add-
      ed as needed]

Graphic arts—*Continued*
- BT   **Art**
- NT   **Clip art**
  - **Drawing**
  - **Engraving**
  - **Painting**
  - **Photography**
  - **Printing**
  - **Prints**
  - **Typography**

Graphic arts—United States   760.0973
- UF   American graphic arts

Graphic fiction
- USE   **Graphic novels**

Graphic methods   001.4; 511
- UF   Flow charts
  - Flowcharting
  - Graphs
- BT   **Drawing**
  - **Geometrical drawing**
  - **Mechanical drawing**
- NT   **Statistics—Graphic methods**

Graphic novels   741.5
- UF   Comic book novels
  - Graphic fiction
- BT   **Comic books, strips, etc.**
  - **Fiction**

Graphics, Computer
- USE   **Computer graphics**

Graphite   553.2
- UF   Black lead
- BT   **Carbon**

Graphology   137; 155.2

Use for materials on handwriting as an expression of the writer's character. General materials on the history and art of writing are entered under **Writing.** Materials on writing with a pen or pencil and practical or prescriptive guides to penmanship are entered under **Handwriting.**
- BT   **Handwriting**
  - **Writing**

Graphs
- USE   **Graphic methods**

Graphs, Theory of
- USE   **Graph theory**

Grass (Drug)
- USE   **Marijuana**

Grasses (May subdiv. geog.)   **584; 633.2**
- BT   **Plants**
- RT   **Feeds**
  - **Forage plants**
  - **Hay**

Lawns

Grasslands (May subdiv. geog.)   **577.4; 578.74**
- BT   **Land use**
- NT   **Prairies**

Gratefulness
- USE   **Gratitude**

Gratitude   179
- UF   Gratefulness
  - Thankfulness
- BT   **Emotions**
  - **Virtue**

Graves
- USE   **Burial**
  - **Cemeteries**
  - **Epitaphs**
  - **Funeral rites and ceremonies**
  - **Mounds and mound builders**
  - **Tombs**

Graveyards
- USE   **Cemeteries**

Gravitation   521; 531

Use for materials on the phenomenon in physics of attraction between masses. Materials on the gravitational pull of the earth or other planets or celestial bodies on objects at or near their surface are entered under **Gravity.**
- BT   **Physics**
- NT   **Gravity**
- RT   **Relativity (Physics)**

Gravity   531

Use for materials on the gravitational pull of the earth or other planets or celestial bodies on objects at or near their surface. Materials on the phenomenon in physics of attraction between masses are entered under **Gravitation.**
- UF   Earth—Gravity
- BT   **Gravitation**

Gravity free state
- USE   **Weightlessness**

Gray Friars
- USE   **Franciscans**

GRE
- USE   **Graduate Record Examination**

Grease
- USE   **Lubrication and lubricants**
  - **Oils and fats**

Great books program
- USE   **Discussion groups**

Great Britain   941

Use for materials on the United Kingdom of Great Britain and Northern Ireland, which

Great Britain—*Continued*
comprises England, Scotland, Wales, and
Northern Ireland, as well as for materials on
the island of Great Britain. May be subdivided
like United States except for *History*. Materials limited to one of the constituent parts of
the United Kingdom, apart from materials relating to history or politics and government,
are entered under that part, e.g. **England.**

NT **England**

Great Britain—**Colonies**   325

UF   British Empire

BT   **Colonies**

RT   **Commonwealth countries**

Great Britain—**History**   941

UF   England—History

English history

Great Britain—**History**—**0-1066**   941.01

NT   **Anglo-Saxons**

Celts

Great Britain—**History**—**1066-1154, Norman period**   941.02

NT   **Domesday book**

**Hastings (East Sussex, Eng-
land), Battle of, 1066**

Normans

Great Britain—**History**—**1066-1485, Medieval period**   941.03

NT   **Hundred Years' War, 1339-
1453**

Great Britain—**History**—**1154-1399, Plan-
tagenets**   941.03

NT   **Magna Carta**

Great Britain—**History**—**1399-1485, Lan-
caster and York**   941.04

Great Britain—**History**—**1455-1485,
Wars of the Roses**   941.04

UF   Wars of the Roses, 1455-1485

Great Britain—**History**—**1485-1603, Tu-
dors**   941.05

NT   **Spanish Armada, 1588**

Great Britain—**History**—**1603-1714, Stu-
arts**   941.06

Great Britain—**History**—**1642-1660, Civil
War and Commonwealth**   941.06

UF   Civil War—England

Commonwealth of England

Great Britain—**History**—**1714-1837**
941.07

NT   **War of 1812**

Great Britain—**History**—**19th century**
941.081

RT   **Industrial revolution**

Great Britain—History—1853-1856, Crimean War

USE   **Crimean War, 1853-1856**

Great Britain—**History**—**20th century**
941.082

Great Britain—**History**—**1945-1952**
941.085

Great Britain—**History**—**1952-**   941.085

Great Britain—**History**—**21st century**
941.086

Great Britain—**Kings and rulers**   920;
941.092

UF   Great Britain—Kings, queens,
rulers, etc.

BT   **Kings and rulers**

Great Britain—Kings, queens, rulers, etc.

USE   **Great Britain**—**Kings and rulers**

Great Britain—Prime ministers

USE   **Prime ministers**—**Great Britain**

Great Britain—Queens

USE   **Queens**—**Great Britain**

Great Depression, 1929-1939 (May
subdiv. geog.)   338.5; 909.82

UF   Business depression, 1929-1939

Depressions—1929

BT   **Depressions**

Economic conditions

Greece   938; 949.5
May be subdivided like United States except for *History*.

Greece, Ancient

USE   **Greece**—**History**—**0-323**

Greece—**Antiquities**   938

BT   **Classical antiquities**

NT   **Delphi (Extinct city)**

Greece—**Biography**   920.038; 920.0495

UF   Classical biography

BT   **Biography**

Greece—**Civilization**   938
Use for materials on the civilization of
Greece, ancient and modern. Materials on the
spread of Greek civilization throughout the
ancient world following the conquests of Al-
exander the Great are entered under **Hellenism.** Materials on both ancient Greek and
Roman civilizations are entered under **Classical civilization.**

UF   Civilization, Greek

Greek civilization

BT   **Classical civilization**

NT   **Hellenism**

Greece—Description

USE   **Greece**—**Description and travel**

Greece—Description—0-323
    USE   **Greece—Description and trav-el—0-323**

Greece—Description and travel   914.95

Use for descriptive materials on modern Greece, including materials for travelers. Descriptive materials on ancient Greece, including accounts by travelers in ancient times, are entered under **Greece—Description and travel—0-323.**

    UF   Greece—Description *[Former heading]*

Greece—Description and travel—0-323 913.8

Use for descriptive materials on ancient Greece including accounts by travelers of ancient times.

    UF   Ancient Greece—Description

          Greece—Description—0-323

          [Former heading]

Greece—Geography   914.95

Use for materials on the geography of modern Greece. Materials on the geography of ancient Greece are entered under **Greece—Historical geography.**

    BT   **Geography**

    NT   **Greece—Historical geography**

Greece—Historical geography   911; 913.8

    UF   Classical geography

    BT   **Ancient geography**

          Greece—Geography

          Historical geography

Greece—History   938; 949.5

Greece—History—0-323   938

    UF   Ancient Greece

          Greece, Ancient

Greece—History—323-1453   949.5

    UF   Medieval Greece

Greece—History—1453-   949.5

    UF   Greece, Modern

Greece—History—20th century   949.507

Greece—History—1967-1974   949.507

Greece—History—1974-   949.507

Greece, Modern
    USE   **Greece—History—1453-**

Greed   178

Use for materials on any excessive desire for food, personal possessions, etc. Materials on an inordinate desire for wealth are entered under **Avarice.**

    BT   **Human behavior**

    RT   **Avarice**

Greek antiquities
    USE   **Classical antiquities**

Greek architecture (May subdiv. geog.)
    722

    UF   Architecture, Greek

    BT   **Ancient architecture**

          Architecture

Greek art   709.38; 709.495

    UF   Art, Greek

          Classical art

    BT   **Ancient art**

          Art

          Classical antiquities

Greek Church
    USE   **Greek Orthodox Church**

Greek civilization
    USE   **Greece—Civilization**

Greek language   480

Use for classical Greek. Modern Greek is entered under **Modern Greek language.** May be subdivided like **English language.**

    UF   Classical languages

    BT   **Language and languages**

    RT   **Modern Greek language**

Greek language, Modern
    USE   **Modern Greek language**

Greek letter societies
    USE   **Fraternities and sororities**

Greek literature   880

May use same subdivisions and names of literary forms as for **English literature.**

    BT   **Literature**

    RT   **Classical literature**

Greek literature, Modern
    USE   **Modern Greek literature**

Greek mythology   292.1

    UF   Mythology, Greek

    BT   **Classical mythology**

Greek Orthodox Church (May subdiv. geog.)   **281.9**

    UF   Greek Church

    BT   **Christian sects**

          Orthodox Eastern Church

Greek philosophy
    USE   **Ancient philosophy**

Greek sculpture   730.938; 730.9495

    UF   Sculpture, Greek

    BT   **Sculpture**

Green movement
    USE   **Environmental movement**

Green technology (May subdiv. geog.)
    363.7

    UF   Earth-friendly technology

          Environmental technology

Green technology—*Continued*
 BT **Technology**
Green tourism
 USE **Ecotourism**
Greenhouse effect (May subdiv. geog.)
 363.738; 551.5; 551.6
 UF Atmospheric greenhouse effect
 Carbon dioxide greenhouse effect
 Global warming
 Greenhouse effect, Atmospheric
 BT **Climate**
 Solar radiation
Greenhouse effect, Atmospheric
 USE **Greenhouse effect**
Greenhouses 631.5
 UF Hothouses
 BT **Flower gardening**
 Gardening
 Horticulture
 RT **Garden rooms**
Greeting cards 741.6; 745.594
 UF Cards, Greeting
 SA types of greeting cards [to be added as needed]
 NT **Christmas cards**
Gregorian chant
 USE **Chants (Plain, Gregorian, etc.)**
Grey Friars
 USE **Franciscans**
Grey market
 USE **Black market**
Grief 152.4; 155.9
 Use for materials on mental suffering or sorrow from causes such as loss or remorse other than the loss of a loved one. Materials on the suffering of those who have lost a loved one are entered under **Bereavement.**
 UF Sorrow
 BT **Emotions**
 RT **Bereavement**
 Consolation
 Joy and sorrow
Grievance procedures (Public administration)
 USE **Ombudsman**
Grill cooking
 USE **Barbecue cooking**
Grinding and polishing 621.9
 UF Buffing
 Polishing
 BT **Machine shop practice**
 RT **Machine tools**

Grist mills
 USE **Flour mills**
Groceries—Packaging
 USE **Food—Packaging**
Groceries—Purchasing
 USE **Grocery shopping**
Grocery shopping 641.3
 Use for materials on food buying. Materials on the principles and methods involved in the transfer of merchandise from producer to consumer are entered under **Marketing.**
 UF Food buying
 Food—Purchasing
 Groceries—Purchasing
 Marketing (Home economics)
 Supermarket shopping
 BT **Home economics**
 Shopping
Grocery trade (May subdiv. geog.)
 338.4
 BT **Food industry**
 NT **Supermarkets**
 RT **Food**
Grooming
 USE types of animals with the subdivision *Grooming* [to be added as needed]
Grooming, Personal
 USE **Personal grooming**
Gross national product (May subdiv. geog.) **339.3**
 UF GNP
 National product, Gross
 BT **Economics**
 Statistics
 Wealth
 RT **Income**
Grottoes
 USE **Caves**
Ground effect machines
 USE **Air-cushion vehicles**
Ground water
 USE **Groundwater**
Grounds maintenance 712
 Use for materials on maintenance of public, industrial, and institutional grounds and large estates.
 BT **Gardening**
 NT **Roadside improvement**
Groundwater (May subdiv. geog.)
 551.49; 553.7
 UF Ground water
 Subterranean water

Groundwater—*Continued*
      Underground water
  BT **Water**
Group decision making   302.3; 658.4
  BT **Decision making**
Group discussion
  USE **Discussion groups**
Group dynamics
  USE **Social groups**
Group homes   362; 363.5
    Use for materials on planned housing for groups of unrelated people needing supervision.
  UF Community based residences
       Group residences
       Residential treatment centers
  BT **Institutional care**
       Social work
  NT **Halfway houses**
  RT **Foster home care**
Group hospitalization
  USE **Hospitalization insurance**
Group identity   302.4
  UF Collective identity
       Community identity
       Social identity
  BT **Identity (Psychology)**
Group insurance   368.3
    Use for materials on group life insurance. Materials on group insurance in other fields are entered under the specific kind of insurance, e.g. **Health insurance.**
  UF Insurance, Group
  BT **Life insurance**
Group living
  USE **Communal living**
Group medical practice
  USE **Medical practice**
Group medical practice, Prepaid
  USE **Health maintenance organizations**
Group medical service
  USE **Health insurance**
Group method in teaching
  USE **Cooperative learning**
Group problem solving   153.4
  UF Brain storming
       Team problem solving
       Think tanks
  BT **Problem solving**
Group relations training   302
  UF Encounter groups
       Sensitivity training

       T groups
  BT **Interpersonal relations**
Group residences
  USE **Group homes**
Group social work
  USE **Social group work**
Group teaching
  USE **Cooperative learning**
Group theory   512
  UF Groups, Theory of
  BT **Algebra**
       Mathematics
       Number theory
  NT **Boolean algebra**
Group travel
  USE **Travel**
Group values
  USE **Social values**
Group work in education
  USE **Cooperative learning**
Group work, Social
  USE **Social group work**
Grouping by ability
  USE **Ability grouping in education**
Groups of persons
  USE **Persons**
Groups, Social
  USE **Social groups**
Groups, Theory of
  USE **Group theory**
Growing of Christmas trees
  USE **Christmas tree growing**
Grown-up abused children
  USE **Adult child abuse victims**
Growth   155; 571.8; 612.6
  SA subjects with the subdivision
       Growth, e.g. **Children—**
       Growth; Cities and towns—
       Growth; Plants—Growth;
       etc. [to be added as needed]
  BT **Physiology**
Growth disorders   616.4
  UF Abnormal growth
       Abnormalities, Human
       Development
       Failure to thrive syndrome
       Human abnormalities
  BT **Metabolism**
  NT **Dwarfism**
       Giantism

Growth disorders—*Continued*
   RT   **Birth defects**
        Fetal alcohol syndrome
Growth retardation
   USE **Dwarfism**
Guaranteed annual income (May subdiv.
     geog.)   **362.5**
   Use for materials on compensation provided
   by a government to anyone whose annual in-
   come falls below a specified level.
   UF   Annual income guarantee
        Guaranteed income
   BT   **Income**
Guaranteed income
   USE **Guaranteed annual income**
Guerillas
   USE **Guerrillas**
Guerrilla warfare (May subdiv. geog.)
     355.02; 355.4
   Use for materials on the military aspects of
   irregular warfare. General and historical mate-
   rials are entered under **Guerrillas.**
   UF   Unconventional warfare
   BT   **Insurgency**
        Military art and science
        Tactics
        War
Guerrillas (May subdiv. geog.)   **356**
   Use for general and historical materials.
   Materials on the military aspects of irregular
   warfare are entered under **Guerrilla warfare.**
   UF   Guerillas
        Partisans
   SA   names of wars with the subdivi-
        sion *Underground movements,*
        e.g. **World War, 1939-**
        1945—Underground move-
        ments [to be added as need-
        ed]
   BT   **National liberation movements**
Guests
   USE **Entertaining**
Guidance
   USE **Counseling**
Guidance counseling, Educational
   USE **Educational counseling**
Guidance counseling, School
   USE **School counseling**
Guidance, Vocational
   USE **Vocational guidance**
Guide dogs   **636.7**
   UF   Dog guides
        Dogs for the blind

       Seeing eye dogs
   BT   **Animals and the handicapped**
        Working dogs
Guidebooks
   USE names of cities (except ancient
        cities), countries, states, etc.,
        with the subdivision *Guide-*
        books, e.g. **Chicago (Ill.)—**
        Guidebooks; United States—
        Guidebooks; etc. [to be add-
        ed as needed]
Guided missiles   **358.1; 623.4**
   UF   Missiles, Guided
   SA   types of missiles and names of
        specific missiles [to be added
        as needed]
   BT   **Bombs**
        Projectiles
        Rocketry
        Rockets (Aeronautics)
   NT   **Antimissile missiles**
        Ballistic missiles
        Nike rocket
Guilt   **152.4**
   BT   **Conscience**
        Emotions
        Ethics
        Good and evil
        Sin
   RT   **Shame**
Guitar
   USE **Guitars**
Guitar music   **787.87**
   BT   **Instrumental music**
Guitars   **787.87**
   UF   Guitar
   BT   **Stringed instruments**
Gulf States (U.S.)   **976**
   BT   **United States**
Gulf War, 1991
   USE **Persian Gulf War, 1991**
Gums and resins   **547; 668**
   UF   Resins
        Rosin
   BT   **Forest products**
        Industrial chemistry
        Plastics
Gun control (May subdiv. geog.)   **323.4;**
     344.05; 363.33
   Use for materials about existing laws gov-
   erning the purchase and use of firearms and

Gun control—*Continued*
for materials about the political controversy over limiting legal access to firearms and stopping the traffic in illegal firearms.

UF   Control of guns
      Firearms control
      Firearms—Law and legislation
      Guns—Control
      Handgun control
      Right to bear arms
BT   **Law**
      Legislation

Gunpowder 623.4
UF   Powder, Smokeless
      Smokeless powder
BT   **Explosives**
      Firearms
RT   **Ammunition**

Guns
USE   **Firearms**
      Ordnance
      Rifles
      Shotguns

Guns—Control
USE   **Gun control**

Gunsmithing
USE   **Firearms industry**

Gymnastics 613.7; 796.44
UF   Calisthenics
BT   **Athletics**
      Exercise
      Sports
RT   **Acrobats and acrobatics**
      Physical education

Gynecology
USE   **Women—Diseases**
      Women—Health and hygiene

Gypsies 305.891
UF   Gipsies
      Romanies

Gypsum 553.6
BT   **Minerals**

Gyroscope 629.135; 681
BT   **Aeronautical instruments**

Habit 152.3
BT   **Human behavior**
      Psychology
NT   **Tobacco habit**
RT   **Instinct**

Habitat (Ecology) (May subdiv. geog.)
    577; 591.7
SA   types of ecology, e.g. **Marine ecology;** and types of animals, plants, and crops with the subdivision *Ecology,* e.g. **Fishes—Ecology** [to be added as needed]
BT   **Ecology**

Habitations
USE   types of animals with the subdivision *Habitations,* for materials on the natural shelters and homes animals build for themselves, such as burrows, dens, lairs, etc., e.g. **Beavers—Habitations** [to be added as needed]

Habitations, Human
USE   **Housing**

Habitations of domestic animals
USE   **Animal housing**

Habitations of wild animals
USE   **Animals—Habitations**

Habits of animals
USE   **Animal behavior**

Hades
USE   **Hell**

Haiku 808.1; 808.81
May be used for collections of haiku by one or several authors or for materials about haiku.
BT   **Poetry**

Hair 612.7; 646.7
Use for general materials on hair as well for as materials on hairdressing and haircutting.
UF   Barbering
      Coiffure
      Haircutting
      Hairdressing
      Hairstyles
      Hairstyling
BT   **Head**
      Personal grooming
NT   **Braids (Hairstyling)**
      Wigs

Haircutting
USE   **Hair**

Hairdressing
USE   **Hair**

Hairstyles
USE   **Hair**

Hairstyling
USE **Hair**
Halftone process
USE **Photoengraving**
Halfway houses (May subdiv. geog.)
362; 365

Use for materials on centers for formerly institutionalized individuals, such as mental patients or drug addicts, that are designed to facilitate their readjustment to private life.

BT **Correctional institutions**
Group homes
Halitosis
USE **Bad breath**
Halley's comet   523.6
BT **Comets**
Hallmarks
UF Marks
Marks on plate
SA types of things with identifying marks, other than plate, with the subdivision *Marks,* e.g. **Pottery—Marks** [to be added as needed]
BT **Plate**
Halloween   394.2646
UF All Hallows' Eve
BT **Holidays**
Hallucinations and illusions   616.85;
616.89
UF Delusions
Illusions
BT **Abnormal psychology**
Parapsychology
Subconsciousness
Visions
NT **Optical illusions**
RT **Apparitions**
Fantasy
Magic
Magic tricks
Personality disorders
Hallucinogenic drugs
USE **Hallucinogens**
Hallucinogenic plants
USE **Hallucinogens**
Hallucinogens   615
UF Consciousness expanding drugs
Hallucinogenic drugs
Hallucinogenic plants
SA types of hallucinogens [to be added as needed]

BT **Drugs**
Psychotropic drugs
Stimulants
Ham radio stations
USE **Amateur radio stations**
Hand shadows
USE **Shadow pictures**
Hand weaving
USE **Weaving**
Handbooks, manuals, etc.
USE subjects, classes of persons, and names of places, corporate bodies, individual literary authors, and sacred works with the subdivision *Handbooks, manuals, etc.,* e.g. **Photography—Handbooks, manuals, etc.; United States. Army—Handbooks, manuals, etc.** [to be added as needed]
Handedness
USE **Left- and right-handedness**
Handgun control
USE **Gun control**
Handguns (May subdiv. geog.)   **683.4**
UF Pistols
Revolvers
BT **Firearms**
Handheld computers
USE **Portable computers**
Handicapped (May subdiv. geog.)
305.9; 362.4
UF Disabled
NT **Architecture and the handicapped**
Discrimination against the handicapped
Handicapped children
Mentally handicapped
Physically handicapped
Sick
Socially handicapped
Sports for the handicapped
Vocational guidance for the handicapped
Handicapped and animals
USE **Animals and the handicapped**
Handicapped and architecture
USE **Architecture and the handicapped**

Handicapped children (May subdiv. geog.) **362.7**
- UF Abnormal children
  - Children, Abnormal
- BT **Children**
  - **Exceptional children**
  - **Handicapped**
- NT **Brain damaged children**
  - **Hyperactive children**
  - **Mainstreaming in education**
  - **Mentally handicapped children**
  - **Physically handicapped children**
  - **Socially handicapped children**

Handicapped—Clothing 646.4
- BT **Clothing and dress**

Handicapped—Legal status, laws, etc. (May subdiv. geog.) **346.01**
- UF Disability law
- BT **Law**

Handicapped—Nazi persecution (May subdiv. geog.) **940.53**
- UF Nazi persecution of the handicapped
- BT **Persecution**
  - **World War, 1939-1945—Atrocities**

Handicapped—Salaries, wages, etc. (May subdiv. geog.) **331.2**
- BT **Salaries, wages, etc.**

Handicapped—Services for (May subdiv. geog.) **362.4**
- UF Services for the handicapped
- BT **Human services**
  - **Social work**

Handicapped—Travel 910.2
- BT **Travel**

Handicraft (May subdiv. geog.) **745.5; 746**

Use for materials on creative work done by hand, sometimes with the aid of simple tools or machines.
- UF Crafts (Arts)
- SA types of handicrafts [to be added as needed]
- BT **Arts**
- NT **Chair caning**
  - **Collage**
  - **Craft shows**
  - **Egg decoration**
  - **Furniture finishing**
  - **Hooked rugs**
  - **Industrial arts**
  - **Leather work**
  - **Models and modelmaking**
  - **Nature craft**
  - **Paper crafts**
  - **Picture frames and framing**
  - **Polymer clay craft**
  - **Scrapbooking**
  - **Toy making**
  - **Weaving**
- RT **Arts and crafts movement**
  - **Creative activities**
  - **Decoration and ornament**
  - **Decorative arts**
  - **Folk art**
  - **Hobbies**
  - **Occupational therapy**

Handling of materials
- USE **Materials handling**

Handwriting 652

Use for materials on writing with a pen or pencil and for practical or prescriptive guides to penmanship. General materials on the history and art of writing are entered under **Writing**. Materials on handwriting as an expression of the writer's character are entered under **Graphology**.
- UF Legibility of handwriting
  - Penmanship
  - Writing—Study and teaching
- BT **Writing**
- NT **Calligraphy**
  - **Graphology**
  - **Writing of numerals**

Hang gliding
- USE **Gliding and soaring**

Hanging
- USE **Capital punishment**

Hanukkah (May subdiv. geog.) **296.4; 394.267**
- UF Chanukah
  - Feast of Dedication
  - Feast of Lights
- BT **Jewish holidays**

Happening (Art)
- USE **Performance art**

Happiness 158
- UF Gladness
- BT **Emotions**
- NT **Mental health**
- RT **Joy and sorrow**
  - **Pleasure**

Harassment, Sexual
USE **Sexual harassment**
Harbors (May subdiv. geog.) **386;
387.1; 627**
UF Ports
BT **Civil engineering
Hydraulic structures
Merchant marine
Navigation
Shipping
Transportation**
NT **Marinas**
RT **Docks**
Hard-of-hearing
USE **Hearing impaired**
Hardanger needlework 746.44
UF Norwegian drawn work
BT **Drawn work
Embroidery
Needlework**
Hardware 683
BT **Iron industry**
NT **Knives**
Hares
USE **Rabbits**
Harlem Renaissance 810.9; 974.7
UF New Negro Movement
BT **African American art
African American music
American literature—African
American authors**
Harmful insects
USE **Insect pests**
Harmony 781.2
BT **Composition (Music)
Music
Music—Theory**
Harry S. Truman Library 026
BT **Presidents—United States—Ar-
chives**
Harvesting machinery 631.3
UF Reapers
BT **Agricultural machinery**
Hashish
USE **Marijuana**
Hasidism (May subdiv. geog.) **296.8**
UF Chasidism
Hassidism
BT **Judaism**
Hassidism
USE **Hasidism**

**Hastings (East Sussex, England), Battle
of, 1066 941.02**
BT **Great Britain—History—1066-
1154, Norman period**
Hate 152.4
BT **Emotions**
Hate crimes (May subdiv. geog.) **364**
UF Bias attacks
Bias crimes
Bigotry-motivated crimes
Crimes of hate
Prejudice-motivated crimes
BT **Crime
Discrimination
Violence**
Hatha yoga 613.7
UF Yoga exercises
Yoga, Hatha
BT **Exercise
Yoga**
Hats (May subdiv. geog.) **391.4; 646.5;
687**
UF Millinery
BT **Clothing and dress
Costume**
Haunted houses (May subdiv. geog.)
133.1
BT **Houses**
RT **Ghosts**
Hawking
USE **Falconry**
Hay 633.2
SA types of hay crops, e.g. **Alfalfa**
[to be added as needed]
BT **Farm produce
Forage plants**
RT **Feeds
Grasses**
Hay fever 616.2
BT **Allergy**
Hazardous materials
USE **Hazardous substances**
Hazardous occupations 331.702
UF Dangerous occupations
BT **Occupations**
RT **Industrial accidents
Occupational diseases
Occupational health and safety**
Hazardous substances 363.17; 604.7
UF Dangerous materials
Hazardous materials

Hazardous substances—*Continued*
    Inflammable substances
    Toxic substances
  BT **Materials**
  NT **Hazardous wastes**
      Poisons and poisoning
Hazardous substances—Transportation
    363.17; 604.7
  BT **Transportation**
Hazardous waste disposal
  USE **Hazardous wastes**
Hazardous waste sites (May subdiv.
    geog.) **363.72; 628.4**
  UF Chemical landfills
    Dumps, Toxic
    Toxic dumps
  BT **Landfills**
  NT **Love Canal Chemical Waste**
      Landfill (Niagara Falls,
      N.Y.)
Hazardous wastes **363.72**
  UF Hazardous waste disposal
    Toxic wastes
    Wastes, Hazardous
  BT **Hazardous substances**
    Industrial waste
    Refuse and refuse disposal
  RT **Medical wastes**
    Pollution
HDTV (Television)
  USE **High definition television**
Head **611; 612**
  BT **Anatomy**
  NT **Brain**
    Ear
    Eye
    Face
    Hair
    Mouth
    Nose
    Phrenology
    Teeth
Head pain
  USE **Headache**
Headache **616.8**
  UF Head pain
  BT **Pain**
  NT **Migraine**
Heads of state (May subdiv. geog.)
    352.23; 920
  UF Rulers
    State, Heads of

  SA names of individual heads of
      state [to be added as needed]
  BT **Executive power**
    Statesmen
  NT **Dictators**
    Kings and rulers
    Presidents
Healing **615.5**
  BT **Therapeutics**
Healing, Mental
  USE **Mental healing**
Healing, Spiritual
  USE **Spiritual healing**
Health **613**
  Use for materials on physical, mental, and
social well-being. Materials on personal body
care are entered under **Hygiene.**
  UF Personal health
  SA parts of the body with the sub-
      division *Care,* e.g. **Foot—**
      Care; classes of persons and
      ethnic groups with the subdi-
      vision *Health and hygiene,*
      e.g. **Women—Health and**
      hygiene; and subjects and
      names of wars with the sub-
      division *Health aspects,* e.g.
      World War, 1939-1945—
      Health aspects [to be added
      as needed]
  BT **Medicine**
    Physiology
    Preventive medicine
  NT **Children—Health and hygiene**
    Diet
    Elderly—Health and hygiene
    Exercise
    Health education
    Health self-care
    Infants—Health and hygiene
    Mental health
    Nutrition
    Physical fitness
    Public health
    Rest
    Sleep
    Stress management
    Women—Health and hygiene
  RT **Diseases**
    Holistic medicine
    Hygiene

Health and hygiene
    USE   classes of persons and ethnic
             groups with the subdivision
             Health and hygiene, e.g.
             **Women—Health and hy-
             giene;** and parts of the body
             with the subdivision *Care,*
             e.g. **Foot—Care; Skin—
             Care;** etc. [to be added as
             needed]
Health aspects
    USE   subjects, industries, and wars
             with the subdivision *Health
             aspects,* e.g. **World War,
             1939-1945—Health aspects**
             [to be added as needed]
Health boards   614.06
    UF   Boards of health
          Public health boards
    BT   **Public health**
Health care
    USE   **Medical care**
Health care delivery
    USE   **Medical care**
Health care facilities
    USE   **Health facilities**
Health care personnel
    USE   **Medical personnel**
Health care reform (May subdiv. geog.)
    362.1
    UF   Health reform
          Health system reform
          Medical care reform
          Reform of health care delivery
          Reform of medical care delivery
    RT   **Health insurance**
          Medical care
Health care, Right to
    USE   **Right to health care**
Health care, Self
    USE   **Health self-care**
Health clubs
    USE   **Physical fitness centers**
Health counseling   362.1; 613
    BT   **Counseling
          Health education**
Health education (May subdiv. geog.)
    372.37; 613.07
    UF   Health—Study and teaching
          Hygiene—Study and teaching

    BT   **Education
          Health**
    NT   **Drug education
          Health counseling
          School hygiene**
    RT   **Children—Health and hygiene
          School nurses**
Health—Environmental aspects
    USE   **Environmental health**
Health examinations
    USE   **Periodic health examinations**
Health facilities (May subdiv. geog.)
    362.11
    UF   Clinics
          Health care facilities
          Medical care facilities
    BT   **Medical care
          Public health**
Health foods
    USE   **Natural foods**
Health, Industrial
    USE   **Occupational health and safety**
Health insurance (May subdiv. geog.)
    368.38
    UF   Group medical service
          Insurance, Health
          Medical insurance
    BT   **Insurance**
    NT   **Health maintenance organiza-
             tions
          Hospitalization insurance
          National health insurance
          Workers' compensation**
    RT   **Health care reform**
Health maintenance organizations (May
    subdiv. geog.)   **362.1; 368.38;
    610.6**
    UF   Comprehensive health care orga-
             nizations
          Group medical practice, Prepaid
          HMOs
          Prepaid group medical practice
    BT   **Health insurance
          Medical practice**
Health personnel
    USE   **Medical personnel**
Health professions
    USE   **Medical personnel**
Health program evaluation
    USE   **Public health—Evaluation**

Health reform
　　USE　**Health care reform**
Health resorts (May subdiv. geog.)　**613**
　　UF　Health resorts, spas, etc.
　　　　Health spas
　　　　Sanatoriums
　　　　Spas
　　　　Watering places
　　BT　**Resorts**
　　RT　**Hydrotherapy**
Health resorts, spas, etc.
　　USE　**Health resorts**
Health sciences personnel
　　USE　**Medical personnel**
Health self-care　**613; 616**
　　UF　Health care, Self
　　　　Medical self-care
　　　　Self-care, Health
　　　　Self-care, Medical
　　　　Self-examination, Medical
　　　　Self health care
　　　　Self-help medical care
　　　　Self-medication
　　BT　**Alternative medicine**
　　　　Health
　　　　Medical care
　　NT　**First aid**
　　　　Physical fitness
　　RT　**Holistic medicine**
　　　　Popular medicine
Health services personnel
　　USE　**Medical personnel**
Health spas
　　USE　**Health resorts**
　　　　Physical fitness centers
Health—Study and teaching
　　USE　**Health education**
Health system reform
　　USE　**Health care reform**
Healths, Drinking of
　　USE　**Toasts**
Hearing　**152.1; 612.8**
　　UF　Acoustics
　　BT　**Senses and sensation**
　　　　Sound
　　NT　**Hearing in animals**
　　RT　**Deafness**
　　　　Ear
　　　　Listening
Hearing aids　**617.8**
　　BT　**Deafness**

Hearing ear dogs　**636.7**
　　UF　Dogs for the deaf
　　BT　**Animals and the handicapped**
　　　　Deaf—Means of communication
　　　　Working dogs
Hearing impaired　**362.4; 617.8**
　　UF　Hard-of-hearing
　　　　Partial hearing
　　　　Partially hearing
　　BT　**Physically handicapped**
　　NT　**Deaf**
Hearing in animals　**573.8**
　　BT　**Hearing**
　　　　Senses and sensation in animals
Heart　**573.1; 611; 612.1**
　　BT　**Cardiovascular system**
　　NT　**Artificial heart**
Heart—Anatomy　**573.1; 611**
　　BT　**Anatomy**
Heart attack　**616.1**
　　UF　Heart—Infarction
　　　　Myocardial infarction
　　BT　**Heart diseases**
Heart disease
　　USE　**Heart diseases**
Heart—Diseases
　　USE　**Heart diseases**
Heart diseases　**616.1**
　　UF　Cardiac diseases
　　　　Coronary heart diseases
　　　　Heart disease
　　　　Heart—Diseases
　　BT　**Diseases**
　　NT　**Angina pectoris**
　　　　Heart attack
Heart diseases—Prevention　**616.1**
　　BT　**Preventive medicine**
Heart—Infarction
　　USE　**Heart attack**
Heart—Physiology　**612.1**
　　BT　**Physiology**
Heart resuscitation
　　USE　**Cardiac resuscitation**
Heart—Surgery　**617.4**
　　UF　Open heart surgery
　　BT　**Surgery**
Heart—Surgery—Nursing　**617.4**
　　BT　**Nursing**

Heart—Transplantation 617.4
    BT   Transplantation of organs, tissues, etc.

Heat 536
    BT   Electromagnetic waves
    NT   Steam
          Thermometers
    RT   Combustion
          Fire
          Temperature
          Thermodynamics

Heat—Conduction 536

Heat engines 621.4
    UF   Hot air engines
    BT   Engines
          Thermodynamics

Heat insulating materials
    USE Insulation (Heat)

Heat pumps 621.4
    BT   Pumping machinery
          Thermodynamics

Heat—Transmission 536

Heathenism
    USE Paganism

Heating 644; 697
    SA   subjects with the subdivision *Heating and ventilation*, e.g. **Houses—Heating and ventilation** [to be added as needed]
    BT   Home economics
    NT   Electric heating
          Fireplaces
          Furnaces
          Hot air heating
          Hot water heating
          Houses—Heating and ventilation
          Insulation (Heat)
          Oil burners
          Radiant heating
          Solar heating
          Space heaters
          Steam heating
          Stoves
    RT   Fuel
          Ventilation

Heating and ventilation
    USE types of buildings with the subdivision *Heating and ventilation*, e.g. **Houses—Heating and ventilation** [to be added as needed]

Heaven 202; 236
    BT   Eschatology
          Future life
    NT   Angels
    RT   Paradise

Heavy water
    USE Deuterium oxide

Hebrew language 492.4
    May be subdivided like **English language.**
    UF   Jewish language
          Jews—Language
    BT   Language and languages

Hebrew literature 892.4
    May use same subdivisions and names of literary forms as for **English literature.**
    UF   Jews—Literature
    BT   Literature
    NT   Bible
          Cabala
          Talmud
    RT   Jewish literature

Hebrews
    USE Jews

Heirs
    USE Inheritance and succession

Helicopters 387.7; 629.133
    UF   Aircraft
    BT   Aeronautics
          Airplanes

Helicopters—Piloting 629.132
    BT   Airplanes—Piloting

Heliports 387.7
    BT   Airports

Helium 546
    BT   Chemical elements
          Gases

Hell 202; 236
    UF   Eternal punishment
          Hades
          Retribution
    BT   Eschatology
          Future life

Hellenism 938
    Use for materials on the spread of Greek civilization throughout the ancient world following the conquests of Alexander the Great. Materials limited to the civilization of Greece, ancient and modern, are entered under **Greece—Civilization.** Materials on both ancient Greek and Roman civilizations are entered under **Classical civilization.**
    BT   Greece—Civilization

Helpful insects
    USE **Beneficial insects**
Helpfulness
    USE **Helping behavior**
Helping behavior 158
    UF   Assistance in emergencies
         Behavior, Helping
         Emergency assistance
         Helpfulness
    BT   **Human behavior**
         Interpersonal relations
    NT   **Counseling**
         Encouragement
    RT   **Altruism**
Hemp 633.5; 677
    BT   **Fibers**
    RT   **Rope**
Heraldry (May subdiv. geog.) **929.6**
    UF   Coats of arms
         Crests
         Devices (Heraldry)
         Emblems
         Pedigrees
    BT   **Archeology**
         Signs and symbols
         Symbolism
    NT   **Flags**
         Insignia
         Mottoes
         Seals (Numismatics)
    RT   **Chivalry**
         Decorations of honor
         Genealogy
         Knights and knighthood
         National emblems
         Nobility
Herb remedies
    USE **Herbs—Therapeutic use**
Herbal medicine
    USE **Herbs—Therapeutic use**
         Medical botany
Herbals
    USE **Herbs**
         Materia medica
Herbaria
    USE **Plants—Collection and preservation**
Herbicides 632; 668
    UF   Defoliants
         Weed killers

    SA   types of herbicides, e.g. **Agent Orange** [to be added as needed]
    BT   **Agricultural chemicals**
         Pesticides
    NT   **Agent Orange**
    RT   **Plants**
         Spraying and dusting
Herbs 581.6; 635
    UF   Herbals
    BT   **Plants**
    NT   **Potpourri**
Herbs—Therapeutic use 615
    UF   Herb remedies
         Herbal medicine
         Medicinal herbs
    BT   **Therapeutics**
Hereditary diseases
    USE **Medical genetics**
Hereditary succession
    USE **Inheritance and succession**
Heredity 576.5
    UF   Ancestry
         Descent
         Genes
         Inheritance (Biology)
    BT   **Biology**
         Breeding
    NT   **Chromosomes**
         DNA
         Variation (Biology)
    RT   **Eugenics**
         Genetics
         Mendel's law
         Natural selection
Heredity of diseases
    USE **Medical genetics**
Hereford cattle 636.2
    BT   **Beef cattle**
Heresies
    USE **Heresy**
Heresies, Christian
    USE **Christian heresies**
Heresy 202
    UF   Heresies
    BT   **Religion**
    NT   **Christian heresies**
Heritage property
    USE **Cultural property**
Heritage tourism
    USE **Cultural tourism**

Hermeneutics, Biblical
   USE **Bible—Criticism**
Hermetic art and philosophy
   USE **Alchemy**
          Astrology
          Occultism
Hermits (May subdiv. geog.)   **920**
   UF Recluses
   BT **Eccentrics and eccentricities**
   RT **Monasticism and religious orders**
Heroes and heroines   **920**
   UF Heroines
         Heroism
   BT **Adventure and adventurers**
   NT **Explorers**
         Martyrs
   RT **Courage**
         Mythology
Heroin   **362.29; 615**
   BT **Morphine**
         Narcotics
Heroines
   USE **Heroes and heroines**
Heroism
   USE **Courage**
          Heroes and heroines
Hertzian waves
   USE **Electric waves**
Hi-fi systems
   USE **High-fidelity sound systems**
Hibernation   **591.56**
   UF Animals—Hibernation
   BT **Animal behavior**
Hidden children (Holocaust)   **940.53**
   BT **Jewish children in the Holocaust**
Hidden economy
   USE **Underground economy**
Hidden treasure
   USE **Buried treasure**
Hides and skins   **636.088; 675**
   UF Pelts
         Skins
   BT **Animal products**
   RT **Fur**
         Leather
         Tanning
Hieroglyphics   **411**
   BT **Inscriptions**
         Writing

   NT **Rosetta stone inscription**
   RT **Picture writing**
High blood pressure
   USE **Hypertension**
High definition television   **621.388**
   UF HDTV (Television)
   BT **Television**
High-fidelity sound systems   **621.389**
   UF Hi-fi systems
   BT **Electronics**
         Sound—Recording and reproducing
   NT **Stereophonic sound systems**
   RT **Phonograph**
High-frequency radio
   USE **Shortwave radio**
High income people
   USE **Rich**
High rise buildings
   USE **Skyscrapers**
High risk students
   USE **At risk students**
High school dropouts
   USE **Dropouts**
High school education
   USE **Secondary education**
High school libraries (May subdiv. geog.)
       027.8
   UF Junior high school libraries
         Secondary school libraries
   BT **School libraries**
High school life
   USE **High school students**
High school students (May subdiv. geog.)
       373
   UF High school life
         High schools—Students
   BT **Students**
High school yearbooks
   USE **School yearbooks**
High schools (May subdiv. geog.)   **373**
   UF Secondary schools
   BT **Public schools**
         Schools
   NT **Commencements**
         Junior high schools
   RT **Secondary education**
High schools, Rural
   USE **Rural schools**
High schools—Students
   USE **High school students**

High society
USE **Upper class**
High speed aerodynamics
USE **Supersonic aerodynamics**
High speed aeronautics   629.132
BT **Aeronautics**
NT **Aerothermodynamics**
Rocket planes
Rockets (Aeronautics)
Supersonic aerodynamics
High tech
USE **Technology**
High technology
USE **Technology**
High treason
USE **Treason**
High-yield junk bonds
USE **Junk bonds**
Higher criticism
USE **Bible—Criticism**
Higher education (May subdiv. geog.)
378
UF Education, Higher
BT **Education**
NT **Adult education**
Colleges and universities
Junior colleges
Professional education
Technical education
University extension
Highland clans
USE **Clans—Scotland**
Highland costume
USE **Tartans**
Highway accidents
USE **Traffic accidents**
Highway beautification
USE **Roadside improvement**
Highway construction
USE **Roads**
Highway engineering (May subdiv. geog.)
625.7
UF Road engineering
BT **Civil engineering**
Engineering
NT **Traffic engineering**
RT **Roads**
Highway safety
USE **Traffic safety**

Highway transportation (May subdiv.
geog.) **388.3**
UF Transportation, Highway
BT **Transportation**
NT **Automobiles**
Buses
Traffic safety
Trucks
Highwaymen
USE **Thieves**
Highways
USE **Roads**
Hijacking of aircraft
USE **Hijacking of airplanes**
Hijacking of airplanes (May subdiv.
geog.) **364.15**
Use same form for the hijacking of other
modes of transportation.
UF Air piracy
Airlines—Hijacking
Airplane hijacking
Airplanes—Hijacking
Hijacking of aircraft
BT **Offenses against public safety**
Hiking (May subdiv. geog.) **796.51**
SA types of hiking, e.g.
Backpacking [to be added as
needed]
BT **Outdoor life**
NT **Backpacking**
Orienteering
RT **Trails**
Walking
Hillbilly music
USE **Country music**
Hindu philosophy   181
UF Philosophy, Hindu
BT **Philosophy**
NT **Yoga**
Hinduism (May subdiv. geog.)   **294.5**
BT **Religions**
NT **Vedas**
Yoga
RT **Brahmanism**
Hindus
Hindus (May subdiv. geog.)   **294.5092**
RT **Hinduism**
Hippies (May subdiv. geog.)   **306**
BT **Bohemianism**
Hippies—United States   306

Hispanic American authors   810.9; 920
  SA   genres of American literature
       with the subdivision *Hispanic*
       American authors [to be add-
       ed as needed]
  BT   **American authors**
  NT   **Mexican American authors**
Hispanic American literature (English)
  USE   **American literature—Hispanic**
        American authors
Hispanic American literature (Spanish)
  USE   **American literature (Spanish)**
Hispanic Americans   305.868; 973
  Use for materials on United States citizens
  of Latin American descent. Materials on citi-
  zens of Latin American countries are entered
  under **Latin Americans.**
  UF   Latinos (U.S.)
  SA   names of groups of United
       States citizens from specific
       countries, e.g. **Mexican**
       Americans [to be added as
       needed]
  BT   **Ethnic groups**
  NT   **Mexican Americans**
Historians (May subdiv. geog.)   907;
       920
  UF   Historiographers
  BT   **Authors**
  NT   **Archeologists**
  RT   **Historiography**
       History
Historians, American
  USE   **Historians—United States**
Historians—United States   907; 920
  UF   American historians
       Historians, American
Historic buildings (May subdiv. geog.)
       363.6; 720.9
  Use for materials on buildings that are asso-
  ciated with notable persons or events in his-
  tory. Materials on buildings that are merely
  old are entered under **Buildings;** or under var-
  ious types of buildings, e.g. **Castles; Church**
  buildings; Theaters; etc.
  UF   Historic houses
  BT   **Buildings**
       Historic sites
       Monuments
  NT   **Literary landmarks**
Historic buildings—Chicago (Ill.)   977.3
  UF   Chicago (Ill.)—Historic buildings
Historic buildings—Ohio   977.1
  UF   Ohio—Historic buildings

Historic buildings—United States   973
  UF   United States—Historic buildings
Historic houses
  USE   **Historic buildings**
Historic preservation (May subdiv. geog.)
       363.6
  Use for materials on identifying and pre-
  serving historically important towns, build-
  ings, sites, etc. Materials on protecting cultur-
  al heritage property from theft, misappropria-
  tion, or exportation are entered under **Cultur-**
  al property—Protection.
  UF   Preservationism (Historic preser-
       vation)
  SA   types of objects, architecture,
       etc., with the subdivision
       Conservation and restoration,
       e.g. **Theaters—Conservation**
       and restoration [to be added
       as needed]
  NT   **Theaters—Conservation and**
       restoration
  RT   **Cultural property—Protection**
Historic sites (May subdiv. geog.)   363.6
  UF   Historical sites
  BT   **Archeology**
       History
  NT   **Historic buildings**
  RT   **National monuments**
Historical atlases   911
  UF   Historical geography—Maps
       History—Atlases
       Maps, Historical
  BT   **Atlases**
  RT   **Historical geography**
Historical chronology   902
  Use for materials in which historical events
  are arranged by date.
  UF   Chronology, Historical
       Dates, Historical
       History—Chronology
  SA   ethnic groups, corporate bodies,
       military services, topics not
       inherently historical, and
       names of places with the sub-
       division *History—Chronology,*
       e.g. **Native Americans—His-**
       tory—Chronology; United
       States—History—Chronolo-
       gy; and names of individual
       persons, wars, sacred works,
       topics that are inherently his-

Historical chronology—*Continued*
torical, and topics not subdivided by *History,* such as art, music, literture, etc., with the subdivision *Chronology,* e.g. **Bible—Chronology** [to be added as needed]
BT **Chronology**
   History
Historical dictionaries
   USE **History—Dictionaries**
Historical drama   808.2; 808.82
   May be used for individual works, collections, or materials about historical drama.
   UF Chronicle history (Drama)
       Chronicle plays
       History plays
   SA historical topics, events, or personages with the subdivision *Drama,* e.g. **United States—History—1861-1865, Civil War—Drama; Napoleon I, Emperor of the French, 1769-1821—Drama** [to be added as needed]
   BT **Drama**
   NT **United States—History—1861-1865, Civil War—Drama**
       United States—History—Drama
       War films
       Western films
Historical fiction   808.3; 808.83
   May be used for individual works, collections, or materials about fiction set during a time significantly prior to the time in which it was written.
   UF Historical novels
       Historical romances
   SA historical topics, events, or personages with the subdivision *Fiction,* e.g. **Slavery—United States—Fiction; United States—History—1861-1865, Civil War—Fiction; Napoleon I, Emperor of the French, 1769-1821—Fiction;** etc. [to be added as needed]
   BT **Fiction**
   NT **Gothic novels**
       Regency novels
       War stories
       Western stories

RT **Biographical fiction**
    History
Historical geography   911
   Use for materials that discuss the extent of territory held by the states or nations at a given period of history. Materials limited to one country or region still existing in modern times are entered under the name of the place with the subdivision *Historical geography.* Materials on the geography of regions or countries of antiquity that no longer exist as such in modern times are entered under the name of the place with the subdivision *Geography.*
   UF Geography, Historical
   SA names of modern countries or regions with the subdivision *Historical geography,* e.g. **Greece—Historical geography; United States—Historical geography;** etc.; and names of places of antiquity with the subdivision *Geography,* e.g. **Gaul—Geography** [to be added as needed]
   BT **Geography**
       History
   NT **Ancient geography**
       Gaul—Geography
       Greece—Historical geography
       Rome—Geography
       United States—Historical geography
   RT **Historical atlases**
Historical geography—Maps
   USE **Historical atlases**
Historical geology (May subdiv. geog.)
   551.7
   BT **Geology**
   NT **Paleontology**
Historical materialism
   USE **Dialectical materialism**
Historical novels
   USE **Historical fiction**
Historical poetry   808.1; 808.81
   May be used for individual works, collections, or materials about historical poetry.
   UF Poetry, Historical
   BT **Narrative poetry**
   NT **United States—History—Poetry**
       World War, 1939-1945—Poetry
Historical records—Preservation
   USE **Archives**

Historical reenactments (May subdiv. geog.) **900**
- UF History—Reenactments
  Reenactment of historical events
- BT **History**

Historical romances
- USE **Historical fiction**

Historical sites
- USE **Historic sites**

Historical societies
- USE **History—Societies**

Historical tourism
- USE **Cultural tourism**

Historiographers
- USE **Historians**

Historiography **907**

Use for materials limited to the study and criticism of sources of history, methods of historical research, and the writing of history. General materials on history as a science, including the principles of history, the influence of various factors on history, and the relation of the science of history to other subjects, are entered under **History**. Materials on the interpretation and meaning of history and on the course of events and their resulting consequences are entered under **History—Philosophy.**
- UF History—Criticism
  History—Historiography
- SA subjects, wars, historical events, and names of countries, cities, etc., with the subdivision *Historiography* [to be added as needed]
- BT **Authorship**
  History
- NT **History—Sources**
  Local history
  Philosophy—Historiography
  United States—Historiography
  United States—History—1861-1865, Civil War—Historiography
- RT **Historians**

History **900**

Use for general materials on history as a science, including the principles of history, the influence of various factors on history, and the relation of the science of history to other subjects. Materials on the interpretation and meaning of history and on the course of events and their resulting consequences are entered under **History—Philosophy.** Materials limited to the study and criticism of sources of history, methods of historical research, and the writing of history are entered under **Histo-**

riography. Materials on past events themselves are entered under **World history;** or under the names of regions, countries, cities, etc., with the subdivision *History.*
- UF Social studies
- SA countries, states, etc., with the subdivisions *Antiquities; Foreign relations; History;* or *Politics and government;* and subjects with the subdivision *History,* or, for literature, film, and music headings, *History and criticism,* e.g. **Art—History; English literature—History and criticism** [to be added as needed]
- BT **Humanities**
  Social sciences
- NT **Archeology**
  Art—History
  Biography
  Chronology
  Church history
  Constitutional history
  Exploration
  Genealogy
  Historic sites
  Historical chronology
  Historical geography
  Historical reenactments
  Historiography
  Local history
  Massacres
  Military history
  Naval history
  Numismatics
  Oral history
  Scandals
  Seals (Numismatics)
  Women—History
  World history
- RT **Civilization**
  Historians
  Historical fiction

History, Ancient
- USE **Ancient history**

History and criticism
- USE types of literature, music, and other arts with the subdivision *History and criticism,* e.g. **English literature—History and criticism** [to be added as needed]

History—Atlases
USE **Historical atlases**
History, Biblical
USE **Bible—History of biblical events**
History—Chronology
USE **Historical chronology**
History—Criticism
USE **Historiography**
History—Dictionaries 903
UF Historical dictionaries
BT **Encyclopedias and dictionaries**
NT **United States—History—Dictionaries**
History—Historiography
USE **Historiography**
History, Military
USE **Military history**
History, Modern
USE **Modern history**
History, Modern—16th century
USE **World history—16th century**
History, Modern—17th century
USE **World history—17th century**
History, Modern—18th century
USE **World history—18th century**
History, Modern—19th century
USE **World history—19th century**
History, Modern—20th century
USE **World history—20th century**
History, Modern—1945-
USE **World history—1945-**
History, Modern—21st century
USE **World history—21st century**
History of doctrines
USE religious topics with the subdivision *History of doctrines,* e.g. **Salvation—History of doctrines** [to be added as needed]
History—Periodicals 905
History—Philosophy 901
Use for materials on the interpretation and meaning of history and on the course of events and their resulting consequences. General materials on history as a science, including the principles of history, the influences of various factors on history, and the relation of the science of history to other subjects, are entered under **History**. Materials limited to the study and criticism of the sources of history, methods of historical research, and the writing of history are entered under **Historiography.**

UF Philosophy of history
BT **Philosophy**
History plays
USE **Historical drama**
History—Reenactments
USE **Historical reenactments**
History—Societies 906
UF Historical societies
BT **Societies**
NT **Chicago (Ill.)—History—Societies**
Ohio—History—Societies
United States—History—Societies
History—Sources 900
Use for collections of documents, records, and other source materials upon which narrative history is based and for materials about such sources.
SA historical subjects, periods of history, individual literary and sacred works, and names of wars with the subdivision *Sources,* e.g. **World War, 1939-1945—Sources;** and subjects, ethnic groups, classes of persons, coporate bodies, and names of countries, states, etc., with the subdivision *History—Sources;* e.g. **United States—History—Sources** [to be added as needed]
BT **Historiography**
NT **Archives**
Charters
History tourism
USE **Cultural tourism**
Hittites 939
BT **Ancient history**
HIV disease
USE **AIDS (Disease)**
HMOs
USE **Health maintenance organizations**
Hoaxes
USE **Impostors and imposture**
Hobbies 790.1
UF Avocations
SA types of hobbies [to be added as needed]

Hobbies—*Continued*
- BT **Amusements**
  Leisure
  Recreation
- NT **Collectors and collecting**
- RT **Handicraft**

Hoboes
- USE **Tramps**

Hockey (May subdiv. geog.)   **796.962**
- UF Ice hockey
- BT **Winter sports**

Hogs
- USE **Pigs**

Hoisting machinery   **621.8**
- UF Lifts
- SA types of hoisting machinery [to be added as needed]
- BT **Machinery**
- NT **Cranes, derricks, etc.**
  Elevators
- RT **Conveying machinery**

Holiday cooking (May subdiv. geog.) **641.5**
- SA cooking for particular holidays, e.g. **Christmas cooking** [to be added as needed]
- BT **Cooking**

Holiday decorations   **394.26; 745.5**
- UF Decorations, Holiday
- BT **Decoration and ornament**

Holidays (May subdiv. geog.)   **394.26**

Use for materials on days of general exemption from work or days publicly dedicated to the commemoration of some person, event, or principle. Materials on occasions other than holidays devoted to festive community observances or to programs of cultural events are entered under **Festivals**.

- UF Legal holidays
  National holidays
- SA names of holidays [to be added as needed]
- BT **Days**
  Manners and customs
- NT **April Fools' Day**
  Christmas
  Fourth of July
  Halloween
  Kwanzaa
  Lincoln's Birthday
  Martin Luther King Day
  Memorial Day
  Mother's Day
  Religious holidays
  Thanksgiving Day
  Valentine's Day
  Veterans Day
- RT **Anniversaries**
  Festivals
  Vacations

Holidays, Jewish
- USE **Jewish holidays**

Holistic health
- USE **Holistic medicine**

Holistic medicine (May subdiv. geog.) **610; 615.5**
- UF Holistic health
  Wholistic medicine
- BT **Alternative medicine**
  Medicine
- RT **Health**
  Health self-care
  Mind and body

Holland
- USE **Netherlands**

Holmes, Sherlock (Fictitious character) 823
- UF Sherlock Holmes (Fictitious character)

Holocaust, 1933-1945   **940.53**
- UF Holocaust, Jewish (1939-1945)
  Jewish Holocaust (1933-1945)
- SA names of concentration camps [to be added as needed]
- BT **Antisemitism**
  Jews—Persecutions
- NT **Holocaust denial**
  Holocaust survivors
  Jewish children in the Holocaust
  Righteous Gentiles in the Holocaust
- RT **World War, 1939-1945—Jews**

Holocaust, 1933-1945—Personal narratives 920
- BT **Autobiographies**

Holocaust denial   **940.53**
- BT **Holocaust, 1933-1945**

Holocaust, Jewish (1939-1945)
- USE **Holocaust, 1933-1945**

Holocaust survivors (May subdiv. geog.) **940.53**

Use for materials on Jews who survived persecution or imprisonment under the Nazis.

Holocaust survivors—*Continued*
Accounts by Holocaust survivors are entered under **Holocaust, 1933-1945—Personal narratives.**
    BT   **Holocaust, 1933-1945**

Holography   774
    UF   Laser photography
          Lensless photography
    BT   **Laser recording**
          Photography
    RT   **Three dimensional photography**

Holstein-Friesian cattle   636.2
    UF   Friesian cattle
    BT   **Dairy cattle**

Holy communion
    USE   **Eucharist**

Holy days
    USE   **Religious holidays**

Holy Ghost
    USE   **Holy Spirit**

Holy Grail
    USE   **Grail**

Holy Office
    USE   **Inquisition**

Holy Roman Empire   943
    BT   **Europe—History**

Holy Scriptures
    USE   **Bible**

Holy See
    USE   **Papacy**
          Popes

Holy Shroud   232.96
    UF   Shroud, Holy
          Shroud of Turin
          Turin Shroud

Holy Spirit   231
    UF   Holy Ghost
    BT   **God—Christianity**
          Trinity
    RT   **Spiritual gifts**

Holy war (Islam)
    USE   **Jihad**

Holy Week   263
    BT   **Church year**
          Lent
    NT   **Easter**
          Good Friday

Home   306.8; 640
    RT   **Family**
          Home economics

Home accidents   363.13
    BT   **Accidents**
    NT   **First aid**

Home and school   371.19
    UF   School and home
    BT   **Education**
    RT   **Parent-teacher associations**
          Parent-teacher relationship

Home-based business (May subdiv. geog.)
    338.6; 658
    UF   At-home employment
          Cottage industry
          Home business
          Home labor
          Work at home
          Working at home
    BT   **Business**
          Self-employed
          Small business

Home-based education
    USE   **Home schooling**

Home business
    USE   **Home-based business**

Home buying
    USE   **Houses—Buying and selling**

Home care
    USE   **Home care services**
          and classes of persons with the subdivision *Home care,* e.g. **Elderly—Home care** [to be added as needed]

Home care services (May subdiv. geog.)
    362.14; 649.8
    UF   Home care
          Home health care
          Home medical care
          Respite care
    SA   classes of persons with the subdivision *Home care,* e.g. **Elderly—Home care** [to be added as needed]
    BT   **Medical care**
    NT   **Elderly—Home care**
          Home nursing

Home computers
    USE   **Microcomputers**

Home conservatories
    USE   **Garden rooms**

Home construction
    USE   **House construction**

Home decoration
USE **Interior design**
Home delivered meals programs
USE **Meals on wheels programs**
Home designs
USE **Domestic architecture—Designs
and plans**
Home economics (May subdiv. geog.)
640
UF Homemaking
Household management
Housekeeping
BT **Family life education**
NT **Consumer education
Cooking
Cost and standard of living
Entertaining
Food
Fuel
Grocery shopping
Heating
House cleaning
Household employees
Household equipment and supplies
Household pests
Interior design
Laundry
Mobile home living
Moving
Sewing
Shopping
Storage in the home
Ventilation**
RT **Home
Homemakers**
Home economics—Accounting
USE **Household budgets**
Home education
USE **Correspondence schools and
courses
Home schooling
Self-instruction**
Home health care
USE **Home care services**
Home instruction
USE **Home schooling**
Home labor
USE **Home-based business**
Home life
USE **Family life**

Home loans
USE **Mortgages**
Home medical care
USE **Home care services**
Home missions, Christian
USE **Christian missions**
Home movies
USE **Amateur films**
Home nursing 649.8
BT **Home care services
Nursing**
RT **Sick**
Home purchase
USE **Houses—Buying and selling**
Home remodeling
USE **Houses—Remodeling**
Home repairing
USE **Houses—Maintenance and repair**
Home repairs
USE **Houses—Maintenance and repair**
Home schooling (May subdiv. geog.)
371.04
Use for materials on the provision of compulsory education in the home as an alternative to traditional public or private schooling. General materials on the instruction of children in the home are entered under **Child rearing.**
UF Home-based education
Home education
Home instruction
Home teaching by parents
Homeschooling
BT **Education**
RT **Education—Parent participation**
Home sharing
USE **Shared housing**
Home storage
USE **Storage in the home**
Home study courses
USE **Correspondence schools and
courses
Self-instruction**
Home teaching by parents
USE **Home schooling**
Home video cameras
USE **Camcorders**
Home video movies
USE **Amateur films**

Home video systems   384.55; 621.388;
   778.59
   BT   Television
   NT   Camcorders
        Videotapes
   RT   Video recording
Homeless
   USE   **Homeless persons**
         Homelessness
Homeless people
   USE   **Homeless persons**
Homeless persons (May subdiv. geog.)
   305.5; 362.5
   UF   Homeless
        Homeless people
        Street people
   BT   **Poor**
   NT   **Refugees**
        Runaway children
        Runaway teenagers
        Tramps
   RT   **Homelessness**
Homeless persons—Government policy
   (May subdiv. geog.)   362.5
   BT   **Social policy**
Homelessness (May subdiv. geog.)
   305.5; 362.5
   UF   Homeless
   BT   **Housing**
        Poverty
        Social problems
   RT   **Homeless persons**
Homemakers   306.85; 640
   UF   Househusbands
        Housewives
   RT   **Home economics**
Homemaking
   USE   **Home economics**
Homeopathy   615.5
   BT   **Alternative medicine**
        Pharmacy
Homes
   USE   **Houses**
         and ethnic groups, classes of
         persons, and names of corpo-
         rate bodies, families, and indi-
         vidual persons with the subdi-
         vision *Homes,* e.g. **English
         authors—Homes;** which may
         be further subdivided geo-

graphically [to be added as
   needed]
Homes for the elderly
   USE   **Elderly—Institutional care**
Homes (Institutions)
   USE   **Charities**
         Institutional care
         Orphanages
Homeschooling
   USE   **Home schooling**
Homework   371.3028
   BT   **Study skills**
Homicide (May subdiv. geog.)   **364.152**
   UF   Manslaughter
        Murder
   BT   **Crime**
        Criminal law
        Offenses against the person
   NT   **Assassination**
        Euthanasia
        Poisons and poisoning
        Serial killers
        Trials (Homicide)
   RT   **Suicide**
Homicide trials
   USE   **Trials (Homicide)**
Hominids
   USE   **Human origins**
Hominids, Fossil
   USE   **Fossil hominids**
Homo sapiens
   USE   **Human beings**
Homonyms
   USE   names of languages with the
         subdivision *Homonyms,* e.g.
         **English language—Hom-
         onyms** [to be added as need-
         ed]
Homosexual marriage
   USE   **Same-sex marriage**
Homosexuality (May subdiv. geog.)
   306.76
   UF   Gay lifestyle
   BT   **Sexual behavior**
   NT   **Gay liberation movement**
        Lesbianism
   RT   **Gay men**
        Lesbians
Homosexuals, Female
   USE   **Lesbians**

Homosexuals, Male
  USE   Gay men
Honesty   179
  UF   Dishonesty
  BT   Ethics
       Human behavior
  NT   Cheating (Education)
  RT   Truthfulness and falsehood
Honey   638; 641.3
  BT   Food
  RT   Bees
Honeybee culture
  USE   Beekeeping
Honorary degrees
  USE   Academic degrees
Hooked rugs   746.7
  BT   Handicraft
       Rugs and carpets
Hoover Dam (Ariz. and Nev.)   627
  UF   Boulder Dam (Ariz. and Nev.)
       Colorado River—Hoover Dam
  BT   Dams
Hope   152.4; 179; 234
  BT   Emotions
       Spiritual life
       Virtue
Hormones   571.7; 573.4; 612.4
  BT   Endocrinology
  RT   Endocrine glands
       Steroids
Hornbooks   028.5; 096; 372.41
  BT   Reading materials
Horology
  USE   Clocks and watches
        Sundials
        Time
Horoscopes   133.5
  BT   Astrology
Horror   152.4
  BT   Emotions
       Fear
Horror—Fiction
  USE   Horror fiction
Horror fiction   808.3; 808.83
  May be used for individual works, collec-
  tions, or materials about horror fiction.
  UF   Horror—Fiction
       Horror novels
       Horror stories
       Horror tales
       Terror tales

  BT   Fiction
  NT   Ghost stories
       Gothic novels
  RT   Fantasy fiction
       Occult fiction
Horror films   791.43
  May be used for individual works, collec-
  tions, or materials about horror films.
  UF   Creature films
       Horror movies
       Monster films
  SA   types of horror films, e.g. Vam-
       pire films [to be added as
       needed]
  BT   Motion pictures
  NT   Vampire films
  RT   Fantasy films
Horror movies
  USE   Horror films
Horror novels
  USE   Horror fiction
Horror plays   808.82
  May be used for individual works, collec-
  tions, or materials about horror plays.
  BT   Drama
Horror radio programs   791.44
  May be used for individual works, collec-
  tions, or materials about horror radio pro-
  grams.
  BT   Radio programs
Horror stories
  USE   Horror fiction
Horror tales
  USE   Horror fiction
Horror television programs   791.45
  May be used for individual works, collec-
  tions, or materials about horror television pro-
  grams.
  BT   Television programs
  RT   Fantasy television programs
Horse breeding
  USE   Horses—Breeding
Horse racing   798.4
  BT   Racing
  RT   Horsemanship
Horse riding
  USE   Horsemanship
Horseback riding
  USE   Horsemanship
Horsebreaking
  USE   Horses—Training

Horsemanship (May subdiv. geog.)
798.2
UF   Coaching
Dressage
Equestrianism
Horse riding
Horseback riding
Riding
BT   **Locomotion**
NT   **Horses—Training**
Trail riding
RT   **Horse racing**
Rodeos
Horses (May subdiv. geog.)   **599.665;**
636.1
UF   Foals
BT   **Mammals**
NT   **Ponies**
Horses—Breeding   636.1
UF   Horse breeding
BT   **Breeding**
Horses—Diseases   636.089
BT   **Animals—Diseases**
Horses—Training   636.1
UF   Horsebreaking
BT   **Horsemanship**
Horses—Wounds and injuries   636.1
Horticulture (May subdiv. geog.)   **635**
Use for materials on the scientific and economic aspects of the cultivation of flowers, fruits, vegetables, etc. Materials on the practical aspects of creating gardens and cultivating plants are entered under **Gardening.** General materials about gardens, the history of gardens, various types of gardens, etc., are entered under **Gardens.**
BT   **Agriculture**
Plants
NT   **Flower gardening**
Fruit culture
Greenhouses
Hydroponics
Landscape gardening
Organic gardening
Plant breeding
Truck farming
Vegetable gardening
RT   **Gardening**
Hosiery   391.4; 687
UF   Stockings
BT   **Clothing and dress**
Textile industry

Hospices (May subdiv. geog.)   **362.17**
BT   **Hospitals**
Social medicine
Terminal care
Hospital libraries (May subdiv. geog.)
027.6
UF   Libraries, Hospital
BT   **Libraries**
Hospital personnel administration
USE   **Hospitals—Personnel management**
Hospital ships   362.1; 623.826
UF   Floating hospitals
BT   **Hospitals**
Ships
Hospital wastes
USE   **Medical wastes**
Hospitality
USE   **Entertaining**
Hospitality industry (May subdiv. geog.)
910.46
BT   **Service industries**
Hospitalization insurance   368.38
UF   Group hospitalization
Insurance, Hospitalization
BT   **Health insurance**
Hospitals (May subdiv. geog.)   **362.11**
UF   Infirmaries
Sanatoriums
SA   types of hospitals and names of individual hospitals [to be added as needed]
BT   **Institutional care**
Public health
NT   **Children's hospitals**
Hospices
Hospital ships
Life support systems (Medical environment)
Long-term care facilities
Military hospitals
Nursing homes
Psychiatric hospitals
RT   **Medical centers**
Medical charities
Hospitals—Personnel management (May subdiv. geog.)   **362.11**
UF   Hospital personnel administration
BT   **Personnel management**
Hospitals—Sanitation   614.4
BT   **Sanitation**

Hospitals—United States 362.110973
Hostage escapes
  USE Escapes
Hostage negotiation 363.3
  BT Hostages
      Negotiation
Hostages (May subdiv. geog.) 920
  SA hostages from a particular coun-
      try, e.g. **American hostages**
      [to be added as needed]
  BT Terrorism
  NT American hostages
      Hostage negotiation
Hot air engines
  USE Heat engines
Hot air heating 697
  UF Warm air heating
  BT Heating
Hot water heating 697
  BT Heating
Hotels and motels (May subdiv. geog.)
      728; 910.46
    Use for materials on public accommoda-
    tions, including inns and guest houses.
  UF Boarding houses
      Inns
      Motels
      Rooming houses
      Tourist accommodations
  BT Service industries
  NT Bed and breakfast accommo-
      dations
      Youth hostels
Hotels and motels—United States 728;
      910.460973
Hothouses
  USE Greenhouses
Hotlines (Telephone counseling) 361;
      362.2
  UF Crisis counseling
      Crisis intervention telephone ser-
      vice
      Switchboard hotlines
      Telephone counseling
  BT Counseling
      Information services
      Social work
  RT Crisis centers
Hours of labor 331.25
  UF Eight-hour day
      Five-day work week
      Overtime

Working day
Working hours
  BT Labor
  NT Absenteeism (Labor)
      Flexible hours of labor
      Leave of absence
      Part-time employment
Hours of labor, Flexible
  USE Flexible hours of labor
House boats
  USE Houseboats
House buying
  USE Houses—Buying and selling
House cleaning 648
  BT Cleaning
      Home economics
      Household sanitation
House construction (May subdiv. geog.)
      690
  UF Construction, House
      Home construction
  SA types of house construction and
      special kinds of houses [to be
      added as needed]
  BT Building
      Domestic architecture
  NT Earth sheltered houses
      House painting
      Houses—Remodeling
      Log cabins and houses
      Prefabricated houses
  RT Houses
House decoration
  USE Interior design
House drainage 690
    Use for materials on house drainage. Mate-
    rials on land drainage are entered under
    Drainage.
  UF Drainage, House
  BT Household sanitation
  NT Sewerage
  RT Plumbing
House flies
  USE Flies
House furnishing
  USE Interior design
House of Representatives (U.S.)
  USE United States. Congress. House
House painting 698
  BT House construction
  RT Industrial painting

House plans
USE **Domestic architecture—Designs and plans**
House plans 635.9
BT **Cultivated plants**
Flower gardening
Plants
Window gardening
RT **Container gardening**
Indoor gardening
House purchase
USE **Houses—Buying and selling**
House repairing
USE **Houses—Maintenance and repair**
House repairs
USE **Houses—Maintenance and repair**
House sanitation
USE **Household sanitation**
House selling
USE **Houses—Buying and selling**
House sharing
USE **Shared housing**
House trailers
USE **Mobile homes**
Travel trailers and campers
Houseboats 728.7
UF House boats
BT **Boats and boating**
Household appliances
USE **Household equipment and supplies**
Household appliances, Electric
USE **Electric household appliances**
Household budgets 640
UF Budgets, Household
Domestic finance
Family budget
Finance, Household
Home economics—Accounting
Household finances
BT **Cost and standard of living**
Personal finance
Household employees 640
UF Domestic workers
Housemaids
Servants
BT **Home economics**
Labor

Household equipment and supplies 643; 683
UF Domestic appliances
Household appliances
Labor saving devices, Household
BT **Home economics**
Implements, utensils, etc.
NT **Electric household appliances**
Kitchen utensils
Household finances
USE **Cost and standard of living**
Household budgets
Household management
USE **Home economics**
Household moving
USE **Moving**
Household pests 648
UF Diseases and pests
Vermin
SA types of pests, e.g. **Flies** [to be added as needed]
BT **Home economics**
Household sanitation
Pests
NT **Flies**
RT **Insect pests**
Household repairs
USE **Houses—Maintenance and repair**
Household sanitation 648
UF House sanitation
Sanitation, Household
BT **Sanitation**
NT **House cleaning**
House drainage
Household pests
Laundry
Ventilation
RT **Plumbing**
Household utensils
USE **Kitchen utensils**
Household violence
USE **Domestic violence**
Househusbands
USE **Homemakers**
Housekeeping
USE **Home economics**
Housemaids
USE **Household employees**
Houses (May subdiv. geog.) 643; 728
Use for general materials on buildings in which people live. Materials on residential

Houses—*Continued*
buildings from the standpoint of style and design are entered under **Domestic architecture.**

   UF   Dwellings
          Homes
          Residences
   SA   types of houses, e.g. **Earth sheltered houses;** types of architectural features, e.g. **Windows; Fireplaces;** etc.; and rooms and parts of the house, e.g. **Kitchens** [to be added as needed]
   BT   **Buildings**
   NT   **Apartment houses**
          Earth sheltered houses
          Garden rooms
          Haunted houses
          Housing
          Kitchens
          Log cabins and houses
          Prefabricated houses
          Rooms
          Solar homes
   RT   **Domestic architecture**
          House construction
Houses—Buying and selling   333.33
   UF   Home buying
          Home purchase
          House buying
          House purchase
          House selling
   BT   **Real estate business**
   NT   **Urban homesteading**
Houses—Heating and ventilation   644; 697
   BT   **Heating**
Houses—Maintenance and repair   643
   UF   Home repairing
          Home repairs
          House repairing
          House repairs
          Household repairs
Houses—Remodeling   643
   UF   Home remodeling
          Remodeling (Architecture)
          Remodeling of houses
   SA   types of houses and parts of houses with the subdivision *Remodeling,* e.g. **Kitchens— Remodeling** [to be added as needed]

   BT   **House construction**
Housewives
   USE   **Homemakers**
Housing (May subdiv. geog.)   **307.3; 363.5**

   Use for materials on the social and economic aspects of housing. Materials on the social and economic aspects of housing as it pertains to specific ethnic groups or classes of persons are entered under that group or class of persons with the subdivision *Housing.* Materials on the residential buildings of ethnic groups or classes of persons from the standpoint of architecture, construction, or ethnology are entered under the name of the ethnic group or class of persons with the subdivision *Dwellings.*

   UF   Affordable housing
          Dwellings
          Habitations, Human
          Housing needs
          Urban housing
   SA   ethnic groups, classes of persons, and domestic animals with the subdivision *Housing;* e.g. **Native Americans— Housing; Physically handicapped—Housing;** etc. [to be added as needed]
   BT   **Houses**
          Landlord and tenant
   NT   **African Americans—Housing**
          Apartment houses
          Blacks—Housing
          Cooperative housing
          Discrimination in housing
          Elderly—Housing
          Homelessness
          Labor—Housing
          Mobile homes
          Native Americans—Housing
          Physically handicapped—Housing
          Public housing
          Shared housing
          Timesharing (Real estate)
          Urban homesteading
   RT   **City planning**
Housing, Cooperative
   USE   **Cooperative housing**
Housing estates
   USE   **Planned communities**
Housing for the elderly
   USE   **Elderly—Housing**

Housing for the physically handicapped
USE **Physically handicapped—Housing**
Housing needs
USE **Housing**
Housing projects, Government
USE **Public housing**
Houston Astros (Baseball team) 796.357
UF Astros (Baseball team)
Houston (Tex.). Baseball Club (National League)
BT **Baseball teams**
Houston (Tex.). Baseball Club (National League)
USE **Houston Astros (Baseball team)**
Hovercraft
USE **Air-cushion vehicles**
How to start a business
USE **New business enterprises**
How-to-stop-smoking programs
USE **Smoking cessation programs**
How to study
USE **Study skills**
HTML (Document markup language) 006.7
UF HyperText Markup Language (Document markup language)
BT **Programming languages**
Hudson River (N.Y. and N.J.)—Bridges
USE **Bridges—Hudson River (N.Y. and N.J.)**
Hugging 158; 302.2; 395
UF Embracing
Hugs
BT **Manners and customs**
Nonverbal communication
Touch
Hugo Award 808.3
BT **Literary prizes**
Science fiction
Hugs
USE **Hugging**
Huguenots (May subdiv. geog.) **284**
BT **Christian sects**
Reformation
NT **Saint Bartholomew's Day, Massacre of, 1572**
Hull House
USE **Hull House (Chicago, Ill.)**

Hull House (Chicago, Ill.) 361.4
UF Hull House
BT **Social settlements**
Human abnormalities
USE **Birth defects**
Growth disorders
Human-alien encounters (May subdiv. geog.) **001.942**
UF Alien encounters with humans
Extraterrestrial encounters with humans
Human encounters with aliens
NT **Alien abduction**
RT **Extraterrestrial beings**
Life on other planets
Unidentified flying objects
Human anatomy 611
SA parts of the body, e.g. **Foot;** and names of organs and regions of the body with the subdivision *Anatomy,* e.g. **Heart—Anatomy** [to be added as needed]
BT **Anatomy**
RT **Human body**
Human anatomy—Atlases 611
BT **Atlases**
Human anatomy in art
USE **Artistic anatomy**
Nude in art
Human artificial insemination 346.01; 618.1
UF Artificial insemination, Human
BT **Artificial insemination**
Reproduction
Human assets
USE **Human capital**
Human behavior 150; 302
UF Behavior
Morals
Social behavior
BT **Character**
Psychology
Social sciences
NT **Aggressiveness (Psychology)**
Bad behavior
Behavior modification
Behaviorism
Cannibalism
Compulsive behavior
Conduct of life

Human behavior—*Continued*
- Consolation
- Curiosity
- Deviant behavior
- Duty
- Eating customs
- Etiquette
- Friendship
- Greed
- Habit
- Helping behavior
- Honesty
- Lifestyles
- Love
- Messiness
- Patience
- Patriotism
- Sexual behavior
- Showing off
- Social adjustment
- Sportsmanship
- Suicide—Psychological aspects
- Temper tantrums
- Truthfulness and falsehood
- Vice
- Virtue

RT   Ethics
     Interpersonal relations
     Life skills

Human beings (May subdiv. geog.)
    128; 599.9

Use for materials on the human species from the point of view of biology or anthropology. Materials on human beings as individuals are entered under **Persons.**

UF   Homo sapiens
     Human race
     Man
BT   Primates
NT   Anthropometry
     Ethnology
     Human body
     Persons
     Prehistoric peoples
RT   Anthropology

Human beings (Theology)   **202; 218; 233**

UF   Man (Theology)
BT   Doctrinal theology
NT   Soul

Human body   **612**

Use for materials on the human body not limited to anatomy or physiology.

UF   Body
SA   parts of the body, e.g. **Foot** [to be added as needed]
BT   **Human beings**
     Self
NT   **Body image**
     Body weight
RT   **Human anatomy**
     Mind and body
     Physiology

Human capital (May subdiv. geog.)
    658.3

Use for materials on investments of capital in training and educating employees to improve their productivity. Materials on the strength of a country in terms of available personnel, both military and industrial, are entered under **Manpower.**

UF   Human assets
     Human resources
BT   **Capital**
RT   **Labor supply**

Human cloning   **571.8; 660.6**
BT   **Cloning**

Human cloning—Ethical aspects   **174**
BT   **Ethics**

Human cold storage
USE   **Cryonics**

Human ecology (May subdiv. geog.)
    304.2

UF   Ecology, Human
     Ecology, Social
     Social ecology
BT   **Sociology**
NT   **Environmental influence on humans**
     Human geography
     Human influence on nature
     Human settlements
     Population
     Social psychology
     Survival skills

Human ecology—Ethical aspects
USE   **Environmental ethics**

Human embryos, Frozen
USE   **Frozen embryos**

Human encounters with aliens
USE   **Human-alien encounters**

Human engineering (May subdiv. geog.)
    620.8

Use for materials on engineering design as related to human anatomical, physiological, and psychological capabilities and limitations.

Human engineering—*Continued*
    UF   Biomechanics
           Ergonomics
    BT   **Applied psychology**
           Engineering
           Industrial design
           Psychophysiology
    NT   **Life support systems (Space environment)**
           Life support systems (Submarine environment)
    RT   **Machine design**
Human experimentation in medicine (May subdiv. geog.)   **174.2**
    UF   Experimentation on humans, Medical
           Medical experimentation on humans
    BT   **Medical ethics**
           Medicine—Research
Human fertility (May subdiv. geog.)   **304.6; 612.6; 616.6**
    UF   Fertility, Human
    BT   **Birth rate**
           Fertility
           Population
    RT   **Birth control**
           Childlessness
Human figure in art
    USE **Artistic anatomy**
           Figure drawing
           Figure painting
           Nude in art
Human fossils
    USE **Fossil hominids**
Human geography (May subdiv. geog.)   **304.2**
    UF   Anthropogeography
           Geographical distribution of people
           Social geography
    BT   **Anthropology**
           Ethnology
           Geography
           Human ecology
           Immigration and emigration
    NT   **African diaspora**
           Environmental influence on humans
           Human settlements
           Jewish diaspora
    RT   **Geopolitics**

Human habitat
    USE **Human settlements**
Human influence on nature (May subdiv. geog.)   **304.2; 363.7**
    UF   Earth, Effect of man on
           Man—Influence on nature
           Nature—Effect of human beings on
    BT   **Human ecology**
    NT   **Pollution**
Human locomotion   **152.3; 612.7**
    UF   Biomechanics
           Human mechanics
           Human movement
    BT   **Locomotion**
           Physiology
    NT   **Kinesiology**
           Walking
    RT   **Musculoskeletal system**
Human mechanics
    USE **Human locomotion**
Human movement
    USE **Human locomotion**
Human origins   **599.9**
    UF   Antiquity of man
           Hominids
           Man—Antiquity
           Man—Origin
           Origin of man
    BT   **Physical anthropology**
    RT   **Evolution**
           Fossil hominids
           Prehistoric peoples
Human paleontology
    USE **Fossil hominids**
Human physiology
    USE **Physiology**
Human race
    USE **Anthropology**
           Human beings
Human records
    USE **World records**
Human relations
    USE **Interpersonal relations**
Human resource management
    USE **Personnel management**
Human resources
    USE **Human capital**
           Manpower

Human rights (May subdiv. geog.)   **323; 341.4**

Use for materials on the rights of persons regardless of their legal, socioeconomic, or cultural status, as recognized by the international community. Materials on citizens' rights as established by law or protected by a constitution are entered under **Civil rights.**

UF   Basic rights

Civil rights (International law)

Fundamental rights

Rights, Human

Rights of man

NT   **Civil rights**

Right to health care

Human services (May subdiv. geog.)   **361**

Use for general materials on the various policies, programs, services, and facilities to meet basic human needs, such as health, education, and welfare. Materials on the methods employed in social work, public or private, are entered under **Social work.** Materials on privately supported welfare activities are entered under **Charities.** Materials on tax-supported welfare activities are entered under **Public welfare.**

SA   ethnic groups and classes of persons with the subdivision *Services for,* e.g. **Handicapped—Services for** [to be added as needed]

NT   **Charities**

Handicapped—Services for

Public health

Public welfare

Social work

Human settlements (May subdiv. geog.)   **307**

UF   Human habitat

BT   **Human ecology**

Human geography

Population

Sociology

RT   **Land settlement**

Human survival skills

USE   **Survival skills**

Human values

USE   **Values**

Humane treatment of animals

USE   **Animal welfare**

Humanism (May subdiv. geog.)   **001.2; 880**

Use for materials on culture founded on the study of the classics, or more narrowly on

Greek and Roman scholarship. Materials on any intellectual or philosophical movement or set of beliefs that promotes human values as separate and distinct from religious doctrines are entered under **Secularism.**

BT   **Culture**

Literature

Philosophy

NT   **Humanities**

RT   **Classical education**

Learning and scholarship

Renaissance

Secularism

Humanism, Secular

USE   **Secularism**

Humanitarians

USE   **Philanthropists**

Humanities (May subdiv. geog.)   **001.3**

BT   **Humanism**

Learning and scholarship

NT   **Arts**

History

Literature

Music

Philosophy

Science and the humanities

RT   **Classical education**

Humanities and science

USE   **Science and the humanities**

Humans in space

USE   **Space flight**

Humidity   **551.57**

UF   Air, Moisture of

Atmospheric humidity

Relative humidity

BT   **Meteorology**

Weather

Humor

USE   **Wit and humor**

and subjects with the subdivision *Humor,* e.g. **World War, 1939-1945—Humor** [to be added as needed]

Humorists (May subdiv. geog.)   **809.7; 920**

BT   **Wit and humor**

Humorous fiction   **808.3; 808.83**

May be used for individual works, collections, or materials about humorous fiction.

UF   Comic novels

Humorous stories

BT   **Fiction**

Wit and humor

Humorous fiction—*Continued*
   RT   **Mock-heroic literature**
Humorous films
   USE   **Comedy films**
Humorous pictures
   USE   **Comic books, strips, etc.**
Humorous plays
   USE   **Comedies**
Humorous poetry   808.1; 808.81
     May be used for individual works, collections, or materials about humorous poetry.
   UF   Comic verse
        Humorous verse
        Light verse
   BT   **Poetry**
        Wit and humor
   NT   **Limericks**
        Nonsense verses
Humorous stories
   USE   **Humorous fiction**
Humorous verse
   USE   **Humorous poetry**
Hundred Years' War, 1339-1453   944
   UF   100 years' war
   BT   **Europe—History—476-1492**
        France—History—1328-1589, House of Valois
        Great Britain—History—1066-1485, Medieval period
Hungary—History   943.9
Hungary—History—1956, Revolution 943.905
   BT   **Revolutions**
Hunger (May subdiv. geog.)   **363.8**
   RT   **Fasting**
        Starvation
Hunger strikes (May subdiv. geog.)   **303.6**
   BT   **Demonstrations**
        Fasting
        Nonviolence
        Passive resistance
        Resistance to government
Hunting (May subdiv. geog.)   **799.2**
   SA   types of hunting, e.g. **Whaling;** and ethnic groups with the subdivision *Hunting,* e.g. **Native Americans—Hunting** [to be added as needed]
   NT   **Big game hunting**
        Bowhunting
        Decoys (Hunting)

        Falconry
        Game protection
        Game reserves
        Native Americans—Hunting
        Tracking and trailing
        Whaling
   RT   **Game and game birds**
        Safaris
        Shooting
        Trapping
Hunting—United States   799.2973
Hurricanes (May subdiv. geog.)   **551.55**
     Use for cyclonic storms originating in the region of the West Indies.
   SA   names of specific hurricanes [to be added as needed]
   BT   **Cyclones**
        Storms
        Winds
   RT   **Typhoons**
Husbands   306.872
   UF   Married men
        Spouses
   BT   **Family**
        Marriage
        Married people
        Men
Husbands, Runaway
   USE   **Runaway adults**
Hybridization
   USE   **Plant breeding**
Hydraulic cement
   USE   **Cement**
Hydraulic engineering (May subdiv. geog.)   **627**
   BT   **Civil engineering**
        Engineering
        Fluid mechanics
        Water power
   NT   **Drainage**
        Dredging
        Drilling and boring (Earth and rocks)
        Flood control
        Hydraulic structures
        Hydrodynamics
        Hydrostatics
        Irrigation
        Pumping machinery
        Reclamation of land
        Wells

Hydraulic engineering—*Continued*
   RT   **Hydraulics**
          Rivers
          Water
          Water supply engineering
Hydraulic machinery   621.2
   BT   **Machinery**
          Water power
   NT   **Turbines**
Hydraulic structures   627
   SA   types of hydraulic structures [to
          be added as needed]
   BT   **Hydraulic engineering**
          Structural engineering
   NT   **Aqueducts**
          Canals
          Dams
          Docks
          Harbors
          Pipelines
          Reservoirs
Hydraulics   621.2; 627
   Use for materials on technical applications
of the theory of hydrodynamics.
   UF   Water flow
   BT   **Fluid mechanics**
          Liquids
          Mechanics
          Physics
   NT   **Hydrodynamics**
          Hydrostatics
          Water
          Water power
   RT   **Hydraulic engineering**
Hydrodynamics   532
   Use for materials on the theory of the mo-
tion and action of fluids. Materials on the ex-
perimental investigation and technical applica-
tion of this theory are entered under **Hydrau-
lics.**
   BT   **Dynamics**
          Fluid mechanics
          Hydraulic engineering
          Hydraulics
          Liquids
          Mechanics
   NT   **Hydrostatics**
          Viscosity
          Waves
Hydroelectric power
   USE   **Water power**

Hydroelectric power plants (May subdiv.
   geog.)   **621.31**
   UF   Power plants, Hydroelectric
   BT   **Electric power plants**
          Water power
Hydrofoil boats   623.82
   BT   **Boats and boating**
Hydrogen   546
   BT   **Chemical elements**
Hydrogen bomb   623.4
   BT   **Bombs**
          Nuclear weapons
   NT   **Radioactive fallout**
   RT   **Atomic bomb**
Hydrogen nucleus
   USE   **Protons**
Hydrology
   USE   **Water**
Hydromechanics
   USE   **Fluid mechanics**
Hydropathy
   USE   **Hydrotherapy**
Hydrophobia
   USE   **Rabies**
Hydroponics   631.5; 635
   UF   Plants—Soilless culture
          Soilless agriculture
          Water farming
   BT   **Horticulture**
Hydrostatics   532
   BT   **Fluid mechanics**
          Hydraulic engineering
          Hydraulics
          Hydrodynamics
          Liquids
          Mechanics
          Physics
          Statics
   NT   **Gases**
Hydrotherapy   615.8
   UF   Hydropathy
          Water cure
   BT   **Physical therapy**
          Therapeutics
          Water
   RT   **Baths**
          Health resorts
Hygiene   613
   UF   Body care
          Personal cleanliness
          Personal hygiene

Hygiene—*Continued*
- SA parts of the body with the subdivision *Care,* e.g. **Foot—Care;** and classes of persons and ethnic groups with the subdivision *Health and hygiene,* e.g. **Women—Health and hygiene** [to be added as needed]
- BT **Medicine**
  Preventive medicine
- NT **Baths**
  Children—Health and hygiene
  Cleanliness
  Diet
  Disinfection and disinfectants
  Elderly—Health and hygiene
  Exercise
  Infants—Health and hygiene
  Military personnel—Health and hygiene
  Personal grooming
  Rest
  School hygiene
  Sexual hygiene
  Sleep
  Ventilation
  Women—Health and hygiene
- RT **Health**
  Sanitation

Hygiene, Military
- USE **Military personnel—Health and hygiene**

Hygiene, Sexual
- USE **Sexual hygiene**

Hygiene, Social
- USE **Public health**

Hygiene—Study and teaching
- USE **Health education**

Hymn books
- USE **Hymnals**

Hymnals 782.27

Use for collections of sacred songs that contain both words and music. Materials about hymns are entered under **Hymns.**
- UF Hymn books
  Hymnbooks
- BT **Church music**
  Hymns
  Songbooks

Hymnbooks
- USE **Hymnals**

Hymnology
- USE **Hymns**

Hymns 264; 782.27

Use for materials about hymns. Collections of hymns that contain both words and music are entered under **Hymnals.**
- UF Hymnology
- BT **Church music**
  Liturgies
  Songs
  Vocal music
- NT **Carols**
  Hymnals
  Spirituals (Songs)
- RT **Religious poetry**

Hyperactive children 155.4; 618.92
- UF Children, Hyperactive
  Hyperkinetic children
- BT **Handicapped children**
- RT **Hyperactivity**

Hyperactivity 616.85; 616.92
- UF Hyperkinesia
- BT **Diseases**
- RT **Hyperactive children**

Hyperkinesia
- USE **Hyperactivity**

Hyperkinetic children
- USE **Hyperactive children**

Hyperspace
- USE **Fourth dimension**

Hypertension 616.1
- UF High blood pressure
- BT **Blood pressure**

Hypertext 005.75

Use for materials on document retrieval networks having text files and dynamic indexes for links among documents.
- UF Hypertext systems
- BT **Multimedia**

HyperText Markup Language (Document markup language)
- USE **HTML (Document markup language)**

Hypertext systems
- USE **Hypertext**

Hypnosis
- USE **Hypnotism**

Hypnotism 154.7
- UF Animal magnetism
  Autosuggestion
  Hypnosis
  Mesmerism

Hypnotism—*Continued*
  BT Mental healing
       Psychophysiology
  RT Mental suggestion
       Mind and body
       Psychoanalysis
       Subconsciousness
       Suggestive therapeutics
IBM 7090 (Computer)   621.39
  BT Computers
ICBM
  USE Intercontinental ballistic mis-
        siles
Ice (May subdiv. geog.)   551.3
  UF Freezing
  BT Cold
       Frost
       Physical geography
       Water
  NT Glaciers
       Icebergs
Ice age   551.7
  UF Glacial epoch
  BT Earth
Ice boats
  USE Iceboats
Ice cream, ices, etc.   637; 641.8
  UF Ices
  BT Desserts
       Frozen foods
Ice (Drug)   362.29; 615
  UF Crank (Drug)
       Crystal meth (Drug)
  BT Designer drugs
       Methamphetamine
Ice hockey
  USE Hockey
Ice skating   796.91
  UF Figure skating
       Skating
  BT Winter sports
Ice sports
  USE Winter sports
Icebergs   551.3
  BT Ice
       Ocean
       Physical geography
Iceboats   623.82
  UF Ice boats
  BT Boats and boating

Icelandic language   439
  BT Language and languages
       Scandinavian languages
Icelandic language—0-1500
  USE Old Norse language
Icelandic literature   839
  UF Icelandic literature, Modern
  BT Literature
       Scandinavian literature
  RT Old Norse literature
Icelandic literature, Modern
  USE Icelandic literature
Ices
  USE Ice cream, ices, etc.
Ichthyology
  USE Fishes
Iconography
  USE Art—Themes
Icons (Religion)   704.9
  BT Christian art
Ideal states
  USE Utopian fiction
       Utopias
Idealism   141
  BT Philosophy
  RT Materialism
       Realism
       Transcendentalism
Identification
  SA subjects with the subdivision
       Identification [to be added as
       needed]
  NT Airplanes—Identification
       Bar coding
       Criminals—Identification
       DNA fingerprinting
       Fingerprints
Identity
  USE Identity (Psychology)
       Individuality
       Personality
       and classes of persons with the
       subdivision *Identity,* e.g.
       Women—Identity; ethnic
       groups with the subdivision
       Ethnic identity, e.g. Mexican
       Americans—Ethnic identity;
       and racial groups with the
       subdivision *Race identity,* e.g.
       African Americans—Race

Identity—*Continued*
        identity [to be added as
        needed]
Identity (Psychology)   126
    UF   Identity
    SA   classes of persons with the sub-
         division *Identity*, e.g. **Wom-
         en—Identity;** ethnic groups
         with the subdivision *Ethnic
         identity*, e.g. **Mexican Ameri-
         cans—Ethnic identity;** and
         racial groups with the subdi-
         vision *Race identity*, e.g.
         **African Americans—Race
         identity** [to be added as
         needed]
    BT   **Personality
         Psychology
         Self**
    NT   **Ethnicity
         Group identity
         Women—Identity**
    RT   **Ego (Psychology)**
Ideology (May subdiv. geog.)   140
    BT   **Philosophy
         Political science
         Psychology
         Theory of knowledge
         Thought and thinking**
    NT   **Political correctness**
Idioms
    USE names of languages with the
         subdivision *Idioms*, e.g. **En-
         glish language—Idioms** [to
         be added as needed]
Idyllic poetry
    USE **Pastoral poetry**
Illegal aliens (May subdiv. geog.)   **323.6;
    325; 342**
    UF   Undocumented aliens
    BT   **Aliens
         Immigration and emigration
         Underground economy**
    RT   **Sanctuary movement**
Illegitimacy (May subdiv. geog.)
    306.874; 346.01
    UF   Illegitimate children
         Legitimacy (Law)
    RT   **Unmarried fathers
         Unmarried mothers**
Illegitimate children
    USE **Illegitimacy**

Illiteracy
    USE **Literacy**
Illness
    USE **Diseases**
Illuminated manuscripts
    USE **Illumination of books and
         manuscripts**
Illumination
    USE **Lighting**
Illumination of books and manuscripts
    (May subdiv. geog.)   **096; 745.6**
    UF   Illuminated manuscripts
         Manuscripts, Illuminated
         Miniatures (Illumination of
         books and manuscripts)
         Ornamental alphabets
    BT   **Art
         Books
         Decoration and ornament
         Illustration of books
         Manuscripts
         Medieval art**
    RT   **Alphabets
         Books of hours
         Initials**
Illusions
    USE **Hallucinations and illusions
         Optical illusions**
Illustration of books (May subdiv. geog.)
    741.6
    UF   Book illustration
    SA   types of illustration, e.g. **Botani-
         cal illustration** [to be added
         as needed]
    BT   **Art
         Books
         Color printing
         Decoration and ornament**
    NT   **Botanical illustration
         Caldecott Medal
         Engraving
         Illumination of books and
         manuscripts
         Photomechanical processes**
    RT   **Drawing
         Picture books for children**
Illustrations
    USE subjects, names, and uniform ti-
         tles with the subdivision *Pic-
         torial works*, e.g. **Animals—
         Pictorial works; United**

Illustrations—*Continued*
States—History—1861-1865,
Civil War—Pictorial works;
etc. [to be added as needed]
Illustrators (May subdiv. geog.)
741.6092; 920
BT **Artists**
Illustrators, American
USE **Illustrators—United States**
Illustrators—United States 741.6092;
920
UF American illustrators
Illustrators, American
Image processing software 006.6
BT **Computer software**
Imagery
USE **Figures of speech**
Imaginary animals
USE **Mythical animals**
Imaginary companions
USE **Imaginary playmates**
Imaginary creatures
USE **Mythical animals**
Imaginary friends
USE **Imaginary playmates**
Imaginary places
USE **Geographical myths**
Imaginary playmates 155.4
UF Imaginary companions
Imaginary friends
Make-believe playmates
BT **Child psychology**
Imagination
Play
Imaginary voyages 808.3; 808.83
May be used for individual works, collections, or materials about imaginary voyages.
UF Space flight (Fiction)
Voyages to the moon
BT **Fantasy fiction**
Science fiction
NT **Robinsonades**
RT **Interplanetary voyages**
Imagination 153.3
BT **Educational psychology**
Intellect
Psychology
NT **Creation (Literary, artistic, etc.)**
Fantasy
Imaginary playmates

Imaging, Magnetic resonance
USE **Magnetic resonance imaging**
Imitations
USE types of literature and names of prominent authors with the subdivision *Parodies, imitations, etc.*, e.g. **Shakespeare, William, 1564-1616—Parodies, imitations, etc.** [to be added as needed]
Immigrants (May subdiv. geog.) **304.8**
Use for materials on foreign-born persons who enter a country intending to become permanent residents or citizens. This heading may be locally subdivided by the names of places where immigrants have settled.
UF Emigrants
Foreign population
Foreigners
SA names of immigrant ethnic groups, e.g. **Mexican Americans;** and, for immigrants who are not citizens, the names of national groups with the appropriate subdivision for the country of their residence, e.g. **Mexicans—United States** [to be added as needed]
BT **Minorities**
RT **Aliens**
Immigration and emigration
Immigrants—United States 325.73
UF United States—Foreign population
NT **Mexican Americans**
RT **United States—Immigration and emigration**
Immigration and emigration 304.8; 325
Use for materials on migration from one country to another. Materials on the movement of population within a country for permanent settlement are entered under **Internal migration.**
UF Emigration
Foreign population
Migration
SA names of countries with the subdivision *Immigration and emigration,* e.g. **United States—Immigration and emigration;** and names of immigrant minorities and national groups, e.g. **Mexican Americans;**

Immigration and emigration—*Continued*

    Mexicans—United States;

      etc. [to be added as needed]

  BT **Population**

  NT **Children of immigrants**

      Human geography

      Illegal aliens

      Naturalization

      Refugees

      Return migration

      United States—Immigration and emigration

  RT **Aliens**

      Americanization

      Colonization

      Immigrants

      Internal migration

Immortality   129

Use for materials on the question of the endless existence of the soul. Materials on the character and form of a future existence are entered under **Future life.** Materials on the philosophical concept of eternity are entered under **Eternity.**

  UF Eternal life

      Life after death

  BT **Eschatology**

      Soul

      Theology

  RT **Future life**

Immune system   616.07

  UF Immunological system

  BT **Anatomy**

      Physiology

  RT **Immunity**

Immunity   571.9; 616.07

  NT **Allergy**

      Immunization

  RT **Immune system**

Immunization (May subdiv. geog.)   **614.4**

Use for materials on any process, active or passive, that leads to increased immunity. Materials on active immunization with a vaccine are entered under **Vaccination.**

  BT **Immunity**

      Public health

  NT **Vaccination**

Immunological system

  USE **Immune system**

Immunology   571.9; 616.07

  BT **Medicine**

Impaired vision

  USE **Vision disorders**

Impartiality

  USE **Fairness**

Impeachment

  USE types of public officials and names of individual public officials with the subdivision *Impeachment,* e.g. **Presidents—United States—Impeachment** [to be added as needed]

Impeachments (May subdiv. geog.)   **342**

  SA types of public officials and names of individual officials with the subdivision **Impeachment** [to be added as needed]

  BT **Administration of justice**

  NT **Recall (Political science)**

Imperialism   325

  UF Colonialism

  SA names of countries with the subdivision *Foreign relations* or *Colonies* [to be added as needed]

  BT **Political science**

  NT **Colonies**

      Colonization

Implements, utensils, etc.   683

  UF Gadgets

      Utensils

  NT **Containers**

      Household equipment and supplies

      Stone implements

      Tools

Imports (May subdiv. geog.)   **382**

  BT **International trade**

Impostors and imposture (May subdiv. geog.)   **364.1**

  UF Charlatans

      Hoaxes

      Pretenders

  BT **Crime**

      Criminals

  NT **Counterfeits and counterfeiting**

      Forgery

      Quacks and quackery

  RT **Fraud**

      Swindlers and swindling

Impressionism (Art) (May subdiv. geog.)
    709.03; 759.05
  UF Neo-impressionism (Art)
  BT **Art**
Imprisonment
  USE **Prisons**
In art
  USE names of persons, families, and
      corporate bodies with the sub-
      division *In art,* for materials
      about the depiction of those
      persons or bodies in works of
      art, e.g. **Napoleon I, Emper-**
      or of the French, 1769-
      1821—In art; and phrase
      headings denoting particular
      themes in art for materials
      about those themes, e.g. **Dogs**
      in art [to be added as need-
      ed]
In-line skating **796.2**
  UF Rollerblading
  BT **Roller skating**
In literature
  USE names of persons, families, and
      corporate bodies with the sub-
      division *In literature,* for ma-
      terials about the depiction of
      those persons or bodies in lit-
      erary works, e.g. **Napoleon I,**
      Emperor of the French,
      1769-1821—In literature; and
      phrase headings denoting par-
      ticular themes in literature for
      materials about those themes,
      e.g. **Dogs in literature** [to be
      added as needed]
In-service training
  USE **Employees—Training**
      and types of employees or per-
      sonnel with the subdivision
      In-service training, e.g. **Li-**
      brarians—In-service training
      [to be added as needed]
In vitro fertilization
  USE **Fertilization in vitro**
Inaudible sound
  USE **Ultrasonics**

Inaugural addresses
  USE types of public officials and
      names of individual public of-
      ficials with the subdivision
      Inaugural addresses, e.g.
      Presidents—United States—
      Inaugural addresses [to be
      added as needed]
Inauguration
  USE types of public officials and
      names of individual public of-
      ficials with the subdivision
      Inauguration, e.g. **Presi-**
      dents—United States—Inau-
      guration [to be added as
      needed]
Incandescent lamps
  USE **Electric lamps**
Incas **985**
  BT **Native Americans—South**
      America
Incendiary bombs **623.4**
  UF Fire bombs
  BT **Bombs**
      Incendiary weapons
Incendiary weapons **623.4**
  BT **Chemical warfare**
  NT **Incendiary bombs**
Incentive (Psychology)
  USE **Motivation (Psychology)**
Incest **306.877; 616.85**
  BT **Sex crimes**
  NT **Child sexual abuse**
Incineration
  USE **Cremation**
      Refuse and refuse disposal
Income (May subdiv. geog.) **331.2;**
      339.3
  UF Fortunes
  BT **Economics**
      Finance
      Property
      Wealth
  NT **Guaranteed annual income**
      Retirement income
      Salaries, wages, etc.
  RT **Gross national product**
      Profit

Income tax (May subdiv. geog.)   **336.24**
     UF   Personal income tax
     BT   **Internal revenue**
        Taxation
     NT   **Tax credits**

Incunabula (May subdiv. geog.)   **093**
     Use for materials on books printed before the year 1501.
     UF   Early printed books—15th century
     SA   subjects with the subdivision *Early works to 1800,* for materials on those subjects written before 1800, e.g. **Political science—Early works to 1800** [to be added as needed]
     BT   **Books**

Indebtedness
     USE   **Debt**

Indentured servants
     USE   **Contract labor**

Independence Day (United States)
     USE   **Fourth of July**

Independent schools
     USE   **Private schools**

Independent study   **371.39**
     Use for materials on individual study that may be directed or assisted by instructional staff through periodic consultations.
     BT   **Study skills**
        Tutors and tutoring

Indeterminism
     USE   **Free will and determinism**

Index librorum prohibitorum
     USE   **Books—Censorship**

Indexes   **016**
     Use for works that list topics or names with references to books, articles, or passages where those topics or names are to be found. Works that list words with references to passages in a text where the exact word occurs are entered under **Concordances.**
     SA   subjects with the subdivision *Indexes,* e.g. **Newspapers—Indexes; Short stories—Indexes; English literature—Indexes;** etc. [to be added as needed]
     BT   **Bibliography**
     NT   **Concordances**
        Subject headings

Indexing   **025.3**
     BT   **Bibliographic control**
        Bibliography

     RT   **Cataloging**
        Files and filing

Indian languages (North American)
     USE   **Native American languages**

Indian literature (East Indian)
     USE   **Indic literature**

Indian missions
     USE   **Native Americans—Christian missions**

Indian removal
     USE   **Native Americans—Relocation**

Indian reservations
     USE   **Native Americans—Reservations**
        and names of native peoples, tribes, etc., with the subdivision *Reservations* [to be added as needed]

Indians
     USE   **Native Americans**

Indians of Canada
     USE   **Native Americans—Canada**

Indians of Central America
     USE   **Native Americans—Central America**

Indians of Central America—Guatemala
     USE   **Native Americans—Guatemala**

Indians (of India)
     USE   **East Indians**

Indians of Mexico
     USE   **Native Americans—Mexico**

Indians of North America
     USE   **Native Americans**
        Native Americans—North America
        Native Americans—United States

Indians of North America—Agriculture
     USE   **Native Americans—Agriculture**

Indians of North America—Antiquities
     USE   **Native Americans—Antiquities**

Indians of North America—Architecture
     USE   **Native American architecture**

Indians of North America—Art
     USE   **Native American art**

Indians of North America—Canada
     USE   **Native Americans—Canada**

Indians of North America—Captivities
     USE   **Native Americans—Captivities**

Indians of North America—Children
     USE   **Native American children**

Indians of North America—Christian missions
    USE **Native Americans—Christian missions**
Indians of North America—Claims
    USE **Native Americans—Claims**
Indians of North America—Costume
    USE **Native American costume**
Indians of North America—Dances
    USE **Native American dance**
Indians of North America—Dwellings
    USE **Native Americans—Dwellings**
Indians of North America—Economic conditions
    USE **Native Americans—Economic conditions**
Indians of North America—Education
    USE **Native Americans—Education**
Indians of North America—First contact with Europeans
    USE **Native Americans—First contact with Europeans**
Indians of North America—Folklore
    USE **Native Americans—Folklore**
Indians of North America—Games
    USE **Native American games**
Indians of North America—Government relations
    USE **Native Americans—Government relations**
Indians of North America—History
    USE **Native Americans—History**
Indians of North America—History—Chronology
    USE **Native Americans—History—Chronology**
Indians of North America—Industries
    USE **Native Americans—Industries**
Indians of North America—Languages
    USE **Native American languages**
Indians of North America—Literature
    USE **Native American literature**
Indians of North America—Medicine
    USE **Native American medicine**
Indians of North America—Music
    USE **Native American music**
Indians of North America—Names
    USE **Native American names**
Indians of North America—Origin
    USE **Native Americans—Origin**

Indians of North America—Politics and government
    USE **Native Americans—Politics and government**
Indians of North America—Psychology
    USE **Native Americans—Psychology**
Indians of North America—Relations with early settlers
    USE **Native Americans—Relations with early settlers**
Indians of North America—Religion
    USE **Native Americans—Religion**
Indians of North America—Reservations
    USE **Native Americans—Reservations**
Indians of North America—Rites and ceremonies
    USE **Native Americans—Rites and ceremonies**
Indians of North America—Schools
    USE **Native Americans—Education**
Indians of North America—Sign language
    USE **Native American sign language**
Indians of North America—Silverwork
    USE **Native American silverwork**
Indians of North America—Social conditions
    USE **Native Americans—Social conditions**
Indians of North America—Social life and customs
    USE **Native Americans—Social life and customs**
Indians of North America—Wars
    USE **Native Americans—Wars**
Indians of North America—Women
    USE **Native American women**
Indians of South America
    USE **Native Americans—South America**
Indians of South America—Peru
    USE **Native Americans—Peru**
Indians of the West Indies
    USE **Native Americans—West Indies**
Indic literature   891.4
    UF Indian literature (East Indian)
    BT **Literature**
Indigenous peoples
    USE **Native peoples**

Indigestion   616.3
   UF Dyspepsia
   BT **Digestion**
Individual retirement accounts   332.024
   UF IRAs (Pensions)
   BT **Pensions**
       Retirement income
Individualism (May subdiv. geog.)   **141;**
       302.5; 330.1
   BT **Economics**
       Equality
       Political science
       Sociology
   RT **Persons**
Individuality   155.2
   UF Identity
   BT **Consciousness**
       Psychology
   NT **Self**
   RT **Conformity**
       Personality
Individualized instruction   371.39
   Use for materials on the adaptation of instruction to meet individual needs within a group. General materials on one-on-one instruction are entered under **Tutors and tutoring.**
   BT **Tutors and tutoring**
   RT **Open plan schools**
Indochina   959
   Use for the area comprising Laos, Cambodia, and Vietnam.
   BT **Southeast Asia**
Indoctrination, Forced
   USE **Brainwashing**
Indolence
   USE **Laziness**
Indoor air pollution (May subdiv. geog.)
       363.739; 628.5
   BT **Air pollution**
Indoor games   793
   BT **Games**
   RT **Amusements**
Indoor gardening   635.9
   BT **Gardening**
   NT **Terrariums**
       Window gardening
   RT **Container gardening**
       House plants
       Miniature gardens
Induced abortion
   USE **Abortion**

Induction coils   537.6; 621.319
   BT **Electric apparatus and appliances**
   NT **Condensers (Electricity)**
Induction (Logic)
   USE **Logic**
Induction motors
   USE **Electric motors**
Industrial accidents (May subdiv. geog.)
       363.11; 658.3
   UF Employees—Accidents
       Industrial disasters
       Industrial injuries
       Labor—Accidents
       Occupational accidents
       Occupational injuries
   SA industries with the subdivision
       Accidents, e.g. **Chemical industry—Accidents** [to be added as needed]
   BT **Accidents**
   NT **Chemical industry—Accidents**
   RT **Hazardous occupations**
Industrial alcohol
   USE **Denatured alcohol**
Industrial antiquities
   USE **Industrial archeology**
Industrial applications
   USE types of scientific phenomena, chemicals, plants, and crops with the subdivision *Industrial applications,* e.g. **Ultrasonic waves—Industrial applications** [to be added as needed]
Industrial arbitration (May subdiv. geog.)
       331.89
   UF Arbitration, Industrial
       Industrial conciliation
       Labor arbitration
       Labor courts
       Labor negotiations
       Mediation, Industrial
       Trade agreements (Labor)
   BT **Industrial relations**
       Labor
       Labor disputes
       Labor unions
       Negotiation
   RT **Collective bargaining**
       Strikes

Industrial archaeology
    USE **Industrial archeology**
Industrial archeology (May subdiv. geog.)
    609

    Use for materials on the study of the physical remains of industries from the eighteenth and nineteenth centuries, including buildings, machinery, and tools.

    UF   Industrial antiquities
          Industrial archaeology
    BT   **Archeology**
          Industries—History
Industrial arts   600
    UF   Mechanic arts
          Trades
    SA   types of industries, arts, and trades; and names of countries, cities, etc., with the subdivision *Industries* [to be added as needed]
    BT   **Handicraft**
    NT   **Arts and crafts movement**
          Engineering
          Industrial arts education
          Manufacturing processes
          Printing
    RT   **Technology**
Industrial arts education (May subdiv. geog.)   **607**
    UF   Education, Industrial
          Industrial education
          Industrial schools
          Manual training
    BT   **Industrial arts**
          Vocational education
    RT   **Technical education**
Industrial arts shops
    USE **School shops**
Industrial buildings (May subdiv. geog.)   **725**
    UF   Buildings, Industrial
    BT   **Buildings**
    NT   **Factories**
Industrial buildings—Design and construction   690
    BT   **Architecture**
          Building
Industrial chemistry   660
    UF   Chemical technology
          Chemistry, Technical
          Technical chemistry

    SA   types of industries and products, e.g. **Clay industry; Dyes and dyeing;** etc. [to be added as needed]
    BT   **Chemistry**
          Technology
    NT   **Alloys**
          Bleaching
          Canning and preserving
          Ceramics
          Corrosion and anticorrosives
          Distillation
          Drying
          Electrochemistry
          Food—Analysis
          Gums and resins
          Synthetic products
          Tanning
          Textile chemistry
          Waste products
    RT   **Chemical engineering**
          Chemical industry
          Chemicals
          Metallurgy
Industrial conciliation
    USE **Industrial arbitration**
Industrial councils
    USE **Participative management**
Industrial counseling
    USE **Employees—Counseling of**
Industrial design (May subdiv. geog.)   **745.2**
    UF   Design, Industrial
    BT   **Design**
    NT   **Automobiles—Design and construction**
          Human engineering
          Systems engineering
Industrial disasters
    USE **Industrial accidents**
Industrial diseases
    USE **Occupational diseases**
Industrial disputes
    USE **Labor disputes**
Industrial drawing
    USE **Mechanical drawing**
Industrial education
    USE **Industrial arts education**
            Technical education

Industrial efficiency (May subdiv. geog.)
   658
   Use for materials on the various means of increasing efficiency and output in business and industries, including time and motion studies and materials on the application of psychological principles to industrial production.
   UF   Efficiency, Industrial
   BT   **Management**
   NT   **Job analysis**
        Labor productivity
        Motion study
        Office management
        Time study
Industrial equipment   621.8
   UF   Capital equipment
        Capital goods
        Industries—Equipment and supplies
        Machinery in industry
   SA   types of industries with the subdivision *Equipment and supplies* [to be added as needed]
   BT   **Machinery**
   NT   **Automation**
        Industrial robots
Industrial exhibitions
   USE   **Trade shows**
Industrial health
   USE   **Occupational health and safety**
Industrial injuries
   USE   **Industrial accidents**
Industrial laws and legislation (May subdiv. geog.)   **343**
   UF   Government regulation of commerce
        Industries—Law and legislation
   SA   types of industries with the subdivision *Law and legislation,* e.g. **Chemical industry—Law and legislation** [to be added as needed]
   BT   **Law**
        Legislation
   NT   **Labor laws and legislation**
Industrial libraries
   USE   **Corporate libraries**
Industrial management
   USE   **Management**
Industrial materials
   USE   **Materials**

Industrial mergers
   USE   **Corporate mergers and acquisitions**
Industrial mobilization (May subdiv. geog.)   **355.2**
   Use for materials on industrial and labor policies and programs for defense mobilization.
   UF   Economic mobilization
        Industry and war
        Mobilization, Industrial
        National defenses
   BT   **Economic policy**
        Military art and science
        War—Economic aspects
   RT   **Military readiness**
Industrial organization
   USE   **Management**
Industrial painting   698
   SA   topics with the subdivision *Painting;* e.g. **Automobiles—Painting** [to be added as needed]
   BT   **Finishes and finishing**
   NT   **Automobiles—Painting**
        Lettering
        Sign painting
   RT   **House painting**
Industrial plants
   USE   **Factories**
Industrial policy (May subdiv. geog.)
   338.9; 354
   UF   Government policy
        Government regulation of industry
        Industries—Government policy
        Industries—Organization, control, etc.
        Industry and state
        State regulation of industry
   BT   **Economic policy**
   NT   **Agriculture—Government policy**
        Consumer protection
        Deregulation
        Energy policy
        Government ownership
        Privatization
        Public service commissions
        Railroads—Government policy

Industrial policy—United States
    338.973; 354
    UF   Industries—Government policy—
          United States
          United States—Industrial policy
Industrial processing
    USE **Manufacturing processes**
Industrial psychology
    USE **Applied psychology**
Industrial relations (May subdiv. geog.)
    331

    Use for general materials on employer-employee relations. Materials on problems of personnel and relations from the employer's point of view are entered under **Personnel management.**

    UF   Capital and labor
          Employer-employee relations
          Labor and capital
          Labor-management relations
          Labor relations
    BT   **Labor**
          Management
    NT   **Collective bargaining**
          Industrial arbitration
          Labor contract
          Labor disputes
          Labor unions
          Participative management
          Personnel management
          Strikes
Industrial research (May subdiv. geog.)
    607; 658.5
    BT   **Research**
    NT   **New products**
    RT   **Inventions**
          Technological innovations
Industrial revolution (May subdiv. geog.)
    330.9; 909.81

    Use for materials on the historical shift from home-based industries to large-scale factory production. Materials on the development of organized productions as industries, especially factory-based industries, are entered under **Industrialization.**

    SA   names of countries with the subdivision *Economic conditions*
          [to be added as needed]
    BT   **Economic conditions**
          Industries—History
    RT   **Great Britain—History—19th century**
          Industrialization
          Technology and civilization

Industrial robots   **629.8**
    UF   Robots, Industrial
          Working robots
    BT   **Automation**
          Industrial equipment
          Robots
Industrial safety
    USE **Occupational health and safety**
Industrial schools
    USE **Industrial arts education**
          Technical education
Industrial secrets
    USE **Trade secrets**
Industrial trusts   **338.8; 658**

    Use for materials on combinations in restraint of trade in which stock ownership is transferred to trustees, who in turn issue trust certificates and dividends and who attempt to achieve monopolistic control over output, prices, or markets.

    UF   Cartels
          Trusts, Industrial
    BT   **Capital**
          Commerce
          Economics
    RT   **Antitrust law**
          Competition
          Corporate mergers and acquisitions
          Corporation law
          Corporations
          Monopolies
          Restraint of trade
Industrial trusts—Law and legislation
    USE **Antitrust law**
Industrial uses of space
    USE **Space industrialization**
Industrial waste   **363.72; 628.4**
    UF   Factory and trade waste
          Factory waste
          Industrial wastes
          Trade waste
    BT   **Refuse and refuse disposal**
          Waste products
    NT   **Hazardous wastes**
    RT   **Pollution**
          Water pollution
Industrial wastes
    USE **Industrial waste**

Industrial welfare (May subdiv. geog.)
   658.3
   UF   Welfare work in industry
   BT   **Labor**
        Management
        Social work
   NT   **Social settlements**
Industrial workers
   USE   **Labor**
         Working class
Industrialization (May subdiv. geog.)
   338
      Use for materials on the development of or-
   ganized productions as industries, especially
   factory-based industries. Materials on the his-
   torical shift from home-based industries to
   large-scale factory production are entered un-
   der **Industrial revolution.**
   BT   **Economic policy**
        Industries
   NT   **Developing countries**
        Space industrialization
   RT   **Industrial revolution**
        Modernization (Sociology)
Industries (May subdiv. geog.)   **338**
      Apart from **Manufacturing industries** and
   Service industries, all headings for types of
   industries are formulated in the singular.
   UF   Industry
        Production
   SA   types of industries, e.g. **Steel in-**
        dustry; and ethnic groups
        with the subdivision *Indus-*
        tries, e.g. **Native Ameri-**
        cans—Industries [to be add-
        ed as needed]
   BT   **Economics**
   NT   **Aerospace industry**
        Agricultural industry
        Automobile industry
        Book industry
        Ceramic industry
        Chemical industry
        Clothing industry
        Commercial fishing
        Computer industry
        Computer software industry
        Defense industry
        Electric products industry
        Firearms industry
        Industrialization
        Internet industry
        Iron industry
        Leather industry

        Management
        Manufactures
        Manufacturing industries
        Motion picture industry
        Native Americans—Industries
        Nuclear industry
        Paper industry
        Petroleum industry
        Pollution control industry
        Radio supplies industry
        Service industries
        Steel industry
        Textile industry
Industries—Chicago (Ill.)   **338.09773**
   UF   Chicago (Ill.)—Industries
Industries—Deregulation
   USE   **Deregulation**
Industries—Equipment and supplies
   USE   **Industrial equipment**
Industries—Government policy
   USE   **Industrial policy**
Industries—Government policy—United
   States
   USE   **Industrial policy—United**
         States
Industries—History (May subdiv. geog.)
   338.09
   NT   **Industrial archeology**
        Industrial revolution
Industries—Law and legislation
   USE   **Industrial laws and legislation**
Industries—Ohio   **338.09771**
   UF   Ohio—Industries
Industries—Organization, control, etc.
   USE   **Industrial policy**
Industries—Social responsibility
   USE   **Social responsibility of business**
Industries—United States   **338.0973**
   UF   United States—Industries
Industry
   USE   **Industries**
Industry and state
   USE   **Industrial policy**
Industry and war
   USE   **Industrial mobilization**
         War—Economic aspects
Inequality
   USE   **Equality**
Infallibility of the Pope
   USE   **Popes—Infallibility**

Infant care
    USE **Infants—Care**
Infant care leave
    USE **Parental leave**
Infant mortality
    USE **Infants—Mortality**
Infant sudden death
    USE **Sudden infant death syndrome**
Infantile paralysis
    USE **Poliomyelitis**
Infants (May subdiv. geog.) **155.42;**
    305.232; 362.7; 618.92
    Use for materials about children in the earliest period of life, usually the first two years only.
    UF Babies
    BT **Children**
Infants and strangers
    USE **Children and strangers**
Infants—Birth defects
    USE **Birth defects**
Infants—Care 649
    UF Baby care
         Infant care
    BT **Child care**
    NT **Babysitting**
Infants—Clothing
    USE **Infants' clothing**
Infants' clothing 646.4
    UF Baby clothes
         Infants—Clothing
    BT **Children's clothing**
         Clothing and dress
Infants—Death 306.9; 618.92
    Use for general materials on the death of infants. Materials on infant death rates and causes are entered under **Infants—Mortality.**
    BT **Death**
    NT **Sudden infant death syndrome**
Infants—Diseases 618.92
    UF Pediatrics
    BT **Diseases**
    RT **Infants—Health and hygiene**
Infants—Education
    USE **Preschool education**
Infants—Health and hygiene 613;
    618.92
    UF Infants—Hygiene
         Pediatrics
    BT **Health**
         Hygiene
    RT **Infants—Diseases**

Infants—Hygiene
    USE **Infants—Health and hygiene**
Infants—Mortality (May subdiv. geog.)
    304.6
    Use for materials on infant death rates and causes. General materials on the death of infants are entered under **Infants—Death.**
    UF Infant mortality
    BT **Mortality**
Infants—Nutrition 613.2; 649
    BT **Nutrition**
    NT **Breast feeding**
Infection and infectious diseases
    USE **Communicable diseases**
Infectious wastes
    USE **Medical wastes**
Infertility 616.6
    Use for materials on infertility in humans and in animals.
    UF Sterility in animals
         Sterility in humans
    BT **Reproduction**
    RT **Birth control**
         Childlessness
         Fertility
         Human fertility
Infinitive
    USE names of languages with the subdivision *Infinitive,* e.g. **English language—Infinitive** [to be added as needed]
Infirmaries
    USE **Hospitals**
Inflammable substances
    USE **Hazardous substances**
Inflation (Finance) (May subdiv. geog.)
    332.4
    BT **Finance**
    NT **Wage-price policy**
    RT **Monetary policy**
         Paper money
Influence
    USE subjects, corporate bodies, individual persons, literary authors, religions, denominations, sacred works, and wars with the subdivision *Influence,* e.g. **World War, 1939-1945—Influence; Shakespeare, William, 1564-1616—Influence** [to be added as needed]

Influenza   616.2

UF   Flu

BT   **Cold (Disease)**

Communicable diseases

Diseases

Informal sector (Economics)

USE   **Underground economy**

Information centers

USE   **Information services**

Information clearinghouses

USE   **Information services**

Information, Freedom of

USE   **Freedom of information**

Information networks   004.6

Use for materials on the interconnection through telecommunications of a geographically dispersed group of libraries or information centers for the purpose of sharing their total information resources.

UF   Information superhighway

Networks, Information

SA   types of information networks and names of specific networks [to be added as needed]

BT   **Information systems**

NT   **Internet**

Library information networks

RT   **Computer networks**

Information resources (May subdiv. geog.)   **025.04**

Use for materials on sources of information in general, not limited to a specific topic or format. Materials on organizations that provide information services are entered under **Information services.**

UF   Information sources

SA   subjects with the subdivision *Information resources,* for general materials about information on a subject, e.g. **Business—Information resources;** subjects with the subdivision *Internet resources,* for materials about information available on the Internet on a subject, e.g. **Business—Internet resources;** subjects with the subdivision *Databases,* for materials about data files on a subject regardless of the medium of distribution, e.g. **Business—Databases;** and

headings for the providers or the users of information with the subdivision *Information services,* for materials about organizations that provide information services, e.g. **United Nations—Information services; Consumers—Information services;** etc. [to be added as needed]

BT   **Information science**

NT   **Business—Information resources**

Databases

Information services

Internet resources

Information retrieval   025.5

UF   Data retrieval

Information storage and retrieval

Retrieval of information

BT   **Documentation**

Information science

NT   **Internet searching**

RT   **Information systems**

Information science (May subdiv. geog.)   **020**

BT   **Communication**

NT   **Documentation**

Information resources

Information retrieval

Information systems

Library science

Information services (May subdiv. geog.)   **025.5**

Use for materials on organizations that provide information services. Materials on sources of information, not limited to a specific topic or format, are entered under **Information resources.**

UF   Information centers

Information clearinghouses

SA   headings for the providers or the users of information with the subdivision *Information services,* for materials about organizatons that provide information services, e.g. **United Nations—Information services; Consumers—Information services;** etc.; subjects with the subdivision *Information resources,* for general

Information services—*Continued*
materials about information on a subject, e.g. **Business—Information resources;** subjects with the subdivision *Internet resources,* for materials about information available on the Internet on a subject, e.g. **Business—Internet resources;** and subjects with the subdivision *Databases,* for materials about data files on a subject regardless of the medium of distribution, e.g. **Business—Databases** [to be added as needed]

BT   **Information resources**

NT   **Archives**
     Business—Information services
     Consumers—Information services
     Electronic publishing
     Hotlines (Telephone counseling)
     Machine readable bibliographic data
     Reference services (Libraries)
     United Nations—Information services

RT   **Documentation**
     Information systems
     Libraries
     Research

Information society (May subdiv. geog.) **303.48**
Use for materials on a society whose primary activity is the production and communication of information by means of computer networks and other advanced technology.

BT   **Sociology**

Information sources
USE   **Information resources**

Information storage and retrieval
USE   **Information retrieval**

Information storage and retrieval systems
USE   **Information systems**

Information superhighway
USE   **Computer networks**
     Information networks
     Internet

Information systems   **025.04**
UF   Computer-based information systems

Data storage and retrieval systems
Information storage and retrieval systems

BT   **Bibliographic control**
     Computers
     Information science

NT   **Data processing**
     Database management
     Digital libraries
     Expert systems (Computer science)
     Information networks
     Machine readable bibliographic data
     Management information systems
     Multimedia
     Teletext systems
     Videotex systems

RT   **Information retrieval**
     Information services
     Libraries—Automation

Information systems—Management **025.04**
Use for materials on the management of information systems.

BT   **Management**

Information technology (May subdiv. geog.) **004; 303.48**
Use for materials on the acquisition, processing, storage, and dissemination of any type of information by microelectronics, computers, and telecommunication.

BT   **Technology**

RT   **Knowledge management**

Infrared radiation   **535.01; 621.36**
BT   **Electromagnetic waves**
     Radiation

Infrastructure (Economics) (May subdiv. geog.) **363**
BT   **Economic development**
     Public works

Inhalant abuse
USE   **Solvent abuse**

Inhalation abuse of solvents
USE   **Solvent abuse**

Inheritance and succession (May subdiv. geog.) **346.05**
UF   Bequests
     Heirs
     Hereditary succession
     Intestacy

Inheritance and succession—*Continued*
      Legacies
  BT **Wealth**
  NT **Executors and administrators**
       Inheritance and transfer tax
       Probate law and practice
  RT **Trusts and trustees**
       Wills
Inheritance and transfer tax (May
    subdiv. geog.) **343.05**
  UF Estate tax
      Taxation of legacies
      Transfer tax
  BT **Estate planning**
       Inheritance and succession
       Internal revenue
       Taxation
Inheritance (Biology)
  USE **Heredity**
Initialisms
  USE **Acronyms**
Initials **745.6**
  NT **Printing—Specimens**
  RT **Alphabets**
       Illumination of books and
         manuscripts
       Lettering
       Monograms
       Type and type-founding
Initiation ceremonies
  USE **Initiation rites**
Initiation rites (May subdiv. geog.) **203;**
    392.1
  UF Initiation ceremonies
      Initiations
  BT **Rites and ceremonies**
  NT **Circumcision**
       Female circumcision
Initiations
  USE **Initiation rites**
Initiative and referendum
  USE **Referendum**
Injunctions (May subdiv. geog.) **331.89**
  BT **Constitutional law**
      Labor unions
  RT **Strikes**
Injuries
  USE **Accidents**
      First aid
      Wounds and injuries
Injurious insects
  USE **Insect pests**

Ink drawing
  USE **Pen drawing**
Inland navigation (May subdiv. geog.)
    386
    May be subdivided by the names of rivers,
    lakes, canals, etc., as well as by countries,
    states, cities, etc.
  BT **Navigation**
       Shipping
       Transportation
  RT **Canals**
      Lakes
      Rivers
      Waterways
Inner cities (May subdiv. geog.) **307.76**
    Use for materials on the densely populated,
    economically depressed, central areas of large
    cities.
  UF Ghettoes, Inner city
      Inner city ghettoes
      Inner city problems
  BT **Cities and towns**
Inner city ghettoes
  USE **Inner cities**
Inner city problems
  USE **Inner cities**
Inner city schools
  USE **Urban schools**
Innovations, Technological
  USE **Technological innovations**
Inns
  USE **Hotels and motels**
Innuit
  USE **Inuit**
Inoculation
  USE **Vaccination**
Inorganic chemistry **546**
  UF Chemistry, Inorganic
  BT **Chemistry**
  NT **Metals**
Input equipment (Computers)
  USE **Computer peripherals**
Inquisition (May subdiv. geog.) **272**
  UF Holy Office
  BT **Catholic Church**
Inquisitiveness
  USE **Curiosity**
Insane
  USE **Mentally ill**
Insanity defense (May subdiv. geog.)
    345
  UF Insanity—Jurisprudence
      Insanity plea

Insanity defense—*Continued*
      Mental illness—Jurisprudence
    BT   **Criminal law**
Insanity—Jurisprudence
    USE   **Insanity defense**
Insanity plea
    USE   **Insanity defense**
Inscriptions (May subdiv. geog.)   **411**
    UF   Epigraphy
    BT   **Ancient history**
         Archeology
    NT   **Brasses**
         Epitaphs
         Graffiti
         Hieroglyphics
         Seals (Numismatics)
Insect-eating plants
    USE   **Carnivorous plants**
Insect pests (May subdiv. geog.)   **632**
    UF   Destructive insects
         Diseases and pests
         Garden pests
         Harmful insects
         Injurious insects
    SA   types of insect pests, e.g. **Lo-**
         custs; etc.; and types of
         crops, plants, trees, etc., with
         the subdivision *Diseases and*
         pests, e.g. **Fruit—Diseases**
         and pests [to be added as
         needed]
    BT   **Economic zoology**
         Insects
         Pests
    NT   **Fruit—Diseases and pests**
         Insects as carriers of disease
         Locusts
    RT   **Agricultural pests**
         Household pests
         Parasites
Insecticides   **632; 668**
    SA   types of insecticides [to be add-
         ed as needed]
    BT   **Agricultural chemicals**
         Pesticides
    NT   **DDT (Insecticide)**
         Fumigation
    RT   **Spraying and dusting**
Insecticides—Toxicology   **615.9**
    BT   **Poisons and poisoning**
Insectivorous plants
    USE   **Carnivorous plants**

Insects (May subdiv. geog.)   **595.7**
    SA   types of insects [to be added as
         needed]
    BT   **Animals**
    NT   **Ants**
         Bees
         Beneficial insects
         Butterflies
         Flies
         Insect pests
         Locusts
         Mosquitoes
         Moths
         Silkworms
         Wasps
Insects as carriers of disease   **614.4**
    BT   **Insect pests**
    RT   **Communicable diseases**
Inservice training
    USE   **Employees—Training**
Insider trading   **346.07; 364.16**
    UF   Securities trading, Insider
         Stocks—Insider trading
    BT   **Commercial law**
         Securities
         Stock exchanges
Insignia   **929.9**
    UF   Badges of honor
         Devices (Heraldry)
         Emblems
    SA   armies, navies, and other appro-
         priate subjects with the subdi-
         vision *Insignia* or *Medals,*
         badges, decorations, etc. [to
         be added as needed]
    BT   **Heraldry**
    NT   **Colleges and universities—In-**
         signia
         United States. Army—Insignia
         United States. Army—Medals,
         badges, decorations, etc.
         United States. Navy—Insignia
         United States. Navy—Medals,
         badges, decorations, etc.
    RT   **Decorations of honor**
         Medals
         National emblems
Insolvency
    USE   **Bankruptcy**

Insomnia   616.8
    UF   Sleeplessness
            Wakefulness
    RT   **Sleep**
Inspection
    USE   topics with the subdivision *In-*
            spection, e.g. **Automobiles—**
            Inspection [to be added as
            needed]
Inspection of food
    USE   **Food adulteration and inspec-**
            tion
Inspection of meat
    USE   **Meat inspection**
Inspection of schools
    USE   **School supervision**
            Schools—Administration
Inspiration
    USE   **Creation (Literary, artistic,**
            etc.)
Inspiration, Biblical
    USE   **Bible—Inspiration**
Installment plan   658.8
    UF   Instalment plan
    BT   **Business**
            Consumer credit
            Credit
            Purchasing
Instalment plan
    USE   **Installment plan**
Instant messaging   004.69; 384.3
    BT   **Data transmission systems**
Instinct   152.3; 156
    UF   Animal instinct
    BT   **Animal behavior**
            Psychology
    RT   **Animal intelligence**
            Comparative psychology
            Habit
Institutional care   361
    UF   Asylums
            Benevolent institutions
            Charitable institutions
            Homes (Institutions)
    SA   classes of persons with the sub-
            division *Institutional care* [to
            be added as needed]
    BT   **Charities**
            Medical charities
            Public welfare

    NT   **Blind—Institutional care**
            Children—Institutional care
            Deaf—Institutional care
            Elderly—Institutional care
            Group homes
            Hospitals
            Mentally ill—Institutional care
            Nursing homes
Institutions, Charitable and philanthropic
    USE   **Charities**
Institutions, Ecclesiastical
    USE   **Religious institutions**
Institutions, Religious
    USE   **Religious institutions**
Instruction
    USE   **Education**
            Teaching
Instructional games
    USE   **Educational games**
Instructional materials
    USE   **Teaching—Aids and devices**
Instructional materials centers (May
            subdiv. geog.)   **027.7**
    UF   Audiovisual materials centers
            Curriculum materials centers
            Educational media centers
            Learning resource centers
            Media centers (Education)
            Multimedia centers
            School media centers
    BT   **Libraries**
    NT   **School libraries**
Instructional supervision
    USE   **School supervision**
Instructional systems analysis
    USE   **Educational evaluation**
Instructional technology
    USE   **Educational technology**
Instructive games
    USE   **Educational games**
Instrument flying   629.132
    BT   **Aeronautical instruments**
            Airplanes—Piloting
Instrumental ensembles
    USE   **Ensembles (Music)**
Instrumental music   784
    SA   types of instrumental music [to
            be added as needed]
    BT   **Music**
    NT   **Band music**
            Chamber music

Instrumental music—*Continued*
      Guitar music
      Orchestral music
      Organ music
      Piano music
  RT **Musical instruments**
Instrumentalists (May subdiv. geog.)
      784
  SA types of instrumentalists, e.g. **Vi-
      olinists** [to be added as need-
      ed]
  BT **Musicians**
  NT **Organists**
      Pianists
      Violinists
      Violoncellists
Instrumentation and orchestration
      781.3; 784.13
  UF Orchestration
  BT **Bands (Music)**
      Composition (Music)
      Music
      Orchestra
  RT **Musical instruments**
Instruments, Aeronautical
  USE **Aeronautical instruments**
Instruments, Astronautical
  USE **Astronautical instruments**
Instruments, Astronomical
  USE **Astronomical instruments**
Instruments, Engineering
  USE **Engineering instruments**
Instruments, Measuring
  USE **Measuring instruments**
Instruments, Meteorological
  USE **Meteorological instruments**
Instruments, Musical
  USE **Musical instruments**
Instruments, Negotiable
  USE **Negotiable instruments**
Instruments, Optical
  USE **Optical instruments**
Instruments, Scientific
  USE **Scientific apparatus and in-
      struments**
Insulation (Heat)   **691; 693.8**
  UF Heat insulating materials
      Thermal insulation
  BT **Heating**
Insulation (Sound)
  USE **Soundproofing**

Insults
  USE **Invective**
Insurance (May subdiv. geog.)   **368**
  SA types of insurance, e.g. **Automo-
      bile insurance** [to be added
      as needed]
  BT **Estate planning**
      Finance
      Personal finance
  NT **Automobile insurance**
      Casualty insurance
      Disability insurance
      Fire insurance
      Health insurance
      Life insurance
      Malpractice insurance
      Marine insurance
      Unemployment insurance
Insurance, Accident
  USE **Accident insurance**
Insurance, Automobile
  USE **Automobile insurance**
Insurance, Casualty
  USE **Casualty insurance**
Insurance, Disability
  USE **Disability insurance**
Insurance, Fire
  USE **Fire insurance**
Insurance, Group
  USE **Group insurance**
Insurance, Health
  USE **Health insurance**
Insurance, Hospitalization
  USE **Hospitalization insurance**
Insurance, Life
  USE **Life insurance**
Insurance, Malpractice
  USE **Malpractice insurance**
Insurance, Marine
  USE **Marine insurance**
Insurance, Professional liability
  USE **Malpractice insurance**
Insurance, Social
  USE **Social security**
Insurance, Unemployment
  USE **Unemployment insurance**
Insurance, Workers' compensation
  USE **Workers' compensation**

Insurgency (May subdiv. geog.)   322.4;
    355.02
  UF   Rebellions
  BT   **Revolutions**
  NT   **Guerrilla warfare**
        Subversive activities
        Terrorism
  RT   **Internal security**
        Resistance to government
Integrated churches
  USE **Church and race relations**
Integrated curriculum
  USE **Interdisciplinary approach in
         education**
Integrated language arts (Holistic)
  USE **Whole language**
Integrated schools
  USE **School integration**
Integration in education
  USE **School integration**
        Segregation in education
Integration, Racial
  USE **Race relations**
Intellect   153.4
  UF   Intelligence
        Mind
        Understanding
  BT   **Psychology**
  NT   **Cognitive styles**
        **Creation (Literary, artistic,
         etc.)**
        Imagination
        Logic
        Memory
        Perception
        Reason
        Senses and sensation
  RT   **Reasoning**
        Theory of knowledge
        Thought and thinking
Intellectual cooperation   327.1; 370.116
  UF   Cooperation, Intellectual
  BT   **International cooperation**
  NT   **Conferences**
        Cultural relations
  RT   **International education**
Intellectual freedom   323.44
  BT   **Freedom**
  NT   **Academic freedom**
        Censorship
        Freedom of information

        Freedom of speech
        Freedom of the press
Intellectual life   001.1
    Use for general materials on learning and
scholarship, literature, the arts, etc. Materials
on literature, art, music, motion pictures, etc.
produced for a mass audience are entered un-
der **Popular culture.**
  UF   Cultural life
  SA   classes of persons, ethnic
        groups, and names of coun-
        tries, cities, etc., with the sub-
        division *Intellectual life* [to be
        added as needed]
  BT   **Culture**
  NT   **African Americans—Intellectu-
         al life**
        Blacks—Intellectual life
        Chicago (Ill.)—Intellectual life
        Cultural policy
        Learning and scholarship
        Ohio—Intellectual life
        Popular culture
        United States—Intellectual life
Intellectual life—Government policy
  USE **Cultural policy**
Intellectual property (May subdiv. geog.)
    346.04
  UF   Literary property
        Proprietary rights
        Rights, Proprietary
  BT   **Property**
  RT   **Copyright**
        Patents
Intellectuals (May subdiv. geog.)   305.5
  UF   Intelligentsia
  SA   ethnic groups, classes of per-
        sons, and names of countries,
        cities, etc., with the subdivi-
        sion *Intellectual life,* e.g.
        **African Americans—Intellec-
        tual life; United States—In-
        tellectual life;** etc. [to be
        added as needed]
  BT   **Persons**
        Social classes
Intelligence
  USE **Intellect**
Intelligence agents
  USE **Spies**
Intelligence of animals
  USE **Animal intelligence**

Intelligence service (May subdiv. geog.)
    327.12; 355.3

Use for materials on a government agency that is engaged in obtaining information, usually about an enemy but sometimes about an ally or a neutral country, and also in blocking the attempts by foreign agents to obtain information about one's own national secrets.

  UF Counterespionage
        Counterintelligence
  BT **Public administration**
        Research
  NT **Espionage**
        Military intelligence
  RT **Secret service**

Intelligence service—United States
    327.1273; 355.3

  UF United States—Intelligence service

Intelligence testing
  USE **Intelligence tests**

Intelligence tests   **153.9**
  UF Intelligence testing
        IQ tests
        Mental tests
  BT **Child psychology**
        Educational psychology
  NT **Ability—Testing**
  RT **Educational tests and measurements**

Intelligentsia
  USE **Intellectuals**

Intemperance
  USE **Alcoholism**
        Temperance

Inter-American relations
  USE **Pan-Americanism**

Interactive CD technology
  USE **CD-I technology**

Interactive media
  USE **Multimedia**

Interactive multimedia
  USE **Multimedia**
        and subjects with the subdivision *Interactive multimedia,* e.g. **Geology—Interactive multimedia** [to be added as needed]

Interactive videotex
  USE **Videotex systems**

Interbehaviorial psychology
  USE **Behaviorism**

Interchange of visitors
  USE **Exchange of persons programs**

Interchurch cooperation
  USE **Interdenominational cooperation**

Intercollegiate athletics
  USE **College sports**

Intercommunication systems   **621.38; 651.7**
  UF Interoffice communication systems
  BT **Electronic apparatus and appliances**
        Telecommunication
  NT **Closed-circuit television**
        Microwave communication systems

Intercontinental ballistic missiles   **623.4**
  UF ICBM
  SA names of specific ICBM missiles, e.g. **Atlas (Missile)** [to be added as needed]
  BT **Ballistic missiles**
  NT **Atlas (Missile)**

Intercultural education
  USE **Multicultural education**

Intercultural relations
  USE **Cultural relations**

Intercultural studies
  USE **Cross-cultural studies**

Interdenominational cooperation (May subdiv. geog.)   **280**

Use for materials on religious activities planned and conducted cooperatively by two or more Christian sects. Materials on unity as one of the marks of the church are entered under **Church—Unity.** Materials on prospective and actual mergers within and across denominational lines are entered under **Christian union.** Materials on a movement originating in the twentieth century aimed at promoting church cooperation and unity are entered under **Ecumenical movement.**

  UF Christian unity
        Cooperation, Interchurch
        Cooperation, Interdenominational
        Interchurch cooperation
  BT **Christian sects**
        Church work

Interdisciplinarity in education
  USE **Interdisciplinary approach in education**

Interdisciplinary approach in education
    375
    UF   Integrated curriculum
          Interdisciplinarity in education
          Interdisciplinary studies
    BT   **Curriculum planning**
Interdisciplinary studies
    USE   **Interdisciplinary approach in**
           education
Interest centers approach to teaching
    USE   **Open plan schools**
Interest (Economics)   332.8
    BT   **Banks and banking**
          Business mathematics
          Capital
          Finance
          Loans
Interest groups
    USE   **Lobbying**
           Political action committees
Interfaces, Computer
    USE   **Computer interfaces**
Interfaith marriage   201; 261.8; 306.84
    UF   Mixed marriage
    BT   **Intermarriage**
Interfaith relations   201; 261.2
    BT   **Cultural relations**
Intergovernmental tax relations (May
    subdiv. geog.)   336.2
    UF   Federal-state tax relations
          State-local tax relations
          Tax relations, Intergovernmental
          Tax sharing
    BT   **Taxation**
    NT   **Revenue sharing**
Interior decoration
    USE   **Interior design**
Interior design (May subdiv. geog.)
    729; 747
    Use for materials on the art and techniques
    of planning and supervising the design and
    execution of architectural interiors and their
    furnishings.
    UF   Home decoration
          House decoration
          House furnishing
          Interior decoration
    BT   **Art**
          Decoration and ornament
          Design
          Home economics

    NT   **Bedspreads**
          Draperies
          Furniture
          Lighting
          Mural painting and decoration
          Paperhanging
          Quilts
          Rugs and carpets
          Tapestry
          Upholstery
          Wallpaper
    RT   **Rooms**
Interlibrary loans (May subdiv. geog.)
    025.6
    BT   **Library circulation**
          Library cooperation
Interlocking signals
    USE   **Railroads—Signaling**
Intermarriage (May subdiv. geog.)
    306.84
    Use for materials that discuss collectively
    marriage between persons of different reli-
    gions, religious denominations, races, or eth-
    nic groups.
    UF   Mixed marriage
    BT   **Marriage**
    NT   **Interfaith marriage**
          Interracial marriage
Intermediate schools
    USE   **Middle schools**
Intermediate state
    USE   **Eschatology**
           Future life
Interment
    USE   **Burial**
Internal combustion engines   621.43
    UF   Gas and oil engines
          Gas engines
          Gasoline engines
          Oil engines
          Petroleum engines
    BT   **Engines**
    NT   **Carburetors**
          Diesel engines
Internal migration   304.8
    Use for materials on the movement of pop-
    ulation within a country for permanent settle-
    ment. Materials on casual or seasonal workers
    who move from place to place in search of
    employment are entered under **Migrant labor.**
    Materials on migration from one country to
    another are entered under **Immigration and**
    emigration.

Internal migration—*Continued*
  UF Migration, Internal
        Rural-urban migration
        Urban-rural migration
  BT **Colonization**
        Population
  NT **Cities and towns—Growth**
        Forced migration
  RT **Immigration and emigration**
        Land settlement
        Migrant labor

Internal revenue 336.2
  BT **Taxation**
  NT **Income tax**
        Inheritance and transfer tax

Internal revenue law (May subdiv. geog.)
     343.04
  BT **Law**

Internal security (May subdiv. geog.)
     353.3; 363.2
  UF Loyalty oaths
        Security, Internal
  RT **Insurgency**
        Subversive activities

Internal security—United States 353.3;
     363.2
  UF United States—Internal security

International agencies (May subdiv.
    geog.) **060**
  UF Associations, International
        International associations
        International organizations
  SA names of individual agencies [to
        be added as needed]
  BT **International cooperation**

International arbitration 327.1
  UF Arbitration, International
        International mediation
        Mediation, International
  BT **International cooperation**
        International law
        International relations
        International security
        Treaties
  NT **League of Nations**
        United Nations
  RT **Arms control**
        Peace

International associations
  USE **International agencies**

International business enterprises
  USE **Multinational corporations**

International competition 337; 382;
     658
  UF Competition, International
        World economics
  BT **International relations**
        International trade
  RT **War—Economic aspects**

International conferences
  USE **Conferences**

International cooperation 327.1; 341.7
  Use for general materials on international
  cooperative activities, with or without the par-
  ticipation of governments.
  SA subjects with the subdivision *In-*
        ternational cooperation, e.g.
        Astronautics—International
        cooperation [to be added as
        needed]
  BT **Cooperation**
        International law
        International relations
  NT **Astronautics—International co-**
        operation
        Conferences
        Cultural relations
        Exchange of persons programs
        Foreign aid
        Intellectual cooperation
        International agencies
        International arbitration
        International police
        League of Nations
        Space sciences—International
        cooperation
        United Nations
  RT **International education**
        International organization
        Reconstruction (1914-1939)
        Reconstruction (1939-1951)
        Technology transfer

International copyright
  USE **Copyright**

International economic relations 382
  UF Economic relations, Foreign
        Foreign economic relations
  BT **Economic policy**
        International relations
  NT **Balance of payments**
        Commercial policy
        Foreign aid
        International trade
        Multinational corporations

International economic relations—*Continued*

    Sanctions (International law)
    Technical assistance
    United States—Foreign economic relations

International education (May subdiv. geog.)   **370.116**

Use for materials on education for international understanding, world citizenship, etc.

  BT   **Education**
  NT   **Student exchange programs**
       Teacher exchange
  RT   **Intellectual cooperation**
       International cooperation
       Multicultural education

International exchange
  USE **Foreign exchange**

International exchange of students
  USE **Student exchange programs**

International exhibitions
  USE **Exhibitions**

International investment
  USE **Foreign investments**

International language
  USE **Universal language**

International law (May subdiv. geog.)   **341**

  UF   Law of nations
  BT   **Law**
  NT   **Asylum**
       Boundaries
       International arbitration
       International cooperation
       Intervention (International law)
       Mandates
       Marine salvage
       Maritime law
       Military law
       Naturalization
       Neutrality
       Pirates
       Political refugees
       Privateering
       Sanctions (International law)
       Slave trade
       Sovereignty
       Space law
       Treaties
       War crimes
  RT   **International organization**
       International relations

    Natural law
    War

International mediation
  USE **International arbitration**

International organization   **341.2**

Use for materials on plans leading towards political organization of nations.

  UF   World government
       World organization
  SA   names of specific organizations, e.g. **United Nations** [to be added as needed]
  BT   **International relations**
       International security
  NT   **European federation**
       International police
       League of Nations
       Mandates
       North Atlantic Treaty Organization
       United Nations
  RT   **International cooperation**
       International law
       World politics

International organizations
  USE **International agencies**

International police   **341.7**

  UF   Interpol
       Police, International
  BT   **International cooperation**
       International organization
       International relations
       International security

International politics
  USE **World politics**

International relations   **327; 341.3**

Use for materials on the theory of international relations. Historical accounts are entered under **World politics; Europe—Politics and government;** etc. Materials on the foreign relations of an individual country are entered under the name of the country with the subdivison *Foreign relations.* Materials limited to diplomatic relations between two countries are entered under the name of each country with the subdivision *Foreign relations* further subdivided by the name of the other country, e.g. **United States—Foreign relations—Iran** and also **Iran—Foreign relations—United States.**

  UF   Foreign affairs
       Foreign policy
       Foreign relations
       Peaceful coexistence
       World order

International relations—*Continued*

SA   names of countries with the subdivision *Foreign relations,*
e.g. **United States—Foreign
relations** [to be added as
needed]

NT   **Arms control**
Balance of power
Boundaries
**Catholic Church—Foreign rela-
tions**
Cultural relations
Diplomacy
**Diplomatic and consular ser-
vice**
Diplomats
East and West
Geopolitics
Globalization
International arbitration
International competition
International cooperation
**International economic rela-
tions**
International organization
International police
International security
Jihad
Mandates
Monroe Doctrine
Nationalism
Neutrality
Peace
Political refugees
Treaties
**United States—Foreign rela-
tions**

RT   **International law**
National security
Technology transfer
World politics

International security   327.1; 341.7

UF   Collective security
Security, International

BT   **International relations**

NT   **Arms control**
Arms race
International arbitration
International organization
International police
Neutrality

RT   **Peace**

International space cooperation

USE   **Astronautics—International cooperation**

**International Standard Bibliographic De-
scription**   025.3

UF   ISBD

BT   **Cataloging**

**International Standard Book Numbers
070.5**

UF   ISBN

BT   **Publishers' standard book
numbers**

**International Standard Serial Numbers
070.5**

UF   ISSN

RT   **Serial publications**

International trade (May subdiv. geog.)
382

   Use for general materials about trade among
nations. Materials on foreign trade of specific
countries, cities, etc., are entered under the
name of the place with the subdivision *Commerce.* Materials limited to trade between two
countries are entered under the name of each
country with the subdivision *Commerce* further subdivided by the name of the other
country, i.e. **United States—Commerce—Japan** and also **Japan—Commerce—United
States.**

UF   Foreign commerce
Foreign trade
Trade, International

BT   **Commerce**
**International economic rela-
tions**

NT   **Arms transfers**
Balance of trade
Exports
Free trade
Imports
International competition

Internationalization

USE   **Globalization**

Internet   004.67

UF   Information superhighway
Internet (Computer network)

BT   **Computer networks**
Information networks

NT   **Internet addresses**
Internet resources
World Wide Web

Internet access providers

USE   **Internet service providers**

Internet addresses 004.67
BT Internet
Internet addresses—Directories 025.04
SA topics, names of places, catego-
ries of persons, ethnic groups,
etc., with the subdivisions
*Internet resources—Directo-
ries,* e.g. **Business—Internet
resources—Directories** [to be
added as needed]
Internet and children 004.678083
UF Children and the Internet
BT **Children**
Internet chat groups
USE **Online chat groups**
Internet commerce
USE **Electronic commerce**
Internet companies
USE **Internet industry**
Internet (Computer network)
USE **Internet**
Internet—Computer software
USE **Internet software**
Internet discussion groups
USE **Electronic discussion groups**
Internet gambling (May subdiv. geog.)
795
UF Online gambling
BT **Gambling**
Internet—Home shopping services
USE **Internet marketing**
Internet shopping
Internet in education (May subdiv. geog.)
004.678071
BT **Education**
Internet industry (May subdiv. geog.)
004.67; 338.7
UF Internet companies
BT **Industries**
NT **Internet service providers**
Internet marketing (May subdiv. geog.)
658.8
UF Internet—Home shopping ser-
vices
Online marketing
Online selling
BT **Electronic commerce**
Marketing
RT **Internet shopping**
Internet newsgroups
USE **Electronic discussion groups**

Internet resources 004.67
UF Computer network resources
SA subjects with the subdivision
Internet resources, for materials about information available on the Internet on a subject, e.g. **Business—Internet
resources;** subjects with the
subdivision *Information resources,* for general materials
about information on a subject, e.g. **Business—Information resources;** subjects with
the subdivision *Databases,* for
materials about data files on a
subject regardless of the medium of distribution, e.g.
Business—Databases; and
headings for the providers or
the users of information with
the subdivision *Information
services,* for materials about
organizations that provide information services, e.g. **United Nations—Information services; Consumers—Informa-
tion services;** etc. [to be added as needed]
BT **Information resources
Internet**
NT **Business—Internet resources
Web sites**
Internet searching 004.67; 025.5
UF Searching the Internet
Web searching
World Wide Web searching
BT **Information retrieval**
NT **Web search engines**
Internet service providers (May subdiv.
geog.) **004.67**
UF Internet access providers
BT **Internet industry**
Internet shopping (May subdiv. geog.)
381; 640
UF Cybershopping
Internet—Home shopping ser-
vices
Online shopping
Shopping—Computer network re-
sources
Shopping—Internet resources

Internet shopping—*Continued*
  BT **Electronic commerce**
      Shopping
  RT **Internet marketing**
Internet software 005.7
  UF Internet—Computer software
  BT **Computer software**
Internment camps
  USE **Concentration camps**
Interoffice communication systems
  USE **Intercommunication systems**
Interpersonal competence
  USE **Social skills**
Interpersonal relations (May subdiv.
      geog.) 158; 302
    Use for materials on group behavior, social relations between persons, and problems arising from organizational and interpersonal relations.
  UF Human relations
  SA relations between particular groups of persons or individuals, e.g. **Jewish-Arab relations; Parent-child relationship;** etc. [to be added as needed]
  BT **Social psychology**
  NT **Conflict of generations**
      Discrimination
      Domestic relations
      Family
      Group relations training
      Helping behavior
      Life skills
      Man-woman relationship
      Personal space
      Prejudices
      Social adjustment
      Social skills
      Teacher-student relationship
      Teasing
      Toleration
  RT **Human behavior**
Interplanetary communication
  USE **Interstellar communication**
Interplanetary visitors
  USE **Extraterrestrial beings**
Interplanetary voyages 808.3; 808.83;
      919.904
    Use for general materials about travel to other planets and for individual works, collections, or materials about imaginary accounts

of such travels. Materials on the physics and technical details of flight beyond the earth's atmosphere are entered under **Space flight.**
  UF Interstellar travel
      Space travel
  BT **Astronautics**
      Fiction
  NT **Outer space—Exploration**
  RT **Fantasy fiction**
      Imaginary voyages
      Rockets (Aeronautics)
      Science fiction
      Space flight
Interplanetary warfare
  USE **Space warfare**
Interpol
  USE **International police**
Interpreting and translating
  USE **Translating and interpreting**
Interpretive dance
  USE **Modern dance**
Interracial adoption (May subdiv. geog.)
      362.73
  BT **Adoption**
      Race relations
Interracial marriage (May subdiv. geog.)
      306.84
  UF Marriage, Interracial
      Racial intermarriage
  BT **Intermarriage**
Interracial relations
  USE **Race relations**
Interscholastic sports
  USE **School sports**
Interstate commerce 381
    Use for materials limited to commerce between states. General materials on foreign and domestic commerce are entered under **Commerce.**
  UF Government regulation of commerce
  BT **Commerce**
Interstate highways
  USE **Express highways**
Interstellar communication 621.382
  UF Extraterrestrial communication
      Interplanetary communication
      Outer space—Communication
      Space communication
      Space telecommunication
  BT **Life on other planets**
      Telecommunication

Interstellar communication—*Continued*
  NT   Astronautics—Communication
          systems
          Radio astronomy
Interstellar travel
  USE Interplanetary voyages
Interstellar warfare
  USE Space warfare
Interurban railroads
  USE Electric railroads
          Street railroads
Intervention (International law)   341.5
  UF   Military intervention
  BT   International law
         War
  NT   Monroe Doctrine
  RT   Neutrality
Interviewing   158
  BT   Applications for positions
         Social psychology
  NT   Talk shows
  RT   Applied psychology
         Counseling
         Interviews
Interviewing (Journalism)
  USE Reporters and reporting
Interviews   920
  Use for materials about interviews and for
  collections of diverse interviews.
  SA   subjects, ethnic groups, classes
         of persons, and names of cor-
         porate bodies and individual
         persons with the subdivision
         Interviews, e.g. **Authors—In-**
         terviews [to be added as
         needed]
  BT   Conversation
  NT   Authors—Interviews
  RT   Interviewing
Interviews, Parent-teacher
  USE Parent-teacher conferences
Intestacy
  USE Inheritance and succession
Intifada, 1987-   956.9405
  UF   Arab-Israeli conflict, 1987-
         Israeli-Arab conflict, 1987-
         Palestinian-Israeli conflict, 1987-
         Palestinian uprising, 1987-
  BT   Israel-Arab conflicts
Intolerance
  USE Fanaticism
         Toleration

Intoxicants
  USE Alcohol
         Alcoholic beverages
         Liquors
Intoxication
  USE Alcoholism
         Temperance
Intranets   004.6; 651.7
  BT   Business enterprises—Comput-
         er networks
Intuition   153.4
  BT   Philosophy
         Psychology
         Rationalism
         Theory of knowledge
  RT   Perception
Inuit (May subdiv. geog.)   970.004
  Use for materials on the native peoples of
  the arctic regions of Alaska, Canada, and
  Greenland. If local usage dictates, libraries
  may establish **Eskimos** as a broader term than
  Inuit; and the names of other groups of Arc-
  tic peoples may be added as needed.
  UF   Eskimos
         Esquimaux
         Innuit
  BT   Native peoples
Inuit—Folklore   398
  BT   Folklore
Invalid cooking
  USE Cooking for the sick
         Diet therapy
Invalids
  USE Physically handicapped
         Sick
Invasion of Cuba, 1961
  USE Cuba—History—1961, Invasion
Invasion of privacy
  USE Right of privacy
Invective   808.88
  UF   Abuse, Verbal
         Insults
         Verbal abuse
  BT   Satire
Inventions (May subdiv. geog.)   608
  Use for materials on original devices or
  processes. Materials on technological improve-
  ments in materials, production methods, pro-
  cesses, organization, or management are en-
  tered under **Technological innovations.**
  BT   Technology
  NT   Creation (Literary, artistic,
         etc.)
         Technological innovations

Inventions—*Continued*
        Technology transfer
RT   Industrial research
        Inventors
        Patents
Inventors (May subdiv. geog.)   609.2; 920
RT   Engineers
        Inventions
Inventory control   658.7
UF   Stock control
BT   Management
        Retail trade
Invertebrates   592
BT   Animals
Investment and saving
USE   Saving and investment
Investment companies
USE   Mutual funds
Investment in real estate
USE   Real estate investment
Investment trusts
USE   Mutual funds
Investments (May subdiv. geog.)   332.6
BT   Banks and banking
        Capital
        Finance
NT   Annuities
        Bonds
        Foreign investments
        Futures
        Mutual funds
        Real estate investment
        Savings and loan associations
        Securities
RT   Estate planning
        Loans
        Saving and investment
        Speculation
        Stock exchanges
        Stocks
Investments, Foreign
USE   Foreign investments
Invincible Armada
USE   Spanish Armada, 1588
Invisible world
USE   Spirits
IQ tests
USE   Intelligence tests
Iran   935; 955
      May be subdivided like United States except for *History*.

UF   Persia
Iran—Foreign relations—United States   327.55073
NT   Iran hostage crisis, 1979-1981
Iran—History—1941-1979   955.05
Iran—History—1979-   955.05
Iran hostage crisis, 1979-1981   327.55073; 327.73055; 955
BT   American hostages—Iran
        Iran—Foreign relations—United States
        United States—Foreign relations—Iran
IRAs (Pensions)
USE   Individual retirement accounts
Iron   669; 672
BT   Chemical elements
        Metals
NT   Iron ores
        Ironwork
        Steel
Iron Age (May subdiv. geog.)   930.1
BT   Civilization
Iron and steel building
USE   Steel construction
Iron curtain countries
USE   Communist countries
Iron industry (May subdiv. geog.)   338.2
UF   Iron industry and trade
BT   Industries
NT   Hardware
RT   Steel industry
Iron industry and trade
USE   Iron industry
Iron ores   553.3
BT   Iron
        Ores
Ironing
USE   Laundry
Ironwork (May subdiv. geog.)   672; 682; 739.4
UF   Wrought iron work
BT   Decoration and ornament
        Iron
        Metalwork
NT   Blacksmithing
        Welding
RT   Forging
Irreversible coma
USE   Brain death

Irrigation (May subdiv. geog.)   **333.91; 627; 631.5**

    BT   **Agricultural engineering**
          Hydraulic engineering
          Water resources development
          Water supply
    RT   **Reclamation of land**

Irrigation—United States   **333.91; 627; 631.5**

ISBD
    USE **International Standard Bibliographic Description**

ISBN
    USE **International Standard Book Numbers**

Islam (May subdiv. geog.)   **297**

    Use for materials on the religion. Materials on the believers in this religion are entered under **Muslims.**
    BT   **Religions**
    NT   **Islam—Relations—Judaism**
          Islamic fundamentalism
          Jihad
          Judaism—Relations—Islam
          Koran
          Mysticism—Islam
    RT   **Islamic law**
          Muslims

Islam—Relations—Judaism   **297**

    Use for materials on the relations between Islam and Judaism. When assigning this heading, provide an additional subject entry under **Judaism—Relations—Islam.** Materials on the conflicts between the Arab countries and Israel are entered under **Israel-Arab conflicts.** Materials that discuss collectively the relations between Arabs and Jews, including religious, ethnic, and ideological relations, are entered under **Jewish-Arab relations.**
    UF   Islamic-Jewish relations
          Jewish-Islamic relations
    BT   **Islam**
          Judaism
    RT   **Jewish-Arab relations**

Islam—Sermons
    USE **Islamic sermons**

Islamic architecture (May subdiv. geog.)   **720.917**

    UF   Architecture, Islamic
          Moorish architecture
          Muslim architecture
    BT   **Architecture**
    NT   **Mosques**

Islamic art (May subdiv. geog.)   **709.1**

    UF   Art, Islamic
          Mohammedan art
          Muslim art
          Saracenic art
    BT   **Art**

Islamic countries   **956**

    UF   Muslim countries
    NT   **Arab countries**

Islamic fundamentalism (May subdiv. geog.)   **297.09; 320.557; 322.1**

    UF   Fundamentalism
    BT   **Islam**
          Religious fundamentalism

Islamic gardens (May subdiv. geog.)   **635.9; 712**

    BT   **Gardens**

Islamic holy war
    USE **Jihad**

Islamic-Jewish relations
    USE **Islam—Relations—Judaism**
          Judaism—Relations—Islam

Islamic law (May subdiv. geog.)   **340.5**

    UF   Muslim law
    BT   **Law**
    RT   **Islam**

Islamic literature   **297**

    UF   Muslim literature
    BT   **Religious literature**
    NT   **Islamic sermons**

Islamic mysticism
    USE **Mysticism—Islam**

Islamic sermons   **297**

    UF   Islam—Sermons
          Muslim sermons
    SA   individual Islamic sects with the subdivision *Sermons* [to be added as needed]
    BT   **Islamic literature**
          Sermons

Islands (May subdiv. geog.)   **551.42**

    SA   names of islands and groups of islands [to be added as needed]
    NT   **Coral reefs and islands**
          Cuba
          Islands of the Pacific

Islands, Imaginary
    USE **Geographical myths**

Islands of the Pacific   **990**

    Use for comprehensive materials on all the islands of the Pacific Ocean. Materials re-

Islands of the Pacific—*Continued*
stricted to comprehensive treatment of the island groups of Melanesia, Micronesia, and
Polynesia are entered under **Oceania.**

  UF   Pacific Islands
         Pacific Ocean Islands
  BT   **Islands**
  NT   **Oceania**
  RT   **Pacific rim**

Isotopes   539.7; 541
  BT   **Atoms**
  NT   **Radioisotopes**

Israel   956.94
May be subdivided like United States ex-
cept for *History.*
  BT   **Middle East**

Israel-Arab conflicts   956.05; 965.04
Use for materials on the conflicts between
the Arab countries and Israel. Materials that
discuss collectively the relations between
Arabs and Jews, including religious, ethnic,
and ideological relations, are entered under
Jewish-Arab relations. Materials on relations
between the religions of Judaism and Islam
are entered under **Judaism—Relations—Islam** and under **Islam—Relations—Judaism.**

  UF   Arab-Israel conflicts
         Arab-Israeli conflicts
         Israeli-Arab conflicts
  BT   **Arab countries—Foreign rela-
          tions—Israel**
         **Israel—Foreign relations—
          Arab countries**
  NT   **Intifada, 1987-
         Israel-Arab War, 1948-1949
         Israel-Arab War, 1967
         Israel-Arab War, 1973
         Lebanon—History—1982-1984,
          Israeli intervention
         Sinai Campaign, 1956**
  RT   **Jewish-Arab relations**

Israel-Arab relations
  USE **Arab countries—Foreign rela-
          tions—Israel**
         **Israel—Foreign relations—
          Arab countries**

Israel-Arab War, 1948-1949   956.04
  UF   Arab-Israel War, 1948-1949
  BT   **Israel-Arab conflicts**

Israel-Arab War, 1956
  USE **Sinai Campaign, 1956**

Israel-Arab War, 1967   956.04
  UF   Arab-Israel War, 1967
         Six Day War, 1967
  BT   **Israel-Arab conflicts**

Israel-Arab War, 1973   956.04
  UF   Arab-Israel War, 1973
         Yom Kippur War, 1973
  BT   **Israel-Arab conflicts**

Israel—Collective settlements
  USE **Collective settlements—Israel**

**Israel—Foreign relations—Arab countries
   956**
  UF   Arab-Israel relations
         Arab-Israeli relations
         Israel-Arab relations
         Israeli-Arab relations
  NT   **Israel-Arab conflicts**
  RT   **Arab countries—Foreign rela-
          tions—Israel**
         Jewish-Arab relations

Israel, Ten lost tribes
  USE **Lost tribes of Israel**

Israeli-Arab conflict, 1987-
  USE **Intifada, 1987-**

Israeli-Arab conflicts
  USE **Israel-Arab conflicts**

Israeli-Arab relations
  USE **Arab countries—Foreign rela-
          tions—Israel**
         **Israel—Foreign relations—
          Arab countries**

Israeli intervention in Lebanon, 1982-1984
  USE **Lebanon—History—1982-1984,
          Israeli intervention**

Israelis (May subdiv. geog.)   **305.892;
   920; 956.94**
  BT   **Jews**

Israelites
  USE **Jews**

ISSN
  USE **International Standard Serial
         Numbers**

Italo-Ethiopian War, 1935-1936   963
  UF   Ethiopian-Italian War, 1935-1936

Italy   945
May be subdivided like United States except for *History.*

Italy—History   945
Italy—History—0-1559   945
Italy—History—1559-1789   945
Italy—History—1789-1815   945
Italy—History—1815-1914   945; 945.09
Italy—History—1914-1945   945.091
Italy—History—1945-1976   945.092
Italy—History—1976-   945.092

Ivory   679
    BT   Animal products
Jails
    USE   Prisons
Japan   952
    May be subdivided like United States except for *History*.
Japan—Commerce—United States   382
Japan—History   952
Japan—History—0-1868   952
Japan—History—1868-1945   952.03
Japan—History—1945-1952, Allied occupation   952.04
Japan—History—1952-   952.04
Japanese aesthetics   111; 701; 801
    UF   Aesthetics, Japanese
    BT   Aesthetics
Japanese color prints   769.952
    UF   Color prints, Japanese
    BT   Color prints
Japanese language   495.6
    May be subdivided like English language.
    BT   Language and languages
Japanese language—Business Japanese   495.6
    Business Japanese is a unique subdivision for Japanese language.
    UF   Business Japanese
Japanese paper folding
    USE   Origami
Jargon
    USE   subjects and names of languages with the subdivision *Jargon*, e.g. English language—Jargon [to be added as needed]
Jazz ensembles   784.4
    BT   Ensembles (Music)
Jazz music (May subdiv. geog.)   781.65; 782.42165
    BT   Music
    RT   Blues music
Jealousy   152.4
    BT   Emotions
Jestbooks
    USE   Chapbooks
Jesters
    USE   Fools and jesters
Jesus Christ   232
    UF   Christ
         Christology

    BT   God—Christianity
    NT   Atonement—Christianity
         Second Advent
    RT   Christianity
Jesus Christ—Art   704.9
    UF   Jesus Christ—Iconography
         Jesus Christ in art
    BT   Christian art
    RT   Bible—Pictorial works
Jesus Christ—Atonement
    USE   Atonement—Christianity
Jesus Christ—Birth
    USE   Jesus Christ—Nativity
Jesus Christ—Crucifixion   232.96
    UF   Crucifixion of Jesus Christ
    RT   Good Friday
Jesus Christ—Divinity   232
    UF   Divinity of Jesus Christ
    RT   Trinity
Jesus Christ—Drama   808.82
    Use for collections of plays about Jesus Christ.
    BT   Religious drama
    NT   Passion plays
Jesus Christ—Historicity   232.9
Jesus Christ—Iconography
    USE   Jesus Christ—Art
Jesus Christ in art
    USE   Jesus Christ—Art
Jesus Christ—Last Supper
    USE   Last Supper
Jesus Christ—Messiahship   232
Jesus Christ—Nativity   232.92
    UF   Jesus Christ—Birth
         Nativity of Jesus Christ
    RT   Christmas
Jesus Christ—Parables   226.8; 232.9
    BT   Bible—Parables
         Parables
Jesus Christ—Prayers   232.9
    NT   Lord's prayer
Jesus Christ—Prophecies   232
    BT   Bible—Prophecies
Jesus Christ—Resurrection   232.9
    UF   Resurrection of Jesus Christ
Jesus Christ—Second Advent
    USE   Second Advent
Jesus Christ—Sermon on the mount
    USE   Sermon on the mount
Jesus Christ—Teachings   232.9
    UF   Teachings of Jesus Christ

Jet airplanes
USE **Jet planes**
Jet lag   616.9
BT **Aviation medicine**
Biological rhythms
Fatigue
Jet planes   629.133
UF Jet airplanes
Jets (Airplanes)
BT **Airplanes**
NT **Supersonic transport planes**
Jet propulsion   621.43
BT **Airplane engines**
RT **Rockets (Aeronautics)**
Jets (Airplanes)
USE **Jet planes**
Jewelry (May subdiv. geog.)   **391.7;**
739.27

Use for general materials on jewelry and for materials on gems in which the emphasis is on the setting. Materials on cut and polished precious stones treated from the point of view of art or antiquity are entered under **Gems.** Materials on gem stones treated from the mineralogical or technological point of view are entered under **Precious stones.**

UF Jewels
SA styles of jewelry and types of
jewelry items [to be added as
needed]
BT **Clothing and dress**
Costume
Decorative arts
RT **Gems**
Jewels
USE **Gems**
Jewelry
Precious stones
Jewish-Arab relations   956

Use for materials that discuss collectively the relations between Arabs and Jews, including religious, ethnic, and ideological relations. Materials on the conflicts between the Arab countries and Israel are entered under **Israel-Arab conflicts.** Materials on relations between the religions of Judaism and Islam are entered under **Judaism—Relations—Islam;** and **Islam—Relations—Judaism.**

UF Arab-Jewish relations
BT **Arabs**
Jews
RT **Arab countries—Foreign rela-**
tions—Israel
Islam—Relations—Judaism
Israel-Arab conflicts

Israel—Foreign relations—
Arab countries
Judaism—Relations—Islam
Palestinian Arabs
Jewish children in the Holocaust (May
subdiv. geog.)   **940.53**
BT **Holocaust, 1933-1945**
NT **Hidden children (Holocaust)**
Jewish-Christian relations
USE **Christianity—Relations—Juda-**
ism
Judaism—Relations—Christian-
ity
Jewish civilization   909
UF Jews—Civilization
BT **Civilization**
Jewish customs
USE **Jews—Social life and customs**
Judaism—Customs and prac-
tices
Jewish diaspora   909
UF Diaspora, Jewish
Jews—Diaspora
SA the heading **Jews** subdivided
geographically, e.g. **Jews—**
France [to be added as need-
ed]
BT **Human geography**
Jews
Jewish doctrines
USE **Judaism—Doctrines**
Jewish ethics   296.3
BT **Ethics**
Jewish folk literature   398.2
BT **Folk literature**
Jewish literature
Jewish folklore
USE **Jews—Folklore**
Jewish holidays   296.4; 394.267
UF Fasts and feasts—Judaism
Holidays, Jewish
Jews—Festivals
SA names of individual holidays,
e.g. **Hanukkah** [to be added
as needed]
BT **Judaism**
Religious holidays
NT **Hanukkah**
Passover
Yom Kippur

Jewish Holocaust (1933-1945)
  USE Holocaust, 1933-1945
Jewish-Islamic relations
  USE Islam—Relations—Judaism
       Judaism—Relations—Islam
Jewish language
  USE Hebrew language
       Yiddish language
Jewish legends   296.1; 398.2
    May be used for individual works, collec-
    tions, or materials about Jewish legends.
  UF Jews—Legends
      Legends, Jewish
  BT Legends
Jewish life
  USE Jews—Social life and customs
       Judaism—Customs and prac-
       tices
Jewish literature   296; 808.8
  UF Jews—Literature
  BT Literature
      Religious literature
  NT Bible
      Cabala
      Jewish folk literature
      Jewish religious fiction
      Talmud
      Yiddish literature
  RT Hebrew literature
Jewish liturgies
  USE Judaism—Liturgy
Jewish men (May subdiv. geog.)
       305.38; 305.892
  BT Men
Jewish religion
  USE Judaism
Jewish religious fiction   808.3; 808.83
    Use for individual works, collections, or
    materials about fiction that promotes Jewish
    teachings or exemplifies a Jewish religious
    way of life.
  BT Fiction
      Jewish literature
      Religious fiction
Jewish theology
  USE Judaism—Doctrines
Jewish wit and humor   808.87
  BT Wit and humor
Jewish women (May subdiv. geog.)
       305.48; 305.892
  BT Women

Jews (May subdiv. geog.)   296.092;
       305.892; 909
  UF Hebrews
      Israelites
  NT Essenes
      Israelis
      Jewish-Arab relations
      Jewish diaspora
      Lost tribes of Israel
      World War, 1939-1945—Jews
  RT Judaism
Jews—Antiquities   933
  BT Antiquities
Jews—Civilization
  USE Jewish civilization
Jews—Customs
  USE Jews—Social life and customs
       Judaism—Customs and prac-
       tices
Jews—Diaspora
  USE Jewish diaspora
Jews—Economic conditions   305.892;
       330.9
  BT Economic conditions
Jews—Encyclopedias   909
  BT Encyclopedias and dictionaries
Jews—Festivals
  USE Jewish holidays
Jews—Folklore   398
  UF Jewish folklore
  BT Folklore
Jews—France   305.892; 944
Jews—Language
  USE Hebrew language
       Yiddish language
Jews—Legends
  USE Jewish legends
Jews—Literature
  USE Hebrew literature
       Jewish literature
Jews—Lost tribes
  USE Lost tribes of Israel
Jews—Persecutions (May subdiv. geog.)
       909; 933
  BT Antisemitism
      Persecution
  NT Holocaust, 1933-1945
      World War, 1939-1945—
       Jews—Rescue
Jews—Political activity   909; 956.94
  BT Political participation

404

Jews—Religion
  USE **Judaism**
Jews—Restoration   956.94
  Use for materials on the belief that the Jews, in fulfillment of Biblical prophecy, would some day return to Palestine.
  RT **Zionism**
Jews—Rites and ceremonies
  USE **Judaism—Customs and practices**
Jews—Ritual
  USE **Judaism—Customs and practices**
       Judaism—Liturgy
Jews—Social conditions   305.892; 909
  BT **Social conditions**
Jews—Social life and customs   305.892
  Use for materials on Jewish social customs. General materials on Jewish religious practices are entered under **Judaism—Customs and practices.** Materials on the forms of public worship in Judaism are entered under **Judaism—Liturgy.**
  UF Jewish customs
       Jewish life
       Jews—Customs
  BT **Manners and customs**
Jigsaw puzzles   793.73
  BT **Puzzles**
Jihad   297.7
  UF Holy war (Islam)
       Islamic holy war
       Muslim holy war
  BT **International relations**
       Islam
Job analysis   658.3
  UF Personnel classification
  BT **Factory management**
       Industrial efficiency
       Management
       Occupations
       Personnel management
       Salaries, wages, etc.
  NT **Motion study**
       Time study
Job applications
  USE **Applications for positions**
Job discrimination
  USE **Discrimination in employment**

Job hunting   650.14
  UF Job searching
  SA fields of knowledge, professions, industries, and trades with the subdivision *Vocational guidance* [to be added as needed]
  BT **Employment agencies**
       Vocational guidance
  NT **Applications for positions**
       Résumés (Employment)
Job performance standards
  USE **Performance standards**
Job placement guidance
  USE **Vocational guidance**
Job résumés
  USE **Résumés (Employment)**
Job retraining
  USE **Occupational retraining**
Job satisfaction   650.1; 658.3
  UF Work satisfaction
  BT **Attitude (Psychology)**
       Employee morale
       Personnel management
       Work
  NT **Burn out (Psychology)**
Job searching
  USE **Job hunting**
Job security   331.25; 650.1; 658.3
  UF Employment security
  BT **Personnel management**
  NT **Employees—Dismissal**
Job sharing   331.2; 658.3
  UF Sharing of jobs
  BT **Part-time employment**
Job stress   158.7; 658.3
  UF Occupational stress
       Organizational stress
       Work stress
  BT **Stress (Physiology)**
       Stress (Psychology)
  NT **Burn out (Psychology)**
Job training
  USE **Occupational training**
Jobless people
  USE **Unemployed**
Joblessness
  USE **Unemployment**
Jobs
  USE **Occupations**
       Professions

Jogging 613.7
  BT Running
Joint custody of children
  USE Child custody
        Part-time parenting
Joint ventures (May subdiv. geog.)
        338.7
  BT Business enterprises
        Partnership
Joke books
  USE Jokes
Jokes 808.7; 808.88
    May be used for collections of jokes and
    for materials about jokes.
  UF Joke books
  BT Wit and humor
  NT Practical jokes
Journaling 808
  BT Authorship
        Diaries
Journalism (May subdiv. geog.) 070.4
    Use for materials on writing for the periodi-
    cal press or on journalism as an occupation.
    Materials limited to the history, organization,
    and management of newspapers are entered
    under Newspapers.
  SA types of journalism, e.g. Scien-
        tific journalism; and topics
        with the subdivision Press
        coverage, e.g. Food contami-
        nation—Press coverage [to
        be added as needed]
  BT Authorship
        Literature
  NT Broadcast journalism
        College and school journalism
        Gossip
        Libel and slander
        Newsletters
        Photojournalism
        Press
        Reporters and reporting
        Scientific journalism
  RT Journalists
        Newspapers
        Periodicals
Journalism—Editing 070.4
  UF Magazine editing
        News editing
        Newspapers—Editing
        Periodicals—Editing
  BT Editing

Journalism—Objectivity 070.4
  UF Slanted journalism
  BT Professional ethics
Journalism, Scientific
  USE Scientific journalism
Journalistic photography
  USE Photojournalism
Journalists (May subdiv. geog.) 070.92;
        920
  UF Columnists
  SA names of wars with the subdivi-
        sion Journalists, e.g. World
        War, 1939-1945—Journalists
        [to be added as needed]
  BT Authors
  NT World War, 1939-1945—Jour-
        nalists
  RT Journalism
Journals
  USE Periodicals
Journals (Diaries)
  USE Diaries
Journeys
  USE Travel
        Voyages and travels
Joy and sorrow 152.4
  UF Affliction
        Sorrow
  BT Emotions
  NT Pleasure
  RT Grief
        Happiness
        Suffering
Judaism (May subdiv. geog.) 296
  UF Jewish religion
        Jews—Religion
  SA names of Jewish sects, e.g. Has-
        idism [to be added as need-
        ed]
  BT Religions
  NT Atonement—Judaism
        Cabala
        Christianity—Relations—Juda-
        ism
        Hasidism
        Islam—Relations—Judaism
        Jewish holidays
        Judaism—Relations—Christian-
        ity
        Judaism—Relations—Islam
        Rabbis

Judaism—*Continued*
     Sabbath
     Talmud
  RT **Jews**
     Synagogues
Judaism—Customs and practices   296.4

Use for materials on Jewish religious practices in general. Materials on the forms of public worship in Judaism are entered under **Judaism—Liturgy.** Materials on Jewish social customs are entered under **Jews—Social life and customs.**

  UF Jewish customs
     Jewish life
     Jews—Customs
     Jews—Rites and ceremonies
     Jews—Ritual
  BT **Rites and ceremonies**
  NT **Seder**
  RT **Judaism—Liturgy**
Judaism—Doctrines   296.3
  UF Jewish doctrines
     Jewish theology
  BT **Doctrinal theology**
Judaism—Liturgy   296.4

Use for materials on the forms of public worship in Judaism. Materials on Jewish religious practices in general are entered under **Judaism—Customs and practices.** Materials on Jewish social customs are entered under **Jews—Social life and customs.**

  UF Jewish liturgies
     Jews—Ritual
  BT **Liturgies**
  RT **Judaism—Customs and practices**
Judaism—Relations—Christianity   261.2; 296.3

Use for materials on the relations between Judaism and Christianity. When assigning this heading, provide an additional subject entry under **Christianity—Relations—Judaism.**

  UF Christian-Jewish relations
     Christianity and other religions—Judaism
     Jewish-Christian relations
  BT **Christianity and other religions**
     Judaism
Judaism—Relations—Islam   296.3

Use for materials on the relations between Judaism and Islam. When assigning this heading, provide an additional subject entry under **Islam—Relations—Judaism.** Materials on the conflicts between the Arab countries and Israel are entered under **Israel-Arab conflicts.** Materials that discuss collectively the relations between Arabs and Jews, including religious,

ethnic, and ideological relations, are entered under **Jewish-Arab relations.**
  UF Islamic-Jewish relations
     Jewish-Islamic relations
  BT **Islam**
     Judaism
  RT **Jewish-Arab relations**
Judges (May subdiv. geog.)   **347; 920**
  UF Chief justices
  BT **Lawyers**
  NT **Women judges**
  RT **Courts**
Judicial investigations
  USE **Governmental investigations**
Judiciary
  USE **Courts**
Judo   796.815
  BT **Martial arts**
     Self-defense
  NT **Karate**
Juggling   793.8
  UF Legerdemain
     Sleight of hand
  BT **Amusements**
     Tricks
July Fourth
  USE **Fourth of July**
Jungle animals (May subdiv. geog.)   **578.734**
  UF Jungle fauna
  BT **Animals**
     Forest animals
Jungle fauna
  USE **Jungle animals**
Jungles (May subdiv. geog.)   **634.9**

Use for materials on impenetrable thickets of second-growth vegetation replacing tropical rain forests that have been disturbed or degraded. Materials on forests of broad-leaved, mainly evergreen trees found in moist climates in the tropics, subtropics, and some parts of the temperate zones, are entered under **Rain forests.**

  UF Tropical jungles
  BT **Forests and forestry**
  RT **Rain forests**
Junior colleges (May subdiv. geog.)   **378.1**
  UF Community colleges
     Two-year colleges
  BT **Colleges and universities**
     Higher education
Junior colleges—Directories   378.1
  BT **Directories**

Junior high school libraries
USE **High school libraries**
Junior high schools (May subdiv. geog.)
373.236
UF Secondary schools
BT **High schools**
Public schools
Schools
RT **Middle schools**
Secondary education
Junk
USE **Waste products**
Junk bonds 332.63
UF High-yield junk bonds
BT **Bonds**
Junk in space
USE **Space debris**
Jurisprudence
USE **Law**
Jurisprudence, Medical
USE **Medical jurisprudence**
Jurists
USE **Lawyers**
Jury 345; 347
UF Trial by jury
BT **Courts**
Criminal law
Justice 340
BT **Ethics**
Law
Virtue
RT **Fairness**
Justice, Administration of
USE **Administration of justice**
Juvenile courts (May subdiv. geog.) 345
UF Children's courts
BT **Courts**
RT **Juvenile delinquency**
Probation
Juvenile delinquency (May subdiv. geog.)
364.3
UF Delinquency, Juvenile
Juvenile delinquents
BT **Crime**
Social problems
NT **Gangs**
Juvenile prostitution
School violence
RT **Child welfare**
Emotionally disturbed children
Juvenile courts

Reformatories
Teenagers—Drug use
Youth—Drug use
Juvenile delinquency—Case studies
364.3
Juvenile delinquents
USE **Juvenile delinquency**
Juvenile drama
USE subjects and names with the
subdivision *Juvenile drama,*
e.g. **Christmas—Juvenile
drama** [to be added as need-
ed]
Juvenile fiction
USE subjects and names with the
subdivision *Juvenile fiction,*
e.g. **Christmas—Juvenile fiction** [to be added as needed]
Juvenile literature
USE **Children's literature**
and subjects and names with
the subdivision *Juvenile liter-
ature,* e.g. **Computers—Juve-
nile literature** [to be added
as needed]
Juvenile poetry
USE subjects and names with the
subdivision *Juvenile poetry,*
e.g. **Christmas—Juvenile po-
etry** [to be added as needed]
Juvenile prostitution (May subdiv. geog.)
176; 306.74; 362.7; 363.4;
364.1
UF Adolescent prostitution
Child prostitution
Teenage prostitution
BT **Juvenile delinquency**
Prostitution
Kabbala
USE **Cabala**
Karate 796.815
BT **Judo**
Martial arts
Self-defense
Kart racing
USE **Karts and karting**
Karting
USE **Karts and karting**
Karts and karting 796.7
UF Carts (Midget cars)
Go-karts

Karts and karting—*Continued*
    Kart racing
    Karting
    Karts (Midget cars)
    Midget cars
  BT **Automobile racing**
Karts (Midget cars)
  USE **Karts and karting**
Kayaking (May subdiv. geog.)   **797.122**
  BT **Canoes and canoeing**
Kempo
  USE **Kung fu**
Kennels 636
  BT **Pets—Housing**
Keyboarding (Electronics) 005.72
  UF Computer keyboarding
    Data processing—Keyboarding
    Word processor keyboarding
  BT **Business education**
    Office practice
  RT **Typewriting**
Keyboards (Electronics) 004.7
  UF Computer keyboards
  BT **Computer peripherals**
    Office equipment and supplies
Keyboards (Musical instruments) 786
  BT **Organs (Musical instruments)**
    Pianos
Keys
  USE **Locks and keys**
Kibbutz
  USE **Collective settlements—Israel**
Kidnapping (May subdiv. geog.)   **364.15**
  UF Abduction
  BT **Criminal law**
    Offenses against the person
Kidnapping, Parental
  USE **Parental kidnapping**
Kindergarten (May subdiv. geog.)
    372.21
  BT **Elementary education**
    Schools
  NT **Creative activities**
    Montessori method of education
  RT **Nursery schools**
    Preschool education
Kinematics 531
  BT **Dynamics**
  NT **Mechanical movements**
  RT **Mechanics**
    Motion

Kinesiology 613.7
  UF Cinesiology
  BT **Human locomotion**
    Physical fitness
Kinetic art (May subdiv. geog.)   **709.04**
  UF Art in motion
    Art, Kinetic
  BT **Art**
  NT **Kinetic sculpture**
Kinetic sculpture 731; 735
  UF Sculpture in motion
  BT **Kinetic art**
    Sculpture
  NT **Mobiles (Sculpture)**
Kinetics
  USE **Dynamics**
    Motion
King Award
  USE **Coretta Scott King Award**
King Philip's War, 1675-1676 973.2
  UF United States—History—1675-
    1676, King Philip's War
  BT **Native Americans—Wars**
    United States—History—1600-
    1775, Colonial period
King William's War, 1689-1697
  USE **United States—History—1689-**
    1697, King William's War
Kings and rulers 352.23; 920; 929.7
    Use for materials on monarchs and other
heads of state not democratically elected.
  UF Kings, queens, rulers, etc.
    Monarchs
    Royal houses
    Royalty
    Rulers
    Sovereigns
  SA names of places with the subdi-
    vision *Kings and rulers,* e.g.
    Great Britain—Kings and
    rulers; and names of individ-
    ual monarchs or rulers [to be
    added as needed]
  BT **Heads of state**
  NT **Emperors**
    Great Britain—Kings and rul-
    ers
  RT **Courts and courtiers**
    Monarchy
    Queens
Kings, queens, rulers, etc.
  USE **Kings and rulers**

Kinship (May subdiv. geog.) **306.83**
  SA ethnic groups with the subdivision *Kinship* [to be added as needed]
  BT **Ethnology**
     Family
  RT **Clans**
Kitchen gardens
  USE **Vegetable gardening**
Kitchen remodeling
  USE **Kitchens—Remodeling**
Kitchen renovation
  USE **Kitchens—Remodeling**
Kitchen utensils 643; 683
  UF Cooking utensils
     Household utensils
     Kitchenware
     Utensils, Kitchen
  SA types of kitchen utensils, e.g. **Bread machines** [to be added as needed]
  BT **Household equipment and supplies**
  NT **Bread machines**
Kitchens 643
  BT **Houses**
     Rooms
Kitchens—Remodeling 643
  UF Kitchen remodeling
     Kitchen renovation
     Remodeling of kitchens
Kitchenware
  USE **Kitchen utensils**
Kites 629.133; 796.1
  BT **Aeronautics**
Kitsch 709.03
  BT **Aesthetics**
Kittens
  USE **Cats**
Knicks (Basketball team)
  USE **New York Knicks (Basketball team)**
Knighthood
  USE **Knights and knighthood**
Knights and knighthood (May subdiv. geog.) **394; 940.1**
  UF Knighthood
  BT **Middle Ages**
     Nobility
  RT **Chivalry**
     Heraldry

Knights of the Round Table
  USE **Arthurian romances**
Knitting 677; 746.43
  BT **Needlework**
Knives 621.9; 623.4
  BT **Hardware**
     Weapons
Knots and splices 623.88
  UF Splicing
  BT **Navigation**
     Rope
Knowledge
  USE names of individual persons with the subdivision *Knowledge,* e.g. **Shakespeare, William, 1564-1616—Knowledge;** which may be further subdivided by the subject known, e.g. **Shakespeare, William, 1564-1616—Knowledge—Animals** [to be added as needed]
Knowledge-based systems (Computer science)
  USE **Expert systems (Computer science)**
Knowledge management (May subdiv. geog.) **658.4**
  UF Management of knowledge assets
  BT **Management**
  RT **Information technology**
Knowledge, Theory of
  USE **Theory of knowledge**
Kodak camera 771.3
  BT **Cameras**
Koran 297.1
  UF Qur'an
  BT **Islam**
     Sacred books
Korea 951.9
  Use for comprehensive materials on all of Korea and for materials on Korea before it was divided in 1948 into two separate republics.
  NT **Korea (North)**
     Korea (South)
Korea (Democratic People's Republic)
  USE **Korea (North)**
Korea (North) 951.93
  Use for materials on the Democratic People's Republic of Korea, established in 1948. May be subdivided like United States except for *History.*

Korea (North)—*Continued*
  UF   Korea (Democratic People's Re-
       public)
       North Korea
  BT   **Korea**
Korea (Republic)
  USE **Korea (South)**
Korea (South)   951.95
  Use for materials on the Republic of Korea,
  established in 1948. May be subdivided like
  United States except for *History.*
  UF   Korea (Republic)
       South Korea
  BT   **Korea**
Korean War, 1950-1953   951.904
Ku Klux Klan   322.4
  UF   Ku-Klux Klan (1866-1869)
       Ku Klux Klan (1915-)
  BT   **Secret societies**
  RT   **Reconstruction (1865-1876)**
Ku-Klux Klan (1866-1869)
  USE **Ku Klux Klan**
Ku Klux Klan (1915-)
  USE **Ku Klux Klan**
Kung fu   796.815
  UF   Kempo
       Wing chun
  BT   **Martial arts**
Kwanzaa   394.2612
  BT   **Holidays**
Labeling
  USE subjects with the subdivision *La-
       beling,* e.g. **Food—Labeling**
       [to be added as needed]
Labor (May subdiv. geog.)   **331**
  Use for materials on the collective human
  activities involved in the production and dis-
  tribution of goods and services in an econo-
  my, especially activities performed by workers
  for wages as distinguished from those per-
  formed by entrepreneurs for profits. Also use
  for general materials on workers. Materials on
  laborers as a social class are entered under
  Working class. Materials on the physical or
  mental exertion of individuals to produce or
  accomplish something are entered under
  Work.
  UF   Blue collar workers
       Factory workers
       Industrial workers
       Labor and laboring classes
       Laborers
       Manual workers
       Workers

  SA   types of laborers, e.g. **Agricul-
       tural laborers; Miners;** etc.
       [to be added as needed]
  BT   **Economics**
       Social conditions
       Sociology
  NT   **Agricultural laborers**
       Alien labor
       Apprentices
       Capitalism
       Child labor
       Church and labor
       Collective bargaining
       Contract labor
       Employees
       Employment
       Employment agencies
       Forced labor
       Hours of labor
       Household employees
       Industrial arbitration
       Industrial relations
       Industrial welfare
       Labor supply
       Labor unions
       Libraries and labor
       Migrant labor
       Miners
       Open and closed shop
       Part-time employment
       Peasantry
       Proletariat
       Skilled labor
       Supplementary employment
       Unskilled labor
  RT   **Labor movement**
       Work
       Working class
Labor absenteeism
  USE **Absenteeism (Labor)**
Labor—Accidents
  USE **Industrial accidents**
Labor and capital
  USE **Industrial relations**
Labor and laboring classes
  USE **Labor**
       Labor movement
       Working class
Labor and libraries
  USE **Libraries and labor**

411

Labor and state
   USE   **Labor policy**
Labor and the church
   USE   **Church and labor**
Labor arbitration
   USE   **Industrial arbitration**
Labor (Childbirth)
   USE   **Childbirth**
Labor contract (May subdiv. geog.)
      331.1; 331.89
   Use for materials on agreements between
   employer and employee in which the latter
   agrees to perform work in return for compen-
   sation from the former.
   UF   Collective labor agreements
         Trade agreements (Labor)
   BT   **Contracts**
         Industrial relations
   NT   **Open and closed shop**
   RT   **Collective bargaining**
Labor courts
   USE   **Industrial arbitration**
Labor disputes (May subdiv. geog.)
      331.89
   UF   Industrial disputes
   BT   **Industrial relations**
   NT   **Collective bargaining**
         Industrial arbitration
         Strikes
Labor—Education (May subdiv. geog.)
      331.25
   UF   Education of workers
   BT   **Education**
Labor force
   USE   **Labor supply**
Labor—Government policy
   USE   **Labor policy**
Labor—Housing (May subdiv. geog.)
      363.5
   BT   **Housing**
Labor—Insurance
   USE   **Unemployment insurance**
Labor laws and legislation (May subdiv.
      geog.)   **344.01**
   UF   Work—Law and legislation
   BT   **Industrial laws and legislation**
   NT   **Employee rights**
Labor-management relations
   USE   **Industrial relations**
Labor market
   USE   **Labor supply**

Labor movement (May subdiv. geog.)
      331.8
   Use for materials on the efforts of organiza-
   tions and individuals to improve conditions
   for labor.
   UF   Labor and laboring classes
   BT   **Social movements**
   RT   **Labor**
         Labor unions
Labor negotiations
   USE   **Collective bargaining**
         Industrial arbitration
Labor organizations
   USE   **Labor unions**
Labor output
   USE   **Labor productivity**
Labor participation in management
   USE   **Participative management**
Labor policy (May subdiv. geog.)   **331**
   UF   Government policy
         Labor and state
         Labor—Government policy
         Manpower policy
   BT   **Economic policy**
Labor productivity (May subdiv. geog.)
      331.11
   UF   Labor output
         Productivity of labor
   SA   types of industries, occupations,
         and processes with the subdi-
         vision *Labor productivity*, e.g.
         **Steel industry—Labor pro-
         ductivity** [to be added as
         needed]
   BT   **Industrial efficiency**
   NT   **Production standards**
         **Steel industry—Labor produc-
         tivity**
Labor relations
   USE   **Industrial relations**
Labor rights
   USE   **Employee rights**
Labor saving devices, Household
   USE   **Electric household appliances**
         **Household equipment and sup-
         plies**
Labor supply (May subdiv. geog.)
      331.11
   UF   Labor force
         Labor market
   BT   **Economic conditions**
         Employment

Labor supply—*Continued*
    Labor
  NT Occupational retraining
    Unemployed
    Unemployment
  RT Employment agencies
    Employment forecasting
    Human capital
    Manpower
Labor turnover 331.12
  BT Personnel management
  NT Employment agencies
Labor unions (May subdiv. geog.)
    331.88
  UF Labor organizations
    Organized labor
    Trade-unions
    Unions, Labor
  SA types of unions and names of
      individual labor unions [to be
      added as needed]
  BT Industrial relations
    Labor
    Societies
  NT Industrial arbitration
    Injunctions
    Librarians' unions
    Open and closed shop
    United Steelworkers of America
  RT Collective bargaining
    Labor movement
    Strikes
Labor unions—United States
    331.880973
Labor—United States 331.0973
Laboratory animal experimentation
  USE **Animal experimentation**
Laboratory animal welfare
  USE **Animal welfare**
Laboratory fertilization
  USE **Fertilization in vitro**
Laboratory manuals
  USE scientific and technical subjects
      with the subdivision *Labora-*
      tory manuals, e.g. **Chemis-**
      try—Laboratory manuals [to
      be added as needed]
Laborers
  USE **Labor**
    Working class

and types of laborers, e.g. **Ag-**
    ricultural laborers; Miners;
    etc. [to be added as needed]
Laboring class
  USE **Working class**
Laboring classes
  USE **Working class**
Lace and lace making (May subdiv.
    geog.) **677; 746.2**
  BT Crocheting
    Needlework
    Weaving
  NT Tatting
Lacquer and lacquering (May subdiv.
    geog.) **667; 745.7**
  BT Decorative arts
    Finishes and finishing
Laissez-faire
  USE **Free enterprise**
Laity 262
    May be subdivided by religion or sect.
  UF Laymen
  BT Church
  RT Lay ministry
Laity—Catholic Church 262
  UF Catholic laity
  BT Catholic Church
Lakes (May subdiv. geog.) **551.48**
  SA names of lakes [to be added as
      needed]
  BT Physical geography
    Water
    Waterways
  RT Inland navigation
Lakes—United States 551.48
Lamaze method of childbirth
  USE **Natural childbirth**
Lambs
  USE **Sheep**
Lamentations
  USE **Elegiac poetry**
Lamps 621.32; 749
  BT Lighting
  NT Electric lamps
Land
  USE **Land use**
    Landforms
Land drainage
  USE **Drainage**
Land forms
  USE **Landforms**

Land grants (May subdiv. geog.)   **333.1**
   UF Land patents
   BT **Colonization**
      Public lands
Land mines (May subdiv. geog.)   **355.8;**
   623.4
   BT **Explosives**
      Ordnance
Land patents
   USE **Land grants**
Land question
   USE **Land tenure**
Land, Reclamation of
   USE **Reclamation of land**
Land reform (May subdiv. geog.)   **333.3**
   UF Agrarian reform
      Reform, Agrarian
   BT **Economic policy**
      Land use
      Social policy
   NT **Land tenure**
   RT **Agriculture—Government policy**
Land settlement (May subdiv. geog.)
   304.8; 325
   UF Resettlement
      Settlement of land
   BT **Colonies**
      Land use
   NT **Colonization**
   RT **Human settlements**
      Internal migration
Land settlement—United States   **304.8;**
   325.73
   UF United States—Land settlement
      Westward movement
Land slides
   USE **Landslides**
Land surveying
   USE **Surveying**
Land surveys
   USE **Surveying**
Land tenure (May subdiv. geog.)   **333.3**
   Use for general and historical materials on systems of holding land. Materials on the legal relationships between landlord and tenant are entered under **Landlord and tenant.**
   UF Agrarian question
      Fiefs
      Land question
      Tenure of land

   BT **Agriculture—Economic aspects**
      Land reform
      Land use
   NT **Farm tenancy**
      Feudalism
      Landlord and tenant
   RT **Peasantry**
      Real estate
Land use (May subdiv. geog.)   **333.73**
   Use for general materials that cover such topics as types of land; the utilization, distribution, and development of land; and the economic factors affecting the value of land. Materials dealing only with ownership of land are entered under **Real estate.**
   UF Land
   BT **Economics**
   NT **Eminent domain**
      Farms
      Grasslands
      Land reform
      Land settlement
      Land tenure
      Landfills
      Pastures
      Public lands
      Real estate
      Reclamation of land
      Regional planning
Landfills (May subdiv. geog.)   **363.72;**
   628.3; 628.4
   Use for materials on places for waste disposal in which waste is buried in layers of earth in low ground.
   UF Earth fills
      Fills (Earthwork)
      Sanitary landfills
   SA names of landfills [to be added as needed]
   BT **Land use**
   NT **Hazardous waste sites**
      Love Canal Chemical Waste Landfill (Niagara Falls, N.Y.)
Landforms (May subdiv. geog.)   **551.41**
   UF Land
      Land forms
   SA types of landforms, e.g. **Mountains; Coasts;** etc. [to be added as needed]
   BT **Earth—Surface**
      Geology
   NT **Coasts**
      Mountains

Landforms—*Continued*

Seashore

Wetlands

Landlord and tenant (May subdiv. geog.)
333.5; 346.04

Use for materials on the legal relationships between landlord and tenant. General and historical materials on systems of holding land are entered under **Land tenure.**

UF   Tenant and landlord

BT   **Commercial law**

      Land tenure

      Real estate

NT   **Housing**

RT   **Farm tenancy**

Landmarks, Literary

USE   **Literary landmarks**

Landmarks, Preservation of

USE   **National monuments**

      Natural monuments

Landscape architecture (May subdiv. geog.)   **712**

Use for materials on modifying or arranging the features of a landscape, urban area, etc., for aesthetic or pragmatic purposes.

UF   Landscape design

BT   **Architecture**

NT   **Garden ornaments and furniture**

      Garden structures

      Parks

      Patios

      Roadside improvement

RT   **Landscape gardening**

      Landscape protection

Landscape design

USE   **Landscape architecture**

Landscape drawing   **743**

BT   **Drawing**

RT   **Landscape painting**

Landscape gardening (May subdiv. geog.) **712**

Use for materials on the design or rearrangement of extensive gardens or estates.

UF   Planting

BT   **Gardening**

      Horticulture

NT   **Evergreens**

      Lawns

      Ornamental plants

      Xeriscaping

RT   **Garden design**

      Landscape architecture

Shrubs

Trees

Landscape painting   **758**

BT   **Painting**

RT   **Landscape drawing**

Landscape protection (May subdiv. geog.) **333.73**

UF   Beautification of landscape

      Natural beauty conservation

      Preservation of natural scenery

      Protection of natural scenery

      Scenery

BT   **Environmental protection**

      Nature conservation

NT   **Natural monuments**

RT   **Landscape architecture**

      Regional planning

Landscape sculpture

USE   **Earthworks (Art)**

Landslides (May subdiv. geog.)   **551.3**

UF   Land slides

BT   **Natural disasters**

Language

USE   **Language and languages**

and disciplines, classes of persons, types of newspapers, and names of individual persons, corporate bodies, and literary works entered under title with the subdivision *Language,* e.g. **Technology—Language; Children—Language;** etc. [to be added as needed]

Language and culture (May subdiv. geog.) **306.44**

BT   **Culture**

      Language and languages

Language and languages   **400**

Use for general materials on the history, philosophy, origin, etc., of language. Materials on the scientific study of speech and comparative studies of language are entered under **Linguistics.**

UF   Language

      Languages

      Philology

SA   names of languages or groups of languages, e.g. **English language; Scandinavian languages; Native American languages;** etc.; disciplines,

Language and languages—*Continued*
classes of persons, types of newspapers, and names of individual persons, corporate bodies, and literary works entered under title with the subdivison *Language,* e.g. **Technology—Language; Children—Language;** etc.; and names countries, cities, etc., with the subdivison *Languages,* for materials on the several languages spoken in a place, e.g. **United States— Languages;** etc. [to be added as needed]
- BT **Anthropology**
   Communication
   Ethnology
- NT **Bilingualism**
   Children—Language
   Conversation
   Danish language
   English language
   French language
   German language
   Grammar
   Greek language
   Hebrew language
   Icelandic language
   Japanese language
   Language and culture
   Latin language
   Linguistics
   Modern Greek language
   Modern languages
   Multilingualism
   Native American languages
   Norwegian language
   Old Norse language
   Phonetics
   Programming languages
   Rhetoric
   Romance languages
   Russian language
   Scandinavian languages
   Semantics
   Sign language
   Sociolinguistics
   Spanish language
   Swedish language
   Translating and interpreting

   Universal language
   Verbal learning
   Vocabulary
   Voice
   Writing
   Yiddish language
- RT **Speech**

Language and languages—Business language
- USE names of languages with unique language subdivisions, e.g. **English language—Business English; Japanese language—Business Japanese;** etc. [to be added as needed]

Language and languages—Comparative philology
- USE **Linguistics**

Language and languages—Etymology 412
- UF Etymology
   Word histories
- SA names of languages with the subdivision *Etymology,* e.g. **English language—Etymology** [to be added as needed]

Language and languages—Political aspects 400
Use for general materials on the political aspects of languages.
- SA names of countries, cities, etc., with the subdivision *Languages,* e.g. **United States— Languages;** or with the two subdivisions *Languages—Political aspects;* and names of individual languages and groups of languages with the subdivision *Political aspects* [to be added as needed]

Language and society
- USE **Sociolinguistics**

Language arts 372.6; 400
Use for materials on language and literature considered comprehensively as a school subject at the elementary level.
- UF Communication arts
- BT **Communication**
- NT **Creative writing**
   Literature
   Reading
   Speech

Language arts—*Continued*
>> **Whole language**
>> **Writing**

Language arts (Holistic)
>> USE **Whole language**

Language arts—**Patterning**   372.6
>> UF   Patterns (Language arts)
>> Reading—Patterning
>> Writing—Patterning

Language disorders   616.85

>> Use for materials on disorders of the central neurological functions affecting the reception, processing, or expression of language. Materials on disorders of the physiological mechanisms required for speech are entered under **Speech disorders.**

>> UF   Dysphasia
>> BT   **Communicative disorders**

Language experience approach in education
>> USE   **Whole language**

Language games
>> USE   **Literary recreations**

Language, International
>> USE   **Universal language**

Language laboratories   407
>> UF   Foreign language laboratories
>> RT   **Modern languages—Study and teaching**

Language of flowers   302.2; 398.24
>> UF   Flower language
>> BT   **Plants—Folklore**

Language, Universal
>> USE   **Universal language**

Languages
>> USE   **Language and languages**
>> and countries, cities, etc., with the subdivision *Languages,* for materials on the several languages spoken in a place, e.g. **United States—Languages;** etc. [to be added as needed]

Languages, Modern
>> USE   **Modern languages**

Languages—Vocabulary
>> USE   **Vocabulary**

LANs (Computer networks)
>> USE   **Local area networks**

Lantern slides
>> USE   **Slides (Photography)**

Laptop computers
>> USE   **Portable computers**

Larceny
>> USE   **Theft**

Large and small
>> USE   **Size**

Large print books   028
>> UF   Books for sight saving
>> Books—Large print
>> Large type books
>> Sight saving books
>> BT   **Blind—Books and reading**
>> RT   **Big books**

Large type books
>> USE   **Large print books**

Laser-beam recording
>> USE   **Laser recording**

Laser photography
>> USE   **Holography**

Laser recording   621.36; 621.38
>> UF   Laser-beam recording
>> Recording, Laser
>> BT   **Optical data processing**
>> NT   **Holography**
>> RT   **Lasers**
>> **Optical storage devices**

Lasers   621.36
>> SA   lasers in particular subjects or fields of endeavor, e.g. **Lasers in aeronautics** [to be added as needed]
>> BT   **Light**
>> NT   **Lasers in aeronautics**
>> RT   **Laser recording**

Lasers in aeronautics   629.13
>> BT   **Aeronautics**
>> **Lasers**

Last rites (Sacraments)
>> USE   **Anointing of the sick**

Last sacraments
>> USE   **Anointing of the sick**

Last Supper   232.9

>> Use for materials on the final meal of Jesus with his apostles, where the sacrament of the Eucharist was instituted.

>> UF   Jesus Christ—Last Supper

Last things (Theology)
>> USE   **Eschatology**

Latchkey children   306.874; 362.7; 640
>> BT   **Children of working parents**

Lateness
>> USE   **Punctuality**

Lathe work
>> USE   **Lathes**
>> **Turning**

Lathes 621.9
  UF Lathe work
  BT **Woodworking machinery**
  RT **Turning**
Latin America 980
  Use for materials that discuss collectively several or all of the countries of the Western Hemisphere south of the United States in which Spanish, Portuguese, or French is the principal language.
  UF Spanish America
  SA names of individual Latin American countries [to be added as needed]
  BT **America**
  NT **Pan-Americanism**
Latin America—Politics and government 980
  BT **Politics**
Latin American literature 860
  Use for materials on the French, Portuguese, or Spanish literature of several Latin American countries. May use same subdivisions and names of literary forms as for **English literature.**
  UF South American literature
      Spanish American literature
  SA names of individual Latin American literatures [to be added as needed]
  BT **Literature**
  NT **Brazilian literature**
      Mexican literature
Latin Americans (May subdiv. geog.) 920; 980
  Use for materials on citizens of Latin American countries. Materials on United States citizens of Latin American descent are entered under **Hispanic Americans.**
Latin language 470
  May be subdivided like **English language.**
  UF Classical languages
  BT **Language and languages**
  RT **Romance languages**
Latin literature 870
  May use same subdivisions and names of literary forms as for **English literature.**
  UF Roman literature
  BT **Literature**
  RT **Classical literature**
      Early Christian literature
Latinos (U.S.)
  USE **Hispanic Americans**

Latitude 526; 527
  UF Degrees of latitude and longitude
  BT **Earth**
      Geodesy
      Nautical astronomy
Latter-day Saints
  USE **Church of Jesus Christ of Latter-day Saints**
Laughter 152.4
  BT **Emotions**
Launching of satellites
  USE **Artificial satellites—Launching**
Laundry 648
  UF Ironing
      Washing
  BT **Cleaning**
      Home economics
      Household sanitation
Law (May subdiv. geog.) 340
  UF Jurisprudence
      Laws
      Statutes
  SA names of particular legal systems, e.g. **Islamic law;** special branches of law, e.g. **Criminal law;** subjects with the subdivision *Law and legislation,* e.g. **Automobiles—Law and legislation;** and ethnic groups and classes of persons with the subdivision *Legal status, laws, etc.,* e.g. **Handicapped—Legal status, laws, etc.** [to be added as needed]
  BT **Political science**
  NT **Abortion—Law and legislation**
      Administration of justice
      Administrative law
      Automobiles—Law and legislation
      Chemical industry—Law and legislation
      Commercial law
      Common law
      Constitutional law
      Constitutions
      Corporation law
      Courts
      Criminal law

Law—*Continued*

    Ecclesiastical law
    Environmental law
    Food—Law and legislation
    Gun control
    Handicapped—Legal status,
        laws, etc.
    Industrial laws and legislation
    Internal revenue law
    International law
    Islamic law
    Justice
    Law reform
    Lawyers
    Libraries—Law and legislation
    Litigation
    Maritime law
    Martial law
    Medicine—Law and legislation
    Military law
    Natural law
    Power of attorney
    Safety regulations
    Space law
    Water rights
  RT Legislation

Law and legislation
  USE subjects with the subdivision
      Law and legislation, e.g. **Automobiles—Law and legislation** [to be added as needed]

Law, Election
  USE **Election law**

Law enforcement (May subdiv. geog.)
    363.2
  BT **Administration of criminal justice**
  NT **Criminal investigation**
       Police

Law—Fiction
  USE **Legal stories**

Law of nations
  USE **International law**

Law of nature
  USE **Natural law**

Law of supply and demand
  USE **Supply and demand**

Law of the sea
  USE **Maritime law**

Law reform (May subdiv. geog.) **340**
  UF Legal reform
  BT **Law**

Law schools (May subdiv. geog.)
    340.071
  BT **Colleges and universities**

Law suits
  USE **Litigation**

Law—United States **349.73**
  UF United States—Law

Law—Vocational guidance **340.023**
  BT **Professions**
       Vocational guidance

Lawmakers
  USE **Legislators**

Lawn tennis
  USE **Tennis**

Lawns **635.9; 712**
  BT **Landscape gardening**
  RT **Grasses**

Laws
  USE **Law**
       Legislation

Lawsuits
  USE **Litigation**

Lawyers (May subdiv. geog.) **340.092; 920**
  UF Attorneys
      Bar
      Barristers
      Jurists
      Legal profession
      Solicitors
  BT **Law**
  NT **Judges**
  RT **Legal ethics**

Lawyers—Fiction
  USE **Legal stories**

Lawyers—Salaries, wages, etc. (May subdiv. geog.) **331.2**
  BT **Salaries, wages, etc.**

Lay ministry **253**
  UF Volunteers in church work
  BT **Church work**
  RT **Laity**

Laymen
  USE **Laity**

Laziness **179**
  UF Indolence
      Sloth
  BT **Personality**

Lead poisoning   615.9
UF   Lead—Toxicology
BT   Occupational diseases
     Poisons and poisoning
Lead—Toxicology
USE   Lead poisoning
Leadership   158; 303.3
BT   Ability
     Executive ability
     Social groups
     Success
NT   Elite (Social sciences)
League of Nations   341.22
BT   International arbitration
     International cooperation
     International organization
     World War, 1914-1918—Peace
League of Nations—Mandatory system
USE   Mandates
Learned institutions and societies
USE   Learning and scholarship
Learned societies
USE   Societies
Learning and scholarship (May subdiv.
   geog.)   001.2
UF   Erudition
     Learned institutions and societies
     Scholarship
BT   Civilization
     Intellectual life
NT   Humanities
     Professional education
RT   Culture
     Education
     Humanism
     Research
Learning center approach to teaching
USE   Open plan schools
Learning disabilities   153.1; 371.9;
   616.85
SA   types of learning disabilities [to
     be added as needed]
BT   Psychology of learning
     Slow learning children
NT   Reading disability
Learning, Psychology of
USE   Psychology of learning
Learning resource centers
USE   Instructional materials centers
Learning, Verbal
USE   Verbal learning

Lease and rental services   333.5
UF   Lease services
     Rental services
BT   Service industries
Lease services
USE   Lease and rental services
Leather   675
BT   Animal products
RT   Hides and skins
     Leather industry
     Tanning
Leather clothing
USE   Leather garments
Leather garments   391; 685
UF   Leather clothing
BT   Clothing and dress
     Leather work
Leather industry (May subdiv. geog.)
   338.4
UF   Leather industry and trade
BT   Industries
NT   Shoe industry
RT   Leather
Leather industry and trade
USE   Leather industry
Leather work   745.53
BT   Decoration and ornament
     Decorative arts
     Handicraft
NT   Leather garments
Leave for parenting
USE   Parental leave
Leave of absence (May subdiv. geog.)
   331.25
BT   Hours of labor
NT   Parental leave
Leaves   575.5; 581.4
UF   Foliage
BT   Plants
Lebanon   956.92
   May be subdivided like United States ex-
   cept for *History.*
Lebanon—History   956.92
Lebanon—History—1975-1976, Civil War
   956.9204
Lebanon—History—1982-1984, Israeli in-
   tervention   956.05
UF   Israeli intervention in Lebanon,
     1982-1984
BT   Israel-Arab conflicts

Lectures and lecturing   808.5

Use for general materials on lectures and the art of delivering speeches on academic subjects. Collections of speeches on several subjects and materials about non-academic speeches are entered under **Speeches.** Collections of lectures on a single subject are entered under that subject.

UF   Addresses

Speaking

BT   **Public speaking**

Rhetoric

Teaching

NT   **Radio addresses, debates, etc.**

RT   **Speeches**

Left and right

USE   **Left and right (Direction)**

Right and left (Political science)

Left and right (Direction)   152.1

Use for children's materials on left and right as indications of location or direction. Materials on political views or attitudes are entered under **Right and left (Political science).** Materials on the physical characteristics of favoring one hand or the other are entered under **Left- and right-handedness.**

UF   Left and right

Right and left

BT   **Direction sense**

Left- and right-handedness   152.3

UF   Handedness

Right- and left-handedness

BT   **Psychophysiology**

Left (Political science)

USE   **Liberalism**

Right and left (Political science)

Legacies

USE   **Inheritance and succession**

Wills

Legal aid (May subdiv. geog.)   **362.5**

Use for materials on legal services to the poor, usually provided under the sponsorship of local bar associations or governmental units.

UF   Legal assistance to the poor

Legal representation of the poor

Legal services for the poor

BT   **Public welfare**

Legal assistance to the poor

USE   **Legal aid**

Legal drama (Films)   791.43

May be used for individual works, collections, or materials about motion pictures dealing with trials or litigations.

UF   Courtroom drama

BT   **Motion pictures**

Legal drama (Radio programs)   791.44

May be used for individual works, collections, or materials about radio programs dealing with trials or litigations.

UF   Courtroom drama

BT   **Radio programs**

Legal drama (Television programs)   791.45

May be used for individual works, collections, or materials about television programs dealing with trials or litigations.

UF   Courtroom drama

BT   **Television programs**

Legal ethics (May subdiv. geog.)   **174; 340**

BT   **Ethics**

Professional ethics

RT   **Lawyers**

Legal fiction (Literature)

USE   **Legal stories**

Legal holidays

USE   **Holidays**

Legal medicine

USE   **Medical jurisprudence**

Legal novels

USE   **Legal stories**

Legal profession

USE   **Lawyers**

Legal reform

USE   **Law reform**

Legal representation of the poor

USE   **Legal aid**

Legal responsibility

USE   **Liability (Law)**

Legal services for the poor

USE   **Legal aid**

Legal status, laws, etc.

USE   ethnic groups and classes of persons with the subdivision *Legal status, laws, etc.,* e.g. **Handicapped—Legal status, laws, etc.** [to be added as needed]

Legal stories   808.3; 808.83

May be used for individual works, collections, or materials about fiction dealing with trials or litigations.

UF   Law—Fiction

Lawyers—Fiction

Legal fiction (Literature)

Legal novels

Legal stories—*Continued*
> Trials—Fiction
>> BT **Fiction**

Legal tender
>> USE **Money**

Legations
>> USE **Diplomatic and consular service**

Legendary characters
>> USE names of individual legendary characters, e.g. **Bunyan, Paul (Legendary character)** [to be added as needed]

Legends (May subdiv. geog.)   **398.2**
> May be used for individual works, collections, or materials about tales coming down from the past, especially those relating to actual events or persons. Collections of tales written between the eleventh and fourteenth centuries and dealing with the age of chivalry or the supernatural are entered under **Romances.**
>> UF Folk tales
>> Stories
>> Tales
>> Traditions
>> SA relgious topics and names of individual persons or sacred works with the subdivision *Legends;* e.g. **Grail—Legends;** legends of particular ethnic or religious groups, e.g. **Jewish legends;** and names of individual legendary characters, e.g. **Bunyan, Paul (Legendary character)** [to be added as needed]
>> BT **Fiction**
>> **Literature**
>> NT **Celtic legends**
>> **Jewish legends**
>> **Norse legends**
>> **Tall tales**
>> RT **Fables**
>> **Folklore**
>> **Mythology**
>> **Romances**

Legends, Jewish
>> USE **Jewish legends**

Legends—United States   **398.20973; 973**

Legerdemain
>> USE **Juggling**
>> **Magic tricks**

Legibility of handwriting
>> USE **Handwriting**

Legislation (May subdiv. geog.)   **328**
> Use for materials on the theory of lawmaking and descriptions of the preparation and enactment of laws.
>> UF Laws
>> SA subjects with the subdivision *Law and legislation* [to be added as needed]
>> BT **Political science**
>> NT **Abortion—Law and legislation**
>> **Automobiles—Law and legislation**
>> **Chemical industry—Law and legislation**
>> **Food—Law and legislation**
>> **Gun control**
>> **Industrial laws and legislation**
>> **Legislative bodies**
>> **Libraries—Law and legislation**
>> **Medicine—Law and legislation**
>> **Parliamentary practice**
>> RT **Law**

Legislation, Direct
>> USE **Referendum**

Legislative bodies (May subdiv. geog.)   **328.3**
> Use for materials on various law making bodies considered collectively.
>> UF Legislatures
>> Parliaments
>> SA names of individual legislative bodies, e.g. **United States. Congress** [to be added as needed]
>> BT **Constitutional law**
>> **Legislation**
>> **Representative government and representation**
>> NT **Parliamentary practice**
>> **Term limits (Public office)**
>> **United States. Congress**
>> **War and emergency powers**

Legislative investigations
>> USE **Governmental investigations**

Legislative reapportionment
>> USE **Apportionment (Election law)**

Legislators (May subdiv. geog.)   **328**
>> UF Lawmakers
>> Members of Parliament
>> BT **Statesmen**

Legislatures
  USE **Legislative bodies**
Legitimacy (Law)
  USE **Illegitimacy**
Leisure (May subdiv. geog.) **790.01**
  UF Free time (Leisure)
       Leisure time
  NT **Hobbies**
       Retirement
  RT **Recreation**
Leisure time
  USE **Leisure**
Lemon
  USE **Lemons**
Lemons **634; 641.3**
  UF Lemon
  BT **Citrus fruits**
Lending
  USE **Loans**
Lending institutions
  USE **Financial institutions**
Lending of library materials
  USE **Library circulation**
Lenses **535**
  SA types of lenses, e.g. **Contact
       lenses** [to be added as need-
       ed]
  BT **Optical instruments**
  NT **Contact lenses**
Lensless photography
  USE **Holography**
Lent **263**
  BT **Church year**
  NT **Good Friday**
       Holy Week
       Lenten sermons
  RT **Easter**
Lent—Meditations **242**
  BT **Meditations**
Lenten sermons **252**
  Use for collections of sermons on any sub-
ject preached during the season of Lent.
  BT **Lent**
       Sermons
Lepidoptera
  USE **Butterflies**
       Moths
Lesbian marriage
  USE **Same-sex marriage**
Lesbianism (May subdiv. geog.) **306.76**
  BT **Homosexuality**
  RT **Lesbians**

Lesbians (May subdiv. geog.) **306.76**
  UF Gay women
       Gays, Female
       Homosexuals, Female
  BT **Women**
  NT **Gays and lesbians in the mili-
       tary**
  RT **Homosexuality**
       Lesbianism
       Lesbians' writings
Lesbians and gays in the military
  USE **Gays and lesbians in the mili-
       tary**
Lesbians in the military
  USE **Gays and lesbians in the mili-
       tary**
Lesbians' writings **808.8**
  Use for collections of lesbians' writings by
more than one author and for materials about
such writings.
  UF Gay women's writings
       Writings of lesbians
  BT **Literature**
  RT **Lesbians**
Less developed countries
  USE **Developing countries**
Letter-sound association
  USE **Reading—Phonetic method**
Letter writing **383; 808.6**
  Use for materials on composition, forms,
and etiquette of correspondence. Materials
limited to business correspondence are entered
under **Business letters**. Collections of literary
letters are entered under **Letters**.
  UF Correspondence
  BT **Etiquette**
       Literary style
       Rhetoric
  NT **Business letters**
Lettering **745.6**
  UF Ornamental alphabets
  BT **Decoration and ornament**
       Industrial painting
       Mechanical drawing
  NT **Monograms**
  RT **Alphabets**
       Initials
       Sign painting
Letters **808.86**
  Use for collections of literary letters. Mate-
rials on the composition, forms, and etiquette
of correspondence are entered under **Letter
writing**. Materials limited to business corre-
spondence are entered under **Business letters**.

Letters—*Continued*
    UF   Correspondence
    SA   ethnic groups, classes of per-
            sons, and names of individual
            persons and families with the
            subdivision *Correspondence,*
            e.g. **Authors—Correspon-**
            dence [to be added as need-
            ed]
    NT   **American letters**
          Authors—Correspondence
          English letters
Letters of credit
    USE **Credit**
          Negotiable instruments
Letters of marque
    USE **Privateering**
Letters of recommendation
    USE **Applications for positions**
Letters of the alphabet
    USE **Alphabet**
Leukemia   616.99
    BT   **Blood—Diseases**
          Cancer
Levant
    USE **Middle East**
Leveraged buyouts   338.8; 658.1
    UF   Buyouts, Leveraged
          Management buyouts
    BT   **Corporate mergers and acqui-**
          sitions
Lewis and Clark Expedition (1804-1806)
    973.4
    BT   **United States—Exploring expe-**
          ditions
          United States—History—1783-
          1809
Liability for environmental damages
    (May subdiv. geog.)   **344**
    UF   Environmental damages, Liability
          for
    BT   **Environmental law**
          Liability (Law)
Liability (Law) (May subdiv. geog.)
    346.02
    UF   Accountability
          Legal responsibility
          Responsibility, Legal
    BT   **Contracts**
    NT   **Liability for environmental**
          damages
          Malpractice

Liability, Professional
    USE **Malpractice**
Libel and slander (May subdiv. geog.)
    346.03
    UF   Character assassination
          Defamation
          Slander (Law)
    BT   **Journalism**
    NT   **Gossip**
    RT   **Freedom of speech**
          Freedom of the press
Liberalism (May subdiv. geog.)   **148;**
    320.5
    UF   Left (Political science)
    BT   **Political science**
          Social sciences
    RT   **Right and left (Political sci-**
          ence)
Liberation movements, National
    USE **National liberation movements**
Liberation theology   261.8
    UF   Theology of liberation
    BT   **Christianity—Doctrines**
          Church and social problems
          Theology
Liberty
    USE **Freedom**
Liberty of conscience
    USE **Freedom of conscience**
Liberty of speech
    USE **Freedom of speech**
Liberty of the press
    USE **Freedom of the press**
Liberty of the will
    USE **Free will and determinism**
Librarians (May subdiv. geog.)   **020.92;**
    920
    NT   **African American librarians**
          Black librarians
          Library technicians
    RT   **Libraries**
Librarians—Collective bargaining
    USE **Collective bargaining—Librari-**
          ans
Librarians—Education
    USE **Library education**
Librarians—Ethics   174
    UF   Librarians—Professional ethics
    BT   **Professional ethics**
Librarians—In-service training   020.71
    BT   **Library education**

Librarians—Professional ethics
  USE **Librarians—Ethics**
Librarians—Rating   023
Librarians—Recruiting   023
  BT **Recruiting of employees**
Librarians—Training
  USE **Library education**
Librarians' unions   331.88
  UF Library unions
  BT **Labor unions**
Librarianship
  USE **Library science**
Libraries (May subdiv. geog.)   027
  SA types of libraries, e.g. **Academic libraries;** names of individual libraries, e.g. **Library of Congress;** libraries and particular groups of people, e.g. **Libraries and African Americans;** and libraries and other subjects, e.g. **Libraries and motion pictures** [to be added as needed]
  BT **Documentation**
  NT **Academic libraries**
    Children's libraries
    Church libraries
    Digital libraries
    Hospital libraries
    Instructional materials centers
    Libraries and community
    Libraries and motion pictures
    Libraries and pictures
    Libraries and schools
    Library architecture
    Library catalogs
    Library cooperation
    Library of Congress
    Library resources
    Library services
    Library technical processes
    Public libraries
    School libraries
    Special libraries
    Young adults' libraries
  RT **Archives**
    Information services
    Librarians
Libraries—Acquisitions   025.2
  UF Acquisitions (Libraries)
    Book buying (Libraries)

Libraries—Order department
  Library acquisitions
  BT **Libraries—Collection development**
    Library technical processes
  NT **Book selection**
Libraries—Administration   025.1
  UF Library administration
    Library policies
  NT **Library finance**
    Library trustees
Libraries and African Americans   027.6
  UF African Americans and libraries
    Afro-Americans and libraries
    Library services to African Americans
  BT **African Americans**
    Library services
Libraries and children
  USE **Children's libraries**
Libraries and community   021.2
  UF Community and libraries
  BT **Libraries**
  NT **Libraries—Public relations**
Libraries and labor   027.6
  UF Labor and libraries
    Library services to labor
  BT **Labor**
    Library services
Libraries and motion pictures   021
  UF Educational films
    Motion pictures and libraries
  BT **Libraries**
    Motion pictures
    Motion pictures in education
Libraries and pictures   021
  BT **Libraries**
    Pictures
Libraries and readers
  USE **Library services**
Libraries and schools   021
  UF Schools and libraries
  BT **Libraries**
    Schools
  NT **Libraries and students**
  RT **Children's libraries**
    School libraries
Libraries and state
  USE **Libraries—Government policy**

Libraries and students   027.62
    UF Students and libraries
    BT **Libraries and schools**
         Library services
         School libraries
Libraries and the elderly   027.6
    UF Elderly and libraries
         Library services to the elderly
    BT **Elderly**
         Library services
Libraries—Automation   025.04
    UF Library automation
    SA names of projects, formats, and
         systems, e.g. **MARC formats**
         [to be added as needed]
    BT **Automation**
    NT **Machine readable bibliographic
         data**
    RT **Information systems**
         Online catalogs
Libraries—Boards of trustees
    USE **Library trustees**
Libraries, Business
    USE **Business libraries**
Libraries—Cataloging
    USE **Cataloging**
Libraries—Catalogs
    USE **Library catalogs**
Libraries—Censorship   025.2
    BT **Censorship**
Libraries—Centralization   021.6
    UF Library systems
Libraries—Circulation, loans
    USE **Library circulation**
**Libraries—Collection development
025.2**
    UF Collection development (Librar-
         ies)
    BT **Library technical processes**
    NT **Book selection**
         Libraries—Acquisitions
Libraries—Collective bargaining
    USE **Collective bargaining—Librari-
         ans**
Libraries—Cooperation
    USE **Library cooperation**
Libraries, Corporate
    USE **Corporate libraries**

**Libraries—Equipment and supplies
022**
    UF Library equipment and supplies
         Library supplies
    BT **Furniture**
Libraries—Federal aid
    USE **Federal aid to libraries**
Libraries—Finance
    USE **Library finance**
Libraries—Government aid
    USE **Government aid to libraries**
Libraries—Government policy (May
    subdiv. geog.)   **021.8**
    UF Libraries and state
    BT **Social policy**
    NT **Federal aid to libraries**
         Government aid to libraries
Libraries, Governmental
    USE **Government libraries**
Libraries, Hospital
    USE **Hospital libraries**
Libraries—Law and legislation (May
    subdiv. geog.)   **344**
    UF Library laws
         Library legislation
    BT **Law**
         Legislation
Libraries—Lighting   022
    BT **Lighting**
Libraries, Music
    USE **Music libraries**
Libraries, National
    USE **National libraries**
Libraries—Order department
    USE **Libraries—Acquisitions**
Libraries, Presidential
    USE **Presidents—United States—Ar-
         chives**
Libraries—Public relations (May subdiv.
    geog.)   **021.7**
    UF Public relations—Libraries
    BT **Libraries and community**
    NT **Book talks**
Libraries, Regional
    USE **Regional libraries**
Libraries—Special collections   026
    May be subdivided by subject or form, e.g.
    **Libraries—Special collections—Science fic-
    tion; Libraries—Special collections—Video-
    tapes;** etc.
    UF Special collections in libraries

Libraries—State aid
USE **Government aid to libraries**
Libraries—Statistics 020
BT **Statistics**
Libraries—Technical services
USE **Library technical processes**
Libraries—Trustees
USE **Library trustees**
Libraries—United States 027.073
Library acquisitions
USE **Libraries—Acquisitions**
Library administration
USE **Libraries—Administration**
Library architecture (May subdiv. geog.)
727
Use for materials on the design of library buildings.
BT **Architecture**
Libraries
Library assistants
USE **Library technicians**
Library automation
USE **Libraries—Automation**
Library boards
USE **Library trustees**
Library book fairs
USE **Books—Exhibitions**
Library cataloging
USE **Cataloging**
Library catalogs 017; 025.3
UF Catalogs
Catalogs, Library
Libraries—Catalogs
SA types of library catalogs, e.g.
Online catalogs [to be added as needed]
BT **Libraries**
NT **Book catalogs**
Card catalogs
Classified catalogs
Online catalogs
Subject catalogs
RT **Cataloging**
Library circulation 025.6
UF Book lending
Circulation of library materials
Lending of library materials
Libraries—Circulation, loans
BT **Library services**
NT **Interlibrary loans**

Library classification 025.4
May be further subdivided by a type of literature or by the subject of the materials classified.
UF Books—Classification
Classification—Books
BT **Cataloging**
Classification
Library technical processes
NT **Dewey Decimal Classification**
RT **Classified catalogs**
Library clerks
USE **Library technicians**
Library consortia
USE **Library cooperation**
Library cooperation (May subdiv. geog.)
021.6
UF Consortia, Library
Libraries—Cooperation
Library consortia
BT **Libraries**
NT **Interlibrary loans**
Library information networks
Library education (May subdiv. geog.)
020.71
Use for materials on the education of librarians. Materials on the instruction of readers in library use are entered under **Bibliographic instruction.**
UF Education for librarianship
Librarians—Education
Librarians—Training
Library science—Study and teaching
BT **Education**
Professional education
NT **Librarians—In-service training**
Library schools
Library education—Audiovisual aids
020.71
BT **Audiovisual education**
Audiovisual materials
Library education—Curricula 020.71
BT **Education—Curricula**
Library equipment and supplies
USE **Libraries—Equipment and supplies**
Library extension 021.6
BT **Library services**
NT **Bookmobiles**

Library finance (May subdiv. geog.)
    025.1
    UF Libraries—Finance
    BT **Finance**
          Libraries—Administration
    NT **Government aid to libraries**
    RT **Federal aid to libraries**
Library information networks (May
    subdiv. geog.)   **021.6**
    Use for materials on networks that facilitate the sharing of information resources among several libraries.
    UF Library networks
          Library systems
    BT **Information networks**
          Library cooperation
Library instruction
    USE **Bibliographic instruction**
Library laws
    USE **Libraries—Law and legislation**
Library legislation
    USE **Libraries—Law and legislation**
Library materials
    USE **Library resources**
Library networks
    USE **Library information networks**
Library of Congress   **027.573**
    UF United States. Library of Congress
    BT **Libraries**
Library orientation
    USE **Bibliographic instruction**
Library policies
    USE **Libraries—Administration**
Library processing
    USE **Library technical processes**
Library reference services
    USE **Reference services (Libraries)**
Library resources (May subdiv. geog.)
    025
    Use for materials on the resources and collections available in libraries for research not limited to a single subject or discipline.
    UF Library materials
    SA subjects, ethnic groups, classes of persons, corporate bodies, individual persons, literary authors, and names of countries, cities, etc., with the subdivision *Library resources,* e.g. **United States—History—Library resources** [to be added as needed]

    BT **Libraries**
    NT **Government publications**
Library resources—Conservation and restoration   **025.8**
    UF Books—Preservation
          Library resources—Preservation
          Preservation of library resources
Library resources—Preservation
    USE **Library resources—Conservation and restoration**
Library schools (May subdiv. geog.)
    020.71
    BT **Library education**
Library science (May subdiv. geog.)
    020
    Use for general materials on the knowledge and skill necessary for the organization and administration of libraries. Materials on services offered by libraries to patrons are entered under **Library services.**
    UF Librarianship
    BT **Documentation**
          Information science
    NT **Cataloging**
          Library surveys
          Library technical processes
    RT **Bibliography**
          Library services
Library science—Study and teaching
    USE **Library education**
Library services (May subdiv. geog.)
    025.5
    Use for materials on services offered by libraries to patrons. General materials on the knowledge and skill necessary for the organization and administration of libraries are entered under **Library science.**
    UF Libraries and readers
          Library services to readers
          Reader services (Libraries)
          Readers and libraries
    SA libraries and specific types of users or specific activities for which services are provided, e.g. **Libraries and the elderly** [to be added as needed]
    BT **Libraries**
    NT **Bibliographic instruction**
          Libraries and African Americans
          Libraries and labor
          Libraries and students
          Libraries and the elderly
          Library circulation

Library services—*Continued*
> Library extension
> Reference services (Libraries)
RT Library science
Library services to African Americans
> USE Libraries and African Americans
Library services to children
> USE Children's libraries
Library services to labor
> USE Libraries and labor
Library services to readers
> USE Library services
Library services to teenagers
> USE Young adults' libraries
Library services to the elderly
> USE Libraries and the elderly
Library services to young adults
> USE Young adults' libraries
Library skills
> USE Bibliographic instruction
Library supplies
> USE Libraries—Equipment and supplies
Library surveys   020
> BT Library science
> Surveys
Library systems
> USE Libraries—Centralization
> Library information networks
Library technical processes   025
Use for materials on the activities and processes concerned with the acquisition, organization, and preparation of library materials for use.
> UF Centralized processing (Libraries)
> Libraries—Technical services
> Library processing
> Processing (Libraries)
> Technical services (Libraries)
> BT Libraries
> Library science
> NT Cataloging
> Libraries—Acquisitions
> Libraries—Collection development
> Library classification
Library technicians (May subdiv. geog.)
020.92
> UF Library assistants
> Library clerks
> Paraprofessional librarians

> BT Librarians
> Paraprofessionals
Library trustees   021.8
> UF Libraries—Boards of trustees
> Libraries—Trustees
> Library boards
> BT Libraries—Administration
> Trusts and trustees
Library unions
> USE Librarians' unions
Library user orientation
> USE Bibliographic instruction
Librettos   780; 780.26
Use for collections of miscellaneous librettos and for materials on the history and criticism of librettos and on writing librettos. Individual librettos and collections of librettos of a specific type are entered under the specific type of libretto.
> SA types of librettos, e.g. Opera librettos [to be added as needed]
> BT Books
> NT Opera librettos
Licenses (May subdiv. geog.)   352.8
Use for general works on legal permissions to engage in business or perform other work or activities.
> SA occupational groups, types of industries, and types of vehicles with the subdivision *Licenses,* e.g. Physicians—Licenses; which may be further subdivided geographically [to be added as needed]
> BT Commercial law
> Public administration
Lie detectors and detection   363.2
> UF Polygraph
> BT Criminal investigation
> Medical jurisprudence
> Truthfulness and falsehood
Life   128
Use for materials on philosophical or religious considerations of life. Materials on life from a scientific point of view are entered under Life (Biology).
> NT Death
> Life expectancy
> RT Life (Biology)
Life after death
> USE Future life
> Immortality

Life (Biology)   570.1

Use for materials on life from a scientific point of view. Materials on philosophical or religious considerations of life are entered under **Life.**

BT   Biology
NT   Gaia hypothesis
     Genetics
     Life cycles (Biology)
     Middle age
     Protoplasm
     Reproduction
RT   Life

Life care communities (May subdiv. geog.)   362.61; 363.5

Use for materials on retirement communities that guarantee services and medical care for the rest of a person's life.

UF   Continuing care communities
     Continuing care retirement communities
BT   Retirement communities

Life cycles
USE   Life cycles (Biology)
      and types of plants or animals with the subdivision *Life cycles* [to be added as needed]

Life cycles (Biology)   571.8

UF   Life cycles
SA   types of plants or animals with the subdivision *Life cycles* [to be added as needed]
BT   Biology
     Cycles
     Life (Biology)

Life expectancy (May subdiv. geog.) 304.6

UF   Expectancy of life
     Expectation of life
BT   Age
     Life
     Vital statistics
NT   Longevity

Life, Future
USE   Future life

Life histories
USE   Biography

Life insurance (May subdiv. geog.) 368.32

UF   Insurance, Life
BT   Insurance
NT   Group insurance
RT   Annuities

Life on other planets   576.8

Use for materials on the possibility of indigenous life in outer space. Materials on the biology of humans or other earth creatures while in outer space are entered under **Space biology.**

UF   Astrobiology
     Extraterrestrial life
BT   Astronomy
     Planets
     Universe
NT   Extraterrestrial beings
     Interstellar communication
RT   Human-alien encounters

Life—Origin   113

UF   Germ theory
     Origin of life
BT   Evolution

Life quality
USE   Quality of life

Life saving
USE   Lifesaving

Life sciences (May subdiv. geog.)   570

UF   Biosciences
BT   Science
NT   Agriculture
     Biology
     Medicine

Life sciences ethics
USE   Bioethics

Life skills (May subdiv. geog.)   158; 640

Use for materials on skills needed by an individual to exist in modern society, including skills related to education, employment, finance, etc.

UF   Basic life skills
     Coping skills
     Functional competencies
     Fundamental life skills
     Life skills guides
     Living skills
     Personal life skills
SA   groups and classes of persons with the subdivision *Life skills guides,* e.g. **Elderly—Life skills guides** [to be added as needed]
BT   Interpersonal relations
     Success
NT   Conduct of life
     Elderly—Life skills guides
     Self-improvement
     Social skills
     Study skills

Life skills—*Continued*
 Survival skills
 RT Human behavior
Life skills guides
 USE Life skills
   and groups and classes of per-
   sons with the subdivision *Life
   skills guides,* e.g. Elderly—
   Life skills guides [to be add-
   ed as needed]
Life span prolongation
 USE Longevity
Life styles
 USE Lifestyles
Life support systems (Medical environ-
   ment) 362.1
 BT Hospitals
   Terminal care
Life support systems (Space environ-
   ment) 629.47
 BT Human engineering
   Space medicine
 NT Apollo project
   Lunar bases
   Space suits
Life support systems (Submarine envi-
   ronment) 627
 BT Human engineering
Lifelong education
 USE Adult education
   Continuing education
Lifesaving 363.1
 UF Life saving
 BT Rescue work
 RT First aid
Lifestyles (May subdiv. geog.) 306
 UF Life styles
 SA types of lifestyles [to be added
   as needed]
 BT Human behavior
   Manners and customs
 NT Alternative lifestyles
   Counter culture
   Unmarried couples
Lifts
 USE Elevators
   Hoisting machinery
Light 535
 BT Electromagnetic waves
   Physics
 NT Color
   Lasers

Lighting
 Luminescence
 Refraction
 RT Optics
   Photometry
   Radiation
   Spectrum analysis
Light and shade
 USE Shades and shadows
Light, Electric
 USE Electric lighting
Light production in animals
 USE Bioluminescence
Light ships
 USE Lightships
Light—Therapeutic use
 USE Phototherapy
Light verse
 USE Humorous poetry
Lighthouses (May subdiv. geog.) 387.1;
   623.89; 627
 BT Navigation
 NT Lightships
Lighting (May subdiv. geog.) 621.32
 UF Illumination
 SA types of lighting and types of
   buildings, structures, rooms,
   installations, etc., with the
   subdivision *Lighting,* e.g. Li-
   braries—Lighting [to be add-
   ed as needed]
 BT Interior design
   Light
 NT Candles
   Electric lighting
   Lamps
   Libraries—Lighting
   Photography—Lighting
   Stage lighting
   Streets—Lighting
Lightning 551.56
 BT Electricity
   Meteorology
   Thunderstorms
Lightships 623.89; 627
 UF Light ships
 BT Lighthouses
   Ships
Limbs, Artificial
 USE Artificial limbs

431

Lime 631.8; 666
    UF   Lime (Mineral)
    BT   **Fertilizers**
          Minerals
Lime (Fruit)
    USE **Limes**
Lime (Mineral)
    USE **Lime**
Limericks 808.1; 808.81
    May be used for collections of limericks by one or several authors or for materials about limericks.
    UF   Rhymes
    BT   **Humorous poetry**
    RT   **Nonsense verses**
Limes 634
    UF   Lime (Fruit)
    BT   **Citrus fruits**
Limitation of armament
    USE **Arms control**
Limited access highways
    USE **Express highways**
Limited companies
    USE **Limited liability companies**
Limited liability companies (May subdiv. geog.) 338.7
    UF   Limited companies
          LLCs (Limited liability companies)
          Private companies
          Private limited companies
    BT   **Corporation law**
          Corporations
Lincoln, Abraham, 1809-1865 92; B
    BT   **Presidents—United States**
Lincoln Day
    USE **Lincoln's Birthday**
Lincoln family 920; 929
Lincoln's Birthday 394.261
    UF   Lincoln Day
    BT   **Holidays**
Line engraving
    USE **Engraving**
Linear algebra 512
    BT   **Algebra**
          Mathematical analysis
    RT   **Topology**
Linear system theory
    USE **System analysis**
Linen 677
    BT   **Fabrics**
          Fibers

    RT   **Flax**
Linguistic science
    USE **Linguistics**
Linguistics (May subdiv. geog.) 410
    Use for materials on the scientific study of speech and for comparative studies of languages. General materials on the history, philosophy, origin, etc., of languages are entered under **Language and languages.**
    UF   Comparative linguistics
          Comparative philology
          Language and languages—Comparative philology
          Linguistic science
          Philology
          Philology, Comparative
    BT   **Language and languages**
    NT   **Grammar**
          Semantics
          Sociolinguistics
          Universal language
Linoleum block printing 761
    UF   Block printing
    BT   **Printing**
          Prints
Linotype 686.2
    BT   **Printing**
          Type and type-founding
          Typesetting
Lip-reading
    USE **Lipreading**
Lipreading 418
    UF   Lip-reading
    BT   **Deaf—Means of communication**
Liquefaction of coal
    USE **Coal liquefaction**
Liqueurs
    USE **Liquors**
Liquid fuel
    USE **Petroleum as fuel**
Liquids 532
    BT   **Fluid mechanics**
          Physics
    NT   **Hydraulics**
          Hydrodynamics
          Hydrostatics
Liquor industry (May subdiv. geog.) 338.4
    BT   **Beverage industry**
    NT   **Bars**
    RT   **Liquors**

Liquor problem
    USE   **Alcoholism**
           Drinking of alcoholic beverages
Liquors   **641.2; 663**
    UF   Cordials (Liquor)
          Drinks
          Intoxicants
          Liqueurs
          Liquors and liqueurs
    SA   types of liquors and liqueurs [to
          be added as needed]
    BT   **Alcoholic beverages**
          Beverages
    RT   **Brewing**
          Distillation
          Liquor industry
Liquors and liqueurs
    USE   **Liquors**
List books
    USE   **Books of lists**
Listening   **153.6; 153.7**
    BT   **Attention**
          Educational psychology
    RT   **Hearing**
Listening devices
    USE   **Eavesdropping**
Lists
    USE   **Books of lists**
          and topics with the subdivision
          Lists, e.g. **Sports—Lists** [to
          be added as needed]
LISTSERV lists
    USE   **Electronic discussion groups**
Literacy (May subdiv. geog.)   **302.2;**
    379.2
    UF   **Illiteracy**
    BT   **Education**
    NT   **Computer literacy**
          Functional literacy
          Media literacy
          Technological literacy
          Visual literacy
Literacy, Visual
    USE   **Visual literacy**
Literary awards
    USE   **Literary prizes**
Literary characters
    USE   **Characters and characteristics
          in literature**

Literary collections
    USE   **Anthologies**
          Literature—Collections
          and form headings for minor
          literary forms that represent
          collections of works of sever-
          al authors, e.g. **Essays;**
          American essays; Parodies;
          Short stories; etc.; major lit-
          erary forms and national liter-
          atures with the subdivision
          Collections, e.g. **Poetry—Col-**
          lections; English literature—
          Collections; etc.; and subjects
          with the subdivision *Literary*
          collections, for collections fo-
          cused on a single subject by
          two or more authors involving
          two or more literary forms,
          e.g. **Cats—Literary collec-**
          tions [to be added as needed]
Literary criticism
    USE   **Criticism**
          **Literature—History and criti-
          cism**
Literary forgeries   **098**
    UF   Frauds, Literary
    BT   **Counterfeits and counterfeiting**
          Forgery
Literary landmarks (May subdiv. geog.)
    809
    UF   Authors—Homes and haunts
          Landmarks, Literary
    BT   **Historic buildings**
          **Literature—History and criti-
          cism**
    NT   **English authors—Homes**
Literary landmarks—United States
    810.9
Literary prizes (May subdiv. geog.)
    807.9
    UF   Book awards
          Book prizes
          Literary awards
          Literature—Prizes
    SA   names of awards, e.g. **Caldecott
          Medal** [to be added as need-
          ed]
    BT   **Awards**
    NT   **Caldecott Medal**
          Coretta Scott King Award

Literary prizes—*Continued*
> **Edgar Allan Poe Awards**
> **Hugo Award**
> **Literature—Competitions**
> **Nebula Award**
> **Newbery Medal**

Literary property
> USE **Copyright**
> **Intellectual property**

Literary recreations   793.73
> UF   Language games
> Recreations, Literary
> BT   **Amusements**
> NT   **Charades**
> **Plot-your-own stories**
> **Rebuses**
> **Riddles**
> **Word games**

Literary style   808
> UF   Style, Literary
> BT   **Literature**
> NT   **Letter writing**
> RT   **Criticism**
> **Rhetoric**

Literary themes
> USE   **Literature—Themes**

Literature   800

Literatures are described by countries or geographic regions. In countries or regions with more than one major language the literature may be further qualified by the language in parentheses, e.g. **Canadian literature (French).** There is no distinction made in subject headings between literary works in their original languages and in translations.

> UF   Belles lettres
> Modern literature
> SA   literatures of countries or of regions larger than a single country, e.g. **English literature; French literature; Scandinavian literature;** etc.; national or regional literatures qualified if needed by the language in which the literature was originally written or subdivided by a sub-set of authors within the literature, e.g. **African literature (English); American literature—African American authors;** etc.; literatures of particular religions, e.g. **Christian literature;** literatures of languages not identified with a particular country, e.g. **Latin literature;** and subjects, themes, and stylistic features in literature, e.g. **Bible in literature; Children in literature; Characters and characteristics in literature; Symbolism in literature;** etc. [to be added as needed]

> BT   **Humanities**
> **Language arts**
> NT   **African literature (English)**
> **American literature**
> **Authorship**
> **Ballads**
> **Bible in literature**
> **Biography as a literary form**
> **Black humor (Literature)**
> **Brazilian literature**
> **Campaign literature**
> **Canadian literature**
> **Catholic literature**
> **Chapbooks**
> **Characters and characteristics in literature**
> **Children's literature**
> **Classical literature**
> **Classicism**
> **Communism and literature**
> **Comparative literature**
> **Criticism**
> **Danish literature**
> **Diaries**
> **Drama**
> **Early Christian literature**
> **English literature**
> **Epic literature**
> **Erotic literature**
> **Essay**
> **Fables**
> **Fiction**
> **Folk literature**
> **French literature**
> **Gay men's writings**
> **German literature**
> **Gothic revival (Literature)**
> **Greek literature**
> **Hebrew literature**
> **Humanism**
> **Icelandic literature**

Literature—*Continued*
>> Indic literature
>> Jewish literature
>> **Journalism**
>> **Latin American literature**
>> **Latin literature**
>> **Legends**
>> **Lesbians' writings**
>> **Literary style**
>> **Medieval literature**
>> **Mexican literature**
>> **Mock-heroic literature**
>> **Modern Greek literature**
>> **Modernism in literature**
>> **Multicultural literature**
>> **Music and literature**
>> **Native American literature**
>> **Norwegian literature**
>> **Old Norse literature**
>> **Parody**
>> **Picaresque literature**
>> **Poetry**
>> **Portuguese literature**
>> **Realism in literature**
>> **Religion in literature**
>> **Religious literature**
>> **Romance literature**
>> **Romances**
>> **Russian literature**
>> **Sagas**
>> **Satire**
>> **Scandinavian literature**
>> **Short story**
>> **Soviet literature**
>> **Spanish literature**
>> **Speeches**
>> **Stories, plots, etc.**
>> **Swedish literature**
>> **Symbolism in literature**
>> **Teenagers' writings**
>> **West Indian literature**
>>   (French)
>> **Wit and humor**
>> **World War, 1939-1945—Liter-**
>>   **ature and the war**
>> **Young adult literature**
> RT **Books**
Literature and communism
> USE **Communism and literature**
Literature and music
> USE **Music and literature**

Literature and the war
> USE names of wars with the subdivi-
>   sion *Literature and the war,*
>   e.g. **World War, 1939-**
>   **1945—Literature and the**
>   **war** [to be added as needed]

Literature—Bio-bibliography   809
> RT **Authors**

Literature—Collections   808.8
> Use for collections of literary works by sev-
> eral authors not limited to a single literature
> or literary form or focused on a single subject.
> UF   Collected works
>   Collections of literature
>   Literary collections
>   Literature—Selections
> SA   form headings for minor literary
>   forms that represent collec-
>   tions of works of several au-
>   thors, e.g. **Essays; American**
>   **essays; Parodies; Short sto-**
>   **ries;** etc.; major literary forms
>   and national literatures with
>   the subdivision *Collections,*
>   e.g. **Poetry—Collections; En-**
>   **glish literature—Collections;**
>   etc.; and subjects with the
>   subdivision *Literary collec-*
>   *tions,* for collections focused
>   on a single subject by two or
>   more authors involving two or
>   more literary forms, e.g.
>   **Cats—Literary collections** [to
>   be added as needed]

Literature, Comparative
> USE **Comparative literature**

Literature—Competitions   807.9
> BT **Contests**
>   **Literary prizes**

Literature—Criticism
> USE **Literature—History and criti-**
>   **cism**

Literature—Dictionaries   803
> BT **Encyclopedias and dictionaries**
> NT **English literature—Dictionaries**

Literature, Erotic
> USE **Erotic literature**

Literature—Evaluation
> USE **Best books**
>   **Book reviewing**
>   **Books and reading**
>   **Criticism**

Literature—Evaluation—*Continued*
   Literature—History and criticism
   Literature—Film and video adaptations
   USE **Film adaptations**
   Television adaptations
Literature—History and criticism   809

   Use for materials that are themselves histories or criticisms of literature in general. Materials on the history, principles, methods, etc., of literary criticism are entered under **Criticism.**

   UF   Appraisal of books
         Books—Appraisal
         Evaluation of literature
         Literary criticism
         Literature—Criticism
         Literature—Evaluation
   NT   **Literary landmarks**
Literature—Indexes   016.8
Literature, Medieval
   USE **Medieval literature**
Literature—Outlines, syllabi, etc.   802
   NT   **English literature—Outlines,
         syllabi, etc.**
Literature—Prizes
   USE **Literary prizes**
Literature—Selections
   USE **Literature—Collections**
Literature—Stories, plots, etc.
   USE **Stories, plots, etc.—Collections**
Literature—Themes   809
   UF   Literary themes
         Themes in literature
   SA   subjects, racial and ethnic
         groups, and classes of persons
         in literature, e.g. **Dogs in lit-
         erature; Women in litera-
         ture;** etc., and names of per-
         sons, families, and corporate
         bodies with the subdivision *In
         art,* e.g. **Napoleon I, Emper-
         or of the French, 1769-
         1821—In literature** [to be
         added as needed]
   NT   **African Americans in litera-
         ture**
         Animals in literature
         Blacks in literature
         Children in literature
         Dogs in literature

**Napoleon I, Emperor of the
   French, 1769-1821—In liter-
   ature**
   Nature in literature
   Travel in literature
   Women in literature
   RT   **Characters and characteristics
         in literature**
Literatures of the Soviet Union
   USE **Soviet literature**
Lithographers (May subdiv. geog.)
   763.092; 920
   BT   **Artists**
Lithography (May subdiv. geog.)   **686.2;
   763; 764**
   UF   Lithoprinting
   BT   **Color printing**
         Printing
         Prints
   NT   **Offset printing**
Lithoprinting
   USE **Lithography**
         Offset printing
Litigation (May subdiv. geog.)   **347**
   UF   Actions and defenses
         Civil law suits
         Defense (Law)
         Law suits
         Lawsuits
         Personal actions (Law)
         Suing (Law)
         Suits (Law)
   BT   **Law**
   NT   **Class actions (Civil procedure)**
         Witnesses
   RT   **Arbitration and award**
         Civil procedure
Littering
   USE **Refuse and refuse disposal**
Little League baseball   796.357
   BT   **Baseball**
Little magazines (May subdiv. geog.)
   050
   BT   **Periodicals**
Little theater movement   792
   UF   Community theater
   BT   **Theater**
   RT   **Amateur theater**
Liturgical year
   USE **Church year**

Liturgics
USE **Liturgies**
Liturgies 203; 264
Use for general materials on the forms of prayers, rituals, and ceremonies used in public worship, including the theological and historical study of liturgies, and for texts of liturgies from more than one religion.
UF Church service books
Liturgics
Liturgy
Ritual
Service books (Liturgy)
SA names of individual religions and denominations with the subdivision *Liturgy* or *Liturgy—Texts;* e.g. **Catholic Church—Liturgy; Catholic Church—Liturgy—Texts** etc. [to be added as needed]
BT **Religion**
Rites and ceremonies
NT **Catholic Church—Liturgy**
Eucharist
Hymns
Judaism—Liturgy
Mass (Liturgy)
RT **Church music**
Liturgy
USE **Liturgies**
and names of individual religions and denominations with the subdivision *Liturgy* e.g. **Judaism—Liturgy; Catholic Church—Liturgy;** etc. [to be added as needed]
Live poliovirus vaccine
USE **Poliomyelitis vaccine**
Livestock
USE **Domestic animals**
Livestock industry
Livestock breeding (May subdiv. geog.) **636.08**
UF Livestock—Breeding
BT **Breeding**
Livestock industry
Livestock—Breeding
USE **Livestock breeding**
Livestock industry (May subdiv. geog.) **636**
Use for materials on stock raising as an industry. General materials on farm and other domestic animals are entered under **Domestic animals.**

UF Animal husbandry
Animal industry
Livestock
Stock raising
BT **Agriculture**
Economic zoology
NT **Dairying**
Livestock breeding
Livestock judging
RT **Domestic animals**
Livestock judging 636
UF Stock judging
BT **Livestock industry**
Living earth theory
USE **Gaia hypothesis**
Living skills
USE **Life skills**
Living together
USE **Unmarried couples**
Living trusts (May subdiv. geog.) **346.05**
BT **Trusts and trustees**
Living wills 344
BT **Wills**
RT **Right to die**
Terminal care
Livres à clef
USE **Romans à clef**
Lizards (May subdiv. geog.) **597.95**
BT **Reptiles**
LLCs (Limited liability companies)
USE **Limited liability companies**
Loan associations
USE **Savings and loan associations**
Loan funds, Student
USE **Student loan funds**
Loans (May subdiv. geog.) **332.7**
UF Borrowing
Lending
BT **Finance**
NT **Capital market**
Government lending
Interest (Economics)
Mortgages
Personal loans
Public debts
Savings and loan associations
Student aid
RT **Credit**
Investments

Loans, Personal
　　USE　**Personal loans**
Lobbying (May subdiv. geog.)　**328.3**
　　Use for materials on groups that promote
　　their own interests with public officials. Mate-
　　rials on special interest groups that support
　　sympathetic candidates for public office
　　through campaign contributions are entered
　　under **Political action committees.**
　　UF　Interest groups
　　　　Lobbying and lobbyists
　　　　Lobbyists
　　　　Pressure groups
　　SA　names of specific lobbying and
　　　　　pressure groups [to be added
　　　　　as needed]
　　BT　**Politics**
　　　　Propaganda
　　RT　**Political action committees**
Lobbying and lobbyists
　　USE　**Lobbying**
Lobbyists
　　USE　**Lobbying**
Lobsters (May subdiv. geog.)　**595.3**
　　BT　**Crustacea**
　　　　Shellfish
Local area networks　004.6
　　UF　LANs (Computer networks)
　　BT　**Computer networks**
Local government (May subdiv. geog.)
　　　　320.8; 352.14
　　Use for materials on the government of dis-
　　tricts, counties, townships, etc. Materials limit-
　　ed to county government only are entered un-
　　der **County government.** Materials limited to
　　the government of cities and towns are en-
　　tered under **Municipal government.**
　　UF　Government, Local
　　　　Town meeting
　　　　Township government
　　BT　**Administrative law**
　　　　Community organization
　　　　Political science
　　NT　**County government**
　　　　Metropolitan government
　　　　Municipal government
　　　　Public administration
　　　　State-local relations
Local history　907
　　Use for materials on the writing and com-
　　piling of local histories. Collective histories of
　　several localities are entered under the coun-
　　try, state, etc., with the subdivision *Local his-
　　tory.* Individual local histories are entered un-
　　der the city, county, or other locality with the
　　subdivision *History.*

　　UF　Community history
　　　　Regional history
　　SA　names of countries, states, etc.,
　　　　　with the subdivision *Local
　　　　　history,* e.g. **United States—
　　　　　Local history; Ohio—Local
　　　　　history;** etc.; and names of
　　　　　cities, counties, or other local-
　　　　　ities with the subdivision *His-
　　　　　tory,* e.g. **Chicago (Ill.)—His-
　　　　　tory** [to be added as needed]
　　BT　**Historiography**
　　　　History
　　NT　**Ohio—Local history**
　　　　United States—Local history
Local-state relations
　　USE　**State-local relations**
Local traffic
　　USE　**City traffic**
Local transit (May subdiv. geog.)　**388.4**
　　Use for materials on the various modes of
　　local public transportation.
　　UF　City transit
　　　　Mass transit
　　　　Municipal transit
　　　　Public transit
　　　　Rapid transit
　　　　Transit systems
　　　　Urban transportation
　　BT　**Traffic engineering**
　　　　Transportation
　　NT　**Buses**
　　　　Street railroads
　　　　Subways
Localism
　　USE　**Regionalism**
Localisms
　　USE　names of languages with the
　　　　　subdivision *Provincialisms,*
　　　　　e.g. **English language—Pro-
　　　　　vincialisms** [to be added as
　　　　　needed]
Lockouts
　　USE　**Strikes**
Locks and keys　683
　　UF　Keys
　　BT　**Burglary protection**
Locomotion　152.3; 388
　　NT　**Aeronautics**
　　　　Animal locomotion
　　　　Flight
　　　　Horsemanship

Locomotion—*Continued*
>> Human locomotion
>> Navigation
>> Transportation
Locomotives (May subdiv. geog.)   625.26
> BT Railroads
> NT Steam locomotives
Locomotives—Models   625.1
> UF Model trains
> BT Models and modelmaking
Locusts   595.7; 632
> BT Insect pests
>> Insects
Log cabins and houses (May subdiv. geog.)   728
> UF Cabins
> BT House construction
>> Houses
Logarithms   513.2
> BT Algebra
>> Mathematics—Tables
>> Trigonometry—Tables
> NT Slide rule
Logging (May subdiv. geog.)   634.9
>> Use for materials on the felling of trees and the transportation of logs to sawmills. Materials on lumber and the preparation of lumber are entered under **Lumber and lumbering.**
> UF Timber—Harvesting
> BT Forests and forestry
Logic   160
> UF Argumentation
>> Deduction (Logic)
>> Dialectics
>> Fallacies
>> Induction (Logic)
> BT Intellect
>> Philosophy
>> Science—Methodology
> NT Certainty
>> Critical thinking
>> Probabilities
>> Symbolic logic
>> Theory of knowledge
> RT Reasoning
>> Thought and thinking
Logic, Symbolic and mathematical
> USE Symbolic logic
Lone Ranger films   791.43
>> May be used for individual works, collections, or materials about Lone Ranger films.
> BT Western films

Loneliness   155.9; 158
> UF Social isolation
> BT Emotions
> RT Solitude
Long distance running
> USE Marathon running
Long distance swimming
> USE Marathon swimming
Long distance telephone service (May subdiv. geog.)   384.6
> UF Telephone—Long distance
> BT Telephone
Long life
> USE Longevity
Long-term care facilities (May subdiv. geog.)   362.16
> UF Extended care facilities
> BT Hospitals
>> Medical care
> NT Nursing homes
Longevity (May subdiv. geog.)   612.6; 613
> UF Life span prolongation
>> Long life
> BT Age
>> Life expectancy
> NT Aging
> RT Middle age
>> Old age
Longitude   526; 527
> UF Degrees of latitude and longitude
> BT Earth
>> Geodesy
>> Nautical astronomy
Looking glasses
> USE Mirrors
Looms   677; 746.1
> BT Weaving
Loran   621.384
> BT Navigation
Lord's Day
> USE Sabbath
Lord's prayer   226.9; 242
> BT Jesus Christ—Prayers
Lord's Supper
> USE Eucharist
Losing things
> USE Lost and found possessions

Lost and found possessions 330.1
   UF Finding things
         Losing things
         Lost possessions
         Lost things
   BT **Property**
Lost architectural heritage
   USE **Lost architecture**
Lost architecture (May subdiv. geog.)
   720
     Use for materials on buildings and structures that have been destroyed or demolished.
   UF Lost architectural heritage
         Lost buildings
   BT **Architecture**
Lost buildings
   USE **Lost architecture**
Lost children
   USE **Missing children**
Lost continents 001.94; 398.23; 551.94
   BT **Continents**
         Geographical myths
   NT **Atlantis**
Lost possessions
   USE **Lost and found possessions**
Lost things
   USE **Lost and found possessions**
Lost tribes of Israel 909
   UF Israel, Ten lost tribes
         Jews—Lost tribes
         Ten lost tribes of Israel
   BT **Jews**
Lotteries (May subdiv. geog.) 336.1
   BT **Gambling**
Louisiana Purchase 973.4; 976.3
   BT **United States—History—1783-1809**
Love 152.4; 177; 306.7
   UF Affection
   BT **Emotions**
         Human behavior
   NT **Courtship**
         Crushes
   RT **Friendship**
**Love Canal Chemical Waste Landfill
(Niagara Falls, N.Y.)** 363.72
   BT **Hazardous waste sites**
         Landfills
Love poetry 808.1; 808.81
     May be used for individual works, collections, or materials about love poetry.

   BT **Poetry**
   RT **Erotic poetry**
Love—Religious aspects 202; 231
   UF Love (Theology)
   RT **Charity**
Love stories 808.3; 808.83
     May be used for individual works, collections, or materials about love stories.
   UF Romance novels
         Romances (Love stories)
         Romantic fiction
         Romantic stories
   BT **Fiction**
   RT **Erotic fiction**
         Gothic novels
         Romantic suspense novels
Love stories—Technique 808.3
   BT **Authorship**
Love (Theology)
   USE **Love—Religious aspects**
Low income housing
   USE **Public housing**
Low sodium diet
   USE **Salt-free diet**
Low temperature biology
   USE **Cryobiology**
Low temperatures 536; 621.5
   UF Cryogenics
   BT **Temperature**
   NT **Cryobiology**
   RT **Cold**
         Refrigeration
Loyalists, American
   USE **American Loyalists**
Loyalty 172
   UF Faithfulness
   BT **Ethics**
         Virtue
   NT **Patriotism**
Loyalty oaths
   USE **Internal security**
Lubrication and lubricants 621.8
   UF Grease
   BT **Machinery**
   RT **Bearings (Machinery)**
         Oils and fats
Lucumi (Religion)
   USE **Santeria**
Luggage 685
   UF Baggage
   BT **Containers**

Lullabies   782.42
- UF   Cradle songs
- BT   **Bedtime**
  Children's poetry
  Children's songs
  Songs

Lumber and lumbering (May subdiv. geog.)   **634.9; 674**

Use for general materials on lumber and the preparation of lumber. Materials on the felling of trees and the transportation of logs to saw-mills are entered under **Logging.**

- UF   Timber
  Woods
- BT   **Forest products**
  Forests and forestry
  Trees
  Wood

Luminescence   535
- BT   **Light**
  Radiation
- NT   **Bioluminescence**
  Phosphorescence

Luminescent books
- USE   **Glow-in-the-dark books**

Luminous books
- USE   **Glow-in-the-dark books**

Lunar bases   629.45
- UF   Moon bases
- BT   **Civil engineering**
  Life support systems (Space environment)

Lunar eclipses   523.3
- UF   Eclipses, Lunar
  Moon—Eclipses
- BT   **Astronomy**

Lunar expeditions
- USE   **Space flight to the moon**

Lunar exploration
- USE   **Moon—Exploration**

Lunar geology   559.9
- UF   Geology, Lunar
  Geology—Moon
  Moon—Geology
- BT   **Astrogeology**
- NT   **Lunar soil**
  Moon rocks

Lunar petrology
- USE   **Moon rocks**

Lunar probes   629.43
- UF   Moon probes
- SA   names of specific lunar probe projects [to be added as needed]
- BT   **Space probes**
- NT   **Project Ranger**

Lunar rocks
- USE   **Moon rocks**

Lunar soil   523.3; 552.0999; 631.4
- UF   Moon soil
  Soils, Lunar
- BT   **Lunar geology**
- RT   **Moon—Surface**

Lunar surface
- USE   **Moon—Surface**

Lunar surface radio communication
- USE   **Radio in astronautics**

Luncheons   642
- BT   **Cooking**
  Menus
- RT   **Entertaining**

Lunchrooms
- USE   **Restaurants**

Lung cancer   616.99
- UF   Lungs—Cancer
- BT   **Cancer**
  Lungs—Diseases

Lungs   611; 612.2
- BT   **Respiratory system**

Lungs—Cancer
- USE   **Lung cancer**

Lungs—Diseases   616.2
- SA   types of lung diseases [to be added as needed]
- BT   **Diseases**
- NT   **Asthma**
  Lung cancer
  Pneumonia
  Tuberculosis

Lying
- USE   **Truthfulness and falsehood**

Lyme disease   616.9
- BT   **Diseases**

Lymphatic system   573.1; 612.4; 616.4
- BT   **Physiology**

Lynching (May subdiv. geog.)   **364.1**
- BT   **Crime**
- RT   **Vigilance committees**

Lyricists (May subdiv. geog.)   **782.0092; 920**
  UF   Songwriters
  BT   **Poets**
Lyrics
  USE   **Popular music—Texts**
Machine design   **621.8**
  UF   Machinery—Construction
        Machinery—Design and construction
  SA   types of machines, equipment, etc., with the subdivision *Design and construction,* e.g. **Airplanes—Design and construction** [to be added as needed]
  BT   **Design**
        Machinery
  NT   **Machinery—Models**
Machine intelligence
  USE   **Artificial intelligence**
Machine language
  USE   **Programming languages**
Machine readable bibliographic data
        025.3
  UF   Bibliographic data in machine readable form
        Cataloging data in machine readable form
  SA   names of projects, formats, and systems, e.g. **MARC formats** [to be added as needed]
  BT   **Cataloging**
        Information services
        Information systems
        Libraries—Automation
  NT   **MARC formats**
Machine readable catalog system
  USE   **MARC formats**
Machine readable dictionaries   **413**
  UF   Dictionaries, Machine readable
  BT   **Encyclopedias and dictionaries**
Machine shop practice   **670.42**
  UF   Shop practice
  NT   **Drilling and boring (Metal, wood, etc.)**
        Grinding and polishing
  RT   **Machine shops**
Machine shops   **670.42**
  RT   **Machine shop practice**

Machine tools   **621.9**
  SA   types of machine tools [to be added as needed]
  BT   **Machinery**
        Tools
  NT   **Planing machines**
  RT   **Drilling and boring (Metal, wood, etc.)**
        Grinding and polishing
        Manufacturing processes
Machinery   **621.8**
  UF   Machines
  BT   **Manufactures**
        Mechanical engineering
        Power (Mechanics)
        Technology
        Tools
  NT   **Agricultural machinery**
        Bearings (Machinery)
        Belts and belting
        Construction equipment
        Conveying machinery
        Electric machinery
        Engines
        Gearing
        Hoisting machinery
        Hydraulic machinery
        Industrial equipment
        Lubrication and lubricants
        Machine design
        Machine tools
        Mechanical drawing
        Metalworking machinery
        Robots
        Simple machines
        Woodworking machinery
  RT   **Mechanics**
        Mills
        Power transmission
Machinery—Construction
  USE   **Machine design**
Machinery—Design and construction
  USE   **Machine design**
Machinery—Drawing
  USE   **Mechanical drawing**
Machinery in industry
  USE   **Industrial equipment**
        Machinery in the workplace
Machinery in the workplace   **338**
    Use for materials on the social and economic aspects of mechanization in the area of work.

Machinery in the workplace—*Continued*
    UF   Machinery in industry
           Technology in the workplace
    BT   **Work environment**
    NT   **Automation**
Machinery—Models   **621.8**
    UF   Mechanical models
           Models, Mechanical
    BT   **Machine design**
           Models and modelmaking
Machines
    USE **Machinery**
Machines, Simple
    USE **Simple machines**
Macintosh (Computer)   **004.165**
    UF   Apple Macintosh (Computer)
    BT   **Computers**
Macroeconomics   **339**
    BT   **Economics**
Made-for-TV movies
    USE **Television movies**
Madonna
    USE **Mary, Blessed Virgin, Saint**
Magazine editing
    USE **Journalism—Editing**
Magazines
    USE **Periodicals**
Maghreb
    USE **North Africa**
Magic (May subdiv. geog.)   **133.4**
    Use for materials on charms, spells, etc., believed to have supernatural power. Materials on types of entertainment involving illusionistic tricks are entered under **Magic tricks.**
    UF   Black art (Magic)
           Black magic (Witchcraft)
           Necromancy
           Sorcery
           Spells
    BT   **Occultism**
    RT   **Hallucinations and illusions**
           Magic tricks
           Witchcraft
Magic lanterns
    USE **Projectors**
Magic tricks   **793.8**
    UF   Conjuring
           Legerdemain
           Prestidigitation
           Sleight of hand
    BT   **Amusements**
           Tricks

    NT   **Card tricks**
    RT   **Hallucinations and illusions**
           Magic
Magna Carta   **342; 942.03**
    BT   **Charters**
           Constitutional law
           Great Britain—History—1154-1399, Plantagenets
Magnet schools (May subdiv. geog.)   **373.24**
    Use for materials on schools offering special courses not available in the regular school curriculum and designed to attract students without reference to the usual attendance zone rules, often as an aid to voluntary school desegregation.
    BT   **Public schools**
           School integration
           Schools
Magnet winding
    USE **Electromagnets**
Magnetic needle
    USE **Compass**
Magnetic recorders and recording   **621.382**
    Use for general materials on audio, computer, and video recording on a magnetizable medium.
    UF   Cassette recorders and recording
           Tape recorders
    BT   **Electronic apparatus and appliances**
Magnetic resonance accelerator
    USE **Cyclotrons**
Magnetic resonance imaging   **616.07**
    UF   Imaging, Magnetic resonance
           MRI (Magnetic resonance imaging)
           Nuclear magnetic resonance imaging
    BT   **Diagnosis**
Magnetism   **538**
    BT   **Physics**
    NT   **Compass**
           Electromagnetism
           Electromagnets
           Geomagnetism
           Magnets
    RT   **Electricity**
Magnets   **538; 621.34**
    BT   **Magnetism**
    NT   **Electromagnets**

Mail-order business (May subdiv. geog.)
658.8; 659.13
  UF Mail order catalogs
  BT **Business**
       Direct selling
       Selling
  NT **Direct marketing**
Mail order catalogs
  USE **Commercial catalogs**
       Mail-order business
Mail service
  USE **Postal service**
Mainstreaming in education (May subdiv.
  geog.) **371.9**
  BT **Education**
       Exceptional children
       Handicapped children
  RT **Special education**
Maintenance and repair
  USE **Repairing**
       and types of things that require
       maintenance with the subdivi-
       sion *Maintenance and repair,*
       e.g. **Automobiles—Mainte-
       nance and repair; Build-
       ings—Maintenance and re-
       pair;** etc.; and types of things
       that require no maintenance
       with the subdivision *Repair-
       ing,* e.g. **Radio—Repairing**
       [to be added as needed]
Maintenance of biological diversity
  USE **Biological diversity conserva-
       tion**
Maize
  USE **Corn**
Make-believe playmates
  USE **Imaginary playmates**
Makeup (Cosmetics)
  USE **Cosmetics**
Makeup, Theatrical
  USE **Theatrical makeup**
Making-choices stories
  USE **Plot-your-own stories**
Maladjusted children
  USE **Emotionally disturbed children**
Maladjustment (Psychology)
  USE **Adjustment (Psychology)**
Malaria (May subdiv. geog.) **616.9**
  BT **Diseases**
       Fever

Male actors (May subdiv. geog.) **791.4;
792; 920**
      Use for materials on several male actors
  that emphasize their identity as men. General
  materials on persons of the acting profession,
  whether male or female, are entered under
  Actors.
  UF Men actors
  BT **Actors**
Male change of life
  USE **Male climacteric**
Male circumcision
  USE **Circumcision**
Male climacteric **612.6**
  UF Change of life in men
       Climacteric, Male
       Male change of life
       Male menopause
       Menopause, Male
  BT **Aging**
Male-female relationship
  USE **Man-woman relationship**
Male menopause
  USE **Male climacteric**
Male role
  USE **Sex role**
Malfeasance in office
  USE **Misconduct in office**
Malformations, Congenital
  USE **Birth defects**
Malignant tumors
  USE **Cancer**
Malls, Shopping
  USE **Shopping centers and malls**
Malnutrition (May subdiv. geog.) **362.1;
616.3**
  BT **Nutrition**
  RT **Starvation**
Malpractice (May subdiv. geog.) **346.03**
  UF Liability, Professional
       Professional liability
       Professions—Tort liability
       Tort liability of professions
  SA types of professional personnel
       with the subdivision *Malprac-
       tice* [to be added as needed]
  BT **Liability (Law)**
  NT **Medical personnel—Malprac-
       tice**
       Physicians—Malpractice

Malpractice insurance (May subdiv. geog.) **368.5**
- UF Insurance, Malpractice
- Insurance, Professional liability
- Professional liability insurance
- BT **Insurance**

Mammals (May subdiv. geog.) **599**
- SA types of mammals, e.g. **Marine mammals; Primates; Bats;** etc. [to be added as needed]
- BT **Animals**
- NT **Bats**
- **Beavers**
- **Bison**
- **Camels**
- **Cats**
- **Cattle**
- **Chipmunks**
- **Deer**
- **Dogs**
- **Elephants**
- **Fossil mammals**
- **Horses**
- **Marine mammals**
- **Mice**
- **Pigs**
- **Primates**
- **Rabbits**
- **Reindeer**
- **Seals (Animals)**
- **Sheep**
- **Squirrels**
- **Whales**
- **Wild cats**

Mammals, Fossil
- USE **Fossil mammals**

Man
- USE **Human beings**

Man—Antiquity
- USE **Human origins**

Man in space
- USE **Space flight**

Man—Influence of environment
- USE **Environmental influence on humans**

Man—Influence on nature
- USE **Human influence on nature**

Man—Origin
- USE **Human origins**

Man power
- USE **Manpower**

Man, Prehistoric
- USE **Fossil hominids**
- **Prehistoric peoples**

Man, Primitive
- USE **Primitive societies**

Man (Theology)
- USE **Human beings (Theology)**

Man-woman relationship (May subdiv. geog.) **306.7**
- UF Female-male relationship
- Male-female relationship
- Men—Relations with women
- Men-women relationship
- Relationships, Man-woman
- Woman-man relationship
- Women-men relationship
- Women—Relations with men
- BT **Interpersonal relations**
- RT **Dating (Social customs)**

Management (May subdiv. geog.) **658**

Use for materials on the theory of management and on the application of management principles to business and industry.
- UF Administration
- Business administration
- Business management
- Industrial management
- Industrial organization
- Management science
- Organization and management
- Scientific management
- SA types of management, e.g. **Office management;** types of businesses and industries, types of industrial plants and processes, and names of individual corporate bodies, with the subdivision *Management,* e.g. **Information systems—Management;** and types of institutions in the spheres of health, education, and social services, and names of individual institutions with the subdivision *Administration,* e.g. **Libraries—Administration; Schools—Administration;** etc. [to be added as needed]
- BT **Business**
- **Industries**

Management—*Continued*
NT Conflict management
Crisis management
Factory management
Farm management
Industrial efficiency
Industrial relations
Industrial welfare
Information systems—Management
Inventory control
Job analysis
Knowledge management
Marketing
Materials handling
Natural resources—Management
Occupational health and safety
Office management
Organizational behavior
Organizational change
Personnel management
Planning
Production standards
Purchasing
Sales management
Time management
RT Operations research
Management buyouts
USE Leveraged buyouts
Management—Employee participation
USE Participative management
Management information systems (May subdiv. geog.) 658.4
UF Computer-based information systems
BT Information systems
Management of conflict
USE Conflict management
Management of knowledge assets
USE Knowledge management
Management science
USE Management
Managers
USE Supervisors
Mandates (May subdiv. geog.) 321
UF League of Nations—Mandatory system
BT International law
International organization
International relations

Mania
USE Manic-depressive illness
Manic depression
USE Manic-depressive illness
Manic-depressive illness 616.89
UF Bipolar depression
Bipolar disorder
Mania
Manic depression
Manic-depressive psychoses
Manic-depressive psychosis
Melancholia
BT Mental illness
RT Depression (Psychology)
Manic-depressive psychoses
USE Manic-depressive illness
Manic-depressive psychosis
USE Manic-depressive illness
Manifest destiny (United States)
USE United States—Territorial expansion
Manikins (Fashion models)
USE Fashion models
Manipulative materials
USE Manipulatives
Manipulatives 371.33
Use for works on educational materials designed to be handled or touched by students in learning mathematical concepts.
UF Manipulative materials
Manipulatives (Education)
BT Audiovisual materials
Mathematics—Study and teaching
Teaching—Aids and devices
Manipulatives (Education)
USE Manipulatives
Manned space flight
USE Space flight
Manned undersea research stations
USE Undersea research stations
Mannequins (Fashion models)
USE Fashion models
Manners
USE Courtesy
Etiquette
Manners and customs 390
UF Ceremonies
Customs, Social
Folkways
Social customs
Social life and customs

Manners and customs—*Continued*
Traditions
SA ethnic groups and names of
countries, cities, etc., with the
subdivision *Social life and
customs* [to be added as need-
ed]
BT **Civilization**
Ethnology
NT **African Americans—Social life
and customs**
Anniversaries
**Blacks—Social life and cus-
toms**
Bohemianism
Caste
**Chicago (Ill.)—Social life and
customs**
Chivalry
Clothing and dress
Costume
Country life
Courts and courtiers
Dating (Social customs)
Dueling
Excuses
Fads
Family traditions
Festivals
Folklore
Funeral rites and ceremonies
Gifts
Holidays
Hugging
Jews—Social life and customs
Lifestyles
Marriage customs and rites
**Native Americans—Social life
and customs**
Ohio—Social life and customs
Seafaring life
Tattooing
Travel
**United States—Social life and
customs**
RT **Etiquette**
Rites and ceremonies
Manpower (May subdiv. geog.)   **331.11**
Use for materials on the strength of a coun-
try in terms of available personnel, both mili-
tary and industrial. Materials on personnel in
specific fields are entered under kinds of

workers, e.g. **Agricultural laborers; Nurses;**
etc. Materials on investments of capital in
training and educating employees to improve
their productivity are entered under **Human
capital.**
UF Human resources
Man power
SA names of wars with the subdivi-
sion *Manpower;* e.g. **World
War, 1939-1945—Manpower**
[to be added as needed]
RT **Labor supply**
Military readiness
Manpower policy
USE **Labor policy**
Manslaughter
USE **Homicide**
Manual training
USE **Industrial arts education**
Manual workers
USE **Labor**
Working class
Manufactures (May subdiv. geog.)
338.4; 670
SA types of manufacturing indus-
tries, e.g. **Textile industry,**
and types of manufactures,
e.g. **Glass manufacture** [to
be added as needed]
BT **Commercial products**
Industries
NT **Brand name products**
Consumer goods
Generic products
Machinery
Mills
Papermaking
Patents
Prices
Trademarks
Waste products
RT **Manufacturing industries**
Manufactures—Chicago (Ill.)   **338.4**
UF Chicago (Ill.)—Manufactures
Manufactures—Defects
USE **Product recall**
Manufactures—Ohio   **338.4**
UF Ohio—Manufactures
Manufactures recall
USE **Product recall**
Manufactures—United States   **338.4**
UF United States—Manufactures

447

Manufacturing in space
  USE **Space industrialization**
Manufacturing industries (May subdiv. geog.) **338.4**
  SA types of manufacturing industries, e.g. **Textile industry,** and types of manufactures, e.g. **Glass manufacture** [to be added as needed]
  BT **Industries**
  RT **Manufactures**
Manufacturing processes (May subdiv. geog.) **658.5; 670**
  UF Industrial processing
       Production processes
  SA types of manufacturing industries, e.g. **Textile industry,** and types of manufactures, e.g. **Glass manufacture** [to be added as needed]
  BT **Industrial arts**
  NT **Forging**
       Founding
       Turning
       Welding
  RT **Machine tools**
       Materials
Manures
  USE **Fertilizers**
Manuscripts (May subdiv. geog.) **091**
  SA subjects, literatures, groups of authors, individual literary authors, literary works entered under title, and sacred works with the subdivision *Manuscripts* [to be added as needed]
  BT **Archives**
       Bibliography
       Books
  NT **Illumination of books and manuscripts**
  RT **Autographs**
       Charters
Manuscripts, Illuminated
  USE **Illumination of books and manuscripts**
Map drawing **526**
  UF Cartography
       Plans

  BT **Drawing**
  RT **Topographical drawing**
Maple sugar **641.3; 664**
  BT **Sugar**
Maps **912**
  Use for general materials about maps and their history. Materials on the methods of map making and the mapping of areas are entered under **Map drawing.** Geographical atlases of world coverage are entered under **Atlases.**
  UF Cartography
       Chartography
       Plans
  SA types of maps, e.g. **Road maps;** subjects with the subdivision *Maps,* e.g. **Geology—Maps;** and names of countries, cities, etc., and names of wars with the subdivision *Maps* [to be added as needed]
  BT **Geography**
  NT **Atlases**
       Automobile travel—Guidebooks
       Chicago (Ill.)—Maps
       Geology—Maps
       Globes
       Moon—Maps
       Nautical charts
       Ohio—Maps
       Road maps
       United States—Maps
       World War, 1939-1945—Maps
  RT **Charts, diagrams, etc.**
Maps, Historical
  USE **Historical atlases**
Maps, Military
  USE **Military geography**
Marathon running **796.42**
  UF Long distance running
  BT **Running**
Marathon swimming **797.2**
  UF Long distance swimming
  BT **Swimming**
Marble **552; 553.5**
  BT **Rocks**
       Stone
MARC formats **025.3**
  UF Machine readable catalog system
       MARC system
  BT **Bibliographic control**
       Machine readable bibliographic data

MARC system
    USE **MARC formats**
Marches (Demonstrations)
    USE **Demonstrations**
Marches (Exercises)
    USE **Marching drills**
Marches for civil rights
    USE **Civil rights demonstrations**
Marches (Music)   783.18
    BT **Military music**
Marching
    USE **Marching drills**
Marching drills   613.7
    UF Drill (Nonmilitary)
        Drills, Marching
        Marches (Exercises)
        Marching
    BT **Physical education**
Mardi Gras
    USE **Carnival**
Mariculture
    USE **Aquaculture**
Marihuana
    USE **Marijuana**
Marijuana   362.29; 613.8; 615; 633.7
    UF Cannabis
        Grass (Drug)
        Hashish
        Marihuana
        Pot (Drug)
    BT **Narcotics**
Marinas (May subdiv. geog.)   **387.1**
    UF Yacht basins
    BT **Boats and boating**
        Harbors
        Yachts and yachting
    NT **Docks**
Marine animals (May subdiv. geog.)
        591.77
    UF Marine fauna
        Sea animals
    BT **Aquatic animals**
    NT **Corals**
        Marine mammals
    RT **Marine biology**
Marine aquaculture
    USE **Aquaculture**
Marine aquariums   597.073; 639.34
    UF Salt water aquariums
        Sea water aquariums

    SA names of specific marine aquari-
        ums [to be added as needed]
    BT **Aquariums**
    NT **Marineland (Fla.)**
Marine architecture
    USE **Naval architecture**
Marine biology   578.77
    UF Ocean life
        Sea life
    BT **Biology**
        Oceanography
    NT **Marine ecology**
        Marine plants
        Marine resources
    RT **Marine animals**
Marine disasters
    USE **Shipwrecks**
Marine drilling platforms
    USE **Drilling platforms**
Marine ecology   578.77
    BT **Ecology**
        Marine biology
Marine engineering (May subdiv. geog.)
        623.8
    Use for materials on engineering as applied
    to ships and their machinery.
    UF Naval engineering
    BT **Civil engineering**
        Engineering
        Mechanical engineering
        Naval architecture
        Naval art and science
        Steam navigation
Marine engines   623.87
    BT **Engines**
        Shipbuilding
        Steam engines
Marine fauna
    USE **Marine animals**
Marine flora
    USE **Marine plants**
Marine geology
    USE **Submarine geology**
Marine insurance   368.2
    UF Insurance, Marine
    BT **Commerce**
        Insurance
        Maritime law
        Merchant marine
        Shipping
Marine law
    USE **Maritime law**

449

Marine mammals (May subdiv. geog.)
    599.5
  SA types of marine mammals [to be
        added as needed]
  BT **Mammals**
       Marine animals
  NT **Seals (Animals)**
       Whales

Marine mineral resources (May subdiv.
  geog.) **333.8; 553**
  UF Mineral resources, Marine
       Ocean mineral resources
  BT **Marine resources**
       Mines and mineral resources
       Ocean bottom
       Ocean engineering
  NT **Ocean mining**
  RT **Ocean energy resources**

Marine painting **758**
  UF Sea in art
       Seascapes
       Ships in art
  BT **Painting** ·

Marine plants (May subdiv. geog.) **579**
  UF Aquatic plants
       Marine flora
       Water plants
  BT **Marine biology**
       Plants
  NT **Algae**
  RT **Freshwater plants**

Marine pollution (May subdiv. geog.)
    363.739
  UF Ocean pollution
       Offshore water pollution
       Sea pollution
  BT **Oceanography**
       Water pollution
  RT **Oil pollution of water**

Marine resources (May subdiv. geog.)
    333.91; 591.77
  UF Ocean—Economic aspects
       Ocean resources
       Resources, Marine
       Sea resources
  BT **Commercial products**
       Marine biology
       Natural resources
       Oceanography
  NT **Aquaculture**
       Marine mineral resources

       Ocean energy resources
       Ocean engineering
       Seafood

Marine salvage **387.5; 627**
  UF Ship salvage
  BT **International law**
       Maritime law
       Salvage
  RT **Shipwrecks**

Marine transportation
  USE **Shipping**

Marineland (Fla.) **597.073; 639.34**
  BT **Marine aquariums**

Mariners
  USE **Sailors**

Mariner's compass
  USE **Compass**

Marionettes
  USE **Puppets and puppet plays**

Marital communication
  USE **Communication in marriage**

Marital counseling
  USE **Marriage counseling**

Marital infidelity
  USE **Adultery**

Maritime discoveries
  USE **Exploration**

Maritime law (May subdiv. geog.)
    341.4; 343.09
  UF Law of the sea
       Marine law
       Merchant marine—Law and leg-
         islation
       Naval law
       Navigation—Law and legislation
       Sea laws
  BT **International law**
       Law
       Shipping
  NT **Freight**
       Marine insurance
       Marine salvage
       Merchant marine
       Pirates
       Ships—Safety regulations
  RT **Commercial law**
       Territorial waters

Market gardening
  USE **Truck farming**

Market surveys (May subdiv. geog.)
  658.8
  BT **Advertising**
      Surveys
  RT **Public opinion polls**
Marketing (May subdiv. geog.) **381;**
  658.8
  Use for materials on the principles and methods involved in the transfer of merchandise from producer to consumer. Materials on food buying are entered under **Grocery shopping.**
  UF Distribution (Economics)
      Merchandising
  SA subjects with the subdivision
      Marketing, e.g. **Farm produce—Marketing** [to be added as needed]
  BT **Business**
      Management
  NT **Direct marketing**
      Direct selling
      Farm produce—Marketing
      Internet marketing
      New products
      Sales management
      Telemarketing
  RT **Advertising**
      Selling
Marketing (Home economics)
  USE **Grocery shopping**
       Shopping
Marketing of farm produce
  USE **Farm produce—Marketing**
Markets (May subdiv. geog.) **381; 658.8**
  Use for materials on places where many buyers and sellers are brought into contract with one another in order to exhange goods and services.
  BT **Business**
      Cities and towns
      Commerce
  NT **Flea markets**
      Stock exchanges
  RT **Fairs**
Marking and grading (Education)
  USE **Grading and marking (Education)**
Marks
  USE **Hallmarks**
       and types of things with identifying marks, other than plate, with the subdivision *Marks,*

e.g. **Pottery—Marks** [to be added as needed]
Marks on plate
  USE **Hallmarks**
Marriage (May subdiv. geog.) **306.81;**
  346.01
  UF Married life
      Matrimony
  BT **Family**
      Sacraments
  NT **Communication in marriage**
      Husbands
      Intermarriage
      Marriage contracts
      Marriage counseling
      Marriage customs and rites
      Married people
      Polygamy
      Remarriage
      Same-sex marriage
      Weddings
      Wives
  RT **Courtship**
      Domestic relations
Marriage—Annulment **262.9; 346.01**
  UF Annulment of marriage
Marriage contracts (May subdiv. geog.)
  306.81; 346.01
  UF Antenuptial contracts
      Premarital contracts
      Prenuptial agreements
      Prenuptial contracts
  BT **Contracts**
      Marriage
Marriage counseling **362.82**
  UF Marital counseling
      Premarital counseling
  BT **Counseling**
      Family life education
      Marriage
  RT **Divorce mediation**
Marriage—Cross-cultural studies
  306.81
Marriage customs and rites (May subdiv. geog.) **392.5**
  UF Bridal customs
  BT **Manners and customs**
      Marriage
      Rites and ceremonies
      Weddings

Marriage, Interracial
USE **Interracial marriage**
Marriage registers
USE **Registers of births, etc.**
Marriage statistics
USE **Vital statistics**
Married life
USE **Marriage**
Married men
USE **Husbands**
Married people (May subdiv. geog.)
306.872
UF Married persons
BT **Family**
Marriage
NT **Husbands**
Wives
Married persons
USE **Married people**
Married women
USE **Wives**
Mars (Planet)   523.43
BT **Planets**
NT **Mars probes**
Mars (Planet)—Exploration   629.43
BT **Planets—Exploration**
Mars (Planet)—Geology   559.9
BT **Astrogeology**
Mars (Planet)—Pictorial works   523.43;
778.3
BT **Space photography**
Mars (Planet)—Satellites   523.9
UF Satellites—Mars
BT **Satellites**
Mars probes   629.43
UF Martian probes
BT **Mars (Planet)**
Space probes
Marshall Plan
USE **Reconstruction (1939-1951)**
Marshes (May subdiv. geog.)   **551.41**
BT **Wetlands**
Martial arts (May subdiv. geog.)   **796.8**
BT **Athletics**
NT **Archery**
Dueling
Judo
Karate
Kung fu
Tai chi

RT **Self-defense**
Self-defense for women
Martial law (May subdiv. geog.)   **342**
BT **Law**
RT **Military law**
Martian probes
USE **Mars probes**
Martin Luther King Day   394.261
BT **Holidays**
Martyrs   200.92; 272.092
BT **Church history**
Heroes and heroines
RT **Persecution**
Saints
Marxian theory
USE **Marxism**
Marxism (May subdiv. geog.)   **335.4**
Use for materials on the system of econom-
ic and political thought developed by Karl
Marx, Friedrich Engels, or their followers.
UF **Marxian theory**
Marxist theory
BT **Economics**
Philosophy
Political science
Sociology
RT **Class consciousness**
Communism
Dialectical materialism
Socialism
Marxist theory
USE **Marxism**
Mary, Blessed Virgin, Saint   232.91
UF Blessed Virgin Mary
Madonna
Virgin Mary
BT **Saints**
Mary, Blessed Virgin, Saint—Art   704.9
BT **Christian art**
Mary, Blessed Virgin, Saint—Prayers
242
BT **Prayers**
Masculine psychology
USE **Men—Psychology**
Masculinity (May subdiv. geog.)   **155.3**
UF Masculinity (Psychology)
BT **Sex (Psychology)**
RT **Men**
Masculinity (Psychology)
USE **Masculinity**

Masers 621.381
  BT Amplifiers (Electronics)
      Electromagnetism
      Microwaves
Masks (Facial) 391.4
  BT Costume
Masks (Plays) 808.2; 808.82
    May be used for individual works, collec-
    tions, or materials about masks.
  UF Masques (Plays)
  BT Drama
      Pageants
      Theater
Masks (Sculpture) (May subdiv. geog.)
      731
  UF Death masks
  BT Sculpture
Masonic orders
  USE Freemasons
Masonry (May subdiv. geog.) 693
  BT Building
      Stone
  NT Cement
      Concrete
      Plaster and plastering
      Stonecutting
  RT Bricklaying
Masons (Secret order)
  USE Freemasons
Masques (Plays)
  USE Masks (Plays)
Mass
  USE Mass (Liturgy)
Mass communication
  USE Communication
      Mass media
      Telecommunication
Mass culture
  USE Popular culture
Mass feeding
  USE Food service
Mass (Liturgy) 264
  UF Mass
  BT Liturgies
  RT Eucharist
Mass media (May subdiv. geog.) 302.23
  UF Mass communication
      Media
  SA topics with the subdivision *Press
      coverage,* e.g. **Food contami-
      nation—Press coverage** [to
      be added as needed]

  BT Communication
  NT Motion pictures
      Newspapers
      Periodicals
      Radio broadcasting
      Sex in mass media
      Television broadcasting
      Violence in mass media
  RT Popular culture
Mass media literacy
  USE Media literacy
Mass political behavior
  USE Political participation
      Political psychology
Mass psychology
  USE Social psychology
Mass spectra
  USE Mass spectrometry
Mass spectrometry 543; 547
  UF Mass spectra
      Mass spectrum analysis
  BT Spectrum analysis
Mass spectrum analysis
  USE Mass spectrometry
Mass transit
  USE Local transit
Massacres (May subdiv. geog.) 179.7;
      904
  SA names of individual massacres,
      e.g. **Saint Bartholomew's
      Day, Massacre of, 1572** [to
      be added as needed]
  BT Atrocities
      History
      Persecution
  NT Saint Bartholomew's Day,
      Massacre of, 1572
Massage 613.7; 615.8
  BT Physical therapy
  NT Acupressure
      Chiropractic
      Electrotherapeutics
  RT Osteopathic medicine
Mastodon 569
  BT Extinct animals
      Fossil mammals
Mate selection in animals
  USE Animal courtship

Materia medica (May subdiv. geog.)
    615
  UF Herbals
       Pharmacopoeias
  SA types of drugs [to be added as
       needed]
  BT **Medicine**
       Therapeutics
  NT **Anesthetics**
       Narcotics
  RT **Drugs**
       Pharmacology
       Pharmacy

Material culture (May subdiv. geog.)
    306; 930.1
  Use for materials on the folk artifacts of a people produced by traditional methods.
  SA ethnic groups with the subdivision *Material culture,* e.g., **Native Americans—Material culture** [to be added as needed]
  BT **Culture**
  RT **Folklore**
       Technology

Materialism (May subdiv. geog.) **146**
  BT **Philosophy**
       Positivism
  RT **Idealism**
       Realism

Materials **620.1**
  Use for comprehensive works on the basic processed materials used in engineering and industry. Works on unprocessed minerals and unprocessed animal and vegetable products are entered under **Raw materials.**
  UF Engineering materials
       Industrial materials
       Strategic materials
  SA types of materials, e.g. **Building materials; Hazardous substances;** etc.; and scientific and technical disciplines and types of equipment and construction with the subdivision *Materials* [to be added as needed]
  NT **Adhesives**
       Airplanes—Materials
       Artists' materials
       Building materials
       Ceramics
       Finishes and finishing

       Hazardous substances
  RT **Engineering**
       Manufacturing processes

Materials handling **388; 658.7**
  UF Handling of materials
       Mechanical handling
  BT **Management**
  NT **Conveying machinery**
       Freight
  RT **Trucks**

Maternity
  USE **Mothers**

Mathematical ability **153.9**
  UF Arithmetical ability
       Number ability
  BT **Ability**

Mathematical analysis **515**
  UF Analysis (Mathematics)
  BT **Mathematics**
  NT **Algebra**
       Calculus
       Functions
       Graph theory
       Linear algebra
       Numerical analysis

Mathematical drawing
  USE **Geometrical drawing**
        Mechanical drawing

Mathematical logic
  USE **Symbolic logic**

Mathematical models **511**
  UF Models
       Models, Mathematical
  SA subjects with the subdivision *Mathematical models,* e.g. **Pollution—Mathematical models** [to be added as needed]
  BT **Mathematics**
  NT **Computer simulation**
       Fractals
       Game theory
       Pollution—Mathematical models
       System analysis

Mathematical notation **510**
  Use for materials on the system of graphic symbols used in mathematics as well as for materials on the process or method of setting these down.
  UF Mathematical symbols
       Mathematics—Notation

Mathematical notation—*Continued*
      Mathematics—Symbols
      Notation, Mathematical
      Symbols, Mathematical
  RT   **Mathematics**
Mathematical readiness   **372.7**
  UF   Arithmetical readiness
      Mathematics readiness
      Number readiness
      Readiness for mathematics
  BT   **Arithmetic—Study and teaching**
      Mathematics—Study and teaching
Mathematical recreations   **793.74**
  UF   Recreations, Mathematical
  BT   **Amusements**
      Puzzles
      Scientific recreations
  NT   **Number games**
Mathematical sequences
  USE **Sequences (Mathematics)**
Mathematical sets
  USE **Set theory**
Mathematical symbols
  USE **Mathematical notation**
Mathematicians (May subdiv. geog.)
      510.92; 920
  BT   **Scientists**
  RT   **Mathematics**
Mathematics (May subdiv. geog.)   **510**
  SA   subjects with the subdivision
      Mathematics, e.g. **Astronomy—Mathematics** [to be added as needed]
  BT   **Science**
  NT   **Algebra**
      Arithmetic
      Astronomy—Mathematics
      Binary system (Mathematics)
      Biomathematics
      Business mathematics
      Calculus
      Dynamics
      Fourth dimension
      Fractions
      Functions
      Game theory
      Geometry
      Group theory
      Mathematical analysis
      Mathematical models

      Measurement
      Metric system
      Number theory
      Patterns (Mathematics)
      Probabilities
      Sequences (Mathematics)
      Set theory
      Symbolic logic
      Trigonometry
      Word problems (Mathematics)
  RT   **Mathematical notation**
      Mathematicians
Mathematics—Computer-assisted instruction   **372.7; 510.78**
  BT   **Computer-assisted instruction**
Mathematics—Notation
  USE **Mathematical notation**
Mathematics readiness
  USE **Mathematical readiness**
Mathematics—Study and teaching
      372.7; 510.7
  NT   **Manipulatives**
      Mathematical readiness
Mathematics—Symbols
  USE **Mathematical notation**
Mathematics—Tables   **510**
  UF   Ready reckoners
  NT   **Logarithms**
      Trigonometry—Tables
Mating behavior
  USE **Animal courtship**
      Sexual behavior in animals
Matrimony
  USE **Marriage**
Matter   **117; 530**
  BT   **Dynamics**
      Physics
  NT   **Dark matter (Astronomy)**
Mausoleums
  USE **Tombs**
Maxims
  USE **Proverbs**
Mayas   **972.004**
  BT   **Native Americans—Central America**
      Native Americans—Mexico
Maze puzzles   **793.73**
  UF   Mazes
  BT   **Puzzles**
Mazes
  USE **Maze puzzles**

Meal planning
USE **Menus**
Nutrition
Meals
USE types of meals, e.g. **Breakfasts;**
Dinners; etc. [to be added as
needed]
Meals for school children
USE **School children—Food**
Meals on wheels programs   362
Use for materials on programs that deliver
meals to the homebound.
UF Home delivered meals programs
BT **Food relief**
Meanness
USE **Bad behavior**
Measurement   389; 530.8
UF Metrology
SA subjects with the subdivision
Measurement, e.g. **Air pollu-**
tion—Measurement [to be
added as needed]
BT **Mathematics**
NT **Air pollution—Measurement**
Geodesy
Measuring instruments
Photometry
Surveying
Volume (Cubic content)
RT **Weights and measures**
Measurements, Electric
USE **Electric measurements**
Measures
USE **Weights and measures**
Measuring instruments   389; 681
UF Instruments, Measuring
BT **Measurement**
Weights and measures
Meat   641.3; 664
SA types of meat [to be added as
needed]
BT **Food**
NT **Beef**
Carving (Meat, etc.)
Meat-eating animals
USE **Carnivorous animals**
Meat industry (May subdiv. geog.)
338.1
UF Meat industry and trade
Meat packing industry
Packing industry
Stockyards

BT **Food industry**
NT **Meat inspection**
Meat industry and trade
USE **Meat industry**
Meat inspection (May subdiv. geog.)
363.19
UF Inspection of meat
BT **Food adulteration and inspec-**
tion
Meat industry
Public health
Meat packing industry
USE **Meat industry**
Mechanic arts
USE **Industrial arts**
Mechanical brains
USE **Cybernetics**
Mechanical drawing   604.2
UF Drafting, Mechanical
Engineering drawing
Industrial drawing
Machinery—Drawing
Mathematical drawing
Plans
Structural drafting
BT **Drawing**
Engineering
Machinery
Patternmaking
NT **Blueprints**
Graphic methods
Lettering
RT **Geometrical drawing**
Mechanical engineering (May subdiv.
geog.)   **621**
Use for materials on the application of the
principles of mechanics to the design, con-
struction, and operation of machnery. Materi-
als on the application of the principles of me-
chanics to engineering structures other than
machinery are entered under **Applied me-**
chanics.
BT **Civil engineering**
NT **Electrical engineering**
Machinery
Marine engineering
Mechanical movements
Power (Mechanics)
Power transmission
RT **Steam engineering**
Mechanical handling
USE **Materials handling**

Mechanical models
    USE   **Machinery—Models**
Mechanical movements   531
    UF   Mechanisms (Machinery)
    BT   **Kinematics**
           Mechanical engineering
           Mechanics
           Motion
    NT   **Robots**
           Simple machines
    RT   **Gearing**
Mechanical musical instruments   786.6
    UF   Musical instruments, Mechanical
    SA   types of instruments, e.g. **Music
           boxes** [to be added as need-
           ed]
    BT   **Musical instruments**
    NT   **Music boxes**
Mechanical properties testing
    USE   **Testing**
Mechanical speech recognition
    USE   **Automatic speech recognition**
Mechanics   530; 531
    BT   **Physics**
    NT   **Applied mechanics**
           Dynamics
           Fluid mechanics
           Hydraulics
           Hydrodynamics
           Hydrostatics
           Mechanical movements
           Power (Mechanics)
           Simple machines
           Soil mechanics
           Statics
           Strains and stresses
           Strength of materials
           Vibration
           Viscosity
           Wave mechanics
    RT   **Force and energy**
           Kinematics
           Machinery
           Motion
Mechanics, Applied
    USE   **Applied mechanics**
Mechanics (Persons)   920
Mechanisms (Machinery)
    USE   **Mechanical movements**
Medallions
    USE   **Medals**

Medals (May subdiv. geog.)   **355.1; 737**
    UF   Badges of honor
           Medallions
    SA   names of military services and
           other appropriate subjects with
           the subdivision *Medals,
           badges, decorations, etc.* [to
           be added as needed]
    NT   **United States. Army—Medals,
           badges, decorations, etc.**
           **United States. Navy—Medals,
           badges, decorations, etc.**
    RT   **Decorations of honor**
           Insignia
           Numismatics
Medals, badges, decorations, etc.
    USE   types of armed forces with the
           subdivision *Medals, badges,
           decorations, etc.,* e.g. **United
           States. Army—Medals,
           badges, decorations, etc.** [to
           be added as needed]
Media
    USE   **Mass media**
Media centers (Education)
    USE   **Instructional materials centers**
Media coverage
    USE   topics with the subdivision *Press
           coverage,* e.g. **Food contami-
           nation—Press coverage** [to
           be added as needed]
Media literacy (May subdiv. geog.)
        302.23
    Use for materials on a person's knowledge
    of and ability to use, interpret, and evaluate
    the mass media.
    UF   Mass media literacy
    BT   **Literacy**
Mediation
    USE   **Arbitration and award**
Mediation, Divorce
    USE   **Divorce mediation**
Mediation, Industrial
    USE   **Industrial arbitration**
Mediation, International
    USE   **International arbitration**
Medicaid (May subdiv. geog.)
        362.10973; 368.4
    UF   Medical care for the poor
    BT   **National health insurance**
           Poor—Medical care
           State medicine

Medicaid—*Continued*
  RT **Medicare**
Medical appointments and schedules
  USE **Medical practice**
Medical botany   581.6
  UF Botany, Medical
      Drug plants
      Herbal medicine
      Medicinal herbs
      Medicinal plants
      Plants, Medicinal
  BT **Botany**
      Medicine
      Pharmacy
Medical care (May subdiv. geog.)   **362.1**
  Use for materials on the organization of
  services and facilities for medical care. Mate-
  rials on the technical and scientific aspects of
  medical care are entered under **Medicine.**
  UF Delivery of health care
      Delivery of medical care
      Health care
      Health care delivery
      Medical services
      Personal health services
  SA ethnic groups, classes of per-
      sons, and names of wars with
      the subdivision *Medical care,*
      e.g. **Native Americans—Med-
      ical care; Elderly—Medical
      care;** etc. [to be added as
      needed]
  BT **Public health**
  NT **Armies—Medical care**
      Dental care
      Elderly—Medical care
      Health facilities
      Health self-care
      Home care services
      Long-term care facilities
      Medical charities
      Mental health services
      **Native Americans—Medical
      care**
      Occupational health services
      Poor—Medical care
      Sports medicine
      Terminal care
      **United States—History—1861-
      1865, Civil War—Medical
      care**

**World War, 1939-1945—Medi-
  cal care**
  RT **Health care reform**
      Medicine
Medical care—Costs   362.1
  UF Cost of medical care
      Medical service, Cost of
      Medicine—Cost of medical care
  BT **Medical economics**
Medical care—Ethical aspects
  USE **Medical ethics**
Medical care facilities
  USE **Health facilities**
Medical care for the elderly
  USE **Elderly—Medical care**
        Medicare
Medical care for the poor
  USE **Medicaid**
        Poor—Medical care
Medical care reform
  USE **Health care reform**
Medical care, Right to
  USE **Right to health care**
Medical care—Social aspects
  USE **Social medicine**
Medical centers (May subdiv. geog.)
        362.11
  RT **Hospitals**
Medical charities (May subdiv. geog.)
        362.1
  UF Charities, Medical
  BT **Charities**
      Medical care
      Public health
  NT **Institutional care**
  RT **Hospitals**
Medical chemistry
  USE **Clinical chemistry**
Medical colleges (May subdiv. geog.)
        610.71
  UF Medical schools
  BT **Colleges and universities**
  RT **Medicine—Study and teaching**
Medical consultation
  USE **Medical practice**
Medical diagnosis
  USE **Diagnosis**
Medical drama (Films)   791.43
  May be used for individual works, collec-
  tions, or materials about medical films.
  UF Doctor films
  BT **Motion pictures**

Medical drama (Radio programs)
791.44

May be used for individual works, collections, or materials about medical radio programs.

UF Doctor radio programs

BT **Radio programs**

Medical drama (Television programs)
791.45

May be used for individual works, collections, or materials about medical television programs.

UF Doctor television programs

BT **Television programs**

Medical economics 338.4

Use for comprehensive materials on the economic aspects of medical service from the point of view of both the practitioner and the public.

SA types of medical services with the subdivision *Costs* [to be added as needed]

BT **Economics**

NT **Medical care—Costs**

Medical education

USE **Medicine—Study and teaching**

Medical electricity

USE **Electrotherapeutics**

Medical errors

USE **Errors**

Medical personnel—Malpractice

Physicians—Malpractice

Medical ethics (May subdiv. geog.)
174.2

UF Medical care—Ethical aspects

Medicine—Ethical aspects

SA types of medical practices and procedures with the subdivision *Ethical aspects,* e.g.

Transplantation of organs, tissues, etc.—Ethical aspects [to be added as needed]

BT **Bioethics**

Ethics

Professional ethics

NT **Euthanasia**

Human experimentation in medicine

Right to die

RT **Social medicine**

Medical examinations

USE **Periodic health examinations**

and subjects, classes of persons, ethnic groups, and military services with the subdivision *Medical examinations,* e.g.

Children—Medical examinations [to be added as needed]

Medical experimentation on humans

USE **Human experimentation in medicine**

Medical fiction

USE **Medical novels**

Medical folklore

USE **Traditional medicine**

Medical genetics (May subdiv. geog.)
616

UF Clinical genetics

Congenital diseases

Hereditary diseases

Heredity of diseases

SA names of diseases with the subdivision *Genetic aspects* [to be added as needed]

BT **Genetics**

Pathology

NT **Birth defects**

Cancer—Genetic aspects

Genetic counseling

Medical inspection in schools

USE **Children—Medical examinations**

Medical insurance

USE **Health insurance**

Medical insurance, National

USE **National health insurance**

Medical jurisprudence (May subdiv. geog.) **614**

Use for materials on the application of medical knowledge to questions of law. Materials on the law as it affects medicine and the medical profession are entered under **Medicine—Law and legislation.**

UF Forensic medicine

Jurisprudence, Medical

Legal medicine

BT **Forensic sciences**

NT **DNA fingerprinting**

Lie detectors and detection

Poisons and poisoning

Suicide

RT **Medicine—Law and legislation**

Medical laws and legislation
    USE   **Medicine—Law and legislation**
Medical malpractice
    USE   **Medical personnel—Malprac-**
          tice
Medical missions (May subdiv. geog.)
      362.1
    UF   Missions, Medical
    BT   **Medicine**
Medical novels   808.3
      May be used for individual works, collec-
    tions, or materials about novels with a medi-
    cal setting.
    UF   Doctor novels
         Medical fiction
         Medicine—Fiction
    BT   **Fiction**
Medical offices
    USE   **Medical practice**
Medical partnership
    USE   **Medical practice**
Medical personnel (May subdiv. geog.)
      610.69
    UF   Health care personnel
         Health personnel
         Health professions
         Health sciences personnel
         Health services personnel
         Medical profession
    BT   **Employees**
    NT   **Nurses**
         Physicians
    RT   **Medicine**
Medical personnel—Malpractice (May
      subdiv. geog.)   **346.03**
    UF   Medical errors
         Medical malpractice
    SA   classes of persons in the medical
         field with the subdivision
         Malpractice; e.g. **Physi-**
         cians—Malpractice [to be
         added as needed]
    BT   **Malpractice**
         Medicine—Law and legislation
Medical photography   621.36; 778.3
    BT   **Photography**
         Photography—Scientific appli-
         cations
Medical practice (May subdiv. geog.)
      610.6
    Use for materials on the organization and
    management of medicine as a profession. Sci-

entific materials on the practice of medicine
are entered under **Medicine.**
    UF   Clinics
         Group medical practice
         Medical appointments and sched-
         ules
         Medical consultation
         Medical offices
         Medical partnership
         Medical profession
         Medicine—Practice
    SA   types of medicine with the sub-
         division *Practice,* e.g. **Nucle-**
         ar medicine—Practice [to be
         added as needed]
    BT   **Medicine**
    NT   **Health maintenance organiza-**
         tions
         Nuclear medicine—Practice
Medical profession
    USE   **Medical personnel**
          Medical practice
          Medicine
Medical research
    USE   **Medicine—Research**
Medical schools
    USE   **Medical colleges**
Medical sciences
    USE   **Medicine**
Medical self-care
    USE   **Health self-care**
Medical service, Cost of
    USE   **Medical care—Costs**
Medical services
    USE   **Medical care**
Medical sociology
    USE   **Social medicine**
Medical technologists (May subdiv. geog.)
      610.69
    BT   **Allied health personnel**
Medical technology (May subdiv. geog.)
      610.28
    BT   **Medicine**
Medical transplantation
    USE   **Transplantation of organs, tis-**
          sues, etc.
Medical waste disposal
    USE   **Medical wastes**
Medical wastes   363.72
    UF   Disposal of medical waste
         Hospital wastes
         Infectious wastes

Medical wastes—*Continued*
      Medical waste disposal
      Wastes, Medical
  BT **Refuse and refuse disposal**
  RT **Hazardous wastes**
Medicare (May subdiv. geog.) **368.4**
  UF Medical care for the elderly
  BT **Elderly—Medical care**
      National health insurance
      State medicine
  RT **Medicaid**
Medication abuse **362.29; 613.8; 616.86**
  Use for materials on the abuse or misuse of therapeutic or medicinal drugs, either prescription or non-prescription.
  UF Abuse of medications
      Abuse of medicines
      Pharmaceutical abuse
      Prescription drug abuse
  BT **Drug abuse**
Medicinal chemistry
  USE **Pharmaceutical chemistry**
Medicinal herbs
  USE **Herbs—Therapeutic use**
      Medical botany
Medicinal plants
  USE **Medical botany**
Medicine (May subdiv. geog.) **610**
  Use for materials on the technical and scientific aspects of medical care. Materials on the organization of services and facilities for medical care are entered under **Medical Care.** Materials on the organization and management of medicine as a profession are entered under **Medical practice.**
  UF Medical profession
      Medical sciences
  SA types of medicine, e.g. **Sports medicine;** and names of diseases and groups of diseases, e.g. **AIDS (Disease); Fever; Nervous system—Diseases;** etc., and traditional medicine of particular ethnic groups, e.g.**Native American medicine** [to be added as needed]
  BT **Life sciences**
      Therapeutics
  NT **Alternative medicine**
      Anatomy
      Aviation medicine
      Biochemistry
      Dentistry
      Diagnosis

      Emergency medicine
      Endocrinology
      Family medicine
      First aid
      Health
      Holistic medicine
      Hygiene
      Immunology
      Materia medica
      Medical botany
      Medical missions
      Medical practice
      Medical technology
      Military medicine
      Mind and body
      Native American medicine
      Nuclear medicine
      Nursing
      Orthopedics
      Osteopathic medicine
      Pathology
      Periodic health examinations
      Pharmacology
      Pharmacy
      Physiology
      Podiatry
      Popular medicine
      Preventive medicine
      Psychiatry
      Psychosomatic medicine
      Quacks and quackery
      Social medicine
      Space medicine
      Sports medicine
      State medicine
      Submarine medicine
      Surgery
      Therapeutics
      Toxicology
      Traditional medicine
      Tropical medicine
      Veterinary medicine
  RT **Diseases**
      Medical care
      Medical personnel
      Physicians
Medicine and religion
  USE **Medicine—Religious aspects**
Medicine—Biography **610.92; 920**
  BT **Biography**

Medicine—Cost of medical care
    USE **Medical care—Costs**
Medicine—Ethical aspects
    USE **Medical ethics**
Medicine—Fiction
    USE **Medical novels**
Medicine—Law and legislation (May
      subdiv. geog.) **344**
    Use for materials on the law as it affects
medicine and the medical profession. Materials on the application of medical knowledge
to questions of law are entered under **Medical jurisprudence.**
    UF Medical laws and legislation
    BT **Law**
          Legislation
    NT **Medical personnel—Malprac-
          tice**
          Physicians—Licenses
          Physicians—Malpractice
          Right to die
    RT **Medical jurisprudence**
Medicine, Military
    USE **Military medicine**
Medicine—Miscellanea **610.2**
    BT **Curiosities and wonders**
Medicine, Pediatric
    USE **Children—Diseases**
Medicine—Physiological effect
    USE **Pharmacology**
Medicine, Popular
    USE **Popular medicine**
Medicine—Practice
    USE **Medical practice**
Medicine, Preventive
    USE **Preventive medicine**
Medicine, Psychosomatic
    USE **Psychosomatic medicine**
Medicine—Religious aspects **201;
      261.5; 615.8**
    UF Medicine and religion
          Religion and medicine
    NT **Spiritual healing**
Medicine—Research **610.7**
    UF Medical research
    BT **Research**
    NT **Human experimentation in
          medicine**
Medicine—Social aspects
    USE **Social medicine**
Medicine, State
    USE **State medicine**

Medicine—Study and teaching **610.7**
    UF Medical education
    RT **Medical colleges**
Medicine—United States **610.973**
Medieval architecture (May subdiv.
      geog.) **723**
    UF Architecture, Medieval
    BT **Architecture**
          Medieval civilization
    NT **Byzantine architecture**
          Gothic architecture
          Romanesque architecture
    RT **Castles**
          Cathedrals
Medieval art (May subdiv. geog.)
    709.02
    UF Art, Medieval
    BT **Art**
          Medieval civilization
    NT **Byzantine art**
          Gothic art
          **Illumination of books and
            manuscripts**
          Romanesque art
Medieval church history
    USE **Church history—600-1500,
          Middle Ages**
Medieval civilization **909.07**
    Use for materials on cultural and intellectual developments in the Middle Ages not limited to a single country or region.
    UF Civilization, Medieval
    BT **Civilization**
    NT **Feudalism**
          Medieval architecture
          Medieval art
          Medieval literature
          Medieval philosophy
          Medieval tournaments
    RT **Chivalry**
          Middle Ages
Medieval Greece
    USE **Greece—History—323-1453**
Medieval literature **809**
    May use same subdivisions as for **Literature.**
    UF Literature, Medieval
    BT **Literature**
          Medieval civilization
    NT **Early Christian literature**
          Old Norse literature

Medieval philosophy   189
UF   Philosophy, Medieval
BT   **Medieval civilization**
      Philosophy
Medieval tournaments (May subdiv.
       geog.)   **394**
   Use for materials on medieval contests in
which mounted and armored contestants
fought for a prize with blunted weapons and
in accordance with certain rules, and for mate-
rials on modern re-enactments of such events.
UF   Tournaments
BT   **Chivalry**
      Medieval civilization
      Pageants
Meditation   158; 204; 248.3; 296.7
   Use for materials on spiritual contemplation
or mental prayer. Collections of personal re-
flections or thoughts for use in meditation are
entered under **Meditations.**
BT   **Devotional exercises**
      Spiritual life
NT   **Transcendental meditation**
RT   **Meditations**
Meditations   204; 242
   Use for collections of personal reflections
or thoughts for use in meditation. Materials on
spiritual contemplation or mental prayer are
entered under **Meditation.**
SA   religious topics, names of indi-
         vidual persons, and titles of
         sacred works with the subdi-
         vision *Meditations,* e.g.
         Lent—Meditations [to be
         added as needed]
BT   **Devotional literature**
      Prayers
NT   **Lent—Meditations**
RT   **Meditation**
Meetings, Public
USE   **Public meetings**
Melancholia
USE   **Depression (Psychology)**
       Manic-depressive illness
Melodrama   808.82
   May be used for individual works, collec-
tions, or materials about melodrama.
BT   **Drama**
Members of Parliament
USE   **Legislators**
Memoirs
USE   **Autobiographies**
       Autobiography
       Biography

Memorabilia
USE   **Collectibles**
Memorial Day   394.262
UF   Decoration Day
BT   **Holidays**
Memorizing
USE   subjects, types of literature, and
          titles of sacred works with
          the subdivision *Memorizing,*
          e.g. **Poetry—Memorizing** [to
          be added as needed]
Memory   153.1
SA   subjects, types of literature, and
          titles of sacred works with
          the subdivision *Memorizing,*
          e.g. **Poetry—Memorizing** [to
          be added as needed]
BT   **Brain**
      Educational psychology
      Intellect
      Psychology
      Psychophysiology
      Thought and thinking
NT   **Attention**
      False memory syndrome
      Forgetfulness
      Psychology of learning
      Recovered memory
RT   **Mnemonics**
Memory devices (Computers)
USE   **Computer storage devices**
Men (May subdiv. geog.)   **305.31**
SA   men of particular racial, reli-
          gious or ethnic groups, e.g.
          African American men;
          Jewish men; and men in var-
          ious occupations and profes-
          sions, e.g. **Male actors** [to be
          added as needed]
NT   **African American men**
      Brothers
      Fathers
      Gay men
      Husbands
      Jewish men
      Single men
      Sons
      Widowers
      Young men
RT   **Masculinity**

Men actors
    USE   **Male actors**
Men—Biography   920
    BT   **Biography**
Men—Clothing
    USE   **Men's clothing**
Men—Diseases   616.0081
    BT   **Diseases**
Men—Education (May subdiv. geog.)
    370.81
    UF   Education of men
    BT   **Education**
    RT   **Coeducation**
Men—Employment   331.11
    BT   **Employment**
Men in business
    USE   **Businessmen**
Men—Psychology   155.3
    UF   Masculine psychology
    BT   **Psychology**
Men—Relations with women
    USE   **Man-woman relationship**
Men—Social conditions   305.32
    BT   **Social conditions**
    NT   **Men's movement**
Men—Societies   367
    UF   Men's clubs
          Men's organizations
    BT   **Clubs**
          Societies
Men-women relationship
    USE   **Man-woman relationship**
Mendel's law   576.5
    BT   **Breeding**
          Variation (Biology)
    NT   **Genetics**
    RT   **Heredity**
Mendicancy
    USE   **Begging**
Mendicant orders
    USE   **Franciscans**
Mending
    USE   **Clothing and dress—Repairing**
          Repairing
Mennonites (May subdiv. geog.)   **289.7**
    BT   **Christian sects**
    NT   **Amish**
Menopause   612.6; 618.1
    UF   Change of life in women
          Climacteric, Female
          Female climacteric

    BT   **Aging**
Menopause, Male
    USE   **Male climacteric**
Men's clothing   646; 687
    UF   Men—Clothing
    BT   **Clothing and dress**
Men's clubs
    USE   **Men—Societies**
Men's liberation movement
    USE   **Men's movement**
Men's movement   305.32
    UF   Men's liberation movement
    BT   **Men—Social conditions**
Men's organizations
    USE   **Men—Societies**
Menstruation   612.6
    BT   **Reproduction**
    NT   **Premenstrual syndrome**
Mental arithmetic   513
    UF   Mental calculation
    BT   **Arithmetic**
Mental calculation
    USE   **Mental arithmetic**
Mental deficiency
    USE   **Mental retardation**
Mental depression
    USE   **Depression (Psychology)**
Mental diseases
    USE   **Abnormal psychology**
          Mental illness
Mental healing   615.8
    Use for materials on psychic or psychological means to treat illness. Materials on the use of faith, prayer, or religious means to treat illness are entered under **Spiritual healing.**
    UF   Healing, Mental
          Mind cure
          Psychic healing
    BT   **Alternative medicine**
    NT   **Hypnotism**
    RT   **Mental suggestion**
          Mind and body
          Psychotherapy
          Spiritual healing
          Subconsciousness
          Suggestive therapeutics
Mental health (May subdiv. geog.)
    362.2
    UF   Mental hygiene
    SA   ethnic groups, classes of persons, and names of individual persons with the subdivision

Mental health—*Continued*
        Mental health, e.g. **Wom-**
        en—Mental health [to be
        added as needed]
  BT **Happiness**
       Health
  NT **Burn out (Psychology)**
       Occupational therapy
       Stress (Psychology)
       Women—Mental health
  RT **Abnormal psychology**
       Mental illness
       Mind and body
       Psychiatry
       Psychology
Mental health care
  USE **Mental health services**
Mental health services (May subdiv.
    geog.) **362.2; 616.89**
  UF Mental health care
       Psychiatric care
       Psychiatric services
  SA ethnic groups, classes of per-
       sons, and names of individual
       educational institutions with
       the subdivision *Mental health
       services* [to be added as need-
       ed]
  BT **Medical care**
  NT **Crisis intervention (Mental
       health services)**
Mental hospitals
  USE **Psychiatric hospitals**
Mental hygiene
  USE **Mental health**
Mental illness (May subdiv. geog.)
    362.2; 616.89
  Use for popular materials and materials on
regional or social aspects of mental disorders.
Materials on clinical aspects of mental disor-
ders, including therapy, are entered under **Psy-
chiatry.** Systematic descriptions of mental
disorders are entered under **Abnormal psy-
chology.**
  UF Mental diseases
       Psychoses
  SA names of specific illnesses, e.g.
       Manic-depressive illness [to
       be added as needed]
  BT **Abnormal psychology**
       Diseases
  NT **Manic-depressive illness**
       Multiple personality

       Neurasthenia
  RT **Mental health**
       Mentally ill
       Personality disorders
       Psychiatry
Mental illness—Drug therapy   **616.89**
  BT **Drug therapy**
Mental illness—Jurisprudence
  USE **Insanity defense**
Mental illness—Physiological aspects
    616.89
  BT **Physiology**
Mental institutions
  USE **Mentally ill—Institutional care**
Mental patients
  USE **Mentally ill**
Mental retardation (May subdiv. geog.)
    362.3; 616.85
  UF Mental deficiency
  BT **Abnormal psychology**
  NT **Down syndrome**
  RT **Mentally handicapped**
Mental stereotype
  USE **Stereotype (Psychology)**
Mental stress
  USE **Stress (Psychology)**
Mental suggestion   **131; 154.7; 615.8**
  UF Autosuggestion
       Suggestion, Mental
  BT **Mind and body**
       Parapsychology
       Subconsciousness
  NT **Brainwashing**
  RT **Hypnotism**
       Mental healing
       Suggestive therapeutics
Mental telepathy
  USE **Telepathy**
Mental tests
  USE **Intelligence tests**
       Psychological tests
Mental types
  USE **Typology (Psychology)**
Mentally depressed
  USE **Depression (Psychology)**
Mentally deranged
  USE **Mentally ill**

Mentally handicapped (May subdiv. geog.) **305.9; 362.2; 362.3**
  UF Mentally retarded
  BT **Handicapped**
  NT **Mentally handicapped children**
  RT **Mental retardation**
Mentally handicapped children (May subdiv. geog.) **155.45; 362.2; 362.3**
  UF Children, Retarded
      Mentally retarded children
      Retarded children
  BT **Child psychiatry**
      Handicapped children
      Mentally handicapped
  RT **Slow learning children**
Mentally handicapped children—Education (May subdiv. geog.) **371.92**
  BT **Education**
      Special education
Mentally ill (May subdiv. geog.) **362.2; 616.89**
  UF Insane
      Mental patients
      Mentally deranged
      Psychotics
  BT **Sick**
  NT **Emotionally disturbed children**
  RT **Mental illness**
Mentally ill children
  USE **Emotionally disturbed children**
Mentally ill—Institutional care 362.2
  UF Mental institutions
  BT **Institutional care**
  RT **Psychiatric hospitals**
Mentally retarded
  USE **Mentally handicapped**
Mentally retarded children
  USE **Mentally handicapped children**
Mentoring 361; 371.102; 658.3
  BT **Counseling**
Menus 642
  UF Bills of fare
      Meal planning
  BT **Cooking**
      Diet
  NT **Breakfasts**
      Dinners
      Luncheons
  RT **Catering**

Mercantile buildings
  USE **Commercial buildings**
Mercantile law
  USE **Commercial law**
Mercenary soldiers (May subdiv. geog.) **355.3**
  UF Mercenary troops
      Soldiers of fortune
  BT **Military personnel**
      Soldiers
Mercenary troops
  USE **Mercenary soldiers**
Merchandise
  USE **Commercial products**
       Consumer goods
Merchandising
  USE **Marketing**
       Retail trade
Merchant marine (May subdiv. geog.) **387.5**
  BT **Maritime law**
      Sailors
      Ships
      Transportation
  NT **Harbors**
      Marine insurance
  RT **Shipping**
Merchant marine—Law and legislation
  USE **Maritime law**
Merchant marine—Safety regulations
  USE **Ships—Safety regulations**
Merchant marine—United States 387.50973
Merchants (May subdiv. geog.) **380.1092; 920**
  BT **Businesspeople**
Mercury 546; 669
  UF Quicksilver
  BT **Chemical elements**
      Metals
Mercy killing
  USE **Euthanasia**
Mergers
  USE **Corporate mergers and acquisitions**
       and types of institutions and types of industries and businesses with the subdivision *Mergers,* e.g. **Railroads—Mergers** [to be added as needed]

Mermaids and mermen   398.21
  BT   Mythical animals
Mesmerism
  USE   Hypnotism
Messages
  USE   types of public officials and
        names of individual public of-
        ficials with the subdivision
        Messages, e.g. **Presidents—**
        United States—Messages [to
        be added as needed]
Messages to Congress
  USE   **Presidents—United States—**
        Messages
Messiness   648
  UF   Disorderliness
        Sloppiness
  BT   Human behavior
Metabolism   572
  BT   Biochemistry
  NT   Growth disorders
Metal finishing
  USE   Metals—Finishing
Metal work
  USE   Metalwork
Metallography   669
      Use for materials on the science of metal
  structures and alloys, especially the study of
  such structures with the microscope. Materials
  on the process of extracting metals from their
  ores, refining them, and preparing them for
  use, are entered under **Metallurgy.**
  UF   Metallurgical analysis
        Microscopic analysis
  BT   Metals
Metallurgical analysis
  USE   Metallography
Metallurgy (May subdiv. geog.)   669
      Use for materials on the process of extract-
  ing metals from their ores, refining them, and
  preparing them for use. Materials on the science of metal structures and alloys, especially
  the study of such structures with the micro-
  scope, are entered under **Metallography.**
  NT   Electrometallurgy
  RT   Alloys
        Chemical engineering
        Industrial chemistry
        Metals
        Ores
        Smelting
Metals   669
  SA   types of metals [to be added as
        needed]

  BT   Inorganic chemistry
        Ores
  NT   Alloys
        Aluminum
        Brass
        Iron
        Mercury
        Metallography
        Pewter
        Precious metals
        Soldering
        Tin
        Zinc
  RT   Metallurgy
        Metalwork
Metals—Finishing   671.7
  UF   Metal finishing
  BT   Finishes and finishing
        Metalwork
Metalwork (May subdiv. geog.)   671;
        739
  UF   Metal work
  BT   Decoration and ornament
  NT   Architectural metalwork
        Art metalwork
        Bronzes
        Copperwork
        Dies (Metalworking)
        Electroplating
        Forging
        Founding
        Goldwork
        Ironwork
        Metals—Finishing
        Plate metalwork
        Sheet metalwork
        Silverwork
        Soldering
        Steel
        Tinwork
        Welding
  RT   Metals
        Metalworking machinery
Metalworking machinery   621.9
  BT   Machinery
  RT   Metalwork
Metaphysics   110
  BT   Philosophy
  NT   Causation
        Change
        Existentialism

Metaphysics—*Continued*
    Space and time
    Theory of knowledge
  RT God
Meteorites 523.5
  BT Astronomy
    Meteors
Meteorological instruments 551.5028
  UF Instruments, Meteorological
  SA types of meteorological instruments [to be added as needed]
  BT **Scientific apparatus and instruments**
  NT **Barometers**
    Thermometers
Meteorological observatories 551.5028
  UF Meteorology—Observatories
    Observatories, Meteorological
    Weather stations
  RT **Meteorology**
Meteorological satellites 551.63
  UF Weather satellites
  SA names of satellites, e.g. **TIROS satellites** [to be added as needed]
  BT **Artificial satellites**
  NT **TIROS satellites**
Meteorology (May subdiv. geog.) 551.5
    Use for scientific materials on the atmosphere, especially weather factors. Materials on climate as it relates to humans and to plant and animal life, including the effects of changes of climate, are entered under **Climate**. Materials on the state of the atmosphere at a given time and place with respect to heat or cold, wetness or dryness, calm or storm, are entered under **Weather**.
  BT **Earth sciences**
  NT **Air**
    Auroras
    Clouds
    Cyclones
    Droughts
    Floods
    Fog
    Frost
    Humidity
    Lightning
    Meteorology in aeronautics
    Precipitation (Meteorology)
    Rainbow
    Seasons
    Solar radiation

    Storms
    Sunspots
    Thunderstorms
    Tornadoes
    Weather control
    Weather—Folklore
    Weather forecasting
    Winds
  RT **Atmosphere**
    Climate
    Meteorological observatories
    Weather
Meteorology in aeronautics 629.132
  BT **Aeronautics**
    Meteorology
Meteorology—Observatories
  USE **Meteorological observatories**
Meteorology—Tables 551.5
Meteors 523.5
  UF Falling stars
    Shooting stars
  BT **Astronomy**
    Solar system
  NT **Meteorites**
Meter
  USE **Musical meter and rhythm**
    Versification
Meters, Electric
  USE **Electric meters**
Meth (Drug)
  USE **Methamphetamine**
Methamphetamine 362.29; 615
  UF Meth (Drug)
    Speed (Drug)
  BT **Amphetamines**
  NT **Ice (Drug)**
Methodology
  USE subjects with the subdivision *Methodology,* e.g. **Science—Methodology** [to be added as needed]
Metric system 389; 530.8
  BT **Arithmetic**
    Mathematics
  RT **Decimal system**
    Weights and measures
Metrical romances
  USE **Romances**
Metrology
  USE **Measurement**
    Weights and measures

Metropolitan areas (May subdiv. geog.)
    307.76
    UF   Urban areas
    SA   names of metropolitan areas, e.g.
          Chicago Metropolitan Area
          (Ill.) [to be added as needed]
    BT   **Cities and towns—Growth**
    NT   **Suburbs**
          Urban renewal
Metropolitan finance   336
    Use for general materials on the public finance of metropolitan areas. Materials on the finance of a particular metropolitan area are entered under **Public finance** with the appropriate geographic subdivision.
    BT   **Municipal finance**
          Public finance
Metropolitan government   **320.8; 352.16**
    SA   names of metropolitan areas
          with the subdivision *Politics and government* [to be added as needed]
    BT   **Local government**
    NT   **Chicago Metropolitan Area (Ill.)—Politics and government**
    RT   **Municipal government**
Metropolitan planning
    USE **Regional planning**
Mexican American authors   **810.9; 920**
    SA   genres of American literature with the subdivision *Mexican American authors* [to be added as needed]
    BT   **Hispanic American authors**
Mexican American literature (English)
    USE **American literature—Mexican American authors**
Mexican American women (May subdiv. geog.)   **305.868**
    UF   Chicanas
    BT   **Mexican Americans**
          Women
Mexican Americans (May subdiv. geog.)
    305.868; 973
    Use for materials on American citizens of Mexican descent. Materials on noncitizens from Mexico are entered under **Mexicans—United States**. Use these same patterns for other ethnic groups in the U.S. and other countries.
    UF   Chicanos
    BT   **Ethnic groups**
          Hispanic Americans

          Immigrants—United States
          Minorities
    NT   **Mexican American women**
    RT   **Mexicans—United States**
Mexican Americans—Ethnic identity
    305.868
Mexican literature   860; M860
    May use same subdivisions and names of literary forms as for **English literature**.
    BT   **Latin American literature**
          Literature
Mexican War, 1846-1848   **973.6**
    UF   United States—History—1845-1848, War with Mexico
    BT   **United States—History—1815-1861**
Mexicans (May subdiv. geog.)   **305.868; 920; 972**
Mexicans—United States   **305.868**
    Use for materials on noncitizens from Mexico. Materials on American citizens of Mexican descent are entered under **Mexican Americans**. Use these same patterns for other ethnic groups in the U.S. and other countries.
    BT   **Aliens—United States**
          Minorities
    RT   **Mexican Americans**
Mexico—Presidents
    USE **Presidents—Mexico**
Mezzotint engraving   766
    BT   **Engraving**
MIAs
    USE **Missing in action**
Mice   599.35; 636.088
    UF   Mouse
    BT   **Mammals**
Microbes
    USE **Bacteria**
          Germ theory of disease
          Microorganisms
          Viruses
Microbial energy conversion
    USE **Biomass energy**
Microbiology   579
    SA   subjects with the subdivision *Microbiology* [to be added as needed]
    BT   **Biology**
    NT   **Air—Microbiology**
          Bacteriology
          Biotechnology
          Cheese—Microbiology
          Fermentation

Microbiology—*Continued*

        Food—Microbiology

        Soil microbiology

  RT   **Microorganisms**

Microbreweries (May subdiv. geog.)

    663

  UF   Boutique breweries

  BT   **Breweries**

Microchemistry   540

  BT   **Chemistry**

Microcomputers   004.16; 621.39

    Use for materials on small, usually desktop-sized computers that have a self-contained central processing unit.

  UF   Desktop computers

       Home computers

       PC computers

       PCs

       Personal computers

  SA   types of personal computers, e.g. **Macintosh (Computer)** [to be added as needed]

  BT   **Computers**

Microeconomics   338.5

  UF   Price theory

  BT   **Economics**

Microelectronics   621.381

  UF   Microminiature electronic equipment

       Microminiaturization (Electronics)

  BT   **Electronics**

       Semiconductors

Microfilming

  USE   **Microphotography**

Microfilms   302.23; 686.4

  BT   **Microforms**

Microforms   302.23; 686.4

  UF   Micropublications

  SA   types of microforms [to be added as needed]

  NT   **Microfilms**

  RT   **Microphotography**

Microminiature electronic equipment

  USE   **Microelectronics**

Microminiaturization (Electronics)

  USE   **Microelectronics**

Microorganisms   579

  UF   Germs

       Microbes

       Microscopic organisms

  NT   **Bacteria**

       Protozoa

       Viruses

  RT   **Microbiology**

Microphotography   686.4

    Use for materials on the photographing of objects of any size to produce minute images. Materials on the photographing of minute objects through a microscope are entered under **Photomicrography.**

  UF   Microfilming

  BT   **Photography**

  RT   **Microforms**

Microprocessors   004.16

    Use for materials on the silicon chip that contains the central processing units of a microcomputer or other electronic device.

  BT   **Computers**

Micropublications

  USE   **Microforms**

Microscope and microscopy

  USE   **Microscopes**

Microscopes   502.8

  UF   Microscope and microscopy

       Microscopic analysis

  BT   **Optical instruments**

  NT   **Electron microscopes**

  RT   **Photomicrography**

Microscopic analysis

  USE   **Metallography**

        Microscopes

Microscopic organisms

  USE   **Microorganisms**

Microsoft Word (Computer software)

    005.5

  UF   Word (Computer software)

  BT   **Computer software**

Microwave communication systems

    621.381

  BT   **Intercommunication systems**

       Shortwave radio

       Telecommunication

  NT   **Closed-circuit television**

Microwave cookery

  USE   **Microwave cooking**

Microwave cooking   641.5

  UF   Microwave cookery

  BT   **Cooking**

Microwaves   537.5

  BT   **Electric waves**

       Electromagnetic waves

       Shortwave radio

  NT   **Masers**

Mid-career changes
USE **Career changes**
Mid-life crisis
USE **Midlife crisis**
Middle age   305.24
BT **Age**
Life (Biology)
NT **Aging**
Midlife crisis
RT **Longevity**
Middle aged persons
Middle aged men (May subdiv. geog.)
305.244
BT **Middle aged persons**
Middle aged persons (May subdiv. geog.)
305.24
BT **Age**
NT **Middle aged men**
Middle aged women
RT **Middle age**
Middle aged women (May subdiv. geog.)
305.244
BT **Middle aged persons**
Middle Ages   909.07
Use for materials on the history of the me-
dieval world not limited to a single country or
region.
UF Dark Ages
Middle Ages—History
BT **World history**
NT **Church history—600-1500,**
Middle Ages
Knights and knighthood
World history—12th century
World history—13th century
World history—14th century
World history—15th century
RT **Europe—History—476-1492**
Medieval civilization
Middle Ages—History
USE **Middle Ages**
Middle Atlantic States
USE **Atlantic States**
Middle child
USE **Birth order**
Middle class (May subdiv. geog.)   **305.5**
UF Bourgeoisie
BT **Social classes**
Middle East   956
Use for materials on the region consisting
of northeastern Africa and Asia west of Af-
ghanistan. Materials on several Arabic-
speaking countries are entered under **Arab
countries.**
UF Levant
Near East
Orient
BT **Asia**
NT **Arab countries**
Israel
Middle East—Strategic aspects   956
BT **Military geography**
Strategy
Middle East War, 1991
USE **Persian Gulf War, 1991**
Middle English language
USE **English language—Middle En-**
glish period
Middle English literature
USE **English literature—Middle En-**
glish period
Middle schools (May subdiv. geog.)
373.236
UF Intermediate schools
BT **Schools**
RT **Elementary schools**
Junior high schools
Middle West   977
UF Central States
Midwest
North Central States
BT **Mississippi River Valley**
United States
RT **Old Northwest**
Midget cars
USE **Karts and karting**
Midlife crisis   305.244
UF Mid-life crisis
BT **Middle age**
Midwest
USE **Middle West**
Midwifery
USE **Midwives**
Midwives (May subdiv. geog.)   **618.2**
UF Birth attendants
Midwifery
Nurse midwives
BT **Childbirth**
Natural childbirth
Nurses
Migraine   616.8
BT **Headache**

Migrant labor (May subdiv. geog.)
   331.5; 362.85
   Use for materials on casual or seasonal workers who move from place to place in search of employment. Materials on the movement of population within a country for permanent settlement are entered under **Internal migration.**
   UF   Migratory workers
   BT   **Employees**
          Labor
   RT   **Agricultural laborers**
          Alien labor
          Internal migration
Migration
   USE   **Animals—Migration**
            Immigration and emigration
            and types of animals with the subdivision *Migration,* e.g.
            Birds—Migration [to be added as needed]
Migration, Internal
   USE   **Internal migration**
Migration of birds
   USE   **Birds—Migration**
Migratory workers
   USE   **Migrant labor**
Military aeronautics (May subdiv. geog.)
   358.4
   UF   Aeronautics, Military
          Air warfare
          Naval aeronautics
   SA   names of wars with the subdivision *Aerial operations,* e.g.
          World War, 1939-1945—Aerial operations [to be added as needed]
   BT   **Aeronautics**
          Military art and science
          War
   NT   **Aerial reconnaissance**
          Air bases
          Air defenses
          Air power
          Aircraft carriers
          Military airplanes
          Parachute troops
          World War, 1939-1945—Aerial operations
Military aid
   USE   **Military assistance**
Military air bases
   USE   **Air bases**

Military airplanes (May subdiv. geog.)
   623.74
   UF   Air warfare
          Airplanes, Military
          Naval airplanes
   SA   types of military airplanes [to be added as needed]
   BT   **Airplanes**
          Military aeronautics
   NT   **Bombers**
Military art and science (May subdiv. geog.)   **355**
   UF   Army
          Fighting
          Military power
          Military science
   NT   **Armed forces**
          Armor
          Artillery
          Battles
          Biological warfare
          Camouflage (Military science)
          Chemical warfare
          Civil defense
          Fortification
          Friendly fire (Military science)
          Guerrilla warfare
          Industrial mobilization
          Military aeronautics
          Military camps
          Military transportation
          Ordnance
          Psychological warfare
          Signals and signaling
          Strategy
          Tactics
          Veterans
   RT   **Armies**
          Drill and minor tactics
          Military personnel
          Naval art and science
          War
          Weapons
Military art and science—Study and teaching
   USE   **Military education**
Military assistance   355
   UF   Arms sales
          Foreign aid program
          Military aid
          Military sales

Military assistance—*Continued*

 Mutual defense assistance program

 SA military assistance from particular countries, e.g. **American military assistance** [to be added as needed]

 BT **Military policy**

 NT **American military assistance**

 RT **Arms transfers**

Military assistance, American

 USE **American military assistance**

Military atrocities

 USE **Atrocities**

 War crimes

Military bases (May subdiv. geog.) 355.7

 UF Army bases

 Army posts

 Military facilities

 Military installations

 Military posts

Military biography

 USE names of armies and navies with the subdivision *Biography,* e.g. **United States. Army—Biography; United States. Navy—Biography;** etc. [to be added as needed]

Military camps 355.7

 UF Camps (Military)

 BT **Military art and science**

 NT **Concentration camps**

Military conscription

 USE **Draft**

Military courts

 USE **Courts martial and courts of inquiry**

Military crimes

 USE **Military offenses**

Military desertion (May subdiv. geog.) 343; 355.1

 UF Army desertion

 Desertion

 Desertion, Military

 SA names of wars with the subdivision *Desertions* [to be added as needed]

 BT **Military offenses**

 NT **World War, 1939-1945—Desertions**

 RT **Draft resisters**

Military desertion—United States 343

 UF United States. Army—Desertions

Military draft

 USE **Draft**

Military drill

 USE **Drill and minor tactics**

Military education (May subdiv. geog.) 355.007; 355.5

 UF Army schools

 Military art and science—Study and teaching

 Military schools

 Military training

 Schools, Military

 SA names of military schools, e.g. **United States Military Academy** [to be added as needed]

 BT **Education**

 NT **Military training camps**

Military engineering (May subdiv. geog.) 623

 SA names of wars with the subdivision *Engineering and construction* [to be added as needed]

 BT **Civil engineering**

 Engineering

 NT **World War, 1939-1945—Engineering and construction**

 RT **Fortification**

Military facilities

 USE **Military bases**

Military forces

 USE **Armed forces**

Military geography 355.4

 UF Maps, Military

 Military maps

 SA areas of the world with the subdivision *Strategic aspects* [to be added as needed]

 BT **Geography**

 NT **Middle East—Strategic aspects**

Military government 341.6; 355.4

 Use for general materials on governments under military regimes, not limited to a single country.

 UF Government, Military

 SA names of countries with the subdivision *Politics and government,* or *History,* with appropriate dates as needed, for

473

Military government—*Continued*

materials on governments of particular countries under military rule; and names of countries occupied by foreign military governments with the appropriate subdivision under *History,* e.g., **Netherlands—History—1940-1945, German occupation; Japan—History—1945-1952, Allied Occupation;** etc. [to be added as needed]

- BT **Public administration**
- RT **Military occupation**

Military health
- USE **Military personnel—Health and hygiene**

Military history   355.009
- UF History, Military
  Wars
- SA names of countries with the subhead *Army* or the subdivision *Military history,* e.g. **United States. Army; United States—Military history;** and names of wars, battles, sieges, etc. [to be added as needed]
- BT **History**
- NT **Battles**
  Military policy
  United States. Army
  United States—Military history
- RT **Naval history**

Military hospitals (May subdiv. geog.) **355.7**
- UF Field hospitals
  Veterans—Hospitals
- SA names of wars with the subdivision *Medical care,* e.g. **World War, 1939-1945—Medical care** [to be added as needed]
- BT **Hospitals**
  Military medicine
- RT **Veterans**

Military installations
- USE **Military bases**

Military intelligence (May subdiv. geog.) **355.3**
- SA names of wars with the subdivision *Military intelligence,* e.g. **World War, 1939-1945—**

Military intelligence [to be added as needed]
- BT **Intelligence service**
- NT **World War, 1939-1945—Military intelligence**

Military intervention
- USE **Intervention (International law)**

Military law (May subdiv. geog.)   **343**
- UF Articles of war
  War, Articles of
- BT **International law**
  Law
- NT **Draft**
  Military offenses
  Veterans—Legal status, laws, etc.
- RT **Courts martial and courts of inquiry**
  Martial law
  War

Military life
- USE **Military personnel**
  and names of countries with the subdivision *Armed forces* or the subheads *Army* or *Navy;* etc., with the subdivision *Military life,* e.g. **United States—Armed forces—Military life; United States. Army—Military life;** etc. [to be added as needed]

Military maps
- USE **Military geography**

Military medicine   616.9
- UF Field hospitals
  Medicine, Military
- SA names of wars with the subdivision *Medical care,* e.g. **World War, 1939-1945—Medical care** [to be added as needed]
- BT **Medicine**
- NT **Armies—Medical care**
  Military hospitals
- RT **Military personnel—Health and hygiene**

Military music   781.5
- SA names of wars with the subdivision *Songs* [to be added as needed]

Military music—*Continued*
- BT **Music**
- NT **Band music**
  Marches (Music)
  World War, 1939-1945—Songs

Military occupation 341.6; 355.4
- UF Occupation, Military
  Occupied territory
- SA names of occupied countries
  with the appropriate subdivision under *History*, e.g.,
  Netherlands—History—1940-1945, German occupation;
  Japan—History—1945-1952, Allied occupation; etc. [to be added as needed]
- BT **War**
- NT **World War, 1939-1945—Occupied territories**
- RT **Military government**

Military offenses (May subdiv. geog.)
  343; 355.1
- UF Crimes, Military
  Military crimes
  Naval offenses
  Offenses, Military
- SA types of military offenses, e.g.
  Military desertion [to be added as needed]
- BT **Criminal law**
  Military law
- NT **Military desertion**

Military offenses—United States 343;
  355.1
- UF United States. Army—Crimes and misdemeanors
  United States—Military offenses

Military pensions (May subdiv. geog.)
  331.25
- UF Naval pensions
  Pensions, Naval
  War pensions
- BT **Pensions**
- RT **Veterans**

Military personnel (May subdiv. geog.)
  355.3
- UF Military life
  Servicemen
  Servicewomen
- SA names of countries with the subdivision *Armed forces* or the subheads *Army* or *Navy*, etc.,
  with the subdivision *Military life* or *Officers*, e.g. **United States—Armed forces—Military life; United States. Army—Officers;** etc. [to be added as needed]
- BT **Armed forces**
  War
- NT **Admirals**
  Armies
  Gays and lesbians in the military
  Generals
  Mercenary soldiers
  Navies
  Recruiting and enlistment
  Sailors
  Soldiers
  United States—Armed forces—Military life
  United States. Army—Military life
  United States. Army—Officers
  United States. Navy—Officers
- RT **Military art and science**
  Veterans

Military personnel—Health and hygiene
  613.6
- UF Hygiene, Military
  Military health
  Soldiers—Hygiene
- SA names of wars with the subdivision *Health aspects* or *Medical care*, e.g. **World War, 1939-1945—Health aspects; World War, 1939-1945—Medical care;** etc. [to be added as needed]
- BT **Hygiene**
- RT **Armies—Medical care**
  Military medicine

Military personnel missing in action
- USE **Missing in action**

Military personnel—United States
  355.30973
- UF United States—Military personnel

Military policy (May subdiv. geog.) 355
- UF Defense policy
  Government policy

Military policy—*Continued*
  BT **Military history**
  NT **Military assistance**
      Military readiness
  RT **National security**
Military policy—United States 355
  UF United States—Military policy
  NT **Strategic Defense Initiative**
Military posts
  USE **Military bases**
Military power
  USE **Armies**
       Military art and science
       Navies
       Sea power
Military preparedness
  USE **Military readiness**
Military readiness 355
    Use for materials on military strength,
  including military personnel, munitions, natu-
  ral resources, and industrial war potential. Ma-
  terials on the implements of war are entered
  under **Ordnance** or **Military weapons.** Mate-
  rials on the industries producing them are en-
  tered under **Defense industry.**
  UF Armaments
      Defense readiness
      Military preparedness
      National defenses
  SA names of countries with the sub-
      division *Defenses,* e.g. **United
      States—Defenses** [to be add-
      ed as needed]
  BT **Military policy**
  NT **United States—Defenses**
  RT **Armed forces**
      Arms control
      Arms race
      Defense industry
      Industrial mobilization
      Manpower
Military research (May subdiv. geog.)
    355
  UF Defense research
  BT **Research**
Military sales
  USE **Arms transfers**
       Defense industry
       Military assistance
Military schools
  USE **Military education**
Military science
  USE **Military art and science**

Military service, Compulsory
  USE **Draft**
Military service, Voluntary
  USE **Voluntary military service**
Military signaling
  USE **Signals and signaling**
Military strategy
  USE **Strategy**
Military supplies industry
  USE **Defense industry**
Military tactics
  USE **Tactics**
Military tanks 358; 623.7
  UF Armored cars (Tanks)
      Tanks (Military science)
  BT **Military vehicles**
  RT **Tank warfare**
Military training
  USE **Military education**
Military training camps (May subdiv.
    geog.) 355.7
  UF Students' military training camps
      Training camps, Military
  BT **Military education**
Military training, Universal
  USE **Draft**
Military transportation 358
  UF Transportation, Military
  SA names of wars with the subdivi-
      sion *Transportation,* e.g.
      **World War, 1939-1945—
      Transportation** [to be added
      as needed]
  BT **Military art and science**
      Transportation
  NT **Military vehicles**
Military uniforms 355.1
  UF Naval uniforms
      Uniforms, Military
      Uniforms, Naval
  SA names of military services with
      the subdivision *Uniforms,* e.g.
      **United States. Army—Uni-
      forms** [to be added as need-
      ed]
  BT **Uniforms**
Military vehicles 355.8
  UF Army vehicles
      Vehicles, Military
  BT **Military transportation**
      Vehicles

Military vehicles—*Continued*
  NT **Military tanks**
Military weapons (May subdiv. geog.)
      355.8; 623.4
  UF Armaments
      Arms sales
      Munitions
  SA names of wars with the subdivision *Equipment and supplies* [to be added as needed]
  BT **Ordnance**
      Weapons
  NT **Nuclear weapons**
      Space weapons
      World War, 1939-1945— Equipment and supplies
  RT **Arms race**
      Defense industry
Militia
  USE names of countries and states with the subdivision *Militia,* e.g. **United States—Militia** [to be added as needed]
Militia movements (May subdiv. geog.)
      303.48
      Use for materials on anti-government paramilitary social movements.
  UF Militias
      Paramilitary militia movements
  BT **Radicalism**
      Social movements
Militias
  USE **Militia movements**
Milk   637; 641.3
  BT **Dairy products**
      Dairying
      Food
  NT **Dried milk**
Milk—Analysis   637; 641.3
Milk supply   338.1
  BT **Food adulteration and inspection**
      Public health
Mill and factory buildings
  USE **Factories**
Millenarianism
  USE **Millennium**
Millennialism
  USE **Millennium**
Millennium   236
  UF Millenarianism
      Millennialism

  BT **Eschatology**
  RT **Second Advent**
Millikan rays
  USE **Cosmic rays**
Millinery
  USE **Hats**
Milling (Flour)
  USE **Flour mills**
Millionaires (May subdiv. geog.)   **920**
  BT **Rich**
Mills (May subdiv. geog.)   **670.42**
  UF Mills and millwork
  SA types of mills [to be added as needed]
  BT **Manufactures**
      Technology
  NT **Flour mills**
  RT **Factories**
      Machinery
Mills and millwork
  USE **Mills**
Mime   792.3
  BT **Acting**
  RT **Pantomimes**
Mind
  USE **Intellect**
      Psychology
Mind and body   128; 150
  UF Body and mind
  BT **Brain**
      Medicine
      Parapsychology
      Philosophy
  NT **Abnormal psychology**
      Biofeedback training
      Body image
      Consciousness
      Mental suggestion
      Psychosomatic medicine
      Sleep
      Temperament
  RT **Holistic medicine**
      Human body
      Hypnotism
      Mental healing
      Mental health
      Phrenology
      Psychoanalysis
      Psychophysiology
      Spiritual healing
      Subconsciousness

Mind control
USE **Brainwashing**
Mind cure
USE **Mental healing**
Mind reading
USE **Telepathy**
Mine surveying 622.028
BT **Mining engineering**
Prospecting
Surveying
Mineral lands
USE **Mines and mineral resources**
Mineral resources
USE **Mines and mineral resources**
Mineral resources, Marine
USE **Marine mineral resources**
Mineralogy
USE **Minerals**
Natural history
Minerals (May subdiv. geog.) **549**
Use for materials on the chemical and geo-
logical aspects of natural compounds extracted
from the earth. Materials on mines and mining
and the potential economic value of minerals
are entered under **Mines and mineral re-
sources.**
UF Mineralogy
SA names of minerals, e.g. **Quartz**
[to be added as needed]
BT **Geology**
NT **Asbestos**
Gems
Gypsum
Lime
Ores
Precious stones
Quartz
RT **Crystals**
Mines and mineral resources
Natural history
Petrology
Miners (May subdiv. geog.) **622.092;
920**
SA types of miners [to be added as
needed]
BT **Labor**
NT **Coal miners**
Miners—Diseases 616.9
UF Miners' diseases
BT **Occupational diseases**
Miners' diseases
USE **Miners—Diseases**

Mines and mineral resources (May
subdiv. geog.) **333.8; 338.2**
Use for materials on mines and mining and
the potential economic value of minerals. Ma-
terials on the chemical or geological aspects
of natural compounds extracted from the earth
are entered under **Minerals.**
UF Mineral lands
Mineral resources
Mining
SA types of mines and mining, e.g.
Coal mines and mining [to
be added as needed]
BT **Economic geology**
Natural resources
Raw materials
NT **Coal mines and mining**
Gold mines and mining
Marine mineral resources
Mining engineering
Precious metals
Prospecting
Silver mines and mining
RT **Minerals**
**Mines and mineral resources—United
States** 333.8; 338.2
Miniature gardens 635.9
UF Gardens, Miniature
Tray gardens
BT **Gardens**
Miniature objects
RT **Container gardening**
Indoor gardening
Terrariums
Miniature objects 688; 745.592
UF Miniatures
Tiny objects
SA types of objects with the subdi-
vision *Models* [to be added as
needed]
BT **Art objects**
NT **Doll furniture**
Dollhouses
Miniature gardens
Miniature painting
Models and modelmaking
RT **Toys**
Miniature painting 751.7; 757
UF Miniatures (Portraits)
Portrait miniatures
BT **Miniature objects**
Painting
RT **Portrait painting**

Miniatures
  USE **Miniature objects**
Miniatures (Illumination of books and
    manuscripts)
  USE **Illumination of books and
        manuscripts**
Miniatures (Portraits)
  USE **Miniature painting**
Minibikes 629.227
  BT **Bicycles
       Motorcycles**
Minimum drinking age
  USE **Drinking age**
Minimum wage (May subdiv. geog.)
      331.2
  BT **Salaries, wages, etc.**
Mining
  USE **Mines and mineral resources
        Mining engineering**
Mining, Electric
  USE **Electricity in mining**
Mining engineering (May subdiv. geog.)
      622
  UF Mining
  BT **Civil engineering
       Coal mines and mining
       Engineering
       Mines and mineral resources**
  NT **Drilling and boring (Earth and
       rocks)
       Mine surveying
       Ocean mining**
  RT **Electricity in mining**
Mining, Ocean
  USE **Ocean mining**
Ministers (Diplomatic agents)
  USE **Diplomats**
Ministers of state
  USE **Cabinet officers**
Ministers of the gospel
  USE **Clergy**
Ministry 206; 253
  UF Clergy—Office
  SA ministries of particular religions,
       e.g. **Christian ministry** [to be
       added as needed]
  BT **Church work
       Pastoral theology**
  NT **Christian ministry**
  RT **Clergy**

Minor arts
  USE **Decorative arts**
Minor planets
  USE **Asteroids**
Minor tactics
  USE **Drill and minor tactics**
Minorites
  USE **Franciscans**
Minorities (May subdiv. geog.)   **305.8;
        323.1**
  UF Foreign population
       Minority groups
  SA names of particular ethnic and
       racial minorities and of na-
       tional groups in a foreign
       country, e.g. **African Ameri-
       cans; Mexican Americans;
       Mexicans—United States;**
       etc.; names of places with the
       subdivision *Race relations,*
       e.g. **United States—Race re-
       lations;** names of places with
       the subdivision *Ethnic rela-
       tions,* e.g. **United States—
       Ethnic relations;** and head-
       ings for minorities in various
       industries and fields of en-
       deavor, e.g., **Minorities in
       broadcasting** [to be added as
       needed]
  NT **Aliens
       Immigrants
       Mexican Americans
       Mexicans—United States
       Minorities in broadcasting
       Minorities in television broad-
       casting
       Minorities on television
       Minority business enterprises
       Minority women
       Minority youth**
  RT **Discrimination
       Ethnic relations
       Race relations
       Segregation**
Minorities in broadcasting 384.5; 791.4
  Use for materials on minority involvement
  in the broadcasting industry.
  UF Minority groups in broadcasting
  SA names of particular minority
       groups in broadcasting or in
       particular broadcast media,

479

Minorities in broadcasting—*Continued*
e.g. **African Americans in television broadcasting** [to be added as needed]
- BT **Broadcasting**
  Minorities
- NT **Minorities in television broadcasting**

Minorities in engineering   620
- UF Minority groups in engineering
- BT **Engineering**

Minorities in television
- USE **Minorities on television**

Minorities in television broadcasting 791.45

Use for materials on all aspects of minority involvement in television. Materials on the portrayal of minorities in television programs are entered under **Minorities on television.**
- UF Minorities in the television industry
- SA names of particular minority groups in television broadcasting, e.g. **African Americans in television broadcasting** [to be added as needed]
- BT **Minorities**
  Minorities in broadcasting
  Television broadcasting

Minorities in the television industry
- USE **Minorities in television broadcasting**

Minorities on television   791.45

Use for materials on the portrayal of minorities in television programs. Materials on all aspects of minority involvement in television are entered under **Minorities in television broadcasting.**
- UF Minorities in television
- SA names of particular minority groups in television, e.g. **African Americans on television** [to be added as needed]
- BT **Minorities**
  Television

Minority business enterprises   338.6
- UF Minority businesses
  Minority-owned business enterprises
- BT **Business enterprises**
  Minorities

Minority business enterprises—Federal aid
- USE **Federal aid to minority business enterprises**

Minority businesses
- USE **Minority business enterprises**

Minority groups
- USE **Minorities**

Minority groups in broadcasting
- USE **Minorities in broadcasting**

Minority groups in engineering
- USE **Minorities in engineering**

Minority-owned business enterprises
- USE **Minority business enterprises**

Minority women   305.48
- BT **Minorities**
  Women

Minority youth   305.235
- BT **Minorities**
  Youth

Minstrels   791.092; 920
- BT **Poets**
- NT **Troubadours**

Mints   332.4
- BT **Money**
- RT **Coinage**

Miracle plays
- USE **Mysteries and miracle plays**

Miracles   202; 212; 231.7

Use for materials on miracles in any or all religious traditions.
- RT **Spiritual healing**
  Supernatural

Mirrors   748.8
- UF Looking glasses
- BT **Furniture**

Miscarriage   618.3
- UF Fetal death
- BT **Pregnancy**

Miscellanea
- USE **Books of lists**
  Curiosities and wonders
  and subjects with the subdivision *Miscellanea,* e.g. **Medicine—Miscellanea** [to be added as needed]

Miscellaneous facts
- USE **Books of lists**
  Curiosities and wonders

Misconduct in office (May subdiv. geog.) **353.4**
- UF Malfeasance in office
  Official misconduct
- SA names of specific incidents and offenses [to be added as needed]

Misconduct in office—*Continued*
- BT **Conflict of interests**
  Criminal law
- NT **Police corruption**
- RT **Political corruption**

Misdemeanors (Law)
- USE **Criminal law**

Misleading advertising
- USE **Deceptive advertising**

Misrepresentation in advertising
- USE **Deceptive advertising**

Missiles, Ballistic
- USE **Ballistic missiles**

Missiles, Guided
- USE **Guided missiles**

Missing children (May subdiv. geog.)
362.82; 363.2
- UF Lost children
- BT **Children**
  Missing persons
- NT **Runaway children**

Missing in action   **341.6; 355.7**
- UF MIAs
  Military personnel missing in action
- SA names of wars with the subdivision *Missing in action* [to be added as needed]
- BT **Prisoners of war**
  Soldiers
- NT **World War, 1939-1945—Missing in action**

Missing persons (May subdiv. geog.)
363.2
- BT **Criminal investigation**
- NT **Missing children**
  Runaway adults
  Runaway teenagers

Missionaries, Christian
- USE **Christian missionaries**

Missions
- USE names of Christian churches, denominations, religious orders, etc., with the subdivision *Missions,* e.g. **Catholic Church—Missions;** and names of peoples evangelized with the subdivision *Christian missions,* e.g. **Native Americans—Christian missions** [to be added as needed]

Missions, Christian
- USE **Christian missions**

Missions, Medical
- USE **Medical missions**

Mississippi River Valley   **977**
- UF Mississippi Valley
- BT **United States**
- NT **Middle West**

Mississippi River Valley—History   **977**
- UF New France—History

Mississippi Valley
- USE **Mississippi River Valley**

Mistakes
- USE **Errors**

Mixed marriage
- USE **Interfaith marriage**
  Intermarriage

Mixed race people
- USE **Racially mixed people**

Mixology
- USE **Bartending**

Mnemonics   **153.1**
- SA subjects, types of literature, and titles of sacred works with the subdivision *Memorizing,* e.g. **Poetry—Memorizing** [to be added as needed]
- NT **Poetry—Memorizing**
- RT **Memory**

Mobile home living   **643; 728.7**
- BT **Home economics**
  Mobile homes
- NT **Trailer parks**

Mobile home parks
- USE **Trailer parks**

Mobile homes   **643; 728.7**

Use for materials on stationary transportable structures designed for year-round living. Materials on structures mounted upon a truck or towed by a truck or automobile for the purpose of temporary dwelling or cargo hauling are entered under **Travel trailers and campers.**

- UF House trailers
  Trailers
- BT **Housing**
- NT **Mobile home living**
- RT **Travel trailers and campers**

Mobiles (Sculpture)   **731**
- BT **Kinetic sculpture**
  Sculpture

Mobilization, Industrial
- USE **Industrial mobilization**

Mobs
  USE Crowds
       Riots
Mock epic literature
  USE Mock-heroic literature
Mock-heroic literature   800
  May be used for individual works, collections, or materials about mock-heroic literature.
  UF Comic epic literature
      Mock epic literature
  BT **Literature**
      Wit and humor
  RT **Epic literature**
      Humorous fiction
Model airplanes
  USE **Airplanes—Models**
Model cars
  USE **Automobiles—Models**
Model making
  USE **Models and modelmaking**
Model ships
  USE **Ships—Models**
Model trains
  USE **Locomotives—Models**
       Railroads—Models
Modeling   731.4; 738.1
  UF Clay modeling
  BT **Clay**
      Sculpture
  NT **Soap sculpture**
  RT **Sculpture—Technique**
Modelmaking
  USE **Models and modelmaking**
Models
  USE **Artists' models**
       Fashion models
       Mathematical models
       Models and modelmaking
       and types of objects with the subdivision *Models,* e.g. **Airplanes—Models** [to be added as needed]
Models and model making
  USE **Models and modelmaking**
Models and modelmaking   688
  UF Model making
      Modelmaking
      Models
      Models and model making

SA types of objects with the subdivision *Models,* e.g. **Airplanes—Models** [to be added as needed]
  BT **Handicraft**
      Miniature objects
  NT **Airplanes—Models**
      Automobiles—Models
      Locomotives—Models
      Machinery—Models
      Motorboats—Models
      Patternmaking
      Railroads—Models
      Ships—Models
Models, Artists'
  USE **Artists' models**
Models, Mathematical
  USE **Mathematical models**
Models, Mechanical
  USE **Machinery—Models**
Models (Persons)
  USE **Artists' models**
       Fashion models
Modern architecture
  USE **Modernism in architecture**
Modern architecture—1600-1799 (17th and 18th centuries)
  USE **Architecture—17th and 18th centuries**
Modern architecture—1800-1899 (19th century)
  USE **Architecture—19th century**
Modern architecture—1900-1999 (20th century)
  USE **Architecture—20th century**
Modern architecture—2000-2099 (21st century)
  USE **Architecture—21st century**
Modern art
  USE **Modernism in art**
Modern art—1800-1899 (19th century)
  USE **Art—19th century**
Modern art—1900-1999 (20th century)
  USE **Art—20th century**
Modern art—2000-2099 (21st century)
  USE **Art—21st century**
Modern church history
  USE **Church history—1500-, Modern period**

Modern civilization   306.09; 909

Use for materials on cultural and intellectual developments since 1453 not limited to a single country or region.

UF   Civilization, Modern

BT   **Civilization**

NT   **Enlightenment**

Modern civilization—1950-   306.09; 909.82

Use for materials on cultural and intellectual developments since 1950 not limited to a single country or region.

Modern dance   792.8

UF   Interpretive dance

BT   **Dance**

Modern Greek language   489

May be subdivided like **English language.**

UF   Greek language, Modern

Romaic language

BT   **Language and languages**

RT   **Greek language**

Modern Greek literature   889

May use same subdivisions and names of literary forms as for **English literature.**

UF   Greek literature, Modern

Neo-Greek literature

Romaic literature

BT   **Literature**

Modern history   909.08

Use for materials covering the period after 1453.

UF   History, Modern

BT   **World history**

Modern history—1800-1899 (19th century)

USE   **World history—19th century**

Modern history—1900-1999 (20th century)

USE   **World history—20th century**

Modern history—1945-

USE   **World history—1945-**

Modern history—Study and teaching   907

NT   **Current events**

Modern languages   410

Use for materials dealing collectively with living literary languages. May be subdivided like **English language.**

UF   Languages, Modern

BT   **Language and languages**

Modern languages—Conversation and phrase books   418

Use for instructional materials or for books of convenient conversations and phrases for travelers.

UF   Conversation and phrase books

Conversation in foreign languages

Conversations and phrases

Foreign language phrases

SA   names of languages with the subdivision *Conversation and phrase books,* e.g. **French language—Conversation and phrase books** [to be added as needed]

Modern languages—Study and teaching   418

RT   **Language laboratories**

Modern literature

USE   **Literature**

Modernism in literature

Modern painting—1800-1899 (19th century)

USE   **Painting—19th century**

Modern painting—1900-1999 (20th century)

USE   **Painting—20th century**

Modern painting—2000-2099 (21st century)

USE   **Painting—21st century**

Modern philosophy   190

Use for materials on developments in Western philosophy since the Middle Ages.

UF   Philosophy, Modern

BT   **Philosophy**

NT   **Enlightenment**

Existentialism

Phenomenology

Modern sculpture

USE   **Modernism in sculpture**

Modern sculpture—1900-1999 (20th century)

USE   **Sculpture—20th century**

Modernism

USE   **Modernism (Aesthetics)**

Modernism (Theology)

Modernism (Aesthetics)   700.1

Use for materials on the philosophy and practice of the arts since the nineteenth century characterized by a self-conscious break with the past and a search for new forms of expression.

UF   Modernism

Modernism (Arts)

BT   **Aesthetics**

NT   **Modernism in architecture**

Modernism in art

Modernism in literature

Modernism (Aesthetics)—*Continued*
>   **Modernism in sculpture**
>   RT   **Postmodernism**

Modernism (Art)
>   USE   **Modernism in art**

Modernism (Arts)
>   USE   **Modernism (Aesthetics)**

Modernism in architecture   724
>   Use for materials on the theory and practice of modernism in the architecture.
>   UF   Architecture, Modern
>   Modern architecture
>   BT   **Architecture**
>   **Modernism (Aesthetics)**

Modernism in art   709.04
>   Use for materials on the theory and practice of modernism in the visual arts.
>   UF   Modern art
>   Modernism (Art)
>   BT   **Art**
>   **Modernism (Aesthetics)**

Modernism in literature   801
>   UF   Modern literature
>   Modernism (Literature)
>   BT   **Literature**
>   **Modernism (Aesthetics)**

Modernism in sculpture   735
>   UF   Modern sculpture
>   Modernism (Sculpture)
>   Sculpture, Modern
>   BT   **Modernism (Aesthetics)**
>   **Sculpture**

Modernism (Literature)
>   USE   **Modernism in literature**

Modernism (Sculpture)
>   USE   **Modernism in sculpture**

Modernism (Theology)   230; 273
>   Use for materials on the movement in the Christian churches that applies modern critical methods to biblical study and the history of dogma, and emphasizes the spiritual and ethical side of religion over historic dogmas and creeds.
>   UF   Modernism
>   Modernist-fundamentalist contro-
>   versy
>   BT   **Christianity—Doctrines**
>   RT   **Christian fundamentalism**

Modernist-fundamentalist controversy
>   USE   **Christian fundamentalism**
>   **Modernism (Theology)**

Modernization
>   USE   **Modernization (Sociology)**

Modernization (Sociology) (May subdiv. geog.)   **303.44**
>   Use for materials on the process by which traditional societies achieve the political, cultural, economic, and social characteristics of modernity.
>   UF   Development
>   Modernization
>   BT   **Social change**
>   RT   **Industrialization**

Mohammedan art
>   USE   **Islamic art**

Mold (Fungi)
>   USE   **Molds (Fungi)**

Molding (Metal)
>   USE   **Founding**

Molds (Botany)
>   USE   **Molds (Fungi)**

Molds (Fungi)   579.5
>   UF   Mold (Fungi)
>   Molds (Botany)
>   BT   **Fungi**

Molecular biochemistry
>   USE   **Molecular biology**

Molecular biology   591.6
>   UF   Biology, Molecular
>   Molecular biochemistry
>   Molecular biophysics
>   BT   **Biochemistry**
>   **Biophysics**
>   NT   **Genetic code**

Molecular biophysics
>   USE   **Molecular biology**

Molecular cloning   572.8
>   UF   DNA cloning
>   BT   **Cloning**
>   **Genetic engineering**

Molecular technology
>   USE   **Nanotechnology**

Molecules   539; 541.2
>   BT   **Physical chemistry**

Molesting of children
>   USE   **Child sexual abuse**

Mollusks   594
>   Use for materials on mollusks and for systematic and comprehensive materials on shells. Popular materials on shells and shell collecting are entered under **Shells.**
>   BT   **Shellfish**
>   RT   **Shells**

Monarchs
>   USE   **Kings and rulers**

Monarchy (May subdiv. geog.) **321; 321.8**
>UF Royal houses
>>Royalty
>>Sovereigns
>
>BT **Constitutional history**
>>**Constitutional law**
>>**Executive power**
>>**Political science**
>
>NT **Empresses**
>>**Queens**
>
>RT **Kings and rulers**

Monasteries (May subdiv. geog.) **255; 271; 726**
>UF Cloisters
>
>BT **Church architecture**
>>**Church history**
>
>NT **Abbeys**
>>**Convents**
>
>RT **Monasticism and religious orders**

Monastic orders
>USE **Monasticism and religious orders**

Monasticism
>USE **Monasticism and religious orders**

Monasticism and religious orders (May subdiv. geog.) **255; 271**

Use for materials on the institution of monasticism and for general materials on religious orders not limited to orders for a single sex. This heading may be subdivided by religion or denomination as needed.
>UF Monastic orders
>>Monasticism
>>Orders, Monastic
>>Religious orders
>
>SA names of monastic and religious orders, e.g. **Franciscans** [to be added as needed]
>
>NT **Franciscans**
>>**Monasticism and religious orders for men**
>>**Monasticism and religious orders for women**
>
>RT **Hermits**
>>**Religious life**

Monasticism and religious orders for men 255; 271

This heading may be subdivided by religion or denomination as needed.

>UF Religious orders for men
>
>BT **Monasticism and religious orders**
>
>RT **Monks**

Monasticism and religious orders for women 255; 271

This heading may be subdivided by religion or denomination as needed.
>UF Religious orders for women
>>Sisterhoods
>
>BT **Convents**
>>**Monasticism and religious orders**
>
>RT **Nuns**

Monetary policy (May subdiv. geog.) **332.4**
>UF Currency devaluation
>>Devaluation of currency
>>Free coinage
>>Government policy
>
>BT **Economic policy**
>
>RT **Finance**
>>**Fiscal policy**
>>**Inflation (Finance)**
>>**Money**

Monetary policy—United States 332.4
>UF United States—Monetary policy

Monetary unions (May subdiv. geog.) **332.4**
>UF Common currencies
>
>BT **Money**

Money (May subdiv. geog.) **332.4**

Use for materials on currency as a medium of exchange or measure of value and for general materials on various types of money.
>UF Currency
>>Legal tender
>>Standard of value
>
>BT **Economics**
>>**Exchange**
>>**Finance**
>
>NT **Barter**
>>**Children's allowances**
>>**Coinage**
>>**Coins**
>>**Counterfeits and counterfeiting**
>>**Credit**
>>**Euro**
>>**Foreign exchange**
>>**Mints**
>>**Monetary unions**
>>**Paper money**

Money—*Continued*
  RT **Banks and banking**
       Gold
       Monetary policy
       Silver
       Wealth

Money-making projects for children
    332.024; 650.1
  UF Children's moneymaking projects
       Moneymaking projects for children
  BT **Business enterprises**
  RT **Children's allowances**

Money raising
  USE **Fund raising**

Moneymaking projects for children
  USE **Money-making projects for children**

Monkeys (May subdiv. geog.) **599.8**
  BT **Primates**

Monkeys—Behavior **599.8**
  UF Monkeys—Habits and behavior
  BT **Animal behavior**

Monkeys—Habits and behavior
  USE **Monkeys—Behavior**

Monks **255; 271**
  RT **Monasticism and religious orders for men**

Monograms **745.6**
  UF Ciphers (Lettering)
  BT **Alphabets**
       Decoration and ornament
       Lettering
  RT **Initials**

Monologues **808.85**
  May be used for individual works, collections, or materials about monologues. Monologues with incidental musical background and musical works in which spoken language is an integral part are entered under **Monologues with music.**
  UF Declamations
       Narrations
  BT **Recitations**
  RT **Monologues with music**

Monologues with music **808.85; 782.2**
  Use for musical scores and for materials about monologues with incidental musical background and musical works in which spoken language is an integral part. Individual monologues without music, collections, and materials about monologues without music are entered under **Monologues.**
  UF Musical declamation
       Narration with music

       Recitations with music
  BT **Recitations**
  RT **Monologues**

Monopolies (May subdiv. geog.) **338.8**
  BT **Commerce**
       Economics
  RT **Competition**
       Corporation law
       Industrial trusts
       Restraint of trade

Monorail railroads **385.5; 625.1**
  UF Railroads, Single rail
       Single rail railroads
  BT **Railroads**

Monotheism (May subdiv. geog.) **211**
  BT **Religion**
       Theism
  RT **God**

Monroe Doctrine **327.73**
  BT **International relations**
       Intervention (International law)
       United States—Foreign relations

Monster films
  USE **Horror films**

Monsters **001.9; 398.2**
  Use for materials on legendary animals combining features of human and animal form or having the forms of various animals in combination. Materials on human abnormalities are entered under either **Birth defects** or **Growth disorders.**
  BT **Animals—Folklore**
       Curiosities and wonders
       Folklore
       Mythology
  NT **Dragons**
       Giants
       Sasquatch
       Yeti

Montessori method of education **371.39**
  BT **Elementary education**
       Kindergarten
       Teaching

Months **529**
  SA names of the months [to be added as needed]
  BT **Calendars**
       Chronology

Monumental brasses
  USE **Brasses**

Monuments (May subdiv. geog.) **725**
    UF   Statues
    SA   ethnic groups, classes of persons, individual persons, families, and wars with the subdivision *Monuments,* e.g. **World War, 1939-1945—Monuments** [to be added as needed]
    BT   **Architecture**
          Sculpture
    NT   **Historic buildings**
          National monuments
          Natural monuments
          Obelisks
          Pyramids
          Tombs
          World War, 1939-1945—Monuments

Moon **523.3**
    BT   **Astronomy**
          Solar system
Moon bases
    USE   **Lunar bases**
Moon—Eclipses
    USE   **Lunar eclipses**
Moon—Exploration **629.45**
    UF   Lunar exploration
    BT   **Space flight to the moon**
Moon—Geology
    USE   **Lunar geology**
Moon (in religion, folklore, etc.)
    USE   **Moon worship**
Moon—Maps **523.3022**
    BT   **Maps**
Moon—Photographs
    USE   **Moon—Pictorial works**
Moon—Pictorial works **523.3; 778.3**
    UF   Moon—Photographs
    BT   **Space photography**
Moon probes
    USE   **Lunar probes**
Moon rocks **552.0999**
    UF   Lunar petrology
          Lunar rocks
    BT   **Lunar geology**
          Petrology
Moon soil
    USE   **Lunar soil**

Moon—Surface **523.3**
    UF   Lunar surface
    RT   **Lunar soil**
Moon, Voyages to
    USE   **Space flight to the moon**
Moon worship **202**
    UF   Moon (in religion, folklore, etc.)
    BT   **Religion**
Moonlighting
    USE   **Supplementary employment**
Moons
    USE   **Satellites**
Moorish architecture
    USE   **Islamic architecture**
Moors
    USE   **Muslims**
Moral and philosophic stories
    USE   **Didactic fiction**
          Fables
          Parables
Moral conditions **301; 306; 900**
    UF   Morals
    SA   names of countries, cities, etc., with the subdivision *Moral conditions* [to be added as needed]
    BT   **Social conditions**
    NT   **Chicago (Ill.)—Moral conditions**
          Ohio—Moral conditions
          United States—Moral conditions
Moral development **155.2; 155.4**
    UF   Ethical development
    BT   **Child psychology**
          Moral education
Moral education (May subdiv. geog.) **370.11**
    UF   Character education
          Ethical education
    BT   **Education**
          Ethics
    NT   **Moral development**
    RT   **Religious education**
Moral philosophy
    USE   **Ethics**
Moral theology, Christian
    USE   **Christian ethics**

Morale   152.4
  SA   types of morale, e.g. **Employee morale** [to be added as needed]
  BT   **Courage**
  NT   **Employee morale**
       Psychological warfare
Moralities
  USE   **Morality plays**
Morality
  USE   **Ethics**
Morality plays   792.1; 808.82
  May be used for individual works, collections, or materials about plays in which the chief characters are personifications of abstract qualities.
  UF   Moralities
  BT   **Drama**
       English drama
       Religious drama
       Theater
  RT   **Mysteries and miracle plays**
Morality stories
  USE   **Didactic fiction**
Morality tales
  USE   **Parables**
Morals
  USE   **Conduct of life**
         Ethics
         Human behavior
         Moral conditions
Moravians (May subdiv. geog.)   284
  UF   United Brethren
  BT   **Christian sects**
Mormon Church
  USE   **Church of Jesus Christ of Latter-day Saints**
Mormons (May subdiv. geog.)   289.3092
  RT   **Church of Jesus Christ of Latter-day Saints**
Morphine   362.29; 615
  BT   **Narcotics**
  NT   **Heroin**
  RT   **Opium**
Morphology   571.3
  UF   Biological form
       Biological structure
       Comparative morphology
       Form in biology
       Structure in biology

  SA   animals, languages, plants, and crops with the subdivision *Morphology* [to be added as needed]
  BT   **Comparative anatomy**
Morse code
  USE   **Cipher and telegraph codes**
Mortality (May subdiv. geog.)   304.6
  UF   Burial statistics
       Death rate
       Mortuary statistics
  SA   ethnic groups, classes of persons, diseases, and animals with the subdivision *Mortality,* for works on the number of deaths during a given time among a particular groups or due to a particular cause, e.g. **Infants—Mortality; Tuberculosis—Mortality;** etc. [to be added as needed]
  BT   **Population**
       Vital statistics
  NT   **Children—Mortality**
       Infants—Mortality
  RT   **Death**
Mortar   666; 691
  BT   **Adhesives**
       Plaster and plastering
Mortgage loans
  USE   **Mortgages**
Mortgages (May subdiv. geog.)   332.63; 332.7
  UF   Home loans
       Mortgage loans
  BT   **Loans**
       Securities
Morticians
  USE   **Undertakers and undertaking**
Mortuary customs
  USE   **Cremation**
         Funeral rites and ceremonies
Mortuary statistics
  USE   **Mortality**
         Vital statistics
Mosaics   729; 738.5; 748.5
  BT   **Decoration and ornament**
       Decorative arts
  RT   **Mural painting and decoration**
Moslems
  USE   **Muslims**

Mosques (May subdiv. geog.) **726**
    BT   **Church architecture**
          Islamic architecture
          Temples
Mosquitoes **595.77**
    BT   **Insects**
Mosquitoes—Control **363.7**
    BT   **Pest control**
Mosses (May subdiv. geog.) **588**
    BT   **Plants**
Motels
    USE   **Hotels and motels**
Mother and child
    USE   **Mother-child relationship**
Mother-child relationship **306.874**
    UF   Child and mother
          Mother and child
    BT   **Children**
          Mothers
          Parent-child relationship
    NT   **Mother-daughter relationship**
          Mother-son relationship
Mother-daughter relationship **305.4;**
    306.874
    UF   Daughters and mothers
          Mothers and daughters
    BT   **Daughters**
          Mother-child relationship
          Mothers
Mother Goddess religion
    USE   **Goddess religion**
Mother-son relationship **306.874**
    UF   Mothers and sons
          Sons and mothers
    BT   **Mother-child relationship**
          Mothers
          Sons
Motherhood **306.874**
    BT   **Parenthood**
    RT   **Mothers**
Mothers (May subdiv. geog.) **306.874**
    UF   Maternity
    BT   **Family**
          Women
    NT   **Mother-child relationship**
          Mother-daughter relationship
          Mother-son relationship
          Stepmothers
          Surrogate mothers
          Teenage mothers
          Unmarried mothers

    RT   **Motherhood**
Mothers and daughters
    USE   **Mother-daughter relationship**
Mothers and sons
    USE   **Mother-son relationship**
Mother's Day **394.2628**
    BT   **Holidays**
Mothers' pensions
    USE   **Child welfare**
Moths (May subdiv. geog.) **595.78**
    UF   Cocoons
          Lepidoptera
    BT   **Insects**
    NT   **Caterpillars**
          Silkworms
    RT   **Butterflies**
Motion **531**
    UF   Kinetics
    BT   **Dynamics**
    NT   **Mechanical movements**
          Speed
    RT   **Force and energy**
          Kinematics
          Mechanics
Motion picture actors and actresses
    USE   **Actors**
Motion picture adaptations
    USE   **Film adaptations**
Motion picture cameras **778.5**
    UF   Movie cameras
    BT   **Cameras**
          Cinematography
    RT   **Amateur films**
Motion picture cartoons
    USE   **Animated films**
Motion picture direction
    USE   **Motion pictures—Production**
            and direction
Motion picture directors
    USE   **Motion picture producers and**
            directors
Motion picture festivals
    USE   **Film festivals**
Motion picture industry (May subdiv.
    geog.) **384; 791.43**
    UF   Film industry (Motion pictures)
    BT   **Industries**
    NT   **African Americans in the mo-**
            tion picture industry
          Blacks in the motion picture
            industry

Motion picture industry—*Continued*
      Motion picture producers and
        directors
      Motion pictures—Production
        and direction
      Women in the motion picture
        industry
  RT **Motion pictures**

Motion picture musicals
  USE **Musical films**

Motion picture photography
  USE **Cinematography**

Motion picture plays 808.2; 808.82
    May be used for individual works, collections, or materials about motion picture plays.
  UF Film scripts
      Motion picture scripts
      Movie scripts
      Screenplays
  BT **Drama**

Motion picture plays—Technique 808.2
  UF Motion pictures—Play writing
      Play writing
      Playwriting
  BT **Drama—Technique**

Motion picture posters
  USE **Film posters**

Motion picture producers
  USE **Motion picture producers and
       directors**

Motion picture producers and directors
  (May subdiv. geog.) 791.43; 920
  UF Film directors
      Film producers
      Motion picture directors
      Motion picture producers
  BT **Motion picture industry**
  RT **Motion pictures—Production
      and direction**

Motion picture production
  USE **Motion pictures—Production
      and direction**

Motion picture projectors
  USE **Projectors**

Motion picture scripts
  USE **Motion picture plays**

Motion picture serials 791.43
    May be used for individual works, collections, or materials about motion picture serials.
  BT **Motion pictures**

Motion pictures (May subdiv. geog.)
      384; 791.43
    Use for general materials on motion pictures, including motion pictures as an art form. Materials on the technical aspects of making motion pictures and their projection onto a screen are entered under **Cinematography.** For materials on motion pictures produced by the motion picture industry of an individual country or on the motion pictures shown in a country, subdivide geographically, e.g. **Motion pictures—United States.**
  UF Cinema
      Films
      Movies
  SA types of motion pictures, e.g.
      **Documentary films; Horror
      films;** motion pictures and
      particular groups of persons,
      e.g., **Motion pictures and
      children;** motion pictures as
      used in various industries or
      fields of endeavor, e.g. **Motion pictures in education;**
      subjects and groups of persons portrayed in motion pictures, e.g. **Animals in motion
      pictures; Women in motion
      pictures;** groups of persons in
      the motion picture industry,
      e.g. **Women in the motion
      picture industry;** and names
      of individual motion pictures
      [to be added as needed]
  BT **Audiovisual materials**
      Mass media
      Performing arts
  NT **Adventure films**
      **African Americans in motion
        pictures**
      Amateur films
      Animals in motion pictures
      Animated films
      Bible films
      Biographical films
      Blacks in motion pictures
      Comedy films
      Documentary films
      Epic films
      Erotic films
      Experimental films
      Fantasy films
      Film adaptations
      Film noir

Motion pictures—*Continued*
       Gangster films
       Horror films
       Legal drama (Films)
       Libraries and motion pictures
       Medical drama (Films)
       Motion picture serials
       Motion pictures and children
       Motion pictures in education
       Musical films
       Mystery films
       Science fiction films
       Sherlock Holmes films
       Short films
       Silent films
       Sports drama (Films)
       Spy films
       Star Wars films
       Television movies
       Three Stooges films
       Vampire films
       War films
       Western films
       Women in motion pictures
       World War, 1939-1945—Motion pictures and the war
  RT   **Motion picture industry**
Motion pictures, American
  USE **Motion pictures—United States**
Motion pictures and children 305.23; 649; 791.43
    Use for materials on the effect of motion pictures on children and youth.
  UF Children and motion pictures
  BT **Children**
       Motion pictures
Motion pictures and libraries
  USE **Libraries and motion pictures**
Motion pictures and the war
  USE names of wars with the subdivision *Motion pictures and the war,* e.g. **World War, 1939-1945—Motion pictures and the war** [to be added as needed]
Motion pictures—Biography 791.43092; 920
  BT **Biography**
Motion pictures—Catalogs 016.79143
  UF Catalogs, Film
      Film catalogs
      Filmography

  SA types of motion pictures with the subdivision *Catalogs,* e.g. **Science fiction films—Catalogs**; and subjects, classes of persons, corporate entities, and names of individual persons with the subdivision *Filmography,* e.g. **Animals—Filmography; Shakespeare, William, 1564-1616—Filmography**; etc. [to be added as needed]
Motion pictures—Censorship (May subdiv. geog.) **791.43**
  BT **Censorship**
Motion pictures—Ethical aspects 791.43
  UF Motion pictures—Moral and religious aspects
  BT **Ethics**
Motion pictures in education 371.33
  UF Educational films
  BT **Audiovisual education**
      Motion pictures
      Teaching—Aids and devices
  NT **Libraries and motion pictures**
Motion pictures—Moral and religious aspects
  USE **Motion pictures—Ethical aspects**
       Motion pictures—Religious aspects
Motion pictures—Play writing
  USE **Motion picture plays—Technique**
Motion pictures—Posters
  USE **Film posters**
Motion pictures—Production and direction 384; 791.4302
  UF Film direction
      Film production
      Filmmaking
      Motion picture direction
      Motion picture production
  BT **Motion picture industry**
  RT **Motion picture producers and directors**
Motion pictures—Religious aspects 204; 248.4; 791.43
  UF Motion pictures—Moral and religious aspects

Motion pictures—Reviews 791.43

Motion pictures—Television adaptations

   USE **Television adaptations**

**Motion pictures—United States
   791.430973**

   Use for materials on motion pictures produced by the motion picture industry of the
United States or on motion pictures shown in
the United States.

   UF American films

       American motion pictures

       Motion pictures, American

Motion study 658.5

   BT **Factory management**

       Industrial efficiency

       Job analysis

       Personnel management

       Production standards

   RT **Time study**

Motivation (Psychology) 153.8

   UF Incentive (Psychology)

   BT **Psychology**

   NT **Achievement motivation**

       Burn out (Psychology)

       Wishes

Motor boats

   USE **Motorboats**

Motor buses

   USE **Buses**

Motor cars

   USE **Automobiles**

Motor coordination

   USE **Movement education**

Motor cycles

   USE **Motorcycles**

Motor trucks

   USE **Trucks**

Motor vehicle industry

   USE **Automobile industry**

Motor vehicles—Drivers' licenses

   USE **Drivers' licenses**

Motorboats 623.82

   UF Motor boats

       Power boats

   BT **Boats and boating**

Motorboats—Models 623.82

   BT **Models and modelmaking**

Motorcycles (May subdiv. geog.)
   629.227

   UF Motor cycles

   SA specific makes and models of
       motorcycles [to be added as
       needed]

   BT **Bicycles**

   NT **Antique and vintage motorcy-
       cles**

       Minibikes

   RT **Motorcycling**

Motorcycling (May subdiv. geog.) **796.7**

   BT **Cycling**

   RT **Motorcycles**

Motoring

   USE **Automobile travel**

Motors

   USE **Electric motors**

       Engines

       and types of engines and mo-
       tors, e.g. **Steam engines;**
       Electric motors; etc., and
       types of vehicles and makes
       and models of vehicles with
       the subdivision *Motors,* e.g.
       Automobiles—Motors [to be
       added as needed]

Motorways

   USE **Express highways**

Mottoes 808.88; 929.8

   May be used for collections of mottoes and
for materials about mottoes.

   UF Emblems

   BT **Heraldry**

   RT **National emblems**

Moulding (Metal)

   USE **Founding**

Mound-builders

   USE **Mounds and mound builders**

Mounds and mound builders (May
   subdiv. geog.) **930.1; 970.004**

   UF Barrows

       Graves

       Mound-builders

   BT **Archeology**

       Burial

       Tombs

   RT **Excavations (Archeology)**

Mount Rainier (Wash.) 979.7

   BT **Mountains**

Mountain animals (May subdiv. geog.)
    591.75
    UF   Alpine animals
          Alpine fauna
          Mountain fauna
    BT   **Animals**
Mountain bicycles
    USE **Mountain bikes**
Mountain bikes   **629.227**
    UF   All terrain bicycles
          Mountain bicycles
    BT   **All terrain vehicles**
          Bicycles
Mountain biking (May subdiv. geog.)
    796.63
    UF   All terrain cycling
    BT   **Cycling**
Mountain climbing
    USE **Mountaineering**
Mountain fauna
    USE **Mountain animals**
Mountain flora
    USE **Mountain plants**
Mountain life (May subdiv. geog.)
    307.72
    BT   **Country life**
Mountain people (May subdiv. geog.)
    307.7
    BT   **Ethnology**
Mountain plants (May subdiv. geog.)
    581.7; 635.9
    UF   Alpine flora
          Alpine plants
          Mountain flora
    BT   **Plant ecology**
          Plants
Mountaineering   **796.522**
    UF   Mountain climbing
          Rock climbing
    BT   **Outdoor life**
    RT   **Trails**
Mountains (May subdiv. geog.)   **551.43**
    SA   names of mountain ranges and
          of individual mountains [to be
          added as needed]
    BT   **Landforms**
          Physical geography
    NT   **Mount Rainier (Wash.)**
          Rocky Mountains
          Volcanoes

Mourning
    USE **Bereavement**
Mourning customs
    USE **Funeral rites and ceremonies**
Mouse
    USE **Mice**
Mouth   **591.4; 612.3**
    BT   **Face**
          Head
Mouth—Diseases   **617.5**
    BT   **Diseases**
    NT   **Bad breath**
Movable books
    USE **Toy and movable books**
Movement education   **152.3; 153.7;**
    372.86
    UF   Creative movement
          Motor coordination
    BT   **Physical education**
Movement, Freedom of
    USE **Freedom of movement**
Movements of animals
    USE **Animal locomotion**
Movie cameras
    USE **Motion picture cameras**
Movie festivals
    USE **Film festivals**
Movie novelizations
    USE **Movie novels**
Movie novels   **808.3**
    May be used for individual works, collec-
    tions, or materials about novels based on
    movies.
    UF   Movie novelizations
          Movie tie-ins
    BT   **Fiction**
    RT   **Radio and television novels**
Movie posters
    USE **Film posters**
Movie scripts
    USE **Motion picture plays**
Movie tie-ins
    USE **Movie novels**
Movies
    USE **Motion pictures**
Moving   **648**
    Use for materials on changing the location
    of possessions, household, office, etc.
    UF   Household moving
          Moving, household
    BT   **Home economics**

Moving, household
USE **Moving**
MP3 players   006.5; 621.389
BT **Computer sound processing**
Sound—Recording and repro-
ducing
MRI (Magnetic resonance imaging)
USE **Magnetic resonance imaging**
Mulattoes
USE **Racially mixed people**
Multi-age grouping
USE **Nongraded schools**
Multicultural diversity in the workplace
USE **Diversity in the workplace**
Multicultural education (May subdiv.
geog.)   370.117
Use for materials on the attempt to eradi-
cate racial and religious prejudices through the
study of various races, creeds, and immigrant
cultures.
UF Intercultural education
BT **Acculturation**
Education
Multiculturalism
NT **Bilingual education**
RT **International education**
Multicultural literature
Multicultural literature   808.8
Use for collections that bring together liter-
atures of various cultures for the purpose of
illustrating racial, religious, or ethnic diversi-
ty.
BT **Literature**
Multiculturalism
RT **Multicultural education**
Multiculturalism (May subdiv. geog.)
305.8; 306.44
Use for materials on policies or programs
that foster the preservation of various cultures
or cultural identities within a unified society.
Materials on the coexistence of several dis-
tinct ethnic, religious, or cultural groups with-
in one society are entered under **Pluralism
(Social sciences)**. Materials on the presence of
two distinct cultures within a single country
or region are entered under **Biculturalism.**
UF Diversity movement
BT **Culture**
Social policy
NT **Diversity in the workplace**
Multicultural education
Multicultural literature
RT **Biculturalism**
Ethnic relations
Ethnicity
Pluralism (Social sciences)

Race relations
Multilingual dictionaries
USE **Polyglot dictionaries**
Multilingual glossaries, phrase books, etc.
USE **Polyglot dictionaries**
Multilingualism (May subdiv. geog.)
306.44
BT **Language and languages**
Multimedia   006.7
Use for materials on computer systems,
software, or data items that allow users to ma-
nipulate diverse integrated media, such as text,
graphics, sound, etc.
UF Computer-based multimedia in-
formation systems
Interactive media
Interactive multimedia
Multimedia computing
Multimedia information systems
Multimedia knowledge systems
Multimedia systems
SA subjects with the subdivision *In-
teractive multimedia*, e.g. **Ge-
ology—Interactive multime-
dia** [to be added as needed]
BT **Computer software**
Information systems
NT **Hypertext**
Multimedia centers
USE **Instructional materials centers**
Multimedia computing
USE **Multimedia**
Multimedia information systems
USE **Multimedia**
Multimedia knowledge systems
USE **Multimedia**
Multimedia materials
USE **Audiovisual materials**
Multimedia systems
USE **Multimedia**
Multinational corporations (May subdiv.
geog.)   338.8; 658
UF Business—International aspects
Corporations, Multinational
International business enterprises
BT **Business enterprises**
Commerce
Corporations
**International economic rela-
tions**
NT **Foreign investments**

Multiple birth   618.2
UF   Birth, Multiple
SA   types of multiple births, e.g.
       Twins [to be added as need-
       ed]
BT   **Childbirth**
NT   **Twins**
Multiple personalities
USE **Multiple personality**
Multiple personality   616.85
UF   Double consciousness
      Multiple personalities
      Personality, Multiple
      Split personality
BT   **Abnormal psychology**
      Mental illness
      Personality disorders
      Psychology
Multiple plot stories
USE **Plot-your-own stories**
Multiplication   513.2
BT   **Arithmetic**
Multiracial people
USE **Racially mixed people**
Mummies (May subdiv. geog.)   393
BT   **Archeology**
      Burial
Municipal administration
USE **Municipal government**
Municipal art (May subdiv. geog.)   711
UF   Art, Municipal
      Civic art
      Municipal improvements
BT   **Art**
      Cities and towns
RT   **City planning**
Municipal civil service
USE **Municipal officials and em-
       ployees**
Municipal employees
USE **Municipal officials and em-
       ployees**
Municipal engineering (May subdiv.
      geog.)   628
BT   **Engineering**
      Public works
NT   **Drainage**
      Refuse and refuse disposal
      Sewerage
      Street cleaning
RT   **Sanitary engineering**

Municipal-federal relations
USE **Federal-city relations**
Municipal finance (May subdiv. geog.)
      336
      Use for general materials on city finance
and, when subdivided by country, state, or region, for general considerations of municipal
finance in those places. Materials on the finance of individual cities, towns, or metropolitan areas are entered under **Public finance**
with the appropriate geographic subdivision.
UF   Cities and towns—Finance
      Finance, Municipal
BT   **Municipal government**
      Public finance
NT   **Metropolitan finance**
Municipal government (May subdiv.
      geog.)   320.8; 352.16
      Use for materials on the government of cit-
ies in general and, when subdivided by country, state, or region, for general consideration
of municipal government in those places. Materials on the government of individual cities,
towns, or metropolitan areas are entered under
the name of the city, town, or area with the
subdivision *Politics and government.*
UF   Cities and towns—Government
      City government
      Government, Municipal
      Municipal administration
      Municipalities
SA   names of cities, towns, and met-
      ropolitan areas with the subdi-
      vision *Politics and govern-
      ment* [to be added as needed]
BT   **Local government**
      Political science
NT   **Chicago (Ill.)—Politics and
      government**
      Federal-city relations
      Municipal finance
      **Municipal government by city
      manager**
      **Municipal government by com-
      mission**
      Public administration
      State-local relations
RT   **Metropolitan government**
      **Municipal officials and em-
      ployees**
**Municipal government by city manager
      320.8; 352.16**
UF   City manager
      Commission government with
      city manager

Municipal government by city manager—
Continued
  BT Municipal government
Municipal government by commission
        320.8; 352.16
  UF Commission government
        Government by commission
  BT Municipal government
Municipal government—United States
        320.8; 352.160973
  UF United States—Municipal gov-
        ernment
Municipal improvements
  USE Cities and towns—Civic im-
        provement
        Municipal art
Municipal officers
  USE Municipal officials and em-
        ployees
Municipal officials and employees
        352.16
  UF Municipal civil service
        Municipal employees
        Municipal officers
        Town officers
  SA names of cities with the subdivi-
        sion *Officials and employees,*
        e.g. **Chicago (Ill.)—Officials
        and employees** [to be added
        as needed]
  BT Civil service
  RT Municipal government
Municipal ownership   338.9; 352.5
  UF Public ownership
  BT Corporations
        Economic policy
        Government ownership
Municipal planning
  USE City planning
Municipal transit
  USE Local transit
Municipalities
  USE Cities and towns
        Municipal government
Munitions
  USE Defense industry
        Military weapons
Mural painting and decoration (May
        subdiv. geog.)   729; 751.7
  UF Fresco painting
        Wall decoration
        Wall painting

  BT Decoration and ornament
        Interior design
        Painting
  RT Mosaics
Murder
  USE Homicide
Murder mysteries
  USE Mystery and detective plays
        Mystery fiction
        Mystery films
        Mystery radio programs
        Mystery television programs
Murder trials
  USE Trials (Homicide)
Muscles   611; 612.7
  BT Musculoskeletal system
Muscular system
  USE Musculoskeletal system
Musculoskeletal system   611; 612.7
  UF Muscular system
  BT Anatomy
        Physiology
  NT Bones
        Muscles
        Skeleton
  RT Human locomotion
Museums (May subdiv. geog.)   069; 708
  SA appropriate subjects and names
        of wars and of corporate bod-
        ies with the subdivision *Mu-
        seums,* e.g. **World War,
        1939-1945—Museums;** and
        names of individual galleries
        and museums [to be added as
        needed]
  NT Art museums
        Museums and schools
        World War, 1939-1945—Muse-
        ums
Museums and schools   069
  UF Schools and museums
  BT Museums
        Schools
Museums—Ohio   708.171
Museums—United States   708.13
Mushrooms   579.6; 635
  UF Toadstools
  BT Plants
  RT Fungi

Music   780
  UF   Classical music
  SA   music of particular countries or
        ethnic groups, e.g. **American
        music; Native American mu-
        sic;** etc.; types of music, e.g.
        Vocal music; and subjects,
        classes of persons, and names
        of individual persons, corpo-
        rate bodies, places, or wars,
        with the subdivision *Songs* for
        collections of songs or materi-
        als about songs pertaining to
        the topic or entity named, e.g.
        **Cowhands—Songs; Surfing—
        Songs; United States Mili-
        tary Academy—Songs** [to be
        added as needed]
  BT   **Humanities**
  NT   **African American music**
        American music
        Black music
        Chamber music
        Church music
        Composition (Music)
        Computer music
        Concerts
        Conducting
        Cowhands—Songs
        Dance music
        Electronic music
        Ensembles (Music)
        Folk music
        Harmony
        Instrumental music
        **Instrumentation and orchestra-
        tion**
        Jazz music
        Military music
        Music and literature
        Musical notation
        Musicians
        Native American music
        Orchestral music
        Organ music
        Piano music
        Popular music
        Radio and music
        Rock music
        Singing
        Violin music

      Vocal music
Music—Acoustics and physics   781.2
  UF   Acoustics
  BT   **Music—Theory**
        Physics
  RT   **Sound**
Music, American
  USE   **American music**
Music—Analysis, appreciation
  USE   **Music appreciation**
         Music—History and criticism
Music and literature   780
  UF   Literature and music
        Music and poetry
        Poetry and music
  BT   **Literature**
        Music
Music and poetry
  USE   **Music and literature**
Music and radio
  USE   **Radio and music**
Music—Anecdotes   780
  UF   Music—Anecdotes, facetiae, sat-
        ire, etc.
  BT   **Anecdotes**
Music—Anecdotes, facetiae, satire, etc.
  USE   **Music—Anecdotes**
         Music—Humor
Music appreciation   781.1
  UF   Appreciation of music
        Music—Analysis, appreciation
        Musical appreciation
  BT   **Music—Study and teaching**
  RT   **Music—History and criticism**
Music box
  USE   **Music boxes**
Music boxes   786.6
  UF   Music box
  BT   **Mechanical musical instru-
        ments**
Music—Cataloging
  USE   **Cataloging of music**
Music, Choral
  USE   **Choral music**
Music—Composition
  USE   **Composition (Music)**
Music conductors
  USE   **Conductors (Music)**
Music—Criticism
  USE   **Music—History and criticism**
Music—Discography   016.78

Music education
    USE **Music—Study and teaching**
Music—Examinations   **780.76**
    UF Music—Examinations, questions, etc.
    BT **Examinations**
Music—Examinations, questions, etc.
    USE **Music—Examinations**
Music festivals (May subdiv. geog.)
    780.79
    BT **Festivals**
    RT **Concerts**
Music, Gospel
    USE **Gospel music**
Music-halls
    USE **Concert halls**
Music—History and criticism   **780.9**
    UF Music—Analysis, appreciation
          Music—Criticism
          Musical criticism
    RT **Music appreciation**
Music—Humor   **780**
    UF Music—Anecdotes, facetiae, satire, etc.
    BT **Wit and humor**
Music—Instruction and study
    USE **Music—Study and teaching**
Music libraries (May subdiv. geog.)   **026**
    UF Libraries, Music
    BT **Special libraries**
Music—Notation
    USE **Musical notation**
Music—Psychological aspects   **781**
    UF Psychology of music
    BT **Psychology**
Music—Publishing (May subdiv. geog.)
    070.5
    BT **Publishers and publishing**
Music—Study and teaching   **780.7**
    UF Music education
          Music—Instruction and study
          Musical education
          Musical instruction
          School music
    NT **Music appreciation**
Music—Theory   **781**
    NT **Composition (Music)**
          Counterpoint
          Harmony
          Music—Acoustics and physics
          Musical form

Musical meter and rhythm
Music—Therapeutic use
    USE **Music therapy**
Music therapy   **615.8; 616.89**
    UF Music—Therapeutic use
          Musical therapy
    BT **Therapeutics**
Music videos   **384.55; 778.59**
    May be used for individual works, collections, or materials about music videos.
    UF Videos, Music
    BT **Television programs**
          Videodiscs
          Videotapes
Musical ability   **780.7**
    UF Musical talent
    BT **Ability**
Musical accompaniment   **781.47**
    UF Accompaniment, Musical
    BT **Composition (Music)**
Musical appreciation
    USE **Music appreciation**
Musical comedies
    USE **Musicals**
Musical composition
    USE **Composition (Music)**
Musical criticism
    USE **Music—History and criticism**
Musical declamation
    USE **Monologues with music**
Musical education
    USE **Music—Study and teaching**
Musical ensembles
    USE **Ensembles (Music)**
Musical films   **791.43**
    May be used for individual works, collections, or materials about musical films.
    UF Motion picture musicals
          Musicals (Motion pictures)
    BT **Motion pictures**
    RT **Musicals**
Musical form   **784.18**
    SA names of musical forms expressed in the singular, to be used both for musical scores and for materials about the musical form, e.g. **Concerto** [to be added as needed]
    BT **Composition (Music)**
          Music—Theory
    NT **Concerto**
          Ensembles (Music)

Musical form—*Continued*
> **Fugue**
> **Opera**
> **Operetta**
> **Oratorio**
> **Sonata**
> **Suite (Music)**
> **Symphony**

Musical instruction
> USE   **Music—Study and teaching**

Musical instruments (May subdiv. geog.)
> **784.19**
> UF   Instruments, Musical
> SA   types of instruments, e.g. **Per-**
>   **cussion instruments** [to be
>   added as needed]
> NT   **Bells**
>   **Drums**
>   **Electronic musical instruments**
>   **Mechanical musical instru-**
>   **ments**
>   **Organs (Musical instruments)**
>   **Percussion instruments**
>   **Stringed instruments**
>   **Wind instruments**
> RT   **Instrumental music**
>   **Instrumentation and orchestra-**
>   **tion**
>   **Orchestra**
>   **Tuning**

Musical instruments, Electronic
> USE   **Electronic musical instruments**

Musical instruments, Mechanical
> USE   **Mechanical musical instru-**
>   **ments**

Musical meter and rhythm   **781.2**
> UF   Meter
> BT   **Music—Theory**
>   **Rhythm**

Musical notation   **780.1**
> UF   Music—Notation
> BT   **Music**

Musical revues, comedies, etc.
> USE   **Musicals**

Musical talent
> USE   **Musical ability**

Musical therapy
> USE   **Music therapy**

Musicals (May subdiv. geog.)   **782.1;**
> **792.6**

Use for scores and for materials about musical comedies and revues.

> UF   Dramatic music
>   Musical comedies
>   Musical revues, comedies, etc.
> BT   **Theater**
> RT   **Musical films**
>   **Operetta**

Musicals (Motion pictures)
> USE   **Musical films**

Musicians (May subdiv. geog.)   **780.92;**
> **920**
> SA   types of musicians and names of
>   individual musicians [to be
>   added as needed]
> BT   **Music**
> NT   **African American musicians**
>   **Black musicians**
>   **Composers**
>   **Conductors (Music)**
>   **Ensembles (Music)**
>   **Instrumentalists**
>   **Singers**

Musicians—Biography   **780.92; 920**
> BT   **Biography**

Musicians, Black
> USE   **Black musicians**

Musicians—Portraits   **780.92**

Musicians—United States   **780.92; 920**
> UF   American musicians

Muslim architecture
> USE   **Islamic architecture**

Muslim art
> USE   **Islamic art**

Muslim countries
> USE   **Islamic countries**

Muslim holy war
> USE   **Jihad**

Muslim law
> USE   **Islamic law**

Muslim literature
> USE   **Islamic literature**

Muslim sermons
> USE   **Islamic sermons**

Muslims (May subdiv. geog.)   **297.092**
> UF   Moors
>   Moslems
> RT   **Islam**

Muslims—United States   **297.092**
> NT   **Black Muslims**

Mutation (Biology)
> USE   **Evolution**
>   **Variation (Biology)**

Mutilation, Female genital
    USE **Female circumcision**
Mutual defense assistance program
    USE **Military assistance**
Mutual funds (May subdiv. geog.)
    332.63
    UF   Investment companies
          Investment trusts
    BT   **Investments**
Mutual support groups
    USE **Self-help groups**
Mutualism (Biology)
    USE **Symbiosis**
Mycology
    USE **Fungi**
Myocardial infarction
    USE **Heart attack**
Myotherapy
    USE **Acupressure**
Mysteries
    USE **Mysteries and miracle plays**
          Mystery and detective plays
          Mystery fiction
          Mystery films
          Mystery radio programs
          Mystery television programs
Mysteries and miracle plays   792.1;
    808.82
    May be used for individual plays, collections, or materials about medieval plays depicting the life of Jesus or legends of the saints.
    UF   Miracle plays
          Mysteries
          Mystery plays
    BT   **Bible plays**
          English drama
          Pageants
          Religious drama
          Theater
    NT   **Passion plays**
    RT   **Morality plays**
Mystery and detective comics
    USE **Mystery comic books, strips, etc.**
Mystery and detective films
    USE **Mystery films**
Mystery and detective plays   808.82
    May be used for individual works, collections, or materials about mystery and detective dramas.
    UF   Crime plays
          Detective and mystery plays

Murder mysteries
Mysteries
Mystery plays
Private eye stories
Whodunits
    BT   **Drama**
Mystery and detective radio programs
    USE **Mystery radio programs**
Mystery and detective stories
    USE **Mystery fiction**
Mystery and detective television programs
    USE **Mystery television programs**
Mystery comic books, strips, etc.   741.5
    May be used for individual works, collections, or materials about mystery and detective comics.
    UF   Crime comics
          Detective and mystery comic
             books, strips, etc.
          Detective comics
          Mystery and detective comics
    BT   **Comic books, strips, etc.**
Mystery fiction   808.3; 808.83
    May be used for individual works, collections, or materials about mystery fiction.
    UF   Crime stories
          Detective and mystery stories
          Detective fiction
          Detective stories
          Murder mysteries
          Mysteries
          Mystery and detective stories
          Mystery stories
          Private eye stories
          Suspense novels
          Whodunits
    BT   **Fiction**
    NT   **Edgar Allan Poe Awards**
    RT   **Ghost stories**
          Horror fiction
          Romantic suspense novels
          Spy stories
Mystery films   791.43
    May be used for individual works, collections, or materials about mystery and detective films.
    UF   Crime films
          Detective and mystery films
          Murder mysteries
          Mysteries
          Mystery and detective films
          Private eye stories
          Suspense films

Mystery films—*Continued*
    Whodunits
    SA   particular kinds of detective and
           mystery films, e.g. **Sherlock**
           Holmes films [to be added as
           needed]
    BT   **Motion pictures**
    NT   **Sherlock Holmes films**
    RT   **Film noir**
          Gangster films
          Spy films
Mystery plays
    USE **Mysteries and miracle plays**
          Mystery and detective plays
Mystery radio programs   791.44
    May be used for individual works, collec-
    tions, or materials about mystery and detective
    radio programs.
    UF   Crime programs
          Detective and mystery radio pro-
            grams
          Murder mysteries
          Mysteries
          Mystery and detective radio pro-
            grams
          Private eye stories
          Suspense programs
          Whodunits
    BT   **Radio programs**
Mystery stories
    USE **Mystery fiction**
Mystery television programs   791.45
    May be used for individual works, collec-
    tions, or materials about mystery and detective
    television programs.
    UF   Crime programs
          Detective and mystery television
            programs
          Murder mysteries
          Mysteries
          Mystery and detective television
            programs
          Private eye stories
          Suspense programs
          Whodunits
    BT   **Television programs**
    RT   **Spy television programs**
Mystical theology
    USE **Mysticism**
Mysticism (May subdiv. geog.)   **204;**
    248.2
    May be subdivided by religion or sect, e.g.
    Mysticism—Islam.

    UF   Dark night of the soul
          Mystical theology
    BT   **Spiritual life**
    NT   **Cabala**
          Theosophy
Mysticism—Comparative studies   204;
    248.2
Mysticism—Islam (May subdiv. geog.)
    297.4
    UF   Islamic mysticism
    BT   **Islam**
    NT   **Sufism**
Mythical animals   398.24
    UF   Animal lore
          Animals, Mythical
          Imaginary animals
          Imaginary creatures
    SA   types of mythical animals [to be
           added as needed]
    BT   **Mythology**
    NT   **Dragons**
          Mermaids and mermen
          Sasquatch
          Yeti
    RT   **Animals—Folklore**
Mythology   201; 398.2
    UF   Myths
    SA   mythology of particular national
           or ethnic groups or of partic-
           ular geographic areas, e.g.
           Celtic mythology [to be add-
           ed as needed]
    NT   **Art and mythology**
          Celtic mythology
          Classical mythology
          Geographical myths
          Monsters
          Mythical animals
          Symbolism
          Totems and totemism
    RT   **Folklore**
          Gods and goddesses
          Heroes and heroines
          Legends
          Religion
Mythology, Celtic
    USE **Celtic mythology**
Mythology, Classical
    USE **Classical mythology**
Mythology, Greek
    USE **Greek mythology**

Mythology in art
  USE **Art and mythology**
Mythology, Roman
  USE **Roman mythology**
Myths
  USE **Mythology**
Name
  USE names of countries, cities, etc., individual persons, dieties, corporate bodies, ethnic groups, wars, etc., with the subdivision *Name,* for materials on the name's origin, history, validity, etc. [to be added as needed]
Names **929.4**
  UF Epithets
        Proper names
  SA types of names, e.g. **Geographic names;** types of objects, domestic animals, events, organization, and institutions with the subdivision *Names,* for materials on the naming of those items, e.g. **Pets—Names;** and names of countries, cities, etc., individual persons, dieties, corporate bodies, ethnic groups, wars, etc., with the subdivision *Name,* for materials on the name's origin, history, validity, etc. [to be added as needed]
  NT **Code names**
        Geographic names
        Native American names
        Personal names
        Pseudonyms
        Terms and phrases
Names, Geographical
  USE **Geographic names**
Names, Personal
  USE **Personal names**
Names—Pronunciation **421**
Nannies **649**
  UF Nursemaids
  BT **Child care**

Nanotechnology (May subdiv. geog.)
  620
  UF Molecular technology
  BT **Technology**
Napkin folding **642**
  UF Folding of napkins
  BT **Table setting and decoration**
Napoleon I, Emperor of the French, 1769-1821—Drama **808.82**
  Use for collections of plays about Napoleon. Materials on Napoleon as a character in drama are entered under **Napoleon I, Emperor of the French, 1769-1821—In literature.**
Napoleon I, Emperor of the French, 1769-1821—Fiction **808.83**
  Use for collections of fiction about Napoleon. Materials on Napoleon as a character in fiction are entered under **Napoleon I, Emperor of the French, 1769-1821—In literature.**
Napoleon I, Emperor of the French, 1769-1821—In art **704.9**
  Use for materials about the depiction of Napoleon in works of art.
  UF Napoleon in art
  BT **Art—Themes**
Napoleon I, Emperor of the French, 1769-1821—In literature **809**
  Use for materials about Napoleon as a character or as he is portrayed in works of fiction, drama, or poetry. Collections in which Napoleon is a character are entered under **Napoleon I, Emperor of the French, 1769-1821—Fiction; Napoleon I, Emperor of the French, 1769-1821—Drama;** or **Napoleon I, Emperor of the French, 1769-1821—Poetry;** as appropriate.
  UF Napoleon in fiction, drama, poetry, etc.
  BT **Literature—Themes**
Napoleon I, Emperor of the French, 1769-1821—Poetry **808.81**
  Use for collections of poetry about Napoleon. Materials on Napoleon as portrayed in poetry are entered under **Napoleon I, Emperor of the French, 1769-1821—In literature.**
Napoleon in art
  USE **Napoleon I, Emperor of the French, 1769-1821—In art**
Napoleon in fiction, drama, poetry, etc.
  USE **Napoleon I, Emperor of the French, 1769-1821—In literature**
Napoleonic Wars, 1800-1815 **940.2**
  BT **Europe—History—1789-1815**
        France—History—1799-1815
Narcotic abuse
  USE **Drug abuse**

Narcotic addiction
    USE   **Drug abuse**
Narcotic addiction counseling
    USE   **Drug abuse counseling**
Narcotic addicts
    USE   **Drug addicts**
Narcotic habit
    USE   **Drug abuse**
Narcotic traffic
    USE   **Drug traffic**
Narcotics   178; 394.1; 615

> Use for materials limited to those drugs that induce sleep or lethargy or deaden pain.

    UF   Opiates
          Soporifics
    SA   types of narcotics [to be added as needed]
    BT   **Drugs**
          Materia medica
          Psychotropic drugs
    NT   **Cocaine**
          Heroin
          Marijuana
          Morphine
          Opium
Narcotics and crime
    USE   **Drugs and crime**
Narcotics and criminals
    USE   **Criminals—Drug use**
Narcotics and teenagers
    USE   **Teenagers—Drug use**
Narcotics and youth
    USE   **Youth—Drug use**
Narration with music
    USE   **Monologues with music**
Narrations
    USE   **Monologues**
          Recitations
Narrative poetry   808.1; 808.81

> May be used for individual works, collections, or materials about narrative poetry. Rhyming stories for very young children are entered under the form heading **Stories in rhyme.**

    BT   **Poetry**
    NT   **Epic poetry**
          Historical poetry
          Stories in rhyme
Nation of Islam
    USE   **Black Muslims**
National anthems
    USE   **National songs**

National Book Week   021.7
    UF   Book Week, National
    BT   **Books and reading**
National characteristics   305.8
    UF   National images
          National psychology
    SA   national characteristics of particular countries, e.g. **American national characteristics** [to be added as needed]
    BT   **Anthropology**
          Nationalism
          Social psychology
    NT   **American national characteristics**
    RT   **Ethnopsychology**
National characteristics, American
    USE   **American national characteristics**
National community service
    USE   **National service**
National consciousness
    USE   **Nationalism**
National dances
    USE   **Folk dancing**
National debts
    USE   **Public debts**
National defenses
    USE   **Industrial mobilization**
          Military readiness
National emblems (May subdiv. geog.) **929.9**
    UF   Emblems
          National symbols
    SA   types of national emblems and national symbols, e.g. **Flags** [to be added as needed]
    BT   **Signs and symbols**
    RT   **Flags**
          Heraldry
          Insignia
          Mottoes
          Seals (Numismatics)
          State emblems
National forests
    USE   **Forest reserves**
National Guard (U.S.)
    USE   **United States. National Guard**

National health insurance (May subdiv.
geog.)   **368.4**
  UF   Government health insurance
        Medical insurance, National
        National health service
        Socialized medicine
  BT   **Health insurance**
  NT   **Medicaid**
        Medicare
  RT   **State medicine**
National health service
  USE   **National health insurance**
         State medicine
National heritage
  USE   **Cultural property**
National holidays
  USE   **Holidays**
National hymns
  USE   **National songs**
National images
  USE   **National characteristics**
National interest
  USE   **Public interest**
National landmarks
  USE   **National monuments**
National liberation movements (May
subdiv. geog.)   **320.5**
  Use for materials on minority or other
  groups in armed rebellion against a colonial
  government or against a national government
  charged with corruption or foreign domina-
  tion, usually in the period since World War II.
  UF   Liberation movements, National
  SA   names of individual liberation
        movements [to be added as
        needed]
  BT   **Nationalism**
        Revolutions
  NT   **Guerrillas**
National libraries (May subdiv. geog.)
027.5
  Use for materials on libraries maintained by
  government funds that serve a country as a
  whole, particularly in collecting and preserv-
  ing that country's publications.
  UF   Libraries, National
  SA   names of individual national li-
        braries [to be added as need-
        ed]
  BT   **Government libraries**
National monuments (May subdiv. geog.)
917.3
  Use for materials on monuments, such as
  historic sites or geographic areas, that are

owned and maintained in the public interest
by a country's government.
  UF   Landmarks, Preservation of
        National landmarks
  SA   names of individual national
        monuments [to be added as
        needed]
  BT   **Monuments**
        National parks and reserves
  RT   **Historic sites**
        Natural monuments
National parks and reserves (May subdiv.
geog.)   **338.78; 363.6; 719**
  SA   names of individual national
        parks [to be added as needed]
  BT   **Parks**
        Public lands
  NT   **National monuments**
  RT   **Conservation of natural re-**
        sources
        Forest reserves
        Natural monuments
        Wilderness areas
**National parks and reserves—United
States**   **719; 917.3**
  UF   United States—National parks
        and reserves
  NT   **Yosemite National Park (Calif.)**
National patrimony
  USE   **Cultural property**
National planning
  USE   **Economic policy**
         Social policy
National product, Gross
  USE   **Gross national product**
National psychology
  USE   **Ethnopsychology**
         National characteristics
National resources
  USE   **Economic conditions**
         Natural resources
         United States—Economic con-
         ditions
National security (May subdiv. geog.)
355
  RT   **Economic policy**
        International relations
        Military policy
National security—United States   **355**
  UF   United States—National security

National self-determination (May subdiv. geog.)   **320.1; 341.26**
   UF   Self-determination, National
   BT   **Nationalism**
   RT   **Sovereignty**
National service   361.2
   UF   Alternative military service
        National community service
   BT   **Public welfare**
   RT   **Volunteer work**
National socialism   320.5; 335.6
   Use for materials limited to fascism in Germany during the Nazi regime.
   UF   Nazism
   BT   **Fascism**
        World War, 1939-1945—Causes
   RT   **Neo-Nazis**
        Socialism
National songs (May subdiv. geog.)   **782.42**
   UF   National anthems
        National hymns
        Patriotic songs
   BT   **Songs**
   NT   **War songs**
   RT   **Folk songs**
        Patriotic poetry
National songs—United States   782.42
   UF   American national songs
        United States—National songs
   BT   **American songs**
National symbols
   USE   **National emblems**
National treasure
   USE   **Cultural property**
Nationalism (May subdiv. geog.)   **320.5**
   UF   National consciousness
   BT   **International relations**
        Political science
   NT   **Ethnocentrism**
        National characteristics
        National liberation movements
        National self-determination
   RT   **Patriotism**
        Regionalism
Nationalism, Black
   USE   **Black nationalism**
Nationalism—United States   320.5
Nationalist China
   USE   **Taiwan**

Nationality (Citizenship)
   USE   **Citizenship**
Nationalization
   USE   **Government ownership**
Nationalization of railroads
   USE   **Railroads—Government policy**
Nationalized companies
   USE   **Government business enterprises**
Native American architecture (May subdiv. geog.)   **720.97; 970.004**
   UF   Indians of North America—Architecture
   BT   **Architecture**
   RT   **Native Americans—Dwellings**
Native American art (May subdiv. geog.)   **704; 709.01**
   UF   Indians of North America—Art
   BT   **Art**
Native American authors   810.9; 920
   UF   American Indian authors
   BT   **Authors**
Native American children (May subdiv. geog.)   **305.23; 970.004**
   UF   Indians of North America—Children
        Native Americans—Children
   SA   children of specific Native American groups, e.g. **Navajo children** [to be added as needed]
   BT   **Children**
   NT   **Navajo children**
Native American costume (May subdiv. geog.)   **970.004**
   UF   Indians of North America—Costume
   BT   **Costume**
Native American dance (May subdiv. geog.)   **793.3; 970.004**
   UF   Indians of North America—Dances
   BT   **Folk dancing**
Native American games (May subdiv. geog.)   **790.1; 970.004**
   UF   Indians of North America—Games
   BT   **Games**
        Native Americans—Social life and customs

Native American languages (May subdiv. geog.) **497**

Use for materials on the several languages of Native Americans.

UF Indian languages (North American)

Indians of North America—Languages

SA names of individual languages, e.g. **Navajo language** [to be added as needed]

BT **Language and languages**

NT **Navajo language**

Native American legends

USE **Native Americans—Folklore**

Native American literature (May subdiv. geog.) **897**

Use for collections or materials about literature written in Native American languages by several Native American authors. Collections or materials about literature written in English by several Native American authors are entered under **American literature—Native American authors.**

UF Indians of North America—Literature

BT **Literature**

Native American medicine (May subdiv. geog.) **615.8**

UF Indians of North America—Medicine

BT **Medicine**

Native American music (May subdiv. geog.) **780.89**

Use for musical transcriptions or for materials about the music of the Native Americans.

UF Indians of North America—Music

BT **Music**

Native American mythology

USE **Native Americans—Folklore**

Native Americans—Religion

Native American names (May subdiv. geog.) **929.4**

UF Indians of North America—Names

BT **Names**

Native American sign language 419

UF Indians of North America—Sign language

BT **Sign language**

Native American silverwork 739.2

UF Indians of North America—Silverwork

BT **Silverwork**

Native American women (May subdiv. geog.) **305.4; 970.004**

UF Indians of North America—Women

Native Americans—Women

SA women of specific Native American groups, e.g. **Navajo women** [to be added as needed]

BT **Women**

NT **Navajo women**

Native Americans (May subdiv. geog.) **970.004**

Use for general materials on the native peoples of the Western Hemisphere. Libraries that prefer not to subdivide by *United States* may also use this heading for materials limited to the native peoples of the United States. Phrase headings derived from this term may be similarly established for other ethnic groups and for specific Native American peoples and linguistic families. Topical subdivisions provided under this heading may also be used under other ethnic groups and under specific Native American peoples and linguistic families.

UF American Indians

Indians

Indians of North America

Native peoples—America

Pre-Columbian Americans

SA names of particular Native American peoples and linguistic families, e.g. **Aztecs; Navajo Indians** etc. [to be added as needed]

BT **Native peoples**

Native Americans—Agriculture (May subdiv. geog.) **338.1; 630**

UF Indians of North America—Agriculture

BT **Agriculture**

Native Americans—Amusements

USE **Native Americans—Social life and customs**

Native Americans—Antiquities (May subdiv. geog.) **970.004**

UF Indians of North America—Antiquities

BT **Antiquities**

Native Americans—Canada 971.004

UF Canadian Indians

First nations

Indians of Canada

Native Americans—Canada—*Continued*
    Indians of North America—Canada

Native Americans—Captivities (May subdiv. geog.) **970.004**
  UF Indians of North America—Captivities
  BT **Frontier and pioneer life**

Native Americans—Central America 972.8004
  UF Indians of Central America
  NT **Mayas**

Native Americans—Children
  USE **Native American children**

Native Americans—Christian missions (May subdiv. geog.) **266**
  UF Indian missions
      Indians of North America—Christian missions
  BT **Christian missions**

Native Americans—Chronology
  USE **Native Americans—History—Chronology**

Native Americans—Claims (May subdiv. geog.) **323.1197; 970.004**
  UF Indians of North America—Claims
      Native Americans—Land claims

Native Americans—Customs
  USE **Native Americans—Social life and customs**

Native Americans—Dwellings (May subdiv. geog.) **728; 970.004**
  UF Indians of North America—Dwellings
  NT **Tepees**
  RT **Native American architecture**

Native Americans—Economic conditions (May subdiv. geog.) **970.004**
  UF Indians of North America—Economic conditions
  BT **Economic conditions**

Native Americans—Education (May subdiv. geog.) **371.829; 970.004**
  UF Indians of North America—Education
      Indians of North America—Schools
  BT **Education**

Native Americans—Ethnobiology 578.6
  BT **Ethnobiology**

Native Americans—Ethnobotany 581.6
  BT **Ethnobotany**

Native Americans—Ethnozoology 591.6
  BT **Ethnozoology**

Native Americans—First contact with Europeans (May subdiv. geog.) **970.004**
  UF Indians of North America—First contact with Europeans
  BT **Native Americans—History**
  RT **Native Americans—Relations with early settlers**

Native Americans—Folklore (May subdiv. geog.) **398**
  Use for collections of Native American legends, myths, tales, etc., and for materials about the folklore and mythology of Native Americans.
  UF Indians of North America—Folklore
      Native American legends
      Native American mythology
  BT **Folklore**

Native Americans—Forced Removal
  USE **Native Americans—Relocation**

Native Americans—Government policy
  USE **Native Americans—Government relations**

Native Americans—Government relations (May subdiv. geog.) **323.1197; 970.004**
  Use for materials on the Indian policy of the United States government and on relations between North American governments and the Native Americans.
  UF Federal-Indian relations
      Indians of North America—Government relations
      Native Americans—Government policy
  RT **Native Americans—Relations with early settlers**

Native Americans—Guatemala 972.81004
  UF Indians of Central America—Guatemala

Native Americans—History 970.004
  UF Indians of North America—History
  NT **Native Americans—First contact with Europeans**
      Native Americans—Relations with early settlers

Native Americans—History—*Continued*
Native Americans—Wars
Native Americans—History—Chronology
970.004
Use for materials that list events and dates in the history of the Native Americans in the order of their occurrence.
UF Indians of North America—History—Chronology
Native Americans—Chronology
Native Americans—Housing (May subdiv. geog.) 307.3; 363.5
BT Housing
Native Americans—Hunting (May subdiv. geog.) 970.004
BT Hunting
Native Americans—Industries (May subdiv. geog.) 338.4; 680; 970.004
UF Indians of North America—Industries
BT Industries
Native Americans—Land claims
USE Native Americans—Claims
Native Americans—Material culture 970.004
Native Americans—Medical care (May subdiv. geog.) 362.1
BT Medical care
Native Americans—Mexico 972.004
UF Indians of Mexico
NT Aztecs
Mayas
Native Americans—North America 970.004
UF Indians of North America
SA names of particular Native American peoples and linguistic families, e.g. **Navajo Indians** [to be added as needed]
Native Americans—Origin 970.004
UF Indians of North America—Origin
Native Americans—Peru 985
UF Indians of South America—Peru
Native Americans—Politics and government (May subdiv. geog.) 970.004
UF Indians of North America—Politics and government
Native Americans—Tribal government

BT Politics
Native Americans—Psychology 155.8
UF Indians of North America—Psychology
BT Ethnopsychology
Native Americans—Relations with early settlers (May subdiv. geog.) 970.004
UF Indians of North America—Relations with early settlers
BT Native Americans—History
RT Native Americans—First contact with Europeans
Native Americans—Government relations
Native Americans—Religion (May subdiv. geog.) 270.089; 299.7; 299.8
UF Indians of North America—Religion
Native American mythology
BT Religion
Native Americans—Relocation (May subdiv. geog.) 970.004
UF Forced removal of Indians
Indian removal
Native Americans—Forced Removal
Native Americans—Removal
Removal of Indians
Native Americans—Removal
USE Native Americans—Relocation
Native Americans—Reservations (May subdiv. geog.) 333.1; 970.004
UF Indian reservations
Indians of North America—Reservations
SA names of native peoples, tribes, etc., with the subdivision *Reservations* [to be added as needed]
Native Americans—Rites and ceremonies 970.004
UF Indians of North America—Rites and ceremonies
BT Rites and ceremonies
NT Powwows
Native Americans—Social conditions (May subdiv. geog.) 970.004
UF Indians of North America—Social conditions
BT Social conditions

Native Americans—Social life and customs (May subdiv. geog.)
970.004
UF   Indians of North America—Social life and customs
Native Americans—Amusements
Native Americans—Customs
BT   **Manners and customs**
NT   **Native American games**
Powwows
Native Americans—South America   980
UF   Indians of South America
NT   **Incas**
Native Americans—Southwestern States
979
NT   **Cliff dwellers and cliff dwellings**
Navajo Indians
Native Americans—Tribal government
USE   **Native Americans—Politics and government**
Native Americans—United States
973.04
UF   Indians of North America
Native Americans—Wars (May subdiv. geog.)   970.004
UF   Indians of North America—Wars
BT   **Native Americans—History**
NT   **Black Hawk War, 1832**
King Philip's War, 1675-1676
Pontiac's Conspiracy, 1763-1765
United States—History—1689-1697, King William's War
United States—History—1755-1763, French and Indian War
Native Americans—West Indies
972.9004
UF   Indians of the West Indies
Native Americans—Women
USE   **Native American women**
Native peoples (May subdiv. geog.)
305.8

Use for materials on indigenous groups within a colonial area or modern state where the group does not control the government. General materials on people bound together by common ancestry and culture are entered under **Ethnic groups.** Materials on the various ethnic groups or native peoples in a particular region or country are entered under **Ethnology** subdivided geographically.

UF   Aborigines
Indigenous peoples
Natives
People
SA   names of individual native peoples e.g. **Yoruba (African people)** [to be added as needed]
BT   **Ethnology**
NT   **Aboriginal Australians**
Inuit
Native Americans
Yoruba (African people)
Native peoples—America
USE   **Native Americans**
Natives
USE   **Native peoples**
Nativity of Jesus Christ
USE   **Jesus Christ—Nativity**
NATO
USE   **North Atlantic Treaty Organization**
Natural beauty conservation
USE   **Landscape protection**
Natural childbirth   618.4
UF   Lamaze method of childbirth
BT   **Childbirth**
NT   **Midwives**
Natural cycles
USE   **Cycles**
Natural disasters (May subdiv. geog.)
904
SA   types of natural disasters [to be added as needed]
BT   **Disasters**
NT   **Earthquakes**
Environmental degradation
Floods
Landslides
Storms
Tsunamis
Natural disasters—United States   973
Natural food cooking
USE   **Cooking—Natural foods**
Natural foods   641.3
UF   Health foods
Organically grown foods
BT   **Food**
RT   **Cooking—Natural foods**
Natural gardening
USE   **Organic gardening**

Natural gas (May subdiv. geog.) 553.2;
  665.7
  BT Fuel
    Gases
Natural gas companies
  USE **Gas companies**
Natural gas utilities
  USE **Gas companies**
Natural history (May subdiv. geog.)
  508

  Use for materials on the unsystematic study
  of zoology, botany, mineralogy, etc., the collecting of specimens, and, with a geographic
  subdivision, the description of nature in a particular place. Materials on the study of animals and plants as an elementary school subject are entered under **Nature study.** General
  and theoretical materials on the natural world
  are entered under **Nature.**

  UF Animal lore
    Mineralogy
  BT **Science**
  NT **Aquariums**
    Bible—Natural history
    Bird watching
    Fossils
    Nature photography
  RT **Biogeography**
    Botany
    Minerals
    Nature
    Zoology
Natural history—United States 508.73
  UF Nature study—United States
Natural law 340
  UF Law of nature
    Natural rights
  BT **Ethics**
    Law
  RT **International law**
Natural monuments (May subdiv. geog.)
  719

  Use for general materials on natural objects
  of historic or scientific interest such as caves,
  cliffs, and natural bridges.

  UF Landmarks, Preservation of
    Preservation of natural scenery
    Protection of natural scenery
    Scenery
  SA names of individual natural
    monuments [to be added as
    needed]
  BT **Landscape protection**
    Monuments

  Nature conservation
  RT **National monuments**
    National parks and reserves
Natural monuments—United States
  719; 917.3
Natural parents
  USE **Birthparents**
Natural pesticides 668
  BT **Pesticides**
Natural religion
  USE **Natural theology**
Natural resources (May subdiv. geog.)
  333.7
  UF National resources
  SA types of natural resources [to be
    added as needed]
  BT **Economic conditions**
  NT **Conservation of natural re-
    sources**
    Energy resources
    Forests and forestry
    Marine resources
    Mines and mineral resources
    Water resources development
    Water supply
  RT **Public lands**
Natural resources—Management 333.7
  BT **Management**
Natural resources—United States 333.7
Natural rights
  USE **Natural law**
Natural satellites
  USE **Satellites**
Natural selection 576.8
  UF Survival of the fittest
  BT **Genetics**
    Variation (Biology)
  RT **Evolution**
    Heredity
Natural steam energy
  USE **Geothermal resources**
Natural theology 210

  Use for materials on the knowledge of
  God's existence obtained by observing the
  visible processes of nature.

  UF Natural religion
  BT **Apologetics**
    Theology
  NT **Creation**
  RT **Religion and science**
Natural therapy
  USE **Naturopathy**

Naturalism in art
    USE **Realism in art**
Naturalism in literature
    USE **Realism in literature**
Naturalists (May subdiv. geog.)
    508.092; 920
    SA   types of naturalists, e.g. **Bota-nists** [to be added as needed]
    BT   **Scientists**
    NT   **Biologists**
        Botanists
Naturalization   **323.6**
    BT   **Immigration and emigration**
        International law
        Suffrage
    RT   **Aliens**
        Americanization
        Citizenship
Nature   **508**
    Use for general and theoretical materials on the natural world. Materials on the study of animals and plants as an elementary school subject are entered under **Nature study.** Materials on the unsystematic study of zoology, botany, mineralogy, etc., the collecting of specimens, and the description of nature in a particular place are entered under **Natural history.**
    RT   **Natural history**
        Nature study
Nature conservation (May subdiv. geog.)
    333.72
    UF   Conservation of nature
        Nature protection
        Preservation of natural scenery
        Protection of natural scenery
    BT   **Conservation of natural re-sources**
    NT   **Endangered species**
        Landscape protection
        Natural monuments
        Plant conservation
        Wildlife conservation
Nature craft   **745.5**
    Use for materials on crafts using objects found in nature, such as leaves, shells, etc.
    UF   Naturecraft
    BT   **Handicraft**
    NT   **Potpourri**
        Sand sculpture
Nature—Effect of human beings on
    USE **Human influence on nature**
Nature in literature   **809**
    BT   **Literature—Themes**

Nature in the bible
    USE **Bible—Natural history**
Nature photography   **778.9**
    UF   Photography of nature
    SA   photography of particular sub-jects in nature, e.g. **Photography of birds** [to be added as needed]
    BT   **Natural history**
        Photography
    NT   **Photography of animals**
        Photography of birds
        Photography of fishes
        Photography of plants
    RT   **Outdoor photography**
Nature poetry   **808.1; 808.81**
    May be used for individual works or collections of poetry about nature.
    UF   Nature—Poetry
    BT   **Poetry**
Nature—Poetry
    USE **Nature poetry**
Nature prints   **761**
    BT   **Printing**
        Prints
Nature protection
    USE **Nature conservation**
Nature study   **372.35; 508.07**
    Use for materials on the study of animals and plants as an elementary school subject. Materials on the unsystematic study of zoology, botany, mineralogy, etc., the collecting of specimens, and the description of nature in a particular place are entered under **Natural history.** General and theoretical materials on the natural world are entered under **Nature.**
    BT   **Education**
        Science—Study and teaching
    RT   **Nature**
        Outdoor education
        Outdoor life
Nature study—United States
    USE **Natural history—United States**
Nature tourism
    USE **Ecotourism**
Nature trails (May subdiv. geog.)   **508**
    BT   **Trails**
Naturecraft
    USE **Nature craft**
Naturopathy   **615.5**
    UF   Natural therapy
    BT   **Alternative medicine**
        Therapeutics
    RT   **Chiropractic**

Nautical almanacs   528
  BT   **Almanacs**
       Navigation
Nautical astronomy   527
  BT   **Astronomy**
  NT   **Latitude**
       Longitude
  RT   **Navigation**
       Time
Nautical charts   623.89
  UF   Charts, Nautical
       Navigation charts
       Navigation maps
       Pilot charts
  BT   **Maps**
       Navigation
Navaho Indians
  USE **Navajo Indians**
Navaho language
  USE **Navajo language**
Navajo children (May subdiv. geog.)
       973.04
  UF   Navajo Indians—Children
  BT   **Native American children**
       Navajo Indians
Navajo Indians   973.04
  UF   Navaho Indians
  BT   **Native Americans—Southwest-**
       ern States
  NT   **Navajo children**
       Navajo women
Navajo Indians—Children
  USE **Navajo children**
Navajo Indians—Women
  USE **Navajo women**
Navajo language   497
  UF   Navaho language
  BT   **Native American languages**
Navajo women (May subdiv. geog.)
       973.04
  UF   Navajo Indians—Women
  BT   **Native American women**
       Navajo Indians
Naval administration
  USE **Naval art and science**
       and names of countries with the
       subhead *Navy,* e.g. **United**
       States. Navy [to be added as
       needed]
Naval aeronautics
  USE **Military aeronautics**

Naval air bases
  USE **Air bases**
Naval airplanes
  USE **Military airplanes**
Naval architecture   623.8
  UF   Marine architecture
  BT   **Architecture**
  NT   **Boatbuilding**
       Marine engineering
       Shipbuilding
       Steamboats
       Warships
Naval art and science (May subdiv.
       geog.)   **359**
  UF   Fighting
       Naval administration
       Naval science
       Naval warfare
       Navy
  SA   names of wars with the subdivi-
       sion *Naval operations,* e.g.
       World War, 1939-1945—Na-
       val operations [to be added
       as needed]
  NT   **Camouflage (Military science)**
       Marine engineering
       Navy yards and naval stations
       Privateering
       Sailors
       Sea power
       Signals and signaling
       Strategy
       Submarine warfare
       Torpedoes
       Warships
  RT   **Military art and science**
       Navies
       Navigation
       War
Naval art and science—Study and teaching
  USE **Naval education**
Naval bases
  USE **Navy yards and naval stations**
Naval battles   359.4; 904
  UF   Naval warfare
  SA   names of countries with the sub-
       division *Naval history;* names
       of wars with the subdivision
       Naval operations, e.g. **World**
       War, 1939-1945—Naval op-
       erations; and names of spe-

Naval battles—*Continued*
cific naval battles [to be added as needed]
- BT **Battles**
- RT **Naval history**

Naval biography
- USE names of navies with the subdivision *Biography*, e.g. **United States. Navy—Biography** [to be added as needed]

Naval education (May subdiv. geog.) **359.007**
- UF Naval art and science—Study and teaching
  Naval schools
- BT **Education**

Naval engineering
- USE **Marine engineering**

Naval history **359.009**
- UF Wars
- SA names of countries with the subhead *Navy* or the subdivision *Naval history* [to be added as needed]
- BT **History**
- NT **Pirates**
  Privateering
  United States—Naval history
- RT **Military history**
  Naval battles
  Sea power

Naval law
- USE **Maritime law**

Naval offenses
- USE **Military offenses**

Naval operations
- USE names of wars with the subdivision *Naval operations*, e.g. **World War, 1939-1945—Naval operations** [to be added as needed]

Naval pensions
- USE **Military pensions**

Naval personnel
- USE **Sailors**

Naval power
- USE **Sea power**

Naval schools
- USE **Naval education**

Naval science
- USE **Naval art and science**

Naval shipyards
- USE **Navy yards and naval stations**

Naval signaling
- USE **Signals and signaling**

Naval strategy
- USE **Strategy**

Naval uniforms
- USE **Military uniforms**

Naval warfare
- USE **Naval art and science**
  Naval battles
  Submarine warfare

Navies **359.3**
- UF Military power
  Navy
  Sea life
- SA names of countries with the subhead *Navy*, e.g. **United States. Navy** [to be added as needed]
- BT **Armed forces**
  Military personnel
- NT **Admirals**
  Sailors
  United States. Navy
- RT **Naval art and science**
  Sea power
  Warships

Navigation (May subdiv. geog.) **623.89; 629.04**
- UF Pilots and pilotage
  Seamanship
- BT **Locomotion**
- NT **Compass**
  Global Positioning System
  Harbors
  Inland navigation
  Knots and splices
  Lighthouses
  Loran
  Nautical almanacs
  Nautical charts
  Ocean currents
  Pilot guides
  Radar
  Shipwrecks
  Signals and signaling
  Steam navigation
  Winds
- RT **Direction sense**
  Nautical astronomy

Navigation—*Continued*
    Naval art and science
    Sailing
    Ship pilots
Navigation (Aeronautics)   629.132
    UF   Aerial navigation
            Aeronautics—Navigation
            Air navigation
    BT   **Aeronautics**
    NT   **Airplanes—Piloting**
            Radio in aeronautics
Navigation (Astronautics)   629.45
    UF   Astronavigation
            Space navigation
    BT   **Astrodynamics**
            Astronautics
    NT   **Astronautical instruments**
            Radio in astronautics
            Space vehicles—Piloting
    RT   **Space flight**
Navigation charts
    USE   **Nautical charts**
Navigation—Law and legislation
    USE   **Maritime law**
Navigation maps
    USE   **Nautical charts**
Navigators
    USE   **Explorers**
            Sailors
Navy
    USE   **Naval art and science**
            Navies
            Sea power
            and names of countries with the
            subhead *Navy,* e.g. **United**
            States. Navy [to be added as
            needed]
Navy Sealab project
    USE   **Sealab project**
Navy yards and naval stations (May
    subdiv. geog.)   **359.7**
    UF   Naval bases
            Naval shipyards
    BT   **Naval art and science**
Nazi persecution
    USE   religious groups and classes of
            persons with the subdivision
            Nazi persecution, e.g. **Handi-**
            capped—Nazi persecution [to
            be added as needed]
Nazi persecution of the handicapped
    USE   **Handicapped—Nazi persecution**

Nazism
    USE   **National socialism**
Near-death experiences   133.9; 155.9
    Use for materials on the paranormal experi-
    ences of those who have survived near death
    or apparent death.
    BT   **Death**
    RT   **Parapsychology**
Near East
    USE   **Middle East**
Neatness
    USE   **Cleanliness**
            Orderliness
Nebula Award   808.3
    BT   **Literary prizes**
            Science fiction
Nebulae, Extragalactic
    USE   **Galaxies**
Necrologies
    USE   **Obituaries**
Necromancy
    USE   **Divination**
            Magic
Needlepoint   746.44
    UF   Canvas embroidery
    BT   **Embroidery**
            Needlework
Needlework   746.4
    SA   types of needlework [to be add-
            ed as needed]
    BT   **Decoration and ornament**
            Decorative arts
    NT   **Appliqué**
            Crocheting
            Drawn work
            Embroidery
            Hardanger needlework
            Knitting
            Lace and lace making
            Needlepoint
            Patchwork
            Quilting
            Samplers
            Tapestry
    RT   **Dressmaking**
            Sewing
Negotiable instruments (May subdiv.
    geog.)   **332.7**
    UF   Bills and notes
            Bills of credit
            Commercial paper
            Instruments, Negotiable

Negotiable instruments—*Continued*
        Letters of credit
    BT   **Banks and banking**
        Commercial law
        Contracts
        Credit
    NT   **Bonds**
Negotiation   158; 302.3
    UF   Bargaining
        Discussion
    BT   **Applied psychology**
    NT   **Collective bargaining**
        Conflict management
        Hostage negotiation
        Industrial arbitration
Negritude
    USE   **Blacks—Race identity**
Negro leagues   796.357
    BT   **Baseball**
Negroes
    USE   **African Americans**
        Blacks
Neighborhood (May subdiv. geog.)
        307.3
    UF   Neighborhoods
    BT   **Community life**
        Social groups
Neighborhood centers
    USE   **Community centers**
        Social settlements
Neighborhood development
    USE   **Community development**
Neighborhoods
    USE   **Neighborhood**
Neo-fascism
    USE   **Fascism**
        Neo-Nazis
Neo-Greek literature
    USE   **Modern Greek literature**
Neo-impressionism (Art)
    USE   **Impressionism (Art)**
Neo-Latin languages
    USE   **Romance languages**
Neo-Nazis (May subdiv. geog.)   **320.5**
    Use for materials on political groups whose social beliefs or political agendas are reminiscent of those of Hitler's Nazis.
    UF   Neo-fascism
        Neo-nazism
    BT   **Fascism**
    RT   **National socialism**

Neo-nazism
    USE   **Neo-Nazis**
Neolithic period
    USE   **Stone Age**
Neon tubes   621.32
    BT   **Electric signs**
Nero, Emperor of Rome, 37-68   92; B
    BT   **Emperors—Rome**
Nerves   611; 612.8
    BT   **Nervous system**
Nerves—Diseases
    USE   **Nervous system—Diseases**
Nervous breakdown
    USE   **Neurasthenia**
Nervous exhaustion
    USE   **Neurasthenia**
Nervous prostration
    USE   **Neurasthenia**
Nervous system   611; 612.8
    UF   Neurology
    BT   **Anatomy**
        Physiology
    NT   **Abnormal psychology**
        Brain
        Nerves
        Psychophysiology
Nervous system—Diseases   616.8
    UF   Nerves—Diseases
        Neuropathology
    BT   **Diseases**
    NT   **Communicative disorders**
        Epilepsy
        Paralysis
Nest building   591.56
    UF   Building nests
        Nesting (Animal behavior)
        Nesting behavior
    SA   types of animals and individual
        species on animals with the
        subdivision *Nests,* e.g.
        Birds—Nests [to be added as
        needed]
    BT   **Animal behavior**
        Animals—Habitations
Nesting (Animal behavior)
    USE   **Nest building**
Nesting behavior
    USE   **Nest building**

Nests
  USE   types of animals and individual
        species of animals with the
        subdivision *Nests,* e.g.
        Birds—Nests [to be added as
        needed]
Netherlands   949.2
  May be subdivided like United States ex-
  cept for *History.*
  UF   Holland
Netherlands—History   949.2
Netherlands—History—1940-1945, Ger-
  man occupation   949.207
  UF   German occupation of Nether-
       lands, 1940-1945
Network theory
  USE   **System analysis**
Networks (Associations, institutions, etc.)
  USE   **Associations**
Networks, Computer
  USE   **Computer networks**
Networks, Information
  USE   **Information networks**
Neurasthenia   616.85
  UF   Nervous breakdown
       Nervous exhaustion
       Nervous prostration
  BT   **Mental illness**
Neurology
  USE   **Nervous system**
Neuropathology
  USE   **Nervous system—Diseases**
Neuroses   616.85
  BT   **Abnormal psychology**
  NT   **Anxiety**
       Depression (Psychology)
       Obsessive-compulsive disorder
       Panic disorders
       Phobias
       Post-traumatic stress disorder
Neurotic children
  USE   **Emotionally disturbed children**
Neutrality (May subdiv. geog.)   **327.1;**
       341.6
  UF   Nonalignment
  BT   **International law**
       International relations
       International security
  RT   **Intervention (International law)**

Neutrality—United States   327.73
  UF   United States—Neutrality
  RT   **United States—Foreign rela-**
       tions
Neutron bomb   623.4
  UF   Neutron bombs
  BT   **Bombs**
       Neutron weapons
Neutron bombs
  USE   **Neutron bomb**
Neutron weapons   623.4
  UF   Enhanced radiation weapons
  BT   **Nuclear weapons**
  NT   **Neutron bomb**
Neutrons   539.7
  BT   **Atoms**
       Particles (Nuclear physics)
New Age movement (May subdiv. geog.)
       130; 131; 299
  Use for materials on any of various post-
  1970 cults and organizations that incorporate
  Eastern or Native American religions, occult
  beliefs and practices, mysticism, or meditation
  techniques in an attempt to enhance con-
  sciousness and develop human potential.
  UF   Aquarian Age movement
  BT   **Cults**
       Occultism
       Social movements
New birth (Theology)
  USE   **Regeneration (Christianity)**
New business enterprises (May subdiv.
       geog.)   **338.7**
  UF   How to start a business
       Starting a business
  BT   **Business enterprises**
New communities
  USE   **Planned communities**
New countries
  USE   **New states**
New Deal, 1933-1939   973.917
  BT   **United States—History—1933-**
       1945
New England   974
  BT   **United States**
New France—History
  USE   **Canada—History—0-1763 (New**
       France)
       Mississippi River Valley—His-
       tory
New nations
  USE   **New states**

New Negro Movement
　USE　**Harlem Renaissance**
New product development
　USE　**New products**
New products (May subdiv. geog.)
　　658.5
　UF　New product development
　　　Product development
　BT　**Commercial products**
　　　Industrial research
　　　Marketing
New states　321
　UF　New countries
　　　New nations
　　　States, New
　BT　**Developing countries**
New Testament
　USE　**Bible. N.T.**
New words　417
　UF　Coinage of words
　　　Words, New
　BT　**Vocabulary**
New York Knicks (Basketball team)
　　796.323
　UF　Knicks (Basketball team)
　BT　**Basketball teams**
New York (N.Y.)—Streets
　USE　**Streets—New York (N.Y.)**
Newbery Award
　USE　**Newbery Medal**
Newbery Medal　028.5
　UF　Newbery Award
　　　Newbery Prize books
　BT　**Children's literature**
　　　Literary prizes
Newbery Prize books
　USE　**Newbery Medal**
News agencies (May subdiv. geog.)
　　070.4
　UF　News services
　　　Wire services
　BT　**Press**
News editing
　USE　**Journalism—Editing**
News photography
　USE　**Photojournalism**
News services
　USE　**News agencies**
Newsgroups, Electronic
　USE　**Electronic discussion groups**

Newsletters　070.1
　BT　**Journalism**
　　　Newspapers
Newspaper advertising　659.13
　　Use for materials on advertising in newspapers. Materials on the advertising of newspapers are entered under **Advertising—Newspapers.**
　UF　Advertising, Newspaper
　BT　**Advertising**
　　　Newspapers
Newspaper clippings
　USE　**Clippings (Books, newspapers, etc.)**
Newspaper work
　USE　**Reporters and reporting**
Newspapers (May subdiv. geog.)　**070**
　　Use for materials limited to the history, organization, and management of newspapers. Materials on writing for the periodical press, on the editing of such writing, and on journalism as an occupation, are entered under **Journalism.**
　SA　names of individual newspapers
　　　[to be added as needed]
　BT　**Mass media**
　　　Serial publications
　NT　**Clippings (Books, newspapers, etc.)**
　　　Newsletters
　　　Newspaper advertising
　　　Reporters and reporting
　RT　**Journalism**
　　　Periodicals
　　　Press
Newspapers—Advertising
　USE　**Advertising—Newspapers**
Newspapers—Editing
　USE　**Journalism—Editing**
Newspapers—Great Britain　072
　UF　English newspapers
Newspapers—Indexes　070.1
Newspapers—Sections, columns, etc.
　　070.4
　SA　types of newspaper columns, e.g.
　　　Advice columns [to be added as needed]
　NT　**Advice columns**
Newspapers—United States　071
　UF　American newspapers
Nicene Creed　238
　BT　**Creeds**

Nicknames   929.4
  UF   Epithets
        Sobriquets
  BT   **Personal names**
Nicotine habit
  USE   **Tobacco habit**
Night   529
  BT   **Chronology**
        Time
  NT   **Bedtime**
  RT   **Day**
Night clubs, cabarets, etc. (May subdiv.
        geog.)   **725**
  UF   Cabarets
  BT   **Theaters**
Night schools
  USE   **Evening and continuation**
          schools
Nike rocket   623.4
  BT   **Guided missiles**
Nineteenth century
  USE   **World history—19th century**
Nitrates   553.6
  BT   **Chemicals**
        Fertilizers
Nitrogen   546; 665
  BT   **Gases**
Nobel Prizes   001.4; 807.9
  BT   **Awards**
Nobility (May subdiv. geog.)   **305.5;**
        929.7
  UF   Peerage
  BT   **Upper class**
  NT   **Knights and knighthood**
  RT   **Aristocracy**
        Heraldry
Noise   363.74
  SA   subjects with the subdivision
        Noise [to be added as needed]
  BT   **Public health**
        Sound
  NT   **Airplanes—Noise**
Noise pollution (May subdiv. geog.)
        363.74
  SA   subjects with the subdivision
        Noise [to be added as needed]
  BT   **Pollution**
  NT   **Airplanes—Noise**
Nomadic peoples
  USE   **Nomads**

Nomads (May subdiv. geog.)   **305.9**
  UF   Nomadic peoples
        Pastoral peoples
  BT   **Primitive societies**
Nomenclature
  USE   types of scientific and technical
          disciplines and types of sub-
          stances, plants, and animals
          with the subdivision *Nomen-*
          clature, for systematically de-
          rived lists of names or desig-
          nations that have been formal-
          ly adopted or sanctioned, and
          for discussions of the princi-
          ples involved in the creation
          and application of such
          names, e.g. **Botany—Nomen-**
          clature; scientific and techni-
          cal disciplines and types of
          animals, plants, and crops
          with the subdivision *Nomen-*
          clature (Popular), for lists or
          materials about popular, non-
          technical names or designa-
          tions of substances, species,
          etc., e.g. **Trees—Nomencla-**
          ture (Popular); and subjects,
          classes of persons, sacred
          works, and religious sects
          with the subdivision *Terminol-*
          ogy, for lists or discussions of
          words and expressions found
          in those works or used in
          those fields, e.g. **Botany—**
          Terminology [to be added as
          needed]
Nomenclature (Popular)
  USE   types of scientific and technical
          disciplines and types of ani-
          mals, plants, and crops with
          the subdivision *Nomenclature*
          (Popular), for lists of popular
          or non-technical names or
          designations of substances,
          species, etc., e.g. **Trees—No-**
          menclature (Popular); and
          scientific and technical disci-
          plines and types of sub-
          stances, plants, and animals
          with the subdivision *Nomen-*
          clature, for systematically de-

Nomenclature (Popular)—*Continued*
rived lists of names or designations that have been formally adopted or sactioned, and for discussions of the principles involved in the creation and application of such names, e.g. **Botany—Nomenclature** [to be added as needed]

Nomination
USE types of public officials and names of individual public officials with the subdivision *Nomination,* e.g. **Presidents—United States—Nomination** [to be added as needed]

Nomination of presidents
USE **Presidents—United States—Nomination**

Non-institutional churches   289.9
UF Avant-garde churches
Churches, Non-institutional
Noninstitutional churches
BT **Christian sects**

Non-professional theater
USE **Amateur theater**

Non-proliferation of nuclear weapons
USE **Arms control**

Non-promotion (School)
USE **Promotion (School)**

Non-victim crimes
USE **Crimes without victims**

Non-wage payments
USE **Fringe benefits**

Nonalignment
USE **Neutrality**

Nonbook materials
USE **Audiovisual materials**

Noncitizens
USE **Aliens**

Nonconformity
USE **Conformity**
Counter culture
Dissent

Nondenominational churches
USE **Community churches**

Nonfiction films
USE **Documentary films**

Nonformal schools
USE **Experimental schools**

Nonfossil fuels
USE **Synthetic fuels**

Nongraded schools (May subdiv. geog.)
371.2
UF Multi-age grouping
Ungraded schools
BT **Ability grouping in education**
Education—Experimental methods
Schools

Noninstitutional churches
USE **Non-institutional churches**

Nonlinguistic communication
USE **Nonverbal communication**

Nonnationals
USE **Aliens**

Nonnutritive sweeteners
USE **Sugar substitutes**

Nonobjective art
USE **Abstract art**

Nonprescription drugs   615
UF Drugs, Nonprescription
Over-the-counter drugs
Patent medicines
BT **Drugs**

Nonprint materials
USE **Audiovisual materials**

Nonprofit corporations
USE **Nonprofit organizations**

Nonprofit organizations (May subdiv. geog.)   **346; 658**
UF Corporations, Nonprofit
Nonprofit corporations
Nonprofit sector
Nonprofits
Not-for-profit organizations
Organizations, Nonprofit
BT **Associations**

Nonprofit sector
USE **Nonprofit organizations**

Nonprofitable drugs
USE **Orphan drugs**

Nonprofits
USE **Nonprofit organizations**

Nonpublic schools
USE **Church schools**
Private schools

Nonsense verses   808.1; 808.81
May be used for individual works, collections, or materials about nonsense verse.

Nonsense verses—*Continued*
- UF Rhymes
- BT **Children's poetry**
  Humorous poetry
  Wit and humor
- NT **Tongue twisters**
- RT **Limericks**

Nonsupport
- USE **Desertion and nonsupport**

Nonverbal communication   153.6; 302.2
- UF Nonlinguistic communication
- BT **Communication**
- NT **Body language**
  Hugging
  Personal space
- RT **Deaf—Means of communication**

Nonvictim crimes
- USE **Crimes without victims**

Nonviolence (May subdiv. geog.)   179;
  303.6
- NT **Hunger strikes**
- RT **Pacifism**
  Passive resistance

Nonviolent noncooperation
- USE **Passive resistance**

Nonwage payments
- USE **Fringe benefits**

Nonword stories
- USE **Stories without words**

Nordic peoples
- USE **Teutonic peoples**

Normal schools
- USE **Teachers colleges**

Normandy (France), Attack on, 1944
  940.54
- UF D Day
- BT **World War, 1939-1945—Campaigns**

Normans (May subdiv. geog.)   941.02
- BT **Great Britain—History—1066-1154, Norman period**
- RT **Vikings**

Norse languages
- USE **Old Norse language**
  Scandinavian languages

Norse legends   398.20893
- BT **Legends**

Norse literature
- USE **Old Norse literature**
  Scandinavian literature

Norsemen
- USE **Vikings**

North Africa   961
  Use for materials dealing collectively with the region of Africa that includes Morocco, Algeria, Tunisia, and Libya.
- UF Africa, North
  Barbary States
  Maghreb
- BT **Africa**

North America   970
- BT **America**
- NT **Central America**
  Northwest Coast of North America
  Pacific Northwest

North Atlantic Treaty Organization
  341.7
- UF NATO
- BT **International organization**

North Central States
- USE **Middle West**

North Korea
- USE **Korea (North)**

North Pole   910.9163; 998
- BT **Polar regions**
- RT **Arctic regions**

Northeast Africa   960
  Use for materials dealing collectively with the region of Africa that includes Sudan, Ethiopia, Eritrea, Somalia, and Djibouti.
- UF Africa, Northeast
- BT **Africa**

Northeast Passage   998
- BT **Arctic regions**
  Exploration
  Voyages and travels

Northern lights
- USE **Auroras**

Northmen
- USE **Vikings**

Northwest Africa   964
  Use for materials dealing collectively with the region of Africa that includes Morocco, Western Sahara, Mauritania, Algeria, Mali, Tunisia, Libya, Niger, and Chad.
- UF Africa, Northwest
- BT **Africa**

Northwest Coast of North America
  979.5
- UF Northwest, Pacific coast
  Pacific Northwest coast
- BT **North America**

Northwest, Old
    USE   **Old Northwest**
Northwest, Pacific
    USE   **Pacific Northwest**
Northwest, Pacific coast
    USE   **Northwest Coast of North America**
Northwest Passage   971.9
    BT   **America—Exploration**
        Arctic regions
Northwest Territory
    USE   **Old Northwest**
Norwegian drawn work
    USE   **Hardanger needlework**
Norwegian language   439.8
    May be subdivided like **English language.**
    BT   **Language and languages**
        Scandinavian languages
    NT   **Danish language**
Norwegian language—0-1350
    USE   **Old Norse language**
Norwegian literature   839.82
    May use same subdivisions and names of literary forms as for **English literature.**
    BT   **Literature**
        Scandinavian literature
Nose   611; 612.2
    BT   **Face**
        Head
    RT   **Smell**
Not-for-profit organizations
    USE   **Nonprofit organizations**
Notation, Mathematical
    USE   **Mathematical notation**
Novelists   809.3; 920
    SA   novelists of particular countries, e.g. **American novelists;** and names of individual novelists [to be added as needed]
    BT   **Authors**
    NT   **American novelists**
Novelists, American
    USE   **American novelists**
Novels
    USE   **Fiction**
Novels in letters
    USE   **Epistolary fiction**
Nuclear bomb shelters
    USE   **Air raid shelters**

Nuclear energy (May subdiv. geog.)
    333.792; 539.7
    UF   Atomic energy
        Atomic power
        Nuclear power
    BT   **Nuclear physics**
    NT   **Nuclear engineering**
        Nuclear propulsion
        Nuclear reactors
    RT   **Nuclear industry**
        Nuclear power plants
Nuclear engineering (May subdiv. geog.)
    621.48
    BT   **Engineering**
        Nuclear energy
        Nuclear physics
    NT   **Nuclear reactors**
        Radioactive waste disposal
        Radioisotopes
Nuclear freeze movement
    USE   **Antinuclear movement**
Nuclear industry (May subdiv. geog.)
    333.792
    UF   Atomic industry
    BT   **Industries**
    RT   **Nuclear energy**
Nuclear magnetic resonance imaging
    USE   **Magnetic resonance imaging**
Nuclear medicine   616.07
    UF   Atomic medicine
    BT   **Medicine**
    RT   **Radiation—Physiological effect**
Nuclear medicine—Practice   616.07
    BT   **Medical practice**
Nuclear non-proliferation
    USE   **Arms control**
Nuclear particles
    USE   **Particles (Nuclear physics)**
Nuclear physics   539.7
    UF   Atomic nuclei
    BT   **Physics**
    NT   **Cosmic rays**
        Cyclotrons
        Nuclear energy
        Nuclear engineering
        Nuclear reactors
        Particles (Nuclear physics)
        Radiobiology
        Transmutation (Chemistry)
    RT   **Physical chemistry**
        Radioactivity

Nuclear pollution
USE **Radioactive pollution**
Nuclear power
USE **Nuclear energy**
Nuclear power plants (May subdiv. geog.)
621.48
UF Atomic power plants
Power plants, Nuclear
BT **Electric power plants**
RT **Nuclear energy**
Nuclear power plants—Accidents
363.17
Nuclear power plants—Environmental
aspects 333.792; 621.48
BT **Environment**
Environmental health
NT **Radioactive waste disposal**
RT **Antinuclear movement**
Nuclear power plants—Fires and fire
prevention 363.37; 628.9
BT **Fire prevention**
Fires
Nuclear power plants—Security mea-
sures 621.48
Nuclear propulsion 621.48
UF Atomic-powered vehicles
SA specific applications of nuclear
propulsion, e.g. **Nuclear sub-**
marines [to be added as
needed]
BT **Nuclear energy**
NT **Nuclear submarines**
RT **Nuclear reactors**
Nuclear reactors 621.48
UF Reactors (Nuclear physics)
BT **Nuclear energy**
Nuclear engineering
Nuclear physics
RT **Nuclear propulsion**
Nuclear submarines (May subdiv. geog.)
623.825
UF Atomic submarines
BT **Nuclear propulsion**
Submarines
Nuclear test ban
USE **Arms control**
Nuclear warfare 355.02
UF Atomic warfare
BT **War**
RT **Nuclear weapons**

Nuclear waste disposal
USE **Radioactive waste disposal**
Nuclear weapons (May subdiv. geog.)
355.8; 623.4
UF Atomic weapons
Weapons, Atomic
Weapons, Nuclear
SA types of nuclear weapons, e.g.
Atomic bomb [to be added
as needed]
BT **Military weapons**
NT **Antinuclear movement**
Atomic bomb
Ballistic missiles
Hydrogen bomb
Neutron weapons
RT **Nuclear warfare**
Nucleic acids 547; 572.8
UF Polynucleotides
BT **Biochemistry**
NT **DNA**
RNA
Nucleons
USE **Particles (Nuclear physics)**
Nude in art 704.9; 743.4
UF Human anatomy in art
Human figure in art
BT **Art—Themes**
NT **Artistic anatomy**
Number ability
USE **Mathematical ability**
Number concept 119; 155.4; 372.7
Use for materials on the apperception and
conceptualization of numbers. Materials on
numbers, numbering, and systems of numera-
tion are entered under **Numbers**. Materials on
counting, including counting books, are en-
tered under **Counting**.
BT **Apperception**
Psychology
RT **Numbers**
Number games 793.74
BT **Arithmetic—Study and teach-**
ing
Counting
Mathematical recreations
Number patterns
USE **Patterns (Mathematics)**
Number readiness
USE **Mathematical readiness**
Number symbolism
USE **Numerology**
Symbolism of numbers

Number systems
USE **Numbers**
Number theory   512.7
   Use for materials on that branch of mathe-
matics that involves the study of integers and
their relation to one another.
   UF   Theory of numbers
   BT   **Algebra**
         Mathematics
         Set theory
   NT   **Group theory**
   RT   **Numbers**
Numbers   119; 513
   Use for materials on numbers, numbering,
and systems of numeration. Materials on the
conceptualization of numbers are entered un-
der **Number concept.** Materials on counting,
including counting books, are entered under
Counting. Materials on the graphic represen-
tation of numbers are entered under **Numer-
als.**
   UF   Number systems
         Numeration
   SA   names of individual numbers,
            e.g. **Three (The number);**
            and systems of numeration,
            e.g. **Decimal system** [to be
            added as needed]
   NT   **Binary system (Mathematics)**
         Decimal system
         Three (The number)
   RT   **Arithmetic**
         Counting
         Number concept
         Number theory
         Numerals
         Symbolism of numbers
Numeral formation
   USE   **Writing of numerals**
Numeral writing
   USE   **Writing of numerals**
Numerals   513
   Use for materials on the graphic representa-
tion of numbers.
   SA   types of numerals, e.g. **Roman
            numerals** [to be added as
            needed]
   NT   **Roman numerals**
         Writing of numerals
   RT   **Numbers**
Numerals, Writing of
   USE   **Writing of numerals**
Numeration
   USE   **Numbers**

Numerical analysis   518
   BT   **Mathematical analysis**
   NT   **Approximate computation**
Numerical sequences
   USE   **Sequences (Mathematics)**
Numerology   133.3
   Use for materials on the occult significance
of numbers. General materials on the symbol-
ism of numbers, as in philosophy, religion, or
literature, are entered under **Symbolism of
numbers.**
   UF   Number symbolism
         Sacred numbers
         Symbolic numbers
   BT   **Occultism**
         Symbolism of numbers
Numismatics (May subdiv. geog.)   737
   Use for materials on coins, paper money,
medals, and tokens considered as works of
art, as historical specimens, or as aids to the
study of history, archeology, etc.
   BT   **Ancient history**
         Archeology
         History
   NT   **Seals (Numismatics)**
   RT   **Coins—Collectors and collect-
            ing**
         Medals
Nunneries
   USE   **Convents**
Nuns (May subdiv. geog.)   255; 271
   UF   Sisters (Religious)
   BT   **Women**
   NT   **Ex-nuns**
   RT   **Monasticism and religious or-
            ders for women**
Nurse clinicians
   USE   **Nurse practitioners**
Nurse midwives
   USE   **Midwives**
Nurse practitioners (May subdiv. geog.)
            610.73092; 920
   UF   Nurse clinicians
   BT   **Allied health personnel**
         Nurses
Nursemaids
   USE   **Nannies**
Nurseries, Day
   USE   **Day care centers**
Nurseries (Horticulture) (May subdiv.
         geog.)   **631.5; 635**
   BT   **Fruit culture**
         Gardening
   NT   **Plant propagation**

Nursery rhymes 398.8

May be used for collections of nursery rhymes or for materials about nursery rhymes.

UF Poetry for children
   Rhymes

BT Children's poetry
   Children's songs
   Folklore

Nursery schools 372.21

BT Elementary education
   Schools

RT Day care centers
   Kindergarten
   Preschool education

Nurses (May subdiv. geog.) 610.73092; 920

SA types of nurses [to be added as needed]

BT Medical personnel

NT Midwives
   Nurse practitioners
   Practical nurses
   School nurses

RT Nursing

Nursing (May subdiv. geog.) 610.73; 649.8

SA types of nursing, e.g. **Home nursing;** and diseases and medical procedures with the subdivision *Nursing* [to be added as needed]

BT Medicine
   Therapeutics

NT Cancer—Nursing
   Cooking for the sick
   First aid
   Heart—Surgery—Nursing
   Home nursing
   Practical nursing

RT Nurses
   Sick

Nursing homes (May subdiv. geog.) 362.1

BT Hospitals
   Institutional care
   Long-term care facilities

Nursing (Infant feeding)

USE Breast feeding

Nutrition (May subdiv. geog.) 613.2

UF Meal planning

SA animals, plants and crops, ethnic groups, and classes of persons with the subdivision *Nutrition,* e.g. **Children—Nutrition;** names of diseases with the subdivision *Diet therapy,* e.g. **Cancer—Diet therapy;** and types of foods with the subdivision *Therapeutic use;* e.g. **Herbs—Therapeutic use** [to be added as needed]

BT Health
   Physiology
   Therapeutics

NT Astronauts—Nutrition
   Children—Nutrition
   Eating customs
   Infants—Nutrition
   Malnutrition
   Plants—Nutrition
   Vitamins

RT Diet
   Digestion
   Food

Nuts 581.4; 634

Names of specific kinds of nuts may be used for materials on the nut or the tree.

SA types of nuts, e.g. **Pecans** [to be added as needed]

BT Food
   Seeds

NT Pecans

Nylon 677

BT Synthetic fabrics

Oak 583

UF Oaks

BT Trees
   Wood

Oaks

USE Oak

Oats 633.1

BT Feeds

Obedience 179

UF Disobedience

BT Virtue

Obelisks (May subdiv. geog.) 721

BT Archeology
   Architecture
   Monuments
   Pyramids

Obesity   613.2; 616.3
   UF   Corpulence
        Fatness
        Overweight
   BT   **Body weight**
Obituaries (May subdiv. geog.)   920
   UF   Death notices
        Necrologies
   SA   ethnic groups and classes of per-
        sons with the subdivision
        Obituaries [to be added as
        needed]
   BT   **Biography**
Objets d'art
   USE   **Art objects**
Obligation
   USE   **Responsibility**
Obscene materials
   USE   **Obscenity (Law)**
         Pornography
Obscenity (Law) (May subdiv. geog.)
        345
   UF   Obscene materials
   BT   **Criminal law**
   RT   **Erotica**
        Pornography
Observatories, Astronomical
   USE   **Astronomical observatories**
Observatories, Meteorological
   USE   **Meteorological observatories**
Obsession (Psychology)
   USE   **Obsessive-compulsive disorder**
Obsessive-compulsive disorder   616.85
   UF   Fixed ideas
        Obsession (Psychology)
        Obsessive-compulsive neuroses
   BT   **Neuroses**
   RT   **Compulsive behavior**
Obsessive-compulsive neuroses
   USE   **Obsessive-compulsive disorder**
Obstetrics
   USE   **Childbirth**
Obstinacy
   USE   **Stubbornness**
Occidental civilization
   USE   **Western civilization**
Occult fiction   808.3; 808.83
     May be used for individual works, collec-
     tions, or materials about fiction dealing with
     supernatural powers.

   BT   **Fiction**
   NT   **Ghost stories**
        Gothic novels
   RT   **Fantasy fiction**
Occult sciences
   USE   **Occultism**
Occultism (May subdiv. geog.)   **130**
   UF   Hermetic art and philosophy
        Occult sciences
        Sorcery
   BT   **Religions**
        Supernatural
   NT   **Alchemy**
        Astrology
        Cabala
        Clairvoyance
        Demonology
        Divination
        Magic
        New Age movement
        Numerology
        Oracles
        Palmistry
        Prophecies
        Spiritualism
        Witchcraft
   RT   **Parapsychology**
Occupation, Military
   USE   **Military occupation**
Occupational accidents
   USE   **Industrial accidents**
Occupational crimes
   USE   **White collar crimes**
Occupational diseases (May subdiv. geog.)
        616.9
   UF   Industrial diseases
        Occupations—Diseases
   SA   occupational groups with the
        subdivision *Diseases,* e.g.
        Miners—Diseases; types of
        industries with the subdivi-
        sions *Employees—Diseases;*
        e.g. **Chemical industry—Em-
        ployees—Diseases;** and names
        of occupational diseases [to
        be added as needed]
   BT   **Diseases**
   NT   **Chemical industry—Employ-
        ees—Diseases**
        Lead poisoning
        Miners—Diseases

Occupational diseases—*Continued*
  RT **Hazardous occupations**
      Occupational health and safety
Occupational forecasting
  USE **Employment forecasting**
Occupational guidance
  USE **Vocational guidance**
Occupational health and safety (May
    subdiv. geog.) **363.11; 658.3**
  UF Health, Industrial
      Industrial health
      Industrial safety
      Safety, Industrial
  BT **Environmental health**
      Management
      Public health
  NT **Burn out (Psychology)**
  RT **Hazardous occupations**
      Occupational diseases
      Occupational health services
Occupational health services (May
    subdiv. geog.) **331.25**
    Use for materials on health services for em-
    ployees, usually provided at the place of
    work.
  UF Employee health services
  BT **Medical care**
  RT **Occupational health and safety**
Occupational injuries
  USE **Industrial accidents**
Occupational literacy
  USE **Functional literacy**
Occupational retraining (May subdiv.
    geog.) **331.25**
  UF Job retraining
      Retraining, Occupational
  BT **Employees—Training**
      Labor supply
      Occupational training
      Technical education
      Unemployed
      Vocational education
Occupational stress
  USE **Job stress**
Occupational therapy **615.8**
  BT **Mental health**
      Physical therapy
      **Physically handicapped—Reha-
        bilitation**
      Therapeutics
  RT **Handicraft**

Occupational training (May subdiv.
    geog.) **331.25; 374**
    Use for materials on teaching people a skill
    after formal education. Materials on teaching
    a skill during the educational process are en-
    tered under **Vocational education.** Materials
    discussing on-the-job training are entered un-
    der **Employees—Training.** Materials on
    retraining are entered under **Occupational
    retraining.**
  UF Job training
      Training, Occupational
      Training, Vocational
      Vocational training
  BT **Technical education**
      Vocational education
  NT **Employees—Training**
      Occupational retraining
Occupations (May subdiv. geog.)
    331.702
    Use for descriptions and lists of
    occupations.
  UF Careers
      Jobs
      Trades
      Vocations
  SA fields of knowledge, professions,
      industries, and trades with the
      subdivision *Vocational guid-
      ance,* and ethnic groups and
      classes of persons with the
      subdivision *Employment,* e.g.
      Women—Employment [to be
      added as needed]
  NT **Hazardous occupations**
      Job analysis
      Paraprofessionals
      Professions
      Vocation
  RT **Employment**
      Vocational guidance
      Work
Occupations—Chicago (Ill.) **331.702**
  UF Chicago (Ill.)—Occupations
Occupations—Diseases
  USE **Occupational diseases**
Occupations—Ohio **331.702**
  UF Ohio—Occupations
Occupations—United States **331.702**
  UF United States—Occupations
Occupied territories
  USE names of wars with the subdivi-
      sion *Occupied territories,* e.g.
      World War, 1939-1945—Oc-

Occupied territories—*Continued*
cupied territories [to be added as needed]

Occupied territory
USE **Military occupation**

Ocean   551.46
UF   Oceans
Sea
SA   names of oceans and seas [to be added as needed]
BT   **Earth**
Physical geography
Water
NT   **Atlantic Ocean**
Icebergs
Ocean bottom
Ocean currents
Ocean waves
Tides
RT   **Oceanography**
Seashore

Ocean bottom   551.46
UF   Ocean floor
Sea bed
BT   **Ocean**
Submarine geology
NT   **Marine mineral resources**

Ocean cables
USE   **Submarine cables**

Ocean currents   551.46
UF   Currents, Ocean
BT   **Navigation**
Ocean
NT   **El Niño Current**

Ocean drilling platforms
USE   **Drilling platforms**

Ocean—Economic aspects
USE   **Marine resources**
Shipping

Ocean energy resources   333.91
BT   **Energy resources**
Marine resources
Ocean engineering
NT   **Geothermal resources**
RT   **Marine mineral resources**

Ocean engineering (May subdiv. geog.)
627
Use for materials on engineering beneath the surface of the ocean.
UF   Deep sea engineering
Submarine engineering
Undersea engineering

BT   **Engineering**
Marine resources
Oceanography
NT   **Drilling platforms**
Marine mineral resources
Ocean energy resources
Ocean mining
Offshore oil well drilling

Ocean farming
USE   **Aquaculture**

Ocean fishing
USE   **Saltwater fishing**

Ocean floor
USE   **Ocean bottom**

Ocean life
USE   **Marine biology**

Ocean mineral resources
USE   **Marine mineral resources**

Ocean mining (May subdiv. geog.)   **622**
UF   Deep sea mining
Mining, Ocean
BT   **Marine mineral resources**
Mining engineering
Ocean engineering

Ocean pollution
USE   **Marine pollution**

Ocean resources
USE   **Marine resources**

Ocean routes
USE   **Trade routes**

Ocean transportation
USE   **Shipping**

Ocean travel   910.4
UF   Cruises
Sea travel
BT   **Transportation**
Travel
Voyages and travels
NT   **Steamboats**
Yachts and yachting

Ocean waves   551.46
UF   Breakers
Sea waves
Surf
Swell
BT   **Ocean**
Waves
NT   **Tsunamis**

Oceania   995
Use for comprehensive materials on the lands and area of the central and southern Pa-

Oceania—*Continued*
cific Ocean, including Micronesia, Melanesia, and Polynesia. Comprehensive works on all the islands of the Pacific Ocean are entered under **Islands of the Pacific.**
- UF South Pacific region
  - South Sea Islands
  - South Seas
  - Southwest Pacific region
- BT **Islands of the Pacific**

Oceanographic research
- USE **Oceanography—Research**

Oceanography (May subdiv. geog.)
551.46
- UF Oceanology
- BT **Earth sciences**
- NT **Marine biology**
  - **Marine pollution**
  - **Marine resources**
  - **Ocean engineering**
  - **Submarine geology**
  - **Underwater exploration**
- RT **Ocean**

Oceanography—Atlantic Ocean   **551.46**
Oceanography—Computer software
551.46
- BT **Computer software**

Oceanography—Research   **551.46**
- UF Oceanographic research
- BT **Research**
- NT **Bathyscaphe**
  - **Undersea research stations**

Oceanology
- USE **Oceanography**

Oceans
- USE **Ocean**

Oddities
- USE **Curiosities and wonders**

Offenses against property (May subdiv. geog.)   **364.16**
- UF Property, Crimes against
  - Property, Offenses against
- SA types of offenses, e.g. **Vandalism** [to be added as needed]
- BT **Crime**
  - **Criminal law**
- NT **Fraud**
  - **Theft**
  - **Vandalism**

Offenses against public safety (May subdiv. geog.)   **364.1**
- UF Crimes against public safety
  - Public safety, Crimes against

- SA types of offenses, e.g. **Hijacking of airplanes** [to be added as needed]
- BT **Crime**
  - **Criminal law**
- NT **Bombings**
  - **Hijacking of airplanes**
  - **Riots**
  - **Sabotage**

Offenses against the person (May subdiv. geog.)   **364.15**
- UF Abuse of persons
  - Assault, Criminal
  - Crimes against the person
  - Criminal assault
- SA types of offenses, e.g. **Kidnapping** [to be added as needed]
- BT **Crime**
  - **Criminal law**
- NT **Homicide**
  - **Kidnapping**
  - **Rape**
  - **Stalking**

Offenses, Military
- USE **Military offenses**

Office buildings (May subdiv. geog.)
725
- UF Buildings, Office
- BT **Buildings**

Office employees
- USE **Office workers**

Office equipment and supplies   **651**
- UF Business machines
  - Office machines
  - Office supplies
- SA types of office equipment and supplies [to be added as needed]
- BT **Bookkeeping**
  - **Office management**
- NT **Calculators**
  - **Copying machines**
  - **Keyboards (Electronics)**
  - **Typewriters**

Office etiquette
- USE **Business etiquette**

Office machines
- USE **Office equipment and supplies**

Office management   651.3
  UF Office procedures
  BT **Business**
       Factory management
       Industrial efficiency
       Management
  NT **Files and filing**
       Office equipment and supplies
       Office practice
       Secretaries
       Word processing
  RT **Personnel management**

Office practice   651.3
  UF Secretarial practice
  BT **Office management**
  NT **Keyboarding (Electronics)**
       Shorthand
       Typewriting
       Word processing
  RT **Office workers**

Office procedures
  USE **Office management**

Office romance
  USE **Sex in the workplace**

Office supplies
  USE **Office equipment and supplies**

Office work—Training
  USE **Business education**

Office workers (May subdiv. geog.)
    331.7; 651.3
  UF Clerical employees
       Clerical personnel
       Clerks
       Commercial employees
       Office employees
  BT **Employees**
  RT **Office practice**

Office workers—Salaries, wages, etc.
  (May subdiv. geog.) **331.2**
  BT **Salaries, wages, etc.**

Officers
  USE names of armed forces with the
       subdivision *Officers,* e.g.
       United States. Army—Offi-
       cers [to be added as needed]

Official misconduct
  USE **Misconduct in office**

Official publications
  USE **Government publications**

Officials and employees
  USE **Civil service**
       Public officers
       and names of countries, states,
       cities, etc., and corporate bod-
       ies with the subdivision *Offi-*
       cials and employees, e.g.
       United States—Officials and
       employees; Ohio—Officials
       and employees; Chicago
       (Ill.)—Officials and employ-
       ees; United Nations—Offi-
       cials and employees; etc. [to
       be added as needed]

Offset printing   686.2
  UF Lithoprinting
  BT **Lithography**
       Printing

Offshore oil industry (May subdiv. geog.)
    338.2
  UF Oil industry, Offshore
  BT **Petroleum industry**
  NT **Offshore oil well drilling**

Offshore oil well drilling (May subdiv.
  geog.) **622**
  UF Deep sea drilling (Petroleum)
       Oil well drilling, Offshore
       Oil well drilling, Submarine
       Submarine oil well drilling
       Underwater drilling (Petroleum)
  BT **Ocean engineering**
       Offshore oil industry
       Oil well drilling
  NT **Drilling platforms**

Offshore water pollution
  USE **Marine pollution**

Ohio   977.1
  The subdivisions under **Ohio** may be used
  under the name of any state of the United
  States or province of Canada. The subdivisions under **United States** may be further
  consulted as a guide for formulating other
  headings as needed.

Ohio—Antiquities   977.1
  BT **Antiquities**

Ohio—Bibliography   015.771; 016.9771

Ohio—Bio-bibliography   012

Ohio—Biography   920.0771
  BT **Biography**

Ohio—Biography—Dictionaries
    920.0771

Ohio—Biography—Portraits   920.0771

Ohio—Boundaries   977.1
  BT   Boundaries
Ohio—Census   317.71
  BT   Census
Ohio—Church history   277.71
  UF   Church history—Ohio
       Ohio—Religious history
  BT   Church history
  RT   Ohio—Religion
Ohio—Civilization   977.1
  BT   Civilization
Ohio—Climate   551.69771
  BT   Climate
Ohio—Commerce   381
  BT   Commerce
Ohio—Constitution
  USE   Constitutions—Ohio
Ohio—Constitutional history
  USE   Constitutional history—Ohio
Ohio—Constitutional law
  USE   Constitutional law—Ohio
Ohio—Description
  USE   Ohio—Description and travel
Ohio—Description and travel   917.71
  UF   Ohio—Description [Former
       heading]
       Ohio—Travel
Ohio—Description and travel—Guidebooks
  USE   Ohio—Guidebooks
Ohio—Description and travel—Views
  USE   Ohio—Pictorial works
Ohio—Directories   917.710025
     Use for lists of names and addresses. Lists
  of names without addresses are entered under
  Ohio—Registers.
  BT   Directories
  RT   Ohio—Registers
Ohio—Economic conditions   330.9771
  BT   Economic conditions
Ohio—Economic policy
  USE   Economic policy—Ohio
Ohio—Employees
  USE   Ohio—Officials and employees
Ohio—Executive departments
  USE   Executive departments—Ohio
Ohio—Executive departments—Reorganiza-
     tion
  USE   Administrative agencies—Reor-
       ganization—Ohio
Ohio—Fiction   808.83; 813
     Use for collections of stories about Ohio.

Ohio—Gazetteers   917.71
  BT   Gazetteers
Ohio—Government employees
  USE   Ohio—Officials and employees
Ohio—Government publications
  USE   Government publications—
       Ohio
Ohio—Guidebooks   917.7104
  UF   Ohio—Description and travel—
       Guidebooks
Ohio—Historic buildings
  USE   Historic buildings—Ohio
Ohio—History   977.1
  NT   Constitutional history—Ohio
Ohio—History—Societies   977.106
  BT   History—Societies
Ohio—History—Sources   977.1
Ohio—Industries
  USE   Industries—Ohio
Ohio—Intellectual life   977.1
  BT   Intellectual life
Ohio—Local history   977.1
  BT   Local history
Ohio—Manufactures
  USE   Manufactures—Ohio
Ohio—Maps   912.771
  BT   Maps
Ohio—Militia   355.3
  BT   Armed forces
Ohio—Moral conditions   977.1
  BT   Moral conditions
Ohio—Occupations
  USE   Occupations—Ohio
Ohio—Officials and employees   351.771
  UF   Ohio—Employees
       Ohio—Government employees
Ohio—Officials and employees—Salaries,
     wages, etc.   331.2
  BT   Salaries, wages, etc.
Ohio—Pictorial works   917.710022
  UF   Ohio—Description and travel—
       Views
Ohio—Politics and government   977.1
Ohio—Population   304.609771
  BT   Population
Ohio—Public buildings
  USE   Public buildings—Ohio
Ohio—Public lands
  USE   Public lands—Ohio
Ohio—Public works
  USE   Public works—Ohio

Ohio—Race relations   305.8009771
   BT   Race relations
Ohio—Registers   917.710025
   Use for lists of names without addresses.
   Lists of names that include addresses are entered under Ohio—Directories.
   RT   Ohio—Directories
Ohio—Religion   277.71
   BT   Religion
   RT   Ohio—Church history
Ohio—Religious history
   USE   Ohio—Church history
Ohio—Rural conditions   307.7209771
   BT   Rural sociology
Ohio—Social conditions   977.1
   BT   Social conditions
Ohio—Social life and customs   977.1
   BT   Manners and customs
Ohio—Social policy
   USE   Social policy—Ohio
Ohio—Statistics   317.71
   BT   Statistics
Ohio—Travel
   USE   Ohio—Description and travel
Oil
   USE   Oils and fats
         Petroleum
Oil burners   697
   BT   Heating
         Petroleum as fuel
Oil drilling platforms
   USE   Drilling platforms
Oil engines
   USE   Internal combustion engines
Oil fuel
   USE   Petroleum as fuel
Oil industry
   USE   Petroleum industry
Oil industry, Offshore
   USE   Offshore oil industry
Oil painting
   USE   Painting
Oil pollution of rivers, harbors, etc.
   USE   Oil pollution of water
Oil pollution of water (May subdiv.
      geog.)   363.739; 628.1
   UF   Oil pollution of rivers, harbors,
         etc.
         Petroleum pollution of water
         Water—Oil pollution

   BT   Water pollution
   NT   Oil spills
   RT   Marine pollution
Oil spills (May subdiv. geog.)   363.738
   BT   Oil pollution of water
Oil well drilling (May subdiv. geog.)
      622
   UF   Drilling, Oil well
         Petroleum—Well boring
         Well drilling, Oil
   BT   Drilling and boring (Earth and
         rocks)
         Petroleum industry
   NT   Offshore oil well drilling
         Oil wells—Blowouts
   RT   Oil wells
Oil well drilling, Offshore
   USE   Offshore oil well drilling
Oil well drilling, Submarine
   USE   Offshore oil well drilling
Oil wells (May subdiv. geog.)   622
   BT   Petroleum industry
   RT   Oil well drilling
Oil wells—Blowouts   622
   UF   Blowouts, Oil well
   BT   Oil well drilling
Oils and fats   665
   UF   Animal oils
         Fats
         Grease
         Oil
         Vegetable oils
   NT   Essences and essential oils
         Petroleum
   RT   Lubrication and lubricants
Old age (May subdiv. geog.)   305.26
   BT   Age
   NT   Aging
         Retirement
   RT   Elderly
         Gerontology
         Longevity
Old age homes
   USE   Elderly—Institutional care
Old age pensions (May subdiv. geog.)
      331.25; 368.3
   UF   Aged—Pensions
         Employees—Pensions
   BT   Pensions
         Retirement income

Old English language
    USE **English language—Old English
          period**
Old English literature
    USE **English literature—Old English
          period**
Old Icelandic language
    USE **Old Norse language**
Old Norse language   439
    UF   Icelandic language—0-1500
          Norse languages
          Norwegian language—0-1350
          Old Icelandic language
          Old Norwegian language
    BT   **Language and languages**
          Scandinavian languages
Old Norse literature   839
    UF   Norse literature
    BT   **Literature**
          Medieval literature
    NT   **Eddas**
          Sagas
    RT   **Icelandic literature**
          Scandinavian literature
Old Northwest   977
    Use for materials on the region between the
    Ohio and Mississippi rivers and the Great
    Lakes.
    UF   Northwest, Old
          Northwest Territory
    BT   **United States**
    RT   **Middle West**
Old Norwegian language
    USE **Old Norse language**
Old Southwest   976
    Use for materials on that section of the
    United States that comprised the southwestern
    part before the cessions of land from Mexico
    following the Mexican War. It included Loui-
    siana, Texas, Arkansas, Tennessee, Kentucky
    and Missouri.
    UF   Southwest, Old
    BT   **United States**
Old Testament
    USE **Bible. O.T.**
Older persons
    USE **Elderly**
Oldest child
    USE **Birth order**
Olympic games   796.48; 796.98
    UF   Olympics
    SA   topical headings for Olympic
          events of a particular year,
          e.g. **Olympic games, 1996**

(Atlanta, Ga.) [to be added
          as needed]
    BT   **Athletics**
          Contests
          Games
          Sports
    NT   **Olympic games, 1996 (Atlanta,
          Ga.)**
          Special Olympics
**Olympic games, 1996 (Atlanta, Ga.)
    796.48**
    BT   **Olympic games**
Olympics
    USE **Olympic games**
Ombudsman (May subdiv. geog.)   **328.3;
    342; 352.8**
    UF   Citizen's defender
          Grievance procedures (Public ad-
          ministration)
    BT   **Administrative law**
          Public interest
On-line sex
    USE **Computer sex**
One act plays   808.82
    May be used for individual works, collec-
    tions, or materials about one-act plays.
    UF   Plays
          Short plays
    BT   **Amateur theater**
          Drama
One parent family
    USE **Single-parent families**
Online books
    USE **Electronic books**
Online catalogs   025.3
    UF   Catalogs, Online
          Online public access catalogs
          OPACs (Online public access
          catalogs)
    BT   **Library catalogs**
    RT   **Libraries—Automation**
Online chat groups   004.69
    Use for materials on services that allow us-
    ers to engage in conversations in real time.
    Materials on services, commonly called news-
    groups or LISTSERV lists, that allow sub-
    scribers to post messages that are then distrib-
    uted to other subscribers are entered under
    Electronic discussion groups. Materials on
    services that allow users to post messages and
    retrieve messages from others who have some
    common interest are entered under **Computer
    bulletin boards.**
    UF   Chat groups, Online
          Chat rooms, Online

Online chat groups—*Continued*
    Internet chat groups
    Online chat rooms
  BT **Conversation**
  RT **Computer bulletin boards**
      Electronic discussion groups
Online chat rooms
  USE **Online chat groups**
Online commerce
  USE **Electronic commerce**
Online discussion groups
  USE **Electronic discussion groups**
Online gambling
  USE **Internet gambling**
Online marketing
  USE **Internet marketing**
Online newsgroups
  USE **Electronic discussion groups**
Online public access catalogs
  USE **Online catalogs**
Online publishing
  USE **Electronic publishing**
Online reference services
  USE **Reference services (Libraries)**
Online selling
  USE **Internet marketing**
Online sex
  USE **Computer sex**
Online shopping
  USE **Internet shopping**
Only child   155.44; 306.874
  UF Single child
  BT **Children**
      Family size
OPACs (Online public access catalogs)
  USE **Online catalogs**
Opaque projectors
  USE **Projectors**
Open and closed shop (May subdiv.
    geog.)   **331.88**
  UF Closed shop
      Right to work
      Union shop
  BT **Labor**
      Labor contract
      Labor unions
Open classroom approach to teaching
  USE **Open plan schools**
Open education
  USE **Open plan schools**
Open heart surgery
  USE **Heart—Surgery**

Open housing
  USE **Discrimination in housing**
Open plan schools (May subdiv. geog.)
    371.2
  Use for materials on schools without interior walls.
  UF Interest centers approach to
        teaching
      Learning center approach to
        teaching
      Open classroom approach to
        teaching
      Open education
  BT **Education—Experimental**
      methods
  RT **Experimental schools**
      Individualized instruction
Open universities
  USE **Free universities**
Opera (May subdiv. geog.)   **782.1; 792.5**
  Use for musical scores and for materials about the opera.
  UF Comic opera
      Dramatic music
      Operas
  BT **Drama**
      Musical form
      Performing arts
      Vocal music
  NT **Operetta**
Opera librettos   **782.1026**
  Use for individual opera librettos and for collections of opera librettos.
  UF Operas—Librettos
  BT **Librettos**
  RT **Opera—Stories, plots, etc.**
Opera plots
  USE **Opera—Stories, plots, etc.**
Opera—Sound recordings   **782.1**
  BT **Sound recordings**
Opera—Stories, plots, etc.   **782.1026**
  UF Opera plots
  RT **Opera librettos**
Operas
  USE **Opera**
Operas—Librettos
  USE **Opera librettos**
Operating systems (Computers)
  USE **Computer operating systems**
Operation Desert Storm
  USE **Persian Gulf War, 1991**

Operational analysis
USE **Operations research**
Operational research
USE **Operations research**
Operations research   658.5
UF   Operational analysis
Operational research
BT   **Research**
System theory
RT   **Management**
Systems engineering
Operations, Surgical
USE   **Surgery**
Operetta (May subdiv. geog.)   782.1;
792.5
Use for musical scores and for materials on
the operetta as a musical form.
UF   Comic opera
Dramatic music
Operettas
BT   **Musical form**
Opera
Vocal music
RT   **Musicals**
Operettas
USE   **Operetta**
Opiates
USE   **Narcotics**
Opinion polls
USE   **Public opinion polls**
Opinion, Public
USE   **Public opinion**
Opium   615
BT   **Narcotics**
RT   **Morphine**
Opium—Physiological effect   615
BT   **Drugs—Physiological effect**
Opposites   153.2
UF   Antonyms
Polarity
BT   **Concepts**
RT   **English language—Synonyms**
and antonyms
Optical data processing   006.4; 621.36;
621.39
BT   **Data processing**
NT   **Laser recording**
Optical discs
USE   **Optical storage devices**

Optical illusions   152.14
UF   Illusions
BT   **Hallucinations and illusions**
Psychophysiology
Vision
Optical instruments   681
UF   Instruments, Optical
BT   **Scientific apparatus and in-**
struments
NT   **Lenses**
Microscopes
Telescopes
RT   **Optics**
Space optics
Optical scanners   006.4; 621.39
BT   **Computer peripherals**
Optical storage devices   004.5; 621.39
Use for materials on data storage devices in
which audio, video, or other data are optically
encoded.
UF   Optical discs
BT   **Computer storage devices**
NT   **CD-I technology**
CD-ROMs
Compact discs
DVDs
Videodiscs
RT   **Laser recording**
Optics   535; 621.36
BT   **Physics**
NT   **Color**
Perspective
Radiation
Refraction
Space optics
Spectrum analysis
Vision
RT   **Light**
Optical instruments
Photometry
Optometry   617.7
RT   **Eye**
Oracles   133.3
BT   **Occultism**
RT   **Divination**
Prophecies
Oral history   907
Use for materials on recording oral recollec-
tions of places, events, etc., from persons
drawing on their own life experiences. Oral
histories that focus on a particular topic or
place are entered under that topic or place.
BT   **History**

Oral interpretation
USE **Recitations**
Orange (Fruit)
USE **Oranges**
Oranges   634 ; 641.3
UF   Orange (Fruit)
BT   **Citrus fruits**
Orations
USE **Speeches**
Oratorio   782.23
Use for musical scores and for materials on the oratorio as a musical form.
UF   Oratorios
BT   **Church music**
Musical form
Vocal music
Oratorios
USE **Oratorio**
Oratory
USE **Public speaking**
Orbital laboratories
USE **Space stations**
Orbital rendezvous (Space flight) 629.45
UF   Rendezvous in space
Space orbital rendezvous
SA   names of projects, e.g. **Apollo project; Gemini project;** etc.; and names of specific space ships [to be added as needed]
BT   **Space flight**
Space stations
Space vehicles
NT   **Apollo project**
Gemini project
Orbiting vehicles
USE **Artificial satellites**
Space stations
Orchards
USE **Fruit culture**
Orchestra   784.2
SA   types of orchestras [to be added as needed]
NT   **Conductors (Music)**
Instrumentation and orchestration
Orchestral music
RT   **Bands (Music)**
Conducting
Ensembles (Music)
Musical instruments

Orchestral music   784.2
SA   types of orchestral music, e.g. **Symphony** [to be added as needed]
BT   **Instrumental music**
Music
Orchestra
NT   **Concerto**
String orchestra music
Suite (Music)
Symphonic poems
Symphony
Orchestration
USE **Instrumentation and orchestration**
Order   117
NT   **Orderliness**
Orderliness   640; 648
UF   Neatness
Tidiness
BT   **Order**
Orders, Monastic
USE **Monasticism and religious orders**
Ordination   262; 265
BT   **Rites and ceremonies**
Sacraments
NT   **Ordination of women**
RT   **Clergy**
Ordination of women   262
UF   Women—Ordination
BT   **Ordination**
RT   **Women clergy**
Ordnance   355.8; 623.4
Use for materials on military supplies including weapons, ammunition, and vehicles, and the task of procuring, testing, storing, and issuing such supplies.
UF   Cannon
Guns
SA   types of military ordnance, e.g. **Bombs;** names of armies with the subdivision *Ordnance,* e.g. **United States. Army—Ordnance;** and names of wars with the subdivision *Equipment and supplies,* e.g. **World War, 1939-1945—Equipment and supplies** [to be added as needed]

Ordnance—*Continued*
   BT   **Military art and science**
   NT   **Ammunition**
        Bombs
        Land mines
        Military weapons
        United States. Army—Ordnance
   RT   **Artillery**
        Defense industry
        Projectiles
Ore deposits (May subdiv. geog.)   **553**
   SA   types of ores, e.g. **Iron ores** [to be added as needed]
   BT   **Geology**
   RT   **Ores**
Ore dressing   **622**
   UF   Dressing of ores
   BT   **Smelting**
Oregon country
   USE   **Pacific Northwest**
Oregon Trail   **978**
   BT   **Overland journeys to the Pacific**
        United States
Ores   **553**
   SA   types of ores, e.g. **Iron ores** [to be added as needed]
   BT   **Minerals**
   NT   **Iron ores**
        Metals
   RT   **Metallurgy**
        Ore deposits
Organ
   USE   **Organs (Musical instruments)**
Organ donation
   USE   **Donation of organs, tissues, etc.**
Organ music   **786.5**
   BT   **Church music**
        Instrumental music
        Music
Organ preservation (Anatomy)
   USE   **Preservation of organs, tissues, etc.**
Organ transplants
   USE   **Transplantation of organs, tissues, etc.**
Organic agriculture
   USE   **Organic farming**
Organic chemicals
   USE   **Organic compounds**

Organic chemistry   **547**
   UF   Chemistry, Organic
   BT   **Chemistry**
   NT   **Organic compounds**
Organic chemistry—Synthesis
   USE   **Organic compounds—Synthesis**
Organic compounds   **547**
   UF   Organic chemicals
   SA   types of organic compounds and individual organic substances [to be added as needed]
   BT   **Chemicals**
        Organic chemistry
Organic compounds—Synthesis   **547**
   UF   Chemistry, Synthetic
        Organic chemistry—Synthesis
        Synthetic chemistry
   NT   **Polymers**
   RT   **Synthetic products**
Organic farming (May subdiv. geog.)   **631.5**
   UF   Farming, Organic
        Organic agriculture
        Organiculture
   BT   **Agriculture**
Organic gardening (May subdiv. geog.)   **635**
   UF   Natural gardening
        Organiculture
   BT   **Gardening**
        Horticulture
   RT   **Compost**
Organic waste as fuel
   USE   **Waste products as fuel**
Organically grown foods
   USE   **Natural foods**
Organiculture
   USE   **Organic farming**
        Organic gardening
Organists (May subdiv. geog.)   **786.5092; 920**
   BT   **Instrumentalists**
Organization and management
   USE   **Management**
Organization development
   USE   **Organizational change**
Organization (Sociology)
   USE   **Organizational sociology**
Organization theory
   USE   **Organizational sociology**

Organizational behavior (May subdiv. geog.) **158.2; 302.3; 658**
  UF Behavior in organizations
  BT **Applied psychology**
      Management
      Social psychology
Organizational change (May subdiv. geog.) **338.7; 658.4**
  UF Change, Organizational
      Organization development
      Organizational development
      Organizational innovation
  BT **Management**
  NT **Downsizing of organizations**
Organizational culture
  USE **Corporate culture**
Organizational development
  USE **Organizational change**
Organizational downsizing
  USE **Downsizing of organizations**
Organizational innovation
  USE **Organizational change**
Organizational retrenchment
  USE **Downsizing of organizations**
Organizational sociology **302.3**
  UF Organization (Sociology)
      Organization theory
      Sociology of organizations
  BT **Sociology**
  RT **Bureaucracy**
Organizational stress
  USE **Job stress**
Organizations
  USE **Associations**
Organizations, Nonprofit
  USE **Nonprofit organizations**
Organized crime (May subdiv. geog.) **364.106**
  UF Crime syndicates
  SA types of organized crime, e.g.
      Racketeering [to be added as needed]
  BT **Crime**
  NT **Gangs**
      Racketeering
Organized labor
  USE **Labor unions**
Organs (Anatomy)—Preservation
  USE **Preservation of organs, tissues, etc.**

Organs, Artificial
  USE **Artificial organs**
Organs (Musical instruments) (May subdiv. geog.) **786.5**
  UF Organ
      Pipe organs
  BT **Musical instruments**
  NT **Keyboards (Musical instruments)**
Organs—Transplantation
  USE **Transplantation of organs, tissues, etc.**
Orient
  USE **Asia**
      East Asia
      Middle East
Oriental architecture
  USE **Asian architecture**
Oriental art
  USE **Asian art**
Oriental civilization
  USE **Asia—Civilization**
Oriental rugs (May subdiv. geog.) **746.7**
  SA types of Oriental rugs [to be added as needed]
  BT **Rugs and carpets**
Orientalism (May subdiv. geog.) **303; 950**
      Use for materials on the depiction or adoption of characteristics of Asian and Middle Eastern cultures by Westerners.
  BT **East and West**
Orientation
  USE **Direction sense**
Orienteering **796.58**
  BT **Hiking**
      Racing
      Running
      Sports
  RT **Direction sense**
      Navigation
Origami **736**
  UF Japanese paper folding
      Paper folding
  BT **Paper crafts**
Origin
  USE subjects, ethnic groups, classes of persons, animals, plants, crops, and religions with the subdivision *Origin,* e.g. **Life—Origin; Native Ameri-**

Origin—*Continued*
>> cans—**Origin;** etc. [to be
>> added as needed]
Origin of life
> USE **Life—Origin**
Origin of man
> USE **Human origins**
Origin of species
> USE **Evolution**
Orlando (Legendary character)
> USE **Roland (Legendary character)**
Ornament
> USE **Decoration and ornament**
Ornamental alphabets
> USE **Alphabets**
>> **Illumination of books and
>> manuscripts**
>> **Lettering**
Ornamental plants (May subdiv. geog.)
> **635.9; 715**
> UF Plants, Ornamental
> BT **Cultivated plants**
>> **Flower gardening**
>> **Landscape gardening**
> RT **Shrubs**
Orphan drugs   615
> Use for materials on drugs that appear to be
> useful for the treatment of rare disorders but
> owing to their limited commercial value have
> difficulty in finding funding for research and
> marketing.
> UF Nonprofitable drugs
> BT **Drugs**
Orphanages (May subdiv. geog.)   **362.73**
> UF Charitable institutions
>> Homes (Institutions)
> BT **Charities**
>> **Children—Institutional care**
> RT **Child welfare**
Orphans (May subdiv. geog.)
> **305.23086; 362.73**
> UF Foundlings
> BT **Children**
> RT **Abandoned children**
>> **Adopted children**
Orthodox Eastern Church (May subdiv.
> geog.)   **281.9**
> BT **Christian sects**
>> **Eastern churches**
> NT **Greek Orthodox Church**
>> **Russian Orthodox Church**

Orthography
> USE **Spelling reform**
>> and names of languages with
>> the subdivision *Spelling,* e.g.
>> **English language—Spelling**
>> [to be added as needed]
Orthopedic apparatus   617
> UF Orthotic devices
> BT **Orthopedics**
> NT **Wheelchairs**
Orthopedic surgery
> USE **Orthopedics**
Orthopedics   616.7; 617.4
> UF Orthopedic surgery
> BT **Medicine**
>> **Surgery**
> NT **Artificial limbs**
>> **Orthopedic apparatus**
> RT **Physically handicapped**
Orthotic devices
> USE **Orthopedic apparatus**
Osteopathic medicine   610; 615.5
> Use for materials on the therapeutic system
> based on the theory that disease is caused by
> loss of a structural integrity that can be re-
> stored by manipulation of the bones and mus-
> cles.
> UF Osteopathy
> BT **Medicine**
> RT **Chiropractic**
>> **Massage**
Osteopathy
> USE **Osteopathic medicine**
Ostrogoths
> USE **Goths**
Out-of-body experiences
> USE **Astral projection**
Out-of-doors education
> USE **Outdoor education**
Out-of-work people
> USE **Unemployed**
Outdoor cooking   641.5
> UF Camp cooking
> BT **Camping**
>> **Cooking**
> NT **Barbecue cooking**
Outdoor education   371.3
> UF Out-of-doors education
> BT **Education**
> RT **Nature study**
>> **Outdoor life**

Outdoor life (May subdiv. geog.)   **796.5**
  UF   Rural life
  SA   types of outdoor life, education,
           or activities [to be added as
           needed]
  NT   **Hiking**
         Mountaineering
         Wilderness survival
  RT   **Camping**
         Country life
         Nature study
         Outdoor education
         Sports
Outdoor photography   **778.7**
  UF   Field photography
  BT   **Photography**
  RT   **Nature photography**
Outdoor recreation (May subdiv. geog.)
           796
  SA   types of outdoor recreation, e.g.
           Camping [to be added as
           needed]
  BT   **Recreation**
  NT   **Camping**
         Cycling
         Recreational vehicles
         Roller skating
         Safaris
Outdoor survival
  USE   **Wilderness survival**
Outer space   **523.1**
  UF   Space, Outer
  BT   **Astronautics**
         Astronomy
         Space sciences
  NT   **Space environment**
         Space warfare
Outer space and civilization
  USE   **Astronautics and civilization**
Outer space—Colonies
  USE   **Space colonies**
Outer space—Communication
  USE   **Interstellar communication**
Outer space—Exploration   **629.4**
  UF   Exploration of space
         Space exploration (Astronautics)
         Space research
  BT   **Exploration**
         Interplanetary voyages
         Space flight

  NT   **Planets—Exploration**
         Space probes
Outlaws
  USE   **Criminals**
         Thieves
Outlines, syllabi, etc.
  USE   subjects with the subdivision
           Outlines, syllabi, etc., e.g.
           English literature—Outlines,
           syllabi, etc. [to be added as
           needed]
Output equipment (Computers)
  USE   **Computer peripherals**
Output standards
  USE   **Production standards**
Over-the-counter drugs
  USE   **Nonprescription drugs**
Overland journeys to the Pacific   **978**
         Use for materials on the pioneers' crossing
         of the American continent toward the Pacific
         by foot, horseback, wagon, etc.
  UF   Transcontinental journeys
           (American continent)
  BT   **Frontier and pioneer life**
         Voyages and travels
  NT   **Oregon Trail**
  RT   **West (U.S.)—Exploration**
Overpopulation   **363.9; 304.6**
  UF   Population explosion
  SA   names of countries, cities, etc.
           with the subdivision *Popula-*
           tion, e.g. **United States—**
           Population [to be added as
           needed]
  BT   **Population**
Overseas study
  USE   **Foreign study**
Oversize books
  USE   **Big books**
Oversized books for shared reading
  USE   **Big books**
Overtime
  USE   **Hours of labor**
Overweight
  USE   **Obesity**
Ownership
  USE   **Property**
Oxyacetylene welding
  USE   **Welding**
Oxygen   **546; 547; 665.8**
  BT   **Chemical elements**
         Gases

Oxygen—*Continued*
NT Ozone
Ozone   665.8
BT Oxygen
Ozone layer   363.738; 551.51
UF Ozonosphere
Stratospheric ozone
BT **Stratosphere**
Ozonosphere
USE **Ozone layer**
Pacific Islands
USE **Islands of the Pacific**
Pacific Northwest   979.5
Use for materials on the old Oregon country, comprising the present states of Oregon, Washington, and Idaho, parts of Montana and Wyoming, and the province of British Columbia.
UF Northwest, Pacific
Oregon country
BT **North America**
United States
West (U.S.)
Pacific Northwest coast
USE **Northwest Coast of North America**
Pacific Ocean Islands
USE **Islands of the Pacific**
Pacific rim   330.99; 990
Use for materials on the periphery of the Pacific Ocean, especially as a region of interdependent economies.
RT **East Asia**
Islands of the Pacific
Pacific States   979
BT **West (U.S.)**
Pacifism   174; 303.6
Use for materials on the renunciation of offensive or defensive military actions on moral grounds. Materials on social movements adovcating peace are entered under **Peace movements.**
BT **War—Religious aspects**
NT **Peace movements**
RT **Conscientious objectors**
Nonviolence
Peace
Peace movements
Pack transportation
USE **Backpacking**
Packaging   658.5
SA types of packaging and packaging materials, and subjects with the subdivision *Packag-*

ing, e.g. **Food—Packaging**
[to be added as needed]
BT **Advertising**
Retail trade
NT **Aluminum foil**
Food—Packaging
Gift wrapping
RT **Containers**
Packing industry
USE **Meat industry**
PACs (Political action committees)
USE **Political action committees**
Paganism (May subdiv. geog.)   **292**
UF Heathenism
BT **Christianity and other religions**
Religions
NT **Goddess religion**
Wicca
Pageants (May subdiv. geog.)   **394; 791.6**
BT **Acting**
NT **Masks (Plays)**
Medieval tournaments
Mysteries and miracle plays
Parades
RT **Festivals**
Pain   152.1; 612.8
BT **Diagnosis**
Emotions
Psychophysiology
Senses and sensation
NT **Chronic pain**
Headache
RT **Anesthetics**
Pleasure
Suffering
Paint   645; 667
BT **Finishes and finishing**
RT **Corrosion and anticorrosives**
Pigments
Paint sniffing
USE **Solvent abuse**
Painted glass
USE **Glass painting and staining**
Painters (May subdiv. geog.)   **759; 920**
BT **Artists**
Painters' materials
USE **Artists' materials**
Painters—United States   759.13; 920
UF American painters

Painting   750
  UF   Oil painting
        Paintings
  SA   painting of particular countries,
        e.g. **American painting;**
        types of painting, e.g. **Land-
        scape painting;** and topics
        with the subdivision *Painting;*
        e.g. **Automobiles—Painting**
        [to be added as needed]
  BT   **Art**
        Graphic arts
  NT   **American painting**
        **Animal painting and illustra-
        tion**
        China painting
        Color
        Figure painting
        Finger painting
        Glass painting and staining
        Landscape painting
        Marine painting
        Miniature painting
        Mural painting and decoration
        Perspective
        Portrait painting
        Scene painting
        Stencil work
        Textile painting
        Watercolor painting
  RT   **Composition (Art)**
        Decoration and ornament
        Drawing
        Pictures
**Painting—15th and 16th centuries
709.02; 709.03**
  UF   Painting, Renaissance
        Renaissance painting
**Painting—17th and 18th centuries
759.04**
  UF   Painting, Modern—17th-18th
        centuries
Painting—19th century   759.05
  UF   Modern painting—1800-1899
        (19th century)
        Painting, Modern—19th century
Painting—20th century   759.06
  UF   Modern painting—1900-1999
        (20th century)
        Painting, Modern—20th century

  SA   types of twentieth-century paint-
        ing, e.g. **Cubism** [to be added
        as needed]
Painting—21st century   759.07
  UF   Modern painting—2000-2099
        (21st century)
        Painting, Modern—21st century
Painting, American
  USE   **American painting**
Painting books
  USE   **Coloring books**
Painting—Color reproductions
  USE   **Color prints**
**Painting—Conservation and restoration
751.6**
Painting, Decorative
  USE   **Decoration and ornament**
Painting, Finger
  USE   **Finger painting**
Painting, Modern—17th-18th centuries
  USE   **Painting—17th and 18th centu-
        ries**
Painting, Modern—19th century
  USE   **Painting—19th century**
Painting, Modern—20th century
  USE   **Painting—20th century**
Painting, Modern—21st century
  USE   **Painting—21st century**
Painting, Renaissance
  USE   **Painting—15th and 16th centu-
        ries**
Painting, Romanesque
  USE   **Romanesque painting**
Painting—Technique   751.4
Paintings
  USE   **Painting**
Pair system
  USE   **Binary system (Mathematics)**
Palaces (May subdiv. geog.)   **728.8**
  BT   **Buildings**
Paleobotany
  USE   **Fossil plants**
Paleolithic period
  USE   **Stone Age**
Paleontology (May subdiv. geog.)   **560**
  UF   Paleozoology
  BT   **Historical geology**
        Zoology
  RT   **Fossils**
Paleozoology
  USE   **Paleontology**

Palestinian Arabs (May subdiv. geog.)
    305.892; 956.94
    UF Arabs—Palestine
          Palestinians
    BT **Arabs**
    RT **Jewish-Arab relations**
Palestinian-Israeli conflict, 1987-
    USE **Intifada, 1987-**
Palestinian uprising, 1987-
    USE **Intifada, 1987-**
Palestinians
    USE **Palestinian Arabs**
Palmistry   133.6
    BT **Divination**
          Fortune telling
          Occultism
Pamphlets   025.17
    UF Street literature
    BT **Press**
    NT **Chapbooks**
Pamphlets—Design   686.2
    BT **Design**
Pan-Africanism   320.5; 327
    Use for materials on the advocacy of either
    political alliance or close economic, cultural,
    and military cooperation among the countries
    of Africa.
    UF African relations
    BT **Africa**
Pan-Americanism   320.5; 327
    Use for materials on the advocacy of either
    political alliance or close economic, cultural,
    and military cooperation among the countries
    of North and South America.
    UF Inter-American relations
    BT **Latin America**
    RT **America—Politics and govern-
          ment**
Pan-Arabism   320.5
    Use for materials on the advocacy of either
    political alliance or close economic, cultural,
    and military cooperation among the Arab
    countries.
    UF Panarabism
    BT **Arab countries—Politics and
          government**
Panama Canal   972.87
    BT **Canals**
Panarabism
    USE **Pan-Arabism**
Panel discussions
    USE **Discussion groups**
Panel heating
    USE **Radiant heating**

Panhandling
    USE **Begging**
Panic disorders   362.2; 616.85
    BT **Abnormal psychology**
          Neuroses
Panics (Finance)
    USE **Financial crises**
Pantomimes   792.3
    BT **Acting**
          Amateur theater
          Drama
          Theater
    NT **Shadow pantomimes and plays**
    RT **Ballet**
          Mime
Papacy   262
    UF Holy See
    BT **Catholic Church**
          Church history
    RT **Popes**
Papal encyclicals   262.9
    UF Encyclicals, Papal
    BT **Christian literature**
Papal visits (May subdiv. geog.)   **262**
    UF Popes—Travel
          Popes—Voyages and travels
    BT **Voyages and travels**
Paper   676
    BT **Fibers**
    NT **Papermaking**
    RT **Paper industry**
Paper airplanes
    USE **Airplanes—Models**
Paper bound books
    USE **Paperback books**
Paper crafts   745.54
    UF Paper folding
          Paper sculpture
          Paper work
          Papier-mâché
    SA types of paper crafts [to be add-
          ed as needed]
    BT **Handicraft**
    NT **Decoupage**
          Gift wrapping
          Origami
    RT **Papermaking**
Paper folding
    USE **Origami**
          Paper crafts

Paper hanging
    USE **Paperhanging**
Paper industry (May subdiv. geog.)
    338.4

    Use for materials on the business of making and selling paper. Materials on the technology and craft of making paper are entered under **Papermaking.**

    UF Papermaking industry
    BT **Industries**
    RT **Paper**
Paper making
    USE **Papermaking**
Paper manufacture
    USE **Papermaking**
Paper money (May subdiv. geog.)   **332.4**
    BT **Money**
    RT **Inflation (Finance)**
Paper sculpture
    USE **Paper crafts**
Paper work
    USE **Paper crafts**
Paperback books   **070.5**
    UF Paper bound books
    BT **Books**
          Editions
Paperhanging   **698**
    UF Paper hanging
    BT **Interior design**
    RT **Wallpaper**
Papermaking (May subdiv. geog.)   **676**

    Use for materials on the technology and craft of making paper. Materials on the business of making and selling paper are entered under **Paper industry.**

    UF Paper making
          Paper manufacture
    BT **Manufactures**
          Paper
    RT **Paper crafts**
Papermaking industry
    USE **Paper industry**
Papier-mâché
    USE **Paper crafts**
Parables   **808**

    May be used for individual works, collections, or materials about parables.

    UF Cautionary tales and verse
          Moral and philosophic stories
          Morality tales
    SA individual parables, e.g. **Prodigal son (Parable)** [to be added as needed]

    NT **Bible—Parables**
          Jesus Christ—Parables
          Prodigal son (Parable)
    RT **Allegories**
          Didactic fiction
          Didactic poetry
          Fables
Parachute troops   **356**
    UF Paratroops
    SA names of armies with the subdivision *Parachute troops,* e.g. **United States. Army—Parachute troops** [to be added as needed]

    BT **Military aeronautics**
          Parachutes
    NT **United States. Army—Parachute troops**
Parachutes   **629.134**
    BT **Aeronautics**
    NT **Parachute troops**
Parade floats
    USE **Parades**
Parades (May subdiv. geog.)   **791.6**
    UF Floats (Parades)
          Parade floats
          Pomp
          Processions
    BT **Festivals**
          Pageants
Paradise   **202; 236**

    Use for materials on the earthly paradise or on a blessed intermediate state in the afterlife.

    UF Earthly paradise
          Eden
          Garden of Eden
    BT **Future life**
    RT **Heaven**
          Utopias
Parallel economy
    USE **Underground economy**
Paralysis   **616.8**
    SA individual organs and regions of the body with the subdivision *Paralysis* e.g. **Foot—Paralysis** [to be added as needed]

    BT **Nervous system—Diseases**
    NT **Foot—Paralysis**
Paralysis, Cerebral
    USE **Cerebral palsy**

Paramedical personnel
USE **Allied health personnel**
Emergency medical technicians
Paramedics, Emergency
USE **Emergency medical technicians**
Paramilitary militia movements
USE **Militia movements**
Paranormal phenomena
USE **Parapsychology**
Paraprofessional librarians
USE **Library technicians**
Paraprofessionals   331.7
UF Paraprofessions and
paraprofessionals
SA types of paraprofessional person-
nel, e.g. **Library technicians;**
and fields of knowledge, pro-
fessions, industries, and trades
with the subdivision *Vocation-
al guidance* [to be added as
needed]
BT **Occupations**
Professions
NT **Library technicians**
Paraprofessions and paraprofessionals
USE **Paraprofessionals**
Parapsychology (May subdiv. geog.)
130
Use for materials on investigations of phe-
nomena that appear to be contrary to physical
laws and beyond the normal sense percep-
tions.
UF Paranormal phenomena
Psi (Parapsychology)
Psychic phenomena
Psychical research
BT **Psychology**
Research
Supernatural
NT **Apparitions**
Astral projection
Extrasensory perception
Hallucinations and illusions
Mental suggestion
Mind and body
Psychics
Psychokinesis
Subconsciousness
Visions
RT **Ghosts**
Occultism
Spiritualism

Parasites   577.8; 578.6
UF Animal parasites
Diseases and pests
Entozoa
Epizoa
SA types of animals and parts of
the body with the subdivision
Parasites [to be added as
needed]
BT **Pests**
NT **Bacteria**
RT **Insect pests**
Symbiosis
Parasols
USE **Umbrellas and parasols**
Paratroops
USE **Parachute troops**
Parcel post
USE **Postal service**
Pardon   364.6
BT **Administration of criminal jus-
tice**
Executive power
RT **Amnesty**
Clemency
Forgiveness
Parent abuse
USE **Elderly abuse**
Parent and child
USE **Parent-child relationship**
Parent-child relationship   306.874
Use for materials on the psychological and
social interaction between parents and their
minor children. Materials on the skills, attri-
butes, and attitudes needed for parenthood are
entered under **Parenting.** Materials on the
principles and techniques of rearing children
are entered under **Child rearing.** Materials re-
stricted to the legal right of parents to visit
their children in situations of separation, di-
vorce, etc., are entered under **Visitation
rights (Domestic relations).**
UF Child and parent
Parent and child
BT **Child-adult relationship**
Children
Family
Parents
NT **Adoption**
Child abuse
Child custody
Child rearing
Children of divorced parents
Children of working parents

Parent-child relationship—*Continued*
> **Conflict of generations**
> **Father-child relationship**
> **Mother-child relationship**
> **Parenting**

Parent participation in children's education
> USE **Education—Parent participation**

Parent-teacher associations (May subdiv. geog.) **371.19**
> UF Parents' and teachers' associations
> PTAs
> BT **Community and school**
> **Education—Societies**
> **Parent-teacher relationship**
> **Societies**
> RT **Home and school**

Parent-teacher conferences **371.103**
> UF Conferences, Parent-teacher
> Interviews, Parent-teacher
> Teacher-parent conferences
> BT **Parent-teacher relationship**

Parent-teacher relationship **371.19**
> UF Parent-teacher relationships
> Parents and teachers
> Teacher-parent relationship
> Teachers and parents
> NT **Parent-teacher associations**
> **Parent-teacher conferences**
> RT **Home and school**

Parent-teacher relationships
> USE **Parent-teacher relationship**

Parental behavior
> USE **Parenting**

Parental custody
> USE **Child custody**

Parental involvement in children's education
> USE **Education—Parent participation**

Parental kidnapping (May subdiv. geog.) **362.82**
> UF Child snatching by parents
> Custody kidnapping
> Kidnapping, Parental
> BT **Child custody**

Parental leave (May subdiv. geog.) **331.25**
> UF Family leave
> Infant care leave
> Leave for parenting

> BT **Leave of absence**

Parenthood **306.874; 649**
> BT **Family**
> NT **Fatherhood**
> **Motherhood**

Parenting (May subdiv. geog.) **306.874; 649**
> Use for materials on the skills, attributes, and attitudes needed for parenthood. Materials on the psychological and social interaction between parents and their minor children are entered under **Parent-child relationship.** Materials on the principles and techniques of rearing children are entered under **Child rearing.**
> UF Parental behavior
> BT **Parent-child relationship**
> NT **Grandparenting**
> **Grandparents as parents**
> **Part-time parenting**
> RT **Child rearing**

Parenting by grandparents
> USE **Grandparents as parents**

Parenting, Part-time
> USE **Part-time parenting**

Parents (May subdiv. geog.) **306.874**
> BT **Family**
> NT **Aging parents**
> **Birthparents**
> **Grandparents**
> **Parent-child relationship**
> **Single parents**
> **Stepparents**
> **Teenage parents**

Parents and teachers
> USE **Parent-teacher relationship**

Parents' and teachers' associations
> USE **Parent-teacher associations**

Parents, Biological
> USE **Birthparents**

Parents' choice of school
> USE **School choice**

Parents, Unmarried
> USE **Unmarried fathers**
> **Unmarried mothers**

Parish libraries
> USE **Church libraries**

Parish registers
> USE **Registers of births, etc.**

Parks (May subdiv. geog.) **363.6; 712**
> BT **Cities and towns**
> **Landscape architecture**
> NT **Amusement parks**
> **Botanical gardens**

Parks—*Continued*
> National parks and reserves
> Zoos
>> RT   Playgrounds

Parks—**United States**   363.6; 712; 917.3

Parkways
> USE   **Express highways**

Parliamentary government
> USE   **Representative government and representation**

Parliamentary practice   060.4
> UF   Rules of order
> BT   **Debates and debating**
> > **Legislation**
> > **Legislative bodies**
> > **Public meetings**

Parliaments
> USE   **Legislative bodies**

Parochial schools
> USE   **Church schools**

Parodies   808.87
> Use for collections of parodies. Materials on the literary form of parody, that is, satirical or humorous imitation of a serious piece of literature, are entered under **Parody.**
> UF   Travesties
> SA   types of literature, individual literary works entered under title, and names of prominent authors with the subdivision *Parodies, imitations, etc.,* e.g. **Shakespeare, William, 1564-1616—Parodies, imitations, etc.** [to be added as needed]
> NT   **Fractured fairy tales**

Parodies, imitations, etc.
> USE   types of literature, individual literary works entered under title, and names of prominent authors with the subdivision *Parodies, imitations, etc.,* e.g. **Shakespeare, William, 1564-1616—Parodies, imitations, etc.** [to be added as needed]

Parody   808.7
> Use for materials about the literary form of parody, that is, satirical or humorous imitation of a serious piece of literature. Collections of parodies are entered under **Parodies.**
> UF   Comic literature
> BT   **Literature**
> > **Satire**
> > **Wit and humor**

Parole (May subdiv. geog.)   364.6
> BT   **Administration of criminal justice**
> > **Corrections**
> > **Punishment**
> > **Social case work**
> RT   **Probation**

Part-time employment   331.25
> UF   Alternative work schedules
> BT   **Employment**
> > **Hours of labor**
> > **Labor**
> NT   **Job sharing**
> > **Supplementary employment**

Part-time parenting   306.874; 649
> Use for materials on parenting skills for separated, divorced, or surrogate parents who live apart from their children and spend less than full time with them.
> UF   Co-parenting
> > Joint custody of children
> > Parenting, Part-time
> > Shared parenting
> BT   **Parenting**
> RT   **Children of divorced parents**

Partial hearing
> USE   **Hearing impaired**

Partially hearing
> USE   **Hearing impaired**

Participative management   331.89; 658.3
> UF   Consultative management
> > Employees' representation in management
> > Industrial councils
> > Labor participation in management
> > Management—Employee participation
> > Workers' participation in management
> > Workshop councils
> BT   **Factory management**
> > **Industrial relations**
> > **Personnel management**
> RT   **Collective bargaining**

Particles (Nuclear physics)   539.7
> UF   Elementary particles (Physics)
> > Nuclear particles
> > Nucleons
> SA   names of particles [to be added as needed]

Particles (Nuclear physics)—*Continued*
- BT **Nuclear physics**
- NT **Electrons**
  - **Neutrons**
  - **Protons**
  - **Quarks**

Parties 793.2
- SA types of parties [to be added as needed]
- BT **Entertaining**
- NT **Children's parties**
  - **Showers (Parties)**

Parties, Political
- USE **Political parties**

Partisans
- USE **Guerrillas**

Partita
- USE **Suite (Music)**

Partnership 338.7
- UF Companies
  - Partnership—Law and legislation
- BT **Business enterprises**
- NT **Joint ventures**

Partnership—Law and legislation
- USE **Partnership**

Parts of speech
- USE names of languages with the subdivision *Parts of speech,* e.g. **English language—Parts of speech** [to be added as needed]

Passion plays 792.1; 808.82
  May be used for individual plays, collections, or materials about medieval plays depicting the Passion of Christ.
- BT **Bible plays**
  - **Jesus Christ—Drama**
  - **Mysteries and miracle plays**
  - **Religious drama**
  - **Theater**

Passions
- USE **Emotions**

Passive resistance (May subdiv. geog.) 303.6; 322.4
- UF Nonviolent noncooperation
- BT **Resistance to government**
- NT **Boycotts**
  - **Hunger strikes**
- RT **Nonviolence**

Passover (May subdiv. geog.) 296.4; 394.267
- UF Pesach
- BT **Jewish holidays**
- NT **Seder**

Pastel drawing 741.2
- BT **Drawing**
- RT **Crayon drawing**

Pastimes
- USE **Amusements**
  - **Games**
  - **Recreation**

Pastoral drama 808.82
  May be used for individual works, collections, or materials about pastoral drama.
- UF Rural comedies
- BT **Drama**

Pastoral fiction 808.3; 808.83
  May be used for individual works, collections, or materials about novels or short stories with a rural setting and a tone of romantic nostalgia.
- UF Pastoral romances
  - Rural comedies
- BT **Fiction**

Pastoral peoples
- USE **Nomads**

Pastoral poetry 808.1; 808.81
  May be used for individual works, collections, or materials about pastoral poetry.
- UF Bucolic poetry
  - Eclogues
  - Idyllic poetry
  - Rural poetry
- BT **Poetry**

Pastoral psychiatry
- USE **Pastoral psychology**

Pastoral psychology 206; 253.5
  Use for materials on the application of psychology and psychiatry by the clergy to the spiritual problems of individuals.
- UF Clerical psychology
  - Pastoral psychiatry
  - Psychology, Pastoral
  - Psychology, Religious
  - Religious psychology
- BT **Applied psychology**
  - **Church work**
  - **Psychology of religion**
- RT **Pastoral theology**

Pastoral romances
- USE **Pastoral fiction**

Pastoral theology (May subdiv. geog.)
    206; 253
    May be subdivided by sect or denomination.
    UF   Pastoral work
    BT   **Theology**
    NT   **Ministry**
          Preaching
    RT   **Church work**
          Clergy
          Pastoral psychology
Pastoral work
    USE **Pastoral theology**
Pastors
    USE **Clergy**
          Priests
Pastry   **641.8**
    BT   **Baking**
          Cooking
    RT   **Cake**
Pastures (May subdiv. geog.)   **333.74**
    BT   **Agriculture**
          Land use
Patchwork   **746.46**
    BT   **Needlework**
Patchwork quilts
    USE **Quilts**
Patent medicines
    USE **Nonprescription drugs**
Patents (May subdiv. geog.)   **608**
    BT   **Manufactures**
    RT   **Intellectual property**
          Inventions
          Trademarks
Pathological psychology
    USE **Abnormal psychology**
Pathology   **616.07**
    UF   Disease (Pathology)
    BT   **Medicine**
    NT   **Birth defects**
          Fever
          Medical genetics
          Therapeutics
    RT   **Diseases**
          Preventive medicine
Patience   **179**
    BT   **Human behavior**
          Virtue
Patience (Game)
    USE **Solitaire (Game)**

Patients   **362.1**
    SA   diseases with the subdivision *Patients,* e.g. **Cancer—Patients;** and organs or regions of the body with the subdivisions *Surgery—Patients,* or *Transplantation—Patients* [to be added as needed]
    NT   **Cancer—Patients**
    RT   **Sick**
Patios   **643**
    UF   Decks (Domestic architecture)
    BT   **Landscape architecture**
Patriotic poetry   **808.1; 808.81**
    May be used for individual works, collections, or materials about patriotic poetry.
    BT   **Poetry**
    RT   **National songs**
Patriotic songs
    USE **National songs**
Patriotism (May subdiv. geog.)   **172**
    BT   **Citizenship**
          Human behavior
          Loyalty
    RT   **Nationalism**
Patristic philosophy
    USE **Fathers of the church**
Patristics
    USE **Fathers of the church**
Patronage of the arts
    USE **Art patronage**
Pattern making
    USE **Patternmaking**
Pattern perception   **152.14**
    UF   Design perception
          Pattern recognition
    BT   **Perception**
Pattern recognition
    USE **Pattern perception**
Patternmaking   **671.2**
    UF   Pattern making
    BT   **Models and modelmaking**
    NT   **Mechanical drawing**
    RT   **Design**
          Founding
Patterns
    USE types of handicrafts and manufactures with the subdivision *Patterns,* e.g. **Dressmaking—Patterns** [to be added as needed]

Patterns (Language arts)
 USE **Language arts—Patterning**
Patterns (Mathematics) 372.7
 UF Geometric patterns
    Number patterns
 BT **Mathematics**
Paul Bunyan
 USE **Bunyan, Paul (Legendary character)**
Pauperism
 USE **Poverty**
Pavements (May subdiv. geog.) **625.8**
 RT **Roads**
    Streets
Pay equity
 USE **Equal pay for equal work**
Pay-per-view television
 USE **Subscription television**
Pay television
 USE **Subscription television**
Payroll taxes
 USE **Unemployment insurance**
PC computers
 USE **Microcomputers**
PCs
 USE **Microcomputers**
Peace 172; 327.1; 341.7
 SA names of wars with the subdivision *Peace* e.g. **World War, 1939-1945—Peace** [to be added as needed]
 BT **International relations**
 NT **World War, 1914-1918—Peace**
 RT **Arms control**
    International arbitration
    International security
    Pacifism
    Peace movements
    War
Peace keeping forces
 USE **United Nations—Armed forces**
Peace movements (May subdiv. geog.)
    327.1
 Use for materials on social movements advocating peace. Materials on the renunciation of offensive or defensive military actions on moral grounds are entered under **Pacifism.**
 UF Antiwar movements
    War protest movements
 SA names of wars with the subdivision *Protest movements,* e.g.
    World War, 1939-1945—

Protest movements [to be added as needed]
 BT **Social movements**
 RT **Demonstrations**
    Peace
Peaceful coexistence
 USE **International relations**
Peacocks 598.6
 UF Peafowl
    Peahens
 BT **Birds**
Peafowl
 USE **Peacocks**
Peahens
 USE **Peacocks**
Pearl fisheries 338.3; 639
 UF Pearlfisheries
 BT **Commercial fishing**
Pearl Harbor (Oahu, Hawaii), Attack on, 1941 940.54
 BT **World War, 1939-1945—Campaigns**
Pearlfisheries
 USE **Pearl fisheries**
Peasant art
 USE **Folk art**
Peasantry (May subdiv. geog.) **305.5; 307.72**
 BT **Feudalism**
    Labor
 RT **Agricultural laborers**
    Land tenure
    Rural sociology
Pecan
 USE **Pecans**
Pecans 583; 634
 UF Pecan
 BT **Nuts**
Pedagogy
 USE **Education**
    Education—Study and teaching
    Teaching
Peddlers and peddling (May subdiv. geog.) **658.8**
 UF Door to door selling
 BT **Direct selling**
    Sales personnel
Pediatric psychiatry
 USE **Child psychiatry**
Pediatric surgery
 USE **Children—Surgery**

Pediatrics
USE **Children—Diseases**
Children—Health and hygiene
Infants—Diseases
Infants—Health and hygiene
Pedigrees
USE **Genealogy**
Heraldry
Peer counseling   158; 361.3
UF Peer counseling in rehabilitation
Peer counseling of students
Peer group counseling
Rehabilitation peer counseling
Student to student counseling
BT **Counseling**
Peer counseling in rehabilitation
USE **Peer counseling**
Peer counseling of students
USE **Peer counseling**
Peer group counseling
USE **Peer counseling**
Peer group influence
USE **Peer pressure**
Peer pressure   303.3; 364.2
UF Peer group influence
BT **Socialization**
Peer pressure in adolescence   303.3
Peerage
USE **Nobility**
Pelts
USE **Hides and skins**
Pen drawing   741.2
UF Ink drawing
BT **Drawing**
Pen names
USE **Pseudonyms**
Penal codes
USE **Criminal law**
Penal colonies (May subdiv. geog.)   **365**
UF Expulsion
Transportation of criminals
BT **Colonies**
Correctional institutions
Penal institutions
USE **Correctional institutions**
Prisons
Reformatories
Penal law
USE **Criminal law**
Penal reform
USE **Prison reform**

Penance (May subdiv. geog.)   **265**
UF Contrition
Reconciliation, Sacrament of
Sacrament of Reconciliation
BT **Sacraments**
RT **Confession**
Forgiveness of sin
Pencil drawing   741.2
BT **Drawing**
Penicillin   615
BT **Antibiotics**
Peninsulas (May subdiv. geog.)   **551.41**
SA names of peninsulas [to be add-
ed as needed]
NT **Arabian Peninsula**
Penitentiaries
USE **Prisons**
Penmanship
USE **Handwriting**
Pennsylvania Dutch   974.8
UF Pennsylvania Germans
Pennsylvania Germans
USE **Pennsylvania Dutch**
Penology
USE **Corrections**
Punishment
Pensions (May subdiv. geog.)   **331.25;**
353.5; 658.3
UF Compensation
SA ethnic groups, classes of per-
sons, and employees in partic-
ular industries with the subdi-
vision *Pensions*, e.g. **Teach-
ers—Pensions; Chemical in-
dustry—Employees—Pen-
sions; etc.** [to be added as
needed]
BT **Annuities**
Retirement income
NT **Individual retirement accounts**
Military pensions
Old age pensions
Social security
Pensions, Naval
USE **Military pensions**
Pentagon (Va.) terrorist attack, 2001
USE **September 11 terrorist attacks,
2001**
Pentecostal churches (May subdiv. geog.)
289.9
Use for general materials on Christian de-
nominations of the Pentecostal type. Materials

550

Pentecostal churches—*Continued*
on Christian movements that stress the personal experience of the Holy Spirit in daily life, with emphasis on personal holiness and spiritual gifts, especially the gift of tongues, are entered under **Pentecostalism.**

BT **Christian sects**
Protestantism
RT **Pentecostalism**

Pentecostal movement
USE **Pentecostalism**

Pentecostalism (May subdiv. geog.)
270.8

Use for materials on Christian movements that stress the personal experience of the Holy Spirit in daily life, with emphasis on personal holiness and spiritual gifts, especially the gift of tongues. General materials on Christian denominations of the Pentecostal type are entered under **Pentecostal churches.**

UF Charismatic movement
Charismatic renewal movement
Pentecostal movement
BT **Christianity**
RT **Catholic charismatic movement**
Glossolalia
Pentecostal churches
Spiritual gifts

Peonage (May subdiv. geog.) **306.3; 331.5**

UF Servitude
BT **Forced labor**
RT **Contract labor**
Slavery

People
USE **Ethnic groups**
Native peoples
Persons
and racial and ethnic groups
and native peoples, e.g.
African Americans; Mexican Americans; Yoruba (African people); etc., and classes of persons, e.g. **Elderly; Handicapped; Explorers; Drug addicts;** etc. [to be added as needed]

People in space
USE **Space flight**

People's banks
USE **Cooperative banks**

People's democracies
USE **Communist countries**

People's Republic of China
USE **China**

Pep pills
USE **Amphetamines**

Percentage **513.2**
BT **Arithmetic**

Perception **152.1; 153.7**
UF Feeling
SA types of concepts and images, e.g. **Size; Shape;** etc. [to be added as needed]
BT **Intellect**
Psychology
Senses and sensation
Theory of knowledge
Thought and thinking
NT **Concepts**
Consciousness
Gestalt psychology
Pattern perception
Shape
Size
RT **Apperception**
Intuition

Percussion instruments **786.8**
SA types of percussion instruments, e.g. **Drums** [to be added as needed]
BT **Musical instruments**
NT **Drums**
Pianos

Perennials **635.9**
BT **Cultivated plants**
Flower gardening
Flowers

Perfectionism (Personality trait) **155.2**
UF Self-expectations, Perfectionist
BT **Personality**

Performance **155.2; 658.4**
UF Competence
BT **Work**
NT **Achievement motivation**
Performance standards

Performance art (May subdiv. geog.)
700

Use for materials on live performances by artists, drawing on literature, theater, music, film, etc., and combining elements of the various arts in untraditional ways.

UF Happening (Art)
BT **Art**
Performing arts

Performance motivation
USE **Achievement motivation**

Performance standards   658.5
- UF Job performance standards
- Rating
- Work performance standards
- SA subjects and classes of persons with the subdivision *Rating*, e.g. **Bonds—Rating; Employees—Rating;** etc. [to be added as needed]
- BT **Performance**

Performing arts (May subdiv. geog.) **790.2**
- UF Show business
- SA specific art forms performed on stage or screen [to be added as needed]
- BT **Arts**
- NT **Ballet**
- **Centers for the performing arts**
- **Dance**
- **Motion pictures**
- **Opera**
- **Performance art**
- **Theater**

Performing arts audiences
- USE **Performing arts—Audiences**

Performing arts—Audiences   791
- UF Performing arts audiences
- BT **Audiences**

Perfumes   391.6; 668
- BT **Cosmetics**
- **Essences and essential oils**
- NT **Potpourri**

Periodic health examinations   616.07
- UF Health examinations
- Medical examinations
- Physical examinations (Medicine)
- SA subjects, classes of persons, ethnic groups, and military services with the subdivision *Medical examinations*, e.g. **Children—Medical examinations** [to be added as needed]
- BT **Medicine**

Periodic law   546.8
- BT **Physical chemistry**
- RT **Chemical elements**

Periodicals (May subdiv. geog.)   **050**
- UF Annuals
- Journals

Magazines
- SA subjects with the subdivision *Periodicals*, e.g. **Engineering—Periodicals;** and names of individual periodicals [to be added as needed]
- BT **Mass media**
- **Serial publications**
- NT **Chapbooks**
- **English periodicals**
- **Fanzines**
- **Little magazines**
- RT **Journalism**
- **Newspapers**
- **Press**

Periodicals—Editing
- USE **Journalism—Editing**

Periodicals—Indexes   050

Periodicals—United States   051
- UF American periodicals *[Former heading]*

Periodicity
- USE **Cycles**

Permanent education
- USE **Continuing education**

Persecution (May subdiv. geog.)   **201; 909**
- UF Persecutions
- Religious persecution
- SA religious groups with the subdivision *Persecutions*, e.g. **Christians—Persecutions; Jews—Persecutions;** etc.; and religious groups and classes of persons with the subdivision *Nazi persecution*, e.g. **Handicapped—Nazi persecution** [to be added as needed]
- BT **Atrocities**
- NT **Christians—Persecutions**
- **Handicapped—Nazi persecution**
- **Jews—Persecutions**
- **Massacres**
- RT **Freedom of religion**
- **Martyrs**

Persecutions
- USE **Persecution**
- and religious groups with the subdivision *Persecutions*, e.g. **Christians—Persecutions; Jews—Persecutions;** etc.; and

Persecutions—*Continued*
    religious groups and classes
    of persons with the subdivi-
    sion *Nazi persecution,* e.g.
    **Handicapped—Nazi persecu-
    tion** [to be added as needed]

Perseverance   179
  BT   **Ethics**
Persia
  USE   **Iran**
Persian Gulf War, 1991   956.7044
  UF   Gulf War, 1991
     Middle East War, 1991
     Operation Desert Storm
  BT   **United States—History—1989-**
Persistence   158
  BT   **Personality**
Persistent pain
  USE   **Chronic pain**
Personal actions (Law)
  USE   **Litigation**
Personal appearance   391.6
  UF   Appearance, Personal
     Beauty, Personal
     Physical appearance
     Self image
  NT   **Personal grooming**
     Tattooing
  RT   **Clothing and dress**
Personal cleanliness
  USE   **Hygiene**
Personal computers
  USE   **Microcomputers**
Personal conduct
  USE   **Conduct of life**
Personal development
  USE   **Personality**
     Self-improvement
     Success
Personal films
  USE   **Amateur films**
     Experimental films
Personal finance (May subdiv. geog.)
    332.024
  UF   Budgets, Personal
     Domestic finance
     Family finance
     Finance, Personal
     Financial planning, Personal
  SA   ethnic groups, classes of per-
     sons, and names of individual
     persons with the subdivision

Personal finance, e.g. **Retir-
    ees—Personal finance** [to be
    added as needed]
  BT   **Finance**
  NT   **Children's allowances**
     Consumer credit
     Estate planning
     Household budgets
     Insurance
     Saving and investment
     Tax planning
Personal freedom
  USE   **Freedom**
Personal grooming   391.6; 646.7
  UF   Beauty, Personal
     Good grooming
     Grooming, Personal
  BT   **Hygiene**
     Personal appearance
  NT   **Cosmetics**
     Hair
     Toiletries
  RT   **Clothing and dress**
Personal growth
  USE   **Self-improvement**
Personal health
  USE   **Health**
Personal health services
  USE   **Medical care**
Personal hygiene
  USE   **Hygiene**
Personal income tax
  USE   **Income tax**
Personal life skills
  USE   **Life skills**
Personal loans   332.7
    Use for materials on loans to individuals for
  personal rather than business uses.
  UF   Consumer loans
     Loans, Personal
     Small loans
  BT   **Consumer credit**
     Loans
  NT   **Cooperative banks**
     Savings and loan associations
Personal names (May subdiv. geog.)
    929.4
  UF   Baby names
     Christian names
     Family names
     First names
     Names, Personal

Personal names—*Continued*
    Surnames
  SA personal names of particular national or ethnic origins regardless of the place where they are found, e.g. **Scottish personal names** [to be added as needed]
  BT **Names**
  NT **Nicknames**
      Pseudonyms
      Scottish personal names
Personal names—United States
    929.40973
  UF American personal names
Personal narratives
  USE **Autobiographies**
      Biography
      and subjects with the subdivision *Biography* or *Correspondence;* and names of diseases, events, and wars with the subdivision *Personal narratives,* e.g. **World War, 1939-1945—Personal narratives** [to be added as needed]
Personal space   153.6; 302.2
    Use for materials on the sense of physical space required for psychological comfort.
  UF Space, Personal
  BT **Interpersonal relations**
      Nonverbal communication
      Space and time
Personal time management
  USE **Time management**
Personality   155.2
  UF Identity
      Personal development
  BT **Consciousness**
      Psychology
  NT **Body image**
      Bossiness
      Character
      Eccentrics and eccentricities
      Ego (Psychology)
      Forgetfulness
      Identity (Psychology)
      Laziness
      Perfectionism (Personality trait)
      Persistence
      Self

      Selfishness
      Stubbornness
      Typology (Psychology)
  RT **Individuality**
      Persons
Personality disorders   616.85
  BT **Abnormal psychology**
  NT **Multiple personality**
  RT **Hallucinations and illusions**
      Mental illness
Personality, Multiple
  USE **Multiple personality**
Personnel administration
  USE **Personnel management**
Personnel classification
  USE **Job analysis**
Personnel management (May subdiv. geog.)   **658.3**
  UF Career development
      Employment management
      Human resource management
      Personnel administration
      Supervision of employees
  SA names of corporate bodies and military services and types of industries, services, and organizations with the subdivision *Personnel management,* e.g. **Hospitals—Personnel management** [to be added as needed]
  BT **Industrial relations**
      Management
  NT **Absenteeism (Labor)**
      Affirmative action programs
      Applications for positions
      Counseling
      Diversity in the workplace
      Employee assistance programs
      Employee morale
      Employees—Dismissal
      Employees—Training
      Employment agencies
      Hospitals—Personnel management
      Job analysis
      Job satisfaction
      Job security
      Labor turnover
      Motion study
      Participative management

Personnel management—*Continued*

      Recruiting of employees

      Supervisors

      Time study

  RT **Employees**

      Factory management

      Office management

Personnel service in education

  USE **Educational counseling**

Persons   **128**

    Use for materials on human beings as individuals. Materials on the human species from the point of view of biology or anthropology are entered under **Human beings.**

  UF Categories of persons

      Classes of persons

      Groups of persons

      People

  SA classes of persons, e.g. **Elderly; Handicapped; Explorers; Drug addicts;** etc. [to be added as needed]

  BT **Human beings**

  NT **Celebrities**

      Intellectuals

      Psychics

  RT **Individualism**

      Personality

Perspective   **701**

  UF Architectural perspective

  BT **Descriptive geometry**

      Geometrical drawing

      Optics

      Painting

  RT **Drawing**

Persuasion (Psychology)   **153.8**

  UF Psychology, Applied

  BT **Communication**

      Conformity

  RT **Propaganda**

Persuasion (Rhetoric)

  USE **Public speaking**

      Rhetoric

Perversion, Sexual

  USE **Sexual deviation**

Pesach

  USE **Passover**

Pest control   **363.7; 628.9; 632**

  UF Extermination of pests

      Pest extermination

      Pests—Biological control

      Pests—Control

      Pests—Extermination

  SA types of pests with the subdivision *Control,* e.g. **Mosquitoes—Control** [to be added as needed]

  BT **Agricultural pests**

      Economic zoology

      Pests

  NT **Mosquitoes—Control**

      Pesticides

Pest extermination

  USE **Pest control**

Pesticide pollution

  USE **Pesticides—Environmental aspects**

Pesticides (May subdiv. geog.)   **632; 668**

  BT **Agricultural chemicals**

      Pest control

      Poisons and poisoning

  NT **Fungicides**

      Herbicides

      Insecticides

      Natural pesticides

Pesticides and wildlife   **590**

  UF Wildlife and pesticides

  BT **Pesticides—Environmental aspects**

      Wildlife conservation

Pesticides—Environmental aspects   **363.7; 632**

  UF Environment and pesticides

      Pesticide pollution

  BT **Environment**

      Pollution

  NT **Pesticides and wildlife**

Pestilences

  USE **Epidemics**

Pests   **591.6; 632**

    Use for materials on detrimental or annoying animals or organisms.

  UF Vermin

  SA types of pests, e.g. **Agricultural pests; Flies;** etc.; and names of crops, trees, etc., with the subdivision *Diseases and pests,* e.g. **Fruit—Diseases and pests** [to be added as needed]

  BT **Economic zoology**

  NT **Agricultural pests**

      Flies

      Fruit—Diseases and pests

Pests—*Continued*
> Fungi
> Household pests
> Insect pests
> Parasites
> Pest control

Pests—Biological control
> USE **Pest control**

Pests—Control
> USE **Pest control**

Pests—Extermination
> USE **Pest control**

Pet-facilitated psychotherapy
> USE **Pet therapy**

Pet therapy   615.8
> UF   Animal-facilitated therapy
> Companion-animal partnership
> Pet-facilitated psychotherapy
> BT   **Animals and the handicapped**
> **Therapeutics**

Petrochemicals   661
> UF   Petroleum chemicals
> BT   **Chemicals**

Petroglyphs
> USE   **Rock drawings, paintings, and**
> **engravings**

Petroleum (May subdiv. geog.)   **553.2;**
665.5
> UF   Coal oil
> Crude oil
> Oil
> BT   **Oils and fats**
> NT   **Coal tar products**
> **Gasoline**
> RT   **Petroleum geology**
> **Petroleum industry**

Petroleum as fuel   338.4; 665.5
> UF   Fuel oil
> Liquid fuel
> Oil fuel
> BT   **Fuel**
> NT   **Oil burners**

Petroleum chemicals
> USE   **Petrochemicals**

Petroleum engines
> USE   **Internal combustion engines**

Petroleum geology (May subdiv. geog.)
553.2
> UF   Geology, Petroleum
> BT   **Economic geology**
> **Prospecting**
> RT   **Petroleum**

Petroleum industry (May subdiv. geog.)
338.2
> UF   Oil industry
> Petroleum industry and trade
> BT   **Industries**
> NT   **Offshore oil industry**
> **Oil well drilling**
> **Oil wells**
> **Service stations**
> RT   **Petroleum**

Petroleum industry and trade
> USE   **Petroleum industry**

Petroleum industry—Deregulation (May
> subdiv. geog.)   **338.2**

Petroleum pipelines (May subdiv. geog.)
338.2; 665.5
> BT   **Pipelines**

Petroleum pollution of water
> USE   **Oil pollution of water**

Petroleum—United States   553.2; 665.5

Petroleum—Well boring
> USE   **Oil well drilling**

Petrology (May subdiv. geog.)   **552**
> SA   types of rocks, e.g. **Granite** [to
> be added as needed]
> BT   **Science**
> NT   **Geochemistry**
> **Moon rocks**
> RT   **Geology**
> **Minerals**
> **Rocks**
> **Stone**

Pets (May subdiv. geog.)   **636.088**
> SA   types of common pets, e.g.
> **Dogs**; and types of animals
> not ordinarily kept as pets,
> e.g. **Snakes as pets** [to be
> added as needed]
> BT   **Animals**
> NT   **Snakes as pets**
> RT   **Domestic animals**

Pets and the handicapped
> USE   **Animals and the handicapped**

Pets—Housing   690
> BT   **Animal housing**
> NT   **Kennels**

Pets—Names   636.088

Petting zoos   590.73
> BT   **Zoos**

Pewter   673; 739.5
  BT   **Alloys**
       Art metalwork
       Metals
Phantoms
  USE   **Apparitions**
        Ghosts
Pharmaceutical abuse
  USE   **Medication abuse**
Pharmaceutical chemistry   615
  UF   Drugs—Chemistry
       Medicinal chemistry
  BT   **Chemistry**
  NT   **Disinfection and disinfectants**
  RT   **Pharmacy**
       Therapeutics
Pharmaceuticals
  USE   **Drugs**
Pharmacies
  USE   **Drugstores**
Pharmacodynamics
  USE   **Pharmacology**
Pharmacology   615
    Use for materials on the action and proper-
  ties of drugs in general. Materials limited to
  the effect of drugs on the functions of living
  organisms are entered under **Drugs—Physio-
  logical effect**. Materials on the art or practice
  of preparing, preserving, and dispensing drugs
  are entered under **Pharmacy**.
  UF   Drugs—Adulteration and analysis
       Medicine—Physiological effect
       Pharmacodynamics
  BT   **Medicine**
  NT   **Drugs—Physiological effect**
       Drugs—Testing
       Toxicology
  RT   **Drug therapy**
       Drugs
       Materia medica
       Pharmacy
Pharmacopoeias
  USE   **Materia medica**
Pharmacotherapy
  USE   **Drug therapy**
Pharmacy   615
    Use for materials on the art or practice of
  preparing, preserving, and dispensing drugs.
  Materials on the action and properties of
  drugs are entered under **Pharmacology**. Mate-
  rials on business establishments that sell drugs
  are entered under **Drugstores**.
  BT   **Chemistry**
       Medicine

  NT   **Drugs**
       Homeopathy
       Medical botany
  RT   **Materia medica**
       Pharmaceutical chemistry
       Pharmacology
Pheasants   598.6; 636.5
  BT   **Birds**
       Game and game birds
Phenomenology   142
  BT   **Modern philosophy**
  NT   **Existentialism**
Philanthropists (May subdiv. geog.)
       361.7092; 920
  UF   Altruists
       Humanitarians
  RT   **Philanthropy**
Philanthropy (May subdiv. geog.)   177;
       361.7
  RT   **Charities**
       Charity organization
       Endowments
       Philanthropists
Philately
  USE   **Stamp collecting**
Philology
  USE   **Language and languages**
        Linguistics
Philology, Comparative
  USE   **Linguistics**
Philosophers (May subdiv. geog.)   180;
       190; 920
  RT   **Philosophy**
Philosophers, American
  USE   **Philosophers—United States**
Philosophers' stone
  USE   **Alchemy**
Philosophers—United States   191; 920
  UF   American philosophers
       Philosophers, American
Philosophy   100
  SA   movements in philosophy, e.g.
       Positivism; philosophy of par-
       ticular countries, e.g.
       American philosophy; philos-
       ophy associated with particu-
       lar religions, e.g. **Christian
       philosophy;** and subjects with
       the subdivision *Philosophy,*
       e.g. **History—Philosophy** [to
       be added as needed]

Philosophy—*Continued*
BT Humanities
NT Aesthetics
  American philosophy
  Ancient philosophy
  Belief and doubt
  Causation
  Christian philosophy
  Comparative philosophy
  Empiricism
  Ethics
  Evolution
  Fate and fatalism
  Free will and determinism
  Gnosticism
  Good and evil
  Hindu philosophy
  History—Philosophy
  Humanism
  Idealism
  Ideology
  Intuition
  Logic
  Marxism
  Materialism
  Medieval philosophy
  Metaphysics
  Mind and body
  Modern philosophy
  Philosophy and religion
  Positivism
  Pragmatism
  Psychology
  Rationalism
  Realism
  Reality
  Skepticism
  Soul
  Theism
  Theory of knowledge
  Transcendentalism
  Truth
RT Philosophers
Philosophy, American
 USE American philosophy
Philosophy, Ancient
 USE Ancient philosophy
Philosophy and religion 210
 Use for materials on the reciprocal relationship and influence between philosophy and religion. Materials on the nature, origin, or validity of religion from a philosophical point of view are entered under **Religion—Philosophy.**

UF Religion and philosophy
BT Philosophy
  Religion
RT Religion—Philosophy
Philosophy—Encyclopedias 103
 BT Encyclopedias and dictionaries
Philosophy, Hindu
 USE Hindu philosophy
Philosophy—Historiography 109
 BT Historiography
Philosophy, Medieval
 USE Medieval philosophy
Philosophy, Modern
 USE Modern philosophy
Philosophy of history
 USE History—Philosophy
Philosophy of religion
 USE Religion—Philosophy
Phobias 616.85
 SA types of phobias, e.g. **Agoraphobia** [to be added as needed]
 BT Fear
   Neuroses
 NT Agoraphobia
Phonetic spelling
 USE Spelling reform
Phonetics 414
 UF Phonics
   Phonology
 SA names of languages with the subdivision *Pronunciation* [to be added as needed]
 BT Language and languages
   Sound
 NT English language—Pronunciation
 RT Reading—Phonetic method
   Speech
   Voice
Phonics
 USE Phonetics
   Reading—Phonetic method
Phonograph 621.389
 UF Gramophone
 NT Compact disc players
 RT High-fidelity sound systems
   Sound—Recording and reproducing
Phonograph records
 USE Sound recordings

Phonology
USE **Phonetics**
and names of languages with
the subdivision *Pronunciation,*
e.g. **English language—Pro-
nunciation** [to be added as
needed]
Phosphates   546; 553.6; 631.8
BT **Fertilizers**
Phosphorescence   535
BT **Luminescence**
Radioactivity
Photo journalism
USE **Photojournalism**
Photocopying   686.4
UF Photocopying processes
Photoduplication
Photographic reproduction
Xerography
BT **Copying processes**
RT **Copy art**
Photocopying machines
USE **Copying machines**
Photocopying processes
USE **Photocopying**
Photoduplication
USE **Photocopying**
Photoelectric cells   537.5; 621.3815
UF Electric eye
Photoengraving   686.2
UF Halftone process
BT **Engraving**
RT **Photomechanical processes**
Photographers (May subdiv. geog.)
770.92
BT **Artists**
Photographic chemistry   771
Use for materials on the chemical processes
employed in photography.
BT **Chemistry**
NT **Photography—Processing**
RT **Photography**
Photographic film
USE **Photography—Film**
Photographic reproduction
USE **Photocopying**
Photographic slides
USE **Slides (Photography)**
Photographic supplies
USE **Photography—Equipment and
supplies**

Photographs   770
Use for materials that discuss photographs
as objects, including their classification, cataloging, copying, coloring, mounting, etc.
UF Photos
Snapshots
SA subjects, classes of persons,
names of wars, and names of
cities, states, countries, and
named entities, such as indi-
vidual parks, structures, etc.,
with the subdivision *Pictorial
works,* e.g. **Animals—Pictori-
al works; United States—
History—1861-1865, Civil
War—Pictorial works;** etc.;
and names of persons or
groups of persons with the
subdivision *Pictorial works,* or
Portraits [to be added as
needed]
BT **Pictures**
RT **Photography**
**Photographs—Conservation and restora-
tion   771**
UF Conservation of photographs
Preservation of photographs
Restoration of photographs
Photographs from space
USE **Space photography**
Photography (May subdiv. geog.)   **770**
SA kinds of photography, e.g. **Por-
trait photography;** photogra-
phy of particular subjects, e.g.
Photography of birds; and
subjects, classes of persons,
names of wars, and names of
cities, states, countries, and
named entities, such as indi-
vidual parks, structures, etc.,
with the subdivision *Pictorial
works* [to be added as need-
ed]
BT **Graphic arts**
NT **Aerial photography**
Artistic photography
Astronomical photography
Cameras
Cinematography
Color photography
Commercial photography
Digital photography

Photography—*Continued*
>> Filmstrips
>> Holography
>> Medical photography
>> Microphotography
>> Nature photography
>> Outdoor photography
>> Photojournalism
>> Photomechanical processes
>> Photomicrography
>> Portrait photography
>> Slides (Photography)
>> Space photography
>> Telephotography
>> Three dimensional photography
>> Underwater photography
> RT Photographic chemistry
>> Photographs

Photography—Aesthetics
> USE **Artistic photography**
Photography, Artistic
> USE **Artistic photography**
Photography, Color
> USE **Color photography**
Photography—Darkroom technique
> USE **Photography—Processing**
**Photography—Developing and developers
771**
> BT **Photography—Processing**
Photography—Digital techniques
> USE **Digital photography**
Photography—Enlarging   771
> UF Enlarging (Photography)
**Photography—Equipment and supplies
771**
> UF Photographic supplies
> NT **Cameras**
Photography—Film   771
> UF Photographic film
**Photography—Handbooks, manuals, etc.
770.2**
Photography in astronautics
> USE **Space photography**
Photography—Lighting   771; 778.7
> BT **Lighting**
Photography—Motion pictures
> USE **Cinematography**
Photography of animals   778.9
>> Use for materials on the technique of photographing animals. Materials consisting of

photographs and pictures of animals are entered under **Animals—Pictorial works.**
> UF Animal photography
>> Animals—Photography
> BT **Nature photography**
> RT **Animal painting and illustration**
>> **Animals—Pictorial works**
Photography of birds   778.9
> UF Bird photography
>> Birds—Photography
> BT **Nature photography**
Photography of fishes   778.9
> UF Fishes—Photography
> BT **Nature photography**
Photography of nature
> USE **Nature photography**
Photography of plants   778.9
> UF Plants—Photography
> BT **Nature photography**
Photography—Printing processes   771
> BT **Photography—Processing**
Photography—Processing   771
> UF Darkroom technique in photography
>> Photography—Darkroom technique
> SA types of photographic processing techniques, e.g. **Photography—Developing and developers; Photography—Printing processes;** etc. [to be added as needed]
> BT **Photographic chemistry**
> NT **Photography—Developing and developers**
>> **Photography—Printing processes**
Photography—Retouching   771
> UF Retouching (Photography)
**Photography—Scientific applications
778.3**
> SA specific applications, e.g. **Medical photography** [to be added as needed]
> NT **Medical photography**
>> **Space photography**
Photography, Stereoscopic
> USE **Three dimensional photography**

Photojournalism (May subdiv. geog.)
    070.4; 779
  UF Journalistic photography
      News photography
      Photo journalism
  BT **Commercial photography**
      Journalism
      Photography

Photomechanical processes   **686.2**
  SA types of photomechanical pro-
      cesses, e.g. **Photoengraving**
      [to be added as needed]
  BT **Illustration of books**
      Photography
  RT **Photoengraving**

Photometry   **535**
  UF Electric light
  BT **Measurement**
  NT **Color**
  RT **Light**
      Optics

Photomicrography   **778.3**
    Use for materials on the photographing of
minute objects through a miscroscope. Materials on the photographing of objects of any
size to produce minute images are entered under **Microphotography.**
  BT **Photography**
  RT **Microscopes**

Photos
  USE **Photographs**

Photosynthesis   **572**
  BT **Botany**

Phototherapy   **615.8**
  UF Electric light
      Light—Therapeutic use
  BT **Physical therapy**
      Therapeutics
  RT **Radiotherapy**
      Ultraviolet rays

Photovoltaic power generation   **621.31**
  UF Solar cells
  BT **Solar energy**
  NT **Solar batteries**

Phrenology (May subdiv. geog.)   **139**
  BT **Brain**
      Head
      Psychology
  RT **Mind and body**
      Physiognomy

Physical anthropology (May subdiv.
    geog.)   **599.9**
  UF Biological anthropology
  BT **Anthropology**
      Ethnology
  NT **Human origins**

Physical appearance
  USE **Personal appearance**

Physical chemistry   **541**
  UF Chemistry, Physical and theoreti-
      cal
      Theoretical chemistry
  BT **Chemistry**
      Physics
  NT **Atmospheric chemistry**
      Atomic theory
      Atoms
      Catalysis
      Colloids
      Crystals
      Electrochemistry
      Molecules
      Periodic law
      Polymers
      Radiochemistry
      Solids
      Thermodynamics
  RT **Nuclear physics**
      Quantum theory

Physical culture
  USE **Physical education**

Physical education (May subdiv. geog.)
    613.7; 796.07
  UF Calisthenics
      Physical culture
      Physical education and training
      Physical training
  SA types of sports activities with
      the subdivision *Training*, e.g.
      Soccer—Training; and names
      of sports and types of physi-
      cal exercise [to be added as
      needed]
  BT **Education**
  NT **Coaching (Athletics)**
      Games
      Marching drills
      Movement education
      Physical fitness
      Soccer—Training

Physical education—*Continued*
RT   Athletics
      Exercise
      Gymnastics
      Sports
Physical education and training
USE   **Physical education**
Physical education—Medical aspects
USE   **Sports medicine**
Physical examinations (Medicine)
USE   **Periodic health examinations**
Physical fitness (May subdiv. geog.)
      613.7
UF   Endurance, Physical
      Fitness
      Physical stamina
      Stamina, Physical
SA   classes of persons with the sub-
      division *Physical fitness,* e.g.,
      Women—Physical fitness [to
      be added as needed]
BT   **Exercise**
      Health
      Health self-care
      Physical education
NT   **Bodybuilding**
      Children—Physical fitness
      Kinesiology
      Physical fitness centers
      Posture
      Women—Physical fitness
Physical fitness centers (May subdiv.
      geog.)   613.7
UF   Health clubs
      Health spas
      Recreation centers
      Spas
BT   **Physical fitness**
Physical geography (May subdiv. geog.)
      910
   Use for materials on the physical features
of the earth's surface and its atmosphere.
General materials, frequently school materials,
describing the surface of the earth and its in-
terrelationship with various peoples, animals,
natural products, and industries are entered
under **Geography.**
BT   **Geography**
      Geology
NT   **Deserts**
      Earthquakes
      Geysers
      Glaciers

Ice
Icebergs
Lakes
Mountains
Ocean
Rivers
Volcanoes
Winds
RT   Earth
Physical geography—United States
      917.3
Physical sciences   500.2
BT   Science
NT   Astronomy
      Chemistry
      Earth sciences
      Physics
Physical stamina
USE   **Physical fitness**
Physical therapy   615.8
UF   Physiotherapy
SA   types of physical therapy, e.g.
      Hydrotherapy; and types of
      disabilities, injuries, or dis-
      eases with the subdivision
      Physical therapy, e.g. **Arthri-
      tis—Physicial therapy** [to be
      added as needed]
BT   **Therapeutics**
NT   **Baths**
      Electrotherapeutics
      Hydrotherapy
      Massage
      Occupational therapy
      Phototherapy
      Radiotherapy
Physical training
USE   **Physical education**
Physically handicapped (May subdiv.
      geog.)   362.4
UF   Crippled people
      Invalids
SA   types of physically handicapped
      persons, e.g. **Blind; Deaf;** etc.
      [to be added as needed]
BT   **Handicapped**
NT   **Blind**
      Deaf
      Hearing impaired
      **Physically handicapped chil-
      dren**

Physically handicapped—*Continued*
  RT **Orthopedics**
Physically handicapped children (May
      subdiv. geog.) **155.45; 362.4**
  UF Children, Crippled
       Crippled children
  BT **Handicapped children**
       Physically handicapped
Physically handicapped—Housing (May
      subdiv. geog.) **362.4**
  UF Housing for the physically hand-
       icapped
  BT **Housing**
Physically handicapped—Rehabilitation
      362.4
  NT **Occupational therapy**
Physicians (May subdiv. geog.) **610.69;**
      920
  UF Doctors
  SA types of medical specialists [to
       be added as needed]
  BT **Medical personnel**
  NT **Radiologists**
       Surgeons
       Women physicians
  RT **Medicine**
Physicians—Directories **610.69**
  BT **Directories**
Physicians—Drug use **362.29; 610.69**
  UF Drug abusing physicians
       Drug addicted physicians
Physicians—Licenses (May subdiv. geog.)
      344
  BT **Medicine—Law and legislation**
Physicians—Malpractice (May subdiv.
      geog.) **346.03**
  UF Medical errors
  BT **Malpractice**
       Medicine—Law and legislation
Physicists (May subdiv. geog.) **530.092;**
      920
  BT **Scientists**
Physics **530**
  BT **Physical sciences**
       Science
  NT **Astrophysics**
       Biophysics
       Electricity
       Electronics
       Gases
       Geophysics
       Gravitation

       Hydraulics
       Hydrostatics
       Light
       Liquids
       Magnetism
       Matter
       Mechanics
       Music—Acoustics and physics
       Nuclear physics
       Optics
       Physical chemistry
       Pneumatics
       Quantum theory
       Radiation
       Radioactivity
       Relativity (Physics)
       Solids
       Sound
       Statics
       Thermodynamics
       Weight
       Weights and measures
  RT **Dynamics**
Physics—Conferences **530**
  UF Physics—Congresses
Physics—Congresses
  USE **Physics—Conferences**
Physics, Terrestrial
  USE **Geophysics**
Physiognomy **138**
  BT **Psychology**
  RT **Face**
       Phrenology
Physiological aspects
  USE types of activities and mental
       conditions with the subdivi-
       sion **Physiological aspects,**
       e.g. **Mental illness—Physio-**
       logical aspects [to be added
       as needed]
Physiological chemistry
  USE **Biochemistry**
Physiological effect
  USE types of drugs, chemicals, or en-
       vironmental phenomena or
       conditions with the subdivi-
       sion *Physiological effect,* e.g.
       Alcohol—Physiological effect;
       Radiation—Physiological ef-
       fect; etc. [to be added as
       needed]

Physiological psychology
USE **Psychophysiology**
Physiological stress
USE **Stress (Physiology)**
Physiology 571; 612

Use for general materials on physiology and for materials on human physiology. Materials on the physiology of other animals or of plants are entered under the appropriate heading with the subdivision *Physiology*.

UF Human physiology
SA names of organs and regions of the body, types of plants and animals, and classes of persons with the subdivision *Physiology,* e.g. **Heart—Physiology; Reptiles—Physiology;** etc.; activities and mental conditions with the subdivision *Physiological aspects,* e.g. **Mental illness—Physiological aspects;** and drugs, chemicals, and environmental phenomena or conditions with the subdivision *Physiological effect,* e.g. **Alcohol—Physiological effect; Radiation—Physiological effect;** etc. [to be added as needed]
BT **Biology**
Medicine
Science
NT **Blood**
Body temperature
Cardiovascular system
Cells
Comparative physiology
Digestion
Fatigue
Glands
Growth
Health
Heart—Physiology
Human locomotion
Immune system
Lymphatic system
Mental illness—Physiological aspects
Musculoskeletal system
Nervous system
Nutrition
Psychophysiology
Reproduction

Reproductive system
Reptiles—Physiology
Respiration
Respiratory system
Senses and sensation
Skin
Stress (Physiology)
RT **Anatomy**
Human body
Physiology, Comparative
USE **Comparative physiology**
Physiology of plants
USE **Plant physiology**
Physiotherapy
USE **Physical therapy**
Physique
USE **Bodybuilding**
Phytogeography
USE **Plants—Geographical distribution**
Pianists (May subdiv. geog.) **786.2092; 920**
BT **Instrumentalists**
Piano
USE **Pianos**
Piano music 786.2
BT **Instrumental music**
Music
Pianos 786.2
UF Piano
BT **Percussion instruments**
NT **Keyboards (Musical instruments)**
Pianos—Tuning 786.2
BT **Tuning**
Picaresque literature 800

May be used for individual works, collections, or materials about episodic accounts of the adventures of an engagingly roguish hero.

UF Picaresque novels
Rogues and vagabonds—Fiction
BT **Fiction**
Literature
Picaresque novels
USE **Picaresque literature**
Picketing
USE **Strikes**
Pickling
USE **Canning and preserving**
Pickup campers
USE **Travel trailers and campers**

Pictographs
USE **Picture writing**
Pictorial works
USE **Pictures**
and subjects, classes of persons,
names of wars, and names of
cities, states, countries, and
named entities, such as individual parks, structures, etc.,
with the subdivision *Pictorial
works,* e.g. **Animals—Pictorial works; United States—
History—1861-1865, Civil
War—Pictorial works; Chi-
cago (Ill.)—Pictorial works;
Yosemite National Park
(Calif.)—Pictorial works;**
etc.; and names of persons or
groups of persons with the
subdivisions *Cartoons and
caricatures; Pictorial works;*
or *Portraits* [to be added as
needed]
Picture books
USE **Pictures**
Picture books for children
BT **Children's literature**
NT **Coloring books**
Glow-in-the-dark books
Stories without words
Toy and movable books
RT **Illustration of books**
Picture books for children, Wordless
USE **Stories without words**
Picture dictionaries 413
UF Dictionaries, Picture
Word books
BT **Encyclopedias and dictionaries**
Picture frames and framing 684; 749
UF Framing of pictures
BT **Decoration and ornament**
Handicraft
Picture galleries
USE **Art museums**
Commercial art galleries
Picture postcards
USE **Postcards**
Picture puzzles 793.73
BT **Puzzles**
Picture telephone
USE **Video telephone**

Picture writing 411
Use for materials on the recording of events
or the expression of messages by pictures representing actions or facts.
UF Pictographs
BT **Writing**
RT **Hieroglyphics**
Pictures 025.17; 760
Use for general materials on the study and
use of pictures and for miscellaneous collections of pictures.
UF Pictorial works
Picture books
SA subjects, classes of persons,
names of wars, and names of
cities, states, countries, and
named entities, such as individual parks, structures, etc.,
with the subdivision *Pictorial
works,* e.g. **Animals—Pictori-
al works; United States—
History—1861-1865, Civil
War—Pictorial works; Chi-
cago (Ill.)—Pictorial works;
Yosemite National Park
(Calif.)—Pictorial works;**
etc.; and names of persons or
groups of persons with the
subdivisions *Cartoons and
caricatures; Pictorial works;*
or *Portraits* [to be added as
needed]
BT **Art**
NT **Cartoons and caricatures**
Engraving
Etching
Libraries and pictures
Photographs
Portraits
Views
RT **Painting**
Pigments 547; 667; 751.2
NT **Dyes and dyeing**
RT **Color**
Paint
Pigs 599.63; 636.4
UF Hogs
Swine
BT **Domestic animals**
Mammals
Pilates method 613.7
BT **Exercise**

Pilgrims and pilgrimages (May subdiv. geog.) **203; 263**
  BT **Voyages and travels**
  RT **Shrines**
Pilgrims (New England colonists) **974.4**
  BT **Puritans**
      United States—History—1600-1775, Colonial period
Pilot charts
  USE **Nautical charts**
Pilot guides **623.89**
  UF Coast pilot guides
  BT **Navigation**
Piloting
  USE types of aircraft with the subdivision *Piloting,* e.g. **Airplanes—Piloting** [to be added as needed]
Piloting (Astronautics)
  USE **Space vehicles—Piloting**
Pilots
  USE **Air pilots**
      Ship pilots
Piiots and pilotage
  USE **Navigation**
      Ship pilots
Pimples (Acne)
  USE **Acne**
Ping-pong
  USE **Table tennis**
Pioneer life
  USE **Frontier and pioneer life**
Pipe fitting **696**
  RT **Plumbing**
Pipe lines
  USE **Pipelines**
Pipe organs
  USE **Organs (Musical instruments)**
Pipelines (May subdiv. geog.) **388.5; 621.8**
  UF Pipe lines
  SA types of pipelines [to be added as needed]
  BT **Hydraulic structures**
      Transportation
  NT **Petroleum pipelines**
Pipes, Tobacco
  USE **Tobacco pipes**
Piracy
  USE **Pirates**

Pirates (May subdiv. geog.) **364.16; 910.4**
  UF Buccaneers
      Corsairs
      Piracy
  BT **Criminals**
      International law
      Maritime law
      Naval history
  NT **Privateering**
Pistols
  USE **Handguns**
Place names
  USE **Geographic names**
Places, Imaginary
  USE **Geographical myths**
Places of retirement
  USE **Retirement communities**
Places of work
  USE **Work environment**
Plague (May subdiv. geog.) **616.9**
  UF Black death
      Bubonic plague
  BT **Communicable diseases**
      Epidemics
Plain chant
  USE **Chants (Plain, Gregorian, etc.)**
Plainsong
  USE **Chants (Plain, Gregorian, etc.)**
Plane crashes
  USE **Aircraft accidents**
Plane geometry **516.22**
  UF Geometry, Plane
  BT **Geometry**
  NT **Triangle**
Plane trigonometry
  USE **Trigonometry**
Planetariums **520.74**
  BT **Astronomy**
Planetary satellites
  USE **Satellites**
Planetoids
  USE **Asteroids**
Planets **523.4**
  SA names of planets, e.g. **Saturn (Planet)** [to be added as needed]
  BT **Astronomy**
      Solar system
  NT **Earth**
      Extrasolar planets

Planets—*Continued*
>> Life on other planets
>> Mars (Planet)
>> Saturn (Planet)
>> RT Asteroids

Planets—Exploration 523.4
>> SA names of planets with the subdivision *Exploration* [to be added as needed]
>> BT Outer space—Exploration
>> NT Mars (Planet)—Exploration

Planets—Satellites
>> USE Satellites

Planing machines 621.9
>> BT Machine tools

Planned communities (May subdiv. geog.) 307.76
>> UF Housing estates
>> New communities
>> Residential developments
>> BT City planning

Planned parenthood
>> USE Birth control

Planning (May subdiv. geog.) 338.9; 658.4
>> SA types of planning, e.g. Curriculum planning; and types of activities, facilities, industries, services, and undertakings with the subdivision *Planning,* e.g. Transportation—Planning [to be added as needed]
>> BT Creation (Literary, artistic, etc.)
>> Executive ability
>> Management
>> NT City planning
>> Curriculum planning
>> Economic policy
>> Estate planning
>> Regional planning
>> Social policy
>> Strategic planning
>> Tax planning
>> Transportation—Planning

Plans
>> USE Geometrical drawing
>> Map drawing
>> Maps
>> Mechanical drawing

Plant anatomy
>> USE Plants—Anatomy

Plant breeding 631.5
>> Use for materials on attempts to produce new or improved varieties of plants through controlled reproduction. Materials on the continuance or multiplication of plants by successive production are entered under **Plant propagation.**
>> UF Hybridization
>> BT Agriculture
>> Breeding
>> Horticulture
>> RT Plant propagation

Plant chemistry
>> USE Botanical chemistry
>> Plants—Analysis

Plant classification
>> USE Botany—Classification

Plant closings
>> USE Plant shutdowns

Plant conservation (May subdiv. geog.) 333.95; 639.9
>> UF Conservation of plants
>> Plants—Conservation
>> Protection of plants
>> Wild flowers—Conservation
>> BT Conservation of natural resources
>> Economic botany
>> Endangered species
>> Nature conservation
>> NT Scarecrows
>> RT Rare plants

Plant defenses 581.4
>> UF Defense mechanisms of plants
>> Self-defense in plants
>> Self-protection in plants
>> BT Plant ecology
>> RT Poisonous plants

Plant diseases (May subdiv. geog.) 571.9; 632
>> UF Botany—Pathology
>> Diseases and pests
>> Diseases of plants
>> Garden pests
>> Plant pathology
>> Plants—Diseases
>> SA types of crops, plants, trees, etc., with the subdivision *Diseases and pests* [to be added as needed]
>> BT Agricultural pests
>> Diseases
>> Fungi

Plant diseases—*Continued*
  NT **Fruit—Diseases and pests**
Plant distribution
  USE **Plants—Geographical distribution**
Plant ecology (May subdiv. geog.) **581.7**
  UF Botany—Ecology
      Plants—Ecology
  SA types of plants and crops with
      the subdivision *Ecology* [to be
      added as needed]
  BT **Ecology**
  NT **Desert plants**
      Forest plants
      Mountain plants
      Plant defenses
  RT **Forest influences**
      Symbiosis
Plant introduction (May subdiv. geog.)
      581.6; 631.5
  BT **Economic botany**
Plant lore
  USE **Plants—Folklore**
Plant nutrition
  USE **Plants—Nutrition**
Plant pathology
  USE **Plant diseases**
Plant physiology **571.2**
  UF Botany—Physiology
      Physiology of plants
  BT **Botany**
  NT **Fertilization of plants**
      Germination
      Plants—Growth
      Plants—Nutrition
Plant propagation **631.5**
  Use for materials on the continuance or
  multiplication of plants by successive produc-
  tion. Materials on attempts to produce new or
  improved varieties of plants through con-
  trolled reproduction are entered under **Plant
  breeding.**
  UF Plants—Propagation
      Propagation of plants
  BT **Fruit culture**
      Gardening
      Nurseries (Horticulture)
  NT **Grafting**
      Seeds
  RT **Plant breeding**

Plant shutdowns (May subdiv. geog.)
      338.6
  UF Closing of factories
      Plant closings
  BT **Factories**
      Unemployment
Plant taxonomy
  USE **Botany—Classification**
Plantation life (May subdiv. geog.)
      307.72
  BT **Country life**
Plantations (May subdiv. geog.) **307.72**
  BT **Farms**
Planting
  USE **Agriculture**
      Gardening
      Landscape gardening
      Tree planting
Plants (May subdiv. geog.) **580**
  Use for nonscientific materials. Materials on
  the science of plants are entered under **Bota-
  ny.** Subdivisions used under this heading may
  be used under the names of orders, classes, or
  individual species of plants.
  UF Flora
      Vegetable kingdom
  SA types of plants characterized by
      their physical characteristics,
      environment, or use, e.g.
      **Climbing plants; Desert
      plants; Forage plants;** etc.;
      and names of botanical cate-
      gories of plants, e.g. **Ferns**
      [to be added as needed]
  NT **Aromatic plants**
      Bulbs
      Carnivorous plants
      Climbing plants
      Cultivated plants
      Desert plants
      Edible plants
      Ferns
      Fertilization of plants
      Flowers
      Forage plants
      Forest plants
      Fossil plants
      Freshwater plants
      Fruit
      Fungi
      Grasses
      Herbs
      Horticulture

Plants—*Continued*
> House plants
> Leaves
> Marine plants
> Mosses
> Mountain plants
> Mushrooms
> Poisonous plants
> Popular plant names
> Rare plants
> Seeds
> Shrubs
> Tobacco
> Trees
> Vegetables
> Weeds
>
> RT   Botany
> > Gardening
> > Herbicides

Plants—Analysis   572
> UF   Plant chemistry
> > Plants—Chemical analysis
>
> BT   Botanical chemistry

Plants—Anatomy   571.3
> UF   Anatomy of plants
> > Botany—Anatomy
> > Botany—Structure
> > Plant anatomy
>
> BT   Anatomy
> > Botany

Plants—Chemical analysis
> USE   Plants—Analysis

Plants—Classification
> USE   Botany—Classification

Plants—Collection and preservation   580.75
> UF   Botanical specimens—Collection and preservation
> > Collections of natural specimens
> > Herbaria
> > Preservation of botanical specimens
> > Specimens, Preservation of
>
> BT   Collectors and collecting
> NT   Flowers—Drying

Plants—Conservation
> USE   Plant conservation

Plants, Cultivated
> USE   Cultivated plants

Plants—Diseases
> USE   Plant diseases

Plants—Ecology
> USE   Plant ecology

Plants, Edible
> USE   Edible plants

Plants, Extinct
> USE   Fossil plants

Plants—Fertilization
> USE   Fertilization of plants

Plants—Folklore   398.24
> UF   Plant lore
> BT   Folklore
> NT   Ethnobotany
> > Language of flowers

Plants, Fossil
> USE   Fossil plants

Plants—Geographical distribution   581.9
> UF   Geographical distribution of plants
> > Phytogeography
> > Plant distribution
>
> SA   types of plants with the subdivision *Geographical distribution* [to be added as needed]
>
> BT   Biogeography

Plants—Growth   571.8
> BT   Plant physiology

Plants in art   704.9
> SA   types of plants in art, e.g. **Flowers in art** [to be added as needed]
>
> BT   Art—Themes
> RT   Botanical illustration

Plants, Industrial
> USE   Factories

Plants, Medicinal
> USE   Medical botany

Plants—Names
> USE   Botany—Nomenclature
> > Popular plant names

Plants—Nomenclature
> USE   Botany—Nomenclature
> > Popular plant names

Plants—Nutrition   575.7; 631.5
> UF   Plant nutrition
> BT   Nutrition
> > Plant physiology

Plants, Ornamental
> USE   Ornamental plants

Plants—Photography
> USE   Photography of plants

Plants—Propagation
USE **Plant propagation**
Plants—Soilless culture
USE **Hydroponics**
Plants—United States   581.973
UF   Botany—United States
Plaster and plastering   693
UF   Plastering
BT   **Masonry**
NT   **Cement**
Concrete
Mortar
Stucco
Plaster casts   731.4
UF   Casting
Casts, Plaster
BT   **Sculpture**
Plastering
USE   **Plaster and plastering**
Plastic industries
USE   **Plastics industry**
Plastic materials
USE   **Plastics**
Plastic surgery   617.9
UF   Cosmetic surgery
Reconstructive surgery
Surgery, Plastic
BT   **Surgery**
Plastics   668.4
UF   Plastic materials
SA   names of specific plastics [to be
added as needed]
BT   **Polymers**
Synthetic products
NT   **Gums and resins**
Synthetic rubber
RT   **Plastics industry**
Plastics industry (May subdiv. geog.)
338.4; 668.4
UF   Plastic industries
BT   **Chemical industry**
RT   **Plastics**
Plate   739.2
UF   Gold plate
Silver plate
BT   **Goldwork**
Silverwork
NT   **Hallmarks**
Sheffield plate

Plate metalwork   671.8
BT   **Metalwork**
Sheet metalwork
Plate tectonics   551.1
BT   **Earth—Crust**
Geophysics
RT   **Continental drift**
Submarine geology
Platforms, Drilling
USE   **Drilling platforms**
Play   790
BT   **Recreation**
NT   **Finger play**
Imaginary playmates
Sports
RT   **Amusements**
Games
Play centers
USE   **Community centers**
Playgrounds
Play direction (Theater)
USE   **Theater—Production and di-
rection**
Play production
USE   **Amateur theater**
**Theater—Production and di-
rection**
Play—Therapeutic use
USE   **Play therapy**
Play therapy   616.89; 618.9
UF   Play—Therapeutic use
BT   **Therapeutics**
Play writing
USE   **Drama—Technique**
**Motion picture plays—Tech-
nique**
Radio plays—Technique
Television plays—Technique
Playbills
USE   **Film posters**
Playgrounds (May subdiv. geog.)   **796.06**
UF   Play centers
Public playgrounds
School playgrounds
BT   **Recreation**
Sports facilities
RT   **Community centers**
Parks
Playhouses
USE   **Theaters**

Playing cards 795.4
  UF Cards, Playing
  NT **Tarot**
  RT **Card games**
Plays
  USE **Drama—Collections**
        One act plays
Plays, Bible
  USE **Bible plays**
Plays for children
  USE **Children's plays**
Playwrights
  USE **Dramatists**
Playwriting
  USE **Drama—Technique**
        Motion picture plays—Technique
        Radio plays—Technique
        Television plays—Technique
Pleasure 152.4
  BT **Emotions**
        Joy and sorrow
        Senses and sensation
  RT **Happiness**
        Pain
Plot-your-own stories 808.3
  UF Choose-your-own story plots
        Making-choices stories
        Multiple plot stories
        Which-way stories
  BT **Children's literature**
        Fiction
        Literary recreations
Plots (Drama, fiction, etc.)
  USE **Stories, plots, etc.**
Plows 631.3
  BT **Agricultural machinery**
Plumbing 696
  BT **Building**
  NT **Sewerage**
  RT **House drainage**
        Household sanitation
        Pipe fitting
Pluralism (Social sciences) (May subdiv. geog.) **305.8**

Use for materials on the coexistence of several distinct ethnic, religious, or cultural groups within one society. Materials on the presence of two distinct cultures within a single country or region are entered under **Biculturalism.** Materials on policies or programs that foster the preservation of various cultures or cultural identities within a unified society are entered under **Multiculturalism.**

  UF Ethnic diversity
  BT **Culture**
  NT **Biculturalism**
  RT **Ethnic relations**
        Ethnicity
        Multiculturalism
        Race relations
Plywood 674
  BT **Wood**
PMS (Gynecology)
  USE **Premenstrual syndrome**
Pneumatic transmission
  USE **Compressed air**
Pneumatics 533; 621.5
  BT **Physics**
  NT **Aerodynamics**
        Compressed air
        Sound
  RT **Gases**
Pneumonia 616.2
  BT **Lungs—Diseases**
Pocket billiards
  USE **Pool (Game)**
Pocket calculators
  USE **Calculators**
Podiatry 617.5
  UF Chiropody
  BT **Medicine**
  NT **Foot—Care**
  RT **Foot—Wounds and injuries**
Poetics 808.1

Use for materials on the art and technique of poetry. General materials on the appreciation, philosophy, etc., of poetry are entered under **Poetry.**

  UF Poetry—Technique
  BT **Poetry**
  NT **Rhyme**
        Rhythm
        Versification
Poetry 809.1

Use for general materials on poetry, not for individual works. Materials on the history and criticism of poetry from more than one literature are entered under **Poetry—History and criticism.** Materials on the art and technique of poetry are entered under **Poetics.** Collections of poetry are entered under **Poetry—Collections; English poetry—Collections;** etc.

  UF Poetry—Philosophy
  SA types of poetry, e.g. **Haiku;** and
        subjects, historical events,
        names of places, ethnic

Poetry—*Continued*

groups, classes of persons, and names of individual persons with the subdivision *Poetry,* to express the theme or subject content of collections of poetry, e.g. **Animals—Poetry; World War, 1939-1945—Poetry; Napoleon I, Emperor of the French, 1769-1821—Poetry;** etc. [to be added as needed]

BT   **Literature**

NT   **American poetry**
     Ballads
     Children's poetry
     Didactic poetry
     Eddas
     Elegiac poetry
     English poetry
     Epistolary poetry
     Erotic poetry
     Fantasy poetry
     Free verse
     French poetry
     Haiku
     Humorous poetry
     Love poetry
     Narrative poetry
     Nature poetry
     Pastoral poetry
     Patriotic poetry
     Poetics
     Religious poetry
     Science fiction poetry
     Sea poetry
     Songs
     War poetry

Poetry and music
   USE   **Music and literature**

Poetry—Collections   808.81
   UF   Poetry—Selections
       Rhymes

Poetry—Editing   070.5
   BT   **Editing**

Poetry for children
   USE   **Children's poetry**
       Nursery rhymes

Poetry, Historical
   USE   **Historical poetry**

Poetry—History and criticism   809.1

Poetry—Memorizing   153.1
   BT   **Mnemonics**

Poetry—Philosophy
   USE   **Poetry**

Poetry—Selections
   USE   **Poetry—Collections**

Poetry—Technique
   USE   **Poetics**

Poets   809.1; 920

Use for materials on the lives of several poets, not limited to a single national literature.

   SA   poets of particular countries, e.g.
       American poets [to be added as needed]
   BT   **Authors**
   NT   **American poets**
       Lyricists
       Minstrels
       Troubadours

Poets, American
   USE   **American poets**

Poison ivy   583
   BT   **Poisonous plants**

Poisonous animals (May subdiv. geog.)   **591.6**
   SA   types of poisonous animals, e.g.
       Rattlesnakes [to be added as needed]
   BT   **Animals**
       Dangerous animals
       Economic zoology
       Poisons and poisoning
   NT   **Rattlesnakes**

Poisonous gases   363.17
   UF   Asphyxiating gases
       Gases, Asphyxiating and poisonous
   BT   **Gases**
       Poisons and poisoning
   NT   **Radon**

Poisonous gases—War use
   USE   **Chemical warfare**

Poisonous plants (May subdiv. geog.)   **581.6**
   UF   Toxic plants
   SA   types of poisonous plants, e.g.
       Poison ivy [to be added as needed]
   BT   **Economic botany**
       Plants
       Poisons and poisoning

Poisonous plants—*Continued*
  NT **Poison ivy**
  RT **Plant defenses**
Poisonous substances
  USE **Poisons and poisoning**
Poisons and poisoning   **363.17; 615.9**

Use for materials on poisonous substances and their use. Materials on the science that treats of poisons and their antidotes are entered under **Toxicology.**

  UF Poisonous substances
      Toxic substances
  SA types of poisons or poisoning,
        e.g. **Lead poisoning;** and
        types of poisonous substances
        with the subdivision *Toxicolo-
        gy,* for materials on the influ-
        ence of particular substances
        on humans and animals, e.g.
        Insecticides—Toxicology [to
        be added as needed]
  BT **Accidents**
      Hazardous substances
      Homicide
      Medical jurisprudence
  NT **Food poisoning**
      Insecticides—Toxicology
      Lead poisoning
      Pesticides
      Poisonous animals
      Poisonous gases
      Poisonous plants
  RT **Toxicology**
Poker   **795.412**
  BT **Card games**
Polar expeditions
  USE **Antarctica—Exploration**
       Arctic regions—Exploration
       Scientific expeditions
Polar lights
  USE **Auroras**
Polar regions   **998**

Use for materials on both the Antarctic and Arctic regions.

  NT **Antarctica**
      Arctic regions
      North Pole
      South Pole
Polarity
  USE **Opposites**
Police (May subdiv. geog.)   **363.2**
  UF Police officers
      Policemen

  BT **Administration of criminal jus-
        tice**
      Law enforcement
  NT **Animals in police work**
      Detectives
      Police brutality
      Police corruption
      Policewomen
      Secret service
      State police
  RT **Crime**
      Criminal investigation
Police brutality (May subdiv. geog.)
      363.2
  UF Police—Complaints against
      Police cruelty
      Police repression
      Police violence
  BT **Police**
Police—Complaints against
  USE **Police brutality**
       Police corruption
Police—Corrupt practices
  USE **Police corruption**
Police corruption (May subdiv. geog.)
      363.2
  UF Corruption, Police
      Police—Complaints against
      Police—Corrupt practices
  BT **Misconduct in office**
      Police
Police cruelty
  USE **Police brutality**
Police, International
  USE **International police**
Police officers
  USE **Police**
Police repression
  USE **Police brutality**
Police, State
  USE **State police**
Police—United States   **363.20973**
  UF United States—Police
Police violence
  USE **Police brutality**
Policemen
  USE **Police**
Policewomen (May subdiv. geog.)   **363.2**
  UF Women police officers
  BT **Police**
      Women

Polio
  USE **Poliomyelitis**
Poliomyelitis 616.8
  UF Infantile paralysis
      Polio
  BT **Diseases**
Poliomyelitis vaccine 614.4; 615
  UF Live poliovirus vaccine
      Sabin vaccine
      Salk vaccine
  BT **Vaccination**
Polishing
  USE **Grinding and polishing**
Politeness
  USE **Courtesy**
       Etiquette
Political action committees (May subdiv.
    geog.) **322.4; 324**
    Use for materials on special interest groups
  that support sympathetic candidates for public
  office through campaign contributions. Materi-
  als on groups that promote their own interests
  with public officials are entered under **Lobby-
  ing.**
  UF Interest groups
      PACs (Political action commit-
        tees)
      Pressure groups
  BT **Political participation**
  RT **Lobbying**
Political activity
  USE **Political participation**
       and classes of persons, types of
       industries, military services,
       and religious denominations,
       and names of corporate bod-
       ies and families with the sub-
       division *Political activity,* e.g.
       Women—Political activity [to
       be added as needed]
Political aspects
  USE subjects with the subdivision *Po-
       litical aspects,* e.g. **Ethnic re-
       lations—Political aspects** [to
       be added as needed]
Political asylum
  USE **Asylum**
Political behavior
  USE **Political participation**
       Political psychology
Political boundaries
  USE **Boundaries**

Political campaign literature
  USE **Campaign literature**
Political campaigns
  USE **Politics**
Political conventions 324.5
  UF Conventions, Political
  BT **Conferences**
  NT **Primaries**
  RT **Political parties**
Political correctness 306
  BT **Ideology**
Political corruption (May subdiv. geog.)
    324; 353.4
  UF Boss rule
      Corruption in politics
      Graft in politics
      Political scandals
      Politics—Corrupt practices
      Spoils system
  BT **Conflict of interests**
      Political crimes and offenses
      Political ethics
      Politics
  NT **Whistle blowing**
  RT **Misconduct in office**
Political crimes and offenses (May
    subdiv. geog.) **364.1**
  UF Crimes, Political
      Sedition
  BT **Criminal law**
      Political ethics
      Subversive activities
  NT **Anarchism and anarchists**
      Assassination
      Bombings
      Concentration camps
      Political corruption
      Political prisoners
      Terrorism
      Treason
Political defectors
  USE **Defectors**
Political economy
  USE **Economics**
Political ethics (May subdiv. geog.) **172**
  BT **Ethics**
      Political science
      Politics
      Social ethics
  NT **Citizenship**
      Conflict of interests

Political ethics—*Continued*
    Political corruption
    Political crimes and offenses
    Resistance to government
Political extremism
  USE **Radicalism**
Political geography
  USE **Boundaries**
        Geopolitics
Political participation (May subdiv. geog.)
    323
  UF Citizen participation
        Civic involvement
        Community action
        Mass political behavior
        Political activity
        Political behavior
  SA subjects designating government
        activity with the subdivision
        Citizen participation, e.g.
        Crime prevention—Citizen
        participation; and corporate
        bodies, families, classes of
        persons, industries, military
        services, and religious denom-
        inations with the subdivision
        Political activity, e.g. **Wom-**
        en—Political activity [to be
        added as needed]
  BT **Politics**
  NT **African Americans—Political**
        activity
        Blacks—Political activity
        City planning—Citizen partici-
        pation
        Clergy—Political activity
        College students—Political ac-
        tivity
        Crime prevention—Citizen par-
        ticipation
        Jews—Political activity
        Political action committees
        Students—Political activity
        Women—Political activity
  RT **Social action**
Political parties (May subdiv. geog.)
    324.2
  UF Parties, Political
  SA names of parties [to be added as
        needed]
  BT **Political science**
        Politics

  NT **Democratic Party (U.S.)**
        Politics
        Republican Party (U.S.)
        Right and left (Political sci-
        ence)
        Third parties (United States
        politics)
  RT **Political conventions**
Political parties—Finance
  USE **Campaign funds**
Political prisoners (May subdiv. geog.)
    365
  UF Prisoners of conscience
  BT **Political crimes and offenses**
        Prisoners
Political psychology 302
  UF Mass political behavior
        Political behavior
        Politics—Psychological aspects
  BT **Political science**
        Psychology
        Social psychology
  NT **Propaganda**
        Public opinion
Political refugees (May subdiv. geog.)
    325
  UF Displaced persons
        Refugees, Political
  SA refugees of particular countries,
        geographic regions, or ethnic
        groups, e.g. **Vietnamese refu-**
        gees; Arab refugees; etc.,
        and names of wars with the
        subdivision *Refugees,* e.g.
        World War, 1939-1945—
        Refugees [to be added as
        needed]
  BT **Asylum**
        International law
        International relations
        Refugees
  NT **Defectors**
        World War, 1939-1945—Refu-
        gees
Political satire 808.7; 808.87
  BT **Satire**
Political scandals
  USE **Political corruption**
Political science (May subdiv. geog.)
    320
    Use for materials on the science of politics.
    Materials on the various aspects of practical

Political science—*Continued*
politics, such as electioneering, political machines, etc., are entered under **Politics.** Materials on the political processes of particular regions, countries, cities, etc., are entered under the place with the subdivision *Politics and government.*

- UF   Civics
  - Civil government
  - Commonwealth, The
  - Government
  - Political theory
- SA   movements in political philosophy, e.g. **Marxism;** topics with the subdivision *Political aspects,* e.g. **Ethnic relations—Political aspects;** and names of continents, areas, countries, cities, etc., and native peoples with the subdivision *Politics and government,* e.g. **United States—Politics and government; Native Americans—Politics and government** [to be added as needed]
- BT   Social sciences
- NT   Anarchism and anarchists
  - Aristocracy
  - Authority
  - Bureaucracy
  - Citizenship
  - Civil rights
  - Civil service
  - Collectivism
  - Communism
  - Comparative government
  - Conservatism
  - Democracy
  - Equality
  - Executive power
  - Federal government
  - Freedom
  - Geopolitics
  - Ideology
  - Imperialism
  - Individualism
  - Law
  - Legislation
  - Liberalism
  - Local government
  - Marxism
  - Monarchy
  - Municipal government
  - Nationalism
  - Political ethics
  - Political parties
  - Political psychology
  - Postcolonialism
  - Power (Social sciences)
  - Progressivism (United States politics)
  - Public administration
  - Public opinion
  - Radicalism
  - Representative government and representation
  - Republics
  - Resistance to government
  - Revolutions
  - Right and left (Political science)
  - Separation of powers
  - Social contract
  - Socialism
  - Sovereignty
  - State governments
  - State rights
  - Suffrage
  - Taxation
  - Totalitarianism
  - United States—Politics and government
  - Utopias
  - World politics
- RT   Politics
  - State, The

Political science—Early works to 1800
(May subdiv. geog.)   **320**

Political science—Religious aspects
- USE   **Religion and politics**

Political theory
- USE   **Political science**

Political violence
- USE   **Sabotage**
  - **Terrorism**

Politicians (May subdiv. geog.) **324.2092; 920**
- BT   Statesmen
- NT   Women politicians

Politicians—United States   **324.2092; 920**
- UF   American politicians
  - United States—Politicians

Politics   324.7

Use for materials on the various aspects of practical politics, such as electioneering, political machines, etc. Materials on the science of politics are entered under **Political science.**

UF   Campaigns, Political
      Electioneering
      Political campaigns
      Politics, Practical
      Practical politics

SA   subjects with the subdivision *Political aspects,* e.g. **Ethnic relations—Political aspects;** names of continents, areas, countries, cities, etc., and native peoples, with the subdivision *Politics and government;* and ethnic groups and classes of persons with the subdivision *Political activity,* e.g. **College students—Political activity** [to be added as needed]

BT   **Political parties**

NT   **Arab countries—Politics and government**
      Asia—Politics and government
      Business and politics
      Campaign funds
      Campaign literature
      Chicago (Ill.)—Politics and government
      Elections
      Latin America—Politics and government
      Lobbying
      Native Americans—Politics and government
      Political corruption
      Political ethics
      Political participation
      Political parties
      Primaries
      Regionalism
      Religion and politics
      Television and politics
      United States—Politics and government

RT   **Political science**

Politics and business
  USE **Business and politics**

Politics and Christianity
  USE **Christianity and politics**

Politics and government
  USE names of continents, areas, countries, cities, etc., and native peoples with the subdivision *Politics and government,* e.g. **United States—Politics and government; Arab countries—Politics and government; Native Americans—Politics and government;** etc. [to be added as needed]

Politics and religion
  USE **Religion and politics**

Politics and students
  USE **Students—Political activity**

Politics and television
  USE **Television and politics**

Politics—Corrupt practices
  USE **Political corruption**

Politics, Practical
  USE **Politics**

Politics—Psychological aspects
  USE **Political psychology**

Politics—Religious aspects
  USE **Religion and politics**

Polity, Ecclesiastical
  USE **Church polity**

Pollination
  USE **Fertilization of plants**

Polls
  USE **Elections**
       Public opinion polls

Pollution (May subdiv. geog.)   **304.2; 363.73**

UF   Chemical pollution
      Contamination of environment
      Environmental pollution

SA   types of pollution, e.g. **Air pollution** [to be added as needed]

BT   **Environmental health**
      Human influence on nature
      Public health
      Sanitary engineering
      Sanitation

NT   **Air pollution**
      Noise pollution

Pollution—*Continued*
        Pesticides—Environmental aspects
        Radioactive pollution
        Space debris
        Water pollution
  RT Environmental protection
        Hazardous wastes
        Industrial waste
        Pollution control industry
        Refuse and refuse disposal
Pollution control
  USE Pollution control industry
Pollution control devices (Motor vehicles)
  USE Automobiles—Pollution control devices
Pollution control industry (May subdiv. geog.) 338.4; 363.73
  UF Pollution control
        Pollution—Prevention
  BT Industries
  NT Automobiles—Pollution control devices
        Recycling
        Refuse and refuse disposal
  RT Pollution
Pollution—Mathematical models 304.2; 363.73
  BT Mathematical models
Pollution of air
  USE Air pollution
Pollution of water
  USE Water pollution
Pollution—Prevention
  USE Pollution control industry
Pollution, Radioactive
  USE Radioactive pollution
Poltergeists
  USE Ghosts
Polygamy (May subdiv. geog.) 306.84
  BT Marriage
Polyglot dictionaries 413
  UF Dictionaries, Multilingual
        Dictionaries, Polyglot
        Multilingual dictionaries
        Multilingual glossaries, phrase books, etc.
        Polyglot glossaries, phrase books, etc.
  BT Encyclopedias and dictionaries
Polyglot glossaries, phrase books, etc.
  USE Polyglot dictionaries

Polygraph
  USE Lie detectors and detection
Polymer clay craft 731.2; 738.1; 745.57
  BT Handicraft
Polymerization
  USE Polymers
Polymers 541; 547; 668.9
  UF Polymerization
  SA types of polymers, e.g. Plastics
        [to be added as needed]
  BT Organic compounds—Synthesis
        Physical chemistry
  NT Plastics
Polynucleotides
  USE Nucleic acids
Pomp
  USE Parades
Ponds (May subdiv. geog.) 551.48
  BT Water
Ponies 636.1
  UF Foals
  BT Horses
Pontiac's Conspiracy, 1763-1765 973.2
  BT Native Americans—Wars
        United States—History—1600-1775, Colonial period
Pony express 383
  BT Express service
        Postal service
Pool (Game) (May subdiv. geog.) 794.73
  UF Pocket billiards
  BT Billiards
Pools
  USE Swimming pools
Poor (May subdiv. geog.) 305.5; 362.5
  UF Poor people
        Poor persons
  BT Poverty
        Public welfare
  NT Begging
        Homeless persons
        Tramps
        Unemployed
Poor—Medical care 362.1
  UF Medical care for the poor
  BT Medical care
  NT Medicaid
Poor people
  USE Poor

Poor persons
USE **Poor**
Poor relief
USE **Charities**
Domestic economic assistance
Public welfare
Pop culture
USE **Popular culture**
Pop-up books
USE **Toy and movable books**
Popes 262; 920
UF Holy See
BT **Church history**
RT **Papacy**
Popes—Infallibility 262
UF Infallibility of the Pope
Popes—Temporal power 262
UF Temporal power of the Pope
BT **Church history**
Popes—Travel
USE **Papal visits**
Popes—Voyages and travels
USE **Papal visits**
Popular arts
USE **Popular culture**
Popular culture (May subdiv. geog.)
306.4

Use for materials on literature, art, music, motion pictures, etc., produced for a mass audience. General materials on learning and scholarship, literature, the arts, etc., are entered under **Intellectual life.**

UF Mass culture
Pop culture
Popular arts
BT **Communication**
Culture
Intellectual life
Recreation
NT **Fads**
Sex in popular culture
Violence in popular culture
RT **Mass media**
Popular culture—Chicago (Ill.) 977.3
UF Chicago (Ill.)—Popular culture
Popular culture—United States 973
UF United States—Popular culture
NT **Americana**
Popular government
USE **Democracy**
Popular medicine 616.02

Use for medical books written for the layman.

UF Medicine, Popular
BT **Medicine**
NT **Traditional medicine**
RT **Health self-care**
Popular music (May subdiv. geog.)
781.64; 782.42164
UF Popular songs
SA types of popular music [to be added as needed]
BT **Music**
Songs
NT **Blues music**
Country music
Gospel music
Rap music
Rock music
Popular music—Texts 782.42164
UF Lyrics
Popular song lyrics
Song lyrics
Popular music—Writing and publishing
070.5; 781.3
UF Song writing
Songwriting
BT **Composition (Music)**
Popular plant names 580.1

Use for materials on the common or vernacular names of plants. Systematically derived lists of names or designations of plants and materials about such names are entered under **Botany—Nomenclature.**

UF Plants—Names
Plants—Nomenclature
SA types of plants with the subdivision *Nomenclature (Popular)*, e.g. **Trees—Nomenclature (Popular)** [to be added as needed]
BT **Plants**
NT **Trees—Nomenclature (Popular)**
RT **Botany—Nomenclature**
Popular song lyrics
USE **Popular music—Texts**
Popular songs
USE **Popular music**
Popularity 158
BT **Social psychology**
Population 304.6; 363.9
UF Demography
Foreign population
SA ethnic groups and names of countries, cities, etc., with the subdivision *Population*, e.g.

Population—*Continued*

        United States—Population
        [to be added as needed]

BT   **Economics**
      Human ecology
      Sociology
      Vital statistics

NT   **Baby boom generation**
      Birth control
      Census
      Chicago (Ill.)—Population
      Cities and towns—Growth
      Eugenics
      Human fertility
      Human settlements
      Immigration and emigration
      Internal migration
      Mortality
      Ohio—Population
      Overpopulation
      United States—Population

RT   **Birth rate**

Population explosion
   USE   **Overpopulation**

Porcelain (May subdiv. geog.)   **738.2**

   Use for materials on chinaware and porcelain for the table or decorative use. Materials on the technology of fired earthen products or on clay products intended for industrial use are entered under **Ceramics.**

UF   China (Porcelain)
      Chinaware
      Dishes

SA   types of porcelain [to be added
      as needed]

BT   **Decorative arts**
      Pottery
      Tableware

NT   **China painting**

Porcelain enamels
   USE   **Enamel and enameling**

Porcelain painting
   USE   **China painting**

Pornography (May subdiv. geog.)   **176;
      363.4; 364.1**

UF   Obscene materials

RT   **Erotica**
      Obscenity (Law)

Portable computers   004.16

UF   Handheld computers
      Laptop computers

BT   **Computers**

Portrait miniatures
   USE   **Miniature painting**

Portrait painting   757

UF   Portraiture

BT   **Painting**
      Portraits

RT   **Figure painting**
      Miniature painting

Portrait photography (May subdiv. geog.)
      778.9; 779

UF   Portraiture

BT   **Photography**
      Portraits

Portraits (May subdiv. geog.)   **704.9;
      757**

SA   headings for collective and individual biography, classes of persons, and names of individuals with the subdivision *Portraits,* e.g. **United States—Biography—Portraits; Musicians—Portraits; Shakespeare, William, 1564-1616—Portraits;** etc. [to be added as needed]

BT   **Art**
      Biography
      Pictures

NT   **Cartoons and caricatures**
      Portrait painting
      Portrait photography

Portraiture
   USE   **Portrait painting**
          Portrait photography

Ports
   USE   **Harbors**

Portuguese literature   869

BT   **Literature**
      Romance literature

Position analysis
   USE   **Topology**

Positivism   146

BT   **Philosophy**
      Rationalism

NT   **Materialism**
      Pragmatism

RT   **Agnosticism**
      Deism
      Realism

Post cards
   USE   **Postcards**

Post-colonialism
  USE **Postcolonialism**
Post-impressionism
  USE **Postimpressionism (Art)**
Post-modernism
  USE **Postmodernism**
Post office
  USE **Postal service**
Post-traumatic stress disorder   616.85
  UF Posttraumatic stress disorder
      Traumatic stress syndrome
  BT **Anxiety**
      Neuroses
      Stress (Psychology)
Postage stamp collecting
  USE **Stamp collecting**
Postage stamps (May subdiv. geog.)
      383; 769.56
  UF Stamps, Postage
  BT **Postal service**
  RT **Stamp collecting**
Postage stamps—Collectors and collecting
  USE **Stamp collecting**
Postal cards
  USE **Postcards**
Postal delivery code
  USE **Zip code**
Postal service (May subdiv. geog.)
      354.75; 383
  UF Mail service
      Parcel post
      Post office
  BT **Communication**
      Transportation
  NT **Air mail service**
      Pony express
      Postage stamps
      Zip code
**Postal service—United States   354.75;
  383**
  UF United States—Mail
      United States—Postal service
Postcards   383; 741.6
  UF Picture postcards
      Post cards
      Postal cards
**Postcards—Collectors and collecting
  790.1**
Postcolonial theory
  USE **Postcolonialism**

Postcolonialism (May subdiv. geog.)   **325**
  UF Post-colonialism
      Postcolonial theory
  BT **Political science**
Posters (May subdiv. geog.)   **741.6**
  SA types of posters, e.g. **Film post-
      ers;** and subjects, ethnic
      groups, classes of persons, in-
      dividual persons, corporate
      bodies, and names of wars
      with the subdivision *Posters*
      [to be added as needed]
  BT **Advertising**
      Commercial art
  NT **Film posters**
  RT **Signs and signboards**
Postimpressionism (Art) (May subdiv.
      geog.)   **709.03**
  UF Post-impressionism
  BT **Art**
Postmodernism (May subdiv. geog.)
      190; 700.1
  UF Post-modernism
  BT **Aesthetics**
  RT **Modernism (Aesthetics)**
Posttraumatic stress disorder
  USE **Post-traumatic stress disorder**
Posture   613.7
  BT **Physical fitness**
Pot (Drug)
  USE **Marijuana**
Potable water
  USE **Drinking water**
Potash   631.8; 668
  BT **Fertilizers**
Potatoes   635; 641.3
  BT **Vegetables**
Potpourri   668; 745.92
  BT **Herbs**
      Nature craft
      Perfumes
Potters (May subdiv. geog.)   **738.092;
      920**
  BT **Artists**
Potters' marks
  USE **Pottery—Marks**
Pottery   666; 738
  Use for materials on pottery for the table or
  for decorative use. Materials on the technolo-
  gy of fired earthen products or on clay prod-
  ucts intended for industrial use are entered un-
  der **Ceramics.**

Pottery—*Continued*
  UF Crockery
        Dishes
        Earthenware
        Faience
        Stoneware
  SA types of pottery and pottery of
          particular countries, e.g.
          American pottery [to be add-
          ed as needed]
  BT **Ceramics**
        Clay industry
        Decoration and ornament
        Decorative arts
        Tableware
  NT **American pottery**
        Glazes
        Porcelain
        Terra cotta
  RT **Vases**

Pottery, American
  USE **American pottery**

Pottery—Marks 738
  UF Potters' marks

Poultry 598.6; 636.5
  SA types of domesticated birds, e.g.
          Ducks [to be added as need-
          ed]
  BT **Birds**
        Domestic animals
  NT **Ducks**
        Geese
        Turkeys

Poverty 305.5; 362.5
  UF Destitution
        Pauperism
  SA names of countries with the sub-
          divisions *Economic conditions*
          and *Social conditions* [to be
          added as needed]
  BT **Economic conditions**
        Social problems
  NT **Homelessness**
        Poor
  RT **Basic needs**
        Domestic economic assistance
        Public welfare
        Subsistence economy

Powder, Smokeless
  USE **Gunpowder**

Powdered milk
  USE **Dried milk**

Power blackouts
  USE **Electric power failures**

Power boats
  USE **Motorboats**

Power failures
  USE **Electric power failures**

Power (Mechanics) 531; 621
    Use for materials on the physics and engi-
    neering aspects of power. Materials on the
    available sources of mechanical power in gen-
    eral are entered under **Energy resources.**
  UF Energy technology
  BT **Mechanical engineering**
        Mechanics
  NT **Compressed air**
        Electric power
        Energy resources
        Force and energy
        Machinery
        Power transmission
        Steam
        Water power
        Wind power

Power of attorney (May subdiv. geog.)
    346.02
  UF Durable power of attorney
  BT **Law**

Power plants
  USE **Electric power plants**

Power plants, Hydroelectric
  USE **Hydroelectric power plants**

Power plants, Nuclear
  USE **Nuclear power plants**

Power politics
  USE **Balance of power**
        Cold war

Power resources
  USE **Energy resources**

Power resources conservation
  USE **Energy conservation**

Power resources development
  USE **Energy development**

Power (Social sciences) (May subdiv.
    geog.) 303.3
  BT **Political science**
  NT **Elite (Social sciences)**

Power stations
  USE **Electric power plants**

Power supply
  USE **Energy resources**

Power tools 621.9
  BT **Tools**

Power transmission   621.8
  UF   Transmission of power
  BT   **Mechanical engineering**
       Power (Mechanics)
  NT   **Cables**
       Electric power distribution
       Gearing
  RT   **Belts and belting**
       Machinery

Power transmission, Electric
  USE **Electric lines**
       Electric power distribution

Powers, Separation of
  USE **Separation of powers**

POWs
  USE **Prisoners of war**

Powwows   394.2; 970.004
  BT   **Festivals**
       Native Americans—Rites and
         ceremonies
       Native Americans—Social life
         and customs

Practical jokes   793
  UF   Pranks
  BT   **Jokes**
       Wit and humor

Practical nurses (May subdiv. geog.)
     610.73; 920
  BT   **Nurses**

Practical nursing   610.73; 649.8
  BT   **Nursing**

Practical politics
  USE **Politics**

Practical psychology
  USE **Applied psychology**

Practice
  USE types of professions with the
       subdivision *Practice*, e.g. **Nu-**
       clear medicine—Practice [to
       be added as needed]

Practice teaching
  USE **Student teaching**

Pragmatism   144
  BT   **Philosophy**
       Positivism
       Realism
       Theory of knowledge
  RT   **Empiricism**
       Reality
       Truth
       Utilitarianism

Prairies (May subdiv. geog.)   577.4;
     578.74
  BT   **Grasslands**

Pranks
  USE **Practical jokes**

Prayer   204; 248.3
     May be subdivided by religion or sect. Use
  for materials about prayer. Collections of
  prayers are entered under **Prayers.**
  UF   Devotion
       Devotional theology
  BT   **Worship**
  RT   **Devotional exercises**
       Prayers

Prayer-books
  USE **Prayers**

Prayer-books and devotions
  USE **Prayers**

Prayer in the public schools (May
     subdiv. geog.)   379.2
     Use for materials on the inclusion of
  prayers or a period for silent prayer or meditation in the daily schedule of public schools.
  Materials on the teaching of religion in the
  public schools or on the religious freedom of
  students and school employees are entered under **Religion in the public schools.**
  UF   Prayers in the public schools
       School prayer
  BT   **Religion in the public schools**

Prayers   204; 242; 264
     Use for collections of prayers. Materials
  about prayer are entered under **Prayer.**
  UF   Collects
       Prayer-books
       Prayer-books and devotions
  SA   names of religions, denomina-
       tions, religious orders, classes
       of persons for whose use the
       prayers are intended, and
       names of saints and deities to
       whom the prayers are directed
       with the subdivision *Prayers,*
       e.g. **Buddhism—Prayers;**
       Sick—Prayers; Mary,
       Blessed Virgin, Saint—
       Prayers; etc. [to be added as
       needed]
  BT   **Devotional literature**
  NT   **Buddhism—Prayers**
       Mary, Blessed Virgin, Saint—
       Prayers
       Meditations
       Sick—Prayers

Prayers—*Continued*
   RT **Prayer**
Prayers in the public schools
   USE **Prayer in the public schools**
Pre-Columbian Americans
   USE **Native Americans**
Pre-Lenten festivities
   USE **Carnival**
Preachers
   USE **Clergy**
Preaching (May subdiv. geog.)   **206; 251**
   Use for materials on the art of writing and delivering sermons. Collections of sermons not limited to a single topic, occasion, or Christian denomination are entered under **Sermons.**
   UF Speaking
   BT **Pastoral theology**
        Public speaking
        Rhetoric
   RT **Sermons**
Precious metals (May subdiv. geog.)   **553.4; 669**
   UF Bullion
   BT **Metals**
        Mines and mineral resources
   NT **Gold**
        Silver
Precious stones (May subdiv. geog.)   **553.8**
   Use for mineralogical or technological materials on gem stones. Materials on cut and polished precious stones treated from the point of view of art or antiquity are entered under **Gems.** Materials on gems in which the emphasis is on the setting are entered under **Jewelry.**
   UF Gemstones
        Jewels
   SA names of precious stones [to be added as needed]
   BT **Minerals**
   NT **Diamonds**
   RT **Gems**
Precipitation forecasting
   USE **Weather forecasting**
Precipitation (Meteorology) (May subdiv. geog.)   **551.57**
   BT **Meteorology**
        Water
        Weather
   NT **Rain**
        Snow
Precocious children
   USE **Gifted children**

Predators
   USE **Predatory animals**
Predatory animals   **591.5**
   UF Predators
   SA types of predatory animals [to be added as needed]
   BT **Animals**
   NT **Birds of prey**
Predestination   **202; 234**
   UF Election (Theology)
        Foreordination
   BT **Theology**
   RT **Fate and fatalism**
        Free will and determinism
Predictions
   USE **Forecasting**
        Prophecies
Prefabricated buildings   **693**
   UF Buildings, Prefabricated
   BT **Buildings**
   NT **Prefabricated houses**
Prefabricated houses   **693; 728**
   BT **Domestic architecture**
        House construction
        Houses
        Prefabricated buildings
Pregnancy   **599; 612.6; 618.2**
   BT **Reproduction**
   NT **Miscarriage**
        Prenatal care
        Teenage pregnancy
   RT **Childbirth**
Prehistoric animals   **560**
   UF Animals, Prehistoric
   BT **Animals**
        Fossils
   NT **Dinosaurs**
   RT **Extinct animals**
Prehistoric art (May subdiv. geog.)   **709.01**
   UF Art, Prehistoric
   BT **Art**
   NT **Rock drawings, paintings, and engravings**
Prehistoric man
   USE **Fossil hominids**
        Prehistoric peoples
Prehistoric peoples (May subdiv. geog.)   **930.1**
   UF Man, Prehistoric
        Prehistoric man

Prehistoric peoples—*Continued*
>   Prehistory
> SA   names of prehistoric peoples,
>   e.g. **Cro-Magnons;** etc.; and
>   names of countries, cities,
>   etc., with the subdivision *An-*
>   *tiquities,* e.g. **United States—**
>   **Antiquities** [to be added as
>   needed]
> BT   **Antiquities**
>   **Archeology**
>   **Human beings**
> NT   **Cave dwellers**
>   **Cro-Magnons**
> RT   **Human origins**

Prehistory
> USE   **Archeology**
>   **Fossil hominids**
>   **Prehistoric peoples**

Prejudice
> USE   **Prejudices**

Prejudice in testing
> USE   **Test bias**

Prejudice-motivated crimes
> USE   **Hate crimes**

Prejudices (May subdiv. geog.)   **152.4;**
>   **177; 303.3**
> UF   Bias (Psychology)
>   Bigotry
>   Prejudice
> SA   types of prejudice [to be added
>   as needed]
> BT   **Attitude (Psychology)**
>   **Emotions**
>   **Interpersonal relations**
> NT   **Antisemitism**
>   **Discrimination**
>   **Ethnocentrism**
>   **Racism**
>   **Sexism**

Prejudicial publicity
> USE   **Freedom of the press and fair**
>   **trial**

Prelude and fugue
> USE   **Fugue**

Preludes and fugues
> USE   **Fugue**

Premarital contracts
> USE   **Marriage contracts**

Premarital counseling
> USE   **Marriage counseling**

Premenstrual syndrome   618.1
> UF   PMS (Gynecology)
>   Premenstrual tension
> BT   **Menstruation**

Premenstrual tension
> USE   **Premenstrual syndrome**

Premiers
> USE   **Prime ministers**

Prenatal care (May subdiv. geog.)   **618.2**
> BT   **Pregnancy**

Prenatal diagnosis   618.3
> BT   **Diagnosis**
> NT   **Amniocentesis**
>   **Genetic counseling**

Prenuptial agreements
> USE   **Marriage contracts**

Prenuptial contracts
> USE   **Marriage contracts**

Prepaid group medical practice
> USE   **Health maintenance organiza-**
>   **tions**

Preparation guides for examinations
> USE   **Examinations—Study guides**

Prepared cereals   641.3; 664
> UF   Breakfast cereals
>   Cereals, Prepared
> BT   **Breakfasts**
>   **Food**

Preprimers
> USE   **Easy reading materials**

Presbyterian Church (May subdiv. geog.)
>   **285**
> BT   **Christian sects**

Presbyterian Church—Sermons   252
> BT   **Sermons**

Preschool children
> USE   **Children**

Preschool education (May subdiv. geog.)
>   **372.21**
> UF   Children—Education
>   Education, Preschool
>   Infants—Education
> BT   **Education**
> NT   **Readiness for school**
> RT   **Kindergarten**
>   **Nursery schools**

Preschool reading materials
> USE   **Easy reading materials**

Prescription drug abuse
> USE   **Medication abuse**

Presents
    USE   **Gifts**
Preservation
    USE   types of foods and other things
            preserved with the subdivision
            Preservation, e.g. **Fruit—**
            Preservation; Wood—Preser-
            vation; etc.; antiquities and
            types of natural objects,
            including animal specimens
            and plant specimens, with the
            subdivision *Collection and*
            preservation, e.g. **Birds—Col-**
            lection and preservation; and
            types of art objects, library
            materials, architecture, and
            land vehicles with the subdi-
            vision *Conservation and res-*
            toration, e.g. **Automobiles—**
            Conservation and restoration
            [to be added as needed]
Preservation of antiquities
    USE   **Antiquities—Collection and**
            preservation
Preservation of biological diversity
    USE   **Biological diversity conserva-**
            tion
Preservation of botanical specimens
    USE   **Plants—Collection and preser-**
            vation
Preservation of buildings
    USE   **Architecture—Conservation**
            and restoration
Preservation of food
    USE   **Food—Preservation**
Preservation of forests
    USE   **Forest conservation**
Preservation of historical records
    USE   **Archives**
Preservation of library resources
    USE   **Library resources—Conserva-**
            tion and restoration
Preservation of natural resources
    USE   **Conservation of natural re-**
            sources
Preservation of natural scenery
    USE   **Landscape protection**
          Natural monuments
          Nature conservation

Preservation of organs, tissues, etc.
    617.9
    UF   Organ preservation (Anatomy)
            Organs (Anatomy)—Preservation
    RT   **Transplantation of organs, tis-**
            sues, etc.
Preservation of photographs
    USE   **Photographs—Conservation**
            and restoration
Preservation of specimens
    USE   **Taxidermy**
Preservation of wildlife
    USE   **Wildlife conservation**
Preservation of wood
    USE   **Wood—Preservation**
Preservation of works of art
    USE   subjects with the subdivision
            Conservation and restoration,
            e.g. **Painting—Conservation**
            and restoration [to be added
            as needed]
Preservation of zoological specimens
    USE   **Zoological specimens—Collec-**
            tion and preservation
Preservationism (Historic preservation)
    USE   **Historic preservation**
Preserving
    USE   **Canning and preserving**
Presidential aides
    USE   **Presidents—United States—**
            Staff
Presidential campaigns—United States
    USE   **Presidents—United States—**
            Election
Presidential libraries
    USE   **Presidents—United States—Ar-**
            chives
Presidents (May subdiv. geog.)   **352.23;**
    920
    SA   names of presidents [to be add-
            ed as needed]
    BT   **Heads of state**
    NT   **Vice-presidents**
    RT   **Executive power**
Presidents—Mexico   **920; 972**
    UF   Mexico—Presidents
Presidents—Powers
    USE   **Executive power**

Presidents' spouses—United States   920
> UF   First ladies—United States
> Presidents—United States—
>   Spouses
> Presidents' wives—United States
> Wives of presidents—United
>   States

**Presidents—United States   352.230973;
920**
> When applicable, the subdivisions under this heading may be used under names of presidents, prime ministers, and other rulers.
> UF   United States—Presidents
> SA   names of presidents [to be add-
>   ed as needed]
> NT   **Lincoln, Abraham, 1809-1865**

**Presidents—United States—Appointment
352.23**

**Presidents—United States—Archives
026**
> UF   Libraries, Presidential
> Presidential libraries
> Presidents—United States—Li-
>   braries
> SA   names of individual libraries [to
>   be added as needed]
> BT   **Archives**
> NT   **Harry S. Truman Library**

**Presidents—United States—Assassination
364.15; 973**
> BT   **Assassination**

Presidents—United States—Burial
> USE   **Presidents—United States—
> Death and burial**

**Presidents—United States—Children
920**

**Presidents—United States—Death and
burial   393; 973**
> UF   Presidents—United States—Buri-
>   al
> Presidents—United States—Fu-
>   neral and memorial services
> Presidents—United States—Me-
>   morial services

**Presidents—United States—Election
324.973**
> May further subdivide by date.
> UF   Campaigns, Presidential—United
>   States
> Electoral college
> Presidential campaigns—United
>   States

> BT   **Elections**

Presidents—United States—Family   920

Presidents—United States—Fathers   920

Presidents—United States—Funeral and
memorial services
> USE   **Presidents—United States—
> Death and burial**

**Presidents—United States—Health
352.23; 920**
> UF   Presidents—United States—Ill-
>   ness

Presidents—United States—Homes   728

Presidents—United States—Illness
> USE   **Presidents—United States—
> Health**

**Presidents—United States—Impeachment
342**

Presidents—United States—Inability to
serve
> USE   **Presidents—United States—
> Succession**

**Presidents—United States—Inaugural ad-
dresses   352.23**
> BT   **Speeches**

**Presidents—United States—Inauguration
352.23**

Presidents—United States—Libraries
> USE   **Presidents—United States—Ar-
> chives**

**Presidents—United States—Medals
352.23**

Presidents—United States—Memorial services
> USE   **Presidents—United States—
> Death and burial**

**Presidents—United States—Messages
352.23**
> UF   Messages to Congress
> Presidents—United States—State
>   of the Union message
> State of the Union messages

**Presidents—United States—Mothers
920**

**Presidents—United States—Nomination
324.50973**
> UF   Nomination of presidents

**Presidents—United States—Portraits
973**

Presidents—United States—Power
> USE   **Executive power—United
> States**

Presents—United States—Press rela-
tions   070.4; 352.230973
Presidents—United States—Protection
352.23
Presidents—United States—Quotations
818
    BT   Quotations
Presidents—United States—Relations
with Congress   328.73; 352.23
Presidents—United States—Religion
920
Presidents—United States—Resignation
352.23
Presidents—United States—Sports   920
Presidents—United States—Spouses
    USE   Presidents' spouses—United
States
Presidents—United States—Staff   352.23
    UF   Presidential aides
    BT   Executive departments—United
States
Presidents—United States—State of the
Union message
    USE   Presidents—United States—
Messages
Presidents—United States—Succession
342; 352.23
    UF   Presidents—United States—In-
ability to serve
Presidents—United States—Tombs
917.3
Presidents—United States—Travel
352.23
    UF   Presidents—United States—Voy-
ages and travels
Presidents—United States—Voyages and
travels
    USE   Presidents—United States—
Travel
Presidents' wives—United States
    USE   Presidents' spouses—United
States
Press (May subdiv. geog.)   070
    SA   topics with the subdivision *Press
coverage,* e.g. **Food contamination—Press coverage** [to
be added as needed]
    BT   **Journalism**
Propaganda
Publicity

    NT   **Alternative press**
Broadcast journalism
Freedom of the press
**Freedom of the press and fair
trial**
News agencies
Pamphlets
    RT   **Newspapers**
Periodicals
Public opinion
Press and government
    USE   **Press—Government policy**
Press censorship
    USE   **Freedom of the press**
Press clippings
    USE   **Clippings (Books, newspapers,
etc.)**
Press coverage
    USE   topics with the subdivision *Press
coverage,* e.g. **Food contami-
nation—Press coverage** [to
be added as needed]
Press—Government policy (May subdiv.
geog.)   323.44
    UF   Government and the press
Press and government
    BT   **Freedom of information**
Press relations
    USE   types of public officials and
names of individual public of-
ficials with the subdivision
Press relations, e.g. **Presidents—United States—Press
relations** [to be added as
needed]
Press working of metal
    USE   **Sheet metalwork**
Pressure groups
    USE   **Lobbying**
Political action committees
Prestidigitation
    USE   **Magic tricks**
Pretenders
    USE   **Impostors and imposture**
Prevention
    USE   types of diseases, medical condi-
tions, and situations to be
avoided with the subdivision
Prevention, e.g. **AIDS (Dis-
ease)—Prevention; Acci-**

Prevention—*Continued*
>> dents—**Prevention;** etc. [to
>> be added as needed]
Prevention of accidents
> USE **Accidents—Prevention**
Prevention of crime
> USE **Crime prevention**
Prevention of cruelty to animals
> USE **Animal welfare**
Prevention of disease
> USE **Preventive medicine**
Prevention of fire
> USE **Fire prevention**
Prevention of smoke
> USE **Smoke prevention**
Preventive medicine   613
> UF Diseases—Prevention
> Medicine, Preventive
> Prevention of disease
> SA names of diseases with the sub-
> division *Prevention,* e.g.
> **AIDS (Disease)—Prevention**
> [to be added as needed]
> BT **Medicine**
> NT **Communicable diseases—Pre-
> vention**
> **Health**
> **Heart diseases—Prevention**
> **Hygiene**
> **Vaccination**
> RT **Pathology**
Price controls
> USE **Wage-price policy**
Price indexes, Consumer
> USE **Consumer price indexes**
Price theory
> USE **Microeconomics**
Price-wage policy
> USE **Wage-price policy**
Prices (May subdiv. geog.)   **338.5**
> SA subjects with the subdivision
> *Prices,* e.g. **Art—Prices** [to
> be added as needed]
> BT **Commerce**
> **Consumption (Economics)**
> **Economics**
> **Finance**
> **Manufactures**
> NT **Art—Prices**
> **Books—Prices**
> **Consumer price indexes**
> **Farm produce—Marketing**

Stock price indexes
Wage-price policy
> RT **Cost and standard of living**
> **Salaries, wages, etc.**
> **Supply and demand**
Pride and vanity   179
> UF Vanity
> BT **Conduct of life**
> **Sin**
Priests (May subdiv. geog.)   **200.92;
270.092**
> UF Pastors
> SA names of church denominations
> with the subdivision *Clergy,*
> e.g. **Catholic Church—Cler-
> gy** [to be added as needed]
> BT **Clergy**
> NT **Catholic Church—Clergy**
> **Ex-priests**
Primaries (May subdiv. geog.)   **324.5**
> UF Direct primaries
> BT **Elections**
> **Political conventions**
> **Politics**
Primary education
> USE **Elementary education**
Primates (May subdiv. geog.)   **599.8**
> SA types of primates, e.g. **Monkeys**
> [to be added as needed]
> BT **Mammals**
> NT **Human beings**
> **Monkeys**
Primates—Behavior   599.8
> UF Primates—Habits and behavior
> BT **Animal behavior**
Primates—Habits and behavior
> USE **Primates—Behavior**
Prime ministers (May subdiv. geog.)
352.23; 920
> May use same subdivisions, following geo-
> graphic subdivision, as for **Presidents—Unit-
> ed States.**
> UF Premiers
> BT **Cabinet officers**
> **Executive power**
**Prime ministers—Great Britain
352.230941; 920**
> UF Great Britain—Prime ministers
Primers
> USE **Easy reading materials**

Primitive Christianity
USE **Church history—30-600, Early church**
Primitive man
USE **Primitive societies**
Primitive societies (May subdiv. geog.) **305.8; 306**
Use for materials on nonliterate, nonindustrialized peoples.
UF Man, Primitive
Primitive man
Primitive society
Society, Primitive
BT **Civilization**
Ethnology
NT **Nomads**
Primitive society
USE **Primitive societies**
Princes (May subdiv. geog.) **920**
UF Princes and princesses
Royalty
BT **Courts and courtiers**
Princes and princesses
USE **Princes**
Princesses
Princesses (May subdiv. geog.) **920**
UF Princes and princesses
Royalty
BT **Courts and courtiers**
Printing (May subdiv. geog.) **686.2**
SA types of printing processes [to be added as needed]
BT **Bibliography**
Book industry
Graphic arts
Industrial arts
Publishers and publishing
NT **Advertising layout and typography**
Color printing
Electrotyping
Linoleum block printing
Linotype
Lithography
Nature prints
Offset printing
Proofreading
Textile printing
Type and type-founding
Typesetting
Typography

RT **Books**
Prints
Printing—Exhibitions **686.2074**
BT **Exhibitions**
Printing—Specimens **686.2**
UF Type specimens
BT **Advertising**
Initials
RT **Type and type-founding**
Printing—Style manuals **686.02**
UF Style manuals
RT **Authorship—Handbooks, manuals, etc.**
Prints **769**
SA prints of particular countries, e.g. **American prints** [to be added as needed]
BT **Graphic arts**
NT **American prints**
Bookplates
Color prints
Linoleum block printing
Lithography
Nature prints
Woodcuts
RT **Printing**
Prints, American
USE **American prints**
Prison escapes
USE **Escapes**
Prison labor
USE **Convict labor**
Prison reform **365**
UF Penal reform
BT **Social problems**
Prison schools
USE **Prisoners—Education**
Prisoners (May subdiv. geog.) **365**
UF Convicts
Prisoners and prisons
BT **Criminals**
NT **Convict labor**
Political prisoners
RT **Prisoners of war**
Prisons
Prisoners and prisons
USE **Prisoners**
Prisoners of war
Prisons
and names of wars with the subdivision *Prisoners and*

Prisoners and prisons—*Continued*
　　　prisons, e.g. **World War,**
　　　1939-1945—Prisoners and
　　　prisons [to be added as need-
　　　ed]
Prisoners—Education (May subdiv. geog.)
　　　365
　　UF　Education of criminals
　　　　Education of prisoners
　　　　Prison schools
　　BT　**Adult education**
　　　　Prisons
Prisoners of conscience
　　USE　**Political prisoners**
Prisoners of war (May subdiv. geog.)
　　　341.6; 355.7
　　UF　Exchange of prisoners of war
　　　　POWs
　　　　Prisoners and prisons
　　SA　names of wars with the subdivi-
　　　　sion *Prisoners and prisons,*
　　　　e.g. **World War, 1939-**
　　　　1945—Prisoners and prisons
　　　　[to be added as needed]
　　BT　**War**
　　NT　**Missing in action**
　　　　United States—History—1861-
　　　　1865, Civil War—Prisoners
　　　　and prisons
　　　　World War, 1939-1945—Pris-
　　　　oners and prisons
　　RT　**Concentration camps**
　　　　Prisoners
　　　　Prisons
Prisons (May subdiv. geog.)　　**365**
　　UF　Imprisonment
　　　　Jails
　　　　Penal institutions
　　　　Penitentiaries
　　　　Prisoners and prisons
　　SA　types of prisons, names of indi-
　　　　vidual prisons, and names of
　　　　wars with the subdivision
　　　　Prisoners and prisons, e.g.
　　　　World War, 1939-1945—
　　　　Prisoners and prisons [to be
　　　　added as needed]
　　BT　**Administration of criminal jus-**
　　　　tice
　　　　Correctional institutions
　　　　Punishment

　　NT　**Escapes**
　　　　Prisoners—Education
　　　　Probation
　　　　Reformatories
　　　　United States—History—1861-
　　　　1865, Civil War—Prisoners
　　　　and prisons
　　　　World War, 1939-1945—Pris-
　　　　oners and prisons
　　RT　**Prisoners**
　　　　Prisoners of war
Prisons—United States　365
　　UF　United States—Prisons
Privacy　323.44
　　BT　**Social psychology**
　　RT　**Secrecy**
　　　　Solitude
Privacy, Right of
　　USE　**Right of privacy**
Private art collections
　　USE　**Art collections**
Private companies
　　USE　**Limited liability companies**
Private enterprise
　　USE　**Free enterprise**
Private eye stories
　　USE　**Mystery and detective plays**
　　　　Mystery fiction
　　　　Mystery films
　　　　Mystery radio programs
　　　　Mystery television programs
Private funding of the arts
　　USE　**Art patronage**
Private limited companies
　　USE　**Limited liability companies**
Private property, Right of
　　USE　**Right of property**
Private schools (May subdiv. geog.)
　　　371.02; 373.2
　　UF　Boarding schools
　　　　Independent schools
　　　　Nonpublic schools
　　BT　**Schools**
　　NT　**Church schools**
　　　　English public schools
Private theater
　　USE　**Amateur theater**
Privateering (May subdiv. geog.)　　**359.4**
　　UF　Letters of marque
　　BT　**International law**
　　　　Naval art and science

Privateering—*Continued*
>> **Naval history**
>> **Pirates**

Privatization (May subdiv. geog.)   **338.9**
> Use for materials on the transfer of public assets and service functions to the private sector.
> UF   Denationalization
> BT   **Economic policy**
>> **Industrial policy**
> RT   **Government ownership**

Prize fighting
> USE   **Boxing**

Prizes (Rewards)
> USE   **Awards**

Pro-abortion movement
> USE   **Pro-choice movement**

Pro-choice movement   **179.7; 363.46**
> UF   Abortion rights movement
>> Freedom of choice movement
>> Pro-abortion movement
>> Right to choose movement
> BT   **Social movements**
> RT   **Abortion—Ethical aspects**
>> **Abortion—Religious aspects**
>> **Women's rights**

Pro-life movement   **179.7; 363.46**
> UF   Anti-abortion movement
>> Antiabortion movement
>> Right-to-life movement (Anti-abortion movement)
> BT   **Social movements**
> RT   **Abortion—Ethical aspects**
>> **Abortion—Religious aspects**
>> **Women's rights**

Probabilities   **519.2**
> UF   Fortune
>> Statistical inference
> BT   **Algebra**
>> **Logic**
>> **Mathematics**
>> **Statistics**
> NT   **Average**
>> **Game theory**
>> **Reliability (Engineering)**
>> **Sampling (Statistics)**
> RT   **Risk**

Probate law and practice (May subdiv. geog.)   **346.05**
> BT   **Civil procedure**
>> **Inheritance and succession**

Probation (May subdiv. geog.)   **364.6**
> UF   Reform of criminals
>> Suspended sentence
> BT   **Corrections**
>> **Criminal law**
>> **Prisons**
>> **Punishment**
>> **Reformatories**
>> **Social case work**
> RT   **Juvenile courts**
>> **Parole**

Problem children
> USE   **Emotionally disturbed children**

Problem drinking
> USE   **Alcoholism**

Problem families—Counseling of
> USE   **Family therapy**

Problem solving   **153.4; 510.76**
> BT   **Psychology**
> NT   **Conflict management**
>> **Crisis management**
>> **Critical thinking**
>> **Group problem solving**
> RT   **Decision making**

Problems, exercises, etc.
> USE   subjects with the subdivision *Problems, exercises, etc.,* for compilations of practice problems or exercises for use in the study of a topic, e.g. **Chemistry—Problems, exercises, etc.** [to be added as needed]

Procedural due process
> USE   **Due process of law**

Processing (Libraries)
> USE   **Library technical processes**

Processions
> USE   **Parades**

Procurement, Government
> USE   **Government purchasing**

Prodigal son (Parable)   **226.8**
> BT   **Parables**

Producers
> USE   types of producers and directors in specific media, e.g. **Motion picture producers and directors; Theatrical producers and directors**; etc. [to be added as needed]

Product development
  USE **New products**
Product recall   658.5
  UF Commercial products recall
      Manufactures—Defects
      Manufactures recall
      Recall of products
  BT **Consumer protection**
Product safety   363.19; 658.5
  UF Unsafe products
  BT **Consumer protection**
Production
  USE **Economics**
       Industries
Production engineering
  USE **Factory management**
Production processes
  USE **Manufacturing processes**
Production standards   658.5

  Use for materials on the unit time value for
  the accomplishment of a work task as determined by work measurement techniques.

  UF Output standards
      Standards of output
      Time production standards
      Work standards
  SA types of industries and processes
      with the subdivision *Produc-*
      tion standards, e.g. **Automo-**
      bile industry—Production
      standards [to be added as
      needed]
  BT **Labor productivity**
      Management
  NT **Automobile industry—Produc-**
      tion standards
      Motion study
      Time study
Productivity of labor
  USE **Labor productivity**
Products, Agricultural
  USE **Farm produce**
Products, Animal
  USE **Animal products**
Products, Commercial
  USE **Commercial products**
Products, Dairy
  USE **Dairy products**
Products, Generic
  USE **Generic products**

Professional associations
  USE **Trade and professional associa-**
       tions
Professional education (May subdiv.
  geog.)   **378**
  SA types of professions with the
      subdivision *Study and teach-*
      ing, e.g. **Medicine—Study**
      and teaching [to be added as
      needed]
  BT **Education**
      Higher education
      Learning and scholarship
  NT **Colleges and universities**
      Library education
  RT **Technical education**
      Vocational education
Professional ethics (May subdiv. geog.)
  174
  SA types of professional ethics, e.g.
      Medical ethics; professions
      and types of professional per-
      sonnel with the subdivision
      Ethics, e.g. **Librarians—Eth-**
      ics; and subjects with the
      subdivision *Ethical aspects* [to
      be added as needed]
  BT **Ethics**
  NT **Business ethics**
      Journalism—Objectivity
      Legal ethics
      Librarians—Ethics
      Medical ethics
Professional liability
  USE **Malpractice**
Professional liability insurance
  USE **Malpractice insurance**
Professional sports (May subdiv. geog.)
  796
  SA types of sports [to be added as
      needed]
  BT **Sports**
Professions (May subdiv. geog.)   **331.702**
  UF Careers
      Jobs
      Vocations
  SA types of professions with the
      subdivision *Vocational guid-*
      ance, e.g. **Law—Vocational**
      guidance [to be added as
      needed]

Professions—*Continued*
 BT **Occupations**
   Self-employed
 NT **College graduates**
   Law—Vocational guidance
   Paraprofessionals
 RT **Vocational guidance**
Professions—Tort liability
 USE **Malpractice**
Professors
 USE **Educators**
   Teachers
Profit 338.5; 658.15
 BT **Business**
   Capital
   Economics
   Wealth
 NT **Capitalism**
 RT **Income**
   Risk
Profit sharing (May subdiv. geog.)
   331.2; 658.3
 BT **Commerce**
   Salaries, wages, etc.
 RT **Cooperation**
Program evaluation in education
 USE **Educational evaluation**
Programmed instruction 371.39
 UF Programmed textbooks
 SA subjects with the subdivision
   Programmed instruction [to
   be added as needed]
 BT **Teaching—Aids and devices**
 NT **Computer-assisted instruction**
   **English language—Pro-
   grammed instruction**
   Teaching machines
Programmed textbooks
 USE **Programmed instruction**
Programming (Computers)
 USE **Computer programming**
Programming languages 005.13
 UF Computer languages
   Computer program languages
   Machine language
   Programming languages (Com-
   puters)
   Programming languages (Elec-
   tronic computers)

 SA names of specific languages, e.g.
   **FORTRAN (Computer lan-
   guage)** [to be added as need-
   ed]
 BT **Computer software**
   Language and languages
 NT **FORTRAN (Computer lan-
   guage)**
   **HTML (Document markup
   language)**
 RT **Computer programming**
Programming languages (Computers)
 USE **Programming languages**
Programming languages (Electronic com-
   puters)
 USE **Programming languages**
Programs, Computer
 USE **Computer software**
Programs, Radio
 USE **Radio programs**
Programs, Television
 USE **Television programs**
Programs, Twelve-step
 USE **Twelve-step programs**
Progress 303.44
 UF Social progress
 BT **Civilization**
 NT **Science and civilization**
Progressive education
 USE **Education—Experimental
   methods**
Progressivism (United States politics)
   320.973
 BT **Political science**
Prohibited books
 USE **Books—Censorship**
Prohibition (May subdiv. geog.) **344**
   Use for materials on the legal prohibition of
  liquor traffic and liquor manufacture.
 BT **Criminal law**
 RT **Temperance**
Project Apollo
 USE **Apollo project**
Project Gemini
 USE **Gemini project**
Project method in teaching 371.3
 BT **Teaching**
Project Ranger 629.43
 UF Ranger project
 BT **Lunar probes**
Project schools
 USE **Experimental schools**

Project Sealab
　USE　**Sealab project**
Project Telstar
　USE　**Telstar project**
Project Voyager　629.43
　UF　Voyager project
　BT　**Astronautics—United States**
Projectiles　623.4
　UF　Shells (Projectiles)
　NT　**Ammunition**
　　　Bombs
　　　Guided missiles
　　　Rockets (Aeronautics)
　RT　**Ordnance**
Projective geometry　516
　UF　Geometry, Projective
　BT　**Geometry**
Projectors　778.2
　UF　Film projectors
　　　Magic lanterns
　　　Motion picture projectors
　　　Opaque projectors
　　　Slide projectors
　　　Stereopticon
Proletariat　305.5
　BT　**Labor**
　　　Socialism
　　　Working class
Proliferation of arms
　USE　**Arms race**
Promises　170
　BT　**Ethics**
Promotion in school
　USE　**Promotion (School)**
Promotion (School)　371.2
　UF　Grade repetition
　　　Grade retention
　　　Non-promotion (School)
　　　Promotion in school
　　　Retention, Grade
　　　School grade retention
　　　School promotion
　　　Student promotion
　BT　**Grading and marking (Education)**
Promptness
　USE　**Punctuality**

Pronunciation
　USE　names of languages with the
　　　subdivision *Pronunciation,* e.g.
　　　English language—Pronunciation [to be added as needed]
Proofreading　070.5; 686.2
　BT　**Printing**
Propaganda　303.3; 327.1
　SA　propaganda of particular countries, e.g. **American propaganda;** and names of wars with the subdivision *Propaganda,* e.g. **World War, 1939-1945—Propaganda** [to be added as needed]
　BT　**Political psychology**
　　　Public opinion
　NT　**American propaganda**
　　　Lobbying
　　　Press
　　　Psychological warfare
　　　World War, 1939-1945—Propaganda
　RT　**Advertising**
　　　Persuasion (Psychology)
　　　Publicity
Propaganda, American
　USE　**American propaganda**
Propagation of plants
　USE　**Plant propagation**
Propellers, Aerial
　USE　**Aerial propellers**
Proper names
　USE　**Names**
Property (May subdiv. geog.)　**330.1**
　UF　Ownership
　BT　**Economics**
　NT　**Airspace law**
　　　Cultural property
　　　Eminent domain
　　　Income
　　　Intellectual property
　　　Lost and found possessions
　　　Real estate
　　　Right of property
　　　Surplus government property
　　　Timesharing (Real estate)
　RT　**Wealth**
Property, Crimes against
　USE　**Offenses against property**

Property, Offenses against
    USE   **Offenses against property**
Property, Right of
    USE   **Right of property**
Property rights
    USE   **Right of property**
Property tax—Assessment
    USE   **Tax assessment**
Prophecies   133.3; 202
    UF   Predictions
          Prophecies (Occult sciences)
          Prophecies (Occultism)
          Prophecy
    SA   subjects, titles of sacred works,
          and names of persons with
          the subdivision *Prophecies,*
          e.g. **Bible—Prophecies** [to be
          added as needed]
    BT   **Occultism**
          Supernatural
    RT   **Divination**
          Oracles
Prophecies (Bible)
    USE   **Bible—Prophecies**
Prophecies (Occult sciences)
    USE   **Prophecies**
Prophecies (Occultism)
    USE   **Prophecies**
Prophecy
    USE   **Prophecies**
Prophets (May subdiv. geog.)   200.92
    BT   **Religious biography**
Proportion (Architecture)
    USE   **Architecture—Composition,
          proportion, etc.**
Proportional representation (May subdiv.
    geog.)   328.3
    UF   Representation, Proportional
    BT   **Constitutional law**
          **Representative government and
          representation**
    RT   **Elections**
Proprietary rights
    USE   **Intellectual property**
Prose literature, American
    USE   **American prose literature**
Prose literature, English
    USE   **English prose literature**
Prosody
    USE   **Versification**

Prospecting (May subdiv. geog.)   **622**
    BT   **Gold mines and mining**
          Mines and mineral resources
          Silver mines and mining
    NT   **Mine surveying**
          Petroleum geology
Prosthesis
    USE   **Artificial limbs**
          Artificial organs
Prostitution (May subdiv. geog.)   **176;
    306.74; 363.4; 364.1**
    BT   **Sexual ethics**
          Social problems
          Women—Social conditions
    NT   **Juvenile prostitution**
Protection
    USE   subjects with the subdivision
          Protection, e.g. **Birds—Pro-
          tection** [to be added as need-
          ed]
Protection against burglary
    USE   **Burglary protection**
Protection of animals
    USE   **Animal welfare**
Protection of birds
    USE   **Birds—Protection**
Protection of children
    USE   **Child welfare**
Protection of environment
    USE   **Environmental protection**
Protection of game
    USE   **Game protection**
Protection of natural scenery
    USE   **Landscape protection**
          Natural monuments
          Nature conservation
Protection of plants
    USE   **Plant conservation**
Protection of wildlife
    USE   **Wildlife conservation**
Protectionism (May subdiv. geog.)   **382**
    UF   Free trade and protection
    BT   **Commercial policy**
    RT   **Free trade**
          Tariff
Proteins   547; 572
    BT   **Biochemistry**
    NT   **Enzymes**
Protest
    USE   **Dissent**

Protest marches and rallies
USE **Demonstrations**
Protest movements (May subdiv. geog.)
303.48
SA names of wars and other objects
of protest with the subdivision
Protest movements, e.g.
**World War, 1939-1945—
Protest movements** [to be
added as needed]
BT **Social movements**
NT **World War, 1939-1945—Pro-
test movements**
RT **Demonstrations**
Protestant churches (May subdiv. geog.)
280
Use for materials on Protestant denomina-
tions treated collectively. Works on Protestant
church buildings are entered under **Church
buildings.**
UF Denominations, Protestant
Protestant denominations
SA names of Protestant churches,
e.g. **Presbyterian Church** [to
be added as needed]
BT **Christian sects
Church history
Protestantism**
Protestant denominations
USE **Protestant churches**
Protestant Episcopal Church in the U.S.A.
USE **Episcopal Church**
Protestant Reformation
USE **Reformation**
Protestant work ethic
USE **Work ethic**
Protestantism (May subdiv. geog.) **280**
BT **Christianity
Church history**
NT **Pentecostal churches
Protestant churches**
RT **Reformation**
Protests, demonstrations, etc.
USE **Demonstrations**
Protons **539.7**
UF Hydrogen nucleus
BT **Atoms
Particles (Nuclear physics)**
Protoplasm **571.6**
BT **Biology
Life (Biology)**

RT **Cells
Embryology**
Protozoa **579.4**
BT **Microorganisms**
Proverbs **398.9**
UF Adages
Maxims
Sayings
BT **Folklore
Quotations**
RT **Epigrams**
**Providence and government of God
202; 214; 231**
UF God—Providence and govern-
ment
God—Sovereignty
BT **God**
Provincialism
USE **Regionalism**
Provincialisms
USE names of languages with the
subdivision *Provincialisms,*
e.g. **English language—Pro-
vincialisms** [to be added as
needed]
Pruning **631.5**
BT **Forests and forestry
Fruit culture
Gardening
Trees**
Pseudonyms **929.4**
UF Anonyms
Fictitious names
Pen names
BT **Names
Personal names**
Psi (Parapsychology)
USE **Parapsychology**
Psychiatric care
USE **Mental health services**
Psychiatric hospitals (May subdiv. geog.)
362.2
UF Mental hospitals
BT **Hospitals**
RT **Mentally ill—Institutional care**
Psychiatric services
USE **Mental health services**
Psychiatrists (May subdiv. geog.) **920;
926**
UF Psychopathologists
BT **Psychologists**

Psychiatry (May subdiv. geog.) **616.89**

Use for materials on clinical aspects of mental disorders, including therapy. Popular materials and materials on regional or social aspects of mental disorders are entered under **Mental illness.** Systematic descriptions of mental disorders are entered under **Abnormal psychology.**

BT **Medicine**

NT **Adolescent psychiatry**
Child psychiatry
Psychotherapy

RT **Abnormal psychology**
Mental health
Mental illness

Psychic healing
USE **Mental healing**

Psychic phenomena
USE **Parapsychology**

Psychical research
USE **Parapsychology**

Psychics **133.8092**

UF Clairvoyants

BT **Parapsychology**
Persons

Psychoactive drugs
USE **Psychotropic drugs**

Psychoanalysis (May subdiv. geog.)
150.19; 616.89

BT **Psychology**

NT **Ego (Psychology)**
Psychosomatic medicine

RT **Abnormal psychology**
Hypnotism
Mind and body
Subconsciousness

Psychogenetics
USE **Behavior genetics**

Psychokinesis **133.8**

UF Telekinesis

BT **Parapsychology**
Spiritualism

Psychological aspects
USE subjects with the subdivision *Psychological aspects,* e.g. **Drugs—Psychological aspects; World War, 1939-1945—Psychological aspects;** etc. [to be added as needed]

Psychological stress
USE **Stress (Psychology)**

Psychological tests **150.28**

UF Mental tests

BT **Psychology**

NT **Ability—Testing**

RT **Educational tests and measurements**

Psychological types
USE **Typology (Psychology)**

Psychological warfare **355.3**

Use for materials on methods used to undermine the morale of the civilian population and the military forces of an enemy country.

UF War of nerves

SA names of wars with the subdivision *Psychological aspects* [to be added as needed]

BT **Applied psychology**
Military art and science
Morale
Propaganda
War

NT **Brainwashing**
World War, 1939-1945—Psychological aspects

Psychologists (May subdiv. geog.)
150.92; 920

NT **Psychiatrists**
School psychologists

RT **Psychology**

Psychology (May subdiv. geog.) **150**

UF Mind

SA religions, theological topics, titles of individual sacred works, types of animals, classes of persons, ethnic groups, and names of individual persons, including individual literary authors, with the subdivision *Psychology,* e.g. **Christianity—Psychology; Women—Psychology; Native Americans—Psychology;** etc.; and subjects with the subdivision *Psychological aspects* for materials on the relationship of particular situations, conditions, activities, environments, or objects to the mental condition or personality of the individual, e.g. **Color—Psychological aspects** [to be added as needed]

Psychology—*Continued*
   BT   Brain
         Philosophy
         Soul
   NT   Adjustment (Psychology)
         Adolescent psychology
         Aggressiveness (Psychology)
         Apperception
         Applied psychology
         Assertiveness (Psychology)
         Attention
         Attitude (Psychology)
         Behavior genetics
         Behaviorism
         Bible—Psychology
         Child psychology
         Choice (Psychology)
         Color—Psychological aspects
         Consciousness
         Criminal psychology
         Developmental psychology
         Dogs—Psychology
         Educational psychology
         Ego (Psychology)
         Emotions
         Ethnopsychology
         Genius
         Gestalt psychology
         Habit
         Human behavior
         Identity (Psychology)
         Ideology
         Imagination
         Individuality
         Instinct
         Intellect
         Intuition
         Memory
         Men—Psychology
         Motivation (Psychology)
         Multiple personality
         Music—Psychological aspects
         Number concept
         Parapsychology
         Perception
         Personality
         Phrenology
         Physiognomy
         Political psychology
         Problem solving
         Psychoanalysis
         Psychological tests

         Psychology of religion
         Psychophysiology
         Reasoning
         Self-acceptance
         Self-consciousness
         Self-control
         Self-esteem
         Self-perception
         Self-realization
         Senses and sensation
         Sex (Psychology)
         Social psychology
         Stress (Psychology)
         Subconsciousness
         Temperament
         Thought and thinking
         Typology (Psychology)
         Values
         Women—Psychology
   RT   Mental health
         Psychologists
Psychology and religion
   USE   Psychology of religion
Psychology, Applied
   USE   Applied psychology
         Persuasion (Psychology)
Psychology, Comparative
   USE   Comparative psychology
Psychology—Computer simulation   150
   BT   Computer simulation
Psychology of color
   USE   Color—Psychological aspects
Psychology of learning   153.1
   UF   Learning, Psychology of
   BT   Animal intelligence
         Child psychology
         Education
         Educational psychology
         Memory
   NT   Behavior modification
         Biofeedback training
         Brainwashing
         Concept learning
         Feedback (Psychology)
         Learning disabilities
         Reading comprehension
         Verbal learning
Psychology of music
   USE   Music—Psychological aspects

Psychology of religion   200.1
- UF   Psychology and religion
  Psychology, Religious
  Religion and psychology
  Religion—Psychological aspects
  Religious psychology
- SA   religious topics, titles of individual sacred works, and names of religions with the subdivision *Psychology* [to be added as needed]
- BT   **Psychology**
  Religion
- NT   **Christianity—Psychology**
  Faith—Psychology
  Pastoral psychology

Psychology, Pastoral
- USE   **Pastoral psychology**

Psychology, Pathological
- USE   **Abnormal psychology**

Psychology, Religious
- USE   **Pastoral psychology**
  Psychology of religion

Psychology, Structural
- USE   **Gestalt psychology**

Psychopathologists
- USE   **Psychiatrists**

Psychopathology
- USE   **Abnormal psychology**

Psychopathy
- USE   **Abnormal psychology**

Psychopharmaceuticals
- USE   **Psychotropic drugs**

Psychophysics
- USE   **Psychophysiology**

Psychophysiology   152
Use for materials on the relationship between psychological and physiological processes.
- UF   Behavioral psychology
  Physiological psychology
  Psychophysics
- BT   **Nervous system**
  Physiology
  Psychology
- NT   **Behaviorism**
  Color sense
  Emotions
  Human engineering
  Hypnotism
  Left- and right-handedness
  Memory

Optical illusions
Pain
Senses and sensation
Sleep
Temperament
- RT   **Mind and body**

Psychoses
- USE   **Mental illness**

Psychosomatic medicine   616.08
- UF   Medicine, Psychosomatic
- BT   **Abnormal psychology**
  Medicine
  Mind and body
  Psychoanalysis

Psychotherapy (May subdiv. geog.)   616.89
- UF   Therapy, Psychological
- BT   **Psychiatry**
  Therapeutics
- NT   **Biofeedback training**
  Family therapy
  Sex therapy
  Transactional analysis
- RT   **Mental healing**
  Suggestive therapeutics

Psychotic children
- USE   **Emotionally disturbed children**

Psychotics
- USE   **Mentally ill**

Psychotropic drugs   615
Use for general materials on the group of drugs that act on the central nervous system to affect behavior, mental activity, or perception, including the antipsychotic drugs, antidepressants, hallucinogenic agents, and tranquilizers.
- UF   Psychoactive drugs
  Psychopharmaceuticals
- SA   types of drugs and names of individual drugs [to be added as needed]
- BT   **Drugs**
- NT   **Hallucinogens**
  Narcotics
  Stimulants

PTAs
- USE   **Parent-teacher associations**

Puberty   612.6
- BT   **Sex (Biology)**
- RT   **Adolescence**

Public accommodations, Discrimination in
- USE   **Discrimination in public accommodations**

Public administration   351

Use for general materials on the conduct of public business not limited to a specific place.

UF   Administration

SA   names of countries, states, cities, etc., with the subdivision *Politics and government,* e.g. **United States—Politics and government** [to be added as needed

BT   **Local government**
     Municipal government
     Political science

NT   **Administrative agencies**
     Bureaucracy
     Civil service
     Intelligence service
     Licenses
     Military government
     United States—Politics and government

RT   **Administrative law**
     Public officers

Public assistance

USE   **Public welfare**

Public buildings (May subdiv. geog.)   **352.5; 725**

Use for materials on buildings owned by the public and maintained at public expense, such as government office buildings, public libraries, public schools, etc. Materials on buildings that are privately owned and maintained and are open to the public for business or entertainment are entered under **Buildings** or under the specific type of building.

UF   Government buildings

SA   names of individual public buildings [to be added as needed]

BT   **Buildings**
     Public works

NT   **Capitols**

Public buildings, American

USE   **Public buildings—United States**

Public buildings—Chicago (Ill.)   725.09773

UF   Chicago (Ill.)—Public buildings

Public buildings—Ohio   725.09771

UF   Ohio—Public buildings

Public buildings—United States   352.5; 725.0973

Use for materials on U.S. federal government buildings located in or outside of the United States, including materials on U.S embassy or consulate buildings abroad.

UF   Public buildings, American
     United States—Government buildings
     United States—Public buildings

Public debts (May subdiv. geog.)   **336.3**

Use for materials on government debts.

UF   Debts, Public
     Federal debt
     Government debts
     National debts

SA   names of wars with the subdivision *Finance,* e.g. **World War, 1939-1945—Finance** [to be added as needed]

BT   **Debt**
     Loans
     Public finance

RT   **Bonds**
     Deficit financing

Public debts—United States   336.3

UF   United States—Public debts

Public demonstrations

USE   **Demonstrations**

Public documents

USE   **Government publications**

Public domain

USE   **Public lands**

Public domain software

USE   **Free computer software**

Public enterprises

USE   **Government business enterprises**

Public figures

USE   **Celebrities**

Public finance (May subdiv. geog.)   **336**

Use for general materials on the raising and expenditure of funds in the public sector, and, with a geographic subdivision, for materials on the public finance of countries, states, localities, cities, etc.

UF   Finance, Public

BT   **Finance**

NT   **Budget**
     Deficit financing
     Federal aid
     Fiscal policy
     Government aid
     Government lending
     Grants-in-aid
     Metropolitan finance
     Municipal finance
     Public debts
     Tariff

Public finance—*Continued*
    Taxation
Public health (May subdiv. geog.)
    362.1; 614
    UF Hygiene, Social
        Public hygiene
        Social hygiene
    BT **Health**
        Human services
        Social problems
        State medicine
    NT **Burial**
        Cemeteries
        Communicable diseases
        Community health services
        Cremation
        Disinfection and disinfectants
        Environmental health
        Epidemics
        Food adulteration and inspection
        Health boards
        Health facilities
        Hospitals
        Immunization
        Meat inspection
        Medical care
        Medical charities
        Milk supply
        Noise
        Occupational health and safety
        Pollution
        Refuse and refuse disposal
        School hygiene
        Sewage disposal
        Social medicine
        Street cleaning
        Vaccination
        Water pollution
    RT **Sanitation**
Public health boards
    USE **Health boards**
Public health—Evaluation   362.1
    UF Health program evaluation
Public health—United States
    362.10973; 614
    UF United States—Public health
Public housing (May subdiv. geog.)
    363.5
    UF Government housing
        Housing projects, Government
        Low income housing

    BT **Housing**
Public hygiene
    USE **Public health**
Public interest (May subdiv. geog.)
    172; 320.01; 344
    UF National interest
    BT **State, The**
    NT **Ombudsman**
        Whistle blowing
Public lands (May subdiv. geog.)   333.1
    UF Crown lands
        Public domain
    BT **Colonization**
        Land use
    NT **Forest reserves**
        Land grants
        National parks and reserves
    RT **Natural resources**
Public lands—Ohio   333.109771
    UF Ohio—Public lands
Public lands—United States   333.10973
    UF United States—Public lands
Public libraries (May subdiv. geog.)
    027.4
    UF County libraries
    BT **Libraries**
    NT **Regional libraries**
Public meetings   302.3
    UF Meetings, Public
    BT **Freedom of assembly**
    NT **Demonstrations**
        Parliamentary practice
Public officers   320
    Use for general materials on elected government officials not limited to a particular jurisdiction.
    UF Elected officials
        Government officials
        Officials and employees
        Public officials
    SA names of countries, states, cities, etc., with the subdivision *Officials and employees* [to be added as needed]
    NT **Term limits (Public office)**
    RT **Civil service**
        Public administration
Public officials
    USE **Public officers**

Public opinion (May subdiv. geog.)
    303.3
    UF   Opinion, Public
    SA   subjects with the subdivision
            Public opinion, e.g. **World
            War, 1939-1945—Public
            opinion;** and names of coun-
            tries with the subdivision *For-
            eign opinion* for materials
            dealing with foreign public
            opinion about the country,
            e.g. **United States—Foreign
            opinion** [to be added as need-
            ed]
    BT   **Freedom of conscience
            Political psychology
            Political science
            Social psychology**
    NT   **Propaganda
            Public opinion polls
            Publicity
            United States—Foreign opinion
            World War, 1939-1945—Public
            opinion**
    RT   **Attitude (Psychology)
            Press
            Public relations**
Public opinion polls   303.3
    Use for general materials and for materials
    on the technique of polling public opinion.
    Materials on polls on a specific topic are en-
    tered under the appropriate heading for the
    topic with the subdivision *Public opinion.* Ma-
    terials on polls taken in a specific place are
    entered **Public opinion** subdivided geographi-
    cally. Materials on polls limited to a specific
    class of persons are entered under the appro-
    priate heading for the class of persons with
    the subdivision *Attitudes.*
    UF   Opinion polls
            Polls
            Straw votes
    BT   **Public opinion**
    RT   **Market surveys**
Public ownership
    USE   **Government ownership
            Municipal ownership**
Public playgrounds
    USE   **Playgrounds**
Public procurement
    USE   **Government purchasing**
Public purchasing
    USE   **Government purchasing**

Public records—Preservation
    USE   **Archives**
Public relations (May subdiv. geog.)
    659.2
    SA   topics with the subdivision *Pub-
            lic relations,* e.g. **Libraries—
            Public relations** [to be added
            as needed]
    NT   **Business entertaining
            Customer relations**
    RT   **Advertising
            Public opinion
            Publicity**
Public relations—Libraries
    USE   **Libraries—Public relations**
Public safety, Crimes against
    USE   **Offenses against public safety**
Public schools (May subdiv. geog.)
    371.01
    Use for materials on preschool, elementary,
    and secondary schools supported by state and
    local government. Materials on British en-
    dowed secondary schools that are open to
    public admission but are not financed or ad-
    ministered by any government body are en-
    tered under **English public schools.**
    BT   **Schools**
    NT   **Evening and continuation
            schools
            High schools
            Junior high schools
            Magnet schools
            Religion in the public schools
            Rural schools
            Summer schools**
Public schools and religion
    USE   **Religion in the public schools**
Public schools, Endowed (Great Britain)
    USE   **English public schools**
Public schools, English
    USE   **English public schools**
Public schools—United States
    371.010973
    UF   United States—Public schools
Public service commissions (May subdiv.
    geog.)   **354.72**
    Use for materials on bodies appointed to
    regulate or control public utilities.
    UF   Public utility commissions
    BT   **Corporation law
            Corporations
            Industrial policy**
Public service corporations
    USE   **Public utilities**

Public shelters
USE **Air raid shelters**
Public speaking   808.5
Use for materials on the art of delivering speeches. Collections of speeches on several subjects and materials about speeches that have already been delivered are entered under **Speeches.** Materials limited to scholarly lectures are entered under **Lectures and lecturing.**
UF   Elocution
Oratory
Persuasion (Rhetoric)
Speaking
BT   **Communication**
NT   **Acting**
Book talks
Chalk talks
Debates and debating
Lectures and lecturing
Preaching
Voice culture
RT   **Speeches**
Voice
Public television (May subdiv. geog.)
384.55
UF   Educational television
BT   **Television broadcasting**
Public transit
USE   **Local transit**
Public utilities (May subdiv. geog.)
343.09; 354.72; 363.6
UF   Public service corporations
Utilities, Public
NT   **Electric utilities**
Gas companies
Telegraph
Telephone
Water supply
Public utility commissions
USE   **Public service commissions**
Public welfare (May subdiv. geog.)
361.6
Use for materials on tax-supported welfare activities. Materials on privately supported welfare activities are entered under **Charities.** Materials on the methods employed in welfare work, public or private, are entered under **Social work.** General materials on the various policies, programs, services, and facilities to meet basic human needs, such as health, education, and welfare, are entered under **Human services.**
UF   Poor relief
Public assistance
Relief, Public

Social welfare
Welfare, Public
Welfare reform
BT   **Human services**
Social work
NT   **Child welfare**
Disaster relief
Food relief
Institutional care
Legal aid
National service
Poor
Social medicine
Volunteer work
Welfare state
RT   **Charities**
Poverty
Public works (May subdiv. geog.)
352.7; 363
BT   **Civil engineering**
Domestic economic assistance
NT   **Infrastructure (Economics)**
Municipal engineering
Public buildings
RT   **City planning**
Public works—Chicago (Ill.)   363.09773
UF   Chicago (Ill.)—Public works
Public works—Ohio   352.7; 363.09771
UF   Ohio—Public works
Public works—United States   352.7;
363.0973
UF   United States—Public works
Public worship   203; 264
May be subdivided by religion or sect.
UF   Church attendance
BT   **Worship**
Publicity   659
BT   **Public opinion**
NT   **Press**
RT   **Advertising**
Propaganda
Public relations
Publishers and authors
USE   **Authors and publishers**
Publishers and publishing (May subdiv.
geog.)   **070.5**
UF   Book trade
Publishing
SA   types of literature, types of published materials, and names of individual corporate bodies

Publishers and publishing—*Continued*
    and religious denominations
    with the subdivision *Publish-*
    ing, e.g. **Music—Publishing**
    [to be added as needed]
NT **Authors and publishers**
    Editing
    Electronic publishing
    Music—Publishing
    Printing
    Publishers' catalogs
    Publishers' standard book
    numbers
    Serial publications
RT **Book industry**
    Books
    Booksellers and bookselling
Publishers and publishing—Exhibitions
USE **Books—Exhibitions**
Publishers' catalogs   015
    Use for catalogs produced by publishers and
    for materials about such catalogs. Retail book
    catalogs and book auction catalogs and mate-
    rials about such catalogs are entered under
    Booksellers' catalogs.
UF Books—Catalogs
    Catalogs
    Catalogs, Publishers'
BT **Publishers and publishing**
Publishers' standard book numbers
    070.5
UF Book numbers, Publishers' stan-
    dard
    Standard book numbers
BT **Publishers and publishing**
NT **International Standard Book**
    Numbers
Publishing
USE **Publishers and publishing**
    and types of literature, types of
    published materials, and
    names of individual corporate
    bodies and religious denomi-
    nations with the subdivision
    Publishing, e.g. **Music—Pub-**
    lishing [to be added as need-
    ed]
Pubs
USE **Bars**
Pugilism
USE **Boxing**
Pulmonary resuscitation
USE **Artificial respiration**

Pulsars   523.8
UF Pulsating radio sources
BT **Astronomy**
Pulsating radio sources
USE **Pulsars**
Pumping machinery   621.6
UF Pumps
SA types of pumping machinery,
    e.g. **Heat pumps** [to be add-
    ed as needed]
BT **Engines**
    Hydraulic engineering
NT **Heat pumps**
Pumps
USE **Pumping machinery**
Punctuality   640
UF Lateness
    Promptness
    Tardiness
BT **Time**
    Virtue
Punctuation   411; 421
UF English language—Punctuation
BT **Rhetoric**
Punishment (May subdiv. geog.)   **364.6**
UF Discipline
    Penology
BT **Administration of criminal jus-**
    tice
    Corrections
NT **Capital punishment**
    Correctional institutions
    Parole
    Prisons
    Probation
    Reformatories
    Torture
RT **Crime**
    Criminal law
Punishment in schools
USE **School discipline**
Puns   808.88
    May be used for collections of puns or for
    materials about puns.
UF Puns and punning
BT **Wit and humor**
Puns and punning
USE **Puns**
Puppets and puppet plays   791.5
UF Marionettes
SA types of puppets or puppet plays
    [to be added as needed]

Puppets and puppet plays—*Continued*
  BT **Drama**
      Folk drama
      Theater
  NT **Shadow pantomimes and plays**
Puppies
  USE **Dogs**
Purchasing (May subdiv. geog.) **658.7**
  Use for general materials on buying and materials on buying by commercial enterprises. Materials on consumer buying are entered under **Shopping.**
  UF Buying
  SA types of products and services with the subdivision *Purchasing,* e.g. **Automobiles—Purchasing** [to be added as needed]
  BT **Management**
  NT **Government purchasing**
      Installment plan
      Shopping
Pure food
  USE **Food adulteration and inspection**
Purgatory **202; 236**
  BT **Eschatology**
Purification of water
  USE **Water purification**
Puritans (May subdiv. geog.) **285**
  BT **Christian sects**
  NT **Pilgrims (New England colonists)**
  RT **Calvinism**
      Church of England—United States
      Congregationalism
Puzzles **793.73**
  SA types of puzzles, e.g. **Crossword puzzles** [to be added as needed]
  BT **Amusements**
  NT **Bible games and puzzles**
      Crossword puzzles
      Jigsaw puzzles
      Mathematical recreations
      Maze puzzles
      Picture puzzles
      Rebuses
  RT **Riddles**

Pyramids (May subdiv. geog.) **722; 909**
  BT **Ancient architecture**
      Archeology
      Monuments
  NT **Obelisks**
Pyrography (May subdiv.geog.) **745.51**
  UF Fire etching
      Wood-burning
  BT **Etching**
      Woodwork
Quacks and quackery **615.8**
  BT **Impostors and imposture**
      Medicine
      Swindlers and swindling
Quakers
  USE **Society of Friends**
Qualitative analysis
  USE **Analytical chemistry**
Quality control **519.8; 658.5**
  SA industries, processes, and materials with the subdivision *Quality control* [to be added as needed]
  BT **Reliability (Engineering)**
      Sampling (Statistics)
  NT **Steel industry—Quality control**
Quality of life (May subdiv. geog.) **303.3**
  Use for materials on the objective standards and subjective attitudes by which individuals and groups assess their life situations.
  UF Life quality
  BT **Economic conditions**
      Social conditions
  NT **Cost and standard of living**
  RT **Basic needs**
Quantitative analysis
  USE **Analytical chemistry**
Quantity cookery
  USE **Quantity cooking**
Quantity cooking **641.5**
  Use for materials limited to the preparation and cooking of food in large quantities. Materials on the preparation, delivery, and serving of ready-to-eat foods in large quantities outside of the home are entered under **Food service.**
  UF Cooking for large numbers
      Quantity cookery
  BT **Cooking**
  RT **Food service**
Quantum mechanics
  USE **Quantum theory**

Quantum theory 530.12
  UF Quantum mechanics
  BT **Dynamics**
       Physics
  NT **Wave mechanics**
  RT **Atomic theory**
       Force and energy
       Physical chemistry
       Radiation
       Relativity (Physics)
       Thermodynamics
Quarantine
  USE **Communicable diseases**
Quarks 539.7
  BT **Particles (Nuclear physics)**
Quarries and quarrying (May subdiv. geog.) 622
  UF Stone quarries
  BT **Economic geology**
  RT **Stone**
Quartz 549
  UF Rock crystal
  BT **Crystals**
       Minerals
Quasars 523.1
  UF Quasi-stellar radio sources
  BT **Astronomy**
       Radio astronomy
Quasi-stellar radio sources
  USE **Quasars**
Québec (Province) 971.4
Québec (Province)—History 971.4
Québec (Province)—History—Autonomy and independence movements 971.4
  UF Québec (Province)—Separatist movement
       Separatist movement in Québec (Province)
Québec (Province)—Separatist movement
  USE **Québec (Province)—History—Autonomy and independence movements**
Queens (May subdiv. geog.) 920; 929.7
  Use for materials on women monarchs as well as on wives or consorts of monarchs.
  UF Royalty
       Rulers
       Sovereigns
  SA names of queens, e.g. **Elizabeth II, Queen of Great Britain, 1926-** ; ethnic groups with the subdivision *Queens,* and countries, cities, etc., with the subdivision *Kings and rulers* [to be added as needed]
  BT **Monarchy**
  RT **Courts and courtiers**
       Empresses
       Kings and rulers
Queens—Great Britain 920; 941
  UF Great Britain—Queens
  SA names of British queens, e.g. **Elizabeth II, Queen of Great Britain, 1926-** [to be added as needed]
  NT **Elizabeth II, Queen of Great Britain, 1926-**
Queries
  USE **Questions and answers**
Questions and answers 793.73
  Use for collections of informal quizzes on various subjects. Informal quizzes on a particular subject are entered under the subject with the subdivision *Miscellanea.* Materials on formal examinations are entered under **Examinations.** Examination questions on a particular subject are entered under the subject with the subdivision *Examinations,* e.g. **Music—Examinations.** Compilations of practice problems or exercises for use in the study of a topic are entered under the topic with the subdivision *Problems, exercises, etc.,* e.g. **Chemistry—Problems, exercises, etc.**
  UF Answers to questions
       Queries
       Quizzes
       Trivia
  SA subjects with the subdivision *Miscellanea,* e.g. **Medicine—Miscellanea** [to be added as needed]
  NT **Examinations**
Quick and easy cookery
  USE **Quick and easy cooking**
Quick and easy cooking 641.5
  Use for materials containing recipes or cooking techniques emphasizing economy of preparation time and the use of readily available ingredients.
  UF Convenience cooking
       Easy and quick cooking
       Quick and easy cookery
       Quick-meal cooking
       Time saving cooking
  BT **Cooking**
Quick-meal cooking
  USE **Quick and easy cooking**

Quicksilver
USE **Mercury**
Quilt designing
USE **Quilts—Design**
Quilting 746.46
BT **Needlework**
Sewing
RT **Quilts**
Quilts (May subdiv. geog.) 746.46
UF Coverlets
Patchwork quilts
BT **Interior design**
RT **Quilting**
Quilts—Design 746.46
UF Quilt designing
BT **Design**
Quintets 785
BT **Chamber music**
Quislings
USE **World War, 1939-1945—Collaborationists**
Quit-smoking programs
USE **Smoking cessation programs**
Quizzes
USE **Questions and answers**
Qumran texts
USE **Dead Sea scrolls**
Quotations 080; 808.88
UF Sayings
SA subjects, classes of persons, ethnic groups, and names of individuals with the subdivision *Quotations* [to be added as needed]
BT **Epigrams**
NT **Presidents—United States—Quotations**
Proverbs
Qur'an
USE **Koran**
Rabbis (May subdiv. geog.) 296.6; 920
BT **Clergy**
Judaism
Rabbits 599.32; 636
UF Bunnies
Bunny rabbits
Hares
BT **Mammals**
Rabies 616.9; 636.089
UF Hydrophobia
BT **Communicable diseases**

Race 599.97
BT **Ethnology**
NT **Ethnocentrism**
Race awareness (May subdiv. geog.) 305.8
UF Race identity
Racial identity
SA names of racial groups with the subdivision *Race identity* [to be added as needed]
BT **Race relations**
NT **African Americans—Race identity**
Blacks—Race identity
Racism
Race discrimination (May subdiv. geog.) 305.8
Use for materials on the restriction or denial of rights, privileges, or choice because of race. Materials on prejudicial attitudes about particular groups because of their race are entered under **Racism**.
UF Racial discrimination
SA types of discrimination, e.g. **Discrimination in education** [to be added as needed]
BT **Discrimination**
Race relations
Racism
Social problems
Race identity
USE **Race awareness**
and names of racial groups with the subdivision *Race identity,* e.g. **Blacks—Race identity; African Americans—Race identity;** etc. [to be added as needed]
Race prejudice
USE **Racism**
Race problems
USE **Race relations**
Race psychology
USE **Ethnopsychology**
Race relations 305.8
UF Integration, Racial
Interracial relations
Race problems
Racial integration
SA names of countries, cities, etc., with the subdivision *Race relations,* e.g. **United States—**

Race relations—*Continued*

      Race relations [to be added as needed]

  BT **Acculturation**
       Ethnology
       Sociology

  NT **Chicago (Ill.)—Race relations**
       Culture conflict
       Discrimination
       Interracial adoption
       Ohio—Race relations
       Race awareness
       Race discrimination
       Racism
       School integration
       Segregation
       South Africa—Race relations
       United States—Race relations
       White supremacy movements

  RT **Ethnic relations**
       Minorities
       Multiculturalism
       Pluralism (Social sciences)

Race relations and the church
  USE **Church and race relations**

Races of people
  USE **Ethnology**

Racial balance in schools
  USE **School integration**
       Segregation in education

Racial bias
  USE **Racism**

Racial discrimination
  USE **Race discrimination**

Racial identity
  USE **Race awareness**

Racial integration
  USE **Race relations**

Racial intermarriage
  USE **Interracial marriage**

Racially mixed people (May subdiv. geog.) **305.8**
  UF Bi-racial people
       Mixed race people
       Mulattoes
       Multiracial people
  BT **Ethnic groups**

Racing **796**
  SA types of racing [to be added as needed]

  BT **Sports**
  NT **Airplane racing**
       Automobile racing
       Bicycle racing
       Boat racing
       Horse racing
       Orienteering
       Soap box derbies
  RT **Running**

Racism (May subdiv. geog.) **305.8; 320.5**

Use for materials on prejudicial attitudes about particular groups because of their race. Materials on the restriction or denial of rights, privileges, or choice because of race are entered under **Race discrimination.**

  UF Race prejudice
       Racial bias
  BT **Attitude (Psychology)**
       Prejudices
       Race awareness
       Race relations
  NT **Race discrimination**
       White supremacy movements

Racketeering (May subdiv. geog.) **364.106**
  UF Crime syndicates
  BT **Crime**
       Organized crime

Radar **621.3848**
  BT **Navigation**
       Radio
       Remote sensing

Radar defense networks **623**
  UF Defenses, Radar
  BT **Air defenses**

Radiant heating **697**
  UF Panel heating
  BT **Heating**

Radiation **539.2**
  BT **Optics**
       Physics
       Waves
  NT **Cosmic rays**
       Electromagnetic waves
       Gamma rays
       Infrared radiation
       Luminescence
       Radioactivity
       Radium
       Sound
       Spectrum analysis
       Ultraviolet rays

Radiation—*Continued*
   X-rays
 RT Light
   Quantum theory
Radiation biology
 USE Radiobiology
Radiation—Physiological effect 612
 RT Atomic bomb—Physiological
   effect
   Nuclear medicine
Radiation—Safety measures 363.1; 612
 BT Accidents—Prevention
Radiation, Solar
 USE Solar radiation
Radiation therapy
 USE Radiotherapy
Radicalism (May subdiv. geog.) 320.5
  Use for materials on extremist social and
 political movements of either the right or the
 left.
 UF Extremism (Political science)
   Political extremism
   Radicals and radicalism
 BT Political science
   Revolutions
   Right and left (Political sci-
   ence)
 NT Militia movements
 RT Counter culture
Radicals and radicalism
 USE Radicalism
Radio 621.384
 UF Wireless
 SA radio and other subjects, e.g.
   Radio and music; and radio
   in various industries or fields
   of endeavor, e.g. Radio in
   aeronautics [to be added as
   needed]
 BT Telecommunication
 NT Radar
   Radio and music
   Radio frequency modulation
   Radio in aeronautics
   Radio in astronautics
   Radio in education
   Shortwave radio
Radio addresses, debates, etc. 384.54;
  808.5; 808.85
 UF Radio lectures
 BT Debates and debating
   Lectures and lecturing

   Radio broadcasting
   Radio scripts
Radio advertising 659.14
 UF Commercials, Radio
   Radio commercials
 BT Advertising
   Radio broadcasting
Radio and music 780; 781.5
 UF Music and radio
 BT Music
   Radio
Radio and television novels 808.3
  May be used for individual works, collec-
 tions, or materials about novels based on radio
 or television programs.
 UF Radio novels
   Television novels
 BT Fiction
 RT Movie novels
Radio astronomy 522
 SA names of celestial radio sources,
   e.g. Quasars [to be added as
   needed]
 BT Astronomy
   Interstellar communication
 NT Quasars
Radio authorship 808
 UF Radio script writing
   Radio writing
 BT Authorship
   Radio broadcasting
 NT Radio plays—Technique
 RT Radio scripts
Radio broadcasting (May subdiv. geog.)
  384.54
 UF Radio industry
 SA radio broadcasting of particular
   kinds of programs, e.g. Radio
   broadcasting of sports [to be
   added as needed]
 BT Broadcasting
   Mass media
 NT Radio addresses, debates, etc.
   Radio advertising
   Radio authorship
   Radio broadcasting of sports
   Radio programs
   Radio stations
Radio broadcasting of sports 070.4
 UF Sports broadcasting
   Sports in radio

Radio broadcasting of sports—*Continued*
- BT   **Broadcast journalism**
-        **Radio broadcasting**

Radio chemistry
- USE **Radiochemistry**

Radio comedies
- USE **Comedy radio programs**

Radio comedy programs
- USE **Comedy radio programs**

Radio commercials
- USE **Radio advertising**

Radio drama
- USE **Radio plays**

Radio—Equipment and supplies 621.384028
- NT   **Radio—Receivers and reception**
- RT   **Radio supplies industry**

Radio equipment industry
- USE **Radio supplies industry**

Radio frequency modulation 621.384
- UF   FM radio
-        Frequency modulation, Radio
- BT   **Radio**
- NT   **Shortwave radio**

Radio in aeronautics 629.135
- BT   **Aeronautics**
-        **Navigation (Aeronautics)**
-        **Radio**

Radio in astronautics 629.4
- UF   Lunar surface radio communication
- BT   **Astronautics—Communication systems**
-        **Navigation (Astronautics)**
-        **Radio**

Radio in education 371.33
- UF   Education and radio
- BT   **Audiovisual education**
-        **Radio**
-        **Teaching—Aids and devices**

Radio industry
- USE **Radio broadcasting**
-        **Radio supplies industry**

Radio journalism
- USE **Broadcast journalism**

Radio lectures
- USE **Radio addresses, debates, etc.**

Radio novels
- USE **Radio and television novels**

Radio operators 621.3841

Radio plays 808.2; 808.82

May be used for individual works, collections, or materials about radio plays.
- UF   Radio drama
-        Scenarios
- BT   **Drama**
-        **Radio programs**
- NT   **Soap operas**
- RT   **Radio scripts**

Radio plays—Technique 808.2
- UF   Play writing
-        Playwriting
- BT   **Drama—Technique**
-        **Radio authorship**
- RT   **Television plays—Technique**

Radio programs 384.54

May be used for individual works, collections, or materials about radio programs.
- UF   Programs, Radio
- SA   types of programs and names of specific programs [to be added as needed]
- BT   **Radio broadcasting**
- NT   **Adventure radio programs**
-        **Biographical radio programs**
-        **Comedy radio programs**
-        **Fantasy radio programs**
-        **Horror radio programs**
-        **Legal drama (Radio programs)**
-        **Medical drama (Radio programs)**
-        **Mystery radio programs**
-        **Radio plays**
-        **Radio serials**
-        **Science fiction radio programs**
-        **Sports drama (Radio programs)**
-        **Spy radio programs**
-        **Talk shows**
-        **Variety shows (Radio programs)**
-        **War radio programs**
-        **Westerns (Radio programs)**
- RT   **Radio scripts**

Radio—Receivers and reception 621.384
- UF   Radio reception
-        Radios
- BT   **Radio—Equipment and supplies**

Radio reception
  USE **Radio—Receivers and reception**
Radio—Repairing   621.384
  UF Radio repairs
       Radio servicing
Radio repairs
  USE **Radio—Repairing**
Radio script writing
  USE **Radio authorship**
Radio scripts   791.44; 808.88
  May be used for individual works, collections, or materials about radio scripts.
  NT **Radio addresses, debates, etc.**
  RT **Radio authorship**
       Radio plays
       Radio programs
Radio serials   791.44
  May be used for individual works, collections, or materials about radio serials.
  BT **Radio programs**
  RT **Soap operas**
Radio servicing
  USE **Radio—Repairing**
Radio stations (May subdiv. geog.)
       384.54
  SA names of specific radio stations
       [to be added as needed]
  BT **Radio broadcasting**
  NT **Amateur radio stations**
Radio supplies industry (May subdiv.
       geog.) **338.4**
  UF Radio equipment industry
       Radio industry
  BT **Industries**
  RT **Radio—Equipment and supplies**
Radio waves
  USE **Electric waves**
Radio writing
  USE **Radio authorship**
Radioactive fallout (May subdiv. geog.)
       539.7
  UF Dust, Radioactive
       Fallout, Radioactive
  BT **Atomic bomb**
       Hydrogen bomb
       Radioactive pollution
Radioactive isotopes
  USE **Radioisotopes**

Radioactive pollution (May subdiv. geog.)
       363.17; 363.73; 621.48
  UF Environmental radioactivity
       Nuclear pollution
       Pollution, Radioactive
  BT **Pollution**
       Radioactivity
  NT **Radioactive fallout**
  RT **Radioactive waste disposal**
Radioactive substances
  USE **Radioactivity**
Radioactive waste disposal (May subdiv.
       geog.) **363.72; 621.48**
  UF Nuclear waste disposal
  BT **Nuclear engineering**
       Nuclear power plants—Environmental aspects
       Radioactivity
       Refuse and refuse disposal
  RT **Radioactive pollution**
Radioactivity   539.7
  UF Radioactive substances
  BT **Physics**
       Radiation
  NT **Cosmic rays**
       Phosphorescence
       Radioactive pollution
       Radioactive waste disposal
       Radiobiology
       Radiochemistry
       Radiotherapy
       Transmutation (Chemistry)
  RT **Nuclear physics**
       Radium
       Radon
       Uranium
Radiobiology   571.4
  UF Radiation biology
  BT **Biology**
       Biophysics
       Nuclear physics
       Radioactivity
Radiocarbon dating   539.7
  UF Carbon 14 dating
       Dating, Radiocarbon
  BT **Archeology**
Radiochemistry   541
  UF Radio chemistry
  BT **Physical chemistry**
       Radioactivity

Radiography
USE **X-rays**
Radioisotopes   621.48
UF   Radioactive isotopes
BT   **Isotopes**
Nuclear engineering
Radiologists (May subdiv. geog.)   920
BT   **Physicians**
RT   **Radiotherapy**
Radios
USE   **Radio—Receivers and recep-**
tion
Radiotherapy   615.8
UF   Radiation therapy
BT   **Electrotherapeutics**
Physical therapy
Radioactivity
Therapeutics
RT   **Phototherapy**
Radiologists
Radium
Ultraviolet rays
X-rays
Radium   546; 661; 669
BT   **Chemical elements**
Radiation
RT   **Radioactivity**
Radiotherapy
Radium emanation
USE   **Radon**
Radon   363.738; 546
UF   Radium emanation
BT   **Poisonous gases**
RT   **Radioactivity**
Rage
USE   **Anger**
Railroad accidents (May subdiv. geog.)
363.12
UF   Collisions, Railroad
Derailments
Railroads—Accidents
Train wrecks
BT   **Accidents**
Disasters
Railroad construction
USE   **Railroad engineering**
Railroad engineering (May subdiv. geog.)
625.1
UF   Railroad construction
BT   **Civil engineering**
Engineering

Railroads
Railroad fares
USE   **Railroads—Rates**
Railroad mergers
USE   **Railroads—Mergers**
Railroad rates
USE   **Railroads—Rates**
Railroad workers
USE   **Railroads—Employees**
Railroads (May subdiv. geog.)   385;
625.1
UF   Railways
Trains
SA   names of individual railroads [to
be added as needed]
BT   **Transportation**
NT   **Cable railroads**
Electric railroads
Express service
Freight
Locomotives
Monorail railroads
Railroad engineering
Street railroads
Subways
Railroads—Accidents
USE   **Railroad accidents**
Railroads and state
USE   **Railroads—Government policy**
Railroads, Cable
USE   **Cable railroads**
Railroads—Consolidation
USE   **Railroads—Mergers**
Railroads—Employees (May subdiv.
geog.)   331.7
UF   Railroad workers
BT   **Employees**
Railroads—Fares
USE   **Railroads—Rates**
Railroads—Finance   385
BT   **Finance**
NT   **Railroads—Rates**
Railroads—Government ownership
USE   **Railroads—Government policy**
Railroads—Government policy (May
subdiv. geog.)   354.6; 385
UF   Government ownership of rail-
roads
Government regulation of rail-
roads
Nationalization of railroads

Railroads—Government policy—*Continued*

    Railroads and state
    Railroads—Government owner-
      ship
    Railroads, Nationalization of
    State and railroads
    State ownership of railroads
  BT **Government ownership**
      Industrial policy
  NT **Railroads—Rates**

Railroads—Mergers (May subdiv. geog.)
    338.8
  UF Railroad mergers
      Railroads—Consolidation
  BT **Corporate mergers and acqui-**
      sitions

Railroads—Models 625.1
  UF Model trains
  BT **Models and modelmaking**

Railroads, Nationalization of
  USE **Railroads—Government policy**

Railroads—Rates (May subdiv. geog.)
    385
  UF Railroad fares
      Railroad rates
      Railroads—Fares
  BT **Railroads—Finance**
      Railroads—Government policy
  RT **Freight**

Railroads—Safety appliances
  USE **Railroads—Safety devices**

Railroads—Safety devices 625.10028
  UF Railroads—Safety appliances
  BT **Accidents—Prevention**
      Safety devices
  NT **Railroads—Signaling**

Railroads—Signaling 625.1
  UF Block signal systems
      Interlocking signals
  BT **Railroads—Safety devices**
      Signals and signaling

Railroads, Single rail
  USE **Monorail railroads**

Railroads—Statistics 385
  BT **Statistics**

Railways
  USE **Railroads**

Rain (May subdiv. geog.) **551.57**
  UF Rain and rainfall
      Rainfall

  BT **Precipitation (Meteorology)**
  NT **Acid rain**
      Floods
  RT **Droughts**
      Forest influences
      Storms

Rain and rainfall
  USE **Rain**

Rain forests (May subdiv. geog.)
    577.34; 634.9
    Use for materials on forests of broad-
leaved, mainly evergreen trees found in moist
climates in the tropics, subtropics, and some
parts of the temperate zones. Materials on impenetrable thickets of second-growth vegetation replacing tropical rain forests that have
been disturbed or degraded are entered under
Jungles.
  UF Rainforests
      Tropical rain forests
  BT **Forests and forestry**
  RT **Jungles**

Rain making
  USE **Weather control**

Rainbow 551.56
  BT **Meteorology**
  RT **Refraction**

Rainfall
  USE **Rain**

Rainfall and forests
  USE **Forest influences**

Rainforests
  USE **Rain forests**

Rallies (Protest)
  USE **Demonstrations**

Ranch life (May subdiv. geog.) **307.72;**
    636
    BT **Farm life**
      Frontier and pioneer life
  NT **Cowhands**

Random sampling
  USE **Sampling (Statistics)**

Ranger project
  USE **Project Ranger**

Rank
  USE **Social classes**

Rap music 782.421649
    UF Rap songs
      Rapping (Music)
    BT **African American music**
      Popular music

Rap songs
  USE **Rap music**

Rape (May subdiv. geog.)   362.883;
        364.15
    UF   Assault, Sexual
            Sexual assault
    BT   **Offenses against the person**
            Sex crimes
    NT   **Date rape**
Rapid reading
    USE   **Speed reading**
Rapid transit
    USE   **Local transit**
Rapping (Music)
    USE   **Rap music**
Rare animals (May subdiv. geog.)
        591.68
    SA   names of specific animals, e.g.
            Bison [to be added as need-
            ed]
    BT   **Animals**
    RT   **Endangered species**
            Extinct animals
            Wildlife conservation
Rare books (May subdiv. geog.)   090
    UF   Antiquarian books
            Bibliography—Rare books
            Book rarities
    BT   **Books**
Rare plants (May subdiv. geog.)   581.68
    BT   **Plants**
    RT   **Endangered species**
            Plant conservation
Rates
    USE   types of services, utilities, trans-
            portation systems, etc., with
            the subdivision *Rates,* e.g.
            Railroads—Rates [to be add-
            ed as needed]
Rating
    USE   **Performance standards**
            and subjects and classes of per-
            sons with the subdivision *Rat-
            ing,* e.g. **Bonds—Rating;**
            Employees—Rating; etc. [to
            be added as needed]
Ratio and proportion   513.2
    BT   **Arithmetic**
            Geometry
Rationalism   149; 211
    BT   **Philosophy**
            Religion
            Secularism

Theory of knowledge
    NT   **Empiricism**
            Enlightenment
            Intuition
            Positivism
            Reason
            Skepticism
    RT   **Agnosticism**
            Atheism
            Belief and doubt
            Deism
            Free thought
            Realism
Rattlesnakes   597.96
    BT   **Poisonous animals**
            Snakes
Raw materials (May subdiv. geog.)
        333.7
    Use for works on unprocessed minerals and
    unprocessed animal and vegetable products.
    Comprehensive works on the basic processed
    materials used in engineering and industry are
    entered under **Materials.**
    BT   **Commercial products**
    NT   **Farm produce**
            Forest products
            Mines and mineral resources
Rayon   677
    BT   **Synthetic fabrics**
Rays, Ultra-violet
    USE   **Ultraviolet rays**
Re-enlistment
    USE   **Recruiting and enlistment**
Reaction (Political science)
    USE   **Conservatism**
Reactions, Chemical
    USE   **Chemical reactions**
Reactors (Nuclear physics)
    USE   **Nuclear reactors**
Reader services (Libraries)
    USE   **Library services**
Readers
    USE   **Reading materials**
Readers and libraries
    USE   **Library services**
Readers' theater   792
    Use for materials on the dramatic reading
    of plays before an audience.
    BT   **Theater**
Readiness for mathematics
    USE   **Mathematical readiness**
Readiness for reading
    USE   **Reading readiness**

Readiness for school   372.21

  UF   School readiness
  BT   **Elementary education**
       Preschool education

Reading   372.4; 418

  Use for materials on methods of teaching
  reading and for general materials on the art of
  reading. Materials on teaching slow readers
  are entered under **Reading—Remedial teaching.** Materials on the cultural or informational
  aspects of reading and general discussions of
  books are entered under **Books and reading.**

  UF   Children's reading
       Reading—Study and teaching
  BT   **Language arts**
  NT   **Books and reading**
       Reading comprehension
       Reading disability
       Reading—Phonetic method
       Reading readiness
       Speed reading
       Word recognition
       Word skills

Reading clinics
  USE   **Reading—Remedial teaching**

Reading comprehension   372.48

  BT   **Psychology of learning**
       Reading
       Verbal learning

Reading disability   371.91

  SA   types of reading disabilities, e.g.
       Dyslexia [to be added as
       needed]
  BT   **Learning disabilities**
       Reading
  NT   **Dyslexia**

Reading interests
  USE   **Books and reading**

Reading interests of children
  USE   **Children—Books and reading**

Reading interests of teenagers
  USE   **Teenagers—Books and reading**

Reading interests of young adults
  USE   **Teenagers—Books and reading**

Reading materials   372.41; 418

  Use for materials in English intended to be
  used in teaching reading or language skills.
  Such materials in other languages are entered
  under the language with the subdivision *Reading materials.*

  UF   English language—Reading ma-
       terials
       Readers

  SA   names of languages other than
       English with the subdivision
       Reading materials, e.g.
       **French language—Reading
       materials** [to be added as
       needed]
  BT   **Children's literature**
  NT   **Basal readers**
       Big books
       Easy reading materials
       Hornbooks
       Recitations
  RT   **Books and reading**

Reading—Patterning
  USE   **Language arts—Patterning**

Reading—Phonetic method   372.46

  UF   Letter-sound association
       Phonics
  BT   **English language—Pronuncia-
       tion**
       Reading
  RT   **Phonetics**

Reading readiness   372.41

  UF   Readiness for reading
  BT   **Reading**

Reading—Remedial teaching   372.43

  UF   Reading clinics
       Remedial reading

Reading—Study and teaching
  USE   **Reading**

Readings and recitations
  USE   **Recitations**

Readings (Anthologies)
  USE   **Anthologies**

Ready reckoners
  USE   **Mathematics—Tables**

Real estate (May subdiv. geog.)   333.3

  Use for materials on land and buildings
  considered as property. Materials on the buying and selling of real property are entered
  under **Real estate business.** General materials
  on land apart from the aspect of ownership
  are entered under **Land use.**

  UF   Real property
       Realty
  BT   **Land use**
       Property
  NT   **Farms**
       Landlord and tenant
       Real estate business
       Real estate investment
  RT   **Land tenure**

Real estate business (May subdiv. geog.)
333.33; 346.04

Use for materials limited to the buying and selling of real property. General materials on land and buildings considered as property are entered under **Real estate.**
- BT **Business**
  Real estate
- NT **Houses—Buying and selling**
  Timesharing (Real estate)

Real estate investment (May subdiv. geog.) **332.63**
- UF Investment in real estate
  Real property investment
- BT **Investments**
  Real estate
  Speculation

Real estate investment—Taxation 343.05
- BT **Taxation**

Real estate timesharing
- USE **Timesharing (Real estate)**

Real property
- USE **Real estate**

Real property investment
- USE **Real estate investment**

Real property tax—Assessment
- USE **Tax assessment**

Realism 149
- BT **Philosophy**
- NT **Pragmatism**
- RT **Idealism**
  Materialism
  Positivism
  Rationalism

Realism in art 709.03
- UF Naturalism in art
- BT **Art**

Realism in literature 809
- UF Naturalism in literature
- BT **Literature**

Reality 111
- BT **Philosophy**
  Truth
- RT **Pragmatism**
  Theory of knowledge

Realty
- USE **Real estate**

Reapers
- USE **Harvesting machinery**

Reapportionment (Election law)
- USE **Apportionment (Election law)**

Reason 128; 160
- BT **Intellect**
  Rationalism
- NT **Reasoning**

Reasoning 153.4; 160
- BT **Psychology**
  Reason
  Thought and thinking
- NT **Critical thinking**
- RT **Intellect**
  Logic

Rebellions
- USE **Insurgency**
  Revolutions

Rebels (Social psychology)
- USE **Alienation (Social psychology)**

Rebirth
- USE **Reincarnation**

Rebuses 793.73
- BT **Literary recreations**
  Puzzles
  Riddles

Recall of products
- USE **Product recall**

Recall (Political science) (May subdiv. geog.) **324.6**
- BT **Impeachments**
  Representative government and representation

Recessions (May subdiv. geog.) **338.5**
- UF Business recessions
  Economic recessions
- SA names of countries, states, cities, etc., with the subdivision *Economic conditions* [to be added as needed]
- BT **Business cycles**

Recipes
- USE **Cooking**

Reciprocity
- USE **Commercial policy**

Recitations 808.85

Use for collections of material written or selected for oral presentation and for materials about recitation.
- UF Declamations
  Narrations
  Oral interpretation
  Readings and recitations
- BT **Reading materials**
  School assembly programs

Recitations—*Continued*
- NT **Choral speaking**
  Monologues
  Monologues with music
- Recitations with music
  - USE **Monologues with music**
- **Reclamation of land** (May subdiv. geog.)
  627; 631.6
  Use for general materials on reclamation, including drainage and irrigation.
  - UF Clearing of land
    Land, Reclamation of
  - BT **Agriculture**
    Civil engineering
    Hydraulic engineering
    Land use
  - NT **Drainage**
  - RT **Irrigation**
- Recluses
  - USE **Hermits**
- **Recombinant DNA   572.8**
  - BT **DNA**
    Genetic engineering
    Genetic recombination
- Recombination, Genetic
  - USE **Genetic recombination**
- Recommendations for positions
  - USE **Applications for positions**
- Reconciliation, Sacrament of
  - USE **Penance**
- Reconnaissance, Aerial
  - USE **Aerial reconnaissance**
- **Reconstruction (1865-1876)   973.8**
  - UF Carpetbag rule
    United States—History—1861-1865, Civil War—Reconstruction
  - BT **United States—History—1865-1898**
  - RT **Ku Klux Klan**
- **Reconstruction (1914-1939)   940.3**
  - UF World War, 1914-1918—Reconstruction
  - RT **Foreign aid**
    International cooperation
    World War, 1914-1918—Economic aspects
- **Reconstruction (1939-1951)** (May subdiv. geog. except U.S.)   **940.53**
  - UF Marshall Plan
    World War, 1939-1945—Reconstruction

- NT **World War, 1939-1945—Civilian relief**
  World War, 1939-1945—Reparations
- RT **Foreign aid**
  International cooperation
  World War, 1939-1945—Economic aspects
- Reconstructive surgery
  - USE **Plastic surgery**
- Recorded books
  - USE **Audiobooks**
- Recording, Laser
  - USE **Laser recording**
- Recordings, Sound
  - USE **Sound recordings**
- Records of achievement
  - USE **World records**
- Records of births, etc.
  - USE **Registers of births, etc.**
    Vital statistics
- Records, Phonograph
  - USE **Sound recordings**
- Records—Preservation
  - USE **Archives**
- Records, Sports
  - USE **Sports records**
- Records, World
  - USE **World records**
- Recovered memories
  - USE **Recovered memory**
- **Recovered memory   616.85**
  - UF Delayed memory
    Recovered memories
    Repressed memory
  - BT **Memory**
  - RT **False memory syndrome**
- **Recovering addicts   362.29; 616.86**
  - BT **Drug addicts**
  - RT **Recovering alcoholics**
- **Recovering alcoholics   362.292; 616.86**
  - BT **Alcoholics**
  - RT **Recovering addicts**
- Recovery of space vehicles
  - USE **Space vehicles—Recovery**
- **Recreation** (May subdiv. geog.)   **790**
  - UF Pastimes
    Relaxation

Recreation—*Continued*
  SA classes of persons with the sub-
      division *Recreation*, e.g. **El-
      derly—Recreation** [to be
      added as needed]
  NT **Camps**
      Community centers
      Elderly—Recreation
      Games
      Hobbies
      Outdoor recreation
      Play
      Playgrounds
      Popular culture
      Resorts
      Sports
      Vacations
  RT **Amusements**
      Leisure
      Sports facilities
Recreation centers
  USE **Community centers**
       Physical fitness centers
Recreational vehicles   629.226
  UF RVs
  SA types of recreational vehicles,
      e.g. **Travel trailers and
      campers** [to be added as
      needed]
  BT **Outdoor recreation**
      Vehicles
  NT **Travel trailers and campers**
Recreations, Literary
  USE **Literary recreations**
Recreations, Mathematical
  USE **Mathematical recreations**
Recreations, Scientific
  USE **Scientific recreations**
Recruiting
  USE **Recruiting and enlistment**
       Recruiting of employees
       and types of employees and
       professions with the subdivi-
       sion *Recruiting*, e.g. **Librari-
       ans—Recruiting**; and names
       of armed forces and of armies
       and navies with the subdivi-
       sion *Recruiting, enlistment,
       etc.* [to be added as needed]
Recruiting and enlistment   355.2
  UF Armed forces—Recruiting, enlist-
      ment, etc.

  Enlistment
  Re-enlistment
  Recruiting
  Recruiting, enlistment, etc.
  SA names of armed forces and of
      armies and navies with the
      subdivision *Recruiting, enlist-
      ment, etc.,* e.g. **United
      States—Armed Forces—Re-
      cruiting, enlistment, etc.;
      United States. Army—Re-
      cruiting, enlistment, etc.;** etc.
      [to be added as needed]
  BT **Armed forces**
      Military personnel
  NT **Draft**
      **United States—Armed
      Forces—Recruiting, enlist-
      ment, etc.**
      **United States. Army—Recruit-
      ing, enlistment, etc.**
      **United States. Navy—Recruit-
      ing, enlistment, etc.**
      Voluntary military service
Recruiting, enlistment, etc.
  USE **Recruiting and enlistment**
       and names of armed forces and
       of armies and navies with the
       subdivision *Recruiting, enlist-
       ment, etc.,* e.g. **United
       States—Armed Forces—Re-
       cruiting, enlistment, etc.;
       United States. Army—Re-
       cruiting, enlistment, etc.;** etc.
       [to be added as needed]
Recruiting of employees   658.3
  UF Recruiting
  SA types of employees and profes-
      sions with the subdivision *Re-
      cruiting,* e.g. **Librarians—Re-
      cruiting** [to be added as
      needed]
  BT **Personnel management**
  NT **Employment agencies**
      Librarians—Recruiting
Rectors
  USE **Clergy**
Recurrent education
  USE **Continuing education**

Recycling (May subdiv. geog.)   **628.4**
   UF   Conversion of waste products
         Recycling (Waste, etc.)
   SA   subjects with the subdivision
         Recycling, e.g. **Aluminum—**
         Recycling [to be added as
         needed]
   BT   **Energy conservation**
         Pollution control industry
         Salvage
   NT   **Aluminum—Recycling**
   RT   **Refuse and refuse disposal**
         Waste products
Recycling (Waste, etc.)
   USE   **Recycling**
Red   **535.6; 752**
   BT   **Color**
Redemption
   USE   **Salvation**
Reducing
   USE   **Weight loss**
Reenactment of historical events
   USE   **Historical reenactments**
Reference books (May subdiv. geog.)
      028.7

    Use for materials about reference books.
Reference books themselves are entered under
Encyclopedias and dictionaries; or under the
appropriate subjects with the subdivisions *Dic-*
tionaries; Bibliography; etc., as needed.
   BT   **Bibliography**
         Books
         Books and reading
   NT   **Encyclopedias and dictionaries**
Reference books—Reviews   **028.1**
Reference services (Libraries) (May
      subdiv. geog.)   **025.5**

    Use for materials on activities designed to
make information available to library users,
including direct personal assistance.
   UF   Library reference services
         Online reference services
         Reference work (Libraries)
   BT   **Information services**
         Library services
Reference work (Libraries)
   USE   **Reference services (Libraries)**
Referendum (May subdiv. geog.)   **328.2**
   UF   Direct legislation
         Initiative and referendum
         Legislation, Direct
   BT   **Constitutional law**
         Democracy

         Elections
Refinishing furniture
   USE   **Furniture finishing**
Reflexology   **615.8**
   BT   **Alternative medicine**
Reforestation (May subdiv. geog.)
        333.75; 634.9
   BT   **Forests and forestry**
   RT   **Tree planting**
Reform, Agrarian
   USE   **Land reform**
Reform of criminals
   USE   **Corrections**
         Probation
         Reformatories
Reform of health care delivery
   USE   **Health care reform**
Reform of medical care delivery
   USE   **Health care reform**
Reform schools
   USE   **Reformatories**
Reform, Social
   USE   **Social problems**
Reformation (May subdiv. geog.)   **270.6**
   UF   Protestant Reformation
   SA   names of religious sects, e.g.
         Huguenots [to be added as
         needed]
   BT   **Christianity**
         Church history—1500-, Mod-
         ern period
   NT   **Calvinism**
         Huguenots
   RT   **Counter-Reformation**
         Protestantism
Reformatories (May subdiv. geog.)   **365**
   UF   Penal institutions
         Reform of criminals
         Reform schools
   BT   **Children—Institutional care**
         Correctional institutions
         Prisons
         Punishment
   NT   **Probation**
   RT   **Juvenile delinquency**
Reformers (May subdiv. geog.)   **920**

    Use for materials about political, social, or
religious reformers.
   NT   **Abolitionists**
         Suffragists

Refraction   535
    UF   Dioptrics
    BT   **Light**
          Optics
    RT   **Rainbow**
Refrigeration   621.5
    UF   Cooling appliances
          Freezing
          Refrigeration and refrigerating
            machinery
          Refrigerators
    BT   **Frost**
    RT   **Air conditioning**
          Cold storage
          Low temperatures
Refrigeration and refrigerating machinery
    USE **Refrigeration**
Refrigerators
    USE **Refrigeration**
Refugees (May subdiv. geog.)   305.9;
    341.4; 362.87
    UF   Displaced persons
          Exiles
    SA   refugees of particular countries,
          geographic regions, or ethnic
          groups, e.g. **Vietnamese refu-**
          gees; Arab refugees; etc.,
          and names of wars with the
          subdivision *Refugees,* e.g.
          World War, 1939-1945—
          Refugees [to be added as
          needed]
    BT   **Aliens**
          Homeless persons
          Immigration and emigration
    NT   **Arab refugees**
          Political refugees
          Vietnamese refugees
    RT   **Sanctuary movement**
Refugees, Arab
    USE **Arab refugees**
Refugees, Political
    USE **Political refugees**
Refuse and refuse disposal (May subdiv.
    geog.)   363.72; 628.4
    UF   Disposal of refuse
          Garbage
          Garbage disposal
          Incineration
          Littering
          Solid waste disposal

          Waste disposal
    SA   types of refuse, e.g. **Industrial**
          waste; types of waste dispos-
          al, e.g. **Radioactive waste**
          disposal; Sewage disposal;
          etc.; and types of industries,
          plants, and facilities with the
          subdivision *Waste disposal,*
          e.g. **Chemical industry—**
          Waste disposal [to be added
          as needed]
    BT   **Municipal engineering**
          Pollution control industry
          Public health
          Sanitary engineering
          Sanitation
    NT   **Chemical industry—Waste dis-**
          posal
          Hazardous wastes
          Industrial waste
          Medical wastes
          Radioactive waste disposal
          Sewage disposal
    RT   **Pollution**
          Recycling
          Salvage
          Street cleaning
          Waste products
Regattas
    USE **Boat racing**
Regency novels   808.3
    May be used for individual works, collec-
    tions, or materials about historical novels set
    during or around the period when the future
    George IV of England acted as Regent for
    George III (1811-1820).
    BT   **Historical fiction**
Regeneration (Christianity)   234; 248.2
    UF   Born again Christianity
          New birth (Theology)
          Regeneration (Theology)
    BT   **Christianity—Doctrines**
          Salvation
    RT   **Conversion**
Regeneration (Theology)
    USE **Regeneration (Christianity)**
Regimental histories
    USE names of wars with the subdivi-
          sion *Regimental histories,* e.g.
          World War, 1939-1945—
          Regimental histories [to be
          added as needed]

Regional development
USE **Community development**
Regional planning
Regional history
USE **Local history**
Regional libraries (May subdiv. geog.)
027.4
Use for materials on public libraries serving several communities, counties, or other regions.
UF County libraries
District libraries
Libraries, Regional
BT **Public libraries**
Regional planning (May subdiv. geog.)
307.1; 711
UF County planning
Metropolitan planning
Regional development
State planning
BT **Land use**
Planning
NT **Coastal zone management**
Rural development
RT **City planning**
Landscape protection
Regionalism (May subdiv. geog.)   **320.4;**
330.9
Use for materials on the political or economic power or interests of geographic areas within nations or beyond national boundaries.
UF Localism
Provincialism
Sectionalism
BT **Geography**
Politics
RT **Nationalism**
Regionalism—United States   917.3; 973
UF Sectionalism (United States)
Registers
USE **Registers of births, etc.**
and subjects, ethnic groups, classes of persons, names of countries, cities, etc., and names of families and of corporate bodies, such as colleges and universities, with the subdivision *Registers,* for lists of persons or organizations without addresses or other identifying data, e.g.
United States—Registers;

United States Military Academy—Registers; etc. [to be added as needed]
Registers of births, etc. (May subdiv. geog.)   **929**
UF Birth records
Births, Registers of
Burial statistics
Deaths, Registers of
Marriage registers
Parish registers
Records of births, etc.
Registers
Vital records
BT **Genealogy**
NT **Wills**
RT **Vital statistics**
Registration of voters
USE **Voter registration**
Regulatory agencies
USE **Administrative agencies**
Rehabilitation
USE classes of persons with the subdivision *Rehabilitation,* e.g.
Drug addicts—Rehabilitation; Physically handicapped—Rehabilitation; etc.
[to be added as needed]
Rehabilitation peer counseling
USE **Peer counseling**
Reign of Terror
USE **France—History—1789-1799, Revolution**
Reincarnation   129
UF Rebirth
BT **Theosophy**
RT **Soul**
Reindeer (May subdiv. geog.)   **599.65; 636.2**
BT **Deer**
Domestic animals
Mammals
Reinforced concrete   691
BT **Building materials**
Concrete
Relations among ethnic groups
USE **Ethnic relations**

Relations with Congress
    USE   names of presidents with the
              subdivision *Relations with*
              Congress [to be added as
              needed]
Relationships, Man-woman
    USE **Man-woman relationship**
Relative humidity
    USE **Humidity**
Relativity (Physics)   **530.11**
    BT   **Physics**
    RT   **Gravitation**
          Quantum theory
          Space and time
Relaxation
    USE **Recreation**
          Rest
Reliability (Engineering)   **620**
    UF   Reliability of equipment
          Systems reliability
    BT   **Engineering**
          Probabilities
          Systems engineering
    NT   **Quality control**
          Structural failures
          Testing
Reliability of equipment
    USE **Reliability (Engineering)**
Relief, Public
    USE **Public welfare**
Religion   **200**
    SA   names of peoples, ethnic groups,
          countries, states, etc., and in-
          dividual persons with the sub-
          division *Religion,* e.g. **Native**
          Americans—Religion;
          African Americans—Reli-
          gion; United States—Reli-
          gion; Shakespeare, William,
          1564-1616—Religion; etc.; re-
          ligious subjects subdivided by
          religion or sect, e.g. **Laity—**
          Catholic Church; and other
          subjects with the subdivision
          Religious aspects, e.g. **Ethnic**
          relations—Religious aspects;
          Love—Religious aspects; etc.,
          which may be further subdi-
          vided by religion or sect [to
          be added as needed]

    NT   **African Americans—Religion**
          Agnosticism
          Ancestor worship
          Art and religion
          Atheism
          Blacks—Religion
          Communism and religion
          Deism
          Faith
          Heresy
          Liturgies
          Monotheism
          Moon worship
          Native Americans—Religion
          Ohio—Religion
          Philosophy and religion
          Psychology of religion
          Rationalism
          Religion and politics
          Religion and science
          Religion and sociology
          Religion in literature
          Religious awakening
          Religious education
          Religious fundamentalism
          Religious institutions
          Religious life
          Santeria
          Sun worship
          Supernatural
          Theism
          United States—Religion
          Visions
          War—Religious aspects
          Worship
    RT   **God**
          Mythology
          Religions
          Theology
Religion and art
    USE **Art and religion**
Religion and communism
    USE **Communism and religion**
Religion and education
    USE **Church and education**
Religion and literature
    USE **Religion in literature**
          Religious literature
Religion and medicine
    USE **Medicine—Religious aspects**

Religion and philosophy
   USE **Philosophy and religion**

Religion and politics (May subdiv. geog.)
     201; 261.7; 322
   UF Political science—Religious aspects
       Politics and religion
       Politics—Religious aspects
       Religion—Political aspects
       Religions—Political aspects
   BT **Politics**
       Religion
   NT **Christianity and politics**

Religion and psychology
   USE **Psychology of religion**

Religion and science (May subdiv. geog.)
     215
   UF Science and religion
       Science—Religious aspects
   BT **Religion**
       Science
   NT **Bible and science**
   RT **Creationism**
       Evolution
       Natural theology

Religion and social problems
   USE **Church and social problems**

Religion and society
   USE **Religion and sociology**

Religion and sociology (May subdiv. geog.) **306.6**

Use for materials on religious sociology in general. Materials on the sociology of Christian denominations and on social theory from a Christian point of view are entered under **Christian sociology.** Materials on the practical treatment of social problems from the point of view of the church are entered under **Church and social problems.**

   UF Religion and society
       Religion—Social aspects
       Religious sociology
       Society and religion
       Society—Religious aspects
       Sociology and religion
       Sociology of religion
   SA sociology associated with particular religions, e.g. **Christian sociology** [to be added as needed]
   BT **Religion**
       Sociology
   NT **Christian sociology**

Religion and state
   USE **Church and state**

Religion and war
   USE **War—Religious aspects**

Religion—Government policy
   USE **Church and state**

Religion in literature **809**
   UF Religion and literature
   BT **Literature**
       Religion
   RT **Bible in literature**

Religion in the public schools (May subdiv. geog.) **379.2**

Use for materials on the teaching of religion in the public schools or on the religious freedom of students and school employees. Materials on the inclusion of prayers or a period for silent prayer or meditation in the daily schedule of public schools are entered under **Prayer in the public schools.**

   UF Bible in the schools
       Fundamentalism and education
       Public schools and religion
   BT **Church and education**
       Church and state
       Public schools
       Religious education
   NT **Prayer in the public schools**

Religion—Philosophy **210**

Use for materials on the nature, origin, or validity of religion from a philosophical point of view. Materials on the reciprocal relationship and influence between philosophy and religion are entered under **Philosophy and religion.**

   UF Philosophy of religion
   RT **Philosophy and religion**

Religion—Political aspects
   USE **Religion and politics**

Religion—Psychological aspects
   USE **Psychology of religion**

Religion—Social aspects
   USE **Religion and sociology**

Religion—Study and teaching
   USE **Theology—Study and teaching**

Religions **200**

Use for materials on the major world religions. Materials on independent religious groups whose teachings or practices fall within the normative bounds of the major world religions are entered under **Sects.** Materials on groups or movements whose beliefs or practices differ significantly from the traditional religions, often focused upon a charismatic leader, are entered under **Cults.**

Religions—*Continued*
   UF   Comparative religion
   SA   names of religions and of sects
          within the major world reli-
          gions [to be added as needed]
   BT   **Civilization**
   NT   **Bahai Faith**
         Brahmanism
         Buddhism
         Christianity
         Christianity and other religions
         Confucianism
         Cults
         Druids and Druidism
         Gnosticism
         Hinduism
         Islam
         Judaism
         Occultism
         Paganism
         Sects
         Shinto
         Taoism
         Theosophy
         Voodooism
   RT   **Gods and goddesses**
         Religion
Religions—Biography
   USE   **Religious biography**
Religions—Political aspects
   USE   **Religion and politics**
Religious and ecclesiastical institutions
   USE   **Religious institutions**
Religious art (May subdiv. geog.)   **203;**
   704.9
   UF   Religious art and symbolism
         Religious painting
         Religious sculpture
         Sacred art
   BT   **Art**
   NT   **Christian art**
   RT   **Art and religion**
Religious art and symbolism
   USE   **Religious art**
Religious aspects
   USE   subjects with the subdivision *Re-*
         ligious aspects, e.g. **Ethnic**
         relations—Religious aspects;
         Love—Religious aspects; etc.,
         which may be further subdi-
         vided by the names of reli-

gions or sects [to be added as
    needed]
Religious awakening (May subdiv. geog.)
   204; 269
   Use for materials on a renewal of interest in
religion.
   UF   Awakening, Religious
         Revival (Religion)
   BT   **Religion**
Religious belief
   USE   **Faith**
Religious biography   **200.92; 920**
   UF   Religions—Biography
   SA   biography of particular religions,
         e.g. **Christian biography** [to
         be added as needed]
   BT   **Biography**
   NT   **Christian biography**
         Prophets
         Saints
Religious ceremonies
   USE   **Rites and ceremonies**
Religious cults
   USE   **Cults**
Religious denominations
   USE   **Sects**
Religious drama   **792.1; 808.82**
   May be used for collections or materials
about religious drama, not for individual
works.
   BT   **Drama**
         Religious literature
   NT   **Bible plays**
         Easter—Drama
         Jesus Christ—Drama
         Morality plays
         Mysteries and miracle plays
         Passion plays
Religious education (May subdiv. geog.)
   207
   Use for materials on the instruction of religion in schools and private life. Materials limited to the instruction of Christian religion in
schools and private life are entered under
Christian education. Materials on the relation
of the church to education and on the history
of the part that the church has taken in secular
education are entered under **Church and education.** Materials on church supported and
controlled elementary and secondary schools
are entered under **Church schools.**
   UF   Theological education
   BT   **Education**
         Religion

Religious education—*Continued*
  NT Christian education
      Religion in the public schools
      Sunday schools
  RT Moral education
      Theology—Study and teaching
Religious festivals
  USE Religious holidays
Religious fiction   808.3; 808.83
    Use for individual works, collections, or
    materials about fiction that promotes religious
    teachings or exemplifies a religious way of
    life.
  SA fiction associated with particular
        religions, e.g. Christian fic-
        tion [to be added as needed]
  BT Fiction
  NT Christian fiction
      Jewish religious fiction
Religious freedom
  USE Freedom of religion
Religious fundamentalism (May subdiv.
    geog.)   200
    Use for religious groups opposed to moder-
    nity and secularism and seeking a revival of
    orthodox or conservative beliefs and practices.
  UF Fundamentalism
      Fundamentalist movements
  SA fundamentalism of various reli-
        gions, e.g. Islamic fundamen-
        talism [to be added as need-
        ed]
  BT Religion
  NT Christian fundamentalism
      Islamic fundamentalism
Religious history
  USE Church history
Religious holidays (May subdiv. geog.)
    263; 394.265
    Use for materials on religious holidays in
    general. Materials on secular holidays are en-
    tered under Holidays. Materials on secular
    festivals other than holidays are entered under
    Festivals.
  UF Church festivals
      Ecclesiastical fasts and feasts
      Fasts and feasts
      Feast days
      Holy days
      Religious festivals
  SA holidays of particular religions,
        e.g. Jewish holidays; and
        names of specific religious

holidays and observances, e.g.
      Christmas; Lent; etc. [to be
      added as needed]
  BT Holidays
      Rites and ceremonies
  NT Christian holidays
      Church year
      Jewish holidays
      Thanksgiving Day
  RT Fasting
      Festivals
Religious institutions (May subdiv. geog.)
    206; 260
  UF Churches
      Congregations
      Ecclesiastical institutions
      Institutions, Ecclesiastical
      Institutions, Religious
      Religious and ecclesiastical insti-
        tutions
      Religious organizations
  BT Associations
      Religion
  NT Synagogues
Religious liberty
  USE Freedom of religion
Religious life   204; 248.4
    Use for materials that describe or promote
    personal or community religious and devotion-
    al life.
  SA groups and classes of persons
        with the subdivision *Religious
        life* [to be added as needed]
  BT Religion
  NT Asceticism
      Celibacy
      Christian life
      Family—Religious life
      Spiritual life
      Teenagers—Religious life
      Women—Religious life
      Youth—Religious life
  RT Monasticism and religious or-
        ders
Religious life (Christian)
  USE Christian life
Religious literature   800
  UF Religion and literature
  SA literatures of particular religions
        or denominations, e.g. Catho-
        lic literature [to be added as
        needed]

Religious literature—*Continued*
  BT Literature
  NT Christian literature
      Devotional literature
      Islamic literature
      Jewish literature
      Religious drama
      Religious poetry
      Sacred books
  RT Bible as literature
Religious music
  USE Church music
Religious orders
  USE Monasticism and religious or-
       ders
Religious orders for men
  USE Monasticism and religious or-
       ders for men
Religious orders for women
  USE Monasticism and religious or-
       ders for women
Religious organizations
  USE Religious institutions
Religious painting
  USE Religious art
Religious persecution
  USE Persecution
Religious poetry   808.1; 808.81
    May be used for collections or materials
    about religious poetry, not for individual
    works.
  BT Poetry
      Religious literature
  RT Hymns
Religious psychology
  USE Pastoral psychology
       Psychology of religion
Religious sculpture
  USE Religious art
Religious sociology
  USE Religion and sociology
Religious summer schools (May subdiv.
    geog.)   207; 268
  UF Bible classes
      Vacation church schools
      Vacation schools, Religious
  BT Schools
      Summer schools
Religious tolerance (May subdiv. geog.)
    261.7
    Use for general materials on religous toler-
    ance. Materials on a particular religion's or

denomination's position on religious tolerance
are entered under this heading subdivided by
the name of the religion or denomination.
  BT Toleration
Relocation
  USE ethnic groups and classes of per-
       sons with the subdivision
       Relocation, e.g. Native Amer-
       icans—Relocation; which
       may be further subdivided
       geographically [to be added
       as needed]
Remarriage (May subdiv. geog.)   306.84
  BT Marriage
Remedial reading
  USE Reading—Remedial teaching
Remedial teaching
  USE school subjects with the subdivi-
       sion *Remedial teaching*, e.g.
       Reading—Remedial teaching
       [to be added as needed]
Remodeling
  USE types of buildings and parts of
       buildings with the subdivision
       Remodeling, e.g. Houses—Re-
       modeling; Kitchens—Remod-
       eling; etc. [to be added as
       needed]
Remodeling (Architecture)
  USE Houses—Remodeling
Remodeling of houses
  USE Houses—Remodeling
Remodeling of kitchens
  USE Kitchens—Remodeling
Remote sensing (May subdiv. geog.)
    621.36
  UF Sensing, Remote
      Terrain sensing, Remote
  BT Aerial photography
  NT Aerial reconnaissance
      Electronic surveillance
      Radar
  RT Space optics
Removal of Indians
  USE Native Americans—Relocation
Renaissance (May subdiv. geog.)   940.2
    Use for materials on cultural and intellectu-
    al developments in the fifteenth and sixteenth
    centuries not limited to a single country or re-
    gion.
  BT Civilization
  RT Humanism

Renaissance architecture
USE **Architecture—15th and 16th centuries**
Renaissance art
USE **Art—15th and 16th centuries**
Renaissance decoration and ornament
USE **Decoration and ornament—15th and 16th centuries**
Renaissance English literature
USE **English literature—16th and 17th centuries**
Renaissance painting
USE **Painting—15th and 16th centuries**
Rendezvous in space
USE **Orbital rendezvous (Space flight)**
Renewable energy resources (May subdiv. geog.) **333.79**
UF Alternate energy resources
Alternative energy resources
SA types of renewable resources [to be added as needed]
BT **Energy resources**
NT **Geothermal resources**
Solar energy
Water power
Wind power
Renown
USE **Fame**
Rental services
USE **Lease and rental services**
Reorganization of administrative agencies
USE **Administrative agencies—Reorganization**
Repairing **620**
UF Fixing
Maintenance and repair
Mending
Repairs
SA types of things that require maintenance with the subdivision *Maintenance and repair,* e.g. **Automobiles—Maintenance and repair; Buildings—Maintenance and repair;** etc.; and types of things that require no maintenance with the subdivision *Repairing,* e.g. **Radio—Repairing** [to be added as needed]

Repairs
USE **Repairing**
Reparations
USE names of wars with the subdivision *Reparations,* e.g. **World War, 1939-1945—Reparations** [to be added as needed]
Report writing **808**
UF Reports—Preparation
Research paper writing
Term paper writing
BT **Authorship**
NT **School reports**
Reporters and reporting (May subdiv. geog.) **070.4**
UF Interviewing (Journalism)
Newspaper work
BT **Journalism**
Newspapers
Reports—Preparation
USE **Report writing**
Reports, Teachers'
USE **School reports**
Representation
USE **Representative government and representation**
Representation, Proportional
USE **Proportional representation**
Representative government and representation (May subdiv. geog.) **321.8**
UF Parliamentary government
Representation
Self-government
BT **Constitutional history**
Constitutional law
Political science
NT **Apportionment (Election law)**
Legislative bodies
Proportional representation
Recall (Political science)
RT **Democracy**
Elections
Republics
Suffrage
Representatives, House of (U.S.)
USE **United States. Congress. House**
Repressed memory
USE **Recovered memory**
Reprint editions
USE **Reprints (Publications)**

Reprints (Publications) 016
   UF   Bibliography—Reprint editions
          Reprint editions
   BT   Books
          Editions
Reproduction 573.6; 612.6
   BT   Biology
          Life (Biology)
          Physiology
   NT   Animal reproduction
          Artificial insemination
          Breeding
          Cells
          Fertility
          Fertilization in vitro
          Fetus
          Genetics
          Human artificial insemination
          Infertility
          Menstruation
          Pregnancy
   RT   Embryology
          Reproductive system
          Sex (Biology)
Reproduction processes
   USE   Copying processes
Reproduction—Technological innovations
   USE   Reproductive technology
Reproductive behavior
   USE   Sexual behavior in animals
Reproductive organs
   USE   Reproductive system
Reproductive system 573.6; 611; 612.6
   UF   Generative organs
          Genitalia
          Reproductive organs
          Sex organs
   BT   Anatomy
          Physiology
          Sex (Biology)
   RT   Reproduction
Reproductive technology (May subdiv. geog.) 612.6
   UF   Assisted reproduction
          Reproduction—Technological innovations
   BT   Biotechnology
Reprographic art
   USE   Copy art
Reprography
   USE   Copying processes

Reptiles (May subdiv. geog.) 597.9
   SA   types of reptiles [to be added as needed]
   BT   Animals
   NT   Alligators
          Crocodiles
          Fossil reptiles
          Lizards
          Snakes
          Turtles
Reptiles, Fossil
   USE   Fossil reptiles
Reptiles—Physiology 597.9
   BT   Physiology
Republic of China, 1949-
   USE   Taiwan
Republic of South Africa
   USE   South Africa
Republican Party (U.S.) 324.2734
   BT   Political parties
Republics 321.8
   UF   Commonwealth, The
   BT   Constitutional history
          Constitutional law
          Political science
   NT   Federal government
   RT   Democracy
          Representative government and representation
Rescue of Jews, 1939-1945
   USE   World War, 1939-1945—Jews—Rescue
Rescue operations, Space
   USE   Space rescue operations
Rescue work (May subdiv. geog.) 363.3
   UF   Search and rescue operations
   BT   Civil defense
   NT   First aid
          Lifesaving
          Space rescue operations
   RT   Survival after airplane accidents, shipwrecks, etc.
Research (May subdiv. geog.) 001.4
   UF   Research and development
   SA   subjects with the subdivision *Research* [to be added as needed]
   NT   Agriculture—Research
          Animal experimentation
          Discoveries in science
          Dissertations

Research—*Continued*
>   Industrial research
>   Intelligence service
>   Medicine—Research
>   Military research
>   Oceanography—Research
>   Operations research
>   Parapsychology
>   Surveys
> RT Information services
>   Learning and scholarship

Research and development
>   USE Research

Research paper writing
>   USE Report writing

Reservations
>   USE names of native peoples, tribes, etc., with the subdivision *Reservations,* e.g. Native Americans—Reservations [to be added as needed]

Reservoirs (May subdiv. geog.)   627; 628.1
>   BT Hydraulic structures

Resettlement
>   USE Land settlement

Residences
>   USE Domestic architecture
>   Houses

Residential developments
>   USE Planned communities

Residential security
>   USE Burglary protection

Residential treatment centers
>   USE Group homes

Resignation
>   USE classes of persons and names of individual persons with the subdivision *Resignation,* e.g. Presidents—United States—Resignation [to be added as needed]

Resins
>   USE Gums and resins

Resistance of materials
>   USE Strength of materials

Resistance to government (May subdiv. geog.)   322.4
>   UF Government, Resistance to
>   BT Political ethics
>   Political science

> NT Civil disobedience
>   Hunger strikes
>   Passive resistance
> RT Insurgency
>   Revolutions

Resistance welding
>   USE Electric welding

Resorts (May subdiv. geog.)   790
>   BT Recreation
>   NT Health resorts
>   Summer resorts
>   Winter resorts

Resource management
>   USE Conservation of natural resources

Resources, Marine
>   USE Marine resources

Respiration   573.2; 612.2
>   UF Breathing
>   BT Physiology
>   RT Respiratory system

Respiration, Artificial
>   USE Artificial respiration

Respiratory organs
>   USE Respiratory system

Respiratory system   573.2; 611; 612.2
>   UF Respiratory organs
>   BT Anatomy
>   Physiology
>   NT Lungs
>   RT Respiration

Respite care
>   USE Home care services

Responsibility   170
>   UF Accountability
>   Obligation
>   BT Ethics

Responsibility, Legal
>   USE Liability (Law)

Rest   613.7
>   UF Relaxation
>   BT Health
>   Hygiene
>   NT Sleep
>   RT Fatigue

Restaurants (May subdiv. geog.)   647.95
>   UF Cafes
>   Coffee shops
>   Lunchrooms
>   Restaurants, bars, etc.

Restaurants—*Continued*
- SA types of restaurants [to be added as needed]
- BT **Food service**
- NT **Coffeehouses**
  Fast food restaurants
  Tearooms
- RT **Bars**

Restaurants, bars, etc.
- USE **Bars**
  Restaurants

Restoration of automobiles
- USE **Automobiles—Conservation and restoration**

Restoration of buildings
- USE **Architecture—Conservation and restoration**

Restoration of furniture
- USE **Furniture finishing**
  Furniture—Repairing

Restoration of photographs
- USE **Photographs—Conservation and restoration**

Restoration of works of art
- USE subjects with the subdivision *Conservation and restoration,* e.g. **Painting—Conservation and restoration** [to be added as needed]

Restraint of trade (May subdiv. geog.) **338.6**
- UF Restrictive trade practices
  Trade, Restraint of
- BT **Commerce**
  Commercial law
- RT **Boycotts**
  Corporation law
  Industrial trusts
  Monopolies
  Unfair competition

Restrictive trade practices
- USE **Restraint of trade**

Résumés (Employment) 650.14
- UF Job résumés
- BT **Applications for positions**
  Job hunting

Resurrection
- USE **Future life**

Resurrection of Jesus Christ
- USE **Jesus Christ—Resurrection**

Resuscitation, Heart
- USE **Cardiac resuscitation**

Resuscitation, Pulmonary
- USE **Artificial respiration**

Retail franchises
- USE **Franchises (Retail trade)**

Retail stores
- USE **Stores**

Retail trade (May subdiv. geog.) **381; 658.8**
- UF Merchandising
- BT **Commerce**
- NT **Advertising**
  Chain stores
  Department stores
  Direct selling
  Discount stores
  Drugstores
  Franchises (Retail trade)
  General stores
  Inventory control
  Packaging
  Sales personnel
  Selling
  Shopping centers and malls
  Stores
  Supermarkets

Retarded children
- USE **Mentally handicapped children**

Retention, Grade
- USE **Promotion (School)**

Retired people
- USE **Retirees**

Retired persons
- USE **Retirees**

Retirees (May subdiv. geog.) **155.67; 305.9**
- UF Retired people
  Retired persons
- RT **Elderly**
  Retirement

Retirees—Personal finance 332.024

Retirement (May subdiv. geog.) **305.26; 306.3**
- BT **Leisure**
  Old age
- NT **Retirement income**
- RT **Elderly—Life skills guides**
  Retirees

Retirement communities (May subdiv. geog.) **307.7; 363.5**

  UF Places of retirement

  BT **Elderly—Housing**

  NT **Life care communities**

Retirement income (May subdiv. geog.) **331.25; 353.5**

  BT **Income**

       Retirement

  NT **Annuities**

       Individual retirement accounts

       Old age pensions

       Pensions

Retouching (Photography)

  USE **Photography—Retouching**

Retraining, Occupational

  USE **Occupational retraining**

Retreats 269

    Use for materials on periods of withdrawal from daily routine for the purpose of prayer, meditation, and study.

  BT **Spiritual life**

Retrenchment of organizations

  USE **Downsizing of organizations**

Retribution

  USE **Future life**

       Hell

Retrieval of information

  USE **Information retrieval**

Return migration (May subdiv. geog.) **304.8**

    Use for materials on the return of emigrants to their country of origin.

  BT **Immigration and emigration**

Reunions, Family

  USE **Family reunions**

Revelation 202; 231.7

  BT **God**

       Supernatural

       Theology

Revenue

  USE **Tariff**

       Taxation

Revenue sharing (May subdiv. geog.) **336.1**

    Use for materials on the practice of returning a percentage of federal tax money to state and local governments for locally directed and controlled public service programs.

  UF Federal revenue sharing

       Tax sharing

  BT **Intergovernmental tax relations**

Reviewing (Books)

  USE **Book reviewing**

Reviews

  USE topics and types of books with the subdivision *Reviews,* e.g. **Motion picture—Reviews; Reference books—Reviews;** etc.; and topics, types of literature, ethnic groups, classes of persons, and names of places with the subdivision *Book reviews;* e.g. **Sociology—Book reviews; Children's literature—Book reviews;** etc., for collections of reviews [to be added as needed]

Revival (Religion)

  USE **Evangelistic work**

       Religious awakening

       Revivals

Revivals (May subdiv. geog.) **204; 269**

  UF Revival (Religion)

  BT **Evangelistic work**

Revivals—Music

  USE **Gospel music**

Revolution, American

  USE **United States—History—1775-1783, Revolution**

Revolution, French

  USE **France—History—1789-1799, Revolution**

Revolutions (May subdiv. geog.) **303.6**

  UF Coups d'état

       Rebellions

       Sedition

  SA names of countries with the appropriate subdivision under *History,* e.g. **France—History—1789-1799, Revolution** [to be added as needed]

  BT **Political science**

  NT **France—History—1789-1799, Revolution**

       Hungary—History—1956, Revolution

       Insurgency

       National liberation movements

       Radicalism

       Slave revolts

Revolutions—*Continued*
      Soviet Union—History—1917-
      1921, Revolution
      United States—History—1775-
      1783, Revolution
  RT **Resistance to government**
Revolvers
  USE **Handguns**
Rewards (Prizes, etc.)
  USE **Awards**
Rh factor
  USE **Blood groups**
Rhetoric 808
  UF Composition (Rhetoric)
      English language—Rhetoric
      Persuasion (Rhetoric)
      Speaking
  SA names of languages with the
      subdivision *Composition and*
      exercises, e.g. **English lan-**
      guage—Composition and ex-
      ercises [to be added as need-
      ed]
  BT **Language and languages**
  NT **Criticism**
      Debates and debating
      Figures of speech
      Lectures and lecturing
      Letter writing
      Preaching
      Punctuation
      Satire
  RT **English language—Composition**
      and exercises
      Literary style
Rheumatism 616.7
  BT **Diseases**
  NT **Gout**
Rhyme 808.1
  SA names of languages with the
      subdivision *Rhyme* [to be add-
      ed as needed]
  BT **Poetics**
      Versification
  NT **English language—Rhyme**
      Stories in rhyme
Rhymes
  USE **Limericks**
      Nonsense verses
      Nursery rhymes
      Poetry—Collections

Rhythm 808.1
  BT **Aesthetics**
      Poetics
  NT **Musical meter and rhythm**
      Versification
  RT **Cycles**
Ribonucleic acid
  USE **RNA**
Ribose nucleic acid
  USE **RNA**
Ribozymes
  USE **Catalytic RNA**
Rich (May subdiv. geog.)   **305.5; 920**
  UF Affluent people
      High income people
      Rich people
      Rich persons
      Wealthy people
  BT **Social classes**
  NT **Millionaires**
Rich people
  USE **Rich**
Rich persons
  USE **Rich**
Riches
  USE **Wealth**
Riddles 398.6; 793.735; 808.88
  Use for collections of riddles considered as folklore, as games, or as literary exercises, by one or several authors, and for materials about riddles.
  UF Conundrums
      Enigmas
  BT **Amusements**
      Literary recreations
  NT **Charades**
      Rebuses
  RT **Puzzles**
Ride sharing
  USE **Car pools**
Riding
  USE **Horsemanship**
Rifles 683.4
  UF Carbines
      Guns
  BT **Firearms**
Right and left
  USE **Left and right (Direction)**
      Right and left (Political sci-
      ence)
Right- and left-handedness
  USE **Left- and right-handedness**

Right and left (Political science)   320.5

Use for general materials on political views or attitudes, i.e. conservative, traditional, liberal, radical, etc. Materials on the physical characteristics of favoring one hand or the other are entered under **Left- and right-handedness.** Materials on left and right as indications of location or direction are entered under **Left and right (Direction).**

   UF   Left and right
          Left (Political science)
          Right and left
          Right (Political science)
   BT   **Political parties**
          Political science
   NT   **Radicalism**
   RT   **Conservatism**
          Liberalism

Right of assembly
   USE   **Freedom of assembly**

Right of association
   USE   **Freedom of association**

Right of asylum
   USE   **Asylum**

Right of privacy (May subdiv. geog.)   **323.44**
   UF   Invasion of privacy
          Privacy, Right of
   BT   **Civil rights**
   NT   **Eavesdropping**
          Trade secrets
          Wiretapping

Right of property   323.4
   UF   Private property, Right of
          Property, Right of
          Property rights
   BT   **Civil rights**
          Property

Right (Political science)
   USE   **Conservatism**
          Right and left (Political science)

Right to a fair trial
   USE   **Fair trial**

Right to bear arms
   USE   **Gun control**

Right to choose movement
   USE   **Pro-choice movement**

Right to die (May subdiv. geog.)   **179.7**
   BT   **Death**
          Medical ethics
          Medicine—Law and legislation

   RT   **Euthanasia**
          Living wills
          Suicide

Right to health care   362.1
   UF   Health care, Right to
          Medical care, Right to
          Right to medical care
   BT   **Human rights**

Right to know
   USE   **Freedom of information**

Right-to-life movement (Anti-abortion movement)
   USE   **Pro-life movement**

Right to medical care
   USE   **Right to health care**

Right to work
   USE   **Open and closed shop**

Righteous Gentiles in the Holocaust (May subdiv. geog.)   **940.53**
   BT   **Holocaust, 1933-1945**
          World War, 1939-1945—Jews—Rescue

Rights, Human
   USE   **Human rights**

Rights of animals
   USE   **Animal rights**

Rights of employees
   USE   **Employee rights**

Rights of man
   USE   **Human rights**

Rights of women
   USE   **Women's rights**

Rights, Proprietary
   USE   **Intellectual property**

Riot control (May subdiv. geog.)   **303.6**
   UF   Riots—Control
   BT   **Crowds**
          Riots

Riots (May subdiv. geog.)   **303.6**
   UF   Civil disorders
          Mobs
   SA   names of institutions with the subdivision *Riots;* and names of specific riots [to be added as needed]
   BT   **Crime**
          Freedom of assembly
          Offenses against public safety
   NT   **Riot control**
   RT   **Crowds**
          Demonstrations

Riots—Control
  USE **Riot control**
Ripoffs
  USE **Fraud**
Risk   338.5; 368
  BT **Economics**
  RT **Probabilities**
      Profit
Rites and ceremonies (May subdiv. geog.)
      390
  UF Ceremonies
      Ecclesiastical rites and ceremo-
        nies
      Religious ceremonies
      Ritual
      Traditions
  SA classes of persons and ethnic
        groups with the subdivision
        Rites and ceremonies, e.g.
        Native Americans—Rites
        and ceremonies; and names
        of individual religions and de-
        nominations with the subdivi-
        sion *Liturgy* or *Customs and*
        practices, e.g. **Catholic**
        Church—Liturgy; Judaism—
        Customs and practices; etc.
        [to be added as needed]
  NT **Catholic Church—Liturgy**
      Funeral rites and ceremonies
      Initiation rites
      Judaism—Customs and prac-
        tices
      Liturgies
      Marriage customs and rites
      Native Americans—Rites and
        ceremonies
      Ordination
      Religious holidays
      Sacraments
      Secret societies
  RT **Manners and customs**
Ritual
  USE **Liturgies**
       Rites and ceremonies
River animals
  USE **Stream animals**
River pollution
  USE **Water pollution**

Rivers (May subdiv. geog.)   **551.48**
  SA names of rivers [to be added as
        needed]
  BT **Physical geography**
      Water
      Waterways
  NT **Stream animals**
      Water power
  RT **Floods**
      Hydraulic engineering
      Inland navigation
RNA   572.8
  UF Ribonucleic acid
      Ribose nucleic acid
  BT **Nucleic acids**
  NT **Catalytic RNA**
Road construction
  USE **Roads**
Road engineering
  USE **Highway engineering**
Road machinery   625.7
  BT **Construction equipment**
Road maps   912
  UF Roads—Maps
  SA names of countries, areas, states,
        cities, etc., with the subdivi-
        sion *Maps* [to be added as
        needed]
  BT **Maps**
  RT **Automobile travel—Guidebooks**
Road safety
  USE **Traffic safety**
Road signs
  USE **Signs and signboards**
Roads (May subdiv. geog.)   **388.1; 625.7**
  UF Construction of roads
      Highway construction
      Highways
      Road construction
      Thoroughfares
  BT **Civil engineering**
      Transportation
  NT **Alaska Highway (Alaska and**
        Canada)
      Express highways
      Roadside improvement
      Street cleaning
      Trails
  RT **Highway engineering**
      Pavements
      Soil mechanics

Roads—*Continued*
    Streets
Roads—Maps
  USE **Road maps**
Roadside improvement (May subdiv.
    geog.) **713**
  UF Highway beautification
  BT **Grounds maintenance**
      Landscape architecture
      Roads
Robbers
  USE **Thieves**
Robins **598.8**
  BT **Birds**
Robinsonades **808.3; 808.83**
    May be used for individual works, collec-
    tions, or materials about fictional works de-
    scribing a character's survival without the aid
    of civilization, as on a desert island.
  UF Apocalyptic fantasies
      End-of-the-world fantasies
  BT **Adventure fiction**
      Imaginary voyages
Robotics
  USE **Robots**
Robots **629.8**
    Use for general materials on robots and
    robotics. Materials limited to robots in indus-
    try are entered under **Industrial robots.**
  UF Automata
      Automatons
      Robotics
  BT **Machinery**
      Mechanical movements
  NT **Industrial robots**
Robots, Industrial
  USE **Industrial robots**
Rock and roll music
  USE **Rock music**
Rock climbing
  USE **Mountaineering**
Rock crystal
  USE **Quartz**
Rock drawings
  USE **Rock drawings, paintings, and**
      engravings
Rock drawings, paintings, and engrav-
    ings (May subdiv. geog.) **759.01**
  UF Petroglyphs
      Rock drawings
      Rock engravings
      Rock paintings

  BT **Archeology**
      Prehistoric art
  NT **Cave drawings and paintings**
Rock engravings
  USE **Rock drawings, paintings, and**
      engravings
Rock gardens (May subdiv. geog.)
    635.9
  BT **Gardens**
Rock music (May subdiv. geog.)
    781.66; 782.42166
  UF Rock and roll music
  BT **Music**
      Popular music
Rock paintings
  USE **Rock drawings, paintings, and**
      engravings
Rock tombs
  USE **Tombs**
Rocket airplanes
  USE **Rocket planes**
Rocket flight
  USE **Space flight**
Rocket planes **629.133**
  UF Airplanes, Rocket propelled
      Rocket airplanes
  SA names of rocket planes, e.g.
      X-15 (Rocket aircraft) [to be
      added as needed]
  BT **High speed aeronautics**
      Space vehicles
  NT **X-15 (Rocket aircraft)**
Rocketry **621.43**
  BT **Aeronautics**
      Astronautics
  NT **Guided missiles**
      Rockets (Aeronautics)
      Space vehicles
Rockets (Aeronautics) **629.133**
  UF Aerial rockets
  SA types of rockets and missiles
      and names of specific rockets
      and missiles [to be added as
      needed]
  BT **Aeronautics**
      High speed aeronautics
      Projectiles
      Rocketry
  NT **Artificial satellites—Launching**
      Ballistic missiles
      Guided missiles

Rockets (Aeronautics)—*Continued*
RT   **Interplanetary voyages**
     Jet propulsion
Rocks (May subdiv. geog.)   **552**
   Use for general materials on naturally oc-
   curring solid minerals. Materials on stone as
   a building material are entered under **Stone.**
   SA   varieties of rock, e.g. **Granite**
        [to be added as needed]
   NT   **Granite**
        Marble
   RT   **Geology**
        Petrology
        Stone
Rocky Mountains   **978**
   BT   **Mountains**
Rodeos (May subdiv. geog.)   **791.8**
   BT   **Sports**
   RT   **Cowhands**
        Horsemanship
Roentgen rays
   USE   **X-rays**
Rogues and vagabonds—Fiction
   USE   **Picaresque literature**
Roland (Legendary character)   **398.22**
   UF   Orlando (Legendary character)
   BT   **Folklore**
**Roland (Legendary character)—Ro-
   mances**   **821**
Role conflict   **302.5**
   Use for materials on the conflict within one
   person who is being called upon to fulfill two
   or more competing roles.
   BT   **Social conflict**
        Social role
Role playing   **302**
   BT   **Social role**
   NT   **Fantasy games**
Role playing games
   USE   **Fantasy games**
Role, Social
   USE   **Social role**
Roller coasters (May subdiv. geog.)
        791.06
   BT   **Amusements**
Roller skating   **796.2**
   UF   Skating
   BT   **Outdoor recreation**
   NT   **In-line skating**
        Skateboarding
Rollerblading
   USE   **In-line skating**

Romaic language
   USE   **Modern Greek language**
Romaic literature
   USE   **Modern Greek literature**
Roman antiquities
   USE   **Classical antiquities**
        Rome—Antiquities
        Rome (Italy)—Antiquities
Roman architecture (May subdiv. geog.)
        722
   UF   Architecture, Roman
   BT   **Ancient architecture**
        Architecture
Roman art (May subdiv. geog.)   **709.37**
   UF   Art, Roman
        Classical art
   BT   **Ancient art**
        Art
        Classical antiquities
Roman Catholic Church
   USE   **Catholic Church**
Roman civilization
   USE   **Rome—Civilization**
Roman emperors
   USE   **Emperors—Rome**
Roman Empire
   USE   **Rome**
Roman literature
   USE   **Latin literature**
Roman mythology   **292.1**
   UF   Mythology, Roman
   BT   **Classical mythology**
Roman numerals   **513**
   BT   **Numerals**
Roman philosophy
   USE   **Ancient philosophy**
Romance languages   **440**
   UF   Neo-Latin languages
   SA   names of languages belonging to
        the Romance group, e.g.
        French language [to be add-
        ed as needed]
   BT   **Language and languages**
   NT   **French language**
        Spanish language
   RT   **Latin language**
Romance literature   **840**
   SA   names of literatures belonging to
        the Romance group, e.g.
        French literature [to be add-
        ed as needed]

Romance literature—*Continued*
- BT **Literature**
- NT **French literature**
  Portuguese literature
  Spanish literature

Romance novels
- USE **Love stories**

Romances   808.8

May be used for individual works, collections, or materials about medieval tales dealing with the age of chivalry or the supernatural. They may be either in verse or in prose and may or may not have a basis in fact. Contemporary romance novels are entered under **Love stories** or **Romantic suspense novels.**
- UF   Chivalry—Romances
  Metrical romances
  Stories
- SA   names of historic persons and legendary characters with the subdivision *Romances,* e.g. **Roland (Legendary character)—Romances** [to be added as needed]
- BT   **Fiction**
  Literature
- NT   **Arthurian romances**
- RT   **Chivalry**
  Epic poetry
  Fables
  Legends

Romances (Love stories)
- USE **Love stories**

Romanesque architecture (May subdiv. geog.)   **723**
- UF   Architecture, Romanesque
- BT   **Architecture**
  Medieval architecture

Romanesque art (May subdiv. geog.)   **709.02**
- UF   Art, Romanesque
- BT   **Medieval art**
- NT   **Romanesque painting**

Romanesque painting (May subdiv. geog.)   **759.02**
- UF   Painting, Romanesque
- BT   **Romanesque art**

Romanies
- USE **Gypsies**

Romans à clef   808.3

May be used for individual works, collections, or materials about novels in which fictional characters and events can be readily identified with real persons and events.

- UF   Livres à clef
- BT   **Fiction**

Romantic crushes
- USE **Crushes**

Romantic fiction
- USE **Love stories**

Romantic stories
- USE **Love stories**

Romantic suspense novels   808.3

May be used for individual works, collections, or materials about modern romantic suspense novels. Medieval tales are entered under **Romances.**
- UF   Suspense novels
- BT   **Adventure fiction**
- RT   **Gothic novels**
  Love stories
  Mystery fiction
  Spy stories

Romanticism (May subdiv. geog.)   **141; 709.03; 809**
- BT   **Aesthetics**

Romanticism in art   709.03
- BT   **Art**

Rome   937

Use for materials about the city of Rome in antiquity or about the Roman Empire. Materials on the modern city of Rome are entered under **Rome (Italy).** Materials on the ruins and remains of ancient Rome, the city and its environs, are entered under **Rome (Italy)—Antiquities.** Materials on Roman antiquities in several countries are entered under **Rome—Antiquities.** Materials on Roman antiquities limited to one modern country, city, etc., are entered under the place with the subdivision *Antiquities.*
- UF   Roman Empire

Rome—Antiquities   937

Use for materials on Roman antiquities in several countries. Materials on Roman antiquities limited to one modern country, city, etc., are entered under the place with the subdivision *Antiquities.* Materials on the ruins and remains of ancient Rome, the city and its environs, are entered under **Rome (Italy)—Antiquities.**
- UF   Roman antiquities
- BT   **Classical antiquities**

Rome—Biography   920.037
- UF   Classical biography
- BT   **Biography**

Rome—Civilization   937

Use for materials on the civilization of ancient Rome. Materials on both ancient Greek and Roman civilizations are entered under **Classical civilization.**

Rome—Civilization—*Continued*
 UF Roman civilization
 BT **Classical civilization**
Rome—Description
 USE **Rome—Description and travel**
Rome—Description and travel   **913.7;**
 937

> Use for descriptive materials on the Roman Empire including accounts by travelers of ancient times.

 UF Rome—Description *[Former heading]*
Rome—Geography   **913.7**

> Use for geographic materials on ancient Rome.

 UF Classical geography
 BT **Ancient geography**
   Historical geography
Rome—History   **937**
Rome (Italy)   **945**

> Use for materials on the modern city of Rome. Materials about the city of Rome in antiquity or about the Roman Empire are entered under **Rome.**

Rome (Italy)—Antiquities   **937**

> Use for materials on the ruins and remains of ancient Rome, the city and its environs. Materials on Roman antiquities in several countries are entered under **Rome—Antiquities.** Materials on Roman antiquities limited to one modern country, city, etc., are entered under the place with the subdivision *Antiquities.*

 UF Roman antiquities
 BT **Classical antiquities**
Rome (Italy)—Description and travel
 914.5
Rome (Italy)—History   **945**
Roofs   **690; 695; 721**
 BT **Architecture—Details**
   Buildings
Rooming houses
 USE **Hotels and motels**
Roommates   **643**
 RT **Shared housing**
Rooms   **643; 645**
 SA types of rooms [to be added as needed]
 BT **Buildings**
   Houses
 NT **Garden rooms**
   Kitchens
 RT **Interior design**
Root crops   **633; 635**
 BT **Vegetables**
 RT **Feeds**

Rope   **677**
 NT **Cables**
   Knots and splices
 RT **Hemp**
Roses (May subdiv. geog.)   **583; 635.9**
 BT **Flowers**
Rosetta stone inscription   **493**
 BT **Hieroglyphics**
Rosin
 USE **Gums and resins**
Rotation of crops
 USE **Crop rotation**
Roughage
 USE **Food—Fiber content**
Round stage
 USE **Arena theater**
Routes of trade
 USE **Trade routes**
Rowing   **797.12**
 UF Crew (Rowing)
   Sculling
 BT **Athletics**
   Boats and boating
   Exercise
   Sports
   Water sports
Royal houses
 USE **Kings and rulers**
   Monarchy
Royalty
 USE **Kings and rulers**
   Monarchy
   Princes
   Princesses
   Queens
Rubber   **678**
 BT **Forest products**
Rubber, Artificial
 USE **Synthetic rubber**
Rubber, Synthetic
 USE **Synthetic rubber**
Rubber tires
 USE **Tires**
Rudeness
 USE **Bad behavior**
Rug cleaning
 USE **Rugs and carpets—Cleaning**
Rugs
 USE **Rugs and carpets**

Rugs and carpets (May subdiv. geog.)
    645; 677; 746.7
    UF   Carpets
           Rugs
    BT   **Decorative arts**
           Interior design
    NT   **Hooked rugs**
           Oriental rugs
Rugs and carpets—Cleaning   **677**
    UF   Carpet cleaning
           Rug cleaning
Ruins
    USE **Antiquities**
          Excavations (Archeology)
          Extinct cities
Rule, Golden
    USE **Golden rule**
Rule of equal time (Broadcasting)
    USE **Equal time rule (Broadcasting)**
Rulers
    USE **Emperors**
          Heads of state
          Kings and rulers
          Queens
Rules of order
    USE **Parliamentary practice**
Runaway adults   **173; 306.88**
    UF   Husbands, Runaway
           Runaway husbands
           Runaway wives
           Wives, Runaway
    BT   **Desertion and nonsupport**
          Missing persons
Runaway children   **305.23086; 362.74**
    BT   **Children**
          Homeless persons
          Missing children
Runaway husbands
    USE **Runaway adults**
Runaway slaves
    USE **Fugitive slaves**
Runaway teenagers   **362.74**
    BT   **Homeless persons**
          Missing persons
          Teenagers
Runaway wives
    USE **Runaway adults**
Running   **796.42**
    BT   **Track athletics**
    NT   **Jogging**
          Marathon running

    Orienteering
    RT   **Racing**
Rural architecture
    USE **Farm buildings**
Rural churches (May subdiv. geog.)
    254
    UF   Churches, Country
           Churches, Rural
           Country churches
    BT   **Church work**
Rural comedies
    USE **Pastoral drama**
          Pastoral fiction
Rural community development
    USE **Rural development**
Rural conditions
    USE names of countries, states, etc.,
          with the subdivision *Rural*
          conditions, e.g. **United**
          States—Rural conditions;
          Ohio—Rural conditions; etc.
          [to be added as needed]
Rural credit
    USE **Agricultural credit**
Rural development (May subdiv. geog.)
    307.1
    UF   Rural community development
    BT   **Agriculture—Government poli-**
          cy
          Community development
          Economic development
          Regional planning
Rural education
    USE **Rural schools**
Rural electrification (May subdiv. geog.)
    621.319
    BT   **Electrification**
    RT   **Electricity in agriculture**
Rural families
    USE **Farm family**
Rural high schools
    USE **Rural schools**
Rural life
    USE **Country life**
          Farm life
          Outdoor life
Rural poetry
    USE **Pastoral poetry**
Rural schools (May subdiv. geog.)   **371**
    UF   Country schools
           District schools

Rural schools—*Continued*
   High schools, Rural
   Rural education
   Rural high schools
   BT   **Public schools**
        Schools
Rural sociology   307.72
   Use for materials on the discipline of rural sociology and the theory of social organization in rural areas. Materials on the rural conditions of particular regions, countries, cities, etc., are entered under the place with the subdivision *Rural conditions.* Descriptive, popular, and literary materials on living in the country are entered under **Country life.**
   UF   Sociology, Rural
   SA   names of countries, states, etc.,
        with the subdivision *Rural
        conditions* [to be added as
        needed]
   BT   **Sociology**
   NT   **Ohio—Rural conditions**
        **United States—Rural condi-
        tions**
        Urbanization
   RT   **Country life**
        Farm family
        Farm life
        Peasantry
Rural-urban migration
   USE   **Internal migration**
Russia   947
   Use for materials on Russia (including the Russian Empire) prior to 1917. Materials on the Union of Soviet Socialist Republics from its inception in 1917 until its dissolution in December 1991 are entered under **Soviet Union.** Materials on the independent republic of Russia since its establishment in December 1991 are entered under **Russia (Federation).**
   UF   Russian Empire
   NT   **Russians**
   RT   **Russia (Federation)**
        Soviet Union
Russia (Federation)   947.086
   Use for materials on the independent republic, established in December 1991. Materials on Russia and the Russian Empire before 1917 are entered under **Russia.** Materials on the Union of Soviet Socialist Republics between 1917 and 1991 are entered under **Soviet Union.**
   NT   **Russians**
   RT   **Commonwealth of Independent
        States**
        Russia
        Soviet Union

**Russia (Federation)—History—1991-
        947.086**
Russia—History   947
   Use for materials on the history of Russia and the Russian empire before 1917.
**Russia—History—1905, Revolution
        947.08**
Russian Church
   USE   **Russian Orthodox Church**
Russian communism
   USE   **Communism—Soviet Union**
Russian Empire
   USE   **Russia**
Russian language   491.7
   May be subdivided like **English language.**
   BT   **Language and languages**
Russian literature   891.7
   Use for materials on literature in the Russian language. Materials on several of the literatures of the Soviet Union are entered under **Soviet literature.** May use same subdivisions and names of literary forms as for **English literature.**
   BT   **Literature**
   RT   **Soviet literature**
Russian Orthodox Church (May subdiv.
        geog.)   **281.9**
   UF   Russian Church
   BT   **Christian sects**
        Orthodox Eastern Church
Russian revolution
   USE   **Soviet Union—History—1917-
        1921, Revolution**
Russian satellite countries
   USE   **Communist countries**
Russians (May subdiv. geog.)   **920; 947**
   Use for materials on the dominant Slavic-speaking ethnic group of Russia. Materials on the citizens of the Soviet Union between 1917 and 1991, not limited to a single national or linguistic group, are entered under **Soviets (People).**
   BT   **Russia**
        Russia (Federation)
        Soviet Union
**Russo-Finnish War, 1939-1940
        948.9703**
   UF   Finno-Russian War, 1939-1940
        Soviet Union—History—1939-
        1940, War with Finland
   BT   **Europe—History—1918-1945**
Russo-Turkish War, 1853-1856
   USE   **Crimean War, 1853-1856**
Rust
   USE   **Corrosion and anticorrosives**

Rustless coatings
USE **Corrosion and anticorrosives**
RVs
USE **Recreational vehicles**
Sabbath 263; 296.4
UF Lord's Day
BT **Judaism**
Sabin vaccine
USE **Poliomyelitis vaccine**
Sabotage (May subdiv. geog.) 331.89;
364.16
UF Political violence
BT **Offenses against public safety**
Strikes
Subversive activities
Terrorism
Sacrament of Reconciliation
USE **Penance**
Sacraments 234; 265
BT **Church**
Grace (Theology)
Rites and ceremonies
NT **Anointing of the sick**
Baptism
Confirmation
Eucharist
Marriage
Ordination
Penance
Sacred art
USE **Religious art**
Sacred books 208
SA names of sacred books [to be
added as needed]
BT **Religious literature**
NT **Bible**
Koran
Vedas
Sacred music
USE **Church music**
Sacred numbers
USE **Numerology**
Symbolism of numbers
Sacrifice 203
UF Burnt offering
BT **Worship**
NT **Atonement—Christianity**
Safaris (May subdiv. geog.) 796.5;
910.2
BT **Adventure and adventurers**
Outdoor recreation

Scientific expeditions
Travel
RT **Hunting**
Safe sex
USE **Safe sex in AIDS prevention**
**Sexually transmitted diseases—
Prevention**
Safe sex in AIDS prevention 613.9;
616.97
Use for materials limited to safe sexual
practices in the prevention of AIDS. Materials
on AIDS prevention in general not limited to
safe sexual practices are entered under **AIDS
(Disease)—Prevention.**
UF Safe sex
BT **AIDS (Disease)—Prevention**
Sexual hygiene
Safety appliances
USE **Safety devices**
Safety devices 363.19; 620.8
UF Safety appliances
Safety equipment
SA subjects with the subdivision
Safety devices, e.g. **Rail-
roads—Safety devices** [to be
added as needed]
NT **Railroads—Safety devices**
RT **Accidents—Prevention**
Safety education (May subdiv. geog.)
363.1; 371.7
BT **Accidents—Prevention**
Safety equipment
USE **Safety devices**
Safety, Industrial
USE **Occupational health and safety**
Safety measures
USE **Accidents—Prevention**
and subjects with the subdivi-
sion *Safety measures,* e.g.
**Aeronautics—Safety mea-
sures** [to be added as needed]
Safety regulations (May subdiv. geog.)
343; 363.1
Use for collections or materials about rules
regarding safety that have the force of law.
SA subjects with the subdivision
Law and legislation or *Safety
regulations,* e.g. **Food—Law
and legislation; Ships—Safe-
ty regulations;** etc. [to be
added as needed]
BT **Accidents—Prevention**
Law

Safety regulations—*Continued*
    NT   Drivers' licenses
          Ships—Safety regulations
          Traffic regulations
Sagas   398.22; 839
    BT   Folklore
          Literature
          Old Norse literature
          Scandinavian literature
Sailboarding
    USE Windsurfing
Sailing (May subdiv. geog.)   623.88;
    797.124
    BT   Ships
          Water sports
    NT   Windsurfing
    RT   Boats and boating
          Navigation
          Yachts and yachting
Sailors (May subdiv. geog.)   387.5092;
    623.88092; 920
    UF   Mariners
          Naval personnel
          Navigators
          Sailors' life
          Sea life
          Seamen
    SA   names of navies, e.g. United
          States. Navy [to be added as
          needed]
    BT   Military personnel
          Naval art and science
          Navies
    NT   Merchant marine
          Ship pilots
    RT   Seafaring life
Sailors—Fiction
    USE Sea stories
Sailors' handbooks
    USE United States. Navy—Hand-
          books, manuals, etc.
Sailors' life
    USE Sailors
          Seafaring life
Sailors' song
    USE Sea songs
Sailplanes (Aeronautics)
    USE Gliders (Aeronautics)
Saint Bartholomew's Day, Massacre of,
    1572   944
    UF   St. Bartholomew's Day, Massa-
          cre of, 1572

    BT   France—History—1328-1589,
          House of Valois
          Huguenots
          Massacres
Saint Francis, Order of
    USE Franciscans
Saint Valentine's Day
    USE Valentine's Day
Saints (May subdiv. geog.)   200.92; 920
    SA   saints of particular religions, e.g.
          Christian saints; and names
          of individual saints [to be
          added as needed]
    BT   Religious biography
    NT   Christian saints
          Mary, Blessed Virgin, Saint
    RT   Martyrs
Salads   641.8
    BT   Cooking
    RT   Cooking—Vegetables
Salamanders   597.6
    BT   Amphibians
Salaries
    USE Salaries, wages, etc.
Salaries, wages, etc. (May subdiv. geog.)
    331.2; 658.3
    Use for materials on all forms of compensa-
tion for work performed or services rendered,
including salaries, wages, fees, commissions,
fringe benefits, and pensions.
    UF   Compensation
          Employees—Salaries, wages, etc.
          Fees
          Salaries
          Wages
    SA   types of professional personnel,
          types of workers, and classes
          of persons with the subdivi-
          sion *Salaries, wages, etc.,* e.g.
          Lawyers—Salaries, wages,
          etc.; Office workers—Sala-
          ries, wages, etc.; Handi-
          capped—Salaries, wages,
          etc.; industries and types of
          institutions with the subdivi-
          sions *Employees—Salaries,*
          wages, etc., e.g. Chemical in-
          dustry—Employees—Sala-
          ries, wages, etc.; Colleges
          and universities—Employ-
          ees—Salaries, wages, etc.;

Salaries, wages, etc.—*Continued*

    and countries, states, cities, etc., with the subdivisions *Officials and employees—Salaries, wages, etc.,* e.g. **Ohio—Officials and employees—Salaries, wages, etc.** [to be added as needed]

  BT **Income**

  NT **Chemical industry—Employees—Salaries, wages, etc.**

        Colleges and universities—Employees—Salaries, wages, etc.

        Equal pay for equal work

        Fringe benefits

        Handicapped—Salaries, wages, etc.

        Job analysis

        Lawyers—Salaries, wages, etc.

        Minimum wage

        Office workers—Salaries, wages, etc.

        Ohio—Officials and employees—Salaries, wages, etc.

        Profit sharing

        Wage-price policy

  RT **Cost and standard of living**

        Prices

Sale of infants

  USE **Adoption—Corrupt practices**

Sales agents

  USE **Sales personnel**

Sales, Auction

  USE **Auctions**

Sales management **658.8**

  BT **Management**

        Marketing

        Selling

Sales personnel (May subdiv. geog.) **381.092; 658.85**

  UF Clerks (Retail trade)

        Sales agents

        Salesmen

        Saleswomen

        Traveling sales personnel

  BT **Retail trade**

  NT **Peddlers and peddling**

Sales tax (May subdiv. geog.) **336.2**

  BT **Taxation**

Salesmanship

  USE **Selling**

Salesmen

  USE **Sales personnel**

Saleswomen

  USE **Sales personnel**

Saline water

  USE **Sea water**

Saline water conversion

  USE **Sea water conversion**

Salk vaccine

  USE **Poliomyelitis vaccine**

Salmon **597.5**

  BT **Fishes**

Saloons

  USE **Bars**

Salt free diet

  USE **Salt-free diet**

Salt-free diet **613.2**

  UF Low sodium diet

        Salt free diet

  BT **Cooking for the sick**

        Diet

        Diet in disease

Salt water

  USE **Sea water**

Salt water aquariums

  USE **Marine aquariums**

Saltwater fishing (May subdiv. geog.) **799.16**

  UF Ocean fishing

        Sea fishing

  BT **Fishing**

Salutations

  USE **Etiquette**

Salvage (May subdiv. geog.) **627; 628.4**

  Use for materials on the recovery of equipment, parts, cargo, merchandise, structures, or waste, not limited to ships or shipwrecks.

  UF Salvage (Waste, etc.)

        Utilization of waste

        Waste reclamation

  NT **Marine salvage**

        Recycling

        Waste products as fuel

  RT **Refuse and refuse disposal**

Salvage (Waste, etc.)

  USE **Salvage**

Salvation **202; 234**

  UF Redemption

  BT **Doctrinal theology**

  NT **Atonement—Christianity**

        Conversion

        Faith

Salvation—*Continued*
>> Grace (Theology)
>> Regeneration (Christianity)
>> Sanctification

Salvation Army   287.9
> BT   Christian missions
>> Christian sects

Salvation—Biblical teaching   234
Salvation history
> USE   Salvation—History of doctrines

Salvation—History of doctrines   202;
> 234
> UF   Salvation history
> BT   Doctrinal theology

Same-sex marriage (May subdiv. geog.)
> 306.81; 346.01
> UF   Gay marriage
>> Homosexual marriage
>> Lesbian marriage
> BT   Marriage

Samplers   746.3
> BT   Embroidery
>> Needlework

Sampling (Statistics)   519.5
> UF   Random sampling
> BT   Probabilities
>> Statistics
> NT   Quality control

Sanatoriums
> USE   Health resorts
>> Hospitals

Sanctification   202; 234
> BT   Salvation

Sanctions (International law)   327.1;
> 341.5
> UF   Economic sanctions
> BT   Economic policy
>> International economic rela-
>> tions
>> International law

Sanctuary (Law)
> USE   Asylum

Sanctuary movement (May subdiv. geog.)
> 261.8

Use for materials on any network of religious congregations or churches that shelter refugees or illegal aliens.

> BT   Asylum
>> Church and social problems
>> Social movements
> RT   Illegal aliens
>> Refugees

Sand dunes (May subdiv. geog.)   551.3
> UF   Dunes
> BT   Seashore

Sand sculpture (May subdiv.geog.)   736
> BT   Nature craft
>> Sculpture

Sandwiches   641.8
> BT   Cooking

Sanitary affairs
> USE   Sanitary engineering
>> Sanitation

Sanitary engineering (May subdiv. geog.)
> 628
> UF   Environmental health engineering
>> Sanitary affairs
> BT   Engineering
> NT   Drainage
>> Pollution
>> Refuse and refuse disposal
>> Sewerage
>> Soil microbiology
>> Street cleaning
> RT   Municipal engineering
>> Sanitation

Sanitary landfills
> USE   Landfills

Sanitation (May subdiv. geog.)   363.72;
> 648
> UF   Sanitary affairs
> SA   subjects, types of industries, and
>> names of individual corporate
>> bodies with the subdivision
>> *Sanitation*, e.g. **Hospitals—
>> Sanitation** [to be added as
>> needed]
> NT   Cemeteries
>> Cleaning
>> Cleanliness
>> Cremation
>> Disinfection and disinfectants
>> Hospitals—Sanitation
>> Household sanitation
>> Pollution
>> Refuse and refuse disposal
>> School hygiene
>> Smoke prevention
>> Ventilation
>> Water purification
> RT   Hygiene
>> Public health
>> Sanitary engineering

Sanitation, Household
USE **Household sanitation**
Santa Claus   394.2663
BT **Christmas**
Santeria   299.6
UF Lucumi (Religion)
BT **Religion**
Saracenic art
USE **Islamic art**
Sasquatch   001.9
UF Big foot
Bigfoot
BT **Monsters**
Mythical animals
SAT
USE **Scholastic Aptitude Test**
Satan
USE **Devil**
Satellite communication systems
USE **Artificial satellites in telecom-**
munication
Satellites   523.9
UF Moons
Natural satellites
Planetary satellites
Planets—Satellites
SA names of planets with the subdi-
vision *Satellites,* e.g. **Mars**
(Planet)—Satellites [to be
added as needed]
BT **Solar system**
NT **Mars (Planet)—Satellites**
Satellites, Artificial
USE **Artificial satellites**
Satellites—Mars
USE **Mars (Planet)—Satellites**
Satire   808.7; 808.87
UF Comic literature
SA satire of particular countries, e.g.
American satire [to be added
as needed]
BT **Literature**
Rhetoric
Wit and humor
NT **American satire**
English satire
Invective
Parody
Political satire
Satire, American
USE **American satire**

Satire, English
USE **English satire**
Saturn (Planet)   523.46
BT **Planets**
Saucers, Flying
USE **Unidentified flying objects**
Sauces   641.8
BT **Cooking**
Saving and investment (May subdiv.
geog.)   **332.024**
UF Capital accumulation
Capital formation
Economy
Investment and saving
Saving and thrift
Thrift
BT **Capital**
Economics
Personal finance
Wealth
NT **Savings and loan associations**
RT **Investments**
Saving and thrift
USE **Saving and investment**
Savings and loan associations (May
subdiv. geog.)   **332.3**
UF Building and loan associations
Loan associations
BT **Banks and banking**
Cooperation
Cooperative societies
Investments
Loans
Personal loans
Saving and investment
RT **Cooperative banks**
Savings banks
USE **Banks and banking**
Saws   621.9
BT **Carpentry tools**
Tools
Sayings
USE **Epigrams**
Proverbs
Quotations
Scandals   302.2
BT **History**

Scandinavian languages   439
  UF   Norse languages
  BT   **Language and languages**
  NT   **Danish language**
       Icelandic language
       Norwegian language
       Old Norse language
       Swedish language
Scandinavian literature   839
  UF   Norse literature
  BT   **Literature**
  NT   **Danish literature**
       Eddas
       Icelandic literature
       Norwegian literature
       Sagas
       Swedish literature
  RT   **Old Norse literature**
Scandinavians (May subdiv. geog.)   920;
  948
  Use for materials on the people of Scandi-
  navia since the tenth century. Materials on
  earlier Scandinavians are entered under **Vi-
  kings.**
  NT   **Vikings**
Scarecrows   632
  BT   **Plant conservation**
Scenarios
  USE   **Radio plays**
        Stories, plots, etc.
        Television plays
Scene painting   792.02
  BT   **Painting**
        **Theaters—Stage setting and
          scenery**
Scenery
  USE   **Landscape protection**
        Natural monuments
        Views
        Wilderness areas
Scenery (Stage)
  USE   **Theaters—Stage setting and
          scenery**
Scented gardens
  USE   **Fragrant gardens**
Scepticism
  USE   **Skepticism**
Scholarship
  USE   **Learning and scholarship**
Scholarship funds
  USE   **Scholarships**

Scholarships (May subdiv. geog.)   371.2;
  378.3
  UF   Bursaries
        Fellowships
        Scholarship funds
        Scholarships, fellowships, etc.
  SA   fields of study, ethnic groups,
        and classes of persons with
        the subdivision *Scholarships,*
        [to be added as needed]
  BT   **Education**
        Endowments
        Student aid
Scholarships, fellowships, etc.
  USE   **Scholarships**
Scholastic achievement
  USE   **Academic achievement**
Scholastic achievement tests
  USE   **Achievement tests**
Scholastic Aptitude Test   378.1
  UF   SAT
  BT   **Colleges and universities—En-
          trance examinations**
        Examinations
School achievement tests
  USE   **Achievement tests**
School administration and organization
  USE   **Schools—Administration**
School-age fathers
  USE   **Teenage fathers**
School-age mothers
  USE   **Teenage mothers**
School and community
  USE   **Community and school**
School and home
  USE   **Home and school**
School architecture
  USE   **School buildings**
School assembly programs   371.8
  UF   Assembly programs, School
        School entertainments
        Schools—Exercises and recre-
          ations
        Schools—Opening exercises
  BT   **Student activities**
  NT   **Commencements**
        Recitations
  RT   **Drama in education**
School athletics
  USE   **School sports**

School attendance (May subdiv. geog.)
   371.2
   UF   Absence from school
         Absenteeism (Schools)
         Attendance, School
         Compulsory school attendance
   BT   **Schools—Administration**
   RT   **Compulsory education**
         Dropouts
School boards (May subdiv. geog.)
   353.8
   UF   Boards of education
   BT   **Schools—Administration**
School books
   USE   **Textbooks**
School buildings (May subdiv. geog.)
   371.6; 727
   UF   Buildings, School
         School architecture
         School houses
         Schoolhouses
   BT   **Buildings**
         Schools
School buildings as recreation centers
   USE   **Community centers**
School busing
   USE   **Busing (School integration)**
         School children—Transportation
School children (May subdiv. geog.)
   155.42; 305.234
   BT   **Children**
         Students
School children—Food   371.7; 642
   UF   Food for school children
         Meals for school children
         School lunches
   BT   **Children—Nutrition**
         Diet
         Food
School children—Medical examinations
   USE   **Children—Medical examinations**
School children—Transportation   371.8
   UF   School busing
   BT   **Transportation**
   NT   **Busing (School integration)**
School choice (May subdiv. geog.)   **379.1**
   Use for materials on choosing a school and on the right of parents to choose their children's school.

   UF   Choice of school
         Parents' choice of school
         Schools—Selection
   BT   **Education**
   NT   **College choice**
School clubs
   USE   **Students—Societies**
School counseling   371.4
   Use for materials on the assistance given to students by schools, colleges, or universities in understanding and coping with adjustment problems. Materials on the assistance given to students in the selection of a program of studies are entered under **Educational counseling.**
   UF   Guidance counseling, School
   BT   **Counseling**
   RT   **Educational counseling**
         School psychologists
School desegregation
   USE   **School integration**
School discipline   371.5
   UF   Discipline of children
         Punishment in schools
   BT   **Schools—Administration**
         Teaching
   NT   **Classroom management**
         Student government
School dropouts
   USE   **Dropouts**
School entertainments
   USE   **School assembly programs**
School excursions
   USE   **Field trips**
School fiction
   USE   **School stories**
School finance
   USE   **Education—Finance**
School furniture
   USE   **Schools—Equipment and supplies**
School grade retention
   USE   **Promotion (School)**
School houses
   USE   **School buildings**
School hygiene   371.7
   BT   **Children—Health and hygiene**
         Health education
         Hygiene
         Public health
         Sanitation
   RT   **School nurses**

School inspection
USE **School supervision**
Schools—Administration
School integration (May subdiv. geog.)
379.2
UF Desegregated schools
Desegregation in education
Education—Integration
Integrated schools
Integration in education
Racial balance in schools
School desegregation
BT **Race relations**
NT **Busing (School integration)**
Magnet schools
RT **Segregation in education**
School journalism
USE **College and school journalism**
School libraries (May subdiv. geog.)
027.8
BT **Instructional materials centers**
Libraries
NT **Elementary school libraries**
High school libraries
Libraries and students
RT **Libraries and schools**
School life
USE **Students**
School lunches
USE **School children—Food**
School management and organization
USE **Schools—Administration**
School media centers
USE **Instructional materials centers**
School music
USE **Music—Study and teaching**
School songbooks
Singing
School newspapers
USE **College and school journalism**
School nurses **371.7**
BT **Nurses**
RT **Health education**
School hygiene
School organization
USE **Schools—Administration**
School playgrounds
USE **Playgrounds**
School plays
USE **Children's plays**
College and school drama

School prayer
USE **Prayer in the public schools**
School principals
USE **School superintendents and**
principals
School promotion
USE **Promotion (School)**
School prose
USE **Children's writings**
School psychologists (May subdiv. geog.)
371.7
BT **Psychologists**
RT **School counseling**
School readiness
USE **Readiness for school**
School reports **371.2**
UF Educational reports
Reports, Teachers'
Teachers' reports
BT **Report writing**
RT **Grading and marking (Educa-**
tion)
School shootings (May subdiv. geog.)
371.7
UF Shootings in schools
BT **Crime**
School violence
School shops **373.2**
UF Industrial arts shops
BT **Technical education**
School songbooks **782.42**
UF School music
BT **Songbooks**
Songs
NT **Children's songs**
School sports (May subdiv. geog.) **371.8**
UF Interscholastic sports
School athletics
BT **Sports**
Student activities
RT **College sports**
School stories **808.83**
May be used for individual works, collec-
tions, or materials about school stories.
UF School fiction
Schools—Fiction
BT **Fiction**
School superintendents and principals
(May subdiv. geog.) **371.2**
UF School principals
Superintendents of schools

School superintendents and principals—
Continued
    BT   Schools—Administration
    RT   School supervision

School supervision   371.2

    Use for materials on the supervision of instruction. Materials on the management and organization of schools and on the administrative duties of educators are entered under **Schools—Administration.**

    UF   Inspection of schools
          Instructional supervision
          School inspection
          Supervision of schools
    BT   Schools—Administration
          Teaching
    RT   School superintendents and
          principals

School surveys
    USE **Educational surveys**
School taxes
    USE **Education—Finance**
School teaching
    USE **Teaching**
School trips
    USE **Field trips**
School verse
    USE **Children's writings**

School violence (May subdiv. geog.)
       371.7
    UF   Student violence
          Violence in schools
    BT   **Juvenile delinquency**
          Violence
    NT   **School shootings**

School vouchers
    USE **Educational vouchers**

School yearbooks   371.8
    UF   Annuals
          College yearbooks
          High school yearbooks
          Student yearbooks
    BT   **Serial publications**
          Yearbooks

Schoolhouses
    USE **School buildings**

Schools (May subdiv. geog.)   **371**
    SA   types of schools, e.g. **Church schools; Rural schools;** etc.; names of individual schools; and subjects with the subdivision *Study and teaching,* e.g.

Science—Study and teaching
    [to be added as needed]
    NT   **Business schools**
          Charter schools
          Church schools
          Colleges and universities
          Correspondence schools and
          courses
          Elementary schools
          Evening and continuation
          schools
          Experimental schools
          High schools
          Junior high schools
          Kindergarten
          Libraries and schools
          Magnet schools
          Middle schools
          Museums and schools
          Nongraded schools
          Nursery schools
          Private schools
          Public schools
          Religious summer schools
          Rural schools
          School buildings
          Single-sex schools
          Summer schools
          Urban schools
    RT   **Education**

Schools—Accreditation (May subdiv. geog.)   **379.1**
    UF   Accreditation (Education)
          Educational accreditation
    SA   types of educational institutions and names of individual institutions with the subdivision *Accreditation,* e.g. **Colleges and universities—Accreditation;** and subjects with the subdivision *Study and teaching,* for accreditation of programs of study in those subjects, e.g. **Mathematics—Study and teaching** [to be added as needed]

Schools—Administration (May subdiv. geog.)   **371.2**
    Use for materials on the management and organization of schools and on the administrative duties of educators. Materials on the supervision of instruction are entered under **School supervision.**

Schools—Administration—*Continued*
   UF   Educational administration
        Inspection of schools
        School administration and organization
        School inspection
        School management and organization
        School organization
        Schools—Management and organization
   NT   **Articulation (Education)**
        School attendance
        School boards
        School discipline
        School superintendents and principals
        School supervision
        Schools—Centralization
        Schools—Decentralization
        Student government
Schools and libraries
   USE   **Libraries and schools**
Schools and museums
   USE   **Museums and schools**
Schools as social centers
   USE   **Community centers**
Schools—Centralization (May subdiv. geog.)   **379.1**
   UF   Centralization of schools
        Consolidation of schools
   BT   **Schools—Administration**
Schools—Curricula
   USE   **Education—Curricula**
Schools—Decentralization (May subdiv. geog.)   **379.1**
   UF   Decentralization of schools
   BT   **Schools—Administration**
Schools—Equipment and supplies **371.6**
   UF   School furniture
   BT   **Furniture**
Schools—Exercises and recreations
   USE   **School assembly programs**
Schools—Fiction
   USE   **School stories**
Schools—Management and organization
   USE   **Schools—Administration**
Schools, Military
   USE   **Military education**
Schools, Nonformal
   USE   **Experimental schools**

Schools—Opening exercises
   USE   **School assembly programs**
Schools—Selection
   USE   **School choice**
Schools—United States   **371.00973**
   UF   American schools
Science (May subdiv. geog.)   **500**
   NT   **Astronomy**
        Bible and science
        Biology
        Botany
        Chaos (Science)
        Chemistry
        Computer science
        Discoveries in science
        Earth sciences
        Environmental sciences
        Forensic sciences
        Fossils
        Geology
        Life sciences
        Mathematics
        Natural history
        Petrology
        Physical sciences
        Physics
        Physiology
        Religion and science
        Science and civilization
        Science and the humanities
        Space sciences
        System theory
        Zoology
   RT   **Scientific apparatus and instruments**
        Scientists
Science and civilization   **306.4**
   UF   Civilization and science
        Science and society
   BT   **Civilization**
        Progress
        Science
Science and religion
   USE   **Religion and science**
Science and society
   USE   **Science and civilization**
Science and space
   USE   **Space sciences**
Science and state
   USE   **Science—Government policy**

Science and the Bible
USE **Bible and science**
Science and the humanities   001.3
UF   Humanities and science
BT   **Humanities**
     Science
Science—Exhibitions   507.4
UF   Science fairs
BT   **Exhibitions**
NT   **Science projects**
Science experiments
USE   **Science—Experiments**
Science—Experiments   507
UF   Experiments, Scientific
     Science experiments
     Scientific experiments
SA   branches of science with the
     subdivision *Experiments,* e.g.
     Chemistry—Experiments [to
     be added as needed]
RT   **Science projects**
Science fair projects
USE   **Science projects**
Science fairs
USE   **Science—Exhibitions**
Science fiction   808.3; 808.83
May be used for individual works, collec-
tions, or materials about fiction based on
imagined developments in science and tech-
nology.
UF   Apocalyptic fantasies
     End-of-the-world fantasies
     Space flight (Fiction)
BT   **Adventure fiction**
     Fiction
NT   **Dystopias**
     Hugo Award
     Imaginary voyages
     Nebula Award
     Utopian fiction
RT   **Fantasy fiction**
     Interplanetary voyages
Science fiction comic books, strips, etc.
     741.5
May be used for individual works, collec-
tions, or materials about science fiction com-
ics.
BT   **Comic books, strips, etc.**
Science fiction films   791.43
May be used for individual works, collec-
tions, or materials about science fiction films.

SA   types of science fiction films,
     e.g. **Star Wars films** [to be
     added as needed]
BT   **Motion pictures**
NT   **Star Wars films**
RT   **Fantasy films**
Science fiction films—Catalogs
     016.79143
Science fiction plays   808.82
May be used for individual works, collec-
tions, or materials about science fiction plays.
BT   **Drama**
Science fiction poetry   808.1; 808.81
May be used for individual works, collec-
tions, or materials about science fiction poet-
ry.
BT   **Poetry**
Science fiction radio programs   791.44
May be used for individual works, collec-
tions, or materials about science fiction radio
programs.
BT   **Radio programs**
Science fiction television programs
     791.45
May be used for individual works, collec-
tions, or materials about science fiction televi-
sion programs.
BT   **Television programs**
RT   **Fantasy television programs**
Science—Government policy (May subdiv.
     geog.)   **353.7; 500**
UF   Science and state
     Science policy
Science journalism
USE   **Scientific journalism**
Science—Methodology   501
UF   Scientific method
NT   **Logic**
Science policy
USE   **Science—Government policy**
Science projects   507.8
UF   Science fair projects
BT   **Science—Exhibitions**
RT   **Science—Experiments**
Science—Religious aspects
USE   **Religion and science**
Science—Societies   506
UF   Scientific societies
BT   **Societies**
Science—Study and teaching   507
UF   Scientific education
NT   **Nature study**
Science—Study and teaching—Audiovisu-
     al aids   507.8

Science—Study and teaching—Evaluation
507.6
Science—United States 509.73
Scientific apparatus and instruments
502.8
  UF Apparatus, Scientific
      Instruments, Scientific
      Scientific instruments
  SA types of instruments, e.g. **Aeronautical instruments;** and
      names of specific instruments
      [to be added as needed]
  NT **Aeronautical instruments**
      Astronomical instruments
      Chemical apparatus
      Electric apparatus and appliances
      Electronic apparatus and appliances
      Engineering instruments
      Meteorological instruments
      Optical instruments
  RT **Science**
Scientific breakthroughs
  USE **Discoveries in science**
Scientific creationism
  USE **Creationism**
Scientific discoveries
  USE **Discoveries in science**
Scientific education
  USE **Science—Study and teaching**
Scientific errors
  USE **Errors**
Scientific expeditions 508
  UF Expeditions, Scientific
      Polar expeditions
  SA names of regions explored with the subdivision *Exploration* for materials on scientific expeditions to regions that are unsettled or sparsely settled and largely unknown to the world at large, e.g. **Antarctica—Exploration;** names of countries, states, etc., with the subdivision *Exploring expeditions* for materials on explorations sponsored by those governments; and names of expeditions [to be added as needed]

  BT **Voyages and travels**
  NT **Antarctica—Exploration**
      Arctic regions—Exploration
      Safaris
  RT **Exploration**
Scientific experiments
  USE **Science—Experiments**
Scientific instruments
  USE **Scientific apparatus and instruments**
Scientific journalism (May subdiv. geog.)
070.4
  UF Journalism, Scientific
      Science journalism
  BT **Journalism**
Scientific management
  USE **Management**
Scientific method
  USE **Science—Methodology**
Scientific names of plants
  USE **Botany—Nomenclature**
Scientific plant names
  USE **Botany—Nomenclature**
Scientific recreations 793.8
  UF Recreations, Scientific
  BT **Amusements**
  NT **Mathematical recreations**
Scientific societies
  USE **Science—Societies**
Scientific writing
  USE **Technical writing**
Scientists (May subdiv. geog.) **509.2;**
920
  SA types of scientists and names of individual scientists [to be added as needed]
  NT **Astronomers**
      Biologists
      Chemists
      Geologists
      Mathematicians
      Naturalists
      Physicists
  RT **Science**
Scottish clans
  USE **Clans—Scotland**
Scottish personal names 929.4
  BT **Personal names**
Scottish tartans
  USE **Tartans**

Scouts and scouting   369.4
   BT   Clubs
          Community life
   NT   Boy Scouts
          Girl Scouts
Scrapbook journaling
   USE   Scrapbooking
Scrapbooking   745.593
   UF   Scrapbook journaling
   BT   Handicraft
Screen printing
   USE   Silk screen printing
Screening for drug abuse
   USE   Drug testing
Screenplays
   USE   Motion picture plays
            Television scripts
Scriptures, Holy
   USE   Bible
Scuba diving (May subdiv. geog.)   797.2
     Use for materials on free diving with the aid of a self-contained underwater breathing apparatus. Materials on free diving with mask, fins, and snorkel are entered under **Skin diving.**
   UF   Free diving
   BT   Deep diving
Sculling
   USE   Rowing
Sculptors (May subdiv. geog.)   730.92; 920
   BT   Artists
Sculptors—United States   730.92; 920
   UF   American sculptors
Sculpture   730
   UF   Statues
   SA   sculpture of particular countries, e.g. **Greek sculpture;** and specific types of sculpture [to be added as needed]
   BT   Art
          Decoration and ornament
   NT   American sculpture
          Brasses
          Bronzes
          Greek sculpture
          Kinetic sculpture
          Masks (Sculpture)
          Mobiles (Sculpture)
          Modeling
          Modernism in sculpture
          Monuments
          Plaster casts

          Sand sculpture
          Soap sculpture
   RT   Carving (Decorative arts)
Sculpture—20th century   735
   UF   Modern sculpture—1900-1999 (20th century)
            Sculpture, Modern—20th century
Sculpture—21st century   735
Sculpture, Greek
   USE   Greek sculpture
Sculpture in motion
   USE   Kinetic sculpture
Sculpture, Modern
   USE   Modernism in sculpture
Sculpture, Modern—20th century
   USE   Sculpture—20th century
Sculpture—Technique   731.4
   RT   Modeling
SDI (Ballistic missile defense system)
   USE   Strategic Defense Initiative
Sea
   USE   Ocean
Sea animals
   USE   Marine animals
Sea bed
   USE   Ocean bottom
Sea farming
   USE   Aquaculture
Sea fisheries
   USE   Commercial fishing
Sea fishing
   USE   Saltwater fishing
Sea food
   USE   Seafood
Sea in art
   USE   Marine painting
Sea laboratories
   USE   Undersea research stations
Sea laws
   USE   Maritime law
Sea life
   USE   Marine biology
            Navies
            Sailors
            Seafaring life
Sea mosses
   USE   Algae
Sea poetry   808.1; 808.81
     May be used for individual works, collections, or materials about poetry about the sea.
   BT   Poetry
   NT   Sea songs

Sea pollution
   USE   **Marine pollution**
Sea power   359
   UF   Dominion of the sea
         Military power
         Naval power
         Navy
   SA   names of countries with the sub-
         head *Navy* or the subdivision
         Naval history, e.g. **United**
         States. Navy; United
         States—Naval history; etc.
         [to be added as needed]
   BT   **Naval art and science**
   NT   **Warships**
   RT   **Naval history**
         Navies
Sea resources
   USE   **Marine resources**
Sea routes
   USE   **Trade routes**
Sea shells
   USE   **Shells**
Sea-shore
   USE   **Seashore**
Sea songs   782.42
   UF   Chanties
         Sailors' song
   BT   **Sea poetry**
         Songs
Sea stories   808.3; 808.83
   May be used for individual works, collections, or materials about sea stories.
   UF   Sailors—Fiction
   BT   **Adventure and adventurers**
         Adventure fiction
         Fiction
Sea transportation
   USE   **Shipping**
Sea travel
   USE   **Ocean travel**
Sea water   551.46
   UF   Saline water
         Salt water
   BT   **Water**
Sea water aquariums
   USE   **Marine aquariums**
Sea water conversion   628.1
   UF   Conversion of saline water
         Desalination of water
         Desalting of water
         Saline water conversion

   BT   **Water purification**
Sea waves
   USE   **Ocean waves**
Seafaring life   910.4
   UF   Sailors' life
         Sea life
   SA   names of countries with the sub-
         head *Navy,* e.g. **United**
         States. Navy [to be added as
         needed]
   BT   **Adventure and adventurers**
         Manners and customs
         Voyages and travels
   RT   **Sailors**
Seafood   641.3
   UF   Sea food
   SA   names of marine fish, shellfish,
         etc., used as food [to be add-
         ed as needed]
   BT   **Food**
         Marine resources
   RT   **Fish as food**
Sealab project   551.46
   UF   Navy Sealab project
         Project Sealab
         United States. Navy—Sealab
         project
   BT   **Undersea research stations**
Seals (Animals) (May subdiv. geog.)
         599.79
   BT   **Mammals**
         Marine mammals
Seals (Numismatics) (May subdiv. geog.)
         737; 929.8
   UF   Emblems
         Signets
   BT   **Heraldry**
         History
         Inscriptions
         Numismatics
   RT   **National emblems**
Seamanship
   USE   **Navigation**
Seamen
   USE   **Sailors**
Search and rescue operations
   USE   **Rescue work**
Searching the Internet
   USE   **Internet searching**
Seascapes
   USE   **Marine painting**

Seashore (May subdiv. geog.)   **551.45**
    UF   Sea-shore
    BT   **Landforms**
    NT   **Beaches**
         Sand dunes
    RT   **Coasts**
         Ocean
Seasons (May subdiv. geog.)   **508.2; 525**
    SA   names of the seasons [to be
         added as needed]
    BT   **Astronomy**
         Climate
         Meteorology
    NT   **Autumn**
Seaweeds
    USE **Algae**
Secession
    USE **United States—History—1861-**
         1865, Civil War—Causes
Seclusion
    USE **Solitude**
Second Advent   **236**
    UF   Jesus Christ—Second Advent
         Second coming of Christ
    BT   **Eschatology**
         Jesus Christ
    RT   **Millennium**
Second coming of Christ
    USE **Second Advent**
Second economy
    USE **Underground economy**
Second hand trade
    USE **Secondhand trade**
Second job
    USE **Supplementary employment**
Second World War
    USE **World War, 1939-1945**
Secondary education (May subdiv. geog.)
         373
    UF   Education, Secondary
         High school education
         Secondary schools
    BT   **Education**
    NT   **Adult education**
         Evening and continuation
         schools
    RT   **High schools**
         Junior high schools
Secondary employment
    USE **Supplementary employment**

Secondary school libraries
    USE **High school libraries**
Secondary schools
    USE **High schools**
         Junior high schools
         Secondary education
Secondhand trade   **381**
    UF   Second hand trade
         Used merchandise
    SA   types of secondhand trade, e.g.
         Garage sales [to be added as
         needed]
    BT   **Selling**
    NT   **Flea markets**
         Garage sales
Secrecy   **158.2; 302.5**
    UF   Concealment
    NT   **Children's secrets**
    RT   **Privacy**
Secret service (May subdiv. geog.)
         363.28
    Use for materials on governmental service
of a secret nature.
    SA   names of wars with the subdivi-
         sion *Secret service* [to be
         added as needed]
    BT   **Police**
    NT   **Espionage**
         World War, 1939-1945—Secret
         service
    RT   **Detectives**
         Intelligence service
         Spies
Secret service—United States   **363.28**
    UF   United States—Secret service
Secret societies (May subdiv. geog.)
         366; 371.8
    SA   names of secret societies, e.g.
         Freemasons [to be added as
         needed]
    BT   **Rites and ceremonies**
         Societies
    NT   **Freemasons**
         Ku Klux Klan
    RT   **Fraternities and sororities**
Secret writing
    USE **Cryptography**
Secretarial practice
    USE **Office practice**
Secretaries (May subdiv. geog.)   **651.3**
    BT   **Office management**

Secrets, Trade
USE **Trade secrets**
Sectionalism
USE **Regionalism**
Sectionalism (United States)
USE **Regionalism—United States**
Sects (May subdiv. geog.)   **209; 280**

Use for materials on independent religious groups whose teachings or practices fall within the normative bounds of the major world religions. Materials on the major world religions are entered under **Religions.** Materials on groups or movements whose beliefs or practices differ significantly from the traditional religions, often focused upon a charismatic leader, are entered under **Cults.**

UF   Church denominations
       Denominations, Religious
       Religious denominations
SA   names of churches and sects
       within the major world reli-
       gions, e.g. **Presbyterian**
       Church; Hasidim; etc. [to be
       added as needed]
BT   **Church history**
       Religions
NT   **Christian sects**
RT   **Cults**
Secular humanism
USE **Secularism**
Secularism (May subdiv. geog.)   **171;**
       211

Use for materials on any intellectual or philosophical movement or set of beliefs that promotes human values as separate and distinct from religious doctrines.

UF   Humanism, Secular
       Secular humanism
BT   **Ethics**
       Utilitarianism
NT   **Atheism**
       Rationalism
RT   **Humanism**
Securities (May subdiv. geog.)   **332.63**
UF   Capitalization (Finance)
       Dividends
SA   types of securities [to be added
       as needed]
BT   **Finance**
       Investments
       Stock exchanges
NT   **Bonds**
       Capital market
       Day trading (Securities)
       Futures

Insider trading
Mortgages
Stocks
Securities exchange
USE **Stock exchanges**
Securities fraud (May subdiv. geog.)
       345; 364.1
UF   Stock fraud
       Stock market fraud
BT   **Fraud**
Securities trading, Insider
USE **Insider trading**
Security, Internal
USE **Internal security**
Security, International
USE **International security**
Security measures
USE   subjects with the subdivision *Se-*
       curity measures, e.g. **Nuclear**
       power plants—Security mea-
       sures [to be added as needed]
Seder   **296.4**
BT   **Judaism—Customs and prac-**
       tices
       Passover
Sedition
USE **Political crimes and offenses**
       Revolutions
Seeds   **581.4**
BT   **Plant propagation**
       Plants
NT   **Nuts**
Seeds—Germination
USE **Germination**
Seeing eye dogs
USE **Guide dogs**
Seeking attention
USE **Showing off**
Segregation (May subdiv. geog.)   **305.8**
UF   Desegregation
SA   segregation in particular areas,
       e.g. **Segregation in educa-**
       tion; and racial and ethnic
       groups and classes of persons
       with the subdivision *Segrega-*
       tion, e.g. **African Ameri-**
       cans—Segregation [to be
       added as needed]
BT   **Race relations**
NT   **African Americans—Segrega-**
       tion

Segregation—*Continued*
      Apartheid
      Blacks—Segregation
      Segregation in education
  RT **Discrimination**
      Minorities
Segregation in education (May subdiv.
  geog.) **379.2**
  UF Education—Integration
      Education—Segregation
      Integration in education
      Racial balance in schools
  BT **Segregation**
  RT **Discrimination in education**
      School integration
Segregation in housing
  USE **Discrimination in housing**
Segregation in public accommodations
  USE **Discrimination in public ac-
      commodations**
Seismic sea waves
  USE **Tsunamis**
Seismography
  USE **Earthquakes**
Seismology
  USE **Earthquakes**
Selection, Artificial
  USE **Breeding**
Selective service
  USE **Draft**
Self **126; 155.2**
  BT **Consciousness**
      Individuality
      Personality
  NT **Ego (Psychology)**
      Human body
      Identity (Psychology)
Self-acceptance **155.2**
  UF Self-love (Psychology)
  BT **Psychology**
  RT **Self-confidence**
      Self-esteem
      Self-perception
Self-actualization
  USE **Self-realization**
Self-assurance
  USE **Self-confidence**
      Self-reliance
Self-awareness
  USE **Self-perception**
Self-care, Health
  USE **Health self-care**

Self-care, Medical
  USE **Health self-care**
Self-concept
  USE **Self-perception**
Self-confidence **155.2**
  UF Self-assurance
  BT **Emotions**
  RT **Assertiveness (Psychology)**
      Self-acceptance
      Self-consciousness
      Self-esteem
      Self-reliance
Self-consciousness **155.2**
  UF Embarrassment
  BT **Psychology**
  RT **Self-confidence**
      Self-esteem
      Self-perception
Self-control **153.8**
  UF Self-discipline
      Self-mastery
      Will power
      Willpower
  BT **Psychology**
Self-culture
  USE **Self-improvement**
      Self-instruction
Self-defense **613.6; 796.8**
  UF Fighting
  NT **Boxing**
      Judo
      Karate
      Self-defense for children
      Self-defense for women
  RT **Martial arts**
Self-defense for children **613.6**
  UF Children—Defense
      Children—Self-defense
  BT **Self-defense**
Self-defense for women **613.6; 796.8**
  UF Fighting
      Women—Self-defense
      Women's self-defense
  BT **Self-defense**
  RT **Martial arts**
Self-defense in animals
  USE **Animal defenses**
Self-defense in plants
  USE **Plant defenses**
Self-determination, National
  USE **National self-determination**

Self-development
    USE   **Self-improvement**
            Self-instruction
Self-discipline
    USE   **Self-control**
Self-education
    USE   **Self-instruction**
Self-employed (May subdiv. geog.)
    331.12
    UF   Freelancers
    BT   **Businesspeople**
    NT   **Entrepreneurs**
            Home-based business
            Professions
Self-employed women (May subdiv. geog.)
    331.4
    UF   Women, Self-employed
    BT   **Women—Employment**
Self-esteem   **155.2**
    UF   Self-love (Psychology)
            Self-respect
    BT   **Psychology**
    RT   **Self-acceptance**
            Self-confidence
            Self-consciousness
            Self-perception
Self-evaluation in education
    USE   **Educational evaluation**
Self-examination, Medical
    USE   **Health self-care**
Self-expectations, Perfectionist
    USE   **Perfectionism (Personality**
             trait)
Self-fulfillment
    USE   **Self-realization**
Self-government
    USE   **Democracy**
            Representative government and
             representation
Self-government (in education)
    USE   **Student government**
Self health care
    USE   **Health self-care**
Self-help groups   **361.4; 616.85**
    UF   Mutual support groups
            Support groups
    BT   **Counseling**
Self-help medical care
    USE   **Health self-care**
Self image
    USE   **Personal appearance**

Self-improvement   **158**
    UF   Personal development
            Personal growth
            Self-culture
            Self-development
    BT   **Life skills**
    RT   **Self-instruction**
Self-instruction   **371.39**
    UF   Home education
            Home study courses
            Self-culture
            Self-development
            Self-education
            Teach yourself courses
    SA   subjects with the subdivision
            Programmed instruction, e.g.
            English language—Pro-
            grammed instruction [to be
            added as needed]
    BT   **Education**
            Study skills
    RT   **Correspondence schools and**
            courses
            Self-improvement
Self-love (Psychology)
    USE   **Self-acceptance**
            Self-esteem
Self-mastery
    USE   **Self-control**
Self-medication
    USE   **Health self-care**
Self-mutilation   **616.85**
    BT   **Abnormal psychology**
Self-perception   **155.2**
    UF   Self-awareness
            Self-concept
    BT   **Psychology**
    NT   **Body image**
    RT   **Self-acceptance**
            Self-consciousness
            Self-esteem
Self-protection in animals
    USE   **Animal defenses**
Self-protection in plants
    USE   **Plant defenses**
Self-realization   **155.2; 158**
    UF   Fulfillment, Self
            Self-actualization
            Self-fulfillment
    BT   **Psychology**
    RT   **Success**

Self-reliance   179
　　UF　Self-assurance
　　RT　**Self-confidence**
　　　　Survival skills
Self-respect
　　USE　**Self-esteem**
Selfishness   179
　　BT　**Personality**
Selling   381; 658.8
　　UF　Salesmanship
　　BT　**Business**
　　　　Retail trade
　　NT　**Auctions**
　　　　Direct selling
　　　　Mail-order business
　　　　Sales management
　　　　Secondhand trade
　　RT　**Advertising**
　　　　Marketing
Selling of infants
　　USE　**Adoption—Corrupt practices**
Semantics   121; 302.2; 401
　　BT　**Language and languages**
　　　　Linguistics
　　NT　**Semiotics**
Semiarid regions
　　USE　**Arid regions**
Semiconductors   621.3815
　　BT　**Electric conductors**
　　　　Electronics
　　NT　**Microelectronics**
　　　　Transistors
Semiotics   302.2; 401
　　Use for materials on the relationship be-
　　tween signs and symbols and whatever it is
　　they stand for.
　　BT　**Semantics**
　　NT　**Visual literacy**
　　RT　**Signs and symbols**
Semitic peoples (May subdiv. geog.)
　　　　305.892
　　BT　**Ethnology**
Senate (U.S.)
　　USE　**United States. Congress. Senate**
Senescence
　　USE　**Aging**
Senior citizens
　　USE　**Elderly**
Sense of direction
　　USE　**Direction sense**

Senses and sensation   152.1; 612.8
　　BT　**Intellect**
　　　　Physiology
　　　　Psychology
　　　　Psychophysiology
　　　　Theory of knowledge
　　NT　**Color sense**
　　　　Gestalt psychology
　　　　Hearing
　　　　Pain
　　　　Perception
　　　　Pleasure
　　　　Senses and sensation in ani-
　　　　　　mals
　　　　Smell
　　　　Taste
　　　　Touch
　　　　Vision
Senses and sensation in animals   573.8
　　SA　particular senses in animals, e.g.
　　　　Hearing in animals [to be
　　　　　　added as needed]
　　BT　**Senses and sensation**
　　NT　**Hearing in animals**
Sensing, Remote
　　USE　**Remote sensing**
Sensitivity training
　　USE　**Group relations training**
Separate development (Race relations)
　　USE　**Apartheid**
Separation anxiety in children   155.4
　　BT　**Anxiety**
　　　　Child psychology
Separation (Law)
　　USE　**Divorce**
Separation of church and state
　　USE　**Church and state**
Separation of powers (May subdiv. geog.)
　　　　320.4; 342
　　UF　Division of powers
　　　　Powers, Separation of
　　BT　**Constitutional law**
　　　　Executive power
　　　　Political science
Separation of powers—United States
　　　　320.473
　　UF　United States—Separation of
　　　　　　powers
Separatism, Black
　　USE　**Black nationalism**

Separatist movement in Québec (Province)
USE **Québec (Province)—History—
    Autonomy and independence
    movements**
**September 11 terrorist attacks, 2001
    973.931**
UF Pentagon (Va.) terrorist attack,
    2001
    Terrorist attacks, September 11,
    2001
    World Trade Center (New York,
    N.Y.) terrorist attack, 2001
BT **Terrorism—United States**
Sepulchers
USE **Tombs**
Sepulchral brasses
USE **Brasses**
Sequences (Mathematics)   510
UF Mathematical sequences
    Numerical sequences
BT **Algebra
    Mathematics**
Serial killers   364.15
UF Serial murderers
BT **Criminals
    Homicide**
Serial murderers
USE **Serial killers**
Serial publications (May subdiv. geog.)
    050

Use for general materials on publications in
any medium issued in successive parts bearing
numerical or chronological designations and
intended to be continued indefinitely.

BT **Bibliography
    Publishers and publishing**
NT **Almanacs
    Newspapers
    Periodicals
    School yearbooks
    Yearbooks**
RT **International Standard Serial
    Numbers**
Serigraphy
USE **Silk screen printing**
Sermon on the mount   226.9
UF Jesus Christ—Sermon on the
    mount
Sermons (May subdiv. geog.)   **204; 252**
Use for collections of sermons of several
religions and for collections of Christian ser-
mons not limited to a single topic, occasion,
or Christian denomination. Materials on the
art of writing and delivering sermons are en-
tered under **Preaching.**
SA sermons of particular countries,
    languages, or religions, e.g.
    **English sermons; Islamic
    sermons;** etc.; sermons
    preached at particular times of
    year or on particular occa-
    sions, e.g. **Lenten sermons;**
    and topics and Christian de-
    nominations with the subdivi-
    sion *Sermons,* e.g. **Christian
    life—Sermons; Presbyterian
    Church—Sermons;** etc. [to
    be added as needed]
BT **Christian literature**
NT **Christian life—Sermons
    English sermons
    Islamic sermons
    Lenten sermons
    Presbyterian Church—Sermons**
RT **Preaching**
Serpents
USE **Snakes**
Servants
USE **Household employees**
Service books (Liturgy)
USE **Liturgies**
Service, Customer
USE **Customer services**
Service (in industry)
USE **Customer services**
Service industries (May subdiv. geog.)
    338.4
SA types of service industries [to be
    added as needed]
BT **Industries**
NT **Food service
    Hospitality industry
    Hotels and motels
    Lease and rental services
    Undertakers and undertaking**
Service stations (May subdiv. geog.)
    629.28
UF Filling stations
    Gas stations
BT **Automobile industry
    Petroleum industry**
Servicemen
USE **Military personnel**

Services, Customer
USE **Customer services**
Services for
USE classes of persons, ethnic
groups, animals, and types of
schools with the subdivision
Services for, e.g. **Handi-**
capped—Services for [to be
added as needed]
Services for the handicapped
USE **Handicapped—Services for**
Servicewomen
USE **Military personnel**
Servitude
USE **Peonage**
Slavery
Servomechanisms   629.8
UF Automatic control
BT **Automation**
Feedback control systems
Set theory   511.3
UF Aggregates
Classes (Mathematics)
Ensembles (Mathematics)
Mathematical sets
Sets (Mathematics)
BT **Mathematics**
NT **Arithmetic**
Boolean algebra
Fractals
Functions
Number theory
Topology
RT **Symbolic logic**
Sets, Fractal
USE **Fractals**
Sets (Mathematics)
USE **Set theory**
Sets of fractional dimension
USE **Fractals**
Settlement of land
USE **Land settlement**
Settlements, Social
USE **Social settlements**
Seven Years' War, 1756-1763   940.2
BT **Europe—History—1492-1789**
NT **United States—History—1755-**
1763, French and Indian
War
Seventeenth century
USE **World history—17th century**

Seville (Spain). World's Fair, 1992
USE **Expo 92 (Seville, Spain)**
Sewage disposal (May subdiv. geog.)
628.3
BT **Public health**
Refuse and refuse disposal
RT **Water pollution**
Sewerage (May subdiv. geog.)   **628**
UF Sewers
BT **House drainage**
Municipal engineering
Plumbing
Sanitary engineering
RT **Drainage**
Sewers
USE **Sewerage**
Sewing   646.2
BT **Home economics**
NT **Embroidery**
Quilting
Soft toy making
RT **Dressmaking**
Needlework
Sex
USE **Sexual behavior**
Sex bias
USE **Sexism**
Sex (Biology)   571.8; 612.6
Use for materials on the physical traits that
distinguish the male and female of a species
and on the physiological aspects of sexuality.
Materials on the social and behavioral aspects
of sexuality are entered under **Sexual behav-**
ior. Materials on the psychology of sexuality
are entered under **Sex (Psychology).**
UF Sex—Physiological aspects
Sexuality
BT **Biology**
NT **Puberty**
Reproductive system
Sexual disorders
RT **Reproduction**
Sexual behavior
Sex change
USE **Transsexualism**
Sex crimes (May subdiv. geog.)   **364.15**
UF Sexual abuse
Sexual crimes
Sexual offenses
SA types of sex crimes [to be added
as needed]
BT **Crime**
Sexual behavior

Sex crimes—*Continued*
    NT   **Child sexual abuse**
           Incest
           Rape
Sex differences (Psychology)   155.3
    BT   **Sex (Psychology)**
    NT   **Androgyny**
           Sex role
Sex discrimination (May subdiv. geog.)
      305.3

    Use for materials on the restriction or denial of rights, privileges, or choice because of one's sex. Materials on prejudicial attitudes toward people because of their sex are entered under **Sexism.**
    BT   **Discrimination**
           Sexism
    NT   **Equal rights amendments**
           Women's rights
Sex disorders
    USE   **Sexual disorders**
Sex education (May subdiv. geog.)
      372.37; 613.9071; 649
    UF   Sex instruction
    BT   **Family life education**
    RT   **Sexual hygiene**
Sex in art
    USE   **Erotic art**
Sex in mass media   302.23
    BT   **Mass media**
Sex in popular culture   306.7
    BT   **Popular culture**
Sex in the office
    USE   **Sex in the workplace**
Sex in the workplace   306.7; 658
    UF   Office romance
           Sex in the office
    BT   **Sexual behavior**
    RT   **Sexual harassment**
Sex instruction
    USE   **Sex education**
Sex organs
    USE   **Reproductive system**
Sex—Physiological aspects
    USE   **Sex (Biology)**
Sex—Psychological aspects
    USE   **Sex (Psychology)**
Sex (Psychology)   155.3

    Use for materials on the psychology of sexuality. Materials on the social and behavioral aspects of sexuality are entered under **Sexual behavior.** Materials on the physiological traits that distinguish the male and female of a species and on the physiological aspects of sexuality are entered under **Sex (Biology).**

    UF   Sex—Psychological aspects
           Sexual behavior, Psychology of
           Sexual psychology
           Sexuality
    BT   **Psychology**
    NT   **Femininity**
           Masculinity
           Sex differences (Psychology)
    RT   **Sexual behavior**
Sex role   305.3

    Use for materials on the patterns of attitudes and behavior that are regarded as appropriate to one sex rather than the other.

    UF   Female role
           Gender identity
           Male role
           Sexual identity
    BT   **Sex differences (Psychology)**
           Sexual behavior
           Social role
    NT   **Androgyny**
           Transsexualism
    RT   **Sexism**
Sex therapy   616.6; 616.85
    BT   **Psychotherapy**
    RT   **Sexual disorders**
Sexism (May subdiv. geog.)   305.3

    Use for materials on prejudicial attitudes toward people because of their sex. Materials on the restriction or denial of rights, privileges, or choice because of one's sex are entered under **Sex discrimination.**

    UF   Sex bias
    BT   **Attitude (Psychology)**
           Prejudices
    NT   **Sex discrimination**
    RT   **Sex role**
Sexual abstinence   176; 306.73

    Use for materials on abstinence from sexual activity. Materials on the virtue that moderates and regulates the sexual appetite in human beings are entered under **Chastity.** Materials on the renunciation of marriage for religious reasons are entered under **Celibacy.**

    UF   Abstinence, Sexual
    BT   **Asceticism**
           Sexual behavior
    RT   **Birth control**
           Celibacy
           Chastity
Sexual abuse
    USE   **Child sexual abuse**
            Sex crimes
            Sexual harassment

Sexual assault
USE **Rape**
Sexual behavior   306.7
   Use for materials on the social and behavioral aspects of sexuality. Materials on the physiological traits that distinguish the male and female of a species and on the physiological aspects of sexuality are entered under **Sex (Biology)**. Materials on the psychology of sexuality are entered under **Sex (Psychology)**.
   UF   Sex
        Sexuality
   SA   social groups and classes of persons with the subdivision *Sexual behavior,* e.g. **College students—Sexual behavior** [to be added as needed]
   BT   **Human behavior**
   NT   **College students—Sexual behavior**
        Computer sex
        Homosexuality
        Sex crimes
        Sex in the workplace
        Sex role
        Sexual abstinence
        Sexual behavior in animals
        Sexual deviation
        Sexual harassment
   RT   **Sex (Biology)**
        Sex (Psychology)
        Sexual disorders
        Sexual ethics
Sexual behavior in animals   591.56
   UF   Animal sexual behavior
        Animals—Sexual behavior
        Breeding behavior
        Mating behavior
        Reproductive behavior
   BT   **Animal behavior**
        Sexual behavior
   NT   **Animal courtship**
Sexual behavior, Psychology of
   USE   **Sex (Psychology)**
Sexual crimes
   USE   **Sex crimes**
Sexual deviation   306.7; 616.85
   UF   Deviation, Sexual
        Perversion, Sexual
        Sexual perversion
   BT   **Sexual behavior**
        Sexual disorders

Sexual disorders   616.6; 616.85
   UF   Sex disorders
   BT   **Sex (Biology)**
   NT   **Sexual deviation**
   RT   **Sex therapy**
        Sexual behavior
Sexual ethics (May subdiv. geog.)   **176**
   BT   **Ethics**
   NT   **Adultery**
        Chastity
        Free love
        Prostitution
        Sexual harassment
   RT   **Sexual behavior**
Sexual harassment (May subdiv. geog.)   **331.13; 344**
   UF   Harassment, Sexual
        Sexual abuse
   BT   **Sexual behavior**
        Sexual ethics
   RT   **Sex in the workplace**
Sexual hygiene   613.9
   UF   Hygiene, Sexual
        Social hygiene
   BT   **Hygiene**
   NT   **Birth control**
        Safe sex in AIDS prevention
        Sexually transmitted diseases— Prevention
   RT   **Sex education**
        Sexually transmitted diseases
Sexual identity
   USE   **Sex role**
Sexual offenses
   USE   **Sex crimes**
Sexual perversion
   USE   **Sexual deviation**
Sexual psychology
   USE   **Sex (Psychology)**
Sexuality
   USE   **Sex (Biology)**
        Sex (Psychology)
        Sexual behavior
Sexually abused children
   USE   **Child sexual abuse**
Sexually transmitted diseases (May subdiv. geog.)   **616.95**
   UF   VD
        Venereal diseases
   SA   types of sexually transmitted diseases [to be added as needed]

Sexually transmitted diseases—*Continued*
>BT Communicable diseases
>NT Syphilis
>RT Sexual hygiene

Sexually transmitted diseases—Prevention 616.95
>UF Safe sex
>BT Sexual hygiene

Shade gardens
>USE Gardening in the shade

Shades and shadows 741.2
>UF Light and shade
>Shadows
>BT Drawing

Shadow economy
>USE Underground economy

Shadow pantomimes and plays 791.5
>BT Amateur theater
>Pantomimes
>Puppets and puppet plays
>Shadow pictures
>Theater

Shadow pictures 793
>UF Hand shadows
>Shadowplay
>BT Amusements
>NT Shadow pantomimes and plays

Shadowplay
>USE Shadow pictures

Shadows
>USE Shades and shadows

Shady gardens
>USE Gardening in the shade

Shaft sinking
>USE Drilling and boring (Earth and rocks)

Shakers (May subdiv. geog.) 289
>BT Christian sects

Shakespeare, William, 1564-1616 822.3

When applicable, the subdivisions provided with this heading may be used for other voluminous authors, e.g. Dante; Goethe; etc. These headings are to be used for materials about Shakespeare and about his writings. The texts of his plays, etc., are not given subject headings.

Shakespeare, William, 1564-1616—Adaptations 822.3

May be used for individual works, collections, or materials about literary, cinematic, video, or television adaptations of Shakespeare's works.

>UF Shakespeare, William, 1564-1616—Paraphrases

Shakespeare, William, 1564-1616—Allusions 822.3

Shakespeare, William, 1564-1616—Anniversaries 822.3

Shakespeare, William, 1564-1616—Authorship 822.3
>UF Bacon-Shakespeare controversy

Shakespeare, William, 1564-1616—Bibliography 016.8223

Shakespeare, William, 1564-1616—Biography—Psychology
>USE Shakespeare, William, 1564-1616—Psychology

Shakespeare, William, 1564-1616—Characters 822.3

Shakespeare, William, 1564-1616—Comedies 822.3

Use for materials about the comedies, not for the texts of the plays.

Shakespeare, William, 1564-1616—Concordances 822.303
>UF Shakespeare, William, 1564-1616—Indexes

Shakespeare, William, 1564-1616—Criticism 822.3

Use for materials discussing the criticism of Shakespeare's works, including historical materials. Criticism of Shakespeare's works in general is entered under Shakespeare, William, 1564-1616. Criticism of the comedies is entered under Shakespeare, William, 1564-1616—Comedies; criticism of the sonnets under Shakespeare, William, 1564-1616—Sonnets; etc. Criticism of an individual play is entered under Shakespeare, William, 1564-1616, followed by the title of the play.

>UF Shakespeare, William, 1564-1616—Criticism, interpretation, etc.
>Shakespeare, William, 1564-1616—Psychological studies

Shakespeare, William, 1564-1616—Criticism, interpretation, etc.
>USE Shakespeare, William, 1564-1616—Criticism

Shakespeare, William, 1564-1616—Dictionaries 822.303
>BT Encyclopedias and dictionaries

Shakespeare, William, 1564-1616—Discography 016.8223

Shakespeare, William, 1564-1616—Dramatic production 822.3
>UF Shakespeare, William, 1564-1616—Stage setting and scenery

Shakespeare, William, 1564-1616—Ethics
822.3
    UF   Shakespeare, William, 1564-
1616—Moral ideas
Shakespeare, William, 1564-
1616—Religion and ethics
Shakespeare, William, 1564-1616—Filmography   016.8223
Shakespeare, William, 1564-1616—Histories 822.3
    Use for materials about the histories, not for
the texts of the plays.
Shakespeare, William, 1564-1616—Indexes
    USE Shakespeare, William, 1564-
1616—Concordances
Shakespeare, William, 1564-1616—Influence 822.3
    Use for materials on Shakespeare's influ-
ence on national literatures, literary movements, or specific persons.
Shakespeare, William, 1564-1616—
Knowledge 822.3
    Use for materials on Shakespeare's knowl-
edge or treatment of specific subjects. May be
subdivided by subject, e.g. Shakespeare, William, 1564-1616—Knowledge—Animals; etc.
Shakespeare, William, 1564-1616—Moral
ideas
    USE Shakespeare, William, 1564-
1616—Ethics
Shakespeare, William, 1564-1616—Para-
phrases
    USE Shakespeare, William, 1564-
1616—Adaptations
Shakespeare, William, 1564-1616—Parodies, imitations, etc. 822.3
    UF   Shakespeare, William, 1564-
1616—Parodies, travesties,
etc.
Shakespeare, William, 1564-1616—Parodies, travesties, etc.
    USE Shakespeare, William, 1564-
1616—Parodies, imitations,
etc.
Shakespeare, William, 1564-1616—Poetic
works 822.3
    Use for materials about the poetic works,
not for the poetic texts themselves.
Shakespeare, William, 1564-1616—Portraits 822.3022
Shakespeare, William, 1564-1616—Psychological studies
    USE Shakespeare, William, 1564-
1616—Criticism

Shakespeare, William, 1564-
1616—Psychology
Shakespeare, William, 1564-1616—Psychology 822.3
    UF   Shakespeare, William, 1564-
1616—Biography—Psychology
Shakespeare, William, 1564-
1616—Psychological studies
Shakespeare, William, 1564-1616—Quotations 822.3
Shakespeare, William, 1564-1616—Religion 822.3
    UF   Shakespeare, William, 1564-
1616—Religion and ethics
Shakespeare, William, 1564-1616—Religion
and ethics
    USE Shakespeare, William, 1564-
1616—Ethics
Shakespeare, William, 1564-
1616—Religion
Shakespeare, William, 1564-1616—Sonnets 822.3
    Use for materials about the sonnets, not for
the texts of the sonnets.
Shakespeare, William, 1564-1616—Stage
history 792; 822.3
    BT   Theater
Shakespeare, William, 1564-1616—Stage
setting and scenery
    USE Shakespeare, William, 1564-
1616—Dramatic production
Shakespeare, William, 1564-1616—Style
    USE Shakespeare, William, 1564-
1616—Technique
Shakespeare, William, 1564-1616—Technique 822.3
    UF   Shakespeare, William, 1564-
1616—Style
Shakespeare, William, 1564-1616—Tragedies 822.3
    Use for materials about the tragedies, not
for the texts of the plays.
Shame 152.4
    BT   Emotions
    RT   Guilt
Shape 516
    UF   Shapes
Size and shape
    SA   types of geometric shapes, e.g.
Square [to be added as need-
ed]

Shape—*Continued*
    BT   **Concepts**
          Geometry
          Perception
    NT   **Square**
Shapes
    USE **Shape**
Sharecropping (May subdiv. geog.)
    333.33
    BT   **Farm tenancy**
Shared custody
    USE **Child custody**
Shared housing (May subdiv. geog.)
    363.5; 643
    Use for materials on two or more single, unrelated adults who live together.
    UF   Home sharing
          House sharing
    BT   **Housing**
    NT   **Unmarried couples**
    RT   **Roommates**
Shared parenting
    USE **Part-time parenting**
Shared reading books
    USE **Big books**
Shares of stock
    USE **Stocks**
Shareware (Computer software)   **005.3**
    Use for materials on computer software offered to consumers on a trial basis with the provision that they pay a voluntary fee if they want to use it.
    UF   Software for sharing
    BT   **Computer software**
Sharing of jobs
    USE **Job sharing**
Sheep   **599.649; 636.3**
    UF   Lambs
    BT   **Domestic animals**
          Mammals
Sheet metalwork   **671.8**
    UF   Press working of metal
    BT   **Metalwork**
    NT   **Plate metalwork**
Sheffield plate   **739.2**
    BT   **Plate**
Shellfish   **594; 641.3**
    BT   **Aquatic animals**
    NT   **Crabs**
          Crustacea
          Lobsters
          Mollusks

Shells (May subdiv. geog.)   **591.47; 594.147**
    Use for popular materials on seashells and shell collecting. Systematic and comprehensive materials on shells are entered under **Mollusks.**
    UF   Sea shells
    RT   **Mollusks**
Shells (Projectiles)
    USE **Projectiles**
Shelterbelts
    USE **Windbreaks**
Shelters, Air raid
    USE **Air raid shelters**
Sherlock Holmes (Fictitious character)
    USE **Holmes, Sherlock (Fictitious character)**
Sherlock Holmes films   **791.43**
    May be used for individual works, collections, or materials about Sherlock Holmes films.
    BT   **Motion pictures**
          Mystery films
Shinto (May subdiv. geog.)   **299.5**
    BT   **Religions**
Ship building
    USE **Shipbuilding**
Ship models
    USE **Ships—Models**
Ship pilots (May subdiv. geog.)   **623.89**
    UF   Pilots
          Pilots and pilotage
    BT   **Sailors**
    RT   **Navigation**
Ship safety
    USE **Ships—Safety regulations**
Ship salvage
    USE **Marine salvage**
Shipbuilding (May subdiv. geog.)   **623.8**
    UF   Ship building
          Ships—Construction
    BT   **Naval architecture**
    NT   **Marine engines**
          Steamboats
    RT   **Boatbuilding**
          Ships
Shipping (May subdiv. geog.)   **387.5**
    UF   Marine transportation
          Ocean—Economic aspects
          Ocean transportation
          Sea transportation
          Water transportation

Shipping—*Continued*
  BT Transportation
  NT Harbors
      Inland navigation
      Marine insurance
      Maritime law
      Territorial waters
  RT Merchant marine
Shipping—United States 387.00973
Ships (May subdiv. geog.) 387.2; 623.82
  UF Vessels (Ships)
  SA types of ships and vessels and
      names of individual ships [to
      be added as needed]
  NT Clipper ships
      Hospital ships
      Lightships
      Merchant marine
      Sailing
      Steamboats
      Submarines
      Warships
      Yachts and yachting
  RT Boats and boating
      Shipbuilding
Ships—Construction
  USE Shipbuilding
Ships in art
  USE Marine painting
Ships—Models 623.82
  UF Model ships
      Ship models
  BT Models and modelmaking
Ships—Safety regulations 341.7; 343
  UF Merchant marine—Safety regula-
      tions
      Ship safety
  BT Maritime law
      Safety regulations
Shipwrecks 363.12; 910.4
  UF Marine disasters
  SA names of wrecked ships [to be
      added as needed]
  BT Accidents
      Adventure and adventurers
      Disasters
      Navigation
      Voyages and travels
  RT Marine salvage
      Survival after airplane acci-
      dents, shipwrecks, etc.

Shoe industry (May subdiv. geog.)
      338.4; 685
  BT Clothing industry
      Leather industry
  RT Shoes
Shoes (May subdiv. geog.) 391.4; 646;
      685
  UF Boots
      Footwear
  BT Clothing and dress
  RT Shoe industry
Shooting (May subdiv. geog.) 799.3
    Use for materials on the use of firearms.
    Materials on shooting game are entered under
    Hunting.
  NT Archery
      Decoys (Hunting)
  RT Firearms
      Hunting
Shooting stars
  USE Meteors
Shootings in schools
  USE School shootings
Shop management
  USE Factory management
Shop practice
  USE Machine shop practice
Shop windows
  USE Show windows
Shoplifting 364.16
  BT Theft
Shoppers' guides
  USE Consumer education
      Shopping
Shopping (May subdiv. geog.) 381; 640
    Use for materials on consumer buying.
    General materials on buying and materials on
    buying by commercial enterprises are entered
    under **Purchasing.**
  UF Buyers' guides
      Marketing (Home economics)
      Shoppers' guides
  SA types of products and services
      with the subdivision *Purchas-
      ing,* e.g. **Automobiles—Pur-
      chasing** [to be added as need-
      ed]
  BT Home economics
      Purchasing
  NT Grocery shopping
      Internet shopping
  RT Consumer education

Shopping centers and malls (May subdiv. geog.)   **381; 658.8**
  UF   Malls, Shopping
        Shopping malls
  BT   **Commercial buildings**
        Retail trade
  RT   **Stores**
Shopping—Computer network resources
  USE   **Internet shopping**
Shopping—Internet resources
  USE   **Internet shopping**
Shopping malls
  USE   **Shopping centers and malls**
Shops
  USE   **Stores**
Short films   **791.43**
   May be used for individual works, collections, or materials about short films.
  BT   **Motion pictures**
Short plays
  USE   **One act plays**
Short stories   **808.83**
   Use for collections of short stories by one author or by several authors. Materials on the short story as a literary form and on the technique of writing short stories are entered under **Short story.**
  UF   Stories
  BT   **Fiction**
Short stories—Indexes   **016.80883**
Short story   **808.3**
   Use for materials on the short story as a literary form and on the technique of writing short stories. Collections of stories are entered under **Short stories.**
  BT   **Authorship**
        Fiction
        Literature
  RT   **Storytelling**
Shorthand   **653**
  UF   Stenography
  BT   **Business education**
        Office practice
        Writing
  RT   **Abbreviations**
Shortwave radio   **621.3841**
  UF   High-frequency radio
        UHF radio
        Ultrahigh frequency radio
        Very high frequency radio
        VHF radio
  BT   **Radio**
        Radio frequency modulation

  NT   **Amateur radio stations**
        Citizens band radio
        Microwave communication systems
        Microwaves
Shotguns   **683.4**
  UF   Guns
  BT   **Firearms**
Show business
  USE   **Performing arts**
Show windows   **659.1**
  UF   Shop windows
        Window dressing
  BT   **Advertising**
        Decoration and ornament
        Windows
Showers (Parties)   **793.2**
  BT   **Parties**
Showing off   **302.5**
  UF   Attention-seeking
        Seeking attention
  BT   **Human behavior**
Shrines (May subdiv. geog.)   **203; 263; 726**
  NT   **Tombs**
  RT   **Pilgrims and pilgrimages**
Shroud, Holy
  USE   **Holy Shroud**
Shroud of Turin
  USE   **Holy Shroud**
Shrubs (May subdiv. geog.)   **582.1; 635.9**
  BT   **Plants**
        Trees
  NT   **Evergreens**
  RT   **Landscape gardening**
        Ornamental plants
Shyness   **155.2**
  UF   Bashfulness
  BT   **Emotions**
Sibling rivalry   **306.875**
  BT   **Child psychology**
        Siblings
Sibling sequence
  USE   **Birth order**
Siblings   **155.44; 306.875**
  UF   Brothers and sisters
        Sisters and brothers
  BT   **Family**
  NT   **Brothers**
        Sibling rivalry

Siblings—*Continued*
    Sisters
    Twins
Sick   305.9; 362.1
  UF Invalids
  BT Handicapped
  NT Church work with the sick
       Cooking for the sick
       First aid
       Mentally ill
       Terminally ill
  RT Diseases
       Home nursing
       Nursing
       Patients
Sick—Prayers   204; 242
  BT Prayers
Sickness
  USE Diseases
SIDS (Disease)
  USE Sudden infant death syndrome
Sieges
  USE Battles
Sight
  USE Vision
Sight saving books
  USE Large print books
Sign language   419
  UF Deaf—Sign language
  BT Language and languages
  NT Native American sign language
  RT Deaf—Means of communica-
       tion
       Signs and symbols
Sign painting   667
  BT Advertising
       Industrial painting
  NT Alphabets
  RT Lettering
       Signs and signboards
Signaling
  USE types of transportation and com-
       munication with the subdivi-
       sion *Signaling,* e.g. **Rail-
       roads—Signaling** [to be add-
       ed as needed]
Signals and signaling   388; 621.382
  UF Coastal signals
       Fog signals
       Military signaling
       Naval signaling

  SA types of transportation and com-
       munication with the subdivi-
       sion *Signaling,* e.g.
       Railraods—Signaling [to be
       added as needed]
  BT Communication
       Military art and science
       Naval art and science
       Navigation
       Signs and symbols
  NT Railroads—Signaling
       Sonar
  RT Flags
Signboards
  USE Signs and signboards
Signed editions
  USE Autographed editions
Signets
  USE Seals (Numismatics)
Signs (Advertising)
  USE Signs and signboards
Signs and signboards   659.13
  UF Billboards
       Road signs
       Signboards
       Signs (Advertising)
  BT Advertising
  NT Electric signs
  RT Posters
       Sign painting
Signs and symbols (May subdiv. geog.)
     302.2; 419
  UF Emblems
       Symbols
  BT Communication
  NT Ciphers
       Cryptography
       Heraldry
       National emblems
       Signals and signaling
       State emblems
  RT Abbreviations
       Semiotics
       Sign language
       Symbolism
Signs and symbols in literature
  USE Symbolism in literature
Silage and silos   633.2
  UF Silos
  BT Feeds
       Forage plants

Silent films (May subdiv. geog.)   **791.43**

    May be used for individual works, collections, or materials about films made before the development of films with sound.

  UF Silent motion pictures

  BT **Motion pictures**

Silent motion pictures

  USE **Silent films**

Silk (May subdiv. geog.)   **677**

  BT **Fabrics**

       Fibers

  RT **Silkworms**

Silk screen printing (May subdiv. geog.)   **764**

  UF Screen printing

       Serigraphy

  BT **Color printing**

       Stencil work

  RT **Textile printing**

Silkworms   **595.78; 638**

  UF Cocoons

  BT **Beneficial insects**

       Insects

       Moths

  RT **Silk**

Silos

  USE **Silage and silos**

Silver (May subdiv. geog.)   **332.4; 669**

  BT **Chemical elements**

       Precious metals

  NT **Silverwork**

  RT **Coinage**

       Money

Silver articles

  USE **Silverwork**

Silver mines and mining (May subdiv. geog.)   **622**

  BT **Mines and mineral resources**

  NT **Prospecting**

Silver plate

  USE **Plate**

       Silverware

Silver work

  USE **Silverwork**

Silversmithing

  USE **Silverwork**

Silverware (May subdiv. geog.)   **642; 739.2**

  UF Flatware, Silver

       Silver plate

  BT **Decorative arts**

       Silverwork

       Tableware

Silverwork (May subdiv. geog.)   **739.2**

  UF Silver articles

       Silver work

       Silversmithing

  BT **Art metalwork**

       Metalwork

       Silver

  NT **Native American silverwork**

       Plate

       Silverware

Simple machines   **621.8**

  UF Machines, Simple

  SA types of simple machines, e.g. **Wheels** [to be added as needed]

  BT **Machinery**

       Mechanical movements

       Mechanics

  NT **Wheels**

Simplicity   **179; 646.7**

  BT **Conduct of life**

Simulation, Computer

  USE **Computer simulation**

Simulation games in education   **371.39**

  UF Educational gaming

       Educational simulation games

       Gaming, Educational

  BT **Education**

       Educational games

       Game theory

Sin   **205; 241**

  BT **Ethics**

       Good and evil

       Theology

  NT **Avarice**

       Guilt

       Pride and vanity

  RT **Forgiveness of sin**

Sin, Forgiveness of

  USE **Forgiveness of sin**

Sinai Campaign, 1956   **956.04**

  UF Anglo-French intervention in Egypt, 1956

       Arab-Israel War, 1956

       Israel-Arab War, 1956

  BT **Egypt—History**

       Israel-Arab conflicts

Singers   **782.0092; 920**

  BT **Musicians**

Singing   782; 783
    UF   School music
    BT   **Music**
    NT   **Songbooks**
          Voice culture
    RT   **Choirs (Music)**
          Vocal music
          Voice
Singing games   796.1
    BT   **Games**
Singing societies
    USE   **Choral societies**
Single child
    USE   **Only child**
Single men (May subdiv. geog.)   155.6;
    306.81
    UF   Unmarried men
    BT   **Men**
          Single people
    NT   **Divorced men**
Single-parent families (May subdiv. geog.)
    306.85
    Use for materials on households in which a
    parent living without a partner is rearing chil-
    dren. Materials on parents who were not mar-
    ried at the time of the birth of their children
    are entered under **Unmarried fathers** or **Un-
    married mothers.**
    UF   One parent family
          Single parent family
    BT   **Family**
    RT   **Single parents**
Single parent family
    USE   **Single-parent families**
Single parents (May subdiv. geog.)
    306.85
    BT   **Parents**
          Unmarried couples
    NT   **Children of single parents**
          Unmarried fathers
          Unmarried mothers
    RT   **Single-parent families**
Single parents' children
    USE   **Children of single parents**
Single people (May subdiv. geog.)
    155.6; 306.81
    UF   Unmarried people
    NT   **Divorced people**
          Single men
          Single women
Single rail railroads
    USE   **Monorail railroads**

Single-sex education
    USE   **Single-sex schools**
Single-sex schools (May subdiv. geog.)
    370
    UF   Single-sex education
    BT   **Schools**
Single women (May subdiv. geog.)
    155.6; 306.81
    UF   Unmarried women
    BT   **Single people**
          Women
    NT   **Divorced women**
Sirius   523.8
    BT   **Stars**
Sisterhoods
    USE   **Monasticism and religious or-
          ders for women**
Sisters   306.875
    BT   **Siblings**
          Women
Sisters and brothers
    USE   **Siblings**
Sisters (Religious)
    USE   **Nuns**
Sit-down strikes
    USE   **Strikes**
Sit-ins for civil rights
    USE   **Civil rights demonstrations**
Sitcoms
    USE   **Comedy television programs**
Site oriented art
    USE   **Earthworks (Art)**
Sitters (Babysitters)
    USE   **Babysitters**
Situation comedies
    USE   **Comedy television programs**
Six Day War, 1967
    USE   **Israel-Arab War, 1967**
Sixteenth century
    USE   **World history—16th century**
Size   530.8
    UF   Large and small
          Size and shape
          Small and large
    BT   **Concepts**
          Perception
Size and shape
    USE   **Shape**
          Size
Skateboarding   796.22
    BT   **Roller skating**

Skating
USE   **Ice skating**
           Roller skating
Skeletal remains
USE   **Anthropometry**
Skeleton   573.7; 611
    Use for materials limited to the morphology
    or mechanics of the skeleton, human or ani-
    mal. Comprehensive and systematic materials
    on the anatomy of bones are entered under
    Bones.
BT   **Musculoskeletal system**
RT   **Bones**
Skepticism   149; 186; 211
UF   Scepticism
          Unbelief
BT   **Free thought**
          Philosophy
          Rationalism
RT   **Agnosticism**
          Belief and doubt
          Truth
Sketching
USE   **Drawing**
Ski resorts (May subdiv. geog.)   **796.93**
BT   **Winter resorts**
Skidoos
USE   **Snowmobiles**
Skiing (May subdiv. geog.)   **796.93**
UF   Skis and skiing
          Snow skiing
BT   **Winter sports**
Skill
USE   **Ability**
Skilled labor (May subdiv. geog.)   **331.7**
BT   **Labor**
Skills
USE   **Ability**
Skin   611; 612.7
BT   **Anatomy**
          Physiology
Skin—Care   616.5; 646.7
UF   Skin care
          Skin—Care and hygiene
Skin care
USE   **Skin—Care**
Skin—Care and hygiene
USE   **Skin—Care**
Skin—Diseases   616.5
UF   Dermatitis
SA   types of skin diseases [to be
          added as needed]

BT   **Diseases**
NT   **Acne**
Skin diving (May subdiv. geog.)   **797.2**
    Use for materials on free diving with mask,
    fins, and snorkel. Materials on free diving
    with the aid of a self-contained underwater
    breathing apparatus are entered under **Scuba
    diving.**
UF   Free diving
          Snorkeling
          Underwater swimming
BT   **Deep diving**
Skinheads
USE   **White supremacy movements**
Skins
USE   **Hides and skins**
Skis and skiing
USE   **Skiing**
Skits   791
BT   **Amusements**
          Theater
Sky   520; 551.5
BT   **Astronomy**
          Atmosphere
NT   **Constellations**
Sky diving
USE   **Skydiving**
Skydiving (May subdiv. geog.)   **797.5**
UF   Sky diving
BT   **Aeronautical sports**
Skyscrapers (May subdiv. geog.)   **690;
          720**
UF   High rise buildings
BT   **Buildings**
**Skyscrapers—Earthquake effects   690;
          725**
BT   **Buildings—Earthquake effects**
          Earthquakes
Slander (Law)
USE   **Libel and slander**
Slang
USE   names of languages with the
          subdivision *Slang*, e.g. **En-
          glish language—Slang** [to be
          added as needed]
Slanted journalism
USE   **Journalism—Objectivity**
Slapstick comedies
USE   **Comedies**
          Comedy films
          Comedy television programs
Slave insurrections
USE   **Slave revolts**

Slave narratives 306.3
  BT **Autobiography**
    Slavery
Slave revolts (May subdiv. geog.) **326;**
  909
  UF Slave insurrections
  BT **Revolutions**
  RT **Slavery**
Slave trade (May subdiv. geog.) **306.3;**
  381
  BT **International law**
    Slavery
Slavery (May subdiv. geog.) **177; 306.3;**
  326; 342
  UF Abolition of slavery
    Antislavery
    Servitude
  BT **Crimes against humanity**
  NT **Slave narratives**
    Slave trade
    Slaves
  RT **Abolitionists**
    Forced labor
    Peonage
    Slave revolts
    Slaves—Emancipation
Slavery—Emancipation
  USE **Slaves—Emancipation**
Slavery—United States 306.3; 326.0973
  RT **Southern States—History**
    Underground railroad
Slavery—United States—Fiction
  808.83; 813
    Use for collections of stories dealing with
  slavery in the United States.
Slaves (May subdiv. geog.) **306.3**
  BT **Slavery**
  NT **Fugitive slaves**
Slaves—Emancipation (May subdiv.
  geog.) **306.3**
  UF Abolition of slavery
    Antislavery
    Emancipation of slaves
    Slavery—Emancipation
  BT **Freedom**
  RT **Abolitionists**
    Slavery
Sledding 796.9
  BT **Winter sports**
  RT **Sleds**
Sledges
  USE **Sleds**

Sleds 688.7
  UF Sledges
    Sleighs and sledges
  BT **Vehicles**
  RT **Sledding**
Sleep 154.6; 612.8; 613.7
  BT **Brain**
    Health
    Hygiene
    Mind and body
    Psychophysiology
    Rest
    Subconsciousness
  NT **Bedtime**
  RT **Dreams**
    Insomnia
Sleeplessness
  USE **Insomnia**
Sleighs and sledges
  USE **Sleds**
Sleight of hand
  USE **Juggling**
    Magic tricks
Slide projectors
  USE **Projectors**
Slide rule 510.28
  BT **Calculators**
    Logarithms
Slides (Photography) 778.2
  UF Color slides
    Lantern slides
    Photographic slides
  BT **Photography**
  RT **Filmstrips**
Sloppiness
  USE **Messiness**
Sloth
  USE **Laziness**
Slovakia 943.73
    May be subdivided like United States ex-
  cept for *History.*
  RT **Czechoslovakia**
Slow learning children 155.4; 371.92
    Use for materials on children with less than
  average intelligence and slow social develop-
  ment who can nonetheless be educated and
  lead a normal life.
  BT **Exceptional children**
  NT **Learning disabilities**
  RT **Mentally handicapped children**
Slum clearance
  USE **Urban renewal**

Small and large
USE **Size**
Small arms
USE **Firearms**
Small business (May subdiv. geog.)
338.6; 658.02
Use for materials on small independent business enterprises.
BT **Business**
NT **Entrepreneurship**
Home-based business
Underground economy
Small cars
USE **Compact cars**
Small loans
USE **Personal loans**
Smell **152.1**
BT **Senses and sensation**
RT **Nose**
Smelting **669**
BT **Furnaces**
NT **Blast furnaces**
Electrometallurgy
Ore dressing
RT **Metallurgy**
Smoke-ending programs
USE **Smoking cessation programs**
Smoke prevention **363.738; 628.5**
UF Prevention of smoke
BT **Sanitation**
Smoke stacks
USE **Chimneys**
Smokeless powder
USE **Gunpowder**
Smoking (May subdiv. geog.) **178;**
613.85
NT **Cigarettes**
Cigars
Tobacco habit
Tobacco pipes
RT **Tobacco**
Smoking cessation programs **613.85**
UF How-to-stop-smoking programs
Quit-smoking programs
Smoke-ending programs
BT **Tobacco habit**
Smuggling **364.1**
UF Contraband trade
BT **Crime**
Tariff
Smuggling of drugs
USE **Drug traffic**

Snack foods **641.5; 642**
UF Snacks
BT **Food**
Snacks
USE **Snack foods**
Snakes (May subdiv. geog.) **597.96**
UF Serpents
Vipers
SA types of snakes, e.g. **Rattlesnakes** [to be added as needed]
BT **Reptiles**
NT **Rattlesnakes**
Snakes as pets
Snakes as pets **636.088**
BT **Pets**
Snakes
Snapshots
USE **Photographs**
Snorkeling
USE **Skin diving**
Snow (May subdiv. geog.) **551.57**
BT **Precipitation (Meteorology)**
RT **Blizzards**
Storms
Snow boarding
USE **Snowboarding**
Snow skiing
USE **Skiing**
Snowboarding (May subdiv. geog.)
796.939
UF Snow boarding
BT **Winter sports**
Snowmobiles **629.22; 796.94**
UF Skidoos
BT **All terrain vehicles**
Soap **668**
BT **Cleaning compounds**
RT **Detergents**
Soap box derbies **796.6**
BT **Racing**
Soap carving
USE **Soap sculpture**
Soap operas **791.44; 791.45**
May be used for individual works, collections, or materials about soap operas.
BT **Radio plays**
Television plays
RT **Radio serials**
Television serials

Soap sculpture 736
  UF Soap carving
  BT **Modeling**
      Sculpture
Soaring flight
  USE **Gliding and soaring**
Sobriquets
  USE **Nicknames**
Soccer (May subdiv. geog.) **796.334**
  BT **Ball games**
      Football
      Sports
Soccer—Training **796.334**
  BT **Physical education**
Social ability
  USE **Social skills**
Social action (May subdiv. geog.) **361.2**
  UF Social activism
  SA subjects with the subdivision
      Citizen participation, e.g. **City**
      planning—Citizen participa-
      tion [to be added as needed]
  BT **Social policy**
  NT **City planning—Citizen partici-**
      pation
  RT **Political participation**
      Social problems
      Social work
Social activism
  USE **Social action**
Social adjustment **158; 303.3**
  UF Adjustment, Social
  BT **Human behavior**
      Interpersonal relations
      Social psychology
  NT **Socially handicapped**
  RT **Deviant behavior**
Social alienation
  USE **Alienation (Social psychology)**
Social anthropology
  USE **Ethnology**
Social aspects
  USE subjects with the subdivision *So-*
       cial aspects, e.g. **Genetic en-**
       gineering—Social aspects [to
       be added as needed]
Social behavior
  USE **Human behavior**
Social case work **361.3**
  UF Case work, Social
      Family social work

  BT **Social work**
  NT **Parole**
      Probation
  RT **Counseling**
Social change (May subdiv. geog.)
      303.4; 909
  UF Change, Social
      Cultural change
      Social evolution
  BT **Anthropology**
      Social sciences
      Sociology
  NT **Community development**
      Modernization (Sociology)
      Urbanization
Social classes (May subdiv. geog.)
      305.5; 323.3
  UF Class distinction
      Rank
      Social distinctions
  BT **Caste**
      Sociology
  NT **Class consciousness**
      Elite (Social sciences)
      Intellectuals
      Middle class
      Rich
      Upper class
      Working class
Social competence
  USE **Social skills**
Social conditions **306.09; 909**
  Use for materials on the social aspects of
  several of the following topics: labor, poverty,
  education, health, housing, recreation, moral
  conditions.
  UF Social history
  SA racial and ethnic groups, classes
      of persons, and names of
      countries, cities, etc., with the
      subdivision *Social conditions*
      [to be added as needed]
  BT **Sociology**
  NT **African Americans—Social**
      conditions
      Blacks—Social conditions
      Chicago (Ill.)—Social condi-
      tions
      Cost and standard of living
      Counter culture
      Economic conditions
      Jews—Social conditions

Social conditions—*Continued*
Labor
Men—Social conditions
Moral conditions
Native Americans—Social conditions
Ohio—Social conditions
Quality of life
Social movements
Social policy
Social problems
United States—Social conditions
Urbanization
Women—Social conditions
Social conflict (May subdiv. geog.)
303.6
UF Class conflict
Class struggle
Conflict, Social
BT **Social psychology**
Sociology
NT **Conflict management**
Conflict of generations
Role conflict
Social conformity
USE **Conformity**
Social contract **320.01; 320.1**
BT **Political science**
Sociology
Social customs
USE **Manners and customs**
Social democracy
USE **Socialism**
Social deviance
USE **Deviant behavior**
Social distinctions
USE **Social classes**
Social drinking
USE **Drinking of alcoholic beverages**
Social ecology
USE **Human ecology**
Social equality
USE **Equality**
Social ethics (May subdiv. geog.) **170**
BT **Ethics**
Sociology
NT **Political ethics**
RT **Social problems**
Social evolution
USE **Social change**

Social geography
USE **Human geography**
Social group work **361.4; 362**
UF Group social work
Group work, Social
Social work with groups
BT **Counseling**
Social work
Social groups **302.3; 305**
UF Group dynamics
Groups, Social
BT **Sociology**
NT **Elite (Social sciences)**
Leadership
Neighborhood
Social psychology
Teams in the workplace
Social history
USE **Social conditions**
Social hygiene
USE **Public health**
Sexual hygiene
Social identity
USE **Group identity**
Social insurance
USE **Social security**
Social isolation
USE **Loneliness**
Social learning
USE **Socialization**
Social life and customs
USE **Manners and customs**
and names of ethnic groups, countries, cities, etc., with the subdivision *Social life and customs,* e.g. **Native Americans—Social life and customs; Jews—Social life and customs; United States—Social life and customs;** etc. [to be added as needed]
Social medicine (May subdiv. geog.)
306.4; 362.1
Use for materials on the study of social, genetic, and environmental influences on human disease and disability, as well as the promotion of health measures to protect both the individual and the community.
UF Medical care—Social aspects
Medical sociology
Medicine—Social aspects
BT **Medicine**
Public health

Social medicine—*Continued*
        Public welfare
        Sociology
  NT Hospices
  RT Medical ethics
Social movements (May subdiv. geog.)
        303.48
  SA types of social movements, e.g.
        Environmental movement [to
        be added as needed]
  BT Social conditions
        Social psychology
  NT Animal rights movement
        Anti-apartheid movement
        Antinuclear movement
        Environmental movement
        Labor movement
        Militia movements
        New Age movement
        Peace movements
        Pro-choice movement
        Pro-life movement
        Protest movements
        Sanctuary movement
        Survivalism
        White supremacy movements
        Youth movement
Social planning
  USE **Social policy**
Social policy (May subdiv. geog.) **361.6**
    Use for materials on the ways a society reg-
ulates the relationships among individuals,
groups, communities, and institutions, and on
systematic procedures for achieving social
goals and managing available resources to at-
tain social change.
  UF Government policy
        National planning
        Social planning
        State planning
  SA ethnic groups, classes of per-
        sons, and topics with the sub-
        division *Government policy,*
        e.g. **Homeless persons—Gov-
        ernment policy;** and types of
        activities, facilities, industries,
        services, and undertakings
        with the subdivision *Planning,*
        e.g. **Transportation—Plan-
        ning** [to be added as needed]
  BT Planning
        Social conditions

  NT Arts—Government policy
        Education—Government policy
        Homeless persons—Govern-
        ment policy
        Land reform
        Libraries—Government policy
        Multiculturalism
        Social action
        Urban policy
        Welfare state
  RT Economic policy
Social policy—Chicago (Ill.) **361.6;
        977.3**
  UF Chicago (Ill.)—Social policy
Social policy—Ohio **361.6; 977.1**
  UF Ohio—Social policy
Social policy—United States **361.6; 973**
  UF United States—Social policy
Social problems (May subdiv. geog.)
        361.1
  UF Reform, Social
        Social reform
        Social welfare
  BT Social conditions
        Sociology
  NT Alcoholism
        Child labor
        Church and social problems
        Crime
        Discrimination
        Drug abuse
        Fetal alcohol syndrome
        Homelessness
        Juvenile delinquency
        Poverty
        Prison reform
        Prostitution
        Public health
        Race discrimination
        Solvent abuse
        Suicide
        Unemployment
  RT Social action
        Social ethics
Social problems and the church
  USE **Church and social problems**
Social problems in education
  USE **Educational sociology**
Social progress
  USE **Progress**

Social psychology (May subdiv. geog.)
302
UF   Mass psychology
BT   **Human ecology**
Psychology
Social groups
Sociology
NT   **Alienation (Social psychology)**
Audiences
Class consciousness
Cooperativeness
Discrimination
Empathy
Interpersonal relations
Interviewing
National characteristics
Organizational behavior
Political psychology
Popularity
Privacy
Public opinion
Social adjustment
Social conflict
Social movements
Social role
Stereotype (Psychology)
Violence
RT   **Applied psychology**
Crowds
Ethnopsychology
Social reform
USE   **Social problems**
Social responsibility of business (May
subdiv. geog.)   **174; 658.4**
UF   Business—Social responsibility
Corporate accountability
Corporate responsibility
Corporations—Social responsibil-
ity
Industries—Social responsibility
BT   **Business**
Business ethics
Social role   302
UF   Role, Social
BT   **Social psychology**
NT   **Role conflict**
Role playing
Sex role
Social sciences (May subdiv. geog.)   **300**
Use for general and comprehensive materi-
als on the various branches of knowledge

dealing with human society, such as sociolo-
gy, political science, economics, etc.
UF   Social studies
BT   **Civilization**
NT   **Anthropology**
Conservatism
Cross-cultural studies
Economics
Gerontology
History
Human behavior
Liberalism
Political science
Social change
Social surveys
Sociology
Social security (May subdiv. geog.)
362; 368.4
UF   Insurance, Social
Social insurance
BT   **Pensions**
NT   **Workers' compensation**
Social service
USE   **Social work**
Social settlements (May subdiv. geog.)
361.7; 362.5
UF   Church settlements
Neighborhood centers
Settlements, Social
SA   names of settlements, e.g. **Hull
House (Chicago, Ill.)** [to be
added as needed]
BT   **Charities**
Industrial welfare
Social work
NT   **Community centers**
Hull House (Chicago, Ill.)
Social skills   302; 646.7
UF   Interpersonal competence
Social ability
Social competence
BT   **Interpersonal relations**
Life skills
Social studies
USE   **Geography**
History
Social sciences
Social surveys (May subdiv. geog.)
300.7
Use for materials on the methods employed
in conducting surveys of social and economic
conditions.

Social surveys—*Continued*
   UF   Community surveys
   SA   names of regions, countries, cit-
         ies, etc., with the subdivision
         Social conditions [to be added
         as needed]
   BT   **Social sciences**
         Surveys
Social surveys—United States   301
Social systems   301
   BT   **Sociology**
         System theory
Social values (May subdiv. geog.)   303.3
   UF   Group values
   BT   **Values**
Social welfare
   USE **Charities**
         Public welfare
         Social problems
         Social work
Social work (May subdiv. geog.)   361.3
   Use for materials on the methods employed
in welfare work, public or private. Materials
on privately supported welfare activities are
entered under **Charities.** Materials on tax-
supported welfare activities are entered under
Public welfare. General materials on the vari-
ous policies, programs, services, and facilities
to meet basic human needs, such as health,
education, and welfare, are entered under **Human services.**
   UF   Social service
         Social welfare
         Welfare work
   SA   social work with particular
         groups of people, e.g. **Social
         work with the elderly;** and
         classes of persons and ethnic
         groups with the subdivision
         Services for, e.g. **Handi-
         capped—Services for** [to be
         added as needed]
   BT   **Human services**
   NT   **Charities**
         Child welfare
         Community organization
         Community services
         Crisis centers
         Group homes
         Handicapped—Services for
         Hotlines (Telephone counseling)
         Industrial welfare
         Public welfare
         Social case work

         Social group work
         Social settlements
         Social work with the elderly
   RT   **Social action**
Social work with groups
   USE **Social group work**
Social work with the elderly   362.6
   BT   **Elderly**
         Social work
Socialism (May subdiv. geog.)   320.5;
      335
   UF   Social democracy
   BT   **Collectivism**
         Economics
         Political science
   NT   **Collective settlements**
         Dialectical materialism
         Government ownership
         Proletariat
         Utopias
   RT   **Communism**
         Marxism
         National socialism
Socialism—United States   320.5;
      335.00973
Socialization (May subdiv. geog.)   303.3
   Use for materials on the process by which
individuals acquire group values and learn to
function effectively in society.
   UF   Children—Socialization
         Social learning
   BT   **Acculturation**
         Child rearing
         Education
         Sociology
   NT   **Americanization**
         Peer pressure
Socialization of industry
   USE **Government ownership**
Socialized medicine
   USE **National health insurance**
         State medicine
Socially handicapped (May subdiv. geog.)
      362
   UF   Culturally deprived
         Culturally handicapped
         Disadvantaged
         Underprivileged
   BT   **Handicapped**
         Social adjustment
   NT   **Socially handicapped children**

Socially handicapped children (May subdiv. geog.)   **362.74**
- UF   Culturally deprived children
  - Culturally handicapped children
  - Disadvantaged children
  - Underprivileged children
- BT   **Handicapped children**
  - **Socially handicapped**
- RT   **At risk students**

Socials
- USE   **Church entertainments**

Societies (May subdiv. geog.)   **060**
- UF   Learned societies
- SA   types of societies, e.g. **Choral societies;** subjects, ethnic groups, classes of persons, corporate bodies, individual persons, and sacred works with the subdivision *Societies,* e.g. **Agriculture—Societies; Women—Societies;** etc.; and names of individual societies [to be added as needed]
- BT   **Associations**
- NT   **Agriculture—Societies**
  - **Boys' clubs**
  - **Chemistry—Societies**
  - **Choral societies**
  - **Cooperative societies**
  - **Education—Societies**
  - **Elderly—Societies**
  - **Girls' clubs**
  - **History—Societies**
  - **Labor unions**
  - **Men—Societies**
  - **Parent-teacher associations**
  - **Science—Societies**
  - **Secret societies**
  - **Students—Societies**
  - **Women—Societies**
- RT   **Clubs**

Society and art
- USE   **Art and society**

Society and language
- USE   **Sociolinguistics**

Society and religion
- USE   **Religion and sociology**

Society of Friends (May subdiv. geog.)   **289.6**
- UF   Friends, Society of
  - Quakers

- BT   **Christian sects**

Society, Primitive
- USE   **Primitive societies**

Society—Religious aspects
- USE   **Religion and sociology**

Sociobiology   **304.5; 577.8; 591.56**

   Use for materials on the biological basis of social behavior, especially as transmitted genetically.
- UF   Biology—Social aspects
- BT   **Comparative psychology**
  - **Sociology**

Sociolinguistics (May subdiv. geog.)   **306.44**

   Use for materials on the study of the social aspects of language, particularly linguistic behavior, as determined by sociocultural factors.
- UF   Language and society
  - Society and language
  - Sociology of language
- BT   **Language and languages**
  - **Linguistics**
  - **Sociology**

Sociology (May subdiv. geog.)   **301**
- SA   sociology of particular religions, e.g. **Christian sociology;** and racial and ethnic groups, classes of persons, and names of countries, cities, etc., with the subdivision *Social conditions,* e.g. **United States—Social conditions** [to be added as needed[
- BT   **Social sciences**
- NT   **Christian sociology**
  - **Cities and towns**
  - **Communication**
  - **Educational sociology**
  - **Equality**
  - **Ethnic relations**
  - **Ethnopsychology**
  - **Family**
  - **Human ecology**
  - **Human settlements**
  - **Individualism**
  - **Information society**
  - **Labor**
  - **Marxism**
  - **Organizational sociology**
  - **Population**
  - **Race relations**
  - **Religion and sociology**
  - **Rural sociology**

Sociology—*Continued*
>> Social change
>> Social classes
>> Social conditions
>> Social conflict
>> Social contract
>> Social ethics
>> Social groups
>> Social medicine
>> Social problems
>> Social psychology
>> Social systems
>> Socialization
>> Sociobiology
>> Sociolinguistics
>> Urban sociology
> RT Civilization
>> Culture

Sociology and art
> USE Art and society

Sociology and religion
> USE Religion and sociology

Sociology—Book reviews 301

Sociology, Christian
> USE Christian sociology

Sociology of language
> USE Sociolinguistics

Sociology of organizations
> USE Organizational sociology

Sociology of religion
> USE Religion and sociology

Sociology, Rural
> USE Rural sociology

Sociology, Urban
> USE Urban sociology

Sodium content of food
> USE Food—Sodium content

Soft toy making 745.592
> UF Stuffed toy making
> BT Sewing
>> Toy making

Softball 796.357
> BT Ball games
>> Baseball

Software, Computer
> USE Computer software

Software for sharing
> USE Shareware (Computer software)

Software viruses
> USE Computer viruses

Soil conservation (May subdiv. geog.)
> 631.4
> UF Conservation of the soil
> BT Conservation of natural resources
>> Environmental protection
> RT Erosion
>> Soil erosion

Soil engineering
> USE Soil mechanics

Soil erosion (May subdiv. geog.) 631.4
> UF Top soil loss
> BT Erosion
> RT Soil conservation

Soil fertility
> USE Soils

Soil mechanics 620.1
> UF Soil engineering
>> Soils (Engineering)
> BT Mechanics
>> Structural engineering
> RT Foundations
>> Roads
>> Soils

Soil microbiology 631.4
> UF Soils—Bacteriology
> BT Microbiology
>> Sanitary engineering
> RT Agricultural bacteriology

Soilless agriculture
> USE Hydroponics

Soils (May subdiv. geog.) 631.4
> UF Soil fertility
> BT Agriculture
>> Economic geology
> NT Clay
>> Compost
>> Fertilizers
> RT Agricultural chemistry
>> Soil mechanics

Soils—Bacteriology
> USE Soil microbiology

Soils (Engineering)
> USE Soil mechanics

Soils, Lunar
> USE Lunar soil

Solace
> USE Consolation

Solar batteries 621.31
> UF Batteries, Solar
>> Solar cells

Solar batteries—*Continued*
> Sun powered batteries
> BT   **Electric batteries**
>   **Photovoltaic power generation**
>   **Solar radiation**

Solar cells
> USE   **Photovoltaic power generation**
>   **Solar batteries**

Solar eclipses   **523.7**
> UF   Eclipses, Solar
>   Sun—Eclipses
> BT   **Astronomy**

Solar energy (May subdiv. geog.)
     333.792; 621.47
> UF   Solar power
> BT   **Energy resources**
>   **Renewable energy resources**
>   **Solar radiation**
>   **Sun**
> NT   **Photovoltaic power generation**
>   **Solar engines**
>   **Solar heating**

Solar engines   **621.47**
> BT   **Engines**
>   **Solar energy**

Solar heating   **621.47; 697**
> SA   types of solar heating applica-
>   tions, e.g. **Solar homes** [to be
>   added as needed]
> BT   **Heating**
>   **Solar energy**
> NT   **Solar homes**

Solar homes   **697; 728**
> BT   **Domestic architecture**
>   **Houses**
>   **Solar heating**

Solar physics
> USE   **Sun**

Solar power
> USE   **Solar energy**

Solar radiation   **523.7; 621.47**
> UF   Radiation, Solar
>   Sun—Radiation
> BT   **Meteorology**
>   **Space environment**
> NT   **Greenhouse effect**
>   **Solar batteries**
>   **Solar energy**
>   **Sunspots**

Solar system   **523.2**
> SA   names of planets, e.g. **Saturn
>   (Planet)** [to be added as
>   needed]
> BT   **Astronomy**
>   **Stars**
> NT   **Asteroids**
>   **Comets**
>   **Earth**
>   **Meteors**
>   **Moon**
>   **Planets**
>   **Satellites**
>   **Sun**

Solder and soldering
> USE   **Soldering**

Soldering   **671.5**
> UF   Solder and soldering
> BT   **Metals**
>   **Metalwork**
> RT   **Welding**

Soldiers (May subdiv. geog.)   **355.0092;
920**
> UF   Army life
>   Soldiers' life
> SA   names of countries with the sub-
>   head *Army* and the subdivi-
>   sion *Military life,* e.g. **United
>   States. Army—Military life**
>   [to be added as needed]
> BT   **Armies**
>   **Military personnel**
> NT   **Mercenary soldiers**
>   **Missing in action**
>   **United States. Army—Military
>   life**
>   **United States. Army—Officers**
> RT   **Veterans**

Soldiers' handbooks
> USE   **United States. Army—Hand-
>   books, manuals, etc.**

Soldiers—Hygiene
> USE   **Military personnel—Health
>   and hygiene**

Soldiers' life
> USE   **Soldiers**
>   and names of countries with the
>   subhead *Army* and the subdi-
>   vision *Military life,* e.g. **Unit-
>   ed States. Army—Military
>   life** [to be added as needed]

Soldiers of fortune
    USE **Mercenary soldiers**
Soldiers' songs
    USE **War songs**
Soldiers—United States   355.0092; 920
    UF GIs
         United States—Soldiers
Solicitors
    USE **Lawyers**
Solid geometry   516.23
    UF Geometry, Solid
    BT **Geometry**
Solid waste disposal
    USE **Refuse and refuse disposal**
Solids   530.4; 531; 541
    BT **Physical chemistry**
         Physics
    NT **Crystals**
Solitaire (Game)   795.4
    UF Patience (Game)
    BT **Card games**
Solitude   155.9
    UF Seclusion
    RT **Loneliness**
         Privacy
Solvent abuse (May subdiv. geog.)
      362.29
    UF Aerosol sniffing
         Glue sniffing
         Inhalant abuse
         Inhalation abuse of solvents
         Paint sniffing
         Substance abuse
    BT **Social problems**
    RT **Drug abuse**
Sonar   621.389
    UF Sound navigation
    BT **Signals and signaling**
Sonata   784.18
    Use for musical scores and for materials on the sonata as a musical form.
    UF Sonatas
    BT **Musical form**
Sonatas
    USE **Sonata**
Song books
    USE **Songbooks**
Song lyrics
    USE **Popular music—Texts**

Song writing
    USE **Composition (Music)**
           Popular music—Writing and publishing
Songbooks   782.42
    Use for general collections of songs that contain both words and music. Similar collections limited to sacred songs are entered under **Hymnals.** Materials about songs are entered under **Songs.** Collections of songs on a single subject are entered under the subject with the subdivision *Songs.*
    UF Song books
    BT **Singing**
         Songs
    NT **Hymnals**
         School songbooks
Songs   782.42
    Use for materials about songs. General collections of songs that contain both words and music are entered under **Songbooks.** Collections of songs that contain the words but not the music are entered under **Poetry—Collections** for classical songs and under **Popular music—Texts** for popular songs.
    SA types of songs, e.g. **Children's Songs;** songs of particular countries, e.g. **American songs;** subjects, classes of persons, and names of persons, corporate bodies, places, or wars, with the subdivision *Songs,* for collections or individual songs about the topic or associated with the entity named, e.g. **Cowhands—Songs; Surfing—Songs; United States Military Academy—Songs; World War, 1939-1945—Songs;** etc.; and names of individual songs [to be added as needed]
    BT **Poetry**
         Vocal music
    NT **African songs**
         American songs
         Ballads
         Carols
         Children's songs
         Cowhands—Songs
         Folk songs
         Hymns
         Lullabies
         National songs
         Popular music

Songs—*Continued*
> School songbooks
> Sea songs
> Songbooks
> State songs
> Students' songs
> Surfing—Songs
> United States. Army—Songs
> War songs

Songs, African
USE **African songs**
Songs, African American
USE **African American music**
Songs and music
USE music of particular countries or ethnic groups, e.g. **American music; Native American music;** etc.; types of music, e.g. **Vocal music;** and subjects, classes of persons, and names of individual persons, corporate bodies, places, or wars, with the subdivision *Songs* for collections of songs or materials about songs pertaining to the topic or entity named, e.g. **Cowhands—Songs; Surfing—Songs; United States Military Academy—Songs** [to be added as needed]
Songs for children
USE **Children's songs**
Songwriters
USE **Composers**
> **Lyricists**
Songwriting
USE **Composition (Music)**
> **Popular music—Writing and publishing**
Sons 306.874
BT **Family**
> **Men**
NT **Father-son relationship**
> **Mother-son relationship**
Sons and fathers
USE **Father-son relationship**
Sons and mothers
USE **Mother-son relationship**
Soothsaying
USE **Divination**
Soporifics
USE **Narcotics**

Sorcery
USE **Magic**
> **Occultism**
> **Witchcraft**
Sororities
USE **Fraternities and sororities**
Sorrow
USE **Bereavement**
> **Grief**
> **Joy and sorrow**
Soul 128; 233
UF Spirit
BT **Future life**
> **Human beings (Theology)**
> **Philosophy**
NT **Immortality**
> **Psychology**
RT **Reincarnation**
Sound 534; 620.2
UF Acoustics
BT **Physics**
> **Pneumatics**
> **Radiation**
NT **Architectural acoustics**
> **Computer sound processing**
> **Hearing**
> **Noise**
> **Phonetics**
> **Sound effects**
> **Soundproofing**
> **Sounds**
> **Ultrasonics**
> **Vibration**
RT **Music—Acoustics and physics**
Sound effects 534; 620.2
BT **Sound**
Sound insulation
USE **Soundproofing**
Sound navigation
USE **Sonar**
Sound processing, Computer
USE **Computer sound processing**
Sound recording
USE **Sound—Recording and reproducing**
Sound—Recording and reproducing 621.389
> Use for materials on the equipment or the process by which sound is recorded. Materials on sound recordings that emphasize the content of the recording rather than the equipment, process, or format are entered under

Sound—Recording and reproducing—
Continued

Sound recordings. Materials about the format are entered under the format, e.g. **Compact discs.**

UF   Sound recording

SA   methods of recording, e.g. **Magnetic recorders and recording** [to be added as needed]

NT   **Compact disc players**
      High-fidelity sound systems
      MP3 players
      Stereophonic sound systems

RT   **Phonograph**
      Sound recordings

Sound recordings (May subdiv. geog.)
     621.389; 780.26

Use for general materials and for materials on sound recordings that emphasize the content of the recording rather than the format. Materials about the format are entered under the format, e.g. **Compact discs.** Materials about the equipment or the process by which sound is recorded are entered under **Sound—Recording and reproducing.**

UF   Audio cassettes
      Audiotapes
      Cassette tapes, Audio
      Discography
      Phonograph records
      Recordings, Sound
      Records, Phonograph
      Tape recordings, Audio

SA   types of sound recordings, e.g. **Compact discs** and types of music with the subdivision *Sound recordings,* e.g. **Opera—Sound recordings** [to be added as needed]

BT   **Audiovisual materials**

NT   **Audiobooks**
      Compact discs
      Opera—Sound recordings

RT   **Sound—Recording and reproducing**

Sound recordings—Copyright
   USE **Copyright—Sound recordings**

Sound waves   534; 620.2
   BT   **Vibration**
       Waves
   NT   **Ultrasonic waves**

Soundproofing   620.2; 693.8
   UF   Insulation (Sound)
       Sound insulation

BT   **Architectural acoustics**
      Sound

Sounds   534; 620.2
   BT   **Sound**

Soups   641.8
   BT   **Cooking**

Sources
   USE historical subjects, periods of history, individual literary and sacred works, and names of wars with the subdivision *Sources,* e.g. **World War, 1939-1945—Sources;** and subjects, ethnic groups, classes of persons, coporate bodies, and names of countries, states, etc., with the subdivisions *History—Sources;* e.g. **United States—History—Sources** [to be added as needed]

South Africa   968

Use for materials on the Republic of South Africa.

UF   Republic of South Africa
      Union of South Africa

BT   **Africa**
      Southern Africa

South Africa—History   968

South Africa—Race relations
     305.800968; 968
   BT   **Race relations**
   NT   **Anti-apartheid movement**
       Apartheid

South African Dutch
   USE **Afrikaners**

South Africans, Afrikaans-speaking
   USE **Afrikaners**

South America   980
   BT   **America**

South American literature
   USE **Latin American literature**

South Atlantic States
   USE **Atlantic States**

South Korea
   USE **Korea (South)**

South Pacific region
   USE **Oceania**

South Pole   998
   BT   **Polar regions**
   RT   **Antarctica**

South Sea Islands
   USE   **Oceania**
South Seas
   USE   **Oceania**
South (U.S.)
   USE   **Southern States**
Southeast Asia   959
   Use for materials dealing collectively with
   the region of Asia that includes Burma, Thai-
   land, Malaysia, Singapore, Indonesia, Viet-
   nam, Cambodia, Laos, and the Philippines.
   UF   Asia, Southeastern
   BT   **Asia**
   NT   **Indochina**
Southern Africa   968
   Use for materials dealing collectively with
   the area south of the countries of Zaire and
   Tanzania. Southern Africa includes the politi-
   cal entities of Angola, Botswana, Comoros,
   Lesotho, Madagascar, Malawi, Mozambique,
   Namibia, South Africa, Swaziland, Zambia,
   and Zimbabwe. Materials on the Republic of
   South Africa are entered under **South Africa.**
   UF   Africa, Southern
   BT   **Africa**
   NT   **South Africa**
Southern cooking   641.5975
   BT   **Cooking**
Southern lights
   USE   **Auroras**
Southern literature
   USE   **American literature—Southern**
         States
Southern States   975
   UF   South (U.S.)
   BT   **United States**
Southern States—African Americans
   USE   **African Americans—Southern**
         States
Southern States—History   975
   BT   **United States—History**
   RT   **Slavery—United States**
Southwest, New
   USE   **Southwestern States**
Southwest, Old
   USE   **Old Southwest**
Southwest Pacific region
   USE   **Oceania**
Southwestern States   979
   Use for materials on that part of the United
   States that corresponds roughly with the old
   Spanish province of New Mexico, including
   the present Arizona, New Mexico, southern
   Colorado, Utah, Nevada, and California.
   UF   Southwest, New
   BT   **United States**

Sovereigns
   USE   **Emperors**
         Kings and rulers
         Monarchy
         Queens
Sovereignty (May subdiv. geog.)   **320.1**
   BT   **International law**
         Political science
   RT   **National self-determination**
Soviet bloc
   USE   **Communist countries**
Soviet communism
   USE   **Communism—Soviet Union**
Soviet literature   890
   Use for materials on several of the litera-
   tures of the Soviet Union. Materials on the in-
   dividual literatures of the republics that made
   up the Soviet Union are entered with the ap-
   propriate adjective, e.g. **Russian literature;**
   etc.
   UF   Literatures of the Soviet Union
         Soviet Union—Literatures
   BT   **Literature**
   RT   **Russian literature**
Soviet people
   USE   **Soviets (People)**
Soviet Union   947.084
   Use for materials on the Union of Soviet
   Socialist Republics between 1917 and 1991.
   Materials on Russia or the Russian empire before 1917 are entered under **Russia.** Materials
   on the independent republic of Russia since
   its establishment in December 1991 are entered under **Russia (Federation).** Materials on
   several or all of the countries that emerged
   from the dissolution of the Soviet Union in
   1991 are entered under **Former Soviet republics.** Material specifically on the federation of
   former Soviet republics, which was established in December 1991 and does not include
   the Baltic states, are entered under **Commonwealth of Independent States.** The Baltic
   states and the other republics of the former
   Soviet Union are: Armenia (Republic); Azer-
   baijan; Belarus; Estonia; Georgia (Republic);
   Kazakhstan; Kyrgyzstan; Latvia; Lithuania;
   Moldova; Tajikistan; Turkmenistan; Ukraine;
   and Uzbekistan; to be added as needed. The
   adjective **Soviet** is used to refer to the Soviet
   Union as a whole between 1917 and 1991,
   e.g. **Soviet literature.** Materials on the citizens of the Soviet Union between 1917 and
   1991 are entered under **Soviets (People).** Materials on topics pertaining to individual republics, nationalities, or ethnic groups of the
   former Soviet Union are to be added as needed with the appropriate qualifier, e.g., **Russians; Russian language;** etc.
   UF   Union of Soviet Socialist Repub-
         lics
         USSR

Soviet Union—*Continued*
  NT   Russians
       Soviets (People)
  RT   Commonwealth of Independent
       States
       Former Soviet republics
       Russia
       Russia (Federation)
Soviet Union—Communism
  USE Communism—Soviet Union
Soviet Union—History   947.084
  UF   Soviet Union—History—1917-
       1991
Soviet Union—History—1917-1921, Revo-
  lution   947.084
  UF   Russian revolution
  BT   Revolutions
Soviet Union—History—1917-1925
  947.084
Soviet Union—History—1917-1991
  USE Soviet Union—History
Soviet Union—History—1925-1953
  947.084
Soviet Union—History—1939-1940, War
  with Finland
  USE Russo-Finnish War, 1939-1940
Soviet Union—History—1953-1985
  USE Soviet Union—History—1953-
       1991
Soviet Union—History—1953-1991
  947.085
  UF   Soviet Union—History—1953-
       1985 *[Former heading]*
       Soviet Union—History—1985-
       1991 *[Former heading]*
Soviet Union—History—1985-1991
  USE Soviet Union—History—1953-
       1991
Soviet Union—Literatures
  USE Soviet literature
Soviets (People)   920; 947.084
    Use for materials on the citizens of the So-
    viet Union between 1917 and 1991, not limit-
    ed to a single national or ethnic group. Mate-
    rials on the individual ethnic groups of the
    former Soviet Union are entered under the
    name for the ethnic group, e.g. **Russians**; etc.
  UF   Soviet people
  BT   Soviet Union
Soybean   633.3
  BT   Forage plants
Space age
  USE Astronautics and civilization

Space and time   115
  UF   Time and space
  BT   Fourth dimension
       Metaphysics
       Space sciences
       Time
  NT   Cyberspace
       Personal space
       Time travel
  RT   Relativity (Physics)
Space-based weapons
  USE Space weapons
Space biology   571.0919; 612
    Use for materials on the biology of humans
    or other earth creatures while in outer space.
    Materials on the possibility of indigenous life
    in outer space are entered under **Life on oth-
    er planets.**
  UF   Astrobiology
       Cosmobiology
  BT   Biology
       Space sciences
  NT   Space medicine
Space chemistry   523
  UF   Astrochemistry
       Cosmochemistry
  BT   Chemistry
Space colonies   629.44; 999
    Use for materials on communities estab-
    lished in space or on natural extraterrestrial
    bodies. Materials on bases established on nat-
    ural extraterrestrial bodies for specific func-
    tions other than colonization are entered under
    Extraterrestrial bases. Materials on manned
    installations orbiting in space for specific
    functions, such as servicing space ships, are
    entered under **Space stations.**
  UF   Colonies, Space
       Communities, Space
       Outer space—Colonies
  BT   Astronautics and civilization
  RT   Extraterrestrial bases
Space commercialization
  USE Space industrialization
Space communication
  USE Astronautics—Communication
       systems
       Interstellar communication
Space debris   629.4
  UF   Debris in space
       Junk in space
       Space pollution
  BT   Pollution
       Space environment

Space environment   629.4
- UF   Environment, Space
  Extraterrestrial environment
  Space weather
- BT   **Astronomy**
  Outer space
- NT   **Cosmic rays**
  Solar radiation
  Space debris

Space exploration (Astronautics)
- USE   **Outer space—Exploration**

Space flight   629.4

Use for materials on the physics and technical details of flight beyond the earth's atmosphere. General materials and imaginary accounts of travel to other planets are entered under **Interplanetary voyages.**

- UF   Humans in space
  Man in space
  Manned space flight
  People in space
  Rocket flight
  Space travel
- SA   names of projects, e.g. **Gemini project;** and space flight to particular places, e.g. **Space flight to the moon** [to be added as needed]
- BT   **Aeronautics—Flights**
  Astronautics
- NT   **Astronauts**
  Extravehicular activity (Space flight)
  Gemini project
  Orbital rendezvous (Space flight)
  Outer space—Exploration
  Space flight to the moon
- RT   **Astrodynamics**
  Interplanetary voyages
  Navigation (Astronautics)
  Space medicine
  Space vehicles

Space flight (Fiction)
- USE   **Imaginary voyages**
  Science fiction

Space flight—Law and legislation
- USE   **Space law**

Space flight—Rescue work
- USE   **Space rescue operations**

Space flight to the moon   629.45
- UF   Flight to the moon
  Lunar expeditions

Moon, Voyages to
Voyages to the moon
- BT   **Astronautics**
  Space flight
- NT   **Apollo project**
  Moon—Exploration

Space heaters   644; 697
- BT   **Heating**
- NT   **Fireplaces**
  Stoves

Space industrial processing
- USE   **Space industrialization**

Space industrialization (May subdiv. geog.)   629.44
- UF   Commercial endeavors in space
  Industrial uses of space
  Manufacturing in space
  Space commercialization
  Space industrial processing
  Space manufacturing
  Space stations—Industrial applications
- BT   **Industrialization**

Space laboratories
- USE   **Space stations**

Space law (May subdiv. geog.)   341.4
- UF   Aerospace law
  Artificial satellites—Law and legislation
  Astronautics—Law and legislation
  Space flight—Law and legislation
  Space stations—Law and legislation
- BT   **Astronautics and civilization**
  International law
  Law

Space manufacturing
- USE   **Space industrialization**

Space medicine   616.9
- UF   Aerospace medicine
  Bioastronautics
- BT   **Medicine**
  Space biology
  Space sciences
- NT   **Life support systems (Space environment)**
  Weightlessness
- RT   **Aviation medicine**
  Space flight

Space navigation
USE **Navigation (Astronautics)**
Space nutrition
USE **Astronauts—Nutrition**
Space optics   535
BT **Optics**
Space sciences
NT **Astronautical instruments**
Astronomical instruments
RT **Optical instruments**
Remote sensing
Space orbital rendezvous
USE **Orbital rendezvous (Space
flight)**
Space, Outer
USE **Outer space**
Space, Personal
USE **Personal space**
Space photography   778.3
UF Photographs from space
Photography in astronautics
SA celestial bodies or objects in
space with the subdivision
Pictorial works [to be added
as needed]
BT **Photography**
**Photography—Scientific appli-
cations**
NT **Mars (Planet)—Pictorial works**
Moon—Pictorial works
Space platforms
USE **Space stations**
Space pollution
USE **Space debris**
Space power
USE **Astronautics and civilization**
Space probes   629.43
Use for materials on space exploration by
remote control from earth.
SA types of probes, e.g. **Lunar
probes; Mars probes;** etc.;
and names of space vehicles
and space projects, e.g.
Project Voyager [to be added
as needed]
BT **Outer space—Exploration**
Space vehicles
NT **Lunar probes**
Mars probes
Space rescue operations   629.45
UF Rescue operations, Space
Space flight—Rescue work

Space vehicles—Rescue work
BT **Rescue work**
Space research
USE **Outer space—Exploration**
Space sciences
Space rockets
USE **Space vehicles**
Space sciences (May subdiv. geog.)
500.5
Use for general materials and for scientific
results of space exploration and scientific ap-
plications of space flight.
UF Science and space
Space research
BT **Science**
NT **Outer space**
Space and time
Space biology
Space medicine
Space optics
RT **Astronautics**
Astronomy
Space sciences—International cooperation
500.5
BT **International cooperation**
Space ships
USE **Space vehicles**
Space shuttles   629.44
SA names of individual space shut-
tles [to be added as needed]
BT **Space vehicles**
NT **Challenger (Spacecraft)**
Space stations   629.44
Use for materials on manned installations
orbiting in space for specific functions, such
as servicing space ships. Materials on bases
established on natural extraterrestrial bodies
for specific functions other than colonization
are entered under **Extraterrestrial bases.** Ma-
terials on communities established in space or
on natural extraterrestrial bodies are entered
under **Space colonies.**
UF Orbital laboratories
Orbiting vehicles
Space laboratories
Space platforms
BT **Artificial satellites**
Astronautics
Space vehicles
NT **Orbital rendezvous (Space
flight)**
Space stations—Industrial applications
USE **Space industrialization**

Space stations—Law and legislation
    USE **Space law**
Space suits 629.47
    UF Astronauts—Clothing
    BT **Life support systems (Space environment)**
Space telecommunication
    USE **Interstellar communication**
Space travel
    USE **Interplanetary voyages**
          Space flight
Space vehicle accidents 363.12; 629.4
    UF Astronautical accidents
          Astronautics—Accidents
          Space vehicles—Accidents
    BT **Accidents**
Space vehicles 629.47
    UF Space rockets
          Space ships
          Spacecraft
    BT **Rocketry**
    NT **Orbital rendezvous (Space flight)**
          Rocket planes
          Space probes
          Space shuttles
          Space stations
    RT **Artificial satellites**
          Astronautics
          Space flight
Space vehicles—Accidents
    USE **Space vehicle accidents**
Space vehicles—Extravehicular activity
    USE **Extravehicular activity (Space flight)**
Space vehicles—Guidance systems 629.47
Space vehicles—Instruments
    USE **Astronautical instruments**
Space vehicles—Piloting 629.45
    UF Piloting (Astronautics)
    BT **Astronauts**
          Navigation (Astronautics)
Space vehicles—Propulsion systems 629.47
Space vehicles—Recovery 629.4
    UF Recovery of space vehicles
Space vehicles—Rescue work
    USE **Space rescue operations**

Space vehicles—Thermodynamics 629.47
    BT **Thermodynamics**
Space vehicles—Tracking 629.4
    UF Tracking of satellites
Space walk
    USE **Extravehicular activity (Space flight)**
Space warfare 358
    Use for materials on interplanetary warfare, attacks on earth from outer space, and warfare among the nations of earth in outer space.
    UF Interplanetary warfare
          Interstellar warfare
          Space wars
    BT **Outer space**
          War
    NT **Space weapons**
          Strategic Defense Initiative
Space wars
    USE **Space warfare**
Space weapons 358
    UF Space-based weapons
          Star Wars weapons
          Weapons, Space
    BT **Military weapons**
          Space warfare
    RT **Strategic Defense Initiative**
Space weather
    USE **Space environment**
Spacecraft
    USE **Space vehicles**
Spain 946
    May be subdivided like United States except for *History*.
Spain—History 946
    NT **Spanish-American War, 1898**
          Spanish Armada, 1588
Spain—History—1898, War of 1898
    USE **Spanish-American War, 1898**
Spain—History—1936-1939, Civil War 946.081
Spain—History—1939-1975 946.082
Spain—History—1975- 946.083
Spanish America
    USE **Latin America**
Spanish American literature
    USE **American literature (Spanish)**
          Latin American literature

Spanish-American War, 1898   973.8
> UF   American-Spanish War, 1898
> > Spain—History—1898, War of 1898
> > United States—History—1898, War of 1898
>
> BT   **Spain—History**
> > **United States—History—1865-1898**
> > **United States—History—1898-1919**

Spanish Armada, 1588   942.05; 946
> UF   Armada, 1588
> > Invincible Armada
>
> BT   **Great Britain—History—1485-1603, Tudors**
> > **Spain—History**

Spanish language   460
> May be subdivided like **English language.**
>
> BT   **Language and languages**
> > **Romance languages**

Spanish literature   860
> May use same subdivisions and names of literary forms as for **English literature.**
>
> BT   **Literature**
> > **Romance literature**

Sparring
> USE   **Boxing**

Spas
> USE   **Health resorts**
> > **Physical fitness centers**

Speaking
> USE   **Debates and debating**
> > **Lectures and lecturing**
> > **Preaching**
> > **Public speaking**
> > **Rhetoric**
> > **Speech**
> > **Voice**

Speaking choirs
> USE   **Choral speaking**

Speaking in tongues
> USE   **Glossolalia**

Speaking with tongues
> USE   **Glossolalia**

Spear fishing   799.1
> BT   **Fishing**

Special collections in libraries
> USE   **Libraries—Special collections**

Special education (May subdiv. geog.)   371.9
> SA   classes of exceptional children with the subdivision *Education* [to be added as needed]
>
> BT   **Education**
> NT   **Mentally handicapped children—Education**
> RT   **Mainstreaming in education**

Special libraries (May subdiv. geog.)   026; 027.6
> Use for materials on libraries covering specialized subjects, containing special format materials, or serving a specialized clientele.
>
> SA   types of special libraries, e.g. **Business libraries** [to be added as needed]
>
> BT   **Libraries**
> NT   **Business libraries**
> > **Corporate libraries**
> > **Government libraries**
> > **Music libraries**

Special Olympics   796.087
> BT   **Olympic games**
> > **Sports for the handicapped**

Specialists exchange programs
> USE   **Exchange of persons programs**

Specie
> USE   **Coins**

Specifications
> USE   types of engineering, construction, industries, products, and merchandise with the subdivision *Specifications,* for works on the particular qualities prescribed for a product to meet specific requirements [to be added as needed]

Specimens, Preservation of
> USE   **Plants—Collection and preservation**
> > **Taxidermy**
> > **Zoological specimens—Collection and preservation**
> > and types of natural specimens with the subdivision *Collection and preservation,* e.g. **Birds—Collection and preservation** [to be added as needed]

Spectacles
> USE   **Eyeglasses**

Specters
  USE **Apparitions**
      Ghosts
Spectra
  USE **Spectrum analysis**
Spectrochemical analysis
  USE **Spectrum analysis**
Spectrochemistry
  USE **Spectrum analysis**
Spectroscopy
  USE **Spectrum analysis**
Spectrum analysis   535.8
  UF Spectra
      Spectrochemical analysis
      Spectrochemistry
      Spectroscopy
  BT **Astronomy**
      Astrophysics
      Chemistry
      Optics
      Radiation
  NT **Mass spectrometry**
  RT **Light**
Speculation (May subdiv. geog.)   **332.64**
  BT **Finance**
  NT **Real estate investment**
  RT **Investments**
      Stock exchanges
Speech   302.2; 372.62; 410; 612.7
  UF Speaking
  BT **Language arts**
  NT **Speech disorders**
      Speech processing systems
      Speech therapy
      Voice culture
  RT **Language and languages**
      Phonetics
      Voice
Speech correction
  USE **Speech therapy**
Speech disorders   616.85
  Use for materials on disorders of the physi-
  ological mechanisms required for speech. Ma-
  terials on disorders of the central neurological
  functions affecting the reception, processing,
  or expression of language are entered under
  Language disorders.
  UF Defective speech
      Speech pathology
      Stammering
      Stuttering
  BT **Communicative disorders**
      Speech

Speech, Freedom of
  USE **Freedom of speech**
Speech pathology
  USE **Speech disorders**
Speech processing systems   006.5
  UF Computer speech processing sys-
        tems
      Electronic speech processing sys-
        tems
      Speech scramblers
  BT **Speech**
  NT **Automatic speech recognition**
      Speech synthesis
  RT **Computer sound processing**
Speech recognition, Automatic
  USE **Automatic speech recognition**
Speech scramblers
  USE **Speech processing systems**
Speech synthesis   006.5
  BT **Speech processing systems**
Speech therapy   616.85
  UF Speech correction
  BT **Speech**
Speeches   808.85
  Use for collections of speeches on several
  subjects and materials about speeches that
  have already been delivered. Materials on the
  art of delivering speeches are entered under
  Public speaking or under **Lectures and lec-
  turing.** Collections of speeches on a single
  subject are entered under that subject.
  UF Addresses
      Orations
      Speeches, addresses, etc.
  SA speeches of particular countries,
        e.g. **American speeches** [to
        be added as needed]
  BT **Literature**
  NT **After dinner speeches**
      American speeches
      English speeches
      **Presidents—United States—In-
        augural addresses**
      Toasts
  RT **Lectures and lecturing**
      Public speaking
Speeches, addresses, etc.
  USE **Speeches**
Speeches, addresses, etc., American
  USE **American speeches**
Speeches, addresses, etc., English
  USE **English speeches**

Speed **531**
    UF   Velocity
    BT   **Motion**
Speed (Drug)
    USE **Methamphetamine**
Speed reading **372.45**
    UF   Accelerated reading
           Faster reading
           Rapid reading
    BT   **Reading**
Speed, Supersonic
    USE **Supersonic aerodynamics**
Speleology
    USE **Caves**
Spellers **418**
    BT   **English language—Spelling**
Spelling
    USE names of languages with the
             subdivision *Spelling,* e.g. **En-**
             glish language—Spelling [to
             be added as needed]
Spelling reform **418**
    UF   English language—Spelling re-
           form
           Orthography
           Phonetic spelling
    BT   **English language—Spelling**
Spells
    USE **Charms**
          Magic
Spherical trigonometry
    USE **Trigonometry**
Spices **641.3**
    SA   types of spices [to be added as
           needed]
    BT   **Food**
Spiders (May subdiv. geog.)   **595.4**
    BT   **Animals**
Spies (May subdiv. geog.)   **327.12;**
          353.1; 355.3
    UF   Intelligence agents
           Spying
    BT   **Espionage**
          Subversive activities
    RT   **Secret service**
Spinning **677; 746.1**
    BT   **Textile industry**
    RT   **Yarn**
Spiral gearing
    USE **Gearing**

Spires **721**
    UF   Steeples
    BT   **Architecture**
          Church architecture
Spirit
    USE **Soul**
Spiritism
    USE **Spiritualism**
Spirits **133.9**
    UF   Invisible world
    BT   **Supernatural**
    NT   **Angels**
          Apparitions
          Ghosts
    RT   **Demonology**
          Spiritualism
Spiritual gifts **234**
    Use for materials on extraordinary phenom-
ena, such as glossolalia, visions, prophecies
and interpretations, healings, discernment of
spirits, etc. Materials dealing collectively with
ordinary spiritual phenomena, such as faith,
hope, love, patience, temperance, etc., are entered under **Virtue.**
    UF   Charismata
           Gifts of grace
           Gifts of the Holy Spirit
           Gifts, Spiritual
    BT   **Grace (Theology)**
    NT   **Glossolalia**
          Spiritual healing
          Visions
    RT   **Catholic charismatic movement**
          Holy Spirit
          Pentecostalism
Spiritual healing **203; 234; 615.8**
    Use for materials on the use of faith,
prayer, or other religious means to treat illness. Materials on psychic or psychological
means to treat illness are entered under **Mental healing.**
    UF   Divine healing
           Evangelistic healing
           Faith cure
           Faith healing
           Healing, Spiritual
    BT   **Medicine—Religious aspects**
          Spiritual gifts
    RT   **Christian Science**
          Mental healing
          Mind and body
          Miracles
          Subconsciousness
          Suggestive therapeutics

Spiritual life   204; 248

    Use for materials on spiritual practices and on the relationship that individuals may attain with the sacred. May be subdivided by religion or sect.

  BT **Religious life**
  NT **Conversion**
        Faith
        Hope
        Meditation
        Mysticism
        Retreats

Spiritualism (May subdiv. geog.)   **133.9**

    Use for materials on extraordinary spiritual phenomena, especially contact with the spirits of the dead.

  UF Spiritism
  BT **Occultism**
        Supernatural
  NT **Psychokinesis**
  RT **Apparitions**
        Parapsychology
        Spirits

Spirituals (Songs)   782.25

  BT **Folk songs—United States**
        Hymns
  RT **African American music**
        Gospel music

Splicing
  USE **Knots and splices**

Splicing of genes
  USE **Genetic engineering**

Split personality
  USE **Multiple personality**

Spoils system
  USE **Political corruption**

Sponges (May subdiv. geog.)   **593.4**

  BT **Aquatic animals**

Sporting equipment
  USE **Sporting goods**

Sporting goods   796.028

  UF Sporting equipment
        Sports—Equipment and supplies
  RT **Sports**

Sports (May subdiv. geog.)   **796**

  SA types of sports and names of sports competitions [to be added as needed]
  BT **Play**
        Recreation
  NT **Aeronautical sports**
        Baseball
        Basketball

        Bullfights
        Coaching (Athletics)
        College sports
        Cycling
        Extreme sports
        Field hockey
        Fishing
        Football
        Gymnastics
        Olympic games
        Orienteering
        Professional sports
        Racing
        Rodeos
        Rowing
        School sports
        Soccer
        Sports cards
        Sports for women
        Sports records
        Sports teams
        Sports tournaments
        Sportsmanship
        Tennis
        Track athletics
        Violence in sports
        Water sports
        Winter sports
  RT **Amusements**
        Athletes
        Athletics
        Games
        Outdoor life
        Physical education
        Sporting goods
        Sports facilities

Sports and drugs
  USE **Athletes—Drug use**

Sports—Audiences
  USE **Sports spectators**

Sports betting (May subdiv. geog.)   **796**

  UF Sports handicapping
  BT **Gambling**

Sports broadcasting
  USE **Radio broadcasting of sports**
          Television broadcasting of sports

Sports cards   769
>   UF   Cards, Sports
>   SA   types of cards for specific
>   sports, e.g. **Baseball cards** [to
>   be added as needed]
>   BT   **Sports**
>   NT   **Baseball cards**

Sports cars (May subdiv. geog.)
>   **629.222**
>   SA   names of specific sports cars [to
>   be added as needed]
>   BT   **Automobiles**

Sports coaching
>   USE   **Coaching (Athletics)**

Sports—Corrupt practices   796
>   UF   Cheating in sports
>   Corruption in sports
>   Sports scandals
>   BT   **Criminal law**

Sports drama (Films)   791.43
>   May be used for individual works, collections, or materials about sports drama on film.
>   BT   **Motion pictures**

Sports drama (Radio programs)   791.44
>   May be used for individual works, collections, or materials about sports drama on the radio.
>   BT   **Radio programs**

Sports drama (Television programs)
>   **791.45**
>   May be used for individual works, collections, or materials about sports drama on television.
>   BT   **Television programs**

Sports—Equipment and supplies
>   USE   **Sporting goods**

Sports events
>   USE   names of specific sports events,
>   e.g. **Super Bowl** [to be added
>   as needed]

Sports facilities (May subdiv. geog.)
>   **796.06**
>   SA   types of sports facilities [to be
>   added as needed]
>   NT   **Golf courses**
>   **Playgrounds**
>   **Stadiums**
>   **Swimming pools**
>   RT   **Recreation**
>   **Sports**

Sports fans
>   USE   **Sports spectators**

Sports—Fiction   808.83
>   Use for collections of sports stories.
>   UF   Sports stories
>   SA   types of sports with the subdivision *Fiction*, e.g. **Baseball—Fiction** [to be added as needed]

Sports for the handicapped   796.01
>   BT   **Handicapped**
>   NT   **Special Olympics**
>   **Wheelchair sports**

Sports for women (May subdiv. geog.)
>   **796**
>   UF   Women—Sports
>   SA   types of sports for women, e.g.,
>   **Basketball for women** [to be
>   added as needed]
>   BT   **Sports**
>   NT   **Basketball for women**

Sports handicapping
>   USE   **Sports betting**

Sports in radio
>   USE   **Radio broadcasting of sports**

Sports in television
>   USE   **Television broadcasting of sports**

Sports—Lists   796

Sports—Medical aspects
>   USE   **Sports medicine**

Sports medicine   613.7; 617.1
>   UF   Athletic medicine
>   Physical education—Medical aspects
>   Sports—Medical aspects
>   BT   **Medical care**
>   **Medicine**

Sports records (May subdiv. geog.)   **796**
>   Use for materials on top performances or achievements.
>   UF   Records, Sports
>   BT   **Sports**
>   RT   **Sports—Statistics**
>   **World records**

Sports scandals
>   USE   **Sports—Corrupt practices**

Sports spectators (May subdiv. geog.)
>   **306.4; 796**
>   UF   Sports—Audiences
>   Sports fans
>   BT   **Audiences**

Sports—Statistics   796

SA   types of sports with the subdivision *Statistics* [to be added as needed]

BT   **Statistics**

RT   **Sports records**

Sports stories

USE   **Sports—Fiction**

Sports teams (May subdiv. geog.)
796.06

SA   types of sports teams, e.g. **Baseball teams,** and names of individual teams, e.g. **New York Knicks (Basketball team)** [to be added as needed]

BT   **Sports**

NT   **Baseball teams**
Basketball teams

Sports tournaments (May subdiv. geog.)
796

UF   Tournaments

SA   types of sports with the subdivision *Tournaments,* e.g. **Tennis—Tournaments;** names of sports tournaments, e.g. **Super Bowl** [to be added as needed]

BT   **Contests**
Sports

NT   **Super Bowl**
Tennis—Tournaments

Sports violence

USE   **Violence in sports**

Sportsmanship   175

UF   Bad sportsmanship

BT   **Human behavior**
Sports

Spot welding

USE   **Electric welding**

Spouses

USE   **Husbands**
Wives

Spraying and dusting   632

UF   Dusting and spraying

BT   **Agricultural pests**
Fruit—Diseases and pests

NT   **Aeronautics in agriculture**

RT   **Fungicides**
Herbicides
Insecticides

Spreadsheet software   005.54

UF   Electronic spreadsheets

BT   **Computer software**

Spun glass

USE   **Glass fibers**

Spy films   791.43

May be used for individual works, collections, or materials about spy films.

UF   Espionage films
Suspense films

BT   **Motion pictures**

RT   **Mystery films**

Spy novels

USE   **Spy stories**

Spy radio programs   791.44

May be used for individual works, collections, or materials about spy radio programs.

UF   Suspense programs

BT   **Radio programs**

Spy stories   808.3; 808.83

May be used for individual works, collections, or materials about spy stories.

UF   Espionage stories
Spy novels

BT   **Adventure fiction**

RT   **Mystery fiction**
Romantic suspense novels

Spy television programs   791.45

May be used for individual works, collection, or materials about spy television programs.

UF   Espionage television programs
Suspense programs

BT   **Television programs**

RT   **Mystery television programs**

Spying

USE   **Espionage**
Spies

Square   516

BT   **Geometry**
Shape

Square dancing   793.3

BT   **Folk dancing**

Square root   513.2

BT   **Arithmetic**

Squirrels   599.36

BT   **Mammals**

NT   **Chipmunks**

SST (Supersonic transport)

USE   **Supersonic transport planes**

St. Bartholomew's Day, Massacre of, 1572

USE   **Saint Bartholomew's Day, Massacre of, 1572**

St. Francis, Order of
    USE **Franciscans**
St. Valentine's Day
    USE **Valentine's Day**
Stabilization in industry
    USE **Business cycles**
Stadia
    USE **Stadiums**
Stadiums (May subdiv. geog.)   **796.06**
    UF   Ballparks
          Stadia
    BT   **Sports facilities**
Staff
    USE   types of institutions, types of
           public officials, and names of
           individual public officials with
           the subdivision *Staff,* e.g.
           Presidents—United States—
           Staff [to be added as needed]
Stage
    USE   **Acting**
           Drama
           Theater
Stage history
    USE   names of dramatists with the
           subdivision *Stage history,* e.g.
           Shakespeare, William, 1564-
           1616—Stage history [to be
           added as needed]
Stage lighting   **792.02**
    UF   Television—Stage lighting
          Theaters—Stage lighting
    BT   **Lighting**
Stage scenery
    USE   **Theaters—Stage setting and**
           scenery
Stage setting
    USE   **Theaters—Stage setting and**
           scenery
Stagecoaches
    USE   **Carriages and carts**
Stained glass
    USE   **Glass painting and staining**
Stalking (May subdiv. geog.)   **364.1**
    UF   Antistalking laws
          Stalking—Law and legislation
    BT   **Offenses against the person**
Stalking—Law and legislation
    USE   **Stalking**
Stamina, Physical
    USE   **Physical fitness**

Stammering
    USE   **Speech disorders**
Stamp collecting (May subdiv. geog.)
      769.56
    Use for materials on the collecting, buying,
    and selling of postage stamps.
    UF   Philately
          Postage stamp collecting
          Postage stamps—Collectors and
           collecting
          Stamps—Collectors and collect-
           ing
    BT   **Collectors and collecting**
    RT   **Postage stamps**
Stamps—Collectors and collecting
    USE   **Stamp collecting**
Stamps, Postage
    USE   **Postage stamps**
Standard book numbers
    USE   **Publishers' standard book**
           numbers
Standard of living
    USE   **Cost and standard of living**
Standard of value
    USE   **Money**
Standard time
    USE   **Time**
Standards
    USE   subjects, types of school and in-
           stitutions, and types of indus-
           tries with the subdivision
           Standards, e.g. **Environmen-**
           tal protection—Standards;
           which may be further subdi-
           vided geographically [to be
           added as needed]
Standards of output
    USE   **Production standards**
Star Wars (Ballistic missile defense sys-
    tem)
    USE   **Strategic Defense Initiative**
Star Wars films   **791.43**
    May be used for individual works, collec-
    tions, or materials about Star Wars films.
    BT   **Motion pictures**
          Science fiction films
Star Wars weapons
    USE   **Space weapons**
Stars   **523.8**
    SA   names of constellations and of
          individual stars, e.g. **Sirius** [to
          be added as needed]

Stars—*Continued*
- NT **Black holes (Astronomy)**
  Galaxies
  Sirius
  Solar system
  Supernovas
- RT **Astronomy**
  Constellations

Stars—Atlases   **523.8022**
- UF Astronomy—Atlases
  Atlases, Astronomical
- BT **Atlases**

Starting a business
- USE **New business enterprises**

Starvation   **363.8**
- NT **Famines**
- RT **Fasting**
  Hunger
  Malnutrition

State aid to education
- USE **Government aid to education**

State aid to libraries
- USE **Government aid to libraries**

State and agriculture
- USE **Agriculture—Government policy**

State and environment
- USE **Environmental policy**

State and railroads
- USE **Railroads—Government policy**

State and the arts
- USE **Federal aid to the arts**

State birds   **598**
- BT **Birds**
  State emblems

State constitutions
- USE **Constitutions**
  Constitutions—United States

State emblems (May subdiv. geog.)
   929.9
- UF Emblems, State
  State symbols
- SA types of state emblems and state symbols, e.g. **State birds; State flowers** [to be added as needed]
- BT **Signs and symbols**
- NT **State birds**
  State flowers
- RT **National emblems**

State encouragement of science, literature, and art
- USE **Cultural policy**

State encouragement of the arts
- USE **Arts—Government policy**
  Federal aid to the arts

State-federal relations
- USE **Federal-state relations**

State flowers   **582.13**
- BT **Flowers**
  State emblems

State governments   **352.13**
> Use for general materials on state government not limited to a single state.
- UF United States—State governments
- SA names of states with the subdivision *Politics and government,* e.g. **Ohio—Politics and government** [to be added as needed]
- BT **Political science**
- NT **Federal-state relations**
  Governors
  State-local relations
- RT **Federal government**

State, Heads of
- USE **Heads of state**

State libraries (May subdiv. geog.)
   027.5
> Use for materials on government libraries, maintained by state funds, that preserve state records and publications.
- BT **Government libraries**

State-local relations (May subdiv. geog.)
   320.4; 320.8; 352.13
- UF City-state relations
  Local-state relations
- BT **Local government**
  Municipal government
  State governments

State-local tax relations
- USE **Intergovernmental tax relations**

State medicine (May subdiv. geog.)
   362.1; 368.4; 614
> Use for general materials on the relations of the state to medicine, public health, medical legislation, examinations of physicians by state boards, etc.
- UF Medicine, State
  National health service
  Socialized medicine

State medicine—*Continued*
    BT   **Medicine**
    NT   **Medicaid**
           Medicare
           Public health
    RT   **National health insurance**
State ministries
    USE **Executive departments**
State of the Union messages
    USE **Presidents—United States—**
          Messages
State ownership
    USE **Government ownership**
State ownership of railroads
    USE **Railroads—Government policy**
State planning
    USE **Economic policy**
          Regional planning
          Social policy
State police   363.2
    UF   Police, State
    BT   **Police**
State regulation of industry
    USE **Industrial policy**
State rights   321.02; 342
    UF   States' rights
    BT   **Political science**
State songs   782.42
    BT   **Songs**
State symbols
    USE **State emblems**
State, The   320.1
    UF   Commonwealth, The
    NT   **Church and state**
          Public interest
          Welfare state
    RT   **Political science**
States, New
    USE **New states**
States' rights
    USE **State rights**
Statesmen (May subdiv. geog.)   920
    NT   **Diplomats**
          Heads of state
          Legislators
          Politicians
Statics   531
    BT   **Mechanics**
          Physics
    NT   **Hydrostatics**
          Strains and stresses
    RT   **Dynamics**

Statistical diagrams
    USE **Statistics—Graphic methods**
Statistical inference
    USE **Probabilities**
Statistics   001.4; 310
    Use for materials on the theory and methods of statistics.
    SA   subjects and names of countries, cities, etc., with the subdivision *Statistics* [to be added as needed]
    BT   **Economics**
    NT   **Agriculture—Statistics**
          Average
          Census
          Chicago (Ill.)—Statistics
          Education—Statistics
          Gross national product
          Libraries—Statistics
          Ohio—Statistics
          Probabilities
          Railroads—Statistics
          Sampling (Statistics)
          Sports—Statistics
          United States—Statistics
          Vital statistics
Statistics—Graphic methods   001.4
    UF   Statistical diagrams
    BT   **Graphic methods**
Statues
    USE **Monuments**
          Sculpture
Statutes
    USE **Law**
Stealing
    USE **Theft**
Steam   536; 621.1
    BT   **Heat**
          Power (Mechanics)
          Water
    RT   **Steam engineering**
Steam engineering (May subdiv. geog.)
          621.1
    BT   **Engineering**
    NT   **Steam engines**
          Steam navigation
          Steam power plants
    RT   **Mechanical engineering**
          Steam
Steam engines   621.1
    BT   **Engines**
          Steam engineering

Steam engines—*Continued*
  NT Condensers (Steam)
      Marine engines
      Steam turbines
Steam heating 697
  BT Heating
Steam locomotives (May subdiv. geog.)
      625.26
  BT Locomotives
Steam navigation 387; 623.89
  BT Navigation
      Steam engineering
      Transportation
  NT Marine engineering
      Steam turbines
  RT Steamboats
Steam power plants 621.1
  BT Electric power plants
      Steam engineering
Steam turbines 621.1
  BT Steam engines
      Steam navigation
      Turbines
Steamboats (May subdiv. geog.) 387.2;
      623.82
  UF Steamships
  BT Boats and boating
      Naval architecture
      Ocean travel
      Shipbuilding
      Ships
  RT Steam navigation
Steamships
  USE Steamboats
Steel 669; 672
  BT Iron
      Metalwork
  NT Structural steel
Steel construction (May subdiv. geog.)
      693
  UF Building, Iron and steel
      Iron and steel building
  BT Building
      Structural engineering
  RT Structural steel
Steel engraving
  USE Engraving
Steel industry (May subdiv. geog.)
      338.4; 672
  UF Steel industry and trade
  BT Industries
  RT Iron industry

Steel industry and trade
  USE Steel industry
Steel industry—Labor productivity
      338.4
  BT Labor productivity
Steel industry—Quality control 338.4;
      672
  BT Quality control
Steel industry—Technological innovations
      338.4
  BT Technological innovations
Steel, Structural
  USE Structural steel
Steeples
  USE Spires
Steers
  USE Beef cattle
Stencil work 686.2; 745.7
  BT Decoration and ornament
      Painting
  NT Silk screen printing
Stenography
  USE Shorthand
Step-parents
  USE Stepparents
Stepfamilies 306.874
  UF Stepfamily
  BT Family
Stepfamily
  USE Stepfamilies
Stepfathers 306.874
  BT Fathers
      Stepparents
Stepmothers 306.874
  BT Mothers
      Stepparents
Stepparents 306.874
  UF Step-parents
  BT Parents
  NT Stepfathers
      Stepmothers
Stereo photography
  USE Three dimensional photogra-
        phy
Stereo sound systems
  USE Stereophonic sound systems
Stereophonic sound systems 621.389
  UF Stereo sound systems
  BT High-fidelity sound systems
      Sound—Recording and repro-
        ducing

Stereophotography
USE **Three dimensional photography**
Stereopticon
USE **Projectors**
Stereoscopic photography
USE **Three dimensional photography**
Stereotype (Psychology) (May subdiv. geog.) **303.3**
UF Mental stereotype
Stereotyped behavior
BT **Attitude (Psychology)**
Social psychology
Thought and thinking
Stereotyped behavior
USE **Stereotype (Psychology)**
Sterility in animals
USE **Infertility**
Sterility in humans
USE **Infertility**
Sterilization (Birth control) (May subdiv. geog.) **363.9; 613.9**
BT **Birth control**
NT **Vasectomy**
Steroids 572; 612
UF Anabolic steroids
BT **Biochemistry**
Drugs
RT **Athletes—Drug use**
Hormones
Stewardesses, Airline
USE **Flight attendants**
Stewards, Airline
USE **Flight attendants**
Stills
USE **Distillation**
Stimulants 613.8; 615
SA types of stimulants, e.g. **Amphetamines;** and names of individual stimulants [to be added as needed]
BT **Drugs**
Psychotropic drugs
NT **Amphetamines**
Hallucinogens
Stock averages
USE **Stock price indexes**
Stock car racing (May subdiv. geog.) **796.72**
BT **Automobile racing**

Stock control
USE **Inventory control**
Stock exchange
USE **Stock exchanges**
Stock exchange crashes
USE **Financial crises**
Stock exchanges (May subdiv. geog.) **332.64**
UF Securities exchange
Stock exchange
Stock market
BT **Finance**
Markets
NT **Bonds**
Insider trading
Securities
Wall Street (New York, N.Y.)
RT **Investments**
Speculation
Stocks
Stock fraud
USE **Securities fraud**
Stock indexes
USE **Stock price indexes**
Stock judging
USE **Livestock judging**
Stock market
USE **Stock exchanges**
Stock market fraud
USE **Securities fraud**
Stock market panics
USE **Financial crises**
Stock price indexes 332.63
UF Stock averages
. Stock indexes
BT **Prices**
Stock raising
USE **Livestock industry**
Stockings
USE **Hosiery**
Stocks (May subdiv. geog.) **332.63**
UF Dividends
Shares of stock
BT **Commerce**
Securities
NT **Corporations**
RT **Bonds**
Investments
Stock exchanges
Stocks—Insider trading
USE **Insider trading**

Stockyards
USE **Meat industry**
Stoics 188
BT **Ancient philosophy**
Ethics
Stomach 612.3
BT **Anatomy**
RT **Digestion**
Stone 553.5; 693

Use for materials on stone as a building material. General materials on naturally occurring solid minerals are entered under **Rocks.**

SA types of stone, e.g. **Marble** [to be added as needed]
BT **Building materials**
Economic geology
NT **Granite**
Marble
Masonry
Stonecutting
RT **Petrology**
Quarries and quarrying
Rocks
Stone Age (May subdiv. geog.) **930.1**
UF Eolithic period
Neolithic period
Paleolithic period
BT **Civilization**
RT **Stone implements**
Stone-cutting
USE **Stonecutting**
Stone implements (May subdiv. geog.)
930.1
UF Flint implements
BT **Implements, utensils, etc.**
RT **Stone Age**
Stone quarries
USE **Quarries and quarrying**
Stonecutting 693
UF Stone-cutting
BT **Masonry**
Stone
Stoneware
USE **Pottery**
Storage
USE types of commodities, foods, materials, industrial products, etc., with the subdivision *Storage,* e.g. **Grain—Storage** [to be added as needed]

Storage batteries 621.31
UF Batteries, Electric
BT **Electric apparatus and appliances**
RT **Electric batteries**
Storage devices, Computer
USE **Computer storage devices**
Storage in the home 648
UF Home storage
BT **Home economics**
Store buildings
USE **Commercial buildings**
Stores (May subdiv. geog.) **381**
UF Retail stores
Shops
SA types of stores, e.g. **Drugstores** [to be added as needed]
BT **Commercial buildings**
Retail trade
NT **Chain stores**
Department stores
Discount stores
Drugstores
General stores
Supermarkets
RT **Shopping centers and malls**
Stories
USE **Anecdotes**
Bible stories
Fairy tales
Fiction
Legends
Romances
Short stories
Stories in rhyme
Stories without words
Storytelling
and national literatures and literary or musical forms with the subdivision *Stories, plots, etc.,* e.g. **Ballet—Stories, plots, etc.; Opera—Stories, plots, etc.;** etc. [to be added as needed]
Stories for children
USE **Children's stories**
Stories in rhyme 808.1; 808.81

Use as a form heading for narrative poems for very young children. Narrative poetry and materials about narrative poetry for older children and for adults are entered under **Narrative poetry.**

Stories in rhyme—*Continued*
  UF   Stories
  BT   **Narrative poetry**
       Rhyme
Stories, plots, etc.   808
  Use for materials that analyze plots or discuss the technique of constructing plots. Collections of plots of a specific literary or musical form are entered under that form with the
subdivision *Stories, plots, etc.* General collec-
tions of literary plots are entered under **Sto-
ries, plots, etc.—Collections.**
  UF   Dramatic plots
       Fictional plots
       Plots (Drama, fiction, etc.)
       Scenarios
  SA   national literatures and literary
       or musical forms with the
       subdivision *Stories, plots, etc.,*
       e.g. **Ballet—Stories, plots,
       etc.; Opera—Stories, plots,
       etc.** [to be added as needed]
  BT   **Literature**
Stories, plots, etc.—Collections   802
  Use for collections of literary plots. Materi-
als that analyze plots or discuss the technique
of constructing plots are entered under **Sto-
ries, plots, etc.**
  UF   Literature—Stories, plots, etc.
  SA   national literatures and specific
       genres of literature with the
       subdivision *Stories, plots, etc.*
       [to be added as needed]
Stories without words
  Use as a form heading for stories for chil-
dren told only through a sequence of pictures.
  UF   Nonword stories
       Picture books for children,
       Wordless
       Stories
       Wordless stories
  BT   **Picture books for children**
Storms (May subdiv. geog.)   **551.55**
  SA   types of storms [to be added as
       needed]
  BT   **Meteorology**
       Natural disasters
       Weather
  NT   **Blizzards**
       Cyclones
       Dust storms
       Hurricanes
       Thunderstorms
       Tornadoes
       Typhoons

  RT   **Rain**
       Snow
       Winds
Storytelling   027.62; 372.67
  UF   Stories
  BT   **Children's literature**
  RT   **Folklore**
       Short story
Storytelling—Collections   808.85
  Use for collections of stories compiled pri-
marily for oral presentation.
  UF   Collected works
       Collections of literature
Stoves   697
  BT   **Heating**
       Space heaters
Strain (Psychology)
  USE   **Stress (Psychology)**
Strains and stresses   531; 620.1; 624.1
  UF   Stresses
  BT   **Mechanics**
       Statics
       **Structural analysis (Engineer-
       ing)**
  RT   **Strength of materials**
Strangers and children
  USE   **Children and strangers**
Strategic aspects
  USE   areas of the world with the sub-
        division *Strategic aspects*, e.g.
        **Middle East—Strategic as-
        pects** [to be added as needed]
Strategic Defense Initiative   358.1
  UF   SDI (Ballistic missile defense
       system)
       Star Wars (Ballistic missile de-
       fense system)
  BT   **Military policy—United States**
       Space warfare
       United States—Defenses
  RT   **Space weapons**
Strategic management
  USE   **Strategic planning**
Strategic materials
  USE   **Materials**
Strategic planning (May subdiv. geog.)
       352.3; 658.4
  UF   Strategic management
  BT   **Planning**
Strategy   355.4
  UF   Military strategy
       Naval strategy

Strategy—*Continued*
- SA   countries and areas of the world with the subdivision *Strategic aspects,* e.g. **Middle East—Strategic aspects** [to be added as needed]
- BT   **Military art and science**
       Naval art and science
- NT   **Middle East—Strategic aspects**
       Tactics

Stratigraphic geology (May subdiv. geog.) **551.7**

May be subdivided by geological period.
- UF   Geology, Stratigraphic
- BT   **Geology**
- NT   **Fossils**

Stratosphere   **551.5**
- BT   **Upper atmosphere**
- NT   **Ozone layer**

Stratospheric ozone
- USE   **Ozone layer**

Straw votes
- USE   **Public opinion polls**

Strawberries   **634**
- BT   **Berries**

Stream animals (May subdiv. geog.) **578.76**
- UF   River animals
       Stream fauna
- BT   **Animals**
       Rivers

Stream fauna
- USE   **Stream animals**

Streamlining
- USE   **Aerodynamics**

Street cars
- USE   **Street railroads**

Street cleaning   **363.72; 628.4**
- BT   **Cleaning**
       Municipal engineering
       Public health
       Roads
       Sanitary engineering
       Streets
- RT   **Refuse and refuse disposal**

Street gangs
- USE   **Gangs**

Street life (May subdiv. geog.)   **307.76**
- UF   Urban street life
- BT   **City and town life**

Street lighting
- USE   **Streets—Lighting**

Street literature
- USE   **Pamphlets**

Street people
- USE   **Homeless persons**

Street railroads (May subdiv. geog.) **388.4; 625.6**
- UF   Interurban railroads
       Street cars
       Trams
       Trolley cars
- BT   **Local transit**
       Railroads
- RT   **Cable railroads**
       Electric railroads

Street traffic
- USE   **City traffic**
        Traffic engineering

Streets (May subdiv. geog.)   **388.4; 625.7**
- UF   Alleys
       Avenues
       Boulevards
       Thoroughfares
- BT   **Cities and towns**
       Civil engineering
       Transportation
- NT   **City traffic**
       Street cleaning
- RT   **Pavements**
       Roads

Streets—Chicago (Ill.)   **977.3**
- UF   Chicago (Ill.)—Streets

Streets—Lighting (May subdiv. geog.) **628.9**
- UF   Cities and towns—Lighting
       Street lighting
- BT   **Lighting**

Streets—New York (N.Y.)   **974.7**
- UF   New York (N.Y.)—Streets
- RT   **Wall Street (New York, N.Y.)**

Strength of materials   **620.1**
- UF   Resistance of materials
- SA   types of materials with the subdivision *Testing,* e.g. **Concrete—Testing** [to be added as needed]
- BT   **Mechanics**
       Structural analysis (Engineering)

Strength of materials—*Continued*
  NT   Concrete—Testing
  RT   Building materials
       Strains and stresses
       Testing
Strength training
  USE   Weight lifting
Stress management   155.9
  BT   Health
Stress (Physiology)   612; 616.8
  UF   Physiological stress
       Tension (Physiology)
  BT   Adaptation (Biology)
       Physiology
  NT   Job stress
Stress (Psychology)   155.9; 616.89
  UF   Emotional stress
       Mental stress
       Psychological stress
       Strain (Psychology)
       Tension (Psychology)
  BT   Mental health
       Psychology
  NT   Anxiety
       Burn out (Psychology)
       Job stress
       Post-traumatic stress disorder
Stresses
  USE   Strains and stresses
Strikes (May subdiv. geog.)   331.892
    This heading may also be subdivided by in-
  dustry or occupation and then geographically,
  e.g. Strikes—Automobile industry—United
  States.
  UF   Lockouts
       Picketing
       Sit-down strikes
       Strikes and lockouts
       Work stoppages
  BT   Industrial relations
       Labor disputes
  NT   Sabotage
  RT   Collective bargaining
       Industrial arbitration
       Injunctions
       Labor unions
Strikes and lockouts
  USE   Strikes
Strikes—Automobile industry—United
       States   331.892
Strikes—United States   331.892

String orchestra music   784.7
  BT   Orchestral music
Stringed instruments   787
  UF   Bowed instruments
  SA   types of stringed instruments [to
         be added as needed]
  BT   Musical instruments
  NT   Guitars
       Violins
       Violoncellos
Strip films
  USE   Filmstrips
Stroke   616.8
  UF   Apoplexy
       Cerebrovascular disease
  BT   Brain—Diseases
Structural analysis (Engineering)   624
  UF   Architectural engineering
       Theory of structures
  BT   Structural engineering
  NT   Strains and stresses
       Strength of materials
Structural drafting
  USE   Mechanical drawing
Structural engineering (May subdiv.
     geog.)   624.1
  UF   Architectural engineering
  BT   Civil engineering
       Engineering
  NT   Building
       Foundations
       Hydraulic structures
       Soil mechanics
       Steel construction
       Structural analysis (Engineer-
         ing)
Structural failures   624.1
  UF   Collapse of structures
       Failures, Structural
  SA   types of structural failures, e.g.
         Building failures [to be add-
         ed as needed]
  BT   Reliability (Engineering)
  NT   Building failures
Structural materials
  USE   Building materials
Structural psychology
  USE   Gestalt psychology

Structural steel   691
    UF   Steel, Structural
    BT   **Building materials**
         Civil engineering
         Steel
    RT   **Steel construction**
Structural zoology
    USE   **Animals—Anatomy**
Structure in biology
    USE   **Morphology**
Structures
    USE   **Buildings**
Structures, Garden
    USE   **Garden structures**
Stubbornness   155.2; 179
    UF   Obstinacy
    BT   **Personality**
Stucco   693
    BT   **Building materials**
         Decoration and ornament
         Plaster and plastering
Student achievement
    USE   **Academic achievement**
Student activities (May subdiv. geog.)
    371.8
    UF   Extracurricular activities
    BT   **Students**
    NT   **After school programs**
         Cheerleading
         College and school drama
         College and school journalism
         College sports
         Field trips
         School assembly programs
         School sports
Student aid (May subdiv. geog.)   **371.2;**
    378.3
    UF   Financial aid to students
         Student financial aid
    BT   **College costs**
         Loans
    NT   **Scholarships**
         Student loan funds
Student busing
    USE   **Busing (School integration)**
Student cheating
    USE   **Cheating (Education)**
Student clubs
    USE   **Students—Societies**
Student councils
    USE   **Student government**

Student dishonesty
    USE   **Cheating (Education)**
Student dropouts
    USE   **Dropouts**
Student evaluation of teachers   371.14
    UF   Student rating of teachers
         Teachers, Student rating of
    BT   **Teacher-student relationship**
Student exchange programs   370.116
    UF   Exchange of students
         Exchange programs, Student
         International exchange of stu-
          dents
    BT   **Exchange of persons programs**
         International education
Student financial aid
    USE   **Student aid**
Student government   371.5
    UF   Self-government (in education)
         Student councils
         Student self-government
    BT   **School discipline**
         Schools—Administration
Student guidance
    USE   **Educational counseling**
Student life
    USE   **College students**
         Students
Student loan funds (May subdiv. geog.)
    371.2; 378.3
    UF   Loan funds, Student
    BT   **College costs**
         Student aid
Student movement
    USE   **Youth movement**
Student promotion
    USE   **Promotion (School)**
Student protests, demonstrations, etc.
    USE   **Students—Political activity**
         Youth movement
Student rating of teachers
    USE   **Student evaluation of teachers**
Student revolt
    USE   **Students—Political activity**
         Youth movement
Student self-government
    USE   **Student government**
Student societies
    USE   **Students—Societies**
Student songs
    USE   **Students' songs**

Student-teacher relationships
    USE **Teacher-student relationship**
Student teaching   **370.71**
    UF Practice teaching
          Teachers—Practice teaching
    BT **Teachers—Training**
          Teaching
Student to student counseling
    USE **Peer counseling**
Student violence
    USE **School violence**
Student yearbooks
    USE **School yearbooks**
Students (May subdiv. geog.)   **371.8**
    UF School life
          Student life
    SA types of students, e.g. **College**
          students [to be added as
          needed]
    NT **At risk students**
          College students
          Dropouts
          Foreign students
          High school students
          School children
          Student activities
          Underachievers
Students and libraries
    USE **Libraries and students**
Students—Counseling
    USE **Educational counseling**
Students, Foreign
    USE **Foreign students**
Students—Grading and marking
    USE **Grading and marking (Education)**
Students' military training camps
    USE **Military training camps**
Students—Political activity   **324; 371.8**
    UF Politics and students
          Student protests, demonstrations,
          etc.
          Student revolt
    BT **Political participation**
          Youth movement
Students—Societies   **371.8**
    UF School clubs
          Student clubs
          Student societies
    BT **Societies**
    NT **Fraternities and sororities**

Students' songs   **782.42**
    UF College songs
          Student songs
    BT **Songs**
    NT **United States Military Academy—Songs**
Students—United States   **371.80973**
Students with problems
    USE **At risk students**
Study abroad
    USE **Foreign study**
Study and teaching
    USE **Education**
          and subjects with the subdivision *Study and teaching*, e.g.
          Science—Study and teaching
          [to be added as needed]
Study, Foreign
    USE **Foreign study**
Study guides
    USE named examinations with the subdivision *Study guides*, e.g.
          Graduate Record Examination—Study guides; and subjects, educational levels, and names of educational institutions with the subdivisions *Examinations—Study guides*, e.g. **English language—Examinations—Study guides** [to be added as needed]
Study guides for examinations
    USE **Examinations—Study guides**
Study methods
    USE **Study skills**
Study overseas
    USE **Foreign study**
Study skills   **371.3028**
    UF How to study
          Study methods
    SA subjects with the subdivision *Study and teaching*, e.g.
          Art—Study and teaching [to be added as needed]
    BT **Education**
          Life skills
          Teaching
    NT **Examinations—Study guides**
          Homework
          Independent study
          Self-instruction

Study-work plan
    USE **Cooperative education**
Stuffed toy making
    USE **Soft toy making**
Stunt flying   797.5
    UF Aerobatics
    BT **Airplanes—Piloting**
Stunt men
    USE **Stunt performers**
Stunt performers (May subdiv. geog.)
      791.4
    UF Stunt men
    BT **Actors**
Stuttering
    USE **Speech disorders**
Style in dress
    USE **Clothing and dress**
           Costume
           Fashion
Style, Literary
    USE **Literary style**
Style manikins
    USE **Fashion models**
Style manuals
    USE **Printing—Style manuals**
Sub-Saharan Africa   960
    UF Africa, Sub-Saharan
           Black Africa
    BT **Africa**
Subconsciousness   127; 154.2
    BT **Parapsychology**
           Psychology
    NT **Hallucinations and illusions**
           Mental suggestion
           Sleep
    RT **Consciousness**
           Dreams
           Hypnotism
           Mental healing
           Mind and body
           Psychoanalysis
           Spiritual healing
Subculture
    USE **Counter culture**
Subgravity state
    USE **Weightlessness**
Subject catalogs   016; 017
    UF Catalogs, Subject
    BT **Library catalogs**
    NT **Subject headings**

Subject dictionaries
    USE **Encyclopedias and dictionaries**
Subject headings   025.4
    UF Thesauri
    BT **Cataloging**
           Indexes
           Subject catalogs
Submarine boats
    USE **Submarines**
Submarine cables   384.1; 384.6
    UF Cables, Submarine
           Ocean cables
    BT **Telecommunication**
           Telegraph
Submarine diving
    USE **Deep diving**
Submarine engineering
    USE **Ocean engineering**
Submarine exploration
    USE **Underwater exploration**
Submarine geology (May subdiv. geog.)
      551.46
    UF Marine geology
           Underwater geology
    BT **Geology**
           Oceanography
    NT **Ocean bottom**
    RT **Plate tectonics**
Submarine medicine   616.9
    UF Underwater medicine
           Underwater physiology
    BT **Medicine**
Submarine oil well drilling
    USE **Offshore oil well drilling**
Submarine photography
    USE **Underwater photography**
Submarine research stations
    USE **Undersea research stations**
Submarine vehicles
    USE **Submersibles**
Submarine warfare   359.9
    UF Naval warfare
           Warfare, Submarine
    BT **Naval art and science**
           War
    NT **Submarines**
           Torpedoes
           World War, 1939-1945—Naval
             operations—Submarine

Submarines (May subdiv. geog.)   **359.9;**
        623.82

Use for materials on submarines only. Materials on other underwater craft are entered under **Submersibles.**

UF   Submarine boats

BT   **Ships**
        Submarine warfare
        Submersibles
        Warships

NT   **Nuclear submarines**

Submersibles   623.82

UF   Submarine vehicles
        Undersea vehicles

SA   types of submersibles [to be
        added as needed]

BT   **Vehicles**

NT   **Bathyscaphe**
        Submarines

Subscription television   384.55

UF   Pay-per-view television
        Pay television
        Television, Subscription

BT   **Television broadcasting**

Subsidies (May subdiv. geog.)   **338.9**

Use for materials on financial or other aid given, without equivalent recompense, by governments or governmental agencies to private enterprises.

UF   Corporate welfare
        Government subsidies
        Grants
        Subventions

SA   types of subsidies, e.g. **Agricultural subsidies;** and federal
        aid to specific endeavors, e.g.
        **Federal aid to minority
        business enterprises** [to be
        added as needed]

BT   **Domestic economic assistance**
        Economic policy

NT   **Agricultural subsidies**
        Federal aid to minority business enterprises
        Transfer payments

Subsistence economy (May subdiv. geog.)
        330.9

BT   **Cost and standard of living**

NT   **Barter**

RT   **Poverty**

Substance abuse

USE   **Drug abuse**
        Solvent abuse

Substantive due process

USE   **Due process of law**

Substitute products   338

SA   types of substitute products, e.g.
        Sugar substitutes [to be added
        ed as needed]

BT   **Commercial products**

NT   **Sugar substitutes**

RT   **Synthetic products**

Subterfuge

USE   **Deception**

Subterranean water

USE   **Groundwater**

Subtraction   513.2

BT   **Arithmetic**

Suburban areas

USE   **Suburbs**

Suburban life (May subdiv. geog.)
        307.74

BT   **Suburbs**

Suburbs (May subdiv. geog.)   **307.76**

UF   Suburban areas
        Suburbs and environs

SA   names of suburban areas, e.g.
        **Chicago Suburban Area
        (Ill.)** [to be added as needed]

BT   **Cities and towns—Growth**
        City planning
        Metropolitan areas

NT   **Suburban life**

Suburbs and environs

USE   **Suburbs**

Subventions

USE   **Subsidies**

Subversive activities (May subdiv. geog.)
        322.4; 327.12

Use for materials on any attempt to subvert, overthrow, or cause the destruction of any established or legally constituted government. Materials on the offense of acting to overthrow one's own government or to harm or kill its sovereign are entered under **Treason.**

UF   Fifth column

BT   **Insurgency**

NT   **Espionage**
        Political crimes and offenses
        Sabotage
        Spies
        Terrorism
        Treason

RT   **Internal security**

Subways (May subdiv. geog.)   **388.4; 625.4**
   UF Underground railroads
   BT **Local transit**
       Railroads
Success **158; 650.1**
   UF Fortune
       Personal development
   BT **Business ethics**
       Wealth
   NT **Academic achievement**
       Leadership
       Life skills
   RT **Ability**
       Self-realization
Succession
   USE presidents, prime ministers, and other rulers with the subdivision *Succession,* e.g. **Presidents—United States—Succession** [to be added as needed]
Sudden death in infants
   USE **Sudden infant death syndrome**
Sudden infant death syndrome **618.92**
   UF Cot death
       Crib death
       Infant sudden death
       SIDS (Disease)
       Sudden death in infants
   BT **Infants—Death**
Suffering **128; 152.1; 214**
   UF Affliction
   RT **Joy and sorrow**
       Pain
Suffrage (May subdiv. geog.) **324.6**
   UF Franchise
       Voting
   SA ethnic groups and classes of persons with the subdivision *Suffrage* [to be added as needed]
   BT **Citizenship**
       Constitutional law
       Democracy
       Elections
       Political science
   NT **African Americans—Suffrage**
       Blacks—Suffrage
       Naturalization
       Voter registration
       Women—Suffrage

   RT **Representative government and representation**
Suffragettes
   USE **Suffragists**
Suffragists (May subdiv. geog.) **324.6; 920**
   UF Suffragettes
   BT **Reformers**
   RT **Feminism**
       Women—Suffrage
Sufism (May subdiv. geog.) **297.4**
   BT **Mysticism—Islam**
Sugar **641.3; 664**
   SA types of sugar [to be added as needed]
   BT **Food**
   NT **Maple sugar**
       Syrups
Sugar substitutes **641.3; 664**
   UF Artificial sweeteners
       Nonnutritive sweeteners
   BT **Substitute products**
Suggestion, Mental
   USE **Mental suggestion**
Suggestive therapeutics **615.8**
   UF Therapeutics, Suggestive
   BT **Therapeutics**
   RT **Hypnotism**
       Mental healing
       Mental suggestion
       Psychotherapy
       Spiritual healing
Suicidal behavior
   USE **Suicide—Psychological aspects**
Suicide (May subdiv. geog.) **179.7; 362.28**
   UF Attempted suicide
       Suicide attempts
   SA classes of persons and ethnic groups with the subdivision *Suicide,* e.g. **Teenagers—Suicide** [to be added as needed]
   BT **Medical jurisprudence**
       Social problems
   NT **Teenagers—Suicide**
   RT **Homicide**
       Right to die
Suicide attempts
   USE **Suicide**

Suicide—Psychological aspects   616.85
  UF   Suicidal behavior
  BT   **Human behavior**
Suing (Law)
  USE   **Litigation**
Suite (Music)   784.18
    Use for musical scores and for materials on
  the suite as a musical form.
  UF   Partita
       Suites
  BT   **Musical form**
       Orchestral music
Suites
  USE   **Suite (Music)**
Suits (Law)
  USE   **Litigation**
Suits of armor
  USE   **Armor**
Sulfa drugs
  USE   **Sulfonamides**
Sulfonamides   615
  UF   Sulfa drugs
  BT   **Drugs**
Sulfur
  USE   **Sulphur**
Sulphur   546; 553.6; 661
  UF   Sulfur
  BT   **Chemical elements**
Summer camps
  USE   **Camps**
Summer employment   331.1
  BT   **Employment**
  RT   **Teenagers—Employment**
       Youth—Employment
Summer resorts   790
  BT   **Resorts**
Summer schools (May subdiv. geog.)
       371.2
  UF   Vacation schools
  BT   **Public schools**
       Schools
  NT   **Religious summer schools**
Sun   523.7
  UF   Solar physics
  BT   **Astronomy**
       Solar system
  NT   **Solar energy**
       Sunspots
Sun-dials
  USE   **Sundials**
Sun—Eclipses
  USE   **Solar eclipses**

Sun (in religion, folklore, etc.)
  USE   **Sun worship**
Sun powered batteries
  USE   **Solar batteries**
Sun—Radiation
  USE   **Solar radiation**
Sun-spots
  USE   **Sunspots**
Sun worship (May subdiv. geog.)   **202**
  UF   Sun (in religion, folklore, etc.)
  BT   **Religion**
Sunday schools (May subdiv. geog.)
       268
  UF   Bible classes
  BT   **Church work**
       Religious education
  NT   **Bible—Study and teaching**
Sundials   681.1
  UF   Horology
       Sun-dials
  BT   **Clocks and watches**
       Garden ornaments and furni-
         ture
       Time
Sunken cities
  USE   **Extinct cities**
Sunken treasure
  USE   **Buried treasure**
Sunspots   523.7
  UF   Sun-spots
  BT   **Meteorology**
       Solar radiation
       Sun
Super Bowl   796.33
  UF   Superbowl
  BT   **Sports tournaments**
Super markets
  USE   **Supermarkets**
Superbowl
  USE   **Super Bowl**
Supercomputers   004.1
    Use for materials on extraordinarily power-
  ful computers.
  BT   **Computers**
Superconducting materials
  USE   **Superconductors**
Superconductive devices
  USE   **Superconductors**
Superconductivity
  USE   **Superconductors**

Superconductors   537.6; 621.3
  UF   Superconducting materials
        Superconductive devices
        Superconductivity
  BT   **Electric conductors**
        Electronics
Superhero comic books, strips, etc.
      741.5
      May be used for individual works, collections, or materials about superhero comics.
  BT   **Comic books, strips, etc.**
Superhero films   791.43
      May be used for individual works, collections, or materials about superhero films.
  SA   films with particular superheroes,
        e.g. **Superman films** [to be
        added as needed]
  BT   **Adventure films**
  NT   **Superman films**
Superhero radio programs   791.44
      May be used for individual works, collections, or materials about superhero radio programs.
  BT   **Adventure radio programs**
Superhero television programs   791.45
      May be used for individual works, collections, or materials about superhero television programs.
  BT   **Adventure television programs**
Superhighways
  USE   **Express highways**
Superintendents of schools
  USE   **School superintendents and
          principals**
Superman films   791.43
      May be used for individual works, collections, or materials about Superman films.
  BT   **Superhero films**
Supermarket shopping
  USE   **Grocery shopping**
Supermarkets (May subdiv. geog.)
      658.8
  UF   Super markets
  BT   **Grocery trade**
        Retail trade
        Stores
Supernatural   133; 202; 398.2
  BT   **Religion**
  NT   **Exorcism**
        Occultism
        Parapsychology
        Prophecies
        Revelation
        Spirits

  Spiritualism
  RT   **Miracles**
Supernovae
  USE   **Supernovas**
Supernovas   523.8
  UF   Supernovae
  BT   **Stars**
Supersonic aerodynamics   629.132
  UF   Aerodynamics, Supersonic
        High speed aerodynamics
        Speed, Supersonic
  BT   **Aerodynamics**
        High speed aeronautics
  NT   **Aerothermodynamics**
Supersonic airliners
  USE   **Supersonic transport planes**
Supersonic transport planes   629.133
  UF   SST (Supersonic transport)
        Supersonic airliners
  BT   **Jet planes**
Supersonic waves
  USE   **Ultrasonic waves**
Supersonics
  USE   **Ultrasonics**
Superstition (May subdiv. geog.)   **001.9;
      398**
  UF   Folk beliefs
        Traditions
  BT   **Folklore**
  NT   **Charms**
  RT   **Errors**
Supervision of employees
  USE   **Personnel management**
Supervision of schools
  USE   **School supervision**
Supervisors   331.7; 658.3
  UF   Foremen
        Managers
  BT   **Factory management**
        Personnel management
Supplementary employment   331.1
  UF   Employment, Supplementary
        Moonlighting
        Second job
        Secondary employment
  BT   **Labor**
        Part-time employment

Supply and demand   332; 338.5; 658.8
   UF   Law of supply and demand
   SA   occupational groups and types of
        employees with the subdivi-
        sion *Supply and demand,* e.g.
        **Unskilled labor—Supply and
        demand; Chemical indus-
        try—Employees—Supply and
        demand** [to be added as
        needed]
   BT   **Economics**
   NT   **Chemical industry—Employ-
        ees—Supply and demand
        Unskilled labor—Supply and
        demand**
   RT   **Competition
        Exchange
        Prices**
Support groups
   USE   **Self-help groups**
Support of children
   USE   **Child support**
Supreme Court—United States
   USE   **United States. Supreme Court**
Surf
   USE   **Ocean waves**
Surf riding
   USE   **Surfing**
Surface of the earth
   USE   **Earth—Surface**
Surfboarding
   USE   **Surfing**
Surfing (May subdiv. geog.)   797.3
   UF   Body surfing
        Surf riding
        Surfboarding
   BT   **Water sports**
Surfing—Songs   782.42
   UF   Surfing—Songs and music
   BT   **Songs**
Surfing—Songs and music
   USE   **Surfing—Songs**
Surgeons (May subdiv. geog.)   617.092;
        920
   BT   **Physicians**
Surgery (May subdiv. geog.)   617
   UF   Operations, Surgical
   SA   classes of persons, names of dis-
        eases, and names of organs
        and regions of the body with

the subdivision *Surgery* [to be
added as needed]
   BT   **Medicine**
   NT   **Artificial organs
        Cancer—Surgery
        Children—Surgery
        Cryosurgery
        Heart—Surgery
        Orthopedics
        Plastic surgery
        Transplantation of organs, tis-
        sues, etc.
        Vivisection**
   RT   **Anesthetics
        Antiseptics**
Surgery, Plastic
   USE   **Plastic surgery**
Surgical transplantation
   USE   **Transplantation of organs, tis-
        sues, etc.**
Surnames
   USE   **Personal names**
Surplus government property (May
        subdiv. geog.)   352.5
   UF   Excess government property
        Government property, Surplus
   BT   **Property**
Surrealism (May subdiv. geog.)   709.04;
        759.06; 809
   Use for the movement or style of surrealism
   in literature or in the visual arts.
   BT   **Arts**
Surrogate mothers   176; 306.874;
        346.01
   BT   **Mothers**
Surveillance, Electronic
   USE   **Electronic surveillance**
Surveying (May subdiv. geog.)   526.9
   UF   Land surveying
        Land surveys
   SA   names of countries, cities, etc.,
        with the subdivision *Surveys,*
        for works containing the re-
        sults of land surveys in those
        places, e.g. **United States—
        Surveys** [to be added as
        needed]
   BT   **Civil engineering
        Geography
        Measurement**
   NT   **Mine surveying
        Topographical drawing**

Surveying—*Continued*
    RT   **Geodesy**
Surveys   001.4
    UF   Government surveys
    SA   types of surveys, e.g. **Market surveys;** and names of countries, cities, etc., with the subdivision *Surveys,* for works containing the results of land surveys in those places, e.g. **United States—Surveys** [to be added as needed]
    BT   **Research**
    NT   **Educational surveys**
          Library surveys
          Market surveys
          Social surveys
Survival after airplane accidents, shipwrecks, etc.   613.6
    UF   Castaways
    RT   **Aircraft accidents**
          Rescue work
          Shipwrecks
          Wilderness survival
Survival of the fittest
    USE **Natural selection**
Survival skills   613.6
    Use for materials on skills needed to survive in a hazardous environment, usually stressing self-reliance and economic self-sufficiency.
    UF   Emergency survival
          Human survival skills
    SA   types of survival, e.g. **Wilderness survival** [to be added as needed]
    BT   **Civil defense**
          Environmental influence on humans
          Human ecology
          Life skills
    NT   **Wilderness survival**
    RT   **Self-reliance**
Survivalism (May subdiv. geog.)   320.5; 613.6
    UF   Survivalist movements
    BT   **Social movements**
Survivalist movements
    USE **Survivalism**
Suspended sentence
    USE **Probation**

Suspense films
    USE **Adventure films**
          Mystery films
          Spy films
Suspense novels
    USE **Adventure fiction**
          Mystery fiction
          Romantic suspense novels
Suspense programs
    USE **Mystery radio programs**
          Mystery television programs
          Spy radio programs
          Spy television programs
Sustainable architecture (May subdiv. geog.)   720
    UF   Environmentally friendly architecture
    BT   **Architecture**
Sustainable development (May subdiv. geog.)   333.71; 338.9
    Use for materials on economic development that satisfies the needs of the present generation without depleting natural resources for the future or having adverse environmental effects. General materials on the environmental impact of economic development are entered under **Economic development—Environmental aspects.**
    UF   Economic sustainability
          Sustainable economic development
    BT   **Economic development**
Sustainable economic development
    USE **Sustainable development**
Swamp animals (May subdiv. geog.)   578.768
    UF   Swamp fauna
    BT   **Animals**
Swamp fauna
    USE **Swamp animals**
Swamps (May subdiv. geog.)   551.41
    BT   **Wetlands**
Swashbucklers
    USE **Adventure fiction**
          Adventure films
Swedish language   439.7
    May be subdivided like **English language.**
    BT   **Language and languages**
          Scandinavian languages
Swedish literature   839.7
    May use same subdivisions and names of literary forms as for **English literature.**
    BT   **Literature**
          Scandinavian literature

Sweets
USE **Candy**
Confectionery
Swell
USE **Ocean waves**
Swimming   797.2
BT **Water sports**
NT **Diving**
Marathon swimming
Synchronized swimming
Swimming pools   690; 725; 797.2
UF Pools
BT **Sports facilities**
Swindlers and swindling (May subdiv.
geog.)   364.16
UF Con artists
Con game
Confidence game
BT **Crime**
Criminals
NT **Counterfeits and counterfeiting**
Credit card fraud
Quacks and quackery
RT **Fraud**
Impostors and imposture
Swine
USE **Pigs**
Switchboard hotlines
USE **Hotlines (Telephone counseling)**
Symbiosis   577.8
UF Mutualism (Biology)
BT **Biology**
Ecology
RT **Parasites**
Plant ecology
Symbolic logic   511.3
UF Logic, Symbolic and mathematical
Mathematical logic
BT **Logic**
Mathematics
NT **Boolean algebra**
RT **Set theory**
Symbolic numbers
USE **Numerology**
Symbolism of numbers
Symbolism (May subdiv. geog.)   203;
302.2; 700
SA symbolism of particular reli-
gions, e.g. **Christian symbol-
ism**;   and symbolism in par-

ticular subjects, e.g. **Symbol-
ism in literature** [to be add-
ed as needed]
BT **Art**
Mythology
NT **Christian symbolism**
Figures of speech
Heraldry
Symbolism in literature
Symbolism of numbers
RT **Signs and symbols**
Symbolism in literature   809
UF Signs and symbols in literature
BT **Literature**
Symbolism
RT **Allegory**
Symbolism of numbers   203; 246; 809
Use for general materials on the symbolism
of numbers, as in philosophy, religion, or lit-
erature. Materials on the occult significance of
numbers are entered under **Numerology.**
UF Number symbolism
Sacred numbers
Symbolic numbers
BT **Symbolism**
NT **Numerology**
RT **Cabala**
Numbers
Symbols
USE **Abbreviations**
Signs and symbols
Symbols, Mathematical
USE **Mathematical notation**
Sympathy
USE **Bereavement**
Consolation
Symphonic poems   784.2
BT **Orchestral music**
Symphonies
USE **Symphony**
Symphony   784.18; 784.2
Use for musical scores and for materials on
the symphony as a musical form.
UF Symphonies
BT **Musical form**
Orchestral music
Symptoms
USE **Diagnosis**
Synagogues (May subdiv. geog.)   296.6;
726
BT **Buildings**
Religious institutions
Temples

Synagogues—*Continued*
RT Judaism
Synchronized swimming   797.2
UF Water ballet
BT **Swimming**
Synods
USE **Councils and synods**
Synonyms and antonyms
USE names of languages with the subdivision *Synonyms and antonyms,* e.g. **English language—Synonyms and antonyms** [to be added as needed]
Synthesizer music
USE **Electronic music**
Synthesizer (Musical instrument)
USE **Synthesizers (Musical instruments)**
Synthesizers (Musical instruments)   786.7
UF Synthesizer (Musical instrument)
BT **Electronic musical instruments**
Synthetic chemistry
USE **Organic compounds—Synthesis**
Synthetic detergents
USE **Detergents**
Synthetic drugs of abuse
USE **Designer drugs**
Synthetic fabrics   677
SA types of synthetic fabrics [to be added as needed]
BT **Fabrics**
Synthetic products
NT **Nylon**
Rayon
Synthetic foods
USE **Artificial foods**
Synthetic fuels   662
UF Artificial fuels
Nonfossil fuels
BT **Fuel**
Synthetic products
Synthetic products   670
SA types of synthetic products and names of specific products [to be added as needed]
BT **Industrial chemistry**
NT **Artificial foods**
Plastics
Synthetic fabrics
Synthetic fuels

Synthetic rubber
RT **Organic compounds—Synthesis**
Substitute products
Synthetic rubber   678
UF Rubber, Artificial
Rubber, Synthetic
BT **Plastics**
Synthetic products
Syphilis (May subdiv. geog.)   **616.95**
BT **Sexually transmitted diseases**
Syrups   641.3
BT **Sugar**
System analysis   003; 004.2; 658.4
UF Flow charts
Flowcharting
Linear system theory
Network theory
Systems analysis
BT **Cybernetics**
Mathematical models
System theory
NT **Fuzzy systems**
System design
Systems engineering
System design   003; 004.2; 621.39
UF Systems design
BT **System analysis**
NT **Database design**
System engineering
USE **Systems engineering**
System theory   003
UF Systems, Theory of
Theory of systems
BT **Science**
NT **Chaos (Science)**
Cybernetics
Operations research
Social systems
System analysis
Systems engineering
Systematic botany
USE **Botany—Classification**
Systematic theology
USE **Doctrinal theology**
Systems analysis
USE **System analysis**
Systems, Database management
USE **Database management**
Systems design
USE **System design**

Systems engineering   620
 UF System engineering
 BT Automation
     Cybernetics
     Engineering
     Industrial design
     System analysis
     System theory
 NT Bionics
     Reliability (Engineering)
 RT Operations research
Systems, Fuzzy
 USE Fuzzy systems
Systems reliability
 USE Reliability (Engineering)
Systems, Theory of
 USE System theory
T groups
 USE Group relations training
T-shirts   391; 687
 UF Tee shirts
 BT Clothing and dress
Table decoration
 USE Table setting and decoration
Table etiquette   395.5
 BT Eating customs
     Etiquette
 RT Dining
Table setting and decoration   642
 UF Table decoration
 BT Decoration and ornament
 NT Flower arrangement
     Napkin folding
     Tableware
Table talk
 USE Conversation
Table tennis   796.34
 UF Ping-pong
 BT Ball games
Tables   645; 749
 BT Furniture
Tables (Systematic lists)
 USE subjects with the subdivision *Ta-
      bles,* e.g. **Meteorology—Ta-
      bles; Trigonometry—Tables**
      etc. [to be added as needed]
Tableware (May subdiv. geog.)   642
 UF Dishes
 BT Table setting and decoration
 NT Glassware
     Porcelain

     Pottery
     Silverware
Tactics   355.4
 UF Military tactics
 BT Military art and science
     Strategy
 NT Biological warfare
     Drill and minor tactics
     Guerrilla warfare
Tadpoles
 USE Frogs
Tai chi   613.7; 796.815
 UF Tai ji quan
     Taichi
 BT Exercise
     Martial arts
Tai ji quan
 USE Tai chi
Taichi
 USE Tai chi
Tailoring   646.4; 687
 UF Garment making
 BT Clothing and dress
     Clothing industry
 RT Dressmaking
Taiwan   951.24
    Use for materials dealing with the island of
 Taiwan, regardless of time period, or with the
 post-1948 Republic of China. Materials deal-
 ing with mainland China, regardless of time
 period, or with the People's Republic of Chi-
 na and comprehensive materials on China
 including Taiwan are entered under **China.**
 May be subdivided like United States except
 for *History.*
 UF China (Republic)
     Formosa
     Nationalist China
     Republic of China, 1949-
Takeovers, Corporate
 USE Corporate mergers and acqui-
      sitions
Talebearing
 USE Tattling
Talent
 USE Ability
     Genius
Talents
 USE Ability
Tales
 USE Fables
     Fairy tales
     Folklore
     Legends

Talismans
    USE   **Charms**
Talk shows (May subdiv. geog.)   **791.44;
791.45**
    BT   **Interviewing**
         Radio programs
         Television programs
Talking
    USE   **Conversation**
Talking books
    USE   **Audiobooks**
Tall tales   **398.2; 808.83**
    May be used for individual works, collections, or materials about tall tales.
    BT   **Folklore**
         Legends
         Wit and humor
Talmud   **296.1**
    BT   **Hebrew literature**
         Jewish literature
         Judaism
Tank tactics
    USE   **Tank warfare**
Tank warfare   **358**
    UF   Antitank warfare
         Tank tactics
    SA   names of individual wars with
         the subdivision *Tank warfare*
         e.g. **World War, 1939-
         1945—Tank warfare** [to be
         added as needed]
    BT   **War**
    NT   **World War, 1939-1945—Tank
         warfare**
    RT   **Military tanks**
Tanks (Military science)
    USE   **Military tanks**
Tanning   **675**
    BT   **Industrial chemistry**
    RT   **Hides and skins**
         Leather
Tantrums, Temper
    USE   **Temper tantrums**
Taoism (May subdiv. geog.)   **299.5**
    BT   **Religions**
Tap dancing   **792.7**
    BT   **Dance**
Tap water
    USE   **Drinking water**
Tape recorders
    USE   **Magnetic recorders and recording**

Tape recordings, Audio
    USE   **Sound recordings**
Tape recordings, Video
    USE   **Videotapes**
Tapestry (May subdiv. geog.)   **677;
746.3**
    BT   **Decoration and ornament**
         Decorative arts
         Interior design
         Needlework
Tardiness
    USE   **Punctuality**
Tariff (May subdiv. geog.)   **336.2; 382**
    UF   Custom duties
         Customs (Tariff)
         Duties
         Revenue
    BT   **Commercial policy**
         Economic policy
         Public finance
    NT   **Smuggling**
    RT   **Free trade**
         Protectionism
Tariff—United States   **336.2; 382**
    UF   United States—Tariff
Tarot   **133.3; 795.4**
    Use for materials on the cards and the
game.
    UF   Tarot (Game)
    BT   **Card games**
         Fortune telling
         Playing cards
Tarot (Game)
    USE   **Tarot**
Tartans   **391; 929.6**
    UF   Highland costume
         Scottish tartans
    BT   **Clans**
Taste   **152.1**
    BT   **Senses and sensation**
Taste (Aesthetics)
    USE   **Aesthetics**
Tatting   **746.43**
    BT   **Lace and lace making**
Tattling   **177; 302.3**
    UF   Talebearing
    BT   **Gossip**
Tattooing (May subdiv. geog.)   **391.6**
    UF   Tattoos (Body markings)
    BT   **Manners and customs**
         Personal appearance

Tattoos (Body markings)
　　USE　**Tattooing**
Taverns
　　USE　**Bars**
Tax assessment (May subdiv. geog.)
　　　　336.2

　　Use for general materials on the valuation of property for determining tax liability. Materials on the assessment of property for tax purposes in a particular place are entered under **Taxation** followed by the appropriate geographical subdivision.

　　UF　Appraisal
　　　　Assessment
　　　　Assessment, Tax
　　　　Property tax—Assessment
　　　　Real property tax—Assessment
　　BT　**Taxation**
　　　　Valuation
　　NT　**Tax exemption**
Tax avoidance
　　USE　**Tax evasion**
　　　　Tax planning
Tax credits (May subdiv. geog.)　**336.2**
　　BT　**Income tax**
Tax evasion　345
　　UF　Tax avoidance
　　　　Tax fraud
　　BT　**Criminal law**
　　　　White collar crimes
Tax exempt status
　　USE　**Tax exemption**
Tax exemption (May subdiv. geog.)
　　　　336.2
　　UF　Exemption from taxation
　　　　Tax exempt status
　　BT　**Tax assessment**
Tax fraud
　　USE　**Tax evasion**
Tax planning (May subdiv. geog.)
　　　　343.04
　　UF　Tax avoidance
　　　　Tax saving
　　BT　**Personal finance**
　　　　Planning
　　　　Taxation
　　RT　**Estate planning**
Tax relations, Intergovernmental
　　USE　**Intergovernmental tax relations**
Tax saving
　　USE　**Tax planning**

Tax sharing
　　USE　**Intergovernmental tax relations**
　　　　Revenue sharing
Taxation (May subdiv. geog.)　**336.2**
　　UF　Direct taxation
　　　　Duties
　　　　Revenue
　　　　Taxes
　　SA　subjects with the subdivision
　　　　Taxation, e.g. **Real estate investment—Taxation** [to be added as needed]
　　BT　**Political science**
　　　　Public finance
　　NT　**Income tax**
　　　　Inheritance and transfer tax
　　　　Intergovernmental tax relations
　　　　Internal revenue
　　　　Real estate investment—Taxation
　　　　Sales tax
　　　　Tax assessment
　　　　Tax planning
　　　　Tithes
Taxation of legacies
　　USE　**Inheritance and transfer tax**
Taxation—United States　336.200973
　　UF　United States—Taxation
Taxes
　　USE　**Taxation**
Taxidermy　590.75
　　UF　Preservation of specimens
　　　　Specimens, Preservation of
　　SA　types of specimens with the subdivision *Collection and preservation,* e.g. **Birds—Collection and preservation** [to be added as needed]
　　RT　**Zoological specimens—Collection and preservation**
Taxonomy (Botany)
　　USE　**Botany—Classification**
Tea　633.7; 641.8
　　Use for materials on the plant or on the beverage. Materials on the meal are entered under **Afternoon teas.**
　　BT　**Beverages**
　　RT　**Afternoon teas**
　　　　Tea industry
Tea houses
　　USE　**Tearooms**

Tea industry (May subdiv. geog.)
    338.1; 338.4
  UF   Tea trade
  BT   **Beverage industry**
  NT   **Tearooms**
  RT   **Tea**
Tea rooms
  USE **Tearooms**
Tea shops
  USE **Tearooms**
Tea trade
  USE **Tea industry**
Teach yourself courses
  USE **Self-instruction**
Teacher exchange   370.116
  UF   Exchange of teachers
       Teacher exchange programs
  BT   **Exchange of persons programs**
       International education
Teacher exchange programs
  USE **Teacher exchange**
Teacher-parent conferences
  USE **Parent-teacher conferences**
Teacher-parent relationship
  USE **Parent-teacher relationship**
Teacher-student relationship   371.1;
    378.1
  UF   Student-teacher relationships
       Teacher-student relationships
  BT   **Child-adult relationship**
       Interpersonal relations
       Teaching
  NT   **Student evaluation of teachers**
Teacher-student relationships
  USE **Teacher-student relationship**
Teacher training
  USE **Teachers—Training**
Teachers (May subdiv. geog.)   **371.1;**
    920
  Use for materials on educators engaged in classroom or other instruction. Materials on people engaged professionally in the field of education in general are entered under **Educators.**
  UF   College teachers
       Faculty (Education)
       Professors
  BT   **Educators**
  NT   **Colleges and universities—Faculty**
  RT   **Teaching**
Teachers and parents
  USE **Parent-teacher relationship**

Teachers colleges (May subdiv. geog.)
    378.1
  Use for general and historical materials about teachers colleges. Materials on their educational functions are entered under **Teachers—Training.**
  UF   Normal schools
       Training colleges for teachers
  SA   names of teachers colleges [to
        be added as needed]
  BT   **Colleges and universities**
       Education—Study and teaching
  RT   **Teachers—Training**
Teachers' institutes
  USE **Teachers' workshops**
Teachers—Pensions (May subdiv. geog.)
    331.25
  SA   types of educational institutions
        and names of individual edu-
        cational insititutions with the
        subdivisions *Faculty—Pen-*
        sions, e.g. **Colleges and uni-**
        versities—Faculty—Pensions
        [to be added as needed]
Teachers—Practice teaching
  USE **Student teaching**
Teachers' reports
  USE **School reports**
Teachers, Student rating of
  USE **Student evaluation of teachers**
Teachers—Training (May subdiv. geog.)
    370.71
  Use for materials on the history and methods of training teachers, including the educational functions of teachers colleges. Materials on the study of education as a discipline are entered under **Education—Study and teaching.** Materials on the art of teaching and methods of teaching are entered under **Teaching.**
  UF   Teacher training
       Teachers—Training of
  BT   **Education—Study and teaching**
       Teaching
  NT   **Student teaching**
       Teachers' workshops
  RT   **Teachers colleges**
Teachers—Training of
  USE **Teachers—Training**
Teachers' workshops   371.1
  UF   Teachers' institutes
       Workshops, Teachers'
  BT   **Teachers—Training**

Teaching (May subdiv. geog.)   **371.102**

Use for materials on the art of teaching and methods of teaching. Materials on the study of education as a discipline are entered under **Education—Study and teaching**. Materials on the history and methods of training teachers, including the educational functions of teachers colleges, are entered under **Teachers—Training**.

UF   Instruction
Pedagogy
School teaching

SA   subjects with the subdivision
Study and teaching, e.g. **Science—Study and teaching**
[to be added as needed]

BT   **Education**

NT   **Classroom management**
Cooperative learning
Educational psychology
Examinations
Lectures and lecturing
Montessori method of education
Project method in teaching
School discipline
School supervision
Student teaching
Study skills
Teacher-student relationship
Teachers—Training
Teaching teams
Tutors and tutoring

RT   **Teachers**

Teaching—Aids and devices   **371.33**

UF   Educational media
Instructional materials
Teaching materials

NT   **Audiovisual materials**
Bulletin boards
Manipulatives
Motion pictures in education
Programmed instruction
Radio in education
Teaching machines
Television in education

RT   **Educational technology**

Teaching—Data processing

USE   **Computer-assisted instruction**

Teaching—Experimental methods

USE   **Education—Experimental methods**

Teaching, Freedom of

USE   **Academic freedom**

Teaching machines   **371.33**

BT   **Programmed instruction**
Teaching—Aids and devices

Teaching materials

USE   **Teaching—Aids and devices**

Teaching teams   **371.14**

UF   Team teaching

BT   **Teaching**

Teachings of Jesus Christ

USE   **Jesus Christ—Teachings**

Teahouses

USE   **Tearooms**

Team problem solving

USE   **Group problem solving**

Team teaching

USE   **Teaching teams**

Team work in the workplace

USE   **Teams in the workplace**

Teams in the workplace (May subdiv. geog.)   **658.4**

UF   Team work in the workplace
Teamwork in the workplace
Work groups
Work teams

BT   **Social groups**
Work environment

Teamwork in the workplace

USE   **Teams in the workplace**

Tearooms (May subdiv. geog.)   **647.95**

Use for materials on public establishments devoted primarily to serving tea.

UF   Tea houses
Tea rooms
Tea shops
Teahouses
Teashops

BT   **Restaurants**
Tea industry

Teas

USE   **Afternoon teas**

Teashops

USE   **Tearooms**

Teasing   **158.2; 302.3**

BT   **Aggressiveness (Psychology)**
Interpersonal relations

Technical assistance (May subdiv. geog.)   **338.91; 361.6**

Use for materials on foreign aid in the form of technical expertise. Materials on the trans-

Technical assistance—*Continued*
fer of innovations in technology from one country to another are entered under **Technology transfer.**
- UF Aid to developing areas
  - Assistance to developing areas
  - Foreign aid program
- SA technical assistance from particular countries, e.g. **American technical assistance** [to be added as needed]
- BT **Foreign aid**
  - **International economic relations**
- NT **American technical assistance**
- RT **Community development**
  - **Technology transfer**

Technical assistance, American
- USE **American technical assistance**

Technical chemistry
- USE **Industrial chemistry**

Technical education (May subdiv. geog.) **370.11; 373.246; 374**
- UF Industrial education
  - Industrial schools
  - Technical schools
  - Trade schools
- SA technical subjects with the subdivision *Study and teaching,* e.g. **Engineering—Study and teaching** [to be added as needed]
- BT **Education**
  - **Higher education**
  - **Technology**
- NT **Apprentices**
  - **Correspondence schools and courses**
  - **Engineering—Study and teaching**
  - **Evening and continuation schools**
  - **Occupational retraining**
  - **Occupational training**
  - **School shops**
- RT **Employees—Training**
  - **Industrial arts education**
  - **Professional education**
  - **Vocational education**

Technical schools
- USE **Technical education**

Technical service
- USE **Customer services**

Technical services (Libraries)
- USE **Library technical processes**

Technical terms
- USE **Technology—Dictionaries**

Technical writing   **808**
- UF Scientific writing
- BT **Authorship**
  - **Technology—Language**

Technique
- USE subjects and names of authors and artists with the subdivision *Technique,* e.g. **Fiction—Technique; Painting—Technique; Shakespeare, William, 1564-1616—Technique;** etc. [to be added as needed]

Technological change
- USE **Technological innovations**

Technological innovations (May subdiv. geog.)   **338**
Use for materials on technological improvements in materials, production methods, processes, organization, or management. Works on original devices or processes are entered under **Inventions.**
- UF Innovations, Technological
  - Technological change
- SA subjects with the subdivision *Technological innovations,* e.g. **Automobiles—Technological innovations; Steel industry—Technological innovations** [to be added as needed]
- BT **Inventions**
  - **Technology**
- NT **Automobiles—Technological innovations**
  - **Steel industry—Technological innovations**
- RT **Industrial research**

Technological literacy (May subdiv. geog.)   **302.2**
Use for materials on a person's comprehension of technological innovation and the ability to use particular innovations appropriately.
- BT **Literacy**

Technological transfer
- USE **Technology transfer**

Technology (May subdiv. geog.)   **600**
- UF Applied science
  - High tech

Technology—*Continued*
    High technology
  SA   technology and other subjects,
       e.g. **Technology and civiliza-**
       tion [to be added as needed]
  NT **Distillation**
      Electronics
      Engineering
      Green technology
      Industrial chemistry
      Information technology
      Inventions
      Machinery
      Mills
      Nanotechnology
      Technical education
      Technological innovations
      Technology and civilization
      Technology transfer
  RT **Industrial arts**
      Material culture
Technology and civilization   303.4
  UF Civilization and technology
  BT **Civilization**
      Technology
  NT **Computers and civilization**
  RT **Industrial revolution**
Technology—Dictionaries   603
  UF Technical terms
  BT **Encyclopedias and dictionaries**
Technology in the workplace
  USE **Machinery in the workplace**
Technology—Language   601; 603
  NT **Technical writing**
Technology transfer (May subdiv. geog.)
     338.9

Use for materials on the transfer of innovations in technology from one country to another. Materials on foreign aid in the form of
technical expertise are entered under **Technical assistance.** May be subdivided by the region or country receiving the technology.
Where applicable, make an additional entry
under this heading subdivided by the region
or country transferring the technology.

  UF Technological transfer
      Transfer of technology
  BT **Inventions**
      Technology
  RT **International cooperation**
      International relations
      Technical assistance
Tee shirts
  USE **T-shirts**

Teen age
  USE **Adolescence**
Teen suicide
  USE **Teenagers—Suicide**
Teenage behavior
  USE **Adolescent psychology**
      Etiquette for children and
      teenagers
      Teenagers—Conduct of life
Teenage consumers
  USE **Young consumers**
Teenage drinking
  USE **Teenagers—Alcohol use**
Teenage dropouts
  USE **Dropouts**
Teenage fathers (May subdiv. geog.)
     306.874; 362.7

Use for materials focusing on fathers who
are teenagers. Materials on fathers who at the
time of a child's birth were not married to the
child's mother are entered under **Unmarried
fathers.** Materials focusing on fathers rearing
children without a partner in the household
are entered under **Single-parent families.**

  UF Adolescent fathers
      School-age fathers
  BT **Fathers**
      Teenage parents
Teenage gangs
  USE **Gangs**
Teenage literature
  USE **Young adult literature**
Teenage mothers (May subdiv. geog.)
     306.874; 362.7; 362.83

Use for materials focusing on mothers who
are teenagers. Materials on mothers who at
the time of giving birth were not married to
the child's father are entered under **Unmarried mothers.** Materials focusing on mothers
rearing children without a partner in the
household are entered under **Single-parent
families.**

  UF Adolescent mothers
      School-age mothers
  BT **Mothers**
      Teenage parents
  RT **Teenage pregnancy**
Teenage parents (May subdiv. geog.)
     306.874; 362.7
  BT **Parents**
      Teenagers
  NT **Teenage fathers**
      Teenage mothers

Teenage pregnancy (May subdiv. geog.)
    362.7; 618.2
  UF   Adolescent pregnancy
  BT   **Pregnancy**
  RT   **Teenage mothers**
Teenage prostitution
  USE **Juvenile prostitution**
Teenage suicide
  USE **Teenagers—Suicide**
Teenagers (May subdiv. geog.)   **305.235**

    Use for materials about teen youth. Materials on the time of life extending from thirteen to twenty-five years, as well as on people in that general age range, are entered under **Youth.** Materials limited to people in the general age range of eighteen through twenty-five years of age are entered under **Young men** or **Young women.** Materials on the process or state of growing up are entered under **Adolescence.**

  UF   Adolescents
       Teens
       Young adults
       Young people
       Young persons
  BT   **Age**
       Youth
  NT   **Runaway teenagers**
       Teenage parents
  RT   **Boys**
       Girls
Teenagers—Alcohol use (May subdiv.
    geog.)   **362.292; 613.81; 616.86**
  UF   Alcohol and teenagers
       Drinking and teenagers
       Teenage drinking
       Teenagers and alcohol
  NT   **Drinking age**
Teenagers and alcohol
  USE **Teenagers—Alcohol use**
Teenagers and drugs
  USE **Teenagers—Drug use**
Teenagers and narcotics
  USE **Teenagers—Drug use**
Teenagers—Attitudes   **155.5; 305.235**
  BT   **Attitude (Psychology)**
Teenagers—Books and reading   **011.62;
    028.5**

    Use for materials on the reading interests of teenagers and for lists of books for teenagers. Collections or materials about literature published for teenagers are entered under **Young adult literature.**

  UF   Books and reading for teenagers
       Books and reading for young
         adults
       Reading interests of teenagers
       Reading interests of young
         adults
       Young adults—Books and reading
  BT   **Books and reading**
Teenagers—Conduct of life   **173**
  UF   Behavior of teenagers
       Teenage behavior
  BT   **Conduct of life**
  NT   **Etiquette for children and
       teenagers**
Teenagers—Development
  USE **Adolescence**
Teenagers—Drug use (May subdiv. geog.)
    362.29; 613.8; 616.86
  UF   Drugs and teenagers
       Narcotics and teenagers
       Teenagers and drugs
       Teenagers and narcotics
  BT   **Youth—Drug use**
  RT   **Juvenile delinquency**
Teenagers—Employment (May subdiv.
    geog.)   **331.3**
  BT   **Age and employment**
       Employment
       Youth—Employment
  RT   **Summer employment**
Teenagers—Etiquette
  USE **Etiquette for children and
        teenagers**
Teenagers—Literature
  USE **Young adult literature**
Teenagers—Psychiatry
  USE **Adolescent psychiatry**
Teenagers—Psychology
  USE **Adolescent psychology**
Teenagers—Religious life   **204; 248.4**
  BT   **Religious life**
       Youth—Religious life
Teenagers—Suicide   **362.28; 616.85**
  UF   Teen suicide
       Teenage suicide
  BT   **Suicide**
Teenagers—United States   **305.2350973**
  UF   American teenagers
  BT   **Youth—United States**

Teenagers' writings   818.8
   UF   Writings of teenagers
   BT   **Literature**
Teens
   USE   **Teenagers**
Teepees
   USE   **Tepees**
Teeth   611; 612.3; 617.6
   BT   **Head**
   RT   **Dentistry**
Teeth—Diseases   617.6
   BT   **Diseases**
Telecommunication (May subdiv. geog.)
      384; 621.382
   UF   Mass communication
   SA   subjects with the subdivision
         Communication systems, e.g.
         Astronautics—Communication systems [to be added as needed]
   BT   **Communication**
   NT   **Artificial satellites in telecommunication**
         Astronautics—Communication systems
         Broadcasting
         Computer networks
         Data transmission systems
         Electronic mail systems
         Fax transmission
         Intercommunication systems
         Interstellar communication
         Microwave communication systems
         Radio
         Submarine cables
         Telecommuting
         Telegraph
         Telephone
         Television
         Wireless communication systems
Telecommuting (May subdiv. geog.)
      331.25; 658.3
   Use for materials on employment at home with computers, word processors, etc., connected to a central work site, permitting employees to substitute telecommunications for transportation.
   UF   Alternate work sites
         Work at home
         Working at home

   BT   **Automation**
         Telecommunication
Teleconferencing   384; 658.4
   UF   Conference calls (Teleconferencing)
         Telephone—Conference calls
   BT   **Telephone**
Telegraph   384.1; 621.383
   BT   **Public utilities**
         Telecommunication
   NT   **Cipher and telegraph codes**
         Submarine cables
Telegraph codes
   USE   **Cipher and telegraph codes**
Telekinesis
   USE   **Psychokinesis**
Telemarketing (May subdiv. geog.)   **381; 658.8**
   Use for materials on the use of electronic media as a form of marketing that bypasses retail outlets in the advertising and selling of goods.
   UF   Electronic marketing
   BT   **Direct selling**
         Marketing
Telepathy   133.8
   UF   Mental telepathy
         Mind reading
   BT   **Extrasensory perception**
   RT   **Clairvoyance**
Telephone   384.6; 621.385
   BT   **Public utilities**
         Telecommunication
   NT   **Cellular telephones**
         Long distance telephone service
         Teleconferencing
         Video telephone
Telephone—Conference calls
   USE   **Teleconferencing**
Telephone counseling
   USE   **Hotlines (Telephone counseling)**
Telephone directories
   USE   names of countries, cities, etc., corporate bodies, classes of persons, ethnic groups, and types of organizations and industries with the subdivision *Telephone directories,* e.g. **Chicago (Ill.)—Telephone directories** [to be added as needed]

Telephone—Long distance
USE **Long distance telephone service**
Telephotography   778.3
BT **Photography**
Telescope
USE **Telescopes**
Telescopes   522; 681
UF Telescope
BT **Astronomical instruments**
Optical instruments
Teletext systems   004.692; 384.3
Use for materials on the one-way transmission of computer-based data, such as weather forecasts or stock quotations, from a central source to a television set.
BT **Data transmission systems**
Electronic publishing
Information systems
Television broadcasting
RT **Videotex systems**
Television (May subdiv. geog.)   **302.23; 384.55; 621.388**
Use for materials on the technology of television. Materials on what is seen on television are entered under **Television programs.**
UF TV
SA television and particular groups of people, e.g. **Television and children;** and television in various industries or fields of endeavor, e.g. **Television in education** [to be added as needed]
BT **Telecommunication**
NT **African Americans on television**
Closed caption television
Closed-circuit television
Color television
High definition television
Home video systems
Minorities on television
Television and children
Television and politics
Television and youth
Television broadcasting
Television in education
Video art
Video telephone
Violence on television
RT **Videodiscs**
Videotapes

Television actors
USE **Actors**
Television adaptations   791.45
May be used for individual works, collections, or materials about television adaptations of material from other media.
UF Adaptations
Literature—Film and video adaptations
Motion pictures—Television adaptations
SA names of authors, titles of anonymous literary works, types of literature, and types of musical compositions with the subdivision *Adaptations,* for individual works, collections, or criticism and interpretation of literary, cinematic, video, or television adaptations, e.g., **Shakespeare, William, 1564-1616—Adaptations; Beowulf—Adaptations; Arthurian romances—Adaptations;** etc. [to be added as needed]
BT **Television plays**
Television programs
Television scripts
Television advertising (May subdiv. geog.)   **659.14**
UF Commercials, Television
Television commercials
BT **Advertising**
Television broadcasting
Television and children   305.23; 384.55; 791.45
Use for materials on the effect of television on children.
UF Children and television
BT **Children**
Television
Television and infrared observation satellite
USE **TIROS satellites**
Television and politics (May subdiv. geog.)   **324**
UF Politics and television
Television in politics
BT **Politics**
Television

Television and politics—*Continued*
  NT   Equal time rule (Broadcasting)
       Fairness doctrine (Broadcast-
         ing)
Television and youth (May subdiv. geog.)
       305.235; 384.55; 791.45
  UF   Youth and television
  BT   Television
       Youth
Television—Audiences
  USE Television viewers
Television authorship   808
  UF   Television writing
  BT   Authorship
  NT   Television plays—Technique
Television broadcasting (May subdiv.
       geog.)   384.55
  UF   Television industry
  SA   television broadcasting of partic-
         ular kinds of programs, e.g.
       Television broadcasting of
       sports [to be added as need-
         ed]
  BT   Broadcasting
       Mass media
       Television
  NT   African Americans in television
         broadcasting
       Cable television
       Minorities in television broad-
         casting
       Public television
       Subscription television
       Teletext systems
       Television advertising
       Television broadcasting of
         news
       Television broadcasting of
         sports
       Television—Production and di-
         rection
       Television programs
       Television scripts
       Television stations
       Videotex systems
Television broadcasting of news   070.4
  UF   Television coverage of news
       Television journalism
       Television news
  BT   Broadcast journalism
       Television broadcasting

Television broadcasting of sports   070.4
  UF   Sports broadcasting
       Sports in television
       Television sports
  BT   Broadcast journalism
       Television broadcasting
Television broadcasting—Vocational
       guidance   384.55
  BT   Vocational guidance
Television cartoons
  USE Animated television programs
Television—Censorship (May subdiv.
       geog.)   384.55
  BT   Censorship
  NT   V-chips
Television, Closed-circuit
  USE Closed-circuit television
Television comedies
  USE Comedy television programs
Television comedy programs
  USE Comedy television programs
Television commercials
  USE Television advertising
Television coverage of news
  USE Television broadcasting of
         news
Television drama
  USE Television plays
Television—Equipment and supplies
       621.388
  NT   Television—Receivers and re-
         ception
       Videodisc players
  RT   Television supplies industry
       Video recording
Television equipment industry
  USE Television supplies industry
Television fans
  USE Television viewers
Television films
  USE Television movies
Television games
  USE Video games
Television in education (May subdiv.
       geog.)   371.33
  UF   Education and television
       Educational television
  BT   Audiovisual education
       Teaching—Aids and devices
       Television

Television in politics
USE **Television and politics**
Television industry
USE **Television broadcasting**
Television supplies industry
Television journalism
USE **Broadcast journalism**
Television broadcasting of news
Television movies   791.45
May be used for individual works, collections, or materials about television movies.
UF Made-for-TV movies
Television films
BT **Motion pictures**
Television programs
Television news
USE **Television broadcasting of news**
Television novels
USE **Radio and television novels**
Television personalities (May subdiv. geog.) **791.45**
UF TV personalities
BT **Celebrities**
Television plays   808.2; 808.82
May be used for individual works, collections, or materials about television plays.
UF Scenarios
Television drama
BT **Drama**
Television programs
NT **Soap operas**
Television adaptations
RT **Television scripts**
Television plays—Technique   808.2
UF Play writing
Playwriting
BT **Drama—Technique**
Television authorship
RT **Radio plays—Technique**
Television—Production and direction
384.55; 791.4502
BT **Television broadcasting**
Television programs (May subdiv. geog.)
791.45
Use for materials on what is seen on television. Materials on the technology of television are entered under **Television.**
UF Programs, Television
SA types of television programs and names of specific programs
[to be added as needed]

BT **Television broadcasting**
NT **Adventure television programs**
Animated television programs
Biographical television programs
Comedy television programs
Fantasy television programs
Horror television programs
Legal drama (Television programs)
Medical drama (Television programs)
Music videos
Mystery television programs
Science fiction television programs
Sports drama (Television programs)
Spy television programs
Talk shows
Television adaptations
Television movies
Television plays
Television serials
Variety shows (Television programs)
Violence on television
War television programs
Westerns (Television programs)
RT **Television scripts**
Television—Receivers and reception
621.388
UF Television reception
Television sets
BT **Television—Equipment and supplies**
NT **V-chips**
Television reception
USE **Television—Receivers and reception**
Television—Repairing   621.388
Television scripts   791.45; 808.88
May be used for individual works, collections, or materials about television scripts.
UF Screenplays
BT **Television broadcasting**
NT **Television adaptations**
RT **Television plays**
Television programs
Television serials   791.45
May be used for individual works, collections, or materials about television serials.

Television serials—*Continued*
    BT   Television programs
    RT   Soap operas
Television sets
    USE Television—Receivers and reception
Television sports
    USE Television broadcasting of sports
Television—Stage lighting
    USE Stage lighting
Television stations   384.55
    BT   Television broadcasting
Television, Subscription
    USE Subscription television
Television supplies industry (May subdiv. geog.)   338.4; 384.55
    UF   Television equipment industry
         Television industry
    RT   Television—Equipment and supplies
Television viewers (May subdiv. geog.)   302.23; 791.4
    UF   Television—Audiences
         Television fans
         Television watchers
    BT   Audiences
Television watchers
    USE Television viewers
Television writing
    USE Television authorship
Telstar project   621.382
    UF   Bell System Telstar satellite
         Project Telstar
    BT   Artificial satellites in telecommunication
Temper tantrums   152.4
    UF   Tantrums, Temper
    BT   Emotions
         Human behavior
Temperament   155.2
    BT   Mind and body
         Psychology
         Psychophysiology
    NT   Typology (Psychology)
    RT   Character
Temperance   178; 241; 613.81
       Use for materials on the virtue of temperance or on the temperance movement.
    UF   Abstinence
         Drunkenness
         Intemperance

         Intoxication
         Total abstinence
    BT   Virtue
    RT   Alcoholism
         Drinking of alcoholic beverages
         Prohibition
Temperature   536
    NT   Low temperatures
    RT   Cold
         Heat
         Thermometers
Temperature, Animal and human
    USE Body temperature
Temperature, Body
    USE Body temperature
Temples (May subdiv. geog.)   203; 726
    BT   Buildings
         Church architecture
    NT   Mosques
         Synagogues
Temporal power of the Pope
    USE Popes—Temporal power
Temporary employment   331.25
    UF   Employment, Temporary
    BT   Employment
Ten commandments   222
    UF   Decalogue
    BT   Bible. O.T.
Ten lost tribes of Israel
    USE Lost tribes of Israel
Tenant and landlord
    USE Landlord and tenant
Tenant farming
    USE Farm tenancy
Tenement houses (May subdiv. geog.)   647
    UF   Tenements (Apartment houses)
    BT   Apartment houses
Tenements (Apartment houses)
    USE Tenement houses
Tennis (May subdiv. geog.)   796.342
    UF   Lawn tennis
    BT   Sports
Tennis—Tournaments (May subdiv. geog.)   796.342
    BT   Sports tournaments
Tenpins
    USE Bowling
Tension (Physiology)
    USE Stress (Physiology)

Tension (Psychology)
    USE **Stress (Psychology)**
Tents   796.54
    BT   **Camping**
Tenure of land
    USE **Land tenure**
Tenure of office
    USE **Civil service**
Tepees   728; 970.004
    UF   Teepees
         Wigwams
    BT   **Native Americans—Dwellings**
Term limitations (Public office)
    USE **Term limits (Public office)**
Term limits (Public office) (May subdiv.
         geog.)   **328**
    UF   Term limitations (Public office)
    BT   **Legislative bodies**
         Public officers
Term limits (Public office)—United
         States   328.73
    UF   United States—Term limits
         (Public office)
Term paper writing
    USE **Report writing**
Terminal care (May subdiv. geog.)
         362.17; 616; 649.8
    UF   Care of the dying
    BT   **Medical care**
    NT   **Hospices**
         Life support systems (Medical
         environment)
    RT   **Death**
         Living wills
         Terminally ill
Terminally ill (May subdiv. geog.)
         362.17; 649.8
    UF   Dying patients
         Fatally ill patients
    BT   **Sick**
    NT   **Terminally ill children**
    RT   **Death**
         Terminal care
Terminally ill children (May subdiv.
         geog.)   **362.17; 649.8**
    UF   Dying children
         Fatally ill children
    BT   **Terminally ill**
    RT   **Children—Death**
Terminals, Computer
    USE **Computer terminals**

Termination of pregnancy
    USE **Abortion**
Terminology
    USE **Terms and phrases**
         and subjects, classes of persons,
         sacred works, and religious
         sects with the subdivision
         Terminology, for lists or dis-
         cussions of words and expres-
         sions found in those works or
         used in those fields, e.g. **Bot-**
         any—Terminology; names of
         languages with the subdivision
         Terms and phrases, e.g. **En-**
         glish language—Terms and
         phrases; scientific and techni-
         cal disciplines and types of
         substances, plants, and ani-
         mals with the subdivision *No-*
         menclature, for systematically
         derived lists of names or des-
         ignations that have been for-
         mally adopted or sanctioned,
         and for discussions of the
         principles involved in the cre-
         ation and application of such
         names, e.g. **Botany—Nomen-**
         clature; and scientific and
         technical disciplines and types
         of animals, plants, and crops
         with the subdivision *Nomen-*
         clature (Popular), for lists or
         materials about popular, non-
         technical names or designa-
         tions of substances, species,
         etc., **Trees—Nomenclature**
         (Popular) [to be added as
         needed]
Terms and phrases   030
    UF   Commonplaces
         Terminology
    SA   names of languages with the
         subdivision *Terms and*
         phrases, e.g. **English lan-**
         guage—Terms and phrases;
         subjects, classes of persons,
         sacred works, and religious
         sects with the subdivision
         Terminology, for lists or dis-
         cussions of words and expres-
         sions found in those works or

Terms and phrases—*Continued*
   used in those fields, e.g. **Bot-**
   any—Terminology; scientific
   and technical disciplines and
   types of substances, plants,
   and animals with the subdivision *Nomenclature,* for systematically derived lists of
   names or designations that
   have been formally adopted
   or sanctioned, and for discussions of the principles involved in the creation and application of such names, e.g.
   Botany—Nomenclature; and
   scientific and technical disciplines and types of animals,
   plants, and crops with the
   subdivision *Nomenclature*
   (Popular), for lists or materi-
   als about popular, non-
   technical names or designa-
   tions of substances, species,
   etc., **Trees—Nomenclature**
   (Popular) [to be added as
   needed]
 BT **Names**
 RT **Allusions**
Terns 598.3
 BT **Birds**
   Water birds
Terra cotta 620.1; 691
 BT **Building materials**
   Decoration and ornament
   Pottery
Terrain sensing, Remote
 USE **Remote sensing**
Terrapins
 USE **Turtles**
Terrariums 635.9
 BT **Indoor gardening**
 RT **Miniature gardens**
Terrestrial physics
 USE **Geophysics**
Territorial expansion
 USE names of countries, regions, etc.,
   with the subdivision *Territori-*
   al expansion, e.g. **United**
   States—Territorial expansion
   [to be added as needed]

Territorial questions
 USE names of wars with the subdivi-
   sion *Territorial questions,* e.g.
   World War, 1939-1945—
   Territorial questions; which
   may be further subdivided
   geographically [to be added
   as needed]
Territorial waters (May subdiv. geog.)
   341.4; 342
 UF Economic zones (Maritime law)
   Three-mile limit
 BT **Shipping**
 RT **Continental shelf**
   Maritime law
Territorial waters—United States
   341.4; 342
 UF United States—Territorial waters
Territories and possessions
 USE names of countries with the sub-
   division *Territories and pos-*
   sessions, or *Colonies,* e.g.
   United States—Territories
   and possessions; Great Brit-
   ain—Colonies; etc. [to be
   added as needed]
Terror, Reign of
 USE **France—History—1789-1799,**
   Revolution
Terror tales
 USE **Ghost stories**
   Horror fiction
Terrorism (May subdiv. geog.) 303.6
 UF Political violence
 BT **Insurgency**
   Political crimes and offenses
   Subversive activities
 NT **Bombings**
   Hostages
   Sabotage
 RT **Anarchism and anarchists**
Terrorism—Prevention 363.32
 UF Anti-terrorism
   Counter-terrorism
Terrorism—United States 303.6; 322.4
 NT **September 11 terrorist attacks,**
   2001
Terrorist attacks, September 11, 2001
 USE **September 11 terrorist attacks,**
   2001

Terrorist bombings
USE **Bombings**
Test bias   371.2601
UF   Bias in testing
Prejudice in testing
BT   **Discrimination in education**
Educational tests and measure-ments
Test pilots
USE   **Air pilots**
Airplanes—Testing
Test preparation guides
USE   **Examinations—Study guides**
Test tube babies
USE   **Fertilization in vitro**
Test tube fertilization
USE   **Fertilization in vitro**
Testing   620
UF   Mechanical properties testing
SA   things tested with the subdivi-sion *Testing*, e.g. **Ability—Testing; Airplanes—Testing; Concrete—Testing;** etc [to be added as needed]
BT   **Reliability (Engineering)**
NT   **Electric testing**
RT   **Strength of materials**
Testing for drug abuse
USE   **Drug testing**
Tests
USE   **Educational tests and measure-ments**
Examinations
Teutonic peoples (May subdiv. geog.)   **305.83**
UF   Nordic peoples
Teutonic race
SA   names of particular Teutonic peoples, e.g. **Goths** [to be added as needed]
NT   **Anglo-Saxons**
Goths
Teutonic race
USE   **Teutonic peoples**
Textbooks   371.3
UF   School books
SA   branches of study with the sub-division *Textbooks*, e.g. **Arith-metic—Textbooks** [to be add-ed as needed]
BT   **Books**

Textile chemistry   677
UF   Chemistry, Textile
BT   **Industrial chemistry**
Textile industry
NT   **Dyes and dyeing**
Textile design (May subdiv. geog.)   **746**
UF   Fabric design
BT   **Commercial art**
Decoration and ornament
Design
NT   **Textile painting**
RT   **Textile printing**
Textile fibers
USE   **Fibers**
Textile industry (May subdiv. geog.)   **338.4; 677**
SA   types of articles manufactured, e.g **Rugs and carpets; Ho-siery;** etc. [to be added as needed]
BT   **Industries**
NT   **Bleaching**
Cotton manufacture
Dyes and dyeing
Hosiery
Spinning
Textile chemistry
Textile printing
Weaving
Textile painting   746.6
BT   **Painting**
Textile design
Textile printing   746.6
UF   Block printing
BT   **Printing**
Textile industry
RT   **Silk screen printing**
Textile design
Textiles
USE   **Fabrics**
Texts
USE   types of lesser-known languages, dialects, early periods of lan-guages, liturgies, and types of vocal music with the subdivi-sion *Texts,* e.g. **Catholic Church—Liturgy—Texts; Popular music—Texts;** etc., for individual texts or collec-tions of texts [to be added as needed]

Thankfulness
USE **Gratitude**
Thanksgiving Day 394.2649
  BT **Holidays**
      Religious holidays
Theater (May subdiv. geog.) 792
    Use for materials on drama as acted on the stage. Materials on drama as a literary form are entered under **Drama; American drama; English drama;** etc. Collections of plays are entered under **Drama—Collections; American drama—Collections;** etc. Materials on theater buildings are entered under **Theaters.**
  UF Stage
  SA names of wars with the subdivision *Theater and the war* e.g.
      World War, 1939-1945— Theater and the war [to be added as needed]
  BT **Amusements**
      Performing arts
  NT **Amateur theater**
      Arena theater
      Ballet
      Children's plays
      Experimental theater
      Little theater movement
      Masks (Plays)
      Morality plays
      Musicals
      Mysteries and miracle plays
      Pantomimes
      Passion plays
      Puppets and puppet plays
      Readers' theater
      Shadow pantomimes and plays
      Shakespeare, William, 1564-1616—Stage history
      Skits
      Vaudeville
      World War, 1939-1945—Theater and the war
  RT **Acting**
      Drama
      Dramatic criticism
      Theaters
Theater and the war
  USE names of wars with the subdivision *Theater and the war,* e.g.
      World War, 1939-1945— Theater and the war [to be added as needed]

Theater criticism
  USE **Dramatic criticism**
Theater-in-the-round
  USE **Arena theater**
Theater—Production and direction 792
  UF Direction (Theater)
      Play direction (Theater)
      Play production
      Theatrical direction
      Theatrical production
  RT **Theatrical producers and directors**
Theater—United States 792.0973
Theaters (May subdiv. geog.) 725
    Use for materials on theater buildings, their architecture, technical fixtures, decoration, etc. Materials on drama as a literary form are entered under **Drama.** Materials on drama as acted on the stage are entered under **Theater.**
  UF Playhouses
  SA types of theaters [to be added as needed]
  BT **Buildings**
      Centers for the performing arts
  NT **Night clubs, cabarets, etc.**
  RT **Theater**
Theaters—Conservation and restoration (May subdiv. geog.) 725
  BT **Historic preservation**
Theaters—Stage lighting
  USE **Stage lighting**
Theaters—Stage setting and scenery 792.02
  UF Scenery (Stage)
      Stage scenery
      Stage setting
      Theatrical scenery
  NT **Scene painting**
Theatrical costume
  USE **Costume**
Theatrical direction
  USE **Theater—Production and direction**
Theatrical directors
  USE **Theatrical producers and directors**
Theatrical makeup 791.43; 791.45; 792
  UF Makeup, Theatrical
  BT **Cosmetics**
      Costume

Theatrical producers
  USE **Theatrical producers and directors**
Theatrical producers and directors (May subdiv. geog.) **792; 920**
  UF Theatrical directors
       Theatrical producers
  RT **Theater—Production and direction**
Theatrical production
  USE **Theater—Production and direction**
Theatrical scenery
  USE **Theaters—Stage setting and scenery**
Theft **364.16**
  UF Larceny
       Stealing
  BT **Crime**
       Offenses against property
  NT **Art thefts**
       Bank robberies
       Shoplifting
  RT **Thieves**
Theism (May subdiv. geog.) **211**
  BT **Philosophy**
       Religion
       Theology
  NT **Monotheism**
  RT **Atheism**
       Deism
       God
Theme parks
  USE **Amusement parks**
Themes in art
  USE **Art—Themes**
Themes in literature
  USE **Literature—Themes**
Theological education
  USE **Religious education**
       Theology—Study and teaching
Theology (May subdiv. geog.) **202; 230**
  NT **Apologetics**
       Atheism
       Church
       Covenants
       Deism
       Doctrinal theology
       Eschatology
       Faith
       Feminist theology

       Good and evil
       Immortality
       Liberation theology
       Natural theology
       Pastoral theology
       Predestination
       Revelation
       Sin
       Theism
       Worship
  RT **God**
       Religion
Theology, Doctrinal
  USE **Doctrinal theology**
Theology of liberation
  USE **Liberation theology**
Theology—Study and teaching **202; 230.07**
  UF Education, Theological
       Religion—Study and teaching
       Theological education
  NT **Catechisms**
  RT **Religious education**
Theoretical chemistry
  USE **Physical chemistry**
Theory of games
  USE **Game theory**
Theory of graphs
  USE **Graph theory**
Theory of knowledge **001.01; 121**
  Use for materials on the origin, nature, methods, and limits of human knowledge.
  UF Cognition
       Epistemology
       Knowledge, Theory of
       Understanding
  BT **Consciousness**
       Logic
       Metaphysics
       Philosophy
  NT **Belief and doubt**
       Certainty
       Cognitive styles
       Empiricism
       Gestalt psychology
       Ideology
       Intuition
       Perception
       Pragmatism
       Rationalism
       Senses and sensation

Theory of knowledge—*Continued*
  RT **Apperception**
      Intellect
      Reality
      Truth
Theory of numbers
  USE **Number theory**
Theory of structures
  USE **Structural analysis (Engineer-ing)**
Theory of systems
  USE **System theory**
Theosophy (May subdiv. geog.) **299**
  BT **Mysticism**
      Religions
  NT **Reincarnation**
      Yoga
Therapeutic systems
  USE **Alternative medicine**
Therapeutic use
  USE subjects with the subdivision *Therapeutic use,* e.g. **Cold—Therapeutic use; Herbs—Therapeutic use** etc. [to be added as needed]
Therapeutics **615.5**
  UF Diseases—Treatment
      Therapy
      Treatment
      Treatment of diseases
  SA types of therapies, e.g. **Hydrotherapy;** diseases with the subdivision *Treatment,* e.g. **AIDS (Disease)—Treatment;** subjects with the subdivision *Therapeutic use,* e.g. **Cold—Therapeutic use; Herbs—Therapeutic use;** etc.; diseases with the subdivision *Diet therapy,* e.g. **Cancer—Diet therapy;** and types of drugs and names of specific drugs [to be added as needed]
  BT **Medicine**
      Pathology
  NT **AIDS (Disease)—Treatment**
      Antiseptics
      Aromatherapy
      Art therapy
      Cold—Therapeutic use
      Diet in disease
      Diet therapy

Drug abuse—Treatment
Drug therapy
Drugs
Electrotherapeutics
Gene therapy
Healing
Herbs—Therapeutic use
Hydrotherapy
Materia medica
Medicine
Music therapy
Naturopathy
Nursing
Nutrition
Occupational therapy
Pet therapy
Phototherapy
Physical therapy
Play therapy
Psychotherapy
Radiotherapy
Suggestive therapeutics
  RT **Pharmaceutical chemistry**
Therapeutics, Suggestive
  USE **Suggestive therapeutics**
Therapy
  USE **Therapeutics**
Therapy, Gene
  USE **Gene therapy**
Therapy, Psychological
  USE **Psychotherapy**
Thermal insulation
  USE **Insulation (Heat)**
Thermal waters
  USE **Geothermal resources**
      Geysers
Thermoaerodynamics
  USE **Aerothermodynamics**
Thermodynamics **536**
  SA subjects with the subdivision *Thermodynamics,* e.g. **Space vehicles—Thermodynamics** [to be added as needed]
  BT **Dynamics**
      Physical chemistry
      Physics
  NT **Aerothermodynamics**
      Heat engines
      Heat pumps
      Space vehicles—Thermodynamics

Thermodynamics—*Continued*
  RT **Heat**
      Heat engines
      Quantum theory
Thermometers 536
  UF Thermometry
  BT **Heat**
      Meteorological instruments
  RT **Temperature**
Thermometry
  USE **Thermometers**
Thesauri
  USE **Subject headings**
      and names of languages with
      the subdivision *Synonyms and
      antonyms,* e.g. **English lan-
      guage—Synonyms and ant-
      onyms** [to be added as need-
      ed]
Theses
  USE **Dissertations**
Thieves (May subdiv. geog.) **364.3**
  UF Bandits
      Brigands
      Burglars
      Highwaymen
      Outlaws
      Robbers
  BT **Criminals**
  RT **Theft**
Think tanks
  USE **Group problem solving**
Thinking
  USE **Thought and thinking**
Third parties (United States politics)
    324.273
  BT **Political parties**
      **United States—Politics and
      government**
Third World
  USE **Developing countries**
Third World War
  USE **World War III**
Thirteenth century
  USE **World history—13th century**
**Thirty Years' War, 1618-1648 909.08;
    940.2**
  BT **Europe—History—1492-1789**
      Germany—History—1517-1740
Thoroughfares
  USE **Roads**
      Streets

Thought and thinking 153.4
  UF Thinking
  BT **Educational psychology**
      Psychology
  NT **Attention**
      Critical thinking
      Ideology
      Memory
      Perception
      Reasoning
      Stereotype (Psychology)
  RT **Intellect**
      Logic
Thought control
  USE **Brainwashing**
Threatened species
  USE **Endangered species**
Three dimensional photography 778.4
  UF 3-D photography
      Photography, Stereoscopic
      Stereo photography
      Stereophotography
      Stereoscopic photography
  BT **Photography**
  RT **Holography**
Three-mile limit
  USE **Territorial waters**
Three Stooges films 791.43
    May be used for individual works, collec-
    tions, or materials about Three Stooges films.
  BT **Comedy films**
      Motion pictures
Three (The number) 513
  BT **Numbers**
Thrift
  USE **Saving and investment**
Thrillers
  USE **Adventure fiction**
      Adventure films
Throat 611; 612; 617.5
  BT **Anatomy**
  NT **Voice**
Thunderstorms (May subdiv. geog.)
    551.55
  BT **Meteorology**
      Storms
  NT **Lightning**
**Tiananmen Square Incident, Beijing
  (China), 1989 951.05**
  UF Beijing Massacre, 1989
      China—History—1989, Tianan-
      men Square Incident

Ticks   595.4
  BT   Animals
Tidal waves
  USE   Tsunamis
Tides (May subdiv. geog.)   551.46
  BT   Ocean
Tidiness
  USE   Orderliness
Tie dyeing   746.6
  BT   Dyes and dyeing
Tiles (May subdiv. geog.)   666; 693;
    738.6
  UF   Ceramic tiles
  BT   Building materials
         Ceramics
Timber
  USE   Forests and forestry
         Lumber and lumbering
         Trees
         Wood
Timber—Harvesting
  USE   Logging
Time   529
  UF   Horology
         Standard time
  NT   Calendars
         Chronology
         Clocks and watches
         Day
         Night
         Punctuality
         Space and time
         Sundials
         Time management
  RT   Cycles
         Nautical astronomy
Time and space
  USE   Space and time
Time management   640; 650.1
  UF   Allocation of time
         Personal time management
  BT   Management
         Time
Time production standards
  USE   Production standards
Time saving cooking
  USE   Quick and easy cooking
Time sharing (Real estate)
  USE   Timesharing (Real estate)

Time study   658.5
  BT   Factory management
         Industrial efficiency
         Job analysis
         Personnel management
         Production standards
  RT   Motion study
Time travel   115
  BT   Fourth dimension
         Space and time
Timesharing (Real estate) (May subdiv.
    geog.)   333.3; 333.5; 643
  UF   Condominium timesharing
         Real estate timesharing
         Time sharing (Real estate)
         Vacation home timesharing
  BT   Condominiums
         Housing
         Property
         Real estate business
Tin   669
  BT   Chemical elements
         Metals
Tinsmithing
  USE   Tinwork
Tinwork (May subdiv. geog.)   673
  UF   Tinsmithing
  BT   Metalwork
Tiny objects
  USE   Miniature objects
Tires   678
  UF   Rubber tires
  BT   Wheels
Tiros (Meteorological satellite)
  USE   TIROS satellites
TIROS satellites   551.5
  UF   Television and infrared observa-
            tion satellite
         Tiros (Meteorological satellite)
  BT   Meteorological satellites
Tissue donation
  USE   Donation of organs, tissues,
            etc.
Tissues—Transplantation
  USE   Transplantation of organs, tis-
            sues, etc.
Tithes (May subdiv. geog.)   248; 254
  BT   Church finance
         Ecclesiastical law
         Taxation

Toadstools
  USE **Mushrooms**
Toasts   808.5; 808.85
  UF Healths, Drinking of
  BT **Epigrams**
      Speeches
  RT **After dinner speeches**
Tobacco (May subdiv. geog.)   **633.7**
  BT **Plants**
  NT **Cigarettes**
      Cigars
  RT **Smoking**
Tobacco habit (May subdiv. geog.)   **178;**
      613.85; 616.86
  UF Addiction to nicotine
      Addiction to tobacco
      Nicotine habit
  BT **Habit**
      Smoking
  NT **Smoking cessation programs**
Tobacco pipes   688
  UF Pipes, Tobacco
  BT **Smoking**
Toilet preparations
  USE **Toiletries**
Toilet training   649
  BT **Child rearing**
Toiletries   646.7
  UF Toilet preparations
  BT **Personal grooming**
  RT **Cosmetics**
Tolerance
  USE **Toleration**
Toleration (May subdiv. geog.)   **179;**
      323
  UF Bigotry
      Intolerance
      Tolerance
  BT **Interpersonal relations**
  NT **Academic freedom**
      Freedom of conscience
      Freedom of religion
      Religious tolerance
  RT **Discrimination**
Toll roads
  USE **Express highways**
Tombs (May subdiv. geog.)   **726**
  UF Graves
      Mausoleums
      Rock tombs
      Sepulchers

Vaults (Sepulchral)
  SA classes of persons, and names of
      families, royal houses,
      dynasties, etc., with the subdi-
      vision *Tombs,* e.g. **Presi-**
      dents—United States—
      Tombs [to be added as need-
      ed]
  BT **Archeology**
      Architecture
      Burial
      Monuments
      Shrines
  NT **Brasses**
      Catacombs
      Epitaphs
      Mounds and mound builders
  RT **Cemeteries**
Tomography   616.07; 621.36
  UF CAT scan
      Computerized tomography
  BT **X-rays**
Tongue twisters   398.8
  BT **Children's poetry**
      Folklore
      Nonsense verses
Tools (May subdiv. geog.)   **621.9**
  SA types of tools [to be added as
      needed]
  BT **Implements, utensils, etc.**
  NT **Agricultural machinery**
      Carpentry tools
      Machine tools
      Machinery
      Power tools
      Saws
      Weapons
Top soil loss
  USE **Soil erosion**
Topographical drawing   526
  BT **Drawing**
      Surveying
  RT **Map drawing**
Topology   514
  UF Position analysis
  BT **Geometry**
      Set theory
  NT **Fractals**
      Graph theory
  RT **Linear algebra**

Tories, American
USE **American Loyalists**
Tornadoes (May subdiv. geog.)   **551.55**
UF   Twisters (Tornadoes)
BT   **Meteorology**
      Storms
      Winds
Torpedoes   623.4
BT   **Explosives**
      Naval art and science
      Submarine warfare
Tort liability of professions
USE   **Malpractice**
Tortoises
USE   **Turtles**
Torture (May subdiv. geog.)   **365**
BT   **Criminal procedure**
      Cruelty
      Punishment
Total abstinence
USE   **Temperance**
Totalitarianism (May subdiv. geog.)
      321.9
UF   Authoritarianism
BT   **Political science**
NT   **Communism**
      Dictators
      Fascism
Totem poles (May subdiv. geog.)   **299.7;**
      704.9; 731
BT   **Totems and totemism**
Totems and totemism (May subdiv.
      geog.)   **202**
BT   **Ethnology**
      Mythology
NT   **Totem poles**
Touch   152.1; 612
UF   Feeling
BT   **Senses and sensation**
NT   **Hugging**
Touring, Bicycle
USE   **Bicycle touring**
Tourism
USE   **Tourist trade**
      Travel
Tourist accommodations
USE   **Hotels and motels**
      Youth hostels
Tourist industry
USE   **Tourist trade**

Tourist trade (May subdiv. geog.)   **338.4**
UF   Tourism
      Tourist industry
      Tourists
      Travel industry
BT   **Commerce**
NT   **Cultural tourism**
      Ecotourism
RT   **Travel**
Tourists
USE   **Tourist trade**
      Travelers
Tournaments
USE   **Medieval tournaments**
      Sports tournaments
      and types of sports and games
         with the subdivision *Tourna-*
         ments, e.g. **Tennis—Tourna-**
         ments [to be added as need-
         ed]
Town life
USE   **City and town life**
Town meeting
USE   **Local government**
Town officers
USE   **Municipal officials and em-**
         ployees
Town planning
USE   **City planning**
Towns
USE   **Cities and towns**
Towns, Abandoned
USE   **Ghost towns**
Township government
USE   **Local government**
Toxic dumps
USE   **Hazardous waste sites**
Toxic plants
USE   **Poisonous plants**
Toxic substances
USE   **Hazardous substances**
      Poisons and poisoning
Toxic wastes
USE   **Hazardous wastes**
Toxicology   571.9; 615.9
   Use for materials on the science that treats
of poisons and their antidotes. Materials on
poisonous substance and their use are entered
under **Poisons and poisoning.**

Toxicology—*Continued*

　　UF　Chemicals—Toxicology

　　SA　types of poisons or poisoning,
　　　　　e.g. **Lead poisoning;** and
　　　　　types of poisonous substances
　　　　　with the subdivision *Toxicolo-*
　　　　　gy, for materials on the influ-
　　　　　ence of particular substances
　　　　　on humans and animals, e.g.
　　　　　Insecticides—Toxicology [to
　　　　　be added as needed]

　　BT　**Medicine**
　　　　　Pharmacology

　　RT　**Poisons and poisoning**

Toy and movable books

　　UF　Movable books
　　　　　Pop-up books

　　BT　**Picture books for children**

　　NT　**Glow-in-the-dark books**

Toy making (May subdiv. geog.)
　　　　745.592

　　BT　**Handicraft**

　　NT　**Soft toy making**
　　　　　Wooden toy making

　　RT　**Toys**

Toys (May subdiv. geog.)　**688.7; 790.1**

　　SA　types of toys [to be added as
　　　　　needed]

　　BT　**Amusements**

　　NT　**Doll furniture**
　　　　　Dollhouses
　　　　　Dolls
　　　　　Electric toys
　　　　　Electronic toys

　　RT　**Miniature objects**
　　　　　Toy making

Track and field
　　USE　**Track athletics**

Track athletics (May subdiv. geog.)
　　　　796.42

　　UF　Field athletics
　　　　　Track and field

　　SA　types of track sports [to be add-
　　　　　ed as needed]

　　BT　**Athletics**
　　　　　Sports

　　NT　**Running**

Tracking and trailing (May subdiv.
　　　　geog.)　**799.2**

　　UF　Trailing

　　BT　**Hunting**

　　NT　**Animal tracks**

　　RT　**Animal behavior**

Tracking of satellites
　　USE　**Artificial satellites—Tracking**
　　　　　Space vehicles—Tracking

Tracks of animals
　　USE　**Animal tracks**

Traction engines
　　USE　**Tractors**

Tractors　**629.225; 631.3**

　　UF　Traction engines

　　BT　**Agricultural machinery**

Trade
　　USE　**Business**
　　　　　Commerce

Trade agreements (Labor)
　　USE　**Industrial arbitration**
　　　　　Labor contract

Trade and professional associations (May
　　　　subdiv. geog.)　**381; 650**

　　UF　Professional associations
　　　　　Trade associations

　　BT　**Associations**

Trade associations
　　USE　**Trade and professional associa-**
　　　　　tions

Trade, Balance of
　　USE　**Balance of trade**

Trade barriers
　　USE　**Commercial policy**

Trade, Boards of
　　USE　**Chambers of commerce**

Trade catalogs
　　USE　**Commercial catalogs**

Trade deficits
　　USE　**Balance of trade**

Trade expositions
　　USE　**Trade shows**

Trade fairs
　　USE　**Trade shows**

Trade, International
　　USE　**International trade**

Trade marks
　　USE　**Trademarks**

Trade, Restraint of
　　USE　**Restraint of trade**

Trade routes (May subdiv. geog.)   **387**
UF   Ocean routes
Routes of trade
Sea routes
BT   **Commerce**
Commercial geography
Transportation
Trade schools
USE   **Technical education**
Trade secrets   **346.04; 658.4**
UF   Business secrets
Commercial secrets
Industrial secrets
Secrets, Trade
BT   **Right of privacy**
Unfair competition
Trade shows (May subdiv. geog.)   **659.1**
UF   Industrial exhibitions
Trade expositions
Trade fairs
BT   **Exhibitions**
Fairs
Trade surpluses
USE   **Balance of trade**
Trade-unions
USE   **Labor unions**
Trade waste
USE   **Industrial waste**
Waste products
Trademarks (May subdiv. geog.)
346.04; 929.9
UF   Company symbols
Corporate symbols
Trade marks
SA   types of industries and products
with the subdivision *Trade-
marks,* for materials on the
words, letters, or symbols
used by the manufacturers or
dealers of those goods to dis-
tinguish them from the goods
of others, e.g. **Glassware—
Trademarks** [to be added as
needed]
BT   **Commerce**
Manufactures
NT   **Glassware—Trademarks**
RT   **Brand name products**
Patents

Trades
USE   **Industrial arts**
Occupations
Trading card games
USE   **Collectible card games**
Trading cards   **741.6**
BT   **Collectibles**
Traditional medicine (May subdiv. geog.)
615.8
UF   Folk medicine
Folklore, Medical
Medical folklore
SA   traditional medicine of particular
ethnic groups, e.g. **Native
American medicine** [to be
added as needed]
BT   **Medicine**
Popular medicine
Traditions
USE   **Folklore**
Legends
Manners and customs
Rites and ceremonies
Superstition
Traffic accidents (May subdiv. geog.)
363.12
UF   Automobile accidents
Automobiles—Accidents
Car accidents
Car wrecks
Highway accidents
BT   **Accidents**
Traffic, City
USE   **City traffic**
Traffic control
USE   **Traffic engineering**
Traffic regulations
Traffic engineering (May subdiv. geog.)
388.4
Use for materials on the planning of the
flow of traffic and related topics, largely as
they concern street transportation in cities and
metropolitan areas.
UF   Street traffic
Traffic control
BT   **Engineering**
Highway engineering
Transportation
NT   **Car pools**
City traffic
Express highways
Local transit

Traffic engineering—*Continued*
> **Traffic safety**
RT **Traffic regulations**
Traffic regulations (May subdiv. geog.)
> 388.4
UF Traffic control
BT **Safety regulations**
RT **Automobiles—Law and legislation**
> **Traffic engineering**
Traffic safety   363.12
UF Highway safety
> Road safety
BT **Highway transportation**
> **Traffic engineering**
Trafficking in drugs
USE **Drug traffic**
Trafficking in narcotics
USE **Drug traffic**
Tragedies   808.82
> May be used for individual works or for collections. Materials about tragedy as a literary form are entered under **Tragedy.**
BT **Drama**
Tragedy   792.1; 809.2
> Use for materials on tragedy as a literary form. Individual works and collections of tragedies are entered under **Tragedies.**
BT **Drama**
Trail riding (May subdiv. geog.)   798.2
BT **Horsemanship**
Trailer camps
USE **Trailer parks**
Trailer parks (May subdiv. geog.)   647;
> 796.54
UF Mobile home parks
> Trailer camps
BT **Campgrounds**
> **Mobile home living**
Trailers
USE **Mobile homes**
> **Travel trailers and campers**
Trailing
USE **Tracking and trailing**
Trails (May subdiv. geog.)   796.51
BT **Roads**
NT **Nature trails**
RT **Hiking**
> **Mountaineering**
Train wrecks
USE **Railroad accidents**

Training
USE types of sports activities, plants and crops, animals, and classes of persons with the subdivision *Training,* e.g. **Soccer— Training; Horses—Training; Teachers—Training;** etc. [to be added as needed]
Training camps, Military
USE **Military training camps**
Training colleges for teachers
USE **Teachers colleges**
Training, Occupational
USE **Occupational training**
Training of animals
USE **Animals—Training**
Training of children
USE **Child rearing**
Training of employees
USE **Employees—Training**
Training, Vocational
USE **Occupational training**
Trains
USE **Railroads**
Traitors (May subdiv. geog.)   364.1
NT **Collaborationists**
RT **Treason**
Tramps (May subdiv. geog.)   305.5
> Use for materials on homeless persons who travel about from place to place and work in occasional jobs.
UF Hoboes
> Vagabonds
> Vagrants
BT **Homeless persons**
> **Poor**
RT **Begging**
> **Unemployed**
Trams
USE **Street railroads**
Transactional analysis   158
BT **Psychotherapy**
Transatlantic flights
USE **Aeronautics—Flights**
Transcendental meditation   158
BT **Meditation**
Transcendentalism   141
BT **Philosophy**
RT **Idealism**

Transcontinental journeys (American continent)
USE **Overland journeys to the Pacific**
Transcultural studies
USE **Cross-cultural studies**
Transfer of technology
USE **Technology transfer**
Transfer payments (May subdiv. geog.) **339.5**
  UF Government transfer payments
  BT **Domestic economic assistance**
     Economic policy
     Subsidies
Transfer tax
  USE **Inheritance and transfer tax**
Transformation (Genetics)
  USE **Genetic transformation**
Transformers, Electric
  USE **Electric transformers**
Transgenics
  USE **Genetic engineering**
Transistor amplifiers   621.3815
  UF Amplifiers, Transistor
     Audio amplifiers, Transistor
     Transistor audio amplifiers
  BT **Amplifiers (Electronics)**
     Transistors
Transistor audio amplifiers
  USE **Transistor amplifiers**
Transistors   621.3815
  BT **Electronics**
     Semiconductors
  NT **Transistor amplifiers**
Transit systems
  USE **Local transit**
Translating and interpreting (May subdiv. geog.)   **418**
  UF Interpreting and translating
  BT **Language and languages**
Transmission of data
  USE **Data transmission systems**
Transmission of power
  USE **Electric lines**
     Electric power distribution
     Power transmission
Transmissions, Automobile
  USE **Automobiles—Transmission devices**
Transmutation (Chemistry)   539.7
  Use for materials on the transmutation of metals in nuclear physics. Materials on medi-

eval attempts to change base metals into gold are entered under **Alchemy.**
  UF Transmutation of metals
  BT **Atoms**
     Nuclear physics
     Radioactivity
  NT **Cyclotrons**
  RT **Alchemy**
Transmutation of metals
  USE **Alchemy**
     Transmutation (Chemistry)
Transplantation
  USE **Transplantation of organs, tissues, etc.**
     and organs of the body with the subdivision *Transplantation,* e.g. **Heart—Transplantation** [to be added as needed]
Transplantation of organs, tissues, etc.   617.9
  UF Medical transplantation
     Organ transplants
     Organs—Transplantation
     Surgical transplantation
     Tissues—Transplantation
     Transplantation
  SA organs of the body with the subdivision *Transplantation,* e.g. **Heart—Transplantation** [to be added as needed]
  BT **Surgery**
  NT **Heart—Transplantation**
  RT **Donation of organs, tissues, etc.**
     Preservation of organs, tissues, etc.
Transplantation of organs, tissues, etc.—Ethical aspects   174
  UF Transplantation of organs, tissues, etc.—Moral and religious aspects
  BT **Bioethics**
Transplantation of organs, tissues, etc.—Moral and religious aspects
  USE **Transplantation of organs, tissues, etc.—Ethical aspects**
     Transplantation of organs, tissues, etc.—Religious aspects

Transplantation of organs, tissues, etc.—
  Religious aspects   201; 241
  UF   Transplantation of organs, tis-
       sues, etc.—Moral and reli-
       gious aspects
Transportation (May subdiv. geog.)   388
  SA   subjects, classes of person, and
       names of wars with the sub-
       division *Transportation,* e.g.
       **Hazardous substances—
       Transportation; School chil-
       dren—Transportation;
       World War, 1939-1945—
       Transportation;** etc. [to be
       added as needed]
  BT   **Locomotion**
  NT   **Bridges**
       Canals
       Car pools
       Commercial aeronautics
       Express service
       Freight
       Harbors
       **Hazardous substances—Trans-
       portation**
       Highway transportation
       Inland navigation
       Local transit
       Merchant marine
       Military transportation
       Ocean travel
       Pipelines
       Postal service
       Railroads
       Roads
       **School children—Transporta-
       tion**
       Shipping
       Steam navigation
       Streets
       Trade routes
       Traffic engineering
       Trucking
       Vehicles
       Waterways
       **World War, 1939-1945—Trans-
       portation**
  RT   **Commerce**
Transportation, Highway
  USE   **Highway transportation**

Transportation, Military
  USE   **Military transportation**
Transportation of criminals
  USE   **Penal colonies**
Transportation—Planning (May subdiv.
  geog.)   338
  BT   **Planning**
Transsexualism   305.3; 616.85
  UF   Change of sex
       Sex change
       Transsexuality
  BT   **Sex role**
Transsexuality
  USE   **Transsexualism**
Trapping (May subdiv. geog.)   639
  NT   **Fur trade**
  RT   **Game and game birds**
       Hunting
Traumatic stress syndrome
  USE   **Post-traumatic stress disorder**
Travel   910
  Use for materials on the art and enjoyment
  of travel and advice for travelers. Descriptions
  of actual voyages are entered under **Voyages
  and travels** or under the name of a place with
  the subdivision *Description and travel.* An ac-
  count of an extinct city or town by a traveler
  in ancient times is entered under the name of
  the extinct city or town, without further subdivision, e.g. **Delphi (Extinct city).**
  UF   Group travel
       Journeys
       Tourism
  SA   names of cities (except extinct
       cities), countries, states, etc.,
       with the subdivision *Descrip-
       tion and travel,* e.g. **United
       States—Description and
       travel;** and ethnic groups,
       classes of persons, and names
       of individuals with the subdi-
       vision *Travel,* e.g. **Handi-
       capped—Travel** [to be added
       as needed]
  BT   **Manners and customs**
  NT   **Automobile travel**
       Bicycle touring
       Handicapped—Travel
       Ocean travel
       Safaris
       Travel in literature
       Voyages around the world
  RT   **Tourist trade**
       Voyages and travels

Travel—Authorship
　USE　**Travel writing**
Travel books
　USE　**Voyages and travels**
　　　　Voyages around the world
Travel guides
　USE　**Automobile travel—Guidebooks**
　　　　and names of cities (except an-
　　　　cient cities), countries, states,
　　　　etc., with the subdivision
　　　　Guidebooks, e.g. **Chicago**
　　　　(Ill.)—Guidebooks; United
　　　　States—Guidebooks; etc. [to
　　　　be added as needed]
Travel in literature　809
　Use for materials about the theme of travel
　in literature. Materials about non-fiction travel
　writing, collections of travel writings, and ac-
　counts of voyages and travels not limited to a
　single place are entered under **Voyages and**
　travels. Accounts of voyages and travels lim-
　ited to a single place are entered under the
　name of the place with the subdivision *De-*
　scription and travel.
　UF　Voyages and travels in literature
　BT　**Literature—Themes**
　　　　Travel
　RT　**Voyages and travels**
Travel industry
　USE　**Tourist trade**
Travel trailers and campers　629.226;
　　　796.7
　Use for materials on structures mounted
　upon a truck or towed by a truck or automo-
　bile for the purpose of temporary dwelling or
　cargo hauling. Materials on stationary trans-
　portable structures designed for year-round
　living are entered under **Mobile homes.**
　UF　Automobiles—Trailers
　　　　Campers and trailers
　　　　House trailers
　　　　Pickup campers
　　　　Trailers
　BT　**Camping**
　　　　Recreational vehicles
　NT　**Vans**
　RT　**Mobile homes**
Travel writing　808
　Use for materials about the art of travel
　writing. Materials about a particular place are
　entered under the name of the place with the
　subdivision *Description and travel,* e.g. **Chi-**
　cago (Ill.)—Description and travel.
　UF　Travel—Authorship
　BT　**Authorship**

Travelers (May subdiv. geog.)　**910.92;**
　　　920
　UF　Tourists
　　　　Voyagers
　SA　travelers from particular coun-
　　　　tries, e.g. **American travel-**
　　　　ers; and ethnic groups, class-
　　　　es of person, and names of
　　　　individuals with the subdivi-
　　　　sion *Travel,* e.g. **Presidents—**
　　　　United States—Travel [to be
　　　　added as needed]
　BT　**Voyages and travels**
　NT　**American travelers**
　RT　**Explorers**
Traveling sales personnel
　USE　**Sales personnel**
Travels
　USE　**Voyages and travels**
Travesties
　USE　**Parodies**
Tray gardens
　USE　**Miniature gardens**
Treason (May subdiv. geog.)　**364.1**
　Use for materials on the offense of acting
　to overthrow one's own government or to
　harm or kill its sovereign. Materials on any
　attempt to subvert, overthrow, or cause the
　destruction of any established or legally con-
　stituted government are entered under **Subver-**
　sive activities.
　UF　High treason
　BT　**Crime**
　　　　Political crimes and offenses
　　　　Subversive activities
　RT　**Traitors**
Treasure trove
　USE　**Buried treasure**
Treaties　**341; 341.3**
　SA　names of countries with the sub-
　　　　division *Foreign relations—*
　　　　Treaties, and names of wars
　　　　with the subdivision *Treaties*
　　　　[to be added as needed]
　BT　**Diplomacy**
　　　　International law
　　　　International relations
　NT　**International arbitration**
　　　　United States—Foreign rela-
　　　　tions—Treaties
　　　　World War, 1939-1945—Trea-
　　　　ties

Treatment
  USE **Therapeutics**
        and types of diseases with the
        subdivision *Treatment,* e.g.
        AIDS (Disease)—Treatment
        [to be added as needed]
Treatment of diseases
  USE **Therapeutics**
Tree houses   690
  BT **Buildings**
Tree planting (May subdiv. geog.)
        635.9
  UF Planting
  BT **Forests and forestry**
  NT **Windbreaks**
  RT **Christmas tree growing**
        Reforestation
        Trees
Trees (May subdiv. geog.)   **582.16; 635.9**
        Names of nuts and tree fruits may be used
        for either the nut or fruit or the tree.
  UF Arboriculture
        Timber
  SA types of trees, e.g. **Oak** [to be
        added as needed], in the sin-
        gular form
  BT **Plants**
  NT **Christmas trees**
        Dwarf trees
        Evergreens
        Fruit culture
        Lumber and lumbering
        Oak
        Pruning
        Shrubs
        Wood
  RT **Forests and forestry**
        Landscape gardening
        Tree planting
Trees—Nomenclature (Popular)   582.16
  BT **Popular plant names**
Trees—United States   582.160973
Trent Affair, 1861   973.7
  BT **United States—History—1861-**
        1865, Civil War
Trial by jury
  USE **Jury**
Trial by publicity
  USE **Freedom of the press and fair**
        trial
Trial marriage
  USE **Unmarried couples**

Trials (May subdiv. geog.)   **345; 347**
        May be qualified by topic, e.g. **Trials
        (Homicide).**
  BT **Criminal law**
  NT **Courts martial and courts of**
        inquiry
        Trials (Homicide)
        War crime trials
        Witnesses
  RT **Crime**
Trials—Fiction
  USE **Legal stories**
Trials (Homicide) (May subdiv. geog.)
        345
  UF Homicide trials
        Murder trials
        Trials (Murder)
  BT **Homicide**
        Trials
Trials (Murder)
  USE **Trials (Homicide)**
Triangle   516.15
  BT **Plane geometry**
Tricks   793.5
  SA types of tricks [to be added as
        needed]
  BT **Amusements**
  NT **Card tricks**
        Juggling
        Magic tricks
Tricycles   629.227; 796.6
  UF Trikes
  BT **Vehicles**
  RT **Cycling**
Trigonometry   516.24
  UF Plane trigonometry
        Spherical trigonometry
  BT **Geometry**
        Mathematics
Trigonometry—Tables   516.24
  BT **Mathematics—Tables**
  NT **Logarithms**
Trikes
  USE **Tricycles**
Trinity   231
  BT **Christianity—Doctrines**
        God—Christianity
  NT **Holy Spirit**
  RT **Jesus Christ—Divinity**
Tripoline War, 1801-1805
  USE **United States—History—1801-**
        1805, Tripolitan War

Tripolitan War, 1801-1805
USE   United States—History—1801-
1805, Tripolitan War

Trivia
USE   Curiosities and wonders
Questions and answers

Trolley cars
USE   Street railroads

Tropes
USE   Figures of speech

Tropical conditions
USE   subjects with the subdivision
Tropical conditions, e.g.
**Building—Tropical condi-
tions** or the subdivision *Tropics,* e.g. **Agriculture—Tropics**
[to be added as needed]

Tropical diseases
USE   **Tropical medicine**

Tropical fish   597.17
BT   **Fishes**

Tropical hygiene
USE   **Tropical medicine**

Tropical jungles
USE   **Jungles**

Tropical medicine (May subdiv. geog.)
614
UF   Diseases, Tropical
Tropical diseases
Tropical hygiene
SA   types of tropical diseases, e.g.
Yellow fever [to be added as
needed]
BT   **Medicine**
NT   **Yellow fever**

Tropical rain forests
USE   **Rain forests**

Tropics   910.913
SA   subjects with the subdivision
Tropics, e.g. **Agriculture—
Tropics** or *Tropical condi-
tions,* e.g. **Building—Tropical
conditions** [to be added as
needed]
BT   **Earth**
NT   **Agriculture—Tropics**

Troubadours   849.1; 920
BT   **French poetry**
Minstrels
Poets

Trout fishing (May subdiv. geog.)   **799.1**
BT   **Fishing**

Truck crops
USE   **Truck farming**

Truck farming (May subdiv. geog.)   **635**
UF   Garden farming
Market gardening
Truck crops
Truck gardening
BT   **Agriculture**
Gardening
Horticulture
RT   **Vegetable gardening**

Truck freight
USE   **Trucking**

Truck gardening
USE   **Truck farming**

Trucking (May subdiv. geog.)   **388.3**
UF   Truck freight
BT   **Freight**
Transportation

Trucks (May subdiv. geog.)   **629.224**
UF   Motor trucks
SA   types of trucks and names of
specific makes and models [to
be added as needed]
BT   **Automobiles**
Highway transportation
RT   **Materials handling**

Trucks—Weight   629.224

Trust   158.2
BT   **Attitude (Psychology)**
Emotions

Trust companies (May subdiv. geog.)
332.2
BT   **Business**
Corporations
RT   **Banks and banking**
Trusts and trustees

Trust funds
USE   **Trusts and trustees**

Trustees
USE   **Trusts and trustees**

Trusts and trustees (May subdiv. geog.)
346.05
UF   Boards of trustees
Fiduciaries
Trust funds
Trustees

Trusts and trustees—*Continued*
- SA types of trustees, e.g. **Library trustees** [to be added as needed]
- BT **Contracts**
- NT **Library trustees**
  - **Living trusts**
- RT **Estate planning**
  - **Executors and administrators**
  - **Inheritance and succession**
  - **Trust companies**

Trusts, Industrial
- USE **Industrial trusts**

Truth 121
- BT **Belief and doubt**
  - **Philosophy**
- NT **Reality**
  - **Truthfulness and falsehood**
- RT **Certainty**
  - **Pragmatism**
  - **Skepticism**
  - **Theory of knowledge**

Truth in advertising
- USE **Deceptive advertising**

Truthfulness and falsehood 177
- UF Credibility
  - Falsehood
  - Lying
  - Untruth
- BT **Human behavior**
  - **Truth**
- NT **Deception**
  - **Lie detectors and detection**
- RT **Honesty**

Tsunamis (May subdiv. geog.) **551.46**
- UF Earthquake sea waves
  - Seismic sea waves
  - Tidal waves
- BT **Natural disasters**
  - **Ocean waves**

Tuberculosis (May subdiv. geog.) **616.9**
- BT **Lungs—Diseases**

Tuberculosis—Mortality (May subdiv. geog.) **616.9**

Tuberculosis—Vaccination (May subdiv. geog.) **614.4**
- BT **Vaccination**

Tugboats **623.82**
- BT **Boats and boating**

Tuition
- USE **College costs**
  - **Colleges and universities—Finance**
  - **Education—Finance**

Tumbling 796.47
- BT **Acrobats and acrobatics**

Tumors 616.99
- NT **Cancer**

Tuning 784.192
- SA types of instruments with the subdivision *Tuning* [to be added as needed]
- NT **Pianos—Tuning**
- RT **Musical instruments**

Tunnels (May subdiv. geog.) **388; 624.1**
- BT **Civil engineering**
- NT **Excavation**
- RT **Drilling and boring (Earth and rocks)**

Turbines 621.406
- BT **Engines**
  - **Hydraulic machinery**
- NT **Gas turbines**
  - **Steam turbines**

Turin Shroud
- USE **Holy Shroud**

Turkeys 598.6; 636.5
- BT **Birds**
  - **Poultry**

Turncoats
- USE **Defectors**

Turning 621.9
- UF Lathe work
  - Wood turning
- BT **Carpentry**
  - **Manufacturing processes**
- RT **Lathes**
  - **Woodwork**

Turnpikes (Modern)
- USE **Express highways**

Turtles (May subdiv. geog.) **597.92**
- UF Terrapins
  - Tortoises
- BT **Reptiles**

Tutoring
- USE **Tutors and tutoring**

Tutors
- USE **Tutors and tutoring**

Tutors and tutoring (May subdiv. geog.)
371.39

Use for general materials on one-on-one instruction. Materials on the adaptation of instruction to meet individual needs within a group are entered under **Individualized instruction.**

UF Tutoring

Tutors

BT **Teaching**

NT **Independent study**

Individualized instruction

TV

USE **Television**

TV personalities

USE **Television personalities**

Twelfth century

USE **World history—12th century**

Twelve-step programs   362.29

UF Programs, Twelve-step

Twelve steps (Self-help)

SA names of specific twelve-step programs [to be added as needed]

BT **Behavior modification**

RT **Alcoholism**

Compulsive behavior

Drug abuse

Twelve steps (Self-help)

USE **Twelve-step programs**

Twentieth century

USE **World history—20th century**

Twenty-first century

USE **World history—21st century**

Twins   155.44; 306.875

BT **Multiple birth**

Siblings

Twisters (Tornadoes)

USE **Tornadoes**

Two-career couples

USE **Dual-career families**

Two-career families

USE **Dual-career families**

Two-career family

USE **Dual-career families**

Two-income families

USE **Dual-career families**

Two-year colleges

USE **Junior colleges**

Type and type-founding (May subdiv. geog.)   **686.2**

UF Type and type founding

BT **Founding**

Printing

NT **Computer fonts**

Linotype

RT **Initials**

Printing—Specimens

Typesetting

Typography

Type and type founding

USE **Type and type-founding**

Type design

USE **Typography**

Type-setting

USE **Typesetting**

Type specimens

USE **Printing—Specimens**

Typefaces

USE **Typography**

Types, Psychological

USE **Typology (Psychology)**

Typesetting   686.2

UF Composition (Printing)

Type-setting

BT **Printing**

NT **Linotype**

RT **Type and type-founding**

Typewriters   652.3; 681

BT **Office equipment and supplies**

Typewriting   652.3

UF Typing

BT **Business education**

Office practice

Writing

RT **Keyboarding (Electronics)**

Typhoid fever   616.9

UF Enteric fever

BT **Diseases**

Fever

Typhoons (May subdiv. geog.)   **551.55**

Use for cyclonic storms originating in the region of the China Seas and the Philippines.

BT **Cyclones**

Storms

Winds

RT **Hurricanes**

Typing

USE **Typewriting**

Typography   686.2
    UF   Type design
          Typefaces
    BT   **Graphic arts**
          Printing
    NT   **Advertising layout and typog-
          raphy**
    RT   **Type and type-founding**
Typology (Psychology)   155.2
    UF   Mental types
          Psychological types
          Types, Psychological
    BT   **Personality**
          Psychology
          Temperament
    NT   **Enneagram**
UFO abduction
    USE **Alien abduction**
UFOs
    USE **Unidentified flying objects**
UHF radio
    USE **Shortwave radio**
Ultrahigh frequency radio
    USE **Shortwave radio**
Ultrasonic waves   534.5
    UF   Supersonic waves
          Waves, Ultrasonic
    BT   **Sound waves**
          Ultrasonics
**Ultrasonic waves—Industrial applications
    620.2**
Ultrasonics   534.5
    UF   Inaudible sound
          Supersonics
    BT   **Sound**
    NT   **Ultrasonic waves**
Ultraviolet rays   535.01; 621.36
    UF   Rays, Ultra-violet
    BT   **Electromagnetic waves**
          Radiation
    RT   **Phototherapy**
          Radiotherapy
Umbrellas and parasols   391.4; 685
    UF   Parasols
    BT   **Clothing and dress**
UN
    USE **United Nations**
Unbelief
    USE **Skepticism**
Unborn child
    USE **Fetus**

Unconventional warfare
    USE **Guerrilla warfare**
Undenominational churches
    USE **Community churches**
**Underachievers (May subdiv. geog.)
    371.28**
    BT   **Students**
Underdeveloped areas
    USE **Developing countries**
Undergraduates
    USE **College students**
**Underground architecture (May subdiv.
    geog.)   624.1; 690; 720**
    UF   Underground design
    BT   **Architecture**
    NT   **Basements**
          Earth sheltered houses
Underground design
    USE **Underground architecture**
**Underground economy (May subdiv.
    geog.)   381**
    Use for materials on goods and services
that are produced and sold legally but not re-
ported or taxed. Materials on illegal trade
aimed at avoiding government regulations,
such as fixed prices or rationing, are entered
under **Black market.**
    UF   Economy, Underground
          Hidden economy
          Informal sector (Economics)
          Parallel economy
          Second economy
          Shadow economy
          Untaxed income
    BT   **Economics**
          Small business
    NT   **Barter**
          Illegal aliens
    RT   **Black market**
Underground films
    USE **Experimental films**
Underground houses
    USE **Earth sheltered houses**
Underground literature
    USE **Alternative press**
Underground movements
    USE names of wars with the subdivi-
          sion *Underground movements,*
          e.g. **World War, 1939-
          1945—Underground move-
          ments** [to be added as need-
          ed]

Underground press
    USE **Alternative press**
Underground railroad (May subdiv.
        geog.) **326**
    RT **Slavery—United States**
Underground railroads
    USE **Subways**
Underground water
    USE **Groundwater**
Underprivileged
    USE **Socially handicapped**
Underprivileged children
    USE **Socially handicapped children**
Underprivileged students
    USE **At risk students**
Undersea engineering
    USE **Ocean engineering**
Undersea exploration
    USE **Underwater exploration**
Undersea research stations   551.46
    UF Manned undersea research sta-
            tions
        Sea laboratories
        Submarine research stations
        Underwater research stations
    SA names of special research
            projects and stations, e.g.
            Sealab project [to be added
            as needed]
    BT **Oceanography—Research**
        Underwater exploration
    NT **Sealab project**
Undersea vehicles
    USE **Submersibles**
Understanding
    USE **Intellect**
        Theory of knowledge
Undertakers and undertaking (May
        subdiv. geog.) **363.7; 393**
    UF Funeral directors
        Morticians
    BT **Service industries**
Underwater diving
    USE **Deep diving**
Underwater drilling (Petroleum)
    USE **Offshore oil well drilling**
Underwater exploration (May subdiv.
        geog.) **551.46; 627**
    UF Submarine exploration
        Undersea exploration

    BT **Exploration**
        Oceanography
    NT **Buried treasure**
        Deep diving
        Undersea research stations
Underwater geology
    USE **Submarine geology**
Underwater medicine
    USE **Submarine medicine**
Underwater photography   778.7
    UF Deep-sea photography
        Submarine photography
    BT **Photography**
Underwater physiology
    USE **Submarine medicine**
Underwater research stations
    USE **Undersea research stations**
Underwater swimming
    USE **Skin diving**
Undocumented aliens
    USE **Illegal aliens**
Unemployed (May subdiv. geog.)   **331.13**
    UF Jobless people
        Out-of-work people
    BT **Labor supply**
        Poor
        Unemployment
    NT **Food relief**
        Occupational retraining
    RT **Domestic economic assistance**
        Tramps
Unemployment (May subdiv. geog.)
        331.13
    UF Joblessness
    BT **Employment**
        Labor supply
        Social problems
    NT **Employment agencies**
        Plant shutdowns
        Unemployed
Unemployment insurance (May subdiv.
        geog.) **368.4**
    UF Insurance, Unemployment
        Labor—Insurance
        Payroll taxes
    BT **Insurance**
Unfair competition   338.6
    UF Competition, Unfair
        Fair trade
        Unfair trade practices

Unfair competition—_Continued_
- BT   **Commercial law**
- NT   **Trade secrets**
- RT   **Restraint of trade**

Unfair trade practices
- USE   **Unfair competition**

Ungraded schools
- USE   **Nongraded schools**

Unidentified flying objects   **001.9**
- UF   Flying saucers
  - Saucers, Flying
  - UFOs
- BT   **Aeronautics**
  - **Astronautics**
- RT   **Human-alien encounters**

Uniforms (May subdiv. geog.)   **391**
- SA   classes of persons and names of individual corporate bodies and military services with the subdivision _Uniforms,_ e.g. **United States. Army—Uniforms** [to be added as needed]
- BT   **Clothing and dress**
  - **Costume**
- NT   **Military uniforms**

Uniforms, Military
- USE   **Military uniforms**

Uniforms, Naval
- USE   **Military uniforms**

Union churches
- USE   **Community churches**

Union of South Africa
- USE   **South Africa**

Union of Soviet Socialist Republics
- USE   **Soviet Union**

Union shop
- USE   **Open and closed shop**

Unions, Labor
- USE   **Labor unions**

Unison speaking
- USE   **Choral speaking**

Unitarianism   **289.1**
- BT   **Christian sects**
  - **Congregationalism**

United Brethren
- USE   **Moravians**

United Nations   **341.23**
- UF   UN
- BT   **International arbitration**
  - **International cooperation**
  - **International organization**

United Nations—Armed forces   **341.23; 355.3**
- UF   Peace keeping forces
- BT   **Armed forces**

United Nations—Employees
- USE   **United Nations—Officials and employees**

United Nations—Finance   **336.09; 341.23**
- BT   **Finance**

United Nations—Information services   **341.23**
- BT   **Information services**

United Nations—Officials and employees   **341.23**
- UF   United Nations—Employees

United States   **973**

The subdivisions under **United States**, with the exception of the period divisions of history, may be used under the name of any country or region. The subdivisions under **Ohio** may be used under names of states, and those under **Chicago (Ill.)** under cities. Corporate name headings for corporate entities within the United States government, such as government agencies and departments, which are used either as authors or as subjects, have a period rather than a dash between the parts, e.g. **United States. Army;** and may be added as needed.

- UF   US
  - USA
- SA   regions of the United States and groups of states, e.g. **New England; Southern States;** etc. [to be added as needed]
- NT   **Atlantic States**
  - **Gulf States (U.S.)**
  - **Middle West**
  - **Mississippi River Valley**
  - **New England**
  - **Old Northwest**
  - **Old Southwest**
  - **Oregon Trail**
  - **Pacific Northwest**
  - **Southern States**
  - **Southwestern States**
  - **West (U.S.)**
- RT   **Americans**

United States—Annexations
- USE   **United States—Territorial expansion**

United States—Antiquities   **973**
- BT   **Antiquities**

United States—Appropriations and expenditures   352.4
  UF Federal spending policy
       Government spending policy
  BT **Budget—United States**
United States—Archives
  USE **Archives—United States**
United States—Armed forces   355.00973
  SA official names and branches of the armed forces, e.g. **United States. Army; United States. Navy;** etc. [to be added as needed]
  BT **Armed forces**
  NT **United States. Army**
       United States. Navy
United States—Armed forces—Gays
  USE **Gays and lesbians in the military**
United States—Armed forces—Military life   355.10973
  BT **Military personnel**
United States—Armed Forces—Recruiting, enlistment, etc.   355.2
  BT **Recruiting and enlistment**
United States. Army   355
Subdivisions used under this heading may be used under armies of other countries as appropriate.
  BT **Armies**
       Military history
       United States—Armed forces
  NT **United States Military Academy**
United States. Army—Appointments and retirements   355.1
  UF United States. Army—Retirements
United States. Army—Biography   920
  BT **Biography**
United States. Army—Chaplains   355.3; 920
  BT **Chaplains**
United States. Army—Crimes and misdemeanors
  USE **Military offenses—United States**
United States. Army—Demobilization   355.2
United States. Army—Desertions
  USE **Military desertion—United States**

United States. Army—Enlistment
  USE **United States. Army—Recruiting, enlistment, etc.**
United States. Army—Examinations   355.1
  UF Army tests
  BT **Examinations**
United States. Army—Handbooks, manuals, etc.   355
  UF Soldiers' handbooks
       United States. Army—Officers' handbooks
       United States. Army—Soldiers' handbooks
United States. Army—Insignia   355.1
  BT **Insignia**
United States. Army—Medals, badges, decorations, etc.   355.1
  BT **Insignia**
       Medals
United States. Army—Military life   355.1
  BT **Military personnel**
       Soldiers
United States. Army—Music
  USE **United States. Army—Songs**
United States. Army—Officers   355.3
  BT **Military personnel**
       Soldiers
United States. Army—Officers' handbooks
  USE **United States. Army—Handbooks, manuals, etc.**
United States. Army—Ordnance   355.8
  UF United States. Army—Ordnance and ordnance stores
  BT **Ordnance**
United States. Army—Ordnance and ordnance stores
  USE **United States. Army—Ordnance**
United States. Army—Parachute troops   356
  UF United States—Parachute troops
  BT **Parachute troops**
United States. Army—Recruiting, enlistment, etc.   355.2
  UF United States. Army—Enlistment
  BT **Recruiting and enlistment**
United States. Army—Retirements
  USE **United States. Army—Appointments and retirements**

United States. Army—Soldiers' handbooks
    USE   **United States. Army—Handbooks, manuals, etc.**
United States. Army—Songs   782.42
    UF   United States. Army—Music
          United States. Army—Songs and music
    BT   **Songs**
United States. Army—Songs and music
    USE   **United States. Army—Songs**
United States. Army—Uniforms   355.1
United States—Atlases
    USE   **United States—Maps**
United States—Bibliography   015.73; 016.973
United States—Bicentennial celebrations
    USE   **American Revolution Bicentennial, 1776-1976**
United States—Bill of rights
    USE   **United States. Constitution. 1st-10th amendments**
United States—Bio-bibliography   012
United States—Biography   920.073
    BT   **Biography**
United States—Biography—Dictionaries 920.073
United States—Biography—Portraits 920.073
    UF   United States—History—Portraits
United States—Boundaries   973
    BT   **Boundaries**
United States—Budget
    USE   **Budget—United States**
United States—Campaign funds
    USE   **Campaign funds—United States**
United States—Census   317.3; 352.7
    BT   **Census**
United States—Centennial celebrations, etc.   973
    NT   **American Revolution Bicentennial, 1776-1976**
United States—Church and state
    USE   **Church and state—United States**
United States—Church history   277.3
    UF   Church history—United States
          United States—Religious history
    BT   **Church history**
    RT   **United States—Religion**

United States—Cities and towns
    USE   **Cities and towns—United States**
United States—Civil defense
    USE   **Civil defense—United States**
United States—Civil service
    USE   **Civil service—United States**
United States—Civilization   973
    BT   **Civilization**
    NT   **Americana**
United States—Civilization—1960-1970 973.92
United States—Civilization—1970- 973.92
United States—Civilization—Foreign influences   973
United States—Climate   551.6973
    BT   **Climate**
United States—Commerce   381; 382.0973
    BT   **Commerce**
United States—Commerce—Japan   382
United States—Commercial policy
    USE   **Commercial policy—United States**
United States. Congress   328.73
    UF   Congress (U.S.)
    BT   **Legislative bodies**
    NT   **United States. Congress. House**
          United States. Congress. Senate
United States. Congress. House   328.73
    UF   House of Representatives (U.S.)
          Representatives, House of (U.S.)
    BT   **United States. Congress**
United States. Congress. Senate   328.73
    UF   Senate (U.S.)
    BT   **United States. Congress**
United States. Constitution   342.73
    Use for the text of the United States Constitution and for materials about that document.
    UF   American constitution
          Constitution (U.S.)
United States. Constitution. 1st-10th amendments   342.73
    Use for the text of the United States Bill of rights and for materials about that document.
    UF   American Bill of rights
          Bill of rights (U.S.)
          United States—Bill of rights
United States—Constitutional history
    USE   **Constitutional history—United States**

United States—Constitutional law
    USE **Constitutional law—United States**
United States—Constitutions
    USE **Constitutions—United States**
United States—Courts
    USE **Courts—United States**
United States—Cultural policy
    USE **Cultural policy—United States**
United States—Declaration of independence 973.3
    UF Declaration of independence (U.S.)
United States—Defenses 355.4
    BT **Military readiness**
    NT **Strategic Defense Initiative**
United States—Description
    USE **United States—Description and travel**
United States—Description and travel 917.3
    UF United States—Description *[Former heading]*
          United States—Travel
    BT **Geography**
United States—Description and travel—Guidebooks
    USE **United States—Guidebooks**
United States—Description and travel—Views
    USE **United States—Pictorial works**
United States—Diplomatic and consular service
    USE **American diplomatic and consular service**
United States—Directories 917.30025
    Use for lists of names and addresses. Lists of names without addresses are entered under **United States—Registers.**
    BT **Directories**
    RT **United States—Registers**
United States—Economic conditions 330.973
    May be subdivided by period using the subdivisions under **United States—History,** e.g. **United States—Economic conditions—1600-1775, Colonial period.**
    UF National resources
    BT **Economic conditions**
United States—Economic policy
    USE **Economic policy—United States**
United States—Elections
    USE **Elections—United States**

United States—Emigration and immigration
    USE **United States—Immigration and emigration**
United States—Employees
    USE **United States—Officials and employees**
United States—Environmental policy
    USE **Environmental policy—United States**
United States—Ethnic relations 305.8
United States—Ethnology
    USE **Ethnology—United States**
United States—Executive departments
    USE **Executive departments—United States**
United States—Executive departments—Reorganization
    USE **Administrative agencies—Reorganization—United States**
United States—Executive power
    USE **Executive power—United States**
United States—Exploration 973
    UF Exploration—United States
    BT **America—Exploration**
          Exploration
    NT **West (U.S.)—Exploration**
United States—Exploring expeditions 910.973; 973
    Use for materials on exploring expeditions sponsored by the United States. Materials on early exploration of a particular place are entered under the name of the place with the subdivision *Exploration.*
    UF American exploring expeditions
    SA names of expeditions, e.g. **Lewis and Clark Expedition (1804-1806)** [to be added as needed]
    BT **Explorers**
    NT **Lewis and Clark Expedition (1804-1806)**
United States—Fiscal policy
    USE **Fiscal policy—United States**
United States—Flags
    USE **Flags—United States**
United States—Foreign economic relations 337.73
    UF Foreign economic relations—United States
    BT **International economic relations**

United States—Foreign opinion (May
   subdiv. geog.)   303.3; 973
   Use for materials on foreign public opinion
   about the United States. May be further subdi-
   vided by the country holding the opinion, e.g.
   United States—Foreign opinion—France.
   UF   Anti-Americanism
        Antiamericanism
        United States—Foreign public
        opinion
   BT   **Public opinion**
United States—Foreign opinion—France
   303.3; 973
   Use for materials on French public opinion
   about the United States.
United States—Foreign policy
   USE   **United States—Foreign rela-
         tions**
United States—Foreign population
   USE   **Aliens—United States
         Immigrants—United States**
United States—Foreign public opinion
   USE   **United States—Foreign opinion**
United States—Foreign relations (May
   subdiv. geog.)   327.73
   When further subdividing geographically,
   provide an additional subject entry with the
   two places in reversed positions, i.e. **United
   States—Foreign relations—Iran** and also
   Iran—Foreign relations—United States.
   UF   United States—Foreign policy
   BT   **Diplomacy
        International relations
        World politics**
   NT   **Monroe Doctrine**
   RT   **Neutrality—United States**
United States—Foreign relations—Iran
   327.73055
   NT   **Iran hostage crisis, 1979-1981**
United States—Foreign relations—Trea-
   ties   327.73; 341.3
   UF   United States—Treaties
   BT   **Treaties**
United States—Gazetteers   917.3003
   BT   **Gazetteers**
United States—Geographic names
   USE   **Geographic names—United
         States**
United States—Geography   917.3
   BT   **Geography**
United States—Government
   USE   **United States—Politics and
         government**

United States—Government buildings
   USE   **Public buildings—United States**
United States—Government employees
   USE   **United States—Officials and
         employees**
United States—Government publications
   USE   **Government publications—
         United States**
United States—Governmental investigations
   USE   **Governmental investigations—
         United States**
United States—Guidebooks   917.304
   UF   United States—Description and
        travel—Guidebooks
United States—Historic buildings
   USE   **Historic buildings—United
         States**
United States—Historical geography
   911
   BT   **Historical geography**
United States—Historical geography—
   Maps   911
   BT   **United States—Maps**
United States—Historiography   973.07
   UF   United States—History—Histori-
        ography
   BT   **Historiography**
United States—History   973
   UF   American history
   NT   **Americana
        Constitutional history—United
        States
        Southern States—History
        West (U.S.)—History**
United States—History—1600-1775, Colo-
   nial period   973.2
   Use for materials on American history from
   the earliest permanent English settlements on
   the Atlantic coast up to the American Revolu-
   tion. Materials on the period of discovery are
   entered under **United States—Exploration.**
   UF   American colonies
        Colonial history (U.S.)
   NT   **Bacon's Rebellion, 1676
        King Philip's War, 1675-1676
        Pilgrims (New England colo-
        nists)
        Pontiac's Conspiracy, 1763-
        1765
        United States—History—1689-
        1697, King William's War**

United States—History—1600-1775, Colonial period—*Continued*

    United States—History—1755-1763, French and Indian War

United States—History—1675-1676, King Philip's War

  USE **King Philip's War, 1675-1676**

United States—History—1689-1697, King William's War 973.2

  UF King William's War, 1689-1697

  BT **Native Americans—Wars**

      United States—History—1600-1775, Colonial period

United States—History—1755-1763, French and Indian War 973.2

  UF French and Indian War

  BT **Native Americans—Wars**

      Seven Years' War, 1756-1763

      United States—History—1600-1775, Colonial period

United States—History—1775-1783, Revolution 973.3

May be subdivided like **United States—History—1861-1865, Civil War.**

  UF American Revolution

      Revolution, American

      War of the American Revolution

  BT **Revolutions**

  NT **American Loyalists**

      Canadian Invasion, 1775-1776

      Fourth of July

United States—History—1775-1783, Revolution—Centennial celebrations, etc.

  USE **American Revolution Bicentennial, 1776-1976**

United States—History—1783-1809 973.3; 973.4

  UF Confederation of American colonies

  NT **Lewis and Clark Expedition (1804-1806)**

      Louisiana Purchase

United States—History—1783-1865 973

  NT **War of 1812**

United States—History—19th century 973.5

United States—History—1801-1805, Tripolitan War 973.4

  UF Tripoline War, 1801-1805

      Tripolitan War, 1801-1805

United States—History—1812-1815, War of 1812

  USE **War of 1812**

United States—History—1815-1861 973.5; 973.6

  NT **Black Hawk War, 1832**

      Mexican War, 1846-1848

United States—History—1845-1848, War with Mexico

  USE **Mexican War, 1846-1848**

United States—History—1861-1865, Civil War 973.7

  UF American Civil War

      Civil War—United States

  NT **Confederate States of America**

      Trent Affair, 1861

United States—History—1861-1865, Civil War—Biography 920; 973.7092

  BT **Biography**

United States—History—1861-1865, Civil War—Campaigns 973.7

  SA names of battles, e.g. **Gettysburg (Pa.), Battle of, 1863** [to be added as needed]

  NT **Gettysburg (Pa.), Battle of, 1863**

United States—History—1861-1865, Civil War—Causes 973.7

  UF Secession

United States—History—1861-1865, Civil War—Centennial celebrations, etc. 973.7

United States—History—1861-1865, Civil War—Drama 808.82; 812

Use for collections of plays dealing with the Civil War.

  BT **Historical drama**

United States—History—1861-1865, Civil War—Fiction 808.83; 813

Use for collections of stories dealing with the Civil War.

United States—History—1861-1865, Civil War—Health aspects 973.7

United States—History—1861-1865, Civil War—Historiography 973.7

  BT **Historiography**

United States—History—1861-1865, Civil War—Medical care 973.7

  BT **Medical care**

United States—History—1861-1865, Civil War—Naval operations 973.7

United States—History—1861-1865, Civil
War—Personal narratives   973.7

Use for collective or individual eyewitness
reports or autobiographical accounts of the
war in general. Accounts limited to a specific
topic are entered under that topic.

BT   Autobiographies
     Biography

United States—History—1861-1865, Civil
War—Pictorial works   973.7022

United States—History—1861-1865, Civil
War—Prisoners and prisons
973.7

BT   Prisoners of war
     Prisons

United States—History—1861-1865, Civil
War—Reconstruction

USE   Reconstruction (1865-1876)

United States—History—1861-1865, Civil
War—Sources   973.7

United States—History—1865-1898
973.8

NT   Reconstruction (1865-1876)
     Spanish-American War, 1898

United States—History—1898-1919
973.9; 973.91

NT   Spanish-American War, 1898

United States—History—1898, War of
1898

USE   Spanish-American War, 1898

United States—History—20th century
973.9

United States—History—1914-1918, World
War

USE   World War, 1914-1918—United
States

United States—History—1919-1933
973.91

United States—History—1933-1945
973.917

NT   New Deal, 1933-1939

United States—History—1939-1945, World
War

USE   World War, 1939-1945—United
States

United States—History—1945-   973.92

United States—History—1945-1953
973.918

United States—History—1953-1961
973.921

United States—History—1961-1974
973.92

NT   Vietnam War, 1961-1975
     Watergate Affair, 1972-1974

United States—History—1974-1989
973.92

United States—History—1989-   973.928

NT   Persian Gulf War, 1991

United States—History—21st century
973.9

United States—History—Bibliography
016.973

United States—History—Chronology
973

United States—History—Dictionaries
973.03

BT   History—Dictionaries

United States—History—Drama
808.82; 812

Use for collections of plays dealing with
American history.

BT   Historical drama

United States—History—Examinations
973.076

UF   United States—History—Exami-
     nations, questions, etc.

BT   United States—History—Study
     and teaching

United States—History—Examinations,
questions, etc.

USE   United States—History—Exam-
      inations

United States—History—Fiction
808.83; 813

Use for collections of stories dealing with
American history.

United States—History—Historiography

USE   United States—Historiography

United States—History—Library resources   973.07

United States—History—Outlines, syllabi,
etc.   973.02

BT   United States—History—Study
     and teaching

United States—History—Periodicals
973.05

United States—History—Poetry   808.81;
811

Use for collections of poetry dealing with
American history.

BT   Historical poetry

United States—History—Portraits
USE United States—Biography—
Portraits
United States—History—Societies
973.06
BT History—Societies
United States—History—Sources 973
United States—History—Study and
teaching 973.07
NT United States—History—Exam-
inations
United States—History—Out-
lines, syllabi, etc.
United States—Immigration and emigra-
tion 325; 325.73
UF United States—Emigration and
immigration
SA names of immigrant groups, e.g.
Mexican Americans; Mexi-
cans—United States [to be
added as needed]
BT Americanization
Immigration and emigration
RT Aliens—United States
Immigrants—United States
United States—Industrial policy
USE Industrial policy—United
States
United States—Industries
USE Industries—United States
United States—Insular possessions
USE United States—Territories and
possessions
United States—Intellectual life 973
BT Intellectual life
United States—Intelligence service
USE Intelligence service—United
States
United States—Internal security
USE Internal security—United
States
United States—Land settlement
USE Land settlement—United States
United States—Land surveys
USE United States—Surveys
United States—Languages 306.44
Use for materials on the several languages
spoken in the United States.
United States—Law
USE Law—United States
United States. Library of Congress
USE Library of Congress

United States—Local history 973
BT Local history
United States—Mail
USE Postal service—United States
United States—Manufactures
USE Manufactures—United States
United States—Maps 912.73
UF United States—Atlases
BT Atlases
Maps
NT United States—Historical geog-
raphy—Maps
United States Military Academy
355.0071
UF USMA
West Point (Military academy)
BT Colleges and universities
United States. Army
United States Military Academy—Regis-
ters 355.0071
United States Military Academy—Songs
782.42
UF United States Military Acade-
my—Songs and music
BT Students' songs
United States Military Academy—Songs
and music
USE United States Military Acade-
my—Songs
United States—Military history
355.00973; 973
BT Military history
United States—Military offenses
USE Military offenses—United
States
United States—Military personnel
USE Military personnel—United
States
United States—Military policy
USE Military policy—United States
United States—Militia 355.3
BT Armed forces
NT United States. National Guard
United States—Monetary policy
USE Monetary policy—United States
United States—Moral conditions 973
BT Moral conditions
United States—Municipal government
USE Municipal government—United
States

United States—National characteristics
USE **American national characteristics**

United States. National Guard 355.3
UF National Guard (U.S.)
BT **United States—Militia**

United States—National parks and reserves
USE **National parks and reserves—United States**

United States—National security
USE **National security—United States**

United States—National songs
USE **National songs—United States**

United States—Naval history 359.00973
BT **Naval history**

United States. Navy 359
Subdivisions used under **United States. Army** may be used under this heading and under navies of other countries as appropriate.
BT **Navies**
United States—Armed forces

United States. Navy—Biography 920
BT **Biography**

United States. Navy—Enlistment
USE **United States. Navy—Recruiting, enlistment, etc.**

United States. Navy—Handbooks, manuals, etc. 359
UF Sailors' handbooks
United States. Navy—Officers' handbooks
United States. Navy—Sailors' handbooks

United States. Navy—Insignia 359.1
BT **Insignia**

United States. Navy—Medals, badges, decorations, etc. 359.1
BT **Insignia**
Medals

United States. Navy—Officers 359.3
BT **Military personnel**

United States. Navy—Officers' handbooks
USE **United States. Navy—Handbooks, manuals, etc.**

United States. Navy—Recruiting, enlistment, etc. 359.2
UF United States. Navy—Enlistment
BT **Recruiting and enlistment**

United States. Navy—Sailors' handbooks
USE **United States. Navy—Handbooks, manuals, etc.**

United States. Navy—Sealab project
USE **Sealab project**

United States—Neutrality
USE **Neutrality—United States**

United States—Occupations
USE **Occupations—United States**

United States—Officials and employees 351.73
UF United States—Employees
United States—Government employees
RT **Civil service—United States**

United States—Parachute troops
USE **United States. Army—Parachute troops**

United States—Peoples
USE **Ethnology—United States**

United States—Pictorial works 917.30022
UF United States—Description and travel—Views

United States—Police
USE **Police—United States**

United States—Politicians
USE **Politicians—United States**

United States—Politics
USE **United States—Politics and government**

United States—Politics and government 973
May be subdivided by period using the subdivisions under **United States—History**, e.g. **United States—Politics and government—1600-1775, Colonial period.**
UF American government
American politics
United States—Government
United States—Politics
BT **Political science**
Politics
Public administration
NT **Third parties (United States politics)**

United States—Popular culture
USE **Popular culture—United States**

United States—Population 304.60973
BT **Population**

United States—Postal service
USE **Postal service—United States**

United States—Presidents
USE **Presidents—United States**

United States—Prisons
    USE   **Prisons—United States**
United States—Public buildings
    USE   **Public buildings—United States**
United States—Public debts
    USE   **Public debts—United States**
United States—Public health
    USE   **Public health—United States**
United States—Public lands
    USE   **Public lands—United States**
United States—Public schools
    USE   **Public schools—United States**
United States—Public works
    USE   **Public works—United States**
United States—Race relations
    305.800973
    BT   **Race relations**
United States—Registers   917.30025
    Use for lists of names without addresses. Lists of names that include addresses are entered under **United States—Directories.**
    RT   **United States—Directories**
United States—Religion   200.973; 277.3
    BT   **Religion**
    RT   **United States—Church history**
United States—Religious history
    USE   **United States—Church history**
United States—Rural conditions
    307.720973
    BT   **Rural sociology**
United States—Secret service
    USE   **Secret service—United States**
United States—Separation of powers
    USE   **Separation of powers—United States**
United States—Social conditions   973
    BT   **Social conditions**
United States—Social life and customs
    973
    BT   **Manners and customs**
United States—Social policy
    USE   **Social policy—United States**
United States—Soldiers
    USE   **Soldiers—United States**
United States—State governments
    USE   **State governments**
United States—Statistics   317.3
    BT   **Statistics**
United States. Supreme Court   347.73
    UF   Supreme Court—United States
    BT   **Courts**

United States. Supreme Court—Biography   920
    BT   **Biography**
United States—Surveys   972
    Use for materials containing the results of land surveys of the United States.
    UF   United States—Land surveys
United States—Tariff
    USE   **Tariff—United States**
United States—Taxation
    USE   **Taxation—United States**
United States—Term limits (Public office)
    USE   **Term limits (Public office)—United States**
United States—Territorial expansion
    973
    UF   Expansion (United States politics)
           Manifest destiny (United States)
           United States—Annexations
           Westward movement
United States—Territorial waters
    USE   **Territorial waters—United States**
United States—Territories and possessions   325; 973
    UF   United States—Insular possessions
United States—Travel
    USE   **United States—Description and travel**
United States—Treaties
    USE   **United States—Foreign relations—Treaties**
United States—Vice-presidents
    USE   **Vice-presidents—United States**
United States—World War, 1914-1918
    USE   **World War, 1914-1918—United States**
United States—World War, 1939-1945
    USE   **World War, 1939-1945—United States**
United States—World War, 1939-1945—Casualties
    USE   **World War, 1939-1945—Casualties—United States**
United States—World War, 1939-1945—Casualties—Statistics
    USE   **World War, 1939-1945—Casualties—United States—Statistics**

United Steelworkers of America   331.88
    BT   **Labor unions**
Universal bibliographic control
    USE **Bibliographic control**
Universal history
    USE **World history**
Universal language   401
    UF   International language
          Language, International
          Language, Universal
          World language
    BT   **Language and languages**
          Linguistics
    NT   **Esperanto**
Universal military training
    USE **Draft**
Universe   113; 523.1
    Use for materials limited to the physical description of the universe. General and theoretical materials on the science or philosophy of the universe are entered under **Cosmology.**
    UF   Cosmogony
          Cosmography
    NT   **Astronomy**
          Cosmology
          Life on other planets
    RT   **Creation**
Universities
    USE **Colleges and universities**
Universities and colleges
    USE **Colleges and universities**
University degrees
    USE **Academic degrees**
University extension (May subdiv. geog.)
    378.1
    BT   **Colleges and universities**
          Distance education
          Higher education
    NT   **Adult education**
          Correspondence schools and courses
University graduates
    USE **College graduates**
University libraries
    USE **Academic libraries**
University students
    USE **College students**
Unmarried couples (May subdiv. geog.)
    306.84
    UF   Cohabitation
          Common law marriage
          Living together

          Trial marriage
          Unmarried people
    BT   **Lifestyles**
          Shared housing
    NT   **Single parents**
Unmarried fathers (May subdiv. geog.)
    306.874; 362.82
    Use for materials on fathers who at the time of childbirth were not married to the child's mother. Materials on fathers rearing children without a partner in the household are entered under **Single-parent families.** Materials on fathers who are teenagers are entered under **Teenage fathers.**
    UF   Parents, Unmarried
          Unmarried parents
          Unwed fathers
    BT   **Fathers**
          Single parents
    RT   **Illegitimacy**
Unmarried men
    USE **Single men**
Unmarried mothers (May subdiv. geog.)
    306.874; 362.83
    Use for materials on mothers who at the time of giving birth were not married to the child's father. Materials on mothers rearing children without a partner in the household are entered under **Single-parent families.** Materials on mothers who are teenagers are entered under **Teenage mothers.**
    UF   Parents, Unmarried
          Unmarried parents
          Unwed mothers
    BT   **Mothers**
          Single parents
    RT   **Illegitimacy**
Unmarried parents
    USE **Unmarried fathers**
          Unmarried mothers
Unmarried people
    USE **Single people**
          Unmarried couples
Unmarried women
    USE **Single women**
Unsafe products
    USE **Product safety**
Unselfishness
    USE **Altruism**
Unskilled labor (May subdiv. geog.)
    331.7
    UF   Unskilled workers
    BT   **Labor**

Unskilled labor—Supply and demand
    331.12
    BT **Supply and demand**
Unskilled workers
    USE **Unskilled labor**
Untaxed income
    USE **Underground economy**
Untruth
    USE **Truthfulness and falsehood**
Unwed fathers
    USE **Unmarried fathers**
Unwed mothers
    USE **Unmarried mothers**
Upholstery   684.1; 747
    BT **Interior design**
    NT **Draperies**
    RT **Furniture**
Upper atmosphere   551.5
    UF Atmosphere, Upper
    BT **Atmosphere**
    NT **Stratosphere**
Upper class (May subdiv. geog.)   **305.5**
    UF Fashionable society
         High society
         Upper classes
    BT **Social classes**
    NT **Aristocracy**
         Nobility
Upper classes
    USE **Upper class**
Uranium   669
    BT **Chemical elements**
    RT **Radioactivity**
Urban areas
    USE **Cities and towns**
         Metropolitan areas
Urban development
    USE **Cities and towns—Growth**
         City planning
         Urbanization
Urban education
    USE **Urban schools**
Urban-federal relations
    USE **Federal-city relations**
Urban folklore (May subdiv. geog.)
    398.2
    UF Urban legends
    BT **Folklore**

Urban homesteading (May subdiv. geog.)
    363.5
    BT **Houses—Buying and selling**
         Housing
         Urban renewal
Urban housing
    USE **Housing**
Urban legends
    USE **Urban folklore**
Urban life
    USE **City and town life**
Urban planning
    USE **City planning**
Urban policy (May subdiv. geog.)
    307.76; 320.8
    UF Urban problems
    BT **City and town life**
         Economic policy
         Social policy
         Urban sociology
    RT **City planning**
         Urban renewal
Urban problems
    USE **Urban policy**
Urban renewal (May subdiv. geog.)
    307.3
    Use for materials on the economic, socio-
logical, and political aspects of urban redevel-
opment. Materials on the architectural and en-
gineering aspects are entered under **City plan-
ning.**
    UF Slum clearance
    BT **Metropolitan areas**
         Urban sociology
    NT **Community development**
         Urban homesteading
    RT **City planning**
         Community organization
         Urban policy
Urban renewal—Chicago (Ill.)   307.3
    UF Chicago (Ill.)—Urban renewal
Urban renewal—United States   307.3
Urban-rural migration
    USE **Internal migration**
Urban schools (May subdiv. geog.)   **371**
    UF City schools
         Inner city schools
         Urban education
    BT **Schools**

Urban sociology (May subdiv. geog.)
    307.76
    UF Sociology, Urban
    BT **Sociology**
    NT **City and town life**
          Urban policy
          Urban renewal
          Urbanization
    RT **Cities and towns**
Urban street life
    USE **Street life**
Urban traffic
    USE **City traffic**
Urban transportation
    USE **Local transit**
Urbanization (May subdiv. geog.)
    307.76
    Use for materials on the process by which town and communities acquire urban characteristics.
    UF Cities and towns, Movement to
          Urban development
    BT **Cities and towns**
          Rural sociology
          Social change
          Social conditions
          Urban sociology
    RT **Cities and towns—Growth**
US
    USE **United States**
USA
    USE **United States**
Usage
    USE names of languages and groups of languages with the subdivision *Usage*, e.g. **English language—Usage** [to be added as needed]
Used merchandise
    USE **Secondhand trade**
Useful insects
    USE **Beneficial insects**
Usenet newsgroups
    USE **Electronic discussion groups**
USMA
    USE **United States Military Academy**
USSR
    USE **Soviet Union**
Utensils
    USE **Implements, utensils, etc.**

Utensils, Kitchen
    USE **Kitchen utensils**
Utilitarianism   **144**
    BT **Ethics**
    NT **Secularism**
    RT **Pragmatism**
Utilities (Computer programs)
    USE **Utilities (Computer software)**
Utilities (Computer software)   **005.4**
    Use for materials on software used to perform standard computer system operations such as sorting data, searching for viruses, copying data from one file to another, etc.
    UF Computer utility programs
          Computers—Utility programs
          Utilities (Computer programs) *[Former heading]*
          Utility programs (Computer software)
    BT **Computer software**
Utilities, Public
    USE **Public utilities**
Utility programs (Computer software)
    USE **Utilities (Computer software)**
Utilization of waste
    USE **Salvage**
Utopian fiction   **808.3; 808.83**
    May be used for individual works, collections, or materials about imaginative accounts of ideal societies. Theoretical materials about ideal societies and accounts of practical attempts to create such societies are entered under **Utopias.**
    UF Ideal states
          Utopian literature
    BT **Fantasy fiction**
          Science fiction
    RT **Dystopias**
          Utopias
Utopian literature
    USE **Utopian fiction**
          Utopias
Utopias   **321; 335**
    Use for theoretical materials on ideal societies and for accounts of practical attempts to create such societies. Imaginative accounts of ideal societies are entered under **Utopian fiction.**
    UF Ideal states
          Utopian literature
    BT **Political science**
          Socialism
    RT **Collective settlements**
          Paradise
          Utopian fiction

V-chips 363.3
> UF Violence chips
> BT **Television—Censorship**
>   **Television—Receivers and re-**
>   **ception**

Vacation church schools
> USE **Religious summer schools**

Vacation home timesharing
> USE **Timesharing (Real estate)**

Vacation schools
> USE **Summer schools**

Vacation schools, Religious
> USE **Religious summer schools**

Vacations (May subdiv. geog.) **331.25;**
>   **658.3**
> BT **Recreation**
> RT **Holidays**

Vaccination (May subdiv. geog.) **614.4**
> Use for materials on active immunization
> with a vaccine. Materials on any process, ac-
> tive or passive, that leads to increased immu-
> nity are entered under **Immunization.**
> UF Inoculation
> SA types of animals and types of
>   diseases with the subdivision
>   *Vaccination,* e.g. **Cattle—**
>   **Vaccination; Tuberculosis—**
>   **Vaccination** [to be added as
>   needed]
> BT **Immunization**
>   **Preventive medicine**
>   **Public health**
> NT **Cattle—Vaccination**
>   **Poliomyelitis vaccine**
>   **Tuberculosis—Vaccination**

Vacuum tubes 537.5; 621.3815
> UF Electron tubes
> BT **Electronic apparatus and ap-**
>   **pliances**
> NT **Cathode ray tubes**
> RT **X-rays**

Vagabonds
> USE **Tramps**

Vagrants
> USE **Tramps**

Valentine's Day 394.2618
> UF Saint Valentine's Day
>   St. Valentine's Day
> BT **Holidays**

Valuation 338.5
> Use for general materials on the appraisal
> of property. Materials on valuation of particu-

lar types of property are entered under the
type of property, e.g. **Real estate.** Materials
on valuation for taxing purposes are entered
under **Tax assessment.**
> UF Appraisal
>   Capitalization (Finance)
> NT **Tax assessment**

Values 121; 170; 303.3
> Use for materials on moral and aesthetic
> values.
> UF Axiology
>   Human values
>   Worth
> BT **Aesthetics**
>   **Ethics**
>   **Psychology**
> NT **Social values**

Vampire films 791.43
> May be used for individual works, collec-
> tions, or materials about vampire films.
> UF Vampires in motion pictures
> BT **Horror films**
>   **Motion pictures**

Vampires (May subdiv. geog.) **398.21**
> BT **Folklore**

Vampires in motion pictures
> USE **Vampire films**

Van pools
> USE **Car pools**

Vandalism 364.16
> UF Destruction of property
> BT **Offenses against property**
> NT **Graffiti**

Vanishing species
> USE **Endangered species**

Vanity
> USE **Pride and vanity**

Vans 728.7
> BT **Travel trailers and campers**

Variation (Biology) 576.5
> UF Mutation (Biology)
> BT **Biology**
>   **Genetics**
>   **Heredity**
> NT **Adaptation (Biology)**
>   **Mendel's law**
>   **Natural selection**
> RT **Evolution**

Variety shows (Radio programs)
>   **791.44**
> May be used for individual works, collec-
> tions, or materials about variety shows on the
> radio.
> BT **Radio programs**

Variety shows (Television programs)
791.45

May be used for individual works, collections, or materials about variety shows on television.

BT   Television programs

Varnish and varnishing   667; 698

BT   Finishes and finishing

Varsity sports

USE   College sports

Vascular system

USE   Cardiovascular system

Vasectomy   613.9

BT   Sterilization (Birth control)

Vases (May subdiv. geog.)   **731; 738**

RT   Glassware

Pottery

Vassals

USE   Feudalism

Vatican City   945.6

Use for geographical and descriptive materials on the independent papal state in Rome. Materials on the central administration of the Roman Catholic Church are entered under **Catholic Church.**

Vatican City—Foreign relations

USE   Catholic Church—Foreign relations

Vatican Council (2nd : 1962-1965)   262

BT   Councils and synods

Vaudeville (May subdiv. geog.)   **792.7**

BT   Amusements

Theater

Vaults (Sepulchral)

USE   Tombs

VCRs

USE   Video recording

VD

USE   Sexually transmitted diseases

Vedas   294.5

BT   Hinduism

Sacred books

Vegetable gardening (May subdiv. geog.)
635

UF   Kitchen gardens

BT   Gardening

Horticulture

RT   Truck farming

Vegetables

Vegetable kingdom

USE   Botany

Plants

Vegetable oils

USE   Essences and essential oils

Oils and fats

Vegetables (May subdiv. geog.)   **635;**
641.3

SA   types of vegetables [to be added as needed]

BT   Food

Plants

NT   Celery

Cooking—Vegetables

Potatoes

Root crops

RT   Vegetable gardening

Vegetables—Canning

USE   Vegetables—Preservation

Vegetables—Preservation   641.4

UF   Vegetables—Canning

BT   Canning and preserving

Vegetarian cookery

USE   Vegetarian cooking

Vegetarian cooking (May subdiv. geog.)
641.5

UF   Vegetarian cookery

BT   Cooking

RT   Cooking—Vegetables

Vegetarianism (May subdiv. geog.)
613.2

BT   Diet

Vehicles   388; 629.2

SA   types of vehicles and names of specific makes and models of vehicles [to be added as needed]

BT   Transportation

NT   Air-cushion vehicles

All terrain vehicles

Automobiles

Bicycles

Carriages and carts

Military vehicles

Recreational vehicles

Sleds

Submersibles

Tricycles

Vehicles, Military

USE   Military vehicles

Velocity

USE   Speed

Veneers and veneering   674; 698
    BT   **Cabinetwork**
         Furniture
Venereal diseases
    USE   **Sexually transmitted diseases**
Ventilation   697.9
    SA   types of buildings with the sub-
         division *Heating and ventila-*
         tion, e.g. **Houses—Heating**
         and ventilation [to be added
         as needed[
    BT   **Air**
         Home economics
         Household sanitation
         Hygiene
         Sanitation
    RT   **Air conditioning**
         Heating
Ventriloquism   793.8
    BT   **Amusements**
         Voice
Verbal abuse
    USE   **Invective**
Verbal learning   153.1; 370.15
    Use for materials on the process of learning
    and understanding written or spoken language,
    ranging from learning to associate two non-
    sense syllables to solving problems presented
    in verbal terms.
    UF   Learning, Verbal
    BT   **Language and languages**
         Psychology of learning
    NT   **Reading comprehension**
Vermin
    USE   **Household pests**
         Pests
Vers libre
    USE   **Free verse**
Verse epistles
    USE   **Epistolary poetry**
Versification   808.1
    UF   English language—Versification
         Meter
         Prosody
    BT   **Authorship**
         Poetics
         Rhythm
    NT   **Rhyme**
Vertebrates (May subdiv. geog.)   596
    BT   **Animals**
Very high frequency radio
    USE   **Shortwave radio**

Vessels (Ships)
    USE   **Ships**
Vesta (Roman deity)   292.2
    BT   **Gods and goddesses**
Veterans (May subdiv. geog.)   305.9;
        920
    UF   War veterans
    BT   **Military art and science**
    RT   **Military hospitals**
         Military pensions
         Military personnel
         Soldiers
Veterans Day   394.264
    UF   Armistice Day
    BT   **Holidays**
Veterans—Education (May subdiv. geog.)
        362.86
    UF   Education of veterans
    BT   **Education**
Veterans—Employment   331.5
    BT   **Employment**
Veterans—Hospitals
    USE   **Military hospitals**
Veterans—Legal status, laws, etc.   343
    BT   **Military law**
Veterans—United States   305.9;
        353.5380973; 920
Veterinary medicine (May subdiv. geog.)
        636.089
    SA   types of animals with the subdi-
         vision *Diseases,* e.g. **Horses—**
         Diseases; or with the subdivi-
         sion *Wounds and injuries,* e.g.
         Horses—Wounds and inju-
         ries [to be added as needed]
    BT   **Medicine**
    RT   **Animals—Diseases**
VHF radio
    USE   **Shortwave radio**
Viaducts
    USE   **Bridges**
Vibration   531; 620.3
    BT   **Mechanics**
         Sound
    NT   **Sound waves**
         Waves
Vicarious atonement
    USE   **Atonement—Christianity**

Vice   170
   UF   Vices
   SA   types of vices [to be added as
            needed]
   BT   **Conduct of life**
         Ethics
         Human behavior
   RT   **Crime**
Vice-presidents (May subdiv. geog.)
         352.23; 920
   BT   **Presidents**
Vice-presidents—United States   352.23;
         920
   UF   United States—Vice-presidents
Vices
   USE   **Vice**
Victimless crimes
   USE   **Crimes without victims**
Victims of atomic bombings
   USE   **Atomic bomb victims**
Victims of crime
   USE   **Victims of crimes**
Victims of crimes (May subdiv. geog.)
         362.88
   UF   Crime victims
         Victims of crime
   BT   **Crime**
   NT   **Abused women**
         Adult child abuse victims
Victorian literature
   USE   **English literature—19th**
            century
Victoriana   745.1; 747.0942
   BT   **Antiques**
         Collectibles
Video art (May subdiv. geog.)   700;
         791.45
      Use for materials on works of art created
   with the use of television and video recording
   technology.
   UF   Electronic art
   BT   **Art**
         Television
         Video recording
Video cameras, Home
   USE   **Camcorders**
Video cassette recorders and recording
   USE   **Video recording**
Video cassettes
   USE   **Videotapes**
Video disc players
   USE   **Videodisc players**

Video discs
   USE   **Videodiscs**
Video display terminals
   USE   **Computer monitors**
Video games   688.7; 794.8
   UF   Electronic games
         Television games
   SA   types of video games and names
            of individual games [to be
            added as needed]
   BT   **Electronic toys**
         Games
Video recording   384.55; 621.388;
         778.59
      Use for materials on either the equipment
   or the process by which video or video and
   audio materials are recorded.
   UF   VCRs
         Video cassette recorders and re-
            cording
         Videorecorders
         Videotape recorders and record-
            ing
   NT   **Camcorders**
         Video art
         Videodiscs
         Videotapes
   RT   **Home video systems**
         Television—Equipment and
            supplies
Video recordings
   USE   **Videodiscs**
         Videotapes
Video recordings, Closed caption
   USE   **Closed caption video record-**
            ings
Video recordings for the hearing impaired
   USE   **Closed caption video record-**
            ings
Video tapes
   USE   **Videotapes**
Video telephone   384.6; 621.386
   UF   Picture telephone
         Videophone
   BT   **Data transmission systems**
         Telephone
         Television
Videocassettes
   USE   **Videotapes**

Videodisc players 384.55; 621.388
  UF Video disc players
  BT **Television—Equipment and supplies**
Videodiscs 384.55; 621.388
  UF Video discs
      Video recordings
  BT **Audiovisual materials**
      Optical storage devices
      Video recording
  NT **Closed caption video recordings**
      Music videos
  RT **Television**
Videophone
  USE **Video telephone**
Videorecorders
  USE **Video recording**
Videos, Music
  USE **Music videos**
Videotape recorders and recording
  USE **Video recording**
Videotapes 384.55; 778.59
  UF Tape recordings, Video
      Video cassettes
      Video recordings
      Video tapes
      Videocassettes
  BT **Audiovisual materials**
      Home video systems
      Video recording
  NT **Closed caption video recordings**
      Music videos
  RT **Television**
Videotex systems 004.69; 384.3
    Use for materials on the transmission of computer-based data from a central source to a television set or personal computer allowing for two-way interactions, such as with home shopping or home banking.
  UF Interactive videotex
      Viewdata systems
  BT **Data transmission systems**
      Information systems
      Television broadcasting
  RT **Teletext systems**
Vietnam War, 1961-1975 959.704
    May use appropriate subdivisions under **World War, 1939-1945.**
  UF Vietnamese Conflict, 1961-1975
      Vietnamese War, 1961-1975

  BT **United States—History—1961-1974**
Vietnamese Conflict, 1961-1975
  USE **Vietnam War, 1961-1975**
Vietnamese refugees (May subdiv. geog.) 305.9
  BT **Refugees**
Vietnamese War, 1961-1975
  USE **Vietnam War, 1961-1975**
Viewdata systems
  USE **Videotex systems**
Views 910.22
    Use for collections of pictures of many places.
  UF Scenery
  SA countries, states, cities, etc., and named entities, such as individual parks, structures, etc., with the subdivision *Pictorial works,* e.g. **Chicago (Ill.)—Pictorial works; United States—Pictorial works; Yosemite National Park (Calif.)—Pictorial works;** etc. [to be added as needed]
  BT **Pictures**
Vigilance committees (May subdiv. geog.) 364.1; 364.4
  UF Vigilantes
  BT **Crime**
      Criminal law
  RT **Lynching**
Vigilantes
  USE **Vigilance committees**
Vikings (May subdiv. geog.) 948
    Use for materials on early Scandinavian people. Materials on the people since the tenth century are entered under **Scandinavians.**
  UF Norsemen
      Northmen
  BT **Scandinavians**
  RT **Normans**
Villages (May subdiv. geog.) 307.76
  BT **Cities and towns**
Vines
  USE **Climbing plants**
Vineyards (May subdiv. geog.) 634.8
  UF Viticulture
  BT **Farms**
  RT **Grapes**
      Wine and wine making

Vintage automobiles
    USE **Antique and classic cars**
Vintage cars
    USE **Antique and classic cars**
Vintage motorcycles
    USE **Antique and vintage motorcycles**
Violence (May subdiv. geog.)   **303.6**
    SA   types of violence [to be added as needed]
    BT   **Aggressiveness (Psychology)**
           Social psychology
    NT   **Domestic violence**
           Hate crimes
           School violence
           Violence in mass media
           Violence in popular culture
           Violence in sports
           Violence in the workplace
           Violence on television
Violence chips
    USE **V-chips**
Violence in mass media   **302.23**
    BT   **Mass media**
           Violence
Violence in popular culture   **306.4**
    BT   **Popular culture**
           Violence
Violence in schools
    USE **School violence**
Violence in sports   **796**
    UF   Sports violence
    BT   **Sports**
           Violence
Violence in television
    USE **Violence on television**
Violence in the workplace   **658.4**
    UF   Workplace violence
    BT   **Violence**
           Work environment
Violence on television   **302.23; 791.45**
    UF   Violence in television
    BT   **Television**
           Television programs
           Violence
Violin
    USE **Violins**
Violin music   **787.2**
    BT   **Music**
Violin players
    USE **Violinists**

Violinists (May subdiv. geog.)   **787.2092; 920**
    UF   Violin players
    BT   **Instrumentalists**
Violins   **787.2**
    UF Fiddle
           Violin
    BT   **Stringed instruments**
Violoncellists (May subdiv. geog.)   **787.4092**
    UF   Cellists
           Cello players
           Violoncello players
    BT   **Instrumentalists**
Violoncello
    USE **Violoncellos**
Violoncello players
    USE **Violoncellists**
Violoncellos   **787.4**
    UF   Cello
           Violoncello
    BT   **Stringed instruments**
Vipers
    USE **Snakes**
Virgin Mary
    USE **Mary, Blessed Virgin, Saint**
Virtual libraries
    USE **Digital libraries**
Virtual reality   **006.8**
    UF   Artificial reality
    BT   **Computer simulation**
    RT   **Computer graphics**
Virtue   **170**
    UF   Virtues
    SA   types of virtues [to be added as needed]
    BT   **Conduct of life**
           Ethics
           Human behavior
    NT   **Charity**
           Chastity
           Courage
           Courtesy
           Faith
           Forgiveness
           Gratitude
           Hope
           Justice
           Loyalty
           Obedience
           Patience

Virtue—*Continued*
        Punctuality
        Temperance
Virtues
    USE   **Virtue**
Viruses   579.2
    UF   Microbes
    BT   **Microorganisms**
    NT   **Chickenpox**
Viruses, Computer
    USE   **Computer viruses**
Visceral learning
    USE   **Biofeedback training**
Viscosity   532; 620.1
    BT   **Hydrodynamics**
        Mechanics
Vision   152.14; 573.8; 612.8; 617.7
    UF   Sight
    BT   **Optics**
        Senses and sensation
    NT   **Color sense**
        Optical illusions
        Vision disorders
    RT   **Eye**
Vision disorders   362.4; 617.7
    UF   Defective vision
        Impaired vision
        Visual handicaps
        Visual impairments
    BT   **Vision**
    NT   **Blind**
        Color blindness
Visions   133.8; 204; 248.2
    BT   **Parapsychology**
        Religion
        Spiritual gifts
    NT   **Dreams**
        Hallucinations and illusions
    RT   **Apparitions**
Visitation rights (Domestic relations)
        (May subdiv. geog.)   306.8
    BT   **Domestic relations**
    RT   **Child custody**
Visitors' exchange programs
    USE   **Exchange of persons programs**
Visual handicaps
    USE   **Vision disorders**
Visual impairments
    USE   **Vision disorders**
Visual instruction
    USE   **Audiovisual education**

Visual literacy   153; 707
    Use for materials on the ability to interpret and evaluate visual objects and symbols, such as television, motion pictures, art works, etc.
    UF   Literacy, Visual
    BT   **Arts**
        Literacy
        Semiotics
Vital records
    USE   **Registers of births, etc.**
Vital statistics   304.6; 310
    UF   Burial statistics
        Death rate
        Marriage statistics
        Mortuary statistics
        Records of births, etc.
    SA   names of countries, cities, etc., and names of ethnic groups with the subdivision *Vital statistics,* for compilations of birth, marriage, and death statistics; and names of wars with the subdivision *Casualities—Statistics,* e.g. **World War, 1939-1945—Casualties—Statistics; World War, 1939-1945—Casualties—United States—Statistics;** etc. [to be added as needed]
    BT   **Statistics**
    NT   **Birth rate**
        Census
        Life expectancy
        Mortality
        Population
    RT   **Registers of births, etc.**
Vitamins   572; 613.2; 615
    BT   **Food**
        Nutrition
Viticulture
    USE   **Grapes**
        Vineyards
        Wine and wine making
Vivisection   179
    BT   **Animal experimentation**
        Surgery
Vocabulary   418
    UF   English language—Vocabulary
        Languages—Vocabulary
        Words

Vocabulary—*Continued*
   BT   **Language and languages**
   NT   **New words**
         Word recognition
Vocal culture
   USE **Voice culture**
Vocal ensembles
   USE **Ensembles (Music)**
Vocal music (May subdiv. geog.)   **782**
   BT   **Music**
   NT   **Cantatas**
         Carols
         Choral music
         Folk songs
         Hymns
         Opera
         Operetta
         Oratorio
         Songs
   RT   **Singing**
Vocation   **158.6; 253**
   BT   **Duty**
         Ethics
         Occupations
         Work
Vocation, Choice of
   USE **Vocational guidance**
Vocational education (May subdiv. geog.)
      370.113; 373.246; 374
   Use for materials on teaching a skill during the educational process. Materials on teaching people a skill after formal education are entered under **Occupational training.** Materials discussing on-the-job training are entered under **Employees—Training.** Materials on retraining are entered under **Occupational retraining.**
   UF   Career education
   SA   types of industries, professions, etc., with the subdivision *Study and teaching,* e.g. **Agriculture—Study and teaching** [to be added as needed]
   BT   **Education**
   NT   **Agriculture—Study and teaching**
         Cooperative education
         Employees—Training
         Industrial arts education
         Occupational retraining
         Occupational training
         Vocational guidance
   RT   **Professional education**
         Technical education

Vocational guidance (May subdiv. geog.)
      331.702; 371.4
   Use for materials on the activities and programs designed to help people plan, choose, and succeed in their careers. Materials on the assistance given to students by schools, colleges, or universities in the selection of a program of studies suited to their abilities, interests, future plans, and general circumstances are entered under **Educational counseling.**
   UF   Career counseling
         Career development
         Career guidance
         Careers
         Choice of profession, occupation, vocation, etc.
         Employment guidance
         Guidance, Vocational
         Job placement guidance
         Occupational guidance
         Vocation, Choice of
   SA   vocational guidance for particular classes of persons, e.g. **Vocational guidance for the handicapped;** and fields of knowledge, corporate bodies, military services, professions, and industries and trades with the subdivision *Vocational guidance* [to be added as needed]
   BT   **Counseling**
         Vocational education
   NT   **Career changes**
         Job hunting
         Law—Vocational guidance
         Television broadcasting—Vocational guidance
         Vocational guidance for the handicapped
   RT   **Educational counseling**
         Employment
         Occupations
         Professions
Vocational guidance for the handicapped (May subdiv. geog.)   **371.4**
   BT   **Handicapped**
         Vocational guidance
Vocational training
   USE **Occupational training**
Vocations
   USE **Occupations**
         Professions

Vodun
USE **Voodooism**
Voice **783**
UF Speaking
BT **Language and languages**
Throat
NT **Automatic speech recognition**
Ventriloquism
RT **Phonetics**
Public speaking
Singing
Speech
Voice culture **808.5**
UF Vocal culture
Voice training
BT **Public speaking**
Singing
Speech
Voice training
USE **Voice culture**
Volatile oils
USE **Essences and essential oils**
Volcanoes (May subdiv. geog.) **551.21**
SA names of volcanoes [to be added
as needed]
BT **Geology**
Mountains
Physical geography
Volleyball **796.325**
BT **Ball games**
Volume (Cubic content) **389; 530.8**
UF Cubic measurement
BT **Geometry**
Measurement
Weights and measures
Volume feeding
USE **Food service**
Voluntarism
USE **Volunteer work**
Voluntary associations
USE **Associations**
Voluntary military service (May subdiv.
geog.) **355.2**
UF Military service, Voluntary
Volunteer military service
BT **Armed forces**
Recruiting and enlistment
Voluntary organizations
USE **Associations**
Volunteer military service
USE **Voluntary military service**

Volunteer work (May subdiv. geog.)
361.3
UF Voluntarism
Volunteering
Volunteerism
Volunteers
SA types of volunteer work and
names of volunteer programs,
e.g. **Meals on wheels pro-**
grams [to be added as need-
ed]
BT **Public welfare**
NT **Caregivers**
Foster grandparents
RT **Charities**
National service
Volunteering
USE **Volunteer work**
Volunteerism
USE **Volunteer work**
Volunteers
USE **Volunteer work**
Volunteers in church work
USE **Lay ministry**
Voodoo
USE **Voodooism**
Voodooism (May subdiv. geog.) **299.6**
UF Vodun
Voodoo
Voudou
Voudouism
BT **Religions**
Voter registration (May subdiv. geog.)
324.6
UF Registration of voters
BT **Elections**
Suffrage
Voting
USE **Elections**
Suffrage
Vouchers, Educational
USE **Educational vouchers**
Voudou
USE **Voodooism**
Voudouism
USE **Voodooism**
Voyager project
USE **Project Voyager**
Voyagers
USE **Explorers**
Travelers

Voyages and travels   910.4

Use for materials about non-fiction travel writing, for collections of travel writings, and for accounts of voyages and travels not limited to a single place. Materials about the theme of travel in literature are entered under **Travel in literature.** Materials on the art and enjoyment of travel and advice for travelers are entered under **Travel.**

UF   Journeys

Travel books

Travels

SA   names of cities (except extinct cities), states, countries, continents, etc., with the subdivision *Description and travel;* e.g. **United States—Description and travel;** names of extinct cities or towns, without further subdivision, for accounts of those places by travelers in ancient times, e.g. **Delphi (Extinct city);** names of individual ships; names of regions, e.g. **Arctic regions;** ethnic groups, classes of persons, and names of individuals with the subidivision *Travel,* e.g. **Handicapped— Travel;** names of countries sponsoring exploring expeditions with the subdivision *Exploring expeditions;* e.g. **United States—Exploring expeditions;** and names of places that were unsettled or sparsely settled and largely unknown to the world at large at the time of exploration, with the subdivision *Exploration,* e.g. **America—Exploration** [to be added as needed]

BT   **Geography**

NT   **Aeronautics—Flights**

Northeast Passage

Ocean travel

Overland journeys to the Pacific

Papal visits

Pilgrims and pilgrimages

Scientific expeditions

Seafaring life

Shipwrecks

Travelers

Voyages around the world

Whaling

Yachts and yachting

RT   **Adventure and adventurers**

Exploration

Explorers

Travel

Travel in literature

Voyages and travels in literature

USE   **Travel in literature**

Voyages around the world   910.4

UF   Circumnavigation

Travel books

BT   **Travel**

Voyages and travels

Voyages to the moon

USE   **Imaginary voyages**

Space flight to the moon

Wage-price controls

USE   **Wage-price policy**

Wage-price policy (May subdiv. geog.) **331.2**

UF   Government policy

Price controls

Price-wage policy

Wage-price controls

BT   **Inflation (Finance)**

Prices

Salaries, wages, etc.

Wages

USE   **Salaries, wages, etc.**

Wagons

USE   **Carriages and carts**

Waiters and waitresses (May subdiv. geog.) **642**

UF   Waitresses

BT   **Food service**

Waitresses

USE   **Waiters and waitresses**

Wakefulness

USE   **Insomnia**

Walking (May subdiv. geog.)   **796.51**

BT   **Aerobics**

Athletics

Human locomotion

RT   **Hiking**

Walking in space

USE   **Extravehicular activity (Space flight)**

Wall decoration
  USE **Mural painting and decoration**
Wall painting
  USE **Mural painting and decoration**
Wall Street (New York, N.Y.)   332.6
  Use for materials on the activities of Wall
  Street as a financial district. Historical and de-
  scriptive materials on Wall Street as a street
  are entered under **Streets—New York (N.Y.).**
  BT **Stock exchanges**
  RT **Streets—New York (N.Y.)**
Wallpaper   676; 747
  BT **Interior design**
  RT **Paperhanging**
Walls   690; 721
  BT **Buildings**
      Civil engineering
Walt Disney World (Fla.)   791.06
  UF Disney World (Fla.)
  BT **Amusement parks**
War   172; 303.6; 355.02
  UF Fighting
      Wars
  SA names of wars, battles, etc., e.g.
      **United States—History—
      1861-1865, Civil War; Get-
      tysburg (Pa.), Battle of,
      1863;** and war and other sub-
      jects, e.g. **War and civiliza-
      tion** [to be added as needed]
  NT **Arms control**
      Battles
      Chemical warfare
      Children and war
      Guerrilla warfare
      Intervention (International law)
      Military aeronautics
      Military occupation
      Military personnel
      Nuclear warfare
      Prisoners of war
      Psychological warfare
      Space warfare
      Submarine warfare
      Tank warfare
      War and civilization
      War and emergency powers
      War crimes
      War—Religious aspects
      World War III
  RT **Armed forces**
      International law

      Military art and science
      Military law
      Naval art and science
      Peace
War and children
  USE **Children and war**
War and civilization   172; 303.4
  UF Civilization and war
  BT **Civilization**
      War
**War and emergency powers (May subdiv.
  geog.)   342**
  UF Emergency powers
      War powers
  BT **Constitutional law**
      Executive power
      Legislative bodies
      War
War and industry
  USE **War—Economic aspects**
War and religion
  USE **War—Religious aspects**
War, Articles of
  USE **Military law**
**War crime trials (May subdiv. geog.)
  341.6; 345**
  BT **Trials**
**War crimes (May subdiv. geog.)   341.6;
  345; 364.1**
  UF Military atrocities
  SA names of wars with the subdivi-
      sion *Atrocities,* e.g. **World
      War, 1939-1945—Atrocities;**
      and names of specific atroci-
      ties [to be added as needed]
  BT **Crimes against humanity**
      International law
      War
**War—Economic aspects (May subdiv.
  geog.)   303.6**
  Use for materials discussing the economic
  causes of war and the effect of war on indus-
  try and trade.
  UF Economics of war
      Industry and war
      War and industry
  SA names of wars with the subdivi-
      sion *Economic aspects* [to be
      added as needed]
  NT **Industrial mobilization**
      **World War, 1939-1945—Eco-
      nomic aspects**

War—Economic aspects—*Continued*
  RT **International competition**
War films 791.43
    May be used for individual works, collections, or materials about war films in general, not limited to a particular war.
  UF Anti-war films
      Apocalyptic fantasies
      End-of-the-world fantasies
  SA names of wars with the subdivision *Motion pictures and the war;* e.g. **World War, 1939-1945—Motion pictures and the war** [to be added as needed]
  BT **Historical drama**
      Motion pictures
  NT **World War, 1939-1945—Motion pictures and the war**
War of 1812 940.2; 973.5
  UF United States—History—1812-1815, War of 1812
  BT **Great Britain—History—1714-1837**
      United States—History—1783-1865
War of nerves
  USE **Psychological warfare**
War of the American Revolution
  USE **United States—History—1775-1783, Revolution**
War pensions
  USE **Military pensions**
War poetry 808.1; 808.81
    May be used for individual works or collections of war poetry, or for materials about war poetry in general, not confined to a particular war.
  UF Anti-war poetry
  SA names of wars with the subdivision *Poetry* [to be added as needed]
  BT **Poetry**
  NT **World War, 1939-1945—Poetry**
  RT **War songs**
War powers
  USE **War and emergency powers**
War protest movements
  USE **Peace movements**
War radio programs 791.44
    May be used for individual works, collections, or materials about war radio programs.
  BT **Radio programs**

War—Religious aspects 201; 261.8
    May be subdivided by religion or sect.
  UF Religion and war
      War and religion
  SA names of wars with the subdivision *Religious aspects,* e.g. **World War, 1939-1945—Religious aspects** [to be added as needed]
  BT **Religion**
      War
  NT **Conscientious objectors**
      Pacifism
War ships
  USE **Warships**
War songs 782.42
  UF Battle songs
      Soldiers' songs
  BT **National songs**
      Songs
  NT **World War, 1939-1945—Songs**
  RT **War poetry**
War stories 808.3; 808.83
    May be used for individual works, collections, or materials about war stories.
  UF Anti-war stories
      Apocalyptic fantasies
      End-of-the-world fantasies
  SA names of wars and battles with the subdivision *Fiction,* e.g. **World War, 1939-1945—Fiction** [to be added as needed]
  BT **Fiction**
      Historical fiction
War television programs 791.45
    May be used for individual works, collections, or materials about war television programs.
  BT **Television programs**
War use
  USE subjects with the subdivision *War use,* e.g. **Dogs—War use** [to be added as needed]
War use of animals
  USE **Animals—War use**
War use of dogs
  USE **Dogs—War use**
War veterans
  USE **Veterans**

War work
USE   names of wars with the subdivi-
       sion *War work,* e.g. **World
       War, 1939-1945—War work**
       [to be added as needed]
Warfare, Submarine
USE   **Submarine warfare**
Warm air heating
USE   **Hot air heating**
Wars
USE   **Military history
       Naval history
       War**
       and ethnic groups with the sub-
       division *Wars,* e.g. **Native
       Americans—Wars** [to be
       added as needed]
Wars of the Roses, 1455-1485
USE   **Great Britain—History—1455-
       1485, Wars of the Roses**
Warships (May subdiv. geog.)   **359.8;
       623.825**
UF   Battle ships
       Battleships
       War ships
SA   names of countries with the sub-
       head *Navy,* e.g. **United
       States. Navy;** and names of
       individual warships [to be
       added as needed]
BT   **Naval architecture
       Naval art and science
       Sea power
       Ships**
NT   **Aircraft carriers
       Submarines**
RT   **Navies**
Washing
USE   **Laundry**
Wasps   595.79
BT   **Insects**
Waste as fuel
USE   **Waste products as fuel**
Waste disposal
USE   **Refuse and refuse disposal**
       and types of waste disposal,
          e.g. **Radioactive waste dis-
          posal; Sewage disposal;** etc.;
       and types of industries, plants,
          and facilities with the subdivi-
          sion *Waste disposal,* e.g.

**Chemical industry—Waste
       disposal** [to be added as
       needed]
Waste (Economics)   339.4
BT   **Economics**
Waste products   628.4
UF   By-products
       Junk
       Trade waste
BT   **Industrial chemistry
       Manufactures**
NT   **Industrial waste**
RT   **Recycling
       Refuse and refuse disposal**
Waste products as fuel   333.793; 662
UF   Energy conversion from waste
       Organic waste as fuel
       Waste as fuel
BT   **Salvage**
RT   **Biomass energy**
Waste reclamation
USE   **Salvage**
Wastes, Hazardous
USE   **Hazardous wastes**
Wastes, Medical
USE   **Medical wastes**
Watches
USE   **Clocks and watches**
Water   551.4; 553.7
UF   Hydrology
BT   **Earth sciences
       Hydraulics**
NT   **Drinking water
       Floods
       Frost
       Geysers
       Groundwater
       Hydrotherapy
       Ice
       Lakes
       Ocean
       Ponds
       Precipitation (Meteorology)
       Rivers
       Sea water
       Steam**
RT   **Hydraulic engineering
       Water rights**
Water—Analysis   546; 628.1
BT   **Analytical chemistry**
RT   **Water pollution**

Water animals
USE **Aquatic animals**
Water ballet
USE **Synchronized swimming**
Water birds (May subdiv. geog.)
598.176
UF Aquatic birds
Water fowl
Wild fowl
SA types of water birds [to be add-
ed as needed]
BT **Birds**
NT **Geese**
Terns
Water conduits
USE **Aqueducts**
Water conservation (May subdiv. geog.)
333.91
UF Conservation of water
BT **Conservation of natural re-
sources**
NT **Xeriscaping**
RT **Water supply**
Water cure
USE **Hydrotherapy**
Water farming
USE **Hydroponics**
Water flow
USE **Hydraulics**
Water fluoridation 628.1
UF Fluoridation of water
Water—Fluoridation
BT **Water supply**
Water—Fluoridation
USE **Water fluoridation**
Water fowl
USE **Water birds**
Water—Oil pollution
USE **Oil pollution of water**
Water plants
USE **Freshwater plants**
Marine plants
Water pollution (May subdiv. geog.)
363.739; 628.1
UF Detergent pollution of rivers,
lakes, etc.
Pollution of water
River pollution
SA types of pollution, e.g. **Oil pol-
lution of water** [to be added
as needed]

BT **Environmental health**
Pollution
Public health
NT **Acid rain**
Marine pollution
Oil pollution of water
RT **Industrial waste**
Sewage disposal
Water—Analysis
Water power 333.9; 621.2
UF Hydroelectric power
Water-power
BT **Energy resources**
Hydraulics
Power (Mechanics)
Renewable energy resources
Rivers
Water resources development
NT **Hydraulic engineering**
Hydraulic machinery
Hydroelectric power plants
Water-power
USE **Water power**
Water—Purification
USE **Water purification**
Water purification 628.1
UF Purification of water
Water—Purification
BT **Sanitation**
Water supply
NT **Sea water conversion**
Water resources development (May
subdiv. geog.) 333.91
BT **Energy development**
Natural resources
NT **Irrigation**
Water power
RT **Water supply**
Water rights (May subdiv. geog.)
333.91; 346.04
BT **Law**
RT **Water**
Water safety 363.14; 797.028
UF Aquatic sports—Safety measures
Drowning prevention
Water sports—Safety measures
BT **Accidents—Prevention**
Water skiing 797.3
BT **Water sports**

Water sports (May subdiv. geog.) **797**
  UF Aquatic sports
  SA types of water sports [to be add-
        ed as needed]
  BT **Sports**
  NT **Boats and boating**
        Canoes and canoeing
        Deep diving
        Diving
        Rowing
        Sailing
        Surfing
        Swimming
        Water skiing
        Yachts and yachting
Water sports—Safety measures
  USE **Water safety**
Water supply (May subdiv. geog.)
      363.6; 628.1
  UF Waterworks
  BT **Natural resources**
        Public utilities
  NT **Aqueducts**
        Dams
        Drinking water
        Forest influences
        Irrigation
        Water fluoridation
        Water purification
  RT **Water conservation**
        Water resources development
        Wells
Water supply engineering (May subdiv.
    geog.) **628.1**
  BT **Civil engineering**
        Engineering
  NT **Drilling and boring (Earth and
        rocks)**
  RT **Hydraulic engineering**
Water transportation
  USE **Shipping**
Watercolor painting (May subdiv. geog.)
    751.42
  UF Watercolors
  BT **Painting**
Watercolors
  USE **Watercolor painting**
Watergate Affair, 1972-1974 **973.924**
    BT **United States—History—1961-
        1974**

Watering places
  USE **Health resorts**
Waterways (May subdiv. geog.) **386**
    Use for materials on rivers, lakes, and ca-
    nals used for transportation.
  BT **Transportation**
  NT **Canals**
        Lakes
        Rivers
  RT **Inland navigation**
Waterwise gardening
  USE **Xeriscaping**
Waterworks
  USE **Water supply**
Wave mechanics **530.12; 531**
  BT **Mechanics**
        Quantum theory
        Waves
Waves **531**
  BT **Hydrodynamics**
        Vibration
  NT **Electric waves**
        Ocean waves
        Radiation
        Sound waves
        Wave mechanics
Waves, Electromagnetic
  USE **Electromagnetic waves**
Waves, Ultrasonic
  USE **Ultrasonic waves**
Wealth (May subdiv. geog.) **330.1**
  UF Distribution of wealth
        Fortunes
        Riches
  BT **Economics**
        Finance
  NT **Cost and standard of living**
        Economic conditions
        Gross national product
        Income
        Inheritance and succession
        Profit
        Saving and investment
        Success
  RT **Capital**
        Money
        Property
Wealthy people
  USE **Rich**
Weaponry
  USE **Weapons**

Weapons (May subdiv. geog.) **355.8; 623.4**
- UF   Arms and armor
- Weaponry
- BT   **Tools**
- NT   **Bow and arrow**
- **Firearms**
- **Knives**
- **Military weapons**
- RT   **Armor**
- **Military art and science**

Weapons, Atomic
- USE   **Nuclear weapons**

Weapons industry
- USE   **Defense industry**
- **Firearms industry**

Weapons, Nuclear
- USE   **Nuclear weapons**

Weapons, Space
- USE   **Space weapons**

Weariness
- USE   **Fatigue**

Weather   551.6

Use for materials on the state of the atmosphere at a given time and place with respect to heat or cold, wetness or dryness, calm or storm. Scientific materials on the atmosphere, especially weather factors, are entered under **Meteorology.** Materials on climate as it relates to humans and to plant and animal life, including the effects of changes of climate, are entered under **Climate.**

- SA   names of countries, cities, etc., with the subdivision *Climate,* e.g. **United States—Climate** [to be added as needed]
- NT   **Humidity**
- **Precipitation (Meteorology)**
- **Storms**
- **Weather control**
- **Weather forecasting**
- **Winds**
- RT   **Climate**
- **Meteorology**

Weather control   551.68
- UF   Artificial weather control
- Cloud seeding
- Rain making
- Weather modification
- BT   **Meteorology**
- **Weather**

Weather—Folklore   398.26
- UF   Weather lore
- BT   **Folklore**
- **Meteorology**
- **Weather forecasting**

Weather forecasting (May subdiv. geog.) **551.63**
- UF   Precipitation forecasting
- BT   **Forecasting**
- **Meteorology**
- **Weather**
- NT   **Weather—Folklore**

Weather lore
- USE   **Weather—Folklore**

Weather modification
- USE   **Weather control**

Weather satellites
- USE   **Meteorological satellites**

Weather stations
- USE   **Meteorological observatories**

Weaving (May subdiv. geog.) **677; 746.1; 746.41**
- UF   Hand weaving
- SA   types of woven articles, e.g. **Rugs and carpets** [to be added as needed]
- BT   **Handicraft**
- **Textile industry**
- NT   **Basket making**
- **Beadwork**
- **Lace and lace making**
- **Looms**
- RT   **Fabrics**

Web databases   005.75; 025.04
- BT   **Databases**

Web pages
- USE   **Web sites**

Web publishing
- USE   **Electronic publishing**

Web search engines   005.75; 025.04
- UF   Web searching
- World Wide Web searching
- SA   names of individual Web search engines [to be added as needed]
- BT   **Internet searching**
- **World Wide Web**

Web searching
- USE   **Internet searching**
- **Web search engines**

Web servers 004.67
  UF   World Wide Web servers
  BT   **World Wide Web**
Web sites 005.7
  UF   Web pages
       Websites
       World Wide Web pages
       World Wide Web sites
  SA   names of individual web sites;
       and topics, geographic names,
       categories of persons, ethnic
       groups, etc., with the subdivi-
       sion *Internet resources* [to be
       added as needed]
  BT   **Internet resources**
Web sites—Design 005.7
  BT   **Design**
Websites
  USE **Web sites**
Weddings (May subdiv. geog.) **392.5;**
     395.2
  BT   **Marriage**
  NT   **Marriage customs and rites**
Weed killers
  USE **Herbicides**
Weeds (May subdiv. geog.) **632**
  BT   **Agricultural pests**
       Economic botany
       Gardening
       Plants
Week **529**
  BT   **Calendars**
       Chronology
  RT   **Days**
Weight **530.8**
  UF   Weight (Physics)
  SA   types of objects and substances
       with the subdivision *Weight,*
       e.g. **Trucks—Weight** [to be
       added as needed]
  BT   **Physics**
  NT   **Body weight**
  RT   **Weights and measures**
Weight control
  USE **Weight loss**
Weight lifting **796.41; 613.7**
  UF   Strength training
       Weight training
       Weightlifting
  BT   **Athletics**
       Exercise

  RT   **Bodybuilding**
Weight loss **613.2**
  UF   Dieting
       Diets, Reducing
       Reducing
       Weight control
  BT   **Body weight**
  RT   **Diet**
       Exercise
Weight (Physics)
  USE **Weight**
Weight training
  USE **Weight lifting**
Weightlessness **531**
  UF   Free fall
       Gravity free state
       Subgravity state
       Zero gravity
  BT   **Environmental influence on**
       humans
       Space medicine
Weightlifting
  USE **Weight lifting**
Weights and measures (May subdiv.
     geog.) **389; 530.8**
  UF   Measures
       Metrology
  SA   types of objects and substances
       with the subdivision *Weight,*
       e.g. **Trucks—Weight** [to be
       added as needed]
  BT   **Physics**
  NT   **Electric measurements**
       Measuring instruments
       Volume (Cubic content)
  RT   **Measurement**
       Metric system
       Weight
Welding **671.5**
  UF   Oxyacetylene welding
  BT   **Blacksmithing**
       Forging
       Ironwork
       Manufacturing processes
       Metalwork
  NT   **Electric welding**
  RT   **Soldering**
Welding, Electric
  USE **Electric welding**
Welfare agencies
  USE **Charities**

Welfare, Public
USE **Public welfare**
Welfare reform
USE **Public welfare**
Welfare state (May subdiv. geog.)
330.12; 361.6
BT **Economic policy**
Public welfare
Social policy
State, The
Welfare work
USE **Charities**
Social work
Welfare work in industry
USE **Industrial welfare**
Well boring
USE **Drilling and boring (Earth and**
rocks)
Well drilling, Oil
USE **Oil well drilling**
Wells (May subdiv. geog.) **551.49; 628.1**
BT **Hydraulic engineering**
RT **Drilling and boring (Earth and**
rocks)
Water supply
West Africa 966
Use for materials dealing collectively with
the southern half of the western bulge of the
African continent, bounded on the north by
the Sahara and on the south and west by the
Atlantic Ocean. The term usually includes Be-
nin, Burkina Faso, Cameroon, Gambia, Gha-
na, Guinea, Guinea-Bissau, Ivory Coast, Libe-
ria, Nigeria, Senegal, Sierra Leone, and Togo,
and sometimes Mali, Mauritania, and Niger as
well.
UF **Africa, West**
BT **Africa**
NT **French-speaking West Africa**
West Germany
USE **Germany (West)**
West Indian literature (French) 840
Use for collections and for materials on
West Indian literature written originally in
French.
BT **Literature**
West Point (Military academy)
USE **United States Military Acade-**
my
West (U.S.) 978
Use for the region west of the Mississippi
River.

UF **Western States**
SA names of individual states in
this region [to be added as
needed]
BT **United States**
NT **Pacific Northwest**
Pacific States
West (U.S.)—Exploration 978
BT **United States—Exploration**
RT **Overland journeys to the Pa-**
cific
West (U.S.)—History 978
UF Westward movement
BT **United States—History**
Western civilization 306.09; 909
Use for materials on the culture and society
stemming from the Greco-Roman traditions of
the occident rather than those of Islam, India,
or the Far East.
UF Civilization, Western
Occidental civilization
BT **Civilization**
East and West
Western comic books, strips, etc. 741.5
May be used for individual works, collec-
tions, or materials about Western comics.
BT **Comic books, strips, etc.**
Western Europe
USE **Europe**
Western films 791.43
May be used for individual works, collec-
tions, or materials about Western films.
UF Westerns
SA types of Western films, e.g.
Lone Ranger films [to be
added as needed]
BT **Adventure films**
Historical drama
Motion pictures
NT **Lone Ranger films**
Western States
USE **West (U.S.)**
Western stories 808.3; 808.83
May be used for individual works, collec-
tions, or materials about post-19th-century fic-
tion set in the 19th-century American West.
UF Westerns
BT **Adventure fiction**
Fiction
Historical fiction
Westerns
USE **Western films**
Western stories
Westerns (Radio programs)

783

Westerns—*Continued*
    Westerns (Television programs)
Westerns (Radio programs)   791.44
    May be used for individual works, collections, or materials about Westerns on the radio.
    UF   Westerns
    BT   **Radio programs**
Westerns (Television programs)   791.45
    May be used for individual works, collections, or materials about Western on television.
    UF   Westerns
    BT   **Television programs**
Westminster Abbey   726.5
    BT   **Abbeys**
        Church buildings
Westward movement
    USE   **Land settlement—United States**
        United States—Territorial expansion
        West (U.S.)—History
Wetlands (May subdiv. geog.)   **551.41**
    SA   types of wetlands, e.g. **Marshes**
        [to be added as needed]
    BT   **Landforms**
    NT   **Bogs**
        Marshes
        Swamps
Whales (May subdiv. geog.)   **599.5**
    BT   **Mammals**
        Marine mammals
Whaling (May subdiv. geog.)   **639.2**
    BT   **Commercial fishing**
        Hunting
        Voyages and travels
Wheat (May subdiv. geog.)   **633.1**
    BT   **Grain**
Wheel chairs
    USE   **Wheelchairs**
Wheelchair basketball   796.32
    BT   **Basketball**
        Wheelchair sports
Wheelchair sports   796.04
    BT   **Sports for the handicapped**
    NT   **Wheelchair basketball**
Wheelchairs   617
    UF   Wheel chairs
    BT   **Chairs**
        Orthopedic apparatus

Wheels   621.8; 629.2
    UF   Car wheels
    BT   **Simple machines**
    NT   **Gearing**
        Tires
Which-way stories
    USE   **Plot-your-own stories**
Whistle blowing (May subdiv. geog.)
        174; 342; 353.4
    Use for materials on the practice of calling public attention to corruption, mismanagement, or waste in government, business, the military, etc.
    UF   Blowing the whistle
        Whistleblowing
    BT   **Political corruption**
        Public interest
Whistleblowing
    USE   **Whistle blowing**
White collar crimes (May subdiv. geog.)
        364.16
    UF   Occupational crimes
    BT   **Crime**
    NT   **Fraud**
        Tax evasion
White supremacist movements
    USE   **White supremacy movements**
White supremacy movements (May
        subdiv. geog.)   **320.5**
    UF   Skinheads
        White supremacist movements
    BT   **Race relations**
        Racism
        Social movements
Whittling
    USE   **Wood carving**
Whodunits
    USE   **Mystery and detective plays**
        Mystery fiction
        Mystery films
        Mystery radio programs
        Mystery television programs
Whole language   372.62
    Use for materials on the integration of listening, speaking, writing, and reading skills in meaningful situations in which children participate actively.
    UF   Integrated language arts (Holistic)
        Language arts (Holistic)
        Language experience approach in education

Whole language—*Continued*
    BT   **Education—Experimental**
            methods
            Language arts
Wholistic medicine
    USE **Holistic medicine**
Wica
    USE **Wicca**
Wicca 133.4
    UF Wica
    BT **Folklore**
         Paganism
    RT **Goddess religion**
         Witchcraft
Wickedness
    USE **Good and evil**
Widowers (May subdiv. geog.) **306.88**
    BT **Men**
Widows (May subdiv. geog.) **306.88**
    BT **Women**
Wife abuse (May subdiv. geog.) **362.82**
    UF Abuse of wives
         Abused wives
         Battering of wives
         Wife battering
         Wife beating
    BT **Domestic violence**
    RT **Abused women**
Wife battering
    USE **Wife abuse**
Wife beating
    USE **Wife abuse**
Wigs 391.5
    BT **Clothing and dress**
         Costume
         Hair
Wigwams
    USE **Tepees**
Wild animal dwellings
    USE **Animals—Habitations**
Wild animals
    USE **Animals**
          Wildlife
Wild cats (May subdiv. geog.) **599.75;**
         636.8
    Use for materials on non-domesticated spe-
cies of cats or domestic cats living in a wild
state. Materials on domestic cats are entered
under **Cats.**
    UF Felidae
         Feral cats
         Wildcats

    SA types of wild cats [to be added
         as needed]
    BT **Mammals**
    RT **Cats**
Wild children (May subdiv. geog.)
        155.45
    Use for materials on children who have
been raised by animals or have lived their
formative years in the wild without contact
with human society.
    UF Feral children
         Wolf children
    BT **Exceptional children**
Wild flowers (May subdiv. geog.)
        582.13
    UF **Wildflowers**
    BT **Flowers**
Wild flowers—Conservation
    USE **Plant conservation**
Wild fowl
    USE **Game and game birds**
          Water birds
Wildcats
    USE **Wild cats**
Wilderness areas (May subdiv. geog.)
        333.78
    UF Scenery
    BT **Forest reserves**
    RT **Conservation of natural re-
         sources**
         National parks and reserves
Wilderness survival (May subdiv. geog.)
        613.6; 796.5
    UF Bush survival
         Outdoor survival
    BT **Camping**
         Outdoor life
         Survival skills
    RT **Survival after airplane acci-
         dents, shipwrecks, etc.**
Wildflowers
    USE **Wild flowers**
Wildlife (May subdiv. geog.) **333.95;**
        639
    Use for materials on wild animals in their
natural environment, especially mammals,
birds, and fishes that are hunted for sport or
food.
    UF Feral animals
         Wild animals
    SA types of wildlife, e.g. **Desert
         animals** [to be added as
         needed]

Wildlife—*Continued*
  BT Animals
  NT Game and game birds
  RT Wildlife conservation
Wildlife and pesticides
  USE Pesticides and wildlife
Wildlife attracting   639.9
  UF Attracting wildlife
  BT Animals
  NT Bird attracting
Wildlife conservation (May subdiv. geog.)
    639.9
  UF Conservation of wildlife
      Preservation of wildlife
      Protection of wildlife
  BT Conservation of natural re-
      sources
      Economic zoology
      Endangered species
      Environmental protection
      Nature conservation
  NT Birdbanding
      Birds—Protection
      Game protection
      Game reserves
      Pesticides and wildlife
      Wildlife refuges
  RT Rare animals
      Wildlife
Wildlife refuges (May subdiv. geog.)
    639.9
  UF Wildlife sanctuaries
  SA names of specific refuges [to be
      added as needed]
  BT Wildlife conservation
Wildlife sanctuaries
  USE Wildlife refuges
Will
  USE Brainwashing
      Free will and determinism
Will power
  USE Self-control
Willpower
  USE Self-control
Wills   346.05
  UF Bequests
      Legacies
  BT Genealogy
      Registers of births, etc.
  NT Living wills
  RT Executors and administrators
      Inheritance and succession

Wind
  USE Winds
Wind instruments   788
  SA types of wind instruments [to be
      added as needed]
  BT Musical instruments
  NT Brass instruments
      Flutes
      Woodwind instruments
Wind power (May subdiv. geog.)   333.9;
    621.4
  BT Energy resources
      Power (Mechanics)
      Renewable energy resources
  RT Windmills
Windbreaks   634.9
  UF Shelterbelts
  BT Tree planting
Windmills (May subdiv. geog.)   621.4
  RT Wind power
Window dressing
  USE Show windows
Window gardening   635.9
  UF Windowbox gardening
      Windowsill gardening
  BT Gardening
      Indoor gardening
  NT House plants
  RT Container gardening
      Flower gardening
Windowbox gardening
  USE Window gardening
Windows   721
  BT Architecture—Details
      Buildings
  NT Show windows
Windows, Stained glass
  USE Glass painting and staining
Windowsill gardening
  USE Window gardening
Winds   551.51
  UF Gales
      Wind
  BT Meteorology
      Navigation
      Physical geography
      Weather
  NT Cyclones
      Hurricanes
      Tornadoes
      Typhoons

Winds—*Continued*
   RT   **Storms**
Windsurfing (May subdiv. geog.)   **797.3**
   UF   Board sailing
         Sailboarding
   BT   **Sailing**
Wine and wine making (May subdiv.
     geog.)   **641.2; 663**
   UF   Viticulture
   BT   **Alcoholic beverages**
   RT   **Grapes**
         Vineyards
Wing chun
   USE   **Kung fu**
Winter gardening   **635.9; 712**
   Use for materials on the culture of decorative plants that bloom outdoors in winter.
   BT   **Gardening**
Winter resorts (May subdiv. geog.)
     796.9
   BT   **Resorts**
   NT   **Ski resorts**
Winter sports (May subdiv. geog.)
     796.9
   UF   Ice sports
   SA   types of winter sports [to be
         added as needed]
   BT   **Sports**
   NT   **Hockey**
         Ice skating
         Skiing
         Sledding
         Snowboarding
Wire services
   USE   **News agencies**
Wireless
   USE   **Radio**
Wireless communication systems   **384.5**
   UF   Communication systems, Wireless
         Wireless information networks
   BT   **Telecommunication**
Wireless information networks
   USE   **Wireless communication systems**
Wiretapping   **363.25**
   BT   **Criminal investigation**
         Right of privacy
   RT   **Eavesdropping**
Wiring, Electric
   USE   **Electric wiring**

Wishes   **153.8**
   BT   **Motivation (Psychology)**
Wit and humor   **808.7; 808.87**
   May be used for individual works, collections, or materials about wit and humor.
   UF   Facetiae
         Humor
   SA   wit and humor of particular
         countries or ethnic groups,
         e.g. **American wit and humor; Jewish wit and humor,**
         etc., and subjects with the
         subdivision *Humor,* e.g. **Music—Humor** [to be added as
         needed]
   BT   **Literature**
   NT   **American wit and humor**
         Black humor (Literature)
         Cartooning
         Chapbooks
         Comedies
         Comedy
         Comic books, strips, etc.
         English wit and humor
         Epigrams
         Humorists
         Humorous fiction
         Humorous poetry
         Jewish wit and humor
         Jokes
         Mock-heroic literature
         Music—Humor
         Nonsense verses
         Parody
         Practical jokes
         Puns
         Satire
         Tall tales
         World War, 1939-1945—Humor
   RT   **Anecdotes**
Witchcraft (May subdiv. geog.)   **133.4**
   UF   Black art (Magic)
         Black magic (Witchcraft)
         Sorcery
   BT   **Folklore**
         Occultism
   NT   **Witches**
   RT   **Magic**
         Wicca

Witches (May subdiv. geog.)   **133.4**
   UF   Covens
   BT   **Witchcraft**
Witnesses (May subdiv. geog.)   **345; 347**
   UF   Cross-examination
   BT   **Litigation**
        Trials
Wives (May subdiv. geog.)   **306.872**
   UF   Married women
        Spouses
   BT   **Family**
        Marriage
        Married people
        Women
Wives of presidents—United States
   USE **Presidents' spouses—United**
          States
Wives, Runaway
   USE **Runaway adults**
Wok cooking   **641.7**
   BT   **Cooking**
Wolf children
   USE **Wild children**
Woman
   USE **Women**
Woman-man relationship
   USE **Man-woman relationship**
Women (May subdiv. geog.)   **305.4**
   UF   Woman
   SA   women of particular racial, reli-
        gious or ethnic groups, e.g.
        Mexican American women;
        Jewish women; women in
        various occupations and pro-
        fessions, e.g. **Women artists;**
        Policewomen; Women in the
        motion picture industry;
        etc.; and names of wars and
        military services with the sub-
        division *Women,* e.g. **World**
        War, 1939-1945—Women [to
        be added as needed]
   NT   **Abused women**
        African American women
        Black women
        Businesswomen
        Daughters
        Jewish women
        Lesbians
        Mexican American women
        Minority women

        Mothers
        Native American women
        Nuns
        Policewomen
        Single women
        Sisters
        Widows
        Wives
        Women air pilots
        Women artists
        Women authors
        Women clergy
        Women in the motion picture
          industry
        Women judges
        Women physicians
        World War, 1939-1945—Wom-
          en
        Young women
   RT   **Femininity**
Women actors
   USE **Actresses**
Women air pilots (May subdiv. geog.)
        629.13092; 920
   BT   **Air pilots**
        Women
Women artists (May subdiv. geog.)
        709.2; 920
   Use for materials on the attainments of sev-
   eral women in the area of art.
   BT   **Artists**
        Women
Women authors   **809; 920**
   Use for collections and for materials on the
   attainments of several women authors not lim-
   ited to a single national literature or literary
   form.
   SA   literary forms and national litera-
        tures with the subdivision
        Women authors, e.g.
        American literature—Wom-
        en authors [to be added as
        needed]
   BT   **Authors**
        Women
Women—Biography   **920**
   BT   **Biography**
Women—Biography—Dictionaries
        920.72
Women, Black
   USE **Black women**
Women—Civil rights
   USE **Women's rights**

Women clergy (May subdiv. geog.)
  200.92; 270.092
  BT Clergy
      Women
  RT Ordination of women
Women—Clothing
  USE Women's clothing
Women—Clubs
  USE Women—Societies
Women—Diseases 616.0082; 618.1
  UF Diseases of women
      Gynecology
  BT Diseases
  NT Breast cancer
  RT Women—Health and hygiene
Women—Dress
  USE Women's clothing
Women—Education (May subdiv. geog.)
  371.822
  UF Education of women
  BT Education
  RT Coeducation
Women—Emancipation
  USE Women's rights
Women—Employment (May subdiv.
  geog.) 331.4
  UF Girls—Employment
      Working women
  SA women in various occupations
      and professions, e.g. **Women
      artists; Policewomen; Wom-
      en in the motion picture in-
      dustry;** etc. [to be added as
      needed]
  BT Employment
  NT Equal pay for equal work
      Self-employed women
Women—Enfranchisement
  USE Women—Suffrage
Women—Equal rights
  USE Women's rights
Women—Health and hygiene   613
  UF Gynecology
      Women—Hygiene
  BT Health
      Hygiene
  NT Women—Mental health
      Women—Physical fitness
  RT Women—Diseases
Women—History 305.409
  Use for comprehensive materials on the history of women, their socio-economic, politi-

cal, and legal position, their participation in historical events, and their contributions to society. Materials dealing specifically with women's social condition and status, including historical discussions of the same, are entered under **Women—Social conditions.**
  BT Feminism
      History
Women—Hygiene
  USE Women—Health and hygiene
Women—Identity   305.4
  UF Female identity
      Feminine identity
  BT Identity (Psychology)
Women in art   704.9
  Use for materials on women depicted in works of art. Materials on the attainments of several women in the area of art are entered under **Women artists.**
  BT Art—Themes
Women in business
  USE Businesswomen
Women in literature   809
  Use for materials on the theme of women in works of literature. Collections and materials on several women authors not limited to a single national literature or literary form are entered under **Women authors.**
  BT Literature—Themes
Women in motion pictures   791.43
  Use for materials discussing the portrayal of women in motion pictures. Materials discussing all aspects of women's involvement in motion pictures are entered under **Women in the motion picture industry.**
  BT Motion pictures
Women in the Bible   220.8
  UF Bible—Women
  BT Bible—Biography
Women in the motion picture industry
  791.43
  Use for materials discussing all aspects of women's involvement in motion pictures. Materials discussing the portrayal of women in motion pictures are entered under **Women in motion pictures.**
  BT Motion picture industry
      Women
Women judges (May subdiv. geog.)
  347; 920
  BT Judges
      Women
Women-men relationship
  USE Man-woman relationship
Women—Mental health   362.2
  BT Mental health
      Women—Health and hygiene
  RT Women—Psychology

Women—Ordination
USE   Ordination of women
Women—Physical fitness   613.7
BT   **Physical fitness**
Women—Health and hygiene
Women physicians (May subdiv. geog.)
610.69; 920
BT   **Physicians**
Women
Women police officers
USE   **Policewomen**
Women—Political activity (May subdiv.
geog.)   **324**
BT   **Political participation**
NT   **Women politicians**
Women politicians (May subdiv. geog.)
324.2092; 920
BT   **Politicians**
Women—Political activity
Women—Psychology   155.3
UF   Feminine psychology
BT   **Psychology**
RT   **Women—Mental health**
Women—Relations with men
USE   **Man-woman relationship**
Women—Religious life   204; 248.4
BT   **Religious life**
RT   **Goddess religion**
Women—Self-defense
USE   **Self-defense for women**
Women, Self-employed
USE   **Self-employed women**
Women—Social conditions (May subdiv.
geog.)   **305.42**
Use for materials dealing specifically with
women's social condition and status, including
historical   discussions   of   the   same.
Comprehensive materials on the history of
women are entered under **Women—History.**
BT   **Social conditions**
NT   **Prostitution**
Women's movement
Women—Societies (May subdiv. geog.)
367
UF   Women—Clubs
Women's clubs
Women's organizations
BT   **Clubs**
Societies
Women—Sports
USE   **Sports for women**

Women—Suffrage (May subdiv. geog.)
324.6
UF   Women—Enfranchisement
Women's suffrage
BT   **Suffrage**
Women's rights
RT   **Suffragists**
Women—United States   305.40973
Women's clothing (May subdiv. geog.)
646
UF   Women—Clothing
Women—Dress
BT   **Clothing and dress**
Women's clubs
USE   **Women—Societies**
Women's friendship
USE   **Female friendship**
Women's liberation movement
USE   **Women's movement**
Women's movement (May subdiv. geog.)
305.42; 323.3
Use for materials on activities aimed at ob-
taining equal rights and opportunities for
women. Materials on the theory of the politi-
cal and social equality of the sexes and wom-
en's perspectives on various subjects are en-
tered under **Feminism.**
UF   Women's liberation movement
BT   **Women—Social conditions**
Women's rights
RT   **Feminism**
Women's organizations
USE   **Women—Societies**
Women's rights (May subdiv. geog.)
323.3; 342
UF   Emancipation of women
Rights of women
Women—Civil rights
Women—Emancipation
Women—Equal rights
BT   **Civil rights**
Sex discrimination
NT   **Women—Suffrage**
Women's movement
RT   **Feminism**
Pro-choice movement
Pro-life movement
Women's self-defense
USE   **Self-defense for women**
Women's suffrage
USE   **Women—Suffrage**
Wonders
USE   **Curiosities and wonders**

Wood (May subdiv. geog.)   **620.1; 674**
    UF   Timber
           Woods
    SA   types of wood, e.g. **Oak** [to be
           added as needed]
    BT   **Building materials**
           Forest products
           Fuel
           Trees
    NT   **Lumber and lumbering**
           Oak
           Plywood
           Woodwork
    RT   **Forests and forestry**
Wood block printing
    USE **Wood engraving**
           Woodcuts
Wood-burning
    USE **Pyrography**
Wood carving   **731.4; 736**
    UF   Carving, Wood
           Whittling
    BT   **Carving (Decorative arts)**
           Decoration and ornament
           Woodwork
Wood engraving   **761**
    UF   Block printing
           Wood block printing
    BT   **Engraving**
Wood finishing   **698**
    BT   **Finishes and finishing**
    NT   **Furniture finishing**
Wood—Preservation   **674**
    UF   Preservation of wood
Wood toy making
    USE **Wooden toy making**
Wood turning
    USE **Turning**
Woodcuts   **761**
    UF   Block printing
           Wood block printing
    BT   **Prints**
Wooden toy making   **745.592**
    UF   Wood toy making
    BT   **Toy making**
           Woodwork
Woods
    USE **Forests and forestry**
           Lumber and lumbering
           Wood

Woodwind instruments   **877.2**
    BT   **Wind instruments**
Woodwork (May subdiv. geog.)   **684**
    BT   **Architecture—Details**
           Decorative arts
           Wood
    NT   **Furniture making**
           Pyrography
           Wood carving
           Wooden toy making
    RT   **Cabinetwork**
           Carpentry
           Turning
Woodworking machinery   **621.9; 684**
    SA   types of woodworking machines
           [to be added as needed]
    BT   **Machinery**
    NT   **Lathes**
Wool (May subdiv. geog.)   **677**
    BT   **Animal products**
           Fabrics
           Fibers
Word books
    USE **Picture dictionaries**
Word building
    USE **Word skills**
Word (Computer software)
    USE **Microsoft Word (Computer
          software)**
Word games   **793.734**
    SA   types of word games, e.g.
           Crossword puzzles [to be
           added as needed]
    BT   **Games**
           Literary recreations
    NT   **Crossword puzzles**
Word histories
    USE **Language and languages—Ety-
          mology**
Word problems (Mathematics)   **510**
    BT   **Mathematics**
Word processing   **005.52**
    BT   **Office management**
           Office practice
    RT   **Desktop publishing**
           Word processing software
Word processing software   **005.52**
    BT   **Computer software**
    RT   **Word processing**
Word processor keyboarding
    USE **Keyboarding (Electronics)**

Word recognition   372.46
  BT   Reading
        Vocabulary
Word skills   372.4; 418
  Use for educational materials on conso-
  nants, blends, vowels, prefixes and suffixes,
  digraphs, syllables, root words, rhyming, and
  alphabet, etc.
  UF   Word building
        Words
  BT   Reading
  RT   English language—Spelling
Wordless stories
  USE   Stories without words
Words
  USE   Vocabulary
         Word skills
Words, New
  USE   New words
Work   158.7; 306.3
  Use for materials on the physical or mental
  exertion of individuals to produce or accom-
  plish something. Materials on the collective
  human activities involved in the production
  and distribution of goods and services in an
  economy, as well as materials on the group of
  workers who render these services for wages,
  are entered under Labor.
  NT   Job satisfaction
        Performance
        Vocation
        Work and family
        Work environment
        Work ethic
  RT   Labor
        Occupations
Work addiction
  USE   Workaholism
Work and family (May subdiv. geog.)
        306.3; 306.87; 646.7
  Use for materials on the conflict or balance
  in people's lives between the demands of
  work and family.
  UF   Family and work
  BT   Family
        Work
  RT   Dual-career families
Work at home
  USE   Home-based business
         Telecommuting
Work-based learning
  USE   Cooperative education

Work environment (May subdiv. geog.)
        331.25; 620.8
  UF   Places of work
        Work places
        Working environment
        Workplace environment
        Worksite environment
  BT   Environment
        Work
  NT   Machinery in the workplace
        Teams in the workplace
        Violence in the workplace
Work ethic (May subdiv. geog.)   174
  UF   Protestant work ethic
  BT   Ethics
        Work
Work groups
  USE   Teams in the workplace
Work—Law and legislation
  USE   Labor laws and legislation
Work performance standards
  USE   Performance standards
Work places
  USE   Work environment
Work satisfaction
  USE   Job satisfaction
Work standards
  USE   Production standards
Work stoppages
  USE   Strikes
Work stress
  USE   Job stress
Work teams
  USE   Teams in the workplace
Workaholic syndrome
  USE   Workaholism
Workaholism   155.2; 616.85
  UF   Addiction to work
        Compulsive working
        Work addiction
        Workaholic syndrome
  BT   Compulsive behavior
Workers
  USE   Employees
         Labor
         Working class
Workers' compensation (May subdiv.
        geog.)   368.4
  UF   Compensation
        Employers' liability

Workers' compensation—*Continued*
        Insurance, Workers' compensa-
           tion
        Workmen's compensation
    BT   **Accident insurance**
        Health insurance
        Social security
Workers' participation in management
    USE **Participative management**
Workforce diversity
    USE **Diversity in the workplace**
Working animals   636.088
    SA   animals in specific working situ-
          ations [to be added as need-
          ed]
    BT   **Animals**
        Domestic animals
        Economic zoology
    NT   **Animals in police work**
        Animals—War use
        Working dogs
Working at home
    USE **Home-based business**
        Telecommuting
Working children
    USE **Child labor**
Working class (May subdiv. geog.)
        305.5
    Use for materials on the social class com-
posed of persons who work for wages, usually
in manual labor.
    UF   Blue collar workers
        Factory workers
        Industrial workers
        Labor and laboring classes
        Laborers
        Laboring class
        Laboring classes
        Manual workers
        Workers
        Working classes
    BT   **Social classes**
    NT   **Proletariat**
    RT   **Labor**
Working classes
    USE **Working class**
Working couples
    USE **Dual-career families**
Working day
    USE **Hours of labor**

Working dogs   362.4; 636.73
    BT   **Dogs**
        Working animals
    NT   **Guide dogs**
        Hearing ear dogs
Working environment
    USE **Work environment**
Working hours
    USE **Hours of labor**
Working parents' children
    USE **Children of working parents**
Working robots
    USE **Industrial robots**
Working women
    USE **Women—Employment**
Workmen's compensation
    USE **Workers' compensation**
Workplace environment
    USE **Work environment**
Workplace violence
    USE **Violence in the workplace**
Workshop councils
    USE **Participative management**
Workshops, Teachers'
    USE **Teachers' workshops**
Worksite environment
    USE **Work environment**
World
    USE **Earth**
World economics
    USE **Commercial geography**
        Commercial policy
        Economic conditions
        International competition
World government
    USE **International organization**
World history   909
    UF   Universal history
    BT   **History**
    NT   **Ancient history**
        Geography
        Middle Ages
        Modern history
World history—12th century   909
    UF   Twelfth century
    SA   names of regions, countries, cit-
          ies, etc., with the subdivision
          History—12th century [to be
          added as needed]
    BT   **Middle Ages**

World history—13th century 909
　UF　Thirteenth century
　SA　names of regions, countries, cit-
　　　ies, etc., with the subdivision
　　　History—13th century [to be
　　　added as needed]
　BT　**Middle Ages**
World history—14th century 909
　UF　Fourteenth century
　SA　names of regions, countries, cit-
　　　ies, etc., with the subdivision
　　　History—14th century [to be
　　　added as needed]
　BT　**Middle Ages**
World history—15th century 909
　UF　Fifteenth century
　SA　names of regions, countries, cit-
　　　ies, etc., with the subdivision
　　　History—15th century [to be
　　　added as needed]
　BT　**Middle Ages**
World history—16th century 909
　UF　History, Modern—16th century
　　　Sixteenth century
　SA　names of regions, countries, cit-
　　　ies, etc., with the subdivision
　　　History—16th century [to be
　　　added as needed]
World history—17th century 909
　UF　History, Modern—17th century
　　　Seventeenth century
　SA　names of regions, countries, cit-
　　　ies, etc., with the subdivision
　　　History—17th century [to be
　　　added as needed]
World history—18th century 909.7
　UF　Eighteenth century
　　　History, Modern—18th century
　SA　names of regions, countries, cit-
　　　ies, etc., with the subdivision
　　　History—18th century [to be
　　　added as needed]
World history—19th century 909.81
　UF　History, Modern—19th century
　　　Modern history—1800-1899
　　　(19th century)
　　　Nineteenth century
　SA　names of regions, countries, cit-
　　　ies, etc., with the subdivision
　　　History—19th century [to be
　　　added as needed]

World history—20th century 909.82
　UF　History, Modern—20th century
　　　Modern history—1900-1999
　　　(20th century)
　　　Twentieth century
　SA　names of regions, countries, cit-
　　　ies, etc., with the subdivision
　　　History—20th century [to be
　　　added as needed]
　NT　**World War, 1914-1918**
　　　World War, 1939-1945
World history—1945- 909.82
　UF　History, Modern—1945-
　　　Modern history—1945-
World history—21st century 909.83
　UF　History, Modern—21st century
　　　Twenty-first century
　SA　names of regions, countries, cit-
　　　ies, etc., with the subdivision
　　　History—21st century [to be
　　　added as needed]
World language
　USE　**Universal language**
World order
　USE　**International relations**
World organization
　USE　**International organization**
World politics 909
　　Use for historical accounts of international
　political affairs. Materials on the theory of in-
　ternational relations are entered under **Inter-
　national relations.**
　UF　International politics
　SA　names of countries with the sub-
　　　divisions *Foreign relations*
　　　and *Politics and government*
　　　[to be added as needed]
　BT　**Political science**
　NT　**United States—Foreign rela-
　　　tions**
　　　World War, 1914-1918
　　　World War, 1939-1945
　　　World War III
　RT　**Geopolitics**
　　　International organization
　　　International relations
World politics—1945- 909.82
World politics—1945-1965 909.82
World politics—1945-1991 909.82
　NT　**Cold war**
World politics—1965- 909.82
World politics—1991- 909.82

World records   030
   UF   Human records
          Records of achievement
          Records, World
          World's records
   BT   **Curiosities and wonders**
   RT   **Sports records**
World Trade Center (New York, N.Y.) terrorist attack, 2001
   USE   **September 11 terrorist attacks, 2001**
World War I
   USE   **World War, 1914-1918**
World War II
   USE   **World War, 1939-1945**
World War, 1914-1918 (May subdiv. geog.)   **940.3; 940.4**
May be subdivided like **World War, 1939-1945.**
   UF   First World War
          World War I
   BT   **Europe—History—1871-1918**
          World history—20th century
          World politics
World War, 1914-1918—Chemical warfare   940.4
   UF   World War, 1914-1918—Gas warfare
   BT   **Chemical warfare**
World War, 1914-1918—Economic aspects   940.3
   RT   **Reconstruction (1914-1939)**
World War, 1914-1918—Gas warfare
   USE   **World War, 1914-1918—Chemical warfare**
World War, 1914-1918—Peace   940.3
   BT   **Peace**
   NT   **League of Nations**
World War, 1914-1918—Reconstruction
   USE   **Reconstruction (1914-1939)**
World War, 1914-1918—Territorial questions (May subdiv. geog.)   **940.3**
   BT   **Boundaries**
World War, 1914-1918—United States   940.3; 940.4; 973.91
   UF   United States—History—1914-1918, World War
          United States—World War, 1914-1918

World War, 1939-1945 (May subdiv. geog.)   **940.53; 940.54**
Subdivisions used under this heading may be used under other wars.
   UF   Second World War
          World War II
   SA   names of battles, campaigns, sieges, etc., e.g. **Ardennes, Battle of the, 1944-1945; Pearl Harbor (Oahu, Hawaii), Attack on, 1941;** etc. [to be added as needed]
   BT   **Europe—History—1918-1945**
          World history—20th century
          World politics
World War, 1939-1945—Aerial operations   940.54
   UF   World War, 1939-1945—Battles, sieges, etc.
   BT   **Military aeronautics**
World War, 1939-1945—African Americans   940.53; 940.54
   BT   **African Americans**
World War, 1939-1945—Amphibious operations   940.54
   BT   **World War, 1939-1945—Naval operations**
World War, 1939-1945—Antiwar movements
   USE   **World War, 1939-1945—Protest movements**
World War, 1939-1945—Armistices   940.53
World War, 1939-1945—Arms
   USE   **World War, 1939-1945—Equipment and supplies**
World War, 1939-1945—Art and the war   940.53
   UF   World War, 1939-1945—Iconography
          World War, 1939-1945, in art
   BT   **Art**
World War, 1939-1945—Atrocities   940.54
   SA   names of specific atrocities and crimes [to be added as needed]
   BT   **Atrocities**
   NT   **Handicapped—Nazi persecution**
World War, 1939-1945—Battlefields   940.54

World War, 1939-1945—Battles, sieges, etc.
    USE   **World War, 1939-1945—Aerial operations**
           World War, 1939-1945—Campaigns
           World War, 1939-1945—Naval operations
World War, 1939-1945—Biography
    920
    BT   **Biography**
World War, 1939-1945—Blockades
    940.54
World War, 1939-1945—Campaigns
    (May subdiv. geog.)   **940.54**
    UF   World War, 1939-1945—Battles, sieges, etc.
    SA   names of battles, campaigns, sieges, etc., **Ardennes, Battle of the, 1944-1945** [to be added as needed]
    NT   **Ardennes, Battle of the, 1944-1945**
           Normandy (France), Attack on, 1944
           Pearl Harbor (Oahu, Hawaii), Attack on, 1941
World War, 1939-1945—Cartoons and caricatures   940.53
    BT   **Cartoons and caricatures**
World War, 1939-1945—Casualties (May subdiv. geog.)   **940.54**
World War, 1939-1945—Casualties—Statistics   940.54
World War, 1939-1945—Casualties— United States   940.54
    UF   United States—World War, 1939-1945—Casualties
World War, 1939-1945—Casualties— United States—Statistics   940.54
    UF   United States—World War, 1939-1945—Casualties—Statistics
World War, 1939-1945—Causes   940.53
    NT   **National socialism**
World War, 1939-1945—Censorship
    940.54
    BT   **Censorship**
World War, 1939-1945—Charities
    USE   **World War, 1939-1945—Civilian relief**

World War, 1939-1945—War work
World War, 1939-1945—Chemical warfare   940.54
    BT   **Chemical warfare**
World War, 1939-1945—Children 940.53
    BT   **Children and war**
World War, 1939-1945—Civilian evacuation
    USE   **World War, 1939-1945—Evacuation of civilians**
World War, 1939-1945—Civilian relief 940.54
    UF   World War, 1939-1945—Charities
    BT   **Charities**
           Food relief
           Foreign aid
           Reconstruction (1939-1951)
           World War, 1939-1945—War work
    RT   **World War, 1939-1945—Refugees**
World War, 1939-1945—Collaborationists 940.53
    UF   Fifth column
           Quislings
    BT   **Collaborationists**
World War, 1939-1945—Conferences 940.53
    UF   World War, 1939-1945—Congresses
    BT   **Conferences**
World War, 1939-1945—Congresses
    USE   **World War, 1939-1945—Conferences**
World War, 1939-1945—Conscientious objectors   940.53
    BT   **Conscientious objectors**
World War, 1939-1945—Correspondents
    USE   **World War, 1939-1945—Journalists**
World War, 1939-1945—Desertions 940.54
    BT   **Military desertion**
World War, 1939-1945—Destruction and pillage   940.54

World War, 1939-1945—Diplomatic history   940.53

   NT   World War, 1939-1945—Governments in exile

World War, 1939-1945—Displaced persons

   USE   World War, 1939-1945—Refugees

World War, 1939-1945—Draft resisters   940.54

   BT   Draft resisters

World War, 1939-1945—Economic aspects   940.53

   Use for materials on the economic causes of the war and the effect of the war on commerce and industry.

   BT   War—Economic aspects

   NT   World War, 1939-1945—Finance

          World War, 1939-1945—Manpower

          World War, 1939-1945—Reparations

   RT   Reconstruction (1939-1951)

World War, 1939-1945—Education and the war   940.53

   BT   Education

World War, 1939-1945—Engineering and construction   940.54

   BT   Military engineering

World War, 1939-1945—Equipment and supplies   940.54

   UF   World War, 1939-1945—Arms

          World War, 1939-1945—Military supplies

          World War, 1939-1945—Military weapons

          World War, 1939-1945—Ordnance

          World War, 1939-1945—Supplies

          World War, 1939-1945—Weapons

   BT   Military weapons

World War, 1939-1945—Ethical aspects   940.53

   UF   World War, 1939-1945—Moral and religious aspects

   BT   Ethics

World War, 1939-1945—Evacuation of civilians   940.54

   UF   Civilian evacuation

          World War, 1939-1945—Civilian evacuation

   BT   Civil defense

          World War, 1939-1945—Refugees

World War, 1939-1945—Fiction   808.83

   Use for collections of stories dealing with the Second World War. Materials about the depiction of the war in literature are entered under World War, 1939-1945—Literature and the war.

World War, 1939-1945—Finance   940.53

   Use for materials on the cost and financing of the war, including war debts, and the effect of the war on financial systems, including inflation.

   BT   World War, 1939-1945—Economic aspects

World War, 1939-1945—Food supply   940.53

   BT   Food relief

World War, 1939-1945—Forced repatriation   940.53

   RT   World War, 1939-1945—Refugees

World War, 1939-1945—Governments in exile   940.53

   BT   World War, 1939-1945—Diplomatic history

World War, 1939-1945—Guerrillas

   USE   World War, 1939-1945—Underground movements

World War, 1939-1945—Health aspects   940.54

World War, 1939-1945—Hospitals

   USE   World War, 1939-1945—Medical care

World War, 1939-1945—Human resources

   USE   World War, 1939-1945—Manpower

World War, 1939-1945—Humor   940.53

   BT   Wit and humor

World War, 1939-1945—Iconography

   USE   World War, 1939-1945—Art and the war

World War, 1939-1945, in art

   USE   World War, 1939-1945—Art and the war

World War, 1939-1945, in literature
　USE　**World War, 1939-1945—Liter-
　　　　ature and the war**
World War, 1939-1945, in motion pictures
　USE　**World War, 1939-1945—Mo-
　　　　tion pictures and the war**
World War, 1939-1945—Influence
　　940.53
World War, 1939-1945—Jews　940.53
　BT　**Jews**
　RT　**Holocaust, 1933-1945**
World War, 1939-1945—Jews—Rescue
　　940.54
　UF　Rescue of Jews, 1939-1945
　BT　**Jews—Persecutions**
　NT　**Righteous Gentiles in the
　　　　Holocaust**
World War, 1939-1945—Journalists
　　940.54
　UF　World War, 1939-1945—Corre-
　　　　spondents
　　　　World War, 1939-1945—War
　　　　correspondents
　BT　**Journalists**
**World War, 1939-1945—Literature and
　　the war　809; 940.53**
　　Use for materials on the depiction of the
　war in literature. Collections of stories dealing
　with the Second World War are entered under
　World War, 1939-1945—Fiction.
　UF　World War, 1939-1945, in litera-
　　　　ture
　BT　**Literature**
World War, 1939-1945—Manpower
　　940.54
　UF　World War, 1939-1945—Human
　　　　resources
　BT　**World War, 1939-1945—Eco-
　　　　nomic aspects**
World War, 1939-1945—Maps　940.53
　BT　**Maps**
World War, 1939-1945—Medical care
　　940.54
　UF　World War, 1939-1945—Hospi-
　　　　tals
　BT　**Medical care**
**World War, 1939-1945—Military intelli-
　　gence　940.54**
　BT　**Military intelligence**
World War, 1939-1945—Military supplies
　USE　**World War, 1939-1945—
　　　　Equipment and supplies**

World War, 1939-1945—Military weapons
　USE　**World War, 1939-1945—
　　　　Equipment and supplies**
**World War, 1939-1945—Missing in ac-
　　tion　940.54**
　BT　**Missing in action
　　　　World War, 1939-1945—Pris-
　　　　oners and prisons**
**World War, 1939-1945—Monuments
　　725**
　BT　**Monuments**
World War, 1939-1945—Moral and reli-
　　gious aspects
　USE　**World War, 1939-1945—Ethi-
　　　　cal aspects
　　　　World War, 1939-1945—Reli-
　　　　gious aspects**
**World War, 1939-1945—Motion pictures
　　and the war　791.43; 940.53**
　　Use for materials about films dealing with
　the Second World War or about the use of
　motion pictures in the war effort.
　UF　World War, 1939-1945, in mo-
　　　　tion pictures
　BT　**Motion pictures
　　　　War films**
**World War, 1939-1945—Museums
　　940.53**
　BT　**Museums**
**World War, 1939-1945—Naval opera-
　　tions　940.54**
　UF　World War, 1939-1945—Battles,
　　　　sieges, etc.
　NT　**World War, 1939-1945—Am-
　　　　phibious operations**
**World War, 1939-1945—Naval opera-
　　tions—Submarine　940.54**
　UF　World War, 1939-1945—Subma-
　　　　rine operations
　BT　**Submarine warfare**
**World War, 1939-1945—Occupied terri-
　　tories　940.54**
　SA　names of occupied countries
　　　　with the appropriate subdivi-
　　　　sion under *History,* e.g.,
　　　　**Netherlands—History—1940-
　　　　1945, German occupation;
　　　　Japan—History—1945-1952,
　　　　Allied occupation;** etc. [to be
　　　　added as needed]

World War, 1939-1945—Occupied territories—*Continued*
  BT Military occupation
      World War, 1939-1945—Territorial questions
World War, 1939-1945—Ordnance
  USE World War, 1939-1945—Equipment and supplies
World War, 1939-1945—Peace   940.53
World War, 1939-1945—Personal narratives   940.53; 940.54
    Use for collective or individual eyewitness reports or autobiographical accounts of the war in general. Accounts limited to a specific topic are entered under that topic.
  BT Autobiographies
      Biography
World War, 1939-1945—Pictorial works   940.53022
World War, 1939-1945—Poetry   808.81
    Use for collections of poetry dealing with the Second World War.
  BT Historical poetry
      War poetry
World War, 1939-1945—Prisoners and prisons   940.54
  BT Concentration camps
      Prisoners of war
      Prisons
  NT World War, 1939-1945—Missing in action
World War, 1939-1945—Propaganda   940.54
  BT Propaganda
World War, 1939-1945—Protest movements   940.53
  UF World War, 1939-1945—Antiwar movements
      World War, 1939-1945—Protests, demonstrations, etc.
  BT Protest movements
World War, 1939-1945—Protests, demonstrations, etc.
  USE World War, 1939-1945—Protest movements
World War, 1939-1945—Psychological aspects   940.53
  BT Psychological warfare
World War, 1939-1945—Public opinion   940.53
  BT Public opinion

World War, 1939-1945—Railroads
  USE World War, 1939-1945—Transportation
World War, 1939-1945—Reconstruction
  USE Reconstruction (1939-1951)
World War, 1939-1945—Refugees   940.53
  UF World War, 1939-1945—Displaced persons
  BT Political refugees
  NT World War, 1939-1945—Evacuation of civilians
  RT World War, 1939-1945—Civilian relief
      World War, 1939-1945—Forced repatriation
World War, 1939-1945—Regimental histories   940.54
World War, 1939-1945—Religious aspects   940.53
  UF World War, 1939-1945—Moral and religious aspects
World War, 1939-1945—Reparations   940.53
  BT Reconstruction (1939-1951)
      World War, 1939-1945—Economic aspects
World War, 1939-1945—Resistance movements
  USE World War, 1939-1945—Underground movements
World War, 1939-1945—Secret service   940.54
  BT Secret service
World War, 1939-1945—Social aspects   940.53
World War, 1939-1945—Social work
  USE World War, 1939-1945—War work
World War, 1939-1945—Songs   782.42
  UF World War, 1939-1945—Songs and music
  BT Military music
      War songs
World War, 1939-1945—Songs and music
  USE World War, 1939-1945—Songs
World War, 1939-1945—Sources   940.53

World War, 1939-1945—Submarine opera-
tions
  USE **World War, 1939-1945—Naval
operations—Submarine**
World War, 1939-1945—Supplies
  USE **World War, 1939-1945—
Equipment and supplies**
**World War, 1939-1945—Tank warfare
940.54**
  BT **Tank warfare**
**World War, 1939-1945—Territorial ques-
tions** (May subdiv. geog.) **940.53**
  BT **Boundaries**
  NT **World War, 1939-1945—Occu-
pied territories**
**World War, 1939-1945—Theater and the
war 792; 940.53**
  BT **Theater**
**World War, 1939-1945—Transportation
940.54**
  UF World War, 1939-1945—Rail-
roads
  BT **Transportation**
**World War, 1939-1945—Treaties
940.53**
  BT **Treaties**
**World War, 1939-1945—Underground
movements 940.54**
  UF Anti-fascist movements
Anti-Nazi movement
World War, 1939-1945—Guerril-
las
World War, 1939-1945—Resis-
tance movements
**World War, 1939-1945—United States
940.53; 940.54; 973.917**
  UF United States—History—1939-
1945, World War
United States—World War,
1939-1945
World War, 1939-1945—War correspon-
dents
  USE **World War, 1939-1945—Jour-
nalists**
**World War, 1939-1945—War work
940.53**
  UF World War, 1939-1945—Chari-
ties
World War, 1939-1945—Social
work

  NT **World War, 1939-1945—Civil-
ian relief**
World War, 1939-1945—Weapons
  USE **World War, 1939-1945—
Equipment and supplies**
**World War, 1939-1945—Women
940.53; 940.54**
  BT **Women**
World War III 355
  UF Third World War
  BT **War
World politics**
World Wide Web 004.67
  UF World Wide Web (Information
retrieval system)
  BT **Internet**
  NT **Web search engines
Web servers**
World Wide Web (Information retrieval
system)
  USE **World Wide Web**
World Wide Web pages
  USE **Web sites**
World Wide Web searching
  USE **Internet searching
Web search engines**
World Wide Web servers
  USE **Web servers**
World Wide Web sites
  USE **Web sites**
World's Fair (1992 : Seville, Spain)
  USE **Expo 92 (Seville, Spain)**
World's fairs
  USE **Exhibitions
Fairs**
World's records
  USE **World records**
Worms 592
  BT **Animals**
Worry 152.4
  BT **Emotions**
  RT **Anxiety**
Worship 203; 248.3; 264
  UF Devotion
  BT **Religion
Theology**
  NT **Church year
Devotional exercises
Prayer
Public worship
Sacrifice**

Worship of the dead
USE **Ancestor worship**
Worth
USE **Values**
Wounded, First aid to
USE **First aid**
Wounds and injuries   617.1
UF   Injuries
SA   classes of persons, animals, organs of the body, and plants and crops with the subdivision *Wounds and injuries,* e.g. **Horses—Wounds and injuries; Foot—Wounds and injuries;** etc. [to be added as needed]
BT   **Accidents**
NT   **Fractures**
Wrapping of gifts
USE **Gift wrapping**
Wrath
USE **Anger**
Wrecks
USE **Accidents**
Wrestling (May subdiv. geog.)   **796.812**
BT   **Athletics**
Writers
USE **Authors**
Writing   411

Use for materials on the process or result of recording language in the form of conventionalized visible marks or signs on a surface. Materials limited to writing with a pen or pencil and practical or prescriptive guides to penmanship or the art of writing are entered under **Handwriting.** Materials on handwriting as an expression of the writer's character are entered under **Graphology.** Materials on the alphabet or writing of a particular language are entered under the name of the language with the subdivisions *Alphabet* and *Writing.*

BT   **Communication**
Language and languages
Language arts
NT   **Abbreviations**
Alphabet
Autographs
Braille
Calligraphy
Cryptography
Graphology
Handwriting
Hieroglyphics
Picture writing
Shorthand

Typewriting
Writing of numerals
RT   **Ciphers**
Writing (Authorship)
USE **Authorship**
Creative writing
Writing of numerals   513
UF   Numeral formation
Numeral writing
Numerals, Writing of
BT   **Handwriting**
Numerals
Writing
Writing—Patterning
USE **Language arts—Patterning**
Writing—Study and teaching
USE **Handwriting**
Writings of gay men
USE **Gay men's writings**
Writings of lesbians
USE **Lesbians' writings**
Writings of teenagers
USE **Teenagers' writings**
Wrought iron work
USE **Ironwork**
X-15 (Rocket aircraft)   629.133
BT   **Rocket planes**
X-rays   539.7
UF   Radiography
Roentgen rays
X rays
BT   **Electromagnetic waves**
Radiation
NT   **Gamma rays**
Tomography
RT   **Radiotherapy**
Vacuum tubes
X rays
USE **X-rays**
Xeriscaping   635.9
UF   Waterwise gardening
BT   **Landscape gardening**
Water conservation
Xerographic art
USE **Copy art**
Xerography
USE **Photocopying**
YA literature
USE **Young adult literature**
Yacht basins
USE **Marinas**

Yachting
　　USE　**Yachts and yachting**
Yachts and yachting (May subdiv. geog.)
　　　　797.1
　　UF　Yachting
　　BT　**Boatbuilding**
　　　　Boats and boating
　　　　Ocean travel
　　　　Ships
　　　　Voyages and travels
　　　　Water sports
　　NT　**Marinas**
　　RT　**Sailing**
Yard sales
　　USE　**Garage sales**
Yarn　677
　　NT　**Cotton**
　　　　Flax
　　RT　**Spinning**
Yearbooks　050
　　UF　Annuals
　　SA　subjects with the subdivision *Pe-
　　　　riodicals,* e.g. **Engineering—
　　　　Periodicals** [to be added as
　　　　needed]
　　BT　**Serial publications**
　　NT　**School yearbooks**
　　RT　**Almanacs**
Yeast　641.3
　　BT　**Fungi**
Yellow fever　616.9
　　BT　**Tropical medicine**
Yeti　001.9
　　UF　Abominable snowman
　　BT　**Monsters**
　　　　Mythical animals
Yiddish language　439
　　May be subdivided like **English language.**
　　UF　Jewish language
　　　　Jews—Language
　　BT　**Language and languages**
Yiddish literature　839
　　May use same subdivisions and names of
　　literary forms as for **English literature.**
　　BT　**Jewish literature**
Yoga　181; 613.7
　　BT　**Hindu philosophy**
　　　　Hinduism
　　　　Theosophy
　　NT　**Hatha yoga**
Yoga exercises
　　USE　**Hatha yoga**

Yoga, Hatha
　　USE　**Hatha yoga**
Yom Kippur　296.4
　　UF　Atonement, Day of
　　　　Day of Atonement
　　BT　**Jewish holidays**
Yom Kippur War, 1973
　　USE　**Israel-Arab War, 1973**
Yoruba (African people)　305.896
　　BT　**Africans**
　　　　Native peoples
**Yosemite National Park (Calif.)　719;
　　　　979.4**
　　BT　**National parks and reserves—
　　　　United States**
**Yosemite National Park (Calif.)—Pictori-
　　al works　979.4**
Young adult literature　808; 808.8; 809
　　Use for collections or materials about litera-
　　ture published for teenage readers. Materials
　　on the reading interests of teenagers and lists
　　of books for teenagers are entered under
　　Teenagers—Books and reading.
　　UF　Books for teenagers
　　　　Teenage literature
　　　　Teenagers—Literature
　　　　YA literature
　　　　Young adults' literature
　　BT　**Literature**
Young adults
　　USE　**Teenagers**
　　　　Youth
Young adults—Books and reading
　　USE　**Teenagers—Books and reading**
Young adults' libraries (May subdiv.
　　　　geog.)　**027.62**
　　UF　Library services to teenagers
　　　　Library services to young adults
　　　　Young adults' library services
　　BT　**Libraries**
Young adults' library services
　　USE　**Young adults' libraries**
Young adults' literature
　　USE　**Young adult literature**
Young consumers　640.73; 658.8
　　UF　Children as consumers
　　　　Teenage consumers
　　　　Youth market
　　BT　**Consumers**
Young men (May subdiv. geog.)　**305.31**
　　Use for materials on men in the general age
　　range of eighteen through twenty-five years.

Young men—*Continued*
Materials on the time of life between thirteen and twenty-five, as well as on people in that greater age range are entered under **Youth.**
BT   **Men**
      Youth
RT   **Boys**
Young people
USE   **Teenagers**
        Youth
Young persons
USE   **Teenagers**
        Youth
Young women (May subdiv. geog.)
        305.4
Use for materials on women in the general age range of eighteen through twenty-five years. Materials on the time of life between thirteen and twenty-five, as well as on people in that greater age range are entered under **Youth.**
BT   **Women**
      Youth
RT   **Girls**
Youngest child
USE   **Birth order**
Youth (May subdiv. geog.)   **305.235**
Use for materials on the time of life between thirteen and twenty-five years, as well as on people in this general age range. Materials limited to teen youth are entered under **Teenagers.** Materials limited to people in the general age range of eighteen through twenty-five years of age are entered under **Young men** or **Young women.** Materials on the process or state of growing up are entered under **Adolescence.**
UF   Young adults
      Young people
      Young persons
SA   youth of particular racial or ethnic groups [to be added as needed]
BT   **Age**
NT   **African American youth**
      Church work with youth
      Dropouts
      Minority youth
      Teenagers
      Television and youth
      Young men
      Young women
Youth—Alcohol use (May subdiv. geog.)
        613.81; 616.86
UF   Alcohol and youth
      Drinking and youth
NT   **Drinking age**

Youth and drugs
USE   **Youth—Drug use**
Youth and narcotics
USE   **Youth—Drug use**
Youth and television
USE   **Television and youth**
Youth—Drug use (May subdiv. geog.)
        613.8; 616.86
UF   Drugs and youth
      Narcotics and youth
      Youth and drugs
      Youth and narcotics
NT   **Teenagers—Drug use**
RT   **Juvenile delinquency**
Youth—Employment (May subdiv. geog.)
        331.3
UF   Boys—Employment
      Girls—Employment
BT   **Age and employment**
      Employment
NT   **Teenagers—Employment**
RT   **Summer employment**
Youth hostels (May subdiv. geog.)
        910.46
UF   Tourist accommodations
BT   **Community centers**
      Hotels and motels
Youth market
USE   **Young consumers**
Youth movement (May subdiv. geog.)
        322.4
UF   Student movement
      Student protests, demonstrations, etc.
      Student revolt
BT   **Social movements**
NT   **Students—Political activity**
Youth—Religious life   204; 248.4
BT   **Religious life**
NT   **Teenagers—Religious life**
Youth—United States   305.230973
UF   American youth
NT   **Teenagers—United States**
Zen Buddhism (May subdiv. geog.)
        294.3
BT   **Buddhism**
Zeppelins
USE   **Airships**
Zero gravity
USE   **Weightlessness**

Zeus (Greek deity)   292.2
   BT   Gods and goddesses
Zinc   669
   BT   Chemical elements
       Metals
Zines
   USE   Fanzines
Zionism (May subdiv. geog.)   320.5
   UF   Zionist movement
   RT   Jews—Restoration
Zionist movement
   USE   Zionism
Zip code (May subdiv. geog.)   383
   UF   Postal delivery code
   BT   Postal service
Zodiac   133.5; 523
   BT   Astrology
       Astronomy
Zoning (May subdiv. geog.)   346.04;
   354.3
   UF   City planning—Zone system
       Districting (in city planning)
   BT   City planning
Zoological gardens
   USE   Zoos
Zoological specimens—Collection and
   preservation   590.75
   UF   Collections of natural specimens
       Preservation of zoological speci-
       mens
       Specimens, Preservation of
   SA   types of specimens with the sub-
       division *Collection and pres-*
       ervation, e.g. **Birds—Collec-**
       tion and preservation [to be
       added as needed]
   BT   Collectors and collecting
   NT   Birds—Collection and preser-
       vation
   RT   Taxidermy

Zoology   590
   Use for materials on the science of animals.
Nonscientific materials on animals are entered
under **Animals.**
   UF   Animal kingdom
       Animal physiology
       Fauna
   SA   names of divisions, classes, etc.,
       of the animal kingdom, e.g.
       Invertebrates; Vertebrates;
       Birds; Mammals; etc.; and
       names of animals [to be add-
       ed as needed]
   BT   Biology
       Science
   NT   Animal behavior
       Animals—Anatomy
       Comparative anatomy
       Comparative psychology
       Economic zoology
       Embryology
       Paleontology
   RT   Animals
       Natural history
       Zoos
Zoology—Anatomy
   USE   Animals—Anatomy
Zoology, Economic
   USE   Economic zoology
Zoology of the Bible
   USE   Bible—Natural history
Zoology—United States
   USE   Animals—United States
Zoos (May subdiv. geog.)   590.73
   UF   Zoological gardens
   SA   names of individual zoos [to be
       added as needed]
   BT   Parks
   NT   Petting zoos
   RT   Animals
       Zoology